THE USED CAR RELIABILITY AND SAFETY GUIDE

ADAM BERLIANT

BETTERWAY BOOKS
CINCINNATI, OHIO

ABOUT THE AUTHOR

Adam Berliant is a former award-winning investigative journalist specializing in database reporting. He currently works for the Microsoft Network as an Internet content expert. He lives in Seattle, Washington.

 Published by Betterway Books, an imprint of F&W Publications, Inc., 1507 Dana Avenue, Cincinnati, Ohio 45207. (800) 289-0963.

Other fine Betterway Books are available from your local bookstore or direct from the publisher.

International Standard Serial Number: 1075-6248
International Standard Book Number: 1-55870-438-8

Production edited by Bob Beckstead
Cover photo by Ron Forth Photography

Betterway Books are available for sales promotions, premiums and fund-raising use. Special editions or book excerpts can also be created to specification. For details, contact: Special Sales Manager, F&W Publications, 1507 Dana Avenue, Cincinnati, Ohio 45207.

Contents

Introduction

For most people, there's nothing easy about buying a used car.

In fact, the decision of whether to buy a used car at all can be one of the most difficult choices to make. After all, it's no secret that a car that's been on the road for a number of years, tallied thousands of miles on unknown roads, earned a number of bumps and bruises and been driven by a complete stranger may be more trouble than it's worth.

Plus, everyone knows the worst part of buying a used car: dealing with the owners and dealers who so obviously want to get rid of their used car or truck, and seem as if they'll say anything to convince you that this particular car is in "perfect shape."

Often, buyers are left with nothing but a test-drive and the completely unreliable word of owners or dealers in order to make a big decision about buying a car that, for all they know, is destined for a short drive straight to the dump.

But there is a solution. Through an innovative use of government and consumer information, the second edition of *The Used Car Reliability and Safety Guide* can warn used car buyers of the specific difficulties that are likely to develop or may have already developed in used cars. And better yet, these warnings don't come from a survey, a competing car company or a laboratory. They come from the same people who are trying to sell you used cars: the owners.

Each year, thousands and thousands of dissatisfied customers who are fed up and angry at faulty parts, annoying features or dangerous characteristics of their cars complain to the National Highway Traffic Safety Administration (NHTSA).

These complaints about poor performance, breaking parts, knocks and pings, vibrations, fires, squeaks and squeals, which come from people just like you, are compiled by NHTSA. This guide is a collection of the complaints to provide you, the used car buyer, with the answers to your most important questions:

What should I do when driving a used car?
What parts should I check when looking at the car?
Is this car safe?
Would I be better off with a different car of similar make?
Is this car reliable and will it last?

Throughout these pages, you will find these questions answered by thousands and thousands of real car owners who file unsolicited complaints with the government.

HOW THIS GUIDE WILL HELP YOU

Safety and reliability are at the forefront of a used car buyer's consideration. You need to pinpoint the problems that will affect the performance of a used car or, worse yet, threaten the safety of its driver and passengers.

This guide provides a better and more complete picture of automobile reliability and safety than any other resource. It uses raw data obtained from NHTSA, the public agency responsible for monitoring automobile safety, issuing recalls and performing crash tests and investigations.

The information in this guide is based entirely on consumer complaints. Unlike a survey, there is no consumer praise to be found in NHTSA's records. This guide lists, categorizes and compares complaints to provide buyers the opportunity to identify those vehicles owners have had the least amount of difficulty with.

The following instructions provide a general outline of how to use the three sections of the guide.

HOW TO USE SECTION I

This Complaint Summary section of this guide is a collection of consumer complaints organized by car make, model and year. There are 736 cars listed, first by make and model (alphabetically), then by year (chronologically).

For example, if the car you think you may want to purchase is a 1989 Ford Taurus, simply turn to the Ford section, then the Taurus section and, finally, look for the year. If you can't find the car you are interested in, it's possible that it is not included in this guide.

This guide only includes automobiles built since 1987 for which NHTSA received at least fifty complaints. If the car you're interested in doesn't appear, there are probably not very many of them on the road, or it's a new model that hasn't accumulated enough problems yet. If you can't find a car that you know is a popular model, and it's not a 1995 or newer, that's great—its absence means the car hasn't received that many complaints.

Important Tips and Explanations

1. What was included and what was excluded? The criteria for a car to appear in the guide were as follows: (1) Any car made since 1987 must have received at least fifty complaints; (2) A component had to have received at least four complaints to qualify for review; (3) "Hot Spots" are those components that received the largest number of complaints.

What's new? In the first edition of *The Used Car Reliability and Safety Guide*, up to but not more than five "Hot Spots" were included for each car. In this edition, more than five "Hot Spots" are listed for those cars that received more than the typical number of total complaints. In other words, if you see a car with six or seven "Hot Spots" instead of four or five, you know that that car received far more complaints than many other vehicles. The reverse is also true.

The records included in this guide were obtained in the winter of 1996. If a 1995 or 1996 vehicle doesn't appear in this guide, it simply means not enough complaints had been filed as of that time.

Only one category of complaints was excluded outright from this guide—tires. Occasionally a vehicle would have tires as a "Hot Spot," but not only were the complaints void of useful information, they almost never had anything to do with the vehicle itself. Most complaints read something like "Goodyear tire had to be replaced," giving no indication of what happened, or even if the tire was issued with the vehicle when it was purchased new. Worse yet, multiple brands of tires would appear under a single model year—imagine reading four or five complaints about tires, each one referring to a different brand! Unfortunately, it simply didn't make sense to include tires in this book.

2. Don't let the complaints scare you! Cars are basically safe and reliable, but eventually they all develop problems. Even the cars with the most renowned manufacturers and reputations will eventually end up a scrap pile in a junkyard. Just because a model receives a lot of complaints doesn't necessarily mean that the car you want to purchase is doomed to have or to develop the exact same problems.

This is a book of likelihood. What the guide will tell you is: If the car is going to develop any problems, here are the problems most likely to develop based on the frequency of owners' complaints. When purchasing a used car, you should check these areas with extra care to make sure the difficulties haven't already developed, and be prepared for them if you do purchase the car.

Remember, there are a lot of cars on the road, which leads to a lot of complaints. Just because someone else's engine caught on fire doesn't mean yours will, but don't be surprised if it does.

3. Check the trends. Although looking at the entries for the particular model year is the first thing you should do, be sure to take some extra time to look at all the years for that model. What you'll notice is that some problems seem to come up year after year, while others come and go, or appear only once.

For example, let's say a particular model year shows brake problems as a "Hot Spot," as well as alignment and fuel injection problems. If you look at the previous model years, you will notice that brakes may have been a problem for seven or eight straight years, while the other two problems may be unique to that particular year. The point is, you can learn more by flipping through the pages.

This is particularly important for newer cars (1994, 1995, 1996) because they haven't been on the road long enough to collect as many complaints as older models.

Examining the Listings

1. The Buyer's Summary. The purpose of the buyer's summary is to, first, review the complaints and, second, give you a helpful hint or two about what to look for when considering a purchase. If there are complaints about seat belts, the buyer's summary will remind you to check the performance and fit of the vehicle's seat belts. It may tell you to test the transmission carefully, to look for leaks, or to expect that the brakes may require frequent trips to the mechanic.

Keep in mind that these recommendations are based solely on hot spot complaints. There may still be other difficulties with the car, so always give a used car your best evaluation.

2. The Complaint Severity Rating. The Complaint Severity Rating is not a NHTSA rating, but is unique to this guide. The rating system was determined by a simple formula: the percentage of complaints to NHTSA that were associated with accidents.

The purpose of the rating is to provide used car buyers with some indication of how worried they should be, in terms of safety, should the listed complaints develop.

What's new? The Complaint Severity Rating is actually the same as the "Accident Rating" in the first edition of this guide. The rating has been made easier to understand by a new method of describing the rating.

The formula, which was applied to every car ever complained about to NHTSA, resulted in these new categories:

Best 3% in Guide: This rating is for automobiles that experienced the fewest problems related to accidents. Usually, cars in this category have had almost no problems that are accident related, or maybe even none at all. Keep in mind, however, that a car had to receive a significant number of complaints to appear in this guide, so the car can't be trouble free.

Harmless: Four percent of the cars in the guide fall in this category representing cars that have had so few accident-related problems that they can be considered relatively harmless. This is not to say that the problems that did occur couldn't result in an accident, but, compared to most other complications, the problems are practically insignificant.

Negligible: Seven percent of all automobiles fall in the Negligible group. These automobiles are likely to have some complaints that are accident related, but not enough to be a significant cause for concern.

Minor: Cars in the Minor category will definitely have some accident-related difficulties. Buyers should note that these difficulties exist, and weigh them in their overall decision, but should not be discouraged. Compared to other cars, these automobiles are still better than average in terms of accident-causing malfunctions. Ten percent of all cars are in this group.

Typical: The largest percentage of cars fall in this category, 42 percent. These cars will have a mixture of accident-related problems and less worrisome problems. One might find, but shouldn't be surprised, that a "typical" car has a significant collection of dangerous difficulties.

Troublesome: These cars have a noticeably greater than average number of complaints that are accident related. Used car buyers should take some extra time to note that these problems may be a safety concern. Again, 13 percent of all the cars in this guide fall in this category.

Serious: The 11 percent of cars that are in the Serious category have more than just a significant number of accident-related complaints. The faulty components in these cars should be given special attention, should someone purchase these automobiles.

Very Serious: In this case, the components car owners have complained about almost always contribute to or are associated with accidents. Seven percent of all cars are in this group. Buyers should be extremely wary of these problems and go out of their way to prevent them.

Dangerous (Worst 3% in Guide): This category is made up of automobiles that have had so many accident-related complaints that they fall among the worst 3 percent in the entire guide. Owners should absolutely consider the problems listed as a threat to their safety and take appropriate measures to prevent them from occurring.

More explanation of the Complaint Severity Rating is included in Section II of this guide.

3. The Theft Alert. The most frequently stolen automobiles will have a theft alert that indicates the vehicle's 1995 ranking. This alert refers to a complete car theft, not just a component.

This information was provided by CCC Information Services in Chicago, which provides automobile information to insurance companies.

4. The Recall Alert. Many people don't realize the frequency with which NHTSA issues recalls. The agency actually uses the same database that makes this guide possible to determine which components should be fixed under recall.

When components fail frequently or dangerously, NHTSA will issue a recall campaign. When a recall is issued, owners are supposed to be notified by mail. They are then able to have the problem corrected at no expense for a limited period of time. All of these recall campaigns are included in this guide in the Recall Index.

If you see a Recall Alert, that means you should check to see what components were recalled and why, and make sure the owner has remedied the problem. Some recalls refer to components by a manufacturer's code. These codes are used by dealers to see if the recall campaign refers to your particular automobile.

By looking at the recalls associated with an automobile, not only will you know more about the trouble associated with the car you are looking at, you will also know to check with the owner or dealer to see if the parts have been replaced. If a campaign is too old, you may have to replace parts at your own expense.

Constantly updated recall campaign information is available from NHTSA through their toll-free hotline [(800) 424-9393], or obtained through their World Wide Web site at http://www.dot.gov/affairs/nhtsain.htm (active as of March 1996).

5. The Hot Spots—Specific Parts, General Trends. What's new? The hot spots have experienced the most significant change in the second edition of *The Used Car Reliability and Safety Guide*.

NHTSA categorized complaints in general and specific categories. In this edition, we chose to use the specific categories rather than the general categories. These specific descriptions will give buyers more detail about what, exactly, people are complaining about. Where once a complaint may have been for brakes, now it is for the disc portion of the brakes.

The only downfall to this specificity is that several minor components of a larger part may be complained about separately, so some Hot Spots may seem redundant. For example, one car may have several categories of complaints about the overall braking system.

To make up for this, the guide now includes more than just five Hot Spots for the cars that have received the most complaints: There now can be up to as many as six Hot Spots for some cars.

6. Controversy! NHTSA takes the complaints they receive very seriously—they use them to decide which cars to investigate for recalls. Car companies and attorneys, however, will not always agree with consumers in regard to certain problems.

Many problems are controversial in the courts because sometimes there is a large gray area between design failure and human error. Is a particular type of car inherently unstable, rolling over at the slightest touch of the brakes, or are the people who own that type of car just bad drivers?

In many cases, this guide gives you a special insight into consumer complaints before NHTSA has launched investigations to answer these questions.

So we opt to recognize that it is possible user error can create a perceived problem. We can't ignore that certain problems are more common in some vehicles than in others. In other words, even if all rollovers for a certain car were caused by human error rather than design error, we still think it's valuable to know if that model had more complaints about stability than anything else. Perhaps design errors make human errors more likely.

Therefore, even the most controversial topics are included in this guide.

7. Please, Be Careful! Just because the guide recommends that you give the brakes a thorough test or test the transmission for performance, you should never compromise safety. Don't go out on the highway slamming on your brakes or driving at high speeds. Do what you can to test the components, but safety is of utmost importance.

Use extreme caution at all times when test-driving an unfamiliar car!

Sudden Accelerations

Imagine yourself sitting in your automobile. It's 7 A.M., and you're getting ready to start your car so you can drive to work, just as you do every morning. You put the key in the ignition, press a little on the gas, turn the key and rev it up. So far so good.

Then you put the car in gear—suddenly, at top speed, the car roars. Before you can react, your car races through the garage door. Slamming on the brakes doesn't help—the car speeds up! The car is now heading into the street. You're out of control. You swerve, but right into a tree. Finally it's over and, if you're lucky, no one has been hurt.

This seemingly implausible scenario is exactly what thousands of drivers have claimed to have experienced in a large variety of automobiles. The NHTSA database contains thousands and thousands of records describing "sudden accelerations," many of which end with accidents, injuries and even deaths. Although sudden accelerations occur in huge numbers, controversy has surrounded the concept.

Many car experts, especially car companies, dealers and service department mechanics, claim that sudden accelerations are the fault of car drivers, not the cars themselves.

One Audi mechanic told us the "whole thing is a hoax," and that the hundreds of complaints filed against the Audi 5000 for sudden accelerations were "just part of a trend in the 1980s."

But NHTSA has compiled a great deal of evidence showing that sudden accelerations not only do happen, but sometimes occur because of component failures or poorly designed automobiles—not human error.

Still, there can be situations where the responsibility for the problem is unclear. An NHTSA spokesperson said sometimes the Audi 5000 accelerator pedal, when pressed to the floor, sticks to the car's plush floor mats. Thus, when the car is next put in gear, the accelerator is stuck in the full throttle position—so a sudden acceleration occurs. So who—or what—is at fault here?

Well, we choose to leave that up to NHTSA and the car companies. The purpose of this guide is to encompass all automobile features that drivers have complained about. Sudden accelerations, regardless of fault, are a reality that must be reckoned with. They are taken very seriously in this guide. Even if sudden accelerations are the fault of drivers, they do tend to occur in some cars and not in others.

You will note that sudden acceleration complaints filed by NHTSA are usually categorized under "throttle linkages and control," a generalized term for the throttle system, which includes the gas pedal. But sometimes you will find the problem described under other categories, such as cruise control, which is a reflection of the confusion surrounding the phenomenon.

So, as a used car buyer, what can you do to test for sudden accelerations? Unfortunately, not much. The best you can do is know how to stop a sudden acceleration once it has started.

Some reference guides suggest tapping on the accelerator to see if it's not just stuck on the floor. But, judging by the thousands of testimonies in NHTSA's records, the most consistent solution seems to be to (1) shift the transmission into neutral, (2) steer to safety and (3) remove the key from the ignition.

If the car will not shift to neutral, or continues to accelerate once in neutral, still remove the key from the ignition—but keep in mind, you may lose steering control over your vehicle, especially if you have power steering.

Once you have come to a stop, check to see if your accelerator pedal isn't simply stuck to the floor. If it isn't stuck, then it's possible that you have a more serious problem. Don't risk it happening again: Call for help.

HOW TO USE SECTION II

Once you know what features car owners have complained about from looking at Section I, you may want to know how the vehicle compares to other, similar cars. This is the purpose of Section II.

You will first find a ranking of the top ten vehicles with the worst accident-to-complaint ratios (see The Complaint Severity Rating). The rest of the section is organized by automobile class, such as pickup trucks, minivans, subcompacts, compacts, intermediate and large cars. The classes were determined by a review of multiple sources, including rental agencies, auto dealers and industry publications.

For each class there will be two comparisons. First, you will find a ranking of all vehicles in the class by the percentage of accidents to total complaints—this is the same percentage used to determine the Complaint Severity Rating. This chart indicates how frequently the systems identified in owners' complaints contributed to accidents, but because the cars are sorted by class, the percentage can be used comparatively.

Second, you will find a comparison of the five vehicles with the worst accident percentages in each category. This second comparison will include two additional pieces of information: (1) the primary causes of component difficulties and (2) the percentage of all the accidents caused by these problems.

This section is helpful for determining the severity of accident-causing problems in the most suspicious vehicles. For example, the Suzuki Samurai has an accident percentage of 52—which means 52 percent of all the complaints were associated with accidents, giving it the highest percentage in its class. The second comparison shows that "Instability" was the cause of more than 80 percent of all the accident-related complaints.

In other words, eight of the ten complaints that comprise the 52 percent of complaints associated with accidents were caused by instability of the vehicle. So you know that instability is by far the most severe complaint.

MISCELLANEOUS

You can call NHTSA and complain about your automobile by dialing (800) 424-9393. If you have complaints about your current automobile, it would be very valuable to the agency as well as future editions of this book to call or mail in information about your problems. A sample complaint form has been included in this guide for your convenience.

This number is the NHTSA's Auto Safety Hotline. In addition to registering complaints, you can obtain valuable information about everything from child car seats to crash tests. They can also provide you with safety information about drunk driving, air bags, odometer fraud and much more.

MINI-GLOSSARY

There are a few component and mechanical terms you may find difficult in this guide. Here are the ones that appear most frequently.

Ball Joint: If you've heard of a ball and socket before, you already have a good idea what a ball joint is. If you haven't, swing your arm around like you're winding up to roll a bowling ball. The bones connecting your shoulder and arm that allow for the windmill movement of your arm are the same thing as a ball and socket joint. Your shoulder is the socket, and the end of your arm is the ball. The connection is the ball joint.

You will often find this component mentioned in complaints about suspensions. That's because the key connections in the suspension that allow your wheels to turn are ball joints. Should your ball joints fail, so does your ability to turn.

Brake Calipers, Pads and Discs: When you press on the brakes, pads (which really are just pads) squeeze and press against discs (which really are just discs). The discs, not the pads, actually stop your car from rolling. Calipers are what hold the pads and discs, and also provide the mechanism to perform the squeezing.

Camshaft: This is tough both to explain and understand, so be glad that all you really need to know is that the camshaft is in charge of opening and closing your intake and exhaust valves. Gas comes in, smoke goes out—a system that you definitely don't want to break, as cars frequently do in this guide.

Catalytic Converter: This device helps take nitrous oxide out of your exhaust. It looks like a muffler under your car.

Clutch: Technically, a clutch connects your wheels to the power system of your car. But a lot of people in this guide say *clutch* when what they really mean is either the clutch assembly (the pedal) or the transmission.

Control Arm: If you read the part about *Ball Joints*, then you know there are a lot of moving parts in a suspension. Something has to hold it all together, and that's where the control arm comes in. The control arm, which is connected to the frame of the car, holds the ball joints and other important suspension components. There can be upper and lower control arms, but all you really need to know is that if your control arm goes, so does your entire suspension.

Crankshaft: Ever wonder how a piston, which goes up and down, can turn a driveshaft, which goes round and round? The crankshaft is your answer. It's a shaft that converts the up and down motion of your pistons into round and round motion.

By the way, if you see "connection rods" in any of the complaints about crankshafts, they are just the parts that connect the crankshaft to the pistons.

Differential: Without getting into the laws of physics, when you turn your car, both axles have to move, but not to the same degree. One axle has to turn a little bit more than the other. The differential is the component that keeps your back wheels from turning as much as your front ones.

Distributor: This is what sparks your spark plugs at the right time. If it doesn't work, neither do your spark plugs.

Drive Train: This is an all-encompassing term for everything that makes your wheels spin: clutch, transmission, etc. If it has something to do with turning your tires, it's a drive train component.

Engine Block: This simply refers to the big thing under the hood that looks like an engine. Technically, it's the metal casting that holds the cylinders of your car.

Fuel Injection System: If a car doesn't have a carburetor, it has one of these. A fuel injection system sprays gas into the car's cylinders.

Idler Arm: This is another one that's tough to explain in a few sentences. The idler arm is a part of the steering system located down by the tire on the opposite side of the driver. It helps support the system—if it breaks, your steering system will be hanging loose.

Master Cylinder: The master cylinder is a container that holds and pumps your brake fluid, which is what makes your brakes function. Should the master cylinder leak and you lose your brake fluid, your brakes will not function properly.

Rack-and-Pinion: Imagine one of those cork screws—the one with the arms and the head—and you have a pretty good image of what a rack-and-pinion steering system looks like. The rack-and-pinion is nothing more than the gear many cars use for turning tires.

Timing Chain or Belt: Before you read this, read *Camshaft*, then read *Crankshaft*.

The camshaft, which is opening and closing, is operated by the crankshaft, which is busy doing its own thing. These two components are connected by a timing belt. The camshaft doesn't work when the timing belt breaks. As a result, all sorts of bad things can happen; most noticeably, your car stops running.

Transaxle: This is a component that holds your transmission and differential.

Universal Joints: Cars have a problem—the engine and driveshaft sit still and are bolted to the frame of the car. The axles, on the other hand, pull, bounce and move all over the place.

So the engine's driveshaft needs something to connect it to the axles. A U-joint is a flexible connection that can adjust to all the different angles. There may be lots of U-joints in a car. Just know that you don't want any of them to give you trouble.

Vapor Lock: When your car gets too hot, the gas in your fuel lines will start to boil. It will suffice to say that boiling fuel does not translate to smooth engine performance. In fact, it can stop your engine completely.

Form Approved: O.M.B. No. 2127-0008

U.S. Department of Transportation
National Highway Traffic Safety Administration

AUTO SAFETY HOTLINE

VEHICLE OWNER'S QUESTIONNAIRE

NATIONWIDE 1-800-424-9393
DC METRO AREA 202-366-0123

FOR AGENCY USE ONLY

DATE RECEIVED

od_or ____
rt_dt ____
od_rt ____
up_ltr ____

REFERENCE NO.

DAY TIME TELEPHONE NO. (AREA CODE)

OWNER INFORMATION (TYPE OR PRINT)

NAME and ADDRESS

Do you authorize NHTSA to provide a copy of this report to the manufacturer of your vehicle? YES ☐ NO ☐
In the absence of an authorization, NHTSA *WILL NOT* provide your name or address to the vehicle manufacturer.

SIGNATURE OF OWNER | DATE

VEHICLE INFORMATION

VEHICLE IDENTIFICATION NO.*	VEHICLE MAKE	VEHICLE MODEL	MODEL YEAR

*LOCATED AT BOTTOM OF WINDSHIELD ON DRIVER'S SIDE

CURRENT ODOMETER READING	DATE PURCHASED ____ ☐ NEW ☐ USED	DEALER'S NAME, CITY & STATE	ENGINE SIZE (CID/CC/L) ___ NO. CYLINDERS___	☐ TURBO ☐ DIESEL ☐ GAS ☐ FUEL INJECTN

TRANSMISSION TYPE	ANTILOCK BRAKES	RESTRAINT SYSTEM	CRUISE CONTROL	DRIVETRAIN	BODY STYLE
☐ MANUAL	☐ YES	☐ DRIVERSIDE AIRBAG ☐ MOTORBELT	☐ YES	☐ FRONT	STAWAG ____ HATCH BK ____
☐ AUTOMATIC	☐ NO	☐ PASSENGERSIDE AIRBAG	☐ NO	☐ REAR	4 DR ____ VAN ____
		☐ 3-POINT BELT ☐ 2-POINT BELT		☐ 4-WHEEL	2 DR ____ PK UP TRK ____ OTHER ____

FAILED COMPONENT(S)/PART(S) INFORMATION (REPORT TIRE INFORMATION ON BACK)

COMPONENT	PART NAME(S)	LOCATION	FAILED PART(S)
		☐ LEFT ☐ RIGHT ☐ FRONT ☐ REAR	☐ ORIGINAL ☐ REPLACEMENT

NO. OF FAILURES

DATE(S) OF FAILURE(S) ____

MILEAGE AT FAILURE(S) ____

VEHICLE SPEED AT FAILURE(S)

MANUFACTURER CONTACTED ☐ YES ☐ NO

NHTSA PREVIOUSLY CONTACTED ☐ YES ☐ NO

APPLICABLE ACCIDENT INFORMATION

ACCIDENT	FIRE	NUMBER PERSONS INJURED	NUMBER OF FATALITIES.	PROPERTY DAMAGE EST$ ____	POLICE REPORTED
☐ YES ☐ NO	☐ YES ☐ NO				☐ YES ☐ NO

NARRATIVE DESCRIPTION OF FAILURE(S), ACCIDENT(S), INJURY(IES)

CONTINUE ON BACK IF NEEDED

The Privacy Act of 1974
Public Law 93-579

This information is requested pursuant to authority vested in the National Highway Traffic Safety Act and subsequent amendments. You are under no obligation to respond to this questionnaire. Your response may be used to assist the NHTSA in determining whether a manufacturer should take appropriate action to correct a safety defect. If the NHTSA proceeds with administrative enforcement or litigation against a manufacturer, your response, or a statistical summary thereof, may be used in support of the agency's action.

HS-Form 350 (Rev. 5-92)

Fold to show Return Address (no stamp needed) Fasten with tape or staple and mail

INFORMATION ON TIRE FAILURE(S) (IF APPLICABLE)

TIRE IDENTIFICATION NO.*

D	O	T											MANUFACTURER/TIRE NAME	SIZE

* The identification number consists of 7 to 10 letters and numerals following the letters DOT. It is usually located near the rim flange on the side opposite the whitewall or on either side of a blackwall tire.

NARRATIVE DESCRIPTION (CONTINUED)

☆ U.S. G.P.O.: 1992 -- 623-897 / 60086

U.S. Department of Transportation

National Highway Traffic Safety Administration

400 Seventh St., S.W.
Washington, D.C. 20590

Official Business
Penalty for Private Use $300

NO POSTAGE NECESSARY IF MAILED IN THE UNITED STATES

BUSINESS REPLY MAIL

FIRST CLASS PERMIT NO. 73173 WASHINGTON, D.C.

POSTAGE WILL BE PAID BY NATL HWY TRAFFIC SAFETY ADMIN.

U.S. Department of Transportation
National Highway Traffic Safety Administration
Auto Safety Hotline, NEF-11 HL
400 7th Street, SW
Washington, DC 20590

SECTION I: Troubleshooter's Guide

Acura

ACURA INTEGRA 1989

Complaint Severity: Troublesome. **Recall Alert:** See Recall Index. **Buyer's Summary:** Test transmission for slipping, locking up and performance. Test the clutch. See "Sudden Accelerations" in Introduction. Make sure air conditioner works properly.

Hot Spots and Owner/NHTSA Comments:

1. Air conditioner: failure, malfunction. • "Air conditioning unit failed." • "Air conditioning inoperative, repairs made under warranty." • "Broken air conditioner system." • "Air conditioner failure." • "Cooling system overheated."

2. Fuel: throttle linkages and control, sudden acceleration. • "Upon backing out of driveway, shifted into reverse, engine revved and car shot across street backwards, resulted in accident, injuries sustained." • "Upon shifting transmission from park to reverse, vehicle suddenly accelerated, went out of control, caused accident." • "On numerous occasions while in drive, vehicle suddenly accelerated, went out of control, and once caused an accident." • "Upon placing in reverse, vehicle surged, then accelerated out of control." • "Sudden acceleration twice, causing accidents/injuries." • "With vehicle slowing down, sudden acceleration. Lost control. Impact 12:00, hitting a tree. Speed unknown."

3. Power train: clutch assembly, premature failure. • "Clutch failed." • "Clutch failed twice." • "Clutch wearing prematurely, may need replacing after only 22,000 miles." • "Clutch nonresponsive in 2nd through 5th gears."

4. Power train: transmission: 5-speed and up, failure, locking up. • "5-speed manual transmission/clutch defective, intermittently refused to go into any gear, locks up while slowing approaching stop or intersection." • "5-speed manual transmission intermittently fails to go into gear, usually occurs when slowing to approach stop or intersection." • "When waiting to make left turn, 5-speed transmission refused to go into gear, occurred 4 times a week." • "Several times transmission has intermittently refused to go into gear, locks up, usually when slowing to approach a stop or an intersection."

ACURA INTEGRA 1990

Complaint Severity: Typical. **Recall Alert:** See Recall Index. **Buyer's Summary:** Check the brakes—listen for noise, look for leaks and feel for vibration. They may fail, perform poorly or require frequent mechanical attention. Test the transmission thoroughly. Make sure seat belts function correctly and fit comfortably. Make sure air conditioner works properly.

Hot Spots and Owner/NHTSA Comments:

1. Interior systems: passive restraint: belts, failure, uncomfortable. • "The seat belt tightens during any kind of movement while driving." • "In accident, automatic shoulder harness retractor failed to operate, after door was opened it tightened severely, pinned driver to seat and choked her." • "When door opened after accident occurred, shoulder harness didn't retract into forward position, instead tightened severely, pinning driver's neck/choking her." • "Location of seat belts seems to get in the way of normal performance inside vehicle." • "Chest safety belt terribly uncomfortable, and dangerous in event of an accident: Strap cuts across throat, and would choke if ever in an accident."

2. Power train: transmission: automatic, vibration, failure. • "Transmission leaked, replaced." • "Severe transmission vibration." • "Unspecified transmission problem." • "Transmission failure." • "Experiencing car shaking violently, so violently a window broke, serviced several times, installed computer part, and worked on transmission, still severe shaking." • "Transmission problems, unable to release park without key."

3. Air conditioner: leaks, failure. • "Defective air conditioner, repaired." • "Air conditioning problem." • "Air conditioning system emitting bad odor and not cooling due to several leaks in hosing setup, finally repaired satisfactorily after 3 times at dealer." • "Air conditioning system defective."

4. Brakes: hydraulic: anti-skid system failure. • "While on curve trying to slow down, brakes very hard, no response, wheel locked up, no control over car, hit curb and into a tree." • "Defective antilock brake modulator." • "Antilock brake system modulator fails allowing brake fluid to leak." • "Antilock brake system: Brakes fail to function at appropriate time resulting in close rear-ending. System fails to warn driver something is wrong."

ACURA INTEGRA 1991

Complaint Severity: Typical. **Recall Alert:** See Recall Index. **Buyer's Summary:** Check the brakes—listen for noise, look for leaks and feel for vibration. They may fail, perform poorly or require frequent mechanical attention.

Hot Spots and Owner/NHTSA Comments:

1. Brakes: hydraulic: anti-skid system failure. • "Wherever antilock brakes are activated, vehicle takes greater distances to stop." • "Antilock brake system malfunctioned." • "Antilock brake system failed 3 times." • "Noisy antilock brake system." • "Antilock brake problem." • "Antilock brake system failed to store pressure."

2. Equipment: speed control, failure to disengage. • "Cruise control didn't go off when brakes were applied." • "With cruise control on, applied brakes, no response and felt as if car accelerated out of control, resulting in accident, totaled." • "Speed cruise control would not disengage upon shutting off cruise control switch or depressing clutch." • "Speed cruise control would not disengage." • "Vehicle failed to decelerate when disengaging cruise control mechanism, repaired/replaced, problem reoccurred."

3. Interior systems: passive restraint: belt, locking up, failure. • "The car was off and the automatic seat belt wrapped around her neck and she could not breathe." • "The driver- and passenger-side seat belt retractors lock up when door opens." • "Automatic shoulder belt catches head/neck." • "Shoulder belt locked and jammed when vehicle was rear-ended." • "The seat belts on driver's and passenger's sides pin occupants to the seat upon opening the door; vehicle accelerates or accident results." • "Automatic seat belt failed to operate."

4. Interior systems: active restraints: belt retractors, failure. • "Passenger-side seat belt retractors are intermittent, either pull too tight or lock half way and leave the passenger unprotected." • "Driver-side seat belt did not work when accident occurred." • "Motorized seat belt retractor failed." • "Upon impact of an accident, the seat belt did not retract."

ACURA INTEGRA 1994

Complaint Severity: Serious. **Recall Alert:** See Recall Index. **Buyer's Summary:** The airbags in this vehicle have experienced failures and malfunctions. You may need a professional evaluation on the condition of the airbags. Make sure the power windows function properly. Also, make sure the radio antenna retracts.

Hot Spots and Owner/NHTSA Comments:

1. Equipment: electric power accessories: windows, failure. • "Power window motor regulator failed." • "Power window motor failed, causing windows not to go up and down evenly." • "Driver's

power window failed." • "Left side power window failed." • "Passenger's power window failed." • "Front right power window hesitates when going up and down." • "Power windows failed twice."
2. Interior systems: passive restraint: airbag: driver, failure. • "Antilock brake system failed to stop vehicle on wet surface. No airbag deployment after collision. Driver made contact with steering wheel." • "During 20-30 mph head-on impact, driver's airbag did not deploy." • "Upon frontal impact at 45 mph, driver's airbag failed to deploy." • "In a frontal collision the driver's airbag did not deploy, causing driver to go through windshield." • "Dual airbags did not deploy during rear-end/front-end collision at 55 mph. Minor injuries."
3. Interior systems: passive restraint: airbag: passenger, failure. • "Dual airbags did not deploy during rear-end/front-end collision at 55 mph. Minor injuries." • "During frontal impact the driver and passenger airbags did not deploy." • "Passenger's airbag did not deploy during frontal collision; hit another vehicle head-on; speed 35 mph; impact 12:00 position." • "During 20-30 mph head-on impact, passenger airbag did not deploy." • "Upon frontal impact at 45 mph, passenger's airbag failed to deploy."
4. Equipment: antenna mast: standard, failure. • "Radio antenna failed." • "Radio antenna failed." • "Antenna failed." • "Radio antenna fails to retract all the way."

ACURA LEGEND 1987

Complaint Severity: Dangerous (Worst 3% in Guide). **Recall Alert:** See Recall Index. **Buyer's Summary:** Test the suspension by feeling for vibration or pulling while driving. Carefully check the brakes—listen for noise, look for leaks and feel for vibration. Brakes may fail, perform poorly or require frequent mechanical attention. Test the transmission thoroughly. See "Sudden Accelerations" in Introduction.

Hot Spots and Owner/NHTSA Comments:
1. Fuel: throttle linkages and control, sudden acceleration. • "Sudden acceleration results in crashing into a parked car." • "Sudden acceleration, with foot on brake, causing accident." • "Upon coming to a stop, car suddenly accelerated to a high rate of speed, with foot on brake; came to rest after hitting a tree." • "After starting car and shifting into drive gear, car surged out of control at full throttle, causing accident." • "Vehicle suddenly accelerated at full throttle, while foot on brake, used emergency brake, engine still revving." • "When driver applied brakes, vehicle suddenly accelerated, resulting in accident on two occasions."
2. Power train: transmission: automatic, difficulty shifting. • "Car accelerated in reverse, injured 2 people." • "When shifting into gear, car trembles." • "Defective transmission, vibrates at speeds of 35-45 mph, problem reoccurred 3 times after work has been done on it ." • "Problem with harsh shifting automatic transmission." • "Developed abnormal slipping and noise as automatic transmission shifted from 1st to 2nd." • "Problem with transmission not shifting properly, repaired/replaced."
3. Suspension: independent front: alignment, vibration. • "Excessive front-end vibration, repaired/replaced tire and realigned front end, all repair attempts to no avail." • "Steering wheel vibrates and pulsates at 50-65 mph, tires balanced and aligned, replaced three sets of new tires, different wheels." • "Constant shimmy in steering wheel, noticeable between 35 and 65 mph." • "Steering wheel shimmy." • "Clicking noise when rounding sharp corners, new axle installed." • "Vibration in front end at 35 mph."
4. Brakes: hydraulic system: noise, failure. • "Squeaky brakes." • "Brakes squeak loud whenever pedal touched." • "Brakes—squealing noise made." • "Brakes failed, accident." • "While braking at low speeds, rear end spun out of control with no warning."
5. Electrical system: ignition: electronic control unit, sudden acceleration. • "Vehicle intermittently accelerates when adjusting gears." • "Engine suddenly accelerated, vehicle was uncontrollable, vehicle ran into wall." • "Unspecified failure of the programmable read-only memory." • "Car accelerated on its own in reverse, brakes did not stop acceleration, turned key off, computer adjustments." • "Intermittent sudden-acceleration problem, causing accident."

ACURA LEGEND 1988

Complaint Severity: Dangerous (Worst 3% in Guide). **Theft Alert:** 46. **Recall Alert:** See Recall Index. **Buyer's Summary:** Check the brakes—listen for noise, look for leaks and feel for vibration. They may fail, perform poorly or require frequent mechanical attention. Test the transmission thoroughly. Test the clutch. See "Sudden Accelerations" in Introduction.

Hot Spots and Owner/NHTSA Comments:
1. Fuel: throttle linkages and control, sudden acceleration. • "While shifting gear from park into reverse vehicle suddenly accelerated, caused multicar collision and injuries to driver and passenger." • "Backed into parking spot and put car in gear, vehicle suddenly accelerated, stepped on brakes but couldn't stop car, hit parked car." • "Vehicle suddenly accelerated in reverse, lost control and hit a house." • "Vehicle accelerated at full speed, brakes failed to operate, brakes stuck in upright position." • "Very lightly touched gas pedal, car roared and took off like a rocket, suddenly accelerated, resulted in accident." • "Backing out of driveway, car raced backward, crashing into neighbor's house."
2. Power train: transmission: automatic, difficulty shifting, failure. • "Transmission failed, vehicle lunged forward, resulting in loss of control/accident." • "The car has a shifting problem and sometimes lurches forward." • "Vehicle experiences transmission problems." • "Clutch disc for transmission failed." • "Transmission shifts abruptly, not smoothly." • "Rough gear changes."
3. Brakes: hydraulic: anti-skid system, failure. • "Antilock brakes failed, causing accident." • "Faulty antilock brake system." • "Antilock brake modulator failed." • "Antilock brake system modulator and pressure hose are leaking." • "The antilock brake system no longer works, and dealer claims it cannot be fixed."
4. Power train: clutch assembly, slipping, failure. • "Clutch failed." • "Replaced clutch, pressure plate and flywheel." • "Faulty clutch assembly resulted in gear slippage." • "Repeated clutch failure; replacement produced burning odor when operated, resulting in burning odor inside car."

ACURA LEGEND 1989

Complaint Severity: Serious. **Recall Alert:** See Recall Index. **Buyer's Summary:** The airbags in this vehicle have experienced failures and malfunctions. You may need a professional evaluation on the condition of the airbags. Check the brakes—listen for noise, look for leaks and feel for vibration. They may fail, perform poorly or require frequent mechanical attention. See "Sudden Accelerations" in Introduction. Make sure the battery has been replaced.

Hot Spots and Owner/NHTSA Comments:
1. Fuel: throttle linkages and control, sudden acceleration. • "Started car, shifted to reverse, car shot out of garage, shifted to drive, car shot forward across divider, accident occurred." • "Problem of sudden acceleration, suffered severe bruising and shock." • "When car was started and put in drive/reverse, strong unintended acceleration resulted, foot on brake, could hardly restrain car." • "While pulling into parking space and removing foot

from accelerator, vehicle accelerated and surged forward, caused accident." • "Sudden acceleration." • "Car in car wash in neutral gear; upon coming out, put car in gear, it immediately accelerated forward 30 feet and hit pole."

2. Brakes: hydraulic system, excessive wear. • "Brakes failed twice, with loss of control of vehicle, resulted in accident." • "Brake problems." • "Braking problems on slick road surfaces, causing accidents." • "Brakes not stopping car without pressing them very hard; when looked into, needed replaced at 30,000 miles." • "Problem with little compression in holding down speed in low gear, caused excessive and dangerous brake wear." • "Worn brakes replaced."

3. Brakes: hydraulic: anti-skid system, failure. • "Antilock brake system experienced brake problem, pedal faded, rear-ended the vehicle in front." • "Antilock brake system in for brake repair, found metal shavings in the fluid, failure of antilock brake system pump." • "Antilock sticks." • "Antilock brake system failed, when brakes applied, car went out of control, resulted in accident." • "Whenever snow/ice is on ground, antilock brakes do not enable car to stop in a reasonable amount of time."

4. Electrical system: battery, failure. • "Electrical system fails if vehicle driven in stop-and-go traffic." • "Frequent battery drain." • "Battery failed."

5. Engine cooling system: thermostat, failure. • "Engine thermostat frozen partially open, causing severe engine overheating, thermostat replaced." • "Thermostat failed." • "Faulty thermostat in engine's cooling system." • "Engine thermostat failed and needed to be replaced." • "Radiator thermostat heat indicator highly irregular."

6. Interior systems: passive restraint: airbag, failure. • "Airbag did not deploy when vehicle was involved in a front-end accident." • "Attorney representing client who suffered personal injury due to failure of airbag to deploy at onset of collision." • "Airbag inflated too rapidly upon accident, sparks and smoke were produced upon inflation." • "During frontal collision at speed of 35 mph, impact 12:00, airbag failed to deploy."

ACURA LEGEND 1990

Complaint Severity: Very Serious. **Recall Alert:** See Recall Index. **Buyer's Summary:** The airbags in this vehicle have experienced failures and malfunctions. You may need a professional evaluation on the condition of the airbags. Check the brakes—listen for noise, look for leaks and feel for vibration. They may fail, perform poorly or require frequent mechanical attention. Test the transmission thoroughly. See "Sudden Accelerations" in Introduction. Also make sure the battery has been replaced.

Hot Spots and Owner/NHTSA Comments:

1. Fuel: throttle linkages and control, sudden acceleration. • "While shifting to drive with transmission in park position, motor instantly went to maximum rpms and vehicle accelerated rapidly, caused accident and injury." • "Sudden acceleration occurred on two occasions, both times vehicle accelerated while in drive." • "Sudden acceleration, causing accident." • "Sudden acceleration, causing 3 accidents." • "While driving vehicle at low speed of 10 mph, vehicle experienced sudden acceleration." • "While attempting to back up, vehicle sped and crashed into bank window."

2. Brakes: hydraulic system, excessive wear, failure. • "Brakes failed, causing accident." • "Brake pedal goes to floor any time while driving, especially at 50-55 mph." • "Brakes failed to hold, causing accident." • "Brakes wear quickly." • "Brakes replaced." • "Brakes failed, causing accident."

3. Interior systems: passive restraint: airbag: driver, failure. • "Upon impact during frontal crash on left front bumper, airbag failed to inflate; instead airbag exploded, causing driver minor burns to left arm." • "Airbag did not deploy." • "Defective driver's side airbag, did not deploy on impact." • "Airbag didn't inflate on impact." • "Driver lost control and struck guard rail several times before stopping. Airbag deployed while vehicle sat motionless."

4. Power train: transmission: automatic, slipping, failure. • "Transmission problems." • "Transmission slips, causing vehicle to vibrate when accelerating between 30 and 35 mph." • "When car stopped and shifted into neutral, if gas pedal pressed, car lurches forward several feet." • "Transmission shifting mechanism fails to shift smoothly." • "Transmission failed, replaced."

5. Brakes: hydraulic: anti-skid system, failure. • "Antilock brake system light comes on, replaced." • "Antilock brake system problem." • "Antilock brake system failure, antilock brake system modulator broke, pedal goes to floor." • "Antilock brake system failure, antilock brake system modulator failed, no indication of antilock brake system defect."

6. Electrical system: battery, failure. • "Battery failure." • "Battery failed, replaced." • "Battery failure." • "Original battery failed, was changed by dealer and failed again on same day."

ACURA LEGEND 1991

Complaint Severity: Troublesome. **Recall Alert:** See Recall Index. **Buyer's Summary:** The airbags in this vehicle have experienced failures and malfunctions. You may need a professional evaluation on the condition of the airbags. Check the brakes—listen for noise, look for leaks and feel for vibration. They may fail, perform poorly or require frequent mechanical attention. Test the transmission thoroughly. See "Sudden Accelerations" in Introduction.

Hot Spots and Owner/NHTSA Comments:

1. Brakes: hydraulic: anti-skid system, locking up, failure. • "While driving, antilock braking system locked up, car began to spin." • "Antilock brake system yellow light comes on during 25-mile drive, dealer can find nothing with 2-mile test-drive. No fix is imminent." • "Antilock brakes malfunctioned." • "Antilock brake failure." • "During panic stop at approximately 20 mph, experienced antilock brake system failure, all wheels locked up."

2. Interior systems: passive restraint: airbag: driver, failure. • "Upon impact, during frontal crash at approximately 20 mph, airbag failed to deploy." • "At 35-40 mph collision at 12:00 position, driver's side airbag did not deploy." • "In a head-on collision with a trailer truck, airbag failed to deploy, driver sustained injuries." • "During a frontal collision, impact 12:00 position, speed 20 mph, airbag did not deploy." • "Airbag did not deploy in accident, impact at 12:00, approximately 35 mph."

3. Fuel: throttle linkages and control, sudden acceleration. • "Upon starting up, vehicle surged and suddenly accelerated out of control, resulted in an accident." • "In cold weather, upon starting the vehicle, it suddenly accelerates." • "After cold start, vehicle suddenly accelerates to 20 mph, no injury occurred, no help from dealer." • "Car was placed in drive with foot on brake, vehicle suddenly surged forward, could not be stopped with full brake application." • "Sudden acceleration, causing accident."

4. Interior systems: instrument panel: speedometer: odometer inaccurate readings. • "Speedometer inaccurate." • "Odometer/speedometer readings faulty." • "Speedometer is 10 percent off at all speeds." • "Speedometer defect."

5. Power train: transmission: automatic, failure. • "Shift kit replaced." • "Shift cable failure." • "Defective transmission shift cable bracket." • "Transmission failure causes vehicle to have extreme vibration."

Audi

AUDI 5000 1987

Complaint Severity: Minor. **Recall Alert:** See Recall Index. **Buyer's Summary:** The steering may be stiff or not working correctly. Test the steering, especially on a cold start. Test the transmission thoroughly. See "Sudden Accelerations" in Introduction.

Hot Spots and Owner/NHTSA Comments:

1. Power train: transmission: automatic, difficulty shifting, failure. • "While driving at highway speed, transmission failed and front wheels completely locked up." • "Car rolls frontwards and backwards when engine on or off, sometimes ten feet or more." • "Automatic transmission fails to shift from 1st to 2nd gear, particularly noticeable in morning; fluid brown and smelled burnt, replaced." • "Complete transmission failure." • "Transmission/differential failed prior to recall." • "Transmission failure."

2. Fuel: throttle linkages and control, sudden acceleration. • "Traveling at approximately 45 mph, vehicle suddenly accelerated out of control, resulted in accident; injuries sustained." • "While driving, accident occurred due to sudden acceleration." • "When shifted into reverse, vehicle accelerated out of control; resulted in an accident." • "Vehicle suddenly accelerated out of control, brakes could not stop car; accident." • "At 55 mph car accelerated to 90 mph, accelerated 3 more times while trying to get car to safe place, finally towed, no problem found."

3. Steering: gear: rack, leaks, failure. • "Steering rack leaks fluid." • "Replaced steering rack." • "Steering rack failed." • "Defective steering racks."

BMW

BMW 318 1991

Complaint Severity: Very Serious. **Recall Alert:** See Recall Index. **Buyer's Summary:** The airbags in this vehicle have experienced failures and malfunctions. You may need a professional evaluation on the condition of the airbags.

Hot Spots and Owner/NHTSA Comments:

1. Interior systems: passive restraint: airbag: driver, failure. • "Frontal collision, hitting a brick wall, impact 12:00 position, speed 40 mph, airbag did not deploy." • "Head-on collision, impact 12:00 position, speed 30-35 mph, airbag did not deploy; resulted in injuries and severe damage." • "No deployment of airbag during accident." • "Indicator light came on and airbag deployed by itself." • "Frontal collision, impact 11:00 position, lost control, hit again at 1:00 position, speed 40 mph, airbag did not deploy." • "No deployment of driver's airbag during two different accidents, resulting in injury."

BMW 325 1987

Complaint Severity: Very Serious. **Recall Alert:** See Recall Index. **Buyer's Summary:** The fuel injection system has been blamed for hesitation and stalling. Be sure the vehicle doesn't die in traffic or at stops. See "Sudden Accelerations" in Introduction. There have been complaints about the windshield shattering. It may be useful to have a professional examine the windshield.

Hot Spots and Owner/NHTSA Comments:

1. Fuel: throttle linkages and control, sudden acceleration. • "Car accelerated suddenly while slowing down to pull into parking space, resulted in accident." • "Vehicle suddenly accelerated in drive, collided with parked car, injuries sustained." • "Idle control valve sticks, car idles too fast and surges forward out of control." • "Car suddenly accelerated forward, lost control; accident resulted." • "Upon starting engine and shifting gear to drive, suddenly accelerated out of control, resulting in accident." • "Engine accelerates on random and frequent basis, races back and forth in neutral, from 1,000 rpm to 2,000 rpm." • "Throttle stuck while making a right turn. Speed 25 mph." • "Engine accelerated. Hit a utility pole."

2. Visual systems: glass: window: rearview back light, breaking, cracking. • "Rear window exploded while driving; caused injury." • "Upon starting, rear windshield shattered." • "Rear window shattered from a malfunctioning defogger." • "Rear window has exploded on two occasions, possibly from defrost wires in window shorting." • "Rear window exploded when rear window defroster used twice, probably due to short in wiring."

3. Fuel: fuel injection system, stalling. • "Stalling/starting problems, driving 35-40 mph." • "Hard start, carbon buildups." • "Particular vehicle prone to carbon buildups, therefore preventive maintenance done, after 25,000 miles car needs carbon blast anyway; also hard starting problem." • "Rpm raises up and down although engine at idle, when rpm increases vehicle accelerates unexpectedly, when decreased vehicle stalls."

4. Heater: water: defroster: defogger: heater core: water, failure. • "Vehicle overheated prior to recall." • "Heater core failed prior to recall." • "Heater core recall repairs refused due to vehicle being imported."

BMW 325 1989

Complaint Severity: Serious. **Recall Alert:** See Recall Index. **Buyer's Summary:** Check the brakes—listen for noise, look for leaks and feel for vibration. They may fail, perform poorly or require frequent mechanical attention. See "Sudden Accelerations" in Introduction. The electronic control unit has been blamed for miscellaneous problems, including sudden accelerations.

Hot Spots and Owner/NHTSA Comments:

1. Electrical system: ignition: electronic control unit, sudden acceleration, failure. • "On-board computer failed." • "Idle speed intermittently unstable, fluctuates up and down, as though gas pedal being depressed/released rapidly, car surges and sometimes stalls." • "Placed foot on brake and shifted into drive from park, engine raced, hit another vehicle despite constant application of pressure to brake pedal." • "Defective on-board computer." • "Problem with check engine light coming on, engine stalls at times and accelerates by itself, resulted in 2 accidents."

2. Fuel: throttle linkages and control, sudden acceleration. • "Attorney requesting information, on behalf of client, regarding rapid acceleration or stuck accelerators." • "Vehicle revved high, when shifted into reverse car took off at very high speed, hit curb and tree, brakes didn't stop car." • "Car in drive, engine surged, hit another vehicle and continued 40-50 yards until key turned off." • "Car experienced sudden acceleration, incident began with idling, engine surge and car lurched forward, resulted in accident." • "Throttle on vehicle stuck open, causing an accident."

3. Brakes: hydraulic: anti-skid system, locking up, failure. • "Antilock brake system sometimes grabs and other times shoots forward." • "Recurring antilock brake malfunction." • "Repeated problems with brake lockup—several pads/rotors repaired/replaced." • "Antilock brake didn't work and car skidded, resulting in accident."

Buick

BUICK CENTURY 1987

Complaint Severity: Typical. **Buyer's Summary:** The electronic control unit has been blamed for performance problems. Make sure the car doesn't stall or hesitate: The fuel injection system has been blamed for hesitation and stalling. Be sure the vehicle doesn't die in traffic or at stops. The steering may be stiff or not working correctly. Be sure to test the steering, especially on a cold start. Check the brakes—listen for noise, look for leaks and feel for vibration. They may fail, perform poorly or require frequent mechanical attention. Test the transmission thoroughly. See "Sudden Accelerations" in Introduction.

Hot Spots and Owner/NHTSA Comments:

1. Fuel: fuel injection system, hesitation, stalling. • "Vehicle is stalling in traffic and losing steering and brakes." • "Vehicle has stalling and surging problems, also cuts off and smells." • "Stalling problem; accident occurred when car went dead—ran stop sign, car went into a ditch, driver injured." • "Vehicle will stall without any warning at high and low speeds." • "Vehicle stalls at idle when warm—engine surges when cold, requiring 15-20 ft pressure on power brakes to keep from moving forward." • "Car hesitates, backfires, dies after proceeding from stop, making turns; replaced crank and cam sensor, fuel pump, module, problem not corrected."

2. Electrical system: ignition: electronic control unit, failure. • "Car loses power on highway, stalls out when at stop light." • "Reoccurring engine stalling problem at highway speeds, replaced ignition module and sensors 3 times." • "Computer went out at 20,000 miles, engine surging when at complete stop, continuous stalling." • "Faulty computer chip, vehicle stalls on coast down, replaced programmable read only memory." • "Engine stalling after long trips, highways, slowing down, turning corner; replaced computer chip or programmable read-only memory." • "Driving on superhighway, engine just quit; also occurred when car slowing down slightly or turning corner; replaced computer chip."

3. Steering: gear: rack-and-pinion, stiffness, failure. • "When cold, steering hard to turn, especially to right, OK after it warms up." • "Power steering lost in early morning or initial start up." • "Gradual loss of power steering at 3,982 miles, sudden loss of power steering at highway speeds." • "Defective power steering system, replaced power steering pump twice, replaced rack-and-pinion." • "Power steering erratic; hard to turn sometimes, then it returns to normal." • "Power steering very sluggish almost nonexistent first thing in morning or after car sits for while without being driven."

4. Fuel: throttle linkages and control, sudden acceleration. • "While driving at approximately 45 mph, suddenly engine surged and raced to 70 mph without prior warning; stopped vehicle by applying both feet to brake pedal." • "Throttle position sensor stuck behind lever, causing throttle to stay open." • "Car took off, went through garage door and out through back wall." • "Car took off at high speed when shifted into drive." • "Started car and shifted from park to drive, accelerated suddenly into neighbor's house; brakes ineffective, car totally ruined."

5. Power train: transmission: automatic, difficulty shifting, failure. • "Premature transmission failure." • "Rough shift in transmission, also experienced periodic downshifting, later started disengaging during acceleration; rebuilt." • "While making left turn on street, car went into reverse, moving backwards striking a vehicle." • "Car started drifting and would not go forward or backwards; replaced fluid pump and shaft, adjusted converter." • "Transmission failure, slips out of gear while in operation and accelerates to fast speed, results in jerking, noises, poor performance." • "Excessive play and jerk in transmission when accelerating and decelerating."

6. Brakes: hydraulic system, noise, locking up. • "Brakes lost effectiveness, and greater distances traveled." • "Brake failure, applied brakes, impact 12:00 position, speed 15 mph, loss of brake effectiveness." • "Vehicle fishtailed when braking, wheels locked on wet roads, skidded, accident occurred." • "Defective brake system, makes squeaky/grinding noise when applied; replaced drums, shoes, rotors and pads." • "Brakes make squealing noise when stopping." • "Inadequate braking system, brakes are marginal."

BUICK CENTURY 1988

Complaint Severity: Typical. **Recall Alert:** See Recall Index. **Buyer's Summary:** The electronic control unit has been blamed for engine performance problems, including stalling and surging. The fuel injection system has been blamed for hesitation and stalling. Be sure the vehicle doesn't die in traffic or at stops. Check the brakes—listen for noise, look for leaks and feel for vibration. They may fail, perform poorly or require frequent mechanical attention. Test the transmission thoroughly. See "Sudden Accelerations" in Introduction.

Hot Spots and Owner/NHTSA Comments:

1. Fuel: throttle linkages and control, sudden acceleration. • "Went to start vehicle; it jumped forward, causing accident." • "While parked with emergency brake on, car accelerated backward and landed inside a showroom." • "Engine speeds up and vehicle surges forward when stopped." • "Accident/injuries due to sudden acceleration in reverse." • "While getting out of parking lot, wheels abruptly turned and enormous acceleration ensued, caused car to rush ahead and hit several other cars." • "Vehicle would suddenly accelerate when driving at 30-50 mph, creating potential accident risk."

2. Fuel: fuel injection system, stalling. • "Vehicle intermittently stalls while driving at 50 mph due to defective mass air flow sensor." • "Engine stalled at a critical time; loss of power steering and power brakes." • "Intermittent stalling." • "Persistent engine stalling, problem oxygen/crank repaired/replaced, rough shifting of transmission; stalling and rough shifting stopped, then condition started again." • "Stalling problem."

3. Electrical system: ignition: electronic control unit, failure. • "While driving, engine suddenly stopped; found defective mass air flow sensor; replaced sensor and electronic control module, which was also defective, car stills stalls and runs rough." • "Electronic control module short caused car to stall." • "Vehicle stalls in traffic and dies out without any prior warning." • "Engine races when car is first started and picks up speed when backing up or parking, cuts out on long run at highway speeds." • "Car stalled going downhill at 35 mph, steering wheel mechanism tightens up, limiting steering ability of vehicle; possible computer chip failure."

4. Brakes: hydraulic: shoe: disc brake system, premature failure. • "Intermittent poor braking, front brakes noisy." • "Front brake pulsation, hard to stop, front rotors warped, repeated failure." • "Premature wear of front brakes." • "Repeated brake failure, brakes failed; pedal was applied and car wouldn't stop, accident resulted from brake failure." • "Recurring problem with front brakes, repaired/replaced front pads and calipers, turned rotors several times." • "Caliper mounting pin had burr on it, causing pin to strip out on casting, turned rotors, installed pads and rebuilt caliper kit."

5. Power train: transmission: automatic, difficulty shifting. • "While driving, transmission jumps out of gear; caused vehicle to stall and buck." • "Transmission will not change from 2nd into high gear when in drive." • "Replaced transmission twice." •

"Cable noisy when shifting from park to drive, repaired/replaced cable." • "Transmission burned out; dealer replaced it."

6. Brakes: hydraulic system, poor performance, failure. • "While driving at 35 mph on suburban road, applied brakes to avoid hitting a car in front of vehicle, brakes failed and pedal went to floor." • "Brakes failed." • "Repeated brake vibration, repaired/replaced since purchase." • "Intermittent poor braking, front brakes noisy, rotors out of round, refaced rotors." • "Brakes did not stop car in usual distance allowed, would not slow down properly." • "Unspecified problems with brakes."

BUICK CENTURY 1989

Complaint Severity: Typical. **Recall Alert:** See Recall Index. **Buyer's Summary:** The engine has experienced a variety of problems. Have it examined by a professional. The electronic control unit has been blamed for engine performance problems, including stalling and surging. Check the brakes—listen for noise, look for leaks and feel for vibration. They may fail, perform poorly or require frequent mechanical attention. Test the transmission thoroughly. See "Sudden Accelerations" in Introduction.

Hot Spots and Owner/NHTSA Comments:

1. Electrical system: ignition: electronic control unit, failure. • "Computer failed while braking for stop light, caused engine to stall; dashboard lights came on, car could not be restarted; constantly loud." • "Faulty electronic control module, dashboard lights came on; replaced." • "Computer failure, engine quits, starts hard; replaced under warranty." • "Engine stalls due to a faulty electronic control module." • "Intermittent stalling due to computer wiring failure."

2. Brakes: hydraulic system, premature failure. • "Brakes squeaking, replaced." • "Brakes have been replaced twice within 34,000 miles." • "Brakes malfunctioning, calipers not working, brake pads approximately half worn down to metal, and both rear wheel cylinders leaking." • "Brakes need excessive pressure to stop, also to keep vehicle from not moving." • "Brakes squeaking." • "Extended stopping distance."

3. Fuel: throttle linkages and control, sudden acceleration. • "When removing foot from gas pedal, car accelerates; while pedal does not stick, excessive braking must be applied to slow or stop engine." • "When put into reverse gear, engine races, need to depress brake pedal harder to slow or stop." • "Accident due to sudden acceleration." • "Failure to decelerate upon release of throttle and increasing acceleration without throttle." • "Backing out of driveway, vehicle went into open throttle position, impact 3:00 position, lost control hitting rock piles, which did underbody damage."

4. Power train: transmission: automatic, difficulty shifting, failure. • "When weather is cold have a hard time starting the car; engine and transmission are noisy year-round." • "Shifting problems in transmission; when accelerating, there's long lag before shifting." • "Transmission sometimes jerks/slaps into place." • "Transmission replaced twice, downshifted from overdrive to first without warning while traveling at 65 mph, transmission burned out." • "Transmission replaced."

5. Engine, miscellaneous problems. • "Main bearing oil seal failed." • "Rear main seal needs replacing." • "Serpentine belts are noisy." • "Bearing knock." • "Engine oil leak."

6. Brakes: hydraulic: disc: rotor: disc hub, vibration. • "Brakes have slight intermittent grabbing, seems like rotors out of round." • "Front disc brake rotor wear excessive and premature." • "Rotors on front brakes warped and caused brakes to shimmy when applied." • "Front brake rotors were out of round, which caused brakes to pulsate when vehicle stopped at a red light or at stop sign." • "Recurring problem with brakes pulsating due to warped rotors; turned rotors down several times, also adjusted brakes and turned drums." • "Brakes are pulsating and squeaking, rotors have been ground twice."

BUICK CENTURY 1990

Complaint Severity: Typical. **Recall Alert:** See Recall Index. **Buyer's Summary:** The electronic control unit has been blamed for engine performance problems, including stalling and surging. Check the brakes—listen for noise, look for leaks and feel for vibration. They may fail, perform poorly or require frequent mechanical attention. Test the transmission thoroughly. Make sure seat belts function correctly and fit comfortably. See "Sudden Accelerations" in Introduction.

Hot Spots and Owner/NHTSA Comments:

1. Fuel: throttle linkages and control, sudden acceleration. • "Car does not decelerate when you take your foot off the accelerator pedal." • "Started vehicle, when put in reverse went crazy, feeding itself gas; accident resulted." • "Throttle stuck, caused unwanted rapid acceleration; resulted in accident." • "Unable to control speed of car due to accelerator sticking, accident resulted." • "Shifted from park to drive, vehicle surged forward." • "Throttle stuck in open position; vehicle surged forward, hitting two parked cars; no prior warning." • "Upon starting, shifted gear from park to drive position with foot on brake pedal, engine surged then suddenly accelerated, hitting cars two car lengths away."

2. Interior systems: passive restraint: belts, poor performance. • "Placements of seat belts in door are wide and block side views in back left across car to right." • "Seat belt crosses at neck; extra pad added to front seat, still crosses at neck, if hit from behind and thrown, belt would choke wearer." • "Bad design of seat belt, both ends attached to door before being used; in accident, if door opens there is loss of protection, wearer could be thrown out." • "Automatic lap/shoulder belts installed in driver/passenger seat are ineffective in restraining a wearer; when door is opened, belts pull wearer toward open door." • "Seat belts are on door; if you were to have an accident, they would not save a life—comes across neck and would break neck."

3. Power train: transmission: automatic, failure. • "Transmission stopped operating twice, which resulted in low mileage." • "Automatic transmission defect." • "When shift lever indicator is in park, the transmission is in drive." • "Transmission slips, or shifts in and out of gears." • "Transmission vibrates when it shifts from one gear to another."

4. Interior systems: shoulder belts, failure. • "The passenger's and driver's seat belts have no tension." • "Shoulder strap belts fit along face and neck of passengers, rub into cheek—uncomfortable and irritating; use can be dangerous in case of accident." • "Shoulder belt mounted too high, rubs side of face and obstructs view." • "Shoulder seat belt on driver's side is poorly designed, improper fit around driver's neck." • "Poor and dangerous location of front seat belt support bracket, belt comes across 5′ 2″ person's body way too high up, edge of belt touches neck—uncomfortable."

5. Electrical system: ignition: electronic control unit, failure. • "Electronic control module failure, car stopped twice." • "While traveling on interstate, vehicle lost all power." • "Vehicle stalls while driving due to defective computer system that has been replaced 4 times." • "Electronic control module failed, causing vehicle to stall." • "Due to defective computer chip programmable read-only memory, vehicle shuts completely down when driving at 60 mph on highway."

6. Brakes: hydraulic system, noise, corrosion. • "Vehicle accelerated at a high rate of speed when driver started vehicle and put into gear. Brakes were applied but did not stop vehicle." •

"Brakes noisy." • "Brakes squeak." • "While driving, ride became very rough; smoke from right side because of locking up of brakes, which was caused by rusting of components."

BUICK CENTURY 1991

Complaint Severity: Typical. **Recall Alert:** See Recall Index. **Buyer's Summary:** Verify that the cruise control system works properly, and that it doesn't cause the engine to surge. Test the suspension by feeling for vibration or pulling while driving. Test the transmission thoroughly. See "Sudden Accelerations" in Introduction. Make sure the seat belts are comfortable.

Hot Spots and Owner/NHTSA Comments:

1. Fuel: throttle linkages and control, sudden acceleration. • "After gear was shifted into reverse, vehicle suddenly accelerated out of control; resulted in an accident." • "Car will not slow down when foot is taken from gas pedal." • "Power surge in engine, slipping into gear, jumped over 2-foot curb." • "Vehicle suddenly accelerated upon leaving idling position to drive, causing loss of control and crashing into 6 other vehicles." • "Went to move rented car, started engine with foot on brake and gear in drive, vehicle suddenly accelerated, went over a brick wall and through a fence." • "After starting up, shifted into drive, engine accelerated to high speed across front yard into lawn furniture. No prior warning."

2. Equipment: speed control, failure. • "The cruise control does not work—vehicle just took off about 80 mph, car was completely out of control." • "Cruise control was inoperable after purchase." • "While driving with cruise control on at 50 mph, pressed brake pedal to slow down, but cruise control failed to disengage and maintained a speed of 50 mph." • "Plastic part of cruise control broke."

3. Interior systems: active seat and shoulder belts and belt anchor, uncomfortable. • "Seat belts fit short people poorly; driver is 5′1″, seat belt extends over neck, chin and cheek, chafes neck and head." • "Seat belts do not fit properly; they cut across the face." • "Front seat belts are attached to the doors, wearer could be ejected from vehicle during a collision or at other times." • "Top anchor of seat belt on door is too high or too far forward."

4. Power train: transmission: automatic, slipping. • "Transmission jumps from gear to gear." • "Noisy transmission." • "Power surge in engine, slipping into gear, jumped over 2-foot curb." • "Vehicle slipped into reverse, causing accident."

5. Suspension: independent front, pulling, alignment. • "Vehicle vibrates when speed is increased." • "Vehicle pulls to the right." • "Vehicle is difficult to control because alignment stays out of specs." • "Vehicle drifts to right."

BUICK CENTURY 1992

Complaint Severity: Serious. **Recall Alert:** See Recall Index. **Buyer's Summary:** Make sure the shoulder belts don't cut across your neck and are well anchored. Check the brakes—listen for noise, look for leaks and feel for vibration. They may fail, perform poorly or require frequent mechanical attention. See "Sudden Accelerations" in Introduction.

Hot Spots and Owner/NHTSA Comments:

1. Interior systems: shoulder belts, uncomfortable. • "Shoulder strap comes across the neck." • "The car was in an accident; the seat belts failed and killed the driver and broke the passenger's neck." • "Shoulder strap has no adjustment." • "Seat shoulder belt cuts into neck."

2. Fuel: throttle linkages and control, sudden acceleration. • "Vehicle suddenly accelerated from 25 mph to unknown high speed, causing loss of vehicle control, and ran into an embankment and a tree." • "Sudden acceleration after stopping at a sign, vehicle hit a pole, impact 12:00 position position, speed 50 mph." • "Experienced sudden acceleration, vehicle went into open throttle position, turned ignition off to stop vehicle." • "Foot on brake, shifted to reverse, vehicle surged rearward." • "While in reverse, the car began to accelerate, tried to apply brakes and vehicle continued to accelerate."

3. Brakes: hydraulic: shoe: disc brake system, failure. • "Left front wheel gets very hot and pulls to the left when braking." • "Premature wear of front brakes." • "Front brakes failed. Warning light never acknowledged failure. Front tires were hot." • "Disc/shoe brakes; brakes will not maintain adjustment. Vehicle has struck rear of another vehicle and a boat due to poor response."

BUICK CENTURY 1993

Complaint Severity: Serious. **Recall Alert:** See Recall Index. **Buyer's Summary:** Check the brakes—listen for noise, look for leaks and feel for vibration. They may fail, perform poorly or require frequent mechanical attention. Test the transmission thoroughly. See "Sudden Accelerations" in Introduction.

Hot Spots and Owner/NHTSA Comments:

1. Power train: transmission: automatic, difficulty shifting, failure. • "Transmission failure." • "Transmission fails to shift." • "Transmission problems." • "Vibration in transmission." • "Transmission intermittently jumps from overdrive into neutral, causing vehicle to roll."

2. Fuel: throttle linkages and control, sudden acceleration. • "Sudden acceleration caused loss of control/accident." • "Experienced sudden acceleration after putting vehicle in drive. Lost control, hitting a palm tree. Impact 12:00 position. Speed unknown. Airbag deployed." • "Consumer was putting car into the garage and car accelerated out of control, resulting in an accident." • "Vehicle suddenly accelerated out of control when engaged in drive, regained control, put it in park and vehicle accelerated forward again."

3. Brakes: hydraulic system, failure. • "Brakes intermittently lock up, causing you to pull off highway and drive in reverse for brakes to release." • "Delayed brake response during panic stopping." • "Brakes do not work properly, pushing pedal very hard slows car slowly. Pedal goes almost to the floor." • "Brake failure, extended stopping distance when brakes applied."

BUICK CENTURY 1994

Complaint Severity: Typical. **Recall Alert:** See Recall Index. **Buyer's Summary:** Make sure the door locks work correctly.

Hot Spots and Owner/NHTSA Comments:

1. Equipment: electric power accessories: locks: door, failure. • "Power door locks not functioning correctly." • "Doors automatically unlock when vehicle put in park." • "Automatic door opener replaced." • "Power door lock recall repairs refused due to unavailability of parts." • "Vehicle fire, originating under the dash, prior to power door lock recall."

BUICK ELECTRA 1987

Complaint Severity: Typical. **Recall Alert:** See Recall Index. **Buyer's Summary:** Verify that the cruise control system works properly, and that it doesn't cause the engine to surge. The electronic control unit has been blamed for engine performance problems, including stalling and surging. The fuel injection system has been blamed for hesitation and stalling. Be sure the vehicle doesn't die in traffic or at stops. Check the brakes—listen for noise, look for leaks and feel for vibration. They may fail, perform poorly or require frequent mechanical attention. See "Sudden Accelerations" in Introduction.

Hot Spots and Owner/NHTSA Comments:

1. Fuel: fuel injection system, stalling. • "Engine stalls under all operating conditions, will restart after few minutes." • "Engine stalling problems occur at all speeds." • "Continuous stalling problem; all repair attempts to no avail." • "Engine stalls and cuts off when braking or coming to a stop." • "Vehicle will cut out, stall while driving on expressway and in traffic; loss of power."

2. Fuel: throttle linkages and control, sudden acceleration. • "Car suddenly accelerated backwards into a building." • "Vehicle jumps forward when approaching a traffic light; problem with the fuel injection system; when the car accelerates there is no control over car." • "Sudden and unanticipated acceleration for no apparent reason." • "Uncontrolled sudden acceleration upon starting vehicle, resulting in accident." • "Upon shifting into drive, car shot forward, rear-ended another vehicle."

3. Electrical system: ignition: electronic control unit, failure. • "Engine dies completely while in motion, no power steering or power brakes." • "Engine stalling problems, stalls at any speed; also idles roughly." • "While traveling, engine just cut off, no warning, all power lost, defect in programmable read-only memory, repaired/replaced; also stalling governor." • "Car cuts off when getting off expressway, almost causing accidents, repaired/replaced chips and air damper motor, readjusted computer to no avail." • "Stalling at any speed, when idling at a full stop, decelerating or accelerating with no steering or brakes; replaced programmable read-only memory and idle control valve."

4. Brakes: hydraulic system, noise, failure. • "Brakes squeal and bind against hub." • "When applying brakes, there is chattering and pulsation; repaired under warranty once, but problem has recurred." • "Car has developed violent shaking whenever brakes are applied." • "Accident due to brake failure, brake pedal went all the way to floor." • "Front brakes repaired every 8,000 miles."

5. Equipment: speed control, sudden acceleration. • "Cruise control causes speed to vary too much, it doesn't hold when it should, when cruise turned off, car accelerated by itself." • "While driving, vehicle suddenly accelerated, slipping into cruise mode." • "Recall notice not received for cruise control problem." • "Cruise control failure; new control installed." • "Part of the cruise control piece fell off, leaving wipers going constantly."

6. Electrical system: ignition, failure. • "Vehicle intermittently stalls." • "Engine stalling problems." • "Engine hesitates and stalls." • "Vehicle stalled without warning." • "Defective modules and sensors caused vehicle to completely die, repaired/replaced."

BUICK ELECTRA 1988

Complaint Severity: Typical. **Buyer's Summary:** Verify that the cruise control system works properly, and that it doesn't cause the engine to surge. The fuel injection system has been blamed for hesitation and stalling. Be sure the vehicle doesn't die in traffic or at stops. The steering may be stiff or not working correctly. Be sure to test the steering, especially on a cold start. Check the brakes—listen for noise, look for leaks and feel for vibration. They may fail, perform poorly or require frequent mechanical attention. Test the transmission thoroughly. See "Sudden Accelerations" in Introduction.

Hot Spots and Owner/NHTSA Comments:

1. Fuel: throttle linkages and control, sudden acceleration. • "Upon starting up vehicle with foot on brake, it suddenly accelerated in reverse out of control, jumped curb and crashed into a school building." • "Shifted from park to reverse; immediately, without applying accelerator, engine raced up, car abruptly, uncontrollably started in reverse very fast." • "Vehicle will continue to run thousands of feet after removing foot from gas pedal with no slowing down." • "When shifting gear from park to drive, car shot forward from zero mph to 50-60 mph, motor raced; applied brakes to stop vehicle." • "Vehicle took off while foot on brake pedal, ran into another car."

2. Power train: transmission: automatic, difficulty shifting. • "Vehicle has harsh up and down shifting in high-altitude areas, especially on slippery pavement." • "Shifting drive lever to reverse would cause dramatic clunk when shifting from park to reverse and when going back from drive to reverse." • "Problem with transmission; adjusted linkage." • "Vehicle exhibits rough shifting pattern, gear continually slips from gear to gear." • "Paint chips found in automatic transmission filter."

3. Equipment: speed control, failure. • "Unspecified cruise control problem." • "Unspecified cruise control malfunction." • "Cruise problem." • "Due to defective servo bail in cruise control assembly, vehicle experiences sudden acceleration when nylon bushing fails; 4 replacements." • "Cruise control would not disengage."

4. Steering: gear: rack-and-pinion, stiffness, failure. • "Cold power steering." • "Power steering seems tight." • "Rack-and-pinion steering binds in cold starts." • "Power steering inoperative if outside temperatures 20 degrees Fahrenheit or below for approximately 2 blocks, until warmed up." • "Severe steering problem due to faulty rack-and-pinion."

5. Brakes: hydraulic: shoe: disc brake system, excessive wear, noise. • "Noisy front brakes." • "Discs brakes out of round." • "Front brakes pulsate, discs wobble, discs have to be turned and new pads added." • "Brakes in front continue to wear excessively."

6. Fuel: fuel injection system, stalling. • "Lack of response, poor mileage, car has no get-up-and-go." • "Stalling problem, sometimes it takes about 40 minutes to get it running." • "Car would just die in traffic or going down steep grade at speed limit, and would not restart." • "Car cut off on 3 different occasions at 72 mph on highway, caused by module/crank sensor failures."

BUICK ELECTRA 1989

Complaint Severity: Typical. **Buyer's Summary:** Verify that the cruise control system works properly, and that it doesn't cause the engine to surge. The electronic control unit has been blamed for engine performance problems, including stalling and surging. See "Sudden Accelerations" in Introduction.

Hot Spots and Owner/NHTSA Comments:

1. Electrical system: ignition: electronic control unit, failure. • "Electronic control module failed." • "Stalling due to electronic control module failure; repaired." • "Computer stopped functioning." • "Engine suddenly stalled while in motion, due to module failure." • "Malfunction in computer chip, causing stalling, backfire, quitting." • "Electronic control module operates erratically, causes vehicle to stall."

2. Equipment: speed control, failure. • "Cruise control failed at 17,000 miles." • "Cruise control does not engage 30 percent of time." • "Cruise control sometimes works fine, other times engages with force, causing jerk; exceeds speed programmed, feels like throttle wide open." • "Defective cruise control module; replacement lasted 2 months and no longer working correctly; upon engagement let speed drop to zero." • "Defective cruise control, cuts out again and again when in use, would cut off while passing other vehicle or going up or down hill."

3. Fuel: throttle linkages and control, sudden acceleration. • "Sudden acceleration and surge while driving at 35 mph." • "Vehicle suddenly accelerated to top rpm upon putting in reverse gear, resulted in accident." • "When car in motion and accelerator pedal released, engine rpm stays at whatever rpm it is using, remains there even if shifted to neutral, until coming to complete stop." • "When brakes were applied, vehicle couldn't stop; vehicle continued to accelerate, which resulted in an accident."

BUICK LESABRE 1987

Complaint Severity: Serious. **Recall Alert:** See Recall Index. **Buyer's Summary:** Verify that the cruise control system works properly, and that it doesn't cause the engine to surge. The electronic control unit has been blamed for engine performance problems, including stalling and surging. The fuel injection system has been blamed for hesitation and stalling. Be sure the vehicle doesn't die in traffic or at stops. Check the brakes—listen for noise, look for leaks and feel for vibration. They may fail, perform poorly or require frequent mechanical attention. Test the transmission thoroughly. See "Sudden Accelerations" in Introduction.

Hot Spots and Owner/NHTSA Comments:

1. Fuel: throttle linkages and control, sudden acceleration. • "From a stop position, vehicle accelerates slowly on its own as if you had 'resume' on cruise control." • "Uncontrolled sudden acceleration upon starting car, pumping brakes would not stop car, resulting in accident." • "Unintended sudden acceleration in reverse gear for about 50 feet." • "Car accelerated backwards at top speed with foot on brakes, after putting into reverse; to stop acceleration, turned off ignition." • "Throttle stuck, car accelerated out of control, causing an accident."

2. Fuel: fuel injection system, stalling. • "Fuel injection system malfunction, engine stops when hot or cold." • "Engine stalls at odd times, always restarts immediately." • "Car stalls frequently while driving and/or idling at traffic light stops." • "Sudden engine stalling, causing loss of brakes and steering at high speed." • "Defective fuel injection, car dies on highway or side street doing 25-55 mph." • "Car occasionally stalls while slowing to make a turn or stopping for traffic lights."

3. Power train: transmission: automatic, difficulty shifting. • "Transmission shifts in a very hard and rough manner; rebuilt transmission 4 times." • "Transmission replaced due to erratic downshifting." • "Transmission suffers occasional lockup, which prevents engagement of reverse gear." • "Transmission shifter sticks and binds, requiring excessive effort." • "Automatic transmission failure at 2,000 miles, shifts extremely rough; replaced."

4. Electrical system: ignition: electronic control unit, failure. • "Vehicle stalls 4 to 5 times within distance of one mile or two, stalls only intermittently after that, programmable read-only memory needed replacing." • "Defective electronics, vehicle stalls; interrupt sensor replaced." • "Engine stalls driving at 65 mph or stopping with engine running, starts again when shift to park and turn key; replaced computer chip didn't solve problem." • "Computer chip failure, motor stopped when driving, in middle of traffic, on freeway or on curves." • "Vehicle accelerates on its own without foot on gas pedal, also stalls, doesn't idle down, replaced electronic control module, same problems with another vehicle."

5. Brakes: hydraulic system, failure. • "Brakes have had low brake pedal, leak brake fluid." • "Brake inoperative, goes all the way to floor." • "Driver couldn't stop car in time, hit car in front." • "Brakes go down too far to floor, allowing only half inch from floor." • "In emergency, braking action is only 70 percent, does not stop properly." • "Vehicle suffers chronic brake failure, with no braking capability at all."

6. Equipment: speed control, sudden acceleration, malfunction. • "While driving at night at 90 mph, cruise control would not disengage, rear-ended another vehicle, finally stopped by turning off ignition." • "While driving, set cruise control, all of sudden without warning car would accelerate, continue to accelerate until brake pressed to shut off cruise control." • "Problem of acceleration when cruise control on and when not pressing gas pedal, especially when in decelerating mode like turning or stopping." • "Cruise control malfunction, power surges, then fails to hold speed." • "Cruise control doesn't hold at speed set, slows down on its own, other times surges forward beyond speed set."

BUICK LESABRE 1988

Complaint Severity: Typical. **Recall Alert:** See Recall Index. **Buyer's Summary:** The fuel pump has received complaints: Make sure it doesn't make excessive noise and that you are experiencing adequate engine performance. Also, look for leaks. Verify that the cruise control system works properly, and that it doesn't cause the engine to surge. The fuel injection system has been blamed for hesitation and stalling. Be sure the vehicle doesn't die in traffic or at stops. The steering may be stiff or not working correctly. Be sure to test the steering, especially on a cold start. Check the brakes—listen for noise, look for leaks and feel for vibration. They may fail, perform poorly or require frequent mechanical attention. See "Sudden Accelerations" in Introduction.

Hot Spots and Owner/NHTSA Comments:

1. Fuel: throttle linkages and control, sudden acceleration. • "Vehicle suddenly accelerated, causing loss of control and resulting in accident." • "Sudden acceleration when starting from parked position." • "Vehicle accelerated forward suddenly, literally out of control, did not respond to braking." • "Shifted into gear, car suddenly accelerated out of control, brakes ineffective; hit another vehicle." • "Backed out of parking space, then put car in drive gear, it sped ahead, applied brakes and turned wheel to left; accident occurred." • "When shifted into reverse, vehicle accelerated and crashed into 2 vehicles."

2. Brakes: hydraulic system, fade, pulsate. • "Brake pedal fades on several occasions, regain pressure by pumping brakes; accident." • "Brakes pulsating badly." • "Pulsating during hard downhill braking." • "Apparently, brakes fade." • "Applied brakes at speed of 20 mph, brake pedal went to floor, vehicle continued to travel with no reduction of speed; resulted in accident."

3. Fuel: fuel injection system, stalling. • "Engine stalls intermittently." • "Recurring problem with motor cutting off while in motion." • "Engine stalls, leaving car without power steering or brakes, restarts after pulling over." • "Engine keeps stalling in traffic while underway, rendering power steering and power brakes useless." • "Poor cold start."

4. Steering: gear: rack-and-pinion, stiffness. • "Rack-and-pinion problems; steering requires excessive physical effort." • "Extensive effort turning steering wheel, cold power steering." • "Rack-and-pinion steering seal was defective; it was difficult to make a hard left turn." • "Replaced rack-and-pinion and pump due to contamination of fuel." • "Rack-and-pinion steering locked in place; crash resulted."

5. Fuel: fuel pump, noise, failure. • "Fuel pump was making a loud humming noise; replaced fuel pump." • "Noisy fuel pump." • "Vehicle stalls and won't restart, has been towed 5 times, 5 fuel pumps have been replaced." • "Faulty fuel pump replaced 5 times." • "Car stalls while driving, hard to start when engine hot, repaired/replaced fuel pump."

6. Equipment: speed control, failure. • "Cruise control works for 12 miles, then it kicks in by itself, cannot be reset, kicks itself in after driving 12 to 15 miles or driving 20 minutes." • "Cruise control defect, engages itself, causing increase in speed." • "While using cruise control, mechanism would accelerate engine without operator touching control." • "Cruise very unreliable, won't shift down to help maintain the speed, mostly occurs when going up hill, will gain or lose speed; repaired many times, never fixed." • "Cruise control disengaged by itself, vehicle began to lose speed."

BUICK LESABRE 1989

Complaint Severity: Typical. **Recall Alert:** See Recall Index. **Buyer's Summary:** Verify that the cruise control system works properly, and that it doesn't cause the engine to surge. The engine has experienced a variety of problems: Have it examined by a professional. The electronic control unit has been blamed for engine performance problems, including stalling and surging. The fuel injection system has been blamed for hesitation and stalling. Be sure the vehicle doesn't die in traffic or at stops. Check the brakes—listen for noise, look for leaks and feel for vibration. They may fail, perform poorly or require frequent mechanical attention. Test the transmission thoroughly.

Hot Spots and Owner/NHTSA Comments:

1. Electrical system: ignition: electronic control unit, failure. • "Computer module replaced. Vehicle will lose power without warning while driving at any speed." • "Computer failure, engine began to miss and vibrate when warmed up, problem eventually traced to diode." • "Motor would stall when tried to go forward; replaced C3 module, and C3 crank sensor hitting." • "Defective computer system causes 'engine service' light to come on after driving approximately 10 miles." • "Defective electrical system, 'check engine' light in dash."

2. Equipment: speed control, failure. • "Cruise control doesn't stay active." • "Cruise control disengages by itself." • "Control switch failure." • "Faulty cruise control system; replaced by dealer." • "Cruise control activated, applied brake and cruise control would not disengage, vehicle lurched forward, resulting in warped and bent front brakes."

3. Fuel: fuel injection system, stalling. • "Intermittent stalling." • "About 5,000 miles, engine just stopped; repaired." • "Fuel injector module failed." • "Vehicle vibration, loss of power." • "Car stalled while in traffic; several repair attempts to no avail."

4. Power train: transmission: automatic, failure. • "After 41,000 miles the transmission froze up. Wouldn't shift out of 2nd gear; automatic. Replaced entire transmission." • "Transmission was completely shot, caused vehicle to stop in right lane of traffic and would not move." • "Transmission seal leaks, repaired." • "Shift cable comes loose; driver can't shift transmission or tell what gear it is in." • "Transmission failure, just stopped in middle of traffic with no prior warning of failure; premature failure."

5. Brakes: hydraulic system, vibration, failure. • "Experiencing recurring brake problem; repairs have been done, problem still unsolved." • "Vibration and/or pulsation experienced when applying brakes, vibration caused brake line to leak by wheel, repaired/replaced rotors and right rear drums, tightened torsion bar, no avail." • "Noisy brake, pedal went to floor on 3 occasions." • "Severe brake fading, grabbed, with severe pulling to right." • "Brakes replaced at 18,000 miles."

6. Engine, miscellaneous problems. • "Continuous air leak and noise from under hood; corrected." • "Vehicle stopped, causing rear-end accident." • "Problem with engine oil leak; all repair attempts to no avail." • "During heavy rain, at highway speeds, loud noise under hood followed by loss of power and speed. Unable to diagnose." • "Loss of power, resulting in loss of brakes and steering, and requiring excessive effort to exit off road."

BUICK LESABRE 1990

Complaint Severity: Typical. **Buyer's Summary:** Verify that the cruise control system works properly, and that it doesn't cause the engine to surge. The electronic control unit has been blamed for engine performance problems, including stalling and surging. Check the brakes—listen for noise, look for leaks and feel for vibration. They may fail, perform poorly or require frequent mechanical attention. Make sure seat belts function correctly and fit comfortably. See "Sudden Accelerations" in Introduction.

Hot Spots and Owner/NHTSA Comments:

1. Interior systems: passive restraint: belts, uncomfortable. • "Shoulder harness for front seat belt becomes slack when either occupant leans forward, turns or makes other minor movements." • "Seat belts not adjustable for 5′ 7″ tall person; driver's side seat belt goes across eyeglasses, while passenger's side belt cuts across neck." • "Due to changes in installing seat belt bracket located in corner of upper window, shoulder portion rides up over driver chin and neck—unsafe and uncomfortable." • "Once seat belt is anchored on body, it starts going around neck area, sometimes almost choking occupant." • "Problem with seat belt installation, can't wear belt while driving, strap goes to side of neck and hurts when buckled up."

2. Brakes: hydraulic system, pulling, failure. • "When starting, vehicle accelerated out of control, hitting building. Brakes smoked when trying to stop vehicle." • "Vehicle pulls to right upon application of the brakes, occurs at any speed." • "Brakes failed through intersection." • "Foot brake kept going to floor, smelled oil burning and heard hissing noise; repaired by bleeding brakes." • "Brakes malfunctioning; required replacing brakes and calipers."

3. Equipment: speed control, failure. • "On several long distance trips, after certain mileage, cruise control would not remain set. Dealership can't find cause, saying 'until it happens in shop.' " • "While cruise control was set at 60 mph, vehicle surged and accelerated to 70 mph plus; applied brakes to stop vehicle." • "Car stalls while cruise control is engaged." • "Cruise control doesn't always work, 'cruise' light comes on, but does not maintain the speed the cruise control has engaged."

4. Fuel: throttle linkages and control, sudden acceleration. • "Gear shifted into park position, with vehicle going open throttle position, losing control, impact 1:00 position, speed unknown." • "Had sudden acceleration in reverse, with no warning." • "When starting, vehicle accelerated out of control, hitting building. Brakes smoked while trying to stop vehicle." • "Shift lever moved to drive position, foot still on brakes, engine immediately raced in full throttle through end wall; injury received to head." • "Placed gear in drive and engine accelerated, moved rapidly straight ahead, hitting 3 parked cars."

5. Electrical system: ignition: electronic control unit, failure. • "Intermittent stalling." • "The vehicle has a stalling problem. Replaced idle air control valve, but vehicle still stalls." • "Brakes malfunctioned due to failed electronic control module, warning lights activated." • "Electronic control module turns off while driving, leaving vehicle with no power; electronic control module was replaced and vehicle continued to stall." • "Vehicle stalled; computer replaced." • "Engine stalls when in traffic and when coasting downhill, causes loss of brake effectiveness; electronic control module replaced."

BUICK LESABRE 1991

Complaint Severity: Typical. **Buyer's Summary:** Make sure the shoulder belts don't cut across your neck and are well anchored. The fuel injection system has been blamed for hesitation and stalling. Be sure the vehicle doesn't die in traffic or at stops. Carefully check the brakes—listen for noise, look for leaks and feel for vibration. They may fail, perform poorly or require frequent mechanical attention.

Hot Spots and Owner/NHTSA Comments:

1. Brakes: hydraulic system, failure. • "Brakes failed, causing accident." • "Brake failure; coming off a ramp and going down grade, pedal completely failed." • "Premature brake wear." • "At 6,000 miles vehicle needed new brakes; dealer said they were worn, replaced brake system." • "Brake failure caused accident."

2. Engine, failure. • "Engine failure." • "Vehicle lacking power on inclines." • "Oil pressure sending unit problems." • "Intermittent stalling." • "Oil sending unit failed."

3. Electrical system: ignition, failure. • "Driving at 45 mph and, without warning, engine died when driver lifted foot off gas pedal; vehicle lost all power." • "Engine stalls without warning in various types of driving conditions, especially in city traffic." • "Vehicle stalls constantly without warning, causes loss of control." • "Vehicle will stall intermittently when driving at any speed."

4. Fuel: fuel injection system, stalling. • "Intermittent stalling." • "Serious stalling problem." • "Intermittent stalling problems." • "Accident/injuries due to sudden acceleration; also severe stalling problem." • "Stalling problem; repaired."

5. Interior systems: shoulder belts, uncomfortable, failure. • "Front right passenger shoulder belt did not restrain passenger in head-on collision, resulting in injuries." • "Shoulder belts too high." • "Top strap of seat belt lays across the neck, not shoulder as it was supposed to." • "Front shoulder restraint cuts into driver's neck." • "Shoulder belt does not fit properly across the chest area; adjustment unavailable."

BUICK LESABRE 1992

Complaint Severity: Serious. **Recall Alert:** See Recall Index. **Buyer's Summary:** Verify that the cruise control system works properly, and that it doesn't cause the engine to surge. The airbags in this vehicle have experienced failures and malfunctions: You may need a professional evaluation on the condition of the airbags. Check the brakes—listen for noise, look for leaks and feel for vibration. They may fail, perform poorly or require frequent mechanical attention. Test the transmission thoroughly.

Hot Spots and Owner/NHTSA Comments:

1. Brakes: hydraulic: anti-skid system, failure. • "Antilock brake system: While exiting expressway ramp, applied brakes, pedal traveled to floor; pumping to no avail; brakes completely failed; no prior warning, speed 25 mph." • "Antilock brake system: Needed to brake for light, applied brakes, with pedal going to floor. Vehicle continued through intersection." • "Consumer was driving on a rainy day and tried to stop at light, car wouldn't stop, antilock brake system failed, resulting in loss of control; accident." • "Antilock brake system failed to stop vehicle, causing front-end collision at 40 mph." • "Antilock brake system brake controller overreacts to brake demands and modulates during slow easy stops. Light comes on, pulls right, wheels lock up: Dealer says no defect."

2. Interior systems: passive restraint: airbag: driver, failure. • "Vehicle was involved in a rear-end accident, the airbag did not deploy. GM doesn't respond to owner's questions." • "No deployment of airbag during collision." • "Airbag did not deploy during frontal collision, impact 12:00 position, speed 30 mph." • "Vehicle was involved in a front-end accident and the airbag did not deploy." • "Entering a construction area, vehicle in front of Buick suddenly stopped; applied brakes and they would not hold; airbag failed to deploy."

3. Brakes: hydraulic system, failure. • "Brake failure; pedal failed after applying brakes, vehicle went out of control, resulting in an accident." • "Parking brake failed, foot brake failed, put car in drive and car rolled into grass. Car rolled over." • "Brakes failed, resulting in loss of control; accident." • "Brakes noisy."

4. Electrical system: ignition, failure. • "While driving, vehicle stalls out with no warning." • "Vehicle will stall at any speed and at any time with no warning." • "Car is stalling for no apparent reason." • "Vehicle will stall at any speed while driving." • "Car stalled out without any warning in traffic on highway."

5. Power train: transmission: automatic, hesitation, difficulty shifting. • "Transmission would not shift gears." • "Vehicle jumped from park into reverse and caused an accident." • "Hole in transmission, causing transmission fluid leak, resulting in stalling and hesitation." • "Loss of power and excessive vibration when going uphill at 35 mph." • "Transmission jumped out of drive into 2nd gear."

6. Equipment: speed control, failure. • "Cruise control failed to operate at all speeds." • "Warning light on with cruise control." • "Speed sensor failed." • "Cruise control was set at 60 mph and vehicle accelerated past set speed without driver's foot on accelerator. Disengaged when turned off at steering wheel."

BUICK LESABRE 1993

Complaint Severity: Typical. **Buyer's Summary:** Look carefully for any kind of leakage, especially under the car. The fuel injection system has been blamed for hesitation and stalling. Be sure the vehicle doesn't die in traffic or at stops. The airbags in this vehicle have experienced failures and malfunctions: You may need a professional evaluation on the condition of the airbags. Check the brakes—listen for noise, look for leaks and feel for vibration. They may fail, perform poorly or require frequent mechanical attention. Test the transmission thoroughly. Leaks may also indicate a problem with the fuel lines.

Hot Spots and Owner/NHTSA Comments:

1. Brakes: hydraulic: anti-skid system, failure. • "Antilock brake system locked up." • "Antilock brake system does not perform to driver's expectations." • "Antilock brake system had 2 complete failures, with pedal going to floor on both occasions, once resulting in an accident." • "Antilock brake system malfunction, loss of braking ability." • "When antilock brake system applied, vehicle pulls to the right."

2. Interior systems: passive restraint: airbag: driver, failure. • "Airbag did not deploy." • "In accident at 30 mph, 12:00 position, driver's side airbag did not deploy, causing severe injuries to driver." • "Frontal collision, failure of antilock brake system, impact 12:00 position position, speed 50 mph, driver's side airbag did not deploy." • "Airbag did not inflate during accident." • "Owner was driving at 30 mph; when vehicle was involved in accident and airbag did not deploy; owner hit the steering wheel and was injured."

3. Brakes: hydraulic system, noise, failure. • "While in park with motor running, when brake pedal is depressed a loud clicking is heard and can be felt in steering column." • "Brake vibration, replaced drum and disc assembly." • "Brakes failed, causing extended stopping distances." • "Automatic transmission: Engine stalls; loss of brakes and power steering; no problem restarting in neutral; cause unknown; never know when problem will occur."

4. Fuel: fuel injection system, hesitation, stalling. • "Poor mileage." • "In for service. Vehicle caught fire after several hours of service. Owner heard popping noise, got out and saw flames on both sides engine block." • "Vehicle hesitation." • "Intermittent stalling and hesitation." • "Vehicle intermittently lacks sufficient power to access highways."

5. Fuel: fuel line fittings and pump, leaks, fire. • "Fuel line rupture on highway." • "Vehicle developed a fuel leak because of a disengaged hose." • "The O-ring and clamps were defective; the speedometer doesn't work." • "Gasoline leak due to weak fuel line clips." • "Vehicle caught on fire after first starting, idling for 5 minutes, due to defective fuel supply line. Vehicle totaled." • "Fuel line failed."

6. Power train: transmission: automatic, leaks, failure. • "Vehicle rolls back on hills." • "Vehicle loses power on incline, then shifts into overdrive." • "Transmission fluid leak caused vehicle fire." • "Automatic transmission: engine stalls; loss of brakes and power steering; no problem restarting in neutral; cause unknown, never know when problem will occur." • "Transmission failure."

BUICK LESABRE 1994

Complaint Severity: Troublesome. **Buyer's Summary:** The airbags in this vehicle have experienced failures and malfunctions: You may need a professional evaluation on the condition of your airbags. Check the brakes—listen for noise, look for leaks and feel for vibration. They may fail, perform poorly or require frequent mechanical attention. Make sure the headrests are in a proper position and are comfortable.

Hot Spots and Owner/NHTSA Comments:

1. Interior systems: passive restraint: airbag: driver, failure. • "Frontal collision impact 12:00 position position, vehicle was at complete stop, airbag did not deploy." • "Airbag did not deploy." • "Upon impact, during frontal crash at approximately 40 mph, 11:00 position, on front bumper, airbag failed to deploy; as a result, hit steering column." • "In a collision, driver's airbag did not deploy." • "No deployment of driver's airbag, resulting in driver hitting head on visor; injury."

2. Interior systems: seat head restraints, poor design. • "Headrests positioned too far back." • "Headrest cannot be adjusted to accommodate a tall person." • "Head restraints do not extend high enough for tall person; 4 inches too low; comes out below ear of 6′1″ occupant; involved in accident, causing injury." • "Headrest does not extend high enough." • "Head restraint not designed to be adjusted, causing discomfort."

3. Brakes: hydraulic system, failure. • "Brake system failed." • "Brakes did not respond when applied, vehicle traveled approximately 50 yards, hitting a building." • "Owner says the steering is defective and the brakes locked up." • "Vehicle shimmies when brakes are applied."

4. Interior systems: passive restraint: airbag: passenger, malfunction, failure. • "In a collision passenger's airbag did not deploy." • "Passenger-side airbag exploded upon impact; driver severely burned; both airbags deployed." • "Passenger's airbag location too close to heated expellent cartridge, causing airbag to overheat and catch fire." • "Passenger's airbag deployment was violent during collision, resulting in injuries."

BUICK PARK AVENUE 1991

Complaint Severity: Troublesome. **Recall Alert:** See Recall Index. **Buyer's Summary:** The airbags in this vehicle have experienced failures and malfunctions: You may need a professional evaluation on the condition of the airbags. Check the brakes—listen for noise, look for leaks and feel for vibration. They may fail, perform poorly or require frequent mechanical attention. Make sure the door locks and other electrical systems work. Test the door locks.

Hot Spots and Owner/NHTSA Comments:

1. Brakes: hydraulic: anti-skid system, failure. • "Antilock brake system completely failed and pedal hit the floor." • "Antilock brakes: Driving along an expressway, went to apply the brakes, pedal went to the floor." • "Coming off highway, applied brakes, pedal went to the floor." • "Antilock brake system: Loss of brake pressure when brakes where applied, failed to stop without warning, vehicle ran off highway to stop; underbody damages." • "The antilock brake system warning light came on; took to dealer; have to replace the whole system."

2. Brakes: hydraulic system, failure. • "Complete brake failure with pedal fading; caused an accident, impact 6:00 position, speed 15 mph and airbag did not deploy." • "When shifting gear from park, a noise was heard, then vehicle jerked and brakes locked up." • "Approaching a stop sign at an intersection, applied brakes and they failed; resulted in an accident; sustained 3 injuries and extensive damage." • "Brake area inside drum fills up with mud and water, causing brakes to malfunction." • "When brakes are depressed, car pulls to the extreme right."

3. Equipment: electric power accessories: locks: door, failure. • "Doors unlock when shifted to park." • "Electronic door lock system repeatedly failed, resulting in being locked out or being locked in. Replaced clip." • "Due to failure of actuator switch, all passenger door locks were inoperative, couldn't be opened or closed." • "Vehicle has electric door locks, driver's door has had problem opening. Now passenger rear door cannot be opened manually or otherwise."

4. Brakes: hydraulic: shoe: disc brake system, noise, failure. • "Following 30,000-mile service at Buick dealer, front brakes had a shrill whistle at 55 mph; when stopping to investigate, brake went to the floor." • "Front brakes grabbed and jerked, causing vehicle to go out of control." • "Experiencing problems with front brakes, metal-to-metal sound; had brakes changed 7 times." • "Defective front disc brakes resulted in extended stopping when applied."

5. Interior systems: passive restraint: airbag: driver, malfunction, failure. • "Airbag did not deploy during front-end collision at 35 mph, causing head injuries to driver." • "In a rear-end collision, airbag did not deploy." • "Frontal collision on wet road surface, impact at 1:00 position, speed 25 mph, airbag deployed practically just before getting out of vehicle." • "Airbag did not deploy during 3-car collision; car 1 was rear-ended and pushed into rear end of car 3; car 2 speed 50 mph, car 1 and 3 were at standstill." • "No deployment of airbag during collision caused injury."

6. Electrical system, miscellaneous problems. • "Intermittent electrical system problem, causing several component failures." • "Electrical problems." • "Continuous electrical problems." • "Electrical problems; oil light, battery failure, door locks, air conditioner and heat control."

BUICK PARK AVENUE 1992

Complaint Severity: Very Serious. **Buyer's Summary:** The airbags in this vehicle have experienced failures and malfunctions: You may need a professional evaluation on the condition of the airbags. Check the brakes—listen for noise, look for leaks and feel for vibration. They may fail, perform poorly or require frequent mechanical attention.

Hot Spots and Owner/NHTSA Comments:

1. Brakes: hydraulic: anti-skid system, failure. • "Vehicle stalls out at various speeds with no warning, and antilock brake system parts prematurely wear." • "Antilock brake system problems." • "Antilock brakes failed twice, causing loss of control." • "Antilock brake system malfunctioned, warning light came on during emergency braking, light went off, noticed fading of the pedal." • "Antilock brakes locked up when emergency parking brake was used in damp or wet weather."

2. Interior systems: passive restraint: airbag: driver, malfunction, failure. • "Airbag did not deploy; shoulder portion of lap and shoulder belt did not hold during impact at 12:00; car 1 rear-ended by car 2; car 1 rear-ended car 3." • "Driver's airbag did not inflate during accident, causing injury." • "Vehicle's driver's-side airbag did not deploy; 11:00 position at 20 mph." • "Airbag did deploy upon impact, but driver was severely burned by the acids that came from the airbag."

BUICK REGAL 1987

Complaint Severity: Minor. **Theft Alert:** 25. **Recall Alert:** See Recall Index. **Buyer's Summary:** Look carefully for any kind of leakage, especially under the car. Verify that the cruise control system works properly, and that it doesn't cause the engine to surge. The fuel injection system has been blamed for hesitation and stalling. Be sure the vehicle doesn't die in traffic or at stops. Check the brakes—listen for noise, look for leaks and feel for vibration. They may fail, perform poorly or require frequent mechanical attention. See "Sudden Accelerations" in Introduction.

Hot Spots and Owner/NHTSA Comments:

1. Brakes: hydraulic system, failure. • "Excessive effort needed to engage braking system due to a defective braking switch, has occurred on numerous occasions, GMC Recall totally inadequate." • "Pulsating brakes." • "Intermittent brake failure." • "Brakes squeaking and do not respond as should." • "Brakes failed numerous times, near-accidents; repaired/replaced 3 electric booster pumps, electronic brake pressure switch fails, drains reservoir, repaired/replaced 3 switches."

2. Brakes: hydraulic: power assist: vacuum system, leaks, failure. • "Power master brake system components failed twice." • "While driving, brakes failed, dashboard warning light came on, stopped car by putting transmission in low gear." • "Vehicle exhibits power brake problem, at various times needed to push hard on brakes to make car stop." • "While driving at various speeds, switch suddenly develops high-pressure leak, brake fluid expels under pressure, can hear fluid coming out of switch." • "Brake fluid reservoir has a hole, causing leakage that resulted in brake failure; repaired/replaced brake power master pump assembly and sensor."

3. Fuel: fuel injection system, stalling. • "Car repaired 5 times, stalling initially only when stopping; resulted in loss of steering and brakes." • "Chronic engine stalling problems, bucking and hesitation." • "Continuous cold condition, problem with lack of throttle response or acceleration until car warms up." • "Stalling of engine in heavy traffic at any speed." • "Intermittent stalling."

4. Fuel: throttle linkages and control, sudden acceleration. • "Vehicle experiences sudden surging, acceleration, lunging forward." • "Engine surging, especially before coming to a complete stop, engine hot, idle speed rough." • "Car suddenly accelerated while in motion, losing brakes, causing accident, brakes did not stop acceleration." • "While driving, vehicle accelerated out of control; driver injured." • "Put key in ignition, vehicle shot backward at a speed of 100 mph in reverse on its own."

5. Brakes: hydraulic: master cylinder, failure. • "The brakes on vehicle failed. Light comes on when pedal is depressed. Power master unit has to be replaced." • "Brakes failed without warning, hit car in front; repaired/replaced defective brake cylinder." • "Failure of master cylinder sensor diaphragm caused brake fluid to be sprayed out of sensor, resulted in complete brake failure." • "Master brake cylinder stopped working, then brake light came on; repaired/replaced master cylinder."

6. Equipment: speed control, sudden acceleration. • "Cruise control has set speed but keeps accelerating; seat belt will not retract." • "Cruise control switch is activated when activating turn signal lights, causing acceleration; resulted accident; installed O-ring to restrict switch action." • "Cruise control inoperative."

BUICK REGAL 1988

Complaint Severity: Typical. **Recall Alert:** See Recall Index. **Buyer's Summary:** The electronic control unit has been blamed for engine performance problems, including stalling and surging. The fuel injection system has been blamed for hesitation and stalling. Be sure the vehicle doesn't die in traffic or at stops. Check the brakes—listen for noise, look for leaks and feel for vibration. They may fail, perform poorly or require frequent mechanical attention.

Hot Spots and Owner/NHTSA Comments:

1. Brakes: hydraulic: disc: caliper, failure, locking up. • "Rear brakes totally gone out due to calipers freezing up; owner discovered brake problem when front brakes failed." • "Calipers close and do not reopen, resulting in loss of braking effectiveness." • "When going down a steep incline at 40 mph, brakes went out because of calipers locking up, causing disc pad to fall out." • "Both rear calipers locked up, making them inoperative; also resulting in possible brake pad fire." • "Calipers were sticking, causing brakes to fail, resulting in an accident."

2. Fuel: fuel injection system, stalling. • "Cold engine stalling and surging problem; when first started, car stalls when put in gear or surges uncontrollably." • "Engine stalls at high speed when accelerating and in reverse." • "Vehicle consistently stalls both while driving and when stopped; replacing crank sensor and valve have not helped." • "Engine stalls with no warning, while driving, sitting at traffic light, turning corner, parking, while moving at some speed, up to 30 mph." • "Car stalls on occasions during acceleration, won't restart without pumping pedal, occurs without warning."

3. Brakes: hydraulic: shoe: disc brake system, corrosion. • "Corroded disc brakes causing reduction in braking ability. Repaired 3 times." • "Corroded rear disc brakes; replaced twice." • "While driving, experienced rear disc brake failure when upon applying brake, pedal went to floor, no prior warning." • "Vehicles' braking systems have to have rotors and pads fixed every month." • "Experienced corrosion of rear brakes drags when brakes are applied, replacement parts calipers and disc pads and drums, and rotors repaired 8 times."

4. Electrical system: ignition: electronic control unit, stalling, malfunction. • "While slowing for stop sign, engine quit; lost braking and steering power." • "Computer chip faulty, engine stalls when driving at any speed, not accelerating or braking (coasting) would stop car." • "While driving, suddenly car loses power and does not stay in gear but cruises whatever direction wheels are in." • "Defective computer system caused repeated problems with digital dash, heater, seat belt, wipers and engine cut off, etc.; all repair attempts to no avail." • "Intermittent problem with car not starting, repaired/replaced programmable read-only memory chip."

BUICK REGAL 1989

Complaint Severity: Minor. **Recall Alert:** See Recall Index. **Buyer's Summary:** The electronic control unit has been blamed for engine performance problems, including stalling and surging. The fuel injection system has been blamed for hesitation and stalling. Be sure the vehicle doesn't die in traffic or at stops. Check the brakes—listen for noise, look for leaks and feel for vibration. They may fail, perform poorly or require frequent mechanical attention. Test the transmission thoroughly.

Hot Spots and Owner/NHTSA Comments:

1. Electrical system: ignition: electronic control unit, stalling, malfunction. • "While traveling on city street at 25 mph, vehicle, without any warning, stopped." • "Computer problems, causing stalling." • "Engine stalling problems, various modules in

computer system changed, stalling problem persists." • "Computer failed 3 times." • "Computer problem caused engine to stall."
2. Brakes: hydraulic system, failure. • "Rear brakes inoperable, causing front brakes to be replaced 5 times." • "During highway driving, applied brakes; pedal goes to floor, no braking effect; nearly caused accident." • "Brakes have poor stopping ability; takes a long time to stop at any speed." • "Driving in snow or rain, brakes get wet, do not hold, have to be pumped to take hold." • "Brake failure; serviced 3 times, problem continues."
3. Brakes: hydraulic: disc: caliper, failure, locking up. • "Rear caliper pins corrode, causing caliper assembly to bond, resulting in brake failure and accident." • "Rear calipers designed without bushing, causing premature brake wear." • "Rear disc brake calipers froze and caused complete brake failure." • "Rear calipers freeze up; front brakes do all the braking; seems to be an ongoing problem with parts; front pads wear out continuously." • "Rear disc calipers inoperative due to guide pin sleeves seizing."
4. Fuel: fuel injection system, stalling. • "Engine sluggish, not enough pickup to drive on expressway, black smoke comes from exhaust pipe, engine sometimes cuts off without warning." • "Intermittent hesitation and stalling." • "Intermittent stalling, idle and programmable read-only memory problems." • "Leak in the fuel injection system caused fire under hood." • "Vehicle continuously stalled on deceleration on highway, causing sudden loss of brakes and steering; problem could cause serious accident."
5. Brakes: hydraulic: shoe: disc brake system, corrosion, failure. • "Front disc brake pads defective, can't get 12,000 miles per set, now on fifth set front pads." • "Outsides of the front discs were rusty and brakes only worked partially." • "Rear disc brake pads and rotors rusted and corroded, causing brakes to become inoperative." • "Rear disc brake corrosion; excessive wear of front brake pads." • "Brakes don't respond to pedal when moving on cold start."
6. Power train: transmission: automatic, noise, slipping. • "Transmission fluid leak, causing failure." • "Noisy transmission when downshifting; replaced 2 times." • "Noisy transmission when shifting, electronic control module replaced." • "Transmission slipping problem keeps recurring."

BUICK REGAL 1990

Complaint Severity: Negligible. **Recall Alert:** See Recall Index. **Buyer's Summary:** Check the brakes—listen for noise, look for leaks and feel for vibration. They may fail, perform poorly or require frequent mechanical attention. Test the transmission thoroughly.

Hot Spots and Owner/NHTSA Comments:
1. Brakes: hydraulic: disc: caliper, corrosion, locking up. • "Rear brake pads rusted through to calipers." • "U frame and slides cause calipers to freeze." • "Corroded rear disc brakes; replaced calipers, pads and rotors." • "Rear brakes lock up without prior warning; replaced caliper and rotor." • "Rear caliper sleeves and retainers corroded and jammed; caused brakes to not work properly; caliper sleeves and retainers replaced."
2. Brakes: hydraulic system, excessive wear, failure. • "During normal driving efforts, depressing brake pedal gives no response." • "Extended stopping distance after repairs." • "Brakes wear excessively, front and back brakes have to be replaced every 5 to 6 months; when brakes applied they squeak." • "Rear brakes seize and/or wear out prematurely unless emergency brake is used when parked."
3. Power train: transmission: automatic, failure, leaks. • "The power transmission has been replaced 2 times, and the window wouldn't work." • "Transmission failure after replacement." • "Transmission oil leaked out, car only 6 months old." • "Problems putting into drive." • "Automatic transmission had only 1st gear."
4. Brakes: hydraulic: anti-skid system, failure. • "Antilock brake system wears excessively." • "Antilock brake system malfunction." • "Rear antilock brakes squeak and fail to stop vehicle effectively when applied at any speed." • "Antilock brake system: Front brakes replaced 4 times because rear brakes were not working." • "Antilock brake system failure, brake pedal went completely down to floor."

BUICK REGAL 1991

Complaint Severity: Minor. **Recall Alert:** See Recall Index. **Buyer's Summary:** Check the brakes—listen for noise, look for leaks and feel for vibration. They may fail, perform poorly or require frequent mechanical attention.

Hot Spots and Owner/NHTSA Comments:
1. Brakes: hydraulic system, failure. • "When brake pedal was applied, it went all the way to the floor without stopping vehicle." • "Brakes failed, causing vehicle to lose control." • "While driving, experienced intermittent brake failure, brake pedal became spongy then went to the floor, after stopping for 10 minutes pedal came back up." • "Stopping distance extended as a result of poor braking performance." • "As driver pulled into driveway, brakes failed, vehicle went out of control; involved in an accident, resulted in injuries and damage."
2. Brakes: hydraulic: shoe: disc brake system, premature failure. • "Master cylinder replacement; caused loss of brakes, experienced pedal fading and wear of calipers." • "Premature wear of front brakes." • "Four-wheel disc brake system has failed 7 times." • "Front brakes replaced every 6 months. Rear brakes rust." • "Disc brake; loose pedal and makes noise when pressing on brake; purchased car used."
3. Brakes: hydraulic: anti-skid system, failure. • "Antilock brake system warning light and brake light came on; total brake failure had occurred." • "Antilock brake system: While driving, experienced complete loss of brake effectiveness; in for repair, faulty, install power kit and seal." • "Antilock brake system malfunctions, warning lights come on and brakes leak." • "Antilock brakes are not stopping properly during normal driving conditions." • "Antilock brakes continuously make noise, also perform sluggishly."

BUICK REGAL 1992

Complaint Severity: Typical. **Recall Alert:** See Recall Index. **Buyer's Summary:** Check the brakes—listen for noise, look for leaks and feel for vibration. They may fail, perform poorly or require frequent mechanical attention. See "Sudden Accelerations" in Introduction.

Hot Spots and Owner/NHTSA Comments:
1. Brakes: hydraulic system, failure. • "Brakes failed, causing loss of control; accident." • "Brake pedal goes to the floor, have to pump to stop." • "Brakes failed, vehicle went through red light; had an accident." • "Brakes failed while driving downhill; steering wheel went erratic; vehicle hit a moving truck." • "Brake pedal went to the floor and caused loss of brake effectiveness when driver was making a right-hand turn at 42 mph. Replaced master cylinder and booster." • " 'Check gauge' light came on, then the steering and power brakes locked up."
2. Interior systems: active restraints: belt retractors, miscellaneous problems. • "Front seat belts do not work; one won't retract, the other will not come out." • "Driver side seat belt will not retract." • "Driver's side seat belt won't retract. Once pulled out of assembly. Dealer says parts are on back order." • "Driver's

seat belt does not retract." • "Driver's seat belt fails to pull out." • "Seat belt sticks in retractor; also, passenger seat shifts when stopping."

3. Fuel: throttle linkages and control, sudden accelerations. • "Vehicle in park position, turned key to on position, vehicle surged forward." • "Sudden acceleration." • "While driving, car suddenly accelerated and crashed." • "When vehicle is started, engine revs very high. Vehicle takes off when put into gear." • "Upon placing gear into drive position, vehicle suddenly surged, then shot out of control. Wheels spinning."

BUICK REGAL 1993

Complaint Severity: Typical. **Recall Alert:** See Recall Index. **Buyer's Summary:** Have the condition of the windshield evaluated by a professional.

Hot Spots and Owner/NHTSA Comments:

1. Visual systems: glass: windshield, miscellaneous problems. • "Slanted windshield causes reflections." • "Windshield vision distorted by dust, dew and outside lights." • "Windshield keeps cracking." • "Windshield brace blocked vision, causing accident."

BUICK RIVIERA 1990

Complaint Severity: Best 3% in Guide. **Recall Alert:** See Recall Index. **Buyer's Summary:** Check the brakes—listen for noise, look for leaks and feel for vibration. They may fail, perform poorly or require frequent mechanical attention. Make sure seat belts function correctly and fit comfortably.

Hot Spots and Owner/NHTSA Comments:

1. Interior systems: passive restraint: belts, uncomfortable. • "Shoulder harness of front seat belts does not fit across shoulder as should, instead comes across neck with a choking effect; unable to wear because uncomfortable." • "Automatic seat belt scrapes neck." • "Seat belt comes across driver's neck; dealer states belt cannot be fixed, no amount of seat adjustment will help." • "Seat belt anchorage is attached to top of seat backrest, behind driver; position causes safety belt to rub and drag across neck."

2. Brakes: hydraulic system, locking up, pulling. • "Brakes squeal when stopping." • "Brakes froze due to an inoperative valve block, causing vehicle to lose control and swerve." • "Brakes pull upon sudden stopping between 45-55 mph, causing loss of control."

3. Brakes: hydraulic: shoe: disc brake system, poor performance, noise. • "Noisy left front brake." • "Weak brakes caused poor brake performance in emergency." • "Noisy brakes, repaired/replaced rotor, calipers and pads; also, emergency brakes inoperative." • "In cold weather the front brakes are inoperative."

4. Steering: pulling. • "While driving and braking, vehicle pulls to left; due to faulty steering assembly." • "Vehicle has been steering to the left, has been worked on by three different dealers, could not find problem." • "Steering problems, car pulls left." • "Unspecified steering problem."

BUICK ROADMASTER 1992

Complaint Severity: Serious. **Recall Alert:** See Recall Index. **Buyer's Summary:** The airbags in this vehicle have experienced failures and malfunctions: You may need a professional evaluation on the condition of the airbags. Check the brakes—listen for noise, look for leaks and feel for vibration. They may fail, perform poorly or require frequent mechanical attention. See "Sudden Accelerations" in Introduction.

Hot Spots and Owner/NHTSA Comments:

1. Visual systems: glass: windshield, visibility poor. • "Reflection of defroster outlet on windshield hampers driver's vision." • "Windshield visibility extremely poor as a result of sunlight glare of dashboard reflection." • "The reflection on the windshield in sunlight and at night under street lights obstructs driver's vision." • "Defroster grid reflects in windshield, restricting vision." • "Sun glare obstructs vision due to improperly designed windshield."

2. Interior systems: passive restraint: airbag: driver, malfunction, failure. • "Airbag did not deploy in front-end collision at high speeds." • "Driver received facial injuries." • "While vehicle was idling in park, gears suddenly shifted from park to reverse, vehicle crashed into a house. Airbag failed to deploy." • "Driver's side airbag did not deploy during front-end collision; broadsided another vehicle during 3-car collision." • "Airbag did not deploy during rear- and front-end collisions; front hit tree; impact 12:00 position, speed 35-40 mph. Six-car collision."

3. Brakes: hydraulic: anti-skid system, poor performance, failure, locking up. • "Antilock brakes operated poorly, pedal went to the floor." • "Antilock brake system malfunctioned and pedal went all the way to the floor." • "Antilock brakes malfunctioned and pedal faded on wet road conditions, vehicle could not stop, hit a guard rail and slid, impact 1:00 position." • "Antilock brake computer failed." • "Owner has several problems: Transmission spring rattles, antilock brake system warning light is on, wiring harness problem, rumble in rear, rear brake shoes are noisy."

4. Interior systems: seat belts: lap: rear, poor design. • "Rear seat belts impossible for average-size adult to buckle." • "Rear passenger's seat belt design length is unusually small, unable to hold passenger over 150 pounds." • "Rear lap and shoulder belt is too short for male of 185 pounds. Also, other passenger cannot get in rear seat without an extender." • "Rear seat belts too short."

5. Fuel: throttle linkages and control, sudden accelerations. • "Three-mile trip, restarted, foot on brake pedal, shifting into reverse, experienced sudden acceleration through a garage door." • "Engine accelerated from 5 to 50 mph making right-hand turn. Lost vehicle control. Vehicle hit mailbox and palm trees along road. Impact 12:00 position. Airbag failed." • "During any style of driving, car will suddenly accelerate. Dealer has not been able to duplicate the fault." • "Sudden acceleration, resulting in accident."

BUICK ROADMASTER 1994

Complaint Severity: Typical. **Recall Alert:** See Recall Index. **Buyer's Summary:** The airbags in this vehicle have experienced failures and malfunctions: You may need a professional evaluation on the condition of the airbags. Check the brakes—listen for noise, look for leaks and feel for vibration. They may fail, perform poorly or require frequent mechanical attention. Test the transmission thoroughly.

Hot Spots and Owner/NHTSA Comments:

1. Visual systems: glass: windshield, visibility problems. • "Windshield produces an eyesight-impairing glare in bright sunlight. Could cause a serious accident." • "Glare on windshield in bright sunlight impairs visibility." • "Due to design or material, when sun reflects on windshield, visibility is poor." • "Dashboard reflects on windshield." • "Reflections on windshield impair visibility." • "Windshield wipers failed during a rainstorm."

2. Brakes: hydraulic: anti-skid system, poor performance, failure, locking up. • "The antilock brake failed." • "Antilock brakes lock up while driving at speeds of 5-60 mph and during panic stops." • "Antilock brakes hesitate and go to the floor." • "On second day after purchase of the car, rear antilock brake system module failed."

3. Power train: transmission: automatic, poor performance, difficulty shifting, slipping. • "This is a brand new car—the Buick dealer put in a rebuilt transmission." • "Transmission linkage disconnected after climbing a hill." • "Transmission reverse gear slips and jerks, causing delayed reaction when put into gear." • "Delayed reaction when transmission is put into reverse gear." • "Reverse gear did not operate."
4. Interior systems: passive restraint: airbag: passenger, malfunction, failure. • "Upon frontal collision, both airbags deployed. Passenger's airbag deployed through windshield, shattering it." • "Deployment was violent, causing passenger's side airbag to tear restraining mesh of airbag lid loose, allowing lid to hit and break windshield." • "Passenger's airbag did not deploy during front-end collision; vehicle hit side of another vehicle." • "Vehicle was rear-ended and passenger's airbag did not deploy."

BUICK SKYHAWK 1987

Complaint Severity: Typical. **Recall Alert:** See Recall Index. **Buyer's Summary:** The fuel injection system has been blamed for hesitation and stalling. Be sure the vehicle doesn't die in traffic or at stops. See "Sudden Accelerations" in Introduction.

Hot Spots and Owner/NHTSA Comments:
1. Fuel: throttle linkages and control, sudden accelerations. • "Car accelerates suddenly especially in reverse." • "Vehicle surged forward uncontrollably, which caused accident." • "Sudden acceleration up to 70 mph with no brakes, stopped by emergency brakes." • "While backing out of driveway, car accelerated, hit another car, ran into a fence and hit a tree." • "Upon shifting gears from park to reverse, vehicle suddenly accelerated, hitting another vehicle. Vehicle placed in park position suddenly accelerated forward."
2. Fuel: fuel injection system, stalling, hesitation. • "Car stalls when stopping or slowing down in cold weather, needs to be warmed up 3 to 5 minutes." • "Stalled at 55 mph when approaching a traffic light, causing accident; unable to restart." • "Accident caused by engine hesitating and surging." • "Experiences hesitation and surging of engine; repaired/replaced module, repaired shorts, shimmed, cleaned points, adjusted throttle position sensor; surging, hesitation and stalling continues." • "Engine difficulty, car lost all pickup and then would buck, went on until car died completely."

BUICK SKYLARK 1987

Complaint Severity: Negligible. **Recall Alert:** See Recall Index. **Buyer's Summary:** The electronic control unit has been blamed for engine performance problems, including stalling and surging. The fuel injection system has been blamed for hesitation and stalling. Be sure the vehicle doesn't die in traffic or at stops. Check the brakes—listen for noise, look for leaks and feel for vibration. They may fail, perform poorly or require frequent mechanical attention. Test the transmission thoroughly. See "Sudden Accelerations" in Introduction.

Hot Spots and Owner/NHTSA Comments:
1. Fuel: fuel injection system, stalling, hesitation. • "Engine stalls suddenly, car hiccupped, leapfrogged and died, engine light constantly on, car would turn over and die, with black exhaust out of tailpipe." • "Engine stalls repeatedly when trying to start, can start only by gunning engine in park or neutral then abruptly shifting to drive, worse in cold weather." • "Engine electronics problem, intermittent stalling, bucking and skipping, and cutting at highway speed." • "Engine loses power and stalls while in motion."
2. Brakes: hydraulic system, failure. • "Brakes operate poorly." • "Brakes get real hard and engage all the way, failing to completely stop car; brakes don't lock up, car not equipped with antilock braking." • "Inadequate performance of brakes, slowly come to stop upon braking, car will not stop fast if you step on brakes hard." • "Brakes failed when applied at speed of 25 mph, resulted in rear-end accident with another car."
3. Electrical system: ignition: electronic control unit, stalling, failure. • "Vehicle will not start, stalls due to failure of electronically controlled emissions/fuel system; repaired/replaced controller, electronic control module, sensor, programmable read-only memory, solenoid and calibrator." • "Car stalls while in motion, without warning, bucks, backfires, and front end vibrates; replaced ignition parts and system several times." • "Stalling problems." • "Problem starting car and losing power on highway, repaired/replaced ignition module, spark plugs, wires, etc., all repair attempts to no avail."
4. Fuel: throttle linkages and control, sudden accelerations. • "When brakes applied, car appeared to be stopping, then surged forward, ending up in rear of vehicle in front; injuries sustained from accident." • "Car idles extremely high, and when pressing on brakes, feels as if car pulls away." • "Car put in reverse, engine idling high, car took off at an excessive speed; lost total control of car, causing accident by hitting a garage." • "Unexplained sudden acceleration, gas pedal pulls away from foot; also idles high."
5. Power train: transmission: automatic, poor performance, difficulty shifting, slipping. • "Shift indicator not aligned, does not read proper gear." • "Gears were slipping." • "Quirk in front-wheel drive causing vibration noise when gas pedal released; speed decreases." • "Gear shift must be dropped 1 position below desired gear, cannot drop gear shift from reverse to drive, must first go to low, then back up to drive."

BUICK SKYLARK 1988

Complaint Severity: Troublesome. **Recall Alert:** See Recall Index. **Buyer's Summary:** Make sure the shoulder belts don't cut across your neck and are well anchored. The electronic control unit has been blamed for engine performance problems, including stalling and surging. Carefully check the brakes—listen for noise, look for leaks and feel for vibration. They may fail, perform poorly or require frequent mechanical attention. See "Sudden Accelerations" in Introduction.

Hot Spots and Owner/NHTSA Comments:
1. Brakes: hydraulic system, failure. • "Brake goes out any time with no warning." • "Brake problem, when pressure put on brake pedal to slow down or stop, feel no stopping power; repaired/replaced front pads, rotors, rear shoes, wheel cylinders and drum." • "Extended braking distance and brake pedal hits floor." • "Left rear brake gave out, brake springs chewed up, line cut, parts missing (factory did not put in)." • "Brakes continuously going out; brake ineffectiveness resulted in accident."
2. Fuel: throttle linkages and control, sudden accelerations. • "When slowing car to come to a stop, engine would maintain a high fast idle, making braking difficult." • "Started car, gear in reverse, accelerated to 40 or 50 mph, spun around, wedged between parked cars before stopping; caused extensive damage." • "Vehicle suddenly accelerated wildly, out of control." • "Upon placing gear in reverse, car suddenly accelerated to 40-50 mph, spun around, wedged itself between 2 parked cars; caused extensive damage, injuries." • "Started car and shifted into reverse, car suddenly accelerated to about 40-50 mph, spun around and wedged itself between 2 parked cars."
3. Electrical system: ignition: electronic control unit, stalling, failure. • "Intermittent stalling." • "Computer failed." • "Defective electronic control module in electrical system has caused several stalling problems for driver; several repairs made to cor-

rect." • "Electronic computer module failed, causing vehicle to stall."

4. Interior systems: shoulder belts, poor design. • "Front passive seat belts restraint inadequate; mounted improperly, causing adjustment problems." • "Design and location of seat belt, hanging from door, is added blind spot; if struck on door, this will cause seat belts to lock in, door cannot be opened." • "Shoulder harness rests on driver's neck, unable to adjust." • "Frontal crash, shoulder belt did not protect against broken foot and broken arm."

5. Brakes: hydraulic: power assist: vacuum system, failure. • "Defective brakes, failed 6 times and caused minor collision twice; installed new booster." • "Vehicle experiences brake problem." • "Brake failure; repaired." • "Problem with braking system, need to apply extreme pressure on brakes during sudden stops, pedal goes to the floor."

6. Engine: failure. • "Engine repaired/replaced after failing 4 times." • "Head gasket failed." • "Engine problem, a constant tapping noise when driving." • "Oil pump burst."

BUICK SKYLARK 1989

Complaint Severity: Negligible. **Recall Alert:** See Recall Index. **Buyer's Summary:** The electronic control unit has been blamed for engine performance problems, including stalling and surging. Check the brakes—listen for noise, look for leaks and feel for vibration. They may fail, perform poorly or require frequent mechanical attention. See "Sudden Accelerations" in Introduction.

Hot Spots and Owner/NHTSA Comments:

1. Brakes: hydraulic system, failure, vibration. • "Insufficient pedal power to effect braking until the pedal is almost to the floor." • "Applied brakes to stop, brakes failed, went to floor, did not stop car; resulted in accident." • "Defective braking system, brake pedal goes to floor, brake did not hold during a panic stop; resulted in accident." • "Defective brakes, slides, especially on wet highways; all repair attempts to no avail; caused an accident." • "Brakes malfunctioning, causing vibration in steering wheel when waiting at stop light in drive gear."

2. Electrical system: ignition: electronic control unit, failure. • "Car would not start, repaired/replaced electronic control module." • "Idle level of engine set unusually high; factory representative verified that no adjustment can be made, runs at a fast and dangerous speed in idle." • "Vehicle accelerated out of control at a high rate of speed, resulting in accident."

3. Fuel: throttle linkages and control, sudden accelerations. • "Car accelerated at high speed out of control, resulting in an accident and damages." • "While driving at low speed, vehicle went out of control, causing severe injuries." • "Vehicle experienced surge of acceleration, without added pressure on accelerator."

BUICK SKYLARK 1990

Complaint Severity: Typical. **Recall Alert:** See Recall Index. **Buyer's Summary:** Look carefully for any kind of leakage, especially under the car. Check the brakes—listen for noise, look for leaks and feel for vibration. They may fail, perform poorly or require frequent mechanical attention. Test the transmission thoroughly. See "Sudden Accelerations" in Introduction.

Hot Spots and Owner/NHTSA Comments:

1. Fuel: throttle linkages and control, sudden accelerations. • "Upon starting vehicle and putting in drive gear, it suddenly accelerated out of control." • "When driver crossed speed bump at almost zero mph, vehicle suddenly accelerated at very high rate; accident occurred with injuries sustained." • "Engine races instead of idles, consequently one needs to keep foot on brake when standing still." • "Upon starting up vehicle and putting it in proper gear, engine suddenly accelerated, power steering and power brakes did not work; resulted in accident." • "Shifted into reverse with foot on brake, car accelerated at full speed in reverse; resulted in accident."

2. Brakes: hydraulic: disc: rotor: disc hub, vibration, failure. • "Front-wheel drive vehicle has rotors that have been replaced twice. Vehicle vibrates and jerks." • "Front rotors were chipping off in pieces, and finally cracked." • "Replaced warped left front brake rotor." • "Warped front brake rotors, pads and calipers, causing front end noise."

3. Electrical system: ignition, stalling. • "Vehicle stalls out intermittently with no warning while driving at any speed." • "Intermittent stalling in traffic causes poor control." • "Ignition replaced." • "Vehicle stalls without warning, causing loss of control."

4. Engine: leaks, failure. • "Oil pump inoperative." • "While driving, vibration inside engine occurs." • "Repeated oil leaks; replaced valve, head gasket and cylinder head, still leaking." • "Complete engine failure."

5. Power train: transmission: automatic, poor performance, difficulty shifting, slipping. • "Transmission problem, no reverse, no 2nd gear and will not upshift manually from 1st to 2nd to drive, skips second speed and goes to drive, causing loss of power and/or speed." • "Automatic transmission hangs up in 1st gear for several seconds before shifting into 2nd gear with a jolting motion, almost causes driver to lose control." • "Transmission constantly failed in reverse; repaired each time but it did not help; continued to fail in reverse." • "Automatic transmission pan leaks."

BUICK SKYLARK 1991

Complaint Severity: Typical. **Recall Alert:** See Recall Index. **Buyer's Summary:** The electronic control unit has been blamed for engine performance problems, including stalling and surging. The steering may be stiff or not working correctly. Be sure to test the steering, especially on a cold start. See "Sudden Accelerations" in Introduction.

Hot Spots and Owner/NHTSA Comments:

1. Fuel: throttle linkages and control, sudden accelerations. • "When key was turned on in ignition, it immediately started to accelerate backward while still in the park position." • "Sudden acceleration caused loss of control and an accident." • "Attorney writing concerning vehicle which proceeded to accelerate rapidly in reverse without any assistance, causing accident." • "Upon shifting gear in reverse, vehicle suddenly accelerated out of control, resulted in accident." • "Accident caused by unexplained acceleration, vehicle was turned upside down and black smoke was coming from exhaust."

2. Electrical system: ignition: electronic control unit, stalling, failure. • "Computer keeps shorting out, causing vehicle to stall." • "Electronic control module fuse blew out while driving; lost all vehicle power and control; happens at any speed; no warning; could cause serious accident." • "Engine stalling in traffic at low speeds; have had to replace the electronic control unit about 9 times."

3. Steering: power assist, noise, stiffness. • "Whenever turning, power steering makes loud grinding noise." • "Power steering makes noise." • "Excessive force to turn steering wheel." • "Power steering vibrates and makes noise." • "Steering hard to turn."

BUICK SKYLARK 1992

Complaint Severity: Minor. **Recall Alert:** See Recall Index. **Buyer's Summary:** Check the brakes—listen for noise, look for leaks, feel for vibration. They may fail, perform poorly or require frequent mechanical attention.

Hot Spots and Owner/NHTSA Comments:

1. Brakes: hydraulic: anti-skid system, poor performance, failure, locking up. • "Antilock brake system was constantly on, causing the brakes to wear; problem is still occurring where antilock brake system light comes on and off." • "Antilock brake system grabbing problem." • "Antilock brakes not functioning properly." • "Antilock brake system-equipped vehicle has had the brake master cylinder, sensor and linkage replaced due to an extensive leak. Cause unknown." • "Antilock brake system: Rear brakes lock up and skid on dirt road, sometimes on pavement; no prior warning."

2. Brakes: hydraulic system, locking up, failure. • "Brake problems." • "Frosty weather, during first 20 minutes brakes lock and release the wheels, brake pedal feels steady with no modulation." • "While driving on interstate, brakes failed; slowed down and coasted to a stop. This was a rental car." • "Brakes overheated, resulting in brake failure."

Cadillac

CADILLAC CIMARRON 1987

Complaint Severity: Troublesome. **Buyer's Summary:** Verify that the cruise control system works properly, and that it doesn't cause the engine to surge. The fuel injection system has been blamed for hesitation and stalling. Be sure the vehicle doesn't die in traffic or at stops. See "Sudden Accelerations" in Introduction.

Hot Spots and Owner/NHTSA Comments:

1. Fuel: fuel injection system, stalling, hesitation. • "Car doesn't start properly, stalls after starting, surges when started then turns off, stalls when making turns." • "Car stalls while driving, turning, at stop signs and stop lights." • "While driving, vehicle stalls without warning." • "Vehicle had power surge in line of traffic, continuous stalling due to incorrect setting of fuel injection system." • "Car hesitates due to buildup of carbon on fuel injectors."

2. Fuel: throttle linkages and control, sudden accelerations. • "Making left-hand turn, car accelerated, could not brake or steer; lost control, went over embankment and sustained injuries." • "Driver was making left turn with foot on brake when car suddenly accelerated; lost control and car went over embankment." • "Accelerator sticks intermittently, even on highway going 40, jumps to 80 mph; throttle linkage checked, no problem found, apply brakes to stop." • "Sudden acceleration." • "Vehicle suddenly accelerated from parked position, resulting in an accident and injury."

3. Equipment: speed control, malfunction, sudden acceleration. • "Speed cruise control engage switch malfunctioned." • "Cruise control engages on its own." • "Cruise control engages on its own, resulting in sudden acceleration."

CADILLAC DEVILLE 1987

Complaint Severity: Troublesome. **Theft Alert:** 28. **Recall Alert:** See Recall Index. **Buyer's Summary:** Verify that the cruise control system works properly, and that it doesn't cause the engine to surge. The steering may be stiff or not working correctly. Be sure to test the steering, especially on a cold start. Check the brakes—listen for noise, look for leaks and feel for vibration. They may fail, perform poorly or require frequent mechanical attention. Test the transmission thoroughly. See "Sudden Accelerations" in Introduction.

Hot Spots and Owner/NHTSA Comments:

1. Fuel: throttle linkages and control, sudden accelerations. • "Driving at 45 mph, the car suddenly accelerated and required shifting into neutral and then park to stop. Cruise had not been used in the last 30 days." • "Sudden acceleration when shifting gear into reverse, vehicle hit a parked car and continued to proceed into store, impact 6:00, 20 mph." • "Vehicle suddenly accelerated, resulting in accidents on 2 occasions when putting gear in drive." • "When shifted into gear, vehicle accelerated unexpectedly, causing accident." • "With car in park and brake on, turned key, car shot forward at full power."

2. Engine: noise, leaks. • "Engine backfires constantly; problem undetermined." • "Engine started using excessive amounts of oil." • "Noise from engine; replaced air pump, problem continues." • "Noise in engine." • "Water leaking into oil."

3. Power train: transmission: automatic, poor performance, difficulty shifting, slipping. • "Transmission failure 4 times." • "As driver stepped out from vehicle, gear shift lever slipped into reverse, car proceeded at high rate of speed, striking driver and knocking her to ground." • "Transmission replaced, still jerks in gear and whines." • "When shifted into gear, makes loud thumping noise and vibrates." • "Transmission leaks fluid."

4. Brakes: hydraulic system, failure. • "Braking system faulty, pedal goes all the way to floor, like air is out." • "Brakes have always been soft, with insufficient pedal." • "Brake problem, requires large amount of foot pressure to stop car." • "Brakes hard and didn't seem to grab when applied; caused accident." • "Brakes do not lock up or stop vehicle properly."

5. Equipment: speed control, malfunction. • "While driving with cruise on, vehicle jerks and surges." • "Cruise control not set or on, driving down highway, it kicks in and goes to high rate of speed, it does not stop by pressing on brake." • "Upon engaging cruise control, vehicle surged forward and began accelerating until cruise control disengaged." • "Cruise control surges, picks up speed and drops speed." • "Cruise control stopped working after purchase."

6. Steering: gear: rack-and-pinion, stiffness, poor performance. • "Rack-and-pinion problem caused steering to lock." • "Power steering rack-and-pinion failed, making steering very difficult; also, there is a leak." • "Rack-and-pinion steering locks up in cold weather or when vehicle is first started." • "Unspecified rack-and-pinion problems." • "Power steering makes serious grinding noises; need to replace."

CADILLAC DEVILLE 1988

Complaint Severity: Typical. **Theft Alert:** 31. **Buyer's Summary:** Verify that the cruise control system works properly, and that it doesn't cause the engine to surge. Check the brakes—listen for noise, look for leaks and feel for vibration. They may fail, perform poorly or require frequent mechanical attention. See "Sudden Accelerations" in Introduction. Make sure air conditioner works properly.

Hot Spots and Owner/NHTSA Comments:

1. Fuel: throttle linkages and control, sudden accelerations. • "Throttle stuck in open position; vehicle control lost." • "Upon starting car and shifting gear to drive position, car leaped forward uncontrollably, resulting in accident." • "Two accidents due to sudden acceleration." • "Car bolted forward suddenly, unable to control, car would not stop, finally stopped after crossing concrete median strip." • "Excessive acceleration of engine, attempted to brake, but would not stop; resulted in accident."

2. Brakes: hydraulic system, vibration. • "Experience pulsating effect when car being braked through lower shift ranges to stop." • "Brake pulsation when stopping, especially noticeable when stopping from 45 mph or higher, pedal pressure required much higher than normal." • "Brakes vibrate." • "Brake springs break, causing grinding noise." • "When stopping slowly or stopped, brakes take hold, then 20-40 seconds later brake pedal drops, takes hold again; repaired/replaced drums, shoes, rotors and brake pedal."
3. Air conditioner: failure. • "Continuous air conditioner failure." • "Repaired air conditioner 6 times." • "Air conditioner failure."
4. Equipment: speed control, sudden acceleration. • "Vehicle accelerated without warning. Rod linkage from speed control to accelerator stuck." • "Vehicle accelerates at any speed when cruise is activated and turn signal indicator engaged." • "Cruise control does not always engage." • "Sudden acceleration, each time had to brake hard to stop with cruise control engaged." • "Cruise control switch on, engine accelerated to 50 mph, gas pedal went down by itself, switch turned off, had no effect until ignition key turned off."
5. Brakes: hydraulic: disc: rotor: disc hub, vibration. • "Pulsation felt when brakes depressed, caused by rotors." • "Brakes get hot and warp brake rotors." • "Brakes noisy; turned rotors." • "Experiencing disc brake noise, causing serious rotor wear and pulsation when brakes applied." • "Disc brakes' rotors warped, results in vibration and pulsation."

CADILLAC DEVILLE 1989

Complaint Severity: Typical. **Buyer's Summary:** Look carefully for any kind of leakage, especially under the car. Check the brakes—listen for noise, look for leaks and feel for vibration. They may fail, perform poorly or require frequent mechanical attention. See "Sudden Accelerations" in Introduction. Make sure air conditioner works properly.

Hot Spots and Owner/NHTSA Comments:
1. Brakes: hydraulic system, noise, failure. • "Applied brakes to stop vehicle and had complete brake failure; reapplied the brakes and they locked up, causing car to skid and hit rear of car in front." • "Vehicle lost braking power; was unable to hold speed down while going down a steep hill; no accident." • "Brake failure occurred twice, which caused accident." • "Brakes squeaky." • "Front brakes relined at 13,000 miles."
2. Fuel: throttle linkages and control, sudden accelerations. • "While putting gear into park, vehicle jumped out of control, striking 4 parked vehicles." • "Vehicle suddenly accelerated, climbed up curb and down and hit another vehicle." • "When gear put in drive, accelerator went to floor, brakes totally ineffective in stopping car; accident." • "Car raced forward uncontrollably; striking two utility poles; owner killed upon impact with second pole." • "Car was in parking lot, turned on, pressed on gas and car fully accelerated."
3. Electrical system: alternator: generator, failure. • "Alternator failure." • "Generator assembly failure." • "Alternator failure."
4. Air conditioner: pulling, poor performance, failure. • "Air conditioning cooling system failure." • "Air conditioning programmer had to be replaced twice, wouldn't heat and/or cool car properly." • "Air conditioner light comes on; repaired air conditioner, problem continues." • "Problem with cooling system, air conditioner light goes on and off." • "Air conditioner odor." • "Air conditioner system failed 4 times due to poor sensing devices."
5. Brakes: hydraulic: power assist: vacuum system, noise, vibration. • "Problem with noisy brakes; repaired/replaced." • "Problem with squeaking brakes since purchase." • "Brakes pulsate, which makes it difficult to stop vehicle." • "Power brakes malfunctioned."
6. Engine: leaks, fire. • "Excessive oil consumption." • "Oil leaks by right front wheel; repaired." • "Spontaneous engine fire erupted while driving—speed at time approximately 25 mph." • "Engine leak, excessive oil consumption." • "Water mixed with oil, resulting in engine failure."

CADILLAC DEVILLE 1990

Complaint Severity: Typical. **Recall Alert:** See Recall Index. **Buyer's Summary:** Make sure the shoulder belts don't cut across your neck and are well anchored. The airbags in this vehicle have experienced failures and malfunctions: You may need a professional evaluation on the condition of the airbags. See "Sudden Accelerations" in Introduction.

Hot Spots and Owner/NHTSA Comments:
1. Fuel: throttle linkages and control, sudden accelerations. • "Vehicle suddenly accelerated to high speeds while driving." • "When driving vehicle at any speed, experience high idle." • "Vehicle went into open throttle position while driving, impact 12:00 position, speed unknown, airbag did deploy." • "Accident caused by sudden acceleration." • "When car built, bolt left in cavity under throttle, causing accelerator to stick; throttle had to be manually released."
2. Interior systems: shoulder belts, uncomfortable. • "Shoulder belts, particularly on driver's side, cut across driver's neck, presenting total discomfort." • "Shoulder strap on seat belt is not properly aligned, fitting is down center of chest instead of across breastplate." • "Seat belt is not properly adjusted, fits poorly, goes around neck." • "Shoulder belt catches short people in the neck, causes discomfort." • "Uncomfortable shoulder belts, rest across throat."
3. Interior systems: passive restraint: airbag: driver, malfunction, failure. • "Airbag did not deploy during left front-end collision, impact at 12:00, speed 25 mph; resulted in severe injury to driver. No deployment of airbag in accident." • "Airbag did not deploy." • "In near-frontal accident, the airbag did not deploy and seat belts did not restrain properly, allowing passenger to be thrown into dashboard."
4. Engine: fire, failure. • "Upon shutting engine off, vehicle suddenly erupted into flames." • "Oil leak and blown rod bearing." • "Excessive use of oil." • "Problem with engine knocking and irregular running; repaired/replaced engine."

CADILLAC DEVILLE 1991

Complaint Severity: Typical. **Recall Alert:** See Recall Index. **Buyer's Summary:** The electronic control unit has been blamed for engine performance problems, including stalling and surging. Check the brakes—listen for noise, look for leaks and feel for vibration. They may fail, perform poorly or require frequent mechanical attention. See "Sudden Accelerations" in Introduction.

Hot Spots and Owner/NHTSA Comments:
1. Engine: noise, poor performance. • "Leased from GMC—continuous knock and whining; unable to find cause and/or cure." • "Valve spring failure." • "Excessive oil consumption; also poor engine performance." • "Engine noise." • "Loud noise from under vehicle." • "Intermittent stalling."
2. Electrical system: ignition: electronic control unit, stalling, failure. • "Computer chip went out and driver lost all control of auto—no steering and no brakes." • "Intermittent stalling." • "Computer problem caused stalling." • "Engine constantly stalled." • "Intermittent loss of engine power at any speed."

3. Fuel: throttle linkages and control, sudden accelerations. • "While parking, vehicle suddenly accelerated in reverse position once foot taken off brake; resulted in an accident." • "Vehicle accelerated out of control when shifted into reverse, accident resulted." • "Throttle sticks, causing engine to idle at excessively high speeds." • "Throttle linkage failed, causing continuous acceleration." • "Vehicle accelerates on its own. When brakes are applied, vehicle will then slow down."
4. Electrical system: ignition, stalling, hesitation. • "Vehicle will stall with no warning, eliminating power for steering and brakes." • "Vehicle will stall without warning; fuel tank design makes a loud noise when driving." • "Vehicle hesitates to start, takes several tries." • "Ignition problems."
5. Brakes: hydraulic system, failure. • "While attempting to stop vehicle in parking area, brakes completely failed, which resulted in an accident." • "Vehicle will stall with no warning, eliminating power for steering and brakes." • "Upon application, brakes malfunctioned, vehicle went out of control, resulting in an accident." • "Computer chip went out and driver lost all control of auto—no steering and no brakes."

CADILLAC DEVILLE 1992

Complaint Severity: Typical. **Recall Alert:** See Recall Index. **Buyer's Summary:** The electronic control unit has been blamed for engine performance problems, including stalling and surging. The airbags in this vehicle have experienced failures and malfunctions: You may need a professional evaluation on the condition of the airbags. Check the brakes—listen for noise, look for leaks and feel for vibration. They may fail, perform poorly or require frequent mechanical attention. See "Sudden Accelerations" in Introduction.

Hot Spots and Owner/NHTSA Comments:

1. Brakes: hydraulic: anti-skid system, poor performance, failure, locking up. • "While driving at approximately 25 mph, suddenly brake action became ineffective to slow or stop vehicle, then pedal went to floor, allowing vehicle to rear end; no warning." • "Antilock brake system: Vehicle in for repairs 6 times due to brakes locking up on wet surfaces. Owner keeps having close calls with poor brakes." • "Random problem with the antilock brake system, the dash-mounted status light stays on and the system does not seem to work properly." • "Antilock brake system-equipped car, brake pedal went to the floor; resulted in a crash." • "Antilock brake system-equipped car takes unreasonably long time to stop at speeds over 50 mph. Dealer said car was OK."
2. Fuel: throttle linkages and control, sudden accelerations. • "Sudden acceleration, causing loss of control." • "Car sails on; after reaching approximately 15-20 mph, warm or cold, and releasing the throttle, the car keeps going at set speed." • "Driving up this incline, vehicle accelerated to 72 mph; stopped vehicle by pressing hard on brakes." • "Sudden acceleration, causing loss of control."
3. Interior systems: passive restraint: airbag: driver, malfunction, failure. • "Airbag failed to deploy during an accident." • "Upon impact, during frontal crash at approximately 25 mph, 12:00 position on front bumper, airbag failed to deploy." • "Airbag did not deploy; 12:00 position at 60 mph." • "Frontal collision, vehicle lost control, hitting another vehicle at 30 mph, airbag did not deploy."
4. Electrical system: ignition, stalling. • "Vehicle constantly stalls." • "Engine intermittently stalls in all types of driving conditions, causes loss of control." • "Vehicle stalled without warning. Will not start in neutral." • "Experiences intermittent engine shutdown, whenever gasoline is at 2-3 gallons and turning right at low speeds." • "Engine intermittently stalls while driving under normal conditions; no prior warning."
5. Electrical system: ignition: electronic control unit, failure, stalling. • "Filled vehicle up with gas, computer shut down and then car caught fire." • "While traveling at 20 mph, vehicle stalled due to electrical and/or computer failure." • "Computer chip replaced." • "Computer failure."
6. Engine: other parts, failure, leaks. • "Oil pump failed." • "Crankshaft bearing failing." • "Engine failure, crankshaft failure and oil pump failure, causing engine seizure." • "Oil pan and transmission leaks. Brakes and defrost system replaced." • "Engine main bearings and crankshaft overheated, causing vehicle to knock and/or stall."

CADILLAC DEVILLE 1993

Complaint Severity: Minor. **Recall Alert:** See Recall Index. **Buyer's Summary:** Test the suspension by feeling for vibration or pulling while driving. The airbags in this vehicle have experienced failures and malfunctions: You may need a professional evaluation on the condition of the airbags. Check the brakes—listen for noise, look for leaks and feel for vibration. They may fail, perform poorly or require frequent mechanical attention. Test the transmission thoroughly.

Hot Spots and Owner/NHTSA Comments:

1. Brakes: hydraulic: anti-skid system, poor performance, failure, locking up. • "Antilock brake system failure." • "Brake module valve replaced." • "Vehicle involved in a frontal collision. Antilock brake system did not stop vehicle. Pedal was applied. Airbag did not deploy." • "The antilock brake system failed 5 or 6 times; the master cylinder was replaced 3 times."
2. Interior systems: passive restraint: airbag: driver, malfunction, failure. • "Had double frontal impact, airbag did not deploy." • "No deployment of airbag during accident, resulting in injury." • "In 2 different accidents, driver's airbag did not deploy; dealer said nothing was wrong during first accident, have not checked for second accident." • "No deployment of driver's airbag during accident."
3. Power train: axle assembly: shaft axle, fire. • "Vehicle caught fire prior to recall." • "Vehicle fire prior to recall." • "Vehicle fire prior to recall." • "Recall repairs on transaxle oil cooler hose refused by dealer."
4. Power train: transmission: automatic, poor performance, difficulty shifting, slipping. • "Upon releasing foot from accelerator, then depressing pedal again, vehicle gives rough, harsh bump when attempting to increase speed." • "Transmission leak." • "Transmission failed." • "Transmission failure."
5. Suspension: independent front, pulling, noise. • "Vehicle pulls to the right, changed tires and had wheel alignment twice, 6 attempts to repair to no avail; dealer said car is designed to steer to the right." • "Noisy front end." • "Front end bottoms out." • "The front suspension is failing."

CADILLAC DEVILLE 1994

Complaint Severity: Minor. **Recall Alert:** See Recall Index. **Buyer's Summary:** Check the brakes—listen for noise, look for leaks and feel for vibration. They may fail, perform poorly or require frequent mechanical attention. Test the transmission thoroughly.

Hot Spots and Owner/NHTSA Comments:

1. Equipment: electric power accessories: locks: door, failure. • "Power door locks failed." • "Passenger's side automatic door lock switch failed." • "Power door lock actuator failed." • "Right rear power door lock failed." • "Remote entry system performs erratically with doors and trunk opening while driving."

2. Power train: transmission: automatic, poor performance, difficulty shifting, slipping. • "Transmission failure." • "Transmission failed." • "At 50,000 miles, oil pan and transmission pan rusted out."
3. Brakes: hydraulic system, failure, vibration. • "Brakes stick when first starting car; does not release until in drive gear." • "Brakes pulsate." • "Brakes pulsate when applied." • "Brakes failed."

CADILLAC ELDORADO 1989

Complaint Severity: Typical. **Recall Alert:** See Recall Index. **Buyer's Summary:** The electronic control unit has been blamed for engine performance problems, including stalling and surging. Check the brakes—listen for noise, look for leaks and feel for vibration. They may fail, perform poorly or require frequent mechanical attention. Make sure air conditioner works properly.

Hot Spots and Owner/NHTSA Comments:
1. Electrical system: ignition: electronic control unit, failure, stalling. • "Defective onboard computer." • "Onboard computer failed." • "Defective onboard computer and ignition system." • "Engine stalled while in motion, continued to stall after restarting, until air conditioner turned off, due to disc motor failure; replaced."
2. Air conditioner: failure, poor performance. • "Problem with cooling system." • "Squeaks and mildew in air conditioning." • "Air conditioner failure." • "Cooling port on driver's side emits little air compared to passenger-side and center of dash, making it difficult to adjust air flow to satisfaction."
3. Brakes: hydraulic: shoe: disc brake system, failure. • "Brake failure; repaired/replaced." • "Front brake failed twice while approaching a stop, pumped pedal to stop car." • "Replaced front brakes twice." • "Front and rear disc brakes failed."

CADILLAC ELDORADO 1990

Complaint Severity: Typical. **Recall Alert:** See Recall Index. **Buyer's Summary:** Make sure seat belts function correctly and fit comfortably. See "Sudden Accelerations" in Introduction.

Hot Spots and Owner/NHTSA Comments:
1. Fuel: throttle linkages and control, sudden accelerations. • "While traveling 40 mph, vehicle began to accelerate. When depressing brakes, pedal was hard and wouldn't respond." • "Sudden acceleration, causing vehicle to hit steel pole and another vehicle." • "While driving, vehicle suddenly accelerated, went out of control and caused accident." • "While driving on freeway, engine started racing at high speed, even though did not have foot on accelerator." • "While driving on freeway at 55 mph, engine raced at high speed even though foot was not on accelerator."
2. Interior systems: passive restraint: belts, uncomfortable. • "Shoulder strap on seat belts for driver and passenger cut across neck, regardless of seat position and/or driver height. Fear danger of neck injury in event of accident." • "Driver and front passenger seat belt shoulder straps cut across neck, causing irritation and fear of strangulation." • "Seat belts cross over occupant's and driver's throats rather than chests, posing serious threat of injury in case of accident." • "Shoulder belts in front improperly positioned, which causes belts to lie firmly against neck of passenger and driver; could cause injury in case of collision."

CADILLAC ELDORADO 1992

Complaint Severity: Best 3% in Guide. **Recall Alert:** See Recall Index. **Buyer's Summary:** Verify that the cruise control system works properly, and that it doesn't cause the engine to surge.

Hot Spots and Owner/NHTSA Comments:
1. Equipment: speed control, no indicator light. • "This model does not have a light or other means to show that cruise control is on." • "Vehicle does not have a light or other means to show that cruise control is on and engaged." • "Vehicle has no light or other means to show that cruise control is on and engaged." • "No cruise control indicator."

CADILLAC FLEETWOOD 1989

Complaint Severity: Troublesome. **Recall Alert:** See Recall Index. **Buyer's Summary:** Check the brakes—listen for noise, look for leaks and feel for vibration. They may fail, perform poorly or require frequent mechanical attention. See "Sudden Accelerations" in Introduction.

Hot Spots and Owner/NHTSA Comments:
1. Fuel: throttle linkages and control, sudden accelerations. • "Shifted into drive, car roared and went forward at very high speed, brakes did not stop car." • "Sudden acceleration; when the vehicle was turned on and put into drive, the vehicle began to accelerate, causing an accident and spinning the vehicle around." • "While sitting at drive-through window, engine surged when shifted from park to drive. Hit building 45 feet away." • "Experienced sudden acceleration; after parked, put vehicle into gear, lost control, hitting a metal building. Impact 12:00 position, speed 25 mph." • "Vehicle suddenly accelerated twice at startup, once resulting in an accident and injury." • "Throttle stuck; hit 3 other cars."
2. Brakes: hydraulic: anti-skid system, poor performance, failure, locking up. • "Antilock brake system pump motor had to be replaced." • "Antilock brake system could not stop vehicle." • "Antilock brake system failed several times." • "Rotors warped and caused brakes to jerk. The vehicle is equipped with antilock brake system." • "After applying brakes, they started chattering and did not bring car to a full halt until car rolled back more."

CADILLAC FLEETWOOD 1990

Complaint Severity: Minor. **Recall Alert:** See Recall Index. **Buyer's Summary:** The electronic control unit has been blamed for engine performance problems, including stalling and surging. Check the brakes—listen for noise, look for leaks and feel for vibration. They may fail, perform poorly or require frequent mechanical attention. See "Sudden Accelerations" in Introduction.

Hot Spots and Owner/NHTSA Comments:
1. Brakes: hydraulic: anti-skid system, poor performance, failure, locking up. • "Antilock brakes malfunctioned, couldn't stop vehicle and ran into the rear of a truck." • "Antilock brakes failed when pedal was pushed down; vehicle pulled to the left and did not stay in its lane." • "Antilock brakes respond, but with minimum performance, causing increased stopping distance." • "Antilock brakes locked up and caused vehicle to skid out of its lane. antilock brake system was replaced."
2. Electrical system: ignition: electronic control unit, stalling, failure. • "While driving, vehicle suddenly started to stall and quickly lost speed." • "Power failure; stalled." • "Onboard computer failed while driving, loss of power assist." • "Computer problems."
3. Fuel: throttle linkages and control, sudden accelerations. • "Acceleration after brakes applied; repaired." • "Throttle body blades cleaned and sensor replaced." • "While driving, vehicle suddenly accelerated, surged to high unknown speed, causing loss of vehicle control. No accident." • "Engine accelerated, surged

forward; foot lightly on gas pedal; vehicle was slowed down by shifting to neutral; no warning."

CADILLAC SEVILLE 1989

Complaint Severity: Troublesome. **Recall Alert:** See Recall Index. **Buyer's Summary:** The electronic control unit has been blamed for engine performance problems, including stalling and surging. Check the brakes—listen for noise, look for leaks and feel for vibration. They may fail, perform poorly or require frequent mechanical attention.

Hot Spots and Owner/NHTSA Comments:

1. Electrical system: ignition: electronic control unit, failure. • "Onboard computer failure." • "Problems with onboard computers." • "Date and time functions failed." • "While driving along, vehicle started losing power; computer problem." • "Vehicle lost all power due to computer problem."

2. Brakes: hydraulic system, stiffness, locking up. • "Brakes slow to respond to pressure; adjusted." • "Extreme leg force required to depress brakes, which results in erratic braking." • "Brakes locked up." • "Had to replace brakes at 24,000 miles." • "Brakes failed to stop vehicle within normal stopping distance; pedal spongy; owner was told brakes too small, inadequate for vehicle; nearly caused accident."

CADILLAC SEVILLE 1990

Complaint Severity: Serious. **Recall Alert:** See Recall Index. **Buyer's Summary:** Verify that the cruise control system works properly, and that it doesn't cause the engine to surge. The airbags in this vehicle have experienced failures and malfunctions: You may need a professional evaluation on the condition of the airbags. Check the brakes—listen for noise, look for leaks and feel for vibration. They may fail, perform poorly or require frequent mechanical attention. Test the transmission thoroughly. See "Sudden Accelerations" in Introduction.

Hot Spots and Owner/NHTSA Comments:

1. Fuel: throttle linkages and control, sudden acceleration, stalling. • "When attempting to slow down, the acceleration will not adjust, causing vehicle to have poor control." • "Engine suddenly raced, driver ran from vehicle, engine caught fire and burned the vehicle." • "Driving on highway across bridge, car took off in reverse, veering to right, hitting bridge and bouncing back across highway, hitting opposite side of bridge." • "Stalling; replaced faulty throttle position sensor per NHTSA hotline; remedied." • "High idle; repaired."

2. Power train: transmission: automatic, poor performance, difficulty shifting, slipping. • "Transaxle shift-control cable failed." • "Gearshift fails to go into park; week later inside transmission noisy; repaired/replaced." • "Car does not stay in gear." • "Transmission appears to be in neutral when in drive, does not move when accelerating." • "Placed gear in reverse and car went forward."

3. Brakes: hydraulic: anti-skid system, poor performance, failure, locking up. • "Antilock brake system seems to respond to different measures, the different impulses may cause pulling and swaying upon braking." • "Antilock brakes failed." • "Antilock brake system failed, resulting in extended stopping distance." • "Antilock brake system: When applying brakes, vehicle has a tendency to veer and/or lunge to the left."

4. Equipment: speed control, failure. • "Problems with cruise control." • "Cruise control not working properly." • "Cruise control does not work." • "Cruise control was stuck in open, causing engine to surge."

5. Interior systems: passive restraint: airbag: driver, malfunction, failure. • "Airbag did not deploy during frontal collision; impact 12:00 position; speed 40 mph; car 1 hit left side door of car 2." • "Vehicle was involved in a head-on collision and the airbag did not deploy." • "Driver's side airbag failed to deploy during front-end collision at 12:00 and approximately 40 mph into a telephone pole." • "In a head-on collision at 25 mph, impact at 12:00, airbag did not deploy."

CADILLAC SEVILLE 1991

Complaint Severity: Very Serious. **Buyer's Summary:** Check the brakes—listen for noise, look for leaks and feel for vibration. They may fail, perform poorly or require frequent mechanical attention. See "Sudden Accelerations" in Introduction.

Hot Spots and Owner/NHTSA Comments:

1. Brakes: hydraulic: anti-skid system, poor performance, failure, locking up. • "Antilock brakes did not function properly, couldn't stop vehicle in adequate time; accident resulted." • "Applied brakes and there was no response, resulted in rear-ending another vehicle; impact at 12:00, speed 35 mph, airbag did not deploy." • "Antilock brakes do not stop vehicle effectively when applied at speeds of 35 mph or more." • "Antilock brakes failed, causing loss of control; accident." • "Antilock brake system: While driving down steep road, applied brakes; pedal went to floor; no brakes at all; shifted to park, kept picking up speed; hit 2 parked cars."

2. Fuel: throttle linkages and control, sudden accelerations. • "Sudden acceleration in reverse, causing accident and injury." • "Sudden acceleration, causing accident and injury." • "Backing out of garage in reverse position, vehicle suddenly shot out, accelerating out of control; hit brick wall." • "Vehicle accelerates due to defective idle speed control unit."

CADILLAC SEVILLE 1993

Complaint Severity: Typical. **Recall Alert:** See Recall Index. **Buyer's Summary:** Make sure air conditioner works properly.

Hot Spots and Owner/NHTSA Comments:

1. Air conditioner: failure. • "Air conditioner failure." • "While driving on freeway, air conditioning stopped working and fire started in engine compartment, totally destroying car." • "Air conditioner computer chip failed." • "Air conditioner failed."

Chevrolet—Cars

CHEVROLET BERETTA 1988

Complaint Severity: Typical. **Recall Alert:** See Recall Index. **Buyer's Summary:** The electronic control unit has been blamed for engine performance problems, including stalling and surging. The fuel injection system has been blamed for hesitation and stalling. Be sure the vehicle doesn't die in traffic or at stops. Check the brakes—listen for noise, look for leaks and feel for vibration. They may fail, perform poorly or require frequent mechanical attention. Test the clutch. See "Sudden Accelerations" in Introduction.

Hot Spots and Owner/NHTSA Comments:

1. Structure: door assembly: hinge and attachments, failure, cracking. • "Door hinges failed to hold door open, causing injury to child." • "Door check sheared off. Once sheared off, passenger's door fell off onto ground. On recall, dealer only lubricated door hinges." • "When door opened, hinge cracked on left side; later, right hinge also broke when door opened." • "Driver's door misaligned, causing difficulty closing door properly." • "Left front (driver's) door hanging on ground, supported by bottom hinge, jams occasionally." • "Driver door has squeaking noise when opened and closed, door hinges rusted; failure."

2. Brakes: hydraulic system, pulling, failure. • "Brakes failed in emergency situation, car pulled to right but would not stop." • "Five different times, while driving on freeway, brake pedal went to floor; brakes stay inoperative for about 5 minutes, gradually come back to normal." • "Brakes spongy, coast to stop instead of promptly stopping; resulted in accident." • "While driving, brakes failed, stopped vehicle by using parking brakes." • "While driving behind truck, needed to stop, had to slam on brakes, car didn't stop; resulted in accident."

3. Fuel: fuel injection system, stalling, hesitation. • "Severe driveability problem, stalls following cold start, backfires, slow throttle response during gear changes, repaired/replaced programmable read-only memory, electronic control module and idle air control to no avail." • "Engine hesitation, stalling on cold start, runs rough, strong sulfur smell." • "Chronic and excessive engine stalling problems; several attempts to repair to no avail." • "Chronic engine stalling, also rough idling." • "Engine hesitates almost to point of stalling, problem only when accelerating from dead stops; repaired." • "Vehicle stalls, stumbles and hesitates while driving."

4. Electrical system: ignition: electronic control unit, surging, stalling. • "Episodes of engine surge and hesitation have been attributed to failed programmable read-only memory and electronic control module computer chips." • "Experiencing mild engine surge when stopped or idling at very low speeds." • "Different disturbances in car, would not idle, gas mileage got low because of computer chip malfunction; chip replaced, symptoms have started reappearing." • "Engine computer failure, causing continuous stalling and surging problems." • "Vehicle excessively accelerated while driver's foot on brake; resulted in accidents on 3 occasions, problem related to defective computer command control." • "Stalling problem; repaired/replaced manifold air pressure sensor, module coils, crank sensor, fuel pump, etc.; all repair attempts to no avail."

5. Fuel: throttle linkages and control, sudden accelerations. • "On acceleration from zero mph, car would jolt to high rate of speed, causing everyone in the car to have a sense of whiplash." • "Any acceleration request to the gas pedal will have the throttle pulling itself wide open." • "Heavy acceleration will cause the throttle to stick open, left-hand turn seems to be worse than straight ahead." • "When engine cold, vehicle experiences sudden acceleration, strong gas odor smelled." • "Vehicle intermittently lurches forward." • "With no warning, car accelerated forward when shift in drive, unable to stop forward accelerating movement, even with pressing brake; resulted in accident."

6. Power train: clutch assembly, difficulty shifting, braking. • "Clutch sticks, had to shift manually to move car out of park." • "Rough shifting in transmission due to a worn-out clutch assembly; syncros in transmission were defective." • "Clutch fork broke, vehicle became inoperative." • "Clutch fork broke when going from 1st to 2nd, engine spun at high idle." • "While driving in rush hour traffic, clutch failed, gears became impossible to shift."

CHEVROLET BERETTA 1989

Complaint Severity: Typical. **Recall Alert:** See Recall Index. **Buyer's Summary:** The electronic control unit has been blamed for engine performance problems, including stalling and surging. The fuel injection system has been blamed for hesitation and stalling. Be sure the vehicle doesn't die in traffic or at stops. Check the brakes—listen for noise, look for leaks and feel for vibration. They may fail, perform poorly or require frequent mechanical attention. See "Sudden Accelerations" in Introduction.

Hot Spots and Owner/NHTSA Comments:

1. Electrical system: ignition: electronic control unit, stalling, poor performance. • "Engine stalling problems; repaired/replaced computer programmable read-only memory, stalling continues after driving a half-hour." • "Intermittent stalling; replaced circuit board." • "Continuous engine stalling problems; updated computer chip, problem still not corrected." • "Computer chip has defect in its programming, causing car to stall when hot and/or on very warm days, occurs when slowing, foot off gas pedal, clutch in or out of gear." • "At stop point, vehicle would accelerate, and when brakes applied, it would rapidly decelerate, idle speed very erratic, defect in electronic control module." • "Power died after extended time on highway; repaired."

2. Brakes: hydraulic system, failure, poor performance. • "While driving down the road, total loss of braking action." • "Defective braking system, while making left turn applied brake, went to floor, pumped and still went to floor." • "Brake system faulty, would not engage until brake pedal pushed to floor, replaced at 12,000 miles." • "Poor braking power when putting foot on brake pedal, response time very poor when trying to stop quickly." • "While driving, brakes malfunctioned; caused accident."

3. Fuel: fuel injection system, stalling, hesitation. • "Vehicle misses, resulting in stalling and/or starting failure." • "Car dies with no warning during operation, also sporadically surges forward while operating." • "Starting and stalling problems; engine cradle bolts replaced." • "Engine stalling problem during first 20 minutes after startup, hesitates and occasionally stalls upon takeoff." • "Car constantly stalls in traffic."

4. Fuel: throttle linkages and control, sudden accelerations. • "Upon starting car and putting in reverse, went into reverse, highly accelerated, brake wouldn't hold." • "On several occasions vehicle wouldn't slow down when foot removed from accelerator; resulted in accident." • "Vehicle suddenly accelerated out of control upon starting and putting gear in reverse." • "When car started, will accelerate by itself no matter whether engine is hot or cold." • "Backing out of parking place, engine suddenly accelerated to high speed; vehicle lurched backwards, hit curb."

5. Interior systems: active seat and shoulder belts and belt anchor, sticking, uncomfortable. • "Front seat belts stick, do not open up." • "Not satisfied with repair work on recall repairs by service department of Chevrolet, repairs for improper locking of seat and shoulder belt." • "Seat belts are attached to the door; in case of an accident where doors come open, there is nothing to hold occupant in." • "Front seat belts scrape neck." • "Customer too short for proper operation of seat belt."

6. Structure: door assembly: hinge and attachments, breaking. • "Driver's side door hinge broke." • "Driver's door not closing properly, because lower door hinge pin broke into two, problem similar to recall in 1987-1988 models." • "Door hinge on driver's side broke." • "Passenger door hinge broke and fell off—told of recall on 1988 Berettas, but not 1989." • "Driver and passenger door pockets nearest door hinges broke 3 times."

CHEVROLET BERETTA 1990

Complaint Severity: Typical. **Recall Alert:** See Recall Index. **Buyer's Summary:** Check the brakes—listen for noise, look for leaks and feel for vibration. They may fail, perform poorly or require frequent mechanical attention.

Hot Spots and Owner/NHTSA Comments:

1. Interior systems: active seat and shoulder belts and belt anchor, malfunction, failure. • "Seat belts are not operating

properly." • "Seat belts and shoulder belts do not work." • "Seat belt failed in accident, causing injury." • "When testing seat belt after corrected in a recall, the feature button that locks seat belt into place became jammed; resulted in lack of restraint to driver." • "Seat belt recall repair prolonged due to unavailability of parts."
2. Electrical system: wiring: harness: under dash, malfunction, failure. • "Electrical short developed in wiring under dash; also, vehicle stalled." • "Smoke comes from steering column into passenger compartment." • "When putting on the cruise control, there is smoke coming from the steering column and odor." • "Smoke comes out steering column during long commuting, releasing an odor." • "Notice smoke coming out of steering column near the horn button." • "Vehicle's steering wheel column smokes."
3. Electrical system: ignition, stalling, hesitation. • "Vehicle stalls in traffic when turning corners." • "Car stalls out in traffic." • "When vehicle gets wet, 'check engine' light comes on and vehicle stalls." • "When car is warm, hesitates upon acceleration—at times minor, other times near to causing accident; repaired/replaced programmable read-only memory, problem not solved." • "Vehicle constantly hesitates."
4. Brakes: hydraulic: power assist: vacuum system, poor performance, failure. • "Vehicle's braking system failed and driver hit curb." • "Inadequate brakes while driving, no pressure upon brakes to slow and/or stop vehicle; resulted in accident." • "Vehicle experiences inadequate braking." • "Vehicle experienced constant brake problem."

CHEVROLET BERETTA 1991

Complaint Severity: Serious. **Recall Alert:** See Recall Index. **Buyer's Summary:** Verify that the cruise control system works properly, and that it doesn't cause the engine to surge. The electronic control unit has been blamed for engine performance problems, including stalling and surging. The airbags in this vehicle have experienced failures and malfunctions: You may need a professional evaluation on the condition of the airbags.

Hot Spots and Owner/NHTSA Comments:
1. Electrical system: wiring: harness: under dash, malfunction, failure. • "Steering column started smoking, dash and steering column became engulfed in flames." • "Smoke came from steering column near the flashers. This occurred twice." • "Wiring harness in steering column failed, filling compartment with smoke." • "Vehicle had smoke coming from top of steering column due to turn signal switch shorting out." • "While driving, noticed smoke coming from steering column." • "Smoke emitted from steering wheel column as a result of a fire."
2. Interior systems: passive restraint: airbag: driver, malfunction, failure. • "Airbag did not deploy upon impact with a tree." • "Driver injured after car came to rest and delayed airbag deployment; hit her head and chest." • "Frontal collision occurred at 30-35 mph. Driver's-side airbag failed to function." • "During frontal crash at approximately 45 mph, airbag failed to deploy. Also, shoulder harness did not retract, resulting in chest hitting steering column." • "In 12:00 position, unknown speed, driver's-side airbag did not deploy and passenger's seat belt did not hold."
3. Lighting: switch: button: ring: turn signal lights, locking up, malfunction. • "Steering wheel locked up due to turn signal catching the yellow wiring harness to airbag." • "Second occasion of turn signal burning, first at 8,000 miles, second at 18,000 miles. Smoke comes out of steering wheel." • "Turn signal light switch failed twice." • "Vehicle had smoke coming from steering column due to turn signal shorting out." • "While driving, noticed white smoke coming from steering column where flasher switch is located; replaced turn signal and flasher switch in 1992, problems back." • "Turn signal switch failed, causing smoke to come out of steering column."
4. Electrical system: ignition: electronic control unit, stalling, failure. • "Electronic control module failed; a new unit was installed." • "Vehicle constantly stalled and engine died out; dealer replaced electronic control module, problem recurred." • "On cold starts, vehicle dies; has also died while traveling at 70 mph on 2 separate occasions."
5. Equipment: speed control, failure, malfunction. • "Cruise failures." • "When on the freeway at speed of 55-60 mph, cruise control engaged, smoke started to come out from steering column." • "A momentary loss of total engine power while at highway speeds; cruise control was engaged at time." • "Cruise control failure due to loose connection."

CHEVROLET BERETTA 1992

Complaint Severity: Very Serious. **Recall Alert:** See Recall Index. **Buyer's Summary:** The airbags in this vehicle have experienced failures and malfunctions: You may need a professional evaluation on the condition of the airbags. Check the brakes—listen for noise, look for leaks and feel for vibration. They may fail, perform poorly or require frequent mechanical attention.

Hot Spots and Owner/NHTSA Comments:
1. Brakes: hydraulic: anti-skid system, poor performance, failure, locking up. • "Antilock braking system failed completely and pedal became hard." • "Antilock brake system doesn't work; also, panel lights turn on on occasion." • "Antilock brakes failed twice, resulting in loss of control." • "Antilock brakes activated at 5 mph, pulsated, causing inability to stop. Also, airbag did not deploy." • "Antilock brake system: Experienced pedal fading after applying brakes. Had complete brake lockup after antilock brake system light came on. Impact 12:00 position. Lost control of vehicle."
2. Interior systems: passive restraint: airbag: driver, malfunction, failure. • "Antilock brakes activated at 5 mph, pulsated, causing inability to stop. Also, airbag did not deploy." • "At 45 mph, 12:00 position, airbag did not deploy." • "Stopped at red light, light turned green; started up, airbag deployed; couldn't see, hit car in front." • "Vehicle was in an accident and the airbag did not deploy." • "Thirty mph crash head-on did not deploy the airbag. Car ran into the side of another car."
3. Electrical system: wiring: harness: under dash, malfunction. • "While driving, turned on air conditioner and smelled smoke, noticed fire coming from dash. Fire department said possibly electrical fire." • "Smoke coming out of steering column. Smells like wire burning." • "Steering column smoked due to signal light switch shorting out." • "Due to area of contact switch, grease is coming in contact and causing steering column to smoke. Dealer looking into it."

CHEVROLET CAMARO 1987

Complaint Severity: Typical. **Theft Alert:** 38. **Recall Alert:** See Recall Index. **Buyer's Summary:** The electronic control unit has been blamed for engine performance problems, including stalling and surging. The fuel injection system has been blamed for hesitation and stalling. Be sure the vehicle doesn't die in traffic or at stops. The steering may be stiff or not working correctly. Be sure to test the steering, especially on a cold start. Check the brakes—listen for noise, look for leaks and feel for vibration. They may fail, perform poorly or require frequent mechanical attention. Test the transmission thoroughly. See "Sudden Accelerations" in Introduction.

Hot Spots and Owner/NHTSA Comments:

1. Steering: power assist: pump, breaking, failure. • "Power steering bracket broke, causing accident." • "Loss of power steering; power steering bracket broke." • "Power steering failure; bolts, brackets and belt coming off due to crack in high-pressure line, caused by crack in power steering pump bracket." • "Broken power steering bracket; made of bad aluminum casting, immediately lose power steering as belt comes off, very hard to drive." • "The power steering pump broke causing unexpected loss of control; repaired a defective steering bracket."

2. Fuel: fuel injection system, stalling, hesitation. • "Vehicle has extremely rough idle, stalls, 'check engine' light comes on, sudden acceleration." • "Severe stalling problem when engine hot." • "Car quits while driving, loses brakes and steering power." • "Stalls without warning and at low speeds, accelerated without warning 20 to 50 mph." • "Car stalls on occasion without warning and refuses to restart." • "Engine hesitates, cuts out in all gears, lunges forward at different speeds."

3. Brakes: hydraulic system, failure, malfunction. • "Front end shudders when applying brake—car purchased at 31,000 miles." • "Brake failure; resulted in accident, vehicle totaled." • "Brake system supplied inadequate fluid pressure to rear wheels, right front tire locked up, lost control; accident occurred." • "Uneven braking action, screeching noise." • "When applying brakes, difficult to stop car." • "Malfunction in brake system, pedal goes to floor when applied."

4. Fuel: throttle linkages and control, sudden accelerations. • "Car suddenly accelerated without warning upon pulling into parking space, engine raced and accelerator moved on its own, resulting in an accident." • "Turning corner, vehicle suddenly accelerated." • "No brake response in sudden acceleration, resulting in an accident." • "Approaching off ramp at 55 mph, throttle engaged on its own wide open, able to control by shifting to neutral." • "Vehicle suddenly accelerated, gaining speed, shut car off on expressway, turned key back, gas pedal went to floor, coasted off expressway."

5. Power train: transmission: automatic, poor performance, difficulty shifting, slipping. • "Transmission shifts back and forth from 3rd to 4th at 50 mph, clunk when gear shifted." • "Transmission slips out of park, vehicle rolls, also does not pull; replaced transmission assembly." • "Auto transmission with overdrive downshifting action sluggish, not quick to respond." • "Jumps out of gear from park to reverse." • "Automatic transmission problem, slips, also shifts erratically."

6. Electrical system: ignition: electronic control unit, stalling, sudden acceleration. • "Vehicle suffers surging and stalling while in operation and upon changing gears." • "Electronic component failed, allowing cruise control to come on when turned off, causing sudden acceleration with loss of braking capability." • "While in motion at any speed, engine will lose power and then surge in rapid succession; while this is happening, 'service engine soon' light keeps flashing." • "Stalling problem, stalls at stops due to defective computer." • "Noticeable lack of power when accelerating or going uphill, misses when idling; replaced computer."

CHEVROLET CAMARO 1988

Complaint Severity: Typical. **Theft Alert:** 19. **Recall Alert:** See Recall Index. **Buyer's Summary:** Look carefully for any kind of leakage, especially under the car. The fuel injection system has been blamed for hesitation and stalling. Be sure the vehicle doesn't die in traffic or at stops. Check the brakes—listen for noise, look for leaks and feel for vibration. They may fail, perform poorly or require frequent mechanical attention. Test the transmission thoroughly.

Hot Spots and Owner/NHTSA Comments:

1. Fuel: fuel injection system, stalling, hesitation. • "Vehicle runs poorly, stalls and dies, engine light keeps coming on." • "Vehicle loses power after engine warm; intermittent problem." • "Ongoing stalling problem, feels like engine was never started." • "Malfunction in fuel injection system, causing stalling problems and posing a safety hazard." • "Car fails to start on first try, excessive grinding required for car to start; serviced more than 6 times to no avail." • "Vehicle stalled while driving at 55 mph, sometimes restarts after a cooling period."

2. Interior systems: active restraints: belt retractors, failure. • "Driver's-side seat belt retractor fails to retract." • "Driver and passenger seat belts do not retract." • "Driver's side seat belt is fully extended and retractor is inoperative." • "Failure of seat belt to retract so that it would fit across the chest and support the occupant from going forward to windshield." • "Front seat belt retractors failed."

3. Power train: transmission: automatic, poor performance, difficulty shifting, slipping. • "Automatic transmission doesn't downshift when warm." • "Transmission will not downshift into 2nd gear below 50 mph." • "Transmission sticks, must force into gear." • "Repeated transmission failure; repaired/replaced, replacement acting up." • "Transmission failed."

4. Brakes: hydraulic system, leaks, failure. • "Right front brakes defective." • "Brake failure, retainer used to secure push rod to brake pedal missing, allowing rod to become disengaged from brake pedal." • "Brakes fading, must step on pedal very hard." • "Brake failure; master cylinder replaced because of leak, brake shoes replaced."

5. Fuel: fuel tank assembly, leaks. • "Pressurization causes gas to be forced out around filler cap, running on side of car; replaced gas tanks, caps, lines, etc., still leaks raw gas and fumes." • "Gasoline leak from various locations, raw gas fumes, steady flow of gas forced out from around cap; also, problems with rough idling, unable to locate problem." • "Leaking gasoline in fuel tank area, associated fumes; unable to locate where leak coming from."

CHEVROLET CAMARO 1989

Complaint Severity: Typical. **Recall Alert:** See Recall Index. **Buyer's Summary:** Verify that the cruise control system works properly, and that it doesn't cause the engine to surge. The electronic control unit has been blamed for engine performance problems, including stalling and surging. The fuel injection system has been blamed for hesitation and stalling. Be sure the vehicle doesn't die in traffic or at stops. Check the brakes—listen for noise, look for leaks and feel for vibration. They may fail, perform poorly or require frequent mechanical attention.

Hot Spots and Owner/NHTSA Comments:

1. Electrical system: ignition, stalling. • "Passkey system in ignition shorted out." • "Intermittent stalling at highway speeds, results in loss of steering and braking controls." • "Repeated stalling—numerous repairs/replacements, including ignition." • "Car shuts off without warning at all speeds and conditions." • "Vehicle periodically stalls at stop signs or idling in traffic, or sometimes at fast stop." • "Ignition system failed, preventing start of engine; bad computer chip."

2. Brakes: hydraulic system, noise, failure. • "Brakes made noise in reverse." • "While driving, brakes locked up." • "Rear brakes worn out at 22,000 miles, rotors warped, front rotors still have 10,000 miles worth of wear on them, brake pedal pulsated while trying to stop car." • "Rotors replaced twice in less than 12,000 miles." • "Continuous brake problems—too soft, pedal goes to floor; unable to resolve."

3. Fuel: fuel injection system, stalling, hesitation. • "Vehicle stalls when stopping at stop sign or red lights." • "Car stalls when stopped." • "Intermittent stalling." • "Stalling problems; repaired several times, problems continue." • "Vehicle stalls intermittently and without notice of intent to stall."
4. Interior systems: active seat and shoulder belts and belt anchor, poor performance. • "Webbing on lap and shoulder belt was too long; during a severe crash, its effectiveness was reduced, resulting in injuries." • "Problem with seat belt hanging loose." • "Seat belt failed to hold driver and passenger upon impact, both occupants thrown from car." • "Seat belt failure, never properly repaired/replaced." • "Left front seat belt is cut badly, either by retractor or by factory during installation."
5. Electrical system: ignition: electronic control unit, stalling, failure. • "Onboard computer failure." • "While driving, vehicle will stall, causing loss of steering and braking power." • "Computer module replaced twice due to intermittent problems." • "Engine stalling; computer chip failed." • "Defective fuel injection computer board caused car to stall in traffic on freeway; repaired."
6. Equipment: speed control, sudden acceleration, malfunction. • "Cruise control shuts off intermittently." • "Engine accelerated to 80 mph while cruise control was set at 60 mph while traveling uphill." • "Accelerates beyond set cruise speed, with difficult braking." • "Cruise control disengages when going over bumps and railroad crossings—tendency to speed when already engaged; repairing." • "Several cruise control repairs for unspecified problem." • "Cruise control set at 60 mph, slowed, reset cruise control, car then proceeded to accelerate out of control, motor made deafening roar; turned ignition switch off."

CHEVROLET CAMARO 1990

Complaint Severity: Minor. **Recall Alert:** See Recall Index. **Buyer's Summary:** The airbags in this vehicle have experienced failures and malfunctions: You may need a professional evaluation on the condition of the airbags. Test the transmission thoroughly.

Hot Spots and Owner/NHTSA Comments:

1. Power train: transmission: automatic, poor performance, difficulty shifting, slipping. • "Transmission not shifting until 60 mph." • "Parking, automatic shift doesn't hold." • "Transmission leak; replaced." • "Transmission makes funny sounds, acts like it's slipping." • "Transmission slips, won't shift from overdrive when passing."
2. Engine; leaks. • "Engine oil leak." • "Main oil seals replaced twice." • "Apparent oil leaks since purchase—unable to find cause." • "Problem with oil leakage."
3. Interior systems: passive restraint: airbag: driver, malfunction, failure. • "Airbag failed to deploy during an accident, impact 12:00 position, while going between 25 and 30 mph." • "Airbag didn't deploy upon frontal collision." • "No deployment of airbag during accidents, causing injuries." • "While driving down the street, airbag deployed, causing injuries to arm and stomach."

CHEVROLET CAMARO 1991

Complaint Severity: Typical. **Recall Alert:** See Recall Index. **Buyer's Summary:** The electronic control unit has been blamed for engine performance problems, including stalling and surging. The airbags in this vehicle have experienced failures and malfunctions: You may need a professional evaluation on the condition of the airbags. See "Sudden Accelerations" in Introduction.

Hot Spots and Owner/NHTSA Comments:

1. Interior systems: passive restraint: airbag: driver, malfunction, failure. • "Deployment was violent, causing fire." • "Had an accident. Airbag did not deploy." • "Car had a frontal crash around 20 mph; airbag did not inflate." • "Car crashed at highway speed, left front impact point, no airbag deployment; driver sustained preventable neck injuries." • "Driver's side airbag failed to deploy upon frontal impact." • "Airbag deployment while driving, no impact involved."
2. Electrical system: ignition: electronic control unit, stalling, failure. • "Computer chip and programmable read-only memory failure; 'service engine' light comes on and car stalls." • "Stalling at intersections and on ramps. Surging in traffic." • "Computer processor malfunctioned, fast idling." • "Onboard computers failed." • "Malfunctioning of the electronic computer module caused stalling."
3. Fuel: throttle linkages and control, sudden accelerations. • "Vehicle was parked on a downward-sloping parking area, put gear in park; after being idle for 15-30 seconds, vehicle accelerated backwards and hit 3 cars." • "While at a stop, vehicle experienced a sudden surge." • "While driving, vehicle accelerated out of control and hit tree, which caused accident and damage." • "High idle, causing vehicle to jump forward then stall; repaired."
4. Fuel: fuel tank assembly: tank, leaks. • "Gas tank leaked due to pinholes in it." • "Driver's side fuel tank leaked from a bottom surface crack, fuel collected in a pan-shaped shield under the tank." • "Fuel tank leaking on exhaust system while driving." • "Took vehicle in, dealer found pinholes, told her they couldn't repair because she had a full tank of gas." • "Strong fuel smell enters vehicle. Gas tank will leak when tank is full. Dealership claims that they cannot find problem."
5. Electrical system: ignition, stalling, failure. • "Computer problem." • "Vehicle stalls, temporary loss of power." • "Several repairs/replacements of ignition system for stalling." • "Ignition switch and starter failure." • "Engine stalling, resulting in loss of steering." • "Intermittent stalling of the vehicle, unknown causes."

CHEVROLET CAMARO 1992

Complaint Severity: Typical. **Recall Alert:** See Recall Index. **Buyer's Summary:** Verify that the cruise control system works properly, and that it doesn't cause the engine to surge. The fuel injection system has been blamed for hesitation and stalling. Be sure the vehicle doesn't die in traffic or at stops. The airbags in this vehicle have experienced failures and malfunctions: You may need a professional evaluation on the condition of the airbags. Test the transmission thoroughly.

Hot Spots and Owner/NHTSA Comments:

1. Electrical system: ignition, stalling, failure. • "Car stalls out in traffic without any warning, resulting in steering lockup." • "Vehicle stalls without warning after making a stop." • "Usually when cold, sometimes warm, engine will stall when new, especially when coming to a stop." • "Vehicle stalls or idles down continuously when driver makes a turn and shifts gears; 5-speed manual transmission." • "While driving on expressway, intermittent stalling occurred at low to high speeds; dealer is unable to reproduce on computer."
2. Interior systems: passive restraint: airbag: driver, malfunction, failure. • "No deployment of airbag during collision, resulting in injury." • "Impact 12:00, during frontal crash approximately 30 mph, airbag failed to deploy; also shoulder and lap belt failed to retract, resulting in hitting steering column." • "Approximately 15 mph head-on crash into a police car; airbag did not deploy." • "The airbag did not deploy in an accident." • "Airbag did not deploy during front-end collision; vehicle hit creek bank; totaled."
3. Power train: transmission: automatic, poor performance, difficulty shifting, slipping. • "Vehicle will roll away once placed

in park; this has happened 4 times." • "Automatic transmission linkage slipping." • "Transmission shifts rough." • "Transmission fails to shift properly, sticks in passing gear, has delayed shifting." • "When shifting gears, vibration comes from inside transmission due to something loose inside transmission." • "Automatic transmission oil pan screw keeps coming loose, allowing oil leakage. Replaced transmission pan gasket 5 times and tightened screw."
4. Fuel: fuel injection system, stalling, hesitation. • "Intermittent stalling." • "Vehicle hesitates."
5. Equipment: speed control, failure, malfunction. • "Cruise control failed." • "Cruise control engages itself, sticks." • "Cruise control inoperative."

CHEVROLET CAMARO 1993

Complaint Severity: Typical. **Recall Alert:** See Recall Index. **Buyer's Summary:** Check the brakes—listen for noise, look for leaks and feel for vibration. They may fail, perform poorly or require frequent mechanical attention. See "Sudden Accelerations" in Introduction.

Hot Spots and Owner/NHTSA Comments:
1. Fuel: throttle linkages and control, sudden accelerations. • "Throttle sticks." • "Throttle stuck, causing loss of control; accident." • "Sudden acceleration, causing accident." • "While driving, engine idles 2,000-3,000 rpm, vehicle travels without pressing gas pedal. Replaced idle air control sensor and oil sending unit to no avail." • "While driving, vehicle accelerated out of control without warning." • "Unwanted acceleration, engine revs to 4,000 rpm when idling, settles in at 2,000 rpm. Won't run slower than 2,000 rpm. Engine light comes on."
2. Brakes: hydraulic system, locking up, pulling. • "Rear end axle assembly replacement caused front brakes to lock up when making a sudden stop, resulting in loud noise; cruise control engages without warning." • "Brake master cylinder, rotors and pads, and steering gear replaced." • "Brakes locked up, causing accident." • "Upon pressing brake pedal, vehicle pulls either right or left severely. Dealer contacted Chevrolet; told there is no fix." • "Throttle sticking in a open position, causing high idle and resulting in hard braking."

CHEVROLET CAMARO 1994

Complaint Severity: Serious. **Recall Alert:** See Recall Index. **Buyer's Summary:** The airbags in this vehicle have experienced failures and malfunctions: You may need a professional evaluation on the condition of the airbags. Check the brakes—listen for noise, look for leaks and feel for vibration. They may fail, perform poorly or require frequent mechanical attention. See "Sudden Accelerations" in Introduction.

Hot Spots and Owner/NHTSA Comments:
1. Interior systems: passive restraint: airbag: driver, malfunction, failure. • "Airbag did not deploy during accident, resulting in an injury." • "No deployment of driver's airbag during accident, resulting in injury." • "Car was in an accident, hit in the front and driver's airbag didn't deploy; baby was in car seat, the seat belt didn't restrain child, who was thrown into front." • "Dual airbags did not deploy." • "Frontal collision impact 12:00 position, speed 50 mph; driver's airbags did not deploy."
2. Brakes: hydraulic: anti-skid system, poor performance, failure, locking up. • "Antilock brakes vibrate and overheat." • "Antilock brakes lock up." • "Antilock brake system failed while going 60-65 mph, resulting in an accident." • "Antilock brake system locked and threw occupant forward, applied brakes, accelerated before stopping." • "Antilock brake system completely failed; caused accident; broadsided by another vehicle; brake pedal solid as rock, did not slow down vehicle."
3. Interior systems: passive restraint: airbag: passenger, malfunction, failure. • "Frontal collision, impact 12:00 position, speed 50 mph, passenger's airbag did not deploy." • "Vehicle 12:00 position at 30 mph, driver and passenger airbags deployed and passenger airbag caught on fire after deployment." • "No deployment of passenger's airbag during accident, resulted in an injury." • "Car was in an accident, hit in the front and passenger's airbag didn't deploy; baby was in car seat, the seat belt didn't restrain child, who was thrown into front." • "In accident when both airbags deployed, passenger airbag caught on fire; delayed opening."
4. Interior systems: instrument panel: glove compartment door, failure, breaking. • "Glove box latch broke." • "Glove compartment door latch failed." • "Glove compartment door hinge and lock failure." • "Glove box lock broke, making it difficult to open glove compartment."
5. Fuel: throttle linkages and control, sudden accelerations. • "Vehicle subject to stalling, hesitating and then surging. Dealer worked on vehicle 5 times." • "When engine is cold, the idle drops way down and then goes way up, causing sudden acceleration." • "When at stop sign, with driver's foot on brake, vehicle surged forward. Engine races. Driver put vehicle in park and applied accelerator in order to stop engine from racing." • "Twelve instances of throttle opening, causing sudden acceleration; last occurrence caused a crash into a pole at 35 mph." • "When vehicle is first started, experience high idle with engine; also when air conditioner is on, vehicle will surge with high idle."
6. Electrical system: ignition, stalling, surging. • "Engine stalls and power shuts off while driving." • "While driving at highway speeds, car loses power and shuts off." • "Driving, car cut off and came on at a stop light, and the airbag deployed."

CHEVROLET CAPRICE 1987

Complaint Severity: Troublesome. **Theft Alert:** 8. **Recall Alert:** See Recall Index. **Buyer's Summary:** The carburetion system could contribute to stalling and hesitation. Verify that the cruise control system works properly, and that it doesn't cause the engine to surge. Check the brakes—listen for noise, look for leaks and feel for vibration. They may fail, perform poorly or require frequent mechanical attention. Test the transmission thoroughly. See "Sudden Accelerations" in Introduction.

Hot Spots and Owner/NHTSA Comments:
1. Fuel: throttle linkages and control, sudden accelerations. • "Police vehicle. Throttle stuck in open position, causing vehicle to surge forward." • "Vehicle involved in 2 sudden-acceleration accidents." • "While parking car, sudden surge of acceleration occurred while foot was on brake; collided with brick wall." • "After release of accelerator, car maintains momentum for about 1,000 feet." • "Vehicle rapidly accelerated in reverse, brakes failed to slow down, car shot across street, broke sidewall and uprooted tree."
2. Equipment: speed control, poor performance, sudden acceleration. • "Problem poor performance of cruise control, no way to cut out memory on cruise; after turning off, when turned on again goes to last resume speed, not current." • "Experienced sudden acceleration while cruise control button on." • "Due to location, cruise control can be easily turned on by mistake when using turn signal because both on same control." • "When cruise control turned on, causes car to surge back to last speed in memory." • "Inoperative cruise control; installed new cruise switch." • "Cruise control hangs up sometimes, will not come on til about 5 miles down road after hit 'resume' button, doesn't release like it should."

3. Power train: transmission: automatic, poor performance, difficulty shifting, slipping. • "Automatic transmission failure after 49,000 miles." • "Vehicle stopped in park position, driver exited to open gate, transmission slipped out of park into reverse, caught door on post before stopping." • "While in park, with engine running, car suddenly jumped into gear and lurched forward, resulting in accident." • "Automatic transmission makes growling noise when warming up." • "While driving 55 mph, suddenly motor racing, car slowed down, at best could do only 20 mph."
4. Engine: fire, leaks. • "Engine caught on fire twice; repaired/replaced." • "Coolant leaks and does not stay in reservoir due to cracked block, blown intake gasket, defective water pump, radiator and belt; repaired/replaced engine." • "Loss of coolant in engine for no explainable reason, engine knocking." • "Losing antifreeze; repaired/replaced block, hesitation began, repaired/replaced plug, still losing antifreeze, repaired/replaced cylinder head; rapping noise." • "Engine compartment fire, cause undetermined."
5. Brakes: hydraulic: shoe: disc brake system, failure, locking up. • "Front brakes failed, vehicle was involved in an accident." • "Burning rubber smell from right front wheel area when brakes applied over extended period." • "Front disc pads, calipers and rotors become very hot while in stop-and-go traffic; service center states calipers not releasing properly." • "Front wheels locked, could not get steering wheel to go straight." • "While driving under rainy conditions, front wheels locked up upon braking, causing loss of control, resulting in accident."
6. Fuel: fuel carburetion, stalling, hesitation. • "When attempting to put car in motion upon starting, engine stalls." • "Fuel system malfunctions, resulting in engine surges; accelerates suddenly and erratically." • "Repeated stalling problems, causing loss of power steering in heavy traffic." • "Continuous stalling problem causes brake and steering loss; repaired/replaced fuel pump (twice), solenoid, converter switch and fuel pump filter." • "Intake manifold ruptured, causing antifreeze to leak into cylinders."

CHEVROLET CAPRICE 1988

Complaint Severity: Typical. **Theft Alert:** 18. **Recall Alert:** See Recall Index. **Buyer's Summary:** Verify that the cruise control system works properly, and doesn't cause the engine to surge. Test the transmission thoroughly. See "Sudden Accelerations" in Introduction.

Hot Spots and Owner/NHTSA Comments:
1. Equipment: speed control, malfunction, surging. • "Cruise control would not disengage, causing unwanted acceleration." • "Cruise control malfunction, lagging and surging at various times, surged to previous cruise control set speeds when slowing to make turns." • "Malfunction of the cruise control caused car to go out of control." • "Engine idles fast after braking when using cruise control, cruise control would not disconnect until ignition switch turned off; replaced automatic choke." • "Driver entered freeway, accelerated to merge with traffic, car failed to slow back to traffic speed, striking police car in rear; injuries sustained."
2. Power train: transmission: automatic, poor performance, difficulty shifting, slipping. • "Transmission would not shift into drive until car reaches 40 mph, drives with 2nd gear, stepping on accelerator brings no response for 5 seconds when overtaking." • "Car would not initially shift out of 1st, suddenly lurched forward with extreme motion into 2nd." • "While driving, transmission went out, locked in 1st gear; transmission replaced." • "Transmission performs badly on upgrades while in overdrive, lags on downshifts, speed decreases." • "Transmission blew up; a small transmission for a large car."
3. Fuel: throttle linkages and control, sudden accelerations. • "Vehicle jumped into drive from reverse and accelerated, causing accident." • "Vehicle speed increases while driving. Must depress the brake pedal hard to resume normal speed." • "Upon putting car in reverse, brakes depressed and car accelerated out of control; resulted in accident." • "Car suddenly accelerated, kept pumping brakes but car would not stop, put on parking brake to finally stop car." • "Turning right, car accelerated out of control; accident resulted, driver killed."

CHEVROLET CAPRICE 1989

Complaint Severity: Typical. **Theft Alert:** 14. **Buyer's Summary:** Make sure the shoulder belts don't cut across your neck and are well anchored. Verify that the cruise control system works properly, and that it doesn't cause the engine to surge. The electronic control unit has been blamed for engine performance problems, including stalling and surging. Test the transmission thoroughly. See "Sudden Accelerations" in Introduction.

Hot Spots and Owner/NHTSA Comments:
1. Fuel: throttle linkages and control, sudden accelerations. • "Vehicle suddenly accelerates by itself." • "Upon shifting from park to drive, vehicle suddenly accelerated, went out of control and hit another vehicle." • "No reduction in speed when gas/pressure pedal was stopped/reduced, causing an accident." • "Gas pedal sticks and/or car engine continues to accelerate after foot removed from pedal; occurred twice." • "Vehicle suddenly accelerated, maintained speed without foot on gas pedal." • "Car accelerated in reverse after being shifted from park." • "Brakes did not stop vehicle; hit another vehicle."
2. Power train: transmission: automatic, poor performance, difficulty shifting, slipping. • "Vehicle rolled backward while in park, causing accident and injury." • "Transmission 'thumping' at gear change, frequently 'ready' to downshift; removing foot from pedal causes engine to momentarily speed; caused accident." • "Bump or hard reaction when shifting into 2nd at acceleration." • "Noise in transmission." • "Transmission slipped from park into reverse, resulting in accident." • "Started vehicle, got out to scrape passenger and rear windows, and when started on windshield, car started rolling backwards, hitting tree across street."
3. Equipment: speed control, failure, malfunction. • "Cruise control sticks; even without cruise control on, car continues at same speed until brakes touched." • "Cruise control failed without any warning." • "Cruise control would not engage while driving uphill." • "Cruise control stopped working without braking." • "Bushing in cruise control servo bail slipped out of place, causing sudden acceleration and accident."
4. Interior systems: shoulder belts, uncomfortable, poor design. • "Shoulder strap ratchet feature, to relieve uncomfortable tension on the chest, has been omitted; seat belt very uncomfortable." • "Poorly designed seat belt, unsafe driving condition due to constant choking effect of shoulder strap on neck." • "Driver's seat belt has tendency to strangle; constant tension on retraction mechanism, impossible to lock seat belt into fixed position." • "Seat belts do not have lock to lock in safe position, cut across neck upon sudden stop." • "Shoulder belt fits across neck instead of across chest area, chokes; also, does not ratchet." • "No slack in shoulder belt, pressure is on chest at all times."
5. Electrical system: ignition: electronic control unit, sudden acceleration, stalling. • "Engine completely shuts off when coming to a stop." • "Repaired computer." • "Sudden acceleration, causing accident." • "Vehicle stalls when raining and windshield wipers are functioning."

CHEVROLET CAPRICE 1990

Complaint Severity: Troublesome. **Recall Alert:** See Recall Index. **Buyer's Summary:** Make sure the shoulder belts don't cut across your neck and are well anchored. Make sure the seat belts function correctly and fit comfortably. See "Sudden Accelerations" in Introduction.

Hot Spots and Owner/NHTSA Comments:

1. Interior systems: passive restraint: belts, uncomfortable, poor design. • "Seat belt shoulder strap comes right over neck and eyes, blocks vision to outside rearview mirror, therefore have to look out window before making turns." • "GMC police-package car equipped with shoulder belts attached to door; position obstructs visibility and causes a safety hazard if door opened in a crash." • "Safety belt fastened to driver's door on window frame, blocks vision to left of driver; if door were to fly open on impact, top of body would be unprotected." • "Shoulder harness rubs neck; door doesn't completely close; mounting harness on upper rear portion of window blocks vision to each side." • "Bad design of door-mounted seat belt restraints; police officer died in similar car when thrown out of car, door opened in collision." • "Malfunction in passive restraint system occurred when door of car opened during accident, resulting in fatality."

2. Interior systems: shoulder belts, uncomfortable, malfunction. • "Seat belts are too high." • "Door-mounted shoulder straps ride across both front occupants' neck areas, safety compromised in the event of an impact." • "Design and location of seat belt hazardous to driver; when turning to left, shoulder belt rubs on cheek and nose, belts are loose, do not secure in seat." • "Front shoulder belts come across neck, causing discomfort." • "Door-mounted seat belt failed to restrain driver when door opened during accident." • "While driving a police-package car, vehicle was struck head-on by another vehicle; shoulder belts failed, driver and passenger sustained serious injuries."

3. Fuel: throttle linkages and control, sudden accelerations. • "Vehicle suddenly accelerated, hitting a brick wall, impact 6:00; putting vehicle into drive, hit again at 12:00 position." • "While pulling out of the breezeway of hotel, throttle stuck in open position; vehicle hit concrete wall." • "Car took off with throttle wide open, accident resulted." • "On 3 occasions after driving at 30-55 mph, the throttle sticks as if cruise control is set; hit brakes and vehicle slows down." • "Upon shifting transmission from park to drive, vehicle suddenly accelerated, went out of control and crashed into a bar."

4. Interior systems: active seat and shoulder belts and belt anchor, poor performance, malfunction. • "Seat belts used on these vehicles are making it hard for officers." • "Seat belt system creates a blind spot to the driver's left, severely restricting vision, noticeable when seat is in the way back position." • "Seat belt system is not adequate; unsatisfied with performance." • "Upon impact, driver was thrown forward onto the steering wheel, only then did seat belt take hold during frontal crash at approximately 30-40 mph." • "Driver swerved and braked to avoid an accident, vehicle struck a telephone pole; upon impact, thrown forward and hit steering wheel, only the seat belt held."

CHEVROLET CAPRICE 1991

Complaint Severity: Serious. **Recall Alert:** See Recall Index. **Buyer's Summary:** The airbags in this vehicle have experienced failures and malfunctions: You may need a professional evaluation on the condition of the airbags. Check the brakes—listen for noise, look for leaks and feel for vibration. They may fail, perform poorly or require frequent mechanical attention. See "Sudden Accelerations" in Introduction.

Hot Spots and Owner/NHTSA Comments:

1. Brakes: hydraulic: anti-skid system, poor performance, failure, locking up. • "When you hit a bump, the antilock brake system does not function properly." • "Antilock brake system locked up immediately after right front wheel hit icy spot in road." • "Brake line from antilock brake system installed improperly, resulting in hole wearing through the brake line and loss of brakes." • "Antilock brake system, when applied during panic stop, allows vehicle to continue; poor response to pedal travel." • "Antilock brakes failed, resulting in loss of control and accident." • "The car has antilock brake system. The brakes do not grab right away when used in a panic stop. This only happens at high speeds."

2. Fuel: throttle linkages and control, sudden accelerations. • "Experienced sudden unexplained acceleration while attempting to put vehicle in garage." • "Driver started to put car into drive, foot still firmly on brake, engine accelerated before being placed in drive; caused accident." • "While gear was still in park, vehicle suddenly accelerated and caused an accident." • "Shifted gear into reverse, vehicle accelerated into a wall; no injuries occurred." • "Started vehicle, shifted car into reverse, accelerator pedal stuck to the floor; hit 4 cars." • "Unintended acceleration when shifting into reverse resulted in an accident."

3. Interior systems: passive restraint: airbag: driver, malfunction, failure. • "Vehicle involved in an accident and the airbag did not deploy." • "Airbag did not deploy during frontal collision, impact 1:00 position, speed 30-35 mph; injury to driver." • "Vehicle involved in a head-on collision and airbag did not deploy." • "Sudden acceleration, vehicle in open throttle position when backing up, hit a tree, impact 6:00 position; airbag failed to deploy." • "Vehicle was rear-ended and shoved into telephone pole. Speed of impact not estimated; airbag did not deploy upon contact." • "Frontal collision, impact 12:00 position, hitting another vehicle going 30 mph. Airbag did not deploy."

4. Brakes: hydraulic system, noise, failure. • "When applying brakes, they disengage; slip when obstruction jars front wheel, brake pedal goes down when this happens." • "Left front brake locked, causing accident." • "Brakes make growling noise and fail to hold in summer weather." • "Bushings not tightened, resulting in worn shims and broken vacuum pump." • "Brakes failed, causing accident and injuries."

5. Interior systems: passive restraint: airbag, failure. • "Airbag did not deploy during accident, causing injuries; 3 others injured while wearing seat belts." • "No deployment of airbag; caused injury in accident." • "Airbag failed to deploy in accident." • "Airbag failure during accident; driver injured." • "During a frontal collision at 25 mph, impact at 12:00, airbag did not deploy."

CHEVROLET CAPRICE 1992

Complaint Severity: Very Serious. **Recall Alert:** See Recall Index. **Buyer's Summary:** The fuel injection system has been blamed for hesitation and stalling. Be sure the vehicle doesn't die in traffic or at stops. Test the suspension by feeling for vibration or pulling while driving. The airbags in this vehicle have experienced failures and malfunctions: You may need a professional evaluation on the condition of the airbags. Check the brakes—listen for noise, look for leaks and feel for vibration. They may fail, perform poorly or require frequent mechanical attention. See "Sudden Accelerations" in Introduction.

Hot Spots and Owner/NHTSA Comments:

1. Interior systems: passive restraint: airbag: driver, malfunction, failure. • "Airbag did not deploy in an accident." • "Frontal collision, impact 12:00 position, speed 35 mph, airbag did not deploy." • "Had accident on front left end of the car and the airbag didn't deploy; $6,000 damage." • "Airbag did not deploy after rear-ending another car; speed 35 mph, impact 11:00 position."

2. Brakes: hydraulic: anti-skid system, poor performance, failure, locking up. • "Antilock brake modulating valve failure."

• "Antilock system causes brakes and rear wheels to lock up." • "Antilock brake system failed while utilizing radio-frequency system; speed 40 mph; no warning; cause unknown; patrolman was responding to a radio call." • "Antilock brake system: Driver applied brakes for stopping. Vehicle did not stop right away. Vehicle sounded like a jackhammer and shook when brakes were applied." • "Antilock brakes failed." • "Owner says antilock brake system went out while driving her 4-year-old to school."

3. Communications: horn assembly: button: ring, poor design. • "Design of horn makes it difficult to locate horn button in event of emergency; resulted in an accident. Airbag failed to deploy." • "Due to location of horn mechanism underneath airbag, takes a lot of effort and pressure to blow horn." • "Horn button will not blow in cold weather unless vehicle compartment is warm." • "Location of horn button makes horn operation difficult." • "Horn buttons are difficult to locate in panic situation."

4. Suspension: independent front, alignment, noise, tire wear. • "Front end alignment problem." • "Loss of control after vehicle went over small bumps." • "Noisy suspension." • "Front end misaligned." • "Suspension problems, causing vehicle to wander, premature wear on tires."

5. Fuel: fuel injection system, stalling, hesitation. • "Intermittent stalling." • "Vehicle stalls during heavy rain." • "Intermittent stalling." • "Engine stalled twice in one day."

6. Fuel: throttle linkages and control, sudden accelerations. • "Vehicle suddenly accelerated, hitting a tree head on, airbag did not deploy upon impact." • "Sudden acceleration caused accident." • "Vehicle went into open throttle position while driving, would not stop; vehicle put into neutral to stop, brakes applied." • "Upon starting, barely touching gas pedal, engine roared, then surged and accelerated out of control through garage at approximately 25 mph. Also, airbag failed to deploy."

CHEVROLET CAPRICE 1993

Complaint Severity: Very Serious. **Buyer's Summary:** The airbags in this vehicle have experienced failures and malfunctions: You may need a professional evaluation on the condition of the airbags. See "Sudden Accelerations" in Introduction.

Hot Spots and Owner/NHTSA Comments:

1. Fuel: throttle linkages and control, sudden accelerations. • "Experienced sudden surge in acceleration." • "While coming out of driveway, car accelerated and hit a fence and other objects ending up hitting a house." • "Antilock brake system: Experienced pedal fading after making sudden stop." • "Brakes became hard, antilock brake system light came on, engine shut off. After restart, experienced sudden acceleration." • "Sudden acceleration." • "Sudden acceleration, resulting in loss of control and accident."

2. Interior systems: passive restraint: airbag: driver, malfunction, failure. • "Driver applied brakes and vehicle flipped over. Airbag did not deploy. Front end of vehicle was pushed back." • "Owner's vehicle hit another vehicle from behind. Airbag did not deploy." • "Estimated speed 50 mph. Driver hit wall 3 feet high. Airbag didn't deploy from impact. Vehicle caught fire from front of vehicle to windshield area." • "Thirty mph crash, seat belts did not restrain occupants and airbag did not come out." • "No deployment of airbag during accident, resulting in injuries."

CHEVROLET CAPRICE 1994

Complaint Severity: Typical. **Recall Alert:** See Recall Index. **Buyer's Summary:** Test the suspension by feeling for vibration or pulling while driving. The airbags in this vehicle have experienced failures and malfunctions: You may need a professional evaluation on the condition of the airbags. Check the brakes—listen for noise, look for leaks and feel for vibration. They may fail, perform poorly or require frequent mechanical attention.

Hot Spots and Owner/NHTSA Comments:

1. Brakes: hydraulic: anti-skid system, poor performance, failure, locking up. • "Antilock brake system: Brakes failed while driving over washboard surface; vehicle kept bouncing over humps; no warning; speed 20 mph." • "Antilock brakes fail when going over bumpy roads and applying brakes." • "Antilock brakes activate when going over bumps or uneven road surfaces, causing brake failures." • "Antilock brakes fail on wet and bumpy roads, causing loss of control and an accident." • "Antilock brake system malfunction, experienced long stopping distance; no part replaced." • "Antilock brake system: When traveling over bumpy surface, vehicle will not respond to brake application."

2. Interior systems: passive restraint: airbag, malfunction, failure. • "Dual airbags did not deploy during frontal accident; impact 12:00 position, speed 30 mph. Rear-ended another vehicle." • "No deployment of airbags during accident, resulting in an injury." • "Airbags failed to deploy during accident, causing injuries." • "Airbag deployment was violent, shattering windshield."

3. Suspension: independent front, alignment, pulling. • "Excessive vibration, causing vehicle to lose control, resulting in an accident." • "Front end misaligned." • "Front end misaligned, causing vehicle to pull to the right." • "Misalignment, causing noise."

CHEVROLET CAVALIER 1987

Complaint Severity: Troublesome. **Recall Alert:** See Recall Index. **Buyer's Summary:** The electronic control unit has been blamed for engine performance problems, including stalling and surging. The fuel injection system has been blamed for hesitation and stalling. Be sure the vehicle doesn't die in traffic or at stops. The steering may be stiff or not working correctly. Be sure to test the steering, especially on a cold start. Check the brakes—listen for noise, look for leaks and feel for vibration. They may fail, perform poorly or require frequent mechanical attention. See "Sudden Accelerations" in Introduction.

Hot Spots and Owner/NHTSA Comments:

1. Fuel: throttle linkages and control, sudden accelerations. • "When shifted into drive, car accelerated at high speed, brakes and steering did not work." • "While traveling about 35 mph, car accelerated, brakes and steering failed; struck utility pole sideways." • "Sudden acceleration, causing accident and injury." • "Vehicle suffered sudden acceleration on 2 separate occasions, loss of control, causing accidents each time with severe injuries." • "Accelerator pedal stuck on several occasions, causing sudden acceleration; brakes inoperative, resulting in accident."

2. Brakes: hydraulic system, failure, pulling. • "Must put foot close to floor before brakes activate." • "Brakes ineffective and require excessive pedal force, appears during cold weather or when car cold, fine after warm-up." • "Car pulled to side upon braking, did not stop until hit truck." • "Car did not slow down, but instead left front wheel locked up throwing car into spin, jerked hard to the right." • "Brake pedal spongy, not stopping car; glazed brakes to correct problem." • "Braking action insufficient, caused driver to lose control of vehicle and hit another car."

3. Electrical system: instrument panel: cluster module, malfunction, failure. • "Dash electrical system not functioning." • "Problems with computerized dash." • "Digital dashboard lights go off unless car is driven for extended period of time without braking." • "Problems with electronic read panel, light disappears and cannot read the instrument readout on the panel." • "Digital dashboard started to fade away while driving, finally completely blanking out."

4. Fuel: fuel injection system, stalling, hesitation. • "While stopping at light or intersection, vehicle constantly stalls." • "Problems with car stalling first thing in morning and also when traveling in stop-and-go traffic." • "Engine constantly hesitates on acceleration, runs poorly and hard to start." • "Engine stalls, worse on cold start in warm weather." • "Continuous stalling when downshifting or stopping; several repairs, idle adjustment, repaired/replaced computer to coolant sensor, problem still exists." • "Excessive idling and stalling upon startup, care must be taken pulling out into traffic to avoid stall."
5. Steering: gear: rack-and-pinion, stiffness, poor performance. • "Power steering difficult to operate in cold weather." • "Steering difficult; replaced rack-and-pinion." • "Steering is difficult when cold due to rack-and-pinion failure; daily." • "Rack-and-pinion steering binds and grabs when vehicle is cold." • "Rack-and-pinion steering unit defective, accident resulted due to failure." • "Steering wheel sometimes stiff even after warming car up, remains stiff for a couple of minutes of driving, problem occurs only during winter months."
6. Electrical system: ignition: electronic control unit, stalling, hesitation. • "Car suffered stalling and hesitating severely and rough idle, 'service engine soon' light coming on, foul odor produced smell of excessive fuel burning." • "Stalling problem disenables power steering; programmable read-only memory needs to be replaced." • "Car stalled and bucked badly due to faulty ignition module." • "Engine stalling with no indications while driving; repaired/replaced controlled emission and fuel system, solenoid, calibrator, programmable read-only memory and injectors, continues to stall."

CHEVROLET CAVALIER 1988

Complaint Severity: Typical. **Recall Alert:** See Recall Index. **Buyer's Summary:** The electronic control unit has been blamed for engine performance problems, including stalling and surging. The fuel injection system has been blamed for hesitation and stalling. Be sure the vehicle doesn't die in traffic or at stops. Check the brakes—listen for noise, look for leaks and feel for vibration. They may fail, perform poorly or require frequent mechanical attention. Test the transmission thoroughly. See "Sudden Accelerations" in Introduction.

Hot Spots and Owner/NHTSA Comments:

1. Fuel: fuel injection system, stalling, hesitation. • "Engine stalled twice driving on highway." • "Vehicle periodically stalls and surges forward." • "Fuel injection stuck in open position, causing erratic idling, intermittent stalling and rough starting." • "Vehicle hard to start on cold morning, hesitates and stalls, also surges forward short distance." • "While driving, car stalls without warning, no restart; now when it restarts it doesn't go anywhere." • "Vehicle stalls while driving 55 mph, without warning, must put car in park to restart; near-accidents."
2. Brakes: hydraulic system, premature failure. • "Brake application doesn't stop the car unless with extreme amount of pressure." • "Brakes failed prematurely at 12,000 miles; repaired/replaced pads, rotors, right rear shoes and wheel cylinders." • "While trying to stop suddenly, brakes failed, resulting in accident." • "Brake pedal sinks to near floor." • "Ineffective braking, pulls hard to left when brakes are applied, does not stop within safe distance; repaired 4 times, problem still not solved." • "When pressing down on brakes, brakes go further than should, left brakes shrink."
3. Electrical system: ignition: electronic control unit, stalling, failure. • "Vehicle periodically shuts down or stalls when driving in traffic due to defective electronic control module. Has been repaired 3 times." • "Experiencing intermittent surging and stalling problems, replaced new programmable read-only memory and exhaust gas recirculation valve." • "Computer malfunction, engine idle just before stalling, hesitates when accelerating with cold engine." • "Car dies after starting when engine cold, replaced programmable read-only memory sensor and module, tightened all connections." • "Vehicle intermittently stalls during all kinds of weather."
4. Fuel: throttle linkages and control, sudden accelerations. • "Throttle cable melted, which caused the car to accelerate with no braking response." • "While backing out of driveway, vehicle accelerated out of control and hit a tree; shifted to neutral, vehicle went into reverse and hit neighbor's house." • "Experienced sudden acceleration while parking in garage, brake did not stop vehicle, crashed into wall." • "Vehicle stalled; sudden acceleration, causing accident, after repairs."
5. Engine: fire, noise, stalling. • "While idling, vehicle caught on fire." • "Vibration from engine, causing front window and rear-view mirror to become loose." • "Engine will stall when turning air conditioner on." • "Engine knocking at idle speed." • "Engine unstable, makes noise and stalls." • "Wrong metal on manifold, pinholes developed and engine became noisy; repaired/replaced engine."
6. Power train: transmission: automatic, poor performance, difficulty shifting, slipping. • "On small hills transmission seems to shift up and down excessively." • "Automatic transmission shifts late, makes banging and/or clinking noise when accelerating and/or braking." • "Second gear went out in transmission—hard time steering, especially on left turn." • "Transmission leaks, loose bolts." • "Automatic transmission, leaking transmission fluid."

CHEVROLET CAVALIER 1989

Complaint Severity: Typical. **Recall Alert:** See Recall Index. **Buyer's Summary:** The electronic control unit has been blamed for engine performance problems, including stalling and surging. The fuel injection system has been blamed for hesitation and stalling. Be sure the vehicle doesn't die in traffic or at stops. Check the brakes—listen for noise, look for leaks and feel for vibration. They may fail, perform poorly or require frequent mechanical attention. Test the transmission thoroughly. See "Sudden Accelerations" in Introduction.

Hot Spots and Owner/NHTSA Comments:

1. Electrical system: ignition: electronic control unit, stalling, failure. • "Five electronic control modules have failed. Car has stalled at all speeds and stranded driver in the stream of traffic." • "Intermittent stalling due to faulty computer chip." • "Computer programmable read-only memory, when not working properly, can cause engine to choke down during normal operation of vehicle." • "Electronic control module malfunctioned 3 times, causing vehicle to stall." • "Intermittent stalling due to short in the electronic control module."
2. Brakes: hydraulic system, failure, premature failure, poor performance. • "Brakes and master cylinder failed, causing brakes to fade." • "Inadequate brake system, does not work properly at times." • "Premature wear of brakes." • "Several times brakes go all way to floor, you have to start pumping them." • "When applying lots of pressure, brakes tend to pull, doesn't occur when using brakes gently." • "Brakes defective, required too much pressure on pedal to stop car properly, vehicle pulsating and/or shaking when brakes applied; repaired/replaced front and rear brakes."
3. Fuel: fuel injection system, stalling, hesitation. • "Car engine hesitates badly when trying to accelerate after engine has warmed up; hesitation causes uneven application of power, loses

traction, also backfires." • "Engine stalling problems; also backfires." • "Fuel carburetion system defective, engine backfires, pops, makes firecracker noises." • "Car stalled out when put in reverse." • "Car hesitates or misses on acceleration and at sustained speeds; installed plugs, deflector kit, coils, programmable read-only memory, intake manifold and coolant sensor, still problem." • "Engine stalling problems; several attempts to solve problem to no avail."

4. Fuel: throttle linkages and control, sudden accelerations. • "After turning on the ignition, throttle stuck in open position; engine accelerated, lurched forward, hitting a wall; no prior warning." • "Car accelerates when it is idling." • "Vehicle continues to accelerate once foot removed from gas pedal." • "When pulling out into traffic, the vehicle stalled out." • "Backing out of the driveway, vehicle surged rearward; resulted in an accident." • "Gas pedal stuck, causing car to accelerate, brakes didn't help; resulted in accident."

5. Electrical system: ignition, stalling, failure. • "Vehicle will stall intermittently at any time." • "Ignition module malfunctioned and vehicle stalled." • "Engine would die for no reason; almost caused accident when making left turn." • "Intermittent stalling at highway speeds." • "Car stalls out while driving, with no warning."

6. Power train: transmission: automatic, poor performance, difficulty shifting, slipping. • "Transmission slips when going into 3rd gear due to burnt clutches." • "Transmission leaking." • "When vehicle is in reverse, gears become locked up and unable to shift gears." • "Transmission popping out of 2nd and 4th gears unexpectedly; serviced 4 times, repaired/replaced gear box; also popping noise on downshifting, serviced 8 times, repaired/replaced programmable read-only memory." • "Car making noise when reaching speed of about 50 mph, louder at 65-70 mph, due to transmission problem."

CHEVROLET CAVALIER 1990

Complaint Severity: Troublesome. **Buyer's Summary:** The electronic control unit has been blamed for engine performance problems, including stalling and surging. Check the brakes—listen for noise, look for leaks and feel for vibration. They may fail, perform poorly or require frequent mechanical attention. Make sure seat belts function correctly and fit comfortably. See "Sudden Accelerations" in Introduction.

Hot Spots and Owner/NHTSA Comments:

1. Electrical system: ignition, stalling. • "Cold stalling in the morning; replaced electronic control module twice, overhauled engine and spark plugs cleaned." • "Unexpected stalls while driving at city speeds; no determination as to what is causing the stalls." • "Vehicle constantly stalls." • "Vehicle has an electrical short in system. When left turn signal was used, driver smelled smoke. Car stalled and won't start." • "Dome light stays on, power door locks." • "Vehicle stalls while driving, lost complete power."

2. Interior systems: passive restraint: belts, uncomfortable, poor design. • "Poor seat belt design, hits left ear and crosses lower left side of face." • "Poor design of automatic seat belt, shoulder harness lies directly over windpipe, heard of incidents where occupants were ejected when door opened in crash." • "Safety belts obstructing view on driver and passenger-sides." • "Passive restraint belt and harness are attached to doors rather than frame, shoulder strap misses shoulder of 5′ 2″ tall person and cuts across throat." • "Car came fitted with automatic restraints, shoulder strap misses shoulder and cuts across throat; could crush windpipe in an accident."

3. Electrical system: wiring: harness: front: under hood, failure, fire. • "Car was idling, electrical fire started in engine compartment." • "After 2 miles of use, engine caught fire as soon as vehicle was parked. Fire department report is available." • "Vehicle caught on fire due to electrical short in engine." • "Under the hood electrical short caused a fire." • "After parked 20 minutes, vehicle caught fire due to possible electrical failure under hood."

4. Fuel: throttle linkages and control, sudden accelerations. • "Cruising at 5 mph, vehicle came to stop while foot was on brake, it then raced and took off, colliding from the rear with another vehicle." • "When gear shifted into reverse, vehicle suddenly accelerated, vehicle lost control; resulted in an accident." • "When put car in drive, shot ahead, striking two other cars." • "While backing out of driveway, car shot across the street, brakes ineffective, car stopped after going over stump; damaged gas tank and blew front tire." • "Started car and shifted into reverse with foot on brake, experienced sudden acceleration in reverse, which resulted in accident and injury to driver."

5. Brakes: hydraulic system, failure, noise. • "Pads disintegrated." • "Delayed braking response resulted from poor brake performance." • "Had complete brake failure going down a mountain, car went over cliff; vehicle totaled." • "Brakes failed on steep hill, also failed without any warning, just disintegrated, almost causing accident; caliper stuck open; destroyed rotors, pads and drum." • "While coming to stop, grinding noise followed, then brake pedal went to floor, caused no brakes; resulted in an accident."

6. Electrical system: ignition: electronic control unit, failure, stalling. • "Electrical system failed, all power lost." • "Cold stalling in the morning; replaced electronic control module twice, overhauled engine and spark plugs cleaned." • "Vehicle stalled on highway without warning in fast lane. Computer module seems to be the problem."

CHEVROLET CAVALIER 1991

Complaint Severity: Serious. **Recall Alert:** See Recall Index. **Buyer's Summary:** The electronic control unit has been blamed for engine performance problems, including stalling and surging. Check the brakes—listen for noise, look for leaks and feel for vibration. They may fail, perform poorly or require frequent mechanical attention. See "Sudden Accelerations" in Introduction.

Hot Spots and Owner/NHTSA Comments:

1. Brakes: hydraulic system, premature failure, noise, poor performance. • "Brakes replaced 5 times." • "Brakes operate poorly, need to step hard on pedal to stop car." • "While driving, vehicle accelerated without applying more pressure to accelerator pedal. Brakes responded with minimum performance." • "Rear brakes locked up 4 times, causing brake failure." • "Squeaking brakes." • "Brakes are inoperative in cold weather."

2. Electrical system: ignition, stalling. • "Intermittent stalling at medium speeds." • "While driving, vehicle intermittently stalls." • "Vehicle constantly stalls." • "Vehicle stalls constantly without warning, causing loss of control." • "Vehicle constantly stalled; tapping sounds and noises appeared while driving; replaced ignition module." • "Engine intermittently stalls under normal driving, especially while in 5th gear; no prior warning."

3. Fuel: throttle linkages and control, sudden accelerations. • "After slightly bumping a parking stopper, the vehicle accelerator stuck open and caused the vehicle to suddenly take off, resulting in an accident." • "Upon applying the brakes, vehicle surged forward." • "Car goes into overdrive when brake is pushed, surges without pushing accelerator pedal." • "Engine accelerated and surged forward at high speed immediately after shifting from park to drive; loss of steering and braking power; resulted in an accident." • "In warm weather, car has sudden acceleration with no warning."

4. Electrical system: ignition: electronic control unit, stalling. • "Intermittent engine stalling at any speed." • "Vehicle intermittently stalled and shut off while in motion in various types of driving conditions and without warning." • "Engine stalled causing accident; electronic control module repaired and programmable read-only sensor replaced." • "While driving in heavy traffic, vehicle would lose power and cut off; when starting and putting it in gear, must restart it 3 or 4 times before it takes off." • "Intermittent stalling and acceleration." • "Car stalls while driving, then loses power."
5. Interior systems: active seat and shoulder belts and belt anchor, breaking, uncomfortable, failure. • "Passenger's seat belt cracked, driver's seat belt failed during accident, resulting in injuries." • "Seat belt failed during accident." • "While driving on highway at 25 mph, another vehicle stopped quickly in front of car, had to come to a complete stop, seat belts did not lock." • "Shoulder belts strike the neck." • "During a head-on collision, seat belts failed to hold passengers; 2 occupants suffered injuries."
6. Brakes: hydraulic: shoe: disc brake system, noise, failure. • "Brakes make a popping noise and the steering wheel vibrates when making turns." • "My daughter applied the brakes and there was no response. She rear-ended another vehicle. A police officer depressed the brake and received no response." • "Brakes make a popping noise when applied and steering wheel vibrates when making turns." • "Front brakes replaced 3 times." • "Noisy right front brake; pads and rotors replaced, problem continues."

CHEVROLET CAVALIER 1992

Complaint Severity: Troublesome. **Recall Alert:** See Recall Index. **Buyer's Summary:** The fuel injection system has been blamed for hesitation and stalling. Be sure the vehicle doesn't die in traffic or at stops. Check the brakes—listen for noise, look for leaks and feel for vibration. They may fail, perform poorly or require frequent mechanical attention. See "Sudden Accelerations" in Introduction.

Hot Spots and Owner/NHTSA Comments:
1. Brakes: hydraulic: anti-skid system, poor performance, failure, locking up. • "Antilock brake system failed, left rear wheel locked up, causing accident." • "While driving, upon making attempt to slow down, pedal went to the floor and continued to go forward on antilock brake system-equipped vehicle, hitting another vehicle." • "Antilock brakes failed to stop vehicle when applied, causing extended stopping. Has been repaired twice." • "Antilock brake system failed when applied; brake warning lights come on periodically; speed 25 mph, impact 12:00 position." • "When heavy braking was applied, the antilock brakes locked up, resulting in a skid; then they released and pedal pulsated to a full stop." • "When vehicle approached a red light, the brake pedal went to the floor and vehicle ran into intersection. Seconds later, the antilock brakes resumed."
2. Electrical system: ignition, stalling, failure. • "While driving at speeds up to 55 mph, vehicle stalls and causes a loss of steering and braking power." • "While driving low to high speeds, engine shuts down; just prior to shutting down vehicle starts hesitating." • "Vehicle stalls constantly without warning causing loss of control; contributed to an accident." • "Ignition module failed, caused the muffler to overheat." • "Vehicle stalls while driving."
3. Brakes: hydraulic system, noise, poor performance. • "When applying the brakes, there's no response from the antilock brake system." • "When brakes are applied, car still rolls an additional 10 feet. Resulted in an accident." • "Brake noise; adjusted rear brakes." • "Brakes noisy and require extended stopping distance." • "Brakes hard when cold."
4. Fuel: fuel injection system, stalling, hesitation. • "Vehicle decelerates by itself." • "Vehicle hesitates when accelerating." • "Intermittent stalling; fuel pump replaced, problem continues." • "Five attempts to fix the leaking fuel lines. O-rings failed." • "Intermittent stalling." • "The vehicle leaks gas out of fuel injector onto engine and exhaust system."
5. Fuel: throttle linkages and control, sudden accelerations. • "Vehicle will not respond to acceleration, intermittently. Other times will accelerate, but may start to buck." • "While slowing down on a highway or at a full stop, the vehicle will accelerate at approximately 40-45 mph and at full stop 12-15 mph; requires heavy braking." • "When vehicle is left at idle speed, vehicle will surge." • "Going down road, shifting from 2nd to 3rd caused throttle to stick open. Dealer changed linkage and computer chip." • "Vehicle suddenly accelerated while backing out of parking lot, causing damage to 2 other vehicles."
6. Equipment: electric power accessories: locks: door, malfunction, failure. • "Automatic power door locks lock and unlock while driving down road. This is a safety hazard. Dealer can't diagnose problem." • "Power door locks failed." • "Power door lock actuators fail continually, causing doors to jam."

CHEVROLET CAVALIER 1993

Complaint Severity: Troublesome. **Recall Alert:** See Recall Index. **Buyer's Summary:** Check the brakes—listen for noise, look for leaks and feel for vibration. They may fail, perform poorly or require frequent mechanical attention.

Hot Spots and Owner/NHTSA Comments:
1. Brakes: hydraulic: anti-skid system, poor performance, failure, locking up. • "Antilock brake system failed, resulting in extended stopping distance." • "Antilock brake system failed twice. Pedal traveled to the floor. No braking effect. No prior warning. Resulted in an accident. Owner will send accident report." • "Front antilock brake system brake pads are wearing out prematurely." • "Antilock brake system caused locking of all wheels, no braking power, resulting in accident." • "Antilock brake system brake pedal got rock hard during slushy driving at 20 mph, car would not stop. Second occasion happened at 10 mph, with normal pedal feel but car not stopping."
2. Brakes: hydraulic system, failure. • "Brakes failed 4 times, once resulting in loss of control and an accident." • "Total loss of braking ability, unknown cause for loss of braking." • "On wet pavement, experienced intermittent brake failure when pedal becomes hard halfway, inadequate brake action allows vehicle to continue to roll forward."
3. Communications: horn assembly: button: ring, failure. • "Horn pops out of steering wheel, hangs by the wiring, causing steering problems; replaced 3 times." • "Horn button in center of steering wheel pops out while turning." • "Horn button fell off 5 times." • "Padding for horn falls off; getting stuck in rings of steering wheel, making it almost impossible to steer. Replaced entire steering wheel 3 times."
4. Interior systems: bucket: back rest, malfunction, failure. • "After being rear-ended, driver was thrown forward, unrestrained seat back flew forward and struck the driver's back and head." • "Vehicle merged into traffic at 25 mph, hit another vehicle, impact 6:00, driver's seat backrest collapsed rearward and broke." • "Driver's and passenger's bucket seats flip forward upon braking, sending occupants forward. Could cause personal injury." • "Passenger's seat does not lock when braking suddenly." • "Was driving on the road, went to sit back and the driver's-side seat back fell into the rear."
5. Brakes: hydraulic: disc: pads and shoes, premature failure. • "Right front brake pad smoking." • "Antilock brake system: Replaced front disc pads at 25,000 miles, brakes began to squeak."

• "Front brake pads failed." • "Front brake pads and rotors failed prematurely twice."
6. Communications: horn assembly, malfunction, failure. • "Horn cap fell off." • "Horn pad fell off 6 times." • "Square section where horn is located popped out twice. Second occurrence, popped out with wire wrapping around steering column, causing driver to lose control." • "Wiring connected to the horn keeps popping out, causing difficulty with steering. Replaced steering wheel twice to no avail."

CHEVROLET CAVALIER 1994

Complaint Severity: Typical. **Recall Alert:** See Recall Index. **Buyer's Summary:** The steering may be stiff or not working correctly. Be sure to test the steering, especially on a cold start. Check the brakes—listen for noise, look for leaks and feel for vibration. They may fail, perform poorly or require frequent mechanical attention. Test the transmission thoroughly.

Hot Spots and Owner/NHTSA Comments:
1. Brakes: hydraulic: anti-skid system, poor performance, failure, locking up. • "Antilock brake system-equipped vehicle has failure of brakes when driven over a period of time. Vehicle responds poorly to pedal travel and there is excessive vibration." • "When braking, antilock brake system is loud and causes extended stopping distances." • "Antilock brake system failed to stop vehicle when applied at 35 mph, causing vehicle to rear-end other vehicle." • "Antilock brake system feels like something clicks and/or snaps while applying brakes; pedal goes to floor; pumped brakes to build up enough pressure to stop; problem has occurred 5 times." • "Antilock brake system light comes on periodically, experience no stopping ability, pedal was hard first time, second time faded to the floor; replaced a part of computer module."
2. Communications: horn assembly: button: ring, failure. • "Horn button falls out of steering wheel, wheel was turned and was jammed by button locking between turn signal and the steering wheel. Car crashed." • "Horn button fell off steering wheel into steering column switches." • "The horn button on steering wheel falls off into lap of driver, or lodges between steering wheel and dash." • "Steering wheel cover with horn buttons falls off while driving, hangs by wires so you can't turn the wheel."
3. Communications: horn assembly, failure. • "While backing out driveway, wheel turned clockwise, horn fixture fell out, wiring wrapped around lever on washer and locked up the wheel, broke the lever and horn." • "Horn assembly fell out while driving at 35 mph." • "Vehicle horn assembly disengages from, and jams itself in, lever controls." • "Steering wheel horn and assembly fell off and disconnected while in motion. Assembly repaired twice, with failure reoccurring again." • "Horn cover continues to fall off, has wire attached, gets stuck in the steering wheel."
4. Power train: transmission: automatic, poor performance, difficulty shifting, slipping. • "Purchased brand new car, replaced transmission mount without finding the problem; more problems with the engine." • "Transmission slips on upshifts." • "Brake, steering failed. Auto transmission locked up at 25 mph."
5. Steering: wheel: handlebar, failure, locking up. • "When driving, steering wheel padding comes off; on one occasion it got stuck between wheel and signal bar." • "Steering wheel hub cover with wiring connected to it falls off into steering wheel while driving, causing steering disability." • "When going downhill, vehicle stalls and steering wheel locks up; dealer can not locate the problem." • "Horn button falls out of steering wheel, wheel was turned and was jammed by button locking between turn signal and the steering wheel. Car crashed."

CHEVROLET CELEBRITY 1987

Complaint Severity: Negligible. **Buyer's Summary:** The electronic control unit has been blamed for engine performance problems, including stalling and surging. The fuel injection system has been blamed for hesitation and stalling. Be sure the vehicle doesn't die in traffic or at stops. The steering may be stiff or not working correctly. Be sure to test the steering, especially on a cold start. Check the brakes—listen for noise, look for leaks and feel for vibration. They may fail, perform poorly or require frequent mechanical attention. See "Sudden Accelerations" in Introduction.

Hot Spots and Owner/NHTSA Comments:
1. Steering: gear: rack-and-pinion, stiffness, poor performance. • "Rack-and-pinion steering binds, makes it very difficult to handle vehicle." • "On cold days while warming up, steering wheel feels stiff or locked up, feels okay after warming up." • "Loss of power steering assist due to fluid leaking from power steering hose, pump and steering rack." • "Defective steering seals on rack-and-pinion steering assembly, sometimes very difficult to steer." • "Steering coupling failed, leaking all fluid and rendering steering useless."
2. Brakes: hydraulic system, failure, vibration, premature failure. • "Partial brake failure, brakes did not grab when applied until pedal fully pressed to floor; caused accident with injuries sustained." • "Recurring problem with pulsating brakes; repaired/replaced proportioning valve with piston kit, front rotors, pads, rear drums and bled brakes several times." • "Defective braking system, front rotors and drums turned at 17,683 miles." • "While moving in traffic, applied brake hard, car kept moving, required very hard pedal pressure, and excessive stopping distance."
3. Fuel: fuel injection system, stalling, hesitation. • "Stalling at any point, warm or hot engine, highway speeds, restarting on own after stalling on highway, hesitation upon pickup." • "Engine seems to buck slightly, hesitate when on highway, also stalls out when making complete stop or at traffic light while foot on gas pedal." • "Car cuts out in the middle of traffic and steering locks for a few seconds." • "When decelerating, engine dies suddenly; just before stalling, 'service engine' light comes on."
4. Electrical system: ignition: electronic control unit, hesitation, malfunction, stalling. • "Vehicle hesitates, balks, surges; replaced computer programmable read-only memory twice, problem continues." • "Electronic control module defective, malfunctions, causing car to stall in middle of driving." • "Vehicle constantly stalls with no prior warning; dealer replaced the electronic control module several times, but it did not solve problem." • "Vehicle idle with or without air conditioner on, even after foot removed from accelerator pedal; replaced several parts on computer, problem still exists." • "Car stalls continually while driving at 30 mph, no warning before stall; repaired/replaced computer, spark plugs and programmable read-only memory."
5. Fuel: throttle linkages and control, sudden accelerations. • "Engine surges; it accelerates without pressing on accelerator pedal." • "Vehicle suddenly accelerated, car goes from 0-40 mph without touching gas pedal." • "Car goes 35-40 mph when accelerator not depressed." • "Vehicle suddenly accelerated and caused an accident." • "Car suddenly accelerated when put in drive, brakes didn't work."

CHEVROLET CELEBRITY 1988

Complaint Severity: Typical. **Recall Alert:** See Recall Index. **Buyer's Summary:** The electronic control unit has been blamed for engine performance problems, including stalling and surging. The fuel injection system has been blamed for hesitation and stalling. Be sure the vehicle doesn't die in traffic or at stops. The steering may be stiff or not working correctly. Be sure to test the steering, especially on a cold start. Check the brakes—listen for noise, look for leaks and feel for vibration. They may fail, perform poorly or require frequent mechanical attention. See "Sudden Accelerations" in Introduction.

Hot Spots and Owner/NHTSA Comments:

1. Fuel: fuel injection system, stalling, hesitation. • "Engine cuts off suddenly under normal driving conditions." • "Car stalling at stops; it goes dead at any speed." • "Engine stalling problems, stalls repeatedly and unpredictably." • "While driving on the expressway at 55 mph, engine shut off; car stalls when making turns."

2. Brakes: hydraulic system, locking up. • "Brakes lock up; replaced rear shoes and turned drums and rotors, no cure." • "Brake booster failed." • "Unspecified cause for brake pulsation, calipers machined twice, sanded pads; with less than 7,000 miles on odometer, pulsation has recurred." • "Attorney representing clients who were injured in accident due to brakes that locked up."

3. Fuel: throttle linkages and control, sudden accelerations. • "Black cloudy smoke came from exhaust system, then vehicle surged forward with great speed, brakes failed; resulted in accident." • "Car intermittently accelerates without foot on gas pedal." • "Driver turned ignition on, placed foot on brake, released hand brake, shifted into reverse, car lunged backwards at a high rate of speed with no control; accident." • "Started car and shifted from park to reverse, accelerated at very high speed, which resulted in accident." • "Continued episodes of car bolting; repaired once; car would die out when first started, then accelerate out of control of driver." • "Engine runaway on 2 occasions while foot on brake pedal; repaired/replaced injectors each time; third time, runaway from dead stop caused accident."

4. Steering: gear: rack-and-pinion, stiffness, poor performance. • "Rack-and-pinion failure, rack binding internally; repaired/replaced rack and resealed." • "Rack-and-pinion steering failed while turning, steering locked, car went off road and hit tree; also, steering was hard in morning previously." • "Power steering fluid leakage; replaced steering rack and pump." • "Rack-and-pinion steering binded when vehicle was cold, resulted in loss of power until vehicle was driven for awhile." • "Power steering fluid leak; replaced rack-and-pinion."

5. Electrical system: ignition: electronic control unit, stalling. • "While driving on highway at 65 mph, vehicle suddenly shut down in traffic." • "While driving, engine completely shut down because of defective electronic computer module." • "Vehicle stalled at various speeds; loss of power due to malfunctioning of the electronic control module." • "While driving on public highway vehicle stopped running; electronic control module was replaced." • "Main computer repaired/replaced due to engine stalling and dying out while in standing position and in traffic; surges forward; problems continued after computer replacement."

CHEVROLET CELEBRITY 1989

Complaint Severity: Minor. **Recall Alert:** See Recall Index. **Buyer's Summary:** The electronic control unit has been blamed for engine performance problems, including stalling and surging. The fuel injection system has been blamed for hesitation and stalling. Be sure the vehicle doesn't die in traffic or at stops. Check the brakes—listen for noise, look for leaks and feel for vibration. They may fail, perform poorly or require frequent mechanical attention. See "Sudden Accelerations" in Introduction.

Hot Spots and Owner/NHTSA Comments:

1. Electrical system: ignition: electronic control unit, stalling, failure. • "Computer in the ignition system went out; replaced." • "Several electronic control modules have been replaced, engine will stall at any temperature and any speed." • "Computer ignition control problems." • " 'Check engine' light came on intermittently; repaired/replaced electronic control module." • "Car totally shuts down, brakes and engine, no warning."

2. Fuel: fuel injection system, stalling, hesitation. • "Recurring engine stalling problem; recommended fuel injection be cleaned." • "Constant engine stalling problem, fuel feeds improperly; repaired/replaced programmable read-only memory, computer chip and idle air control several times, all to no avail." • "Engine misses when first started after sitting for long time." • "While driving, either getting off exit from highway or accelerating from restarted conditions, car stalls out." • "While driving, vehicle stalls out with no warning due to malfunction with fuel injection system."

3. Brakes: hydraulic system, premature failure. • "Rotors turned and/or replaced at 15,000, 19,000 and 21,000 miles." • "Car has totally lost all brakes twice. Brake pedal sometimes gets very soft. Brakes come back after car sits for a half-hour. Dealer can't find problem." • "Brake drums need replacing." • "Front brakes grabbing, after being rotated for same problem at 4,000 miles." • "Brakes faded and failed to stop car, except over extended stopping distance; required pumping brakes in order to stop effectively."

4. Electrical system: ignition, stalling. • "Engine intermittently stalls without warning in various types of driving conditions, results in complete loss of power." • "While driving between 35-40 mph, vehicle stalled, resulted in no power steering." • "Intermittent stalling while driving at low speeds." • "While driving on highway at approximately 55-60 mph, upon application of brake, engine stalls with no prior warning." • "After a 10-minute drive, the car will stall repeatedly at low speed or when moving from a stopped condition."

5. Fuel: throttle linkages and control, sudden accelerations. • "Engine ran 10 minutes, was shut off 10 minutes, upon restart and shifting into reverse, it suddenly accelerated backwards til ignition switch was turned off." • "Vehicle suddenly accelerates when driving over 40 mph, causing an uncontrollable risk of accident to occur when driving at high speeds." • "Vehicle continues to idle at 40 mph, accelerates on its own between 25 and 45 mph." • "Gear placed in drive and car took off at high speed, lost power steering and brakes." • "Shifted gear into reverse and car suddenly accelerated, jumped two curbs and grazed tree; engaged brake pedal."

CHEVROLET CORSICA 1988

Complaint Severity: Typical. **Recall Alert:** See Recall Index. **Buyer's Summary:** The electronic control unit has been blamed for engine performance problems, including stalling and surging. Check the brakes—listen for noise, look for leaks and feel for vibration. They may fail, perform poorly or require frequent mechanical attention. See "Sudden Accelerations" in Introduction.

Hot Spots and Owner/NHTSA Comments:

1. Brakes: hydraulic system, excessive wear, poor performance. • "Brakes not adequate, inability to stop in reasonable distance." • "Brakes needed to be replaced due to excessive pressure and wearing on brakes as per recall campaign; problem not corrected, repair service denied by dealer." • "Braking system inadequate and unsafe; accident due to inability to stop car with maximum pressure to brakes." • "Poor performance of brakes, fail at very low speed and in reverse; accident occurred due to brake failure." • "Rotors out of round every 3,000 miles, drums cracked."

2. Structure: hood assembly: latches, failure. • "Hood blew up and destroyed the hood hinges while driving at 55 mph." • "After recall work, hood latch failed, causing the hood to fly open, obstructing driver's view." • "Hood latch failed, causing hood to fly into windshield, loss of visibility and control; accident." • "While driving, hood broke, flew open and blocked visibility; resulted in an accident." • "Hood latch problem, while driving, hood suddenly shot up, hitting windshield with great force; windshield shattered, hood difficult to close back."

3. Electrical system: ignition: electronic control unit, stalling, sudden acceleration. • "Intermittent stalling problem, engine cuts off completely; replaced module and computer." • "Recurring stalling problem, car shuts down while in motion, at stop signs, traffic lights, etc.; repaired/replaced programmable read-only memory and idle air control, problem recurred after 2,000 miles." • "Vehicle experiencing repeated stalling problem, engine would not start back up; replaced 4 computers to no avail." • "Car accelerated without engaging the gas pedal, stopped car by use of emergency brakes and turning off ignition; computer malfunction." • "Electronic computerized ignition would cause motor to shut off; repaired, engine now unexpectedly increases as much as 4,000 rpm while stopped in drive."

4. Fuel: throttle linkages and control, sudden accelerations. • "Vehicle suddenly accelerated, engine races up to 50-60 mph." • "Vehicle suddenly accelerated, when brakes were applied they malfunctioned." • "Intermittent stuck throttle." • "Shifted gear into drive, gas pedal stuck, vehicle accelerated and ran through garage door." • "Upon shifting from park to reverse, the vehicle suddenly accelerated backwards."

CHEVROLET CORSICA 1989

Complaint Severity: Typical. **Recall Alert:** See Recall Index. **Buyer's Summary:** Make sure the shoulder belts don't cut across your neck and are well anchored. The electronic control unit has been blamed for engine performance problems, including stalling and surging. Check the brakes—listen for noise, look for leaks and feel for vibration. They may fail, perform poorly or require frequent mechanical attention. See "Sudden Accelerations" in Introduction.

Hot Spots and Owner/NHTSA Comments:

1. Interior systems: active seat and shoulder belts and belt anchor, uncomfortable, poor performance. • "Seat belt fits across throat; hazardous even in minor accident." • "Anchor of front seat belts too high on doors, causing seat beat to cut across passenger chin and throat." • "Seat belt attached to door; during an accident when door opens, seat belt becomes detached and person slides out." • "Seat belts cut across neck, causing irritation to neck and discomfort; not adjustable." • "Front seat belts improperly installed, lack adjustability."

2. Brakes: hydraulic system, poor performance, failure. • "Repeated brake failure; work with pumping action." • "When attempted to stop for changing signal, traveling 30 mph, brakes failed to stop vehicle despite full braking pressure; accident occurred." • "While driving 25 mph, applied brakes, car did not respond; resulted in accident." • "Defective braking system, no response upon braking application." • "Defective braking system, brakes soft, do not stop car beyond required distance, power booster does not work properly."

3. Interior systems: shoulder belts, uncomfortable, breaking. • "Front shoulder straps are mounted too high on front doors, strap rubs on side of neck, causing irritation." • "Seat belts and cables repaired/replaced, original belts pulled too tight across neck, could choke person in accident." • "Seat belt shoulder strap should be repositioned so that it will not cut across face." • "Seat belts failed to lock up during a crash on driver's side." • "Car was in an accident, seat belt broke."

4. Electrical system: ignition: electronic control unit, stalling, failure. • "Vehicle had a tendency to stop dead in traffic while going 30-55 mph." • "Engine stalled; electronic control unit replaced." • "Vehicle in dealership 6 times for the same repair; at 65 mph the engine will stall." • "Recurring stalling problem, total loss of control, steering wheel and brakes locked up; repaired/replaced electronic control module, idle air control, etc., to no avail." • "While driving, vehicle started to die and engine light kept coming on."

5. Fuel: throttle linkages and control, sudden accelerations. • "When pulling in parking space at 3 mph, car lurched forward suddenly at high speed; resulted in collision." • "Throttle stuck, vehicle suddenly accelerated forward and crashed." • "When started vehicle and shifted gear into drive, vehicle accelerated out of control after being driven prior to that time." • "Vehicle suddenly accelerated when moving gears from park to drive." • "Vehicle suddenly accelerated out of control when started and put in reverse gear."

CHEVROLET CORSICA 1990

Complaint Severity: Troublesome. **Recall Alert:** See Recall Index. **Buyer's Summary:** Check the brakes—listen for noise, look for leaks and feel for vibration. They may fail, perform poorly or require frequent mechanical attention. See "Sudden Accelerations" in Introduction.

Hot Spots and Owner/NHTSA Comments:

1. Interior systems: active seat and shoulder belts and belt anchor, malfunction, failure. • "Seat belt did not restrain occupant from making contact with steering wheel, impact was 12:00 position." • "During a 3-vehicle collision, car door came open with seat belts attached to the door, caused driver to hit steering wheel, which resulted in injuries." • "Seat belt recall refused due to unavailability of parts." • "Recalled due to faulty seat belt; however, after adjustment, seat belt does not ride across shoulder but behind ear and neck." • "Sudden stop experiences intermittent failure of retractor assembly on passenger's side. Also, upon release must feed belt by hand into assembly." • "The seat belt on driver's side will not retract into receptacle without forcing belt. Recall repair was performed already."

2. Fuel: throttle linkages and control, sudden accelerations. • "Upon shifting gear into reverse, vehicle accelerated and caused accident." • "Sudden acceleration problem, engine surged, rear-ending 2 cars, brakes ineffective." • "Brake pedal went to the floor during sudden acceleration emergency; car hit a wall." • "When shifting from park to reverse, brake pedal fully applied, sudden acceleration occurred and ignition had to be turned off." • "Throttle stuck while going through an intersection, hit a bump in road and vehicle suddenly accelerated."

3. Electrical system: wiring: harness: under dash, malfunction, failure. • "Smoke comes out of steering column when turning wheel hard. Dealer cannot detect what's causing the problem." • "Steering column started to smoke about 5 minutes after car was started, experienced smell of burning electrical wiring." • "Steering column smoke." • "Smoke intermittently coming from steering column with turn signal on."

4. Brakes: hydraulic system, noise, failure. • "Noisy and grabbing brakes." • "Brakes have a tendency to fade when applied, and even with force will not lock up." • "Non-antilock brake system brake pedal went to the floor during sudden acceleration emergency; car hit a wall."

5. Interior systems: seat tracks and anchors, breaking, failure. • "Driver's seat track mounting bolt comes loose." • "Driver's seat bracket that's bolted to floor broke. This allows seat to move in any direction." • "Driver's seat broke while driving, experienced seat back failure." • "Had frontal collision, driver's seat came completely off of track." • "Front seats are sliding out of brackets."

CHEVROLET CORSICA 1991

Complaint Severity: Serious. **Recall Alert:** See Recall Index. **Buyer's Summary:** The steering may be stiff or not working correctly. Be sure to test the steering, especially on a cold start. The airbags in this vehicle have experienced failures and malfunctions: You may need a professional evaluation on the condition of the airbags. Check the brakes—listen for noise, look for leaks and feel for vibration. They may fail, perform poorly or require frequent mechanical attention.

Hot Spots and Owner/NHTSA Comments:

1. Interior systems: passive restraint: airbag: driver, malfunction, failure. • "Vehicle was involved in a head-on collision and airbag did not deploy." • "Airbag failed to deploy during front-end collision, impact 12:00 position, approximately 25-30 mph; resulted in injuries to driver wearing seat belt." • "Rear-ended at 45 mph into other vehicle at 12:00 position, airbag did not deploy; driver's side front seat broke and fell off." • "Upon impact at approximately 35-40 mph, the airbag failed to deploy during frontal crash at 12:00." • "Frontal collision, vehicle impact 12:00 position position, speed 40 mph, airbag did not deploy."

2. Electrical system: wiring: harness: under dash, malfunction, failure. • "White smoke emitting from steering column on several occasions." • "Turned on ignition, smoke came from location of the turn signal indicator. Resulted in fire." • "Tilt steering column smokes and has a smell like electrical wires burning when speed is 55 mph and over." • "Driving at 60 mph, smoke started coming from the steering." • "Smoke comes out of steering; possibly a wiring problem."

3. Lighting: switch: button: ring: turn signal lights, fire, failure. • "Smoke came out of steering column due to a short in turn signal switch." • "Turn signal dimmer is situated too closely to steering wheel; at night when lights are bright and going into a curve, it is impossible to dim lights." • "Electrical fire in turn signal." • "Turn signal switch failed."

4. Steering: wheel and column, locking up, failure. • "While driving on turnpike, middle of steering wheel fell in my lap." • "Steering wheel fell off." • "Steering column locked up, causing accident; prior to recall." • "Steering wheel fell off car into lap while backing out of driveway; repaired/replaced steering wheel nut."

5. Brakes: hydraulic system, poor performance, locking up. • "Poor braking performance." • "Brakes do not work properly, extended stopping distance." • "No antilock brake system, speeds greater than 30 mph have reduced stopping power. At speeds under 30 mph, brakes are sufficient." • "Brakes locked up, causing loss of control." • "Takes a lot of effort to stop vehicle because of brakes."

CHEVROLET CORSICA 1992

Complaint Severity: Troublesome. **Recall Alert:** See Recall Index. **Buyer's Summary:** The airbags in this vehicle have experienced failures and malfunctions: You may need a professional evaluation on the condition of the airbags. Check the brakes—listen for noise, look for leaks and feel for vibration. They may fail, perform poorly or require frequent mechanical attention.

Hot Spots and Owner/NHTSA Comments:

1. Brakes: hydraulic: anti-skid system, poor performance, failure, locking up. • "Brakes intermittently pull to left; bumping and jerking noise; rough stop, as if something was hindering braking; antilock brake system lights constantly come on." • "While driving, experienced intermittent brake failure where pedal goes to floor, without prior warning, on antilock brake system-equipped vehicle; dealer has repaired several times." • "Antilock brake system responds poorly to pedal application. Responding with intermittent braking action. Dealer has made 3 attempts to fix, with cause still unknown." • "Brakes failed to stop vehicle when applied, causing extended stopping." • "While coming down a steep grade, antilock brake system began to fade until brakes completely failed and touched floor. Brakes remained inoperative."

2. Interior systems: passive restraint: airbag: driver, malfunction, failure. • "Frontal collision, impact 12:00 position, speed 50 mph, driver's-side airbag did not deploy." • "Frontal collision, impact 12:00 position, speed 65 mph, airbag did not deploy." • "Airbag did not deploy during right front-end collision; impact 1:00 position; speed 40 mph; vehicle totaled." • "In 12:00 position at 45 mph, driver's-side airbag did not fully inflate." • "Frontal collision, impact 12:00 position, speed 25 mph, hitting another vehicle, airbag did not deploy."

3. Electrical system: wiring: harness: under dash, fire, malfunction. • "Owner's vehicle caught fire from the inside and melted the steering column." • "Possible wiring problems, causing turn signal switch and hazard light flashers to fail intermittently; also, burning smell from steering column." • "While driving, smoke and odor come from steering column; no visible fire; cause unknown." • "Strong odor and smoke coming out of steering column."

4. Brakes: hydraulic system, vibration, failure. • "Brake system failure, intermittently the brake pedal goes to the ground." • "When making a stop, brakes pulsate. When hitting a bump the antilock brake light comes on." • "Entered entrance to highway, car in front stopped; driver stopped on brake pedal, but there was no response—brakes failed, slammed into car in front." • "Brakes will fail when applying and then return with no known cause."

5. Lighting: switch: button: ring: turn signal lights, malfunction, failure. • "After using turn signal, noticed smoke coming out of steering column." • "Directional signal would function intermittently. Smoke came out of steering column by hazard switch. Cause undetected by dealer." • "Turn signal switch malfunctioned, causing smoke to emit from steering column." • "The turn signal switch burned. When making turns, smoke came from the steering column."

CHEVROLET CORSICA 1993

Complaint Severity: Troublesome. **Buyer's Summary:** The airbags in this vehicle have experienced failures and malfunctions: You may need a professional evaluation on the condition of the airbags. Check the brakes—listen for noise, look for leaks and feel for vibration. They may fail, perform poorly or require frequent mechanical attention.

Hot Spots and Owner/NHTSA Comments:

1. Interior systems: passive restraint: airbag: driver, malfunction, failure. • "Frontal collision impact, 12:00 position, speed 35 mph. Airbag did not deploy. Shoulder belt did not properly retract." • "Airbag did not deploy" • "Owner says at 45 mph he ran into a parked car and airbag not deploy. Contacted the dealer, with no recourse." • "Vehicle hit a telephone pole at 25 mph and airbag did not deploy."

2. Brakes: hydraulic: anti-skid system, poor performance, failure, locking up. • "Antilock brake system malfunction, brakes lock up constantly at any speed." • "Antilock brake system does not work; when road is wet antilock brake system locks up." • "Antilock brake system brake pedal went to the floor at 20 mph in rainy weather. Car in frontal crash. Pedal was spongy after the accident." • "Antilock brake system light came on when vehicle was idling and when brake was applied. Wheels locked and caused accident." • "Antilock brake system locked up, causing front-end collision at 20 mph."

3. Lighting: switch: button: ring: high/low beam dimmer, poor design. • "High-beam switch hitting steering, not allowing beams to be turned off." • "High-beam/low-beam dimmer switch difficult to operate." • "Dimmer switch becomes inoperative when making a turn." • "Designed location of dimmer switch allows steering wheel to hit switch." • "Dimmer switch becomes inoperative when driving in a curve or making a turn."

4. Interior systems: bucket: backrest, poor design. • "Passenger's seat back is loose and latch is not repairable." • "Loose passenger's seat back." • "Top portion of passenger's seat has a variance of 8-10″." • "Passenger side seat back has 5 inches of play in it. Could cause seat back to collapse during accident."

CHEVROLET CORVETTE 1988

Complaint Severity: Very Serious. **Recall Alert:** See Recall Index. **Buyer's Summary:** The steering may be stiff or not working correctly. Be sure to test the steering, especially on a cold start. See "Sudden Accelerations" in Introduction.

Hot Spots and Owner/NHTSA Comments:

1. Fuel: throttle linkages and control, sudden accelerations. • "Faulty accelerator caused sudden acceleration, brakes failed to slow speed when applied; resulted in accident." • "When shifted from park to drive, vehicle accelerated uncontrollably, resulting in accident." • "While driving at night between 30 and 35 mph, at apex of a curve, vehicle accelerated forward, couldn't control vehicle, spun 180 degrees into a curb and damaged back rim." • "Upon shifting from park to drive, with foot on brake, car began full acceleration, back end lifted with tires spinning, struck tree, shut engine off." • "Car suddenly accelerated to high rpm, took off uncontrollably; resulted in accident."

2. Steering: linkages: tie rod: end, premature failure. • "While traveling, right rear wheel began pulling car off road to right; rear tie rod assembly broke due to design or material." • "Broken right rear tie rod assembly damaged rear wheel, caused right rear wheel to pull vehicle off road to right; replaced tie rod and wheel." • "Recall campaign due to fatigue which could cause fracture in the rear wheel tie rod assembly; problem also exists in 1989 models." • "While traveling at speed of 45-50 mph, when brakes applied hard and fast, rear wheel tie rod broke, caused loss of control; hit curve and car overturned." • "Recall on 1988-1989 model, rear wheel tie rod assembly may fatigue and could fracture, resulting in loss of control."

CHEVROLET CORVETTE 1989

Complaint Severity: Minor. **Recall Alert:** See Recall Index. **Buyer's Summary:** The electronic control unit has been blamed for engine performance problems, including stalling and surging. The steering may be stiff or not working correctly. Be sure to test the steering, especially on a cold start. Check the brakes—listen for noise, look for leaks and feel for vibration. They may fail, perform poorly or require frequent mechanical attention.

Hot Spots and Owner/NHTSA Comments:

1. Electrical system: ignition: electronic control unit, stalling, failure. • "Experienced computer and fuel pump failures, engine wouldn't start." • "Computer failed, electrical problems." • "On-board computer problem." • "Stalling; onboard computer replaced." • "Defective computer circuit board causes engine to stall at idle and low speed."

2. Steering: linkages: tie rod: end, tire wear, premature failure. • "Driver completely lost control of vehicle due to a defect in rear wheel tie rod assembly; accident." • "Recall on rear wheel tie rod." • "Car has excessive tire wear on the rear end, wear due to defected tie rod assembly on rear end." • "Received recall on rear tie rod that can cause crash." • "Recall notice received on rear wheel tie rod assembly that may fatigue and could fracture; parts unavailable for repairs."

3. Emergency parking brake: mechanical, failure. • "Ratchet on emergency brake failed; repaired/replaced." • "Emergency brakes failed." • "Parking brake failed." • "Emergency brake problems; recall."

4. Brakes: hydraulic system, malfunction, failure. • "Brakes malfunction." • "Brakes too sensitive when engaging or making sudden stops." • "Defective brakes; 3 times when brakes were applied car went out of control and almost resulted in accident." • "Serious brake problems."

5. Brakes: hydraulic: power assist: booster, failure, leaks. • "Power booster failure." • "Brake booster failed." • "Defective power brake booster, diaphragm has pinhole." • "Power brake leaks and makes air noise, sometimes need more pressure on brakes; repaired, problem recurred."

CHEVROLET CORVETTE 1990

Complaint Severity: Troublesome. **Recall Alert:** See Recall Index. **Buyer's Summary:** The steering may be stiff or not working correctly. Be sure to test the steering, especially on a cold start. Test the suspension by feeling for vibration or pulling while driving. Check the brakes—listen for noise, look for leaks and feel for vibration. They may fail, perform poorly or require frequent mechanical attention. Test the transmission thoroughly. See "Sudden Accelerations" in Introduction.

Hot Spots and Owner/NHTSA Comments:

1. Brakes: hydraulic system, failure, pulling. • "Twice vehicle suddenly went into a spin; wet weather caused the brakes to grab intermittently; second incident resulted in an accident." • "Uneven brake wear." • "Brake failure on 3 separate occasions, causing 3 separate accidents." • "Vehicle experienced brake failure." • "During brake application, vehicle pulls violently to the left."

2. Fuel: throttle linkages and control, sudden accelerations. • "Sudden acceleration, applied brakes and vehicle would not stop; resulted in an accident." • "Sudden acceleration." • "Throttle linkage failure." • "Upon starting, engine surged then suddenly accelerated into garage, causing extensive structural damage to garage and house." • "Problems with accelerator sticking, causing to accelerate at high rate of speed, applied brakes, but car went out of control, smashing into tree."

3. Suspension: independent front, vibration, failure. • "Computer-controlled suspension system failed." • "Vibration and skidding on turns." • "Vehicle spun to the left during light rain, causing accident and injuries." • "Vehicle went out of control on wet pavement, causing accident and injury." • "Loss of control in wet weather conditions resulted in accident and injuries."

4. Interior systems: active seat and shoulder belts and belt anchor, failure. • "Seat belts failed prior to recall." • "Problems with safety belts." • "Driver's side seat belt failed." • "Seat belt failed."

5. Power train: transmission: automatic, poor performance, difficulty shifting, slipping. • "Transmission shift module replaced." • "Defective transmission seal." • "Problem with the transmission."

6. Steering: power assist, noise, failure. • "Problem with steering noise when turning wheel left or right or when car is stationary; 4 repair attempts, still a problem." • "Power steering failure; accident." • "Power steering gasket; intake and hose replaced." • "Steering problem."

CHEVROLET CORVETTE 1991

Complaint Severity: Very Serious. **Recall Alert:** See Recall Index. **Buyer's Summary:** Check the brakes—listen for noise, look for leaks and feel for vibration. They may fail, perform poorly or require frequent mechanical attention. See "Sudden Accelerations" in Introduction.

Hot Spots and Owner/NHTSA Comments:

1. Brakes: hydraulic: anti-skid system, poor performance, failure, locking up. • "Antilock brake system light failed." • "Antilock brake system active warning light on." • "Antilock brake system failure." • "Brake failure on antilock brake system, light came on and pedal faded; caused an accident." • "Brakes locked up, causing loss of control and an accident."

2. Fuel: throttle linkages and control, sudden accelerations. • "On several occasions vehicle accelerated out of control when foot was removed from accelerator pedal." • "Upon taking foot of the accelerator pedal in order to pull out onto highway, vehicle accelerated, hit patch of ice, jumped curve and hit concrete sound barrier." • "Throttle linkage that holds up pedal broke, causing pedal to fade, resulting in vehicle veering to the left, hitting a wall." • "Sudden acceleration caused accident." • "Antilock brake system light has flickered since car was new; owner feels this may relate to sudden acceleration when he tried to drive slowly in reverse."

CHEVROLET LUMINA 1990

Complaint Severity: Minor. **Recall Alert:** See Recall Index. **Buyer's Summary:** Check the brakes—listen for noise, look for leaks and feel for vibration. They may fail, perform poorly or require frequent mechanical attention.

Hot Spots and Owner/NHTSA Comments:

1. Brakes: hydraulic: shoe: disc brake system, excessive wear. • "Front brakes have been replaced at least 5 times during 2-year period; exact cause of problem unknown." • "Brakes wear out, make a grinding noise; replaces brakes continually every 8,000 miles, only front pads." • "Rear brakes inoperable, causing premature front brake wear." • "Brakes will fail intermittently; they respond poorly, with pedal traveling to the floor or it may fade." • "Vehicle has replaced 4 sets of brakes, rotors and pads due to signs of rust and corrosion."

2. Brakes: hydraulic: disc: caliper, corrosion, premature failure. • "Brakes failed, complete loss of brakes due to faulty slides that rusted, causing brake fluid to overheat." • "Rear brake calipers seized on slide pins due to design, resulting in ineffective braking." • "Left front brake caliper fell off vehicle while driving at 20-25 mph due to defective bolt." • "Brakes failed while driving on highway. Rear brakes failed, then the front." • "Rear brake calipers corroded, causing burning smell."

3. Brakes: hydraulic system, corrosion, failure, excessive wear. • "Brake pedal went to floor, resulting in complete brake failure. No prior warning; speed 55 mph." • "Excessive corrosion of power brakes; failed to stop vehicle effectively when applied at any speed. Repaired 3 times." • "Third brake replacement resulting from excessive brake wear." • "Excessive brake wear, resulting in total loss of braking capability." • "Rear brakes stick, causing excessive wear of front brakes."

4. Brakes: hydraulic: shoe and drum system, corrosion, excessive wear. • "Rear disc brakes freeze, putting all braking pressure on front; replaced unit of rear brakes." • "Corroded rear brakes, excessive wear on front brakes." • "Excessive brake failure; wear prematurely; had brakes replaced in 3 years." • "Rear disc brake rusted and came completely off vehicle; no rear brakes." • "Owner has problem with rear disc brakes rusting out; also reduction in brake."

5. Brakes: hydraulic: disc: rotor: disc hub, locking up, poor performance. • "Disc brakes fail to stop vehicle effectively when applied. Brake pads fell off and brake rotor rusted." • "Brake rotors warped, causing calipers to lock up with grinding noise." • "Brake failure, continued wear of disc pads, rotors and calipers." • "Rear brakes work poorly, rotors were damaged irregularly; repaired/replaced rotors and pads." • "Brake pedal went to floor, failure resulted in accident; repaired/replaced rotors."

6. Brakes: hydraulic: disc: pads and shoes, corrosion, excessive wear. • "Rear brake pad fell off while driving, also master cylinder and rotors failed." • "While driving, experienced reduction in brake effectiveness due to corroded rear pads, which were found frozen in open position." • "Brake failure, continued wear of disc pads, rotors and calipers." • "Vehicle has premature rear disc brake corrosion." • "Replaced pad assembly." • "Disc brakes fail to stop vehicle effectively when applied. Brake pads fell off and brake rotor rusted."

CHEVROLET LUMINA 1991

Complaint Severity: Typical. **Recall Alert:** See Recall Index. **Buyer's Summary:** Check the brakes—listen for noise, look for leaks and feel for vibration. They may fail, perform poorly or require frequent mechanical attention.

Hot Spots and Owner/NHTSA Comments:

1. Brakes: hydraulic: disc: caliper, corrosion, premature failure. • "Continuous warping of rear brake calipers. Has been repaired 3 times." • "Rear disc brakes corroded and rusted, causing brakes to freeze and leaving only front brakes operative; extended stopping." • "Rear disc brake failure due to rusted rear caliper guide pins." • "Rear rotors warped, causing caliper slides to fail, wear on pads." • "Brake calipers rusted, causing brake failure."

2. Brakes: hydraulic: shoe: disc brake system, poor performance, excessive wear, corrosion. • "The brakes on vehicle are not working properly. Rotors have been replaced 7 times. Brakes heat up and warp rotors. Spongy brakes. Brakes lock up." • "Disc brakes wear excessively, causing lack of braking ability. Repaired twice." • "Antilock brake system rear brake not working; there is a service bulletin on the brake, but changed brake pad at 2,200 miles and cleaned the rotor." • "Brakes difficult to apply above 40 mph; caused accident." • "Corroded rear brakes, excessive wear on front brakes."

3. Brakes: hydraulic system, excessive wear, failure. • "While driving, made attempt to brake, pedal went to the floor; on 3 prior occasions this occurred, but was able to get pedal to come back after pumping." • "Brakes failed 3 times, resulting in an accident and injuries." • "Had 3 sets of the brakes on the car since February 1993." • "During pedal application brakes appear to grind; caused by corrosion." • "Had to replace brake system 3 times because of premature wear."

4. Brakes: hydraulic: shoe and drum system, corrosion, excessive wear. • "Antilock brake system: Driver heard clicking noise; rear brakes rotted; fell apart." • "Antilock brake system became completely inoperative. Pedal went to floor, left rear wheel was smoking. Rear brakes were inoperative." • "The rear brakes have just been replaced because they were totally corroded, causing extra wear on the front brakes." • "Rear brakes have premature wear due to front brakes absorbing stopping pressure."

5. Brakes: hydraulic: disc: pads and shoes, excessive wear, corrosion. • "Hit brakes and the rear pad came off." • "Replaced rusted rear pads." • "During normal and emergency stopping, pedal gets hard and brake does not respond; replaced brake pad." • "Pads not making contact with rotors, causing rotors to warp." • "Excessive wear of front brakes every 8,000 miles."

6. Brakes: hydraulic: disc: rotor: disc hub, vibration, rust, noise. • "Under service bulletin, replaced caliper on 4-wheel disc brakes, pedal vibrates when pressed, need to replace all 4 rotors." • "Rotors are rusted; pads are not contacting rotors; causes vibration; decreased stopping ability." • "Antilock brake system: Heard noise when applying brakes; rear caliper froze; rust developed on rotor; pads rub on rust, not touching rotor; causes excessive braking effect." • "Front brake discs and steering become inoperative when driving through water." • "Rear disc brake rotors freeze up, burn the brake shoes and destroy the brakes."

CHEVROLET LUMINA 1992

Complaint Severity: Typical. **Recall Alert:** See Recall Index. **Buyer's Summary:** Check the brakes—listen for noise, look for leaks and feel for vibration. They may fail, perform poorly or require frequent mechanical attention.

Hot Spots and Owner/NHTSA Comments:

1. Brakes: hydraulic: anti-skid system, poor performance, failure, locking up. • "Front brake pads wear excessively, producing a squeal. Pads have been replaced with low mileage. Vehicle equipped with antilock brakes." • "Antilock brake system: Complete loss of brake effectiveness. Replaced disc pads and rotors. When driving down an incline, brakes will lock up." • "Antilock brake system: Defect in front brake rotors causes brake pads to wear prematurely, causing brakes to heat up; pedal travels to the floor; extended stopping distances." • "The antilock brake system locked up on vehicle. Pedal went to the floor and vehicle slid into another vehicle. Replaced rear calipers, pads and antilock brake system sensor." • "Antilock brake system: Excessive wear of front brake pads; replaced every 13 months and 12,000 to 13,000 miles."
2. Brakes: hydraulic: disc: pads and shoes, excessive wear, corrosion. • "Brake pads wear prematurely." • "Four-wheel disc brake system front pads wore out in 4,600 miles. Rear brakes are inoperative due to corrosion. Definite safety hazard." • "Antilock brake system: Brake pads wear out prematurely every 3,000 to 5,000 miles; causes failure of antilock braking system; feels like brakes aren't working. Slipping." • "Antilock brake system: Excessive wear of front brake pads; replaced every 13 months and 12,000 to 13,000 miles." • "Have experienced total brake loss and the front brake pads have been replaced several times."
3. Brakes: hydraulic: shoe: disc brake system, excessive wear, corrosion, noise. • "Difficult to push brake pedal, extended stopping distance." • "Excessive brake wear, resulting in front-end vibration and poor braking ability." • "Continuous brake noise due to rotors, pads, calipers and rear sleeves." • "Corroded rear disc brakes; replaced both rear calipers and 4 rotors and pads." • "Corroded rear disc brakes cause reduction in braking ability when applied. Repaired twice."
4. Brakes: hydraulic: disc: caliper, corrosion, excessive wear. • "Four-wheel disc antilock brakes, rear calipers have corroded and rendered rear brakes inoperative, front brakes wear out prematurely. Definitely a safety hazard." • "Caliper froze up and brakes overheated, resulting in no brakes." • "The front disc brake calipers are worn, rotors need to be replaced." • "Vehicle's right and left rear brake calipers are freezing due to corrosion." • "Left front brake pad wore through, ruining front rotors." • "Replaced pads, rotors, and installed rear slide kit."
5. Brakes: hydraulic system, failure. • "Non-antilock brakes will not stop the car at an acceptable distance; one crash has resulted." • "Brakes: Loss of brake effectiveness. Experienced pedal fading when applied. Intermittently grabs. Impact 12:00 position, hitting a tree; speed 15 mph." • "Front and rear brakes replaced." • "While driving, lost brakes upon application."
6. Brakes: hydraulic: disc: rotor: disc hub, corrosion, vibration. • "Defective brake rotors due to corrosion." • "Brake pedal pulsates when applying brakes; caused by warped rotors; back rotors corroded; back pads half worn; rotors turned; pads replaced." • "Left front brake pad wore through ruining front rotors." • "Replaced pads, rotors, and installed rear slide kit." • "The front disc brake calipers are worn, rotors need to be replaced." • "Brake rotors need to be replaced."

CHEVROLET LUMINA 1993

Complaint Severity: Minor. **Recall Alert:** See Recall Index. **Buyer's Summary:** Check the brakes—listen for noise, look for leaks and feel for vibration. They may fail, perform poorly or require frequent mechanical attention.

Hot Spots and Owner/NHTSA Comments:

1. Brakes: hydraulic system, failure. • "While driving at speed of 15 mph, applied brakes and experienced pedal fading. Impact 12:00 position." • "While driving, experienced intermittent brake failure; brake action seems ineffective upon applying brake and vehicle rolls forward, rear-ending another car." • "Power brakes fail to stop vehicle effectively when applied at any speed, causing extended stopping distance." • "Intermittent extended stopping distance when applying the brakes."
2. Brakes: hydraulic: anti-skid system, poor performance, failure, locking up. • "Replaced 3 sets of shoes and rotor; antilock brake system malfunctioned, causing excessively long stopping distance and brake loss." • "Antilock brakes have failed several times, antilock brake light stays on. Most parts have been changed, but problem persists." • "Antilock brakes fail to stop vehicle when applied, causing extended stopping distance. Brake pedal periodically goes to floorboard; use emergency brake to stop." • "Erratic operation of antilock brakes when applied. Pedal goes to floor. Increased stopping distance." • "Antilock brake system failure with loss of effectiveness, vibration when brakes are applied and loud grinding noise."
3. Brakes: hydraulic: shoe: disc brake system, corrosion, locking up. • "The rear brakes are corroded and are causing the front brakes to go out." • "Right brake calipers slide pins froze up, causing rotor to corrode." • "While driving, upon making attempt to stop, brakes seem ineffective and cause extended stopping distance; dealer replaced pads and turned rotors at 11,000 miles." • "Four-wheel disc brakes, experienced extended stopping distance and glazing of brakes." • "Antilock brake system front brakes will lock up. Three dealers can't detect failure. Owner had accident."
4. Brakes: hydraulic: disc: pads and shoes, noise, excessive wear, failure. • "Rear brakes clunk and brake pads fell off; replacement pads smoke and squeak." • "Faulty disc brakes cause front brakes to wear prematurely and squeal, causing antilock brake failure and loss of control." • "Purchased car new, the disc rotor was replaced at 30,000 miles and have had 5 sets of pads." • "Rear brakes make a loud noise when applied; in for repair, turn brake rotors and replace disc pads." • "Brake pedal hard in the morning, also experiencing long stopping distance; replaced front pads and turned front rotors."
5. Brakes: hydraulic: disc: rotor: disc hub, excessive wear, noise, corrosion. • "Brake rotors wear prematurely, causing brakes to squeal and fade." • "Rear brake rotors were rusted and pitted due to improper rear caliper function." • "Rear brakes make a loud noise when applied; in for repair, turn brake rotors and replace disc pads." • "Brake pedal hard in the morning, also experiencing long stopping distance; replaced front pads and turned front rotors." • "Front brake rotors failed prematurely."
6. Brakes: hydraulic: shoe and drum system, corrosion, locking up. • "Rear brakes pop and snap when being applied.

Vehicle in for service 4 times. Cause is still unknown." • "Corroded rear brakes, causing excessive wear of the front pads." • "Rear brakes freeze; shuddering when brakes are applied due to only front brakes stopping vehicle. Rear brakes corroded." • "The rear brakes are corroded and no longer work." • "The rear brakes are corroded and are causing the front brakes to go out."

CHEVROLET MONTE CARLO 1987

Complaint Severity: Typical. **Recall Alert:** See Recall Index. **Buyer's Summary:** Check the brakes—listen for noise, look for leaks and feel for vibration. They may fail, perform poorly or require frequent mechanical attention. Test the transmission thoroughly. See "Sudden Accelerations" in Introduction.

Hot Spots and Owner/NHTSA Comments:

1. Power train: transmission: automatic, poor performance, difficulty shifting, slipping. • "Vehicle jumped out of gear and hit car; accident." • "Automatic transmission with overdrive failed while in motion, engine stopped running; repaired/replaced transmission." • "Upon starting up vehicle, it took a while to put transmission in reverse, but after a while it wouldn't go into reverse at all." • "Automatic transmission cooler lines loose, rubbing noise; also, leak in transmission." • "Transmission leaked; repaired."

2. Brakes: hydraulic system, failure. • "Power brake has poor stopping power when brakes applied; when roads are wet/damp, extreme caution used in braking." • "Brakes failed when stepped on lightly to stop for red light, within seconds car completely turned around, almost out of control." • "Brakes do not stop right away, click when depressed; replaced, still not working properly." • "Improper fluid put in braking system, caused all rubber parts to be badly eroded and distorted; resulted in total brake failure while driving."

3. Fuel: throttle linkages and control, sudden accelerations. • "Gear shift from park to drive, car suddenly accelerated at incredible speed, unable to stop; resulted in accident." • "Vehicle accelerated forward, causing accident." • "While driving, vehicle suddenly accelerates, goes out of control; resulted in an accident." • "Accident caused by sudden acceleration."

CHEVROLET NOVA 1987

Complaint Severity: Typical. **Buyer's Summary:** Check the brakes—listen for noise, look for leaks and feel for vibration. They may fail, perform poorly or require frequent mechanical attention. Test the transmission thoroughly.

Hot Spots and Owner/NHTSA Comments:

1. Brakes: hydraulic system, noise, vibration. • "Defective brakes, rattle constantly, make loud and irritating noise." • "Experiencing trouble with brakes." • "Problem with pulsating brakes."

2. Power train: transmission: automatic, poor performance, difficulty shifting, slipping. • "While in motion, car locks up; transmission defect from factory." • "Vehicle's transmission malfunctions; locked-up engine and front wheel." • "Automatic transmission shifts hard at different intervals, same acceleration." • "Transmission failure."

CHEVROLET NOVA 1988

Complaint Severity: Typical. **Buyer's Summary:** Test the transmission thoroughly. See "Sudden Accelerations" in Introduction.

Hot Spots and Owner/NHTSA Comments:

1. Fuel: throttle linkages and control, sudden accelerations. • "Started car, foot on brake, put gear in reverse, shot backwards, hitting car in back; put in drive, foot still on brake, shot forward, hitting porch." • "Coming down incline, applied brakes, depressed brake pedal, engine raced, car actually accelerated, crossed 4 lanes of rush-hour traffic, jumping curb." • "Accelerator stuck wide open, turned ignition off but car was still accelerating." • "Car malfunctioned when shifted into reverse, leaped about 5 feet to curb out of control, went forward, hit building, no warning of high acceleration." • "Sudden acceleration, causing loss of control."

2. Power train: transmission: automatic, poor performance, difficulty shifting, slipping. • "Several incidences of rolling after engine shut off and car left in gear." • "Transfer filter had hole too small, in pickup vehicle would overheat and fail." • "Problems with automatic transmission, hesitation when accelerating during engine warm-up.

CHEVROLET SPECTRUM 1987

Complaint Severity: Troublesome. **Recall Alert:** See Recall Index. **Buyer's Summary:** Look carefully for any kind of leakage, especially under the car. Problems with the timing gear and chain can cause serious problems. Have the engine checked by a professional. The fuel injection system has been blamed for hesitation and stalling. Be sure the vehicle doesn't die in traffic or at stops. Check the brakes—listen for noise, look for leaks and feel for vibration. They may fail, perform poorly or require frequent mechanical attention.

Hot Spots and Owner/NHTSA Comments:

1. Brakes: hydraulic system, noise, excessive wear, failure. • "Brakes squeaking loudly; resurfaced rotors, repaired/replaced front brake pads and shoes." • "Brake system failed 5 times and replaced; manufacturer problem with valves causing brakes to malfunction quickly." • "Brakes wear out prematurely." • "Hydraulic brake system failed, brake shoes caught fire; hit telephone pole." • "Brakes went to floor and would not stop vehicle."

2. Engine: noise, leaks, failure. • "Engine was running hot, stalled when stopped for lights and oil was burning rapidly." • "Noise and odor from engine—does not say if problem was present prior to non-defect—caused accident to front end." • "Engine seized up solid." • "Oil leakage covering engine caused engine to catch fire during the winter." • "Engine failure due to 'non-freewheeling' design of engine, which causes parts to bind when timing belt fails."

3. Engine: timing gear and chain, failure. • "Timing belt broke, causing vehicle to stall." • "Engine timing belt broke and engine immediately failed." • "Timing belt broke and stalled vehicle in heavy-traffic situation." • "Vehicle's timing belt melted and vehicle became inoperative."

4. Fuel: fuel injection system, stalling, hesitation. • "Vehicle stalled and caused front-end accident." • "Car died in middle of road with no warning or indication lights on, no rough idle." • "Engine idles extremely high after driving 55 mph; stopped at signal light, car acts as though foot on accelerator." • "Stalling problem, misses on hot days and when car is warm."

Chevrolet—Trucks

CHEVROLET TRUCK ASTRO 1987

Complaint Severity: Troublesome. **Recall Alert:** See Recall Index. **Buyer's Summary:** Look carefully for any kind of leakage, especially under the car. The steering may be stiff or not working correctly. Be sure to test the steering, especially on a cold start. Check the brakes—listen for noise, look for leaks and feel for vibration.

They may fail, perform poorly or require frequent mechanical attention. See "Sudden Accelerations" in Introduction.

Hot Spots and Owner/NHTSA Comments:

1. Fuel: throttle linkages and control, sudden accelerations. • "When starting vehicle, the car was at full throttle, went out of control and crashed into light pole." • "Upon shifting from park to drive, vehicle suddenly accelerated, which resulted in an accident." • "Vehicle suffered sudden acceleration, apparently due to sticking and binding of throttle linkage; an accident resulted." • "Upon moving gears from park to drive, vehicle suddenly accelerated, went out of control; passenger was thrown into front windshield and suffered head injury." • "While pulling out of garage, vehicle suddenly accelerated out of control; resulted in an accident."

2. Steering: linkages: arm: idler and attachment, tire wear, excessive wear. • "Problem with idler arms; due to design defect, this part of steering mechanism starts falling apart." • "Two sets of tires worn out in 35,000 miles, cannot keep front wheels in alignment; repaired/replaced one idler arm." • "Idler arm is defective, causing severe tire wear and constant replacements." • "Erratic wear on tires on front end is caused by the excessive play in idler arms." • "Unspecified steering problem; replaced idler arm."

3. Power train: axle assembly: seal: axle shaft, leaks, failure. • "Rear axle seals leaking at 25,000 miles, rear drum brakes damp with rear axle fluid." • "Fluid leak from rear wheels; repaired/replaced both rear axle shaft oil seals." • "Rear axle seal failed, transaxle fluid spilled onto brakes; stopping time at speeds of 30 mph increased, it was hard to stop." • "Both rear axle seals leaking, while driving rear wheels started smoking and drums got too hot to touch; replaced seals, started leaking again." • "Rear seals are defective, seals begin to fall apart and leak, which causes major damage to rear drive mechanism."

4. Steering: power assist: pump, leaks, breaking. • "Power steering bracket broken and complete front engine bracket assembly cracked." • "Power steering bracket ¼" metal broke, causing loss of control." • "Two bolts from power steering pump mounting to block broke off." • "The power steering pump bracket broke, causing vehicle to lose power." • "Eleven power steering hoses have been replaced after leaking because the power steering bracket failed."

5. Steering: power assist, failure. • "Several power steering problems with cracked brackets, hoses, etc." • "Faulty steering, causing vehicle to wander when speed exceeds 30 mph." • "Two bolts connecting power steering pump to vehicle sheared off, caused loss of power steering. Later, bracket around 2 bolts broke again." • "While making left turn, wheel locked into a position that caused vehicle to veer to right; hit telephone pole; impact 1:00 position; 2 of 3 bolts became loose and fell out." • "Steering bracket replaced, prior to recall."

6. Brakes: hydraulic system, locking up, poor performance. • "Consumer states that the brakes of the van are designed poorly thus fail to provide adequate braking; resulted in 1 accident." • "While driving, brakes suddenly locked up, causing loss of control; accident due to faulty brakes." • "Brakes: Vehicle does not stop quick enough; accident due to brakes not stopping van." • "Brake loss on sudden stop, causing accident; repaired, problem persists." • "When conditions are wet or slippery, front brakes lock up when applied firmly, rear brakes ineffective."

CHEVROLET TRUCK ASTRO 1988

Complaint Severity: Typical. **Recall Alert:** See Recall Index. **Buyer's Summary:** The steering may be stiff or not working correctly. Test the steering, especially on a cold start. Test the transmission thoroughly. See "Sudden Accelerations" in Introduction.

Hot Spots and Owner/NHTSA Comments:

1. Steering: linkages: arm: idler and attachment, premature failure, tire wear. • "Idler arm problem, worn and loose at 36,980 miles." • "Idler arms faulty, caused van to pull to right, making it extremely difficult to steer vehicle; repaired/replaced idler arms." • "Idler arm wears, causing both front tires to wear out quickly on outside edge." • "Original steering idler arms have worn out (left and right sides), premature failure, caused excessive and premature tread wear in tires." • "Defective idler arms causing tires to wear out and need replacement at 20,000 miles; replaced both idler arms."

2. Steering: power assist: pump, failure. • "Power steering pump bracket bolt cracked. Caused overheating and loss of power steering assist." • "Bolts came loose from steering pump bracket getting sheared off, causing serpentine belt to fall off." • "Vehicle exhibited loss of power steering capability, power steering pump inoperative and bracket broke." • "Bolts holding power steering pump have sheared off twice, and another was found to be missing." • "Bolts holding power steering pump sheared off twice and were replaced."

3. Fuel: throttle linkages and control, sudden accelerations. • "Upon putting vehicle in reverse, took off wide open in reverse, brakes wouldn't stop; went over hill, resulted in accident and damages." • "High-speed acceleration, brake and parking brake unable to stop vehicle." • "Vehicle continued to accelerate in spite of heavy application of brakes, auto zigzagged uncontrollably; resulted in collision." • "Van suddenly accelerated, hitting a parked car and a pole before stopping, brakes did not operate, resulting in accident." • "After shifting to reverse, engine accelerated, lurched forward. Turned off ignition. Engine still running. Accelerated again, lurched backwards. No warning."

4. Power train: axle assembly: seal: axle shaft, leaks. • "Rear axle seals leak, causing grease to build up on brakes and brake drums." • "Rear axle seals leaked badly, soaking rear brakes making them unusable in emergency stop." • "Approached stop sign, applied brakes, didn't stop, went through sign and was hit; told later rear axle seal leaked fluid on rear brake, causing no rear brake." • "Rear wheel grease seals leaking, right rear at 15,000 miles and 26,000 miles; when seals fail, grease coats brake shoes and drums, which affects stopping of vehicle in quick stops." • "Left and right axle oil seals failed 3 times; rear end could run dry and lock up if not replaced."

5. Power train: transmission: automatic, poor performance, difficulty shifting, slipping. • "Engine runs excessively in lower transmission gears, sometimes does not want to shift up when vehicle is cold." • "Automatic transmission at highway speed, vibrations and poor shifting." • "Transmission sometimes will shift at 35 mph, sometimes bypass to go into overdrive." • "Hot transmission fluid spewed out of the filler or dipstick tube onto hot engine while driving on highway, resulting in engine compartment fire." • "Transmission fluid leaked onto exhaust system, causing fire."

6. Structure: door assembly, breaking, failure. • "Door handles broke off 3 times." • "Double door leaks; unable to repair." • "Doors would not shut properly til slammed." • "All door handles are broken, including sliding door; doors could open on their own while driving, allowing occupants to fall out onto street." • "Sliding door hangs when opening/closing; repaired/replaced lock, repair rods twisted."

CHEVROLET TRUCK ASTRO 1989

Complaint Severity: Typical. **Recall Alert:** See Recall Index. **Buyer's Summary:** Look carefully for any kind of leakage, especially under the car. The steering may be stiff or not working correctly.

Be sure to test the steering, especially on a cold start. Test the suspension by feeling for vibration or pulling while driving. See "Sudden Accelerations" in Introduction.

Hot Spots and Owner/NHTSA Comments:

1. Steering: linkages: arm: idler and attachment, premature failure. • "Both idler arms worn out, causing vehicle to wander and tires to wear out excessively." • "Both idler arms needed to be replaced at 34,000 miles." • "Excessive play in idler arms." • "Loose steering due to premature wear of the idler arms." • "Worn idler arms replaced, problems continue."

2. Engine: leaks, premature failure. • "Cracked engine block." • "Oil seals leak." • "Engine froze, causing smoke to emanate into vehicle, impairing vision." • "Rear main seal leaked." • "Experiencing consistent and ongoing coolant leaks; repaired/replaced manifold, thermostat, gaskets, radiator and tightened hoses, still leaks; repaired/replaced intake gasket and cleaned valve covers."

3. Fuel: throttle linkages and control, sudden accelerations. • "While driving, vehicle accelerated by itself; used emergency brake to stop." • "Throttle stuck in open position; applied brakes to slow down for potholes in road; applied gas pedal; engine accelerated to high speed; speed 20 mph." • "Engine surged, had to turn vehicle off to stop. Replaced throttle body." • "From a stop, vehicle suddenly accelerated to full throttle without pressing on accelerator pedal." • "Van suddenly accelerated full length of garage, crashed through front wall."

4. Suspension: independent front, alignment, tire wear. • "Front end of van does not stay in alignment; faulty front end alignment." • "Faulty front end alignment caused premature wear of front tires." • "Misalignment of suspension ruined tire." • "Defect in suspension caused one tire to wear." • "Upper and lower control arms were replaced."

5. Electrical system: alternator: generator, premature failure. • "Premature failure of alternator." • "While driving on freeway, motor died, alternator froze up; replaced, along with fan belt." • "Alternator defective." • "Fire originated in alternator." • "Alternator out of order, stuck; replaced."

6. Suspension: single axle: rear, leaks, excessive wear. • "While driving, right rear tire blew out, tires show irregular tread wear; problems with suspension." • "Rear axle seal malfunctioned." • "Rear axle suspension not properly lubricated." • "Rear axle seals leak fluid into the drum area (common in Astros and Safaris)." • "Rear axle seals leak onto brake system, causing loss of braking power."

CHEVROLET TRUCK ASTRO 1990

Complaint Severity: Typical. **Recall Alert:** See Recall Index. **Buyer's Summary:** The steering may be stiff or not working correctly. Be sure to test the steering, especially on a cold start. Check the brakes—listen for noise, look for leaks and feel for vibration. They may fail, perform poorly or require frequent mechanical attention. Test the transmission thoroughly. See "Sudden Accelerations" in Introduction.

Hot Spots and Owner/NHTSA Comments:

1. Brakes: hydraulic: anti-skid system, poor performance, failure, locking up. • "Left front wheel sensor replaced, light kept coming on for antilock brakes." • "Problem with brakes grinding during routine stopping; repaired/replaced antilock brake shield and brake sensor." • "Defect in antilock brake system, left front sensor failed causing loss of brake pedal; brakes had to be pumped to stop vehicle." • "Computer from antilock brake system malfunctioning, antilock brake lights came on and stayed on." • "Antilock brakes failed to stop vehicle effectively, causing extended stopping distance. Has been repaired twice."

2. Brakes: hydraulic system, failure. • "Antilock brake system light came on and vehicle completely lost brakes, hit a wall, impact 12:00 position, and caused damages on the underbody of vehicle." • "Power brakes failed to stop vehicle when applied at any speed, causing extended stopping or no braking ability." • "Complete braking failure without warning." • "While performing routine braking evolution with no forewarning, pedal moves forward to the floor and van lurches forward; recurring problem, repaired 4 times."

3. Fuel: throttle linkages and control, sudden accelerations. • "When transmission shifted on its own from park to reverse, vehicle suddenly accelerated." • "When moving from park to reverse, the vehicle suddenly accelerated, vehicle did not stop when brakes were applied; resulted in an accident." • "While in park, vehicle accelerated forward, went out of control, hit a tree and stopped." • "While applying the brakes, vehicle suddenly accelerated, went out of control; resulted in an accident." • "Accident caused by sudden acceleration."

4. Steering: linkages: arm: idler and attachment, premature failure, alignment, tire wear. • "Vehicle has been in the shop 4 times for replacement of idler arms." • "Front idler arm became loose, causing premature tire wear." • "Idler arm seized, causing vehicle to pull to the right, misalignment and sidewall disintegration." • "Owner has had to replace the idler arms on both front sides twice in the last 5 years, and has ruined a number of tires." • "Idler arm, front end failure; being replaced by factory."

5. Power train: transmission: automatic, poor performance, difficulty shifting, slipping. • "Transmission leaking fluid; serviced 3 times." • "Experienced transmission boiling over; additional exterior transmission cooler installed; problem solved." • "Vehicle caught fire in engine compartment; caused by transmission fluid." • "Transmission failed pulling trailer." • "Transmission jumps out of gear."

6. Structure: door assembly, breaking, failure. • "Son opened sliding door upon departure from a convenience store, the sliding door fell off." • "Weld on inside passenger door side collision bar broke, causing bar to detach at that end." • "Side sliding door defective." • "Sliding door came off twice." • "Side door opening difficult; adjusted."

CHEVROLET TRUCK ASTRO 1991

Complaint Severity: Troublesome. **Recall Alert:** See Recall Index. **Buyer's Summary:** The steering may be stiff or not working correctly. Be sure to test the steering, especially on a cold start. Check the brakes—listen for noise, look for leaks and feel for vibration. They may fail, perform poorly or require frequent mechanical attention. See "Sudden Accelerations" in Introduction.

Hot Spots and Owner/NHTSA Comments:

1. Brakes: hydraulic: anti-skid system, poor performance, failure, locking up. • "Antilock brake system light comes on; system replaced. Brake failure resulted in 2 accidents." • "Antilock brake system failed, vehicle went out of control, which resulted in an accident." • "Several brake failures from day one—several inspections before sensor problem found." • "Antilock brake system failed twice due to chafed harness wire to right front wheel speed sensor." • "Antilock brake system failed at 15 mph. All 4 wheels locked up. Brake warning lights came on after problem."

2. Brakes: hydraulic system, locking up, vibration. • "Brakes failed, caused driver to run into ditch to avoid hitting another vehicle." • "Brakes continue to lock up after servicing due to a defective brake system." • "Brake cable failed." • "Antilock brake system front brake rotors warp after driving 5,000-7,000 miles and pads replaced; causes vibration in steering wheel and brake pedal. Rear drums resurfaced at 9,000 miles."

3. Fuel: throttle linkages and control, sudden accelerations. • "While passing another vehicle, car accelerated and remained at high speed." • "Upon shifting gears from park to drive, vehicle suddenly accelerated, crashing into brick wall of garage." • "After vehicle had been sitting for 3-4 minutes, it was started and accelerated out of control in gas station." • "Vehicle accelerates when at a stop position when foot is on brake." • "Upon coming to a stop, vehicle intermittently will accelerate forward; a very firm hold-down of brakes is necessary at all stops."
4. Steering: linkages: arm: idler and attachment, tire wear, premature failure. • "When applying brakes, front end shimmies, resulting in tire wear; replaced idler arm in 1992 and 1994." • "Vehicle's idler arm is loose and causes tire, shock and suspension problems." • "Excessive play in idler arms, causing tire wear." • "Due to vehicle front end design, excessive wear on front tires." • "Loose idler arm replaced due to steering problems, replacement arms became loose after 24,000 miles."
5. Structure: door assembly, premature failure. • "Sliding door won't shut; dealer replaced lock, and now says door needs to be replaced." • "Front doors loose and misaligned, causes rattling and sticking." • "Sliding door lock inoperable." • "Problems with sliding door." • "Internal body weld passenger door separated."

CHEVROLET TRUCK ASTRO 1992

Complaint Severity: Serious. **Recall Alert:** See Recall Index. **Buyer's Summary:** Look carefully for any kind of leakage, especially under the car. Make sure the shoulder belts don't cut across your neck and are well anchored. Check the brakes—listen for noise, look for leaks and feel for vibration. They may fail, perform poorly or require frequent mechanical attention. Test the transmission thoroughly.

Hot Spots and Owner/NHTSA Comments:

1. Brakes: hydraulic: anti-skid system, poor performance, failure, locking up. • "Brake failure; pedal faded, causing an accident with frontal impact at 6:00 position." • "Antilock brakes failed to stop vehicle effectively when applied at 40 mph, causing extended stopping." • "Antilock brakes failed, causing accident." • "Applied slow pressure to brake pedal; no response from antilock braking system." • "Antilock brake system: When stopping during wet weather or on wet surface, antilock brake system will kick in; vehicle will continue to move at normal speed, increasing stopping distance."
2. Brakes: hydraulic system, locking up, failure. • "The accelerator stuck, causing the truck to go out of control, and the brakes would not stop vehicle." • "Owner applied brakes and had difficulty, used excessive effort." • "Gel forming in brake fluid, causing brake seals to break down, resulting in brakes locking up." • "Brakes self-apply while vehicle is in motion, causing brakes to overheat with burning smell; vehicle slows down regardless of attempts to accelerate." • "Poor brake performance and loss of rear brakes."
3. Power train: transmission: automatic, poor performance, difficulty shifting, slipping. • "Transmission slipping/shifting problem." • "Transmission failed." • "Transmission spring and/or ball valve failure." • "Transmission problems." • "When driving, the car cut off at stop light, transmission made a noise."
4. Engine: leaks, failure. • "Engine replaced." • "Engine idles rough, leaking." • "Motor will race and accelerate forward when stopping; will die while idling." • "Engine failed, causing vehicle to stall."
5. Interior systems: shoulder belts, uncomfortable, poor design. • "Passenger shoulder belt comes across face and throat." • "Seat belt button on shoulder harness failed." • "Seat belts don't fit properly." • "Bench seat in rear of vehicle lap and shoulder belt latch female end is too long."

CHEVROLET TRUCK ASTRO 1993

Complaint Severity: Typical. **Recall Alert:** See Recall Index. **Buyer's Summary:** Make sure the shoulder belts don't cut across your neck and are well anchored. Check the brakes—listen for noise, look for leaks and feel for vibration. They may fail, perform poorly or require frequent mechanical attention. Test the transmission thoroughly.

Hot Spots and Owner/NHTSA Comments:

1. Brakes: hydraulic: anti-skid system, poor performance, failure, locking up. • "Antilock brakes failed to stop vehicle, resulting in loss of control and an accident." • "Antilock brake system on rear driver's side locks up at 55 mph. Pressure was not applied, rear brakes overheated." • "Antilock brake system: When applying brakes, experienced complete brake lockup. Vehicle slid to a stop, losing control. Brakes made a loud grinding noise." • "Antilock brake system brake pedal intermittently travels to the floor with no braking effect; no prior warning; could cause accident. At one time, brake module was replaced." • "Antilock brake system does not work properly. Antilock brake system warning light came on. Brakes grind when applied and feel spongy. Wire shorted out."
2. Power train: transmission: automatic, poor performance, difficulty shifting, slipping. • "Bolts in automatic transmission were loose, causing knocking in rear end; tightened bolts." • "Transmission does not shift in 1st and 2nd gears properly." • "When driving, transmission would downshift into neutral." Also, locks up in 2nd gear due to an electrical short in the speed sensor harness." • "Transmission failed." • "Transmission stuck in park; replaced."
3. Electrical system: ignition, stalling. • "Vehicle stalled." • "In cold weather conditions, vehicle stalls and is very hard to keep running." • "While driving down mountain, engine shut down, rendering power steering and brakes inoperative, almost went over cliff; experiences intermittent stalling." • "Vehicle stalls after car has been running for a while. It's like a vapor lock. Dealer cannot duplicate the problem."
4. Interior systems: active seat and shoulder belts and belt anchor, breaking, failure. • "Driver's seat belt and all belts for benches broke, ejecting 5 passengers from vehicle." • "Driver's seat belt failed during sudden stop, resulting in injury." • "Bench seat belt is too long, causing belt to be in wrong position when fastened." • "Front seat belts of insufficient length to fasten."
5. Interior systems: instrument panel: speedometer: odometer, poor performance, failure. • "Odometer defective." • "Odometer failure." • "Speedometer failed." • "While sitting in park, engine revs, digital dashboard mileage indicator turned over miles."
6. Interior systems: shoulder belts, uncomfortable, failure. • "Driver's side seat belt does not fit occupant properly. Belt is not long enough, but with extender the belt hits stomach vs. hips." • "Seat belts do not retract or restrain." • "Third rear shoulder and lap seat belt does not properly restrain occupant due to looseness." • "Poor fit of rear seat belt assembly. Upon vehicle accident, could cause child to be thrown from seat."

CHEVROLET TRUCK ASTRO 1994

Complaint Severity: Serious. **Recall Alert:** See Recall Index. **Buyer's Summary:** The airbags in this vehicle have experienced failures and malfunctions: You may need a professional evaluation on the condition of the airbags. Check the brakes—listen for noise, look for leaks and feel for vibration. They may fail, perform poorly or require frequent mechanical attention. Test the transmission thoroughly. Make sure air conditioner is working properly.

Hot Spots and Owner/NHTSA Comments:

1. Brakes: hydraulic: anti-skid system, poor performance, failure, locking up. • "Antilock brakes failed, causing accident and injuries." • "Antilock brake system failed to stop vehicle when applied, becoming inoperative, brake pedal went completely to floorboard." • "Antilock brake system: After slowing down to make turn, brakes applied, pedal went to floor; extended stopping; vehicle skidded before stopping." • "Antilock brakes failed twice, causing vehicle to lose control and veer to the left, resulting in accidents." • "When applying and driving, the brakes make noise/ vibrate and the brakes lock up; antilock brake system."

2. Interior systems: passive restraint: airbag: driver, malfunction, failure. • "Airbag did not deploy during frontal collision; speed 35 mph; impact 12:00 position; entire subframe replaced; car 1 broadsided car 2." • "During head-on collision, driver's-side airbag did not deploy; totaled." • "Truck struck broadside and went frontal into utility pole. Neither shoulder belt nor airbag activated." • "Frontal collision, impact 12:00 position, speed 35 mph, airbag did not deploy or inflate." • "At 12:00 position at 35-40 mph, hit a concrete bridge embankment and airbag did not deploy."

3. Electrical system: alternator: generator, failure. • "Alternator to air conditioning line failed." • "Alternator failed." • "Alternator failed twice."

4. Air conditioner: failure. • "Air conditioner failed." • "Air conditioner emits odor." • "Air conditioner failed."

5. Electrical system: ignition, stalling. • "While driving, vehicle stalled out. Replaced electronic control module first time, fuel pump second time, to no avail." • "Vehicle periodically stalls when driving at any speed." • "Engine stalls when driving down road. Problem is intermittent. Could cause accident." • "Stalling occurs without warning." • "When starting vehicle, engine outputs black smoke; when driving uphill has a loss of power."

6. Power train: transmission: automatic, poor performance, difficulty shifting, slipping. • "Transmission problems." • "Transmission failed." • "Transmission failure, loss of engine power." • "Transmission failed to shift into upper gears."

CHEVROLET TRUCK BLAZER 1987

Complaint Severity: Typical. **Buyer's Summary:** Look carefully for any kind of leakage, especially under the car. The electronic control unit has been blamed for engine performance problems, including stalling and surging. The steering may be stiff or not working correctly. Be sure to test the steering, especially on a cold start. Check the brakes—listen for noise, look for leaks and feel for vibration. They may fail, perform poorly or require frequent mechanical attention. Test the transmission thoroughly.

Hot Spots and Owner/NHTSA Comments:

1. Brakes: hydraulic system, failure, malfunction. • "Intermittent brake failure; repaired, problems continued." • "Brakes failed intermittently while driving, pedal became hard." • "Brake malfunctions, produces excessive noise and squeal and grabbing." • "Defect occurs when braking suddenly, panic stop, brake pedal becomes hard as a rock, no vacuum assist, does not move down, car does not stop." • "Brakes defective, pedal won't go to floor when depressed."

2. Steering: power assist: pump, malfunction, failure. • "Bracket that holds the steering pump broke, lodged a bolt in the water pump, at which time the steering pump slipped and forced unilateral belt off." • "Two mounting bolts on exhaust manifold to brace on bracket of steering pump were found to be sheared; broke while driving." • "Power steering pump support broke; repaired/replaced pump, brackets and high-pressure hose." • "Bracket housing steering fluid box broke 3 times; one replaced under recall."

3. Power train: transmission: automatic, poor performance, difficulty shifting, slipping. • "Transmission locked up; failed twice." • "Transmission case and front seal leaking; rear axle rebuilt at 3,300 miles, because pinion nut came loose, caused uncontrollable steering." • "Transmission leaks; replaced front pump cover." • "While in motion, vehicle stalled, almost caused an accident, caused by failure of the entire transmission; unrepairable." • "Automatic transmission problems, intermittent difficulties with transmission."

4. Engine: leaks. • "Experiencing problem with low oil pressure on vehicle." • "Engine problem, leaking motor and radiator overflow bottle." • "Engine oil leak, due to blow-by; replaced short block." • "Engine rear main seal and valve cover gaskets leaking; replaced gaskets and seals."

5. Fuel: fuel tank assembly: tank, leaks, malfunction. • "Loose baffle inside tank destroyed inner components, vehicle hesitates, sags and stumbles when starting or pulling out in traffic; replaced air sensor and ignition coil." • "Poor location for fuel tanks." • "Vehicle has a leak in the gas tank due to rust." • "Gas tank seams are separating, allowing puddles to accumulate quickly." • "Leaky gas tank."

6. Electrical system: ignition: electronic control unit, stalling, malfunction, sudden acceleration. • "Stalling problems; electronic control module replaced, problem continues." • "Car accelerates, computer control system apparently not working correctly." • "Stalls while braking due to faulty electronic control module." • "Unspecified computer programmable read-only memory failure." • "Engine lost power after sudden surge and had trouble with instrument panel."

CHEVROLET TRUCK BLAZER 1988

Complaint Severity: Typical. **Recall Alert:** See Recall Index. **Buyer's Summary:** Verify that the cruise control system works properly, and that it doesn't cause the engine to surge. Check the brakes—listen for noise, look for leaks and feel for vibration. They may fail, perform poorly or require frequent mechanical attention. See "Sudden Accelerations" in Introduction.

Hot Spots and Owner/NHTSA Comments:

1. Brakes: hydraulic system, pulling, locking up. • "Brakes failed, causing driver to pull off road." • "When braking, vehicle pulls to left." • "Vehicle's brakes unable to hold 4-wheel drive; while backing down steep grade, struck another vehicle, operator lost control when gear was put into reverse." • "When applying brakes at any speed, vehicle severely pulls to right, causing lane change." • "Steadily and increasingly applying pressure on brakes, wheels will lock, causing rear end of vehicle to pass front of vehicle."

2. Fuel: throttle linkages and control, sudden accelerations. • "Intermittent engine acceleration while stopping at lights." • "Vehicle suddenly accelerates repeatedly, gas pedal goes to floor then releases, always occurred when clutch was depressed." • "Engine surges temporarily, loss of pressure when brake pedal is depressed." • "Upon shifting from park to overdrive, vehicle suddenly accelerated into a van." • "Vehicle suddenly accelerated, foot on brakes did not work; resulted in accident."

3. Power train: axle assembly, excessive wear, breaking. • "Rear end spins out easily, even on dry pavement and worse on wet surfaces, with normal driving." • "While driving, heard loud noise, could not control vehicle as right rear axle broke." • "Left and right axles sheared off, causing vehicle to swerve into tree;

vehicle skidded off icy road into ditch, ripping out rear axle." • "Axle broke off, causing accident." • "Drive axle broke, causing accident."

4. Electrical system: ignition, stalling, high idle. • "Engine shuts off in traffic while applying brakes; no warning." • "Vehicle constantly stalls." • "Vehicle kept stalling on highway. Owner replaced ignition system and flywheel." • "Idles too fast; repaired/replaced computer."

5. Equipment: speed control, malfunction, failure. • "Cruise control at times will not work right." • "Cruise control doesn't operate properly, always up 3 mph lower than set, it resumes when it wants to, also sticks, going as high as 80 mph." • "Cruise control shuts off and does not resume to correct speed; replaced servo valve 3 times." • "Due to the location of cruise control on turn signal arm, the mechanism can be activated without knowing it; this has resulted in the vehicle accelerating."

6. Interior systems: active restraints: belt retractors, malfunction, failure. • "Rear seat belt replaced because it wouldn't retract to hold infant car seat." • "Seat belts failed during an accident; caused injury." • "Seat belts won't retract." • "The driver's-side seat belt does not work properly; the retractor does not work all the time."

CHEVROLET TRUCK BLAZER 1989

Complaint Severity: Typical. **Recall Alert:** See Recall Index. **Buyer's Summary:** Look carefully for any kind of leakage, especially under the car. Verify that the cruise control system works properly, and that it doesn't cause the engine to surge. Test the suspension by feeling for vibration or pulling while driving. Check the brakes—listen for noise, look for leaks and feel for vibration. They may fail, perform poorly or require frequent mechanical attention. Test the transmission thoroughly. See "Sudden Accelerations" in Introduction.

Hot Spots and Owner/NHTSA Comments:

1. Suspension: independent front, alignment, tire wear. • "Front end failed, torsion bar mounts broke; repaired." • "Replaced camber bushings in front suspension, improper front tire wear, feathering of the outer edge tire tread." • "Front wheels realigned, continued poor tire wear despite repairs." • "Car out of alignment, 2 front tires worn." • "Two front tires wear excessively."

2. Fuel: throttle linkages and control, sudden accelerations. • "Upon shifting from park to drive, vehicle suddenly accelerated and crashed into another vehicle; caused death of driver." • "Sudden throttle surging resulted in frontal collision and total loss of control and braking ability." • "Upon putting vehicle into drive, motor revved loudly, suddenly accelerated and crashed into brick wall." • "Started engine, vehicle took off like a rocket, gear selector in park position, steering in lock position; resulted in accident." • "Accelerator hesitated then accelerated; backed into stone wall and damaged tailgate."

3. Brakes: hydraulic system, malfunction, excessive wear, pulling. • "Brake system malfunction, brakes overheating; inherent weakness in system, causing excessive strain on front brakes, resulting in premature wear and failures." • "Front brakes replaced twice, rear brakes replaced." • "Front brakes replaced." • "Vehicle pulls severely to the right when brakes are applied." • "Vehicle pulls to right when braking at highway speeds."

4. Equipment: speed control, failure, malfunction. • "Defect in cruise control." • "Cruise control failed." • "Cruise control works intermittently." • "Cruise control came on and accelerated, hitting a pickup truck." • "Information requested regarding cruise control system defect in 1989-1991 Blazer."

5. Power train: transfer case (4-wheel drive): leaks, noise. • "Defective transfer case caused fluid to leak; repaired/replaced seal in tail shaft, yoke on driveshaft, case and seal." • "Defective chain in 4-wheel drive transfer case is cause of grinding noise when vehicle is in high 4-wheel drive." • "Transfer case in transmission leaked; replaced seal." • "Vacuum switch wouldn't disengage front hubs to freewheeling rotors when vehicle was put into 4-wheel drive." • "Defective chain in 4-wheel drive transfer case, grinding noise when in high 4-wheel drive."

6. Power train: transmission: automatic, poor performance, difficulty shifting, slipping. • "Transmission failure." • "Erratic automatic transmission system." • "Transmission problem." • "Problem with transmission slipping; repaired/replaced gears, clutches, seals, etc., slippage continued." • "Transmission seals failed."

CHEVROLET TRUCK BLAZER 1990

Complaint Severity: Harmless. **Recall Alert:** See Recall Index. **Buyer's Summary:** Look carefully for any kind of leakage, especially under the car. Test the suspension by feeling for vibration or pulling while driving. Check the brakes—listen for noise, look for leaks and feel for vibration. They may fail, perform poorly or require frequent mechanical attention. Test the transmission thoroughly.

Hot Spots and Owner/NHTSA Comments:

1. Brakes: hydraulic system, pulling, premature failure. • "Since purchased, vehicle pulls dangerously to side when brakes steadily applied; engineers have tried to correct problem to no avail." • "Brake dump valve failed; replaced." • "Driver contends vehicle unsafe because it pulls to right upon braking, claims manufacturing defect and arbitrator ruled in his favor." • "Premature brake failure, vehicle drifts or veers to right whenever brakes applied firmly; replaced rear shoes, front pads, drums turned." • "With hard braking, vehicle pulls markedly to right; fails to brake in straight line with hard braking."

2. Power train: transmission: automatic, poor performance, difficulty shifting, slipping. • "Transmission failed to shift from low gear at stop sign." • "Terrible noise, clunking and rough shifting." • "Vehicle rolls back and forth while shifting gears." • "Transmission fluid fire." • "Vehicle jumped out of gear while on a slight grade in a parking lot."

3. Suspension: independent front, alignment, tire wear. • "Front upper and lower ball joints replaced twice." • "Front end would not stay aligned, vibration at high speeds, wore outer edges of tires down." • "Front end alignment problems caused excessive wear of tires." • "When vehicle makes a full turn or U-turn, tires click and appear to be wearing unevenly."

4. Brakes: hydraulic: anti-skid system, poor performance, failure, locking up. • "Poor performance of antilock braking system; repaired by resetting computer error codes, unit failed again." • "Isolation pump valve in rear wheel antilock brake system failed; also, 'brake service' light in dash stays on." • "Front brakes failed." • "Antilock brakes malfunction constantly." • "Antilock brakes failed, causing vehicle to pull to left."

5. Engine: leaks, failure. • "Engine failure." • "Engine overheats." • "Oil leaks." • "Engine compartment burned."

6. Brakes: hydraulic: shoe: disc brake system, pulling, locking up. • "Front brakes defective, need to be checked/corrected." • "Right front brake pulled to the right." • "When braking hard, the vehicle pulls to the right; if uncorrected, at highway speeds the front end of vehicle will change lanes." • "Antilock brake system front brakes locked up while driving, causing jerking when applying brakes."

CHEVROLET TRUCK BLAZER 1991

Complaint Severity: Typical. **Recall Alert:** See Recall Index. **Buyer's Summary:** Check the brakes—listen for noise, look for leaks and feel for vibration. They may fail, perform poorly or require frequent mechanical attention. Test the transmission thoroughly. See "Sudden Accelerations" in Introduction.

Hot Spots and Owner/NHTSA Comments:

1. Brakes: hydraulic: anti-skid system, poor performance, failure, locking up. • "Antilock brakes engaged and released, causing vehicle to lurch forward into a second vehicle twice." • "Antilock brake system and brake light came on dashboard; when owner brought vehicle into shop, she was told ground tubing corroded, causing antilock brake system unit not to work at all." • "Replaced antilock brakes; also, antilock brake system lights come on intermittently." • "Antilock brakes fail when stopping on slick and/or dry surfaces, causing loss of control and antilock brake system warning light to come on." • "Antilock brake system failed, resulting in excessively long stopping distances."

2. Fuel: throttle linkages and control, sudden accelerations. • "Truck may experience uncontrollable acceleration at any time." • "Upon startup, experienced high idle flare, and surging when decelerating or stopping, causing 3-vehicle accident." • "When shifted into gear, truck accelerated out of control, hitting construction tractor and a pile of lumber." • "When gear was shifted into drive, vehicle accelerated and ran into garage." • "Accident and injury caused by sudden acceleration." • "Throttle sticks."

3. Power train: transmission: automatic, poor performance, difficulty shifting, slipping. • "Transmission failed to shift gears." • "Vehicle experiences transmission problems, including loss of low and 2nd gears." • "Transmission caught on fire." • "Transmission engages very hard, vehicle jerks." • "Intermittent transmission failure, does not shift out of 2nd gear and at times does not engage or respond to acceleration."

4. Brakes: hydraulic system, locking up, failure. • "Numerous brake problems occurring, including brakes locking up when driving; repaired/replaced calipers, rotors, master cylinder and pads, problem still exists." • "Brakes completely failed without any warning, vehicle went out of control and caused an accident." • "Hydraulic braking system is inadequate in stopping vehicle in emergency situations as well as in non-emergency situations; one accident already happened." • "Preventional brake gasket has failed, resulting in brakes reducing to a minimum with pedal down to floor."

5. Interior systems: active restraints: belt buckles, malfunction, failure, breaking. • "Rear seat belts do not work; once latched, will not release with button." • "Rear seat belt locking mechanism sticks." • "Front lap belt buckle will not lock when pulled forward." • "Rear seat belt buckle not functioning." • "Front passenger seat belt buckle broke; replaced."

6. Engine: vibration, failure. • "Oil sending gauge failure." • "Engine light comes on erratically." • "Engine parts replaced due to blown gasket." • "Oil pressure gauge sending unit failed." • "At idle and running speeds, engine vibrates."

CHEVROLET TRUCK BLAZER 1992

Complaint Severity: Troublesome. **Recall Alert:** See Recall Index. **Buyer's Summary:** The electronic control unit has been blamed for engine performance problems, including stalling and surging. Check the brakes—listen for noise, look for leaks and feel for vibration. They may fail, perform poorly or require frequent mechanical attention. See "Sudden Accelerations" in Introduction.

Hot Spots and Owner/NHTSA Comments:

1. Brakes: hydraulic: anti-skid system, poor performance, failure, locking up. • "Antilock brakes respond erratically and may shudder when applied. Warning light came on for a short time before failing." • "Antilock brake system: Complete brake failure, pedal faded and light sensor came on." • "Antilock brakes failed to stop vehicle effectively when applied." • "Antilock brake system failed; caused brakes to lock up and pedal to fade; also, light comes on." • "During wet weather conditions, the antilock brake system lights came on, rendering brakes inoperative."

2. Brakes: hydraulic system, noise, failure. • "While driving at 20 mph, driver moved foot from accelerator to brakes and vehicle went full throttle. Driver shifted into neutral and pulled off." • "Brakes fail intermittently. Brake pedal goes completely to floor. No warning lights come on." • "Poor directional control when braking; also, extended stopping distance." • "Applied brakes and then released them, pedal went to the floor with a grinding sound." • "Vehicle had sudden acceleration and brake would not override."

3. Fuel: throttle linkages and control, sudden accelerations. • "Driver turned off engine due to high idling, causing accident." • "Experienced sudden acceleration while backing out of parking lot and putting vehicle in gear." • "Just before coming to a complete stop, the engine races and the vehicle jumps forward." • "Vehicle surged forward when taken from neutral to drive position. Driver did not have foot on accelerator." • "While driving at 20 mph, driver moved foot from accelerator to brakes and vehicle went full throttle. Driver shifted into neutral and pulled off."

4. Brakes: hydraulic: master cylinder, premature failure. • "Master cylinder replaced." • "Antilock brake system; brake pedal went to the floor." • "Master cylinder failed." • "Brake master cylinder failed." • "Owner says she was driving in wet weather when another driver pulled in front of her—she applied brakes and found that master cylinder had gone out."

5. Brakes: hydraulic: disc: pads and shoes, excessive wear. • "Brakes wear prematurely." • "Antilock brake system continues to wear; replaced brake pads that were making a loud noise." • "Replaced front brake pads." • "Antilock brake system: Brake system warning light inoperative; as a result, brakes wore through pads, unknown to owner."

6. Electrical system: ignition: electronic control unit, stalling, failure, sudden acceleration. • "Replaced electronic control module." • "Intermittent stalling." • "Computer module failed." • "Sudden acceleration from stop, causing loss of control."

CHEVROLET TRUCK BLAZER 1993

Complaint Severity: Very Serious. **Recall Alert:** See Recall Index. **Buyer's Summary:** Test the suspension by feeling for vibration or pulling while driving. Check the brakes—listen for noise, look for leaks and feel for vibration. They may fail, perform poorly or require frequent mechanical attention. Test the transmission thoroughly. See "Sudden Accelerations" in Introduction.

Hot Spots and Owner/NHTSA Comments:

1. Brakes: hydraulic: anti-skid system, poor performance, failure, locking up. • "Antilock brake system wheel cylinder and backing plate broke while driving." • "Antilock brake system failed for the second time. After the first repair, the second failure resulted in an accident in which driver hit a tree." • "Antilock brake system brake pedal travels to floor with no braking effect; no warning." • "Antilock brake system: When making a sudden stop, front brakes stop vehicle, rear brakes have loss of brake effectiveness, causing vehicle to slide." • "Antilock brake system: 4-wheel drive; when applying brakes, engine would shut off, idle rough."

2. Brakes: hydraulic system, premature failure. • "Premature brake failure, consumer had a hard time stopping at low speed." • "Coming up to an intersection, went to step on brakes and they went to the floorboard. Brakes are in and out." • "Pedal fades during wet weather, brakes feel like they go completely out; replaced rotor to no avail." • "Brakes failed, causing loss of control and an accident." • "Regular brakes perform erratically, needing to be pumped until antilock brakes interact."

3. Fuel: throttle linkages and control, sudden accelerations. • "Estimated speed 20 mph or less. Had brief acceleration. Applied brakes and had a delayed response. Two occasions, one accident." • "Accelerator pedal stuck, causing sudden acceleration in reverse for 62 feet. Rammed into a tree with rear bumper." • "While backing out of garage with gear in reverse, engine accelerated. Vehicle lurched backwards at high speed. Stopped by shifting to park and excessive braking." • "Upon placing vehicle into drive position, suddenly engine surged, overpowering brake, resulting in hitting a wall."

4. Power train: transmission: automatic, poor performance, difficulty shifting, slipping. • "Transmission problems prior to recall notification; recall work refused due to part unavailability." • "Transmission started shifting from 2nd to neutral after repairs." • "New vehicle had shifting problems and new transmission installed; 4 months later sudden acceleration, resulting in 3-car crash."

5. Suspension: independent front, alignment, vibration. • "Shocks and ball joints failed." • "Front end alignment unstable." • "Low-speed front end vibration; aligned front end." • "Owner was going under 30 mph when other car ran stop sign and hit her; Blazer flipped all the way over and landed back on its wheels." • "The front end shakes and vibrates so bad that it is hard to steer and control the vehicle."

6. Interior systems: active restraints: belt retractors, malfunction, failure. • "Vehicle hit at 6:00 position while at a complete stop, lap and shoulder belt did not retract on driver's side." • "Front seat belts are too loose." • "Difficulty retracting seat belt." • "Seat belt retractor failed." • "Shoulder harness will not retract its own webbing."

CHEVROLET TRUCK BLAZER 1994

Complaint Severity: Very Serious. **Recall Alert:** See Recall Index. **Buyer's Summary:** Check the brakes—listen for noise, look for leaks and feel for vibration. They may fail, perform poorly or require frequent mechanical attention. See "Sudden Accelerations" in Introduction.

Hot Spots and Owner/NHTSA Comments:

1. Brakes: hydraulic: anti-skid system, poor performance, failure, locking up. • "Antilock brake system failure, going through intersection. Antilock brake system failed on icy surface, impact 12:00 position, speed 3 mph." • "Antilock brake system became inoperative with pedal to floor at 25 mph; had accident." • "Antilock brakes fail and grab, causing loss of control and accident." • "Antilock brake system: Applied brakes at 35 mph and truck failed to respond, with extended stopping distance." • "Vehicle's antilock brake system intermittently locks up with no warning. Hard pedal. Prior to lockup a loud knocking noise is heard."

2. Interior systems: active restraints: belt retractors, malfunction, failure. • "Front right and rear left seat belts fail to retract." • "Driver's seat belt tensioning device malfunctioned, allowing slack in shoulder strap. Replaced seat belt mechanism 2 times." • "Both front seat belt retractors are inoperative. No parts available in United States; factory doesn't know when it will be available." • "Driver's shoulder harness wouldn't retract to fit snugly over chest; hangs loosely." • "Driving vehicle at 25 mph, impact 9:00 position, lap and shoulder belts failed and did not retract in vehicle, causing injuries."

3. Brakes: hydraulic system, failure, noise. • "During brake application, brakes make a ticking noise and pedal goes to the floor." • "When attempting to stop, brakes had no response and sudden acceleration then initiated." • "Brake failure."

4. Fuel: throttle linkages and control, sudden accelerations. • "Vehicle accelerated by itself; equipped with antilock brake system." • "Sudden acceleration, causing accident and injury." • "When attempting to stop, brakes failed, vehicle suddenly accelerated out of control, resulting in an accident." • "Vehicle accelerated without driver applying accelerator pedal. His foot was on brakes. Vehicle was in drive."

CHEVROLET TRUCK BLAZER 1995

Complaint Severity: Troublesome. **Recall Alert:** See Recall Index. **Buyer's Summary:** The airbags in this vehicle have experienced failures and malfunctions: You may need a professional evaluation on the condition of the airbags. Check the brakes—listen for noise, look for leaks and feel for vibration. They may fail, perform poorly or require frequent mechanical attention. See "Sudden Accelerations" in Introduction.

Hot Spots and Owner/NHTSA Comments:

1. Brakes: hydraulic: anti-skid system, poor performance, failure, locking up. • "The antilock brake system did not function properly, causing the wheels to lock up and a vehicle accident." • "Antilock brake system: When brakes applied, vehicle does not respond, and pedal goes to the floor during regular stopping." • "Antilock brake system: Premature wear of front brake pads and turning of rotors." • "Vehicle's antilock brake system malfunctions intermittently, pedal gets spongy and long, extended stopping occurs." • "Problem with brake pedal going to the floor on antilock brake system."

2. Electrical system: ignition, stalling, failure. • "The main wiring harness shorts out repeatedly while driving and causes the vehicle to stall without warning." • "Vehicle stalls when slowing down, turning or removing foot from accelerator. Computer at dealer unable to detect fault code." • "While driving, upon reaching intersection, while applying brakes, engine suddenly shuts down, no warning."

3. Brakes: hydraulic system, poor performance, failure. • "Brakes failed, causing an accident." • "While driving, suddenly vehicle began to accelerate, throttle seemed to be stuck, brake action was inadequate; dealer can't reproduce problem." • "When brakes get wet they do not stop vehicle adequately."

4. Fuel: throttle linkages and control, sudden accelerations. • "While driving, suddenly vehicle began to accelerate, throttle seemed to be stuck, brake action was inadequate; dealer can't reproduce problem." • "Vehicle rpm races up to 3,000 before shifting." • "Fuel throttle stuck on 2 occasions, tachometer register went beyond 6,000 rpm." • "Had problem with vehicle stalling when pressing on the accelerator, which caused an accident."

5. Interior systems: passive restraint: airbag: driver, malfunction, failure. • "Consumer was driving, the brakes locked up (antilock brake system); to avoid hitting another vehicle, consumer hit pole; driver's airbag didn't deploy and shoulder harness didn't restrain." • "Driver side airbag did not deploy during head-on impact." • "Riding on a city street, rear-ended other vehicle at 20 mph and airbag didn't deploy." • "Upon frontal impact, estimated speed 35-40 mph, front crumbled, with airbag not deploying."

CHEVROLET TRUCK C SERIES (LIGHT) 1988

Complaint Severity: Typical. **Buyer's Summary:** Test the suspension by feeling for vibration or pulling while driving. Check the brakes—listen for noise, look for leaks and feel for vibration. They may fail, perform poorly or require frequent mechanical attention. Test the transmission thoroughly.

Hot Spots and Owner/NHTSA Comments:

1. Power train: transmission: automatic, poor performance, difficulty shifting, slipping. • "Overheated transmission fluid overflowed onto breather vent of transmission and spilled onto cross member exhaust pipe, causing fire prior to recall." • "Transmission fluid caught fire prior to recall." • "Transmission slips and leaks." • "Vehicle fire prior to recall repairs." • "Transmission fluid fire prior to recall, resulting in damaged torque converter."

2. Brakes: hydraulic: disc: rotor: disc hub, failure, noise. • "Front brake rotors and pads failed prior to recall." • "Brake problems after recall repairs." • "Front brake rotors failed, causing accident prior to recall." • "Composite brake rotor separated from the cast outer rotor prior to recall." • "Brake rotors failed prior to recall, causing loud noise and vehicle to veer sharply."

3. Suspension: independent front control arm: unknown type: ball joint, excessive wear, failure. • "Ball joint separated, resulting in an accident; also, premature wear of tires." • "Recall repairs refused." • "Loose ball joints replaced." • "Ball joints failed."

CHEVROLET TRUCK C SERIES (LIGHT) 1989

Complaint Severity: Minor. **Buyer's Summary:** Test the suspension by feeling for vibration or pulling while driving. Test the transmission thoroughly.

Hot Spots and Owner/NHTSA Comments:

1. Power train: transmission: automatic, poor performance, difficulty shifting, slipping. • "Transmission failed prior to recall." • "Transmission leaked fluid, causing fire." • "Transmission leak prior to recall; transmission repairs refused." • "Transmission failure." • "Vehicle fire caused by transmission fluid leak onto exhaust pipe."

2. Suspension: independent front control arm: unknown type: ball joint, failure, tire wear. • "Ball joints failed prior to recall." • "Ball joint failed, causing premature tire wear." • "Replaced ball joints." • "Ball joint separated, resulting in an accident; also, premature wear of tires."

CHEVROLET TRUCK C SERIES (LIGHT) 1993

Complaint Severity: Typical. **Buyer's Summary:** Check the brakes—listen for noise, look for leaks and feel for vibration. They may fail, perform poorly or require frequent mechanical attention.

Hot Spots and Owner/NHTSA Comments:

1. Brakes: hydraulic: anti-skid system, poor performance, failure, locking up. • "Disc brakes locked up." • "Antilock brakes failed." • "Right rear wheel locks up when wet and brakes applied."

2. Interior systems: active seat and shoulder belts and belt anchor, premature failure. • "Center passenger's seat belt failed." • "Seat belt failed." • "Passenger seat belt failed." • "Right front seat belt failure."

CHEVROLET TRUCK C SERIES (LIGHT) 1994

Complaint Severity: Harmless. **Buyer's Summary:** Test the suspension by feeling for vibration or pulling while driving. Check the brakes—listen for noise, look for leaks and feel for vibration. They may fail, perform poorly or require frequent mechanical attention. Test the transmission thoroughly.

Hot Spots and Owner/NHTSA Comments:

1. Power train: transmission: automatic, poor performance, difficulty shifting, slipping. • "Transmission failure." • "Automatic transmission failure." • "Transmission has clunking noise when stopping vehicle." • "Transmission jumps forward when shifting into reverse and drive gears." • "Transmission makes excessive noise after 5 repair attempts."

2. Suspension: independent front, pulling, alignment, tire wear. • "Vehicle pulls to right, causing tire damage." • "Front end misaligned; also, wheel out of balance." • "Front end misaligned." • "Misalignment, causing excessive tire wear." • "Front end misaligned."

3. Brakes: hydraulic: master cylinder, failure, leaks. • "Master cylinder reservoir failed." • "Master cylinder failure." • "Master brake cylinder leak." • "Master cylinder replaced."

4. Interior systems: active seat and shoulder belts and belt anchor, premature failure. • "Seat belt failure." • "Driver's side seat belt failure." • "Passenger's seat belt failed."

5. Brakes: hydraulic system, locking up, failure. • "Brakes failed, causing an accident." • "Brake failure." • "Brakes failed; locked up, causing accident." • "Brakes replaced due to noise, problem continues."

6. Engine: stalling, poor performance. • "Intermittent stalling." • "Vehicle not powerful enough to tow." • "Intermittent stalling." • "Engine replaced due to knocking."

CHEVROLET TRUCK C10 1987

Complaint Severity: Negligible. **Buyer's Summary:** Look carefully for any kind of leakage, especially under the car.

Hot Spots and Owner/NHTSA Comments:

1. Fuel: fuel tank assembly: tank, leaks, corrosion. • "Fuel tank has rusted, causing fuel leak due to sand accumulation between tank and factory-installed fuel tank shield." • "Rusted fuel tanks caused leakage." • "Poor location of fuel tanks." • "Tank mounted on side of vehicle leaks; accumulation of moisture and dirt trapped by plastic seal around tank caused rust and corrosion at bottom of mounting bracket." • "Gas tank leak caused by the tanks being corroded at bracket assembly."

CHEVROLET TRUCK C10 1988

Complaint Severity: Typical. **Recall Alert:** See Recall Index. **Buyer's Summary:** Verify that the cruise control system works properly, and that it doesn't cause the engine to surge. Check the brakes—listen for noise, look for leaks and feel for vibration. They may fail, perform poorly or require frequent mechanical attention.

Hot Spots and Owner/NHTSA Comments:

1. Brakes: hydraulic system, locking up, poor performance. • "Brakes grab, front wheels lock and slide traveling at any speed." • "Inadequate brake performance caused extended stopping distance and loss of vehicle control." • "Inadequate brake performance, doesn't stop properly, front pads wore into rotors; installed rear brakes, larger booster, new pads, still bad brakes." • "Accident due to inadequate brake power, brake lights inoperative at times." • "Very difficult to stop vehicle, requires excessive effort and is worse at higher speeds."

2. Equipment: speed control, malfunction, failure. • "Cruise control fails when windshield wipers in operation." • "Intermittent problems with cruise control; when speed set between 55 and 70 mph, loses 5-10 mph then rapidly picks up to speed set, throwing head against rear window." • "Cruise control comes on by itself, control handle too close to steering wheel and switch too easy to accidentally turn on." • "Cruise control requires excessive brake pressure to disengage, accelerated on own, out of control, cruise sticks throttle open; disconnected cruise linkage."

3. Lighting: general or unknown component: brake lights, malfunction. • "Brake lights come on when vehicle is off; emergency lights blinking at dash." • "Electrical short in brake lights causes tail lights to melt." • "Rear brake lights are inoperative on an intermittent basis." • "Rear brake lights stay on after brake pedal is released; causes hazardous driving conditions."

CHEVROLET TRUCK C10 1989

Complaint Severity: Harmless. **Recall Alert:** See Recall Index. **Buyer's Summary:** Verify that the cruise control system works properly, and that it doesn't cause the engine to surge. Test the transmission thoroughly.

Hot Spots and Owner/NHTSA Comments:

1. Equipment: speed control, malfunction, failure. • "Cruise switch failed." • "Speed cruise control did not engage; had to be replaced." • "Cruise control will not engage; repaired." • "Vehicle surges while using cruise."

2. Power train: transmission: automatic, poor performance, difficulty shifting, slipping. • "Defective cooling lines to transmission; repaired 3 times." • "Vehicle's transmission slipped when shifting from park to reverse on flat surface, went out of control and rolled 6 feet; caused accident." • "Drive shaft splines to transmission bang at stop-and-go driving; GMC says unable to repair." • "Transmission failure."

CHEVROLET TRUCK C15 1988

Complaint Severity: Negligible. **Buyer's Summary:** Test the suspension by feeling for vibration or pulling while driving. Check the brakes—listen for noise, look for leaks and feel for vibration. They may fail, perform poorly or require frequent mechanical attention. See "Sudden Accelerations" in Introduction.

Hot Spots and Owner/NHTSA Comments:

1. Brakes: hydraulic system, noise, stiffness, failure. • "Approaching a stop sign at an intersection at approximately 20 mph, applied brakes normally and brakes did not react as usual. Had to push the pedal hard." • "Approaching a stop light, another vehicle in front pulled out, vehicle's brakes were inoperative and could not stop in time; resulted in an accident." • "Defective braking system, performs poorly, brake light stays on." • "Brakes don't keep truck stopped when at fast idle, make groaning noise at low speeds, brake pedal becomes very spongy at times." • "Brake pedal feels soft; while sitting at stop signs, must hold firm downward pressure, pedal goes to floor in traffic."

2. Suspension: independent front, pulling, excessive wear, tire wear. • "Ball joints broke and were replaced by dealer." • "Front end pulls to right, turns hard to left, vibrates in steering wheel and noise from right front when turning hard to right and braking." • "Front end pulls to left, bumping noise in left front; alignment kit installed, secured front stabilizer bracket." • "Replaced upper and lower ball joints, installed kit to adjust alignment." • "Front end suspension problem, tires worn til tubes had to be put in, rotated often, still cut through, 2 blowouts on highway; almost caused accident."

3. Brakes: hydraulic: switch: brake light, malfunction, failure. • "A defective brake switch caused the brake lights to stay on; repaired." • "Brake light switch is inoperative; however, remains lit regardless of brake pedal action. Drains battery." • "Brake light switch fails to release after releasing brake pedal, causing brake lights to stay on, resulting in tail light assembly melting." • "Brake light switch does not stay in adjustment, light stays on and melts brake light housing." • "Brake light switch sticks, causes brake lights to stay on constantly."

4. Suspension: independent front control arm: lower: ball joint, tire wear, excessive wear. • "Lower ball joint failure, front wheel shimmy, right front tire began to wear on inside, ball joints found to be excessively worn." • "Traveling, made left turn, went through slight dip in road, at which point right side of truck took nosedive into the ground; lower ball joint failure." • "Traveling, when left front end hit pavement, truck skidded to the left, lower ball joint failure, front end dragging the ground." • "Ball joints separate, causing front wheel to fold under—accident imminent when this event occurs." • "Lower ball joints in suspension system seem to be going bad prematurely."

5. Brakes: hydraulic: anti-skid system, poor performance, failure, locking up. • "Antilock brake system defect, necessary to make quick stop, hit pothole and bounced out, rear wheels locked, computer took over, brake pedal went to floor, no control." • "Driving down slight grade, applied brakes, vehicle did not slow down, front brakes would not lock, antilock brakes work fine on wet and/or snowy conditions." • "Experiences inadequate brake action upon attempt to stop, pedal gets hard and truck will not stop as it should. Vehicle tends to fade, then catches." • "Antilock brake system: Failure of brake master cylinder, causing pedal to fade."

6. Fuel: throttle linkages and control, sudden accelerations. • "At idle and at speeds up to 50 mph, motor surges and runs rough." • "Engine rpm runs at speed that makes standing start difficult, runs at 20-25 mph without pressure on accelerator, requiring constant braking." • "Vehicle surges hard, cannot hold speed from 35-45 mph, cuts out or misses on hard pulls; repaired many times, to no avail." • "While driving, accelerator pedal went to floor and brake pedal froze in upright position; caused accident."

CHEVROLET TRUCK C15 1989

Complaint Severity: Harmless. **Buyer's Summary:** Look carefully for any kind of leakage, especially under the car. Test the suspension by feeling for vibration or pulling while driving. Check the brakes—listen for noise, look for leaks and feel for vibration. They may fail, perform poorly or require frequent mechanical attention. Test the transmission thoroughly. Make sure air conditioner works properly.

Hot Spots and Owner/NHTSA Comments:

1. Power train: transmission: automatic, poor performance, difficulty shifting, slipping. • "Problem with transmission slipping." • "Automatic transmission continues to shift violently after coming to complete stop." • "Automatic transmission failure." • "Transmission had only 1st and 2nd gears." • "Replaced transmission 3 times."

2. Brakes: hydraulic system, failure, leaks. • "Brakes replaced twice." • "Brake failure." • "Claims brake pedal goes to floor at times; dealer unable to duplicate." • "Brakes spongy, soft." • "Brake seal broke, causing leak."

3. Suspension: independent front, pulling, alignment, tire wear. • "Front end shakes and pulls to the right." • "Vehicle pulls to the right, front end vibration; hard to control." • "Front wheel alignment parts kit defective; due to failure, tires have been worn." • "Suspension does not have an adjustment to wheel alignment, caused all tires to be out of round." • "Premature tire wear due to a faulty front end suspension system."

4. Suspension: independent front control arm: unknown type: ball joint, excessive wear, failure. • "Ball joint wears prematurely, causing collapse of wheel and loss of steering." • "Front ball joint failed, caused tires to be badly worn; recall repair." • "Defect in ball joints." • "Four ball joints failed, caused idler arm to wear prematurely, impossible to replace ball joints." • "Ball joint failure."

5. Air conditioner: leaks, failure. • "Air conditioning system developed leaks; repaired." • "Defective air conditioning unit." • "Air conditioning unit quit working." • "Driver choked, cause being air conditioner and vent seals dried up."

CHEVROLET TRUCK C15 1990

Complaint Severity: Negligible. **Theft Alert:** 37. **Recall Alert:** See Recall Index. **Buyer's Summary:** Look carefully for any kind of leakage, especially under the car. Check the brakes—listen for noise, look for leaks and feel for vibration. They may fail, perform poorly or require frequent mechanical attention. Test the transmission thoroughly.

Hot Spots and Owner/NHTSA Comments:

1. Power train: transmission: automatic, poor performance, difficulty shifting, slipping. • "Vehicle caught on fire in transmission. Car was totaled." • "Transmission not operative due to metal chips left in transmission when assembled." • "With air conditioner on, transmission downshifts by itself about 50-60 mph; need to slow down to resume normal action and smooth operation." • "Shifting mechanism was blocked by a piece of tubing, made it impossible to shift to 2nd or 1st gear; adjusted." • "Faulty automatic transmission; repaired under warranty."

2. Brakes: hydraulic: anti-skid system, poor performance, failure, locking up. • "Trouble braking at low speeds since purchase; replaced master cylinder—later had 10-mph accident." • "Antilock brake system failure, brake system operates normally otherwise." • "Antilock brake system did not react fast enough to avoid hitting a slow-moving truck; resulted in accident." • "Problem with antilock brake system." • "Antilock brake system brake light comes and will go off."

3. Engine: leaks, fire. • "Main engine oil seal failure." • "Two front main bearings burned out, causing knocking in engine." • "Fire started in engine compartment; total loss for client." • "Engine oil/coolant leak." • "Engine oil leaks."

4. Brakes: hydraulic system, malfunction, failure. • "Brakes malfunctioned, act as if there is no vacuum booster." • "Brakes on truck do not appear to have enough stopping action." • "Brake problems." • "Brakes malfunctioning, with warning light staying on; when standing on pedal with both feet, vehicle still continues to move."

CHEVROLET TRUCK C15 1991

Complaint Severity: Typical. **Buyer's Summary:** Test the transmission thoroughly.

Hot Spots and Owner/NHTSA Comments:

1. Power train: transmission: automatic, poor performance, difficulty shifting, slipping. • "Transmission seal failed." • "Transmission failed 5 times." • "Transmission failure." • "Shavings left in the transmission cause it to slip."

CHEVROLET TRUCK C15 1992

Complaint Severity: Typical. **Buyer's Summary:** Test the transmission thoroughly.

Hot Spots and Owner/NHTSA Comments:

1. Power train: transmission: automatic, poor performance, difficulty shifting, slipping. • "Transmission failed while hauling 5th-wheel trailer." • "Transmission failed." • "Transmission overheated while towing trailer." • "Transmission locked up while driving, caused loss of control."

CHEVROLET TRUCK C25 1989

Complaint Severity: Harmless. **Buyer's Summary:** Check the brakes—listen for noise, look for leaks and feel for vibration. They may fail, perform poorly or require frequent mechanical attention. Test the transmission thoroughly.

Hot Spots and Owner/NHTSA Comments:

1. Power train: transmission: automatic, poor performance, difficulty shifting, slipping. • "Transmission overheated and pushed fluid out through dipstick and onto fire wall, engine, exhaust manifold and catalytic converter, causing fire." • "Transmission fluid leaked on engine, causing fire." • "The transmission: The 2nd gear and reverse went out." • "Automatic transmission going into 3rd gear, occasionally winds up before it kicks in; rebuilt transmission." • "Transmission jiggles when in 4th gear under load, when moving at 35-45 mph."

2. Brakes: hydraulic system, excessive wear, failure. • "Brakes replaced at 15,000 miles—would have caused extensive rotor damage." • "Certain times brakes grab, squeal, scrape; no brakes at all on several occasions." • "Brakes failed traveling downhill, causing accident." • "Brakes went out at about 11,000 miles."

CHEVROLET TRUCK G SERIES 1993

Complaint Severity: Harmless. **Buyer's Summary:** Make sure the shoulder belts don't cut across your neck and are well anchored. Check the brakes—listen for noise, look for leaks and feel for vibration. They may fail, perform poorly or require frequent mechanical attention. Test the transmission thoroughly.

Hot Spots and Owner/NHTSA Comments:

1. Interior systems: active seat and shoulder belts and belt anchor, uncomfortable, poor design. • "Seat belts too short for conversion van." • "Driver's seat belt does not fit properly when seat is all the way in forward position; when positioned for a larger person, the belt is too tight." • "Seat belts do not fit passengers, require extensions." • "Front seat belts too short to fasten." • "Driver's side seat belt fits poorly."

2. Brakes: hydraulic: anti-skid system, poor performance, failure, locking up. • "Dashboard light stays on." • "Antilock brakes lock up, causing loss of control." • "Brake pedal goes to the floor followed by antilock brake system warning light coming on; also, flutter in brake pedal." • "Antilock brakes failed, also antilock brake light came on." • "Antilock brake system failed; rear brake drums out of round." • "Noisy antilock brakes."

3. Interior systems: shoulder belts, uncomfortable, poor design. • "Shoulder belts are too short." • "Shoulder harness comes across neck and armpit, also seat belts not long enough." • "Driver's shoulder belt comes across neck." • "Driver's shoulder belt comes across face and upper neck."

4. Power train: transmission: automatic, poor performance, difficulty shifting, slipping. • "Transmission problems." • "Transmission fails to shift into gear after starting and depressing brake pedal." • "Transmission can be placed into gear without applying brake due to recall modification." • "Transmission failed."

CHEVROLET TRUCK LUMINA APV 1990

Complaint Severity: Typical. **Recall Alert:** See Recall Index. **Buyer's Summary:** Check the brakes—listen for noise, look for leaks and feel for vibration. They may fail, perform poorly or require frequent mechanical attention.

Hot Spots and Owner/NHTSA Comments:

1. Brakes: hydraulic system, excessive wear, noise. • "Excessive wear of brakes; dealer says no problem, but brakes have been replaced 3 times in the last year." • "Vehicle's braking system becomes inoperative with no warning, with pedal to floor. Had to be pumped to get some pedal back." • "Brake pedal would go to floor while trying to brake; had fixed, happened again, had accident." • "Poor brake design is causing extended stopping distances and caused an accident." • "Noisy brakes; repaired, problem continues."

2. Interior systems: active restraints: belt retractors, malfunction, failure. • "Lap and shoulder belt retractor will not retract." • "Left front seat belt failure." • "Driver's seat and middle end seat positions have failed seat belt retractors. No spring tension pulling the belts against occupant's torso." • "Driver's side rear seat belt no longer retracts or restrains." • "The driver's seat belt will not retract."

3. Interior systems: bucket: backrest, breaking, malfunction. • "Driver side seat back collapsed upon side impact." • "Driver side seat back broke and collapsed during rear-end impact." • "Driver's seat back broke at the hinge and bolt, allowing seat back to collapse." • "Seat backs on front seats keep ratcheting down to a horizontal position. Seats are coming apart. Could be safety hazard in an accident."

CHEVROLET TRUCK S10 1987

Complaint Severity: Typical. **Recall Alert:** See Recall Index. **Buyer's Summary:** The fuel injection system has been blamed for hesitation and stalling. Be sure the vehicle doesn't die in traffic or at stops. The steering may be stiff or not working correctly. Be sure to test the steering, especially on a cold start. Check the brakes—listen for noise, look for leaks and feel for vibration. They may fail, perform poorly or require frequent mechanical attention. Test the transmission thoroughly. See "Sudden Accelerations" in Introduction.

Hot Spots and Owner/NHTSA Comments:

1. Fuel: throttle linkages and control, sudden accelerations. • "Vehicle suffered sudden acceleration due to apparent fuel linkage sticking; an accident resulted." • "Upon accelerating from a stop, suddenly accelerated, skidded to stop." • "Engine would rev high, have to apply brakes or engage clutch to slow down." • "Truck surges and idles on own without applying gas pedal, computer reads 1,750 rpm at idle." • "Acceleration problem, engine light came on and off, while driving behind vehicle it lurches forward, almost causing accident."

2. Steering: power assist: pump, noise, vibration. • "Two studs that hold the power steering pump attached to engine at the exhaust manifold sheared off." • "Noise from under hood, caused by broken, cracked, missing or stripped power steering pump brace or bracket bolts; bolt broke off in the water pump housing." • "Power steering bracket broke, leaving vehicle without power steering in middle of driving." • "Bracket that holds power steering pump broke, allowed the pump to vibrate and rub a hole in pipe, which resulted in fluid leak." • "Power steering pump was ruptured when mounting bolt punctured it; power steering belt also separated upon failure of mounting bracket bolt."

3. Power train: transmission: automatic, poor performance, difficulty shifting, slipping. • "Transmission overhauled at 30,000 miles." • "Transmission vibrates at 55-65 mph." • "Transmission experiencing grinding noise in 2nd gear and overdrive." • "Automatic transmission defective, has been replaced twice in less than 7,650 miles, excessive noise from transmission." • "Vehicle in parked position, automatic transmission slipped out from park gear to reverse, rolled down driveway; accident occurred."

4. Steering: power: gear box, weak bracket assembly. • "Power steering bracket failed, resulting in truck losing steering. Defect was corrected once before." • "While driving at approximately 55 mph, power steering bracket broke, causing loss of power steering capability." • "Power steering bracket broke, throwing the one-piece fan belt off and resulting in a loss of power steering." • "Upon starting vehicle, heard a pop sound, pulled hood up and found belt detached and power steering bracket broken." • "As vehicle was coming to a stop, power steering bracket broke, and the single belt accessory drive, the serpentine drive, came off and became entangled."

5. Brakes: hydraulic system, malfunction, failure. • "Loses all braking power after a hard and quick acceleration." • "Brakes malfunction, possibly in vacuum, causing very hard action when applying." • "Unspecified brake failure, brake pedal goes to floor on hard brake application, panic stop not possible." • "Brakes very inconsistent, sometimes don't engage properly and other times don't disengage completely." • "Brakes failed, causing accident and injury."

6. Fuel: fuel injection system, stalling, hesitation. • "Fuel injector malfunctioned." • "Severe hesitation problems when accelerating from a stop." • "Problem with frequent stalling and loss of power, 'service engine' light flickers on and off; all repair attempts unsuccessful." • "Poor idle, sometimes stalls when foot taken from gas pedal, sometimes idles too high, had emissions part repaired/replaced twice but didn't solve problem." • "Stalling problem, engine shuts down, causing total loss of steering and brakes."

CHEVROLET TRUCK S10 1988

Complaint Severity: Negligible. **Buyer's Summary:** The engine has experienced a variety of problems. Have it examined by a professional. The electronic control unit has been blamed for engine performance problems, including stalling and surging. The steering may be stiff or not working correctly. Be sure to test the steering, especially on a cold start. Test the suspension by feeling for vibration or pulling while driving. Test transmission for slipping, locking up and performance. See "Sudden Accelerations" in Introduction.

Hot Spots and Owner/NHTSA Comments:

1. Fuel: throttle linkages and control, sudden accelerations. • "Vehicle suddenly surged forward, various factory welds became loose." • "Vehicle engine continues to race even after accelerator is released, takes several seconds to slow down." • "Engine surges in rpm and accelerates when vehicle is in drive or overdrive after foot is removed from gas pedal." • "Problem of excessive fast idle and missing and surging." • "Engine speeds up and slows down by itself, lunges forward without stepping on accelerator."

2. Electrical system: ignition: electronic control unit, malfunction, failure. • "Master computer system resets itself several times per minute, resulting in decreased fuel economy, pollution and very hard starting when warm." • "Electronic control module failed." • "Electronic control module malfunctioned and vehicle would continually quit." • "Engine starts to cut out; 'service engine' light comes on, vehicle stalls, jerks and shakes; replaced electronic control module and cleaned injectors." • "Turning to the right may cause a short in the electronic control module circuit, which could cause the vehicle to stall or respond erratically."

3. Power train: transmission: 5-speed and up, malfunction, failure. • "Five-speed manual transmission replaced 3 times; owner recommended replacement of 5-speed transmission with automatic." • "Five-speed manual transmission malfunction, grinds in all gears, pops out of 2nd, won't go into reverse." • "Five-speed manual transmission has slack in drive line." • "Standard transmission occasionally pops out of 1st gear." • "Transmission/clutch system malfunction, transmission stopped working; repaired; again transmission pops out when put reverse, clanking noise when shifting, accelerating, etc."

4. Suspension: independent front, alignment, premature failure. • "Front end misaligned from factory; repaired/replaced transfer case housing." • "Defective ball joints." • "Ball joints failed on 4 different occasions." • "Front idler arm and ball joints broke." • "Front suspension malfunction, defective ball joints and tie rod ends."

5. Engine: miscellaneous problems. • "Smoke coming from under hood when in motion." • "Head gaskets replaced." • "Engine burning oil." • "Driving, engine started smoking, then flames started coming from engine." • "Oil pressure drops when engine warms up."

6. Steering: linkages: arm: idler and attachment, excessive wear, failure. • "Replaced idler arms twice." • "Replaced idler arm." • "Idler arms malfunctioned." • "Replaced idler arm and ball joints twice."

CHEVROLET TRUCK S10 1989

Complaint Severity: Minor. **Recall Alert:** See Recall Index. **Buyer's Summary:** Look carefully for any kind of leakage, especially under the car. The electronic control unit has been blamed for engine performance problems, including stalling and surging. Test the suspension by feeling for vibration or pulling while driving. Check the brakes—listen for noise, look for leaks and feel for vibration. They may fail, perform poorly or require frequent mechanical attention. See "Sudden Accelerations" in Introduction.

Hot Spots and Owner/NHTSA Comments:

1. Electrical system: ignition: electronic control unit, poor performance, failure. • "Problem with computer; serviced." • "Electronic control module malfunctioned; replaced twice." • "Computer replaced twice." • "Onboard computer problem." • "Engine races when in gear or going downhill; after letting up on accelerator, there is substantial lag before engine rpm will back off or reduce."

2. Fuel: throttle linkages and control, sudden accelerations. • "Vehicle would suddenly accelerate when foot is removed from brake at all times." • "Stepped on gas pedal, vehicle lurched forward. Resulted from screw breaking in throttle body housing." • "Uncontrollable sudden acceleration, vehicle traveled up to 50 mph with no warning or ability to stop." • "Vehicle jerks and surges, engine idle varies at times, stays up at very high idle, worse in cold until warm-up; unable to identify problem." • "Vehicle engine races at speeds up to 30 mph with no gas applied."

3. Engine: vibration, leaks, fire. • "Problem with engine vibration; all repair attempts to no avail." • "Defective head gasket." • "Engine oil leak; repaired." • "Engine sensor and temperature sensor problems." • "Defective engine caught fire while driving; destroyed."

4. Suspension: independent front, alignment, excessive wear. • "Ball joints of the 4-wheel drive vehicles are not safe; they are loose and could fall off." • "Steering wandering, wheel not straight and tight as should be; front end tire vibration due to problem with alignment." • "Ball joints failed and were replaced." • "Misalignment caused truck to sway and pull." • "Excessive ball joint wear resulted in wheel wobble."

5. Brakes: hydraulic system, locking up, pulling. • "Brakes lock up easily." • "Brake light flashing; module replaced." • "Brakes lock up, causing vehicle to turn to left." • "Hydraulic brakes light switch disconnected from dashboard and fell away, there was no way to put light on." • "Brakes locked at 65 mph, causing driver to hit steering wheel."

6. Engine cooling system: fan, breaking. • "Traveling at 55 mph, the fan blade broke and punctured the radiator." • "Fan blades broke prior to recall, causing vehicle to overheat." • "Fan blade recall repairs refused because of factory-installed air conditioning."

CHEVROLET TRUCK S10 1990

Complaint Severity: Typical. **Recall Alert:** See Recall Index. **Buyer's Summary:** Check the brakes—listen for noise, look for leaks and feel for vibration. They may fail, perform poorly or require frequent mechanical attention.

Hot Spots and Owner/NHTSA Comments:

1. Brakes: hydraulic: anti-skid system, poor performance, failure, locking up. • "Antilock brakes constantly lock up and there is no control of the vehicle." • "Antilock brake system malfunctioned while in drive, low speed, wheels locked up, vehicle skidded down driveway at low speeds." • "Loss of antilock braking system." • "Rear wheels lock when braking." • "Antilock brake system malfunctions and fails to perform effectively when brakes are applied, causing interior light to stay on. Replaced valve."

CHEVROLET TRUCK S10 1991

Complaint Severity: Troublesome. **Theft Alert:** 35. **Recall Alert:** See Recall Index. **Buyer's Summary:** The electronic control unit has been blamed for engine performance problems, including stalling and surging. Check the brakes—listen for noise, look for leaks and feel for vibration. They may fail, perform poorly or require frequent mechanical attention. Test the transmission thoroughly. See "Sudden Accelerations" in Introduction.

Hot Spots and Owner/NHTSA Comments:

1. Brakes: hydraulic: anti-skid system, poor performance, failure, locking up. • "Antilock brake system locked up in snow going 10-15 mph, pedal faded." • "Antilock brake system failed to stop vehicle when applied, causing rear-end collision at 25-30 mph; second accident." • "Antilock brake system fails to stop vehicle effectively, dashboard brake light comes on and stays on while driving." • "Antilock brake system makes grinding noise then gives way resulting in loss of brakes." • "Dealer tried fixing antilock brake system 4 times, including replacement of antilock brake system module. Last problem was no brake fluid. Replaced brake shoes and brake calipers."

2. Electrical system: ignition: electronic control unit, stalling, sudden acceleration. • "Electronic control module failure caused idle air control to open up and allow engine to increase rpm." • "Electronic control module operates erratically, resulting in engine stalling." • "While driving at normal speed, vehicle experienced sudden engine shutoff." • "Onboard computer and ignition gauge replaced." • "Electronic control module malfunctioned, caused vehicle to increase speed without notice."

3. Engine: vibration, failure. • "Motor vibration eventually caused oil cooling line and brake line to wear through. This caused oil to spray underneath transmission housing and behind area." • "Belt tensioner pulley replaced." • "Cylinder head, fan belts and thermostat problem." • "Excessive oil use, required one quart of oil at 1,142 miles." • "Oil pressure gauge not registering properly; engine blew up 3 times."

4. Power train: transmission: automatic, poor performance, difficulty shifting, slipping. • "Automatic transmission refuses to engage or sticks in 1st gear at 10-20 mph, car revs and lunges forward; transmission replaced twice, needed third replacement." • "Transmission slips on acceleration." • "Valve failure in transmission caused erratic gear shifting." • "Transmission failure, would not change gears; repaired."

5. Brakes: hydraulic system, locking up, failure. • "Brakes locked up, truck slid and hit another vehicle." • "Brakes didn't slow vehicle (hauling less than ½ ton) down enough to avoid accident." • "Brakes failed, causing accident." • "Cable to computer controlling antilock brake system broke." • "Upon applying brakes, vehicle has difficulty in stopping."

6. Fuel: throttle linkages and control, sudden accelerations. • "After starting vehicle and putting it into drive, vehicle accelerated forward and hit a wall." • "When cold and engaged in drive or reverse, vehicle surges; replaced throttle position sensor to no avail." • "Engine idles too high when cold; surges in reverse; idles and surges at traffic stops in gear; surges at and over 35 mph." • "The accelerator of vehicle stuck even though driver applied the brakes, causing an accident."

CHEVROLET TRUCK S10 1992

Complaint Severity: Troublesome. **Recall Alert:** See Recall Index. **Buyer's Summary:** The electronic control unit has been blamed for engine performance problems, including stalling and surging. Check the brakes—listen for noise, look for leaks and feel for vibration. They may fail, perform poorly or require frequent mechanical attention. See "Sudden Accelerations" in Introduction.

Hot Spots and Owner/NHTSA Comments:

1. Brakes: hydraulic: anti-skid system, poor performance, failure, locking up. • "While driving, front brakes locked on antilock brake system-equipped vehicle, caused vehicle to go into an embankment." • "Antilock brake system locked up during wet weather conditions. No warning." • "Antilock brake system failed. Backup system of regular brakes failed." • "Complete loss of braking ability. Both brake lights came on panel moments before failure." • "While driving, experienced intermittent brake ineffectiveness. When applied, pedal becomes hard and vehicle continues to roll forward; dealer can't reproduce." • "Antilock brake system totally inoperative; failed during wet weather; normal braking stopped vehicle; antilock brake system warning light came on after braking; speed 35 mph."

2. Brakes: hydraulic: power assist: lines: vacuum, failure. • "Vacuum hose on power brake booster fell off."

3. Fuel: throttle linkages and control, sudden accelerations. • "While driving, experienced throttle sticking when vehicle suddenly accelerated out of control, hit another car." • "Engine accelerated to high speed while exiting parking lot; brakes applied; gear in drive; vehicle hit 3 other vehicles, flipped on side." • "Vehicle cannot be controlled. Vehicle idles too fast, races and takes off quickly." • "Cold start, backed out of garage, when put into drive vehicle surged forward with foot on brakes, hitting a retaining wall. Vehicle surged again when restarted." • "Vehicle suddenly accelerates or surges forward periodically, causing loss of vehicle control."

4. Brakes: hydraulic system, locking up, malfunction. • "While driving, experienced intermittent brake ineffectiveness, when applied pedal becomes hard and vehicle continues to roll forward; dealer can't reproduce." • "Red antilock brake system warning light came on and brake pedal went to the floor, but vehicle would not stop, rear-ending another car." • "Brakes lock up when roads are damp from rain." • "While driving down a highway, made an attempt to stop, brakes malfunctioned and brake pedal went to the floor, resulting in an accident." • "Power brakes engage intermittently."

5. Electrical system: ignition: electronic control unit, stalling, failure. • "Computer programmable read-only memory for transmission failed." • "Intermittent stalling." • "Electronic control module failed, causing vehicle to decelerate and stall." • "Defective computer programmable read-only memory, causing knocking and pinging." • "Fuel/air mixture forms moisture on exhaust, causing exhaust problems due to wrong programmable read-only memory installed."

6. Brakes: hydraulic: disc: caliper, locking up, excessive wear. • "Binding brake calipers caused worn rotors and pads." • "Front right caliper locks up due to premature wear." • "Right front caliper froze, causing brakes to squeak, premature wear on pads and rotors." • "Truck has 33,000 miles; had to replace front pads and cut the caliper." • "Passenger side front brake line wearing rotor and caliper out, replaced rotor and caliper twice."

CHEVROLET TRUCK S10 1993

Complaint Severity: Troublesome. **Recall Alert:** See Recall Index. **Buyer's Summary:** Check the brakes—listen for noise, look for leaks and feel for vibration. They may fail, perform poorly or require frequent mechanical attention. Test the transmission thoroughly. See "Sudden Accelerations" in Introduction.

Hot Spots and Owner/NHTSA Comments:

1. Brakes: hydraulic: anti-skid system, poor performance, failure, locking up. • "Have had to have the antilock brake system replaced numerous times starting at only 8,000 miles." • "Noticed long stopping distance, must pump antilock brake system for response; dealer cannot locate problem." • "Antilock brake system: During wet weather when coming to stop, press on brakes, pedal goes to floor; makes grinding sound, followed by extended stopping; nearly caused accident." • "Antilock brake system failed, extended stopping distance, causing vehicle to skid; lost control and vehicle rolled over."

2. Fuel: throttle linkages and control, sudden accelerations. • "In reverse, vehicle intermittently has sudden acceleration without warning." • "Throttle stuck open and would not close. Had to put car in neutral, coast to side of road and turn key off. Could cause serious accident." • "Engine surges and has sudden acceleration at all temperatures and drive times. Dealer has not been able to correct problem." • "Throttle stuck/jammed; caused full acceleration with brakes applied; vehicle was stopped by turning off ignition." • "Vehicle suddenly accelerated while braking, causing loss of control and accident."

3. Brakes: hydraulic system, locking up, failure. • "The brakes failed twice when applied, once resulting in loss of control; accident and injuries." • "Upon applying the brakes, vehicle did not stop, resulting in rear-end collision." • "Vehicle has antilock brake system on the back of vehicle and regular brakes on front of vehicle. Front brakes lock up while rear brakes allow wheels to keep spinning." • "While trying to stop, brakes went all the way to the floor; accident."

4. Power train: transmission: automatic, poor performance, difficulty shifting, slipping. • "Transmission incompatible with vehicle type, causing transmission to shift into low gear and/or disengage." • "Transmission throwout bearings failed." • "Transmission sticks in gear. Also transmission overheated, spit fluid out of overflow tube. Resulted in under hood fire." • "Replaced transmission." • "Transmission replaced twice due to slipping, vehicle sticking in 1st gear."

5. Brakes: hydraulic: shoe: disc brake system, locking up, excessive wear, malfunction. • "Antilock brake system: In wet weather, front brakes have tendency to lock up, causing loss of vehicle control; vehicle skidded, spun around off road into a field." • "Front brakes wear excessively with low mileage accumulation. All 4 shocks are leaking fluid, throwing off balance." • "Resurfaced front rotors and replaced front pads." • "Antilock brake system malfunction, resulting in excessively long stopping distance; replaced front pads and rotor."

6. Electrical system: alternator: generator, fire, failure. • "Alternator failure." • "Faulty alternator shorted out, causing fire." •

"Three alternators failed." • "While driving, noticed lights dimming, looked to rear, saw sparks, smoke came in through vent, found alternator had caught fire and belt was gone."

CHEVROLET TRUCK S10 1994

Complaint Severity: Serious. **Recall Alert:** See Recall Index. **Buyer's Summary:** Look carefully for any kind of leakage, especially under the car. Check the brakes—listen for noise, look for leaks and feel for vibration. They may fail, perform poorly or require frequent mechanical attention. Test the transmission thoroughly. See "Sudden Accelerations" in Introduction.

Hot Spots and Owner/NHTSA Comments:
1. Brakes: hydraulic: anti-skid system, poor performance, failure, locking up. • "Antilock brake system fails to stop vehicle when applied, causing extended stopping, or inoperative. Repaired 5 times." • "Antilock brake system pressed down, brake went to the floor; hit someone from the back because of brake failure." • "Vehicle antilock brake system is malfunctioning and has long, extended stopping distance and a lot of grabbing." • "Antilock brake system failed, causing extended stopping distance, resulting in accident and injuries."
2. Fuel: throttle linkages and control, sudden accelerations. • "While driving, experience intermittent engine surges, 40-50 mph, without touching gas pedal; dealer can't fix problem, manufacturer has advised dealer to take back as trade." • "Consumer was going in a parking garage, pressed on the gas, truck accelerated." • "Car goes 50 mph without touching the accelerator." • "On heavy acceleration the throttle stuck open on 2 occasions."
3. Brakes: hydraulic system, failure. • "Applied brakes at stop sign, pedal went to the floor and kept going." • "Vehicle's braking system acts erratically, with intermittent failures using a combination of pedal pressures. Warning light comes on during failure." • "Applied brakes, vehicle does not respond and the pedal vibrates; second time this happened resulted in accident." • "Power brakes freeze in cold weather, causing brakes to be inoperative." • "While driving at approximately 15-20 mph, suddenly pedal became spongy and unresponsive, then warning light came on, then continued to roll forward, hitting vehicle in front."
4. Electrical system: ignition, stalling. • "Vehicle backfires when pulling into traffic, and stalls." • "While driving, at any speed, experience intermittent sudden engine shutdown without prior warning; dealer replaced several parts." • "Vehicle stalls out while driving at 40-55 mph." • "Engine will stall without prior warning."
5. Engine: leaks, failure, fire. • "Motor locked up and vehicle caught on fire." • "Had 2 engines in truck." • "Had total engine failure; had to have it replaced." • "Engine replacement due to loose wrist pins." • "Oil leak on top of engine."
6. Power train: transmission: automatic, poor performance, difficulty shifting, slipping. • "When first starting vehicle and motor is cold, transmission sticks in low gear." • "Transmission vibrates." • "Sudden reverse acceleration while vehicle was in park gear, resulting in accident and injury." • "Transmission gears failed to shift automatically."

CHEVROLET TRUCK S10 1995

Complaint Severity: Very Serious. **Recall Alert:** See Recall Index. **Buyer's Summary:** The airbags in this vehicle have experienced failures and malfunctions: You may need a professional evaluation on the condition of the airbags. Check the brakes—listen for noise, look for leaks and feel for vibration. They may fail, perform poorly or require frequent mechanical attention.

Hot Spots and Owner/NHTSA Comments:
1. Interior systems: passive restraint: airbag: driver, malfunction, failure. • "Frontal collision, impact 12:00 position, airbag did not deploy, speed 35 mph." • "In a head-on collision at approximately 40 mph, the driver's-side airbag did not deploy, and the driver's-side seat belt did not function properly." • "In a head-on collision at 45 mph, the driver's-side airbag did not deploy." • "Frontal collision at 50 mph and the airbag did not deploy." • "Steering wheel lockup, causing loss of vehicle control; went into embankment, hitting a wall, speed 45 mph, impact 12:00 position, airbag did not deploy."
2. Brakes: hydraulic: anti-skid system, poor performance, failure, locking up. • "Antilock brake system: Antilock braking system engages at inappropriate times; dry surfaces; small pothole or bridge transition; speeds 10-15 mph; caused accident." • "The brake makes noise when brakes are applied, it happens sometimes and the brake pedal goes down to the floor." • "Antilock brakes failed, causing loss of control and an accident." • "Antilock brake system failed 6 times, once resulting in an accident." • "Brake pedal fades to the floor, brake did not respond to stopping, resulting in accident; dealer cannot locate the problem."

CHEVROLET TRUCK SUBURBAN 1987

Complaint Severity: Minor. **Buyer's Summary:** The fuel pump has received complaints. Make sure it doesn't make excessive noise and that you are experiencing adequate engine performance. Also, look for leaks. Check the brakes—listen for noise, look for leaks and feel for vibration. They may fail, perform poorly or require frequent mechanical attention.

Hot Spots and Owner/NHTSA Comments:
1. Brakes: hydraulic system, locking up, pulling, failure. • "Brake pedal hits floor, no braking power; installed master cylinder and booster." • "Hard and very ineffective braking, necessary to pump brake several times." • "Approaching stop sign at 20 mph, applied brakes, brakes failed, collided with truck; foreign matter in brake fluid had eaten gasket, whole brake system ruined." • "Vehicle's brakes are prone to sudden lockup, resulting in skids." • "Brakes pull right when applied in normal driving." • "Brakes not very effective when stopping; machined front rotors, adjusted rear brakes and replaced master cylinder."
2. Fuel: fuel tank assembly: tank, stalling, corrosion, leaks. • "Gas line disconnected inside gas tank, vehicle went dead instantaneously." • "Baffles inside gas tank broke, destroyed tank sender and fuel pump; caused vehicle to die." • "Baffle in gas tank came loose, knocked out fuel pump and level gauge mechanism, plugged filter on gas line to motor, repaired." • "Failure of fuel pump and baffles, causing stalling while driving." • "Gas tank on vehicle has corroded on top and side, which allows fuel leakage."
3. Fuel: fuel pump, stalling, failure. • "Baffles inside tank broke loose, damaging fuel pump." • "Failure of fuel pump and baffles, causing stalling while driving." • "Engine shuts off at any speed, at any time, power failure to fuel pump." • "Fuel pump and other parts within fuel tank breaking apart, no fuel from fuel tank."
4. Fuel: fuel tank assembly, miscellaneous problems. • "Pressure buildup in fuel tank, expels fuel from filler pipe upon removing gas cap." • "Faulty fuel gauge, erratic performance, plastic baffle tray in bottom of tank loose from brass posts, sieve of pump gauge frayed from rubbing against tray." • "Extreme pressure builds up in fuel tank in high-temperature driving situations, forcing fuel out of fill tube when gas cap removed to refill tank." • "Vehicle suddenly lost power, baffles inside tank broke loose inside tank, bending fuel quantity sender and electric fuel pump." • "Baffle inside fuel tank came loose and dislodged the fuel pump, causing it to become inoperable; engine would not run."

CHEVROLET TRUCK SUBURBAN 1988

Complaint Severity: Typical. **Recall Alert:** See Recall Index. **Buyer's Summary:** Verify that the cruise control system works properly, and that it doesn't cause the engine to surge. Check the brakes—listen for noise, look for leaks and feel for vibration. They may fail, perform poorly or require frequent mechanical attention.

Hot Spots and Owner/NHTSA Comments:

1. Equipment: speed control, sudden acceleration, malfunction. • "Driver applies accelerator pedal and vehicle accelerates out of control. When brakes are applied the vehicle will not stop." • "Cruise control turns on by itself in cold weather, when intentionally reset, vehicle comes back at greater speed than the original setting." • "Cruise control occasionally turns on by itself, usually in cold weather, when turned back on after braking vehicle accelerates on past set speed." • "While cruise control on, car will accelerate, will not stop until brakes applied." • "With windshield wipers activated, cruise control also activated at 65 mph, causing engine to go into hard acceleration until deactivated by brake pedal."

2. Brakes: hydraulic system, pulling, poor performance. • "Brakes operated poorly, vehicle pulled to the right while braking." • "Brakes very weak, when slowing for turn or stop, stopping improper." • "While driving, upon braking, brakes pull to right, loss of control braking on snow-covered roads; repaired/replaced rotors, pads, right front brake hose, calipers and brake valve." • "Brakes grab at all speeds, vehicle pulls to right on heavy braking application; resulted in accident; replaced brakes."

3. Fuel: fuel tank assembly: tank, corrosion, miscellaneous problems. • "Fuel tank baffle disconnected, jammed float, causing indicator to fail." • "Inner wall of fuel tank collapsed onto sender, causing fuel gauge to give false readings." • "Seals in gas tank broke; resulted in fuel pump failure." • "Fuel tank, between the skid plate and form, absorbs water and rots out the fuel tank."

4. Interior systems: bucket: backrest, breaking, failure. • "Driver's seat bolt broke and seat back fell backwards." • "Driver's seat back fell back; dealer said vehicle was not included in recall." • "Left front bucket seat back collapsed due to sheared bolt." • "While driving, driver's seat back collapsed due to bolt breakage." • "Manual driver's seat back collapsed when starting truck."

CHEVROLET TRUCK SUBURBAN 1989

Complaint Severity: Typical. **Recall Alert:** See Recall Index. **Buyer's Summary:** Test the suspension by feeling for vibration or pulling while driving. Check the brakes—listen for noise, look for leaks and feel for vibration. They may fail, perform poorly or require frequent mechanical attention. Test the transmission thoroughly.

Hot Spots and Owner/NHTSA Comments:

1. Interior systems: bucket: backrest, breaking, failure. • "Front seat back bracket bolt broke, seat back fell backwards, causing injury." • "Driver's seat back broken, fully reclined on 2 occasions while driving, driver fell backwards into rear seat, almost caused complete loss of control of car." • "While accelerating up on an access ramp, driver leaned right to access control on console, seat back flopped down onto rear seat." • "Rear-ended at 70 mph and both front passenger seat backs fell; due to complications, passenger died." • "Driver's seat back bolt sheared, causing seat back to fall backwards and injury."

2. Brakes: hydraulic system, premature failure, vibration. • "Front and rear brakes worn out prematurely; repaired/replaced several times." • "Defective braking system, fails to stop or slow car at different times, almost causing accident." • "Brake overheated, warping front rotors at 25,000 miles; needed complete brake job." • "Brake system malfunction, inherent weakness in brake system causing excessive strain on front brakes, resulting in premature wear and failures." • "Brakes squeaking, vibrating and pulsating; replaced on several occasions, problem continues."

3. Power train: transmission: automatic, poor performance, difficulty shifting, slipping. • "Vehicle rolled backwards while still in park position, pinned person under front tire." • "Automatic transmission not shifting properly." • "Transmission has been repaired/replaced 2 times within 25,000 miles." • "Transmission went because of metal flakes inside; has been in the shop 3 times for the same problem."

4. Brakes: hydraulic: shoe: disc brake system, pulling, locking up, vibration. • "Brakes cause vehicle to pull to the right when applied in sudden stops." • "Problem with front brake locking up on wet pavement under normal braking conditions, causes uncontrollable skid; resulted in 2 minor accidents." • "When braking under medium or hard braking conditions at over 30 mph, front wheels lock up, truck loses traction and slides; resulted in accidents." • "Front brake system exhibits vibration and noise, pads and discs need servicing in 6,000-mile intervals." • "Front disc brakes replaced."

5. Suspension: independent front, noise, pulling, tire wear. • "Noise in front suspension when driving over bumps." • "Problems with suspension." • "Clunk in front suspension when full turn over bumps." • "Vehicle consistently pulls to the right; all repair and modification attempts to no avail."

6. Air conditioner: compressor, malfunction, failure. • "Defective air conditioner compressor." • "Air conditioner compressor clutch and bearing failed twice." • "Air conditioner compressor malfunctioned." • "Air conditioner compressor bearing replaced."

CHEVROLET TRUCK SUBURBAN 1990

Complaint Severity: Harmless. **Recall Alert:** See Recall Index. **Buyer's Summary:** Check the brakes—listen for noise, look for leaks and feel for vibration. They may fail, perform poorly or require frequent mechanical attention. Test the transmission thoroughly.

Hot Spots and Owner/NHTSA Comments:

1. Power train: transmission: automatic, poor performance, difficulty shifting, slipping. • "Transmission vibrates when accelerating, shifts hard." • "Leak in transmission, repaired, blew oil, transmission rebuilt, finally transmission burned up." • "Transmission slips when taking off." • "Truck was in park idling for several minutes, suddenly jumped out of gear after making a humming sound." • "Transmission slippage at 12,000 miles; transmission problem repaired."

2. Brakes: hydraulic system, locking up, failure. • "Pad out of round, causing brake lockup." • "Brakes jerked while stopping on incline; repaired." • "Upon applying the brakes, pedal went to the floor." • "Right rear brakes stick and/or lock up with normal braking conditions." • "Brake pedal failed during braking; took car in twice before problem was found."

3. Brakes: hydraulic: anti-skid system, poor performance, failure, locking up. • "Antilock brake system failed on 5 occasions." • "Left side dump valve sticking, causing light to come on." • "Antilock braking system computer failed; repaired." • "When road is slippery, vehicle loses control due to front wheel lockup." • "Antilock brake system malfunctioned when stopping at stop sign with foot on pedal, vehicle still rolled; replaced master cylinder, power booster and antilock brake system control module."

4. Equipment: electric power accessories: windows, malfunction, failure. • "Power windows inoperative." • "Actuator switch for rear window failed." • "Power windows malfunctioned." • "Right passenger power window rolls down slowly."

5. Interior systems: seat track anchors and seats, breaking, failure. • "Driver's seat broke while driving." • "May 1993, seat bolt broke and driver fell back. March 3, 1994, recalled bolt replaced. March 11, 1994, seat fell backwards again." • "Driver's seat back broke after recall. Seat fixed 4 times." • "Driver's seat collapsed prior to and twice after recall repairs."

CHEVROLET TRUCK SUBURBAN 1991

Complaint Severity: Minor. **Recall Alert:** See Recall Index. **Buyer's Summary:** Check the brakes—listen for noise, look for leaks and feel for vibration. They may fail, perform poorly or require frequent mechanical attention. Test the transmission thoroughly.

Hot Spots and Owner/NHTSA Comments:

1. Power train: transmission: automatic, poor performance, difficulty shifting, slipping. • "Vehicle caught on fire while driving. Fluid leaked near heated catalytic converter and ignited." • "Transmission replaced, as 4th gear went out." • "Transmission computer chip failure." • "Transmission overhauled." • "Automatic transmission sticks in gear."

2. Brakes: hydraulic: anti-skid system, poor performance, failure, locking up. • "Accident caused by lockup of antilock brake system." • "One-mile trip, antilock brake system brake pedal went to floor and clunked, pedal still going to floor." • "Antilock brake system locks up only on wet surface. In one situation, truck rear-ended another vehicle. Dealers can't find cause." • "Antilock brakes and on-slip differential. Brake lockup upon applying the brakes." • "Calipers, rotors and disc pads failed, causing disc pads to wear, vehicle to pull to left and brake squealing."

3. Brakes: hydraulic: shoe: disc brake system, noise, locking up. • "Front brakes noisy due to worn pads; replaced, problem continues." • "Right front brake locked up, causing it to overheat and resulting in vehicle having to be towed." • "Vehicle's power brakes inoperative." • "Brakes fade, burning smell, squeaking. Replaced front pads and machined rotors."

4. Brakes: hydraulic system, failure, noise. • "Factory omitted pins in caliper assembly, resulted in movements and noise when braking; also, caliper not attached to mounting." • "Brake booster failed." • "Brake pedal fades and brakes grab." • "Brakes failed."

CHEVROLET TRUCK SUBURBAN 1992

Complaint Severity: Serious. **Recall Alert:** See Recall Index. **Buyer's Summary:** Check the brakes—listen for noise, look for leaks and feel for vibration. They may fail, perform poorly or require frequent mechanical attention. Test the transmission thoroughly.

Hot Spots and Owner/NHTSA Comments:

1. Brakes: hydraulic: anti-skid system, poor performance, failure, locking up. • "Antilock brake system light came on and when brakes were applied, they made a grinding noise; pedal faded, the only way to stop vehicle was to use emergency brake." • "While driving, antilock brake system completely failed, pedal went to floor; warning light came on after accident." • "Antilock brakes failed twice, causing loss of control, 2 accidents and injuries." • "Antilock brake system: Brakes don't respond to application resulting in rear-ending." • "Antilock brake system failure if moisture is present, will experience pedal fading and brake lockup."

2. Power train: transmission: automatic, poor performance, difficulty shifting, slipping. • "Vehicle caught on fire due to transmission fluid leaking." • "Transmission gears failed." • "Transmission failed." • "While driving, engine surged then began to lose rpm, pulled to side, noticed puff of smoke, looked at underside and found transmission on fire." • "Transmission overheated after recall repairs."

3. Brakes: hydraulic system, locking up, pulling. • "Brakes did not activate when applied, driver was coming to a stop, speed 10 mph." • "Brake pedal felt normal, but vehicle would not stop." • "Brake cylinder failed." • "Brakes either lock up, pull to the left or right, or they feel spongy." • "When passengers are in the back, they come forward when brakes are applied."

CHEVROLET TRUCK SUBURBAN 1993

Complaint Severity: Typical. **Buyer's Summary:** Look carefully for any kind of leakage, especially under the car. Check the brakes—listen for noise, look for leaks and feel for vibration. They may fail, perform poorly or require frequent mechanical attention.

Hot Spots and Owner/NHTSA Comments:

1. Brakes: hydraulic: anti-skid system, poor performance, failure, locking up. • "Antilock brakes failed to stop vehicle when applied, causing front-end collision at 30 mph." • "Antilock brake system locked without brake pedal being applied. Driver could not control vehicle. Brake fluid is also being lost." • "Brakes failed twice due to antilock brake system computer not being calibrated, causing loss of control; 2 accidents and injuries." • "Brakes make grinding sound, feels like pedal goes to the floor. No response from antilock braking system." • "Experience intermittent antilock brake system failure when front wheels lock up under normal application of brake, wet or dry conditions."

2. Brakes: hydraulic system, locking up, pulling, failure. • "Heavy stopping causes front wheels to lock and makes steering uncontrollable." • "Vehicle pulls to left or right when braking." • "Intermittent problem. Depressed pedal, brakes went to the floor, resulting in extended stopping distance." • "Brakes became spongy at intersection and brake pedal went to the floor."

3. Interior systems: active restraints: belt retractors, failure. • "Driver's- and passenger's-side shoulder and lap seat belts do not retract, causing potential risk of injuries. Twice for driver's side and once for passenger's side." • "Seat belt does not retract properly; also, driver's-side seat belt gets caught between arm and door." • "Driver's seat belt failed to retract." • "Retractor failed."

4. Interior systems: active seat and shoulder belts and belt anchor, failure. • "Seat belts failed." • "Seat belts didn't lock on sudden stop." • "Seat belts twisted, parts missing."

5. Brakes: hydraulic: shoe and drum system, locking up, noise, failure. • "Rear brakes lock up, causing vehicle to skid." • "Rear disc brakes squeal." • "Extended stopping distance at low speed, and rear locked up." • "Rear brake seal broke and leaked brake fluid over rear brakes."

6. Engine: leaks, failure, fire. • "Engine oil leak." • "Engine belt/tensioner pulley failed." • "Oil seal failure." • "Engine fire."

CHEVROLET TRUCK SUBURBAN 1994

Complaint Severity: Serious. **Buyer's Summary:** Check the brakes—listen for noise, look for leaks and feel for vibration. They may fail, perform poorly or require frequent mechanical attention. Test the transmission thoroughly.

Hot Spots and Owner/NHTSA Comments:

1. Brakes: hydraulic: anti-skid system, poor performance, failure, locking up. • "Antilock brake system had complete failure, causing 2-car accident." • "Antilock brake system failure; at a high speed, driver unable to make sudden stop." • "Antilock brake system: Upon application vehicle continued forward, rear-ending other vehicle. No airbag deployment." • "Antilock brake system: Pedal goes to floor with no braking effect when coming to stop and on bumpy surface." • "Traveling between 40 and 45 mph and hit slight bump, the antilock brake system engaged. Resulted in an accident."

2. Brakes: hydraulic system, failure. • "Brakes on vehicle are inadequate, excessive long stopping distance." • "In driving, the brake pedal travels 3 to 4 inches before brakes will catch." • "While driving, experienced spongy brake pedal when made attempt to stop; result inadequate brake action." • "Delayed brake response and extended stopping distance during emergency situations." • "Brake pedal gives out; when completely depressed, car does not stop."

3. Interior systems: active restraints: belt retractors, malfunction, failure. • "Both driver and passenger shoulder belts do not retract." • "Front driver and passenger shoulder and lap belts won't retract, belt continues to come out of assembly." • "Owner has had to replace the driver's-side seat belt, which would not lock into place." • "Seat belt retractors failed." • "Vehicle's driver's-side shoulder belt has been replaced 3 times due to nonretraction."

4. Power train: transmission: automatic, poor performance, difficulty shifting, slipping. • "Automatic transmission: While driving highway, transmission overheated; ruptured seal; sprayed transmission fluid; caused a fire." • "Automatic transmission failed after 7,000 miles." • "Transmission slips upon acceleration." • "Transmission fails to shift." • "While in park position, with engine running, suddenly vehicle jumped out of gear into reverse."

5. Air conditioner: compressor, failure. • "Air conditioner compressor failed." • "Air conditioner compressor failed." • "Air conditioner compressor failed twice."

6. Brakes: hydraulic: master cylinder, failure, fade. • "Master cylinder failed." • "Antilock brake system failed completely with no power. Master cylinder and other components replaced, with no change in condition." • "Brakes fade out, resulting in accident; replaced brake line and master cylinder system, antilock brake system." • "After going over bump, experienced complete antilock brake system loss for a brief moment."

Chrysler—Cars and Trucks

CHRYSLER CONCORDE 1993

Complaint Severity: Typical. **Buyer's Summary:** Verify that the cruise control system works properly, and that it doesn't cause the engine to surge. The airbags in this vehicle have experienced failures and malfunctions: You may need a professional evaluation on the condition of the airbags. Check the brakes—listen for noise, look for leaks and feel for vibration. They may fail, perform poorly or require frequent mechanical attention. Test the transmission thoroughly.

Hot Spots and Owner/NHTSA Comments:

1. Brakes: hydraulic: anti-skid system, poor performance, failure, locking up. • "Antilock brakes failed 3 times." • "Brakes are mushy and antilock brake system warning light comes on." • "Antilock brake system failure; when brakes applied vehicle skidded at speed of 35 mph, lost control, antilock brake system locked up, impact 6:00 position." • "Antilock brake system: When applying brakes, experienced pedal fading. Impact 12:00 position, 25 mph." • "The antilock brake system fails on an intermittent basis. Driver applied brakes and pedal went to the floor. Vehicle did not stop."

2. Power train: transmission: automatic, poor performance, difficulty shifting, slipping. • "Vehicle automatic transmission jumps out of control when vehicle gets down to 5 mph; replaced computer to no avail." • "Transmission shifts erratically before and after repair work." • "Transmission difficult to shift." • "Computer-controlled automatic transmission sometimes fails to shift into drive. Engine must be turned off to get it to shift again."

3. Brakes: hydraulic system, noise, failure. • "Noisy brakes." • "Brakes failed prior to and after repairs." • "Brakes replaced 3 times due to squealing." • "Brakes failed, causing accident." • "Brake failure."

4. Interior systems: passive restraint: airbag, malfunction, failure. • "Dual airbags didn't deploy in collision; impact 11:00 position; car 1 rear-ended by car 2 at 55-65 mph; car 1 rear-ended car 3; car 1 at standstill. Airbag did not deploy." • "Airbag did not deploy." • "Owner complains of the airbag light staying on; dealer is not sure why this is happening."

5. Equipment: speed control, malfunction, failure. • "Cruise control problems." • "Cruise control operated sporadically." • "Speed increases while going downhill when cruise control is used." • "Cruise control is very erratic."

6. Lighting: general or unknown component: headlights, poor performance. • "Headlights aren't sufficient for night vision." • "Headlights are inadequate, not penetrating darkness. Poor visibility." • "Left rear headlight misaligned, affecting night visibility." • "Lighting visibility is insufficient for driving at night. Too dim for use. Front windshield visibility is distorted."

CHRYSLER CONCORDE 1994

Complaint Severity: Typical. **Recall Alert:** See Recall Index. **Buyer's Summary:** Check the brakes—listen for noise, look for leaks and feel for vibration. They may fail, perform poorly or require frequent mechanical attention. Test the transmission thoroughly.

Hot Spots and Owner/NHTSA Comments:

1. Lighting: general or unknown component: headlights, poor performance. • "When driving, headlights are very dim, causing vision problems." • "Headlights don't provide sufficient lighting." • "Vehicle's headlight design is poor, light is very dim, design does not allow lighting on either side of front." • "Headlights operating at only 25 percent intensity, causing poor visibility." • "Headlights have blind spots, do not produce enough light." • "Can't see yellow line on right."

2. Brakes: hydraulic: anti-skid system, poor performance, failure, locking up. • "Antilock brake system failure; applied the brakes and experienced extended stopping distance." • "The antilock brake system went out on the car. The lights came on and would not go off. Had to replace the antilock brake system module." • "The car has antilock brakes. They have experienced total brake failure. The pedal went to the floor." • "Antilock brake system: Hydraulic unit replaced due to brakes failing completely." • "When brakes applied in wet weather, brake pedal pulsates badly, resulting in long stopping distance; dealer cannot locate problem."

3. Power train: transmission: automatic, poor performance, difficulty shifting, slipping. • "Transmission downshifts to a lower gear when braking at 2-7 mph." • "Transmission does not change gears, stays in low gears until vehicle warms up." • "Transmission would not shift." • "Transmission slipped." • "Transmission went out at 13,351 miles, causing vehicle to shimmy."

4. Lighting: lamp or socket: headlights, poor performance. • "Front headlight design is poor, not supplying enough illumination." • "Headlight design insufficient for night driving, causing poor visibility." • "Headlights insufficient for night driving." • "Right front low-beam headlight bulb failed."

5. Visual systems: glass: windshield, miscellaneous problems. • "Windshield angle allows accumulation of road debris, impairing visibility." • "Severe glare from windshield due to reflections off dashboard; cannot see out of windshield due to direct sunlight." • "Back rear window shattered when driver's-side door was opened." • "Water flows across driver's-side front window, obliterating visibility."

CHRYSLER FIFTH AVENUE 1987

Complaint Severity: Negligible. **Buyer's Summary:** The carburetion system could contribute to stalling and hesitation. The fuel injection system has been blamed for hesitation and stalling. Be sure the vehicle doesn't die in traffic or at stops. Test the suspension by feeling for vibration or pulling while driving. Check the brakes—listen for noise, look for leaks and feel for vibration. They may fail, perform poorly or require frequent mechanical attention. Test the transmission thoroughly. See "Sudden Accelerations" in Introduction.

Hot Spots and Owner/NHTSA Comments:

1. Power train: transmission: automatic, poor performance, difficulty shifting, slipping. • "After parking car and placing gear in park, rolls about 6 or 7 feet; could cause injury to someone." • "Car surges and jerks when shifting gears; rear axle repairs to no avail." • "On 2 occasions car rolled several feet with shift lever engaged in park; took to dealer, found nothing wrong with park mechanism." • "Automatic transmission: Put in park, car rolled backwards, transmission jumped out of gear from park to reverse; repeated use of emergency brake stopped car." • "Transmission leaks in front, transmission gasket and bands blown."

2. Brakes: hydraulic system, locking up, poor performance. • "Improper performance of brakes, lock up when applied, pull left on hard braking; replaced front and rear brakes, K-frame, problem still exists." • "When applying brakes in emergency situation on wet pavement, car goes into slide rather than stopping." • "While driving at 20 mph and making right turn, power brakes locked up, causing vehicle to crash into a truck. No injuries." • "Brakes have developed an unidentified malfunction that causes skidding and fishtailing." • "On a wet surface, when brakes are applied, vehicle will go into a skid."

3. Fuel: fuel carburetion, stalling, hesitation. • "Car stalls repeatedly." • "Very little power, sluggish and slow when traveling uphill or on a grade, no pickup." • "Engine stalls on acceleration, turning corners, slowing down for red light; 4 repair attempts to no avail, adjusted carburetor, repaired/replaced computer and coil wire." • "Carburetor malfunctioned 7 times; had it fixed but vehicle still hesitates." • "Defective carburetor, engine runs irregularly after 24,000 miles, clicking noise, lack of power with engine."

4. Fuel: fuel injection system, stalling, hesitation. • "When vehicle is cold, car hesitates and stalls when first starting to drive." • "Upon starting, car continuously stalls; on first stop after starting car stalls." • "Engine stalls and also surges while driving, without warning." • "Engine dies on acceleration from stop and when backing up."

5. Suspension: independent front, alignment, tire wear. • "Continuous front-end alignment problem, pulls to left, uneven wear on front tires; repaired/replaced K-frame, problem not corrected." • "When brakes applied, hands loose on steering wheel, car pulls left; tires badly worn on sides." • "Alignment problems, resulting in premature and uneven tire wear; vehicle veers to left side of road." • "Noise from front torsion bar straps."

6. Fuel: throttle linkages and control, sudden accelerations. • "Engine idles too high; adjusted carburetor; second incident car stalled, restarted, accelerated through red light, brakes failed to operate." • "Car surges and idles too fast." • "Car suddenly accelerated and could not be controlled." • "Vehicle suddenly accelerates out of control while driving, resulting in an accident." • "Engine suddenly accelerated, resulting in an accident."

CHRYSLER FIFTH AVENUE 1988

Complaint Severity: Typical. **Recall Alert:** See Recall Index. **Buyer's Summary:** The fuel injection system has been blamed for hesitation and stalling. Be sure the vehicle doesn't die in traffic or at stops. Check the brakes—listen for noise, look for leaks and feel for vibration. They may fail, perform poorly or require frequent mechanical attention. Test the transmission thoroughly.

Hot Spots and Owner/NHTSA Comments:

1. Fuel: fuel injection system, stalling, hesitation. • "Constant engine stalling and cutting out." • "Vehicle experiences stalling problems, when slowing down or making turns." • "Car cutting off from time to time, idled roughly to continue driving." • "Vehicle surging, hesitation on slight acceleration, poor gas mileage, stalls in damp weather." • "Intermittent stalling, hesitation and starting problems."

2. Brakes: hydraulic system, pulling, locking up. • "When brakes were applied, car pulled drastically to one side and spun into ditch; problem caused by left front wheel grabbing, repaired/replaced all brakes." • "Very poor braking system; replaced brake shoe, rotor and booster 3 times." • "When brakes were applied, vehicle traveled beyond a reasonable distance, went out of control, resulting in an accident." • "Braking system ineffective; in attempt to apply, brakes locked up, causing vehicle to spin out of control; serious defect in system." • "Intermittent lockup on front brakes upon application of brake pedal in routine stopping situations."

3. Power train: transmission: automatic, poor performance, difficulty shifting, slipping. • "Car rolls easily when in park." • "While parked, vehicle started to move backwards, struck with rear end of other car." • "Vehicle may roll when put into park." • "Unspecified failure of spider gear; also, accident occurred."

CHRYSLER FIFTH AVENUE 1990

Complaint Severity: Harmless. **Recall Alert:** See Recall Index. **Buyer's Summary:** The electronic control unit has been blamed for engine performance problems, including stalling and surging. Test the transmission thoroughly.

Hot Spots and Owner/NHTSA Comments:

1. Power train: transmission: automatic, poor performance, difficulty shifting, slipping. • "Unspecified transmission problem." • "Transmission failed." • "Defective transmission; repaired/replaced several times to no avail." • "Automatic transmission system not functioning properly." • "Automatic transmission jerks or jumps, sometimes slams into gear with horrendous chatter, clutch plate and disc engagement clutch system failure."

2. Electrical system: battery, failure. • "Recurring electrical problem in starting car, needs to be jump-started." • "Bad battery; replaced." • "Failed battery; replaced." • "Battery failed; replaced."

3. Electrical system: ignition: electronic control unit, premature failure. • "Computer replaced." • "Computer memory failed." • "Computer failed twice." • "Vehicle not running properly due to a defective power module."

CHRYSLER IMPERIAL 1990

Complaint Severity: Typical. **Recall Alert:** See Recall Index. **Buyer's Summary:** Check the brakes—listen for noise, look for leaks and feel for vibration. They may fail, perform poorly or require frequent mechanical attention. Test the transmission thoroughly.

Hot Spots and Owner/NHTSA Comments:

1. Brakes: hydraulic: anti-skid system, poor performance, failure, locking up. • "Brakes failed on vehicle several times. Vehicle has antilock brake system and was part of a recall." • "Antilock brakes cause extended stopping when applied. Has been

repaired 8 times." • "Antilock brake system pedal traveled to the floor with no braking effect. Speed 55 mph. No prior warning." "Antilock brakes failed; replaced rear brake pads and turned rotor." • "Antilock brake system: Loss of braking effectiveness; rolled through stop sign; antilock brake system booster pump, front brake pads and master cylinder have all been replaced."
2. Electrical system: battery, failure. • "Battery failed." • "Battery failed 2 times." • "Defective battery replaced." • "Defective battery in electrical system."
3. Power train: transmission: automatic, poor performance, difficulty shifting, slipping. • "Transmission fluid leak caused by factory-defective transmission parts." • "Slight noise from lower gears when in drive." • "Transmission leaks. Replaced rear main seal." • "Vehicle experienced 2 transmission failures."

CHRYSLER IMPERIAL 1991

Complaint Severity: Typical. **Recall Alert:** See Recall Index. **Buyer's Summary:** Check the brakes—listen for noise, look for leaks and feel for vibration. They may fail, perform poorly or require frequent mechanical attention. Test the transmission thoroughly.

Hot Spots and Owner/NHTSA Comments:

1. Brakes: hydraulic: anti-skid system, poor performance, failure, locking up. • "Antilock brake system: When making a sudden stop, loss of brake effectiveness." • "Compete pedal fading." • "Recall repairs refused due to unavailability of parts." • "Antilock brake system failure, loss of effectiveness; in for repair, replaced pump and hydraulic system." • "Vehicles antilock brake system pump malfunctioned, causing long extended stopping distances." • "Brake wear due to internal hydraulic system leaking."
2. Power train: transmission: automatic, poor performance, difficulty shifting, slipping. • "Automatic transmission: System in shop several times due to transmission not shifting when accelerating." • "Transmission failed." • "Transmission failed." • "Transmission problem." • "Transmission slips to low gear at 50-55 mph."
3. Exhaust system: manifold: oxygen sensor, failure, poor performance. • "Experiencing power loss due to faulty manifold air pressure sensors; repaired/replaced 4 times, repair shop unable to give explanation of failing condition." • "Manifold air pressure sensor unit failed 5 times, unit keeps breaking down, auto will not start or run." • "Engine running rough, plastic bucket and papers on floor of trunk over muffler area partially melted; manifold air pressure sensor needed replacing." • "Starting or rough engine ride or idle."
4. Fuel: throttle linkages and control, sudden accelerations. • "Vehicle was completely stopped, after taking foot off brake experienced sudden acceleration. Impact 12:00 position. Hit a wall at speed of 20 mph." • "Throttle went into open position after starting, vehicle went out of control, hitting a wall, impact 11:00 position on rear fender." • "Accelerator stuck full-throttle position while driving uphill, applied brakes." • "While driving, vehicle surged forward and hit 3 parked vehicles." • "Vehicle surge at speed of 45 mph."
5. Electrical system: instrument panel: cluster module, premature failure. • "Digital dashboard burned out—no speedometer, gas gauge, temperature, rpm, oil pressure, voltage, mileage, turn indicator, high beam indicator." • "Digital cluster board failed, front power windows inoperative, ignition problem." • "Intermittent electrical shortage in dashboard resulted in poor driver information." • "Digital instrument panel blacked out." • "Dashboard in car went blank due to defect in digital dashboard cluster; repaired/replaced, problem reoccurred at 40,000 miles."
6. Steering: gear: rack-and-pinion, stiffness, poor performance. • "Rack-and-pinion steering came loose, almost contributed to an accident." • "Rack-and-pinion bolts got loose, causing damage to cross member and also contributing to leak in power steering hose." • "Rack-and-pinion system malfunctioned, steering works very tight." • "At 42,000 miles developed a severe power steering problem, leakage in the rack-and-pinion system." • "One of the bolts holding the rack-and-pinion steering system was loose, and 3 were missing."

CHRYSLER LE BARON 1987

Complaint Severity: Typical. **Recall Alert:** See Recall Index. **Buyer's Summary:** The fuel injection system has been blamed for hesitation and stalling. Be sure the vehicle doesn't die in traffic or at stops. The steering may be stiff or not working correctly. Be sure to test the steering, especially on a cold start. Test the transmission thoroughly. See "Sudden Accelerations" in Introduction.

Hot Spots and Owner/NHTSA Comments:

1. Fuel: fuel injection system, stalling, hesitation. • "Car died while driving; replaced fuel pump, fixed crimped fuel lines." • "Engine sputters; numerous repairs made to correct the problem, including replacement of throttle body." • "Engine stalls when coming to stop, cuts off at highway speeds and hesitates on start." • "Engine sputters and/or hesitates, especially when automatic transmission shifts." • "Vehicle has unexpected power loss while driving, stalls, will not restart; due to defective mapping system sensor, replaced twice; also, exhaust manifold leaks."
2. Power train: transmission: automatic, poor performance, difficulty shifting, slipping. • "The transmission gear sometimes goes into park, can't get it out." • "Gearshift lever defect, car shifted by itself from park position to reverse, accelerating backward into concrete wall." • "In parked position with key removed, shifting lever can be shifted freely and car rolls." • "Able to remove key from ignition with transmission in drive, car rolled 20 feet." • "Experiencing ongoing problem with transmission slipping out of gear."

CHRYSLER LE BARON 1988

Complaint Severity: Troublesome. **Buyer's Summary:** The fuel injection system has been blamed for hesitation and stalling. Be sure the vehicle doesn't die in traffic or at stops. The steering may be stiff or not working correctly. Be sure to test the steering, especially on a cold start. The airbags in this vehicle have experienced failures and malfunctions: You may need a professional evaluation on the condition of the airbags. Test the transmission thoroughly. See "Sudden Accelerations" in Introduction.

Hot Spots and Owner/NHTSA Comments:

1. Steering: gear: rack-and-pinion, stiffness, poor performance. • "Rack-and-pinion steering separated from engine cradle." • "Bolts that hold rack-and-pinion together broke, caused looseness in steering system; claimed repairs covered under warranty, dealer denied it." • "Defective rack-and-pinion steering system; repaired/replaced." • "Rack-and-pinion mounting bolts caused steering mechanism to become loose when driving/steering the vehicle." • "Rack-and-pinion mounting bolts loosened; rack binds up; causes loss of steering control."
2. Fuel: fuel injection system, stalling, hesitation. • "Intermittent shuddering and stalling of vehicle while coming to stop." • "Engine misfires, sometimes difficult to move car quickly from a stop light." • "Engine backfires, misses, stalls frequently in traffic and when decelerating." • "Numerous problems with vehicle missing or hesitation in engine, trying to merge on freeway, creating severe safety hazard." • "Engine stalls at release of accelerator, when slowing to turn corner or stop."

3. Power train: transmission: automatic, poor performance, difficulty shifting, slipping. • "Upon starting car and shifting gears, vehicle became wedged in garage wall and door exit." • "When engine was running in park, transmission suddenly engaged in reverse and took off; resulted in an accident." • "Automatic transmission leak, erratic shifting of gears unexpectedly, skidding at startup." • "Key can be removed when auto not in park, drifts away; malfunction of automatic transmission." • "Car was first started and ran for 3 minutes, stopped in park with no parking brake applied, the vehicle self-shifted into reverse and backed into a tree."
4. Interior systems: passive restraint: airbag: driver, malfunction, failure. • "Upon head-on collision, airbag inflated partially, resulting in injuries to driver." • "Airbag caused burns during accident." • "While driving, was cut off by unknown vehicle; as brake applied, airbag blew up, scaring driver and causing to hit guardrail." • "During collision, instead of inflating, airbag emitted black acrid-smelling material, hitting face and hand of driver; caused first and second degree burns." • "During a minor accident, airbag engaged/exploded with a lot of force, fracturing driver's elbow and causing other injuries."
5. Fuel: throttle linkages and control, sudden accelerations. • "When accelerating, rpm skyrocketed at low speed; repairs rendered, problem continues." • "Idles 30 mph at all times; dealer installed new computer, second dealer tuned engine, still has high idle." • "While driving at moderate speed, with no warning vehicle accelerated full throttle. First occurrence dealership replaced throttle sensor. Vehicle caught fire." • "The head gaskets have had to be replaced on numerous occasions, and the throttle gets stuck in the open position." • "Any temperature, any terrain, the car may stall when trying to accelerate; the last episode caused a crash."
6. Steering: gear: rack, noise, breaking, failure. • "Power steering intermittently goes out while making turns; exact cause unknown." • "Bolts on K-frame periodically loosen, which causes dangerously excessive play in steering wheel; repaired/replaced entire K-frame/rack-and-pinion, bolts continue to loosen." • "Extra play and noise in steering, problem due to breakage of 3 out of 4 bolts holding rack to frame, leaving only 1 to hold mechanism." • "Coming to abrupt stop, slid into vehicle; this has happened twice, steering wheel pulls left when applying brakes in panic situation, steering rack came loose."

CHRYSLER LE BARON 1989

Complaint Severity: Typical. **Recall Alert:** See Recall Index. **Buyer's Summary:** Look carefully for any kind of leakage, especially under the car. The airbags in this vehicle have experienced failures and malfunctions: You may need a professional evaluation on the condition of the airbags. Check the brakes—listen for noise, look for leaks and feel for vibration. They may fail, perform poorly or require frequent mechanical attention.

Hot Spots and Owner/NHTSA Comments:

1. Brakes: hydraulic system, excessive wear, poor performance. • "Defective front brakes, excessive and premature wear." • "Computer chip that controls front brake went out and front brakes locked, resulted in front brake pads, rotors and other parts being replaced." • "Braking performance poor, brakes go too far to floor, close calls of almost hitting other cars." • "Replaced brakes in front after 4,000 miles; system defect." • "Brakes lock up and pull to right; replaced front pads, noticed only half of brake pad touching rotor, brakes improperly installed."
2. Brakes: hydraulic: disc: pads and shoes, noise, premature failure. • "Rear brakes replaced prior to recall, front pads replaced 3 times." • "Recall done. Eleven thousand miles later heard noise coming from rear antilock brakes. While driving, rear brakes dropped out of vehicle." • "Front brake pads wore out; repaired/replaced pads, calipers and rotors; at 22,000 miles, pads started grinding again; repaired/replaced front pads." • "When applying brakes, a loud bang and grinding sound from rear brake system occurs; brake pad fell off vehicle." • "Experiencing hard/soft pedal after 5,000 miles, found brake pad in driveway as result of both left pads not being connected to shoes."
3. Interior systems: passive restraint: airbag: driver, malfunction, failure. • "Defective airbag, did not release at time of impact when accident occurred; passenger sustained injuries." • "During an accident, while going at approximately 35 mph, vehicle impacted with a truck on passenger's side front bumper at 12:00, airbag failed to deploy." • "At approximately 2-5 mph vehicle hit a bump in road, the airbag deployed, causing facial and chest injuries." • "Airbag deployed, driver received burns on neck and chin area; 20 mph; impact 12:00 position; rear-ended another vehicle; chest area may have hit steering wheel before deployment." • "Defective airbag; upon impact car released airbag, which caused second degree burns due to gaseous substance used to release/inflate airbag."
4. Brakes: hydraulic: shoe: disc brake system, vibration, failure. • "Front brakes rubbing and grinding, unsafe to drive; replaced rotor, caliper and pads, problem not cured." • "Brake lining separates from pads." • "Problem with front brakes; repaired/replaced left front disc rotor and resurfaced right front disc rotor." • "Installed front disc brake calipers, rotors in front brake system; front calipers sticking." • "Front and rear rotors are destroyed. Causes pulsation in braking."
5. Engine: gaskets: valve cover, leaks, fire. • "Engine drips, faulty oil seal; gasket and valve cover defective." • "Received recall notice on defective valve cover, problem not corrected due to unavailability of parts." • "Engine valve cover gasket replaced." • "After valve cover recall work was performed, more valve cover oil leaked, causing engine compartment fire." • "Valve gasket cover disconnected; leaking oil onto engine block after recall repairs."
6. Interior systems: passive restraint: airbag, malfunction, failure. • "Airbag did not deploy during head-on." • "During a front-end collision with rear of another vehicle, airbag failed, speed at impact was 30 mph." • "Driver's airbag inflated with gas during accident, causing second and third degree burns on driver's arm due to vent holes on airbag being placed in unsafe position.

CHRYSLER LE BARON 1990

Complaint Severity: Serious. **Recall Alert:** See Recall Index. **Buyer's Summary:** The airbags in this vehicle have experienced failures and malfunctions: You may need a professional evaluation on the condition of the airbags. Check the brakes—listen for noise, look for leaks and feel for vibration. They may fail, perform poorly or require frequent mechanical attention. Test the transmission thoroughly.

Hot Spots and Owner/NHTSA Comments:

1. Power train: transmission: automatic, poor performance, difficulty shifting, slipping. • "Vehicle parked in driveway, rolled down driveway through chain link fence and into garage, driveway on very slight incline." • "Transmission shifts into 2nd gear while driving at various speeds, remains in that gear until car brought to complete stop." • "Automatic transmission problem, motor could not be started in park position but could be started in neutral; problem corrected." • "Automatic transmission tends to slip on occasion, then jerk forward after quick stops at intersections." • "Automatic transmission slipped out of gear and locked up."

2. Interior systems: passive restraint: airbag: driver, malfunction, failure. • "During frontal crash, impact 12:00 position, at approximately 60-65 mph, airbag deployed, with white smoke and fumes coming out causing chemical burns and injury." • "Frontal collision. Impact 12:00 position, speed 50 mph. Lost control of vehicle, hitting an embankment; airbag did not deploy." • "Frontal collision, impact 12:00 position, speed 35 mph, airbag did not deploy. Lap and shoulder belt did not retract." • "Airbag deployed during front-end collision at 8-10 mph, causing burns to driver's hands and fingers." • "Airbag did not inflate during accident, also filled vehicle with black smoke affecting visibility."
3. Brakes: hydraulic system, excessive wear, failure. • "Brakes, when applied, go almost to floor." • "Replaced pads and brake shoes because of wear." • "Front brake rotors warped 3 times. Left rear disc pad separated from backing while moving, causing momentary brake failure." • "To avoid a serious frontal collision, stepped on brakes but they failed; vehicle spun and hit a light pole, which collapsed on top of car; caused minor injury." • "Sitting still, engine running, brake pedal goes to floor in 5 seconds; problem persists."
4. Interior systems: passive restraint: airbag, malfunction, failure. • "Severe crash on the passenger's side did not trigger the airbag to deploy." • "False deployment of airbag, causing accident and burns." • "Driving at approximately 45 mph, vehicle was in head-on collision and hit a lamp pole, airbag failed to deploy." • "While traveling at 35 mph, a collision occurred at 12:00 position, airbag deployed but did not inflate." • "Wearing seat belt, upon impact received an airbag first degree burn injury; question safety of fabric type."
5. Electrical system: ignition, stalling, failure. • "Ignition key lock assembly fell out; received recall on part." • "Ignition switch inoperative." • "Part holding ignition key block fell out." • "Vehicle intermittently stalls out at any speed." • "The car will cut off while in motion when driving with the air conditioner on."
6. Brakes: hydraulic: disc: pads and shoes, rust, noise, excessive wear. • "Pin on brake pad rusted, causing pad to fall off." • "Brake pads failed." • "Front and rear brake pads fell off; 2 days prior, driver heard loud noise; brake light came on." • "While driving, rear brake pads fell off, experienced loss of brake effectiveness. Also, 4 times rearview mirror replaced." • "Premature wear of brake pads and shoes caused braking problems."

CHRYSLER LE BARON 1991

Complaint Severity: Serious. **Recall Alert:** See Recall Index. **Buyer's Summary:** The electronic control unit has been blamed for engine performance problems, including stalling and surging. The airbags in this vehicle have experienced failures and malfunctions: You may need a professional evaluation on the condition of the airbags. Check the brakes—listen for noise, look for leaks and feel for vibration. They may fail, perform poorly or require frequent mechanical attention. Test the transmission thoroughly. See "Sudden Accelerations" in Introduction.

Hot Spots and Owner/NHTSA Comments:
1. Power train: transmission: automatic, poor performance, difficulty shifting, slipping. • "Brass bushings in transmission failed, resulting in extensive damage." • "Transmission slips due to faulty torque converter/clutch, also shifts erratically due to faulty pressure regulator valve." • "Transmission hesitates and lurches, does not shift smoothly." • "Automatic transmission jerks when depressing accelerator pedal." • "Vehicle jerks when transmission shifts."
2. Interior systems: passive restraint: airbag: driver, malfunction, failure. • "Frontal collision, vehicle hit a telephone pole, impact 12:00 position, 25 mph, airbag did not deploy." • "No deployment of driver's airbag during accident, resulting in injury." • "Airbag did not deploy in a frontal collision at 12:00, speed approximately 35 mph." • "Airbag did not deploy, nor did seat belt restrain occupant, in frontal collision." • "Airbag did not deploy in a frontal collision, impact 12:00 position, speed 25 mph; passenger seat belt latch opened, allowing occupant to fall forward."
3. Fuel: throttle linkages and control, sudden accelerations. • "Child was able to start car without clutch being applied and car accelerated, running over 2 bikes and crashing." • "Upon shifting gear from park into drive and also into reverse, vehicle suddenly surged out of control, resulting in an accident." • "While driving, vehicle suddenly accelerated." • "On several driving occasions, experienced intermittent throttle sticking, without prior warning." • "Accident due to sudden acceleration."
4. Brakes: hydraulic system, noise, failure. • "Brake problems." • "Brake failure." • "Noisy brakes." • "Intermittent stalling problem. Motor quits, power steering and brakes stop functioning." • "Noise in brakes or gearshift."
5. Electrical system: ignition, stalling, failure. • "Vehicle will stall without warning while driving; in for repair, no problem found." • "Engine stalled 4 times in traffic during various types of driving conditions; no prior warning; on one occasion, caused an accident." • "Rotor and distributor cap wires failed." • "Intermittent stalling problem. Motor quits, power steering and brakes stop functioning." • "When driving vehicle in hot weather and with air conditioner turned on, vehicle will stall without warning."
6. Electrical system: ignition: electronic control unit, stalling, premature failure. • "Erratic idling of the computer module causes vehicle to stall." • "Computer failure." • "Onboard computer problem." • "Computer indicates oil pressure and temperature high or low."

CHRYSLER LE BARON 1992

Complaint Severity: Typical. **Recall Alert:** See Recall Index. **Buyer's Summary:** The airbags in this vehicle have experienced failures and malfunctions. You may need a professional evaluation on the condition of the airbags. Test the transmission thoroughly.

Hot Spots and Owner/NHTSA Comments:
1. Power train: transmission: automatic, poor performance, difficulty shifting, slipping." • "Transmission went down in 1st or 2nd gear and stuck, car jolted 3 times." • "Transmission and torque converter replaced." • "Transmission downshifts on its own while on freeway; speed 50 mph; presents safety hazard." • "Vehicle rolled backwards when touched slightly, resulting in accident." • "While driving, transmission went out; car stopped and had to be towed."
2. Interior systems: passive restraint: airbag: driver, malfunction, failure. • "No airbag deployment, 25 mph, right front headlamp impact, tore headlight wire harness. Steering wheel bent, key is jammed." • "Airbag did not deploy during front-end collision; impact 1:00 position; speed 10-20 mph; vehicle was hit by another vehicle traveling 60 mph." • "Frontal collision, impact 12:00 position, speed 35 mph, hit another vehicle that was stopped, airbag did not deploy." • "Skidding on wet road caused the airbag to deploy, driver's face was injured. Driver said airbag did not inflate til several minutes after deployment."

CHRYSLER LE BARON 1993

Complaint Severity: Typical. **Buyer's Summary:** The airbags in this vehicle have experienced failures and malfunctions: You may need a professional evaluation on the condition of the airbags. Check the brakes—listen for noise, look for leaks and feel for vibration.

They may fail, perform poorly or require frequent mechanical attention. Test the transmission thoroughly.

Hot Spots and Owner/NHTSA Comments:

1. Electrical system: ignition, stalling, failure. • "Vehicle stalls out while driving at any speed." • "While driving, car stalls out, with loss of all control mechanisms." • "Vehicle stalls out in summertime—defect seems to be related to hot weather—causing loss of all control." • "Vehicle stalls out at any speed, resulting in steering and braking control loss; replaced air injection system motor to no avail." • "Vehicle stalls out at any speed; replaced air injection system motor and adjusted throttle to no avail."

2. Interior systems: passive restraint: airbag: driver, malfunction, failure. • "Driver airbag did not deploy after pulling in parking lot and vehicle accelerated out of control." • "Driver's airbag did not deploy upon impact, resulting in an injury." • "Going 25 mph, impact 12:00 position, airbag did not deploy." • "Airbag deployment was violent, causing irritation, burns and itching to driver." • "Frontal collision, impact 12:00 position, speed 55, mph airbag deployed, causing second degree burns on wrist and chest and burning jacket."

3. Brakes: hydraulic: anti-skid system, poor performance, failure, locking up. • "Antilock brake system locks up when applied at 40 mph or more, causing vehicle to fishtail/spin." • "Antilock brake system brake pedal goes to the floor on wet surfaces." • "Replaced antilock brake system; also antilock brake system light comes on and off."

4. Power train: transmission: automatic, poor performance, difficulty shifting, slipping. • "While driving, the vehicle put itself into park without driver's help." • "Automatic transmission locked while traveling 65 mph; sounded like metal grinding against metal." • "Automatic transmission downshifts violently. Throws occupants into windshield. Dealer thinks problem is sensor or computer related." • "Transmission failure."

CHRYSLER NEW YORKER 1987

Complaint Severity: Typical. **Recall Alert:** See Recall Index. **Buyer's Summary:** The fuel injection system has been blamed for hesitation and stalling. Be sure the vehicle doesn't die in traffic or at stops. The steering may be stiff or not working correctly. Be sure to test the steering, especially on a cold start. Test the suspension by feeling for vibration or pulling while driving. Test the transmission thoroughly.

Hot Spots and Owner/NHTSA Comments:

1. Fuel: fuel injection system, stalling, hesitation. • "Engine stalling problem, vehicle suffers from poor acceleration, low power, steering wheel stiffens, stalls, then leaps forward instead of smooth pickup." • "Severe problem of engine stalling, dying out; all you have to do is put on brakes or turn wheel and it dies." • "Gasoline odor in passenger compartment when vehicle is started in cold temperatures; also, sluggish performance." • "Fuel injection problem, loss of power, on highway car completely stalled out and died, no warning when engine lost power."

2. Suspension: independent front, malfunction, noise, poor performance. • "Malfunction in front end, left turn feels like front wheels are coming off, severe wiggle in front wheel." • "Lower ball joint defective." • "Front end grinds constantly." • "Front end makes noise on turns; repaired/replaced struts, constant velocity joints and steering rack, all repair attempts unsuccessful." • "Malfunction in front suspension, uncomfortable, rough ride, front end plunges up and down, bottoms out on large bumps, bounces enough to lose steering control."

3. Steering: gear: rack-and-pinion, stiffness, poor performance. • "Rack-and-pinion replaced twice." • "Vehicle wouldn't turn right; repaired/replaced rack-and-pinion mounts." • "While driving, lost power steering 3 times due to rack-and-pinion failure; replaced 3 times." • "Rack-and-pinion steering noise when turning left or right." • "Steering safety defect, major repairs to constant velocity joint, steering rack struts and bearings, all to no avail."

4. Power train: transmission: automatic, poor performance, difficulty shifting, slipping. • "Transmission slipped from park into reverse, vehicle went out of control, rolled into gate." • "Automatic transmission clunks and hard to shift, grabbing between gears." • "Transmission jumped out of park into 1st gear, causing accident." • "Car leaps forward or in reverse when started in cold or warm weather." • "When vehicle is in park position, it rolls away with no warning."

5. Electrical system: ignition, stalling, poor performance. • "Engine shuts off at highway speed after stalling; replaced speed cluster, module, distributor." • "Power indicator light flashed on and lost all power; replaced starter relay, manifold air pressure sensor, distributor plate, logic module." • "Vehicle stalls intermittently." • "Hairline crack in rotor, causing intermittent stalling; replaced rotor, noticed some improvement but also some rough idle."

6. Equipment: electric power accessories: windows, malfunction, failure. • "Power door locks shorting out; inoperative." • "Driver's side window motor broke down and window would not roll down." • "Broken gear caused driver's electric window to stop working." • "Electrical problem caused power window motors to burn out; repaired/replaced."

CHRYSLER NEW YORKER 1988

Complaint Severity: Minor. **Buyer's Summary:** Look carefully for any kind of leakage, especially under the car. Verify that the cruise control system works properly, and that it doesn't cause the engine to surge. The fuel injection system has been blamed for hesitation and stalling. Be sure the vehicle doesn't die in traffic or at stops. Check the brakes—listen for noise, look for leaks and feel for vibration. They may fail, perform poorly or require frequent mechanical attention. Test the transmission thoroughly.

Hot Spots and Owner/NHTSA Comments:

1. Brakes: hydraulic: anti-skid system, poor performance, failure, locking up. • "Brakes failed without warning approaching intersection, pumping did not help, drifted to stopping point." • "While driving, vehicle would vibrate and wobble when antilock brakes were applied." • "Two brake failures resulted from defective antilock brake system sensor; first was partial with warning light, second was a complete failure with no warning." • "Pressed on gas pedal, no response from the braking system." • "Antilock brake light comes on intermittently. Replaced brake motor and computer." • "Brakes pulsate, then antilock brake system and brake lights come on; had to have accumulator replaced."

2. Fuel: fuel injection system, stalling, hesitation. • "Problem with vehicle stalling; repaired/replaced fuel injector and related parts." • "Car stalls, shuts off at high or low speeds." • "Vehicle experiencing stalling and hesitation problems." • "Intermittent hesitation when accelerating." • "Intermittent stalling." • "Experiencing hesitation while pressing accelerator, then all power goes; repaired/replaced pickup coil distributor, fuel injectors, all to no avail."

3. Power train: transmission: automatic, poor performance, difficulty shifting, slipping. • "Lockup of transmission, abrupt jerk engaging gears, vibration of car; repaired twice." • "Jerky, rough operation of transmission when shifting from park to drive or reverse, when shifting through various speeds and from regular drive to overdrive." • "Transmission slipped from park to reverse, caused vehicle to lose control; resulted in an accident." • "Vehicle slipped from park into drive gear; resulted in accident." • "The

transmission hesitates, and it bucks and jumps in and out of the gears while driving."
4. Equipment: speed control, malfunction, failure. • "Cruise control cuts in by itself intermittently." • "With switch on but not engaged, the speed cruise control will kick in automatically if lever is touched." • "Cruise control will not hold speed of vehicle, varying as much as 8-10 mph, particularly at speeds around 40 mph." • "When speed indicator reactivates with speed control engaged while driving, car would suddenly accelerate." • "Sudden acceleration due to cruise control engagement, sometimes cruise control does not engage at all."
5. Brakes: hydraulic system, noise, failure. • "Brakes shudder/squeal." • "Unspecified problems with braking system." • "Brakes squeak, when applying in rain there's little traction; front end pulls to right and back end fishtails when driving over 45 mph." • "Vehicle seems to be experiencing total brake failure; dealer unable to repair it." • "Braking distance fades. Pumped brakes, but still had an accident."
6. Engine: vibration, leaks, failure. • "Engine failure." • "Engine fluctuates and vibrates." • "Unspecified fire." • "Oil leak." • "Vehicle overheats, oil under hood."

CHRYSLER NEW YORKER 1989

Complaint Severity: Negligible. **Buyer's Summary:** The electronic control unit has been blamed for engine performance problems, including stalling and surging. Test the suspension by feeling for vibration or pulling while driving. Check the brakes—listen for noise, look for leaks and feel for vibration. They may fail, perform poorly or require frequent mechanical attention. Test the transmission thoroughly.

Hot Spots and Owner/NHTSA Comments:

1. Power train: transmission: automatic, poor performance, difficulty shifting, slipping. • "Transmission failed; despite the fact that vehicle should have been recalled, Chrysler refused to fix it." • "While driving, vehicle suddenly downshifted, almost to a halt, shifted from 3rd to 1st gear instead of overdrive; caused serious neck injuries." • "Transmission would not shift down when stopping; rebuilt." • "When driving at 50-60 mph, car will drop into low gear with no warning." • "Vehicle was left unattended, in park, on an incline. Jumped out of gear and rolled forward, hitting the driver and house."
2. Electrical system: ignition: electronic control unit, malfunction, failure. • "Body computer failed, caused failure of electronic instrumental panel, temperature control system, door locks, etc." • "Electrical equipment failure, onboard computer failure." • "After driving, vehicle cuts off due to a bad electrical system; have to let stand for an hour to restart." • "Engine light comes on frequently. Dealer has replaced parts with no corrective response." • "Engine computer module giving false information; need to replace."
3. Brakes: hydraulic: anti-skid system, poor performance, failure, locking up. • "High-pressure pump of antilock brake system failed, brake pedal went to floor, took half a block to stop car from low speed." • "Antilock brakes jerk and grab, cause loss of brake effectiveness." • "Antilock braking system defective, almost complete loss of braking power; pump repaired/replaced, problem still not solved." • "Antilock warning light comes on, pedal goes to the floor, no response from braking system. This is the fifth incident." • "Antilock brake system pump that controls the disc brake assembly was inoperative, resulting in loss of brakes."
4. Suspension: independent front, vibration, tire wear, excessive wear. • "During replacement of defective suspension parts, bumper misalignment resulted, causing car to sag to one side." • "Problem with front end causes loss of control; resulted in accident." • "Front end suspension problem, left and right front wheel bearings both failed at 31,000 miles." • "Vibration experienced when traveling at any speed, but worse between 42 and 55 mph." • "Factory defect in front suspension, severe tire wear, brake pulsation; repaired several times, problem never corrected."
5. Brakes: hydraulic system, noise, failure. • "Antilock brake system warning light comes on when brakes applied." • "Sudden and total brake failures, brakes failed to stop vehicle; repaired, problem not corrected." • "Badly scored brake piston caused pad failure." • "Repeated repairs to brakes for noise." • "Vehicle's braking system failed, causing vehicle to go out of control, hitting an embankment."
6. Electrical system: battery, premature failure. • "Battery failed; replaced by dealer." • "While parked, electrical part kept running, battery went dead." • "Battery has bad cell, would not take a charge." • "If car is not driven within 10 days, the battery goes dead, defect in electrical system." • "Battery failed."

CHRYSLER NEW YORKER 1990

Complaint Severity: Negligible. **Recall Alert:** See Recall Index. **Buyer's Summary:** Look carefully for any kind of leakage, especially under the car. The electronic control unit has been blamed for engine performance problems, including stalling and surging. Check the brakes—listen for noise, look for leaks and feel for vibration. They may fail, perform poorly or require frequent mechanical attention. Test the transmission thoroughly.

Hot Spots and Owner/NHTSA Comments:

1. Power train: transmission: automatic, poor performance, difficulty shifting, slipping." • "Defective transmission, ceased to move; repaired/replaced oil pump, valve body, torque converter, etc., problem reoccurred; repaired/replaced transmission, computer and electrical harness." • "Automatic transmission failure, car would not move forward or reverse, engine would run but race in place, or run rough for a mile then shift gears." • "Transmission stuck in 1st gear." • "When you are slowing down or coming to a stop, car downshifts abruptly."
2. Brakes: hydraulic: anti-skid system, poor performance, failure, locking up. • "Antilock brake system fails to stop vehicle effectively causing system to shut down and lock up." • "Antilock brake system difficult to activate; brake pedal hard; extended stopping." • "The antilock brake system has failed on the car. The hydraulic system went out also." • "Antilock brake system brake pedal traveled to the floor; complete brake failure; speed 40 mph; brake warning light came on prior to failure." • "Six sets of brakes replaced at 56,000 miles, brakes smoke after normal driving in city."
3. Electrical system: ignition, locking up, stalling. • "Ignition switch locks up." • "Total lockup, ignition key will not turn." • "While driving at a high speed, engine suddenly cuts off." • "Difficulty in removing key from ignition; also, difficulty turning key to start car." • "Vehicle stalls in highway traffic."
4. Electrical system: battery, leaks, failure. • "Premature battery failure." • "Replaced 2 batteries due to leaking acid from caps (vent holes)." • "Faulty original battery." • "Short in electrical system caused battery to go dead, car wouldn't start in morning; replaced battery." • "Battery premature failure."
5. Brakes: hydraulic system, noise, failure. • "Squeaky left rear brake." • "Brakes." • "Brakes failed; replaced." • "Brakes fail to stop vehicle effectively when applied, causing extended stopping and front-end collision."
6. Electrical system: ignition: electronic control unit, malfunction, failure. • "The ignition system is causing the car to lose electrical power, and the computer keeps going down." •

"Computer chip malfunctioned." • "Electronic control module failed." • "Computer failure."

CHRYSLER NEW YORKER 1991

Complaint Severity: Typical. **Recall Alert:** See Recall Index. **Buyer's Summary:** Check the brakes—listen for noise, look for leaks and feel for vibration. They may fail, perform poorly or require frequent mechanical attention. Test the transmission thoroughly.

Hot Spots and Owner/NHTSA Comments:

1. Power train: transmission: automatic, poor performance, difficulty shifting, slipping. • "While vehicle was idling in park, gear shifted into reverse; caused accident that resulted in an injury and property damage." • "Transmission will not change gears, also will not accelerate. Had replaced once." • "Transmission replaced after 2 unsuccessful repairs." • "Transmission leaks fluid, shifts gears and fails to go into overdrive." • "Vehicle jumped out of gear, causing accident, injury." • "Transmission valve body failure."

2. Brakes: hydraulic: anti-skid system, poor performance, failure, locking up. • "Antilock brakes malfunctioned; brake pedal locked and would not depress, and then went all the way to the floor." • "Antilock brakes failed to stop vehicle when applied; repaired twice." • "Antilock brake system light within dashboard came on. Brakes vibrated, causing hazardous driving." • "When applying the brakes, pedal goes to the floor due to antilock brake pump failure." • "Vehicle's antilock brake system had to be completely replaced at 69,000 miles."

CHRYSLER NEW YORKER 1994

Complaint Severity: Minor. **Recall Alert:** See Recall Index. **Buyer's Summary:** Check the brakes—listen for noise, look for leaks and feel for vibration. They may fail, perform poorly or require frequent mechanical attention. Test the transmission thoroughly.

Hot Spots and Owner/NHTSA Comments:

1. Lighting: general or unknown component: headlights, poor performance. • "Headlights do not provide sufficient lighting for night driving in rainy or foggy weather, causing lack of proper visibility when driving." • "Headlights on vehicle are not adequate for illuminating the roadside." • "Headlights have very poor pattern and coverage; causes poor illumination and poor visibility." • "Headlights fail to illuminate left and right sides of roadway, impairing visibility of curves, dividers and pedestrians." • "Headlights don't illuminate road enough, poor visibility; manufacturer aware but no fix." • "Headlights do not illuminate the road adequately. Owner questions that this car meets the federal standards. Neither high nor low beam is properly bright."

2. Lighting: lamp or socket: headlight, poor performance. • "On low beam, light pattern very dim and poorly focused; have to use high beam while driving back streets; impairs vision of oncoming traffic." • "Visibility." • "Design of headlights causes lamps not to be bright enough for night driving, decreasing driver's visibility." • "Headlight system provides poor visibility for night driving, the lenses put in headlights dim and throw beam off to the sides; have had the lights adjusted." • "Headlights aren't bright." • "Inadequate headlights for right and left turns; also, inadequate illumination when driving downhill."

3. Power train: transmission: automatic, poor performance, difficulty shifting, slipping. • "Antilock brake system: Experienced failure of rear brakes. Automatic transmission will downshift while driving." • "Traveling 30 mph, transmission went out on freeway due to kickdown/reverse band failure." • "Vehicle downshifted by itself, causing loss of acceleration." • "Transmission sticks in low."

4. Brakes: hydraulic: anti-skid system, poor performance, failure, locking up. • "Antilock brakes fail to engage upon hard stopping; also, soft brake pedal." • "Antilock brake system failed, vehicle went out of control, resulting in an accident." • "Antilock brake system warning light came on; had computer replaced." • "Antilock brake system warning signal came on, then experienced brake lockup." • "Antilock brake system intermittently fails to stop vehicle when applied on very slippery roads."

5. Brakes: hydraulic: disc: rotor: disc hub, excessive wear, premature failure. • "The rotors are warped and do not work properly." • "Front brake rotors failed." • "Replaced rotors twice." • "All 4 brake rotors warped prematurely due to high temperatures generated during numerous emergency braking situations."

6. Communications: horn assembly: button: ring, poor location. • "Location and size of horn buttons on steering wheel cause difficulty accessing buttons in emergencies; also, excessive effort required to press buttons." • "Difficulty accessing horn buttons during emergency situations due to location." • "Horn location and design are insufficient for an emergency, unable to locate." • "Due to location and size of horn, impossible to locate during an emergency."

CHRYSLER TRUCK TOWN AND COUNTRY 1992

Complaint Severity: Typical. **Recall Alert:** See Recall Index. **Buyer's Summary:** Check the brakes—listen for noise, look for leaks and feel for vibration. They may fail, perform poorly or require frequent mechanical attention. Test the transmission thoroughly.

Hot Spots and Owner/NHTSA Comments:

1. Brakes: hydraulic: anti-skid system, poor performance, failure, locking up. • "Antilock brake system malfunction, resulting in loss of braking ability and resulting in accident." • "Driver reached over to turn on lights, instead the antilock brake system light came on and the brakes locked up. Vehicle came to halt on freeway." • "Antilock brake system malfunctioned, light comes on and stays on, excessively long stopping distance; manufacturer said no parts available." • "Antilock brake system failed 3 times and prior to failure warning system lights came on briefly. Twice partial loss of effectiveness. Once completely stopped, brakes not applied." • "The antilock brake system has to be replaced after 16,000 miles."

2. Power train: transmission: automatic, poor performance, difficulty shifting, slipping. • "Transmission shifts erratically." • "Transmission shifts irregularly." • "Transmission hums in reverse." • "Transmission leaks." • "Transmission grinds in reverse."

CHRYSLER TRUCK TOWN AND COUNTRY 1993

Complaint Severity: Best 3% in Guide. **Recall Alert:** See Recall Index. **Buyer's Summary:** Check the brakes—listen for noise, look for leaks and feel for vibration. They may fail, perform poorly or require frequent mechanical attention.

Hot Spots and Owner/NHTSA Comments:

1. Brakes: hydraulic: anti-skid system, poor performance, failure, locking up. • "Hard braking, excessive stopping distance, excessive force." • "Antilock brakes do not release until foot is completely off gas pedal or car slows down to 15-20 mph." • "Brakes become totally ineffective in reaction time and stopping distance in wet area." • "Antilock brake system: Hard to step on brakes, takes excessive effort to hold brakes, increased stopping distances." • "Antilock brake system: Frontal collision. Applied brakes and experienced pedal fading. Speed 35 mph. Impact 12:00 position. Airbag deployed."

2. Structure: hatchback locks and latches, malfunction, failure. • "Having difficulty closing rear door, have to slam several times to close." • "Rear liftgate opened by itself while driving." • "Upon coming to a stop, rear back latch flew open, allowing item to fly out the rear door." • "Latch gate opens while car is in motion or when door is unlocked." • "Sometimes when driving, the rear hatch latch comes open; no one was hurt."

3. Brakes: hydraulic system, poor performance. • "Brakes are ineffective on wet roads." • "Experiencing extended stopping distance." • "It appears power brakes and engine are turned off during brake application." • "Brake failure."

Dodge—Cars

DODGE ARIES 1987

Complaint Severity: Typical. **Buyer's Summary:** The fuel injection system has been blamed for hesitation and stalling. Be sure the vehicle doesn't die in traffic or at stops. Check the brakes—listen for noise, look for leaks and feel for vibration. They may fail, perform poorly or require frequent mechanical attention. See "Sudden Accelerations" in Introduction.

Hot Spots and Owner/NHTSA Comments:

1. Fuel: fuel injection system, stalling, hesitation. • "When slowing down, rpm drops, car vibrates, hood shakes; replaced idle speed motor and speed sensor." • "Fuel injection system; recurring stalling when backing up." • "Injector recall refused by dealers not connected with car's purchase." • "Replaced fuel injector." • "Loss of power, intermittent hesitation."

2. Exhaust system: manifold: oxygen sensor, malfunction, failure. • "Manifold air pressure sensor failed, caused engine to shut down, sensor prevents pressurized fuel from being pumped into intake manifold when fuel is consumed." • "Repeated failure of manifold air pressure sensor; replaced several times." • "Manifold air pressure sensor replaced 6 times under 83,000 miles; towed on 2 occasions." • "Manifold air pressure sensor failed at least 7 times; when this happens, car stops with no warning or power." • "Manifold air pressure sensor failed 5 times."

3. Fuel: throttle linkages and control, sudden accelerations. • "Sudden acceleration, causing accident." • "Downshifted on its own from park to reverse, with sudden acceleration causing accident." • "Sudden acceleration in drive, brakes useless, driver lost control; accident resulted." • "Driver's foot removed from gas pedal and on the brake pedal, car had surge of power, could only stop by turning off the ignition and putting car in reverse." • "Engine idles too high without application to accelerator."

4. Exhaust system: catalytic converter system, malfunction, failure. • "Catalytic converter gave off sulfur smell; replaced converter." • "While driving, vehicle gives off rotten egg smell; replaced catalytic converter." • "Catalytic converter gives off rotten egg smell, bites tongue and burns eyes." • "Car emits foul odor throughout entire car, contaminating air conditioning vents and embedding itself in upholstery, pungent odor like rotten egg."

5. Exhaust system: converter, malfunction. • "Catalytic converter releases a strong sulfur smell inside car when windows are up and vent fan is on." • "Sulfuric odor present in interior of car, very pronounced when stopping at traffic signs." • "Hydrogen sulfide smell emits inside car when in operation, moving very slowly, or after ignition turned off." • "Sulfur smell from exhaust emission system."

6. Brakes: hydraulic system, failure. • "Brakes failed while traveling on high-speed highway." • "Master cylinder failed." • "Unspecified brake problems." • "Brakes went out, which caused accident."

DODGE ARIES 1988

Complaint Severity: Minor. **Buyer's Summary:** The fuel injection system has been blamed for hesitation and stalling. Be sure the vehicle doesn't die in traffic or at stops. The steering may be stiff or not working correctly. Be sure to test the steering, especially on a cold start. Check the brakes—listen for noise, look for leaks and feel for vibration. They may fail, perform poorly or require frequent mechanical attention. Test the transmission thoroughly.

Hot Spots and Owner/NHTSA Comments:

1. Fuel: fuel injection system, stalling, hesitation. • "While driving at 55 mph on highway, car just cut off; stalls out in traffic." • "Intermittent stalling." • "Engine hesitates, idles up and down." • "Vehicle stalls out continuously; checked throttle position sensor, repaired/replaced fuel filter, checked wires to and from distributor, problem still exists." • "While driving at 45-50 mph, power surges or misses, repaired 5 times, problem still not solved."

2. Power train: transmission: automatic, poor performance, difficulty shifting, slipping. • "Excessive ring gear whine; replaced transfer shaft gear." • "Transmission malfunctioned, car rolled out of garage." • "All 4 wheels partially locked up when transmission failed, vehicle responded in an erratic fashion." • "Transmission replaced 3 times." • "Transmission jumps into different gears when idling."

3. Steering: gear: rack-and-pinion, stiffness, poor performance. • "Fluid leaks coming from steering column area; fluid hose to rack-and-pinion loose." • "Defective rack-and-pinion causing squeak in front end." • "Steering intermittent when first started." • "Nuts that hold steering are tack-welded and broke loose, with subsequent loss of steering. Could cause accident." • "Mounting bolts for rack-and-pinion steering came loose, caused difficulty steering and controlling vehicle."

4. Brakes: hydraulic system, noise, locking up, failure. • "Brakes making excessive noises due to glaze built up on rotor, related to metal components of brakes; sanded pads, turned rotors." • "Brakes have been repaired 10 times." • "Brakes failed, worn out, making grinding sound when applied or making left turns; accident occurred." • "While driving, brakes locked up, which caused flat spin and loss of control." • "Brakes failed twice; repaired/replaced, problem continues."

5. Engine: gaskets: valve cover, leaks. • "Valve cover gasket replaced." • "Head gasket replaced." • "Valve cover gasket leaked oil, problems with new seal." • "Valve cover leaks oil." • "Unspecified problems with valve cover gasket."

6. Brakes: hydraulic: shoe: disc brake system, noise, uneven wear. • "Unspecified brake problem, noisy sounds when brake applied; front pads replaced, rotors cut down." • "Front brakes failed due to uneven brake wear, makes grinding noises; repaired/replaced rotor, caliper, brake pads." • "Brakes developed real problems, left caliper stuck, pads went out." • "Front brakes problem; repairs unsatisfactory."

DODGE ARIES 1989

Complaint Severity: Typical. **Recall Alert:** See Recall Index. **Buyer's Summary:** Check the brakes—listen for noise, look for leaks and feel for vibration. They may fail, perform poorly or require frequent mechanical attention.

Hot Spots and Owner/NHTSA Comments:

1. Engine: gaskets: valve cover, leaks. • "Faulty oil seal gaskets on engine valve cover; pronounced oil leak vaporized by hot engine surfaces permeated interior of car, creating odor." • "Excessive oil consumption due to defect in valve cover and valve cover gasket; oil creeping along wires behind engine and odor from oil being burned." • "Problem with oil leak; repaired/replaced valve cover 5 times to no avail; recall campaign initiated." • "Valve cover gasket leaking." • "Problem with oil leakage; received recall letter on valve cover gasket, problem getting recall repair done."

2. Brakes: hydraulic system, poor performance, failure. • "Vehicle periodically goes at a constant speed of 30-40 mph, surging, failing to stop when brakes are applied. Repaired 3 times." • "When applying brakes to make a complete halt, brakes did not respond." • "Brake problems."

DODGE CHARGER 1987

Complaint Severity: Harmless. **Recall Alert:** See Recall Index. **Buyer's Summary:** The carburetion system could contribute to stalling and hesitation. Look carefully for any kind of leakage, especially under the car. The fuel injection system has been blamed for hesitation and stalling. Be sure the vehicle doesn't die in traffic or at stops. Check the brakes—listen for noise, look for leaks and feel for vibration. They may fail, perform poorly or require frequent mechanical attention.

Hot Spots and Owner/NHTSA Comments:

1. Fuel: fuel carburetion, stalling, hesitation. • "While driving, car keeps jerking and stalling out without any warning." • "Carburetor leaking internally caused stalling, hesitation." • "Vehicle would not start occasionally, also consistent stalling; carburetor rebuilt." • "Vehicle experiencing engine stalling and hesitation." • "Car stalls out, leaks gas from carburetor and hesitates when idling."

2. Fuel: fuel injection system, stalling, hesitation. • "Vehicle dies when accelerating from stop, surges up and down in speed while trying to steady speed; acceleration chokes." • "Hard start; 3 distributors replaced." • "Vehicle hesitates when accelerated." • "Intermittent stalling." • "While parked, vehicle caught on fire; subsequently received 3 recall notices concerning fuel pressure regulator leaking fuel into engine compartment."

3. Brakes: hydraulic: shoe: disc brake system, noise, premature failure. • "Car started to make dragging noise, grinding in front end; front brake job done." • "Defective brake system, front brake overheated and burned; replaced several times." • "Front brake failure at less than 30,000 miles; replaced pads, rotors and calipers." • "Front brakes, calipers, rotor and pad erode quickly, giving off burning smell, grinding metal noise."

4. Fuel: fuel systems, stalling, fire, fuel odor. • "Pressure builds up in gas tank, strong odor of gasoline throughout, stalls when started, runs rough; repaired/replaced O_2 sensor, carburetor." • "Vehicle emitting extremely strong gasoline fumes into passenger compartment while in motion." • "Gas tank sometimes builds up pressure, interior of car smells of gasoline, hard to start and restart, dies when started and/or driving, runs rough; unsuccessful repair." • "Vehicle caught fire due to fuel pressure regulator failing." • "Vapor locking, (flood out) causing vehicle to stall completely or to decrease takeoff speed; replaced carburetor, added electric fuel pump and antivapor-lock kit."

5. Fuel: fuel injection: unknown type: regulator, leaks, fire. • "Carburetor replaced due to fire caused by defective fuel pressure regulator leaking." • "Gasoline fumes caused by failure of fuel pressure regulator, prior to recall." • "Fuel regulator replaced prior to recall." • "Vehicle caught fire due to faulty regulator prior to recall." • "Driving down the highway, fuel pressure regulator leaked, causing a fire prior to service recall."

6. Engine, fire, hesitation, leaks. • "Engine fire." • "Vehicle engine caught on fire. Owner received a recall notice 1 week later." • "Noisy engine and coolant leak; possible water pump defect." • "Missing/hesitation." • "Oil plug on pan loose, leaking; repaired/replaced piston rings, oil pump, rear main seal, crankshaft, lifters, timing belt, cam bearing seal; engine completely rebuilt."

DODGE COLT 1987

Complaint Severity: Negligible. **Recall Alert:** See Recall Index. **Buyer's Summary:** Look carefully for any kind of leakage, especially under the car. Problems with the timing gear and chain can cause serious problems. Have the engine checked by a professional. Test the transmission thoroughly. See "Sudden Accelerations" in Introduction.

Hot Spots and Owner/NHTSA Comments:

1. Fuel: throttle linkages and control, sudden accelerations. • "Upon accelerating to pass vehicle, accelerator jammed, vehicle accelerated to high speed, was able to stop by turning off ignition." • "Vehicle constantly surges forward and out of control." • "Vehicle accelerates on its own." • "Throttle stuck; vehicle sped up until key was turned off." • "Upon placing gear into drive position, vehicle suddenly accelerated, causing injury to driver and passenger when both hit windshield after impact with stump."

2. Power train: transmission: automatic, poor performance, difficulty shifting, slipping. • "Automatic transmission failure; also, problem with torque converter." • "Transmission problem causes surging and hesitation in car." • "Transmission failure." • "Problem with transmission leak." • "Transmission still jerky when accelerating from low to high speeds."

3. Exhaust system, leaks, failure. • "Extensive heat from exhaust system caused right rear end of bumper to catch on fire, bumper melted out and fell to ground." • "Problem with exhaust leak." • "Sulfur smell. Catalytic converter replaced, along with corroded muffler, tailpipe." • "Entire exhaust system failure." • "Exhaust system collapsed, catalytic converter clogging."

4. Interior systems: active restraints: belt buckles, malfunction, failure. • "Driver's seat belt buckle failed to latch." • "Driver's seat belt release button cracked, preventing seat belt from entering buckle." • "Driver's side seat belt release button will not properly fasten for occupant restraint due to chipped pieces." • "One front and one rear seat belt will not latch, stick." • "At one time, driver's shoulder and lap belt would catch and not release; now does not catch at all; cause unknown."

5. Engine: leaks, fire, failure. • "Purchased new, drove car for two years, was driving on the freeway and car stalled; needed a new engine and the rotor was replaced." • "Engine compartment fire." • "Replaced timing belt 3 times." • "Engine failure." • "Problem with oil leak."

6. Engine: timing gear and chain, breaking. • "Timing belt broke; repaired." • "Timing belt broke prematurely while in motion." • "Timing belt failed due to oil leak." • "Defective timing belt; broke on 2 occasions."

DODGE COLT 1988

Complaint Severity: Typical. **Recall Alert:** See Recall Index. **Buyer's Summary:** Make sure seat belts function correctly. The engine has experienced problems. Have it examined by a professional.

Hot Spots and Owner/NHTSA Comments:

1. Interior systems: active restraints: belt buckles, breaking, poor performance. • "The driver and passenger-side seat belt buckle came loose." • "Seat belt buckle in lock position, it will not release." • "Orange plastic piece where push to release belt broke on driver/passenger-side, no longer catches; no longer holds seat belt together; does not work at all." • "Driver's side seat belt red plastic in-latch broke, causing latch to jam."

2. Engine: noise, fire. • "Loss of power while in motion, car began to smoke, caught on fire and flames engulfed car." • "Engine making clicking noise, overheating within less than 10 miles of starting." • "Defective engine, makes tapping noise, 'check engine' light stays on, slows down going uphill and downhill, overheats within 5 minutes of ignition." • "Air filter under hood caught fire while driving; only warning was smell of smoke right before; vehicle totaled."

3. Electrical system: wiring: harness: front: under hood, stalling, fire. • "While going uphill vehicle stalled, then noticed white smoke coming from engine compartment, resulting in fire; totaled." • "Vehicle was rear-ended and stuck under another vehicle and pulled for 110 yards, then caught on fire; occupants were trapped." • "Driving at 20 mph, saw smoke and found a fire under the hood, low rear on driver's side of engine." • "While driving out of parking lot, noticed smoke emanating from under the hood; stopped car and extinguished fire."

DODGE COLT 1989

Complaint Severity: Minor. **Recall Alert:** See Recall Index. **Buyer's Summary:** Look carefully for any kind of leakage, especially under the car. The fuel injection system has been blamed for hesitation and stalling. Be sure the vehicle doesn't die in traffic or at stops. Make sure seat belts function correctly and fit comfortably.

Hot Spots and Owner/NHTSA Comments:

1. Interior systems: active restraints: belt buckles, breaking, malfunction. • "Vehicle's front passenger seat belt buckle release button is partially broken off." • "Takata seat belt jammed; would not release; occupant kept pushing hard to release; pieces of particles were found inside release button." • "Driver's side seat belt buckle broke and trapped the driver." • "Seat belt buckle has broken 2 times, making it inoperative." • "Front passenger's seat buckle fastener will not fasten to retain occupant."

2. Engine: leaks, failure. • "Engine locked up and leaked oil. Valve cover gasket and crankshaft replaced." • "Engine problem." • "Complete loss of engine power due to seized engine components; reason unknown." • "Oil leaks."

3. Fuel: fuel injection system, stalling, hesitation. • "Fuel injection system malfunction; car started out with rough idle, sometimes won't start; also backfires." • "Hesitating, repaired, problem continues." • "Engine idles at varying speeds, sometimes very slowly." • "Vehicle stalling and/or sputtering continuously, then caught on fire; repaired many times to no avail."

4. Interior systems: passive restraint: belts, malfunction, uncomfortable. • "Shoulder belt does not retract properly when front seat adjusted fully backward, shoulder belt binds between guide ring and retractor." • "Automatic seat belts do not release enough belt to adequately restrain occupant; tightens around neck and chokes occupant." • "While driving on a major 3-lane highway, automatic seat belt began moving, propelled passenger quickly and violently forward into dashboard." • "Automatic shoulder belt will either tighten and/or lock, preventing exit. Failure has repeated itself, same conditions."

5. Structure: door assembly: hinge and attachments, failure. • "Door hinges disconnected." • "Driver's-side door fell off while driving." • "Door hinges failed."

DODGE DAYTONA 1987

Complaint Severity: Typical. **Recall Alert:** See Recall Index. **Buyer's Summary:** The fuel injection system has been blamed for hesitation and stalling. Be sure the vehicle doesn't die in traffic or at stops. Test the transmission thoroughly.

Hot Spots and Owner/NHTSA Comments:

1. Fuel: fuel injection system, stalling, hesitation. • "Vehicle started trembling and stalls; replaced sensor, exhaust gas recirculation, fuel injector and plugs." • "Engine sags, hesitates in taking gas until motor is fully warmed up, when touch gas pedal or let it idle in park, rpm drops off, runs rough and/or stalls until it warms up." • "Intermittent surging and stalling." • "Fuel injection system faulty." • "Gas fumes inside vehicle when turning corner."

2. Exhaust system: miscellaneous problems. • "Exhaust system overheated, burning hole in carpet in hatchback area." • "Rear driver's side of hatchback trunk gets extremely hot when driving, can't put anything in back due to melting, burning or destroying items." • "Overheated exhaust system, exhaust pipe from engine to tailpipe including all parts of the catalytic converter, get cherry red glow; heat burns wiring in starter." • "When accelerating on gas pedal, slight backfire noise can be heard out of motor, black smoke coming out of exhaust pipe."

3. Power train: transmission: automatic, poor performance, difficulty shifting, slipping. • "Automatic transmission failure." • "Transmission slips out of drive into reverse or drive, depending on which way it strikes; does not lock properly when in gear." • "Endless problems with transmission, including torque converter and burnt clutch; both replaced; metal chips in transmission." • "Automatic floor shift jumped out of park to reverse; accident resulted, car hit wooden fence."

DODGE DAYTONA 1988

Complaint Severity: Typical. **Buyer's Summary:** The steering may be stiff or not working correctly. Be sure to test the steering, especially on a cold start. Check the brakes—listen for noise, look for leaks and feel for vibration. They may fail, perform poorly or require frequent mechanical attention.

Hot Spots and Owner/NHTSA Comments:

1. Brakes: hydraulic system, failure. • "Replacement of new disc pads in front brakes needed, also needed to adjust rear brakes." • "While driving, brakes felt spongy and failed to stop vehicle, vehicle spun out of control, resulting in accident." • "Brake pedal went to floor, causing poor performance." • "Continuous brake failure, brakes spongy, pedal fades to floor upon application; repaired/replaced master cylinder 3 times, brake booster 2 times." • "Entire brake system failed and pedal went to the floor."

2. Exhaust system: muffler: resonator, heat buildup. • "Muffler overheated, burning hole through carpet." • "Muffler overheating, melting carpeting in hatch." • "Heat shield not installed, causing plastic to burn when muffler area overheated." • "Muffler lacks heat shield." • "Excessive heat is coming from the trunk above the muffler and it has melted the carpet in the trunk."

3. Brakes: hydraulic: shoe: disc brake system, locking up, excessive wear. • "Front brakes defective; calipers repaired/replaced, disc turned at 22,500 miles." • "Defective front brakes; replaced." • "Front left and right brakes lock up, rivets ground 3 grooves about 2 millimeters deep into rotors; replaced rotors, shoes, discs and pads; continue to grab and squeal." • "Brake system failures; calipers sticking, brake pads prematurely worn; applied brakes, slid more than 6 car lengths into another vehicle."

4. Exhaust system: malfunction. • "Malfunction in exhaust system, driver's side of cargo area gets extremely hot during normal operation." • "Faulty exhaust system." • "Hot spot over muffler, odor from exhaust." • "Heat shield not installed in area of trunk at factory." • "Exhaust system overheated around trunk floor, burning hole in carpet the size of a quarter."

5. Fuel: fuel systems, malfunction, fire. • "Rotten odor and fumes." • "Smoke came from driver's side under hood, pulled to side; shortly after, vehicle completely engulfed in flames and totally destroyed." • "Smoke under hood over left front tire, gauges read normal, engine sparked, consequently burst into flames; burned entire vehicle."

6. Steering: gear: rack-and-pinion, stiffness, poor performance. • "Bolts that hold rack-and-pinion are too tight; rack-and-pinion moves in clamps; causes loss of steering control." • "Rack-and-pinion steering problem." • "Rack-and-pinion failed, bolts holding rack on frame came out, making car impossible to steer." • "Rack-and-pinion plate nut fell off."

DODGE DAYTONA 1989

Complaint Severity: Serious. **Recall Alert:** See Recall Index. **Buyer's Summary:** Look carefully for any kind of leakage, especially under the car. The airbags in this vehicle have experienced failures and malfunctions: You may need a professional evaluation on the condition of the airbags. Check the brakes—listen for noise, look for leaks and feel for vibration. They may fail, perform poorly or require frequent mechanical attention.

Hot Spots and Owner/NHTSA Comments:

1. Brakes: hydraulic: disc: pads and shoes, malfunction, failure. • "Brake pads separated from backing plate, resulting in loss of brakes." • "In reverse, brake pedal went to floor; later found brake pad in street; pad had separated from backing plate, spot weld did not hold." • "While driving, the brake pad tore out of its mounting." • "The right rear brake pads have been glued together and are separating from the metal plate." • "Brake makes grinding noise and vehicle had extended stopping distances 3 times."

2. Brakes: hydraulic system, premature failure. • "Front and rear brake pads fell off the metal backings, caused the pads to fall out of the car." • "All 4 brakes replaced 4 times in first 11,000 miles." • "While coming to a stop, brake pedal went to floor; unable to stop, downshifted and coasted to a stop." • "Brakes grab when applied during wet weather conditions." • "Brakes grabbed intermittently prior to recall."

3. Interior systems: passive restraint: airbag: driver, malfunction, failure. • "Vehicle hit a dip in the road at 12:00 position and airbag deployed, causing injuries to driver on face, chest and arm." • "Airbag deployed when the vehicle came to a quick stop; warning light would flash on from time to time." • "Driver rear-ended another vehicle at speed of 50 mph, airbag did not deploy." • "Airbag did not completely deploy during front-end collision at 30 mph; caused neck and burn injuries to driver." • "Had an accident, airbag deployed; received second degree burns from chemicals inside airbag." • "Frontal collision, impact 1:00 position, speed 50 mph, driver's-side airbag did not inflate, gases came out of bag, causing burns."

4. Brakes: hydraulic: shoe: disc brake system, excessive wear, locking up. • "While driving, stepped on brake pedal and heard a clunk, the brake went to the floor; front brake pads, shoes, lining and rotors were worn out." • "Front wheels locked during braking; resulted in accident with property damage." • "Constant brake problems, brake pedal goes to floor when applying brakes; repaired/replaced 7 times, with problem still existing." • "Front right disc and brake pad wear out easily; it happened 3 times in two years." • "Poor disc brake ventilation caused by discs standing on rotors and drums. Air is being emitted, causing brakes to become spongy." • "Brake rotors and pads replaced prior to recall."

5. Engine: gaskets: valve cover, leaks, failure. • "Valve cover gasket leaked, prior to recall." • "Received recall on the engine gasket valve cover; having the same problem: The right rear pads broke and came out of the wheel." • "Recall on valve cover that could cause a leak and result in engine compartment fire; parts not available for repair because vehicle purchased elsewhere." • "Valve cover gasket leaking oil, oil cap blowing oil over engine." • "Valve cover gasket failed, causing vehicle to leak prior to recall; repairs refused due to vehicle identification number."

6. Interior systems: passive restraint: airbag, malfunction, failure. • "Airbag popped out from steering wheel, black smoke burned driver's hands." • "Driver's-side airbag failure; airbag deployed and instantly blinded driver." • "Airbag safety device very vague and works only in specific instance, whereas the option gives false security that any frontal collision will activate airbag." • "Airbag failed to work properly, and passenger heads smashed into the windshield." • "Airbag clock spring was repaired and replaced by dealer; airbag deployed after impact and horn did not work."

DODGE DAYTONA 1990

Complaint Severity: Serious. **Recall Alert:** See Recall Index. **Buyer's Summary:** The fuel injection system has been blamed for hesitation and stalling. Be sure the vehicle doesn't die in traffic or at stops. The airbags in this vehicle have experienced failures and malfunctions: You may need a professional evaluation on the condition of the airbags. Test the transmission thoroughly.

Hot Spots and Owner/NHTSA Comments:

1. Interior systems: passive restraint: airbag: driver, malfunction, failure. • "Person in vehicle in front hit brakes, owner hit him from behind at 36 mph and airbag did not deploy." • "Made a sudden stop, frontal collision, impact 12:00 position going 40 mph, airbag did not deploy." • "Vehicle involved in front-end collision. Airbag deployed, causing second and third degree burns on wrist and fingers. Vehicle filled up with smoke." • "Another vehicle crossed yellow lines, hit first vehicle, impact 11:00 position, speed 35 mph, airbag did not deploy." • "During an accident while driving at 35 mph, impact at 12:00, airbag did not deploy."

2. Power train: transmission: automatic, poor performance, difficulty shifting, slipping. • "Transmission failed 3 times." • "Goes into gear even when there is no key in the ignition." • "Automatic transmission slips out of gears and into gears." • "Transmission failed; replaced."

3. Fuel: fuel injection system, stalling, hesitation. • "Stalls and/or hesitates." • "Vehicle will stall without warning, with difficulty in restarting." • "Engine surges and runs rough." • "Intermittent stalling."

4. Interior systems: instrument panel: speedometer: odometer, malfunction, failure. • "Speed variation from speedometer." • "Odometer malfunctioned and dealer could not repair it." • "Speedometer reading error, reads about 10 miles above actual speed traveling." • "Tachometer failure."

5. Interior systems: passive restraint: airbag, malfunction, failure. • "Airbag did not deploy during accident." • "False deployment of airbag, causing injury." • "Problem with airbag in steering column, feeling of something loose and snapping against plastic steering column housing." • "Airbag deployed after hitting small manhole."

DODGE DYNASTY 1988

Complaint Severity: Best 3% in Guide. **Buyer's Summary:** The steering may be stiff or not working correctly. Be sure to test the steering, especially on a cold start. Check the brakes—listen for noise, look for leaks and feel for vibration. They may fail, perform poorly or require frequent mechanical attention. Test the transmission thoroughly.

Hot Spots and Owner/NHTSA Comments:

1. Power train: transmission: automatic, poor performance, difficulty shifting, slipping. • "Continuous engine stalling at stop lights when put in park or reverse." • "Difficulty shifting." • "After starting car, when shifted into reverse or drive, car does not move for up to 30 seconds." • "Unspecified transmission failure." • "Shift lever linkage resists movement from park to reverse or drive, movement especially difficult when parked on incline, front or rear elevated."

2. Brakes: hydraulic system, noise, failure. • "Brakes dragged when pedal released; brakes bled to solve problem." • "Brake failure; replaced master cylinder to no avail." • "Vehicle experienced brake failure." • "Antilock brake light on dash came on and there was a clicking noise when brakes were applied; second time when light came on, brakes did not work."

3. Brakes: hydraulic: anti-skid system, poor performance, failure, locking up. • "Defect in antilock brake system, both antilock brakes and brake light remained on at all times; several repair efforts to no avail." • "Applied brake pedal, pedal fade, antilock brake system light came on, resulting in complete brake loss, then brakes started failing intermittently; pump motor needs replacing." • "Attempted to brake, had to continuously pump before it stopped. Had antilock brake system part replaced." • "Antilock brake system: When applying brakes, excessive effort is necessary to stop. System replaced several times."

4. Steering: gear: rack-and-pinion, stiffness, poor performance. • "Rack-and-pinion steering in vehicle went out due to leak." • "Rack-and-pinion steering makes loud noise and leaks fluid on both ends." • "Rack-and-pinion failure." • "Unspecified rack-and-pinion failure, power assist failing, power steering fluid leaking; repairs."

DODGE DYNASTY 1989

Complaint Severity: Best 3% in Guide. **Recall Alert:** See Recall Index. **Buyer's Summary:** Look carefully for any kind of leakage, especially under the car. The fuel pump has received complaints. Make sure it doesn't make excessive noise and that you are experiencing adequate engine performance. Also, look for leaks. Check the brakes—listen for noise, look for leaks and feel for vibration. They may fail, perform poorly or require frequent mechanical attention. Test the transmission thoroughly. Make sure air conditioner works properly.

Hot Spots and Owner/NHTSA Comments:

1. Power train: transmission: automatic, poor performance, difficulty shifting, slipping. • "Every time car was stopped at low speed, every stop sign or red light, car lunged forward; repaired/replaced defective transmission sending unit." • "Automatic transmission slams into gear when stopping." • "Transmission will not shift out of low gear, sometimes will shift down, but not all the way to 2nd." • "Between 50 and 55 mph, when ultradrive transmission shifts into 4th gear, jolt is felt and entire car vibrates until car reaches minimum of 55 mph." • "While driving, transmission seized, fluid leaked out into engine compartment, which started a fire."

2. Engine: gaskets: valve cover, leaks. • "Oil leak at valve cover gasket." • "Engine valve cover gasket leaks oil down toward the exhaust system." • "Vehicle recalled regarding defective valve cover gasket that leaks." • "Valve cover gasket leaked prior to recall." • "Six fuel pumps, 3 fuel lines; gas leaking into engine, engine valve cover gaskets replaced; caused oil leaks; seat belts didn't lock in accident."

3. Brakes: hydraulic system, locking up, failure. • "While traveling 30 mph, brakes failed to stop; accident." • "Brakes failed completely due to lockup; brake components have been replaced." • "Brake repairs." • "Replaced brakes 4 times." • "Brakes failed, causing accident and injuries."

4. Fuel: fuel pump, leaks, failure. • "Replaced fuel pump twice." • "Six fuel pumps, 3 fuel lines; gas leaking into engine, engine valve cover gaskets replaced; caused oil leaks; seat belts didn't lock in accident." • "Vehicle lost power while traveling at 40 mph; caused by fuel pump failure." • "Fuel pump failed without warning, unable to restart car."

5. Air conditioner: vibration, stalling, poor performance. • "Vehicle vibrated when air conditioner was running." • "Air conditioner repaired twice and still not working." • "Engine dies when air conditioner is turned on." • "Vehicle stalls when air conditioner is on." • "Air conditioner not blowing cold air."

6. Brakes: hydraulic: anti-skid system, poor performance, failure, locking up. • "Antilock brake system failed, resulting in 60 percent failure." • "The antilock brake system fails." • "Antilock brakes continually make grinding noises when applied." • "Antilock brake system brake pedal has gone to the floor twice. Last episode prompted the Chrysler factory to supply a new hydraulic assembly." • "Replacement of brake shoes, pads and calipers after driving vehicle for 2,000 miles; pedal faded, antilock brake system."

DODGE DYNASTY 1990

Complaint Severity: Typical. **Recall Alert:** See Recall Index. **Buyer's Summary:** The airbags in this vehicle have experienced failures and malfunctions: You may need a professional evaluation on the condition of the airbags. Check the brakes—listen for noise, look for leaks and feel for vibration. They may fail, perform poorly or require frequent mechanical attention. Test the transmission thoroughly.

Hot Spots and Owner/NHTSA Comments:

1. Power train: transmission: automatic, poor performance, difficulty shifting, slipping. • "Transmission slips into neutral while driving." • "Automatic transmission does not shift up as intended; remains in low gear at 35 mph; causes hazardous driving." • "Automatic transmission sticks in 2nd gear; downshifts on its own at any speed; no warning. Replaced once." • "Transmission jerks and shifts rough when shifting gears." • "Automatic transmission would not shift into forward gears, only into low gears, noticed whining sound."

2. Brakes: hydraulic: anti-skid system, poor performance, failure, locking up. • "Brake/antilock brake system not functioning properly; warning light comes on repeatedly; brakes harder and harder to use; total brake failure." • "Antilock brake cables allow water to enter lines, causing short and failure." • "Pressed down on brakes to stop or to slow down for stopping, antilock brakes malfunctioned and pedal went to the floor; resulted in an accident." • "Antilock brake system failed at 25,000 miles and 50,000 miles, resulting in complete brake loss; also, antilock brake system light goes on and off." • "Antilock brake system: Rotors warp; brakes make noise, jerky; pedal goes almost to floor before it catches."

3. Interior systems: passive restraint: airbag: driver, malfunction, failure. • "Premature deployment of the airbag, resulting in control loss and injury." • "Airbag did deploy but did not inflate when vehicle hit back of another vehicle. There was smoke coming from the airbag." • "During a frontal collision, impact at 12:00, speed 30-35 mph, airbag failed to deploy." • "Airbag did not deploy during front-end impact at 12:00, speed 55 mph; resulted in personal injury to driver." • "During a frontal collision at 65

mph, airbag deployed but driver suffered burns."
4. Brakes: hydraulic system, malfunction, failure, locking up. • "Worn-out brake shoes caused brakes to fail, nearly causing accident." • "Brakes malfunctioned, vehicle lost control and ran into side of tractor trailer." • "Brakes failed when backing into a parking space; hit another car." • "Brakes keep locking up." • "Vehicle developed a metal scraping sound due to malfunctioning of one side of crisscross brake system; dealer refused to acknowledge a defect."
5. Electrical system: ignition, stalling, failure. • "Car dies out while driving. Will not start back up." • "Ignition cylinder rekeyed due to vehicle not starting." • "Door chimes with key out of ignition, alarm light flashes, power doors inoperable." • "Unable to turn key." • "Vehicle stalls while in traffic."
6. Interior systems: passive restraint: airbag, malfunction, failure. • "Attorney for client states airbag burned driver's hands after inflated in collision." • "During an accident, airbag was deployed; however, driver received a burn from airbag." • "Vehicle sustained a front-end collision and airbag did not deploy. No serious injury at 45 mph." • "Airbag light stays on." • "Airbag module appears to interfere with electrical system, resulting in loss of power from battery. Airbag light illuminated before failure."

DODGE DYNASTY 1991

Complaint Severity: Typical. **Recall Alert:** See Recall Index. **Buyer's Summary:** Check the brakes—listen for noise, look for leaks and feel for vibration. They may fail, perform poorly or require frequent mechanical attention. Test the transmission thoroughly.

Hot Spots and Owner/NHTSA Comments:
1. Power train: transmission: automatic, poor performance, difficulty shifting, slipping. • "Transmission slips out of drive into neutral at 40 mph." • "The transmission jumps out of gear; sometimes it won't go back into gear." • "Automatic downshifts at high and various speeds without warning." • "Automatic transmission (3-speed) sticks in 2nd gear; will not shift to 3rd." • "Upon acceleration from stop, transmission jerks as it shifts into 2nd gear, transmission very rough, engages so violently it feels like being hit from behind."
2. Electrical system: ignition, sudden acceleration, stalling. • "Car accelerates while foot is on brake pedal. Also, vehicle stalls out; cannot find problem." • "Vehicle stalls without warning, causing loss of control." • "Ignition cable failed." • "Vehicle stalls intermittently while driving, parked, and right after startup; exact cause unknown." • "Entire ignition system separated from steering column."
3. Brakes: hydraulic: anti-skid system, poor performance, failure, locking up. • "Had antilock brake system replaced less than a year ago, experiencing failure again." • "Antilock brake system warning light/brake light came on, had to replace the antilock brake system." • "The antilock brake system in the vehicle failed. In a panic stop the brakes and the antilock brake system did not activate, and the vehicle did not stop." • "Antilock brake control unit failed." • "Antilock brake system: Experienced extended stopping distance; replaced master cylinder, pump."
4. Engine: cracking, fire, leaks. • "Popping and cracking were heard when key was turned off." • "Engine problems." • "While driving, engine caught on fire." • "Vehicle hesitates and oil pressure too high. Replaced oil pressure sending unit." • "Water pump and oil pan gasket leak."
5. Interior systems: passive restraint: airbag: malfunction, failure. • "Airbag deployed but did not inflate during accident; driver struck open plastic lid that encloses airbag; caused injuries." • "Airbag and seat belt failure in accident caused injury." • "Violent deployment." • "Airbag deployment was violent on impact, causing injury." • "Airbag did not inflate in accident, causing bodily injuries to driver."
6. Interior systems: instrument panel: speedometer: odometer, failure. • "Speedometer intermittently fails, giving false readings." • "Speedometer intermittently does not work." • "Speedometer defected, needle spun and dropped from 60 mph to 0 while car was still going." • "Speedometer pinion failed, causing false readings."

DODGE DYNASTY 1992

Complaint Severity: Minor. **Recall Alert:** See Recall Index. **Buyer's Summary:** The airbags in this vehicle have experienced failures and malfunctions: You may need a professional evaluation on the condition of the airbags. Check the brakes—listen for noise, look for leaks and feel for vibration. They may fail, perform poorly or require frequent mechanical attention. Test the transmission thoroughly.

Hot Spots and Owner/NHTSA Comments:
1. Brakes: hydraulic: anti-skid system, poor performance, failure, locking up. • "Antilock brake system brake pump failed, caused pedal to fade and vibration occurred when applying brakes." • "Antilock brake system brake controller has failed and allowed the brake pedal to go to the floor 3 times. Pumping starts the electric antilock brake system pump and stops the vehicle." • "Antilock brake system: Entire antilock brake system went out; could hear and feel vibration when applied; antilock brake system warning light stayed on; pedal very hard; used excess pressure." • "Antilock brake system experiences pedal fading when brakes are applied, antilock brake system light comes on and will not go off."
2. Engine cooling system: belts, breaking. • "For unknown reason, fan belt broke 4 times within 27,000 miles." • "Drive belt, belt tensioner and water pump replaced." • "Fifth-toothed power steering belt is shaving the edge of belt down to failure stage. Female driver fears loss of control if belt fails during critical driving mode." • "Fan and equipment belts have failed multiple times, resulting in loss of power steering and engine overheating."
3. Power train: transmission: automatic, poor performance, difficulty shifting, slipping. • "Transmission jumps out of gear when pushing on gas pedal after coming to a full stop; when shifting into reverse, it launches backwards." • "Harsh jolting with ultradrive transmission when coming to a stop." • "Transmission snap ring broke, causing inability to downshift; also differential gears and constant velocity joint failed, and rear axle seal was replaced 5 times." • "The transmission has had to be replaced." • "Transmission won't change gears, stays in low; also leaks."
4. Interior systems: passive restraint: airbag: driver, malfunction, failure. • "Airbag did not inflate completely upon deployment." • "Had an accident, airbag burned chest area." • "Vehicle entered an intersection and was hit from an 11:00 position, airbag did not deploy, speed 10 mph." • "Four-car accident, vehicle 3 stopped, hit vehicle 2 in rear, airbag did not deploy; caused head injuries." • "The airbag deployed when driver hit a dog. Smoke engulfed the vehicle compartment, occupant could not breathe or get out of vehicle easily."
5. Brakes: hydraulic system, noise, poor performance. • "Brakes make a lot of noise when applied; dealer greased calipers and adjusted rear brakes, problem still persists." • "Problem with brakes." • "Brakes had numerous repairs performed due to excessive grinding noise. Dealers unable to detect cause." • "The bolt in the idle pulley broke, causing loss of steering and braking."
6. Brakes: hydraulic: shoe: disc brake system, noise, fade. • "Front brakes overheat and are noisy." • "Replaced front brakes." • "Front brake rotors and disc pads continue to wear causing pedal

to fade; frontal collision, impact 12:00 position position, speed 10 mph. Airbag failed to deploy." • "Brakes on left front side grind. Dealer has had in the shop several times, but the cause is still unknown."

DODGE INTREPID 1993

Complaint Severity: Typical. **Recall Alert:** See Recall Index. **Buyer's Summary:** Check the brakes—listen for noise, look for leaks and feel for vibration. They may fail, perform poorly or require frequent mechanical attention. Test the transmission thoroughly.

Hot Spots and Owner/NHTSA Comments:

1. Lighting: general or unknown component: headlights, poor performance. • "Headlights have poor illumination when used. Headlights have a single-bulb halogen design." • "Headlight lenses on vehicle do not disperse light effectively. There are dark spots in the headlight beam." • "Headlights do not give sufficient lighting, even when using high beams." • "Headlights don't illuminate road enough. Focus is basically in center of road. Does not spread out over road." • "Headlights don't illuminate sufficiently for the vehicle size. Had adjusted several times and dealer can't correct problem."

2. Brakes: hydraulic: anti-skid system, poor performance, failure, locking up. • "Antilock brakes failed, causing extended stopping distance." • "Antilock brakes locked up on wet roads, causing vehicle to slide; lost control." • "Antilock brake system light came on; pulsating and loss of braking." • "Vehicle's antilock brake system fails upon passing, dip in road and turning right." • "Antilock brake system brake pedal freezes when applying brakes; vibration on pedal; vehicle becomes erratic and uncontrollable."

3. Lighting: lamp or socket: headlights, poor performance. • "Both high and low beams are lacking in quality and focus of light for safe driving; big difference between this and all other cars tested." • "Headlight beams don't provide sufficient light." • "Poor visibility due to headlight design." • "The headlights do not illuminate an area large enough to see what is in front of vehicle." • "Headlight lens not angled toward the road, causing poor night visibility."

4. Power train: transmission: automatic, poor performance, difficulty shifting, slipping. • "Transmission locks up in 2nd gear, also noisy when downshifting." • "Automatic transmission does not shift into any gear; towed to mechanic; parts not available because of large volume of repairs." • "The automatic transmission, when shifting is very erratic, and at times does not downshift." • "Transmission downshifts into 1st gear before stopping and/or shifting."

5. Brakes: hydraulic system, vibration, failure. • "Vehicle vibrates between 65 and 70 mph, noisy; front and rear brakes replaced." • "Horn went off, trunk flies open while driving, obstructing driver's vision. Also, vehicle loses power, brakes lock up and car dies." • "Brake failure twice in one year; pedal went to the floor. Also, pin failure in rear axle causing vehicle to fishtail." • "Vehicle braking system had delayed reaction, causing extended stopping distances." • "Failure of the cruise control; went into high rpm, applied brakes, which caused overheating and warping of brakes."

6. Brakes: hydraulic: disc: rotor: disc hub, vibration, excessive wear. • "Antilock brake system: Front brake rotors warped when applying brakes, causing vibrations. Vibration stops after releasing brakes." • "Rotors are warped, only have 14,000 miles on vehicle." • "Needs front rotors under 12,000 miles. Electrical system will fail in different components." • "Vehicle is subject to vibrating due to rotors warping, continually burning brake pads." • "Purchased car new; had to take car to dealer for worn-out rotor." • "Front brake rotors have been replaced 9 times in 12,000 miles."

DODGE INTREPID 1994

Complaint Severity: Typical. **Recall Alert:** See Recall Index. **Buyer's Summary:** The airbags in this vehicle have experienced failures and malfunctions: You may need a professional evaluation on the condition of the airbags. Check the brakes—listen for noise, look for leaks and feel for vibration. They may fail, perform poorly or require frequent mechanical attention. Test the transmission thoroughly.

Hot Spots and Owner/NHTSA Comments:

1. Lighting: general or unknown component: headlights, poor performance. • "Design of headlights does not provide sufficient lighting for driving at night in rural areas; poor visibility when driving expressway; nearly caused an accident." • "Headlights are out of adjustment; only time headlights show any brightness is on side roads; vehicle doesn't get light on sign until it is on top of sign." • "Headlight design does not provide adequate amount of beam for night driving, making it hard to see." • "Headlights: When making a sharp right or left turn, vehicle has poor visibility." • "Driving, must use high beams." • "Headlight intermittently fails to turn off; also, taillights leak water."

2. Power train: transmission: automatic, poor performance, difficulty shifting, slipping. • "Automatic transmission went out twice while driving; speed 35-45 mph; no warning." • "While traveling 50 mph, vehicle will downshift into 1st. Failure is repeated with instructions to shut off to reset computer. Driver hit steering wheel." • "Automatic transmission dropped out while driving; seemed as though brakes had been slammed on; transmission went into limp mode; has occurred 3 times." • "When engine is cold, while driving vehicle suddenly without warning jumps out of gear, from drive into neutral." • "While driving, due to transmission lockout, vehicle won't shift from 3rd to 4th gear, suddenly at 40 mph it acts as though in neutral gear, rendering it inoperative."

3. Lighting: lamp or socket: headlights, poor performance. • "Headlights are too weak, causing poor visibility when driving at night." • "Headlight high beams do not illuminate as well as the low beams, creating a visibility problem." • "Poor illumination/visibility with headlights when driving at night." • "Design of headlights is inadequate for night driving, causing poor visibility." • "Headlights do not provide sufficient light on country or unlighted roads."

4. Brakes: hydraulic: anti-skid system, poor performance, failure, locking up. • "Antilock brake system: After warming up, applied brakes; brakes grabbed; pedal went to floor; vehicle started to roll until coasting to stop; no warning; faulty master cylinder?" • "Antilock brake system failed 3 times within 6 weeks; pedal traveled to floor; no prior warning; at road and freeway speeds." • "The control unit had to be replaced on the antilock brake system on the car." • "Antilock brake system failure on wet surface while driving, causing loss of control; hit a curb, causing under body damages." • "Antilock brake system wheel sensor failed, antilock brake system light also comes on."

5. Interior systems: passive restraint: airbag: driver, malfunction, failure. • "In frontal collision, driver's side airbag failed to deploy." • "Head-on collision and driver's airbag did not deploy." • "Driver's airbag split from top to bottom after driver hit head on airbag during collision, causing injury." • "Consumer impacted at 12:00 position at 45 mph, airbag failed to deploy." • "Dual airbag did not deploy in accident."

6. Brakes: hydraulic system, noise, poor performance. • "Brakes squeak." • "When pedal is pressed it goes to the floor, but only after it has warmed up for a few minutes." • "Antilock brake system: Hard brake pedal with no braking effect; antilock braking system not needed during hard braking." • "When brake applied, the wheel shimmies back and forth; replaced rotor 3 times, replacement solved the problem for 15,000 miles." • "Brakes failed."

DODGE LANCER 1987

Complaint Severity: Typical. **Recall Alert:** See Recall Index. **Buyer's Summary:** The fuel injection system has been blamed for hesitation and stalling. Be sure the vehicle doesn't die in traffic or at stops. Test the transmission thoroughly.

Hot Spots and Owner/NHTSA Comments:

1. Electrical system: ignition, stalling, poor performance. • "While driving, vehicle stalls out, leaving driver without power steering and brakes." • "Vehicle stalled and was rear-ended." • "At highway speed when ambient temperature is high, engine dies." • "Vehicle stalled on the road every few months."

2. Fuel: fuel injection system, stalling, hesitation. • "When engine heats up, or in warm weather, idle drops to 500 rpm, stalls at slow speed in traffic, causes loss of power steering and brakes." • "Vehicle missing at 35-50 mph." • "Intermittent stalling." • "Intermittent stalling."

3. Power train: transmission: automatic, poor performance, difficulty shifting, slipping. • "No warning to alert owner of key in ignition, transmission in drive." • "Key can be removed from automatic transmission when in any gear." • "Can take key out of ignition in any gear; car rolled down; accident." • "Automatic transmission: Can turn off motor without key, got 1 foot out of car, noticed car was rolling, slammed on brakes; resulted in accident."

DODGE MONACO 1990

Complaint Severity: Typical. **Recall Alert:** See Recall Index. **Buyer's Summary:** The electronic control unit has been blamed for engine performance problems, including stalling and surging.

Hot Spots and Owner/NHTSA Comments:

1. Electrical system: ignition: electronic control unit, stalling, failure. • "Poor acceleration resulted from computer problems." • "Computer problems; repaired." • "Vehicle cuts off in transit, with total loss of power." • "Intermittent engine stalling at highway speeds."

DODGE MONACO 1991

Complaint Severity: Harmless. **Recall Alert:** See Recall Index. **Buyer's Summary:** Heater core could cause visibility problems, or may not work. Have the constant velocity joint checked professionally.

Hot Spots and Owner/NHTSA Comments:

1. Heater: water: defroster: defogger: heater core: water, poor performance, failure. • "Heater core failed, causing excessive heat around legs; recall repairs refused." • "Heater core bypass, recall repairs refused due to unavailability of parts." • "Heater core failure, causing film on windshield and poor visibility; prior to recall." • "Heater core failed, causing fumes and odor to enter into vehicle; prior to and after recall repairs." • "Heater core bypass is defective."

2. Power train: driveline universal joint: constant velocity, excessive wear, failure. • "Replaced torn inner left constant velocity boot." • "Constant velocity boots and joints failed." • "Four constant velocity boots replaced." • "Crack in constant velocity joint caused leak."

DODGE NEON 1995

Complaint Severity: Very Serious. **Recall Alert:** See Recall Index. **Buyer's Summary:** The airbags in this vehicle have experienced failures and malfunctions: You may need a professional evaluation on the condition of the airbags. Check the brakes—listen for noise, look for leaks and feel for vibration. They may fail, perform poorly or require frequent mechanical attention. See "Sudden Accelerations" in Introduction.

Hot Spots and Owner/NHTSA Comments:

1. Brakes: hydraulic: anti-skid system, poor performance, failure, locking up. • "Antilock brakes failed, causing an accident and injury; prior to recall; also extended stopping distance." • "Antilock brake system failed 5 times due to brake fluid being pushed out of master cylinder cap; once resulting in an accident; also, brake warning light failed." • "Antilock brakes failed 3 times, resulting in extended stopping distance and noise." • "Antilock brake system locked up, causing vehicle to lose control and resulting in an accident and injury." • "The antilock brake system locks when trying to make a quick stop."

2. Interior systems: passive restraint: airbag: driver, malfunction, failure. • "Had an accident, driver's airbag deployed and shattered both door windows." • "Driver's airbag did not deploy during 3-car collision; car rear-ended at 60 mph; rear-ended van at 30 mph." • "Going across intersection, hit a truck in side, airbags did not deploy." • "Frontal collision, impact 12:00 position, speed 25 mph, airbag deployed, caught on fire and burned." • "Frontal collision, impact 12:00 position, speed 25 mph, airbag deployed but did not deflate; caused severe burns on hands and arms."

3. Brakes: hydraulic system, noise, failure. • "Traveling 30 mph, applied the brakes, no response. Resulted in rear-end collision." • "When releasing brakes after applying, noise is heard. Replaced pads, rotors and wheel bearing." • "Applied brakes, pedal went to the floor. Vehicle went over an embankment." • "The brakes, when applied, do not work all the time and they squeak." • "When the brakes were applied the vehicle lost control; caused an accident."

4. Fuel: throttle linkages and control, sudden accelerations. • "Acceleration governor sticks, resulting in sudden acceleration." • "Vehicle will accelerate by itself." • "Vehicle continued to accelerate when brakes applied, causing loss of control and 2 accidents." • "On the throttle linkages there were missing and loose bolts." • "Car in sudden acceleration; stalling."

5. Interior systems: passive restraint: airbag: passenger, malfunction, failure. • "Car was in an accident, airbag on passenger-side deployed but caught on fire." • "Passenger's side airbag did not deploy during rear-end collision." • "During emergency turning, lost steering control; also, passenger airbag blew out the passenger window." • "Vehicle broadsided another vehicle at 25 mph, passenger's airbag did not deploy." • "Car was involved in accident and passenger's airbag deployed; chemical burns were experienced."

6. Lighting: general or unknown component: headlights, poor performance. • "The headlights blink when the air compressor is turned on, and when shifting from 3rd through 5th gears." • "Headlights blink upon startup and when driving." • "At night the headlights and the light on the dash are blinking." • "Manufacturer issued a service bulletin stating not to attempt to repair headlight for blinking; problem still exists, causing visual problem." • "Headlights flicker while driving; dealer gave a service bulletin concerning headlight flicking, saying do not attempt repairs."

DODGE OMNI 1987

Complaint Severity: Harmless. **Recall Alert:** See Recall Index. **Buyer's Summary:** The carburetion system could contribute to stalling and hesitation. Look carefully for any kind of leakage, especially under the car. The fuel injection system has been blamed for hesitation and stalling. Be sure the vehicle doesn't die in traffic or at stops. Test transmission for slipping, locking up and performance.

Hot Spots and Owner/NHTSA Comments:
1. Fuel: fuel carburetion, stalling, hesitation. • "Carburetor overhauled at 52,000 miles, choke adjusted twice." • "Fuel leaks from carburetor resulted in engine fire." • "Engine stalling problems, won't stay running, poor idle when running, blows out black smoke, hard to restart; repaired/replaced fuel pump to no avail." • "Car misses and stalls on freeway from 0-65 mph; vapor canister and other parts connected to fuel system replaced twice." • "Carburetor caused vehicle to hesitate, stall, fluctuates when idling, hard start, high idle, replaced carburetor."
2. Fuel: fuel injection system, stalling, hesitation. • "Vehicle experiences recurring stalling problems; near-accident on several occasions due to a faulty fuel injection system." • "Fuel pressure regulator failure caused fire; prior to recall." • "Vehicle idles rough and surges after fuel pressure regulator repair." • "Fuel line leakage twice; prior to recall." • "Engine hesitates, cold hard start, rough idle, stalls during acceleration at low and high speeds, accelerates and doesn't go anywhere; replaced fuel foaming kit."
3. Fuel: fuel systems, stalling, leaks. • "When gas cap removed, hot pressurized vaporized gas expels from tank, hot enough to cause burns; installed fuel pump in gas tank and rerouted fuel lines." • "Recall repair refused due to unavailability of parts." • "Vehicle suffers chronic stalling due to elusive and unspecified fuel delivery system failures." • "Gas odor from car after shutdown; when driving, burning odor and smoke appeared, engine caught fire due to faulty fuel system." • "Fuel leakage occurred at fuel pressure regulator, with fuel falling over hot manifold; a potential fire hazard."
4. Fuel: fuel injection: unknown type: regulator, leaks, fire. • "Problem with leaking fuel pressure regulator; found gasoline on floor, noticed gas odor; possible fire and life hazard condition." • "Defective fuel pressure regulator caused engine fire; prior to recall." • "Recall repair refused due to unavailability of part, resulting in fire." • "Recall repair refused." • "Fuel injection regulator failed prior to recall, resulting in a fire; recall repairs refused due to model year."
5. Electrical system: ignition, stalling, failure. • "Hard starting car when cold, must turn starter 6-8 times to get engine to catch; defect in ignition system, replaced starter twice." • "Intermittent stalling." • "Computer has been replaced, pickup coil defect, can suddenly lose all power on hot engine." • "Vehicle stalls while in traffic, loss of steering and power." • "Replaced ignition system and many more parts in fuel system."
6. Power train: transmission: 5-speed and up, difficulty shifting, malfunction. • "Five-speed transmission sometimes won't shift from 1st to 2nd gear, nor will it go in reverse; also, noise in drive train." • "Manual transmission's 5th gear grinds, hard to shift in all gears." • "Five-speed transmission malfunction, fails to shift into reverse and 1st gear, hard to shift and clashing gears." • "Manual 5-speed transmission shifts hard; also, shifter broke off while driving." • "Gearshift has to be pushed hard to change gears, no clear feel between 1st and 3rd gears."

DODGE OMNI 1989

Complaint Severity: Harmless. **Recall Alert:** See Recall Index. **Buyer's Summary:** Look carefully for any kind of leakage, especially under the car.

Hot Spots and Owner/NHTSA Comments:
1. Engine: leaks, vibration, failure. • "Continuous oil leaks; repaired/replaced rear main seal, valve cover gasket." • "Engine failed, smoked and burned heavily; repaired several times." • "When first started, car runs fine; after engine is warm, experiencing pronounced vibration." • "Engine overheated due to noise when cold." • "Engine components failed."
2. Engine: gaskets: valve cover, leaks. • "Engine valve gasket failed twice." • "Valve cover gasket leaked prior to and after recall." • "Oil leakage in valve cover gasket, car caught fire in engine area." • "Defective engine cylinder head cover gasket leaks oil from rear of engine, near or from intake bolt, dripping on manifold; smokes, smells." • "After having recall regarding engine gaskets taken care of, a repetition of the same problem occurred; leaks appeared after 11,000 miles."

DODGE SHADOW 1987

Complaint Severity: Troublesome. **Recall Alert:** See Recall Index. **Buyer's Summary:** The electronic control unit has been blamed for engine performance problems, including stalling and surging. The fuel injection system has been blamed for hesitation and stalling. Be sure the vehicle doesn't die in traffic or at stops. The steering may be stiff or not working correctly. Be sure to test the steering, especially on a cold start. Check the brakes—listen for noise, look for leaks and feel for vibration. They may fail, perform poorly or require frequent mechanical attention. See "Sudden Accelerations" in Introduction.

Hot Spots and Owner/NHTSA Comments:
1. Fuel: throttle linkages and control, sudden accelerations. • "Vehicle does not idle down at stops." • "Intermittent extremely high idle in neutral, when driving must keep using brake to stay in speed limit, once car is hot valves get very noisy." • "Intermittent sticking throttle, engine warm; depressing clutch to change gears or stop engine, rpm increases on its own, slow to return to idle speed." • "Car continuously would lurch forward; when entering garage, would hit brakes immediately to stop." • "When shifted into drive, 'power loss' light illuminated and vehicle accelerated out of control. Brakes had no impact on speed." • "Vehicle suddenly accelerated forward, crashing into garage, while idling in park gear."
2. Electrical system: ignition: electronic control unit, malfunction, stalling, sudden acceleration. • "Computer malfunction, idle races at times at 1,000 rpm higher than normal for no apparent reason, and for no apparent reason it stops on its own." • "Continuous engine stalling problem; replaced pickup plate and logic/power module." • "Vehicle stalls intermittently without warning, causing loss of control." • "Vehicle idles extremely high, sudden acceleration when putting car in gear, also dies out while driving; replaced logic module."
3. Exhaust system: manifold: oxygen sensor, malfunction, failure. • "Problem with car not starting; repaired/replaced manifold air pressure sensor." • "Recurring problem with no start and loss of power while in motion; repaired/replaced manifold air pressure sensor several times." • "Manifold air pressure sensor repeatedly failed 3 times." • "Manifold air pressure, speed control failed, vehicle would stall while in operation." • "Engine has erratic idle, dies and/or races up to 3,000 rpm; repaired/replaced manifold air pressure sensor, throttle position sensor, idle motor, to no avail; stalling persisted."
4. Steering: gear: rack-and-pinion, stiffness, poor performance. • "Defective rack-and-pinion system failed while turning steering column." • "Steering area leaking fluid and making loud noise, loss of power steering; replaced rack-and-pinion." • "Bolts that connect the rack-and-pinion to body of car worked out, causing poor control of steering." • "Internal seal failure of rack-and-pinion, causing loss of power steering."
5. Fuel: fuel injection system, stalling, hesitation. • "Engine racing when shifting gears with clutch depressed and off; re-

paired/replaced fuel injection body and speed sensor." • "Engine trouble, black smoke billows out of exhaust pipe when car starts; repaired/replaced manifold air pressure sensor, fuel injector, temperature/oxygen sensor, and fuel regulator." • "Vehicle intermittently stalls out, difficulty in restarting; gas pedal fails to respond, finally engine cuts off." • "Vehicle completely halted in mid-travel, gas light on dashboard indicates no fuel although gas tank full, loss of power steering and brakes." • "Chronic and excessive idling problem, dies at stops and when put in park, engine races to 3,000 rpm or more; several attempts to repair, all to no avail." • "Intermittent stalling."

6. Brakes: hydraulic system, vibration, locking up, failure. • "Brake pads worn; replaced pads, rotors, calipers." • "Pulsating brake pedal from 10 mph down to zero." • "Defective brake system, brakes stick; serviced brakes." • "Brake failure; when applying brakes car does not stop." • "While applying brakes left front brake locked, causing car to slide into another car."

DODGE SHADOW 1988

Complaint Severity: Typical. **Recall Alert:** See Recall Index. **Buyer's Summary:** Look carefully for any kind of leakage, especially under the car. The fuel injection system has been blamed for hesitation and stalling. Be sure the vehicle doesn't die in traffic or at stops. The steering may be stiff or not working correctly. Be sure to test the steering, especially on a cold start. Make sure seat belts function correctly and fit comfortably. See "Sudden Accelerations" in Introduction.

Hot Spots and Owner/NHTSA Comments:

1. Interior systems: passive restraint: belts, malfunction, poor performance. • "Automatic shoulder belts inoperative, not moving on tracks." • "Motorized seat belts stop halfway upon starting car." • "Passenger's side automatic seat belt fails occasionally; driver's-side automatic seat belt failed completely." • "The safety restraint motor is on recall and the dealer is having a problem getting the part."

2. Steering: gear: rack-and-pinion, stiffness, poor performance. • "Improper mounting of rack-and-pinion to cross member, causing steering failure." • "The rack-and-pinion bolts have stripped loose from subframe and driver cannot steer vehicle." • "Vehicle has improper bolting in rack-and-pinion steering, has only 1 bolt on." • "Weld holding nuts for bolts to secure rack to frame broken, permitting nuts to loosen; entire rack floating on frame caused unstable steering when turning." • "Steering problems; rack-and-pinion replaced due to too much play in steering wheel."

3. Interior systems: active restraints: belt retractors, breaking, failure. • "When accident occurred, seat belt exploded at latch and threw child's car seat forward into back of driver's seat, which in turn threw driver's seat forward." • "Automatic seat belt retractor failed to retract." • "Automatic shoulder belt on driver's-side fails to retract completely on door track, intermittently moves slowly when activated." • "The seat belt housing track broke, would not retract, resulting in inability to lubricate seat belt." • "Driver's automatic seat belt failed, prior to recall."

4. Engine cooling system: radiator, leaks, failure. • "Radiator failed." • "Hole in radiator." • "Radiator is starting to leak." • "Car lost some power, gauge red hot, radiator burst at seams on passenger side." • "Problem with leaking radiator; repaired/replaced."

5. Fuel: fuel injection system, stalling, hesitation. • "Engine stalls, idle fluctuates between 50 and 75 rpm while stopped with engine in drive; suggested design flaw in Chrysler engines." • "Hesitation and loss of power." • "Vehicle hard starting, chugs at 300 rpm when initially starting, blows black smoke, rpm accelerates on its own, driver applied brake to maintain moderate speed." • "Motor home has continuous idle problem, persistent stalling problem, cannot be resolved; replaced fuel injection module, distributor, fuel pump." • "Trouble getting engine started; when started, would stall halfway down drive."

6. Fuel: throttle linkages and control, sudden accelerations. • "Vehicle suddenly accelerated, throttle seems to stick, engine races, accelerates without notice." • "On highway, car jerked and then started to pick up speed, brakes could not slow down speed." • "When releasing foot from accelerator, car does not slow down, continues traveling at same speed until applying brakes." • "Car traveling 5 mph, throttle stuck, caused collision; before accident rpm high while idling." • "Vehicle accelerated with high idle when coming to a stop; applied extra brake pressure. When foot let off brake pedal, vehicle surged forward."

DODGE SHADOW 1989

Complaint Severity: Typical. **Recall Alert:** See Recall Index. **Buyer's Summary:** Look carefully for any kind of leakage, especially under the car. Make sure the shoulder belts don't cut across your neck and are well anchored. Make sure seat belts function correctly and fit comfortably.

Hot Spots and Owner/NHTSA Comments:

1. Engine: gaskets: valve cover, leaks, fire. • "Oil leaking around engine's cylinder head cover and drain plug; later, engine caught fire and gasket was replaced; recurring valve cover and seal leak." • "Received recall notice on engine valve cover gasket, may dislocate and allow engine oil leak, possibly cause fire." • "Defective engine cylinder head cover gasket; replaced." • "Engine fluid leaks continue to plague vehicle, defective engine gaskets, brought vehicle to dealer 10 times." • "Vehicle destroyed by fire due to faulty valve covering gasket letting oil leak onto hot manifold."

2. Interior systems: passive restraint: belts, uncomfortable, malfunction. • "Motorized shoulder belt problems, prior to and after recall." • "Automatic seat belts too high, scrape neck and sometimes do not lock." • "Both front seat belts no longer move when ignition is turned on. Waiting for parts since June 1993."

3. Interior systems: active seat and shoulder belts and belt anchor, malfunction, failure. • "Upon impact and during frontal crash, driver and passenger shoulder harness and lap belts failed to hold, sustained injuries from steering column and dashboard." • "Seat belt mechanisms have been lubricated under recall; mechanisms have now failed with no offer of repair." • "Inoperative seat belt." • "Driver's-side passive seat belt motor failed, only front seat belts are operative."

4. Interior systems: shoulder belts, poor performance, failure. • "Seat belt fit improperly." • "Inoperative shoulder harness passive restraint." • "Seat belt shoulder harness inoperative during an accident." • "Front automatic shoulder restraint system will not retract; occupants operate the system manually to prevent increased risk of injury."

5. Engine: leaks, fire, failure. • "Second occasion of engine seizing and stopping the car in the middle of heavy traffic, risking a rear-end collision." • "Engine oil leak; repaired, problem continues." • "Engine compartment defect." • "Defective seal." • "Driving down highway without difficulty, 'oil' and 'check engine' lights came on, seconds later flames were coming from engine area and entire car."

6. Interior systems: active restraints: belt retractors, failure, malfunction. • "Passenger's side seat belt retractor does not work." • "Driver's seat belt failed, motor replaced." • "Frontal collision, impact 12:00 position, lap and shoulder belt did not retract." • "Shoulder restraints stick intermittently." • "Seat belt retractor failed."

DODGE SHADOW 1990

Complaint Severity: Very Serious. **Recall Alert:** See Recall Index. **Buyer's Summary:** Look carefully for any kind of leakage, especially under the car. The airbags in this vehicle have experienced failures and malfunctions. You may need a professional evaluation on the condition of the airbags. Check the brakes—listen for noise, look for leaks and feel for vibration. They may fail, perform poorly or require frequent mechanical attention.

Hot Spots and Owner/NHTSA Comments:

1. Interior systems: passive restraint: airbag: driver, malfunction, failure. • "When traveling at speed of 45 mph, vehicle had a frontal collision, airbag deployed. Driver's clothes were burned from contact." • "Upon impact during frontal crash at approximately 30-40 mph beneath underside of truck at right angle, 2:00 position, airbag failed to deploy." • "Had an accident, airbag deployment was delayed; hit head on windshield, hand was burned by airbag." • "During front-end collision at 30 mph, airbag deployment particles and gas hit driver neck, causing burns and injury." • "Steering wheel locked up, causing loss of vehicle control, front-end collision at 15-20 mph. Airbag did not deploy. Total loss of vehicle."

2. Interior systems: passive restraint: airbag, malfunction, failure. • "Driver's-side airbag deployed, with hot gas causing serious burns to driver during accident." • "Went over a dip in road at 25 mph, airbag deployed." • "While making a U-turn, airbag deployed without impact." • "Small frontal impact resulted in airbag deployment with an explosion; driver received facial and arm burns." • "Airbag deployment was violent, causing severe burns to face and body."

3. Brakes: hydraulic: shoe: disc brake system, malfunction, locking up, noise. • "Brakes malfunctioned and brake pedal went to the floor twice before wiring burned up." • "Front right rotor and shoes worn, wheel cylinders on both sides leaking." • "Steering wheel and brakes locked up when avoiding a deer, vehicle ended in ditch after rolling." • "Front disc brakes, made of metal, squeak on occasion and tend to heat up." • "Due to worn-out rotors and brake pads that fell off, extended stopping occurred, which finally resulted in an accident."

4. Engine: gaskets: valve cover, leaks, failure. • "Valve cover gasket leaked oil prior to and after recall repair." • "Valve cover gasket leaks; replaced 3 times." • "Cracked head gasket causing a potential risk of fire." • "Continuous oil leak problems prior to and after recall." • "Failure of engine valve cover gasket, prior to recall, resulted in vehicle fire."

5. Brakes: hydraulic system, locking up, failure. • "Car braked at 30-40 mph; then skidded when brakes were applied approximately one-quarter to one-half block." • "Vehicle experienced brake failure." • "Frequent brake failure, sticks and locks up." • "Brakes need repair." • "Brakes failed."

6. Electrical system: battery, failure. • "Battery died." • "Battery failed." • "Battery replaced." • "Upon attempting to start vehicle, found battery to be dead."

DODGE SHADOW 1991

Complaint Severity: Serious. **Recall Alert:** See Recall Index. **Buyer's Summary:** Look carefully for any kind of leakage, especially under the car. The airbags in this vehicle have experienced failures and malfunctions: You may need a professional evaluation on the condition of the airbags. Test the transmission thoroughly. See "Sudden Accelerations" in Introduction.

Hot Spots and Owner/NHTSA Comments:

1. Fuel: throttle linkages and control, sudden accelerations. • "Dealer attempted 7 repairs in 2 years; car will leap forward from an idle position, speedometer will show 30 mph." • "Vehicle periodically accelerates suddenly or surges when driving, causing loss of vehicle control." • "While sitting at a light with foot on the brake, vehicle starts to surge." • "Seventh time the throttle stuck while braking; dealer tried repairs twice. Foot off the gas pedal and the car will accelerate." • "Vehicle suddenly accelerated when changing lanes at 30 mph to high unknown rpm."

2. Interior systems: passive restraint: airbag: driver, malfunction, failure. • "Driver's-side airbag did not deploy upon 12:00 collision at 15-20 mph." • "Lost control of vehicle, hit embankment; airbag did not deploy." • "Vehicle rear-ended vehicle in front. Airbag deployed but only on the right side, allowing left side to contact steering wheel." • "Airbag failed to deploy and seat belts did not work properly in an accident, which allowed injuries to the driver." • "Airbag did not deploy during side impact accident at 30 mph."

3. Electrical system: ignition, stalling, sudden acceleration. • "Vehicle stalls at highway speeds without warning." • "Vehicle will stall with no warning. Dealer unable to detect failure." • "Vehicle stalls constantly without warning at speeds above 50 mph, causing loss of steering and braking power." • "Problem with sudden acceleration, stalling and dying on the road." • "Consumer was driving on highway at 45 mph, car decelerated to zero; 4-cycle, 2.5L engine."

4. Interior systems: bucket: backrest, breaking, failure. • "Driver seat back broke while sitting in reclining position." • "Driver and passenger bucket seat backs fell backwards intermittently with the slightest movement from occupants." • "Driver's-side seat back did not hold during an accident but flopped back and forth." • "Driver's seat back fell because bolt that secures back broke." • "When driving, driver seat falls backward."

5. Structure: body roof: convertible top, leaks, visual problems. • "Owner is having problems seeing out of the back of rear window that is made of plastic." • "Convertible top obstructs vision when in down position." • "Convertible top leaks." • "Top of vehicle leaks in rainy weather, fogging interior, causing poor visibility." • "Plastic convertible top rear window is all distorted, causing poor visibility."

6. Power train: transmission: automatic, poor performance, difficulty shifting, slipping. • "Transmission failures." • "Transmission oil leak." • "Transmission lever shifted by child, without key in ignition; vehicle rolled backwards into park." • "Transmission burned up, causing drive train failure."

DODGE SHADOW 1992

Complaint Severity: Very Serious. **Recall Alert:** See Recall Index. **Buyer's Summary:** The airbags in this vehicle have experienced failures and malfunctions: You may need a professional evaluation on the condition of the airbags. Check the brakes—listen for noise, look for leaks and feel for vibration. They may fail, perform poorly or require frequent mechanical attention. Test the transmission thoroughly. See "Sudden Accelerations" in Introduction.

Hot Spots and Owner/NHTSA Comments:

1. Interior systems: passive restraint: airbag: driver, malfunction, failure. • "No deployment of airbag during accident, resulted in a fatality." • "Upon frontal collision, driver's lap and shoulder belt didn't restrain occupant from hitting windshield. No airbag deployment." • "Frontal collision, impact 12:00 position, speed 15 mph; could not breathe due to fumes which were inhaled, and received injuries." • "Owner was driving down the road, other driver jumped in front of him and he hit her at 30 mph with airbag deploying but not fully inflating." • "While driving, airbag deployed for no reason, lost control of vehicle."

2. Interior systems: bucket: backrest, breaking, failure. • "Driver's seat back does not stay up; flops backwards, does not stay vertical; propped up by suitcase." • "Heard a popping noise and plastic piece fell off, causing driver seat back to shift to the right 5 to 6 inches." • "Experienced seat back failure while driving, seat is very loose." • "Power seat track and seat back portion failed twice." • "Driver seat back broke, due to sheared bolt, resulting in collapsing."

3. Power train: transmission: automatic, poor performance, difficulty shifting, slipping. • "Transmission shifts harshly and jumped out of gear when placed in reverse, also hesitates when going uphill." • "Vehicle will downshift while driving at any speed." • "Torn transmission mounts, overdrive surge." • "Transmission linkage out of adjustment." • "Transmission failed 3 times."

4. Interior systems: passive restraint: airbag, malfunction, failure. • "Airbag did not inflate during accident, causing injury." • "No deployment of driver's and passenger's airbags during accident, causing injuries." • "Frontal impact resulted in airbag deployment but no inflation of airbag." • "Brakes locked trying to avoid collision. Shoulder belt didn't restrain from hitting steering wheel and windshield. Airbag deployed after collision had happened." • "No deployment of airbags during accident, resulting in injury."

5. Brakes: hydraulic system, locking up, failure. • "During brake application, occupants are thrust forward and backwards." • "Brakes locked trying to avoid collision. Shoulder belt didn't restrain from hitting steering wheel and windshield. Airbag deployed after collision had happened." • "Vehicle's brakes locked up with no warning, and the steering wheel would not turn." • "Brake failure caused accident and injury."

6. Fuel: throttle linkages and control, sudden accelerations. • "After pulling out of car wash, throttle stuck open, causing car to accelerate. Driver hit pickup in the rear, airbag did not deploy." • "Intermittent sudden acceleration." • "Vehicle does not slow down when removing foot from accelerator." • "Throttle sticks in open position; causes high acceleration; no warning."

DODGE SHADOW 1993

Complaint Severity: Very Serious. **Buyer's Summary:** The airbags in this vehicle have experienced failures and malfunctions: You may need a professional evaluation on the condition of the airbags. Check the brakes—listen for noise, look for leaks and feel for vibration. They may fail, perform poorly or require frequent mechanical attention. Test the transmission thoroughly.

Hot Spots and Owner/NHTSA Comments:

1. Interior systems: passive restraint: airbag: driver, malfunction, failure. • "Airbag came out upon impact, letting off cloudy fumes, resulting in poor visibility." • "Driver seat shoulder belt did not restrain driver and airbag did not deploy upon accident." • "While driving on the highway, owner rear-ended another driver at 20 or 25 mph and his airbag did not deploy." • "Airbag deployment was violent, resulting in injury." • "Driving vehicle at speed of 30 mph, went into gravel, lost control, hit an embankment, vehicle flipped and rolled; airbag did not deploy."

2. Brakes: hydraulic system, noise, locking up. • "A loud grinding noise in braking system is heard while driving." • "Brake pedal went near the floor. Two miles at 20 mph, car pulled to the left, spun and bumped into telephone pole; bent rim of right front wheel." • "Driver applied brakes (not antilock brake system) and they locked up. Vehicle was heading south and slid east into a ditch." • "Holding vehicle on hills with foot on brake has pedal going to the floor. Dealer claims this is standard to all Dodge Shadows, non-antilock brake system vehicle."

3. Power train: transmission: automatic, poor performance, difficulty shifting, slipping. • "While parked with engine running, vehicle suddenly jumped out of gear into reverse, hitting a pole." • "Automatic transmission failure." • "Small metal chips were in transmission line; had to have replaced." • "Transmission was rebuilt and still having the same problem; warranty is expired, purchased car new."

4. Interior systems: passive restraint: airbag, failure. • "Short in the switch, causing the airbag light to stay on." • "Airbag did not deploy." • "Rear-ended vehicle. Airbag did not deploy nor did belts restrain." • "Antilock brakes failed to stop vehicle when applied, causing front-end collision at 35 mph. Airbag did not deploy."

DODGE SHADOW 1994

Complaint Severity: Serious. **Buyer's Summary:** The airbags in this vehicle have experienced failures and malfunctions: You may need a professional evaluation on the condition of the airbags. Check the brakes—listen for noise, look for leaks and feel for vibration. They may fail, perform poorly or require frequent mechanical attention.

Hot Spots and Owner/NHTSA Comments:

1. Brakes: hydraulic system, failure. • "While driving slight incline, applied brakes; total brake failure; rear-ended vehicle in front." • "Brakes compress when stopping or when traffic is bumper to bumper." • "Brake pedal goes to the floor and driver has to pump brake pedal in order to restore brake functions." • "When on an incline, the brake pedal goes all the way to the floor and barely stops the car."

2. Interior systems: passive restraint: airbag: driver, malfunction, failure. • "Airbag did not deploy." • "Car was hit in the rear by a semitrailer. Driver's seat latch broke allowing driver to be injured severely. Airbag did not deploy." • "Driver's-side airbag did not deploy during impact at 12:00 position at 8 mph." • "Car involved in head-on collision and driver's-side airbag did not deploy." • "During a head-on collision, the driver's-side airbag did not deploy."

3. Engine: noise, stalling, failure. • "Engine noise." • "Intermittent stalling." • "Replaced engine." • "Engine failure."

4. Interior systems: bucket: backrest, malfunction, failure. • "Seat backs don't latch. Could be hazardous in an accident." • "Seat back failure, upon rear-end collision seat back collapsed backward." • "Driver and passenger seat backrests do not lock in place." • "Car was stopped when another car coming at 40 mph rear-ended stopped car; passenger seat completely collapsed."

DODGE SPIRIT 1989

Complaint Severity: Typical. **Recall Alert:** See Recall Index. **Buyer's Summary:** Look carefully for any kind of leakage, especially under the car. Check the brakes—listen for noise, look for leaks and feel for vibration. They may fail, perform poorly or require frequent mechanical attention. Test the transmission thoroughly. See "Sudden Accelerations" in Introduction.

Hot Spots and Owner/NHTSA Comments:

1. Engine: gaskets: valve cover, leaks, premature failure. • "Valve cover seal defective; replaced." • "Vehicle had valve cover gasket replaced 4 times due to leakage." • "Head gasket leaks after recall repairs." • "Defective valve cover gasket replaced by dealer." • "Engine oil accumulation in air cleaner, coolant leaks internally into engine; possible blown head gasket."

2. Fuel: throttle linkages and control, sudden accelerations. • "Attempting to park, car accelerated over curb, foot on brakes." • "While engine was running in park, car accelerated backwards and collided." • "While stopping at a stoplight, vehicle suddenly accelerated forward." • "Sudden acceleration after putting vehicle in gear, impact 12:00 position, hit a parked vehicle, speed 25 mph." • "Car slammed into post; afterwards moved into drive, acted normally."

3. Power train: transmission: automatic, poor performance, difficulty shifting, slipping. • "Transmission problems; won't shift, downshifts without warning, leaks and hard downshifts." • "Transmission malfunctioned twice; repaired by dealer; however, transmission still malfunctioning." • "Transmission has been replaced 3 times." • "Automatic transmission defective." • "Transmission failed."

4. Brakes: hydraulic system, malfunction, noise. • "Brake system malfunctioned, caused brakes to stay engaged." • "Brakes squeak; tried to repair twice, problem still exists." • "When brakes applied at full stop, pedal went to floor and front end vibrated, vehicle spun sideways with snow on road." • "Brakes make noise when applied; replaced left front rotors."

DODGE SPIRIT 1990

Complaint Severity: Troublesome. **Recall Alert:** See Recall Index. **Buyer's Summary:** Look carefully for any kind of leakage, especially under the car. The electronic control unit has been blamed for engine performance problems, including stalling and surging. The airbags in this vehicle have experienced failures and malfunctions. You may need a professional evaluation on the condition of the airbags. Check the brakes—listen for noise, look for leaks and feel for vibration. They may fail, perform poorly or require frequent mechanical attention. Test the transmission thoroughly. See "Sudden Accelerations" in Introduction.

Hot Spots and Owner/NHTSA Comments:

1. Power train: transmission: automatic, poor performance, difficulty shifting, slipping. • "Automatic gearshift on floor defective; when key removed while transmission still in drive, car rolled backwards 70 feet and caused accident." • "Tried to put gear in park prior to shutting off motor, gearshift did not move beyond neutral; repositioned pin that slipped out of reverse lockout mechanism." • "Transmission slipped out of park into reverse and rolled freely down a hill." • "Continuous transmission failures and repairs." • "Vehicle would not shift out of 2nd gear; also, vehicle could not go over 35 mph."

2. Interior systems: passive restraint: airbag: driver, malfunction, failure. • "Entire front end totaled, with airbag not deploying." • "Driver's-side airbag deployed on vehicle, impact 30 mph, knocked out front teeth." • "Airbag deployed while driving, had not struck anything." • "In a frontal accident, impact at 11:00 while going 20 mph, airbag deployed and stayed inflated; caused driver second degree burns." • "Airbag did not deploy during a rear-end collision."

3. Brakes: hydraulic: disc: pads and shoes, excessive wear, failure. • "Epoxy adhesive broke loose, causing brake pad to fall off vehicle." • "Brake pad is separating from backing plate; has occurred twice after being repaired." • "Front brake pads delaminated from backing plate." • "Premature brake wear; serviced 4 times, problem continues." • "Driver's-side brake pads separated from the metal, causing brake failure. Owner claims vehicle has defective front pads."

4. Electrical system: ignition: electronic control unit, stalling, failure. • "Computer module failed, causing vehicle to stall." • "Faulty computer module." • "Intermittent engine shuddering." • "Computer failure."

5. Engine: gaskets: valve cover, leaks, fire. • "Defective valve cover gasket, on recall." • "Oil leaking from valve cover gasket." • "Engine valve cover gaskets failed, prior to recall." • "Vehicle caught on fire, prior to recall."

6. Fuel: throttle linkages and control, sudden accelerations. • "Vehicle is subject to stalling at any speed intermittently without warning. Dealer has made attempts with no correction." • "Car stalls when slowing down or making a turn. Engine will not idle." • "Vehicle started in reverse on slight grade and suddenly accelerated into street, lost control and caused injury and property damage." • "While pulling into angled parking stall, vehicle suddenly accelerated out of control and crashed through front of post office, airbag deployed."

DODGE SPIRIT 1991

Complaint Severity: Typical. **Recall Alert:** See Recall Index. **Buyer's Summary:** Problems with the timing gear and chain can cause serious problems. Have the engine checked by a professional. The airbags in this vehicle have experienced failures and malfunctions: You may need a professional evaluation on the condition of the airbags. Test the transmission thoroughly. See "Sudden Accelerations" in Introduction.

Hot Spots and Owner/NHTSA Comments:

1. Fuel: throttle linkages and control, sudden accelerations. • "Vehicle constantly surges forward." • "While slowing down, vehicle will accelerate." • "Car experiences sudden power surges at low speeds; requires constant braking." • "Engine intermittently races to twice the idle speed, causes vehicle to surge forward." • "Engine surged forward while stopped; brakes applied; excessive effort applied to stop vehicle; no prior warning."

2. Electrical system: ignition, stalling, failure. • "Five- to thirty-minute drive, accelerating will bring about a total stall. Usually the engine will restart. Dealer cannot find the problem." • "Key was removed in drive position and car rolled away." • "Ignition key could be removed in any gear; resulted in vehicle rolling away."

3. Interior systems: passive restraint: airbag: driver, malfunction, failure. • "Upon being forced off the road, car hit an embankment on front left side, airbag didn't deploy." • "At 12:00 position and 20 mph, airbag deployed after driver struck steering wheel. Black smoke consumed the car and burned clothing and skin of driver." • "Frontal collision, impact 11:00 position, 30 mph. Airbag did not deploy until after impact, inflated halfway." • "No deployment of airbag during accident." • "Vehicle's driver's-side airbag deployed for no reason while driving."

4. Power train: transmission: automatic, poor performance, difficulty shifting, slipping. • "Automatic transmission: Snap rings broke; transmission jumps out of gear; does not shift as intended; speed 55 mph; replaced; problem has reoccurred." • "Automatic transmission: Driving downhill; shifted from overdrive to drive; after reaching 2,100 rpms, transmission automatically went into high gear; rapidly picked up speed." • "Shift lever left in drive position when removing key from ignition, causing vehicle to move; would not shift into park." • "Loud grinding noise, transmission was hanging down almost to ground; reassembled transmission." • "Gear slipped from park to reverse, and then vehicle rolled into parked car."

5. Engine: timing gear and chain, breaking. • "Timing belt broke twice." • "Timing belt failed 4 times, causing loss of control." • "Timing belt broke at 45 mph." • "At 19,000 miles the timing belt has gone out without warning."

DODGE SPIRIT 1992

Complaint Severity: Typical. **Recall Alert:** See Recall Index. **Buyer's Summary:** Check the brakes—listen for noise, look for leaks and feel for vibration. They may fail, perform poorly or require frequent mechanical attention. Test the transmission thoroughly.

Hot Spots and Owner/NHTSA Comments:

1. Brakes: hydraulic: anti-skid system, poor performance, failure, locking up. • "The antilock brake system has failed. When braking the pedal goes down and keeps moving and making a grinding noise." • "Antilock brakes failure, resulting in extended stopping distances." • "Brake pedal was harder and higher than normal, cruise control would not turn off, no brakes from 55 mph. Ignition had to be turned off. Power lines nearby." • "While driving, experienced intermittent brake failure; when pedal applied, it went to the floor on antilock brake system-equipped vehicle." • "Antilock brake light stays on due to main sensing unit failure, causing antilock brake system failure."

2. Power train: transmission: automatic, poor performance, difficulty shifting, slipping. • "Automatic transmission keeps slipping and car drifts after putting into park; it takes extra effort to put car into park position." • "Transmission slipping during cold start; feels like car is in 2nd gear." • "Transmission failed; vehicle would start but was not able to go into gears." • "Vehicle jumped from park to reverse while idling, hitting garage wall and door." • "Vehicle in driveway in park in idle position, jumped into reverse, impact 6:00 position, speed unknown, causing damages to house."

Dodge—Trucks

DODGE TRUCK CARAVAN 1987

Complaint Severity: Typical. **Recall Alert:** See Recall Index. **Buyer's Summary:** The carburetion system could contribute to stalling and hesitation. Look carefully for any kind of leakage, especially under the car. The fuel injection system has been blamed for hesitation and stalling. Be sure the vehicle doesn't die in traffic or at stops. Test the transmission thoroughly.

Hot Spots and Owner/NHTSA Comments:

1. Power train: transmission: automatic, poor performance, difficulty shifting, slipping. • "Transmission sticks in low gear and then jumps from gear to gear." • "Transmission shifting with faulty plate design; newly installed replacement slips about 15-17 mph from low into 2nd." • "Car sluggish, no pep, transmission not engaging in drive, then popping in with jerk, hard to shift." • "Transmission malfunctioning, slipping into high gear; repaired/replaced transaxle assembly and torque converter." • "Car shifted from park to reverse, will not engage fully upon starting, over revs, jerks, and stays in lower gear too long; transaxle failure."

2. Engine: mounts, premature failure, noise. • "Two broken motor mounts in under 30,000 miles." • "Engine mount broke twice, extreme vibration occurred in reverse gear." • "Faulty engine mounts; 1 broke at 17,000 miles; noisy valve lifters when engine cold." • "Front motor mount completely failed, with engine resting on transmission." • "Defective motor mount bolt, causing rocking and noises when shifting into gears or during stopping, acceleration or deceleration."

3. Fuel: fuel carburetion, stalling, hesitation. • "Stalling after engine is warmed up, causing loss of power steering and brakes." • "Intermittent stalling, fuel dumping into carburetor, uneven fuel mileage." • "Stalling due to vapor lock." • "Vehicle suffers chronic stalling due to fuel delivery system." • "Van lost power going up hills; constant stalling; problem with the fuel carburetion system."

4. Structure: hatchback locks and latches, malfunction, failure. • "Rear latch pops open while driving, without impact; bolts come loose and hatch comes open." • "Rear latch popped open after being hit on the left rear panel." • "Car was in a rear-end crash and the hatch latch opened." • "While driving and when car is parked, rear hatch latch opens." • "Rear latch gate came open during an accident."

5. Fuel: fuel injection system, stalling, hesitation. • "Engine stalling problems; defect in fuel injection system." • "Intermittent stalling, vapor lock." • "Have had lots of problems with engine hesitating, almost stalling; had dealer check it out 3 times." • "Engine stalls periodically without warning, primarily due to a faulty fuel injection system." • "Vehicle bogs down or stalls after a hot restart; also emits noxious odors and smokes occasionally."

6. Engine: leaks, failure. • "The 'overheat' light for engine reading constantly came on; replacement." • "Engine problems; overheating and cracked head." • "Head gasket leak." • "Engine oil leak; replaced gaskets." • "Engine blew soft plug, throwing oil all over engine."

DODGE TRUCK CARAVAN 1988

Complaint Severity: Minor. **Recall Alert:** See Recall Index. **Buyer's Summary:** The fuel pump has received complaints. Make sure it doesn't make excessive noise and that you are experiencing adequate engine performance. Also, look for leaks. The fuel injection system has been blamed for hesitation and stalling. Be sure the vehicle doesn't die in traffic or at stops. The steering may be stiff or not working correctly. Be sure to test the steering, especially on a cold start. Check the brakes—listen for noise, look for leaks and feel for vibration. They may fail, perform poorly or require frequent mechanical attention. Test the transmission thoroughly.

Hot Spots and Owner/NHTSA Comments:

1. Power train: transmission: automatic, poor performance, difficulty shifting, slipping. • "Vehicle shakes between 50 and 60 mph; problems with transmission, universal joints, drive shafts and torque converter." • "Transmission defect; problem with automatic shifting into reverse from neutral or drive position, car jumps and makes clanging noise." • "Automatic transmission failed at 5,000 miles, slipping occasionally." • "Problem with transmission slipping out of gear; left van with gear in park and ignition on, van moved backwards and stopped after smashing into a tree." • "Runaway vehicle when transmission slipped out of park and van collided with house across street."

2. Steering: gear: rack-and-pinion, stiffness, poor performance. • "Lost all power steering fluid; complete steering rack-and-pinion unit damaged internally." • "Steering malfunctioning due to fluid leaking from rack-and-pinion steering unit; repaired." • "Repeated failure of rack-and-pinion unit; has been repaired/replaced 3 times; also, power steering pump has failed twice." • "Two bolts supporting rack-and-pinion steering were missing, and 2 were loose; caused leakage of seal and loose steering." • "Rack-and-pinion on power steering failed prematurely, oil seal leak letting air into hydraulic system."

3. Fuel: fuel pump, stalling, malfunction. • "Stalling problem; replaced faulty fuel pump, upon inspection found electrical connections on fuel pump body scorched black." • "Fuel pump malfunctioned 4 times and was replaced." • "Fuel pump vapor locks." • "Electric fuel pump noisy; found electrical connection to electric motor not insulated, but just friction-fitted together." • "Vehicle shuts down due to faulty fuel pump."

4. Structure: hatchback locks and latches, malfunction, failure. • "Rear hatch latch failed, causing liftgate to open with no warning while driving, sending all cargo out." • "While driving, experience intermittent liftgate latch failure when latch suddenly disengages; once this happens it's very difficult to lock." • "The rear hatch latch makes noise, rattles when going over bumps, indicating that the latch is not holding it tight." • "While driving, noticed rattling sound coming from rear, indicating liftgate was loose; finally had to have dealer replace latch mechanism at own expense." • "Rear tailgate will not open with key or force, but when driving along and hit a bump, gate comes open."

5. Brakes: hydraulic system, corrosion, failure. • "When at a stop, brake pedal pumps itself down to the floorboard and brake light sometimes comes on." • "Experiencing brake problems, vehicle unsafe to drive; repaired/replaced front rotors and rear brakes." • "Brake suddenly became weak; rubber parts of brake system had corroded due to contamination of system." • "Complete brake repair 4 times in 2 years." • "Under wet conditions braking not effective, does not stop without several applications of brakes, works fine in dry weather."

6. Fuel: fuel injection system, stalling, hesitation. • "Engine revs wide open when started normally, whether engine warm or cold." • "Engine not running properly, quitting in cold weather; malfunction in fuel system." • "Intermittent stalling and/or hesitation." • "Recurring engine stalling problem with complete loss of steering and brakes due to electronic fuel injection failure." • "In hot weather, after a half-hour driving, engine goes out if decelerate and then try to accelerate."

DODGE TRUCK CARAVAN 1989

Complaint Severity: Negligible. **Recall Alert:** See Recall Index. **Buyer's Summary:** Look carefully for any kind of leakage, especially under the car. Check the brakes—listen for noise, look for leaks and feel for vibration. They may fail, perform poorly or require frequent mechanical attention. Test the transmission thoroughly.

Hot Spots and Owner/NHTSA Comments:

1. Power train: transmission: automatic, poor performance, difficulty shifting, slipping. • "When driving at 55 mph, vehicle would downshift into 1st or 2nd gear, causing high rpm without driver manually shifting." • "Transmission locks up periodically when driving at any speed or after being parked." • "Transmission shifted into 2nd gear and will not shift out of it until engine is shut off or vehicle stops." • "Vehicle will downshift while driving; also, transmission will lock up in 1st gear." • "Gear sheared off in the automatic transmission, resulting in vehicle being inoperative, replaced once, needs to be replaced again."

2. Engine: fire, premature failure. • "Defective engine gaskets and valve cover; recall related." • "Water entered engine air intake, broke pistons, causing engine failure." • "Vehicle caught fire while parked and burned beyond repairs." • "Vehicle lost all oil while driving; incorrect filter used, was too loose, Chrysler filter should have been used; engine destroyed." • "Replacement of engine gasket, valve cover and gasket on a continuing basis."

3. Engine: gaskets: valve cover, leaks, fire. • "Owner was driving along when all of the lights came on and vehicle stalled. Later, owner found that a head gasket had blown." • "Dislocation of engine cylinder head gasket allows engine oil leakage; repaired/replaced valve cover gasket, recall campaign initiated." • "Faulty valve cover seal leaking oil in engine, causing fire; recall notice received two weeks after car burned." • "Recall for 1989 4-cylinder 2.5L engine, defective cylinder head gasket; oil leaking from gasket, should be repaired, chance of fire." • "Oil leak from engine gasket creates potential risk of fire."

4. Structure: hatchback locks and latches, malfunction, failure. • "Rear hatch latch pops open without warning while driving." • "Driving along when rear hatch popped open; contents spilled on the highway." • "When hit even a bump the latch would disengage, allowing rear hatch to fly up; latch has been replaced 3 times." • "Rear liftgate problems. When hatch is closed it appears to be locked, but is not." • "Consumer was driving at 45 mph and rear hatch latch came open."

5. Structure: door assembly, malfunction, failure. • "Right passenger-side door opens when driving at any speed. Repaired 13 times. • "Side sliding door fell off at 3 rollers on the corners, being held on by 1 roller." • "Having difficulty opening side door, will not open from inside or outside." • "The sliding door doesn't close well; has almost fallen off and cannot be opened." • "Front door passenger-side door jams, will not open inside or outside with handles."

6. Brakes: hydraulic system, locking up, noise, excessive wear. • "Brakes locked up when driving above 15 mph; resulted in an accident." • "Brakes lock prematurely upon application, resulting in skidding and long stopping distances." • "Brakes noisy; repaired, problem continues." • "Rear wheel cylinders leaked, master cylinder failed." • "Front and rear brakes wear excessively, causing erratic operation."

DODGE TRUCK CARAVAN 1990

Complaint Severity: Typical. **Recall Alert:** See Recall Index. **Buyer's Summary:** Look carefully for any kind of leakage, especially under the car. Check the brakes—listen for noise, look for leaks and feel for vibration. They may fail, perform poorly or require frequent mechanical attention. Test the transmission thoroughly.

Hot Spots and Owner/NHTSA Comments:

1. Power train: transmission: automatic, poor performance, difficulty shifting, slipping. • "Auto transmission failure; rebuilt and replaced 5 times since purchasing new in 1990." • "Automatic transmission (4-speed): After 36,000 miles, transmission slipped from drive to neutral; would not downshift; at times violently downshifts at various speeds." • "Automatic transmission failure; has been rebuilt 3 different times." • "Automatic transmission: While driving, any speed, gear will downshift to 1st gear on its own; locks up; abruptly slows down vehicle; could cause accident." • "Automatic transmission failure; when shifting into gear, vehicle lurches forward."

2. Structure: hatchback locks and latches, malfunction, failure. • "Rear liftgate has opened while driving due to latch failure." • "Rear liftgate doesn't stay up in open position." • "While driving at 55 mph, back latch popped open." • "While driving, experienced rear liftgate failure; when latch mechanism disengages, hatch pops open; as a result child strollers were flung out onto road 2 times."

3. Structure: door assembly, failure. • "Sliding passenger door fell off while trying to close it." • "The sliding door bolt came off." • "Side sliding door fell off." • "Side sliding door fell off completely; put it back on the track and replaced a screw." • "Side sliding door fell off the rail."

4. Brakes: hydraulic system, locking up, failure. • "Van suddenly spun around while braking; loss of control, accident 2 times." • "Rear brakes would overheat and lock." • "Right front and left rear wheels lock up upon application of brakes in emergency situations, occurs only under light vehicle loads." • "Brake failure caused accident." • "Brakes spongy, pedal goes to floor."

5. Structure: hatchback assembly, malfunction, failure. • "Rear liftgate opened on it own, while driving on the highway." • "Vehicle's tailgate tends to open while driving on bumpy surfaces, cargo falling out." • "Rear hatch has opened completely 4 times. Dealer tightened latch mechanism. Owner describes popping and/or rattling sound." • "While driving 20 mph on 2 occasions, suddenly rear hatchback popped open." • "Rear liftgate opened on its own while driving over railroad track; warning light did not come on; speed 20 mph."

6. Engine: leaks, fire. • "The engine light keeps going on; dealer can't find problem." • "Engine leaks oil and overheats." • "While parked in driveway, engine caught on fire, cause unknown; van was totaled." • "Unit supposed to be tow vehicle, but with a boat and trailer, which weighs about 1,300 pounds, car heats up."

DODGE TRUCK CARAVAN 1991

Complaint Severity: Typical. **Recall Alert:** See Recall Index. **Buyer's Summary:** The airbags in this vehicle have experienced failures and malfunctions: You may need a professional evaluation on the condition of the airbags. Check the brakes—listen for noise, look for leaks and feel for vibration. They may fail, perform poorly or require frequent mechanical attention. Test the transmission thoroughly.

Hot Spots and Owner/NHTSA Comments:

1. Brakes: hydraulic: anti-skid system, poor performance, failure, locking up. • "Antilock brake system failure resulted in extremely hard braking, pedal pressure needed to stop vehicle." • "High-pressure hose failed, leaking all brake fluid." • "Driving down steep hill with 1½-inch snow, antilock brakes failed, ran into house at bottom of hill; recall work done on antilock brake system hose." • "When brakes were applied, they locked up, could not depress the pedal." • "While driving at 30 mph, driver suddenly applied brakes and only received response from the left front brake."

2. Power train: transmission: automatic, poor performance, difficulty shifting, slipping. • "Transmission; replaced 3 transmissions at 35,000 miles, second at 76,000 miles." • "Four-speed overdrive. Transmission slips out of gear, it will not go over 40-45 mph." • "Transmission slips upon acceleration, also locks in 2nd gear." • "The transmission locks up. When it goes into 2nd gear it gets rough and starts to work erratically."

3. Brakes: hydraulic system, premature failure. • "While driving, brakes malfunctioned because connection to master cylinder blew off, with immediate loss of brake fluid." • "First time brakes are applied nothing happens, have to pump brakes." • "Applied brakes, no response from the braking system." • "Brake pedal would not depress." • "Complete brake failure on 6 different occasions."

4. Interior systems: passive restraint: airbag: driver, malfunction, failure. • "Airbag did not deploy during a front-end collision at 55 mph." • "While driving at approximately 2 mph, no impact, airbag deployed. Noticed airbag light coming on intermittently a few days prior." • "Vehicle was involved in a head-on collision and the airbag did not open." • "Airbag did not deploy in an accident." • "Airbag did not deploy during front-end collision; impact 12:00 position; speed 30 mph; driver injured."

5. Structure: hatchback locks and latches, malfunction, failure. • "Rear hatch latch came loose while driving; dealer said switch needs to be rewired." • "Rear latch failure while riding over rough roads or railroad tracks; attempt to repair did not work." • "In a rear-end collision the rear hatch door popped open, spilling contents on the road." • "Rear hatch door fails to latch. Latches after pushing and releasing lock button and slamming hatch." • "Rear latch mechanism is weak, allowing rear door to bounce around."

6. Structure: door assembly, premature failure. • "Sliding side door fell off track upon closing." • "Sliding door fell from vehicle." • "Passenger sliding door fell off onto ground as child shut door; parts seem to be missing from roller and track assembly; no rust involved." • "Front side passenger doors failed." • "Sliding door fell off." • "Misaligned sliding door tread replacement." • "Front passenger's door locks from outside; able to open doors from inside."

DODGE TRUCK CARAVAN 1992

Complaint Severity: Typical. **Recall Alert:** See Recall Index. **Buyer's Summary:** The airbags in this vehicle have experienced failures and malfunctions: You may need a professional evaluation on the condition of the airbags. Check the brakes—listen for noise, look for leaks and feel for vibration. They may fail, perform poorly or require frequent mechanical attention. Test the transmission thoroughly.

Hot Spots and Owner/NHTSA Comments:

1. Brakes: hydraulic: anti-skid system, poor performance, failure, locking up. • "Both antilock brake system and brake light came on, acknowledging failure with no power to brakes." • "On 2 occasions when vehicle was going downhill on wet pavement and brakes were applied, antilock brakes locked up and it was difficult to stop." • "First day of driving experienced brake failure, antilock brake system and red brake lights came on, no stopping when pushing the pedal. Also, speedometer is limited to 47 mph." • "Antilock brake system failed to stop vehicle when applied, crashing into another vehicle at 25 mph. Airbag did not deploy." • "Antilock brakes locked up, causing vehicle to skid sideways during wet conditions."

2. Power train: transmission: automatic, poor performance, difficulty shifting, slipping. • "Transmission fails to shift into gear, also engine revs before 1st gear engages." • "Transmission failed; shifts roughly upon acceleration and/or deceleration." • "Transmission locked up, causing vehicle to come to a sudden stop; accident." • "Transmission intermittently fails to engage when shifted to reverse." • "Transmission locked up and vibrated; replaced, problem continues."

3. Brakes: hydraulic system, poor performance, failure. • "Complete brake failure, had to employ emergency brake to stop vehicle." • "Brakes are not strong enough to provide adequate stopping distance." • "Lost total braking power when applying the brakes." • "Red brake and orange antilock brake system lights come on; 30 seconds later, vehicle has no stopping power. Takes tremendous pushing on brake pedal to stop." • "Brake failure; master cylinder and booster failed, causing accident, impact 12:00 position."

4. Interior systems: passive restraint: airbag: driver, malfunction, failure. • "Airbag did not deploy during front-end collision; impact 12:00 position; speed 30-40 mph; hit a steel light pole." • "Vehicle was involved in a frontal collision and the airbag did not deploy. The rear seat came loose and landed in the middle seat." • "Antilock brake system failed to stop vehicle when applied, crashing into another vehicle at 25 mph. Airbag did not deploy." • "Vehicle was involved in a frontal collision and the driver's-side airbag did not deploy." • "During a frontal collision at approximately 20-25 mph, impact 12:00 position, airbag failed to deploy; driver suffered injuries and vehicle sustained heavy damage."

5. Structure: door assembly, failure. • "Passenger door welds broken; the hinges will not allow door to close all the way, making it hard to open or close." • "Side door of vehicle comes off the track and won't close." • "Sliding door fell off the van while backing out of parking lot." • "Rear gate of the van opened while vehicle was in motion; child fell out and suffered injuries." • "Sliding door has fallen off twice, will not close properly or latch."

6. Interior systems: restraint: belt anchor and attachment, failure. • "Middle right seat belt anchor in van disengaged from floor during accident, resulting in injuries." • "Clip on end of middle seat belt is not anchored properly and comes unclipped, leaving passenger unrestrained." • "Middle seat belt attachment to floor will not stay latched, rendering seat belt unsafe." • "In center section of seats on right-hand side, seat belt disengages at anchor point, allowing passenger to become unrestrained unknowingly."

DODGE TRUCK CARAVAN 1993

Complaint Severity: Typical. **Recall Alert:** See Recall Index. **Buyer's Summary:** The airbags in this vehicle have experienced failures and malfunctions: You may need a professional evaluation on the condition of the airbags. Check the brakes—listen for noise, look for leaks and feel for vibration. They may fail, perform poorly or require frequent mechanical attention. Test the transmission thoroughly.

Hot Spots and Owner/NHTSA Comments:

1. Brakes: hydraulic: anti-skid system, poor performance, failure, locking up. • "Antilock brake system caused extended stopping or became inoperative when applied. Has been serviced 3 times." • "Antilock brake system does not perform effectively when applied, causing extended stopping. Repaired 4 times." • "Erratic operation of braking system caused brakes to stick and sometimes lock up." • "Antilock brake system experienced extended stopping distance when applying brakes." • "Antilock brake system experienced extended stopping distance when slowing down to prevent an accident, impact 12:00 position, speed 20 mph. Airbag did not deploy."

2. Power train: transmission: automatic, poor performance, difficulty shifting, slipping. • "When you pull away from a stop, transmission slips, causing vehicle to hesitate; jerks forward and resumes running." • "The transmission failed after 37,000 miles." • "While traveling 55 mph, automatic transmission downshifted into low gear, slinging occupants forward." • "Automatic transmission out of alignment, causing motor to shift, steering problems, and accelerator gets stuck."

3. Brakes: hydraulic system, noise, pulling, locking up. • "Had to have brake system replaced 4 times within 3 months." • "Antilock brake system: Brake light comes on and off with clicking noise; brakes hard; pulls to left and right; feel of metal to metal; extended stopping; speed normally 40 mph." • "Experienced brake lockup while driving 5-10 mph, impact 1:00 position, airbag deployed, but could not turn wheel to avoid hitting oncoming vehicle." • "Brakes locked up while attempting to brake. Had brake fluid contamination." • "When driving, brake warning light came on, brakes malfunctioned, resulting in excessive stopping distance and in some cases complete brake loss."

4. Interior systems: passive restraint: airbag: driver, malfunction, failure. • "Frontal collision impact, 12:00 position, 40 mph, airbag fumes came out, airbag did not deploy." • "Vehicle was involved in frontal collision, impact 12:00 position position, speed 25 mph; driver's-side airbag did not deploy." • "Airbag partially deployed during front-end collision; speed 35 mph; impact 11:00 position." • "At 35 mph, vehicle hit another vehicle in a frontal collision. Airbag did not deploy. Impact 12:00 position." • "Estimated speed 30 mph upon rear collision. Airbag deployed partially, spewing powdery residue onto driver."

5. Structure: hatchback locks and latches, premature failure. • "In 8:00 position during an accident, rear hatch latch failed, hatch gate opened and everything fell out of car." • "Car was hit in the front, the rear hatch latch came open." • "Consumer was driving and the rear hatch latch failed, hatch popped open; no one was hurt." • "While driving, noticed rattle sound, which meant latch mechanism was loose; dealer fixed once but problem persists." • "Interior light comes on periodically, indicating that rear hatch door is open." • "Rear hatchback latch failed, popped open while driving; no impact involved, child fell out."

6. Electrical system: ignition, stalling, hesitation. • "Vehicle periodically shuts down when making a turn at any speed or degree. Antilock brake system fails to stop vehicle effectively, causing extended stopping, or inoperative." • "Vehicle stalls out without any warning, resulting in no steering and braking ability; replaced cam and crank sensor fuel pump assembly and electrical system to no avail." • "The van hesitates when pulling out from a complete stop." • "Vehicle frequently hesitates, dies, shuts down when driving at any speed. Repaired 5 times." • "While the vehicle is engaged in gear, vehicle will hesitate or totally die."

DODGE TRUCK CARAVAN 1994

Complaint Severity: Very Serious. **Recall Alert:** See Recall Index. **Buyer's Summary:** The airbags in this vehicle have experienced failures and malfunctions: You may need a professional evaluation on the condition of the airbags. Check the brakes—listen for noise, look for leaks and feel for vibration. They may fail, perform poorly or require frequent mechanical attention.

Hot Spots and Owner/NHTSA Comments:

1. Brakes: hydraulic: anti-skid system, poor performance, failure, locking up. • "Antilock brake system failed to stop vehicle effectively while driving 65 mph, causing loss of control, with vehicle flipping over onto right side." • "Antilock brake system: Failure of brakes—don't function as expected. Impact 12:00 position, low speed (5 mph), no deployment of airbag." • "Experiencing long stopping distance after antilock brake system light comes on; dealer cannot locate the problem." • "Vehicle's antilock brake system has had complete brake failure 5 times. On occurrence pedal goes to floor and brake light comes on." • "Antilock brake system: Pedal gets hard with no brakes; on 1 occasion left rear locked up."

2. Interior systems: passive restraint: airbag: driver, malfunction, failure. • "Antilock brake system: Failure of brakes, doesn't function as expected. Impact 12:00 position, low speed (5 mph), no deployment of airbag." • "Frontal collision, impact 11:00 position, speed 30 mph, airbag did not deploy." • "Frontal collision, impact 12:00 position, vehicle was at stop, driver's lap and shoulder belt did not retract, dual airbags did not deploy." • "Dual airbags did not deploy." • "Rear-ended another vehicle, airbag did not deploy. Seat belts did not restrain."

3. Structure: hatchback locks and latches, poor performance, failure. • "Indicator light does not come on when gates open, rear tailgate flew open, ejecting a wheelchair out of the back." • "The rear latch failed, causing rear liftgate to pop open for no apparent reason, causing owner to lose items on the road." • "During rear-end side collision at 15-20 mph, rear tailgate latch failed, causing tailgate door to fly open; belongings inside of vehicle fell out." • "Rear liftgate opened twice when sitting still while opening passenger door without touching rear latch." • "Rear hatchback liftgate latch very hard to latch intermittently; problem with latch."

4. Structure: hatchback assembly, failure. • "Rear liftgate switch on dash failed." • "Rear liftgate popped open while vehicle was still." • "Rear hatchback opened upon an impact from the rear." • "Rear tailgate flew open upon a side impact on passenger rear side; item flew out of the rear of the vehicle." • "The back door continues to stay open and causes the warning chime to keep ringing."

5. Brakes: hydraulic system, failure. • "The brakes failed for the second time in a year, causing the vehicle to roll into a lake." • "When approaching a stop at low speed the brake pedal gives way." • "Was involved in accident due to brake failure." • "While driving at approximately 20 mph, made attempt to slow down, noticed braking power was inoperative, used emergency brakes to stop from hitting another vehicle." • "Owner has problems stopping vehicle; she has to floor the brakes and also use emergency brakes to stop vehicle; Chrysler will not offer her any assistance."

6. Interior systems: passive restraint: airbag: passenger, failure. • "Rear-ended another vehicle, airbag did not deploy. Seat belts did not restrain." • "Passenger's airbag did not deploy during head-on collision." • "Passenger's airbag did not deploy." • "Passenger's airbag on vehicle did not deploy upon head-on collision." • "Head-on collision at 30 mph and passenger's airbag did not deploy."

DODGE TRUCK DAKOTA 1987

Complaint Severity: Typical. **Recall Alert:** See Recall Index. **Buyer's Summary:** Look carefully for any kind of leakage, especially under the car. Test the transmission thoroughly. Test transmission for slipping, locking up and performance. Test the clutch.

Hot Spots and Owner/NHTSA Comments:

1. Power train: transmission: 5-speed and up, difficulty shifting, failure. • "Defective transmission and clutch, no reverse, jumps out of 3rd gear; repaired/replaced gear and 9 others, clutch noise and pedal out, repaired/replaced throwout bearing and 5 parts." • "Five-speed transmission makes noise, won't shift properly while truck in gear and emergency brakes on; vehicle rolled, hit a car." • "Clutch pedal squeaks and slips; replaced; jumps out of 3rd gear, oil leak in transmission case, pops out of reverse; replaced rear housing; hard shifting." • "Difficult to shift transmission into 1st and reverse gears, must shut off first. Replaced 3 clutches, 2 transmissions, 2 pressure plates, 2 bearings, problem still exists." • "Irregular shifting in 5-speed transmission, doesn't shift properly, gears grind going from 1st to 2nd, extremely difficult to get into 3rd gear."

2. Power train: transmission: automatic, poor performance, difficulty shifting, slipping. • "Unattended truck left in park. Jumped out of gear into reverse. Accident." • "Transmission in park, left idling, transmission slipped into reverse; truck proceeded out driveway." • "Transmission makes loud noises when shifting to reverse." • "Malfunction in transmission, bumped gearshift, truck went out of park and rolled down driveway." • "Parked truck moved backwards with transmission in park."

3. Power train: clutch assembly, difficulty shifting, excessive wear. • "Transmission would not shift without grinding noise, shifting of gears, worse in cold; replaced clutch and throwout bearings." • "Malfunction in clutch assembly, clutch stiff after sitting 4 days in cold weather, clutch assembly popped and fell off in attempt to shift gears." • "Continuous clutch problem, experienced difficulty shifting until clutch progressed to total decay, debris from clutch throwout bearing fouled starter." • "Vehicle requires constant shifting, causing wear on clutch, U-joints and gears; overdrive useless." • "Clutch had a problem engaging; repaired/replaced."

4. Engine, noise, leaks, failure. • "Oil pump failure caused engine to blow out; replaced valves." • "Vehicle lost power due to blown motor." • "Engine has loud knocking noise when engine cold." • "Oil leaks; repaired/replaced new valve cover, oil pan gasket and new timing chain gasket."

DODGE TRUCK DAKOTA 1988

Complaint Severity: Typical. **Recall Alert:** See Recall Index. **Buyer's Summary:** The fuel injection system has been blamed for hesitation and stalling. Be sure the vehicle doesn't die in traffic or at stops. Check the brakes—listen for noise, look for leaks, feel for vibration. They may fail, perform poorly or require frequent mechanical attention. Test the transmission thoroughly. Test transmission for slipping, locking up and performance.

Hot Spots and Owner/NHTSA Comments:

1. Fuel: fuel injection system, stalling, hesitation. • "Vehicle has no power from stop signs or park, whether truck is warm, cold or in between." • "Motor stalls without warning, will not start for a few minutes, will then start and stall again, intermittent problem; changing computer chips hasn't helped." • "Truck producing very low mileage; problem with fuel injection system." • "Vehicle loses power steering when engine stalls; it just fades out."

2. Power train: transmission: automatic, poor performance, difficulty shifting, slipping. • "Problem with vehicle moving while transmission is in park; parked truck in front of garage, about an hour later it rolled into the garage door." • "Transmission jumps out of gear; won't go into reverse 50 percent of time." • "Jumps out of gear when lever indicator still on park with engine running." • "When shifting from park to reverse and from reverse through neutral to drive, not smooth as should be, clunks hard." • "Vehicle jumps from park position; lockup converter replaced."

3. Electrical system: ignition, stalling, hesitation. • "Ignition module failed." • "Ignition system problems; electronic control module and distributor replaced after much irritation." • "Vehicle stalling in traffic when coming to a stop or when accelerating, taking 2 to 20 minutes to restart; serviceman states needs pickup plate." • "Engine shuts itself off, causing the steering to lock up." • "Engine hesitation problems, 'check engine' light comes on and engine just cuts out."

4. Engine, noise, poor performance, leaks. • "Poor performance of engine, engine lacked power, acceleration rough." • "Problem with noises in motor." • "Valve tapping reoccurring sporadically; engine idle is rougher after having been repaired." • "Engine was clicking, missing and running erratically with severe loss of power; discovered leak in engine head cylinder valve guide; head needed to be replaced."

5. Brakes: hydraulic: shoe: disc brake system, vibration, noise, premature failure. • "Front brake rotors and pads wore out, causing pulsation. Rotors and pads were replaced." • "While making a fast stop, brakes failed, pedal went all the way to the floor." • "Front brake system had to be replaced, loud squealing noise, rotors developed grooves; cannot be fixed due to metallic brake pads." • "Front disc brakes freeze on constant pressure, causing brake to wear until broken; accident resulted due to brake failure."

6. Power train: transmission: 5-speed and up, difficulty shifting, poor performance. • "Transmission pops out of 3rd gear, mostly when decelerating; hard shifting and grinds going into reverse; replaced clutch assembly." • "Chronic problems with manual transmission during cold mornings, shift lever would not stay in 1st or 3rd gear, requires holding until fluid warms." • "Vehicle jumped out of reverse gear when towing small camper; repaired several times, still jumps out of 1st and reverse gears." • "Truck hard to shift from 1st to 2nd, 2nd to 3rd gear; intermittent; replaced contaminated clutch assembly."

DODGE TRUCK DAKOTA 1989

Complaint Severity: Minor. **Recall Alert:** See Recall Index. **Buyer's Summary:** Look carefully for any kind of leakage, especially under the car. The electronic control unit has been blamed for engine performance problems, including stalling and surging. Check the brakes—listen for noise, look for leaks and feel for vibration. They may fail, perform poorly or require frequent mechanical attention. Test the transmission thoroughly.

Hot Spots and Owner/NHTSA Comments:

1. Power train: transmission: automatic, poor performance, difficulty shifting, slipping. • "Rebuilt transmission, repaired transfer case twice." • "Differential seal and transmission cooler failed, lost fluid on freeway." • "Numerous problems with transmission and drive train." • "Transmission will downshift while vehicle is operating at high speed; defect shows the same character while cruise control is being used." • "Transmission failure; repaired."

2. Brakes: hydraulic system, excessive wear, noise, leaks. • "Calipers failed." • "Brakes acting up, sticking; brake pedal is all the way up, won't push down when applied." • "While driving in traffic, 35 mph, went to apply brakes, pedal went to floor; rear-end collision occurred." • "Brake system problems, squeal in rear brakes, leak at rear axle; replaced brakes and rear shoes and turned drums to no avail." • "Premature wear of calipers and rotors due to materials used."

3. Brakes: hydraulic: anti-skid system, poor performance, failure, locking up. • "All 4 wheels locked up upon application of the brakes, vehicle was equipped with Antilock brake system; accident resulted." • "Antilock brakes malfunctioning." • "Antilock brake system failure." • "Antilock brake system failure in the rear; replaced master cylinder and in for repair, wheel cylinder and other broken." • "Rear brakes failure, there is very little braking from the rear brakes, equipped with antilock brake system."

4. Engine: gaskets: valve cover, leaks, fire. • "Valve cover gasket failed prior to and after recall repairs." • "Valve cover gasket replaced twice due to leak, oil sending unit failed; also idler pulley failed, causing vibration." • "Soon after engine cylinder head gasket was repaired/replaced under recall, engine caught fire, resulting in a total loss." • "Engine valve cover gasket cracked, causing oil to leak and resulting in fire in engine compartment." • "Valve cover problem."

5. Electrical system: ignition, stalling, malfunction. • "Vehicle will stall without warning when air conditioning is turned on." • "Malfunction in ignition system." • "Intermittent stalling in traffic." • "Truck will stall randomly while operating. Various dealers have tried to resolve with no satisfaction."

6. Electrical system: ignition: electronic control unit, fire, stalling. • "Vehicle had been driven about 15 miles, under-hood fire after vehicle was parked for 10 minutes. Electronic control module causing electrical short." • "Problem with engine running rough and stalling; serviced fuel injector and replaced computer, all repair attempts to no avail." • "Recurring problem with rough idle, loss of engine power, etc., repaired/replaced throttle position sensor, coolant sensor, etc.; all repair attempts to no avail." • "Computer failure."

DODGE TRUCK DAKOTA 1990

Complaint Severity: Negligible. **Recall Alert:** See Recall Index. **Buyer's Summary:** Look carefully for any kind of leakage, especially under the car. The steering may be stiff or not working correctly. Be sure to test the steering, especially on a cold start. Check the brakes—listen for noise, look for leaks and feel for vibration. They may fail, perform poorly or require frequent mechanical attention. Test the transmission thoroughly. See "Sudden Accelerations" in Introduction.

Hot Spots and Owner/NHTSA Comments:

1. Power train: transmission: automatic, poor performance, difficulty shifting, slipping. • "Transmission does not shift properly." • "Automatic transmission shifting dangerously; when placing gear selector in drive or reverse, produces rapid movement forward or reverse without stepping on accelerator." • "While in overdrive, vehicle seems to downshift at least amount of speed reduction, seems to occur when in cruise control and when driving manually." • "Vehicle gearshift slipped from park to reverse while idling." • "Transmission failed, replaced, replacement transmission leaks."

2. Engine: gaskets: valve cover, leaks, failure. • "Valve cover gaskets leak; recall repairs refused for model date." • "Valve cover gasket defective, leaks out; repaired by dealer." • "Valve cover gasket failed prior to recall." • "Upper and lower head gaskets were replaced." • "Head gasket leak."

3. Brakes: hydraulic: anti-skid system, poor performance, failure, locking up. • "Antilock brake system failed, causing accident." • "Antilock rear brakes; actual skid, did lock and left small skid marks, no safety failure involved, acted like regular brakes; fixed under warranty." • "Noisy antilock brake system; serviced, problem continues." • "Antilock brake system intermittently locks up without warning; locks up and/or slides when coming to stop; nearly caused accident." • "Rear antilock brake system failure, loss of braking at low speeds."

4. Fuel: throttle linkages and control, sudden accelerations. • "Erratic engine rpm; set differently and too high." • "Throttle sticking, ups speed by itself; if left, throttle would start to sputter but keep on going until engine shut off, started back to up." • "Throttle sticks and vehicle accelerates." • "Truck doesn't decelerate fast enough; slows down if gear is put in neutral and hit the brake, but engine still revs too high." • "Upon starting up, vehicle accelerated in reverse, went out of control and hit another vehicle."

5. Steering: gear: rack-and-pinion, stiffness, poor performance. • "Rack-and-pinion came apart from frame while driving." • "While driving, rack-and-pinion ripped loose from the frame; resulted in no steering." • "Rack-and-pinion steering pulled out of K-member, resulting in loss of steering." • "While driving, rack-and-pinion broke, steering was difficult."

DODGE TRUCK DAKOTA 1991

Complaint Severity: Typical. **Recall Alert:** See Recall Index. **Buyer's Summary:** Test the suspension by feeling for vibration or pulling while driving. Check the brakes—listen for noise, look for leaks and feel for vibration. They may fail, perform poorly or require frequent mechanical attention. Test the transmission thoroughly.

Hot Spots and Owner/NHTSA Comments:

1. Power train: transmission: automatic, poor performance, difficulty shifting, slipping. • "Transmission leaking oil." • "The transmission blew up; had to rebuild the transmission at 73,000 miles." • "The truck was in park and shifted into reverse; vehicle lost control, resulting in an accident." • "Transmission will downshift at any speed without warning, some occurrences have caused vehicle to go out of control." • "Automatic transmission jumped out of park into reverse, causing accident."

2. Brakes: hydraulic system, pulling, failure. • "Vehicle pulls to the right upon application of the brakes, problem is more pronounced when brakes are applied." • "When brakes were applied, vehicle pulled to the left." • "Vehicle experienced complete brake failure; with no prior warning, pedal went to the floor." • "When driving on wet surface, brakes, when applied, will cause loss of control." • "Vehicle pulls when brakes applied; also, excessive pressure required to apply brakes."

3. Brakes: hydraulic: anti-skid system, poor performance, failure, locking up. • "The antilock brake system brakes failed at low speed; truck slid on wet road." • "The truck has antilock brake system brakes and has experienced failure. The pedal goes to the floor and has caused an accident." • "Antilock brake system: After backing up, shifting from reverse to drive, brakes locked up. No warning. Releases only after excessive effort." • "Antilock brake on right-hand side of rear wheel locked up." • "Rear antilock brake system will fail between 2,000 and 5,000 miles, repeatedly, causing brakes to lock up."

4. Suspension: independent front, alignment, tire wear. • "Misalignment, causing premature wear of left front tire." • "Muffler rubbed drive shaft." • "Steering pulls when brakes are applied in rain or snow." • "Front suspension bottoms out when on country roads."

5. Brakes: hydraulic: shoe: disc brake system, locking up, excessive wear, vibration. • "Front brakes will pulsate at speeds between 30 and 40 mph." • "Recall repair refused." • "Front brakes lock up and rear wheels would continue to turn." • "Front brakes were crumbling and had to be replaced." • "Antilock brake system worn out prematurely; metal-to-metal rubbing; all brake parts replaced at 33,000 miles."

6. Brakes: hydraulic: disc: rotor: disc hub, vibration, excessive wear. • "Front disc brake rotors are so warped that they cannot be turned. Front end shakes hard when stopping quickly. Could cause accident." • "Brakes pulsate when applied." • "The rotors are laminated and the seals are real bad." • "Front brake rotors failed."

DODGE TRUCK DAKOTA 1992

Complaint Severity: Typical. **Recall Alert:** See Recall Index. **Buyer's Summary:** Verify that the cruise control system works properly, and that it doesn't cause the engine to surge. Check the brakes—listen for noise, look for leaks and feel for vibration. They may fail, perform poorly or require frequent mechanical attention. Test the transmission thoroughly.

Hot Spots and Owner/NHTSA Comments:

1. Power train: transmission: automatic, poor performance, difficulty shifting, slipping. • "Transmission slips and/or drops into low gear." • "Transmission would not shift from 1st gear until warm." • "Transmission slipped out of gear, causing vehicle to roll backwards, resulting in injuries." • "Vehicle moves forward when first started while transmission is in park." • "Vehicle was parked on flat surface, jumped out of gear into reverse, impact 6:00 position, hitting a fence and telephone pole."

2. Brakes: hydraulic: anti-skid system, poor performance, failure, locking up. • "Service lights stayed on, wiring above tires on driver's-side broke, causing fire. Bouncing when braking, antilock brake system. Leaking oil from underneath car." • "When brakes are applied, vehicle literally pulls to left; causes loss of control." • "Vehicle has had continual brake problems. Keeps pulling to the left. Has antilock brake system." • "Antilock brake system is defective, causing long and extended stopping distances and reoccurring pedal going to floor." • "Antilock brake system locked up when applied. Caused very little braking action. Vehicle slid into another vehicle. Impact 12:00 position. Speed 35 mph."

3. Equipment: speed control, malfunction, failure. • "Speed sensor failed twice." • "Cruise control failure." • "Cruise control kicks in on its own, increasing (unwanted) speed; repaired 6 times; could cause accident; difficulty stopping." • "Cruise control engages and disengages by itself with no warning." • "Driving on highway, put cruise control on and the car accelerated; stepped on brake, car still went to 60 mph."

4. Brakes: hydraulic system, noise, locking up, failure. • "When braking, vehicle makes a popping noise and severely vibrates; front brake rotors and pads have been replaced twice, rear drums once." • "A new mirror, seat belt, a muffler and 4 sets of brakes replaced; and grinding noise from rear end." • "Continuous braking failures, causing brakes to lock up, loss of control." • "Brakes repaired 4 times, problem continues."

5. Brakes: hydraulic: shoe: disc brake system, pulling, locking up. • "When brakes are applied, vehicle pulls to left; the pull increases as stops are increasingly violent; dealer could not find problem, is working on it." • "Front brakes stick." • "Brake sticks on right front; repaired, problem continues." • "Truck has been in dealers 15 times due to front brakes locking up and pulling to the right, especially when applied with pulling load." • "Front brake rotors and pads failed, causing vehicle pulsation."

6. Electrical system: ignition, stalling, failure. • "Truck will stall with no warning. Once this happens, vacuum pump and steering is lost. This also caused wheels to lock up. Dealer replaced air injection system part." • "Vehicle stalls after being driven for a period of one hour." • "When slowing down, vehicle will completely lose power." • "Vehicle will not start, intermittently. Dealer bulletin for defect." • "Engine dies while driving at high speed."

DODGE TRUCK DAKOTA 1993

Complaint Severity: Typical. **Recall Alert:** See Recall Index. **Buyer's Summary:** Look carefully for any kind of leakage, especially under the car. Test the suspension by feeling for vibration or pulling while driving. Check the brakes—listen for noise, look for leaks and feel for vibration. They may fail, perform poorly or require frequent mechanical attention. Test the transmission thoroughly.

Hot Spots and Owner/NHTSA Comments:

1. Brakes: hydraulic: anti-skid system, poor performance, failure, locking up. • "Antilock brakes lock up periodically when driving at any speed." • "Rear brakes do not work when there is weight in the truck, resulting in skidding; antilock brake system." • "Front right antilock brake system locked up, causing truck to skid and lose control." • "Antilock brakes locked up 5 times on slick, wet roads, once resulting in an accident." • "Owner complains that the antilock brake system became inoperative without warning on a rain-covered street; the brakes went to the floor, forcing owner into a ditch."

2. Power train: transmission: automatic, poor performance, difficulty shifting, slipping. • "Transmission would not shift into gear after starting. Must be put back into park, then into gear. Also, transfer case (4-wheel drive) broke 4 times." • "Vehicle does not shift into drive gear until shift lever is moved into another gear and then into drive." • "Transmission leak." • "Vehicle stalls and/or surges when shifting into reverse." • "Transmission has been repaired 5 times; truck will not go into gear from park to reverse, makes vehicle difficult to operate."

3. Brakes: hydraulic: shoe: disc brake system, locking up, pulling. • "Front antilock brake system, 2-wheel drive system locks up and fails to stop vehicle effectively when applied. Has been repaired 6 times." • "Front brakes wore out." • "Front brakes on this antilock brake system-equipped truck will smoke after driving 5 miles at 40 mph. Dealer says no problem. Truck does not roll easily." • "Front brakes cause car to pull right while driving and brakes become very hard when braking." • "Front brakes locked up on wet roads, causing loss of control and an accident."

4. Suspension: independent front, alignment, poor performance. • "Left front upper control arm and ball joint separated; speed 65 mph; no prior warning; caused minimum loss of steering control." • "Vehicle lost control in heavy snow, causing accident." • "Poor alignment, causing premature tire wear." • "Front suspension is loose, affects steering ability."

5. Wheels: lugs: nuts: bolts, poor performance. • "Wheel studs are too short, causing insufficient thread engagement." • "Wheel nuts can only be screwed on by one-half of thread length." • "Rear wheel lug nuts too short." • "Wheel studs too short." • "Lug nuts do not hold."

6. Brakes: hydraulic system, stalling, leaks, failure. • "Brakes failed." • "Brakes failed 6 times." • "Upon applying brakes at certain times, brakes fail completely. Brakes also lose brake fluid." • "When decelerating in 2nd gear, vehicle stalls out, causing power steering and brake failure; replaced pickup on the distributor to no avail."

DODGE TRUCK DAKOTA 1994

Complaint Severity: Typical. **Recall Alert:** See Recall Index. **Buyer's Summary:** The steering may be stiff or not working correctly. Be sure to test the steering, especially on a cold start. Test the suspension by feeling for vibration or pulling while driving. The airbags in this vehicle have experienced failures and malfunctions: You may need a professional evaluation on the condition of the airbags. Check the brakes—listen for noise, look for leaks and feel for vibration. They may fail, perform poorly or require frequent mechanical attention.

Hot Spots and Owner/NHTSA Comments:

1. Interior systems: passive restraint: airbag: driver, malfunction, failure. • "During head-on collision, driver airbag did not deploy." • "Airbag did not deploy during frontal head-on collision, speed 35 mph; impact 12:00 position." • "Frontal collision impact 12:00 position, speed 20 mph, airbag did not deploy." • "Upon frontal collision at 45 mph, airbag failed to deploy." • "Car was in an accident; the steering locked up, the airbag didn't deploy in the accident." • "Airbag did not deploy during an accident."

2. Steering: wheel and column, difficulty steering. • "Two steering wheel back cover plugs failed." • "While exiting driveway onto roadway, key became jammed in steering wheel plug rubber grommet hole, locking steering wheel; prior to recall." • "Open groove on steering column catches dangling keys on key ring, switching vehicle ignition off." • "Steering wheel column plugs failed; prior to recall." • "Received recall notice a few weeks after steering problem mentioned in recall occurred; seeking reimbursement, charged by dealer to look at vehicle."

3. Brakes: hydraulic: anti-skid system, poor performance, failure, locking up. • "Antilock brake system: When applying, system fails to stop. Brakes replaced twice." • "Rear antilock brake system malfunction; while going downhill, brake pedal faded to the floor; dealer cannot locate problem." • "Antilock brake system: When applying brakes, experience a very hard pull to left and front wheel locks up." • "Steering wheel lockup while driving; no response from the antilock braking system." • "While driving at approximately 10-20 mph, in panic stop front wheel locked up, caused vehicle to swerve and hit a parked vehicle; during accident antilock brake system light came on."

4. Electrical system: ignition, stalling, failure. • "Truck has been in the shop about 10 times; it backfires, will not start, truck just dies." • "Truck will stall with no warning. Problem evaluated and repaired numerous times with no change in condition." • "Vehicle stalls without warning when going from reverse to drive." • "Truck has complete engine failure, shutting down at any time; problem not replicated by dealer."

5. Suspension: independent front, pulling, alignment, noise. • "Vehicle pulls to the right." • "When vehicle is at idle speed and at complete stop, it experiences vibration and poor acceleration when taking off." • "Front end misaligned." • "Noisy front suspension." • "Traveling 20 to 25 mph, vehicle vibrates, causing poor steering control."

6. Steering: column, locking up, failure. • "Steering wheel column locks up with no warning." • "There was a recall on steering column; recall done and still experienced the same problem." • "Steering column failed after recall repairs; plug sent by dealer did not remedy defect, vehicle was almost involved in an accident." • "Key jammed in steering column, shutting ignition off due to ignition switch being too closely situated to wheel; prior to and after recall repairs."

DODGE TRUCK RAM 1987

Complaint Severity: Troublesome. **Buyer's Summary:** Test the transmission thoroughly. See "Sudden Accelerations" in Introduction.

Hot Spots and Owner/NHTSA Comments:

1. Power train: transmission: automatic, poor performance, difficulty shifting, slipping. • "Problem with van rolling after it has been placed in park and ignition turned off; happens almost daily." • "Transmission does not lock when key out of ignition, 5-year-old put truck into drive, went forward and crashed." • "Automatic transmission failure at 53,000 miles." • "Transmission slips going into high gear; repaired/replaced transaxle assembly and torque converter." • "Stopped to put vehicle into garage, vehicle jumped gear from park to reverse; knocked down driver, who sustained injuries."

2. Fuel: throttle linkages and control, sudden accelerations. • "Problem of sudden acceleration, cannot stop truck with brakes, need to put gear in park and take out keys." • "When shifted into drive, vehicle shot forward at high rate of speed; hit parked car." • "Accelerator pedal sticks for up to 60 seconds intermittently." • "Uncontrollable acceleration, takes 15 to 20 minutes for engine to cool down."

3. Visual systems: glass: window: rearview back light, poor performance. • "Rear window appears to show images not actually there, cars in front appear to be in back when looking through rear window, also appears in rearview mirror." • "Rear windows create 3-dimensional effect in rearview mirror." • "Rear window reflects light onto rearview mirror; poor visibility." • "Rear window reflects objects from front of vehicle into rearview mirror, making it very confusing."

DODGE TRUCK RAM 1988

Complaint Severity: Typical. **Buyer's Summary:** Test the transmission thoroughly.

Hot Spots and Owner/NHTSA Comments:

1. Power train: transmission: automatic, poor performance, difficulty shifting, slipping. • "Transmission slipped out of park into reverse; crushed person's leg against wall." • "Three transmission repair jobs in 5 months." • "Transmission slipped into reverse after idling for 10 minutes in park." • "Ignition locks in park, does not have to be in park to turn ignition off, can turn it off to lock, with shifting lever in any gear." • "Transmission jumped out of gear, causing accident and injuries."

DODGE TRUCK RAM 1989

Complaint Severity: Negligible. **Recall Alert:** See Recall Index. **Buyer's Summary:** Test the suspension by feeling for vibration or pulling while driving. Test the transmission thoroughly.

Hot Spots and Owner/NHTSA Comments:

1. Suspension: independent front attaching mechanisms: stabilizer bar, premature failure. • "Stabilizer bar bolt loose." • "Bracket connecting right side stabilizer bar to frame broke."

2. Power train: transmission: automatic, poor performance, difficulty shifting, slipping. • "Transmission engages harshly when shifting from park or neutral to drive, with engine at normal curb idle; repaired 5 times to no avail." • "Transmission lunges van with every shift." • "Transmission failed." • "The transmission quit while driving."

DODGE TRUCK RAM 1990

Complaint Severity: Typical. **Recall Alert:** See Recall Index. **Buyer's Summary:** Test the transmission thoroughly.

Hot Spots and Owner/NHTSA Comments:

1. Power train: transmission: automatic, poor performance, difficulty shifting, slipping. • "Transmission problems." •

"Transmission automatically shifted from park to reverse 3 times, once resulting in an accident." • "Gear indicator jumped from park to reverse while vehicle was parked on level ground and unattended; rolled backwards into a fence." • "Engine running, transmission in park, truck moved forward, hitting tree; found lever in reverse position." • "Transmission slipped out of drive into 2nd while driving; in park for 1-2 minutes, suddenly moved forward, hitting tree; found in reverse."

DODGE TRUCK RAM 1991

Complaint Severity: Harmless. **Recall Alert:** See Recall Index. **Buyer's Summary:** The fuel pump has received complaints. Make sure it doesn't make excessive noise and that you are experiencing adequate engine performance. Also, look for leaks. Verify that the cruise control system works properly, and that it doesn't cause the engine to surge. Test the suspension by feeling for vibration or pulling while driving. Check the brakes—listen for noise, look for leaks and feel for vibration. They may fail, perform poorly or require frequent mechanical attention. Test the transmission thoroughly.

Hot Spots and Owner/NHTSA Comments:

1. Fuel: fuel pump, failure, poor performance. • "Fuel pump in vehicle engine has metal shavings getting into fuel lines and clogging them. Tow package. Lights melt wiring harness." • "Fuel gauge not reading the same as tank. Replaced fuel pump first time, other problems happened 7 more times relating to fuel pump." • "Fuel pump failed, causing starting difficulty." • "Recall repairs for diesel fuel pump; failed 4 times due to use of rebuilt pumps." • "Diesel fuel pump failed 4 times after recall repairs."

2. Power train: transmission: automatic, poor performance, difficulty shifting, slipping. • "Transmission repaired 3 times; also leaks fluid." • "Vehicle was parked with ignition shut off and keys removed, 2-year-old shifted gear from park to reverse; truck rolled, hitting a vehicle." • "Transmission lunges forward, causing injuries." • "Defective speed sensor on automatic transmission."

3. Brakes: hydraulic: anti-skid system, poor performance, failure, locking up. • "Antilock brake system light comes on. Once illuminated, brakes lose 80 percent capability. Dealer is aware of problem, but doesn't know the cause." • "Antilock brake system failed while vehicle was climbing snow-covered hill." • "Intermittent antilock brake system failure." • "Brakes lock on and off when stepping on the brake pedal; antilock brake system." • "When driving at speeds lower than 45 mph, the brakes fade and the lights come on."

4. Brakes: hydraulic system, premature failure. • "Owner complains of brake problems since February 1994." • "Continuous brake failures; hard pedal during cold weather, also brake light and antilock lights come on." • "Master cylinder failed." • "Complete brake failure while backing out of driveway."

5. Equipment: speed control, malfunction, failure. • "Intermittent failure of cruise control, decelerating vehicle abruptly." • "Cruise control failure." • "Speed control sensor replaced." • "Problems with speed sensor."

6. Suspension: independent front, pulling, alignment. • "When driving the vehicle veers to the left or right." • "Front end has a defect; vehicle leans by cab." • "Cushion keeping metal from contacting metal not properly installed."

DODGE TRUCK RAM 1992

Complaint Severity: Harmless. **Recall Alert:** See Recall Index. **Buyer's Summary:** The fuel pump has received complaints. Make sure it doesn't make excessive noise and that you are experiencing adequate engine performance. Also, look for leaks. Check the brakes—listen for noise, look for leaks and feel for vibration. They may fail, perform poorly or require frequent mechanical attention. Test the transmission thoroughly.

Hot Spots and Owner/NHTSA Comments:

1. Brakes: hydraulic: anti-skid system, poor performance, failure, locking up. • "The pressure pump that holds the main cylinder was defective, resulting in antilock brake system and brake light staying on and loss of brakes." • "Overheating of brakes, antilock brake light stays on; finally brakes were completely gone." • "Antilock brake system, when applied, don't respond, letting truck continue forward." • "Applied brake pedal, went to the floor; no response from antilock braking system, resulting in extended stopping distance."

2. Power train: transmission: automatic, poor performance, difficulty shifting, slipping. • "Transmission leaking in park." • "Transmission, torque converter and overdrive failed." • "Overdrive transmission fails periodically." • "Transmission became inoperable." • "Magnum 8 engine. Transmission does not shift into gear."

3. Fuel: fuel pump, stalling, failure. • "Recall for injector pump has not been done." • "Fuel pumps failed; also exhaust gas recirculation valve and intake manifold seal replaced." • "Diesel fuel pump recall work not performed due to unavailability of special tools." • "Vehicle stalled, mechanic discovered that fuel pump wiring was smoldering, grommet was not in place."

DODGE TRUCK RAM 1994

Complaint Severity: Typical. **Recall Alert:** See Recall Index. **Buyer's Summary:** Look carefully for any kind of leakage, especially under the car. Test the suspension by feeling for vibration or pulling while driving. The airbags in this vehicle have experienced failures and malfunctions: You may need a professional evaluation on the condition of the airbags. Check the brakes—listen for noise, look for leaks and feel for vibration. They may fail, perform poorly or require frequent mechanical attention. See "Sudden Accelerations" in Introduction.

Hot Spots and Owner/NHTSA Comments:

1. Brakes: hydraulic: anti-skid system, poor performance, failure, locking up. • "Antilock brake system locked up, resulting in accident, and driver airbag did not deploy." • "The gear in the rear end was altered, which affected the speedometer and caused antilock brake system to burn out." • "Replaced master cylinder, the front rotor was replaced; antilock brake system, when pressing on brake, you can feel the wheel locking up." • "Owner says while driving about 85 mph, antilock brakes fail, squeak and feel soft; also, master cylinder leaks." • "While driving, experienced intermittent brake failure; upon applying brake, action seems to be inadequate, vehicle continues to roll forward and wheels lock."

2. Suspension: independent front, leaks, alignment, pulling. • "Vehicle shimmies and leaks. If struck from the rear could result in vehicle fire." • "Steering wheel locked up while attempting to make a right turn, causing loss of control and accident; prior to recall due to suspension failure." • "Front end misalignment, causing premature wear of tires." • "Auto pulls to the right when brakes are applied and could cause an accident if someone is driving close." • "Vehicle rides very rough; when turning wheels to right or left, can hear noise, can feel in hands and arms when driving over uneven surface; entire replacement needed."

3. Visual systems: glass: windshield, cracking. • "Front windshield cracked due to stress." • "Stress cracks occurred on windshield." • "Windshield replaced twice due to distortion, causing poor visibility." • "Front windshield cracked very easily; hit by a small stone thrown up by another vehicle; speed 35 mph." • "Front windshield cracked; replaced 2 times within 1 year; caused by stress, according to auto mechanic; no other apparent reason."

4. Interior systems: passive restraint: airbag: driver, malfunction, failure. • "Upon impact, during frontal crash at approximately 45 mph, 12:00 position on front bumper, airbag failed to deploy; note second accident, frontal crash, in which airbags failed to deploy." • "Airbag did not deploy during front-end collision at 45 mph." • "Antilock brake system locked up, resulting in accident, and driver airbag did not deploy." • "Upon impact, during frontal crash at approximately 35 mph, 12:00 position on front bumper, airbag failed to deploy when vehicle hit broadside."

5. Brakes: hydraulic system, pulling, failure. • "Brakes are spongy, also fail intermittently." • "Vehicle pulls to right when brakes are applied." • "Vehicle slipped into cruise control without cruise control engaged, resulting in it being hard to stop the vehicle; no accident." • "Headlight switch overheats and melts; causes headlights to go out while driving; also, brakes are too small for truck, either overrated or underrated." • "Ongoing braking problems, causing insufficient braking ability; vehicle to pull towards the left."

6. Fuel: throttle linkages and control, sudden accelerations. • "Engine races when braking; appears vehicle is idling high." • "Passing gear would not disengage, which resulted in loss of antilock brake system." • "Vehicle accelerated backwards when put in drive position, resulting in an accident." • "Driving the vehicle at low speed of 10 mph, vehicle went to high idle position, open throttle; to stop the vehicle, turned off the ignition." • "Throttle will stick; cause can't be determined by dealer other than saying it's the floor mat."

DODGE TRUCK RAM 1995

Complaint Severity: Troublesome. **Recall Alert:** See Recall Index. **Buyer's Summary:** The airbags in this vehicle have experienced failures and malfunctions: You may need a professional evaluation on the condition of the airbags. Check the brakes—listen for noise, look for leaks and feel for vibration. They may fail, perform poorly or require frequent mechanical attention.

Hot Spots and Owner/NHTSA Comments:

1. Brakes: hydraulic: anti-skid system, poor performance, failure, locking up. • "Experienced extended stopping distance due to defective antilock brake system." • "The antilock brake system light came on, and the next day the antilock brake system failed, resulting in an accident." • "Antilock brake system: When braking, front wheels lock up; very dangerous during rainy weather; lost control; vehicle skidded." • "While driving, brake action seems inadequate; upon braking, pedal goes almost all the way down before vehicle comes to a halt, extending stopping distance." • "Antilock brake system locked up; vehicle ran into ditch; seat belt did not hold; airbag did not deploy; vehicle totaled."

2. Interior systems: passive restraint: airbag: driver, malfunction, failure. • "Frontal collision, impact 12:00 position, speed 55 mph, airbag did not deploy." • "Broadsided oncoming vehicle and airbag did not deploy." • "Antilock brake system locked up; vehicle ran into ditch; seat belt did not hold; airbag did not deploy; vehicle totaled." • "Driver airbag did not deploy during head-on collision with a tree." • "Involved in a head-on collision and the airbag did not deploy."

Eagle

EAGLE MEDALLION 1988

Complaint Severity: Harmless. **Recall Alert:** See Recall Index. **Buyer's Summary:** Check the brakes—listen for noise, look for leaks and feel for vibration. They may fail, perform poorly or require frequent mechanical attention.

Hot Spots and Owner/NHTSA Comments:

1. Brakes: hydraulic system, noise, premature failure. • "High-pitched metal-on-metal sound when braking in morning, brakes squeal all day; replaced front and rear brake pads, turned rotors." • "Brakes screeching when applied, loud noise continues after disengagement." • "Numerous brake problems; finally brakes failed completely, which caused accident." • "Vehicle fails when stopped during brake applications, almost causing accidents, due to brakes being too small to stop vehicle; components come loose."

EAGLE MEDALLION 1989

Complaint Severity: Negligible. **Recall Alert:** See Recall Index. **Buyer's Summary:** Look carefully for any kind of leakage, especially under the car. Check the brakes—listen for noise, look for leaks and feel for vibration. They may fail, perform poorly or require frequent mechanical attention. Test the transmission thoroughly. See "Sudden Accelerations" in Introduction.

Hot Spots and Owner/NHTSA Comments:

1. Brakes: hydraulic system, excessive wear, noise, failure. • "Brake pedal hard at times and at other times extremely soft; when held down for any length of time, would suddenly drop to floor; continually failing." • "Replaced brakes several times because of wear on rotors; replaced every 10,000 to 15,000 miles. Brake line had been cut; never reconnected wires." • "Braking system defective, brakes stick, squeal, and stopping performance poor; several attempts to repair all to no avail." • "Vehicle experiences a brake problem, brakes were replaced 4 times but still continue to malfunction." • "Wheel cylinders and constant velocity boot broken and leaking, causing brake failure." • "Attorney representing client who has experienced brake problems is requesting information."

2. Brakes: hydraulic: shoe: disc brake system, noise, excessive wear, failure. • "Brakes noisy, grinding; repaired/replaced on 6 occasions, pads, rotors, calipers." • "Caliper, both brake pads and rotors wore out, twice caused front brake failures." • "Design of front brake system is poor, replaced every 7,000 miles." • "Front brake pads worn down to metal, rotors turned; brakes needed repairing again after only 5,000 miles." • "Defective front brakes needed repair, rotors scarred and pads worn down to metal."

3. Fuel: throttle linkages and control, sudden accelerations. • "Accelerator cable defect; cylinder came apart and increased engine rpm instantly." • "Upon starting engine and putting in reverse, accelerated rapidly immediately in reverse, stopping only when it collided with another parked car." • "When shifting into reverse, there was no problem, but in drive, vehicle suddenly accelerated; resulted in an accident." • "Car suddenly accelerated in reverse, rode over 3 railroad ties to top of a bank, rolled over and backed up on its wheels; was in park gear when it landed." • "While engaging vehicle in drive, gear shift locked in reverse and vehicle suddenly accelerated, hitting a pole."

4. Fuel: throttle linkages: accelerator, sudden accelerations. • "Throttle cable broke and was replaced." • "Owner complaining of unavailability of parts for recalled throttle cable; pedal damper replaced at owner's expense for stiff throttle." • "Problem with accelerator cable getting stuck; repaired by dealer." • "Throttle cable malfunctioned when vehicle put into gear to go forward, accelerated at high speed; caused accident." • "Recall notice received for faulty throttle cable; repairs not made due to parts out of stock."

5. Engine: gaskets: valve cover, leaks, failure. • "Problem with numerous oil leaks from valve cover gasket." • "Engine head gasket blown, oil leaking from right side of block onto exhaust pipes; repaired." • "Oil leak problem; head gasket repaired/replaced." • "Engine experienced overheating and oil leakage problems due to blown head gasket; repaired/replaced thermostat, coolant cap and head gasket." • "Replaced head gasket; oil leaking into the coolant caused engine to burn."

6. Power train: transmission: automatic, poor performance, difficulty shifting, slipping. • "Gearshift sticking; repaired." • "Intermittent transmission locked up; many repairs to no avail." • "Transmission rebuilt, main oil seals replaced." • "Transmission slips on hills, leaks." • "Transmission blew up; repaired but still does not change gears properly."

EAGLE PREMIER 1988

Complaint Severity: Harmless. **Recall Alert:** See Recall Index. **Buyer's Summary:** Look carefully for any kind of leakage, especially under the car. Check the brakes—listen for noise, look for leaks and feel for vibration. They may fail, perform poorly or require frequent mechanical attention. Test the transmission thoroughly. See "Sudden Accelerations" in Introduction.

Hot Spots and Owner/NHTSA Comments:

1. Power train: transmission: automatic, poor performance, difficulty shifting, slipping. • "Vehicle shifts irregularly, especially in stop-and-go traffic on flat terrain, difficulties shifting into 4th gear." • "Hesitation upon acceleration, no upshifts; filings in filter, replaced transaxle." • "Internal problems in transmission, vehicle broke down on highway, suddenly lost speed and stopped; whole transmission system replaced." • "Transmission failure occurs, more so in morning than other times. Automatic transmission has a delayed reaction once gear is shifted."

2. Brakes: hydraulic system, premature failure. • "The gas pedal got stuck on the freeway and the brake would not stop the car." • "Defective rotor and hoses." • "Three-car accident; upon braking with both feet at 45 mph with 500 feet stopping distance, brakes never lurched, slid into car; found brakes were completely glazed." • "Replaced brake lines." • "Brakes defective, rotors turned, car pulls when brakes are given full pressure under a stop condition."

3. Interior systems: instrument panel: speedometer: odometer, malfunction, failure. • "Speedometer periodically quits working; repeated service, including replacing wiring harness." • "Electronic speedometer would drop to zero for a period of time no matter what speed vehicle is traveling." • "Vehicle experiences intermittent speedometer/odometer operation problems." • "Speedometer operates erratically, from no reading to fluctuations and improper readings." • "Since new, car has been at dealer's for erratic odometer complaints. Odometer failed at 76,000 miles and has been wrong by over 10 percent. Dealer would not repair."

4. Fuel: throttle linkages and control, sudden accelerations. • "The gas pedal got stuck on the freeway and the brake would not stop the car." • "Vehicle suddenly accelerated, causing loss of vehicle control. Car crashed into an embankment. Throttle stuck open." • "Vehicle suddenly accelerated on its own to an uncontrolled speed; finally threw gear into park and turned off ignition to stop car." • "Sudden unintended acceleration while backing out, engine overpowered brakes for about 40 feet; revving out of control while in park." • "While driving, accelerator stuck in open throttle position, and brakes almost inoperative; no accident."

5. Heater: water: defroster: defogger: heater core: water, leaks, failure. • "Fumes in passenger compartment due to heater core leakage. Recall related, previously repaired." • "Owner received a recall notice for the heater core, but he had no problem with it until he had it serviced for the recall; outcome, heat does not work at all." • "Heater core failed, causing antifreeze fumes and fog to enter passenger compartment." • "Took vehicle in for recall of the cooling system; vehicle has been running hot since then and the air conditioner stays on the blink." • "Heater bypass hose failed, prior to recall, causing vehicle to overheat."

6. Brakes: hydraulic: master cylinder, poor performance, failure. • "Master cylinder defective, affects braking power." • "Master cylinder defective." • "When brake depressed for long periods, pedal goes clear to floor, poor performance of brakes." • "Replaced faulty master brake cylinder." • "Master cylinder failure, brakes keep going downward at stops, hard to keep brakes adjusted."

EAGLE PREMIER 1989

Complaint Severity: Harmless. **Recall Alert:** See Recall Index. **Buyer's Summary:** Look carefully for any kind of leakage, especially under the car. Check the brakes—listen for noise, look for leaks and feel for vibration. They may fail, perform poorly or require frequent mechanical attention. Test the transmission thoroughly. Make sure seat belts function correctly and fit comfortably. See "Sudden Accelerations" in Introduction.

Hot Spots and Owner/NHTSA Comments:

1. Power train: transmission: automatic, poor performance, difficulty shifting, slipping. • "Shifts up and down during deceleration." • "Transmission malfunctioned twice." • "Transmission jerks when put in reverse." • "Vehicle jerks when downshifting while accelerating at steady speed." • "Automatic transmission slips out of gear while driving. Could result in accident.

2. Heater: water: defroster: defogger: heater core: water, leaks, poor performance. • "Windshield has an oily film on inside caused by a leak in the heater core, which also caused antifreeze level to drop." • "Hot coolant leaked into passenger compartment, causing burns to occupants' legs." • "The heater core is leaking; has a recall for heater core bypass, but the heater core is already leaking and dealer won't fix it." • "Owner took vehicle in for recall of the heater core bypass; vehicle began to give trouble; when owner took it back he was asked to pay for the work." • "Heater core bypass failed, prior to recall."

3. Brakes: hydraulic system, vibration, noise, malfunction. • "Severe vibration when brakes applied at speeds of about 45-50 mph; vibration appears to be coming from front wheels, getting progressively worse." • "Repeated problems with brakes fading and grabbing." • "Brake light was on, later brakes malfunctioned which resulted in leaking brake fluid; accident occurred." • "Brakes malfunctioned and were replaced; they still squeak, must apply lots of foot power even when traveling at moderate speeds." • "Received recall on front brake hoses and left rear brake tube; unavailable parts delaying completion of repairs."

4. Power train: driveline universal joint: constant velocity, excessive wear, premature failure. • "Replaced constant velocity joints/boots." • "Right/left constant velocity boot failed prematurely; replaced." • "Constant velocity boot problem, because of structural error, which causes tire wear and alignment problems." • "Front axle joints and wheel bearings went bad; caused by the malfunctioning of the constant velocity boot." • "Replaced right and left outer constant velocity boots, which tore due to leakage."

5. Interior systems: passive restraint: belts, malfunction, poor performance. • "Passenger's motorized seat belt fails to retract; also, seat belt warning light stays on." • "Driver belt stuck, passive restraint will not travel; needs seat motor." • "Driver's automatic safety belt is stuck in restraining position; to release belt must be manually disconnected, making 2 manual connections needed with lap belt." • "Clip that holds buckle onto trolley fails due to possible fatigue. Clips break, affecting operation of shoulder

belt." • "Passenger's side automatic seat belt failed to move into forward position when door was opened."
6. Fuel: throttle linkages and control, sudden accelerations. • "Runaway vehicle; heater control valve hoses stopped the throttle from returning, throttle was fully open, difficulty stopping vehicle." • "Upon putting vehicle in reverse, went forward with force and struck steel post, brakes would not work when applied." • "Engine revved up unusually fast when car was started, shifted into drive, speed was almost uncontrollable during the 5-mile drive." • "When starting up, vehicle initially stalls, then accelerates up to 4,000-5,000 rpm." • "Vehicle suddenly accelerated in reverse, causing an accident."

EAGLE PREMIER 1990

Complaint Severity: Typical. **Recall Alert:** See Recall Index. **Buyer's Summary:** Look for any kind of leakage, especially under the car. Check the brakes—listen for noise, look for leaks and feel for vibration. They may fail, perform poorly or require frequent mechanical attention. Test the transmission thoroughly. Make sure seat belts function correctly and fit comfortably.

Hot Spots and Owner/NHTSA Comments:
1. Heater: water: defroster: defogger: heater core: water, leaks, poor performance. • "Heater core failed, causing engine to leak coolant, prior to recall; also, heater failed to work properly after recall repairs." • "Vehicle involved in recall, dealer repaired the vehicle but did not correct problem." • "Heating system failed, allowing coolant steam into compartment, fogging windows. Driver hit curb while avoiding another vehicle." • "Experiencing fog on windshield and a bad odor inside vehicle after recall repair was done." • "Heater core failed, allowing steam to enter passenger compartment, fogging windshield, resulting in poor visibility and an accident."
2. Power train: transmission: automatic, poor performance, difficulty shifting, slipping. • "Transmission failure." • "Oil leaking from transmission." • "One and a half hours drive time, went into 6-lane intersection and lost the transmission." • "Transmission malfunctioned 3 times; transmission locks up in warm weather." • "Erratic transmission up/downshift, causing power surge or deceleration."
3. Brakes: hydraulic system, failure. • "Repeated brake failure—pedal to floor—replaced master cylinder and tubing but still a problem." • "Brakes failed, causing accident, after hose replaced per recall." • "Rotors replaced." • "Brake problems." • "Brake pedal faded 6 times."
4. Electrical system: ignition, premature failure. • "Ignition relay failed." • "Turning on ignition, it began to smoke and almost caught on fire. Ignition switch and harness had to be replaced." • "Turning on ignition, it began to smoke and almost caught on fire. Ignition and starter had to be replaced." • "Ignition key is designed so that it can be removed without vehicle being in park."
5. Interior systems: passive restraint: belts, uncomfortable, failure. • "Poor design of restraint system; shoulder belt rides up and chafes neck." • "Front shoulder belts poorly designed, strap comes across neck." • "Driver's automatic shoulder belt failed in open position; passenger's failed in closed position; no warning."

EAGLE PREMIER 1991

Complaint Severity: Harmless. **Recall Alert:** See Recall Index. **Buyer's Summary:** Check the brakes—listen for noise, look for leaks and feel for vibration. They may fail, perform poorly or require frequent mechanical attention. Test the transmission thoroughly. Make sure seat belts function correctly and fit comfortably.

Hot Spots and Owner/NHTSA Comments:
1. Brakes: hydraulic: anti-skid system, poor performance, failure, locking up. • "Vehicle experiences intermittent brake lockup on antilock brake system-equipped vehicle; potential for brake failure." • "Antilock brake system intermittently locks, causing vehicle to slide forward." • "Antilock brake system brake failure; on wet surface one wheel locks up, vehicle has no control." • "Car with no warning failed to stop; when antilock brakes were applied, vehicle only slowed down." • "Antilock hydraulic unit, pump and motor failed."
2. Interior systems: passive restraint: belts, poor performance, malfunction. • "Driver's-side motorized belt does not work; have been waiting 5 months for part." • "Passive restraint motor broke, driver's belt does not work." • "Lap and shoulder, motorized shoulder belt will not retract." • "Motorized safety belt retracts when stopping at stop sign. Replaced seat belt system 2 times." • "Driver's automatic shoulder belt is stuck in restraining position."
3. Power train: transmission: automatic, poor performance, difficulty shifting, slipping. • "Transmission failure." • "Transmission failed in the middle of traffic without warning while making a turn; almost caused an accident." • "Automatic transmission slips, sticks in gear, and locks up." • "Transmission failed." • "Transmission has been slipping."

EAGLE TALON 1990

Complaint Severity: Minor. **Recall Alert:** See Recall Index. **Buyer's Summary:** Look carefully for any kind of leakage, especially under the car. Problems with the timing gear and chain can cause serious problems. Have the engine checked by a professional. Check the brakes—listen for noise, look for leaks and feel for vibration. They may fail, perform poorly or require frequent mechanical attention.

Hot Spots and Owner/NHTSA Comments:
1. Engine: timing gear and chain, breaking, premature failure. • "Timing belt broke, causing valves and cylinder head to fail." • "Timing belt broke while driving, causing engine to lock up." • "Timing belt broke twice." • "Timing belt has broken 2 times." • "Broken timing belt caused engine problems."
2. Brakes: hydraulic: disc: rotor: disc hub, excessive wear, vibration. • "Rotors turned." • "Front brake rotors became warped due to defective calipers." • "Rotors have been replaced several times because when brakes are applied, steering shakes." • "Front disc hub failure, extreme vibration upon braking." • "Front brake rotors failed twice."
3. Engine: leaks, noise, fire. • "Front crank seal leaks." • "Oil pump nut failed." • "Grinding and clicking noise in the engine." • "Vehicle caught on fire while it was parked; exact cause of fire unknown."

EAGLE VISION 1993

Complaint Severity: Typical. **Recall Alert:** See Recall Index. **Buyer's Summary:** Check the brakes—listen for noise, look for leaks and feel for vibration. They may fail, perform poorly or require frequent mechanical attention. Test the transmission thoroughly.

Hot Spots and Owner/NHTSA Comments:
1. Power train: transmission: automatic, poor performance, difficulty shifting, slipping. • "Upon stopping at stop light, vehicle will not move in any gear." • "Automatic transmission shifted out of gear while parked." • "While holding foot on brakes, the gear slips." • "Emergency parking brake didn't hold on a hill; car will roll if the transmission is in neutral." • "The transmission failed at 47,000 miles just past the factory warranty."

2. Brakes: hydraulic: disc: rotor: disc hub, excessive wear, vibration. • "Rotors are prematurely warped due to excessive heat; need to be replaced; steering column vibrates when braking from high speed." • "Brakes pulsate due to warping of the brake rotors." • "The front brake rotors keep warping at 10,000 or 11,000 miles, causing loss of control of the vehicle when braking." • "The rotors keep warping and have to be replaced constantly; the metal is too thin." • "Warped front brake rotor."

3. Electrical system: ignition, stalling, premature failure. • "Owner is having problems with the electrical system. It shuts down without warning and comes back without warning." • "Vehicle stalled at least 3 times." • "Key gets stuck in ignition." • "When starting car, it will start on the first and second attempt, but when car turned off and try to start, it will not start; when stopped at light, car started to make noise."

Fleetwood

FLEETWOOD BOUNDER 1990

Complaint Severity: Typical. **Recall Alert:** See Recall Index. **Buyer's Summary:** Test the windsheild wipers. Make sure they work.

Hot Spots and Owner/NHTSA Comments:

1. Visual systems: windshield wiper, poor performance, failure. • "Windshield wipers inoperative." • "Windshield wipers extend too far." • "Windshield wiper failed." • "Windshield wiper fails to clear windshield."

Ford—Cars

FORD CROWN VICTORIA 1987

Complaint Severity: Troublesome. **Recall Alert:** See Recall Index. **Buyer's Summary:** Look carefully for any kind of leakage, especially under the car. Verify that the cruise control system works properly, and that it doesn't cause the engine to surge. The fuel injection system has been blamed for hesitation and stalling. Be sure the vehicle doesn't die in traffic or at stops. Test the suspension by feeling for vibration or pulling while driving. See "Sudden Accelerations" in Introduction.

Hot Spots and Owner/NHTSA Comments:

1. Fuel: throttle linkages and control, sudden accelerations. • "Sudden acceleration; vehicle was in park; when put in gear, vehicle surged forward, hit 2 parked vehicles, impact 12:00 position position." • "Car parked in parking lot; driver turned on ignition; engine accelerated; surged forward, hitting a concrete wall." • "Vehicle had sudden acceleration, slipping from park to reverse and hitting a tree." • "Upon exiting parking lot, car crept up to 55 mph without driver touching accelerator." • "Sudden unexplained acceleration due to defective throttle system, driver lost control and hit wall."

2. Equipment: speed control, malfunction, failure. • "Cruise control engaged and set at approximately 63 mph, brakes failed to disengage until key turned off to shut motor off." • "Second time speed control system fails to disengage when brakes are applied; first repair unsuccessful." • "Cruise control at 55 mph, brake to disengage, surge of speed to 70 mph." • "Gas pedal goes to floor when button pressed, vehicle accelerates quickly." • "While driving at 55 mph, cruise control failed to disengage."

3. Exhaust system, leaks, premature failure. • "Exhaust system not properly aligned, causing spring to wear hole in tailpipes; needs muffler assembly repaired/replaced." • "Police vehicles' carbon monoxide exposure showed higher levels of carbon monoxide while idling, causing headaches and dizziness." • "Seven police vehicles experience exhaust system problems, leakage causing excessive fumes to seep inside vehicle, irritating drivers." • "Significant problems with exhaust system of the 7 patrol cars purchased by sheriff's department; carbon monoxide leak, strong odor and fumes." • "Significant problem with exhaust system, carbon monoxide leak; additional vehicles having similar problem."

4. Suspension: independent front, vibration, alignment. • "Shake and shimmy between 35 and 65 mph." • "Front end alignment problems, resulting in steering problems." • "Steering pulled to the right; aligned front end." • "Suspension problem; front end checked for vibration 4 times, front tire wear." • "Front end seems to be out of line, car wanders left and right; had 3 alignments to no avail."

5. Fuel: fuel injection system, stalling, hesitation. • "Engine failed on different occasions while driving between 45 and 55 mph, restarts after 10-15 minutes." • "Repeated engine stalling at 40 mph and over." • "Engine stalls and cuts out very often; problem supposedly repaired several times, only to come back again." • "Defective fuel sensor."

6. Fuel: fuel systems, fire, stalling. • "The car caught fire in the garage for no reason." • "While parked, approximately 10 minutes later vehicle was on fire; completely destroyed." • "Stalls; no cause and/or cure." • "Engine fire due to defect in fuel system."

FORD CROWN VICTORIA 1988

Complaint Severity: Typical. **Recall Alert:** See Recall Index. **Buyer's Summary:** Verify that the cruise control system works properly, and that it doesn't cause the engine to surge. See "Sudden Accelerations" in Introduction.

Hot Spots and Owner/NHTSA Comments:

1. Fuel: throttle linkages and control, sudden accelerations. • "Vehicle accelerated to approximately 75 mph from 20 mph without warning." • "Accelerator stuck, causing sudden acceleration, no response from brakes; resulted in accident." • "Upon shifting from drive to neutral in parked position, vehicle roared, then surged forward suddenly accelerating out of control; hit a brick building." • "Throttle plate became stuck in wide open position, causing car to accelerate, and only emergency brakes stopped the car." • "Car has sudden acceleration, especially after running for several hours. Idle speed is erratic and will make the car go out of control if shifted into drive."

2. Equipment: speed control, malfunction, failure. • "Cruise control sticks, button fails to stop cruise control." • "Upon starting engine, car accelerated, pressure on brake to control; problem continued when set cruise at 55 mph." • "Unexplained acceleration at under 10 mph, brakes failed when applied." • "Four different occurrences, after stepped on brakes, pressed 'off' switch, vehicle accelerated; cruise control defect." • "Cruise control will not disengage when brakes are applied."

FORD CROWN VICTORIA 1989

Complaint Severity: Typical. **Recall Alert:** See Recall Index. **Buyer's Summary:** Verify that the cruise control system works properly, and that it doesn't cause the engine to surge. Test the suspension by feeling for vibration or pulling while driving. Check the brakes—listen for noise, look for leaks, feel for vibration. They may fail, perform poorly or require frequent mechanical attention.

Test the transmission thoroughly. See "Sudden Accelerations" in Introduction.

Hot Spots and Owner/NHTSA Comments:

1. Power train: transmission: automatic, poor performance, difficulty shifting, slipping. • "Transmission complete failure, doesn't make 3rd to 4th shift properly; received letter from Ford stating transmission will self-destruct if shift pattern not corrected." • "Factory recall on transmission." • "Leak in automatic transmission system." • "Transmission not upshifting into 3rd gear or overdrive." • "Automatic transmission malfunctioned, lost power in traffic."

2. Fuel: throttle linkages and control, sudden accelerations. • "Throttle stuck in open position, causing accident and injuries." • "Car in park position, pulled lever to drive, immediately lunged to a high rate of speed, striking a tree." • "While driving, vehicle suddenly accelerated and went into another car; stopped it by putting gear into park." • "Thirty-minute drive, engine off for 10 minutes, restarted and shifted into reverse, brought sudden acceleration, causing a crash." • "Upon starting car and putting in gear, suddenly accelerated out of control, striking parked car."

3. Brakes: hydraulic system, excessive wear, failure. • "Defective brakes, went to make stop and brakes went to floor, have to pump them part of the time." • "Intermittent brake fade, erratic response occurs, hear vacuum leak near feet, noise changes with varying pressures applied; when noise not present, brakes function correctly." • "Brake pedal would go down to floor/hit bottom when depressed, especially when sitting at light or stop sign." • "Problem with brake cable return spring, resulting in dragging." • "Braking system too small for vehicle size, causing premature brake wear."

4. Electrical system: wiring: harness: under dash, fire, malfunction. • "Internal steering column fire while driving." • "Fire started in the steering column, just below the ignition switch, caused by a short in electrical harness." • "Fire broke out in steering column just below ignition switch." • "Puncture in harness, causing short in system." • "While parked over weekend, horn and windshield wipers activated. Vehicle began to burn from under dash; possible that electrical system under dash triggered fire."

5. Equipment: speed control, malfunction, failure. • "Cruise control would not disconnect when brake was applied." • "Cruise control does not release when brakes are engaged; accelerates without pushing accelerator at times." • "Speed cruise control will not disengage once switch is turned off." • "Intermittent sudden accelerations due to faulty cruise control, which will engage on its own." • "Unexplained acceleration when owner was pulling vehicle into garage. The cruise control engaged and caused vehicle to hit owner's home."

6. Suspension: independent front, tire wear, alignment. • "Problem with front end wandering." • "Front tires wearing down to steel cord within 14,000 miles, required front end alignment." • "Right front tire wearing out, caused by alignment, which does not stay within specification." • "Front end will not hold alignment, tires wear excessively; also, vehicle shimmies." • "Excessive front-end tire wear on outside tread of tire."

FORD CROWN VICTORIA 1990

Complaint Severity: Very Serious. **Recall Alert:** See Recall Index. **Buyer's Summary:** The airbags in this vehicle have experienced failures and malfunctions: You may need a professional evaluation on the condition of the airbags. Check the brakes—listen for noise, look for leaks and feel for vibration. They may fail, perform poorly or require frequent mechanical attention. Test the transmission thoroughly. See "Sudden Accelerations" in Introduction.

Hot Spots and Owner/NHTSA Comments:

1. Fuel: throttle linkages and control, sudden accelerations. • "When shifting into reverse, vehicle accelerated and went out of control, caused accident." • "While approaching light with foot off gas pedal, car accelerated violently; resulted in serious accident." • "When shifting from park into drive, vehicle accelerated. Driver hit vehicles in parking lot." • "While making attempt to back out in reverse, vehicle accelerated out of control, hitting two vehicles." • "Upon putting key into ignition, vehicle suddenly accelerated and crashed into a truck in front; shifted into reverse and stopped vehicle."

2. Brakes: hydraulic system, pulling, locking up. • "Brakes locked up, causing vehicle to go into a skid." • "Vehicle pulls to right when brakes applied." • "Power brakes failed to stop vehicle when applied, causing extended stopping." • "Foot on brake, turned ignition on, vehicle surged forward through a garage." • "Warped front rotor."

3. Interior systems: passive restraint: airbag: driver, malfunction, failure. • "Upon head-on collision at 25-30 mph, driver's airbag deployed but did not inflate; injuries sustained." • "Airbag deployed during accident, leaking fluid into driver's eye." • "Piece off the trailer in front struck the grill area; airbag deployed. Questioned whether airbag came out too easily." • "Airbag deployment was violent, causing driver's arm to be thrown into windshield, shattering windshield and causing injury."

4. Interior systems: passive restraint: airbag, malfunction, failure. • "Airbag deployment was violent in accident, causing injury to face and chest." • "Attorney for consumer says airbag deployment caused hearing loss." • "Only the right portion of airbag inflated on impact, resulting in injuries to driver, impact 10 mph, 12:00 position." • "While driving at approximately 45 mph, vehicle collided with another car, airbag failed to deploy; inspector concluded that it was not a system failure."

5. Power train: transmission: automatic, poor performance, difficulty shifting, slipping. • "When shifting into reverse, vehicle accelerated and went out of control, resulting in accident." • "Hard shifting transmission (clunking noise)." • "Difficult to shift gear to park." • "Problem with transmission shifting roughly; adjusted throttle to no avail." • "Rough shift into overdrive."

6. Communications: horn assembly: horn, poor location. • "Difficult to locate horn in emergency situations." • "Horn buttons are inconveniently located, hard to find in emergency situation." • "Two design failures, the horn and 4-way flashers; main problem can't find horn automatically while turning, when entering intersection and making a turn."

FORD CROWN VICTORIA 1991

Complaint Severity: Very Serious. **Recall Alert:** See Recall Index. **Buyer's Summary:** The airbags in this vehicle have experienced failures and malfunctions. You may need a professional evaluation on the condition of the airbags. Check the brakes—listen for noise, look for leaks and feel for vibration. They may fail, perform poorly or require frequent mechanical attention. Test the transmission thoroughly. See "Sudden Accelerations" in Introduction.

Hot Spots and Owner/NHTSA Comments:

1. Fuel: throttle linkages and control, sudden accelerations. • "Upon shifting gear from park to drive with foot on brake, vehicle suddenly accelerated out of control; caused accident, which resulted in injuries and damage." • "When shifting to drive with foot on brake pedal, car accelerated, jumped curve, hit tree and 2 parked cars." • "Upon shifting gear from park to drive, vehicle suddenly accelerated, causing a front-end collision." • "When attempting to leave from a parking space, car suddenly accelerated and hit another vehicle." • "Car in parking space. Started vehicle, with foot on brake, and shifted into reverse. Vehicle surged 143 feet into a building."

2. Interior systems: passive restraint: airbag: driver, malfunction, failure. • "Car was hit from left rear and airbag did not deploy." • "Airbag deployed, and caused acute bronchitis." • "While driving at approximately 25 mph, rear-ended a stopped car, impact at 12:00, airbag did not deploy; vehicle sustained substantial front-end damage." • "Three police vehicles were involved in head-on collision with impact at 12:00, speed 30-40 mph, airbags did not deploy." • "Frontal collision, speed 20 mph, faulty airbag deployment, airbag deployed a few minutes after the impact."

3. Brakes: hydraulic system, excessive wear, locking up. • "Brakes needed replacing every 3,000 to 5,000 miles due to excessive wear." • "Under hard braking, calipers seem to give to outside, pads wearing on outside from toe to heel; repaired/replaced front pads twice, and rear brakes at 15,000 miles." • "When driving at 60 mph or more, power brakes will lock up when applied, causing loss of vehicle control." • "When shifted into drive, vehicle began to idle and then accelerated, running through wall of garage. Brakes had no effect, but left skid marks through garage." • "Brakes failed twice."

4. Brakes: hydraulic: shoe: disc brake system, pulling, noise, fade. • "When brake pedal is depressed, the front brakes grab." • "Front brakes too small for vehicle size, causing brakes to overheat and fade." • "Front brakes fail to lock, causing extended stopping distance and skidding." • "Car pulls to left when front brakes activated." • "Brake pads separated from the metal, causing a grinding noise, and rotors had to be turned down."

5. Brakes: hydraulic: disc: pads and shoes, vibration, poor performance. • "Under hard braking, calipers seem to give to outside, pads wearing on outside from toe to heel; front brake pads replaced twice." • "Vibration occurs when brakes are applied, problem caused by warped pads; repaired, problem lessened but not eliminated, brake also grabs."

6. Power train: transmission: automatic, poor performance, difficulty shifting, slipping. • "Transmission jumps out of gear and brakes grind." • "Automatic transmission leak." • "Vehicle in park and unoccupied, rolled across 6 lanes of traffic, striking 2 vehicles." • "Transmission is not functioning properly, hard to shift from gear to gear and it is noisy."

FORD CROWN VICTORIA 1992

Complaint Severity: Typical. **Recall Alert:** See Recall Index. **Buyer's Summary:** Check the brakes—listen for noise, look for leaks and feel for vibration. They may fail, perform poorly or require frequent mechanical attention. Test the transmission thoroughly. See "Sudden Accelerations" in Introduction.

Hot Spots and Owner/NHTSA Comments:

1. Brakes: hydraulic: anti-skid system, poor performance, failure, locking up. • "Antilock brake system: Brakes lock up when applied, causing front end to shake and grab, also drag." • "Antilock brake system: When applying brakes, they will not release, causing lockup; to release, stop vehicle and turn engine off." • "While driving, experienced intermittent brake failure when brake pedal went to floor without prior warning; avoided collision with another car, hit a pole." • "Antilock brake system sensor ring and power booster failed." • "Antilock brake system failure due to location of sensor wiring bundles, wheel stops, additional vehicles in fleet with similar problem."

2. Fuel: throttle linkages and control, sudden accelerations. • "After years of sudden acceleration, in a recent attempt to start engine, heard series of clicks, rough idle, then smooth idle. Shifting to reverse caused runaway." • "Automatic transmission: While parked, gear lever in park; got inside car; closed door; car suddenly lurched backwards; stopped after pumping brakes." • "Consumer went to put car into the garage, shifted gear into drive, car accelerated out of control and hit a brick wall." • "Immediately after shifting gear into reverse and brakes applied, vehicle accelerated out of control, resulting in an accident." • "During a 5-minute drive, made a sweeping right turn into a smooth parking lot; no turn signal, no foot on the brake, engine accelerated."

3. Brakes: hydraulic system, pulling, failure. • "Brakes failed, causing accident and injury." • "Vehicle pulls to the right when brakes are applied in a sudden stop, causing loss of vehicle control." • "Brakes malfunctioned; had to pump brakes hard." • "While driving from slow to moderately fast speeds, the brake suddenly engages and quickly decelerates the speed of the car." • "Brake line that goes from master cylinder to rear brakes rubbed against firewall; caused a hole in brake line."

4. Brakes: hydraulic: disc: pads and shoes, excessive wear, vibration, failure. • "Vehicle has experienced excessive premature disc pad failure." • "Brakes pulsating when applied." • "Antilock brake system disc rotors and pads on rear repaired/replaced." • "Right front brake outer pad had improper wear." • "The brakes are failing."

5. Brakes: hydraulic: shoe: disc brake system, excessive wear, locking up, failure. • "Brake rotors and pads wear prematurely." • "At various times, vehicle would suddenly start to downspeed and the brakes would lock up, this would last until stepping on brakes and unlocking them." • "Front brake pads and rotors warped, causing vehicle to shake and rattle as if it had a flat tire; different speeds; no warning." • "Front brake rotors and pads failed." • "Defective brake design caused front disc to hit spindle arm."

6. Power train: transmission: automatic, poor performance, difficulty shifting, slipping. • "Vehicle experienced transmission problems, difficulty in shifting from gear to gear." • "When driving at speed of 20 mph, experience vibration before changing gears." • "Downshift mechanism failed, causing vehicle to prematurely downshift; also surges between 40-45 mph." • "Automatic transmission failure at 47,000 miles." • "Rough transmission, jerks in and out of gears."

FORD CROWN VICTORIA 1993

Complaint Severity: Harmless. **Recall Alert:** See Recall Index. **Buyer's Summary:** Check the brakes—listen for noise, look for leaks and feel for vibration. They may fail, perform poorly or require frequent mechanical attention. See "Sudden Accelerations" in Introduction.

Hot Spots and Owner/NHTSA Comments:

1. Fuel: throttle linkages and control, sudden accelerations. • "Police vehicle oversteering when making rapid turns caused vehicle to skid." • "Sudden acceleration." • "Vehicle speed does not decrease when foot is removed from gas." • "Throttle position sensor failed, causing vehicle to hesitate, buck, jerk and surge."

2. Brakes: hydraulic system, vibration, noise. • "Worn rear brakes scored rotors, causing pulsation." • "The brakes grind and are very noisy." • "Brake pedal went to floor and vehicle jerked." • "Brakes soft and they stick."

3. Brakes: hydraulic: disc: rotor: disc hub, vibration, failure. • "Front brake rotors failed." • "Antilock brake system failure; replaced disc rotors and pads, calipers in front and rear." • "Front brake rotors failed, causing vibration." • "Defective brake rotors caused vehicle to vibrate when braking."

FORD CROWN VICTORIA 1994

Complaint Severity: Typical. **Recall Alert:** See Recall Index. **Buyer's Summary:** The airbags in this vehicle have experienced failures and malfunctions: You may need a professional evaluation on the condition of the airbags. Check the brakes—listen for noise, look for leaks and feel for vibration. They may fail, perform poorly or require frequent mechanical attention. See "Sudden Accelerations" in Introduction.

Hot Spots and Owner/NHTSA Comments:

1. Brakes: hydraulic: shoe and drum system, excessive wear, premature failure. • "Four caliper backing plate bolts loosened, prior to recall." • "Rear brake bushings replaced." • "Nuts and bolts attaching rear brake adapter to axle housing flange loosened and separated, prior to recall." • "Recall repairs refused for rear brake backing plate adapter fasteners due to unavailability of parts." • "Loose backing plate bolts caused rear-end antilock brake system failure."

2. Fuel: throttle linkages and control, sudden accelerations. • " 'Check engine' light comes on, vehicle goes high rpm and into open throttle position." • "Vehicle experienced sudden acceleration 4 times." • "Sudden acceleration." • "While driving, acceleration idler pulley throttle went open throttle position, lost control of vehicle, hitting a brick wall, impact 12:00 position, speed 50 mph."

3. Brakes: hydraulic: shoe and drum wheel cylinders, excessive wear, failure. • "Loose backing plate bolts, causing antilock brake system to fail." • "Dealer doesn't have the parts." • "Backing plate bolts malfunctioned prior to manufacturer's recall." • "Seven police cars. Backing plate bolt came off, shearing remaining bolts and twisted backing plate; destroyed axle housing, brake line."

4. Interior systems: passive restraint: airbag: driver, malfunction, failure. • "Driver's airbag did not deploy." • "Car was in an accident and airbag didn't deploy." • "Police vehicle. Brake light came on, applied brakes driver's-side airbag deployed. Resulted in rear-end collision." • "Driver's-side airbag failed to deploy at right time, impact at 12:00."

5. Interior systems: passive restraint: airbag: passenger, malfunction, failure. • "The airbag on the passenger side came out with such force that the occupant's wrist is broken and her face is badly cut." • "Passenger-side airbag failed to deploy at the right time, impact at 12:00 position." • "Police vehicle. Brake light came on, applied brakes, passenger-side airbag deployed. Resulted in rear-end collision."

FORD ESCORT 1987

Complaint Severity: Typical. **Recall Alert:** See Recall Index. **Buyer's Summary:** The fuel pump has received complaints. Make sure it doesn't make excessive noise and that you are experiencing adequate engine performance. Also, look for leaks. The fuel injection system has been blamed for hesitation and stalling. Be sure the vehicle doesn't die in traffic or at stops. Test the transmission thoroughly. See "Sudden Accelerations" in Introduction.

Hot Spots and Owner/NHTSA Comments:

1. Fuel: fuel injection system, stalling, hesitation. • "When engine is warm it misses, stalls, backfires and dies, it seems upon acceleration not to be getting enough gas." • "Engine would stall without warning and then completely die." • "Repeated fuel injector and line failure, flooding engine with gas, causing engine to stall." • "A short in electrical wire that connects to the injector caused massive fuel component failures." • "Fuel injection system malfunctioning, stalling, hesitation; results in loss of steering."

2. Fuel: throttle linkages and control, sudden accelerations. • "Sudden acceleration; replaced throttle position. Sensor, cleaned shaft and tubes of right rear throttle body, and throttle linkage cable; also stalls between gears." • "Vehicle suddenly accelerated when shifted into drive, hit two parked cars and came to rest." • "Vehicle experiences sudden acceleration when foot off gas pedal, have to brake or clutch to bring rpm down." • "Car spontaneously accelerated on its own with foot off accelerator; replaced throttle position sensor, problem continues." • "Shifted from park to reverse and car accelerated out of control; stopped after hitting a post, knocked driver unconscious."

3. Fuel: fuel pump, stalling, premature failure. • "Defective fuel pump sensing unit failed; caused stalling while in operation, would not restart." • "When driving on highway, engine quit, would not start until cooled off; replaced solenoid twice, fuel pump and regulator." • "Fuel pump failed, possibly due to tank of bad fuel that had clogged fuel filter; replaced." • "Experienced failure of fuel pump while driving, presented rather precarious situation; design flaw of fuel pump." • "While driving, car cuts off; short in electrical fuel pump that is mounted inside fuel tank."

4. Fuel: fuel systems, stalling, fire. • "Engine stalling and strong sulfuric odor both indicate poor fuel and exhaust system malfunctions." • "Car destroyed by fire, was parked in front of residence, received recall notice after fire for fuel line clips." • "Vehicle stalls intermittently, hesitation and/or bucking while driving, usually in 5th gear; fuel shutoff switch replaced, problem back after few months." • "Raw gasoline fumes permeating inside of vehicle while operating at idle or increased speeds, engine cannot be operated with windows opened when air conditioner on." • "Gasoline fumes in the inside of automobile."

5. Power train: transmission: automatic, poor performance, difficulty shifting, slipping. • "Leaking automatic transmission pan gasket." • "Automatic transmission stopped working." • "Automatic transmission slipping." • "Problem with slipping transmission." • "Automatic transmission has erratic shifting problem, shifts like standard transmission."

6. Engine: fire, leaks. • "Excessive oil consumption." • "After acceleration, car began smoking due to fire in engine compartment." • "Head bolt broke, causing antifreeze to come out of engine head." • "Experienced numerous engine problems, engine caught fire while in motion." • "Continual oil leak under hood and in back behind rear seat."

FORD ESCORT 1988

Complaint Severity: Typical. **Recall Alert:** See Recall Index. **Buyer's Summary:** The fuel injection system has been blamed for hesitation and stalling. Be sure the vehicle doesn't die in traffic or at stops. The steering may be stiff or not working correctly. Be sure to test the steering, especially on a cold start. Test the transmission thoroughly. Make sure seat belts function correctly and fit comfortably. See "Sudden Accelerations" in Introduction.

Hot Spots and Owner/NHTSA Comments:

1. Fuel: fuel injection system, stalling, hesitation. • " System malfunctioning, engine stalls at any speed, time and weather; loss of power steering occurs." • "High idling of engine at times, skips, jerks, jumps from 1 rpm to 2 rpm." • "Engine bogs down as though not enough gas from fuel injection, then suddenly revs up very high." • "Fuel injection system failed, car skips, hesitates." • "Defective fuel system, engine stalls intermittently when braking to stop, bucks upon acceleration, surge of speed when fuel system linkage sticks."

2. Fuel: throttle linkages and control, sudden accelerations. • "While driving, engine raced at full throttle, brakes malfunctioned, causing accident." • "After starting, engine revs up to 3,500 rpm, then drops to 700 rpm, engine stalls out." • "While driving, vehicle surges forward." • "When placed in reverse, vehicle accelerated backwards, causing accident."

3. Interior systems: passive restraint: belts, malfunction, failure. • "Automatic shoulder belt for passenger has quit working; failed in closed-door position." • "Driver's automatic shoulder restraint failed in accident, causing injury." • "Automatic shoulder belt stops on track; possible electrical short." • "When accident occurred at speed of 25 mph, seat belts that automatically wrap around failed to hold driver from being thrown against steering wheel." • "Automatic shoulder harness seat belts; involved in accident with sudden deceleration, passive seat belt, shoulder harness didn't catch."

4. Interior systems: active seat and shoulder belts and belt anchor, uncomfortable, malfunction, failure. • "Seat belts were defective; during an accident door flew open, seat belt disengaged, passenger was thrown out of car and killed." • "Automatic shoulder belt fails to open when car stopped, door opened and ignition key turned off; only way to get out of car is to lift belt manually." • "Front seat belts rub against neck, rear seat belts (lap) are too high." • "During an accident, driver's-side seat belt did not restrain her, causing head injuries." • "Seat belt broke in upper right-hand corner during accident."

5. Power train: transmission: automatic, poor performance, difficulty shifting, slipping. • "Transmission slipped from park position, rolled backwards, causing accident." • "Welds broke on two small gears around transmission planetary gear, resulting in transmission failure." • "Seals failed on transmission." • "Was losing transmission fluid; dealer replaced fluid filter and gasket." • "Automatic transmission shifts hard, slips between 10 and 25 mph, 2nd and 3rd gears, and when engaging passing gear."

6. Steering: linkages: tie rod: end, premature failure, tire wear. • "Tie rod ends replaced, which caused tires to wear so badly that they needed replacing." • "Premature failure of front tie rods; replaced." • "Outer tie rods are not lubricated and caused breakage; no grease fittings." • "Tie rod ends required replacing after 19,000 miles due to no grease fitting on original parts." • "Tie rod ends failing, causes early wearing out of tires; total failure resulted in loss of steering."

FORD ESCORT 1989

Complaint Severity: Typical. **Buyer's Summary:** The fuel pump has received complaints. Make sure it doesn't make excessive noise and that you are experiencing adequate engine performance. Also, look for leaks. The fuel injection system has been blamed for hesitation and stalling. Be sure the vehicle doesn't die in traffic or at stops. Check the brakes—listen for noise, look for leaks and feel for vibration. They may fail, perform poorly or require frequent mechanical attention. Test the transmission thoroughly. See "Sudden Accelerations" in Introduction.

Hot Spots and Owner/NHTSA Comments:

1. Fuel: fuel injection system, stalling, hesitation. • "Fuel injection system malfunctioned and vehicle stalled." • "Vehicle bucks and/or stalls at highway speeds and in cold weather." • "Defective fuel injectors cause stalling when going into reverse." • "Engine dies out at low speeds." • "Fuel injection system malfunctioned and vehicle won't start; had to be replaced."

2. Brakes: hydraulic system, failure. • "While driving at approximately 45 mph, made attempt to slow down and suddenly brake pedal went to floor, without prior warning; as a result, hit another vehicle." • "Brakes started dragging, then noticed fire coming from the right front wheel; replaced brake assembly." • "Uneven brake wear and rotors replaced." • "Front brakes defective; rebuilt calipers, replaced pads and rotors, brakes still spongy." • "Upon applying brakes to slow down, suddenly rear end slid to left, attempted to control wheel, rear end swerved to right; car rolled over and stopped."

3. Fuel: throttle linkages and control, sudden accelerations. • "Car suddenly accelerated, upon shift into reverse, without driver touching accelerator car shot backwards; resulted in accident." • "Acceleration evident with foot removed from gas, traveling as fast as 35 mph." • "Throttle stuck while on expressway doing 55 mph, and would not release; accident occurred." • "Engine surging up to 35 mph, have to put clutch in and apply brakes to decelerate speed; few very close calls experienced." • "Car went out of control, speed 35 mph, took foot off gas, applied brakes; ended up overturning car."

4. Fuel: fuel pump, malfunction, failure. • "Driving up a hill and the fuel pump went out." • "Fuel pump failed; replaced 3 times." • "Fuel pump malfunctioned." • "Fuel pump shutoff switch not easily accessible to driver." • "Fuel pump quit without warning; vehicle towed off freeway."

5. Power train: transmission: automatic, poor performance, difficulty shifting, slipping. • "Hard shifting and vibration at 55 mph." • "Transmission kit replaced due to oil leak causing difficult shifting." • "Automatic transmission failure; when transmission was in drive it would not move forward." • "Transmission slipped gears, causing accident and loss of control." • "Automatic transmission hesitates in passing gear."

6. Engine: noise, fire. • "Engine off after a short drive, engine compartment burst into fire and destroyed the car." • "Engine check light came on, loss of engine power, white smoke appeared. Five minutes after parking, engine compartment caught on fire." • "Car failed due to engine drawing water up through air supply system for fuel injectors." • "Loud engine valves noise."

FORD ESCORT 1990

Complaint Severity: Typical. **Recall Alert:** See Recall Index. **Buyer's Summary:** The fuel pump has received complaints. Make sure it doesn't make excessive noise and that you are experiencing adequate engine performance. Also, look for leaks. Test the transmission thoroughly. Make sure seat belts function correctly and fit comfortably.

Hot Spots and Owner/NHTSA Comments:

1. Fuel: fuel pump, noise, stalling. • "Noise was coming from fuel pump, then vehicle died out in heavy traffic; dealer replaced fuel pump." • "While driving, vehicle stalled with no warning because of a faulty fuel pump." • "Fuel pump failed while driving on a major highway; resulted in engine dying and loss of power steering control." • "Fuel pump makes noise; mechanic told owner vehicle may stop at any time."

2. Interior systems: passive restraint: belts, malfunction, failure. • "Automatic shoulder belt: Where it bolts in place, it unscrews itself; occupants subject to increased risk of injury in event of sudden impact or accident." • "Owner was rear-ended and driver's seat back fell backwards. Seat belt broke and driver was thrown into passenger seat." • "Safety belt failed when vehicle was involved in a rollover accident. Harness portions of driver's and passenger's belts did not catch." • "Automatic seat belts did not hold during an accident at approximately 15 mph, passenger suffered severe rib injury and driver bruised head."

3. Power train: transmission: automatic, poor performance, difficulty shifting, slipping. • "Transmission slips while in 1st gear, will not shift, also leaks." • "Transmission has not been operating properly, grinds loudly, hesitates." • "Vehicle stalls and surges erratically, does not downshift properly." • "Transmission problems, low power on acceleration, consistent ongoing fluid leaks; several attempts to repair halfshaft assembly/different oil seal, still leaking." • "While riding on street, automatic transmission and parts began to disconnect and fall onto road in pieces. Vehicle failed to stop and began smoking."

4. Electrical system: ignition, fire, stalling. • "Ignition fire, causing dash to melt and steering column damage." • "Electrical fire originating from under dash." • "While driving, vehicle shut off. Owner restarted and vehicle began to smoke and caught fire." • "Intermittent stalling results in loss of brakes and steering controls, also rapid acceleration from throttle up to 3,000 rpm with pedal application."

5. Interior systems: active seat and shoulder belts and belt anchor, malfunction, failure. • "During an accident, seat belt failed; driver hit steering wheel and was injured." • "During an accident, shoulder and lap belts failed upon impact, tracking system went forward and lap belt latch broke simultaneously." • "Upper portion of driver's seat belt did not restrain occupant upon braking." • "Seat belts are not functioning correctly." • "Screw missing on driver's and passenger's seat belts."

6. Engine: stalling, fire. • "Timing belt and head gasket problem." • "Intermittent stalling; also engine failed 3 times." • "Engine fire caused vehicle to explode." • "Defective engine, caught on fire twice." • "Unspecified cause of fire."

FORD ESCORT 1991

Complaint Severity: Minor. **Recall Alert:** See Recall Index. **Buyer's Summary:** The fuel pump has received complaints. Make sure it doesn't make excessive noise and that you are experiencing adequate engine performance. Also, look for leaks. Check the brakes—listen for noise, look for leaks and feel for vibration. They may fail, perform poorly or require frequent mechanical attention. Test the transmission thoroughly. Make sure seat belts function correctly and fit comfortably. See "Sudden Accelerations" in Introduction.

Hot Spots and Owner/NHTSA Comments:

1. Fuel: fuel pump, fire, malfunction. • "Electrical short occurred while driving at 65-70 mph on highway, melting and burning all wires due to poor location of fuel pump, with wires rubbing on insulation." • "Fuel pump shorted out, causing fumes and wiring to burn, blowing out fuses." • "Wiring harness melted, causing smoke to come into passenger compartment from under seat and dashboard due to failure of fuel pump." • "While driving, noticed burning smell, noticed smoke coming from dash and vents, engine shut down, then caught fire; fuel pump and electrical. Wire harness shorted." • "Fuel pump leak rusted/corroded plate, causing gasoline to enter into rear passenger seating area, creating a fire risk."

2. Brakes: hydraulic system, noise, premature failure. • "While driving brakes faded making stopping ability difficult. Replaced brakes twice, second time pin fell out." • "Complete brake failure, pedal went to floor." • "When driving vehicle at any speed, brakes failed to stop vehicle when applied." • "Continuous squealing and screeching, brakes grab and are spongy; unable to resolve the problem." • "Brakes wore out prematurely, causing vibration in front."

3. Interior systems: passive restraint: belts, malfunction, failure. • "Automatic seat belts failed to restrain passenger at 35 mph; passenger hit windshield." • "Motor track defective; seat belt does not come back on driver; upon impact, driver could be thrown forward into dashboard and/or windshield." • "After release of motorized seat belts, with engine running and doors open, passenger's front belt reactivated and began to tighten around child." • "Motorized shoulder belt may stick with belt loose, or choke occupant when activated."

4. Fuel: throttle linkages and control, sudden accelerations. • "Throttle position sensor failed, causing vehicle to become stuck in 3rd gear and high rpms when driving 60-65 mph." • "Throttle position sensor failed, causing engine light to come on." • "Upon coming to a stop, car accelerated and shot forward, went down 2,500-foot embankment; accident occurred." • "Throttle stuck; resulted in an accident." • "Throttle jammed in wide-open position when accelerator pedal was floored to induce automatic transmission downshift."

5. Power train: transmission: automatic, poor performance, difficulty shifting, slipping. • "Transmission slips from neutral to drive." • "Transmission gear sticks at 30 mph; ringing and/or grinding noise." • "Automatic transmission locks up completely while driving; need to replace transmission." • "At 39,000 miles the vehicle just stopped, the engine kept running but the vehicle would not move; the transmission froze up." • "Transmission leak with erratic shifting; repaired, problem continues."

6. Electrical system: ignition: switch, locking up, failure. • "Ignition lock fell out of steering column housing. Could not get key into ignition to engage transmission." • "Ignition lock fell out of column, causing steering wheel to lock up." • "As vehicle was pulling away from a stop and beginning a left turn, the ignition switch fell out of the steering column, caused steering to lock up." • "Ignition lock came out while turning key to start vehicle."

FORD ESCORT 1992

Complaint Severity: Typical. **Recall Alert:** See Recall Index. **Buyer's Summary:** Look carefully for any kind of leakage, especially under the car. The fuel pump has received complaints. Make sure it doesn't make excessive noise and that you are experiencing adequate engine performance. Also, look for leaks. Check the brakes—listen for noise, look for leaks and feel for vibration. They may fail, perform poorly or require frequent mechanical attention. Make sure seat belts function correctly and fit comfortably. See "Sudden Accelerations" in Introduction.

Hot Spots and Owner/NHTSA Comments:

1. Fuel: throttle linkages and control, sudden accelerations. • "When coming to a stop, rpm goes up to 3,000-4,000; does not come down until vehicle is turned off." • "When attempting to decelerate by removing foot from accelerator, vehicle continued with high rpm." • "Vehicle fails to slow down and sometimes speeds up after removing foot from accelerator on an incline." • "Vehicle will accelerate intermittently with no warning with rpm running 4,500. Vehicle has 5-speed transmission." • "Driver floored the throttle to pass, throttle stuck requiring a shift to neutral and maximum use of brakes to gain control. Restart had normal throttle."

2. Interior systems: passive restraint: belts, malfunction, failure. • "Driver's automatic shoulder harness did not hold upon impact; driver fell forward; vehicle was rear-ended during bumper-to-bumper traffic." • "Vehicle hit tree; driver's and passenger's automatic shoulder harnesses and lap belts did not hold." • "Upon impact, passive restraint belts didn't lock or restrain, allowing front occupants to hit dashboard." • "Automatic shoulder belt failed during accident; also, shoulder belt rubbed against eye, causing injury."

3. Fuel: fuel pump, leaks, failure. • "Entire wiring harness in car had to be replaced when wiring from fuel pump in tank shorted out." • "Recall related; fuel system, fuel pump replaced 3 times, vapor line breaks, leaking, smell of fumes." • "Fuel pump failed, prior to recall; repaired, problem continues." • "Fuel pump on vehicle is leaking gas. This was a recall from previous year. Owner had recall work performed, but fuel pump started leaking again." • "Fuel pump failed twice."

4. Fuel: fuel tank assembly: tank, leaks, cracking. • "Twice gasoline poured out of gas tank resulting in a leak." • "Plastic fuel tank leaks gasoline due to cracks. Dealer replaced tank and pump gasket several times; tank has begun to leak again." • "Gas tank leaks when filled above three-quarters full." • "Found big puddle under rear of car due to gas tank leak, took off pressure by opening gas cap." • "Fuel tank leaked from under right-hand side of vehicle."

5. Brakes: hydraulic system, noise, excessive wear. • "Brakes failed to stop effectively when applied; pedal goes to the floor and there is a grinding noise, causing extended stopping. Repaired 6 times." • "Premature wear of rotors, power booster, pads." • "After driving for approximately 40 minutes, there was a brake failure; unable to stop vehicle by applying the brakes after the car has been idle for 5 hours or more." • "When turning corner, burning odor emits from brakes." • "Brake pedal goes all the way to the floor."

FORD ESCORT 1993

Complaint Severity: Typical. **Recall Alert:** See Recall Index. **Buyer's Summary:** Check the brakes—listen for noise, look for leaks and feel for vibration. They may fail, perform poorly or require frequent mechanical attention. Test the transmission thoroughly. Make sure seat belts function correctly and fit comfortably. See "Sudden Accelerations" in Introduction.

Hot Spots and Owner/NHTSA Comments:

1. Fuel: throttle linkages and control, sudden accelerations. • "Throttle sticks in open position, causing sudden acceleration." • "After driving 20-25 miles at 55 mph, engine accelerates on its own until ignition is turned off; no warning." • "Owner says that the idle went very fast, she had to put vehicle in neutral in order to stop." • "Owner is having problems with high acceleration; brakes have to go to the floor or vehicle won't stop." • "Vehicle accelerates out of control, possibly due to a throttle position sensor malfunction."

2. Interior systems: passive restraint: belts, malfunction, failure. • "Driver's seat belt did not lock into place upon impact as intended. Driver ended up face down on floor. Speed 35 mph. Car rear-ended by another car. Impact 6:00 position." • "Driver's-side shoulder harness seat belt did not retract during sudden stopping, causing injuries to driver at 35 mph. No accident." • "Driver's automatic seat belt did not restrain driver during accident, resulting in injuries." • "Experience intermittent motorized seat belt failure when closing door, belt won't go around; also, while driving, suddenly belt comes around with no warning."

3. Brakes: hydraulic system, noise, failure. • "Brakes overheat, rub, causing noise. Replaced front pads and rear shoes." • "When car is cold, brake system doesn't stop vehicle until fully warmed up." • "Owner is having problems with high acceleration; brakes have to go to the floor or vehicle won't stop." • "Brake calipers, rotors, and brake sensor problem." • "Vehicle stopped. Hit from 6:00 position. Applied brakes to stop vehicle, complete loss of brake effectiveness. Experienced seat back failure on passenger's side."

4. Exhaust/crankcase emission control devices: failure. • "Twelve vehicles are having sudden acceleration with warm engines and slowing down to turn, park or maneuver. Ford replaced air bypass valve with a new-design part."

5. Power train: transmission: automatic, poor performance, difficulty shifting, slipping. • "Replaced transmission mount." • "After idling for 1 minute, vehicle suddenly jumped forward with transmission in neutral, breaking driver's wrist." • "Transmission will not shift from park to drive intermittently." • "Purchased car as a program car and the transmission went out twice; the first time at 32,000 miles, and right now the transmission is at 52,000 miles." • "When shifting transmission into reverse, vehicle pulls forward."

6. Electrical system: battery, failure. • "Battery failure." • "Battery failure." • "Battery replaced."

FORD ESCORT 1994

Complaint Severity: Typical. **Recall Alert:** See Recall Index. **Buyer's Summary:** Problems with the timing gear and chain can cause serious problems. Have the engine checked by a professional. The airbags in this vehicle have experienced failures and malfunctions: You may need a professional evaluation on the condition of the airbags. Check the brakes—listen for noise, look for leaks and feel for vibration. They may fail, perform poorly or require frequent mechanical attention. Test the transmission thoroughly. Make sure seat belts function correctly and fit comfortably.

Hot Spots and Owner/NHTSA Comments:

1. Brakes: hydraulic system, noise, failure. • "Brake pedal soft, little power, needs long distance to stop." • "Experienced brake failure when pedal went to floor and heard metal-to-metal sound upon braking; also, brake light comes on intermittently while driving." • "Brake system failure, loss of braking ability." • "Brake pedal goes completely hard and vehicle can't be stopped." • "Had to have front brakes replaced because of grinding; still not stopping properly."

2. Interior systems: passive restraint: airbag: driver, malfunction, failure. • "Airbag did not deploy, lost control, steering wheel didn't drop." • "Driver's-side airbag did not deploy during accident." • "Frontal collision, impact 12:00 position, speed 50 mph, airbag partially deployed." • "Frontal collision, impact 12:00 position, speed 45 mph, airbag did not deploy." • "Consumer was in an accident. Airbag didn't deploy during accident, resulting in an injury."

3. Power train: transmission: automatic, poor performance, difficulty shifting, slipping. • "Transmission fails to shift from 2nd to 3rd gear." • "Automatic transmission shifts harshly." • "Transmission mounts misaligned, causing noise when shifting." • "Vehicle shifts harshly, also gets into 4th gear too early." • "Vehicle jumped into park while going 50 mph and slammed into a ditch."

4. Engine: timing gear and chain, failure. • "Timing belt overtensioned, causing noise when braking or shifting." • "Replaced timing belt." • "Timing belt too tight." • "Timing chain adjuster failed." • "Timing belt failure."

5. Interior systems: passive restraint: belts, uncomfortable, malfunction, failure. • "Driver and passenger front automatic shoulder harness and lap belts do not properly restrain occupants when driving. Too much slack." • "Consumer was in an accident; the driver's-side automatic seat belt failed to restrain driver." • "Automatic shoulder harness has poor fit." • "The front seat belt retractor was retracting back, caught consumer hand." • "The automatic seat belt in the car has caught people's hair, hands and also occupant's elbow."

6. Interior systems: passive restraint: airbag, malfunction, failure. • " 'Airbag needs service' indicator light comes on." • "No deployment of airbag during accident, causing injury." • "Airbag did not deploy." • "No deployment of airbag during accident, causing injury."

FORD FESTIVA 1988

Complaint Severity: Troublesome. **Recall Alert:** See Recall Index. **Buyer's Summary:** Test the suspension by feeling for vibration or pulling while driving.

Hot Spots and Owner/NHTSA Comments:

1. Interior systems: active restraints: belt buckles, breaking, failure. • "Vehicle passenger front seat belt will not stay latched." • "Driver's-side lap and shoulder belt will not retract, rear lap belt will not fasten." • "Passenger-side seat belt buckle will not fasten, orange plastic is broken inside." • "Driver's seat belt buckle re-

lease button sticking, causing inability to engage and/or disengage." • "The driver's-side seat belt female receptacle button has broken off and will not latch."
2. Suspension: independent front, vibration, pulling. • "Steering failure after violent vibration in front end; attempting to stop with no steering resulted in rear-end accident with another vehicle." • "Front end shimmies at highway speed, vibration felt in steering wheel." • "While driving on highway in rain at 50 mph, car went into left lane, spun around and stopped, facing traffic, due to front end extremely loose." • "When driving over metal grate surface, car moves sideways, experiences loss of control."
3. Wheels: noise, failure. • "Rear passenger tire came off while driving, lost brakes and almost had accident." • "While driving down highway, the right wheel and assembly disconnected; vehicle was in shop for brake repair." • "Noise in rear wheels; replaced wheel seals and rear shoes." • "Entire rear wheel on driver's-side fell off while driving on highway."

FORD FESTIVA 1989

Complaint Severity: Typical. **Recall Alert:** See Recall Index. **Buyer's Summary:** Check the brakes—listen for noise, look for leaks and feel for vibration. They may fail, perform poorly or require frequent mechanical attention.

Hot Spots and Owner/NHTSA Comments:
1. Brakes: hydraulic system, poor performance, vibration. • "Brakes failed." • "Poor braking performance." • "Brake system noisy when applied." • "Complete front and rear brakes wore out and replaced at 24,000 miles." • "Brakes vibrate and do not engage well."
2. Interior systems: active restraints: belt buckles, breaking, malfunction. • "Shoulder and lap belt buckle red push-button tab is inoperative, due to plastic broken piece that has fallen into latch mechanism; male won't go into female." • "Seat belt buckle failure, unable to latch seat belt." • "The passenger-side seat belt will not latch until you press the button." • "Vehicle's seat belt buckle red push-in button has fallen in and rendered seat belt inoperative; is under recall." • "Driver's seat belt red plastic release button cracked; caused seat belt to become inoperative."
3. Interior systems: active seat and shoulder belts and belt anchor, breaking, failure. • "Seat belt broke during an accident; driver died and a passenger suffered injuries." • "Seat belt does not lock to secure driver and/or passengers on impact; occupant went into windshield, which shattered." • "Seat belts failed." • "Seat belts lock up and don't retract in back seat."

FORD MUSTANG 1987

Complaint Severity: Troublesome. **Recall Alert:** See Recall Index. **Buyer's Summary:** The electronic control unit has been blamed for engine performance problems, including stalling and surging. The fuel injection system has been blamed for hesitation and stalling. Be sure the vehicle doesn't die in traffic or at stops. See "Sudden Accelerations" in Introduction.

Hot Spots and Owner/NHTSA Comments:
1. Fuel: throttle linkages and control, sudden accelerations. • "While driving, suddenly engine surged to 3,000 rpm without touching gas pedal and with foot on brake pedal; vehicle jumped 15 feet forward and hit a brick wall." • "When shifted into drive, vehicle suffered sudden acceleration and loss of control. An accident resulted, injuring driver." • "Car suddenly accelerated backwards, driver lost control; accident resulted." • "Vehicle stumbles, stalls and misses; also suddenly accelerates to 3,000-3,500 rpm." • "Defective throttle position sensor caused uncontrollable acceleration of vehicle in reverse, which resulted in accident."
2. Fuel: fuel injection system, stalling, hesitation. • "Vehicle exhibits severe stalling, rough idling, backlashing, surging upon deceleration; occurs at all speeds." • "While driving, vehicle hesitates and stalls on deceleration; loss of power steering when it stalls." • "Recurring stalling, hesitating, surging and intermittent bucking problems; replaced exhaust gas recirculation solenoid, idle curb processor; surges forward when downshifting." • "Intermittent hesitation, stalling moderate, heavy acceleration." • "Vehicle loses power."
3. Lighting: switch: button: ring: headlights, malfunction, failure. • "Headlight switch overheats when fog lights turned on with headlights; loss of headlights." • "Broken headlight switch causing headlight malfunction." • "Faulty headlight switch, headlights would short out and shut off while driving." • "Switch wiring melts when both headlights and fog lights are turned on." • "Headlight switch overheats, melting wires and plugs; also causes headlights to go out."
4. Electrical system: ignition: electronic control unit, stalling, sudden acceleration. • "Engine speed rises from idle to 2,500 rpm with no driver input, no warning, difficult to control on slippery road." • "Vehicle experiencing stalling and accelerating problems; repaired/replaced processor several times, exhaust gas recirculation solenoid, problem still exists." • "Replaced ignition module." • "While in motion, car suddenly accelerated out of control, brakes ineffective; resulted in accident with injury."
5. Lighting: general or unknown component: headlights, malfunction, leaks. • "Headlights periodically go out when driving at night, causing lack of visibility when driving." • "Headlamps may flicker on and off when fog lamps are used for extended time due to overheating of headlamp circuit #15, as per service bulletin." • "Continuous problem with water getting into headlight on driver's side; may cause some electrical problems too." • "Headlights gone 8 times; headlights repaired, still not working right, lights keep blinking on and off." • "Problem with water getting into headlight on driver's side; repaired several times to no avail."
6. Electrical system: wiring: harness: under dash, malfunction, fire. • "Under-dash fire ignited while driving highway; no prior warning." • "Electrical fire totaled vehicle." • "Under-dashboard fire; smoke escaped from under dash before bursting into flames." • "Vehicle caught on fire due to electrical short under the dashboard in the passenger compartment."

FORD MUSTANG 1988

Complaint Severity: Typical. **Buyer's Summary:** Look carefully for any kind of leakage, especially under the car. The fuel injection system has been blamed for hesitation and stalling. Be sure the vehicle doesn't die in traffic or at stops. See "Sudden Accelerations" in Introduction.

Hot Spots and Owner/NHTSA Comments:
1. Fuel: throttle linkages and control, sudden accelerations. • "While driving at a steady slow speed, the car suddenly accelerated. Had to turn off the ignition switch to stop the engine." • "Problem with throttle position sensor, engine stops when decelerating at low speed, causing all power functions to cease; replaced throttle position sensor." • "Engine surging problem, engine revs by itself up to 2,500 rpm, lurches forward, cruises for miles between 30 and 50 mph without touching gas pedal." • "Upon starting up engine and shifting gear selector to drive, suddenly car leaped forward, completely out of control." • "Accelerator hung wide open, car ran out of control; accident resulted; replaced throttle position sensor, problem continues."
2. Lighting: general or unknown component: headlights, malfunction, premature failure. • "Headlight flickers on and

off at about 3-minute interval, usually only when fog lights are on." • "Driving with fog lamps on over 20 minutes at night, headlight starts blinking on and off, almost causing accident; if left on, headlight switch catches fire." • "Headlights burn out intermittently." • "Headlight emits very distorted beam, creates severe blinding glare to oncoming traffic; adjustments and replacements done." • "Headlights go out when using fog lights due to faulty wires and/or circuits."

3. Fuel: fuel injection system, stalling, hesitation. • "Engine hesitation problem; hesitates when pulling out, loss of power on hills and when air conditioner or heater is on." • "Vehicle stalled while traveling down roadway at some speed, lost all power and control; struck a tree." • "Intermittent stalling; replaced several fuel injection parts, problem continues." • "After driving 16 miles, rpm revving up and down, smelled fuel, car stopped twice; flushed fuel system and replaced throttle position sensor." • "While driving, engine suddenly rose above 7,000 rpm, turned engine off; intake manifold replaced."

4. Electrical system: stalling, fire, failure. • "Having electrical problems; headlights suddenly go off, windshield wipers don't work in sleet and snow, tachometer is off, won't idle in cold weather." • "Vehicle stalling with no warning while driving at 45-50 mph. Replaced starter once, alternator 6 times." • "Flames and gray smoke came from under dashboard, smelled of plastic, appeared to be electrical and toxic smell; resulted in electrical fire." • "Electrical defect, car cab caught fire; vehicle totaled."

5. Exhaust system: catalytic converter system, leaks, noise, failure. • "Catalytic converter came loose inside of pipe." • "Catalytic converter system has deteriorated and has been replaced once. Failure has repeated itself and may need replacement a second time." • "Catalytic converter cracked, causing exhaust leaks." • "Noise from engine and exhaust; replaced catalytic converter."

6. Electrical system: wiring: harness: under dash, failure, fire. • "Fire started due to electrical failure under the dashboard." • "When parked and tried to start vehicle, fire broke out under the dash." • "Electrical fire under dash on driver's-side caused vehicle to become filled with toxic smoke." • "Driving, smoke coming in defrost vents, pulled over, heard a pop and car engulfed in flames." • "Steering column smoked and caught on fire. Vehicle had previously been repaired for similar situation. Vehicle parked and engine off."

FORD MUSTANG 1989

Complaint Severity: Typical. **Buyer's Summary:** The fuel pump has received complaints. Make sure it doesn't make excessive noise and that you are experiencing adequate engine performance. Also, look for leaks. Test the suspension by feeling for vibration or pulling while driving. Test the transmission thoroughly. See "Sudden Accelerations" in Introduction.

Hot Spots and Owner/NHTSA Comments:

1. Fuel: throttle linkages and control, sudden accelerations. • "When driving or parking, vehicle goes to a high-idle pitch, sometimes suddenly accelerates; had be repaired and sensors were replaced at least 6 times." • "Car takes off on its own; when going at 60 mph, car accelerates to 85 mph without using gas pedal, will stick until hit brakes very hard or downshifted." • "Experienced sudden acceleration while driving, speed was increased more than 50 mph; resulted in accident." • "Engine began racing to 4,000 rpm, vehicle accelerated to 40-45 mph; must constantly use brakes to stop vehicle." • "Sudden acceleration, impact 12:00 position, accelerator stuck, vehicle speed at 35 mph, hitting a house."

2. Interior systems: active restraints: belt retractors, malfunction, failure. • "Defective front seat belts do not retract, thus provide no restraint and/or protection; replacement needed." • "Both front seat belts do not retract properly; seat belt replaced but problem still exists." • "Rear seat belt is difficult to retract, frequently jams up." • "Driver's seat belt retractor fails to retract or hold tension, causing belt to become too loose." • "Driver's- and passenger-side lap and shoulder belt failed, did not retract, impact 1:00 position, speed 35 mph."

3. Fuel: fuel pump, stalling, malfunction. • "Electrical wiring snapped off inside of fuel pump due to stress on wire because of fuel pump movement; wiring was not properly anchored to bracket." • "Fuel pump malfunctioned while driving." • "Electronic fuel pump failed." • "Faulty fuel pump replaced." • "Fuel pump failed, causing vehicle to stall."

4. Engine: noise, premature failure. • "Engine light constantly turns on." • "Cylinder head cracked." • "Engine started knocking and losing oil pressure." • "Engine had to be replaced at 7,600 miles due to oil consumption problem." • "Temperature sensor for engine failed, causing interior heater on vehicle to stall, with rpm below 1,500."

5. Power train: transmission: automatic, poor performance, difficulty shifting, slipping. • "While driving, transmission would only shift into reverse gear, causing it to jerk." • "Premature transmission failure at 12,000 miles." • "Transmission rattles; all repair attempts to no avail." • "Transmission hard to go into 1st gear." • "Washer between the center support and direct drum broke, resulting in transmission failure."

6. Suspension: independent front, pulling, noise, alignment. • "Vehicle pulls extremely to the left, cannot be driven without force, jerks to the left when hitting bumps, front tires grind on fenders when car moving." • "Cracking noise on front left side of car when brakes were applied and when accelerating from a stop; probably caused fatal accident." • "Front end out of alignment at 4,000 and 12,000 miles, tires started wearing on outer edge." • "Problem with misalignment of front suspension caused 4 sets of tires to wear."

FORD MUSTANG 1990

Complaint Severity: Serious. **Buyer's Summary:** The fuel pump has received complaints. Make sure it doesn't make excessive noise and that you are experiencing adequate engine performance. Also, look for leaks. Verify that the cruise control system works properly, and that it doesn't cause the engine to surge. The electronic control unit has been blamed for engine performance problems, including stalling and surging. The airbags in this vehicle have experienced failures and malfunctions: You may need a professional evaluation on the condition of the airbags. Test the transmission thoroughly. See "Sudden Accelerations" in Introduction.

Hot Spots and Owner/NHTSA Comments:

1. Fuel: throttle linkages and control, sudden accelerations. • "Recurring problem with accelerator pedal going to the floor; resulted in accident." • "Intermittent stuck throttle resulted in high idle speeds." • "Vehicle suddenly accelerated while driving." • "Engine surged forward at high speed, nearly causing an accident." • "Vehicle throttle advances on its own, vehicle is in high idle."

2. Interior systems: passive restraint: airbag: driver, malfunction, failure. • "Vehicle's airbag deployed for no apparent reason while driving on highway, causing the driver to lose control momentarily and run off the road." • "Airbag did not deploy in accident at 12:00 position, speed 25-30 mph." • "During a frontal collision, impact at 12:00, speed 35 mph, airbag failed to deploy." • "Airbag did not deploy upon impact at 12:00, speed 60-70 mph; driver suffered broken neck and shoulder."

3. Fuel: fuel pump, stalling, noise, failure. • "Fuel pump failure resulted in engine stalling in highway traffic." • "While waiting for a traffic light, engine stalled and then died, caused by a malfunctioning fuel pump." • "Fuel pump replaced twice in 21,000 miles." • "Noisy fuel pump." • "Fuel pump started to make noise, didn't fail to function; replaced by manufacturer."

4. Electrical system: ignition: electronic control unit, failure. • "Power loss; defective microprocessor replaced." • "At times, engine will race instead of idle with no pressure on gas pedal, usually occurs after cold starts; condition corrected by turning engine on and off." • "Onboard computer failed; repaired." • "Sensors, electrical computer problems." • "Computer chip and sensor faulty."

5. Equipment: speed control, malfunction, failure. • "Inoperative cruise control." • "Cruise control failed to engage; replaced clutch switch." • "Speed cruise control will not disengage." • "Defective cruise control." • "Cruise control switch inoperative."

6. Power train: transmission: automatic, poor performance, difficulty shifting, slipping. • "Automatic transmission leak due to a faulty transmission system." • "Automatic transmission makes clunking sound when shifting into parking gear." • "Transmission failure, unable to put car in park." • "Automatic transmission with overdrive will pop out of gear into neutral while traveling. Dealer rebuilding transmission a second time."

FORD MUSTANG 1991

Complaint Severity: Serious. **Recall Alert:** See Recall Index. **Buyer's Summary:** The airbags in this vehicle have experienced failures and malfunctions: You may need a professional evaluation on the condition of the airbags. Test the transmission thoroughly. See "Sudden Accelerations" in Introduction.

Hot Spots and Owner/NHTSA Comments:

1. Interior systems: passive restraint: airbag: driver, malfunction, failure. • "No deployment of driver's airbag during accident, resulting in injury." • "Airbag failed to deploy at speed of 25 mph." • "Airbag did not deploy during a rear-end collision at 30 mph; also, seat belt failed to hold; driver suffered injuries." • "Airbag did not deploy properly in an accident, causing injury to the driver." • "Automatic transmission with cruise control has history of sudden accelerations, downhill on ice it resulted in crash. Airbag failed to deploy." • "No deployment of airbag during accident, causing injury."

2. Structure: hood assembly: latches, failure. • "While driving at 55 mph on a major interstate, the hood suddenly flew up and totally covered the windshield." • "Hood latch failure at interstate speed, loss of control and vehicle damage." • "Complete hood latch failure resulted in total visual loss; hood contacted the windshield." • "Hood flew up and blocked vision when it wrapped around the windshield." • "While traveling on interstate, hood latch failed, hood flew open without warning and hit windshield and roof."

3. Electrical system: wiring: harness: under dash, failure, fire. • "Vehicle's dashboard electrical wiring shorted out and caught dash on fire while parked with ignition off." • "Vehicle fire due to electrical short under dash while vehicle was sitting in driveway." • "On 3 occasions, vehicle dashboard wiring burned, and the last time ignition switch burst into flames, due to electrical failure." • "Steering column started smoking and within 2 minutes car was totally engulfed in flames." • "While driving the vehicle, smelled smoke; under-dash fire cause by electrical short."

4. Fuel: throttle linkages and control, sudden accelerations. • "Throttle stuck wide open while in drive, brakes stopped vehicle after 200 feet and locked wheels up, engine continued to surge forward." • "Half-hour drive, parked for half hour, restarted and ran for 5 minutes, car suddenly accelerated. Floor mat OK; standard shift transmission with cruise control." • "Sticking throttle." • "Automatic transmission with cruise control has history of sudden accelerations; downhill on ice, this sudden acceleration resulted in crash." • "Vehicle went to full throttle without warning."

5. Interior systems: passive restraint: airbag, malfunction, failure. • "Driver received chemical burns from airbag during accident." • "Vehicle slid on curve and went end over end; no airbag deployment." • "Had an accident. Driver's-side seat belt did not restrain. Airbag did deploy." • "Airbag did not deploy." • "Airbag sensor was defective; replaced."

6. Power train: transmission: automatic, poor performance, difficulty shifting, slipping. • "Transmission serviced 3 times." • "Transmission slips." • "Transmission failed." • "Interior seal on transmission failed." • "Automatic transmission with cruise control has history of sudden accelerations, downhill on ice, this acceleration resulted in a crash."

FORD MUSTANG 1992

Complaint Severity: Serious. **Buyer's Summary:** The airbags in this vehicle have experienced failures and malfunctions: You may need a professional evaluation on the condition of the airbags. Check the brakes—listen for noise, look for leaks and feel for vibration. They may fail, perform poorly or require frequent mechanical attention.

Hot Spots and Owner/NHTSA Comments:

1. Interior systems: passive restraint: airbag: driver, malfunction, failure. • "In an accident at 30 mph, impact at 12:00, airbag did not deploy." • "Airbag deployed after impact during a front-end collision at 30 mph, causing injuries to driver." • "Airbag failed to deploy upon frontal impact, estimated speed 50 mph." • "Upon frontal impact, airbag failed to deploy." • "Frontal collision, impact 12:00 position, speed 30 mph, airbag did not deploy, fuel line shutoff valve did not work."

2. Brakes: hydraulic: disc: rotor: disc hub, cracking, vibration. • "Cracked front brake rotors." • "Warped brake rotors and drums, causing vehicle to pulsate and chatter." • "Front brake rotors vibrate when brakes applied at high speeds." • "Both front brake rotors, from the hub to outside edge, have developed cracks due to inferior metal."

3. Visual systems: windshield wiper, premature failure. • "Windshield wiper will cease to function with no warning. Replaced parts 7 times. • "Windshield wipers will cease to operate without warning. Driver has been caught in heavy rains several times with no visibility." • "Windshield wipers failed during rainstorm; motor replaced, wipers now perform erratically." • "Windshield wipers fail intermittently."

FORD MUSTANG 1993

Complaint Severity: Serious. **Theft Alert:** 36. **Recall Alert:** See Recall Index. **Buyer's Summary:** The airbags in this vehicle have experienced failures and malfunctions: You may need a professional evaluation on the condition of the airbags. Check the brakes—listen for noise, look for leaks and feel for vibration. They may fail, perform poorly or require frequent mechanical attention.

Hot Spots and Owner/NHTSA Comments:

1. Brakes: hydraulic system, locking up, failure. • "Brakes locked up, causing vehicle to slide." • "Brakes failed, causing vehicle to lose control on wet road; also, noise." • "Brakes failed with steering lockup. Applied brakes at speed of 15 mph, hitting a wet spot in highway, lost control, going over median strip; underbody damages." • "Vehicle would not stop when brakes were applied, veered to the right to avoid hitting car in front; instead, hit rubber road marker."

2. Brakes: hydraulic: disc: rotor: disc hub, breaking, premature failure. • "Front brake rotors replaced 3 times." • "Left front brake rotor broke into pieces and fell off, causing the wheel to lock up and loss of control, hitting a wall." • "Brake rotor fractured, causing accident and injury." • "Front brakes do not operate correctly in panic stops."
3. Interior systems: passive restraint: airbag: driver, malfunction, failure. • "Airbag did not deploy during frontal collision; speed 30 mph; impact 12:00 position; car 1 slid into car 2." • "Upon frontal collision, airbag didn't deploy completely." • "During a rear-end collision, the airbag deployed and burned driver's arm." • "Involved into a frontal collision and the airbag did not deploy."

FORD MUSTANG 1994

Complaint Severity: Very Serious. **Theft Alert:** 43. **Recall Alert:** See Recall Index. **Buyer's Summary:** The airbags in this vehicle have experienced failures and malfunctions: You may need a professional evaluation on the condition of the airbags. Check the brakes—listen for noise, look for leaks and feel for vibration. They may fail, perform poorly or require frequent mechanical attention.

Hot Spots and Owner/NHTSA Comments:
1. Brakes: hydraulic: anti-skid system, poor performance, failure, locking up. • "Brakes periodically lock up while driving, causing accident at 15 mph." • "In rainy weather, no response from the antilock braking system." • "Consumer was driving, tried to stop, the antilock brake system locked up; caused accident." • "Antilock brake system: Driver applied brake. Pedal modulated when antilock brake system activated and went to floor. Vehicle slid to left on a right-hand curve. Possible that wheels locked." • "When applying antilock brakes, pedal went to floor, not responding to pedal travel. No dual airbag deployment."
2. Interior systems: passive restraint: airbag: driver, malfunction, failure. • "Dual airbags did not inflate." • "Dual airbags did not deploy." • "When applying antilock brake system, pedal went to floor, not responding to pedal travel. No driver airbag deployment." • "Driver's airbag did not deploy upon impact." • "Driver's-side airbag did not deploy upon 2:00 collision."
3. Interior systems: passive restraint: airbag: passenger, failure. • "Passenger's airbag failed." • "Passenger's airbag did not deploy upon impact." • "Dual airbags did not inflate." • "Dual airbags did not deploy." • "When applying antilock brake system, pedal went to floor, not responding to pedal travel. No passenger airbag deployment."

FORD PROBE 1989

Complaint Severity: Typical. **Recall Alert:** See Recall Index. **Buyer's Summary:** Check the brakes—listen for noise, look for leaks and feel for vibration. They may fail, perform poorly or require frequent mechanical attention. Test the transmission thoroughly. See "Sudden Accelerations" in Introduction.

Hot Spots and Owner/NHTSA Comments:
1. Fuel: throttle linkages and control, sudden accelerations. • "While turning ignition on, wheels began spinning swiftly, vehicle went in reverse at high speed, shift still in park position; hit wall at 60 mph." • "Shifted car out of park with foot on brake, car suddenly accelerated and went through fence; stopped after hitting fence post." • "While in reverse, vehicle rapidly accelerated, went out of control, which resulted in an accident." • "Car put in reverse, immediately shot backwards at high speed; attempts to stop with brakes failed; resulted in accident before coming to stop." • "Car put in reverse to back out and immediately shot backwards at high speed; repeated attempts at applying brakes failed to stop."
2. Power train: transmission: automatic, poor performance, difficulty shifting, slipping. • "Transmission slips and/or hesitates in 1st and 2nd gears before and after repairs." • "Transmission struggles to make first shift when car is cold, moves back and forth between gears with too much frequency." • "Recurring problem with transmission slipping; repaired." • "Oil leaks from transmission." • "Manual shift light on dash would come on and off frequently; feel a change in power when this happens."
3. Equipment: electric power accessories: windows, premature failure. • "Electric window switch location gets wet due to design and shape of window and door, with no gutters to catch water. Switch is corroded." • "Power window regulator problems." • "Power window problems; repaired." • "Power windows fail intermittently." • "Power window motor failed."
4. Brakes: hydraulic system, locking up, pulling. • "The braking system locks up very easily, resulting in numerous skid situations." • "Front brakes fixed twice." • "Brakes replaced." • "Brake application pulls steering wheel to right from left position, car wanders all over road; resulted in accident."
5. Electrical system: alternator: generator, premature failure. • "Voltage regulator/alternator failed." • "Alternator ruined battery." • "Alternator caused a power surge, which shorted out entire electrical system and components throughout." • "Alternator replaced twice, battery also replaced." • "Every 12,000 miles the electrical system alternator needs to be replaced; this is the fourth complaint about the same problem."
6. Engine, noise, premature failure. • "Cracked motor mounts." • "Engine noisy when accelerated, hard sounds, clunking noise—possibly underside rear of car—especially noticeable in tight turns, going up and down driveways." • "Engine block cracked." • "While driving, car smoked, burning smell, hood very hot, engine light on and oil level dropped, flashing 'hot,' vehicle accelerated to 100 mph; accident occurred."

FORD PROBE 1990

Complaint Severity: Minor. **Recall Alert:** See Recall Index. **Buyer's Summary:** The electronic control unit has been blamed for engine performance problems, including stalling and surging. Check the brakes—listen for noise, look for leaks and feel for vibration. They may fail, perform poorly or require frequent mechanical attention. Test the transmission thoroughly. Make sure seat belts function correctly and fit comfortably. See "Sudden Accelerations" in Introduction.

Hot Spots and Owner/NHTSA Comments:
1. Interior systems: passive restraint: belts, uncomfortable, malfunction. • "Mechanized shoulder belt entangled and severed tendons of right hand while driving. Was fighting choking action of belt." • "Front driver's-side automatic seat belt retracting system jammed. Could not be operated electrically or manually." • "Driver's motorized shoulder harness is inoperative; it won't move on track." • "The driver's seat belt fell right out of the automatic seat belt track." • "Driver's passive restraint system pulls too tight with no warning, or may not complete cycle."
2. Interior systems: active restraints: belt retractors, malfunction, failure. • "Driver's-side seat belt track broke at midpoint, also problems with passenger's seat belt." • "Seat belt does not retract or release at all times; replaced seat belt retractor mechanism." • "The driver's- and passenger-side seat retractors will not move forward when opening the door." • "Driver's-side motorized shoulder belt caught in middle of track; caused by defective retractor; could cause personal injury in event of accident." • "The seat

belt retractor intermittently jammed due to a manufacturer's defect."

3. Power train: transmission: automatic, poor performance, difficulty shifting, slipping. • "Problem with transmission shifting hard, feels like it's slipping upon downshift on incline, or hard downshifting with lag time in between gears." • "Automatic transmission is not shifting properly between 1st and 2nd gears, very violent with severe difficulty at low speeds; transmission replaced." • "Problem with transmission not shifting properly between 1st and 2nd gear." • "Automatic transmission struggles to make first shift when car cold, moves back and forth between gears with too much frequency."

4. Brakes: hydraulic system, noise, locking up. • "Brakes low and spongy when applied." • "Brakes squeal, and also lock up upon quick stop from about 35 mph, car then slides about 7 feet on dry concrete." • "Front brakes failed twice; replaced." • "Brakes squeak when applied." • "Replaced brake rotors, pads and shoes."

5. Electrical system: ignition: electronic control unit, stalling, malfunction. • "Recall notice regarding malfunctioning of computer processor which was replaced." • "Emission control computer module recalled, engine idles too high when cold." • "Engine cuts off at stops, cuts off when turned headlights on; repaired/replaced processor." • "Computer system malfunctioning, car vibrates and won't start properly." • "While exiting from the throughway and applying the brakes, vehicle slowed down and then engine went dead."

6. Fuel: throttle linkages and control, sudden accelerations. • "Vehicle's idle speed is extremely high after microprocessor was replaced for a recall." • "Car revs high and then shuts off." • "Engine stalls and surges; replaced throttle position sensor." • "Engine surges violently when idling, sometimes stalling." • "Throttle sticks in open position."

FORD PROBE 1991

Complaint Severity: Minor. **Recall Alert:** See Recall Index. **Buyer's Summary:** Make sure the shoulder belts don't cut across your neck and are well anchored. Check the brakes—listen for noise, look for leaks and feel for vibration. They may fail, perform poorly or require frequent mechanical attention. Make sure seat belts function correctly and fit comfortably. See "Sudden Accelerations" in Introduction.

Hot Spots and Owner/NHTSA Comments:

1. Interior systems: passive restraint: belts, malfunction, failure. • "Driver's-side lap and shoulder belt will not retract, froze in the track and will not move." • "Motorized shoulder belt stopped working. Motor went out." • "Front seat belt automatic retractor bracket assembly jams or sticks, resulting in no occupant protection in event of an accident." • "Motorized seat belt did not restrain occupant during a collision with impact at 12:00, while driving at 35 mph." • "Driver's motorized shoulder belt stopped in middle of door jamb. Passenger's side locks, pinning occupant against seat."

2. Interior systems: active restraints: belt retractors, uncomfortable, failure. • "Automatic shoulder belt will not completely go down to end of track, causing a pressured feeling on person's shoulder, must manually disengage belt." • "Automatic shoulder belt sticks and squeezes driver." • "Driver seat belt retractor stops working when door is closed; can hear motor click and go back halfway." • "Belt retractor fails to release enough belt to allow the belt to move along the track to its final drive position; belt stops across throat area."

3. Brakes: hydraulic system, vibration, failure. • "Master cylinder failed." • "Replaced all brakes." • "Brakes failed at high speed." • "When vehicle at idle speed and brakes applied, vibration in front end of vehicle."

4. Electrical system: battery, premature failure. • "Battery failure." • "Replaced battery." • "Battery failure."

5. Fuel: throttle linkages and control, sudden accelerations. • "Sudden acceleration occurred with no warning. Car was put in park and turned off to stop." • "Engine accelerates to high speed regardless of gear position; engine makes a roaring sound while surging; goes up to 4,000 and 5,000 rpm; brakes applied to stop." • "Sudden acceleration, impact 11:00 position, speed 20 mph." • "Sudden acceleration, causing accident."

6. Interior systems: shoulder belts, uncomfortable, malfunction. • "Shoulder belt sometimes chokes and is loose." • "While driving, experienced driver's- and passenger-side shoulder harness belts tightening on automatic seat belt system on several occasions; dealer cannot fix." • "Motorized shoulder belt will either lock up so that the emergency brake release switch must be used to get out, or tighten driver to seat." • "Driver's-side shoulder harness fits too tightly; need to release it manually and reconnect it to prevent strangulation."

FORD PROBE 1993

Complaint Severity: Serious. **Buyer's Summary:** The airbags in this vehicle have experienced failures and malfunctions: You may need a professional evaluation on the condition of the airbags. Check the brakes—listen for noise, look for leaks and feel for vibration. They may fail, perform poorly or require frequent mechanical attention. Test the transmission thoroughly.

Hot Spots and Owner/NHTSA Comments:

1. Brakes: hydraulic: anti-skid system, poor performance, failure, locking up. • "Trying to stop, the brake pedal went to the floor, engine was idling too fast to stop. Struck a garage." • "While driving at low speed, brakes failed to work." • "While driving at approximately 40-50 mph, brakes locked up in rear wheels on antilock brake system-equipped system. Results in a spin when locked up." • "Antilock brake system locks up while driving at any speed. Transmission gears periodically stick in park or neutral. Steering wheel sticks often when making turns."

2. Interior systems: passive restraint: airbag: driver, malfunction, failure. • "Airbag did not deploy and antilock brakes remained locked up; front-end impact at 11:00; speed 55 mph; driver lost control of vehicle." • "Airbag did not deploy during front-end collision; speed 35 mph; vehicle struck a deer crossing highway." • "While driving at 55 mph, lost control, with vehicle hitting a ditch. Airbag deployed, but did not inflate, causing injury." • "Airbag deployed after driver had impacted the steering wheel during front-end collision at approximately 35 mph." • "Airbag did not deploy during front-end collision at 55 mph when vehicle struck a concrete culvert; minor injuries."

3. Brakes: hydraulic system, failure. • "Continuous brake failures." • "Brakes failed, causing accident." • "Brake booster and master cylinder failed." • "While driving, experience intermittent brake failure when brake pedal becomes spongy, then goes to the floor and vehicle continues to roll forward." • "When driving at about 60 mph, motor acts like it's out of gas and quits, with loss of steering and brakes. Has almost caused several serious accidents."

4. Power train: transmission: automatic, poor performance, difficulty shifting, slipping. • "Antilock brake system locks up while driving at any speed. Transmission gears periodically stick in park or neutral. Steering wheel sticks often when making turns." • "Transmission makes vehicle shake while driving." • "Automatic transmission shifts from one gear to another; stalls; corrected; problem has reoccurred; jumps out of gear; shudders to a stop."

• "Transmission has been rebuilt twice by dealer; car was in accident and the antilock brakes failed." • "Transmission failure."
5. Steering: pulling, stiffness. • "Engine shuts off by itself, causing the brakes and power steering to fail." • "Loss of steering control; diagnosis not complete. System has unpredictable steering loss. Steering wheel becomes very hard to turn, requires much effort." • "While driving at 55 mph, lost control, with vehicle hitting a ditch. Airbag deployed, but did not inflate, causing injury." • "When driving at about 60 mph, motor acts like it's out of gas and quits with loss of steering and brakes. Has almost caused several serious accidents." • "At 55-60 mph vehicle pulled to left uncontrollably and brakes became hard; not able to stop vehicle, causing accident."
6. Electrical system: ignition, stalling, failure. • "Vehicle periodically dies and/or shuts down when driving at any speed." • "Ignition system failed, causing vehicle to stall." • "Engine shuts off by itself, causing the brakes and power steering to fail." • "In cold weather, car stalls and dies when driving on highway."

FORD TAURUS 1987

Complaint Severity: Negligible. **Recall Alert:** See Recall Index. **Buyer's Summary:** Look carefully for any kind of leakage, especially under the car. The fuel injection system has been blamed for hesitation and stalling. Be sure the vehicle doesn't die in traffic or at stops. Check the brakes—listen for noise, look for leaks and feel for vibration. They may fail, perform poorly or require frequent mechanical attention. Test the transmission thoroughly. See "Sudden Accelerations" in Introduction.

Hot Spots and Owner/NHTSA Comments:
1. Power train: transmission: automatic, poor performance, difficulty shifting, slipping. • "Transmission lunges forward after stopping; replaced 4 times." • "After starting and warming up, the car just dies out in any gear. Possibly due to transmission." • "Transmission failed, causing vehicle to stall." • "Transmission failure at 43,000 miles due to improper throttle pressure." • "After sitting for a while, sometimes has delayed engagement after gearshift has been moved to drive or reverse gear."
2. Fuel: fuel injection system, stalling, hesitation. • "Intermittent stalling; repaired, problem continues." • "Car stalls intermittently due to improper fuel injection system, partial loss of power steering and brakes." • "Fuel injection problem, when gas tank one-quarter full, car hesitates; stalls when starting from stoplight and when shifting from 1st to 2nd gear." • "Fuel injection problem, suddenly accelerated at full throttle; also, continuous stalling problem, surges at stop signs and traffic lights." • "Fuel tank assembly problem, car hesitates or stalls when one-fourth and one-half full of gas, then with a full tank of gas."
3. Fuel: throttle linkages and control, sudden accelerations. • "Automatic transmission: Throttle sticks in open position; causing uncontrollable speed; surges forward at intersections from stop position; no prior warning." • "Engine surges, idles high and races when depressing clutch, causing vehicle not to decelerate when accelerator released; excessive oil use and stalling." • "Vehicle accelerated to speeds up to 60-65 mph, would not stop after ignition turned off, driver had no control of vehicle." • "Vehicle suddenly surged rapidly forward upon turning ignition on; resulted in accident." • "Severe problems of rapid acceleration, cutting off, loss of power and unintended acceleration while in motion; many attempts to repair to no avail."
4. Brakes: hydraulic system, failure. • "While driving, experienced sudden acceleration when throttle opened and brakes were ineffective; had to place vehicle in neutral to stop while engine raced." • "Brake pedal goes to floorboard when braking at low speeds, does not have solid cushion when braking; spongy, soft brake pedal." • "Upon applying brakes at highway speed, control of car was lost. Vehicle crashed through a guardrail, running into a ditch." • "While driving, attempting to reduce speed, applied brakes lightly, car started skidding, fishtailing and slid into guardrail."
5. Engine: poor performance, leaks, overheating. • "Engine problems; repaired/replaced head gasket, water pump and thermostat." • "Car displayed excessive oil consumption along with sluggish performance; repaired/replaced head gasket, no improvement." • "Excessive consumption of oil, leak from hole in block that holds capscrew for the outer end of starter bracket." • "Constant problem with engine leaking oil; repaired/replaced seals and gaskets, oil still dripping on garage floor." • "Engine overheats; head gasket and water pump replaced, problem still exists."
6. Brakes: hydraulic: disc: rotor: disc hub, locking up, pulling, excessive wear. • "Brakes locked up due to defective front brake calipers and rotors. This is the second incident." • "Rotor failed, pulling vehicle to one side, causing accident; prior to recall." • "While driving, front driver's-side disc rotor separated with no warning, passenger-side rotor is severely corroded." • "Rotors replaced twice and turned 9 times due to warping."

FORD TAURUS 1988

Complaint Severity: Minor. **Recall Alert:** See Recall Index. **Buyer's Summary:** Look carefully for any kind of leakage, especially under the car. The fuel injection system has been blamed for hesitation and stalling. Be sure the vehicle doesn't die in traffic or at stops. Check the brakes—listen for noise, look for leaks and feel for vibration. They may fail, perform poorly or require frequent mechanical attention. Test the transmission thoroughly. See "Sudden Accelerations" in Introduction.

Hot Spots and Owner/NHTSA Comments:
1. Engine: mounts, vibration, premature failure. • "Had engine mounts replaced. Only lasted 10,000 miles before breaking again." • "Defective motor mount caused engine to drop; wheels locked up; loss of steering; motor mount replaced; problem has reoccurred." • "While vehicle was being serviced for defective power switch, it was discovered that one motor mount was missing and the other broke off." • "Two motor mounts broke; resulted in engine vibrating." • "Engine mounts repaired 6 times; problem keeps reoccurring; problem still exists; Ford has offered owner $1,000 voucher; next owner will have same problem."
2. Fuel: throttle linkages and control, sudden accelerations. • "Vehicle failed to decelerate when foot was removed from accelerator pedal, resulting in loss of control and an accident." • "Engine surged forward at a very high speed without warning while vehicle stopped at traffic light." • "Vehicle accelerated from 35 to 70 mph without driver pressing accelerator pedal." • "Throttle stuck right after shifting from park to reverse; accelerated to high rpm; no warning; caused accident; speed 20 mph; impact 5:00." • "Car put in drive, rapidly accelerated into retaining wall; brakes also failed to operate."
3. Power train: transmission: automatic, poor performance, difficulty shifting, slipping. • "Four-speed automatic transmission with floor-mounted selector does not lock in park position when key removed from ignition, jumps out of park when car not running." • "Car slams into gear going from 1st to 2nd, usually occurs when decelerating down to 1st gear, followed by acceleration; repeated adjustments have failed." • "The transmission went out at 82,000 miles, at first transmission slipped, then vehicle completely stopped; no power in forward/reverse gears." • "Had to have transmission replaced 7 times. Vehicle would not move." • "Transmission continually slipped; replaced 3 times."

4. Brakes: hydraulic: disc: rotor: disc hub, vibration, excessive wear. • "Front brake pulsation; rotors replaced at 15,000 miles; also, steering is difficult when braking hard." • "Warped front brake rotors resulted in constant vibration, especially when braking in a straight line." • "Front brake rotors snapped, causing a loss of braking power, which was reduced to a minimum." • "Vibration when brakes applied, prior to recall; repairs refused due to unavailability of parts." • "Brakes pulsate when applied, turned and replaced rotors."
5. Brakes: hydraulic system, noise, leaks, failure. • "Brake failure, brake pedal bottoms out at stop lights." • "Brake problems; rotors are warped and cylinders leak." • "Repeated failure of brakes, constantly grind, squeak, wheel cylinder bent." • "Extreme noise is observed when brakes are applied." • "Loss of vehicle control upon application of the brakes."
6. Fuel: fuel injection system, stalling, hesitation. • "Stalls unexpectedly at stop lights, stop signs or when driving at very slow speeds." • "Vehicle cuts off, losing all acceleration and power; happens without warning at both highway speeds and in city traffic." • "With no warning, car just shut down, everything stopped." • "Frequent engine stalling during stops and under slow-moving conditions." • "Engine cuts out periodically while driving at 60-65 mph, then difficult to restart."

FORD TAURUS 1989

Complaint Severity: Minor. **Recall Alert:** See Recall Index. **Buyer's Summary:** Check the brakes—listen for noise, look for leaks and feel for vibration. They may fail, perform poorly or require frequent mechanical attention. Test the transmission thoroughly. See "Sudden Accelerations" in Introduction.

Hot Spots and Owner/NHTSA Comments:
1. Interior systems: active restraints: belt buckles, malfunction, failure. • "Driver's and passenger's lap and shoulder belts are fastened with excessive effort and difficulty, disconnecting on their own. Recall." • "Frontal collision, impact 12:00 position, lap and shoulder belt buckle unlatched, speed 55 mph." • "Seat belt locks do not remain fastened on driver's and passenger's sides." • "Front passenger's seat belt buckle became disengaged with the slightest pressure or motion." • "Driver's seat belt release button is stuck in down position; will not release; excessive effort; sometimes will hold, other times comes right back out."
2. Brakes: hydraulic system, excessive wear, vibration, failure. • "Brake wore excessively and prematurely at 8,000 miles." • "Repeated brake failure; brakes go to floor upon application, do not stop car." • "Brakes intermittently stop functioning; seconds later, start functioning again; fade out completely; reason unknown." • "Vibrations when braking; seized calipers and out-of-round rotors; repeated problem."
3. Power train: transmission: automatic, poor performance, difficulty shifting, slipping. • "At 55 mph, transmission shifted without warning from high gear to 1st gear, causing vehicle to decelerate; transmission finally failed." • "Car was stopped at light and accelerator pedal went to the floor by itself. Vehicle was turned off twice in order to bring idle to normal. Transmission was burned out." • "Purchased car used; have had to replace the transmission 4 times, replaced every 20,000 miles." • "Automatic transmission failed at 76,000 miles. Started jerking at traffic light and was slipping, growing worse, destroying gears." • "The automatic transmission lurches forward when slowing down to come to a complete stop."
4. Brakes: hydraulic: disc: rotor: disc hub, vibration, excessive wear. • "Experiencing pulsation in wheel when brakes applied; replaced front brakes, rotor and drum at 25,000 miles." • "Brake failure at 12,000 miles; vibrate when applied; rotors need to be turned." • "Front rotors warped; had them turned; new pads installed at 29,000 miles, warped again; when applying brakes, makes car hard to control." • "Warped front rotors cause heavy vibration when brakes are applied at cruising speed; repaired/ replaced rotors, problem recurred after 4,000 miles." • "Vibration while braking due to warped rotors."
5. Fuel: throttle linkages and control, sudden accelerations. • "Upon starting and putting in reverse, vehicle accelerated to top speed, going out of driveway down an embankment." • "While driving out of a parking spot and turning left, vehicle suddenly accelerated out of control, hit telephone pole on right side; suffered injuries." • "Problem with sticking throttle body, experienced sudden acceleration, applied brakes to no avail; resulted in accident with injury and property damage." • "While in reverse position, vehicle shot out of control; resulted in hitting a bus stop." • "Engine accelerated from 0 to 35 mph while stopping with brakes applied."
6. Engine: mounts, premature failure. • "Vehicle has had 3 replacements of motor mounts within 60,000 miles. Excessive movement and vibration." • "Replaced 2 front motor mounts at 32,000 miles; possibly dangerous manufacturing design defect and/or installation flaw." • "Engine motor mount broke at only 31,000 miles." • "While driving, noticed that motor mount near right front radiator broke." • "Broken motor mounts cause a loud noise and vehicle lurches forward when coming to a stop all the time."

FORD TAURUS 1990

Complaint Severity: Typical. **Recall Alert:** See Recall Index. **Buyer's Summary:** The airbags in this vehicle have experienced failures and malfunctions: You may need a professional evaluation on the condition of the airbags. Check the brakes—listen for noise, look for leaks and feel for vibration. They may fail, perform poorly or require frequent mechanical attention. Test the transmission thoroughly. See "Sudden Accelerations" in Introduction.

Hot Spots and Owner/NHTSA Comments:
1. Fuel: throttle linkages and control, sudden accelerations. • "Sudden acceleration caused the vehicle to hit a pole, impact 1:00 position, speed 25 mph." • "Engine accelerated and surged forward at rapid speed while vehicle was fully stopped and gear in park position; resulted in an accident." • "Recurring problem with engine racing and surging forward when brake depressed; repaired/replaced fuel pump, processor, electronic control unit, throttle position sensor, etc., all repairs to no avail." • "Driver turned on ignition; shifted gear into reverse; engine suddenly accelerated; lurched backward into garage door; damaged trunk; airbag did not deploy." • "Vehicle periodically suddenly accelerates while idling at stop or driving."
2. Brakes: hydraulic: disc: rotor: disc hub, excessive wear, vibration. • "Front brake rotors warped and caused brake pads to wear excessively with low mileage accumulation of 15,000." • "Rotors worn prematurely, causing vibration and loss of brakes." • "Due to premature wear of front brake rotors, vehicle vibrated when stopping." • "Warped front brake rotors caused vehicle to vibrate; rotors replaced 3 times under warranty." • "When brakes were applied, vehicle vibrated; dealer replaced 2 front rotors at owner's expense."
3. Interior systems: passive restraint: airbag: driver, malfunction, failure. • "In accident at 12:00 position, speed 15 mph, airbag did not deploy; car was completely lost." • "Estimated speed 20-30 mph, airbag failed to deploy upon contact. Impact 11:00 position." • "Frontal collision, impact 12:00 position, speed 65 mph, hitting a guardrail airbag did not deploy." • "Vehicle was rear-ended and hit car in front, estimated speed 35 mph, airbag did not

deploy." • "Airbag deployment was violent on impact, resulting in injuries to head, chest and other parts of body."
4. Power train: transmission: automatic, poor performance, difficulty shifting, slipping. • "Automatic transmission gasket leaking; noticed oil leak when tires realigned." • "Automatic transmission does not shift down smoothly; repaired 3 times." • "Transmission slipping, causing car to jump forward when accelerating." • "Transmission hesitates before engaging in gear while accelerating." • "Automatic transmission has vibration and missing and/or delayed reaction switching gears."
5. Brakes: hydraulic system, failure. • "Experienced brake failure when applied, pushed right to floor with no braking whatsoever; resulted in accident." • "With absolutely no warning, experienced complete brake failure momentarily on 2 occasions." • "While completely stopped, foot on brake, feels like car being rear-ended and car moved forward 2-3 inches, but nobody is behind; possible brake failure." • "Brakes failed. Experienced pedal fading. Frontal collision. Impact 12:00 position. Speed 25 mph. Airbag did not deploy." • "Intermittent brake failure; master cylinder replaced, problem continues."
6. Engine: mounts, premature failure. • "Main motor mount broke; does not support motor, supported by other 2 mounts; could cause motor to drop out while driving; made squeaking, grinding noise." • "The motor mount went out at 36,000 miles, and it is starting the same problem now." • "Two of the 3 motor mounts broke sometime before 20,000 miles." • "Vehicle motor mounts broke; vehicle not involved in recall." • "Engine mount bolts loosen, causing dangerous shifting of engine and uncontrollable acceleration."

FORD TAURUS 1991

Complaint Severity: Typical. **Recall Alert:** See Recall Index. **Buyer's Summary:** The steering may be stiff or not working correctly. Be sure to test the steering, especially on a cold start. The airbags in this vehicle have experienced failures and malfunctions: You may need a professional evaluation on the condition of the airbags. Check the brakes—listen for noise, look for leaks and feel for vibration. They may fail, perform poorly or require frequent mechanical attention. Test the transmission thoroughly. See "Sudden Accelerations" in Introduction.

Hot Spots and Owner/NHTSA Comments:
1. Power train: transmission: automatic, poor performance, difficulty shifting, slipping. • "While in park with key out of ignition, vehicle rolled down driveway, hitting the garage." • "While making a left-hand turn and accelerating, vehicle will change gears from drive to neutral and back." • "Transmission difficult to shift from park to drive; caught fire." • "Automatic transmission seize-up; has been replaced 3 times and caused condenser and speed sensor burnout." • "Vehicle experiences delay in engaging when shifting from neutral into drive and upon acceleration."
2. Brakes: hydraulic: disc: rotor: disc hub, excessive wear, vibration. • "Front rotors warped, front pads also cracked, causing brakes to pulsate when depressed." • "Brakes did not stop vehicle properly due to warped rotors, which had to be replaced." • "Brake pedal pulsates during braking; steering wheel shakes; and tires wear on the outside in a cupped fashion; repaired rotors and replaced tires." • "Fourth set of front brake rotors in 31,000 miles. Brakes suddenly vibrate at highway speeds. Vibration felt throughout front end and steering wheel." • "Vibration, extended stopping or reduced brake effectiveness occur due to corrosion or defective rotors. Replaced 4 times."
3. Engine: mounts, premature failure. • "Left side motor mount fell out, apparently was not tightened when left factory and vibrated out of engine; resulted in poor performance." • "Bolt came out of motor mount twice, shifting engine into radiator fan." • "Bolt on motor mount fell off while driving, causing engine to shift and resulting in shutdown." • "Bolt holding front engine mount broke, causing excessive movement in engine." • "Clicking sound when accelerating due to worn or broken motor mount."
4. Interior systems: passive restraint: airbag: driver, malfunction, failure. • "Airbag deployed during front-end collision at 35 mph, causing burns and abrasion to driver." • "No deployment of driver's-side airbag during accident, resulting in an injury." • "Upon impact, during frontal crash at 12:00 on right front bumper, passenger's airbag failed to deploy." • "At 12:00 position, 35 mph, driver's-side airbag did not deploy." • "In accident at 20 mph, at 11:00 position, airbag had a delayed deployment."
5. Steering: linkages: tie rod: inner, failure. • "Outer tie rod broke while driving out of parking lot, causing loss of steering." • "Inner tie rod broke and ruptured the fuel line." • "Tie rods separated from rack-and-pinion while driving at 5-10 mph, causing loss of steering control." • "Inner tie rod broke on the passenger side; after completion of repair, frontal collision, impact 12:00 position, speed 25, airbag did not deploy." • "Left tie rod broke and replaced on driver side (inner) while driving. Right tie rod replaced."
6. Fuel: throttle linkages and control, sudden accelerations. • "While backing out of parking lot very slowly, engine accelerated; vehicle shot backwards; hit 3 other vehicles, resulting in accident and injury." • "From park, shifted into drive and experienced sudden acceleration, crashing into 2 other cars." • "Three-mile trip, restart brought a sudden acceleration when driver shifted into reverse, subsequent shifting into drive caused sudden acceleration into a crash." • "Vehicle at stoplight, pushed accelerator pedal to drive and vehicle downshifted into reverse. Experienced sudden acceleration." • "Accelerator stuck, fuel injectors defective; put into reverse, put into drive, lost control, impact 11:00 position, speed unknown, airbag did not deploy."

FORD TAURUS 1992

Complaint Severity: Troublesome. **Recall Alert:** See Recall Index. **Buyer's Summary:** The airbags in this vehicle have experienced failures and malfunctions: You may need a professional evaluation on the condition of the airbags. Check the brakes—listen for noise, look for leaks and feel for vibration. They may fail, perform poorly or require frequent mechanical attention. Test the transmission thoroughly. See "Sudden Accelerations" in Introduction.

Hot Spots and Owner/NHTSA Comments:
1. Engine: mounts, breaking, premature failure. • "Three motor mounts were broken; damaged other parts of vehicle." • "The front left side of engine mount is broken, causing the engine to move." • "Motor mounts failed; they have broken 2 different times." • "Motor mounts broke, causing vehicle to jerk." • "Motor mount bolts sheared off, leaving engine loose."
2. Interior systems: passive restraint: airbag: driver, malfunction, failure. • "Frontal collision, impact 12:00 position position, speed 35 mph, driver's-side airbag did not deploy." • "Driver's airbag did not deploy during side and front-end impact; hit by another vehicle, ended up hitting road sign and an embankment." • "Head-on crash at 40 mph, seat belts did not restrain and driver's head hit visor, with chest hitting steering wheel. Airbag did not deploy." • "During a head-on collision, impact at 12:00, speed 31 mph, airbag did not deploy." • "During a rear-end collision at approximately 55 mph, car jammed into another vehicle, impact at 1:00 on front bumper, airbag failed to deploy."
3. Fuel: throttle linkages and control, sudden accelerations. • "While driving at 50 mph, high rpm caused vehicle to suddenly accelerate to 90 mph; near-misses of accidents." • "Vehicle was at a stoplight, impact 3:00 position, at a low speed of 3 mph, vehicle

went into open throttle position, throttle was stuck." • "When vehicle coming to a stop, engine goes into high idle; to stop vehicle, turn engine off." • "Vehicle has very high idle and does not decelerate quickly." • "Sudden acceleration caused loss of control and an accident."

4. Power train: transmission: automatic, poor performance, difficulty shifting, slipping. • "Automatic transmission; when engaged on slight incline, transmission pops out of gear." • "Erratic operation of transmission sensors, not shifting into gear properly." • "While driving, vehicle surges forward about 10 miles over vehicle speed due to problem with transmission computer." • "Transmission doesn't shift into overdrive or downshifts into 2nd gear." • "Vehicle was parked in gear with engine in parked position on an incline, vehicle jumped out of gear, hitting a building, impact 12:00 position position, speed unknown."

5. Brakes: hydraulic: disc: rotor: disc hub, vibration, excessive wear. • "Defective rotors cause vehicle vibration; also, pads replaced." • "Front brakes. Disc rotors warped and replaced. Vibration felt when brakes are applied." • "Premature brake rotor failure." • "Front brake rotors failed; replaced twice."

6. Brakes: hydraulic: anti-skid system, poor performance, failure, locking up. • "Antilock brake system: Slowly approached intersection; applied brakes; drifted through intersection as if on ice; intended stopping; no warning." • "Antilock brake system. When driver applies brakes, vehicle takes longer to stop. Brakes don't have full stopping power. They had to be pumped before they return." • "Antilock brake system malfunctions when brakes applied, pedal does not release, leaving brakes engaged; replaced rack-and-pinion twice, dealer cannot find problem." • "Antilock brake system malfunction, pedal fades to the floor, then pressure comes back with full braking ability; dealer cannot find problem." • "Brakes fail to stop vehicle effectively when applied, causing extended stopping and vibration. Repaired 5 times."

FORD TAURUS 1993

Complaint Severity: Typical. **Recall Alert:** See Recall Index. **Buyer's Summary:** The airbags in this vehicle have experienced failures and malfunctions: You may need a professional evaluation on the condition of the airbags. Check the brakes—listen for noise, look for leaks and feel for vibration. They may fail, perform poorly or require frequent mechanical attention. Test the transmission thoroughly. See "Sudden Accelerations" in Introduction.

Hot Spots and Owner/NHTSA Comments:

1. Brakes: hydraulic: disc: rotor: disc hub, vibration, excessive wear. • "Front brake rotors wearing within 15,000 miles, causing shaky steering." • "Rotors failed, causing pulsation when brakes applied." • "Warped front brake rotors and pads, causing vehicle to vibrate when braking." • "Rotors are warped, brakes pulsate; had replaced 8 times and repaired once." • "When rotors get warm they warp, which causes vibration and handling problem; also, excessive brake wear."

2. Interior systems: passive restraint: airbag: driver, malfunction, failure. • "Driver's-side airbag deployed but did not inflate completely at 40 mph." • "The car was in a frontal collision and the driver's airbag did not deploy." • "Airbag did not deploy upon front-end impact; vehicle rear-ended another vehicle that suddenly stopped; vehicle 1 slid into vehicle 2." • "Airbag deployment was violent, burning inner right arm and knee during accident."

3. Fuel: throttle linkages and control, sudden accelerations. • "Vehicle periodically accelerates to high speed and rpm." • "Vehicle suddenly accelerates out of control, regained control, brakes did not respond." • "On trying to accelerate in passing or starting out at an intersection, vehicle hesitates and flutters." • "Engine accelerated in an uncontrollable manner while coming to stop. After stopping, vibrated violently. Speed 45 mph. No prior warning."

4. Power train: transmission: automatic, poor performance, difficulty shifting, slipping. • "While driving, vehicle lurches and surges forward, cruise not engaged; dealer suspects transmission malfunction." • "Vehicle left in park with engine running, and transmission slipped from park into reverse." • "Fully electronic automatic transmission has a 2-4 second delay when turning either direction." • "Car does not accelerate properly. Transmission is slipping." • "The transmission sensor went out for the third time since January."

5. Brakes: hydraulic: anti-skid system, poor performance, failure, locking up. • "Antilock brake system has the pedal going to the floor, and the vehicle either locks up the wheels or does not stop." • "Antilock brakes failed on vehicle. Front of vehicle hit rear of other vehicle and airbag did not deploy." • "Vehicle was involved in an accident because antilock brake system did not work properly. In addition, airbag failed to deploy." • "Vehicle suddenly accelerates out of control; regained control, brakes did not respond." • "Vehicle's antilock brake system has a severe shake when applying brakes, causing difficulty in stopping."

6. Brakes: hydraulic system, failure. • "Vehicle stalls out over 30 and under 50 mph, resulting in steering and braking ability loss; dealer cannot locate problem." • "Brakes failed, causing loss of control and an accident." • "Brake interlock switch disengaged while vehicle was parked; vehicle rolled backwards; resulted in an accident." • "Frontal collision, experienced brake failure and pedal fading, impact 12:00 position, 50 mph. Also, airbag failed to deploy."

FORD TAURUS 1994

Complaint Severity: Typical. **Recall Alert:** See Recall Index. **Buyer's Summary:** The airbags in this vehicle have experienced failures and malfunctions: You may need a professional evaluation on the condition of the airbags. Check the brakes—listen for noise, look for leaks and feel for vibration. They may fail, perform poorly or require frequent mechanical attention. Test the transmission thoroughly. See "Sudden Accelerations" in Introduction.

Hot Spots and Owner/NHTSA Comments:

1. Interior systems: passive restraint: airbag: driver, malfunction, failure. • "Owner hit deer between 40 and 45 mph and airbag did not deploy, resulting in an injury." • "Airbag light stays on, only when engine is hot." • "Had a frontal collision and the airbag did not deploy." • "In a low-speed collision the driver's airbag deployed." • "Driver's-side airbag deployed and broke driver's arm."

2. Electrical system: ignition, stalling, fire. • "Vehicle suddenly lost power and caught on fire." • "Ignition suppresser failed." • "Ignition module failed, causing vehicle to stall." • "Vehicle stalls out at high speeds."

3. Brakes: hydraulic system, noise, failure. • "Noisy brakes." • "Brake problems." • "Vehicle surges forward with the brakes on." • "Upon start, with foot applied to brake, suddenly vehicle accelerated without warning out of control, rendering brake ineffective." • "Brakes went out completely; warning light came on; pedal traveled to the floor."

4. Fuel: throttle linkages and control, sudden accelerations. • "Upon start, with foot applied to brake, suddenly vehicle accelerated without warning out of control, rendering brake ineffective." • "Vehicle surging." • "Vehicle surges forward with the brakes on." • "Turned the ignition and vehicle accelerated backwards through garage door."

5. Power train: transmission: automatic, poor performance, difficulty shifting, slipping. • "Shifted from drive to park, opened door and stepped out; gear jumped from park to reverse; rolled backward into ditch." • "Transmission failure." • "Transmission sticks in 2nd gear, causing engine to rev if going over 40 mph." • "Bought brand new in 1994, a few days ago transmission blew up; had back to dealer, casing was changed but have nothing but jerking starts and slipping out of gear."

FORD TEMPO 1987

Complaint Severity: Minor. **Recall Alert:** See Recall Index. **Buyer's Summary:** The carburetion system could contribute to stalling and hesitation. The fuel pump has received complaints. Make sure it doesn't make excessive noise and that you are experiencing adequate engine performance. Also, look for leaks. The electronic control unit has been blamed for engine performance problems, including stalling and surging. The fuel injection system has been blamed for hesitation and stalling. Be sure the vehicle doesn't die in traffic or at stops. Test the transmission thoroughly. See "Sudden Accelerations" in Introduction.

Hot Spots and Owner/NHTSA Comments:

1. Fuel: throttle linkages and control, sudden accelerations. • "Vehicle is subject to accelerating without warning." • "Upon shifting into reverse, car idling high, took off by itself; resulted in accident." • "Car accelerates in reverse and in 1st without depressing accelerator; forced to jam on brakes to stop." • "Vehicle suffers sudden acceleration due to sticking and binding of fuel linkage assembly."

2. Fuel: fuel injection system, stalling, hesitation. • "Fuel injection system replaced under recall notice; also, fuel tank and fuel pump replaced." • "Continuous stalling problem; installed injector, repaired/replaced processor, throttle position sensor, integrated circuit actuator assembly and throttle." • "Several repairs made to improve performance of fuel injection system to no avail; engine races, hunts for speed before settling." • "Dangerous intermittent stalling problem at stop signals or in stop-and-go traffic." • "Stalling; repaired/replaced fuel injectors, sensors, spark plugs and exhaust gas recirculation valve, problem continues."

3. Power train: transmission: automatic, poor performance, difficulty shifting, slipping. • "Transmission gasket leaked oil; repaired/replaced transmission gasket, planetary and gear assembly." • "Pan gasket leaks transmission fluid; resulted in total failure." • "Transmission jerks and constantly shifts hard, shifts gear in a rough and loud manner." • "Vehicle has failed to shift gears properly, has run rough, overheated and stalled frequently under power; problems associated with faulty transmission." • "Transmission mounts failed; also, transmission fluid leak."

4. Electrical system: ignition: electronic control unit, stalling, sudden acceleration. • "Engine experiencing excessive surging problem, rpm has been as high as 45 on rpm dial; repaired to no avail." • "Engine dies while driving; replaced starter and ignition module, problem still existed; microprocessor/computer chips failed." • "Defective electronic processor control box; vehicle loses power suddenly, lights go out." • "Defect in electronic computer module, engine races, also bucks, pings and loses power." • "Electronic computer idle sensor failed; shifted into drive, car rocketed forward; resulted in accident."

5. Fuel: fuel pump, stalling, premature failure. • "Replaced electric fuel pump after 37,000 miles." • "Engine stalling at speeds of 50 mph; replaced fuel pump." • "Engine loses power while driving, slows and dies intermittently; suspect bad fuel pump." • "On 2 occasions while driving, engine suddenly quit due to a faulty fuel pump; repaired/replaced." • "Cold day, driving 25 mph, the electric fuel pump will fail and bring the vehicle to a stall. Several occasions."

6. Fuel: fuel carburetion, stalling, hesitation. • "Constant problems with the engine cutting off, stalling when driving; carburetor malfunctioned, filter clogged." • "Fuel carburetion system faulty, problems with power surges; adjusted base idle, problem still continues." • "Carburetor became disconnected, jammed accelerator rod and kept throttle open; sudden acceleration resulted." • "Car stalls at different speeds; replaced carburetor." • "Vehicle stalls unexpectedly, also decelerates occasionally."

FORD TEMPO 1988

Complaint Severity: Typical. **Recall Alert:** See Recall Index. **Buyer's Summary:** The fuel pump has received complaints. Make sure it doesn't make excessive noise and that you are experiencing adequate engine performance. Also, look for leaks. The fuel injection system has been blamed for hesitation and stalling. Be sure the vehicle doesn't die in traffic or at stops. The steering may be stiff or not working correctly. Be sure to test the steering, especially on a cold start. See "Sudden Accelerations" in Introduction.

Hot Spots and Owner/NHTSA Comments:

1. Fuel: fuel pump, stalling, failure. • "Intermittent fuel pump failure resulted in vehicle stalling and loss of steering control." • "Fuel pump failed, causing vehicle to stall, prior to and after recall repairs." • "Continuing problem with vehicle sputtering and/or stalling in heavy traffic, will literally choke down after acting like starving for fuel, fuel pump hums loudly." • "While driving, driver was unable to keep car running due to faulty fuel pump; problem not corrected due to unavailable part." • "While driving, experienced intermittent deceleration due to fuel pump malfunction; dealer about to replace it with the ninth fuel pump."

2. Fuel: fuel injection system, stalling, hesitation. • "Problems with stalling and hesitation due to dirty positive crankcase ventilation valves and fuel pump; dealer replaced processor chips and cleaned fuel injectors." • "Car has exhibited idling problem, hesitates, stalls and sometimes surges forward." • "Engine stalling problems experienced; also has timing problems." • "Intermittent stalling; many repairs, problem eventually identified as faulty fuel pump." • "Intermittent stalling and surge problem; fuel pump replaced." • "Intermittent stalling; replaced fuel injection pump to no avail."

3. Fuel: throttle linkages and control, sudden accelerations. • "Car accelerated backward for 10-15 feet and could not be stopped by brakes; crashed into guardrail." • "Throttle stuck; caused loss of control and resulted in an accident." • "Vehicle would suddenly accelerate when moving from a stop position into drive. Repaired numerous times." • "Vehicle surged forward and out of control; resulted in an accident." • "Vehicle idling in park position, upon releasing emergency brake, vehicle suddenly lurched forward, smashing garage door, then turning on its side."

4. Steering: linkages: tie rod: end, alignment, tire wear, excessive wear. • "Defective inner and end tie rods, cause misalignment of front end, resulting in premature tire failure; repaired/replaced tie rod and 4 sets of tires." • "Approaching a stop, sudden loss of steering function occurred, left side tie rod found to have fractured transition area between ball and rod inner joint." • "Tie rods were worn too loose; caused tires to wear out and alignment problems." • "Left outer tie rod end was in poor condition; caused steering to feel loose while driving." • "Front right tie rod broke, right front wheel turned completely sideways; repaired/replaced."

5. Steering: linkages: tie rod: inner, pulling, premature failure. • "Noticed vehicle pulling to right; inner tie rods worn." • "Problem with loose steering; repaired/replaced right inner tie rod end." • "Left inner tie rod broke at ball pivot due to rusting."

• "Both tie rod ends were replaced on 3 different occasions." • "Front inner tie rods in steering linkage became worn; made clunking noises whenever it was driven over bumps or turning corners."
6. Engine: leaks. • "Engine defect; excessive oil consumption." • "Engine problems; oil leak on motor, and head gasket leak." • "Engine oil leak; front crankshaft seal replaced." • "Excessive oil leak from both ends of crankshaft; many repairs, problem continues."

FORD TEMPO 1989

Complaint Severity: Typical. **Buyer's Summary:** The fuel pump has received complaints. Make sure it doesn't make excessive noise and that you are experiencing adequate engine performance. Also, look for leaks. The fuel injection system has been blamed for hesitation and stalling. Be sure the vehicle doesn't die in traffic or at stops. The steering may be stiff or not working correctly. Be sure to test the steering, especially on a cold start. Check the brakes—listen for noise, look for leaks and feel for vibration. They may fail, perform poorly or require frequent mechanical attention. Make sure seat belts function correctly and fit comfortably. See "Sudden Accelerations" in Introduction.

Hot Spots and Owner/NHTSA Comments:
1. Fuel: fuel pump, hesitation, stalling. • "Electric fuel pump malfunctioned; engine would not accelerate after stopping for light; stalled, gas pedal went to floor when tried to accelerate again." • "Fuel pump failed, causing vehicle to hesitate and/or stall, prior to and after recall." • "Vehicle's fuel pump shut off, causing stalling and resulting in loss of steering and brakes." • "Fuel pump failure while in operation; vehicle just shut down entirely." • "Recurring stalling problem; repaired/replaced fuel pump, fuel filter, retainer tube, throttle position sensor, etc., all repair attempts to no avail."
2. Fuel: throttle linkages and control, sudden accelerations. • "Sudden acceleration. Engine temperature sensor gave false reading to throttle position sensor, which kept engine idling faster than it should." • "While pulling into a parking space at a supermarket, throttle stuck, vehicle suddenly accelerated forward and out of control and went into store window." • "Throttle position sensor malfunction caused sudden acceleration." • "Sudden acceleration upon shifting from park to reverse; accident resulted." • "Vehicle was started, put into gear, then accelerated at a high rate of speed while driver's foot was on brake."
3. Fuel: fuel injection system, stalling, hesitation. • "When driving car for a while during daytime, car gets hot and chokes off; car sits for a day or so, then OK; also, gas fumes entering through air conditioner; repaired." • "Engine stalls, then surges after stopping or at low speed." • "Vehicle hesitates and stalls when pulling out from stop sign or traffic light." • "Defective fuel injection system causes continual stalling problem; car broke down twice."
4. Interior systems: passive restraint: belts, breaking, malfunction. • "The passenger's front automatic retractable seat belt does not run along the track." • "Seat belt track failed; seat belt is locked in position." • "During an accident, shoulder belt strap broke; passenger suffered an injury." • "Motorized shoulder belt broke off the track." • "Driver's-side passive restraint. When closing the door, belt hesitates 5 to 6 seconds. May not restrain in vehicle accident."
5. Brakes: hydraulic system, locking up, noise, failure. • "Front right brake locked." • "Clinking, rattling noise in front brakes; hesitation in stopping; anti-rattling device causing noise, per mechanic; also, replaced pads, shoes, rotors." • "Vehicle does not stop when brakes are applied; brakes malfunctioned and have been replaced at least 3 times." • "Brakes failed and were replaced both in front and back." • "Uneven brake wear."
6. Steering: linkages: tie rod: inner, breaking, failure. • "Tie rods failed, causing accident." • "Tie rod broke, causing loss of control." • "Inner tie rod ends replaced." • "Loose inner tie rods."

FORD TEMPO 1990

Complaint Severity: Typical. **Recall Alert:** See Recall Index. **Buyer's Summary:** The steering may be stiff or not working correctly. Be sure to test the steering, especially on a cold start. Check the brakes—listen for noise, look for leaks and feel for vibration. They may fail, perform poorly or require frequent mechanical attention. Test the transmission thoroughly. Make sure seat belts function correctly and fit comfortably. See "Sudden Accelerations" in Introduction.

Hot Spots and Owner/NHTSA Comments:
1. Fuel: throttle linkages and control, sudden accelerations. • "Car in park position, put foot on brake and car into drive, there was roar and car took off, brakes failed to stop, causing accident with injuries sustained." • "Fast idle, vehicle goes to 30 mph without touching accelerator." • "Throttle position sensor recalled; awaiting repairs." • "While putting vehicle in garage, it suddenly accelerated, went through entire back end of the garage and hit steel fence pole and was stopped by a tree." • "Backing out of parking space, upon placing into forward gear, engine surged, then suddenly accelerated out of control. Resulted in hitting another vehicle."
2. Brakes: hydraulic system, locking up, failure. • "Was cut off by another vehicle and had to stop short, brakes locked, causing vehicle to skid sideways; could not regain control and hit guardrail head on." • "Experienced brake failure, pedal fading, master cylinder failure. Brake drums, shoes, pads, and rotors replaced." • "Brakes do not always want to grab hold, at times brakes must be pumped continuously." • "Brakes lock and jerk vehicle; brake pedal fades."
3. Electrical system: ignition, stalling, malfunction. • "Electric system: Terminal on distributor cap and on coil completely corroded; prevents electricity from going through; causes delayed start-ups." • "While driving, low to high speeds, engine suddenly shuts down, causing loss of power steering and brakes, no prior warning." • "Vehicle stalls out upon pulling off from a stop; replaced sensor twice to no avail." • "Almost every time vehicle comes to a stop, it hesitates, and sometimes stalls completely."
4. Power train: transmission: automatic, poor performance, difficulty shifting, slipping. • "Transmission will not upshift." • "Transmission noise and poor performance." • "Transmission mount failure." • "Transmission would not shift out of low gear." • "Transmission does not shift smoothly, when driven over 50 mph feels like it is in 2nd gear, not in drive."
5. Interior systems: passive restraint: belts, malfunction, failure. • "During accident, automatic seat belt didn't work; caused injury." • "Design of passive restraint seat belt capable of wrapping around passenger's neck upon rapid exit from vehicle, delaying or preventing exit and causing injury." • "Seat belt design performance questionable; after an accident, does chest belt release or remain locked; if locked, how does passenger make hasty exit." • "Driver's and passenger's shoulder harnesses froze in open position." • "Automatic seat belts failed in an accident."
6. Steering: linkages: tie rod: inner, premature failure. • "Inner tie rods broke on vehicle; loss of steering." • "Power steering inner tie rod broke nearly at the ball. Owner can see a flaw in the metal. Parts will be sent to NHTSA." • "Steering rod failures due to reverse bending fatigue through tapered portion of rod, just below ball end fillet, which causes rod to wear and break." • "Two inner tie rods replaced; premature failure of critical part, especially

on a 2-year-old car with less than 20,000 miles." • "Defective left inner tie rod replaced."

FORD TEMPO 1991

Complaint Severity: Typical. **Buyer's Summary:** The fuel injection system has been blamed for hesitation and stalling. Be sure the vehicle doesn't die in traffic or at stops. Check the brakes—listen for noise, look for leaks and feel for vibration. They may fail, perform poorly or require frequent mechanical attention. Test the transmission thoroughly. Make sure seat belts function correctly and fit comfortably. See "Sudden Accelerations" in Introduction.

Hot Spots and Owner/NHTSA Comments:

1. Electrical system: ignition, stalling. • "Vehicle is subject to stalling at any time without warning. Dealer has made several repairs, with no change in condition, only temporary." • "While driving at reduced speeds, experiences intermittent stalling upon start-up and stop at intersections." • "Vehicle stalls on acceleration from a stopped position." • "Ignition failed, causing vehicle to stall."

2. Power train: transmission: automatic, poor performance, difficulty shifting, slipping. • "Car jumped into gear from park; automatic transmission." • "Transmission linkage misadjusted, causing incorrect gear selection." • "Intermittent shifting problem." • "Automatic transmission sticks in 1st gear, then engine revs to high rpm; almost in serious accidents, dealer said they rebuilt the transmission to no avail." • "While driving down the road, transmission jerks."

3. Fuel: fuel injection system, stalling, hesitation. • "Fuel vapor; leaks fumes inside of vehicle." • "Intermittent stalling and sudden acceleration." • "Intermittent stalling; serviced 5 times, problem continues." • "Intermittent stalling." • "Vehicle is subject to shutting off when driver accelerates from stopping. Vehicle has been in shop 11 times with no defect correction."

4. Fuel: throttle linkages and control, sudden accelerations. • "Vehicle sitting in driveway; started vehicle, shifted into gear, vehicle raced and surged forward." • "While traveling, vehicle suddenly accelerated; attempted to brake and brakes did not work, lost control and went into a ditch, where vehicle stopped." • "After vehicle in drive, vehicle went open throttle position, impact 12:00 position, speed unknown." • "While backing out of driveway with gearshift in reverse and foot lightly on brake, vehicle suddenly accelerated out of control and hit a parked car." • "While driving, suddenly accelerated, went out of control, hit a tree and traveled another 30 to 40 feet and became lodged atop a telephone pole."

5. Brakes: hydraulic system, noise, premature failure. • "Brakes failed to lock properly, causing accident." • "Rear brakes wore out at 13,000 miles and front brakes at 20,060; brakes became spongy, immediately followed by loss of braking effectiveness." • "Front and rear brakes failed." • "Noisy brakes." • "Brake pedal goes to floor; repaired, problem continues."

6. Interior systems: passive restraint: belts, uncomfortable, malfunction, failure. • "Automatic shoulder belt did not restrain driver in an automobile accident." • "Automatic shoulder belt stretches across driver's neck." • "Seat belts get stuck in track, do not work properly." • "Automatic shoulder belt does not hold passenger tightly." • "Automatic shoulder belt does not retract when opening the door."

FORD TEMPO 1992

Complaint Severity: Typical. **Buyer's Summary:** Make sure the shoulder belts don't cut across your neck and are well anchored. Test the transmission thoroughly. See "Sudden Accelerations" in Introduction.

Hot Spots and Owner/NHTSA Comments:

1. Electrical system: ignition, stalling. • "Lost power while driving; after waiting a few seconds, engine will restart." • "When driving, vehicle stalls out and idles roughly prior to shutdown. Very difficult to start." • "Car will stall while driving at any speed up to 65 mph. Will restart after a short interval. Dealer has not been able to repair." • "'Return for service' light came on, and then the vehicle stalled out 3 feet from the edge of a cliff." • "Car constantly stalls."

2. Interior systems: shoulder belts, malfunction, failure. • "Lap and shoulder belts failed, driver and passenger seats; on driver's seat belt locked up while driving, impact 6:00 position, vehicle at a complete stop." • "Shoulder straps in the front on both sides do not work; has been on back order since September." • "Driver's-side shoulder harness will not retract to position to restrain driver in event of an accident or sudden stop." • "Right front shoulder restraint failed." • "Shoulder belts failed during accident, causing injuries."

3. Engine: stalling, premature failure. • "Rocker arms failed." • "Engine vibrates and/or stalls." • "Engine fire." • "Vehicle will seize without any prior warning while driving." • "Car was ticking; bolt from the engine came off."

4. Fuel: throttle linkages and control, sudden accelerations. • "Vehicle will jerk upon acceleration, stalls and rough idle." • Engine light comes on intermittently." • "Air bypass valve sticks, causing sudden acceleration to high rpm when driving on highway." • "When driving, accelerator pedal sticks in closed position, vehicle will stall." • "Idle surge." • "Fast idle."

5. Interior systems: bucket: backrest, breaking, poor performance. • "During collision driver's seat back broke; replacing seat, moving foot off brake pedal, hit vehicle in front." • "Driver's seat collapsed, bending track and breaking hinge. Driver sustained injuries and unconsciousness." • "Front driver's seat back bent and/or broke during accident, causing injuries." • "Vehicle was rear-ended at a red traffic light, the backs of front seats became bent and were flattened against the rear seat cushion."

6. Power train: transmission: automatic, poor performance, difficulty shifting, slipping. • "Transmission gasket or seals failed." • "Stopped on flat surface, put vehicle in neutral and left car; vehicle jumped out of gear and hit a truck." • "Transmission not shifting." • "Automatic transmission locks up, causing vehicle to downshift, resulting in an accident." • "Transmission leak."

FORD TEMPO 1993

Complaint Severity: Typical. **Buyer's Summary:** Look carefully for any kind of leakage, especially under the car. Check the brakes—listen for noise, look for leaks and feel for vibration. They may fail, perform poorly or require frequent mechanical attention. Test the transmission thoroughly. Make sure seat belts function correctly and fit comfortably. See "Sudden Accelerations" in Introduction.

Hot Spots and Owner/NHTSA Comments:

1. Power train: transmission: automatic, poor performance, difficulty shifting, slipping. • "No acceleration over 30 mph, other times not over 10 mph." • "When vehicle is cold, transmission sticks in 1st gear." • "Transmission stuck in 2nd gear intermittently." • "The car gets stuck in 1st gear and will not shift out of 1st gear; only way to rectify is to pull over, turn off the car and start again." • "Automatic transmission failure; replaced transmission 4 times."

2. Brakes: hydraulic system, leaks, noise, excessive wear. • "Experienced brake grinding; had replaced 4 times." • "Vehicle slides when brakes applied; calipers and rotors replaced." • "Brake fluid leak." • "Brakes pulsate and are noisy." • "Power brakes continually warp, causing brakes not to perform effectively when applied."

3. Interior systems: passive restraint: belts, malfunction, failure. • "Front automatic seat belts replaced 6 times within an 8-month period; seat belts were off track; did not retract as intended." • "Automatic seat belts on both driver and passenger-sides do not work properly. When brakes are applied, they lock. When doors are opened, belts do not release." • "Left front motorized front seat belt retracts too tight. Sticks intermittently." • "Driver's-side seat belt unwinds, not preventing occupant from hitting interior." • "Motor and track assembly failed due to teeth on track being stripped."

4. Fuel: throttle linkages and control, sudden accelerations. • "Sudden acceleration, causing accident and injuries." • "Vehicle loses power and intermittently stalls with no warning." • "Car accelerates on its own. And sometimes, vehicle won't accelerate at all." • "When slowing to a stop, engine will surge and stall. Dealer attempted 5 repairs." • "Once vehicle is started up, it continues to accelerate on its own. Dealer says if they can't duplicate the problem, it can't be fixed."

5. Brakes: hydraulic: disc: rotor: disc hub, vibration, failure. • "Front brake rotors failed, causing vehicle to pulsate when braking at high speeds." • "Replaced rotors due to vehicle vibration." • "Brakes shimmy upon application. Dealer installed shoes, hubs and rotors. Every couple of months dealer replaces same components." • "Brake rotors out of round, causing failure."

6. Electrical system: ignition, stalling. • "While driving on highway at approximately 55 mph, engine suddenly shuts down without prior warning; dealer can't reproduce problem on computer; 4 times." • "Vehicle will stall at any speed while driving." • "Vehicle stalls in traffic intermittently." • "Random loss of engine power while driving; creates bucking stop-and-go motion; nearly caused accident."

FORD THUNDERBIRD 1987

Complaint Severity: Typical. **Recall Alert:** See Recall Index. **Buyer's Summary:** The fuel injection system has been blamed for hesitation and stalling. Be sure the vehicle doesn't die in traffic or at stops. Test the suspension by feeling for vibration or pulling while driving. Check the brakes—listen for noise, look for leaks and feel for vibration. They may fail, perform poorly or require frequent mechanical attention. Test the transmission thoroughly. See "Sudden Accelerations" in Introduction.

Hot Spots and Owner/NHTSA Comments:

1. Fuel: throttle linkages and control, sudden accelerations. • "Fuel module failed, causing car to stall; also, accelerator pedal stuck, causing car to speed out of control; accident resulted." • "Upon starting car and putting gear into drive, car suddenly accelerated uncontrollably, colliding with another vehicle." • "Started ignition, put car into drive, it jolted forward at a high speed; applying brakes, vehicle would not stop." • "Vehicle suddenly accelerated while slow moving, no response from brakes; resulted in slamming into concrete block." • "Vehicle has sudden bursts of acceleration that can only be stopped by turning off the engine."

2. Interior systems: active restraints: belt buckles, breaking, failure. • "The driver's- and passenger-side seat belt buckles come loose, seat belts don't tighten up; retractor fell out of track." • "Driver's-side seat belt buckle failure, unable to latch seat belt." • "Driver's seat belt buckle does not lock." • "Driver's seat belt buckle spring broke inside buckle." • "Driver's seat belt buckle fails to fasten and/or latch."

3. Power train: transmission: automatic, poor performance, difficulty shifting, slipping. • "Rough automatic transmission shifting." • "Rear transmission seal leaks onto hot catalytic converter, flashed vapor and smoke; potential fire hazard." • "Rumbling vibration when stopped with car in drive, also noticed noise when accelerating." • "Automatic transmission shifter failure; sticks in reverse when shifting into park from drive; other transmission problems, does not work properly." • "Auto transmission gears don't adjust at appropriate speeds, noisy at speeds of 15-30 mph; problems began after repairs (thermostat, intake, radiator)."

4. Brakes: hydraulic system, noise, excessive wear. • "Brakes squeal and grab, resulting in poor performance." • "Brakes malfunctioning; locks upon application, pulls to right." • "Defective braking system; have had to repair/replace 5 sets of brakes." • "Brakes grind and groan." • "Squeaking noise when releasing pressure from foot brake."

5. Suspension: independent front, vibration, tire wear. • "Steering column and vehicle vibrate constantly at highway speeds, steering pulls to right and left; replacing struts, brake system and so on has not helped." • "Vehicle vibration at 45-50 mph." • "Defect in suspension system; tires wear excessively." • "Loud creaking noise when turning at any speed; replaced MacPherson struts and coils." • "When driving, noticed it wandered from left to right; front wheel had negative camber, did not steer properly."

6. Fuel: fuel injection system, stalling, hesitation. • "Fuel injection failure; runaway engine, jam brakes to stop car, replaced exhaust gas recirculation solenoid, throttle position sensor." • "Engine surges, runs rough, hesitates, stalls and bucks; replaced throttle position and manifold air pressure sensors, idle speed control, problem continues." • "Engine bucks and surges." • "Vehicle not starting, stalling on freeway and in traffic." • "Vehicle starts losing power on steep inclines; changing spark plugs seemed to alleviate problem for a while, hesitation reappeared."

FORD THUNDERBIRD 1988

Complaint Severity: Typical. **Recall Alert:** See Recall Index. **Buyer's Summary:** The fuel injection system has been blamed for hesitation and stalling. Be sure the vehicle doesn't die in traffic or at stops. Test the suspension by feeling for vibration or pulling while driving. Check the brakes—listen for noise, look for leaks and feel for vibration. They may fail, perform poorly or require frequent mechanical attention. Test the transmission thoroughly. See "Sudden Accelerations" in Introduction.

Hot Spots and Owner/NHTSA Comments:

1. Fuel: throttle linkages and control, sudden accelerations. • "Barely touching accelerator, engine accelerated to near maximum rpm; unable to stop car before hitting wooden guardrail." • "Throttle went open position; after putting in gear, vehicle locked in reverse, impact 3:00 position, lost control." • "While passing another vehicle, during acceleration, pedal became stuck and vehicle continued to accelerate." • "Engine has intermittent surging problems, engine speed increases by itself from 1,200-2,400 rpm, accelerator pedal results in car maintaining and/or increasing speed." • "While vehicle travels smoothly through traffic, or stopping at traffic light or stop sign, vehicle will suddenly surge to over 3,000 rpm."

2. Interior systems: active restraints: belt buckles, malfunction, failure. • "Claims has a defective driver's-side seat belt; went to dealer to obtain recall information and was rebuffed." • "Internal springs of driver and passenger seat belts do not latch, making inoperative." • "Driver's front shoulder and lap belt buckles inoperative; when snap male portion into female, buckle comes undone." • "Seat belt buckle broken, causing fastening failure." • "Driver's-side seat belt failure; latch on seat belt failed."

3. Suspension: independent front, tire wear, alignment. • "Excessive wear on outside edge of front tires; rotated tires from front to rear." • "Right front wheel rejects proper alignment, causing vibration and shimmy actions, resulting in accident." • "Defect in front suspension; steering pulls badly to left." • "Front end shimmies between 40 and 60 mph; tried to balance tires, car still shimmies." • "Front end struts have been replaced and front-end alignment could not be properly adjusted; vehicle shakes and rattles."

4. Fuel: fuel injection system, stalling, hesitation. • "Engine stalling occurs at various speeds in 20s, 30s, 40s and 60s, accompanied by violent lurching or bucking; very difficult to regain speed." • "O-rings of one of the fuel injectors failed; fuel dripped over hot metal parts, causing a minor fire, which was contained." • "Hesitation when starting, black smoke from tailpipe, loss of power, sluggish, smell gas fumes, metal tapping in engine." • "Vehicle stalls, no warning, causing poor performance." • "Car began running rough, engine began bucking and stalling; new camshaft, lifters, timing chain, gaskets and starter were put in."

5. Brakes: hydraulic system, excessive wear, noise. • "Premature wear of brakes increases stopping distances and reduces their effectiveness; replaced 6 times." • "Brakes lock at high speed, causing car to skid (completely around) on dry surfaces." • "Noisy disc failed." • "Brakes replaced." • "Brakes failed to slow or stop vehicle."

6. Power train: transmission: automatic, poor performance, difficulty shifting, slipping. • "Transmission failure while in operation." • "Vehicle in park position, jumped into gear, rolled away and picked up speed until someone was able to turn off ignition key; injuries sustained." • "Experiencing heaviness and rough shifting of automatic transmission at premature mileage." • "Stopped car and placed gear in park, heard it jump into gear and it began picking up speed; hurled a person to the ground while trying to stop it." • "Transmission would not go into park occasionally; remains in neutral when parking."

FORD THUNDERBIRD 1989

Complaint Severity: Troublesome. **Recall Alert:** See Recall Index. **Buyer's Summary:** Check the brakes—listen for noise, look for leaks and feel for vibration. They may fail, perform poorly or require frequent mechanical attention. Test the transmission thoroughly. See "Sudden Accelerations" in Introduction.

Hot Spots and Owner/NHTSA Comments:

1. Brakes: hydraulic: disc: rotor: disc hub, vibration, pulling, excessive wear. • "Disc brake rotors warp or distort, causing front end to vibrate violently to point of nearly jerking steering wheel from hand; repaired/replaced, problem reoccurred." • "Experiencing rotor warpage and pad failures in front brakes." • "Front brake rotors distort due to heat buildup when brakes are applied, as a result severe vibration in the front end." • "Brake rotors completely warped, causes car to pull and vibrate excessively." • "Experiencing brake problems; 3 sets of rotors replaced, problems still not corrected, first replacement occurred at approximately 1,500 miles."

2. Fuel: throttle linkages and control, sudden accelerations. • "Throttle stuck; while driving, vehicle suddenly accelerated and in order to stop vehicle, shifted gear into neutral." • "While driving at 55 mph, engine surged to 85-90 mph, had to apply brakes to stop vehicle." • "Upon shifting into reverse, car suddenly accelerated at full throttle; resulted in accident." • "Throttle cable sticks, vehicle intentionally accelerated to full throttle, when gas pedal released, throttle remained wide open, engine revved to maximum." • "Started car with foot on brakes and shifted gear into reverse, accelerator stuck open and vehicle skidded at high rate of speed; accident with injury."

3. Brakes: hydraulic system, vibration, poor performance. • "Experienced front brake problems at 28,000 miles; replaced front brake pads, problem still exists at 49,000 miles, all due to design problem." • "Brakes not good for model car, needed to be redone at 11,000 miles." • "Continuing intermittent problem with brakes; pedal goes all way to floor and not stopping car properly." • "Front disc brakes warped, causing vibration in steering wheel." • "Recall notice of brakes received before dealers received theirs, repair kits not included; notice and parts should be received before customers receive notice."

4. Brakes: hydraulic: shoe: disc brake system, vibration, poor performance. • "Recall notice received of potential reduced braking capacity; right and left front brake caliper contacts front suspension, extended brake travel occurs; parts not available." • "Front brake system unable to properly dissipate the heat generated under braking, causing brake rotors to distort and friction pads to overheat." • "Brake pedal pulsates, causing car to vibrate and steering wheel to shake at speeds over 30 mph; repaired using Ford's front brake rotor and pad service kit." • "Experiencing front brake vibration due to front rotors being warped; consumer received recall notification on brakes."

5. Power train: transmission: automatic, poor performance, difficulty shifting, slipping. • "Problem with leaking transmission; failure of universal joint." • "Internal transmission failure." • "Transmission sometimes slips." • "After parking with cruise control on, 1 hour later started engine with foot on brake, vehicle accelerated, resulting in accident; replaced transmission." • "While starting vehicle, transmission jumped from park to reverse and engine surged to maximum speed."

6. Fuel: fuel tank assembly: gauge: fuel, failure. • "Fuel gauge gives incorrect reading." • "Defective fuel gauge sender." • "Gas gauge and sensor replaced." • "Fuel gauge inoperative when full." • "When filling up fuel tank, fuel gauge sticks on full."

FORD THUNDERBIRD 1990

Complaint Severity: Typical. **Recall Alert:** See Recall Index. **Buyer's Summary:** Check the brakes—listen for noise, look for leaks and feel for vibration. They may fail, perform poorly or require frequent mechanical attention. Test the transmission thoroughly. See "Sudden Accelerations" in Introduction.

Hot Spots and Owner/NHTSA Comments:

1. Fuel: throttle linkages and control, sudden accelerations. • "Vehicle was idling while in park, when shifted into drive the vehicle suddenly accelerated out of control; resulted in an accident." • "When shifting gear from park to drive, vehicle surged into a brick wall." • "Sitting in a parking lot at a restaurant, upon releasing brakes, car shot forward somewhat uncontrollably; also, at stoplights, car tries to keep moving." • "Throttle sticking presenting very unsafe driving conditions, in that acceleration is sudden and unintentional." • "Accelerator stuck wide open; car exiting parking space, sped across lot, brakes unable to stop car; striking curb and tree."

2. Brakes: hydraulic: disc: rotor: disc hub, vibration, excessive wear. • "Rotors being replaced, but car still has the same problem; dealer not willing to repair the problem." • "Recall related. Warped rotors replaced by Ford for free." • "Rotors are warped again. When brakes are applied, steering wheel vibrates." • "Front rotors out of round, causing vibration in steering when brakes applied; replaced rotors 3 times." • "Front brake rotors were wearing unevenly; causes car to vibrate and steering wheel to shake during brake application; need to repair/replace front brake rotors and pads." • "Brake rotors warped, causing severe front wheel shimmy when braking."

3. Brakes: hydraulic system, vibration, poor performance. • "While driving, car accelerated; brake slowed acceleration but did not stop vehicle." • "Upon braking, pedal traveled to floor, brakes were pumped, they re-engaged and locked up; vehicle slid across road into an embankment." • "Vehicle vibrates when brakes are applied at low speeds of 40 mph or less." • "While depressing brakes at 30-55 mph, steering wheel shimmies from left to right without warning." • "Most of the time, brakes allow vehicle to continue to travel before slowing, causing front end to shake."

4. Brakes: hydraulic: shoe: disc brake system, vibration, poor performance. • "Antilock brake system brake pedal goes to the floor and vibrates. Replaced right rear caliper and rotor, front brake pads and rotors." • "Front brakes defective, front wheels vibrate at slow to stop speeds, and drive shaft vibrates at 65 mph and above." • "Vehicle contains poorly designed rotors." • "Front rotors and pads defective." • "Front disc brakes pulsed and vibrated; recalled."

5. Brakes: hydraulic: anti-skid system, poor performance, failure, locking up. • "While driving, experienced hard brake pedal; resulted in ineffective brake action." • "Vehicle has antilock brake system, antilock brake system warning light illuminates; shortly after the brake pedal becomes very hard to push, makes vehicle hard to stop." • "Antilock brake system failed to stop vehicle when applied at 40 mph, causing extended stopping distance. Driver coasted vehicle to a stop." • "Antilock brake system warning light came on and with brake application, pedal would not go down."

6. Power train: transmission: automatic, poor performance, difficulty shifting, slipping. • "Transmission would not shift into 4th gear; rebuilt." • "Transmission stuck in 2nd gear." • "Transmission fails to shift properly, seems jerky." • "Automatic transmission failed prematurely at 170 miles, vehicle switched into neutral while driving." • "Automatic transmission failed prematurely at 1,000 miles."

FORD THUNDERBIRD 1991

Complaint Severity: Minor. **Recall Alert:** See Recall Index. **Buyer's Summary:** Check the brakes—listen for noise, look for leaks and feel for vibration. They may fail, perform poorly or require frequent mechanical attention. Test the transmission thoroughly.

Hot Spots and Owner/NHTSA Comments:

1. Brakes: hydraulic: disc: rotor: disc hub, vibration, excessive wear. • "Front brakes disc rotor overheated and caused front-end vibration when brakes were applied." • "Front brake rotors warped, causing vehicle to vibrate." • "Front brake rotors' inside hole is too small and will cause brakes to pulsate severely, and possibly wheel to fall off." • "Owner says rotors are damaged prematurely." • "The vehicle is not stopping due to bad rotors, and the calipers are stuck in the front brakes."

2. Brakes: hydraulic system, noise, pulling. • "Brakes failed to stop vehicle when applied at 40 mph, causing a front-end collision." • "Brakes grab and make loud scrubbing noise when applied, causing steering wheel to vibrate." • "When attempting to stop, brakes fade and vehicle tends to pull to the side." • "Hearing noises, thought something lodged in rear tire; caused by new environmentally acceptable material used for brakes; brakes deglazed, noise started again."

3. Brakes: hydraulic: shoe: disc brake system, vibration, excessive wear. • "Increased stopping distance, brake pedal pulsated and rotors heated up and warped." • "Front disc brakes worn on right side of vehicle with no abnormality of other brake pads." • "Left front brake calipers jam, causing wear of rotors and brake pads." • "Brake failure. Warped rotors and disc pads. Vibration when applying brakes." • "Premature wear of front pads, rotors and calipers."

4. Power train: transmission: automatic, poor performance, difficulty shifting, slipping. • "When driver changes gears, vehicle hesitates and stumbles." • "Driving up a hill and applying the brakes, the vehicle jumped out of gear and rolled backwards, both feet had to be used to start driving again." • "Gearshift will not release from park position." • "Transmission gears lock up in drive, preventing driver from shifting or changing gears." • "Transmission locks up in drive."

5. Brakes: hydraulic: anti-skid system, poor performance, failure, locking up. • "Antilock braking system failed repeatedly." • "Brake pedal goes to floor." • "Antilock brake system has failed 6 times since vehicle purchased." • "Antilock brake system failure; sporadic failure of the brakes, partial loss of braking."

6. Equipment: electric power accessories: windows, failure. • "Right front power window failed." • "Power window failed." • "Power window problems."

FORD THUNDERBIRD 1992

Complaint Severity: Typical. **Buyer's Summary:** Check the brakes—listen for noise, look for leaks and feel for vibration. They may fail, perform poorly or require frequent mechanical attention. Test the transmission thoroughly. See "Sudden Accelerations" in Introduction.

Hot Spots and Owner/NHTSA Comments:

1. Brakes: hydraulic: disc: rotor: disc hub, vibration, poor performance. • "Antilock brake system: Front and rear rotors replaced twice in 6 months due to warping, causing vibration when stopping." • "Antilock brake system, 4-wheel disc rotors; continuous warping causing extensive vibration." • "Rotors warp, causing excessive vibration and misalignment, also wears out pads prematurely." • "Warped rotors have caused pulsation; upon braking, steering wheel had to be held tightly to keep control of vehicle." • "Brake failure; corrosion of rotors, and pads are not touching; vehicle vibrates when applying brakes."

2. Emergency parking brake: mechanical, failure. • "Parking brake needed adjustment; replaced linkage." • "Parking brake failed." • "Parking brake locking panel spring failed." • "Emergency brake failed." • "Emergency brake will not set at all."

3. Brakes: hydraulic: anti-skid system, poor performance, failure, locking up. • "Antilock brake system pulsated when first started vehicle, experienced pedal fading." • "Antilock brake system: Replaced rotors and pads; when applying brakes, steering wheel shook. When making a left turn, made a loud noise." • "Antilock brake system vibrates when brakes are applied. Vehicle in for repairs before. Owner was told by dealer this is normal. Vibration increased with higher speeds." • "Antilock brake system failed, antilock brake system light came on/off." • "Antilock brake system relay malfunctioned and pump would not turn on intermittently; had no brakes."

4. Brakes: hydraulic system, vibration, noise, locking up. • "When brakes are applied, vehicle vibrates; pads, rotors and linings were replaced." • "Touching the pedal does not release the cruise control. Car pulled off the road into a ditch. Cruise control knob had to be manually turned off." • "Vibrating and/or squeaking brakes." • "After slowing down to 5 mph, pressed accelerator and got stuck to the floor; slammed on brakes; vehicle continued to move forward with tires spinning; hit curb." • "Brakes lock up, have had them repaired 4 times."

5. Fuel: throttle linkages and control, sudden accelerations. • "While driving, experienced intermittent surging; engine suddenly accelerated out of control, hitting another vehicle and went through garage." • "After slowing down to 5 mph, pressed accelerator and got stuck to the floor; slammed on brakes; vehicle continued to move forward with tires spinning; hit curb." • "Experienced sudden acceleration in reverse; backing the vehicle out of parking, vehicle surged forward, hitting concrete pillar, impact 6:00 position, speed unknown." • "Unintended acceleration; possible problem with the throttle position sensor or idle control valve." • "Car would not decelerate while driving due to stuck throttle."

6. Power train: transmission: automatic, poor performance, difficulty shifting, slipping. • "Transmission failed." • "Transmission downshifts by itself." • "Transmission problems." • "While driving up grade in drive, car vibrates. In overdrive, vehicle is smooth." • "Transmission slips and does not shift correctly."

FORD THUNDERBIRD 1993

Complaint Severity: Negligible. **Buyer's Summary:** Look carefully for any kind of leakage, especially under the car. Check the brakes—listen for noise, look for leaks and feel for vibration. They may fail, perform poorly or require frequent mechanical attention. Make sure air conditioner works properly.

Hot Spots and Owner/NHTSA Comments:

1. Brakes: hydraulic: disc: rotor: disc hub, excessive wear, failure. • "Brakes on vehicle keep going out. Rotors have had to be resurfaced and brought to Ford specifications. Pedal went to the floor when brakes were applied." • "Premature wear of front brake rotors, pads and calipers, causing vehicle to grind." • "Warped front brake rotors, causing vehicle to shimmy." • "Excessive wear of front brake rotors. This is the sixth occurrence." • "Rotors are wearing prematurely; turned rotors at 30,000 miles and replaced at 55,000 miles."

2. Air conditioner: leaks, failure. • "Air conditioner leaks water onto driver's feet." • "Air conditioning leak." • "Compressor leak." • "Air conditioner water leak." • "Air conditioner failed."

3. Brakes: hydraulic system, poor performance. • "Brake switch underneath steering column breaks, rendering brake lights inoperative." • "Upon braking, vehicle continues to roll forward due to inadequate brake action; resulted in extended stopping distance." • "Car shudders when braking." • "The engine is making a tapping noise; has been replaced with new motor and brake has been replaced 3 times."

4. Brakes: hydraulic: disc: pads and shoes, vibration, pulling, excessive wear. • "Antilock brake system failure; continued wear of rotors and disc pads; replaced 4 times." • "Brake shoe and lining failed." • "Vehicle vibrated and pulled to right when brakes applied." • "Premature wearing of brake pads causes noisy brakes; also replaced master cylinder and booster." • "Antilock brake system: Experienced rear wheel cylinder leaks, replaced twice." • "Replaced brake rotors and disc pads. Engine leaks; locking up." • "Oil leak." • "Engine lockup; induction system under the body, large amount of water to go through engine." • "Excessive use of oil." • "Rocker arm failed." • "At 18,000 miles had to replace the brakes, and at 31,000 miles antilock brake." • "Antilock brake system: Applied brakes and had complete loss of brake effectiveness. Used the emergency brake to stop vehicle." • "Brakes failed." • "Antilock brake system: Vibration when brakes are applied, making a loud noise; replaced disc pads and rotors, loss of effectiveness, continued pedal fading." • "Antilock brakes fail to stop vehicle effectively when applied at any speed, causing extended stopping distance, inoperative. Repaired 4 times."

FORD THUNDERBIRD 1994

Complaint Severity: Typical. **Buyer's Summary:** Check the brakes—listen for noise, look for leaks and feel for vibration. They may fail, perform poorly or require frequent mechanical attention. Test the transmission thoroughly.

Hot Spots and Owner/NHTSA Comments:

1. Brakes: hydraulic: disc: rotor: disc hub, premature failure. • "Defective rotors warped prematurely." • "Warped disc brake rotors." • "Front brake rotors failed twice." • "Left front brake rotor failed." • "Front brake disc rotors replaced after 15,000 miles due to grinding when braking."

2. Brakes: hydraulic: anti-skid system, poor performance, failure, locking up. • "Applied brakes, pedal went to the floor, no response from the antilock braking system." • "Antilock brake system malfunction, resulting in long stopping distance." • "Antilock brake system malfunction; during emergency stop, brakes locked up; skidded into another vehicle." • "Vehicle's antilock brake system has had 2 brake jobs; first time at 6,000 and second at 10,000 miles." • "Antilock brake system experiencing long stopping distance and also complete brake loss; resulted in accident."

3. Power train: transmission: automatic, poor performance, difficulty shifting, slipping. • "Transmission slipped 3 times at stop sign; revved as if in neutral, then accelerated when slipping into drive." • "Transmission failed twice." • "Transmission seal leak." • "Transmission shifts late when put in reverse." • "Transmission stuck in 2nd gear."

4. Brakes: hydraulic system, vibration, locking up, noise. • "Vibration when braking." • "Brakes failed, causing vehicle to shimmy." • "Brakes locked up, causing vehicle to skid, resulting in an accident." • "Brake failure; making a loud noise when making stop; in for repair 3 times."

5. Brakes: hydraulic: disc: pads and shoes, excessive wear, vibration. • "Premature wear of front brake pads." • "Brake pads failed." • "Brake pads and rotors failed, resulting in extended stopping distance." • "Steering wheel shimmies at highway speeds; also, vehicle wanders left and right due to brake pad and rotor failure." • "Antilock brake system: Brakes have vibration in front end; replaced disc pads and rotors."

6. Brakes: hydraulic: shoe: disc brake system, locking up, vibration, failure. • "Brakes locked up, causing loss of control and an accident." • "Brakes; when applying, front of vehicle vibrates extensively. Two new brake systems replaced with no change in condition." • "Brake failure; when brakes are applied, pull very hard, causing lockup; replaced rotors and pads; also experienced pedal fading." • "Under certain braking conditions, front end goes down, and there is a cracking noise at high speeds."

Ford—Trucks

FORD TRUCK AEROSTAR 1987

Complaint Severity: Negligible. **Recall Alert:** See Recall Index. **Buyer's Summary:** Look carefully for any kind of leakage, especially under the car. Check the brakes—listen for noise, look for leaks and feel for vibration. They may fail, perform poorly or require frequent mechanical attention. Test the transmission thoroughly.

Hot Spots and Owner/NHTSA Comments:

1. Power train: transmission: automatic, poor performance, difficulty shifting, slipping. • "Transmission failure; rebuilt, including torque converter." • "Vehicle parked and locked on slight incline; about an hour later, rolled from parking place three-quarters of block and caused accident." • "Transmission rough when shifting into or out of low gear; during cold weather, vehicle must reach 45 mph before shifting out of low gear." • "Transmission hangs up between drive and overdrive when air conditioner on." • "Complete transmission failure at 19,000 miles; replaced."

2. Brakes: hydraulic system, pulling, vibration, locking up. • "Upon application, front brakes grab and pull sharply to right; brakes fade and require excessive pedal pressure; van fishtailed when stopping." • "Brakes had pedal vibration, would grab, had to pump to stop vehicle, causing vehicle to slide; replaced rotors, rods, calipers, cylinder, pads and booster." • "When brakes applied in cold or damp weather, they lock up, causing vehicle to fishtail." • "Brake failure, very slow to stop vehicle; resulted in an accident." • "Defective braking system, completely locks up at times."

3. Engine: pulley: crankshaft, breaking, premature failure. • "Crankshaft pulley broke free from engine; 4 studs sheared off; loud noise." • "Crankshaft pulley belts sheared off, caused engine to overheat, radiator overflow hose popped off spraying antifreeze; repaired/replaced crankshaft pulley, damper and belts." • "Pulley that holds belts for power steering and water pump came off, bolts that hold pulley broke off." • "Engine belts and crank pulley broken at 23,940 miles; oil light beeps and is very erratic." • "Metal parts of crankshaft pulley warped; 4 steel bolts snapped in half, causing pulley to fall off."

4. Engine: leaks, noise, failure. • "Engine overheats, antifreeze leaking, engine making excessive noise due to defective head bolts; replaced head gasket and other items." • "Overheating occurred and engine had to be shut off to prevent further damage." • "Engine leaking oil, blew up; repaired rear main and lower part of engine." • "Water in engine oil, vapor in exhaust; also, radiator coolant disappears." • "Front and rear main seal leaks, threw crankshaft pulley."

5. Brakes: hydraulic: shoe: disc brake system, locking up, noise. • "Ongoing brake problem, front brakes constantly malfunctioned due to worn-out pads and rotors; repaired 9 times." • "Front brakes grind and groan, also lock up in wet weather." • "Right front brakes lock up below 30 mph; grinding sound in brakes before locking." • "While driving, brakes started grinding and making loud noises; replaced brake pads and other adjustments."

6. Brakes: hydraulic: shoe and drum system, locking up, pulling. • "Rear brakes lock up when moderate pressure applied to brakes, worse when raining or when brakes warmed up; brake composition problem, front rotors warped." • "While vehicle was in for service, noticed complete brake deterioration due to excess water entering rear brake system, causing an accumulation of rust." • "Grind and grab feeling in rear brakes in cold; complete brake job done." • "Rear brakes lock upon first use, then at other times depending on how hard they are depressed." • "Rear brakes locked up; replaced entire brake system."

FORD TRUCK AEROSTAR 1988

Complaint Severity: Typical. **Recall Alert:** See Recall Index. **Buyer's Summary:** The engine has experienced a variety of problems. Have it examined by a professional. Check the brakes—listen for noise, look for leaks and feel for vibration. They may fail, perform poorly or require frequent mechanical attention. Test the transmission thoroughly. See "Sudden Accelerations" in Introduction.

Hot Spots and Owner/NHTSA Comments:

1. Power train: transmission: automatic, poor performance, difficulty shifting, slipping. • "Transmission failed at 15,000 miles; had to be rebuilt." • "Vehicle experienced transmission problems; at first, transmission shifted hard, then it slipped, and at last started to vibrate; dealer refused to fix it." • "When 45 mph reached, transmission would slip before going into overdrive; transmission had to be completely rebuilt." • "Parked vehicle jumped out of gear, rolling backwards and causing an accident." • "Vehicle was parked with engine off, rolled backwards out of driveway, impact 6:00 position."

2. Brakes: hydraulic system, rust, locking up, leaks. • "Brake shoes and pad are rusted, rear brakes nearly frozen and brake trouble light indicator is on; front brakes compensate for problem and were worn and unsafe." • "Rear brakes locked up, resulting in an accident; prior to accident, had new rotor put on." • "Brakes grab, causing passenger to lurch forward when applied, mostly when weather is humid or brakes wet." • "When shifting into gear to pull out, vehicle accelerated and brakes became insufficient to stop vehicle." • "Braking problems, leak around master cylinder; many repairs, problem continues."

3. Fuel: throttle linkages and control, sudden accelerations. • "Van instantly accelerated, leaping forward and striking another car, brakes hard; upon stopping, accelerator pedal stuck to floorboard." • "Upon starting vehicle and placing into gear, vehicle suddenly accelerated out of control through garage door." • "Vehicle surges without advance notice while transmission disengaged; resulted in accident." • "When transmission placed into drive, vehicle accelerated out of control, collided with an interior warehouse wall; resulted in injury and damage." • "Car suddenly accelerated in reverse, brakes applied but failed; accident resulted."

4. Brakes: hydraulic: shoe and drum system, locking up. • "Brakes locked up and skidded 1 car length; vehicle was rear-ended at approximately 30-35 mph." • "Intermittent rear brake lockup in wet conditions; they also lock up in cold conditions." • "Rear brakes locked, rear end skidded around to right side on two wheels; resulted in accident." • "Problems with rear brakes locking with very little pedal pressure applied under damp or wet conditions; accident resulted as result of brake lockup." • "When applying brakes at speed as slow as 2 mph and as fast as 32 mph, rear brakes lock up at random, putting van into rear-end slide."

5. Engine: miscellaneous problems. • "Engine problems; main bearing cap bolt broke, master cylinder leak, and oil pressure gauge inoperative." • "Excessive loss of engine oil leaking from rear main seal at high speed." • "After driving for about an hour, saw blue-gray smoke, vehicle caught on fire; gas tank did not explode, car behind saw spray of liquid on its windshield." • "Temperature gauge in red zone, smell of antifreeze." • "Broken crankshaft pulley bolts, main bearing bolts, head bolts."

6. Engine: pulley: crankshaft, premature failure. • "Four bolts holding bottom pulley broke at same time, pulley fell on road, all belts came off." • "While driving, bolts sheared off crankshaft pulley, causing loss of power steering, fan, alternator and fuel pump, and severe damage to harmonic balancer." • "Notice received concerning crankshaft defect, may loosen and break, causing pulley to detach." • "Pulley bolts snapped off in high-speed traffic; loss of power steering and brakes." • "Bolts holding pulley on the crankshaft sheared, causing pulley to fall off onto the highway."

FORD TRUCK AEROSTAR 1989

Complaint Severity: Troublesome. **Recall Alert:** See Recall Index. **Buyer's Summary:** Look carefully for any kind of leakage, especially under the car. Check the brakes—listen for noise, look for leaks and feel for vibration. They may fail, perform poorly or require frequent mechanical attention. Test the transmission thoroughly. See "Sudden Accelerations" in Introduction. Make sure air conditioner works properly.

Hot Spots and Owner/NHTSA Comments:

1. Power train: transmission: automatic, poor performance, difficulty shifting, slipping. • "Transmission does not lock when key removed, can put car in any gear without key; vehicle rolled back, collision occurred." • "Recurring problem of automatic transmission not shifting properly; takes off in 2nd gear, continuous use will cause transmission to burn up." • "Pieces of metal in bottom of transmission case caused transmission to go out." • "Vehicle rolled backwards from parked position, causing accident and injury." • "Vehicle started in drive, causing it to lurch forward, resulting in accident."

2. Fuel: throttle linkages and control, sudden accelerations. • "The throttle stuck and caused the vehicle to go out of control while in reverse, hitting another car." • "Upon shifting gears from park to drive, vehicle suddenly accelerated to unknown high speed, causing vehicle to crash into a brick wall." • "While shifting into reverse, vehicle accelerated out of control; ran into a bank and caused minor injuries." • "Van suddenly and unexpectedly accelerated in reverse gear; caused serious injury when it pinned person in the door." • "Vehicle experienced power surge when put into drive, went out of control, striking another car; possibility of throttle sticking."
3. Brakes: hydraulic system, locking up, failure. • "Brakes lock up at any speed, causing vehicle to turn right, slide sideways and start to roll over; repaired/replaced 8 times." • "Rear brakes became very sensitive and locked up with the slightest application of brake pedal, front brakes did not work at all; resulted in an accident." • "Accident caused when brakes failed while driving in reverse." • "Brakes lock up at times and van skids into oncoming traffic." • "In wet or damp weather, vehicle would not stop when brakes were applied."
4. Air conditioner: leaks, failure. • "Defective air conditioner; repaired/replaced compressor." • "Air conditioner sustained severe coolant leak." • "Air conditioning system failed to operate." • "Air conditioner accumulator assembly replaced." • "Air conditioner repair."
5. Brakes: hydraulic: shoe and drum system, locking up. • "When brake was applied, went into 180-degree spin twice; rear brake pads were recalled." • "When it is damp or raining, rear brakes will lock up." • "Rear brakes will lock up sometimes, one time it caused an accident; after being fixed, they still lock up." • "Rear brakes locked up in damp weather; master cylinder loses fluid; problem happened under warranty, dealer refuses to repair." • "Rear brakes appear to lock, causing car to skid; on two occasions car has gone into 360-degree spin upon slow stops."
6. Equipment: electric power accessories: windows, premature failure. • "Defective power window motor goes out often." • "Left and right power window motors defective." • "Power window on driver's-side does not roll down; repaired/replaced switch, still does not work." • "Problem with right power window; wiring bad." • "Vehicle's front electrical windows have a slow and stumbling effect when in use."

FORD TRUCK AEROSTAR 1990

Complaint Severity: Very Serious. **Recall Alert:** See Recall Index.
Buyer's Summary: Look carefully for any kind of leakage, especially under the car. Check the brakes—listen for noise, look for leaks and feel for vibration. They may fail, perform poorly or require frequent mechanical attention. Test the transmission thoroughly. See "Sudden Accelerations" in Introduction. Make sure air conditioner works properly.

Hot Spots and Owner/NHTSA Comments:
1. Fuel: throttle linkages and control, sudden accelerations. • "Intermittent sudden acceleration upon shifting from park into reverse; resulted in an accident." • "While driving in parking lot, vehicle suddenly accelerated, lost control and flipped over on its roof." • "Engine raced to full throttle when gearshift lever was placed in reverse, struck another car; brakes ineffective." • "Placed in drive gear, engine made loud revving noise, propelled forward with foot on brake, did not slow impact down; crashed into parked cars." • "Truck accelerated out of control. Two fatalities and 9 injuries sustained."
2. Power train: transmission: automatic, poor performance, difficulty shifting, slipping. • "Traveling at 65 mph, transmission disengaged, losing all forward power motion, coasted to edge of road; previously replaced transmission at 33,000 miles for same reason." • "Transmission jumped out of gear while in parked position, resulted in an accident." • "While in park, vehicle rolled down hill, hitting a retaining wall."
3. Brakes: hydraulic: anti-skid system, poor performance, failure, locking up. • "Rear antilock brakes and master cylinder problems." • "Antilock braking system malfunction, causing brakes to lock up intermittently." • "Antilock brake system grabbed, causing vehicle to skid; repaired, problem continues." • "Antilock brake system brake pedal will go to the floor and stay there for a count of 5. Dealer has installed 5 new master cylinders." • "Antilock brake system failure during wet conditions causes complete brake lockup; also, pedal fades."
4. Brakes: hydraulic: master cylinder, leaks, excessive wear. • "Owner complains of having to replace the master cylinder 4 times." • "Defective master cylinder replaced; brake light on instrument panel, dealer said it was a short, found out master cylinder was defective again." • "Master brake cylinder problem caused manufacturer to recall models." • "Master brake cylinder replaced due to leakage around the plastic." • "Master cylinder replaced twice in 36,000 miles."
5. Brakes: hydraulic system, locking up, rust. • "Brakes inoperable in wet conditions; caused accident." • "Brakes grab and lock up after driving on wet pavement." • "While driving in parking lot, vehicle suddenly lost control, applied brakes but they did not work, vehicle flipped over on its roof." • "Loss of brake fluid when brakes applied." • "Complete brake failure due to rust."
6. Air conditioner: noise, failure. • "Air conditioner frosting up front window; repaired at dealers, part of air conditioner was defective, worked but was noisy." • "Air conditioner doesn't cool." • "Cooling system failed." • "Air conditioner failed." • "Air conditioner malfunctioned; had to replace condenser, evaporator and belts."

FORD TRUCK AEROSTAR 1991

Complaint Severity: Very Serious. **Recall Alert:** See Recall Index.
Buyer's Summary: Check the brakes—listen for noise, look for leaks and feel for vibration. They may fail, perform poorly or require frequent mechanical attention. Test the transmission thoroughly. See "Sudden Accelerations" in Introduction. Make sure air conditioner works properly.

Hot Spots and Owner/NHTSA Comments:
1. Power train: transmission: automatic, poor performance, difficulty shifting, slipping. • "Vehicle rolls forward when placed in park position." • "Transmission jumped out of park and went into reverse, rolled down hill; caused property damage." • "Vehicle rolled backwards from parked position, causing accident." • "Vehicle rolled down from incline while in parked position, causing accident." • "Automatic transmission park mechanism replaced; cable and shifting mechanism failed."
2. Fuel: throttle linkages and control, sudden accelerations. • "When starting, the vehicle suddenly accelerated out of control, resulting in an accident and injury." • "While stepping on the brake, vehicle kept on surging; rolled over and kept going, hitting edge of concrete and left side of wooden door; caused damage." • "From park to drive, engine raced and surged forward, applied brakes to no avail; accident." • "Sudden acceleration upon shifting from park into reverse; resulted in an accident." • "Started vehicle with foot on brake; put transmission into reverse and vehicle accelerated backward, brakes were inoperative; vehicle went over a pole."
3. Brakes: hydraulic: anti-skid system, poor performance, failure, locking up. • "Antilock brakes failed, pedal went to floor; also, master cylinder/rotors failed." • "Antilock brake system

brake pedal traveled to the floor upon braking while pulling trailer down mountainside. No warning. Started fading out until completely to the floor." • "When applying antilock brakes, pedal may go to the floor, even after pumping. Braking doesn't respond to pedal travel." • "Anti-skid system locks up during wet weather; causes rear end to skid in a fishtail-like motion." • "Antilock brake system sensor light comes on, failure within the master cylinder; continual replacement of cylinder."

4. Brakes: hydraulic system, locking up, failure. • "Brake pedal occasionally goes to floor and becomes very soft; rear brakes squeal." • "Brake pedal was pushed and felt like vehicle should slow down, but no braking force stopped truck before it crashed." • "Brake sensor failure." • "Complete brake failure; replaced front and rear brakes, hubs, rotors, wheel cylinders, drums and backing plates." • "Continuous brake problems; locking up and extended stopping distance."

5. Air conditioner: failure. • "Compressor failed." • "Air conditioner failed." • "Air conditioner vacuum hose failed." • "Air conditioner hose failure." • "Air conditioner fades in and out."

FORD TRUCK AEROSTAR 1992

Complaint Severity: Troublesome. **Buyer's Summary:** The airbags in this vehicle have experienced failures and malfunctions: You may need a professional evaluation on the condition of the airbags. Check the brakes—listen for noise, look for leaks and feel for vibration. They may fail, perform poorly or require frequent mechanical attention. Test the transmission thoroughly.

Hot Spots and Owner/NHTSA Comments:

1. Interior systems: passive restraint: airbag: driver, malfunction, failure. • "Twelve o'clock position, unknown mph, driver's-side airbag had delayed opening." • "Airbag deployed and filled van with stinging odor that burned eyes. Vehicle struck a deer at 60 mph." • "When avoiding accident, vehicle began to accelerate out of control. Upon impact, hitting pole head-on, airbag failed to deploy." • "While parked on roadside, oncoming vehicle hit other vehicle head on at approximately 60 mph. Airbag of vehicle struck did not deploy." • "Van was in a front-end crash; the airbag deployed after the driver hit the steering wheel, and white material came out of the bag."

2. Brakes: hydraulic: anti-skid system, poor performance, failure, locking up. • "Frontal collision, impact 12:00 position, 25 mph, brake failure; antilock brake system lockup on wet surface; airbag on driver's side partially deployed; also, lap and shoulder belt failed." • "Vehicle pulls to the right during heavy braking, causing loss of vehicle control." • "Intermittent brake problems; antilock brake system light on and pedal feels spongy." • "Antilock brake system: In rainy wet conditions. First time brakes were applied, extended stopping distance. The second time brakes were applied in panic situation, the brakes failed." • "Having brake problems; had to take it in 4 times, replaced rear shoes, cylinders, drums and front rotors."

3. Brakes: hydraulic system, pulling, locking up. • "Upon application of brakes, vehicle intermittently pulls to right, must steer to left to compensate; dealer cannot correct problem." • "While driving at 35-40 mph, attempted to slow down to avoid hitting a car in front, applied brakes but they failed, vehicle surged and hit entrance to street." • "Antilock brake system: All brake parts have been replaced 2 times within 2 years, including master cylinder; pedal goes to floor; extended stopping; caused accident." • "Braking system failure; wet conditions make brake extremely sensitive." • "Right rear wheel locked up, causing vehicle to skid into intersection."

4. Power train: transmission: automatic, poor performance, difficulty shifting, slipping. • "The water pump was replaced twice; the air conditioner has not worked in three years; the rack-and-pinion, transmission and the power steering pump repaired/replaced." • "The transmission slips in hot weather only." • "Gear jumped out of park into reverse; shift cable seized." • "Gearshift locked in park." • "While parked on a hill, vehicle rolled backwards, causing accident."

5. Air conditioner: compressor, failure. • "Air conditioner compressor clutch failed." • "Air conditioner compressor failed." • "Air conditioner hose installed on top of rack-and-pinion and rubs against it; put a hole into the hose."

6. Brakes: hydraulic: disc: rotor: disc hub, excessive wear, vibration, pulling. • "The third time in 20,000 miles, and they had to replace rotors, calipers and shoes." • "Antilock brake system: Brake failure; continued wear of disc rotors and pads, in front and rear; replaced 7 times." • "Antilock brake system: Front brakes make vibration; turn rotors in for repair 6 times." • "Antilock brake system: Warping of disc rotor. Replaced 3 times; front wheels making noise." • "Antilock brake system: Right front rotor broke away from mounting hub; fractured clear around radius and separated; vehicle pulls to the left when applying brakes."

FORD TRUCK AEROSTAR 1993

Complaint Severity: Typical. **Buyer's Summary:** Test the suspension by feeling for vibration or pulling while driving. The airbags in this vehicle have experienced failures and malfunctions: You may need a professional evaluation on the condition of the airbags. Check the brakes—listen for noise, look for leaks and feel for vibration. They may fail, perform poorly or require frequent mechanical attention. Test the transmission thoroughly.

Hot Spots and Owner/NHTSA Comments:

1. Interior systems: passive restraint: airbag: driver, malfunction, failure. • "When coming to a stop, antilock brakes locked up and airbag deployed, filling vehicle with smoke." • "Driver's-side airbag failed to deploy at a 12:00 position collision while traveling at 30 mph." • "Airbag did not deploy during a front-end collision; impact 12:00 position; speed 25 mph." • "No deployment of airbag during collision, resulting in injuries." • "Airbag partially deployed during front-end collision at 30 mph."

2. Brakes: hydraulic: anti-skid system, poor performance, failure, locking up. • "After an hour's drive, while parking in reverse, vehicle made whining noise then accelerated, going through house. Antilock brake system did not stop vehicle's acceleration." • "When coming to a stop, antilock brakes locked up and airbag deployed, filling vehicle with smoke." • "Antilock brake system: Antilock brake light comes on intermittently; twice, whole braking system failed; no tension in brake pedal, went completely to floor; car coasted to a stop." • "While driving at approximately 55 mph, made attempt to slow down; upon pressing brake pedal, antilock brake system light appeared, noticed brake action was inadequate."

3. Suspension: independent front, noise, leaks. • "Unknown thump is heard, more so when applying brakes. Antilock brake system performs erratically, having poor response to pedal." • "Vehicle lost control, skidded and turned over twice, resulting in accident." • "Vehicle shimmies." • "Replaced inner seals that are leaking grease." • "Replaced axle grease from right front wheel."

4. Brakes: hydraulic system, pulling, locking up, vibration. • "Brakes failed on left side of vehicle, causing consumer to go off the main road down an embankment." • "Brakes grab and lock due to brake leakage; needs heavy pedal pressure for brake response. May cause loss of brakes and an accident." • "Foot on brake pedal, shifted from park to drive, vehicle went into full throttle." • "Vehicle vibrates when brakes applied." • "Power steering, transmission and brake not working."

5. Power train: transmission: automatic, poor performance, difficulty shifting, slipping. • "Power steering, transmission and brake not working." • "Car stalls out intermittently with no warning. Five transmissions replaced by manufacturer." • "When driving at low speed, there is sometimes a loud noise." • "Transmission shifts in a jerky manner." • "Transmission failed twice."
6. Structure: door assembly, failure. " • "Sliding panel door fell off while attempting to open it." • "Sliding door jams." • "Rear fiberglass doors cracking 12 inches from top down." • "Sliding door won't open." • "The side sliding door caught a child's fingers; the door jammed and couldn't be opened."

FORD TRUCK AEROSTAR 1994

Complaint Severity: Typical. **Buyer's Summary:** Check the brakes—listen for noise, look for leaks and feel for vibration. They may fail, perform poorly or require frequent mechanical attention.

Hot Spots and Owner/NHTSA Comments:

1. Brakes: hydraulic: anti-skid system, poor performance, failure, locking up. • "No response from braking system when applying brakes in parking lot." • "Antilock brake system failure; intermittent failure of antilock brake system when it's raining." • "Antilock brake system: When applying brakes, vehicle vibrates. Front brake pads replaced 10 times, along with rotors turned." • "Antilock brake system: Vibration in front; replaced disc pads and rotors." • "After applying antilock brakes, had complete loss of brake effectiveness, lost control, went into embankment."

FORD TRUCK BRONCO 1987

Complaint Severity: Typical. **Recall Alert:** See Recall Index. **Buyer's Summary:** The engine has experienced a variety of problems. Have it examined by a professional. Test the suspension by feeling for vibration or pulling while driving. Check the brakes—listen for noise, look for leaks and feel for vibration. They may fail, perform poorly or require frequent mechanical attention. Test the transmission thoroughly. See "Sudden Accelerations" in Introduction.

Hot Spots and Owner/NHTSA Comments:

1. Brakes: hydraulic system, pulling, locking up, fading. • "Brakes pull left when cold, after warm might pull right or left." • "Brakes spongy, locked up and smoking; brake system module and valve replaced." • "Vehicle pulls to right, brakes lock when braking, front brakes caught on fire; malfunction in computer box caused too much pressure on front brakes." • "Antilock brake system experiences pedal fading when brakes get very hot, causes complete loss of brake; emergency brake applied to stop vehicle."
2. Suspension: independent front, tire wear, vibration. • "Front end bounces, wanders terribly, causing premature wear of tires; hard to control on highway." • "Front end shaking, steering wheel shakes excessively at 60 mph." • "Vehicle has excessive camber, causing vibration and poor handling; also, excessive tire wear; camber angle was off 2 degrees." • "Serious vibration; tires balanced and replaced, front end aligned, problem continues." • "Heat appears to radiate from front brake discs through to manually controlled front hubs; hubs get so hot that they have burned 2 people."
3. Brakes: hydraulic: shoe: disc brake system, locking up, excessive wear. • "When brakes applied, weaves from side to side, veered suddenly to left." • "Truck equipped with antilock rear brakes only; front brakes lock front wheels on slippery road conditions, cannot steer." • "In operation, vehicle started going side to side and up and down; right front brakes locked, vehicle turned over; right brake rotor warped, pads overheated, grabbing." • "While driving, front brakes locked up, causing vehicle to slide 65 yards, causing rear-ender into truck." • "Excessive wear on the front brake, rotors, pads, calipers; first failure at 21,000 miles, again at 33,000 miles."
4. Fuel: throttle linkages and control, sudden accelerations. • "Throttle cable worn, causing sudden acceleration." • "Car suddenly accelerates when shifted to overdrive, control lost; accident resulted." • "Accelerator pedal sticks to floor, causing engine to run at full throttle." • "Truck bounces forward when idling at high rate, suddenly accelerated; resulted in accident." • "Episodes of chronic hesitation and sudden acceleration have been attributed to sticking and binding of throttle linkage controls."
5. Power train: transmission: automatic, poor performance, difficulty shifting, slipping. • "While in operation, without warning, automatic transmission would slip very strongly, then bump." • "Automatic transmission slips hard, strong bump throws head back." • "Transmission failed at 40,000 miles; replaced." • "Transmission overdrive replaced." • "While trying to control vehicle on mountainous terrain with normal braking procedures, transmission does not provide enough low gear to hold back vehicle."
6. Engine: miscellaneous problems. • "Vehicle fire." • "Number 2 cylinder fouling, causing engine misfire." • "Gutted engine, replacing all seals and gaskets." • "Excessive oil consumption, burning quart every 1,000 miles, sometimes 2 quarts." • "Engine has low oil pressure, low oil consumption; replaced oil gauge."

FORD TRUCK BRONCO 1988

Complaint Severity: Typical. **Recall Alert:** See Recall Index. **Buyer's Summary:** The engine has experienced a variety of problems. Have it examined by a professional. The fuel injection system has been blamed for hesitation and stalling. Be sure the vehicle doesn't die in traffic or at stops. Test the suspension by feeling for vibration or pulling while driving. Check the brakes—listen for noise, look for leaks and feel for vibration. They may fail, perform poorly or require frequent mechanical attention.

Hot Spots and Owner/NHTSA Comments:

1. Brakes: hydraulic system, pulling, locking up, failure. • "Vehicle pulls to left when braking at 45-50 mph; braking system defect." • "Brake problem on right front wheel; vehicle pulls left, difficult stopping any speed, front wheels lock, loss of control; repaired/replaced rear sensor and antilock brakes." • "Defective braking system; master cylinder loses fluid and pedal goes to floor, anti-skid warning lights also come on." • "Vehicle would pull to the right when braking because of defective braking equipment."
2. Brakes: hydraulic: anti-skid system, poor performance, failure, locking up. • "Antilock brakes lock up intermittently, resulting in front end swerving." • "Anti-skid brakes lock up during all wet weather, causing vehicle to jerk and lurch forward." • "Right rear antilock brake spring broke." • "Antilock brakes failed, vehicle veered into center lane, then into right lane, veered again into center lane, where it hit another vehicle and rolled over." • "Antilock brakes lock up and vehicle skids."
3. Engine: miscellaneous problems. • "Engine head cracked." • "Loud knocking noise from engine, engine ripped down with 186 miles because of factory defect." • "Smoke and fumes entering cab through ventilation; caused by oil leaking onto exhaust system; replaced rear main oil seal." • "Crankshaft, valve, engine rod and bearings failed; also, oil pump replaced." • "Vehicle uses 1 to 2 quarts of oil between 3,000-mile changes."
4. Suspension: independent front, pulling, alignment. • "Defective front suspension system, causing vehicle to pull to one side when brakes applied; replaced vehicle, second vehicle has same defect in design." • "Upon braking, vehicle pulls to left very badly, continuous alignment problem." • "Vehicle pulls toward left upon braking." • "Representing client killed as result of rollover; while

traveling expressway, vehicle veered to right and left then right again, and rolled over down highway."

5. Brakes: hydraulic: shoe: disc brake system, pulling, failure. • "Left front brakes pull vehicle to left when brakes applied." • "Front brakes malfunctioning; front hubs and wheels become very hot to touch during normal driving." • "Failure of front disc brakes caused extended stopping distance." • "Front left brake failure; repaired."

6. Fuel: fuel injection system, stalling, hesitation. • "Intermittent stalling." • "Intermittent stalling." • " 'Check engine' light comes on when on inclines; engine cuts off when coming to stop or slowing; also, noise under hood when accelerating." • "Vehicle would begin to run rough, then stall and would not restart."

FORD TRUCK BRONCO 1989

Complaint Severity: Typical. **Recall Alert:** See Recall Index. **Buyer's Summary:** Look carefully for any kind of leakage, especially under the car. The fuel pump has received complaints. Make sure it doesn't make excessive noise and that you are experiencing adequate engine performance. Also, look for leaks. Check the brakes—listen for noise, look for leaks and feel for vibration. They may fail, perform poorly or require frequent mechanical attention. Test the transmission thoroughly.

Hot Spots and Owner/NHTSA Comments:

1. Brakes: hydraulic system, pulling, poor performance. • "When applied, brakes pull left and right, mostly left, very sharply, making truck hard to control and dangerous." • "Vehicle pulls to left into opposing traffic at all times; when applying brakes it pulls to left, but sometimes to right." • "Vehicle drifts anywhere from 4-18 feet when applying brakes." • "Applying brakes over 55 mph causes loss of control." • "Loss of braking ability while coming downhill with tow caused driver to rear-end another vehicle."

2. Power train: transmission: automatic, poor performance, difficulty shifting, slipping. • "Transmission transfer case failed." • "Transmission shifting rough and jerky." • "While driving, vehicle feels as if something is dragging on or within rear drive train of vehicle." • "Transmission failure." • "Automatic gearshift lever doesn't move clearly in or out of gear—muddy and imprecise feel to it—trouble quickly putting into gear."

3. Brakes: hydraulic: shoe: disc brake system, locking up, pulling. • "When brakes were applied, it locked up and skidded, resulted in loss of steering power, causing an accident." • "Front brake system overheats, causing piston to enlarge with heat." • "When applying brakes in emergency manner to slow down, car veered from direction of travel to left, front wheel locked up and skidded." • "Intermittent brake problem; front disc brakes pull to the right/left when applied; repaired/replaced and lubricated caliper piston, all repair attempts to no avail." • "Front brakes lock up in wet weather and at low speeds."

4. Fuel: fuel pump, fire, failure. • "Fuel pump shorted, resulting in fire." • "Fuel pump design results in failure, losing steering and braking controls while driving." • "Fuel pump failure." • "Premature failure of fuel pump at 32,000 miles."

5. Structure: body, cracking, leaks. • "Whenever anyone seated in passenger seat, floor buckets' metal fatigues, sooner or later will split and seat will become unsecured." • "Floor pan where driver's seat bolted developed split, caused seat to crack floor pan because brackets used to hold seat not long enough to support seat." • "Leaks underneath dash; repaired 4 times, still leaks." • "Driver's seat went through floorboard where it mounts; hole in floorboard." • "While driving, seat went through floorboard where it's mounted; hole in floorboard is very close to where seat belt fastens to floor."

6. Engine cooling system: pump: water, leaks, premature failure. • "Water pump went out twice at 4,000 miles." • "Water pump failure." • "Problem with water pump in engine cooling system." • "Water pump leaking badly—vehicle overheating."

FORD TRUCK BRONCO 1990

Complaint Severity: Typical. **Recall Alert:** See Recall Index. **Buyer's Summary:** Look carefully for any kind of leakage, especially under the car. Check the brakes—listen for noise, look for leaks and feel for vibration. They may fail, perform poorly or require frequent mechanical attention. Test the transmission thoroughly.

Hot Spots and Owner/NHTSA Comments:

1. Power train: transmission: automatic, poor performance, difficulty shifting, slipping. • "Automatic transmission failed to move truck when in gear." • "Replacement of transmission—only few days after purchasing vehicle." • "Transmission slips when cold." • "When putting transmission into reverse when engine is cold, it takes about 45-60 seconds to catch." • "Transmission rear seal failed."

2. Brakes: hydraulic system, pulling, poor performance. " • "Brake pads, rotor, caliper, master cylinder and brake booster sensor replaced." • "Front brakes defective; repeated attempts to repair, problem still exists." • "Vehicle pulls sharply to right when brakes are applied; repaired/replaced complete braking system, problem caused by faulty equipment installed at factory." • "Experiencing inadequate braking when brakes applied at highway speeds." • "Vehicle pulled to reverse when braking; was not alignment."

3. Interior systems: seat tracks and anchors, breaking, malfunction. • "Mounting bolt on driver's seat broke, causing seat to break off from base of vehicle." • "Driver's seat bolt mount disconnected from floorboard." • "Power adjusting front seat tracks and anchors malfunction; driver's seat loose and passenger's seat never locks into place." • "Passenger seat does not stay locked when allowing people into back seat." • "Driver and passenger seat mounting bolts tend to vibrate loose every 1,000 to 2,000 miles."

4. Structure: body, miscellaneous problems. • "Poor engineering of steering member; when vehicle turns sharply, tires will rub on movable turning members; could cause excessive wear to tires." • "Floor shakes and vibrates at 60-65 mph; installed part reinforcing floor." • "Reinforcement floor pan fractured; recalled." • "Seat continued to come loose due to floorboard fracture; repaired 5 times before problem discovered, repairs not satisfactory to owner." • "Problem with flooring under driver and passenger seats cracking."

5. Brakes: hydraulic: anti-skid system, poor performance, failure, locking up. • "Brake calipers replaced on 5 occasions." • "While driving down a mountain road at low speed, noticed strong acrid burning odor and smoke coming from front brakes." • "During a sudden stop, vehicle did not stop immediately when the antilock brakes were applied; extended stopping distance resulted in a rear-end accident." • "Antilock brake system failure. Experienced extended stopping distance; replaced master cylinder." • "Defective master cylinder on antilock brakes, rendering inability to stop."

6. Engine: leaks, poor performance. • "While driving, engine loses all compression; had replaced 3 times." • "Incomplete information obtained from insurance carrier, smelled smoke while driving, Ford dealer repaired immediately." • "Unspecified engine problems." • "Oil leaks from front main seal of engine."

FORD TRUCK BRONCO 1991

Complaint Severity: Typical. **Recall Alert:** See Recall Index. **Buyer's Summary:** See "Sudden Accelerations" in Introduction.

Hot Spots and Owner/NHTSA Comments:

1. Fuel: throttle linkages and control, sudden accelerations. • "Sudden acceleration in reverse, causing accident." • "The vehicle suddenly accelerated while owner was driving on highway. He put vehicle in neutral and pulled over to side of the road, and vehicle idled down." • "Vehicle suddenly accelerated 3 times; once resulting in an accident." • "Was driving in automatic overdrive; accelerated, had to pull over and cut overdrive off." • "Sudden acceleration, causing accident."

FORD TRUCK BRONCO 1992

Complaint Severity: Minor. **Recall Alert:** See Recall Index. **Buyer's Summary:** Check the brakes—listen for noise, look for leaks and feel for vibration. They may fail, perform poorly or require frequent mechanical attention. See "Sudden Accelerations" in Introduction.

Hot Spots and Owner/NHTSA Comments:

1. Fuel: throttle linkages and control, sudden accelerations. • "Throttle stuck, causing high idle. Vehicle will surge forward." • "Started engine in neutral, pressed the brake pedal and shifted from neutral to reverse; vehicle accelerated and rammed into a pickup truck." • "On icy conditions, throttle stuck when driver depressed pedal." • "Throttle sticks in open position; to disengage, shift gear to neutral and wait." • "Engine light comes on; when this occurs truck will either stall or accelerate out of control. Dealer can only detect problem if light stays on."

2. Brakes: hydraulic: shoe: disc brake system, excessive wear, vibration, pulling. • "Frozen caliper, warped rotors and premature and uneven wear of pads causing vibration." • "Vehicle pulls to the left while braking, pulls to the right intermittently." • "Antilock brake system grabs and locks up when applied in wet road conditions." • "Brakes always pull to the left; hard stop will throw the truck off the road." • "Brake pads and calipers failed."

3. Structure: door assembly: latches and locks, malfunction, failure. • "Door latch failed, resulting in accident prior to and after recall." • "Door latches failed." • "Door latches will open while driving and will not catch." • "Door latch and lock may cause driver's door to stick, and possibly open if leaned against."

4. Brakes: hydraulic: anti-skid system, poor performance, failure, locking up. • "When antilock brakes are applied, vehicle will pull to the left." • "When antilock brakes are applied, vehicle pulls to the left and often into traffic." • "When brakes are applied, they lock up and truck skids." • "Antilock brake system-equipped brake pedal locks at full pedal height; vehicle will not stop."

FORD TRUCK BRONCO 1994

Complaint Severity: Harmless. **Recall Alert:** See Recall Index. **Buyer's Summary:** Check the brakes—listen for noise, look for leaks and feel for vibration. They may fail, perform poorly or require frequent mechanical attention.

Hot Spots and Owner/NHTSA Comments:

1. Brakes: hydraulic: anti-skid system, poor performance, failure, locking up. • "Intermittent braking failure; equipped with antilock brake system brakes." • "Antilock brake system: On wet surfaces, or surface changes, brakes will lock up. Owner has had several occurrences of locking." • "The antilock brake system got mushy and the brakes were smoking." • "Antilock brake system: Continued wear of disc brakes and rotors, and vibration in the front end; in for repair 4 times." • "When driving at highway speed and applying brakes, vehicle will pull to left into oncoming traffic."

2. Brakes: hydraulic: disc: rotor: disc hub, vibration, excessive wear. • "Brake rotor out of round, causing steering wheel to vibrate when brakes applied." • "Vehicle's antilock brake system rotors are warping prematurely; changed 4 times and resurfaced 2 times within 1 year. • "Front and rear brakes, rotors and drums failed twice." • "Front brake rotors warp; replaced the rotors 6 times in a year."

3. Brakes: hydraulic system, pulling, noise, vibration. • "In for repair; when driving and brakes are applied, pulls very hard to left." • "When brakes are applied, vehicle pulls to the extreme right, pulls out of lane." • "Brakes rub and squeak; when applying brake nothing happens." • "Vehicle developed a vibration problem due to brakes overheating. This occurs every 3,000 miles." • "The entire truck vibrates when brakes are applied."

FORD TRUCK BRONCO II 1987

Complaint Severity: Serious. **Recall Alert:** See Recall Index. **Buyer's Summary:** Test the suspension by feeling for vibration or pulling while driving. Check the brakes—listen for noise, look for leaks and feel for vibration. They may fail, perform poorly or require frequent mechanical attention. Test the transmission thoroughly. See "Sudden Accelerations" in Introduction.

Hot Spots and Owner/NHTSA Comments:

1. Brakes: hydraulic: anti-skid system, poor performance, failure, locking up. • "Antilock brake system: Front wheels lock up when applying brakes on slippery pavement; causes loss of steering control." • "Anti-skid system problem; brakes malfunctioned, allowing vehicle to strike rear of another vehicle; accident occurred during rain." • "Antilock brake system allows rear brakes to release when front wheels are sliding; accident resulted." • "Antilock brake lights on periodically, antilock brakes spongy and hesitate when stopping; repairs." • "Antilock rear brakes lock up whenever brakes applied hard."

2. Suspension: poor performance. • "Unstable vehicle rolled over at 40 mph; started to swerve, tried to steady wheel, braked hard, vehicle went out of control; trapped victim inside." • "While stopped on slight hill, vehicle rolled over on its top; vehicle was completely stopped, then tipped over; poor stability." • "While driving on highway, tire blew out, vehicle started to swerve, tried to control, it rolled over due to poor stability." • "When driving at normal 2-wheel drive, vehicle skids over small bumps or small objects, causing loss of control." • "While driving 60 mph on freeway, turned wheel to make quick lane change, vehicle swerved out of control, then turned over 2 times."

3. Suspension: independent front, alignment, tire wear. • "Dealer rotated tires and performed front-end alignment; tires worn on front end." • "Lost complete control of vehicle, hit guardrail and rolled due to possible broken right shock and faulty front-end alignment." • "Front alignment off, pulls to left or right; brake makes car hard to control." • "Chronic front-end misalignment results in excessive tire wear." • "Vehicle rollover, causing death."

4. Engine: noise, fire. • "Vehicle caught on fire while owner was driving down street. Sparks were coming from underneath vehicle." • "While traveling, experienced loss of power, noise and smoke from engine; engine compartment completely gutted by fire." • "Engine misses, smokes from under hood when starting, burning coolant smell, oil level rising 1 quart higher; continual repairs on valves, gaskets." • "Cracked engine heads." • "At higher rpm, engine develops excessive whining noises."

5. Fuel: throttle linkages and control, sudden accelerations. • "Turned ignition key, vehicle immediately accelerated backwards at full throttle, struck a tree; when it jumped curb back into street, it stalled." • "Vehicle throttle accelerated by itself; hit throttle hard, it unstuck by itself." • "While driving in commute traffic, throttle stuck wide open, causing vehicle to suddenly increase speed." • "Vehicle accelerated by itself on 4 different occasions; throttle just pulled away from foot and floor, could be unstuck by hitting throttle and letting up." • "Throttle stuck wide open while in motion, resulting in sudden acceleration."

6. Power train: transmission: automatic, poor performance, difficulty shifting, slipping. • "Transmission sprung a leak, and car rolled backwards when accelerator hit." • "Automatic transmission; reverse does not engage properly at times, shifting into other gears not smooth." • "Transmission leakage, causing transmission to slip and not shift, resulting in deceleration; overhauled transmission." • "Defective transmission seal causes terrible vibration and noise when in motion."

FORD TRUCK BRONCO II 1988

Complaint Severity: Very Serious. **Buyer's Summary:** The fuel injection system has been blamed for hesitation and stalling. Be sure the vehicle doesn't die in traffic or at stops. Check the brakes—listen for noise, look for leaks and feel for vibration. They may fail, perform poorly or require frequent mechanical attention. Test the transmission thoroughly. See "Sudden Accelerations" in Introduction.

Hot Spots and Owner/NHTSA Comments:

1. Suspension: poor performance. • "Vehicle overturned while doing approximately 25-30 mph on residential road; injuring 2." • "Truck overturned after hitting a slick spot in the road at 40-45 mph." • "Vehicle wants to tuck and roll when turning and braking simultaneously; power steering too sensitive for short-coupled vehicle." • "Attempted to make left turn, turned back in southbound lane; in attempt to avoid collision, drove to reverse, then turned left to avoid pole; vehicle rolled over." • "While trying to avoid head-on accident by swerving off road, vehicle rolled over."

2. Fuel: throttle linkages and control, sudden accelerations. • "Recurring sudden acceleration problem; can stop car only by turning off ignition." • "While slowing down, throttle went to floored position and stuck there." • "Throttle stuck in open position, causing vehicle to accelerate out of control." • "Throttle sticks wide open due to aluminum and steel, which causes electrolysis in the two different metals." • "The throttle stuck, causing the vehicle to speed out of control, on 2 separate occasions."

3. Power train: transmission: automatic, poor performance, difficulty shifting, slipping. • "While engine was off and with transmission in drive, vehicle rolled into traffic and caused accident." • "Automatic transmission locked up; caused loss of control and resulted in an accident." • "Vehicle jumped out of gear." • "Leak developed in automatic transmission." • "Automatic transmission; while standing in the driveway, vehicle jumped from park to reverse."

4. Engine: gaskets: valve cover, leaks. • "Valve cover leaking oil on exhaust manifold; possible fire hazard; gaskets replaced twice, problem persists." • "Head gasket inoperative, affects proper functioning of engine." • "Lack of oil could cause head gasket to crack resulting in engine failure." • "Valve cover leaks at bolts; runs up threads and runs out over exhaust manifold; gaskets replaced but still leaks." • "Valve cover gaskets leaked."

5. Fuel: fuel injection system, stalling, hesitation. • "Vehicle sometimes stalls and sometimes races wildly without warning at highway speeds, hard brake pressure needed to slow down." • "Vehicle stalls at any time, any speed, without warning; able to maintain control of vehicle." • "Vehicle will stall while driving; will not start up for several minutes." • "Vehicle stalls at highway speeds; repaired/replaced thick-film integrated module, problem continues."

6. Brakes: hydraulic: anti-skid system, poor performance, failure, locking up. • "Braking to pass slow vehicle, brakes locked, sending truck out of control, due to malfunction of antilock brake system; repaired 6 times to no avail." • "When brake linings cold, front brakes grab, pull left; antilock rear brakes lock up when wet, caused loss of control." • Antilock brake system pressure valve failed, right rear wheel locked up when pressure applied to slow vehicle on wet road, spun 180 degrees and flipped on right side." • "During wet weather, antilock brake system did not respond, resulting in running a stop sign; after pumping, system brake responded later."

FORD TRUCK BRONCO II 1989

Complaint Severity: Typical. **Recall Alert:** See Recall Index. **Buyer's Summary:** Look carefully for any kind of leakage, especially under the car. The fuel injection system has been blamed for hesitation and stalling. Be sure the vehicle doesn't die in traffic or at stops. Check the brakes—listen for noise, look for leaks and feel for vibration. They may fail, perform poorly or require frequent mechanical attention.

Hot Spots and Owner/NHTSA Comments:

1. Fuel: fuel tank assembly: tank, rust, leaks. • "Gas tank rusted, causing leak onto the exhaust pipe, creating a potential fire risk." • "Fuel leaking when full. Fuel leaks onto exhaust pipe." • "Gas tank rusted from the outside in, causing leakage near exhaust system. Needs to be replaced." • "Fumes enter the vehicle when gas tank is full. Resulting from rusted fuel tank." • "Fuel tank rusted from top and leaked on the exhaust pipe."

2. Wheels: noise, vibration. • "Excessive noise and/or vibration in wheels; wheel came loose from vehicle on 1 occasion." • "Safety defect recall on left front wheel bearing nut retaining key; may not have been installed on vehicle, must be installed." • "Recall notice for missing retaining key for wheel bearing nut." • "Rattle in front driver's-side tire." • "Right rear wheel locks up when brakes are applied; it will unlock only in reverse."

3. Brakes: hydraulic system, malfunction, poor performance. • "Installed brake caliper pin for both front wheels, adjusted rear brakes; heard noise every time applied brakes." • "Brake light and antilock brake light stayed on all the time; repaired 3 times." • "Vehicle pulled out in front, applied brakes but did not stop, hit vehicle broadside; brakes making noise each time applied them." • "When braking, loud pop and/or thump noise under front floorboard; repaired/replaced calipers, rotors and pads, loud noise continues." • "Pads keep falling apart."

4. Fuel: fuel injection system, stalling, hesitation. • "While traveling at 65 mph, vehicle started to sputter, hesitated and stalled out." • "After start, engine surges up and down, hesitates when accelerating." • "When engine warms up, vehicle hesitates as if about to stall." • "Fuel injectors replaced at 9,000 miles; very noisy." • "Intake manifold malfunction caused vehicle to stall."

5. Suspension: instability. • "Vehicle fails when boat and trailer attached; sways with boat and fishtails at varying speed because front wheels come up off ground." • "In attempt to escape a car accident, vehicle started rolling over. Flipped 12 times." • "Vehicle traveling at 40 mph, struck on passenger's side, spun one-quarter turn, rolled onto roof and back onto its wheels; due to lack of stability." • "Loss of control of steering and traction, with 2 and 4 wheels off road; when vehicle hits washboarded roads, potholes, rear end is thrusted toward front driver side." • "Driver was killed in accident because of rollover propensity, instability of vehicle."

6. Engine: leaks, fire, premature failure. • "Replaced head, block and gaskets." • "Vehicle suddenly caught on fire while driving at 60 mph. During damp, rainy weather, vehicle collects water in passenger compartment periodically." • "Water leaks into engine via front grill, which causes stalling and missing." • "Engine replaced 3 times out of warranty over 3,000 miles—dealer doesn't want to work with consumer."

FORD TRUCK E150 1987

Complaint Severity: Best 3% in Guide. **Buyer's Summary:** Look carefully for any kind of leakage, especially under the car.

Hot Spots and Owner/NHTSA Comments:

1. Fuel: fuel tank assembly, leaks, pressure buildup. • "Fuel indicator not operating properly; fuel tank gives off very strong fumes, making passengers sick." • "Inadequate fuel tank; leaks and smells." • "Fuel tank overpressurizes when temperature reaches 90 degrees or above, regardless of amount of fuel in tank; upon opening filler cap, gas spurts out." • "When fuel in main and auxiliary (rear) tanks, it becomes pressurized; due to driving, fuel will shoot out filler neck with great pressure when cap is removed."

2. Fuel: fuel tank: auxiliary selector and switch, failure. • "Rear fuel tank switch not engaging rear fuel tank; problem not corrected." • "Dual gas tank system useless; selector switch from main to auxiliary gas tank failed due to fuel system being overpressurized." • "When front tank selected, transfer valve fills up rear tank. When rear tank is full, valve leaks." • "Faulty fuel selector switch."

FORD TRUCK E150 1988

Complaint Severity: Typical. **Buyer's Summary:** See "Sudden Accelerations" in Introduction.

Hot Spots and Owner/NHTSA Comments:

1. Fuel: throttle linkages and control, sudden accelerations. • "Engine accelerated while in motion; went over a curb and continued in a circular motion, hit 2 parked cars in parking lot." • "Upon starting, van lurched backward, vehicle remained in park, did not actually move; if park did not hold, it would have raced backward." • "Applied brakes to stop, the accelerator kicked in, brakes applied clear to the floor but van did not stop." • "Surging; accelerator stuck; cables sprayed with lube."

FORD TRUCK E150 1989

Complaint Severity: Best 3% in Guide. **Recall Alert:** See Recall Index. **Buyer's Summary:** Look carefully for any kind of leakage, especially under the car. Test the suspension by feeling for vibration or pulling while driving. Check the brakes—listen for noise, look for leaks and feel for vibration. They may fail, perform poorly or require frequent mechanical attention. Test the transmission thoroughly.

Hot Spots and Owner/NHTSA Comments:

1. Suspension: independent front, tire wear, vibration, alignment. • "Defect in front end; tires wearing unevenly, cupping; improper handling of steering." • "Tires have excessive tread wear on outside; had several alignments and frame adjustments." • "Vibration in front end." • "Problem with front end alignment causes excessive tire wear; repaired/replaced 2 tires." • "Stud that holds the kingpin on the front axle broke."

2. Fuel: fuel tank: auxiliary selector and switch, leaks, failure. • "Fuel leak in front tank while driving. Rear tank pumped approximately 5 gallons of fuel to front tank." • "Dual fuel tank selector valve leaks and allows one tank to bleed over to the second tank, causing overfilling and expelling fuel onto the expressway." • "Dual fuel tank selector valve failed." • "Dual tank; gas flows, pumping gasoline continuously." • "Dual fuel tanks, when switching from one to the other, fuel leaks on the highway."

3. Power train: transmission: automatic, poor performance, difficulty shifting, slipping. • "Transmission has severe vibration and noise; many repairs, problem continues." • "Transmission slips between gears; many repairs, problem continues." • "Knocking noise in transmission around 35-45 mph; got worse at 8,000 miles; repaired, noise persists when releasing gas pedal." • "Transmission sometimes will not downshift into passing gear at about 50 mph."

4. Brakes: hydraulic: shoe: disc brake system, excessive wear, fade. • "The front brake still makes heat; the rear-end axle was replaced." • "Front disc brake expansion pin on caliper accumulates dirt, caliper doesn't retract when releasing brake, which causes excessive brake wear." • "Brakes began to fade and brake shoes began smoking." • "The retaining pin that holds the brake caliper for the disc brakes fell off."

FORD TRUCK E350 1987

Complaint Severity: Minor. **Recall Alert:** See Recall Index. **Buyer's Summary:** This vehicle may experience trouble with stalling and hesitation. Fuel system has caused fires.

Hot Spots and Owner/NHTSA Comments:

1. Fuel: fuel tank assembly, stalling, fire, malfunction. • "Problem with fuel tank assembly; while driving, pressure builds up in gas tank; upon removing filler cap, gas floods out, smell gas fumes in cab." • "Fuel tank assembly suffers overheating; this causes overpressurization of fuel tank, producing fuel expulsion and resulting in fire; vehicle is ambulance." • "Engine stalls, pressure builds up, gas spilling out of tank; gas spewed out upon removal of cap." • "Excessive amount of pressure in gas tank; also, engine backfiring with flames from exhaust; problems occur when temperature near 90 degrees and using air conditioner." • "Problem fuel tank assembly; while driving, pressure builds up in tank; caused engine to stumble and stall; when cap removed, jet stream of raw gas released."

2. Fuel: fuel systems, stalling, fire. • "Overfueling; vehicle getting too much fuel in combustion chambers, causing huge backfires, flaming from tail pipe, engine cutting out." • "Inadequate fuel system, causing flooding of engine with diesel fuel; could cause fire." • "Gas tank overheats, causing boiling gas, fumes, erratic idle, backfires; expels gas when filler caps are removed." • "Gasoline smell evident when vehicle stopped, then smoke came from under hood; resulted in fire." • "Van stalls continually, hissing sounds when preparing to uncap gas tank."

FORD TRUCK E350 1988

Complaint Severity: Typical. **Recall Alert:** See Recall Index. **Buyer's Summary:** The vehicle may leak oil. Look for leaks and smell for burning oil. Vehicle may have acceleration trouble.

Hot Spots and Owner/NHTSA Comments:

1. Engine: gaskets: valve cover, leaks. • "Engine head gaskets leaking oil and compression; repaired twice, leaking again." • "Head gaskets of diesel engine leaking both oil and compression, left gasket presents more problem; repaired/replaced both gaskets several times, no improvement."

2. Fuel: fuel injection: unknown type: accumulator, failure. • "Fuel lift pump failed; vehicle began to run rough, would not accelerate properly, fuel injector lost pressure; fuel not injected into cylinder properly." • "Fuel injector pump; fuel lift pump lost pressure, stopped pumping fuel into cylinders; vehicle runs rough and would not accelerate properly." • "Fuel injection pump lost pressure; fuel not injected into cylinders, governor cage loose; copper shavings around head and rotor; vehicle ran rough and/or hesitated."

FORD TRUCK E350 1989

Complaint Severity: Negligible. **Recall Alert:** See Recall Index. **Buyer's Summary:** The fuel injection system has been blamed for hesitation and stalling. Be sure the vehicle doesn't die in traffic or at stops. Check the brakes—listen for noise, look for leaks and feel for vibration. They may fail, perform poorly or require frequent mechanical attention. Test the transmission thoroughly.

Hot Spots and Owner/NHTSA Comments:

1. Brakes: hydraulic system, premature failure. • "Brake pedal goes to floor, pumping brings brakes part way back." • "After sustained and frequent use of brakes, they apparently overheat and pedal goes to the floor." • "Brakes fail and pedal fades while driving an emergency medical service ambulance." • "Brakes failed 3 times." • "Brakes will not respond to pedal application, more so on inclined areas."

2. Power train: transmission: automatic, poor performance, difficulty shifting, slipping. • "Transmission leaks; failed." • "Transmission malfunctioned." • "Transmission problems; replaced seal and pump." • "Snap ring broke; resulted in vehicle freewheeling down an incline." • "Failure of transmission park gear (clip); 5 out of 6 buses have had parking gear fail."

3. Brakes: hydraulic: shoe: disc brake system, failure. • "Prolonged use of front brakes caused overheating and failure." • "While driving, brake pedal went to the floor; resulted in total brake failure on antilock brake system." • "Vehicle had complete brake failure, and the front brakes caught on fire." • "Vehicle may experience intermittent fading or complete loss of brakes." • "Front brake pads are dragging on rotors, resulting in heat buildup."

4. Fuel: fuel injection system, stalling, hesitation. • "Vehicle exploded during collision, causing death." • "Vehicle experiencing continual loss of power and stalling." • "Fuel-injected engine defect; loss of engine power indirect cause of accident." • "Motorhome with Econoline 350 7.5L fuel-injected engine malfunction; loss of power indirect cause of accident; motor died while going down steep incline." • "Repeated failure of fusible link to electronic fuel injection."

5. Brakes: hydraulic: disc: caliper, failure, fire. • "Brakes have had 2 complete failures due to hot calipers." • "Front brakes overheat due to calipers seizing, causing brake failure." • "Front brake failure due to calipers overheating, causing brake fluid to catch on fire." • "Front brake failure (caliper overheats); the brake fluid caught on fire."

6. Brakes: hydraulic: pedal, failure. • "While coming down mountain road, brakes began to feel soft and pedal began descending to the floor." • "When applying brakes, they fade to the floor; after waiting 45 minutes of cooldown period, brakes are fine." • "Brake pedal traveled to the floor with no braking effect; emergency brakes were applied to stop vehicle; no prior warning." • "On a 2-lane narrow road, prior to starting a downgrade, touched the brake pedal and it went down all the way to the floor."

FORD TRUCK E350 1990

Complaint Severity: Minor. **Recall Alert:** See Recall Index. **Buyer's Summary:** Check the brakes—listen for noise, look for leaks and feel for vibration. They may fail, perform poorly or require frequent mechanical attention.

Hot Spots and Owner/NHTSA Comments:

1. Brakes: hydraulic: anti-skid system, poor performance, failure, locking up. • "Brakes failed to stop vehicle while driving downhill at 20 mph." • "Antilock brake system pedal moves to the floor when pressed; brakes inoperative." • "While pulling into rest stop, bus lost all braking ability. Driver pumped brakes with no reaction. Vehicle is equipped with antilock brake system." • "Upon applying the brakes, there was no response."

2. Brakes: hydraulic system, vibration, failure. • "Brakes failed; had to use emergency brakes to stop vehicle." • "Brakes fade, with pedal going all the way to the floor." • "Brakes fail to stop vehicle effectively during sudden stops." • "When applying brake, experience vibration and pedal fading." • "When brakes get hot and driver applies brake pedal, pedal goes to the floor. When brakes cool down they become responsive again."

FORD TRUCK ECONOLINE 1987

Complaint Severity: Typical. **Recall Alert:** See Recall Index. **Buyer's Summary:** Look carefully for any kind of leakage, especially under the truck.

Hot Spots and Owner/NHTSA Comments:

1. Fuel: fuel tank assembly, malfunction, leaks. • "Defective fuel system causing tanks to spew heated gas out of filler cap, or causing fuel vapor in vicinity of muffler and catalytic converter to ignite." • "Electric-operated gas valve assembly erratic; while operating vehicle on front gas tank, gas returned to rear tank; pressurized gas forced out of tank." • "After engaging front fuel tank, gas smell occurs and pressure builds up in tanks, causing gas to be sprayed out when cap removed." • "Dual gas tanks; gas siphoning from front tank into rear tank causing rear tank to overfill, gas leaking from filler tube into tank venting system."

FORD TRUCK ECONOLINE 1989

Complaint Severity: Minor. **Recall Alert:** See Recall Index. **Buyer's Summary:** Check the brakes—listen for noise, look for leaks and feel for vibration. They may fail, perform poorly or require frequent mechanical attention.

Hot Spots and Owner/NHTSA Comments:

1. Brakes: hydraulic system, failure. • "Brakes failed at 10,000 miles." • "Front disc brakes, rotors, and calipers repaired/replaced at low mileage." • "Brakes overheated, causing failure and fading." • "Rebuilt front brakes." • "Brake pedal went to the floor after descending a hill. After waiting 45 minutes, brakes normal."

2. Brakes: hydraulic: shoe: disc brake system, pulling, noise, locking up. • "Brake fluid overheated, causing front brakes to catch on fire." • "Upon entering Yellowstone Park, applied brakes to go into a turnout, brake pedal went all the way to the floor." • "Front brakes have been pulling and squealing since 5,000 miles; rotors replaced and vehicle was realigned." • "Traveling down a hill, the brakes heated up; lost total braking ability." • "On wet pavement, applied brakes, wheels locked up and vehicle went into a skid; caused an accident."

3. Brakes: hydraulic: anti-skid system, poor performance, failure, locking up. • "While coming down a grade, brakes failed and pedal went all the way to the floor." • "While driving at 25 mph, brakes failed to stop vehicle when applied." • "Going down a winding road, brakes became soft and pedal went close to the floor." • "While driving down a slight grade, brakes heat up, pedal becomes soft and goes to floor."

4. Fuel: fuel tank: auxiliary selector and switch, malfunction, leaks. • "Switch-over system for dual tank malfunctioned." • "Dual fuel tank expels fuel." • "Had recall work done, now there are strong fuel fumes in vehicle." • "Fuel tank auxiliary selector switch failed, causing gasoline to leak onto exhaust pipe; prior to recall."

FORD TRUCK ECONOLINE 1990

Complaint Severity: Minor. **Recall Alert:** See Recall Index. **Buyer's Summary:** Check the brakes—listen for noise, look for leaks and feel for vibration. They may fail, perform poorly or require frequent mechanical attention. Test the transmission thoroughly.

Hot Spots and Owner/NHTSA Comments:

1. Brakes: hydraulic system, malfunction, failure. • "Brake problems; extended stopping distance and fluid spilling out of master cylinder." • "Brakes failed; pumping brakes would bring them back." • "While going up a long, steep mountain, brakes malfunctioned and pedal went to the floor." • "Complete brake failure under severe braking while driving through mountainous country; emergency brakes and shifting to low gear used to get off steep slope."

2. Brakes: hydraulic: anti-skid system, poor performance, failure, locking up. • "Loss of brake effectiveness in wet weather conditions causes loss of control." • "While driving downgrade on mountainous terrain, downshifted to low gear and applied brakes, brakes started to lose effectiveness and pedal went to the floor." • "Antilock brakes failed." • "Antilock brakes locked up, vehicle lost control and had an accident."

3. Power train: transmission: automatic, poor performance, difficulty shifting, slipping. • "Transmission malfunctioned; vehicle just stopped running and had no gears." • "Recurring transmission failure." • "Transmission jumps out of gear." • "Whenever in cruise or overdrive position going uphill, transmission jumps out of gear at 35-40 mph, as if in neutral position."

FORD TRUCK ECONOLINE 1992

Complaint Severity: Harmless. **Recall Alert:** See Recall Index. **Buyer's Summary:** The steering may be stiff or not working correctly. Be sure to test the steering, especially on a cold start. Test the suspension by feeling for vibration or pulling while driving. Test the transmission thoroughly.

Hot Spots and Owner/NHTSA Comments:

1. Power train: transmission: automatic, poor performance, difficulty shifting, slipping. • "Transmission occasionally slips and/or jerks into gear." • "Transmission hesitates when shifting out of 1st gear; also surges when shifting." • "Transmission accelerates to high speed without applying brake pedal." • "Transmission does not shift properly." • "Transmission downshifts out of overdrive too quickly."

2. Suspension: independent front, pulling, alignment. • "Vehicle pulls to the left." • "Upper and lower ball joints failed, causing vehicle to pull to the right; also replaced tires." • "Front end misaligned, causing rubbing noise, vibration and excessive tire wear." • "Frame and body were not properly connected, causing vehicle to sway." • "Front spring rubs against front bracket."

3. Steering: wheel and column. • "Friction in steering column when driving." • "Excessive play in steering." • "Consistent steering wheel pull to right after several alignments."

4. Suspension: independent front control arm: unknown type: ball joint, alignment, pulling, tire wear. • "Ball joints failed twice." • "Upper ball joint failure." • "Misalignment, causing vehicle to pull to the right; also replaced ball joints and spindle; premature wear of tires." • "Loose ball joints replaced."

5. Visual systems: mirrors: rearview: exterior, vibration, poor performance. • "Rearview mirror vibrates." • "Remote side mirrors vibrate, distorting visibility; also, dirt accumulates on mirrors, affecting visibility." • "Driver's rearview mirror vibrates excessively." • "Driver's outside rearview mirror vibrates, impairing visibility."

FORD TRUCK ECONOLINE 1993

Complaint Severity: Negligible. **Recall Alert:** See Recall Index. **Buyer's Summary:** Test the suspension by feeling for vibration or pulling while driving. Check the brakes—listen for noise, look for leaks and feel for vibration. They may fail, perform poorly or require frequent mechanical attention.

Hot Spots and Owner/NHTSA Comments:

1. Brakes: hydraulic: anti-skid system, poor performance, failure, locking up. • "Antilock brake system: Experienced lockup when applying brakes. Vehicle slides and pedal fades." • "Antilock brakes failed 3 times, causing vehicle to pull left or right." • "When driving on wet/icy gravel roads, vehicle will not stop; with antilock brake system rear brakes, all braking is on front brakes, causing front brakes to lock up." • "Antilock brake system: While driving, when applying the brakes vehicle pulls very hard to right; continued wear of front disc rotors and pads."

2. Suspension: independent front, vibration, poor performance. • "Front end vibration." • "Camber caster failed." • "Front end vibrates; looseness when encountering rough roads." • "Vehicle sways at speeds over 50 mph."

FORD TRUCK EXPLORER 1991

Complaint Severity: Typical. **Recall Alert:** See Recall Index. **Buyer's Summary:** Look carefully for any kind of leakage, especially under the car. Test the suspension by feeling for vibration or pulling while driving. Check the brakes—listen for noise, look for leaks and feel for vibration. They may fail, perform poorly or require frequent mechanical attention. Test the transmission thoroughly. See "Sudden Accelerations" in Introduction.

Hot Spots and Owner/NHTSA Comments:

1. Power train: transmission: automatic, poor performance, difficulty shifting, slipping. • "Automatic transmission park mechanism does not hold vehicle in parked position." • "Driving 55 mph, car was in drive, proceeded to shift into overdrive, transmission locked up in reverse; vehicle lost control, and as result had an accident." • "Transmission parking gear failed 3 times after recall repairs." • "Consumer had the master booster cylinder and transmission rebuilt and the antilock brake system module replaced."

2. Fuel: throttle linkages and control, sudden accelerations. • "Consumer was driving, started to accelerate and tried to stop; the antilock brake system could not stop the car; hit a wall and broke back." • "While driving, throttle stuck, accelerator pedal stayed in full throttle after pedal force was removed; braking was ineffective, had to shut off engine to stop." • "Accelerator pedal stays in throttle position, causing vehicle to surge or suddenly accelerate to high speeds." • "Upon leaving a stoplight, vehicle suddenly accelerated." • "While accelerating beyond 50 mph, owner released accelerator pedal, but truck continued speed. Owner lost control and truck rolled."

3. Brakes: hydraulic: anti-skid system, poor performance, failure, locking up. • "At approximately 15-20 mph began to apply brakes, felt vehicle skid in rear; antilock brake system malfunctioned; caused vehicle to hit a tree." • "While driving at 30-50 mph, the brakes would lock up when applied; caused vehicle to skid and lose control; vehicle had rear antilock brakes." • "Rear antilock brakes lock up during rainy weather; serviced several

times, problem continues." • "Antilock brake system: Driver experienced extended stopping distances while applying brakes. Caused accident. Speed 50 mph. Impact 12:00 position." • "Antilock brakes locked up, causing loss of control, resulting in an accident and injuries; also, warning light failed."
4. Brakes: hydraulic system, leaks, pulling, vibration. • "Brake fluid leak at clutch cylinder on firewall, causing clutch failure." • "While driving, brakes failed, warning light did not function; missing part in brake system caused failure." • "When applying brakes, car will pull either to the left or right, causing difficulty when driving." • "Front left brake grabs intermittently; braking system replaced, problem persists." • "Brakes have a tendency to vibrate and show excessive wear at low mileage due plastic piston, which melts, not releasing caliper."
5. Brakes: hydraulic: shoe: disc brake system, excessive wear, noise. • "Brake pads worn and replaced 6 times, rotors 1 time." • "Vehicle experiences constant noise from front brakes; replaced pads and realigned rotors." • "Front brakes make loud grinding noise when applied; decreased braking capability." • "Front brake pads wear excessively; replaced and brake rotors resurfaced every 12,000 miles." • "Antilock brake system: When applying brakes, they make loud grinding noise; replaced rotors and calipers. Brakes do not release."
6. Suspension: independent front, vibration, poor performance. • "Front-end vibrations make steering difficult." • "Vibration in steering wheel and front end." • "Vehicle delivered with out-of-tolerance parts in front end; front end could not be properly aligned, pulled hard right." • "Unable to align front end—pulls right." • "Front brakes replaced 6 times and dealer rebuilt front end at 1,000 miles; vehicle still pulls to the right above 60 mph. Wet pavement makes steering dangerous."

FORD TRUCK EXPLORER 1992

Complaint Severity: Typical. **Recall Alert:** See Recall Index. **Buyer's Summary:** Test the suspension by feeling for vibration or pulling while driving. Check the brakes—listen for noise, look for leaks and feel for vibration. They may fail, perform poorly or require frequent mechanical attention. Test the transmission thoroughly.

Hot Spots and Owner/NHTSA Comments:
1. Brakes: hydraulic system, pulling, locking up. • "Vehicle pulls to right when brakes applied, resulting in an accident." • "Car had sudden acceleration and complete brake failure at 60 mph, 12:00 position; accident resulted." • "Brakes pull to right when applied in wet conditions." • "Started vehicle and put foot on brakes, brakes malfunctioned and vehicle accelerated out of control." • "Brakes fail to stop vehicle effectively, causing extended stopping; inoperative. Repaired 5-6 times." • "Brakes lock up, causing vehicle to pull to left or right when braking."
2. Brakes: hydraulic: anti-skid system, poor performance, failure, locking up. • "Antilock brake system: Low pedal and soft, with vibration and extended stopping. Brake pads replaced yearly." • "Antilock brakes failed; locked up, causing loss of control and accident." • "While driving at 40 mph, rear wheel locked; vehicle spun around and hit a fence post, then flipped over on antilock brake system-equipped vehicle without prior warning." • "Antilock brakes fail to stop vehicle when applied, causing vehicle to pull to right; loss of vehicle control, crashing into telephone pole while driving at 30 mph." • "Antilock brakes fail continually; master cylinder replaced twice, replaced shoes and pads; antilock brake system light still stays on."
3. Power train: transmission: automatic, poor performance, difficulty shifting, slipping. • "Transmission failed, resulting in loss of steering control and stalling." • "Transmission slipped and gears completely disengaged." • "Transmission jumped out of gear; also, loose gearshifter." • "Transmission slipped out of gear and locked up." • "Transmission sticks in park, and when placed in park rolls 6-8 inches."
4. Suspension: independent front, vibration, noise, alignment. • "Front driver and passenger's bushings failed, causing vehicle to bounce; also, makes noise." • "Lateral vibration on rough road under 45 mph, and high-speed vibration at 55-65 mph." • "Misalignment, causing front-end vibration; also, tires rotated and balanced." • "While driving at speed of 65 mph, experience vibration in the front of vehicle; in for repair, no problem found." • "Vehicle front end shimmies and shakes while driving."
5. Brakes: hydraulic: disc: rotor: disc hub, excessive wear, noise. • "Antilock brake system front brake pads have to be replaced every 10,000 miles; rotors also." • "Front brake rotors prematurely wear; third set at only 35,000 miles." • "Inside surfaces on both front rotors are disintegrating, causing brakes and pedal to pulsate." • "When applied, brakes made loud squeaking and/or grinding noise; rotors have been turned, brakes relined; problem still exists." • "The front brake pads and rotor had to be replaced at 7,000 or 8,000 miles."
6. Brakes: hydraulic: shoe: disc brake system, excessive wear, pulling, failure. • "Premature wear of front brake rotors, pads and calipers; causing noise when braking." • "While traveling on dirt gravel road at 35 mph, front wheels locked up, vehicle lost control and slid, resulting in an accident." • "Brake failure; complete loss of brakes, pedal faded, making loud grinding noise; could not stop vehicle, shifted gear into neutral and used emergency brake." • "Vehicle pulls to right when going downhill; brake shoes and rotors replaced, problem continues." • "Applied brakes at highway speeds and vehicle pulled to the right or left violently; vehicle demonstrated intermittent brake problem."

FORD TRUCK EXPLORER 1993

Complaint Severity: Typical. **Recall Alert:** See Recall Index. **Buyer's Summary:** Test the suspension by feeling for vibration or pulling while driving. Check the brakes—listen for noise, look for leaks and feel for vibration. They may fail, perform poorly or require frequent mechanical attention. See "Sudden Accelerations" in Introduction.

Hot Spots and Owner/NHTSA Comments:
1. Brakes: hydraulic: anti-skid system, poor performance, failure, locking up. • "Antilock brake system, when applied on wet surfaces, cause vibrations, and directional control is affected." • "Antilock brake system: Experience pedal fading when brakes are applied. Vehicle will pull to the left or right intermittently." • "Antilock brake system locks up; vehicle will stop, then skid; nearly caused accident; various speeds; no warning." • "Antilock brake system fails, locking right front wheel and pulling truck off road. Problem corrected by taking out of alignment and making pull to left." • "Four-wheel antilock brake equipped; vehicle fishtailed in either direction upon more severe stops."
2. Suspension: independent front, pulling, vibration, noise. • "Vehicle jumps and/or pulls to the right when going over small bumps." • "Front suspension; noise and vibration in front drive at speeds of 35 and 65 mph." • "When brakes applied, notice vehicle pulls to the left and right; dealer aligned front end, bled brakes and replaced rotors and shoes." • "Vibration of front end at speeds beyond 65 mph." • "Front end shimmies at 63 or 64 mph; steering wheel goes from side to side; stops when slowing down and over 65 mph."
3. Brakes: hydraulic system, locking up, pulling, failure. • "While driving approximately 15 mph, made attempt to brake and pedal went to the floor, without prior warning; hit another vehicle."

• "Brake system failure; brakes would lock when stopping at low speeds." • "The truck has had several brake jobs. When applying the brakes, the vehicle goes all over the road." • "During emergency stopping, twice brake pedal faded to the floor, resulting in two different accidents; replaced pad, shoes and rotor to no avail." • "Repeated brake problems; pulling to the left very violently. Front wheel bearings failed."

4. Fuel: throttle linkages and control, sudden accelerations. • "Vehicle throttle stuck wide open when accelerating from stop position." • "Vehicle suddenly accelerated at very high speed without warning." • "Vehicle goes into open-throttle position while driving. When vehicle is at stop, experienced sudden acceleration." • "Engine surged, brakes would not stop vehicle; hit another vehicle." • "While driving, suddenly engine surged, pedal went to the floor, then accelerated, overpowering brakes. While having emissions tested, vehicle went through garage."

5. Emergency parking brake: mechanical, failure. • "While parked, emergency brake applied, brake released, allowing vehicle, with 2 children in car seats, to roll down onto driveway and hit a fence." • "Vehicle was parked in driveway with emergency brake on, rolled back and hit a tree, impact 6:00 position." • "Emergency parking brake slips; ratchets down very fast." • "Parking brake does not hold vehicle, causing the vehicle to roll freely." • "Emergency parking brake failure."

6. Suspension: twin: I-beam: solid: front: radius arm, noise, premature failure. • "Radius arm failed, causing front end noise when vehicle goes over bumps." • "Front-end radius arm bushings failed." • "Front end made groaning noise when subjected to bumps." • "Noisy rubber insulators replaced on front radius arms." • "Radius arm spacers failed."

FORD TRUCK EXPLORER 1994

Complaint Severity: Troublesome. **Recall Alert:** See Recall Index. **Buyer's Summary:** Look carefully for any kind of leakage, especially under the car. Test the suspension by feeling for vibration or pulling while driving. Check the brakes—listen for noise, look for leaks and feel for vibration. They may fail, perform poorly or require frequent mechanical attention.

Hot Spots and Owner/NHTSA Comments:

1. Brakes: hydraulic: anti-skid system, poor performance, failure, locking up. • "Antilock brake system: Vehicle constantly wants to pull to right from high-speed brake applications; 50 mph and higher; 1 brake wheel locks up; happens wet or dry weather; no warning." • "Antilock brake system failure; loss of effectiveness and brake pressure when brakes are applied; when driving could not stop vehicle, causing injuries." • "Antilock brake system: When applying brakes at low speed, brakes grind, steering wheel and whole front of vehicle vibrates; rotors warped; replaced 4 times, problem still exists." • "Equipped with antilock brake system; brakes are low and have poor potential for stopping. Front pads replaced and rotors turned." • "When driving and come to a stop sign, brakes go down to the floor; went through the stop sign; van has been back to dealer twice; there is no warning."

2. Brakes: hydraulic: disc: rotor: disc hub, excessive wear, failure. • "Driver's-side rotor and both front brake pads worn prematurely, causing pads to rub and squeak." • "Antilock brake system failure; experienced overheating of disc rotors, causing warping and loss of effectiveness." • "Vehicle's brake rotors prematurely warped and master brake cylinder was leaking; rotors had to be replaced at 11,000 miles, cylinder at 12,000 miles." • "Rotors on right and left side of the vehicle are cracked for the second time; replaced rotors once, need to be replaced again." • "The brake rotor had extreme, excessive wear on one side, so severely that it cut into the rotor, requiring having the rotor resurfaced."

3. Brakes: hydraulic system, failure. • "Brakes failed while moving up at stoplight, which caused an accident; no one was hurt." • "While driving, touched brakes and there were none; had to apply emergency brakes to stop." • "The braking is not as sharp as it used to be." • "During brake application, pedal went to the floor." • "Truck was put in reverse, engine accelerated, both feet on brake would not stop it. Caused accident."

4. Brakes: hydraulic: master cylinder, leaks, malfunction. • "Vehicle's antilock brake system has 2 failures, with pedal to floor and grinding metal-to-metal sound." • "Antilock brake system became inoperative due to defective master cylinder; 1 week after replacement, second failure occurred." • "Antilock brake system malfunction on several occasions; light came on periodically; replaced master cylinder, rotor, caliper and antilock controller." • "Master cylinder leaking, causing brakes to lose their effectiveness." • "Vehicle master brake cylinder was leaking and had to be replaced at 11,000 miles, rotors for cylinder at 12,000 miles."

5. Brakes: hydraulic: shoe: disc brake system, excessive wear, pulling, vibration. • "Premature and uneven wear of front brakes, causing brakes to fail." • "Front disc brake rotors, pads and calipers warped, causing vehicle to pull to the right, resulting in accident and injuries." • "Excessive wear of front braking system. This is the second incident." • "Rotors out of round; warped pads and calipers, causing vibration." • "During inclement weather, front brakes lock up and vehicle skids the first few times brakes are applied."

6. Suspension: independent front, alignment, pulling. • "Misalignment, causing vehicle to pull to the right." • "Misalignment, causing premature tire wear." • "Vehicle has severe vibration and cannot be driven at highway speeds." • "Front suspension failure causes difficulty steering and uneven tire wear." • "When driving at 60 or 65 mph, there is a front vibration in the truck."

FORD TRUCK F SERIES (LIGHT) 1987

Complaint Severity: Typical. **Recall Alert:** See Recall Index. **Buyer's Summary:** The carburetion system could contribute to stalling and hesitation. Look carefully for any kind of leakage, especially under the car. The fuel injection system has been blamed for hesitation and stalling. Be sure the vehicle doesn't die in traffic or at stops. Test the suspension by feeling for vibration or pulling while driving.

Hot Spots and Owner/NHTSA Comments:

1. Suspension: independent front, alignment, vibration, tire wear. • "Excessive shimmying in front end." • "Front end misaligned, vibration in front end, front tires worn unevenly." • "Front tires worn out due to truck pulling to right." • "Front end misaligned, caused tires to wear excessively; aligned front end twice." • "Front suspension, shimmy; replaced tire for rubber separation, balanced, rotated and aligned."

2. Fuel: fuel carburetion, stalling, hesitation. • "While traveling, vehicle died; loud pop from under hood, flames coming from under carburetor; destroyed, previously had carburetor rebuilt." • "Truck cuts out when it goes above 4,000 feet, when pulling trailer; flames shoot out of exhaust pipe, gas spills, engine stalls." • "Engine stalls, causes hesitation; engine belts squeal; poor performance." • "Repeated stalling problem."

3. Fuel: fuel injection system, stalling, hesitation. • "While traveling 30 to 35 mph, engine seems to run out of fuel, stalls, dies." • "Vehicle continues to stall; extremely difficult to maneuver at slow speeds because of the stalling." • "Upon entering traffic from ramps, at stops, in icy conditions or slowing to stop, truck loses power." • "Engine stalling and dying out, especially on inclines, while stopping or in a slight roll."

4. Fuel: fuel lines fittings and pump, leaks, fire. • "Recall on fuel lines; dealer refuses to repair." • "Fuel line came off, sprayed gas into engine compartment; explosion occurred; upon attempting to start vehicle, fire resulted." • "Fuel line couplings failure; dealer wrote to repair/replace because of possibility of fire; experiencing engine dying out." • "Fuel line leaks."

FORD TRUCK F SERIES (LIGHT) 1987

Complaint Severity: Negligible. **Buyer's Summary:** Test the suspension by feeling for vibration or pulling while driving.

Hot Spots and Owner/NHTSA Comments:

1. Suspension: tire wear, alignment. • "Vehicle shimmies; tires worn out, prior to and after recall repairs." • "Suspension failure, prior to recall; repairs unsatisfactory." • "Suspension failure, causing premature wear on tires and alignment; recall repairs refused." • "Suspension failure, prior to recall; repairs refused due to unavailability of parts." • "Suspension failed, prior to recall repairs, causing loss of control and an accident; recall repairs refused."

FORD TRUCK F SERIES (LIGHT) 1988

Complaint Severity: Minor. **Buyer's Summary:** Look carefully for any kind of leakage, especially under the car. Check the brakes—listen for noise, look for leaks and feel for vibration. They may fail, perform poorly or require frequent mechanical attention.

Hot Spots and Owner/NHTSA Comments:

1. Suspension: alignment, tire wear. • "Front-end shimmy, prior to recall notification; recall repairs refused due to lack of dealer notification." • "Suspension recall repairs refused." • "Suspension failure caused misalignment and premature wear of tires, prior to recall; tire replacement refused."

2. Brakes: hydraulic system, failure. • "Brake problems." • "Brake problems." • "Brake problems."

3. Engine: leaks, failure. • "Cylinder heads, piston rings and valves failed." • "Engine replaced." • "Vehicle leaked oil and water." • "Engine consumed excessive amount of fuel and oil."

FORD TRUCK F SERIES (LIGHT) 1989

Complaint Severity: Harmless. **Buyer's Summary:** Check the brakes—listen for noise, look for leaks and feel for vibration. They may fail, perform poorly or require frequent mechanical attention. The engine may experience stalls, and there have been complaints of fire.

Hot Spots and Owner/NHTSA Comments:

1. Brakes: hydraulic: shoe and drum system: linings, failure. • "Brake linings failed, prior to recall." • "Recall repairs refused due to unavailability of parts." • "Brakes failed, prior to and after recall." • "Brake fluid overheated, causing brake failure, prior to recall." • "Brakes fade when climbing uphill, prior to recall."

2. Engine: stalling, fire. • "When crankcase is filled with oil, smoke gets into engine, causing spontaneous combustion and a runaway engine; also excessive oil usage and starting difficulty." • "Valve cover gaskets and rear main seal failed." • "Excessive oil consumption." • "Vehicle fire." • "Engine stalls when cold; also, rpm increases at stops."

3. Fuel: fuel tank: auxiliary selector and switch, malfunction, failure. • "Front tank overflowed into rear tank, prior to recall; recall repairs refused." • "Auxiliary selector switch failed, prior to recall. Recall repairs refused due to model." • "Fuel tank selector switch failed." • "Dual tank selector valve failed; after recall campaign—was never notified about recall." • "Auxiliary tank switch failed, causing front tank to siphon fuel out of rear tank prior to recall; repairs refused due to month vehicle was manufactured."

4. Brakes: hydraulic: anti-skid system, poor performance, failure, locking up. • "Antilock brake system failed." • "Rear antilock brakes lock up, causing vehicle to skid." • "Calipers and rotors failed, causing brakes to overheat, fail; recall refused due to vehicle type." • "Antilock brakes failed, prior to recall."

5. Interior systems: active restraints: belt retractors, failure. • "Driver's-side seat belt retractor failed." • "Seat belts do not retract properly." • "Seat belt retractors failed." • "Seat belt fails to retract; hangs out when getting out of vehicle; belt gets caught in door when entering vehicle."

FORD TRUCK F SERIES (LIGHT) 1990

Complaint Severity: Minor. **Buyer's Summary:** Look carefully for any kind of leakage, especially under the car. Check the brakes—listen for noise, look for leaks and feel for vibration. They may fail, perform poorly or require frequent mechanical attention. Test the transmission thoroughly.

Hot Spots and Owner/NHTSA Comments:

1. Fuel: fuel tank assembly, malfunction, fire. • "Fuel tank delivery module recall work not performed due to part unavailability by dealer." • "Short fuel line within fuel tank assembly broke, leaking fuel onto engine." • "Gasoline expulsion from rear fuel tank." • "Fuel tank assembly short-circuited, resulting in a fire." • "Fuel tank assembly failed, causing fuel to overflow."

2. Brakes: hydraulic system, noise, excessive wear. • "Brakes failed 3 times." • "Noisy brakes; pads replaced, problem continues." • "Brakes overheated; failed." • "Premature wear of brakes." • "Brakes overheated."

3. Power train: transmission: automatic, poor performance, difficulty shifting, slipping. • "Vehicle vibrates, noise during shifting; U-joints replaced, problem continues." • "Transmission failed." • "Transmission problems." • "Transmission failed; replaced twice."

4. Fuel: fuel tank assembly: tank, leaks. • "Rear fuel tank module failed after recall repair." • "Gas tank fell apart, causing gas leakage." • "Problems getting recall work performed by dealer due to replacement dual fuel tank unavailability." • "Vehicle leaks gas." • "Dual fuel tanks leak."

5. Brakes: hydraulic: anti-skid system, poor performance, failure, locking up. • "Right and left rear wheels lock up when brakes applied." • "Vehicle continued to roll after brakes applied, resulting in accident." • "Antilock brakes locked up, causing vehicle to skid during bad weather." • "Brake failure due to rear wheel lockup, causing vehicle to veer and increasing stopping distance."

6. Power train: axle assembly: seal: axle shaft, leaks, locking up. • "Rear axle seals leaking." • "Rear axle seal leaked, causing rear brakes to lock up, resulting in loss of control." • "Front and rear axle seals failed." • "Axle seals failed, causing rear brake failure due to brake shoes being saturated with grease."

FORD TRUCK F SERIES (LIGHT) 1991

Complaint Severity: Harmless. **Buyer's Summary:** Look carefully for any kind of leakage, especially under the car. The fuel pump has received complaints. Make sure it doesn't make excessive noise and that you are experiencing adequate engine performance. Also, look for leaks. Check the brakes—listen for noise, look for leaks and feel for vibration. They may fail, perform poorly or require frequent mechanical attention. Test the transmission thoroughly.

Hot Spots and Owner/NHTSA Comments:
1. Power train: transmission: automatic, poor performance, difficulty shifting, slipping. • "Transmission solenoid failed." • "Transmission failure." • "Transmission stuck in passing gear." • "Transmission leaks oil." • "Transmission shudders when changing gears."
2. Fuel: fuel pump, leaks, failure. • "Fuel pump failed after recall work completed on fuel tanks, causing leak." • "Dual fuel pumps failed, causing vehicle to stall." • "Both fuel pumps failed, causing loss of control." • "Fuel pump failure caused rear tank to overflow into front tank."
3. Engine: noise, leaks, stalling. • "Engine fire." • "Engine oil leak and noise." • "Engine overheats when pulling up long, moderate to steep grades." • "Intermittent stalling; leaky valve cover gaskets."
4. Fuel: fuel tank assembly: tank, leaks, failure. • "Front fuel tank developed leak in the seam." • "Gas gushes from fuel tank." • "Dual gas tanks leak." • "Fuel system quantity indicator sending unit from front fuel tank failed twice." • "Dual gas tanks recall repairs refused."
5. Brakes: hydraulic system, locking up, excessive wear. • "Brakes lock up and/or grab." • "Brake failure." • "Brakes grab." • "Brakes wear out prematurely."

FORD TRUCK F SERIES (LIGHT) 1992

Complaint Severity: Troublesome. **Buyer's Summary:** Check the brakes—listen for noise, look for leaks and feel for vibration. They may fail, perform poorly or require frequent mechanical attention. Test the transmission thoroughly.

Hot Spots and Owner/NHTSA Comments:
1. Power train: transmission: automatic, poor performance, difficulty shifting, slipping. • "Transmission downshifts rough when vehicle decelerates." • "Transmission does not shift properly." • "Transmission does not shift properly; noisy." • "Transmission jumps out of gear." • "Transmission shifting roughly."
2. Brakes: hydraulic: anti-skid system, poor performance, failure, locking up. • "Antilock brakes failed, causing loss of control; also, antilock brake system light stays on." • "Antilock brakes overheat, causing front brake failure." • "Antilock brakes locked up, causing loss of control and an accident." • "Antilock brakes grip, causing rear wheels to lock up in wet or damp weather." • "Antilock brake light came on and brakes locked up, causing brake failure."
3. Emergency parking brake: mechanical, failure. • "Parking brake failed, causing vehicle to roll backwards, resulting in an accident and injury." • "Emergency brake failed twice while parked on an incline; vehicle rolled forward, resulting in accidents." • "Parking brake failed, causing vehicle to roll backwards, resulting in accident." • "Parking brake failed to set and/or reset." • "Emergency brake failed, causing accidents."
4. Engine cooling system: belts, breaking, failure. • "Broken serpentine belt caused loss of all power controls to the vehicle." • "Fan belt failed." • "Alternator belt that turns vacuum pump broke, causing vehicle to lose control." • "Serpentine belt failed."
5. Brakes: hydraulic: disc: rotor: disc hub, vibration, locking up, pulling. • "Gravel from roadway lodges against rotor, causing wheels to drag and squeal." • "Brakes pulsate when applied due to cracked rotors." • "Front discs warped." • "Vehicle pulls to side when braking; serviced 3 times, problem continues." • "Brakes locked up, causing loss of control and an accident."

FORD TRUCK F SERIES (LIGHT) 1993

Complaint Severity: Negligible. **Buyer's Summary:** Check the brakes—listen for noise, look for leaks and feel for vibration. They may fail, perform poorly or require frequent mechanical attention.

Hot Spots and Owner/NHTSA Comments:
1. Brakes: hydraulic system, pulling, failure. • "Brakes failed, causing vehicle to swerve to the left." • "Brakes failed, causing vehicle to pull to the left." • "Vehicle pulls to the right when braking." • "Vehicle pulls to left or right when braking." • "Brakes failed while traveling downgrade on a mountainous highway."
2. Power train: transmission: automatic, poor performance, difficulty shifting, slipping. • "Transmission slipped, causing accident and injuries." • "Transmission replaced 3 times." • "Automatic transmission failed to hold while in park, causing accident." • "Transmission vibrates; noisy."
3. Brakes: hydraulic: anti-skid system, poor performance, failure, locking up. • "Antilock brakes lock up in wet weather." • "Antilock brakes fail intermittently, causing extended stopping distance." • "Antilock brakes locked up while traveling downhill, causing loss of control, accident and injuries." • "Antilock brake system, drums, master cylinder failed." • "Antilock brakes lock up on wet roads, causing loss of control and extended stopping distance."
4. Brakes: hydraulic: disc: rotor: disc hub, vibration, locking up, excessive wear. • "Brakes pulsate." • "Rotors and drums replaced; also, noise when brakes applied." • "Brake rotors continue to warp." • "Brake rotors out of round, causing front wheels to lock up and vibrate." • "Brake rotors, calipers, pads, master cylinder and antilock valve failed." • "Warped brake rotors."
5. Emergency parking brake: mechanical, failure. • "Emergency brakes failed." • "Emergency brake slips." • "Parking brake disengaged while vehicle was parked with transmission in neutral." • "Emergency brake popped out of gear, resulting in an accident." • "Intermittent emergency brake failure."
6. Brakes: hydraulic: disc: caliper, locking up, failure. • "Caliper slides binding, causing brakes to lock up." • "Calipers stick, causing brakes to overheat." • "Calipers replaced." • "Front brake calipers failed."

FORD TRUCK F SERIES (LIGHT) 1994

Complaint Severity: Negligible. **Buyer's Summary:** Check the brakes—listen for noise, look for leaks and feel for vibration. They may fail, perform poorly or require frequent mechanical attention.

Hot Spots and Owner/NHTSA Comments:
1. Brakes: hydraulic system, pulling, vibration, locking up. • "Brakes failed." • "When brakes applied, vehicle intermittently pulls to the right or left." • "Brakes vibrate." • "Wheels lock up when brakes applied, causing loss of control."
2. Brakes: hydraulic: disc: rotor: disc hub, excessive wear. • "Brake rotors and pads failed twice." • "Warped drums and right front rotor, causing uneven wear and cupped tires." • "Brake rotors, pads and calipers replaced 3 times due to erratic braking problems." • "Brake rotors turned; also, rear drums replaced." • "Plastic caliper piston stuck, causing rotors to warp and brake shudder."
3. Engine cooling system: belts, breaking, failure. • "Flat belt that holds everything together broke (this is a brand new truck—belt broke once already, this is the second time)." • "Engine fan belt fell off, causing engine to overheat and thermostat to fail." • "Fan belt jumped off pulley, resulting in overheated engine and stalling." • "Engine fan belt failed." • "Fan belt broke 5 times."

FORD TRUCK F150 1987

Complaint Severity: Minor. **Recall Alert:** See Recall Index. **Buyer's Summary:** The fuel injection system has been blamed for hesitation and stalling. Be sure the vehicle doesn't die in traffic or at stops. The steering may be stiff or not working correctly. Be sure to test the steering, especially on a cold start. Check the brakes—listen for noise, look for leaks and feel for vibration. They may fail, perform poorly or require frequent mechanical attention. Test the clutch. See "Sudden Accelerations" in Introduction.

Hot Spots and Owner/NHTSA Comments:

1. Fuel: fuel systems, hesitation, malfunction. • "Repeated problems starting truck, possibly due to fuel injector processor; gauge shows rear tank full and front tank empty, but truck running on front tank." • "Hesitation while accelerating, pinging sound while accelerating, fan that cools fuel in injectors not working; gas foaming causing vapor lock." • "Strong smell of gas inside cab of truck." • "Fuel system recall; repairs done, still have problem starting." • "Truck had been driven 3-4 miles and then parked; approximately 25 minutes later, smoke and flames were coming out from under the hood."

2. Fuel: throttle linkages and control, sudden accelerations. • "Engine races and runs out of control going through stop signs and in traffic." • "Engine idles very rough, especially after engine gets warm; also, on deceleration at lower speeds, engine sometimes dies." • "Fast idling of engine; when driving, you have to be on guard every minute in anticipation of racing engine." • "Motor idles too fast, to 2,000 rpm by itself; sometimes gas pedal sticks down after passing or at top of hill, almost causing accidents." • "Accelerator stuck, vehicle accelerated forward; before wife could react, truck hit a pole on opposite driveway. Wife sustained injury."

3. Power train: clutch assembly, excessive wear, stalling. • "Plastic hydraulic line that connects master/slave cylinder contacted hot exhaust pipe when shifting; pressure ruptured line; not protected from heat." • "Clutch would not disengage; clutch completely depressed, vehicle lunged, without warning lost control, disengaging clutch caused stalling." • "Defective clutch assembly caused pedal not to go in when pressed." • "Clutch would not disengage because the bolts in the brake master cylinder mounted on fire wall cracked." • "Replaced 3 slave clutches and 1 bracket on slave clutch within 38,000 miles."

4. Steering: linkages: tie rod: end, excessive wear, failure. • "End tie rod broke twice." • "Loose steering resulting from premature wear of both tie rod end assemblies." • "Tie rod ends worn out at 28,000 miles." • "Outer tie rod ends on both sides broke and were replaced." • "Two thousand miles since installing aftermarket tie rod ends, right front tie rod end pulled apart and allowed front wheels to turn wrong direction for correct steering control."

5. Fuel: fuel injection system, stalling, hesitation. • "Fluctuation of miles per gallon of fuel; repaired/replaced manifold air pressure sensor, oil sending unit and spark plugs, fuel injectors cleaned; repair successful, but later problem reoccurred." • "Engine has irregular miss and stalls when at idle or low speed; after servicing, car idles fast and will not slow down; several repair attempts to no avail." • "Vehicle bucked, spit and spurted before finally moved." • "Several components of fuel system have been replaced: throttle bodies, fuel injection valves, processors; engine still races, fast idle, bucks and stalls."

6. Brakes: hydraulic system, locking up, vibration, failure. • "Braking system defective; continues to fail in spite of many attempts to repair." • "Brakes malfunctioned and antilock brakes locked up totally; hubs out of round from factory; resulted in accident." • "Pulls to left severely when brakes applied; brakes pulsate upon application." • "Defect in brake system; right side brake keeps wearing; replaced pads, rotors and piston wheel cylinder." • "Braking system defective; repaired/replaced left front rotor and caliper, right front brake pad."

FORD TRUCK F150 1988

Complaint Severity: Typical. **Recall Alert:** See Recall Index. **Buyer's Summary:** Look carefully for any kind of leakage, especially under the car. Check the brakes—listen for noise, look for leaks and feel for vibration. They may fail, perform poorly or require frequent mechanical attention. Test the transmission thoroughly. See "Sudden Accelerations" in Introduction.

Hot Spots and Owner/NHTSA Comments:

1. Brakes: hydraulic system, pulling, vibration, locking up. • "Persistent brake problems; front brakes pull in both left and right direction; rear antilock brakes lock up; vibration in front." • "Brakes have not performed up to standards, have to stand on them to stop; repaired several times, never got fixed." • "Brake failure; when applied, pull severely toward oncoming traffic; repaired 12 times to no avail." • "Both rear brakes show rust where shoes don't contact; front brakes are locking wheels; 3 accidents have resulted; valve changed, not fixed." • "Brakes lock up on rear wheel when applied; also, wheel squealed when making turn."

2. Brakes: hydraulic: anti-skid system, poor performance, failure, locking up. • "Antilock brake system had complete brake failure and front wheels locked up." • "Antilock brake system failed and pedal hit the floor." • "Brake pedal spongy and travels to floor causing loss of braking ability." • "Antilock brake system had extended stopping distance, resulting in getting rear-ended by another vehicle." • "Antilock brake system locked up in the rear. Accident occurred; frontal collision. Fuel shutoff switch did not stop fuel from fuel injectors."

3. Fuel: throttle linkages and control, sudden accelerations. • "Intermittent throttle sticking resulted in uncontrolled engine surging while driving." • "Engine experiences uncontrollable and unexplained acceleration." • "Step on the clutch with left foot, raise right foot off accelerator, motor speeds up and tachometer shoots up additional 2,000 to 6,000 rpm." • "Serious surge problem at idle speed; sudden acceleration resulted in accident." • "While in motion, took foot off gas pedal and applied brakes, vehicle accelerated and was stopped by shifting into neutral; could hear engine racing."

4. Power train: transmission: automatic, poor performance, difficulty shifting, slipping. • "Malfunction in transmission; seemingly forgets to shift from 2nd to 3rd." • "Erratic operation of transmission in drive and overdrive; accelerating from 35 mph, transmission slows down, other times it seems to freewheel, no engine braking." • "Automatic transmission malfunction; when shifting up or down, loud noise, jerks rather hard; repaired/replaced rear end and transfer case." • "Defective transmission; engine revving and roaring while forward motion disproportionately low; repair attempts unsuccessful."

5. Fuel: fuel tank assembly: gauge: fuel, malfunction, failure. • "Gas gauge works intermittently." • "Front fuel gauge quit registering, pump continued to work properly." • "Rear fuel tank gauge will move and state false reading due to possible electrical sending unit short." • "Fuel gauge gives a faulty reading, especially when fuel tank is not full." • "Fuel tank gauges became inoperable; they read full until there was a quarter tank of gas, then gauge moved off full."

6. Fuel: fuel tank assembly: tank, corrosion, leaks, fire. • "Leakage in front fuel tank was caused by rust and corrosion." • "Gas was dripping from front gas tank. When front tank is empty, it stops leaking." • "Owner smelled gas odor coming from tank. Gas is leaking from top of front tank. Electrical power surge when accelerating and lights are on." • "Vehicle caught on fire; driver burned to death; shortly after impact of accident, truck equipped with 2 factory-installed gas tanks." • "Gas tank exploded, bursting seams. Wiring and fuel pump burned."

FORD TRUCK F150 1989

Complaint Severity: Negligible. **Recall Alert:** See Recall Index. **Buyer's Summary:** Look carefully for any kind of leakage, especially under the car. The engine has experienced a variety of problems. Have it examined by a professional. Check the brakes—listen for noise, look for leaks and feel for vibration. They may fail, perform poorly or require frequent mechanical attention. Test the transmission thoroughly.

Hot Spots and Owner/NHTSA Comments:

1. Brakes: hydraulic: anti-skid system, poor performance, failure, locking up. • "Loss or lack of braking power when brakes are applied; brakes often lock up." • "Whenever driving under extreme heavy rain, brakes tend to lock up on vehicle equipped with antilock brake system without prior warning." • "Rear antilock brake system locks up when first starting vehicle or driving at high speeds, causing extended stopping or becoming inoperative." • "Loss of vehicle control forced vehicle to go into a ravine; caused by loss of brake effectiveness when brakes were applied." • "Antilock brakes intermittently fail and/or grab."

2. Brakes: hydraulic system, noise, locking up. • "Problem with soft brake pedal; repaired/replaced master cylinder and vacuum power booster repeatedly." • "Brakes are noisy and lock up in rear." • "Brakes pull and squeal upon application." • "Vehicle's brakes squeal when applied; sanded and cleaned brakes, noise persists." • "Brakes crunch, barely stop truck, and smell hot; replaced front calipers, turned rotors, adjusted rear brakes, still have problem."

3. Engine: miscellaneous problems. • "Excessive engine oil consumption." • "Truck is leaking fuel, oil, coolant and freon. Potential safety hazard. Dealer won't fix." • "Water pump failed; oil pan and valve cover leaks." • "Problem with truck running cool; repaired/replaced temperature sender in block to no avail." • "Oil consumption—uses approximately 1 quart of oil to 450 miles."

4. Fuel: fuel tank: auxiliary selector and switch, malfunction, failure. • "Dual fuel tank selector valve recall repairs delayed due to faulty computer reading." • "Fuel runs from one tank to the other, then overflows." • "Dual fuel tank: Front fuel tank is pumping gas into the rear tank, resulting in fuel leakage." • "Gasoline expulsion due to a defective switch over valve in the auxiliary fuel tank assembly."

5. Power train: transmission: automatic, poor performance, difficulty shifting, slipping. • "Transmission makes whining noise driving on highway; clunking noise." • "After coming to stop or park position, vehicle on incline, shift lever in apparent park position, ignition off, vehicle begins to roll away." • "Automatic transmission stopped working; vehicle wouldn't move forward at regular speed; replaced complete transmission." • "It is difficult to shift transmission into overdrive from 4th gear." • "At about 30 mph, when vehicle is in overdrive, transmission slips into neutral when trying to accelerate."

6. Fuel: fuel tank: auxiliary, leaks, tank pressure. • "When switched to back tank, fuel is transferred to front and tank overflows onto ground." • "When front tank is full, back tank leaks; when cap is removed, fuel will shoot out." • "The rear fuel tank would overflow at the cap." • "Leakage from front tank when transferring gas from auxiliary tank." • "When switched to front gas tank, remaining gas from rear tank pumped into front tank, causing overflow and splash onto left rear tire."

FORD TRUCK F150 1990

Complaint Severity: Negligible. **Recall Alert:** See Recall Index. **Buyer's Summary:** The fuel pump has received complaints. Make sure it doesn't make excessive noise and that you are experiencing adequate engine performance. Also, look for leaks. Test the suspension by feeling for vibration or pulling while driving. Test the transmission thoroughly.

Hot Spots and Owner/NHTSA Comments:

1. Power train: transmission: automatic, poor performance, difficulty shifting, slipping. • "Transmission slipping gears. Fuel system causes vehicle to stall. Brakes cause car to pull left to right." • "Electronic automatic transmission will shift into neutral or high gear." • "While idling, vehicle gears self-shifted and vehicle suddenly accelerated out of control; no driver." • "Vehicle was parked in gear; rolled backwards, hitting a building. Impact 6:00 position." • "There is a long delay when shifting into reverse before transmission engages."

2. Brakes: hydraulic: antiskid, poor performance, locking up. • "Truck uses excessive brake pads; replaced rotors and calipers." • "Front antilock brake system locks up on slick or icy roads, causing loss of steering control." • "The rear antilock brake system keeps locking up in cold, damp weather." • "Driver only taps brake pedal lightly in order for brake to lock up. Metallic dust settles in brake area." • "When antilock brakes were applied in a sudden stop, the pedal went all the way to the floor and did not stop the vehicle; resulted in an accident."

3. Brakes: hydraulic system, locking up, vibration, excessive wear. • "During the winter, when it is cold, the brakes grab and lock up, causing vehicle to slide on icy streets and on gravel." • "Sending and fuel pump unit inside fuel tank failed; caused engine to quit running; also, front disc brake pedal pulsates when applied; causes severe vibration." • "When he steps on the brake pedal, it lurches so hard it throws him through the windshield." • "Transmission slipping gears. Fuel system causes vehicle to stall. Brakes cause car to pull left to right." • "Premature wear on front and back brakes; repaired 5 times."

4. Fuel: fuel pump, stalling, malfunction. • "Poor fuel circulation, causing vehicle to stall. Replaced fuel pump on back tank; now the front tank went out." • "Owner had recall work performed on his vehicle for the check valve but it did not solve the problem. Fuel tank still spills between tanks when full." • "Sending and fuel pump unit inside fuel tank failed; caused engine to quit running; also, front disc brake pedal pulsates when applied; causes severe vibration." • "Fuel pumps failed due to broken fuel line connectors."

5. Suspension: independent front, pulling, tire wear, failure. • "Brakes lock up on vehicle when weather is damp. There is also a surging, lunging and vibration in the front end." • "Vehicle pulls to either side when driven on uneven wet surface." • "Front left brake pulls to the left; all repair attempts to no avail." • "Vehicle purchased with poor wheel alignment, pulls to right on highway when steering and/or braking; front tires wearing excessively." • "Tie rod ends and ball joints have failed; needed replacement at 32,000 miles."

6. Electrical system: ignition, stalling. • "Experienced high idle when stopping vehicle, or intermittently stalls without warning." • "At low rpm, engine runs rough, sometimes stopping." • "Vehicle constantly stalls; stalls whether switching gears, or during hot or cold weather in summer and winter." • "Experiencing intermittent stalling on downshift and stops; condition exists without warning; several components replaced; fuel sensor and new processor, still a problem." • "Vehicle has intermittent missing and rough idling problem."

FORD TRUCK F150 1991

Complaint Severity: Typical. **Recall Alert:** See Recall Index. **Buyer's Summary:** Look carefully for any kind of leakage, especially under the car. The fuel pump has received complaints. Make sure it doesn't make excessive noise and that you are experiencing adequate engine performance. Also, look for leaks. Check the brakes—listen for noise, look for leaks and feel for vibration. They may fail, perform poorly or require frequent mechanical attention. Test the transmission thoroughly.

Hot Spots and Owner/NHTSA Comments:

1. Brakes: hydraulic system, pulling, locking up, poor performance. • "Brakes pull to the left when applied, causing loss of control." • "Brakes locked, causing truck to hit a tree; repaired/ replaced pads, rotors and calipers." • "Squeaking noise when brake pedal is applied; brakes grab and driver is thrown forward. Windshield had to be replaced because of this problem." • "Brake failure; pedal faded on wet surface, causing accident; vehicle ran into a ditch, impact 1:00 position, speed 30 mph." • "When braking, vehicle veers to the left, causing poor performance."

2. Power train: transmission: automatic, poor performance, difficulty shifting, slipping. • "Vehicle was in park and jumped out of gear, went out of control; caused 3 fatalities." • "When vehicle in reverse, it rolls forward." • "When in park and ignition is on and vehicle is bumped slightly, it jumps out of gear into drive. Caused a collision with another vehicle. No one was in vehicle." • "Transmission doesn't seem to downshift; there's a vibration from driver's-side dash." • "Transmission shifts from overdrive into drive at wrong speeds."

3. Brakes: hydraulic: anti-skid system, poor performance, failure, locking up. • "Brakes do not respond when pedal travel is at its fullest application." • "Applied brakes and pedal locked up; vehicle lost control and skidded 20 feet, then hit a car that was in front of vehicle." • "Rear antilock brakes lock up first thing in the morning every time the brakes are applied when the weather is wet." • "Brake pedal will decrease in depth, getting softer until hitting floorboard. Truck is equipped with antilock brake system." • "Antilock brake system on rear wheels locks up after sitting overnight in wet weather; caused vehicle to skid. When first starting vehicle, hard stopping when brakes applied."

4. Brakes: hydraulic: shoe and drum system, locking up. • "Rear brakes locked up, resulting in an accident and injury." • "Rear brake lockup occurs in rainy weather." • "Rear brakes lock up in wet weather, causing sliding." • "Rear antilock brake system locks up and front end shimmies." • "Rear antilock brakes lock up periodically when brakes are applied at any speed."

5. Fuel: fuel pump, failure. • "In the fuel tank, the fuel pumps kept on running after engine was turned off; dealer installed a small relay to remedy situation." • "Recall related; correction for dual fuel tank did not remedy the problem. Replaced both fuel pumps to correct problem." • "Malfunctioning check valve within the fuel pump." • "Noise in gas tank dealership diagnosis: electronic fuel pump." • "Fuel pumps in tanks are defective, potential for fuel spillage."

6. Fuel: fuel tank: auxiliary selector and switch, leaks, malfunction. • "Fuel pumps do not shut off and the leaky fuel tank selector valve allows one tank to overflow onto the exhaust system." • "On dual fuel tank system, the rear tank is siphoning fuel from the front tank, causing the rear one to overflow onto the ground." • "Large stream of gas was leaking out of front fuel tank filler pipe due to a faulty valve in front fuel pump." • "Malfunctioning check valve causes leakage and spillage in dual fuel tanks." • "Dual fuel tanks exchange fuel without touching switch."

FORD TRUCK F150 1992

Complaint Severity: Typical. **Recall Alert:** See Recall Index. **Buyer's Summary:** Test the suspension by feeling for vibration or pulling while driving. Check the brakes—listen for noise, look for leaks and feel for vibration. They may fail, perform poorly or require frequent mechanical attention. Test the transmission thoroughly.

Hot Spots and Owner/NHTSA Comments:

1. Brakes: hydraulic: anti-skid system, poor performance, failure, locking up. • "Severe sudden pull to right when brakes are applied in wet highway conditions resulted in loss of control and poor direction." • "Antilock brake system front brakes will vibrate when applied due rotors being warped. Braking performance has decreased." • "Rear antilock brake system will lock when slamming on brakes while moving intermittently. Dealer has made numerous attempts, with no solution." • "Rear antilock brake system locks up in damp or rainy weather, causing lack of braking ability."

2. Emergency parking brake: mechanical, failure. • "Emergency brake failed to hold on hill (prior to recall), causing loss of control and an accident." • "Emergency parking brake released while vehicle was parked on incline; hit a parked vehicle. Impact 6:00 position." • "Parking brake disengaged and vehicle rolled; hit a tree, denting bumper. Dealer refused to do anything about problem." • "Emergency brake released, allowing truck to roll down highway." • "Loss of power steering at low engine rpm or while making series of quick turning movements; also, emergency parking brake failed to engage when applied."

3. Power train: transmission: automatic, poor performance, difficulty shifting, slipping. • "Gear jumped from park to reverse with no warning." • "Vehicle was parked with shift lever in park position; upon starting, it surged forward and parking prawl engaged, keeping van from striking the car in front." • "Transmission shifting rough; replaced, problem continues." • "Transmission not shifting properly when put into gear."

4. Suspension: independent front, pulling, failure. • "Front suspension bolts were loose; while driving, it felt as if front suspension was dislocated from the chassis." • "Hit uneven road surface. Lost control. When brakes where applied, experienced instability in front suspension. Hit an embankment. Impact 12:00 position. Speed 50 mph." • "Vehicle pulls very hard to the right while driving." • "Owner has been having front-end problems due to upper and lower ball joint failure." • "While driving, car changed directions, very poor stability; dealer said there is a defect in front end. Replaced front end, problem still exists."

5. Structure: door assembly: latches and locks, malfunction, failure. • "Door will not latch in freezing weather, opens while driving." • "Door latch fails to engage, door fails to securely lock from inside when closing." • "Door locking and latching mechanism freezes due to redesign of cable." • "Door lock assembly will not latch properly in cold weather, prior to and after recall repairs." • "Door locks failed."

6. Brakes: hydraulic system, pulling, locking up, failure. • "Vehicle pulls to left or right while braking." • "Brakes make truck pull to the left upon braking." • "Antilock brake system: When applying brakes have low brake pressure; also, pedal faded." • "Brakes keep locking up, especially when it rains." • "While driving, brakes failed; had to coast until vehicle stopped."

FORD TRUCK F150 1993

Complaint Severity: Troublesome. **Recall Alert:** See Recall Index. **Buyer's Summary:** Check the brakes—listen for noise, look for leaks and feel for vibration. They may fail, perform poorly or require frequent mechanical attention. See "Sudden Accelerations" in Introduction.

Hot Spots and Owner/NHTSA Comments:

1. Brakes: hydraulic: anti-skid system, poor performance, failure, locking up. • "Antilock brake system brake pedal traveled to the floor with no braking effect; speed 35 mph; caused accident; hit 2 other cars; impact 12:00 position." • "Antilock brake system failure in wet road conditions; brake grabs real hard." • "Antilock brake system left front brake locks up. In wet conditions, brakes will not hold." • "Antilock brake system: Owner has lost brakes, pedal went to the floor and brakes were smoking. Vehicle pulls to the right when brakes are applied." • "Antilock brake system: Brakes replaced numerous times, front and rear. When applying brakes, skidded to right." • "Front disc brakes, rear antilock brake system fails to stop vehicle effectively when applied."

2. Brakes: hydraulic: shoe: disc brake system, pulling, excessive wear. • "The front disc brake and bearing went out." • "When braking, vehicle pulls to the right intermittently." • "Vehicle pulls to the right and left when braking. Replaced front end to no avail." • "Antilock brake system will lock up on wet or icy surfaces; vehicle skidded and lost control; replaced disc rotors on front." • "Antilock brake system front discs have been replaced 3 times in 35,000 miles: pads, rotors and calipers. Dealer says pads are no good."

3. Fuel: throttle linkages and control, sudden accelerations. • "Engine accelerates on its own; no prior warning." • "When vehicle was taken from park to reverse, it jumped about 5 feet at full throttle." • "When backing in reverse, truck accelerated out of control, leaving 37 feet of skid marks. Rear tires were smoking from friction of braking." • "Engine idles fast, car will drive at 20 mph with no foot pressure on accelerator pedal." • "Experienced sudden acceleration, resulting in accident. Accelerator stuck at 60 mph."

4. Brakes: hydraulic system, pulling, locking up. • "Applying brakes while going down 6 percent grade, experienced front wheel shimmy and loss of control. Vehicle not responding to steering wheel, leading to a crash." • "When applying the brake, vehicle pulls to the right and shudders." • "Brakes lock up during wet or damp weather, resulting in skidding and extended stopping distances." • "When brake is applied, the truck loses control." • "Front subframe where shocks are mounted is loose; causing loss of suspension, steering and brakes."

5. Brakes: hydraulic: disc: rotor: disc hub, excessive wear, noise, vibration. • "Disc rotors on front prematurely wear; vehicle surges forward. Rotor out of round." • "Front brake rotors overheat, turning discolored. Front rotors are replaced continualy." • "Noticed squeaking noise coming from brake rotor; replaced pad and cut rotor twice with 15,000 miles to no avail." • "Front brake rotors, pads and calipers failed, causing vibration and noise upon braking." • "Brake system failure; rotors are warping."

6. Brakes: hydraulic: disc: caliper, locking up, noise, malfunction. • "Front driver's-side wheel locking up when making sudden stops on wet surface; replaced caliper and new brakes to no avail." • "Brake system failure; replaced calipers." • "Calipers make clinging noise." • "Antilock brake system malfunction; caliper pin locked up, causing vehicle to pull to left or right, possibly due to rusting out; replaced pin 3 times and pad twice."

FORD TRUCK F150 1994

Complaint Severity: Troublesome. **Recall Alert:** See Recall Index. **Buyer's Summary:** The airbags in this vehicle have experienced failures and malfunctions: You may need a professional evaluation on the condition of the airbags. Check the brakes—listen for noise, look for leaks and feel for vibration. They may fail, perform poorly or require frequent mechanical attention. Test the transmission thoroughly.

Hot Spots and Owner/NHTSA Comments:

1. Brakes: hydraulic: anti-skid system, poor performance, failure, locking up. • "Antilock brake system fails repeatedly; replaced system 5 times. Brakes will not respond to application." • "Vehicle's antilock brake system front brakes: In damp road conditions the front wheels lock up prematurely. This is the second truck with problem. A bad vibration occurs prior to lockup." • "Antilock brake system failure; on wet road surface, experience a very hard pull to left and vibration when brakes are applied; also, makes loud noise." • "Antilock brake system, when applied, will grab, possibly due to rotors warping." • "Antilock brake system: When applied, either left or right front brakes will lock up, vibrate or have very poor response to pedal travel."

2. Brakes: hydraulic: disc: rotor: disc hub, excessive wear, vibration. • "Antilock brake system: Failure of disc rotors, causing warping and wear of pads; replaced once." • "Front brake rotors warp after 2,000 miles; replaced several times." • "Antilock brake system, when applied, will grab, possibly due to rotors warping." • "The front brake rotors have had to be turned at least 3 times; the vehicle vibrates when the brakes are applied because of warped rotors." • "Frontal collision, impact 12:00 position; disc rotors failed; vehicle equipped with antilock brake system, speed 30 mph."

3. Brakes: hydraulic: shoe: disc brake system, excessive wear, locking up, vibration. • "Excessive wear of front brake pads and rotors, causing vehicle to vibrate when braking." • "Right front brakes lock up during wet, rainy weather, causing vehicle to pull to the right." • "Front brakes have shuddering at high speeds." • "Front brake pads and rotors failed, causing vibration when brakes are applied." • "Front brakes are locking up only when wet; equipped with antilock brake system in rear wheels."

4. Interior systems: passive restraint: airbag: driver, malfunction, failure. • "After replacing engine, had an accident; driver airbag did not deploy." • "Airbag did not deploy during a frontal collision." • "Frontal collision, impact 12:00 position, speed 35 mph, airbag deployed with a delay." • "In a frontal collision, the driver's-side airbag did not deploy." • "In accident at 35 mph, 12:00 position, hit a pole when rear antilock brake system locked up; driver's-side airbag did not deploy."

5. Brakes: hydraulic system, pulling, vibration, excessive wear. • "When brakes are applied, truck pulls to the left." • "Experiencing pulling to left when braking; replaced pad, master cylinder, brake lock and turned rotor." • "Brakes pulsate every time applying brakes, worst at faster speeds." • "When pressure was applied to the brake, vehicle lost control and pulled to the right, resulting in injuries." • "Brakes grind and vehicle pulls to the right when braking, causing premature wear on brake drums, pads, calipers and rotors."

6. Power train: transmission: automatic, poor performance, difficulty shifting, slipping. • "The vehicle came out of the park gear and rolled over driver." • "Vehicle has harsh reverse motion and operation, intermittently stalling when placed in reverse." • "Owner has had 2 episodes of vehicle slipping out of park into reverse; once resulting in an accident." • "Automatic transmission has grinding noise that increases as rpm is higher." • "Solenoid wire was crossed, causing transmission to slip from park to reverse, hitting brick wall."

FORD TRUCK F150 1995

Complaint Severity: Typical. **Buyer's Summary:** Test the suspension by feeling for vibration or pulling while driving. Check the brakes—listen for noise, look for leaks and feel for vibration. They may fail, perform poorly or require frequent mechanical attention.

Hot Spots and Owner/NHTSA Comments:

1. Brakes: hydraulic: anti-skid system, poor performance, failure, locking up. • "Vehicle's antilock brake system is operating erratically with soft pedal; very difficult to stop, and a popping sound occurred at one point." • "Front brakes, when applied, pull very hard to the right or left; in for repair 3 times." • "Antilock brake system front brakes twice developed distinct shimmy due to warping of rotors." • "Driving vehicle at 15 mph, applied brakes, brakes locked up, impact 12:00 position (antilock brake system)." • "Antilock brake system malfunction; pedal fades to the floor, experienced long stopping distance; resulted in accident."

2. Suspension: independent front, vibration, pulling. • "Front end vibrates." • "In a sudden stop the vehicle turns to the left." • "Three attempts by dealer to correct drifting. Dealer now says drift is normal." • "The truck pulls to the left, and it pulls even more when the brakes are applied."

FORD TRUCK F250 1987

Complaint Severity: Typical. **Recall Alert:** See Recall Index. **Buyer's Summary:** Check the brakes—listen for noise, look for leaks and feel for vibration. They may fail, perform poorly or require frequent mechanical attention. Test the clutch. See "Sudden Accelerations" in Introduction.

Hot Spots and Owner/NHTSA Comments:

1. Brakes: hydraulic: anti-skid system, poor performance, failure, locking up. • "Intermittent brake failure; pedal gets hard, truck will not stop, antilock light comes on and brake will be working again; all repair attempts to no avail." • "Brakes ineffective on quick stop or on downhill grade, antilock braking system disconnected; parts replaced to no avail." • "Antilock brake system failed to stop vehicle coming down mountain, resulting in accident; repaired/replaced master cylinder; when brakes get wet, problems magnified." • "Brakes failed numerous times at city driving coming to normal stop; lubricated caliper slides; seemed to help, but did not solve problem." • "While driving down a steep hill, 15 percent grade, for approximately half a mile, brakes lost their effectiveness and pedal went to the floor."

2. Brakes: hydraulic system, locking up, failure. • "Brake fluid boiled over; brakes completely failed, pedal went to the floor." • "Vehicle has complete brake loss and pedal goes to the floor." • "Roll pins in front disc brakes hanging up due to inadequate lubrication, thus brake pedal hard, does not stop; sometimes pedal soft with no response." • "Front and rear brakes faded to the floor, resulting in rear lockup, allowing vehicle to side-slide, almost turning over."

3. Fuel: fuel systems, fire, malfunction. • "Coming down side of mountain, truck backfired once, gas pedal went to floor, smoke began pouring from under hood, smelled gas immediately." • "Experiencing loss of power and backfiring; replaced fuel separator valve with low-return valve." • "Parked vehicle with engine idling, suddenly entire vehicle became engulfed in flames; total loss, cause undetermined." • "When truck was parked after hour drive, noticed smoke, flames started under truck, caught fire at gas line or canister; inadequate fuel system." • "Passenger-side exhaust manifold cracked at #5 plug; also, fuel line clips recalled; installed new clips and replaced manifold."

4. Brakes: hydraulic: shoe: disc brake system, vibration, fade. • "Upon applying front brakes, vehicle would pulsate; replaced rotors and pads several times, but vehicle continues to pulsate." • "Vehicle experienced loss of brake effectiveness while coming down an incline." • "Vehicle may experience fading under prolonged braking." • "While coming down a mountain road, brakes began to fade until completely inoperative." • "Vehicle experienced loss of brake effectiveness."

5. Fuel: throttle linkages and control, sudden accelerations. • "Sudden acceleration caused driver to lose control, resulting in an accident." • "Vehicle suddenly accelerated at full power; driver losing control resulted in collision with tree, killing driver and injuring occupant." • "Experiencing sudden acceleration of vehicle upon applying brakes and exiting highway." • "Throttle went into open position while driving vehicle; flex ring failed, injection pump plastic parts melted."

6. Power train: clutch assembly, difficulty shifting, poor performance. • "Standard shift clutch master cylinder pushrod slips at its adjustment fitting, and the clutch engages for sudden acceleration." • "Four-speed; improper shifting of clutch assembly." • "Three complete clutch systems since owning truck; needs replacing approximately every 8,000 miles." • "Manual clutch failure; while driving, it was impossible to shift gears." • "Clutch plate poorly fastened to firewall; plate breaks, causing clutch to go to floor, losing control of vehicle."

FORD TRUCK F250 1988

Complaint Severity: Typical. **Recall Alert:** See Recall Index. **Buyer's Summary:** Look carefully for any kind of leakage, especially under the car. The fuel injection system has been blamed for hesitation and stalling. Be sure the vehicle doesn't die in traffic or at stops. Check the brakes—listen for noise, look for leaks and feel for vibration. They may fail, perform poorly or require frequent mechanical attention. Test the transmission thoroughly.

Hot Spots and Owner/NHTSA Comments:

1. Brakes: hydraulic: anti-skid system, poor performance, failure, locking up. • "While coming down a mountain road, brakes began to lose power and overheated." • "Antilock brake system failed to stop vehicle effectively, causing extended stopping or becoming inoperative when applied. Recall related." • "Complete loss of foot brakes while driving down grade; had to use hand brake to stop vehicle (antilock brake system)." • "Driving, tried to stop, the antilock brake system failed." • "Brakes performed poorly, pedal faded; going down steep hill with load, vehicle will not stop."

2. Brakes: hydraulic system, leaks, locking up, failure. • "Brakes failed; when applied, brake pedal goes all the way down to the floor." • "Possible leakage of seals caused brakes to malfunction; resulted in an accident." • "When brakes were applied the vehicle pulled to left, causing lack of control." • "Rear brakes lock up, front brakes won't catch when rear brakes lock up." • "Brake pedal goes to floor in 10 seconds when excessive pressure is applied."

3. Brakes: hydraulic: shoe: disc brake system, locking up, failure. • "Brake pedal began to fade and lose pressure when coming down steep grade; brakes returned when cooled." • "While traveling on wet surface, front brakes lock up and steering is impossible to maneuver." • "Front brake wheel cylinders froze up; caused brakes to lock up." • "Front disc brakes grab securely, not lock, long before drum brakes with antilock go into effect; light pressure on brake pedal puts front end into a skid." • "After recall, front disc brakes are still inadequate, resulting in extended stopping distance."

4. Fuel: fuel injection system, stalling, hesitation. • "Fuel injector pump failed twice, causing loss of power and fuel leak." • "Problem with fuel injector pump leak; oil pressure problems." • "Recurring stalling problem; repaired/replaced electronic fuel injection processor; soon after replacement, malfunction reappears; all repair attempts to no avail." • "Vehicle stalling problems, with loss of power steering."

5. Structure: body, cracking, failure. • "Fire wall weakened; it moves approximately 1 to 1½ inches when clutch is depressed." • "Defective design in fire wall, part loose on left side, allowing to move forward." • "Fire wall is not strong enough; as a result, the clutch will not shift gears." • "Sheet metal used for fire wall structure not strong enough to handle pressure, causing cracks; spot welds; master clutch cylinder forced away from fire wall." • "Man-

ual transmission: floor shifted; 5-speed. Fire wall cracked." • "Vehicle is very hard to start. Shifting of gears very difficult."
6. Power train: transmission: automatic, poor performance, difficulty shifting, slipping. • "While parked on incline, vehicle rolled down; caused damage and injury." • "Automatic transmission malfunctioned; cannot shift to lower gear." • "While in park, vehicle jumped into drive, crashing into iron post." • "Automatic transmission defect; automatic drive, high gear will not remain engaged."

FORD TRUCK F250 1989

Complaint Severity: Minor. **Recall Alert:** See Recall Index. **Buyer's Summary:** Look carefully for any kind of leakage, especially under the car. Check the brakes—listen for noise, look for leaks and feel for vibration. They may fail, perform poorly or require frequent mechanical attention. Test the transmission thoroughly.

Hot Spots and Owner/NHTSA Comments:
1. Brakes: hydraulic: anti-skid system, poor performance, failure, locking up. • "While driving down a long, fairly steep hill, the brakes became hot, started smoking and became spongy." • "Total brake failure resulted in poor braking performance; spongy and extended pedal travel." • "While driving down a mountain road and not going too fast, brakes totally failed, pedal went to floor; had to use emergency brake to stop." • "While driving, brakes failed and pedal went all the way to the floor." • "Rear antilock brakes respond poorly, putting pressure on front brakes."
2. Power train: axle assembly: seal: axle shaft, leaks, breaking, failure. • "Rear axle seals leaked on rear brake shoes." • "Both rear wheel seals blew, causing rear brake failure; due to grease-soaked brake lining." • "Rear seals broke, allowing grease to get onto brake shoes, causing brakes not to hold; resulted in accident." • "Rear axle seals go out and spill oil on rear brake shoes; by time shows up, brakes are gone; Ford has redesigned seals 3 times, does not seem to fix problem." • "Rear axle seals leak oil onto the brakes, causing loss of rear brakes."
3. Power train: transmission: automatic, poor performance, difficulty shifting, slipping. • "Transmission seal leaks." • "Engine rpm increases momentarily at approximately 40 mph when automatic transmission downshifting." • "Vehicle on recall due to output shaft snap ring that could break inside transmission; owners state truck moves when placed in park position." • "Transmission races when running 55 mph on freeway, and uses excessive amounts of oil." • "Transmission makes lots of noise."
4. Brakes: hydraulic: disc: caliper, locking up, malfunction. • "Front calipers stick due to brake fluid overheating, causing loss of brakes." • "Disc brake caliper seized on brake rotor, causing front wheel to lock up; control lost." • "Brakes failed while towing trailer; caused by ceramic front brake calipers." • "Defective front brake calipers overheat to the point of ineffectiveness." • "Front brake calipers froze and were not releasing when not braking; dealer overhauled 4 caliper pistons and brake pads."

FORD TRUCK F250 1990

Complaint Severity: Minor. **Recall Alert:** See Recall Index. **Buyer's Summary:** Look carefully for any kind of leakage, especially under the car. Check the brakes—listen for noise, look for leaks and feel for vibration. They may fail, perform poorly or require frequent mechanical attention. Test the transmission thoroughly.

Hot Spots and Owner/NHTSA Comments:
1. Brakes: hydraulic: anti-skid system, poor performance, failure, locking up. • "Loss of brakes while descending a grade, had to use hand brake to stop." • "Hauling a camper on a mountain in 2nd gear, brakes failed; managed to stop by pulling off road." • "Brakes faded going down incline, burning smell filled cab; vehicle free-flying, slowed by downshifting." • "Going down a hill on gravel road with a loaded camper towing a boat at 20 mph, lost brakes completely."
2. Brakes: hydraulic system, failure. • "While driving, vehicle had complete brake failure with pedal going to the floor." • "Brakes repaired 4 times prior to recall; problems continue." • "Experienced brake inadequacy when pedal became spongy and continued to go to the floor, even after recall repair has been done; dealer cannot correct." • "Brakes failed to stop vehicle effectively when applied at any speed, caused extended stopping. Has been recalled and repaired previously." • "Upon applying the brakes, there is extended stopping distance."
3. Power train: transmission: automatic, poor performance, difficulty shifting, slipping. • "Transmission leaks fluid." • "Automatic transmission started overheating with load on, slipped and cut off while hauling 5th-wheeler; due to transmission body valve failure." • "Vehicle caught on fire; caused by foaming transmission fluid overflowing and dripping on catalytic converter." • "Transmission slipping and burning while driving." • "Vehicle leaks and transmission caught on fire."
4. Power train: axle assembly: seal: axle shaft, leaks, failure. • "Rear axle seal leaked on rear brake shoes, causing failure." • "Brakes perform ineffectively when applied due to leakage in rear seals." • "Rear axle seals leak." • "Rear axle seals leak fluid on brake shoes, causing extended stopping and loss of control." • "Rear axle seals leak oil onto brake shoes and cause sudden loss of brakes. Dealer has made several repair attempts."
5. Brakes: hydraulic: shoe and drum system, leaks, malfunction. • "Rear brakes grabbed due to oil hose seals leaking onto pad and lining." • "Rear brake seal went out, resulting in oil leak and brake loss." • "Rear brake system malfunction; rear brakes have stopped working." • "While applying brakes from medium to speed braking, rear brakes shimmy and shudder, creating rear wheel hop while braking to a stop." • "Rear brake system's seals leaking causes brakes to malfunction."

FORD TRUCK F250 1991

Complaint Severity: Negligible. **Recall Alert:** See Recall Index. **Buyer's Summary:** Look carefully for any kind of leakage, especially under the car. Check the brakes—listen for noise, look for leaks and feel for vibration. They may fail, perform poorly or require frequent mechanical attention. Test the transmission thoroughly. See "Sudden Accelerations" in Introduction.

Hot Spots and Owner/NHTSA Comments:
1. Brakes: hydraulic: anti-skid system, poor performance, failure, locking up. • "While parked in driveway, vehicle experienced brake failure when the pedal went to the floor; later the pedal came back up." • "Total brake failure resulted in rear-end collision at speed around 20 mph." • "Brakes faded while driving downhill and on flat surfaces; vehicle jumps when brakes are applied." • "Brake ineffectiveness while driving down grade; pedal dropped to the floor; used emergency brake to stop vehicle." • "While driving down a steep, winding dirt road in mountainous terrain, antilock brakes failed to stop vehicle; truck was stopped by using parking brake."
2. Power train: transmission: automatic, poor performance, difficulty shifting, slipping. • "Transmission slips." • "Torque converter failure." • "Vehicle has experienced transmission problems; vehicle downshifts very rough." • "Transmission jumped into gear, causing accident." • "Transmission failed when shifted into reverse."

3. Brakes: hydraulic system, malfunction, noise, failure. • "Stepped on brake pedal to disconnect cruise control and pedal went all the way to the floor." • "Serpentine belt broke and caused loss of braking ability." • "Going down a mountain and pulling 5th-wheel travel trailer, stopped for 5 minutes, then restarted, but there were no brakes, with pedal going to the floor." • "Brakes are noisy and grabbing." • "Was driving down steep hill, brakes went out completely."

4. Brakes: hydraulic: master cylinder, failure. • "Brake failure while towing 5th-wheel recreational vehicle; master cylinder replaced prior to recall." • "Failure of master cylinder caused brake pedal to travel to floor and complete brake failure, speed 35 mph while slowing down to make a turn." • "Brakes failed while towing 5th-wheel recreational vehicle; prior to recall." • "Vehicle experienced complete brake failure because of defective master cylinder."

5. Fuel: throttle linkages and control, sudden accelerations. • "Unwanted acceleration." • "Consumer was driving, stopped at a stoplight, car accelerated from 600 to 1,000 rpm for 3 to 4 seconds went back down to 600 for 10 seconds and jumped back up." • "Vehicle intermittently surges while driving at high speeds." • "Vehicle surges from 700 to 1,300 rpm during deceleration, causing rear wheels to lock up."

FORD TRUCK F250 1992

Complaint Severity: Typical. **Recall Alert:** See Recall Index. **Buyer's Summary:** Check the brakes—listen for noise, look for leaks and feel for vibration. They may fail, perform poorly or require frequent mechanical attention. Test the transmission thoroughly.

Hot Spots and Owner/NHTSA Comments:

1. Brakes: hydraulic: anti-skid system, poor performance, failure, locking up. • "When braking, antilock brakes did respond with pedal travel; brake pedal went to floor." • "Antilock brake system performed poorly; resulted in vibrations and increased stopping distance." • "Antilock brake system locked up when applied; vehicle skidded through intersection; speed 40 mph; no prior warning." • "Antilock brake system locked up while driving, causing truck to spin in traffic while raining. When tested, no problem found." • "Antilock brake system failure; when applying brake, had complete loss of brake; pedal goes to the floor."

2. Power train: transmission: automatic, poor performance, difficulty shifting, slipping. • "Vehicle was parked unattended for 5 minutes, motor running, gear in parked position, emergency brakes not applied; rolled backwards into boat and storage shed." • "Transmission jerks when shifting; repaired/replaced 4 times, problem continues." • "Automatic transmission; system being replaced for the third time after becoming inoperative in middle of road." • "Automatic transmission; vehicle vibrates in 1st gear when towing campers or any other piece of equipment and when carrying heavy loads; cause of vibration unknown." • "Transmission jumps out of gear; can be riding along and find yourself in neutral."

3. Brakes: hydraulic system, excessive wear, failure. • "Brakes and power steering failed while driving at 55 mph; both components tied to 1 belt-pulley system." • "Brake problems." • "Brake failure." • "Cruise control would not disengage, momentarily slowed down, then began to speed up. Brakes became inoperative due to malfunction of pump switch valve." • "Front brake rotors replaced 4 times, pads 2 times, and rear brake shoes replaced 2 times; due to warping."

4. Engine cooling system: belts, breaking, failure. • "Vehicle has had 3 failures of the belt breaking, causing loss of power assist and other functions." • "The belts break in the pulley, causing loss of power steering and brakes." • "The fan belt fell off about 10 to 12 times; keep taking it back to be fixed." • "Serpentine belt continually fails, interrupting other engine functions." • "Engine belt that operates steering and braking functions broke 15 times; replaced."

5. Emergency parking brake: mechanical, failure. • "Parking brake fails to release properly; prior to recall, recall repairs refused." • "Emergency parking brake failure." • "Parking brake on vehicle doesn't catch when applied, it goes all the way down to the floor." • "Parking brake pedal will slip and go to the floor. Requires recycling until assembly catches."

FORD TRUCK F250 1993

Complaint Severity: Typical. **Recall Alert:** See Recall Index. **Buyer's Summary:** Check the brakes—listen for noise, look for leaks and feel for vibration. They may fail, perform poorly or require frequent mechanical attention.

Hot Spots and Owner/NHTSA Comments:

1. Engine cooling system: belts, breaking, failure. • "Experiences intermittent power steering loss when serpentine fan belt slips upon acceleration or deceleration." • "Serpentine belt popped off, causing loss of steering control and sending vehicle into embankment. Repaired 5 times." • "Belt drive keeps coming off, causing power brake and steering failure. Repaired 3 times to no avail." • "Engine drive belt to cooling system continues to break; design problem."

2. Brakes: hydraulic: anti-skid system, poor performance, failure, locking up. • "Rear antilock brake system will lock up on wet pavement intermittently. On 2 occasions, owner has driven through intersections, not able to stop." • "Antilock brakes cause vehicle to vibrate when applied at any speed." • "Antilock brakes disengage in hard stopping at any speed." • "Antilock brake system causes vehicle to vibrate at any speed when brakes are applied. Has been repaired 5 times." • "Antilock brake system brake drums are out of round; when applying brakes, vehicle shakes."

3. Brakes: hydraulic system, vibration, malfunction. • "Upon applying the brakes, they bumped real badly." • "Upon applying the brakes, vehicle had heavy vibrations." • "Dealer repaired brakes, but did not fix problem. Recall related." • "When brakes are applied, the truck shimmies."

4. Emergency parking brake: mechanical, malfunction, failure. • "Parking brake does not hold the vehicle. Vehicle did roll away and crash into something. Brake had been replaced once before from earlier complaints." • "Emergency brake may disengage allowing truck to roll. Assembly was replaced, but did not prevent truck from rolling downhill while in neutral and hitting a car." • "Parking brake on the vehicle sometimes will hold and sometimes it will not. Parking brake didn't hold vehicle and caused an accident." • "Parking emergency brake released while in park; vehicle rolled backwards and smashed into a tree."

FORD TRUCK F350 1987

Complaint Severity: Minor. **Recall Alert:** See Recall Index. **Buyer's Summary:** The carburetion system could contribute to stalling and hesitation. Test the suspension by feeling for vibration or pulling while driving. Check the brakes—listen for noise, look for leaks and feel for vibration. They may fail, perform poorly or require frequent mechanical attention. Test the clutch.

Hot Spots and Owner/NHTSA Comments:

1. Suspension: independent front, alignment, tire wear. • "Front end of truck has shimmy; must stop completely to stop shimmy; cannot drive over 35 mph, pulls steering wheel out of hand; purchased 4 sets of tires." • "Entire front end; front suspension defective, shimmies; aligned front end, repaired/replaced left

inner and outer tie rods." • "Suspension system may not adequately control steering-type wobble, allowing the front end to shimmy." • "Aligned front end due to shimmy and tire cupping wear problem in the front end; recall initiated, 7 repair attempts to no avail." • "Severe front-end shimmy or side-to-side movement of truck that could result in chassis damage, loss of steering; repaired under recall, still having problem."
2. Power train: clutch assembly, stiffness, failure. • "Clutch replaced 3 times due to slippage." • "Casing enclosing clutch assembly fell apart." • "Clutch hard to disengage, hard shifting gears, grinding, clutch would not release; repaired/replaced master cylinder and slave cylinder." • "Vehicle's clutch failed; flimsy fire wall caused clutch to burn out; installed clutch kit, consisting of plate with 4 bolts attached to firewall for reinforcement." • "Problems experienced with clutch system."
3. Suspension: vibration, poor performance. • "Truck recalled for steering suspension; front-end suspension replaced, still unstable; tires are popping out in holes, toe-in and toe-off causing wear." • "Violent vibration at 40-45 mph, to the extent of possible loss of control if allowed to continue; tires are badly worn." • "Upon driving 50 mph, truck would shimmy and bounce until driver no longer in control." • "While driving, vehicle shakes, there is a recall that relates to 2-wheel drive, but not 4-wheel drive. Sometimes shakes so bad that truck has to be stopped to regain control."
4. Brakes: hydraulic system, locking up, failure. • "Brakes locked up; driver lost control, skidded into guardrail." • "Brake pedal fades all the way to floor." • "Brakes would release after having been applied without letting foot off pedal, and wouldn't re-engage or reapply." • "Malfunction in braking system; on wet pavement, when brakes applied, front wheels lock up and rear wheels do nothing."
5. Fuel: fuel carburetion, stalling, hesitation. • "Carburetor failure; repairs and replacement done." • "Carburetor surge problem." • "Faulty carburetor system caused engine fire." • "Vehicle stalls, then would only go 10-15 mph." • "Automatic transmission linkage became disconnected and gets stuck in gears."

FORD TRUCK F350 1988

Complaint Severity: Typical. **Recall Alert:** See Recall Index. **Buyer's Summary:** Test the suspension by feeling for vibration or pulling while driving. Check the brakes—listen for noise, look for leaks and feel for vibration. They may fail, perform poorly or require frequent mechanical attention. Test the transmission thoroughly.

Hot Spots and Owner/NHTSA Comments:
1. Brakes: hydraulic: anti-skid system, poor performance, failure, locking up. • "While driving down grade, made an attempt to slow vehicle and pedal went to the floor." • "Partial brake failure; brake pedal went to the floor, couldn't stop vehicle in a reasonable distance; resulted in an accident." • "While driving, experienced total brake fade, pedal went to the floor, noticed brake fluid was boiling; resulted in an accident." • "Brakes failed to stop vehicle when applied during wet weather conditions." • "When driving downhill at 5 mph, the brakes failed to stop immediately; caused extended stopping distance."
2. Suspension: independent front, tire wear, vibration. • "Defect in front suspension, causing shimmying through steering wheel and pulling dramatically to right." • "Poor suspension system, front-end shimmy, damaged and worn tires due to front-end problem; repaired/replaced front suspension." • "Received recall notice for front-end shimmy; took long time to receive parts." • "Vibration in front end, while driving, magnified to point where dangerous driving over road deviations at various speeds; excessive inner tire wear." • "Poor suspension system; violent vibration in front end causing excessive wear on tires; repaired/replaced shock absorbers."
3. Brakes: hydraulic system, locking up, failure. • "Entire braking system defective; several attempts to repair but remain spongy; totally failed on 3 separate occasions." • "While driving vehicle down incline, brakes overheated, causing pedal to fade and lock up." • "Brakes caught on fire after recall service as a result of thickness of replacement shield. With thickness of brake pad and metal shield, brakes didn't release." • "Defective brake system; 7 repeated and ongoing repair attempts; rear wheels lock, causes skidding, fishtailing and sliding while locked up on wet pavement."
4. Power train: transmission: automatic, poor performance, difficulty shifting, slipping. • "Clutch problem; has a cracked firewall." • "Premature transmission failure." • "Transmission does not shift properly during cold weather; also, loose part in bottom of automatic transmission oil pan." • "Transmission failed." • "Transmission slips when towing; jumps out of gear; shifting is stiff."
5. Suspension: tire wear, poor performance. • "Steering and suspension systems do not adequately control steering wobble, causing front end to shimmy; tire wear is excessive." • "Shimmy problem; recall campaign initiated, but dealer performed partial repair."
6. Brakes: hydraulic: shoe: disc brake system, fade, failure. • "Front disc brakes fading." • "While driving, vehicle experienced intermittent fade of brake system; resulting in total brake failure on antilock brake system." • "Front brakes failed, prior to recall."

FORD TRUCK F350 1989

Complaint Severity: Typical. **Recall Alert:** See Recall Index. **Buyer's Summary:** Look carefully for any kind of leakage, especially under the car. Test the suspension by feeling for vibration or pulling while driving. Check the brakes—listen for noise, look for leaks and feel for vibration. They may fail, perform poorly or require frequent mechanical attention. Test the transmission thoroughly.

Hot Spots and Owner/NHTSA Comments:
1. Brakes: hydraulic: anti-skid system, poor performance, failure, locking up. • "Antilock brake system: When brakes were applied, pedal faded; continued to move, and stopped vehicle by using emergency brake." • "Brakes failed to stop vehicle while driving downhill at 10 mph." • "Antilock brake system completely failed; pedal hit the floor; emergency brake used to stop." • "Braking ability is inadequate in emergency stopping situations; brakes have completely failed on numerous occasions, whole fleet has problem." • "While towing 5th-wheel trailer, brake pedal went to the floor; also rear seals went out; the dealer found oil on the brake drums."
2. Power train: axle assembly: seal: axle shaft, leaks, failure. • "Rear seals leaked, causing brake failure." • "Rear axle seal leaked, prior to recall." • "Right rear axle seal fell off." • "Rear axle seals failed; grease leaked onto brake shoes; loss of brake and lubrication to bearings." • "Rear axle seal leaked; greased brakes, caused brakes to lock up and slide, almost causing accidents."
3. Suspension: independent front, alignment, tire wear, pulling. • "Van weaves, front end needs alignment; misaligned at factory." • "Faulty front-end suspension causes premature front tire wear." • "Front end pulls hard to right and shimmies, has been replaced, but problem still occurs." • "Truck pulls to right; Ford claims alignment on truck is set to specs; however, tires are worn and truck stills pulls to right." • "Problem with front end pulling from side to side, bounces like diving board, difficult to drive; repaired."

4. Brakes: hydraulic: shoe and drum system, leaks, locking up, failure. • "Rear brakes failed, causing accident; repaired, problem continues." • "Vehicle rear grease seals leaked, causing the loss of brake effectiveness. Impact 6:00 position. Speed 15 mph. Wet road surface." • "Rear dual wheel antilock brake system will lock prematurely in intervals. Seals had no links to stop oil from leaking onto system." • "Brake failure; drums got very hot and broke seals, vehicle had no rear brakes."
5. Power train: transmission: automatic, poor performance, difficulty shifting, slipping. • "Rpm loss between shifts causes power loss, clutch slippage during gear change; broken front snap ring allows transmission to disengage." • "Had continuous problem with transmission shifting from 3rd to 4th overdrive." • "Vehicle is a diesel truck and it caught on fire. Transmission fluid leaked out of vent tube and dipstick." • "Can't tell what gear transmission is in; low clutch band went out."

FORD TRUCK F350 1990

Complaint Severity: Negligible. **Recall Alert:** See Recall Index. **Buyer's Summary:** Check the brakes—listen for noise, look for leaks and feel for vibration. They may fail, perform poorly or require frequent mechanical attention. Test the transmission thoroughly.

Hot Spots and Owner/NHTSA Comments:
1. Brakes: hydraulic: anti-skid system, poor performance, failure, locking up. • "When driving in heavy traffic and continued use of antilock brake system, had complete loss of brake effectiveness." • "While going down a hill or steep grade, antilock brakes failed twice; was able to stop vehicle using emergency brakes." • "Antilock brakes fail to stop vehicle when applied at 50 mph while driving down incline. Driver coasted/drove vehicle until it stopped." • "Extreme brake fading and overheating while braking on steep incline." • "Brake pedal traveled to floor without warning; resulted in loss of brake effectiveness."
2. Brakes: hydraulic system, poor performance, failure. • "Brakes performed poorly; when applied brake pedal pressure, there was no increase in brake effectiveness; resulted in an accident." • "Since new parts were installed on the brakes, braking distance has increased." • "Brakes perform poorly and pedal goes to the floor." • "Brakes failed 5 times; once at stopping, and 4 times when vehicle started in the mornings."
3. Power train: transmission: automatic, poor performance, difficulty shifting, slipping. • "Automatic transmission gears shift out of position constantly." • "Automatic transmission shifts from overdrive to drive to overdrive; dealer serviced vehicle 3 times and replaced an electrical switch, but problem remains." • "Automatic transmission began to fail about 6,000 miles, recently at 9,500 miles transmission fluid leaking in amounts sufficient to spray onto adjacent exhaust pipe." • "Transmission malfunctioned; grinds in 4th gear, not in 5th gear, and pops out of 1st gear."
4. Brakes: hydraulic: power assist: vacuum system, noise, failure. • "Ambulances: When brake pedal is pumped 3-4 times, loss of assist from power brake booster." • "Twice brakes failed and pedal went to the floor." • "While driving at approximately 35 mph, attempted to slow down, brake pedal first went down two-thirds, continued to pump and brakes malfunctioned; ran into ditch." • "Since time of purchase, heard loud shattering noise from brakes each time applied; rotors warped." • "Brakes chatter."

FORD TRUCK F350 1991

Complaint Severity: Minor. **Recall Alert:** See Recall Index. **Buyer's Summary:** Check the brakes—listen for noise, look for leaks and feel for vibration. They may fail, perform poorly or require frequent mechanical attention. Test the transmission thoroughly.

Hot Spots and Owner/NHTSA Comments:
1. Brakes: hydraulic: anti-skid system, poor performance, failure, locking up. • "Antilock brake system failed to stop vehicle on incline; vehicle has been repaired numerous times." • "Antilock brakes failed to stop vehicle on incline; vehicle has been repaired 5 times, but problem persists." • "Front brakes fail to stop vehicle effectively when applied; has been repaired 4 times." • "Brake pedal went completely to floor with vehicle pulling slightly to right when applied at 40 mph; inoperative. Braking ability resumed 30 minutes later." • "When attempting to make a quick or emergency stop, brakes did not function properly; vehicle slid into the trunk of another vehicle."
2. Power train: transmission: automatic, poor performance, difficulty shifting, slipping. • "Transfer case failed." • "Transmission malfunctioned 4 times. (Ford refused to honor warranty. Won decision on 'lemon law'; Ford appealed decision; jury trial 930525. This is second truck.)" • "Owner complains of transmission control processor going out. Shifts to neutral." • "Broken gear." • "Transmission malfunctioned."

FORD TRUCK F350 1992

Complaint Severity: Best 3% in Guide. **Recall Alert:** See Recall Index. **Buyer's Summary:** Check the brakes—listen for noise, look for leaks and feel for vibration. They may fail, perform poorly or require frequent mechanical attention.

Hot Spots and Owner/NHTSA Comments:
1. Engine cooling system: belts, breaking, failure. • "The belt keeps coming off; dealer replaced a dozen times, but will not replace this one." • "Belt from 2 main pulleys which supply power to alternator and brake booster snapped while driving down a hill and exiting the highway." • "Fan belt comes off, causing loss of power steering and brakes; snapped bolt that holds idler pulley." • "Single serpentine belt causes power steering to become inoperative."
2. Brakes: hydraulic: anti-skid system, poor performance, failure, locking up. • "Antilock brake system failed ; when coming to stop, rear wheel went over a bump and automatically activated the antilock brake system, which caused the brakes to release." • "Antilock brake system failed; ruined pads, rotors and calipers." • "Upon applying the brakes, rear brakes locked up; no response from the antilock brake system." • "Antilock brake system will not hold vehicle when applied in wet or damp weather, causing extended stopping." • "Antilock brake system brake pedal goes to the floor with little or no braking effect, mostly while pulling trailer. No warning."

FORD TRUCK F350 1993

Complaint Severity: Typical. **Recall Alert:** See Recall Index. **Buyer's Summary:** Check the brakes—listen for noise, look for leaks and feel for vibration. They may fail, perform poorly or require frequent mechanical attention.

Hot Spots and Owner/NHTSA Comments:
1. Brakes: hydraulic: anti-skid system, poor performance, failure, locking up. • "Antilock brake system failed, causing pulsation; also, antilock brake system light comes on." • "Brake system failure; equipped with antilock brake system." • "Truck has antilock brake system in rear. Truck vibrates when brakes are applied." • "Antilock brake system locks up on wet, damp and snowy road conditions. Often overheats, causing vibrations, warping and ineffective braking. Repaired 6 times." • "Antilock brake

system on rear only. When brakes are applied, the vehicle veers to the left with moderate load. When vehicle is empty, intermittent problem."

2. Engine: cooling system: belts, breaking, failure. • "Eight serpentine belts failed and disabled steering and brakes when diesel lost hydraulic pump. Ford is buying vehicle back. Oil pours over engine when belt fails." • "There is 1 belt that runs all the belt-driven parts, and when this breaks you lose all control of the vehicle." • "Serpentine belt comes off and/or fails, causing loss of steering and brakes." • "Serpentine belt came off 5 times while driving."

FORD TRUCK RANGER 1987

Complaint Severity: Typical. **Recall Alert:** See Recall Index. **Buyer's Summary:** The fuel injection system has been blamed for hesitation and stalling. Be sure the vehicle doesn't die in traffic or at stops. Check the brakes—listen for noise, look for leaks and feel for vibration. They may fail, perform poorly or require frequent mechanical attention. Test the transmission thoroughly. Test transmission for slipping, locking up and performance. See "Sudden Accelerations" in Introduction.

Hot Spots and Owner/NHTSA Comments:

1. Power train: transmission: 5-speed: lever and linkage: floor shift, difficulty shifting, locking up. • "When shifting 5-speed manual transmission to 1st gear from stop, floor-shift lever became limp, won't respond; repaired/replaced new plastic linkage mount and rubber boot." • "Transmission shifter locked up in 3rd and 4th gear; repaired." • "Gearshift lever loose; will not go in gear." • "While merging onto expressway, upon shifting into 4th gear, shifter came out of housing into hand; unable to shift." • "Proceeding to move from stopped position, gearshift lever on 5-speed manual transmission broke while engaged in 1st gear."

2. Fuel: fuel injection system, stalling, hesitation. • "Engine bucks upon acceleration, stalls, high idle; obnoxious odor inside vehicle." • "Engine stalls intermittently; repaired, problem continues." • "Intermittent stalling; replaced oxygen sensor, problem continues." • "Vehicle hesitates when cold, dies upon acceleration, bucks and jumps when shifting gears." • "Car stalls, rpm low when cold; replaced sensors and brain, problem continues.

3. Power train: transmission: automatic, poor performance, difficulty shifting, slipping. • "Signs of leakage are noticeable in vehicle's automatic transmission system; possible defect internally." • "Automatic transmission defective; key can be removed while not in park; does not lock; vehicle rolled back while unoccupied; minor accident resulted." • "Transmission locks up while driving, believed to be caused by broken crankshaft." • "Will not go in reverse; repaired/replaced transmission, overhauled converter and replaced worn-out seals." • "Transmission changes gear when not supposed to; jerks real bad and vibrates just before stopping."

4. Brakes: hydraulic system, locking up, noise. • "Brakes do not release; lock up under normal driving conditions." • "Defective braking system; brakes lock up in damp weather, causing back end to veer to side; brakes also very noisy." • "Engine speed increases without warning; after brakes are applied vehicle slows down." • "Brakes grab or sometimes lock up on wet or snowy surfaces; also will squeak." • "Brakes became temperamental shortly after warranty expired; lock up at various speeds and under all conceivable weather conditions, regardless of brake pedal pressure."

5. Fuel: throttle linkages and control, sudden accelerations. • "Vehicle suddenly accelerated, started to speed up on its own; applied brakes; accident occurred." • "Accelerator pedal became stuck and vehicle could be stopped only by coasting to side of road; problem of sudden acceleration." • "When turned over key, truck made deafening roar, much as a race car, shot across parking lot, crashing into support pillar at bank." • "While traveling at approximately 50 mph, vehicle suddenly accelerated to 65 mph and continued to surge until taking foot off brake." • "While driving, throttle body plate seized in wide-open position from 50 mph to 100 mph."

6. Engine: malfunction, fire, leaks. • "Engine blowing oil everywhere; 2 cylinders flooded with oil; replaced 2 pistons and gasket." • "After being parked for 5 minutes, noticed smoke coming from engine compartment." • "After turning off ignition, vehicle exploded under hood; fire completely engulfed under hood." • "Vehicle stuck in ditch, revved engine in attempt to move; caught fire and burned completely." • "Engine leaks oil or burns oil excessively."

FORD TRUCK RANGER 1988

Complaint Severity: Typical. **Recall Alert:** See Recall Index. **Buyer's Summary:** Look carefully for any kind of leakage, especially under the car. The fuel injection system has been blamed for hesitation and stalling. Be sure the vehicle doesn't die in traffic or at stops. Check the brakes—listen for noise, look for leaks and feel for vibration. They may fail, perform poorly or require frequent mechanical attention. See "Sudden Accelerations" in Introduction.

Hot Spots and Owner/NHTSA Comments:

1. Brakes: hydraulic system, locking up, pulling, noise. • "Front wheel locks up when brakes are applied, usually on wet or slippery pavement." • "While passing a truck pulling a trailer, saw another vehicle approaching, applied brakes to get over again when brakes locked up, pulling car into trailer." • "Brakes are unpredictable; lock up, vehicle pulls and slides sideways in road at different speeds when brakes are applied." • "Brakes grab and/or squeal, causing skidding effect." • "Brakes lock up on first few applications whenever any kind of moisture present."

2. Brakes: hydraulic: shoe and drum system, locking up, noise. • "Driving 40-45 mph, rear brakes locked up when barely applied, resulting in accident and injuries." • "Rear brakes start to lock up when pulling boat or when applied at higher speeds." • "Heavy metal noise from rear brakes when backing also grab with slight pressure." • "Rear brakes have a tendency to lock up at all speeds under light or heavy brake pressure, causing loss of control." • "Rear brakes have tendency to lock up when weather is rainy."

3. Engine: leaks, poor performance. • "Vehicle underpowered for size and weight; engine additionally has manufacturing defect." • "Excessive oil consumption due to leak in engine; repaired leak but problem persists; all repair attempts to no avail." • "Excessive oil consumption." • "Continuous engine oil leak." • "Engine leaks oil from rear main seal, pan gasket and valve cover."

4. Fuel: throttle linkages and control, sudden accelerations. • "Foot removed from throttle, engine continues at speed for 4 to 7 seconds, then starts to slow down; could cause disastrous skid on slippery surfaces." • "Throttle sticks open and causes vehicle to surge." • "Twice accelerator on vehicle stuck with throttle wide open, unable to slow vehicle sufficiently by braking; turned off ignition to slow down." • "Throttle stuck on numerous occasions." • "Upon putting truck in drive gear, suddenly accelerated out of control, hitting another vehicle in rear."

5. Fuel: fuel systems, stalling, hesitation, fire. • "Vehicle smoking from hood; opened hood, observed gas line into fuel injection system on fire; metal fuel line burned completely." • "While vehicle was parked after drive, within 12 minutes caught on fire; resulted in total loss." • "Fuel injection fuel system defective; fire developed; several attempts to repair." • "Stalling and/or hesitation."

6. Fuel: fuel injection system, stalling, hesitation. • "Vehicle stalls when accelerator pressed and while driving at low speed; will not idle correctly, tries to stall; repaired 5 times to no avail." • "Vehicle does not idle correctly, stalls at stops; at times, when accelerator pressed, refused to accept gas; shakes terribly, stalls while driving." • "Engine stalls when cold or hot, stops on highway accelerating or slowing down." • "Problem with engine idling rough; replaced sensor boards 3 times, problem still not corrected." • "During normal driving, noticed smoke coming from engine area; erupted into fire; determined after inspection that a leak present at or near fuel rail ignited."

FORD TRUCK RANGER 1989

Complaint Severity: Negligible. **Recall Alert:** See Recall Index. **Buyer's Summary:** The fuel injection system has been blamed for hesitation and stalling. Be sure the vehicle doesn't die in traffic or at stops. Check the brakes—listen for noise, look for leaks and feel for vibration. They may fail, perform poorly or require frequent mechanical attention. Test the transmission thoroughly.

Hot Spots and Owner/NHTSA Comments:

1. Brakes: hydraulic: anti-skid system, poor performance, failure, locking up. • "Antilock braking system defective; accident resulted twice due to defect; rear brakes did not release, causing severe heat wear to braking system." • "Antilock brake wheel sensor malfunctioned." • "Antilock brakes failed, caused brake pedal to pulsate, which in turn reduced brake effectiveness." • "Brakes failed due to lack of braking power; caused extended stopping in sudden stops or overheating of brakes with no brake power going downhill." • "Failure developed in antilock brake system."

2. Brakes: hydraulic system, locking up, failure. • "Complete brake failure; needs rotors and all other parts of brake system." • "Brake system defective; antilock brake light and brake light come on; pads wore too much and scored drums; repaired." • "Brakes not working properly while driving on damp or wet roads." • "Brakes slow to respond; especially under wet conditions, it is very hard to stop vehicle." • "After starting vehicle, the first 5 to 6 times and the brakes are applied, the rear wheels will lock up."

3. Fuel: fuel tank assembly: gauge: fuel, malfunction, failure. • "Fuel gauge reading inaccurate due to bad sending unit." • "Gas gauge stopped working; replaced fuel sender in gas tank." • "Fuel gauge failed; repaired." • "Fuel gauge malfunctioned." • "Gas gauge malfunctioned and vehicle ran out of gas on freeway."

4. Power train: transmission: automatic, poor performance, difficulty shifting, slipping. • "Shifting cable wouldn't shift." • "Transmission was shifting to overdrive and back to drive again; dealer repaired/replaced an electronic part, problem solved." • "Automatic transmission inoperative, vehicle would not move." • "Vehicle hesitates while shifting automatic transmission into reverse." • "Transmission shifts rough; driveshaft bolts come loose."

5. Engine: gaskets: valve cover, leaks. • "Valve cover gasket leaks; potential fire hazard." • "Defective head gasket and seal valve cover." • "Blown head gasket." • "Faulty valve cover gasket in engine." • "Head gasket leaks." • "Engine valve covers continuously leak oil; resealed with new gasket and valve covers replaced."

6. Fuel: fuel injection system, stalling, hesitation. • "Intermittent stalling, fluctuation of oil pressure." • "Locked and walked away from vehicle, came back approximately 25 minutes later and vehicle was totally engulfed in flames; fire department was on scene." • "When slowing down to approximately 15 mph or making turn at corners, engine would stall; lost control of power brakes and steering." • "Vehicle bucks and hesitates when climbing uphill." • "Engine stalling problems; vehicle cuts off when slowing or turning, also when coming to a stop."

FORD TRUCK RANGER 1990

Complaint Severity: Typical. **Recall Alert:** See Recall Index. **Buyer's Summary:** Test the suspension by feeling for vibration or pulling while driving. Check the brakes—listen for noise, look for leaks and feel for vibration. They may fail, perform poorly or require frequent mechanical attention. Test the transmission thoroughly. See "Sudden Accelerations" in Introduction.

Hot Spots and Owner/NHTSA Comments:

1. Power train: transmission: automatic, poor performance, difficulty shifting, slipping. • "Transmission modulator replaced." • "Transmission would not shift out of 1st gear." • "Vehicle rolled while in parked position, causing injury." • "Difficulty getting transmission recall repair." • "Transmission doesn't engage into park completely."

2. Brakes: hydraulic: anti-skid system, poor performance, failure, locking up. • "Antilock brake light comes on and off." • "After a 30-minute drive, unloaded truck and it would not stop when brake pedal went to the floor." • "Rear brakes drag when wet." • "Loss of brake effectiveness while traveling downhill." • "When brakes were applied, the rear antilock brakes locked up, causing vehicle to skid sideways."

3. Engine, vibration, noise. • "Engine knocked several times." • "Engine knocking; repair attempts 6 times, repaired/replaced." • "At certain rpm there is rattling and/or vibration from the engine." • "Vehicle has severe engine knock and other noises, also excessive oil consumption." • "Excessive engine piston-to-cylinder clearance."

4. Fuel: throttle linkages and control, sudden accelerations. • "Accelerator pedal sticks, causing engine to race; after shifting, remove foot from pedal; pedal does not return to idle; lurched forward at high rpm." • "Uncontrolled acceleration caused an accident; vehicle rolled over." • "Vehicle suddenly accelerated on its own; caused an accident." • "Engine races randomly at excessive rpm, must turn key off to stop. Dealer tried 20 times to fix." • "While backing out, brakes were applied and truck accelerated; gas pedal was not being used."

5. Suspension: independent front, vibration, tire wear, alignment. • "While driving on freeway, left front camber tire blew out; bad cambers, realigned." • "When driving approximately 30 mph, vehicle vibrates." • "Problem with front-end alignment." • "Tires worn out; dealer rotated them." • "Tires misaligned, causing vibration."

6. Visual systems: mirrors: rearview: exterior, vibration, poor performance. • "Driver and passenger-side exterior rearview mirrors can be moved by the force of the wind." • "Outside rearview mirrors fold down at high speed." • "Left and right rearview mirrors vibrate real bad; images in mirrors very distorted due to constant blur of lights behind; difficult to estimate distance of auto behind." • "Driver's-side rearview mirror fell out; repaired/replaced."

FORD TRUCK RANGER 1991

Complaint Severity: Typical. **Recall Alert:** See Recall Index. **Buyer's Summary:** Verify that the cruise control system works properly, and doesn't cause the engine to surge. The fuel injection system has been blamed for hesitation and stalling. Be sure the vehicle doesn't die in traffic or at stops. Check the brakes—listen for noise, look for leaks and feel for vibration. They may fail, perform poorly or require frequent mechanical attention. Test the transmission thoroughly. See "Sudden Accelerations" in Introduction.

Hot Spots and Owner/NHTSA Comments:

1. Fuel: throttle linkages and control, sudden accelerations. • "Unknown cause of vehicle's sudden acceleration; sometimes occurs with cruise control on, other times when it is not." • "Throttle sticking in open position caused vehicle to lose control, which resulted in serious injuries to driver and passenger." • "While driving at 30 mph, vehicle suddenly accelerated, crashing into a pile of logs." • "On highway, throttle stuck in open position, which caused driver to hit a brick building." • "Vehicle surges forward at a high rate of speed."

2. Power train: transmission: automatic, poor performance, difficulty shifting, slipping. • "Transmission failed, prior to recall." • "Transmission will not lock in park; vehicle, which was parked in driveway, rolled into house and broke stairs and upper deck." • "Transmission slips from park or neutral into reverse or drive." • "Transmission slips."

3. Brakes: hydraulic system, locking up, pulling, noise. • "When brakes are applied at high speeds, the vehicle moves into another lane." • "Left front brakes stuck, causing vehicle to slide out of control." • "Left rear tire locks upon hard braking." • "Brake system; before vehicle's completely warmed up, brakes pull very hard to left while driving." • "Brakes grab and squeal."

4. Equipment: speed control, malfunction, failure. • "Cruise control failure; difficulty disengaging the cruise control." • "Cruise control did not disengage when brakes were pressed due to blown fuse." • "When cruise control is activated and driver attempts to engage clutch to downshift position, it does not turn off cruise control as intended." • "Cruise control doesn't cancel when brake pedal is depressed due to a faulty brake switch." • "Problems with cruise control kicking off often, and passenger seat not latching again."

5. Electrical system: ignition, stalling, failure. • "Processor assembly problem." • "While driving, vehicle will stall and then regain speed." • "Ignition failure." • "Truck has been repaired 8 to 10 times to correct for stalling. Problem reoccurs intermittently." • "Series of engine stalls when weather is 25 degrees or colder."

6. Fuel: fuel injection system, stalling, hesitation. • "Vehicle stalls; rough idle." • "Engine stalls." • "Fuel injection intake valve location caused vehicle to stall in shallow water." • "Vehicle does not get gas." • "Vacuum feedback system for fuel injection failure."

FORD TRUCK RANGER 1992

Complaint Severity: Typical. **Recall Alert:** See Recall Index. **Buyer's Summary:** Check the brakes—listen for noise, look for leaks and feel for vibration. They may fail, perform poorly or require frequent mechanical attention. Test the transmission thoroughly. See "Sudden Accelerations" in Introduction.

Hot Spots and Owner/NHTSA Comments:

1. Brakes: hydraulic: anti-skid system, poor performance, failure, locking up. • "Brakes pull to the right when applied causing loss of control." • "Antilock brakes smell, smoke and overheat periodically when applied, at any speed on long- or short-distance drive." • "Antilock brake system on rear of vehicle locked up and has caused the owner to have 2 accidents. Brakes have not functioned properly since day one." • "Antilock brake system: Loss of brake effectiveness when applying brakes." • "Replaced brake drums. • "Antilock brakes locked up, causing vehicle to skid." • "Antilock brake system: When surface wet or vehicle sits for 6 hours, experience brake lockup."

2. Power train: transmission: standard: manual, difficulty shifting, locking up. • "Transmission stuck in 4th gear." • "Transmission stuck in 4th gear." • "Fourth gear lockup." • "Transmission problems." • "Transmission stuck in 4th gear."

3. Brakes: hydraulic system, pulling, noise, locking up. " • "Vehicle pulls to the left when brakes are applied." • "Upon braking, vehicle pulls to left without turning steering wheel." • "Noisy brakes." • "When traveling at 35 mph, steering wheel column and brakes locked up." • "Soft brakes."

4. Power train: transmission: automatic, poor performance, difficulty shifting, slipping. • "Transmission oil leak." • "Transmission shift cable disconnected from holding bracket." • "Transmission locked up." • "Adjusted shift linkages." • "Vehicle suddenly accelerated upon shifting gears from park to neutral, causing loss of vehicle control. Transmission locked in 1st gear."

5. Fuel: throttle linkages and control, sudden accelerations. • "Vehicle was in gear, then it rolled backwards and caused injuries." • "Rough idling and engine racing at 2,300 rpm." • "Vehicle was being driven down dirt road in reverse when driver touched brake pedal, vehicle accelerated out of control." • "Sudden acceleration, causing accident." • "Throttle sticks at a high rpm intermittently."

6. Brakes: hydraulic: lines: hose: nonmetallic, leaks. • "Brake hose leaks; replaced." • "Front brake hoses leaked."

FORD TRUCK RANGER 1993

Complaint Severity: Typical. **Recall Alert:** See Recall Index. **Buyer's Summary:** Look carefully for any kind of leakage, especially under the car. Test the suspension by feeling for vibration or pulling while driving. Check the brakes—listen for noise, look for leaks and feel for vibration. They may fail, perform poorly or require frequent mechanical attention. See "Sudden Accelerations" in Introduction.

Hot Spots and Owner/NHTSA Comments:

1. Emergency parking brake: mechanical, poor performance, failure. • "Emergency brake does not work. You can push truck with it on. Dealer says that's the way brake is supposed to be." • "Applied the emergency brake and vehicle rolled backwards; vehicle lost control, hitting wire to service pole." • "Emergency parking brake failed, prior to and after recall repairs." • "Parking brake failed to hold vehicle on incline." • "Had to replace emergency brake, but it still does not work."

2. Brakes: hydraulic: anti-skid system, poor performance, failure, locking up. • "After 15-minute drive, 35-mph stop will cause a severe swerve in either direction. Antilock brake system." • "Vehicle antilock brake system is erratic, causing vehicle to veer to the right when braking." • "Braking system failure; vehicle surges forward when braking; equipped with antilock brake system." • "Possibly equipped with antilock brake system; when brakes applied, noticed vibration and pulsation in brake pedal." • "Antilock brakes lock up, causing loss of control and skidding."

3. Suspension: independent front, vibration, pulling, failure. • "Front end vibrates between 55 and 75 mph." • "Front suspension failed." • "Vehicle pulls to right; pulls to left when straightened, causing accident." • "Truck loses control on rough surfaces or bumps." • "Replaced front-end components."

4. Engine: other parts, leaks, failure. • "Oil leak." • "Rear main engine seal failure." • "Oil pump failure." • "Oil leak." • "Starter shorted out while trying to change oil filter due to close proximity."

5. Fuel: throttle linkages and control, sudden accelerations. • "While driving at 50 mph on highway, vehicle suddenly accelerated to 75 mph, causing loss of vehicle control." • "Truck used on mountain highways. Truck has poor acceleration efficiency. Dealer is aware, but can't determine and/or correct problem. 'Check engine' light comes on." • "While driving, vehicle went into open-throttle position, lost control and flipped over, impact 1:00 position, speed 62 mph." • "Vehicle's accelerator sticks when air conditioning is on." • "Vehicle raced forward after putting gear in drive, causing loss of control and an accident."

6. Power train: transmission: unknown type, leaks, difficulty shifting. " • "Manual transmission sticks when shifting gears." • "Transmission fluid leak." • "Standard transmission failure." • "Transmission does not shift properly from 1st to 2nd gear." • "Lack of power, and gearing is too high."

FORD TRUCK RANGER 1994

Complaint Severity: Typical. **Recall Alert:** See Recall Index. **Buyer's Summary:** Test the suspension by feeling for vibration or pulling while driving. Check the brakes—listen for noise, look for leaks and feel for vibration. They may fail, perform poorly or require frequent mechanical attention. Test the transmission thoroughly.

Hot Spots and Owner/NHTSA Comments:

1. Emergency parking brake: mechanical, failure. • "While parked on steep incline with emergency brake applied, brake disengaged, allowing vehicle to roll downhill, hitting a tree; received recall notice next day." • "Truck parked on hill, put into neutral with emergency parking brake on; truck backed up and hit another car; consumer received recall today on the same problem." • "Parking brake failed to hold, resulting in vehicle rolling downhill; accident; prior to recall." • "Emergency brakes engaged on vehicle in gear, vehicle was parked on incline, rolled backwards, hitting a house. Impact 6:00 position, speed unknown." • "Emergency brake does not work; truck rolls when brake is on."

2. Brakes: hydraulic: anti-skid system, poor performance, failure, locking up. • "Antilock brake system: Upon applying brakes, all 4 wheels locked up, resulting in skidding 60 feet into rear end of another vehicle. No airbag." • "Rear antilock brake system malfunctioned and had rear wheel lockup." • "Clutch assembly has faulty spring that hangs until braking. Gears failed to respond, grinding gears." • "Antilock brake system: When applying brakes, pedal goes to floor." • "Rear antilock brake system locks up when driving during wet or damp conditions." • "Rear antilock brake system malfunctioned and had rear wheel lockup."

3. Suspension: independent front, pulling, vibration. • "Front end pulls to right; goes off road while driving straight forward; low or high speed; no warning." • "Vehicle shimmies when driving over cracks, bumps or holes." • "When going over bumps in road at 45 mph, vehicle pulls; feels like it's losing control." • "Vehicle vibrates when engine is operating at high rpm."

4. Brakes: hydraulic: shoe and drum system, locking up, malfunction. • "Brakes grab when pedal is pushed lightly, intermittently." • "Lost brakes while driving twice—back wheels lock." • "Involved in 2 accidents with cause not clear; rear locking up and brakes not activating." • "Rear brakes are locking up."

5. Power train: transmission: automatic, poor performance, difficulty shifting, slipping. • "Transmission failure." • "When parked on an incline, truck will roll backwards." • "When cold-starting vehicle, rpm picks up when transmission is shifted into reverse from park; rpm also picks up when shifting from park into drive."

FORD TRUCK WINDSTAR 1995

Complaint Severity: Minor. **Recall Alert:** See Recall Index. **Buyer's Summary:** Check the brakes—listen for noise, look for leaks and feel for vibration. They may fail, perform poorly or require frequent mechanical attention. Test the transmission thoroughly.

Hot Spots and Owner/NHTSA Comments:

1. Brakes: hydraulic: anti-skid system, poor performance, failure, locking up. • "Malfunction with antilock brake system; during normal stopping, experience long stopping distance, pedal fades and then gets hard; dealer cannot locate problem." • "Rear antilock brake system fails to stop vehicle effectively when applied, causing extended stopping." • "Antilock brake system failure; loss of effectiveness while driving, brakes make a loud noise; in for repair 2 times, replaced pad, shoes and disc rotors in front." • "Brake system failure; brakes are spongy, pedal goes all the way to floor when braking." • "Antilock brake system makes loud grinding noises; hard to stop vehicle; now, antilock brake system has gone out."

2. Brakes: hydraulic system, premature failure. • "Have experienced 3 brake failures. Dealer cannot find problem." • "Brakes failed, brake pedal went to the floor." • "Poor braking; if making a quick stop, experience pedal fading." • "On 3 occasions, loss of brakes at low speeds; pedal gets hard, brakes don't grab and can't stop vehicle." • "Brakes failed in nonemergency situations; brakes also make noise."

3. Power train: transmission: automatic, poor performance, difficulty shifting, slipping. • "Slowing down, applied brakes, vehicle jerked, shifted into neutral and transmission caused vehicle to stall." • "Transmission slipped from neutral to drive and from park into reverse, causing loss of control and an accident." • "Transmission failed, causing vehicle to become stuck in park position." • "Transmission slips." • "Problem with automatic transmission; vehicle not stopping as it should."

4. Electrical system: ignition, stalling, noise, locking up. • "The vehicle dies in the middle of traffic at highway speeds of 55 mph and up." • "When making left-hand turns, car stalls out." • "Traveling 60 mph, front end made loud noise and vehicle locked up due to an electrical problem." • "Vehicle periodically stalls or shuts down upon leaving idling position or driving."

5. Electrical system: wiring: harness: front: under hood, malfunction, fire. • "Engine compartment fire." • "Engine compartment fire: Fire started on left side of engine; vehicle not moving; parked for 10 minutes; cause unknown." • "Consumer was driving, shut off van; there was smoke under the hood, fire around the power control box and wire was burning."

6. Equipment: electric power accessories: windows, malfunction. • "The passenger front power window caught an occupant and the dog's neck in the window. The way the button is placed, it is dangerous and there's no lockout mechanism." • "Electrical windows intermittently operate." • "Left side power window switch inoperative." • "Driver's power window only goes all the way down; cannot get it to stop at desired locations."

Geo

GEO METRO 1989

Complaint Severity: Very Serious. **Recall Alert:** See Recall Index. **Buyer's Summary:** Test the suspension by feeling for vibration or pulling while driving.

Hot Spots and Owner/NHTSA Comments:

1. Structure: hood assembly: latches, breaking, vibration, malfunction. • "Hood latch broke while driving; hood flew up; shattered front windshield; fragments of glass hit face and neck of driver." • "Front hood would raise slightly, fall slightly and vibrate at speeds of 25 mph. Due to detachment of a piece of metal that secures hood to frame." • "Hood popped up while driving at 45 mph. Manufacturer mailed no notification, but verified vehicle was involved in recall." • "Hood latch failed, causing hood to pop up and crack windshield, prior to recall." • "Ring on inside of hood latch developed stress cracks."

2. Suspension: independent front, alignment, rust, failure. • "Loose suspension." • "Faulty alignment caused tires to wear out prematurely." • "While driving the front axle broke, car lost control and flipped over, and passenger-side seat belt broke." • "Shocks and struts failed." • "While driving, the right front suspension collapsed due to frame rusting."
3. Suspension: single axle: rear: control arm, breaking, failure. • "Rear control arm broke, causing accident and injury." • "Rear control arm broke, causing accident and injury." • "Left rear control arm broke, causing accident and injury." • "Loss of control resulted in car crossing lanes and hitting guardrail; caused by broken left rear suspension control rod."

GEO METRO 1990

Complaint Severity: Very Serious. **Recall Alert:** See Recall Index. **Buyer's Summary:** Check the brakes—listen for noise, look for leaks and feel for vibration. They may fail, perform poorly or require frequent mechanical attention.

Hot Spots and Owner/NHTSA Comments:
1. Structure: hood assembly: latches, failure. • "Hood latch failed, causing hood to fly backwards, cracking windshield; prior to recall." • "Hood flew up while driving. Vehicle involved with recall, but dealer says failure due to latch not being lubricated." • "Hood flew up while driving; received recall for hood three days before. Dealer will not fix." • "Hood latch failed, prior to recall, causing hood to fly up, cracking windshield. Recall repairs refused for windshield; only hood repaired." • "Hood latch failed, resulting in hood release; prior to recall, owner was never notified."
2. Brakes: hydraulic system, noise, malfunction, failure. • "Wet road, brakes froze and vehicle skidded and slid into a car in front." • "Brakes became inoperative and caused accident." • "Grinding sound occurs in front passenger-side brakes upon quick stops." • "Brakes went out; brake pedal nearly goes to floor when applying; repaired/replaced, continual problems." • "While driving at approximately 25 mph and attempting to stop, brakes malfunctioned; resulted in an accident."

GEO METRO 1991

Complaint Severity: Very Serious. **Recall Alert:** See Recall Index. **Buyer's Summary:** The airbags in this vehicle have experienced failures and malfunctions: You may need a professional evaluation on the condition of the airbags. Make sure seat belts function correctly and fit comfortably.

Hot Spots and Owner/NHTSA Comments:
1. Structure: hood assembly: latches, failure. • "Hood latch failed, causing hood to come off vehicle; prior to recall, recall refused due to prior damage to vehicle."
2. Interior systems: passive restraint: airbag: driver, malfunction, failure. • "Airbag did not deploy during front-end collision; impact 1:00 position; speed 15-20 mph; driver lost control; hit a brick wall." • "Lost control of vehicle on wet road, hitting a telephone pole. Impact 12:00 position. Speed 35 mph. Airbag did not deploy." • "In 12:00 position at 40 mph, car hit a bus and airbag did not deploy." • "Airbag did not deploy during an accident" • "In frontal collision at 45 mph, impact at 12:00, airbag did not deploy and seat belt did not retract."
3. Interior systems: passive restraint: belts, malfunction, failure. • "Automatic seat belt disengaged when door opened during accident, causing death." • "Manufacturer states that an infant restraint belt is needed in order to have baby in front seat with automatic seat belts. Dealer can't get part."

GEO METRO 1992

Complaint Severity: Serious. **Recall Alert:** See Recall Index. **Buyer's Summary:** Check the brakes—listen for noise, look for leaks and feel for vibration. They may fail, perform poorly or require frequent mechanical attention. See "Sudden Accelerations" in Introduction.

Hot Spots and Owner/NHTSA Comments:
1. Brakes: hydraulic system, noise, locking up, failure. • "Noisy brakes." • "Left rear brakes lock up when braking is applied, causing vehicle to fishtail and loss of vehicle control." • "Rear-ended vehicle due to brake failure in cold weather." • "Brakes failed, causing accident and injuries."
2. Fuel: throttle linkages and control, sudden accelerations. • "Sudden acceleration, resulting in injury." • "Engine runaway after engine warms up." • "Erratic idle caused the car to suddenly accelerate." • "Vehicle loses power; fuel pressure regulator of fuel throttle body. 'Check engine' light comes on." • "Vehicle surged backward out of control, causing an accident."
3. Interior systems: active restraints: belt buckles, malfunction, failure. • "Seat belt buckle unlatched on impact, resulting in injuries." • "The front seat belts do not engage." • "Driver's seat belt will not stay attached; dealer used special spray, which only lasted a few days and they were back to not working." • "Rear-ended another vehicle at red light at about 30-35 mph, seat belt buckle became unraveled; driver sustained injuries."
4. Interior systems: active restraints: belt retractors, malfunction, failure. • "Seat belt retractors failed." • "During frontal crash at approximately 30 mph, 10:00 position on front bumper, airbag failed to deploy, shoulder harness failed to retract, resulting in hitting windshield." • "Driver's shoulder and lap belt does not retract as intended. Hangs loose after releasing buckle."
5. Structure: hood assembly: latches, failure. • "Hood flew open while vehicle was in motion; cracked windshield; shattered little pieces of glass at bottom of windshield; decreased driver's vision." • "Hood assembly fly-up occurred while driving on highway at 55 mph, breaking windshield, denting roof and damaging interior dome light. Recall related." • "Hood latches failed, causing hood to separate from vehicle."

GEO METRO 1993

Complaint Severity: Serious. **Recall Alert:** See Recall Index. **Buyer's Summary:** The airbags in this vehicle have experienced failures and malfunctions: You may need a professional evaluation on the condition of the airbags. Check the brakes—listen for noise, look for leaks and feel for vibration. They may fail, perform poorly or require frequent mechanical attention.

Hot Spots and Owner/NHTSA Comments:
1. Brakes: hydraulic system, locking up, malfunction. • "When air conditioner is running, brakes don't seem to be very responsive, especially in stop-and-go traffic; caused accident; hit another vehicle at standstill." • "Driving vehicle at 55 mph. Steering locked up, causing loss of control. Brakes locked up; hit a tree. Impact 12:00 position. Heat coil fell out." • "Loss of brake effectiveness after applying brakes. Pedal faded." • "Engine has sudden acceleration; brakes will not hold the car. Dealer has been working on problem since vehicle was new and says there is no problem."
2. Electrical system: ignition, stalling, malfunction. • "Engine stalls out; vehicle jerks spasmodically." • "Vehicle stalls out while driving with no warning." • "There is a sensor in the engine which freezes in zero-degree weather and causes the vehicle to buck, stall and die." • "Vehicle will stall; poor idling, intermittently. After starting and moving forward, vehicle runs very poorly for the first 10 minutes of operation."

3. Exhaust system: manifold: oxygen sensor, stalling, failure. • "Poor shifting of transmission due to manifold air pressure sensor." • "Airflow manifold air pressure sensor defective, causing stalling problems when driving in cold weather." • "The manifold air pressure sensor in vehicle collects moisture and breaks, causing vehicle to stall in traffic." • "Manifold air pressure sensor failed, causing sluggishness, starting problems and temperature indicator failure; also caused 'check engine' and 'door lock' lights to stay on."

4. Interior systems: passive restraint: airbag: driver, malfunction, failure. • "Airbag did not deploy during front-end collision at 35 mph. Driver received minor injuries." • "Car was rear-ended in an accident; the airbag didn't deploy." • "Car hit tree at 40 mph; airbag did not deploy." • "When airbag opened, it burst open, causing burns to driver's arms."

GEO METRO 1994

Complaint Severity: Very Serious. **Buyer's Summary:** Check the brakes—listen for noise, look for leaks and feel for vibration. They may fail, perform poorly or require frequent mechanical attention.

Hot Spots and Owner/NHTSA Comments:

1. Brakes: hydraulic system, noise, failure. • "Brakes did not stop vehicle, resulting in rear-end collision." • "Rear brakes make noise when depressing brake pedal." • "Brakes failed, resulting in an accident." • "Applied brakes, pedal went to floor, vehicle started spinning, eventually hit divider; vehicle extremely lightweight, does not hold to road."

GEO PRIZM 1990

Complaint Severity: Typical. **Buyer's Summary:** The electronic control unit has been blamed for engine performance problems, including stalling and surging. The fuel injection system has been blamed for hesitation and stalling. Be sure the vehicle doesn't die in traffic or at stops. Check the brakes—listen for noise, look for leaks and feel for vibration. They may fail, perform poorly or require frequent mechanical attention. Test the transmission thoroughly. See "Sudden Accelerations" in Introduction.

Hot Spots and Owner/NHTSA Comments:

1. Fuel: fuel injection system, stalling, hesitation. • "Intermittent stalling." • "Stalling and surging problems." • "Engine power weak, especially when going up slightest incline, car strains." • "Car stalls out during starts and while in operation." • "Intermittent stalling."

2. Brakes: hydraulic system, vibration, malfunction. • "Continue to wear disc rotors, pads and drums of rear and front brakes. When applying brakes, experience jerks and vibration in front end." • "Front brakes were resurfaced once and warped once. Rear brakes were resurfaced once." • "While making a stop, brakes malfunctioned; vehicle slid into guardrail." • "When applying the brakes at 45 mph, the brakes pulsate." • "While driving, hit the brakes going downhill and brakes locked up. Hit curb and flipped over."

3. Electrical system: ignition: electronic control unit, stalling, malfunction. • "Engine misses and sometimes stalls; electronic control module installed but failed shortly after installment; second electronic control module installed but still shows stalling problems." • "Electronic control module failure; starting malfunctions, popping sounds under hood and strong fuel fumes, behaved as if choke was sticking; dealer said chip on back order." • "Problem with engine bucking; repaired/replaced electronic control module and oxygen sensing unit, solved problem temporarily." • "Computer problem caused car to stall and lose power."

4. Power train: transmission: automatic, poor performance, difficulty shifting, slipping. • "Transmission jerks after 40 mph." • "Transmission seals leaked; repaired." • "The automatic transmission is very noisy." • "Transmission vibrates." • "Automatic transmission: While driving 60 mph, transmission froze; wheels locked up; started making unfamiliar sounds; several loud thumps, then froze."

5. Electrical system: ignition, stalling, failure. • "Engine automatically shuts off without warning while driving; excessive effort to start back up." • "Vehicle stalls and the engine cuts off without warning while driving along; resulted in loss of control." • "Vehicle stalls when coming to a stop, and also idles high." • "Ignition problems."

6. Fuel: throttle linkages and control, sudden accelerations. • "Upon shifting into reverse, car engine raced wildly, loudly; without success, shifted to drive, then park. Car continued in reverse; resulted in accident." • "Car accelerated without pressure on gas pedal and hit a tree." • "While gear was in reverse, vehicle accelerated at a high rate of speed." • "Intermittent stalling."

GEO PRIZM 1991

Complaint Severity: Serious. **Recall Alert:** See Recall Index. **Buyer's Summary:** The exhaust manifold has received complaints. Have the exhaust system checked thoroughly by a professional.

Hot Spots and Owner/NHTSA Comments:

1. Structure: door assembly: handle: inside, breaking, poor performance. • "When pulling on inside door release handle, plate behind it broke twice, disabling door release." • "Inside handles break off; unable to exit vehicle." • "Vehicle's inside door handles are breaking prematurely; had 5 handles replaced." • "The inner door latches have broken and fallen apart; cannot get out of car on one side." • "All four door handles inside of vehicle are broken."

2. Exhaust system: manifold: engine, noise, cracking. • "Loud noise from under the hood; dealer states cracked exhaust manifold." • "The exhaust manifold that goes back to the exhaust system has cracked; this is the second owner." • "Exhaust manifold cracked in 2 places." • "Original and replacement exhaust manifold cracked." • "While driving at 65 mph, vehicle made noise; exhaust manifold split in half."

GEO PRIZM 1993

Complaint Severity: Very Serious. **Buyer's Summary:** Test the suspension by feeling for vibration or pulling while driving. The airbags in this vehicle have experienced failures and malfunctions: You may need a professional evaluation on the condition of the airbags. Test the transmission thoroughly.

Hot Spots and Owner/NHTSA Comments:

1. Interior systems: passive restraint: airbag: driver, malfunction, failure. • "Frontal collision, impact 12:00 position, airbag did not deploy; lap and shoulder belt did not retract." • "Frontal collision, impact 12:00 position, speed 35 mph, airbag did not deploy." • "Upon right front impact, shoulder and lap belt failed to restrain driver from making contact and no airbag deployment." • "Frontal collision, impact 12:00 position, speed 30 mph, hitting another vehicle; airbag did not deploy."

2. Equipment: electric power accessories: windows, malfunction, failure. • "Automatic window sticks shut; sprayed with silicone on 2 occasions, third repair, replaced front passenger and driver window regulators." • "Window regulator; while driving down highway, passenger front window fell into door." • "While pushing button to roll down window, window came off regulator and flipped over on its side." • "Front power window regulators failed 5 times." • "On 2 occasions, motor for electric windows failed. Part on national back order."

3. Power train: transmission: automatic, poor performance, difficulty shifting, slipping. • "Vehicle wouldn't shift into 3rd gear before 60 mph." • "Transmission shifts into 3rd gear." • "Transmission will not downshift to lower gears after highway driving." • "Transmission piece broke off, fell into front wheels, causing vehicle to stall."

4. Suspension: independent front, pulling, vibration, noise. • "Vehicle pulls to right." • "Vehicle vibration." • "Car pulled to right driving on straight 2-lane road; lost control; hit top of embankment; car hydroplaned; impact 6:00 position, speed 45 mph; totaled." • "Flutter noise in left front end when turning left."

GEO PRIZM 1994

Complaint Severity: Very Serious. **Recall Alert:** See Recall Index. **Buyer's Summary:** The airbags in this vehicle have experienced failures and malfunctions: You may need a professional evaluation on the condition of the airbags.

Hot Spots and Owner/NHTSA Comments:

1. Interior systems: passive restraint: airbag: driver, malfunction, failure. • "Airbag did not inflate during accident." • "No deployment of driver's airbag during accident, resulting in an injury." • "Driver's airbag deployment was violent, resulting in injury." • "Airbag deployed; hoses detached sprayed chemicals on driver's neck, resulting in burns and breaking driver's jaw." • "Had frontal accident, airbag did not deploy."

2. Interior systems: passive restraint: airbag: passenger, failure. • "Upon impact, during frontal crash at approximately 35 mph, 12:00 position on front bumper, both driver and passenger airbags failed to deploy; no prior warning." • "No deployment of passenger's airbag during accident, resulting in an injury." • "Consumer was leasing this car when she rear-ended another driver at 35 mph and passenger's airbag did not deploy." • "In a frontal collision, the passenger's airbag did not deploy."

3. Interior systems: active restraints: belt retractors, malfunction. • "Right rear seat belt retractor does not work, and left rear is malfunctioning." • "The driver seat belt retractor will not come out." • "Driver's-side seat belt will not release from the retractor housing." • "Driver's seat belt will not extend out of retractor."

GEO STORM 1990

Complaint Severity: Dangerous (Worst 3% in Guide). **Recall Alert:** See Recall Index. **Buyer's Summary:** The steering may be stiff or not working correctly. Be sure to test the steering, especially on a cold start. The airbags in this vehicle have experienced failures and malfunctions: You may need a professional evaluation on the condition of the airbags. Check the brakes—listen for noise, look for leaks and feel for vibration. They may fail, perform poorly or require frequent mechanical attention.

Hot Spots and Owner/NHTSA Comments:

1. Interior systems: passive restraint: airbag: driver, malfunction, failure. • "Frontal collision, impact 12:00 position, speed 20 mph, airbag did not deploy." • "Airbag failed to deploy during front-end collision between 10:00 and 11:00 positions at approximately 30 to 40 mph; vehicle went into a concrete wall." • "Airbag deployment during accident resulted in chemical burns." • "Frontal collision occurred at 20 mph and airbag did not deploy." • "During front-end collision at 25 mph, airbag failed to deploy."

2. Steering: wheel and column, vibration, failure. • "Steering column became so loose that the wheel could have snapped off because the bolts had no seal." • "Steering not in proper working order, causing accident." • "Loose steering column bracket." • "Steering wheel vibration after recall repair." • "Steering failed after initial collision, causing second collision and injuries."

3. Brakes: hydraulic system, noise, failure. • "While coming to a stop sign, brakes failed, resulting in an accident." • "Brake failure." • "Noisy brakes." • "Brakes making squealing noise shortly after purchasing vehicle." • "Brakes failed several times; dealer can't fix them."

4. Electrical system: alternator: generator, failure. • "Engine overheated; alternator replaced." • "Alternator and regulator failed." • "Lights on instrument panel stay on and heater/air conditioner blower fan turns on or doesn't operate due to alternator." • "Alternator fails intermittently." • "Replaced alternator 4 times; possibly because a heat shield is needed; results in vehicle stalling out."

GEO STORM 1991

Complaint Severity: Dangerous (Worst 3% in Guide). **Recall Alert:** See Recall Index. **Buyer's Summary:** The fuel injection system has been blamed for hesitation and stalling. Be sure the vehicle doesn't die in traffic or at stops. The steering may be stiff or not working correctly. Be sure to test the steering, especially on a cold start. The airbags in this vehicle have experienced failures and malfunctions: You may need a professional evaluation on the condition of the airbags.

Hot Spots and Owner/NHTSA Comments:

1. Interior systems: passive restraint: airbag: driver, malfunction, failure. • "Airbag did not deploy during a front-end collision at 20 mph. Driver received head injuries." • "Head-on crash at 50 mph, with no airbag deployment." • "Airbag deployment during a front-end collision caused a chemical to leak out and resulted in driver receiving second degree burns on chin and arm." • "Vehicle had an accident during which airbag did not deploy upon impact." • "Airbag did not deploy on frontal impact at 12:00, speed 35 mph."

2. Interior systems: passive restraint: airbag, malfunction, failure. • "Steering wheel became completely separated from steering column during an accident, immediately after airbag deployed; cause unknown at this time." • "During a front-end collision, airbag did not deploy; caused neck injuries." • "During frontal collision with impact at 9:00, speed 30 mph, airbag failed to deploy; seat belt failed to lock, driver hit head on steering wheel. Injuries." • "Airbag failed during accident, causing injury."

3. Exhaust system: manifold: engine, cracking, failure. • "Crack in exhaust manifold extends through opening for oxygen sensor." • "Exhaust manifold cracked in half." • "Exhaust manifold is cracked. Vehicle hesitates, bucks and jerks." • "Exhaust manifold is split, causing car to die." • "Engine exhaust manifold replaced."

4. Steering: wheel and column, miscellaneous problems. • "Steering wheel became completely separated from steering column during an accident, immediately after airbag deployed; cause unknown at this time." • "Driving to dealer for recall repairs, steering wheel failed and the car crashed." • "Defective steering wheel center hub." • "Recall repairs refused due to unavailability of parts." • "Steering wheel turns by itself after recall repairs."

5. Electrical system: ignition, stalling, hesitation. • "Vehicle stalled while driving; turning into intersection and vehicle hit from a 3:00 position, speed 20 mph." • "Vehicle started up by itself with no keys in ignition and no driver, and went uphill, resulting in accident." • "Car was parked in the driveway and was off; it cut itself back on and off, and tire was turning." • "Five-speed automatic transmission; engine deceleration resulted in stalling and loss of steering and brake control." • "Vehicle stalls and hesitates in traffic."

6. Fuel: fuel injection system, stalling, hesitation. • "Intermittent stalling." • "Inconsistent stalling and idle fluctuation problems." • "Stalling and high idle problems." • "Vehicle caught fire during accident."

GEO STORM 1992

Complaint Severity: Dangerous (Worst 3% in Guide). **Recall Alert:** See Recall Index. **Buyer's Summary:** The airbags in this vehicle have experienced failures and malfunctions: You may need a professional evaluation on the condition of the airbags.

Hot Spots and Owner/NHTSA Comments:

1. Interior systems: passive restraint: airbag: driver, malfunction, failure. • "During a frontal collision, impact at 10:00, airbag did not deploy." • "Airbag did not deploy during a head-on 30-mph crash. Seat belts bruised the driver and caused back injury." • "Airbag did not deploy during a front-end collision at 20 mph; vehicle hit a tree and driver received head and facial injuries." • "No deployment of driver's airbag during accident, resulting in injury." • "Airbag did not deploy during frontal impact into a telephone pole at 45 mph. Driver received injuries."

GMC

GMC C1500 1988

Complaint Severity: Typical. **Recall Alert:** See Recall Index. **Buyer's Summary:** Check the brakes—listen for noise, look for leaks and feel for vibration. They may fail, perform poorly or require frequent mechanical attention.

Hot Spots and Owner/NHTSA Comments:

1. Brakes: hydraulic system, vibration, failure. • "Problems with brake system." • "Loose 1¼ inch hexhead bolt found in left rear brake; did not belong to any part of brake or backing plate." • "Brakes failed continuously; replaced 3 times." • "Brake vibration, drums out of round and high spots on brake shoes; repaired/replaced brake shoes and refaced shoes and drums."

GMC JIMMY 1989

Complaint Severity: Troublesome. **Buyer's Summary:** See "Sudden Accelerations" in Introduction.

Hot Spots and Owner/NHTSA Comments:

1. Fuel: throttle linkages and control, sudden accelerations. • "While shifting from park to drive, vehicle (S15 model) suddenly accelerated; first occasion resulted in an accident." • "When about to back up, engine throttle stuck wide open, went backwards, spinning tires into side of school building." • "Engine started racing very loud and fast; almost resulted in accident when brakes failed to stop car." • "Stopped in traffic but engine surged forward into a truck's tailgate." • "Upon shifting gear into reverse, vehicle suddenly accelerated, which resulted in an accident."

GMC JIMMY 1991

Complaint Severity: Troublesome. **Recall Alert:** See Recall Index. **Buyer's Summary:** Check the brakes—listen for noise, look for leaks and feel for vibration. They may fail, perform poorly or require frequent mechanical attention. Make sure the seat belts are firmly anchored.

Hot Spots and Owner/NHTSA Comments:

1. Brakes: hydraulic: anti-skid system, poor performance, failure, locking up. • "Brake and antilock brake system warning lights came on as brake pedal traveled to floor; resulted in total loss of brakes." • "While driving, antilock brake system completely failed; pedal faded to the floor with no prior warning." • "Brake pedal goes all the way to floor; brake light constantly flashes; brakes are equipped with antilock system." • "Brakes failed to stop vehicle when applied and caused front-end collision at 11:00 position going 10 mph." • "Applying antilock brakes, did not feel any pedal modulation; truck swerved and rolled over 3 times. Disconnecting battery hid codes stored in computer."

2. Interior systems: active seat and shoulder belts and belt anchor, breaking, failure. • "Brought truck 3 years ago new; had to replace rear driver's-side belt twice, front passenger belt replaced once and about to replace the rear passenger belt." • "Seat belt broke during accident, causing injuries." • "Driver's seat belt failed during accident, causing injury." • "Seat belt failure."

GMC JIMMY 1992

Complaint Severity: Serious. **Buyer's Summary:** Check the brakes—listen for noise, look for leaks and feel for vibration. They may fail, perform poorly or require frequent mechanical attention.

Hot Spots and Owner/NHTSA Comments:

1. Brakes: hydraulic: anti-skid system, poor performance, failure, locking up. • "Antilock brake system malfunctioned; pedal faded to the floor during normal stop, resulting in accident; dealer cannot find problem." • "Antilock brake system: When applying brakes, rear pulls to either direction, fishtails or poor response to application." • "Antilock brakes make noise and pull toward the right when stopping and turning, especially when raining, causing partial brake loss." • "When driving in wet weather, the antilock brakes slide." • "Antilock brakes make noise when turning and lock up in wet weather."

2. Brakes: hydraulic: disc: pads and shoes, excessive wear, failure. • "Antilock brake system: Outer brake pads wear excessively; replaced every 21,000 miles (replaced twice)." • "Front brake system had to be replaced twice; pads and disc wear prematurely." • "Front brake pads wear out prematurely." • "Brakes; wear of disc pads, and experience extended pedal fading." • "Brake computer chip replaced; also, brake pads, rotors and calipers failed, causing brake failure and loss of control."

3. Interior systems: bucket: backrest, breaking, poor performance. • "Vehicle struck from rear; driver's seat collapsed." • "Bench seat will not lock in place; will fall forward while driving." • "After rear-end collision, the front seats collapsed backwards."

GMC JIMMY 1993

Complaint Severity: Very Serious. **Recall Alert:** See Recall Index. **Buyer's Summary:** Check the brakes—listen for noise, look for leaks and feel for vibration. They may fail, perform poorly or require frequent mechanical attention. Test the transmission thoroughly.

Hot Spots and Owner/NHTSA Comments:

1. Brakes: hydraulic: anti-skid system, poor performance, failure, locking up. • "Antilock brake system malfunctions; during sudden stopping, noticed excessively long stopping distance; replaced brake booster to no avail." • "Antilock brake system: Replacement of brake rotors and disc pads, rear axle seals replacement; experienced extended stopping distance." • "While driving at approximately 5-10 mph, upon application of brake, vehicle continued to roll forward, as a result went through intersection, hitting another car; no warning." • "Antilock brake system/hydraulic system failed 8 times; once causing an accident and loss of control." • "While driving at approximately 20 mph, made attempt to brake, brake pedal became hard; continued to roll forward, hitting another vehicle; no prior warning."

2. Brakes: hydraulic system, excessive wear, failure. • "Brakes wear out prematurely at less than 20,000 miles." • "When brakes are applied, there is a delay in actual braking, especially at slower speeds and when backing up." • "Applied the brakes while traveling at 25 mph and truck didn't stop, causing an accident." • "Firm brake pedal application causes the front end of vehicle to shimmy." • "Brakes failed 6 times on wet roads."

3. Power train: transmission: automatic, poor performance, difficulty shifting, slipping. • "Automatic transmission leaks fluid onto catalytic converter. Could cause fire. GMC said to install transmission cooler." • "Transmission hesitates in 3rd gear." • "Transmission shifts into neutral; between shifts hangs up in lower gears." • "Transmission defect repaired."

GMC JIMMY 1994

Complaint Severity: Serious. **Recall Alert:** See Recall Index. **Buyer's Summary:** Check the brakes—listen for noise, look for leaks and feel for vibration. They may fail, perform poorly or require frequent mechanical attention.

Hot Spots and Owner/NHTSA Comments:

1. Brakes: hydraulic: anti-skid system, poor performance, failure, locking up. • "During brake application, pedal goes to the floor; no response from the antilock braking system." • " 'Check engine' light comes on, then antilock brake system fails, resulting in long stopping distance." • "Brakes appeared to be inadequate; substandard to stop vehicle; vehicle lost control, resulting in an accident." • "Antilock brake system: During wet weather or damp air, antilock brakes make noise; pedal goes to floor; extended stopping distance; 20-30 mph; no warning." • "Antilock brake system went into anti-skid mode upon coming to a stop on dry pavement; failed 3 times, once resulting in an accident."

2. Brakes: hydraulic system, noise, pulling, failure. • "After parking vehicle, then starting up, car accelerated at high speed; brake did not stop vehicle." • "When brakes are applied, there's a loud sound and the truck slides." • "Brake cable grinds." • "When brakes are applied, vehicle pulls to the left." • "Noisy brakes."

GMC SAFARI 1987

Complaint Severity: Minor. **Recall Alert:** See Recall Index. **Buyer's Summary:** Look carefully for any kind of leakage, especially under the car. Verify that the cruise control system works properly, and that it doesn't cause the engine to surge. The steering may be stiff or not working correctly. Be sure to test the steering, especially on a cold start.

Hot Spots and Owner/NHTSA Comments:

1. Power train: axle assembly: seal: axle shaft, leaks, pulling, locking up. • "Rear brakes grabbed; rear axle seals leaked onto brakes." • "Rear axle seal leak." • "Rear seal failure, causing rear axle oil to leak onto rear brakes, making vehicle difficult to stop." • "Leak on right and left rear axle seals saturated brake shoes; clunking noise from rear brake shoes; repaired/replaced axle, seals, bearings." • "Brakes lock up; caused by rear axle seal leak."

2. Steering: linkages: arm: idler and attachment, tire wear, alignment. • "Problem with front end; excessive wear of idler arms and ball joint." • "Noticed tires wearing badly on front end; right idler arm badly worn." • "Front-end alignment; excessive outer-edge tire wear; very weak idler arms were problem." • "Defect in idler arms; could cause excessive tire wear." • "Idler arm worn excessively at 19,000 miles."

3. Engine: other parts, miscellaneous problems. • "Number 1 left cylinder essentially dead and has never worked." • "Connecting rod bearings failed due to lack of lubrication at crankshaft." • "Broken mounting bolts on the fan pulley bracket." • "Poor engine oil consumption."

4. Equipment: speed control, malfunction, failure. • "Cruise control will drop from set speed; if 'resume' is pushed, will regain speed lost." • "Cruise control suddenly quit while driving at 65 mph." • "Cruise control malfunction; while traveling on highway at approximately 65 mph, cruise control suddenly quit." • "Cruise control defect; while driving, cruise control will go off without having touched button; also engages itself sometimes."

5. Interior systems: active restraints: belt retractors, malfunction, failure. • "Frequent problem when children sitting in back; managed to twist seat belt, causing it to lock up, then no pullout or retraction." • "Seat belt retractors fail to hold." • "Front shoulder belt retractor not adjusting properly." • "Passenger safety belt would not release; replaced."

6. Interior systems: active seat and shoulder belts and belt anchor, malfunction, failure. • "Seat belts on bucket seats do not retract when pulled completely out; cannot safely fasten child seat." • "Driver's and passengers' seat belts are always loose." • "Driver's seat belt assembly does not retract after being extended; safety compromised in the event of an accident." • "Seat belt failed to prevent child seat from sliding off seat."

GMC SAFARI 1988

Complaint Severity: Typical. **Recall Alert:** See Recall Index. **Buyer's Summary:** The steering may be stiff or not working correctly. Be sure to test the steering, especially on a cold start.

Hot Spots and Owner/NHTSA Comments:

1. Steering: linkages: arm: idler and attachment, tire wear, alignment. • "Left front idler arm bad; caused excessive wear on front tires." • "Alignment impossible due to worn-out idler arms in steering linkage." • "Idler arms have too much movement to be lined up properly; pull to one side, throwing steering off and causing tires to wear excessively." • "Not able to align front end on vehicle due to excess tolerance in 2 idler arms; tires wear out prematurely." • "Idler arms need replacement; vehicle has low mileage."

2. Steering: power assist: pump, failure. • "Bolts that hold power steering pump broke off, losing steering and brake capabilities." • "Power steering bracket and bolts cracked twice." • "Power steering pump failure." • "Power steering pump bolts and bracket broke and fell off 4 times."

GMC SAFARI 1990

Complaint Severity: Typical. **Recall Alert:** See Recall Index. **Buyer's Summary:** Look carefully for any kind of leakage, especially under the car. Test the suspension by feeling for vibration or pulling while driving. Check the brakes—listen for noise, look for leaks and feel for vibration. They may fail, perform poorly or require frequent mechanical attention.

Hot Spots and Owner/NHTSA Comments:

1. Brakes: hydraulic: anti-skid system, poor performance, failure, locking up. • "While driving recently, brakes failed twice; however, earlier they were working properly." • "Replaced electronic control unit and bled entire brake system." • "Intermittent antilock brake failure." • "Problem with antilock brake locking up and pulling under heavy braking; all repair attempts to no avail." • "Antilock brake system: Brake system fails, with condition repeating itself yearly."

2. Brakes: hydraulic system, noise, failure. • "Broken brake lines, causing squealing and grabbing." • "Once truck did a panic stop. Two brake warning lights came on." • "Brakes faded when applied, with no brake warning. Brakes controlled by computer. Replaced." • "Brakes have repeated problems; repairs and replacements have only lasted temporarily." • "Brake pedal goes completely to floor; when holding the pressure, brake valve failed; rear drums out of round too." • "While foot was on brake, van was put into drive; it accelerated, went out of control and ran into brick house, causing injury."

3. Suspension: independent front, vibration, tire wear, pulling. • "Vehicle vibrates; repaired/replaced tires, shocks and wheels, problem continues." • "Excessive tire wear due to front end." • "Van pulls to the right frequently due to a faulty suspension system." • "Front suspension; vehicle pulled very hard to left, causing loss of control, impact 2:00 position, speed 30 mph." • "Front end suspension causing excessive tire wear."

4. Fuel: fuel lines: hoses: nonmetallic, leaks, noise. • "Recall work on faulty fuel return hose." • "Recall notice for faulty fuel return hose." • "Fuel line leak between pump (in tank) and engine." • "Noticed noise from underneath vehicle at 50-70 mph; fuel line broke after receiving recall notice concerning fuel line breakage that may cause fire."

5. Structure: door assembly, noise, failure. • "Rear doors aren't properly aligned." • "Door rattles." • "Door latch repaired." • "The sliding door on the side of the vehicle is faulty."

GMC SAFARI 1994

Complaint Severity: Troublesome. **Recall Alert:** See Recall Index. **Buyer's Summary:** The airbags in this vehicle have experienced failures and malfunctions: You may need a professional evaluation on the condition of the airbags. Check the brakes—listen for noise, look for leaks and feel for vibration. They may fail, perform poorly or require frequent mechanical attention.

Hot Spots and Owner/NHTSA Comments:

1. Interior systems: passive restraint: airbag: driver, malfunction, failure. • "Driver's-side airbag did not inflate in a front-end crash, resulting in injuries." • "During frontal collision, driver's-side airbag did not deploy, resulting in a fatality." • "Driver's airbag did not inflate during accident, resulting in injury." • "During rear-end impact, the airbag did not deploy." • "Driver's-side airbag did not deploy upon frontal collision."

2. Electrical system: alternator: generator, failure. • "Alternator failure." • "Replaced alternator and wire to starter." • "Alternator failure." • "Replaced generator and alternator."

3. Brakes: hydraulic system. • "Brakes failed due to battery malfunctioning when too much power was drawn from battery for radio." • "Intermittent loss of brakes while driving. Dealer has not been able to duplicate the problem." • "Pulls hard to the right when brakes applied; dealer aligned, tightened idler arm, all to no avail." • "During brake application, pedal goes to the floor."

GMC SONOMA 1994

Complaint Severity: Typical. **Buyer's Summary:** Check the brakes—listen for noise, look for leaks and feel for vibration. They may fail, perform poorly or require frequent mechanical attention. Test the clutch. See "Sudden Accelerations" in Introduction.

Hot Spots and Owner/NHTSA Comments:

1. Brakes: hydraulic: anti-skid system, poor performance, failure, locking up. • "Antilock brakes are subject to intermittent failure, causing extended stopping. On other occasions, brakes make grinding sound while initiating right-hand turns." • "Antilock brake system failure; makes a loud noise when applying brakes; also, extended pedal fade; suspension system vibration in front causing wear of tires." • "Antilock brake system failed in dry weather; driving 25-30 mph, pressed on brake, heard a noise, car went through stop sign." • "Rear antilock brake system will continually lock in wet weather. Dealer has adjusted brakes several times with no change in condition." • "Antilock brakes failed, vehicle lost control, resulting in an accident and injuries."

2. Fuel: throttle linkages and control, sudden accelerations. • "While driving, throttle system stuck and antilock brake system failed; almost resulting in accident." • "Accelerator sticks, when going 55-65 mph with automatic transmission." • "Vehicle had sudden acceleration in drive and reverse; braking system did not operate with extreme hard pedal." • "Fuel emission systems causing high idle and engine acceleration."

3. Power train: clutch assembly, noise, difficulty shifting, stalling. • "Clutch assembly became inoperative while driving at 60 mph; made car come to complete halt." • "Clutch actuator has been replaced 3 times; vehicle stalling. Component made of plastic." • "Noise in rear of vehicle when shifting or braking." • "Clutch failed." • "Manual shift 5-speed; when clutch is depressed, vehicle will stall and lose all power."

GMC SUBURBAN 1989

Complaint Severity: Typical. **Recall Alert:** See Recall Index. **Buyer's Summary:** Check the brakes—listen for noise, look for leaks and feel for vibration. They may fail, perform poorly or require frequent mechanical attention.

Hot Spots and Owner/NHTSA Comments:

1. Brakes: hydraulic system, pulling, noise, malfunction. • "Brake pedal very spongy; under heavy application cannot lock wheels on dry pavement." • "Brakes pull to right; making noises." • "Brakes malfunctioning; vehicle drifts to right when braking hard on flat road." • "Load-adjusting rear brake system trips over bumps, causing excessive brake wear." • "Rotors failed."

2. Interior systems: bucket: backrest, breaking, malfunction. • "When entering and sitting on driver seat, the seat back fell backwards." • "Driver's seat back collapsed 3 times, causing injury." • "Bolts holding seat back in place broke, causing seat to collapse." • "Driver's seat back bolt broke, causing seat back to fall backward, resulting in injuries." • "Bucket seat back bolt broke, throwing driver into prone position."

GMC SUBURBAN 1993

Complaint Severity: Serious. **Buyer's Summary:** Check the brakes—listen for noise, look for leaks and feel for vibration. They may fail, perform poorly or require frequent mechanical attention.

Hot Spots and Owner/NHTSA Comments:

1. Brakes: hydraulic: anti-skid system, poor performance, failure, locking up. • "Antilock brake system does not stop vehicle. Brakes are applied and vehicle slows but does not stop. Driver slid through intersection." • "Antilock brake system: When coming to a complete stop, experienced pedal fading. To avoid accident, ran off highway." • "Car did a 360, then a 180 and came to a complete stop. The tire fell off. Antilock brake system malfunction, causing a lockup." • "Antilock brake system failed; caused extended stopping; resulted in rear-end collision; speed 15 mph." •

"Antilock brake system: On numerous occasions, brakes fail to respond upon application; on wet surface, driver maneuvered to avoid rear-end collision."

2. Brakes: hydraulic system, poor performance, failure. • "Brakes perform erratically." • "Periodically, brake pedal has to be pushed to the floor to stop." • "Have to use extreme effort to stop vehicle; brakes are locking up." • "Upon applying brakes, pedal went to the floor." • "Brake failure; extended stopping distance."

GMC SUBURBAN 1994

Complaint Severity: Typical. **Buyer's Summary:** Check the brakes—listen for noise, look for leaks and feel for vibration. They may fail, perform poorly or require frequent mechanical attention.

Hot Spots and Owner/NHTSA Comments:

1. Brakes: hydraulic: anti-skid system, poor performance, failure, locking up. • "Vehicle's antilock brake system is causing excessive wear of pads and equipment, especially the right-hand side." • "Antilock-brake car has 3,000 miles; was driving, trying to stop, pedal went down to the floor, pushed up and pressed down, car stopped; damaged passenger-side mirror." • "Antilock brakes failed, causing brakes to lock and vehicle to skid." • "Antilock brake system: When braking at hard stop, vehicle keeps on rolling; vehicle too heavy for brake design."

2. Interior systems: active restraints: belt retractors, failure. • "Front seat belt retractors failed." • "Seat belt retractors failed." • "Driver and passenger lap and shoulder seat belts will not retract." • "Both front seat belts do not retract." • "Seat belt shoulder harness will not retract. This is the second incident."

3. Brakes: hydraulic system, pulling, premature failure. • "Brakes pull to the right; also, pedal fades out intermittently; disabled antilock brake system to no avail." • "Intermittent brake failures after repairs, causing loss of control; 1 accident and injuries." • "When applying the brakes, pedal goes to the floor." • "The brakes have failed all around on the vehicle, which is 5 months old with 20,000 miles." • "Brakes failed 3 times; once resulting in an accident."

4. Brakes: hydraulic: shoe: disc brake system, locking up, vibration. • "At 7 mph or less, the front wheel locked up when braking." • "Warped front brake calipers, pads and rotors, causing vehicle to vibrate upon braking." • "When brakes are applied, front right wheel locks up." • "Antilock brake system in low speed has front wheel lockup occur on dry and wet pavement." • "Antilock brakes are locking up, front left or right (or both). GMC and dealer can't fix."

Honda

HONDA ACCORD 1987

Complaint Severity: Dangerous (Worst 3% in Guide). **Theft Alert:** 41. **Recall Alert:** See Recall Index. **Buyer's Summary:** Check the brakes—listen for noise, look for leaks and feel for vibration. They may fail, perform poorly or require frequent mechanical attention. Test the transmission thoroughly. See "Sudden Accelerations" in Introduction.

Hot Spots and Owner/NHTSA Comments:

1. Fuel: throttle linkages and control, sudden accelerations. • "When put in gear, vehicle spontaneously accelerated, slamming into a cement wall; brakes failed." • "Upon parking, shifted in reverse position with foot on brake, car suddenly accelerated by itself; resulted in accident." • "Upon putting car in reverse and proceeding to back up, vehicle suddenly accelerated out of control with no braking response, resulting in accident." • "Vehicle started, gear placed in reverse, unexplained acceleration propelled car out of garage into a fence." • "Started car, foot on brake, placed gear in reverse, suddenly accelerated, car raced out of control; collision."

2. Brakes: hydraulic system, vibration, poor performance. • "Vibration while braking." • "Brakes do not respond properly; extended stopping distance." • "Brake failure due to poorly designed brake cylinders." • "When braking at stops, red lights and curves, vehicle vibrates." • "Severe vibration from braking experienced."

3. Interior systems: active restraints: belt buckles, breaking, malfunction. • "Driver's seat belt release button broke; seat belt does not latch." • "Right front seat belt buckle released latch plate on several occasions." • "Driver's and passenger's manual seat belts buckle with difficulty. Dealer sprayed, and now they're easier to unfasten." • "Passenger shoulder and lap belt buckles inoperative; won't latch due to brittle plastic chips that have fallen inside." • "The driver's-side seat belt buckle broke."

4. Fuel: fuel tank assembly: pipe: filler: neck, corrosion, failure. • "Rust developed on filler neck; chipping of metal in fuel tank could cause stalling problems." • "Fuel filler pipe: Manufacturer says notification in a few months; it's been 10 months. Recall related." • "Fuel filler pipe failed, prior to recall." • "Fuel filler pipe was sprayed, not replaced, to repair corrosion. Recall related." • "Gasoline filler tube broke and was replaced."

5. Power train: transmission: automatic, poor performance, difficulty shifting, slipping. • "Stopped vehicle in garage, turned off the ignition and took out key, left gear in drive; vehicle rolled into driveway." • "Spring on gear selector is weak, allows transmission to slip into reverse if engine started with selector partially out of park." • "Vehicle jumping gear from neutral to reverse, then accelerating out of control." • "Transmission gear selector malfunction caused unintended acceleration; accident." • "Shifting from reverse to park causes a grinding noise."

6. Brakes: hydraulic: shoe: disc brake system, vibration, excessive wear. • "Brakes; front disc repaired twice (not to owner's satisfaction), mechanic says brakes are defective but Honda won't replace them." • "Brakes started grabbing, which sounded like metallic pads were gone; steel brake pad plate grinding rotor." • "Pulsation in steering wheel when braking at highway speeds; rotors out of round." • "Excessive brake wear; repaired/replaced rotors and pads." • "Brakes prematurely worn at 19,000 miles, front disc brakes at 23,482."

HONDA ACCORD 1988

Complaint Severity: Dangerous (Worst 3% in Guide). **Theft Alert:** 4. **Recall Alert:** See Recall Index. **Buyer's Summary:** Check the brakes—listen for noise, look for leaks and feel for vibration. They may fail, perform poorly or require frequent mechanical attention. Test the transmission thoroughly. See "Sudden Accelerations" in Introduction.

Hot Spots and Owner/NHTSA Comments:

1. Fuel: throttle linkages and control, sudden accelerations. • "Without warning, vehicle suddenly accelerated out of control and hit a house." • "After shifting gear into park, vehicle accelerated and surged forward at very high speed without prior warning." • "Parked vehicle in driveway and shifted gear into park, vehicle suddenly accelerated backwards approximately 30 feet; driver suffered injuries." • "Upon starting car, foot on brake, shift in reverse, car surged backward; sudden acceleration; braked hard to stop." • "Started engine, foot on brakes, shifted into reverse, vehicle suddenly accelerated, brakes failed; collision occurred."

2. Brakes: hydraulic system, noise, excessive wear, poor performance. • "Upon brake application, brakes chatter, steering shudders." • "Brakes squeal and grind on heavy braking." • "Brakes squeak and make grinding noise." • "Spongy brakes; premature wear." • "When depressing brake pedal, a knocking or clunking sound is audible; also felt in brake system, same sounds when pedal released."

3. Power train: transmission: automatic, poor performance, difficulty shifting, slipping. • "Transmission jumps from park to reverse while unattended." • "Changed gears to reverse vehicle, but vehicle jerked into drive and then again into reverse, impact 6:00 position, speed unknown." • "Rolls after placed in park and parking brake applied." • "Extended time shifting from 1st to 2nd." • "Transmission has clunking noise when shifting from park into reverse."

4. Interior systems: active restraints: belt buckles, malfunction, failure. • "The driver's-side seat belt doesn't lock; comes out when driving." • "Driver and passenger shoulder and lap belts; male won't click into female; also, rear center lap belt comes undone." • "The car was in an accident where the driver's shoulder harness did not restrain him; therefore he hit the window and now has seizures due to injury." • "The front and passenger-side seat belt buckles are not working." • "Experiences difficulty in latching front passenger lap and shoulder harness buckle."

5. Brakes: hydraulic: shoe: disc brake system, noise, vibration, excessive wear. • "When brakes are applied, front end of car shakes." • "Brakes are noisy and vibrate when applied." • "Upon applying the brakes, experienced vibration; told by dealer that rotors were worn out and needed replacement; after replacement, vibration continued." • "Hard braking conditions resulted in wheel vibrations and extended braking distances." • "Premature wear of front brakes increased stoppage distance."

6. Brakes: hydraulic: disc: rotor: disc hub, premature failure. • "Rotors warping every 1,500 miles (3 times) and at 3,000 miles (1 time), causing longer stopping distance, vibration of steering wheel and fading of brakes." • "Warped front brake rotors; repaired/replaced." • "Brake rotors warped after replacement." • "Rotors resurfaced 3 times within 33,000 miles." • "Premature warping of brake rotors."

HONDA ACCORD 1989

Complaint Severity: Typical. **Theft Alert:** 15. **Recall Alert:** See Recall Index. **Buyer's Summary:** Verify that the cruise control system works properly, and that it doesn't cause the engine to surge. Check the brakes—listen for noise, look for leaks and feel for vibration. They may fail, perform poorly or require frequent mechanical attention. Test the transmission thoroughly. See "Sudden Accelerations" in Introduction.

Hot Spots and Owner/NHTSA Comments:

1. Brakes: hydraulic system, excessive wear, noise, poor performance. • "Vehicle shimmies when applying the brakes." • "Premature brake wear." • "Brakes bad; constant squeaking; also, fluid leaks in front." • "Inadequate braking performance." • "Brakes squeaked a few months after purchase; repaired/replaced, problem still exists; unsatisfied with brake performance." • "Brakes malfunctioned, couldn't stop vehicle; resulted in an accident."

2. Fuel: throttle linkages and control, sudden accelerations. • "Vehicle suddenly accelerated, it was like accelerator hung wide open; applied brakes to no avail; resulted in accident." • "Apparent throttle sticking, causing vehicle to suddenly accelerate and resulting in accident." • "Put car in drive and drove slowly to reach main highway; as entered highway, vehicle suddenly took off by itself." • "Alleged engine surging while parking resulted in frontal damage; no injuries." • "Coming to an intersection, applied brakes, vehicle surged forward." • "Had a accident because of sudden acceleration; problem is recurring."

3. Power train: transmission: automatic, poor performance, difficulty shifting, slipping. • "Governor assembly broke in half." • "Transmission lurches at speed of 10 mph, resulting in accident." • "Transmission slippage, resulting from fluid overheating, caused unsafe vehicle control." • "Transmission malfunctioned; car parked on 20 percent grade, hand brake not on, car moved backward even though shift engaged in park; caused accident." • "Automatic transmission suddenly ceased to operate; new transmission installed."

4. Electrical system: battery, failure. • "Battery defective upon purchase." • "Battery replaced under warranty." • "Faulty battery in the electrical system." • "Defective battery; failed." • "Battery failed."

5. Interior systems: active restraints: belt retractors, failure. • "Seat belt retractors failed." • "Door-mounted shoulder belt does not retract into door if unbuckled." • "The driver's-side seat belt retractor sometimes retracts halfway; it is a slow process." • "Seat belt spontaneously releases." • "Seat belts don't retract, causing metal connector to catch between the door; caused severe door panel damage."

6. Equipment: speed control, malfunction, failure. • "Cruise control does not always hold, especially going uphill." • "Speed cruise control exceeds preset speed by 3-5 mph after negotiating a hill or crest on the road." • "Cruise control will not hold its speed, varies constantly 2 to 3 miles per hour in 30-second intervals." • "Cruise control didn't disengage when brakes were applied; car experienced sudden acceleration, which resulted in accident." • "While driving along a highway at 55 mph with cruise control on, coming into traffic, hit brakes, but cruise control did not disengage; caused an accident."

HONDA ACCORD 1990

Complaint Severity: Typical. **Theft Alert:** EX, 9; LX, 30. **Recall Alert:** See Recall Index. **Buyer's Summary:** Check the brakes—listen for noise, look for leaks and feel for vibration. They may fail, perform poorly or require frequent mechanical attention. Test the transmission thoroughly. Make sure seat belts function correctly and fit comfortably. See "Sudden Accelerations" in Introduction.

Hot Spots and Owner/NHTSA Comments:

1. Power train: transmission: automatic, poor performance, difficulty shifting, slipping. • "When placed in gear, does not engage until you hit accelerator." • "Experiencing delay from reverse to drive." • "Problem with transmission delay in shifting when going from park to drive or reverse." • "Transmission hard to place into reverse." • "Hesitation on shifting gears."

2. Structure: door assembly: latches and locks, malfunction, failure. • "Ninety-five percent of time occupant can't get out from driver's front door because of a faulty door lock actuator." • "Passenger-side front door does not open due to disconnected latch." • "Driver's-side door, once closed, could not be opened; dealer had to remove door panel and replace response parts." • "Driver's-side door lock failed to unlock." • "Driver's-side door lock mechanism has failed; locked."

3. Interior systems: passive restraint: belts, uncomfortable, failure. • "Automatic passive restraint seat belt dangerous to short persons; cuts across neck instead of shoulder." • "After being struck from behind, passive restraint started to tighten up, thus pinning driver to seat; tension generated, system jammed and driver unable to exit car for minutes." • "Driver's seat belt locks, fails to release." • "Driver's-side seat belt gets stuck on track;

chokes driver." • "Faulty seat belts fit very poorly; have to release emergency release to prevent crushing occupant."

4. Brakes: hydraulic system, poor performance, locking up, noise. • "Performance of brakes poor; feel soft and sluggish." • "Both rear brake cylinders leaking." • "Continuous warping of brakes; brakes have been repaired 3 times." • "Brakes lock up intermittently." • "Noisy brakes; serviced twice, problem continues."

5. Electrical system: ignition: distributor, stalling, failure. • "Ignition distributor failed and showed signs of melting. Vehicle would stall with no warning." • "Igniter within distributor died while driving 35 mph; no warning." • "Igniter unit in distributor failed." • "Igniter malfunctioned, causing vehicle to stall." • "Several instances of electronic igniter failure with engine stalling in traffic, causing threat of collision."

6. Fuel: throttle linkages and control, sudden accelerations. • "Car was in drive; accelerated on its own, crashed; put in reverse and car accelerated again. Inspected; no faulty part identified." • "When backing vehicle out of driveway, vehicle went into open-throttle position; applied brakes, put into drive and went into sudden acceleration; no problem found." • "Vehicle surged backward, causing an accident." • "While driving, vehicle suddenly accelerated; resulted in an accident." • "Ten-minute drive, automatic transmission, 5 mph in drive, steering straight ahead, sudden acceleration; crashed the car into a pole and a parked car."

HONDA ACCORD 1991

Complaint Severity: Typical. **Theft Alert:** EX, 7; LX, 24. **Recall Alert:** See Recall Index. **Buyer's Summary:** Make sure the shoulder belts don't cut across your neck and are well anchored. Test the suspension by feeling for vibration or pulling while driving. Test the transmission thoroughly. Make sure seat belts function correctly and fit comfortably. Make sure air conditioner works properly.

Hot Spots and Owner/NHTSA Comments:

1. Power train: transmission: automatic, poor performance, difficulty shifting, slipping. • "Transmission would not engage in gear properly." • "Automatic transmission hesitates and causes a feeling of almost stalling." • "Transmission was replaced by dealer; 186 miles later, vehicle caught on fire; dealer states cause is unknown." • "Automatic transmission failed; stranded vehicle on rural road." • "Vehicle hesitates and lunges forward when put in drive."

2. Suspension: independent front, tire wear, alignment, vibration. • "Suspension is too light for vehicle, causing excessive wear on tires and misalignment." • "Left side front axle assembly is worn, and is causing steering and tire problems." • "Vehicle pulls to right." • "Poor alignment caused tire wear." • "Vehicle vibration over 55 mph."

3. Air conditioner: poor performance. • "Odor when air conditioner is on." • "Musty odor emitted through air conditioner." • "Odor coming from air conditioner." • "Air conditioner won't cool." • "Strong odor from air conditioner."

4. Interior systems: shoulder belts, uncomfortable, failure. • "Shoulder belt presses against driver's neck, making it very uncomfortable; poorly designed." • "Automatic shoulder belts activate intermittently; tighten when turning off car." • "Shoulder belt too tight on driver." • "Shoulder and lap belts failed in accident." • "Shoulder harness cuts across neck area."

5. Interior systems: passive restraint: belts, malfunction, failure. • "Passive restraint; motorized shoulder belt jammed and locked against passenger's chest; breathing was impaired." • "Vehicle was at complete stop, impact 6:00 position, lap and shoulder belt overretracted, trapping the driver in the seat." • "The seat belt retractor light comes on and keeps beeping, even though seat belt is buckled—when unbuckled, it should only beep 6 seconds; the beep will not stop." • "Passenger's motorized shoulder belt stuck in sun visor. This prevented occupant from exiting." • "Driver's seat belt failed in accident, causing injury."

6. Electrical system: ignition, premature failure. • "Vehicle shuts down when driving at any speed, or while idling, due to electrical short. Rattling noise in front of vehicle." • "Vehicle periodically shuts down when driving at any speed." • "Distributor failures." • "Car won't start on occasion due to ignition problem." • "Distributor replaced."

HONDA ACCORD 1992

Complaint Severity: Very Serious. **Theft Alert:** EX, 9; LX, 13. **Recall Alert:** See Recall Index. **Buyer's Summary:** Make sure the shoulder belts don't cut across your neck and are well anchored. The airbags in this vehicle have experienced failures and malfunctions: You may need a professional evaluation on the condition of the airbags. Check the brakes—listen for noise, look for leaks and feel for vibration. They may fail, perform poorly or require frequent mechanical attention. Test the transmission thoroughly. See "Sudden Accelerations" in Introduction.

Hot Spots and Owner/NHTSA Comments:

1. Fuel: throttle linkages and control, sudden accelerations. • "Foot on brake, pulled into parking space, vehicle surged forward at high speed. This is the fifth occurrence. Also, airbag failed to deploy." • "Engine accelerated while slowing down to park; vehicle rear-ended a parked vehicle; impact 12:00 position; speed 3 mph." • "Vehicle suddenly accelerates when trying to hold at steady pace. Vehicle jerks forward and is hard to control. Replaced throttle body, but it did not help." • "Engine accelerated from 5 to 30 mph while entering parking lot; brakes applied; vehicle surged forward, hitting wire fence; heard roaring sound from engine." • "Owner had vehicle in neutral, idling, his foot on brake, vehicle suddenly accelerated by itself. Airbag deployed."

2. Power train: transmission: automatic, poor performance, difficulty shifting, slipping. • "At 55 mph on highway, experienced transmission failure; suddenly vehicle began to lose power and decelerated; upon pressing gas pedal there was no response." • "The transmission went out after 42,000 miles." • "Loose transmission cable, causing constant engagement and disengagement of the lockup torque converter." • "While driving car at 30 mph, gear shifted into neutral." • "Transmission case cracked, causing oil leak."

3. Brakes: hydraulic system, noise, failure. • "Loss of brake effectiveness without warning resulted in a frontal accident." • "Brakes make squeaking noise." • "Vehicle experienced extreme brake problems; brakes squeak and had difficulty stopping vehicle; was told by dealer this was typical of Honda vehicles." • "While driving, brakes failed completely and pedal went to floor twice." • "Frontal collision, impact 11:00 position, hit cement curb, caused by the loss of brake effectiveness with pedal fading, speed 20 mph. Airbag failed to deploy."

4. Interior systems: passive restraint: airbag, failure. • "Frontal collision, impact 12:00 position, speed 40 mph. Hitting another vehicle. Airbag did not deploy." • "Airbag failed to deploy during front-end collision at 35 mph into another vehicle at 12:00. Resulted in injuries to driver." • "Airbag did not deploy during accident." • "Airbag did not deploy."

5. Interior systems: shoulder belts, failure. • "Had a head-on collision; seat belts did not restrain occupants." • "Airbag did not deploy and seat belts did not restrain in collision." • "Airbag did not deploy during frontal crash; impact 12:00 position; speed 35 mph; rear-ended another vehicle that stopped abruptly. Also,

shoulder harness did not hold." • "The driver's seat belt (material) was broken when involved in an accident; it broke from impact." • "Vehicle was impacted at 6:00 position; vehicle was at complete stop, driver's-side lap and shoulder belt failed."
6. Interior systems: passive restraint: airbag: driver, malfunction, failure. • "Frontal collision, impact 10:00 position; lost control, hitting a light pole; lap and shoulder belt did not restrain and airbag did not deploy at 40-45 mph." • "Airbag did not deploy during front-end collision; vehicle rear-ended another vehicle; skid marks 10-12 feet; impact 12:00 position; speed 25 mph." • "Airbag did not deploy during frontal collision. Impact 1:00, speed 25 mph. Car 2 hit car 1 on right rear; car 1 lost control, hit concrete median." • "Upon impact, during frontal crash at approximately 70 mph, 10:00 position on front bumper, airbag failed to deploy." • "When rear-ended by minivan, vehicle was pushed forward with force into vehicle in front. No airbag deployment. Driver received stomach and leg bruises."

HONDA ACCORD 1993

Complaint Severity: Dangerous (Worst 3% in Guide). **Theft Alert:** SE, 32; LX, 48. **Recall Alert:** See Recall Index. **Buyer's Summary:** Make sure the shoulder belts don't cut across your neck and are well anchored. Test the suspension by feeling for vibration or pulling while driving. The airbags in this vehicle have experienced failures and malfunctions: You may need a professional evaluation on the condition of the airbags. Check the brakes—listen for noise, look for leaks, feel for vibration. They may fail, perform poorly or require frequent mechanical attention. See "Sudden Accelerations" in Introduction.

Hot Spots and Owner/NHTSA Comments:
1. Fuel: throttle linkages and control, sudden accelerations. • "While parking, vehicle began to accelerate until out of control, going through store window. No airbag deployment." • "Vehicle was at complete stop, with engine idling; when put in gear, vehicle jerked forward real hard, hitting guardrail; impact 12:00 position, no airbag deployment." • "Vehicle will not accelerate in moving traffic; pushing accelerator hard, vehicle suddenly accelerated, which caused the vehicle to skid." • "Engine will intermittently stall and stumble, followed by sudden acceleration strong enough to spin the tires. Dealer cannot replicate situation." • "Sudden acceleration, resulting in an accident."
2. Brakes: hydraulic: anti-skid system, poor performance, failure, locking up. • "Antilock brake system failed to stop vehicle when driver applied brakes." • "Antilock brake system: When coming to complete stop, vehicle appears to go into antilock brake system; no braking effect on wet or dry pavement." • "Antilock brake system failed." • "Applied brake pedal; went to the floor with no response from antilock brakes. Also, airbag did not deploy." • "Antilock brake system did not stop vehicle."
3. Interior systems: shoulder belts, malfunction, failure. • "Shoulder belt failed during accident, causing injuries." • "Clunk is heard when vehicle is being turned either left or right. There is condensation building up in the turn signal area. Seat belt fails to lock on driver's-side." • "Driver's-side shoulder harness and lap belt detached during front-end collision at 60 mph, causing driver to spring forward, hitting knee. Airbag did deploy." • "Vehicle was involved in an accident and the front seat shoulder belts did not hold passengers; also, airbag failed to deploy." • "Front and rear seat belts failed to hold driver and passengers in position during collision, causing injuries."
4. Interior systems: passive restraint: airbag, malfunction, failure. • "While traveling at estimated speed of 35 mph, vehicle had frontal collision. Airbag did not deploy on driver's or on passenger's side." • "Both driver's and passenger's airbags deployed prematurely when tire hit curb, causing driver to lose control." • "Hit brakes to avoid a car; brakes failed. Had an accident. Airbag did not deploy." • "Airbag did not deploy."
5. Suspension: independent front, pulling, vibration, alignment. • "Steering pulls to the extreme left when doing 50 mph or more." • "Alignment problems." • "Vehicle vibrates excessively." • "Vehicle shimmies or shakes when driving over 50 mph. Vehicle shuts down when driving at 50-60 mph." • "Vehicle vibrates while stopping at red light or stop sign."
6. Interior systems: passive restraint: airbag: driver, malfunction, failure. • "In a single-car wreck, driver's-side airbag did not deploy." • "Driver's airbag failed to deploy upon impact." • "Consumer was in a front-end collision and the driver's-side airbag didn't deploy." • "Frontal collision, impact 12:00 position, speed 50 mph, airbag did not deploy." • "While parking, vehicle began to accelerate until out of control, going through store window. No airbag deployment."

HONDA ACCORD 1994

Complaint Severity: Serious. **Theft Alert:** EX, 1; LX, 29. **Recall Alert:** See Recall Index. **Buyer's Summary:** The airbags in this vehicle have experienced failures and malfunctions: You may need a professional evaluation on the condition of the airbags. Check the brakes—listen for noise, look for leaks, feel for vibration. They may fail, perform poorly or require frequent mechanical attention. Test the transmission thoroughly. See "Sudden Accelerations" in Introduction.

Hot Spots and Owner/NHTSA Comments:
1. Fuel: throttle linkages and control, sudden accelerations. • "Experienced sudden acceleration after slowing vehicle down by applying brakes." • "Upon acceleration from a stop or low speed, vehicle would idle and/or coast at low speed while accelerator remained depressed." • "Car lurched forward while attempting to drive." • "Pulling in a parking space in parking garage, car accelerated and hit a wall."
2. Power train: transmission: automatic, poor performance, difficulty shifting, slipping. • "From park to drive or reverse gear, transmission hesitates as if in neutral; also, driving 65 mph, suddenly transmission decelerates without prior warning." • "Transmission has extreme delay when shifting from park into drive or reverse gear." • "Transmission jerks when vehicle takes off." • "Vehicle does not engage when put in drive for about 5 seconds; also, loses speed on freeways, dropping from 55 to 30 mph." • "Transmission shifts quickly from 3rd gear to 4th gear after long hesitation between 2nd/3rd gears."
3. Interior systems: passive restraint: airbag: driver, malfunction, failure. • "Right front tire blew and vehicle rolled over; airbag did not deploy." • "Frontal collision, impact 12:00 position, speed 40 mph, airbag on driver's side did not deploy." • "Vehicle was involved in a frontal collision; driver's airbag deployed. Gases in airbags filled passenger compartment, making it difficult to see and breathe." • "In 11:00 position at 60 mph, driver's-side airbag did not deploy; impact was above bumper level." • "Airbag did not deploy during front-end collision at 30 mph. No injuries."
4. Interior systems: passive restraint: airbag: passenger, failure. • "In 11:00 position at 60 mph, passenger-side airbag did not deploy; impact was above bumper level." • "Passenger's airbag did not deploy after hitting a tree." • "At 12:00 position at 40 mph, passenger airbag did not deploy due to underride." • "Driving about 30 mph in the snow, hit a person and passenger airbag didn't deploy." • "No deployment of passenger's airbag during accident."
5. Brakes: hydraulic system, excessive wear, noise, failure. • "Electrical wiring to rear wheels was too short and broke, causing brakes to fail; also, after repairs brakes grabbed." • "Premature

wear of brakes." • "Brakes failed twice; once resulting in an accident." • "When trying to stop, the brake pedal goes to the floor." • "Noisy brakes."
6. Brakes: hydraulic: anti-skid system, poor performance, failure, locking up. • "Purchased car 7 months ago; had to change the brake calipers and disc rotor twice in 7 months and car is still not working properly." • "Antilock brake failure." • "Premature wear of antilock brakes." • "Antilock brake light comes on; also, leak under chassis." • "Antilock brake system failed to stop when applied, causing loss of vehicle control."

HONDA CIVIC 1987

Complaint Severity: Very Serious. **Recall Alert:** See Recall Index. **Buyer's Summary:** Check the brakes—listen for noise, look for leaks and feel for vibration. They may fail, perform poorly or require frequent mechanical attention. Test the transmission thoroughly. See "Sudden Accelerations" in Introduction.

Hot Spots and Owner/NHTSA Comments:
1. Fuel: fuel systems, sudden acceleration, hesitation, fire. • "Sudden acceleration while vehicle is in park gear." • "Six occurrences of sudden acceleration, finally resulting in accident; cause unknown." • "Engine hesitates to start when cold." • "While warming up car, engine caught on fire; caused a death."
2. Fuel: throttle linkages and control, sudden accelerations. • "Sudden acceleration occurred frequently, eventually resulting in an accident; poor performance of throttle linkages and controls." • "Vehicle suffered sudden acceleration and loss of control when shifted into reverse; an accident resulted with extensive damage." • "Pulled into parking space, car suddenly accelerated forward, jumped curb and hit utility pole." • "Upon starting car and shifting gear to reverse, immediately accelerated uncontrollably in reverse, striking tree." • "When shifter placed in reverse, vehicle suddenly accelerated out of control, resulting in accident."
3. Interior systems: active restraints: belt buckles, malfunction, failure. • "Left rear seat belt seems to be locked, but it comes unfastened." • "Rear left seat belt buckle loose." • "Seat belt buckle failed during an accident, resulting in an injury; prior to recall." • "The driver's-side seat belt buckle, when locked, comes loose." • "Driver's-side impact caused passenger's seat belt buckle and infant car seat to fail, resulting in ejection."
4. Brakes: hydraulic system, failure. • "Two accidents happened as a result of inferior brakes." • "Brakes went bad due to failure of warranted parts; front pads and rotors turned, and back brake shoes." • "While backing up in reverse position, engine suddenly surged then accelerated out of control, hitting 2 other vehicles; foot was on brake pedal." • "Brakes inoperative when hot or cold, pedal sinks to floor; accident."
5. Interior systems: seat tracks and anchors, breaking, poor performance. • "Seat dislodged from mountings while putting pressure against foot brake and seat to stop acceleration." • "Driver's seat base broke; metal frame that attaches to the sliding seat rail broke away from the nut flange by which it is attached." • "Driver's seat anchors repaired." • "Right front seat lever spring, which holds the lever down and keeps the seat from moving, broke, allowing the seat to move freely." • "Seat bottom broke from the seat track mounts. Seat wobbles and slides during braking."
6. Power train: transmission: automatic, poor performance, difficulty shifting, slipping. • "Transmission failed twice." • "Transmission oil leak." • "Transmission popped out of reverse, into drive; this occurred as a result of an accident."

HONDA CIVIC 1988

Complaint Severity: Troublesome. **Recall Alert:** See Recall Index. **Buyer's Summary:** The electronic control unit has been blamed for engine performance problems, including stalling and surging. The fuel injection system has been blamed for hesitation and stalling. Be sure the vehicle doesn't die in traffic or at stops. Check the brakes—listen for noise, look for leaks and feel for vibration. They may fail, perform poorly or require frequent mechanical attention. Test the transmission thoroughly. See "Sudden Accelerations" in Introduction.

Hot Spots and Owner/NHTSA Comments:
1. Fuel: fuel injection system, stalling, hesitation. • "Continual engine stalling problem; when put in neutral or after starting, rough idling when stopped for lights; sometimes lunges slightly at intersection." • "Poor acceleration with or without air conditioner on, more pronounced when air conditioner in use; engine stalls intermittently." • "Defect in fuel injection system; gas fumes." • "Engine would not idle right; stalled in intersections, occasionally speeds up at stop." • "Defect in emission valve in fuel injection system; vehicle accelerates on its own, then cuts off completely."
2. Electrical system: ignition: electronic control unit, stalling, failure. • "Vehicle would stall for no apparent reason." • "Vehicle suddenly raced while at light; replaced electronic computer unit." • "Computer failure." • "Ignition control module failed while driving 40 mph. Lost all power." • "Failure of ignition control module causes sudden stalling; engine will not start back up; no warning; could cause an accident."
3. Power train: transmission: automatic, poor performance, difficulty shifting, slipping. • "From curb, car shifted itself from park to reverse and throttle went open; car suddenly crashed into a rearward object." • "Car moves forward uphill in neutral after sitting overnight; condition experienced when cold is not abnormal due to close tolerances inside the transmission." • "Key can be removed from transmission even though car is still in drive." • "Vehicle stuck in snow; rocked vehicle from drive to reverse to get out, causing reverse gear to break." • "Vehicle slips out of 1st gear when on incline." • "Ignition can be turned off without automatic transmission in parked position."
4. Brakes: hydraulic system, excessive wear, vibration, failure. • "Repeated rotor warping." • "Excessive wear on front brakes." • "Brakes hanging and/or grabbing, then vibration." • "Brake failure; caused vehicle to impact rear of stopped truck." • "Vehicle fails to come to a complete stop when brakes applied."
5. Brakes: hydraulic: disc: rotor: disc hub, excessive wear, vibration. • "Defect in braking system; rotors warped at 14,000 miles of use." • "Front brake rotors resurfaced because of excessive runout and pulsating pedal; problem recurred and causes increased pedal travel." • "Both front brake rotors wore out prematurely due to inferior alloys that manufacturer incorporated into metal cast." • "Defective rotors cause car to vibrate on braking at highway speed." • "Excessive front rotor wear; also, vibration when brakes are engaged."
6. Fuel: throttle linkages and control, sudden accelerations. • "Placed gearshift in drive, car accelerated into brick wall; no control over acceleration." • "Upon shifting into reverse and then into drive, vehicle suddenly accelerated out of control; caused an accident that resulted in injury and property damage." • "Vehicle will intermittently increase in speed without touching accelerator pedal. Temperature sensor replaced." • "When vehicle is at stop or idling, vehicle suddenly accelerates and surges forward." • "Vehicle exhibits high idling condition, causing the vehicle to surge."

HONDA CIVIC 1989

Complaint Severity: Typical. **Recall Alert:** See Recall Index. **Buyer's Summary:** The fuel injection system has been blamed for hesitation and stalling. Be sure the vehicle doesn't die in traffic or at stops. Test the suspension by feeling for vibration or pulling while driving. Check the brakes—listen for noise, look for leaks and feel for vibration. They may fail, perform poorly or require frequent mechanical attention. See "Sudden Accelerations" in Introduction.

Hot Spots and Owner/NHTSA Comments:

1. Fuel: fuel injection system, stalling, hesitation. • "Vehicle stalls." • "Ignition failed." • "Recurring stalling problem in all weather conditions; all repair attempts to no avail, common problem with 1989 Hondas." • "Car began decelerating no matter how much gas pedal pushed until engine died; after 5 minutes, ran like normal." • "Fire in engine compartment; possible throttle problem."

2. Fuel: throttle linkages and control, sudden accelerations. • "Upon shifting gear into reverse and touching gas pedal lightly, vehicle accelerated out of control; after several minutes, vehicle decelerated and stopped." • "Vehicle suddenly accelerated when started, hit several cars while shift lever remained in park position." • "While parking the vehicle with foot on brake and shifting gear into park, vehicle lunged forward; hit a parked car in front." • "Vehicle was idling normally when put into park the first time. After getting back inside and shifting, vehicle accelerated, with brakes having minimum response." • "The accelerator stuck and the car went under the car in front."

3. Electrical system: battery, failure. • "Battery failed; needed replacement." • "Battery, original, needed replacement." • "Defective battery; repaired/replaced." • "Battery failed twice; replaced." • "Battery failed."

4. Suspension: independent front, alignment, tire wear. • "Misalignment causing excessive tire wear." • "Vehicle pulls to left; alignment performed but problem continues." • "While driving at about 48 mph, independent front-end suspension shimmy; repaired several times." • "Rapid tire wear, front tires; wheel alignment and/or suspension problem, type of tires unknown." • "Tire sidewall breakdown caused by alignment problem."

5. Brakes: hydraulic system, noise, premature failure. • "Vehicle was idling normally when put in park first time. After getting back inside and shifting, vehicle accelerated, with brakes having minimum response." • "Brakes failed twice while trying to stop the vehicle." • "Defective brakes." • "Brakes went out prematurely; accident." • "Noisy brakes."

6. Engine: stalling, failure. • "Oil plug threads stripped, causing plug to come out; loss of oil, causing engine failure." • "While driving at 50 mph, engine seized without prior warning." • " 'Check engine' light comes on; experienced power loss, car failed to run at expected speed; repaired/replaced sensor in engine system." • "Engine sounds like diesel, surges and/or stalls at times; repaired, problem reoccurred." • "Both ends of engine heat shield broke off."

HONDA CIVIC 1990

Complaint Severity: Typical. **Recall Alert:** See Recall Index. **Buyer's Summary:** Test the suspension by feeling for vibration or pulling while driving. Check the brakes—listen for noise, look for leaks and feel for vibration. They may fail, perform poorly or require frequent mechanical attention. Test the transmission thoroughly. Make sure seat belts function correctly and fit comfortably.

Hot Spots and Owner/NHTSA Comments:

1. Electrical system: ignition: distributor, stalling, failure. • "Since recall performed on igniter, vehicle is subject to severe stalling. Vehicle will start on some occasions." • "While driving down the freeway at high speed, igniter module went bad and car came to a complete stop." • "Igniter fails, causing the vehicle to stall without warning." • "After pulling out of parking lot onto street, engine quit without warning. Caused by defective igniter." • "Has problem starting vehicle; at times it would start right away, and sometimes it wouldn't start at all due to malfunctioning of igniter."

2. Suspension: independent front, alignment, tire wear. • "Vehicle misaligned, causing premature tire wear." • "Defective front-end suspension system caused 1 right front tire to go flat, and left to be worn; both problems occurred at 7,000 miles." • "Both wheels were out of alignment, wore to the thread, tire had a 1-inch slice on the inside." • "While driving at 50 mph, front suspension became noisy and began to vibrate, which resulted in loss of steering control and caused an accident." • "Uneven wear on tires due to a faulty suspension system."

3. Brakes: hydraulic system, noise, vibration, failure. • "Applied brakes to avoid rear-end collision, brakes failed, neither stopped or slowed down; unable to press brake pedal to maximum force." • "Brakes noisy; dealer uncooperative about repairs." • "Brakes too slow to avoid collision when applied." • "Vibrations in steering wheel and in brake pedal when applying brakes." • "Front brakes replaced due to wear."

4. Electrical system: ignition, stalling, failure. • "Ignition system malfunctioned 4 times; always had difficulty starting vehicle." • "Car is stalling when coming to a stop." • "Engine shuts off while driving down the road. Won't start again. Had recall on ignition done; problem started after that. Has intermittent electrical problem." • "Vehicle experienced restart problem after intermittent stalling." • "The ignition on vehicle cut out at highway speed. The catalytic converter became extremely hot, and insulation around fire wall caught on fire."

5. Interior systems: passive restraint: belts, malfunction, failure. • "Automatic seat belts failed to restrain passenger and driver from interior impact, resulting in chest injuries." • "In a head-on collision, door-mounted passive restraint did not lock upon impact; driver was not properly restrained and was thrust upon steering wheel." • "When door closed, automatic shoulder seat belt wouldn't move, leaving only the lap belt for protection." • "Motorized seat belts froze up in safety position." • "The automatic seat belt gets stuck in the front or rear of the track; does not tighten when the brakes are applied."

6. Power train: transmission: automatic, poor performance, difficulty shifting, slipping. • "Shift lock release fails to release transmission out of park unless brake pedal is depressed; to correct, restart car, placing gear in neutral with brake pedal depressed." • "Problem with loud whine in transmission." • "Transmission problems." • "Transmission does not engage when accelerating." • "Automatic transmission performance erratic; problem occurs in slowing down process, will downshift very hard, hard enough to cause passenger to jerk forward."

HONDA CIVIC 1991

Complaint Severity: Typical. **Theft Alert:** 34. **Recall Alert:** See Recall Index. **Buyer's Summary:** Check the brakes—listen for noise, look for leaks and feel for vibration. They may fail, perform poorly or require frequent mechanical attention. Make sure seat belts function correctly and fit comfortably.

Hot Spots and Owner/NHTSA Comments:

1. Interior systems: active restraints: belt buckles, breaking, malfunction. • "Upon impact, during side impact, rear lap and shoulder belt detached at buckle, allowing child safety seat to flip over." • "The passenger front seat belt latch part has broken and the pieces have fallen in." • "Driver seat belt buckle will not engage in lock position." • "Impact 3:00 position; passenger's passive shoulder belt released during collision." • "Shoulder belt buckle disengaged during side impact. Belt came apart as if door was opened and belt opened to allow consumer to exit."

2. Brakes: hydraulic system, noise, pulling. • "Car pulls to one side and shakes upon moderate application of brakes; resurfaced rotor, remedied problem for a short time." • "Vehicle experienced braking problems; brakes were noisy and squeaky." • "When applied, brakes make noise." • "Brakes failed and vehicle lost control; crashed against concrete median barriers and driver suffered multiple injuries." • "Noisy rear brakes."

3. Exhaust system: leaks. • "Tailpipe problem." • "Oxygen sensor failure." • "Strong exhaust fumes in passenger area of vehicle." • "Heat shields failed." • "Heat shield failed." • "Cabin of car fills up with exhaust fumes on long climbs up medium to steep hills or upon acceleration."

4. Interior systems: active seat and shoulder belts and belt anchor, malfunction, failure. • "Lap belt does not secure driver in seat; shoulder belt comes across chest." • "Passenger's 3-point safety belt replaced." • "Seat belt warning buzzer wouldn't go off after fastening; buckle replaced." • "Driver safety belt broke during accident, causing injury." • "Seat belt on driver's-side failed to connect and, as a result, was unusable."

5. Interior systems: passive restraint: belts, malfunction, failure. • "Descending a hill in 4th gear at 40 mph, vehicle fishtailed on icy road; front passenger automatic seat belt did not operate properly." • "Driver's-side seat belt failure." • "Automatic seat belt sticks in 'off' position." • "Injury received from passenger-side motorized seat belt buckle; finger lacerated." • "Waiting at stoplight for a green light, vehicle was sideswiped by car from left-hand side that crossed red light; automatic seat belt failed."

6. Brakes: hydraulic: disc: rotor: disc hub, excessive wear, vibration, noise. • "Premature brake wear; 2 times." • "Vibration in steering wheel when braking; rotors were resurfaced and vibration disappeared." • "Brake failure warping disc rotors in front; vehicle will pull very hard, causing wearing of pads and resulting in vibration." • "Noisy brakes; replaced rotors." • "Front brake rotors are warping; cause pulsation when braking and vibration in steering wheel."

HONDA CIVIC 1992

Complaint Severity: Dangerous (Worst 3% in Guide). **Recall Alert:** See Recall Index. **Buyer's Summary:** Test the suspension by feeling for vibration or pulling while driving. The airbags in this vehicle have experienced failures and malfunctions: You may need a professional evaluation on the condition of the airbags. Check the brakes—listen for noise, look for leaks and feel for vibration. They may fail, perform poorly or require frequent mechanical attention.

Hot Spots and Owner/NHTSA Comments:

1. Interior systems: passive restraint: airbag: driver, malfunction, failure. • "Upon accident, neither passenger's nor driver's airbag deployed." • "Vehicle was involved in a frontal collision and the airbag did not deploy." • "In course of a frontal collision, airbag failed to deploy; driver suffered injury and vehicle had extensive damage." • "Airbag did not deploy during a front-end collision at 25 mph into a pole." • "Airbag failed to deploy at 55 mph. Shoulder belt did not restrain driver from making contact with windshield and rearview mirror."

2. Brakes: hydraulic system, vibration, failure. • "Vehicle had complete brake loss; couldn't stop vehicle, it went out of control and hit a house." • "Pulsating brakes." • "Antilock brake system failure on wet road condition and pedal faded; also, slid when brakes were applied." • "Brakes failed, causing an accident, and airbag did not deploy; going at 45 mph, hit a vehicle from the rear." • "Brakes failed, causing accident."

3. Interior systems: passive restraint: airbag, failure. • "Airbag failed in accident." • "No deployment of airbag." • "No deployment of airbag during collision." • "Airbag did not deploy."

4. Steering: noise, stiffness, pulling. • "While driving at 45 mph, vehicle spun out of control, resulting in accident." • "Hard steering, squeaking noise. Dealer repaired properly." • "Hard steering, having to use excessive force to turn wheel, squeaking noise. Dealer refused to repair vehicle under warranty." • "Vehicle pulls to left when roads are wet."

5. Suspension: independent front, pulling. • "Suspension problem, causing car to drift." • "Upon making right turn, rear end swings around to left, causing accident and injury." • "Vehicle continually pulls to left." • "Constant veering motion and pulling to right in front end."

HONDA CIVIC 1993

Complaint Severity: Very Serious. **Recall Alert:** See Recall Index. **Buyer's Summary:** The airbags in this vehicle have experienced failures and malfunctions: You may need a professional evaluation on the condition of the airbags. Check the brakes—listen for noise, look for leaks and feel for vibration. They may fail, perform poorly or require frequent mechanical attention. Test the transmission thoroughly. See "Sudden Accelerations" in Introduction.

Hot Spots and Owner/NHTSA Comments:

1. Interior systems: passive restraint: airbag: driver, malfunction, failure. • "Airbag did not deploy during front-end impact; speed 35-40 mph; car 1 rear-ended car 2; impact 11:00 position." • "Upon impact, during frontal crash at approximately 30 mph, 2:00 position on front bumper, airbag failed to deploy." • "Vehicle had sudden acceleration and went through fence, hitting a retaining wall. Driver's-side airbag did not deploy." • "Car hit car in front at 35 mph. Airbag did not deploy." • "Downshifting vehicle into 3rd gear, vehicle shifted into 4th gear, impact 12:00 position, speed 35 mph; airbag did not deploy."

2. Brakes: hydraulic system, locking up, failure. • "Automatic transmission: Engine surged while pulling into parking space with brakes applied; vehicle went forward about 10 feet; hit fence; low speed; impact 11:00 position." • "Vehicle goes into sideways skid when brakes are applied on wet surfaces." • "Brake failed, vehicle went out of control, resulting in accident and injury." • "Vehicle was parked. Changed gears into reverse, experienced sudden acceleration with brakes applied; brakes would not stop vehicle." • "Brakes pull and are sluggish."

3. Fuel: throttle linkages and control, sudden accelerations. • "Vehicle was parked. Changed gears into reverse, experienced sudden acceleration with brakes applied; brakes would not stop vehicle." • "Driver pulled vehicle into parking space, went to straighten out vehicle and it suddenly accelerated. Emergency brake was used to stop vehicle." • "Slowed vehicle down to stop, frontal collision, impact 12:00 position, speed 30 mph; vehicle surged forward." • "Vehicle had sudden acceleration and went through fence, hitting a retaining wall. Driver's-side airbag did not deploy." • "Automatic transmission: Engine surged while pulling into parking space with brakes applied; vehicle went forward about 10 feet; hit fence; low speed; impact 11:00 position."

4. Steering: locking up, noise. • "While driving, steering locked up; had an accident." • "Steering locked up and made noise; took it to the dealer; they said it was fixed, but still having this problem." • "Difficulty in steering releasing." • "Loss of steering control while driving on highway; no prior warning; cause unknown; speed 65 mph; vehicle almost hit guardrail."

5. Interior systems: passive restraint: airbag, failure. • "Driver and passenger-side airbags did not deploy in front-end collision at 25 mph; vehicle crashed into another vehicle." • "No deployment of airbag during collision." • "Airbag failed to deploy."

• "Airbag did not inflate during accident, causing injury." • "Airbag did not deploy."
6. Power train: transmission: automatic, poor performance, difficulty shifting, slipping. • "Automatic transmission failed." • "Dipstick in the transmission was installed incorrectly, which damaged the transmission." • "Automatic transmission linkage clip failed, prior to recall." • "Transmission jerks and is rough when downshifting into 2nd and 4th gears." • "Transmission clip failed."

HONDA CIVIC 1994

Complaint Severity: Very Serious. **Recall Alert:** See Recall Index. **Buyer's Summary:** The airbags in this vehicle have experienced failures and malfunctions: You may need a professional evaluation on the condition of the airbags. Check the brakes—listen for noise, look for leaks and feel for vibration. They may fail, perform poorly or require frequent mechanical attention. See "Sudden Accelerations" in Introduction.

Hot Spots and Owner/NHTSA Comments:
1. Interior systems: passive restraint: airbag: driver, malfunction, failure. • "Airbags did not deploy upon head-on collision at 35 mph." • "Driver's-side airbag did not deploy upon frontal collision at 50 mph." • "Frontal collision, impact 12:00 position, speed 40 mph; airbag did not deploy." • "Driver's airbag did not deploy during frontal collision; rear-ended another vehicle; speed approximately 40 mph; impact 12:00 position." • "Frontal collision, impact 12:00 position, 35 mph; hitting another vehicle, airbag did not deploy on driver's side."
2. Interior systems: passive restraint: airbag: passenger, failure. • "Passenger's airbag did not deploy during rear-end collision; car rear-ended by another car while stopped; impact 5:00 position." • "Vehicle was involved in a frontal collision and passenger's airbag did not deploy." • "Passenger's airbag did not deploy during frontal collision; rear-ended another vehicle; speed approximately 40 mph; impact 12:00 position." • "At 12:00 position at standstill; hit car in front after being hit from behind at 40 mph; passenger's airbag failed to deploy, resulting in an injury."
3. Fuel: throttle linkages and control, sudden accelerations. • "Experienced sudden acceleration; vehicle went into open throttle position and high idle; to stop, put into low gear and emergency brake on; in for repair, no problem found." • "Vehicle suddenly accelerated from a stopped position while brake was engaged and transmission in park gear." • "After accelerating to pass, driver took foot off gas pedal. Vehicle continued to accelerate, even after braking. After gaining control, vehicle accelerated again." • "Throttle stuck in full-open position; brakes applied; driver heard roaring noise; vehicle collided with 4 other vehicles before stopping."
4. Brakes: hydraulic: anti-skid system, poor performance, failure, locking up. • "Antilock brake system: When applying, brakes will lock up. On 1 occasion driver lost control due to locking, having accident." • "Antilock brakes failed, causing loss of control, accident and injuries." • "Antilock brake system failure; rear cable sticking, causing vibration; also, pedal faded 4 times." • "Antilock brake system failed to stop vehicle with hard effort." • "Antilock brake system failed to stop vehicle effectively when applied, causing extended stopping distances on icy road at stop sign."
5. Brakes: hydraulic system, failure. • "Brakes did not stop vehicle." • "The brakes failed and caused an accident." • "Failure of braking system; when on wet surface, experienced brake lockup, impact 12:00 position." • "In rainy weather, driver applied brakes and vehicle would not stop. Driver slid through intersection, applied brakes and almost hit another vehicle; had accident."
6. Interior systems: passive restraint: airbag, failure. • "Airbag did not deploy." • "No deployment of airbag during accident, causing injury." • "No deployment of driver's or passenger's airbag during collision, causing injury." • "Dual airbags did not deploy."

HONDA PRELUDE 1988

Complaint Severity: Very Serious. **Recall Alert:** See Recall Index. **Buyer's Summary:** Look carefully for any kind of leakage, especially under the car. The steering may be stiff or not working correctly. Be sure to test the steering, especially on a cold start. Test the transmission thoroughly. See "Sudden Accelerations" in Introduction.

Hot Spots and Owner/NHTSA Comments:
1. Fuel: throttle linkages and control, sudden accelerations. • "Vehicle suddenly accelerated; once engaged in reverse with brakes on; resulted in hitting a tree; once stopped; gear was in 1st or 2nd." • "Accelerator pedal stuck behind pedal stop; applied full braking force to no avail traveling 60-70 mph; became airborne for 30 yards, landed in field." • "Upon changing gear from park to reverse, vehicle accelerated uncontrollably in reverse at approximately 80 mph, resulting in accident." • "Upon shifting gear into reverse and a second time into drive, vehicle suddenly accelerated out of control; hit a rock across driveway." • "Car accelerated in reverse; put in neutral, it accelerated forward; car didn't stop when brakes applied; control lost; accident resulted."
2. Power train: transmission: automatic, poor performance, difficulty shifting, slipping. • "Gear solenoid that electronically changes the gear failed; car was starting in 3rd and 4th gears; dealer put transmission together without mount bushing." • "Defective automatic transmission throttle valve; vehicle moves slowly regardless of pedal location; difficult changing gears, continues until downshift gear engaged." • "Problem with automatic transmission; when pulling onto highway, car very sluggish, does not pick up speed." • "Rebuilt transmission twice; slips when changing gears."
3. Power train: driveline universal joint: constant velocity, vibration, leaks, failure. • "Noticed vibration; needed left constant velocity joint; joint felt excessive play, saw lubrication leak of inner joint." • "Constant velocity joints failed, causing accident and injuries." • "Both front constant velocity boots ruptured." • "Both constant velocity joints failed simultaneously." • "Right and left outer constant velocity boots failed."
4. Interior systems: active restraints: belt buckles, malfunction, failure. • "Passenger-side seat belt unlatches by itself with no warning." • "Seat belt buckle failure on driver and passenger seats will not latch." • "Both front passenger- and driver's-side seat belt buckles sometimes lock up when using; hard to unlock." • "The driver's-side seat belt will not retract back when released; buckle is hard to lock; passenger seat belt warning whether it is locked or not." • "Seat belt buckle is broken (release button is broken)."
5. Steering: power assist: hose: fluid, leaks, fire, failure. • "Power steering hose failed." • "Power steering hose rests on manifold, causing a fire; prior to recall." • "Power steering fluid leaked onto manifold, causing a fire; prior to recall." • "Power steering hose cracked in several places; caused fluid to spill onto manifold and smoke."

Hyundai

HYUNDAI ELANTRA 1992

Complaint Severity: Typical. **Buyer's Summary:** Problems with the timing gear and chain can cause serious problems. Have the engine checked by a professional. Test the transmission thoroughly.

Hot Spots and Owner/NHTSA Comments:

1. Engine: timing gear and chain, breaking, failure. • "Timing belt came off retainer lip of oil pump sprocket, causing all valves to be bent." • "Timing belt was adjusted." • "Timing belt broken twice." • "Timing belt failed twice, causing engine to blow up." • "Timing belt broke from being dry and cracked."

2. Power train: transmission: automatic, poor performance, difficulty shifting, slipping. • "Vehicle would not move forward in drive gear; also, difficulty shifting from park to drive." • "While driving, gear downshifts to speed of 20 mph." • "Purchased as a demo, has 900 miles on it and the transmission blew." • "Automatic transmission failed." • "Transmission was jerking, had to have replaced twice. Inspected, only had one gear."

3. Electrical system: ignition, stalling, hesitation. • "Vehicle will stall at any speed." • "Vehicle hesitated due to a faulty ignition system." • "Vehicle will not start unless you lift hood and slam it shut." • "Vehicle warms up, experience stalling and racing of the motor; in for repair."

HYUNDAI EXCEL 1987

Complaint Severity: Troublesome. **Recall Alert:** See Recall Index. **Buyer's Summary:** The carburetion system could contribute to stalling and hesitation. Look carefully for any kind of leakage, especially under the car. Test the suspension by feeling for vibration or pulling while driving. Check the brakes—listen for noise, look for leaks and feel for vibration. They may fail, perform poorly or require frequent mechanical attention. Test the transmission thoroughly: Test transmission for slipping, locking up and performance.

Hot Spots and Owner/NHTSA Comments:

1. Power train: transmission: 5-speed and up, difficulty shifting, leaks. • "Transmission seized while shifting from 1st to 2nd gear. Car slid to a stop." • "Driver heard clicking noise; unintended decrease in speed; shifted to 1st gear; pulled to side of road; transmission fluid was leaking from under vehicle." • "While driving at 55 mph, manual 5-speed transmission failed, causing wheels to lock up; came to a halt." • "Manual transmission lockup while driving at 5 mph when shifting gears from 2nd to 1st."

2. Brakes: hydraulic system, poor performance, premature failure, pulling. • "Defective brakes; car would not stop on dry road, even when going only 10 to 15 mph or less; repaired/replaced." • "Poor performance of brakes; premature failure." • "Brakes failed when applied; had to put on brakes about 4 to 5 car distances away in order to stop at desired position." • "While driving, vehicle starting swerving side to side uncontrollably; eased off gas, touched brake lightly; car pulled left and hit guardrail." • "Brake problems; had to downshift with clutch to slow car, causing clutch to wear out."

3. Engine: leaks, fire. • "While driving, car suddenly lost power; smoke coming from engine, engine on fire; caused by oil leaking on hot engine parts." • "Oil pressure switch seal burst, causing no indication light to appear." • "Seal was leaking around oil sending unit, causing oil to be thrown back on exhaust system." • "Engine problems; oil and water leaking; overheating; repaired/replaced thermostat and radiator switch." • "Oil sending unit failed and oil spilled onto highway, causing engine to overheat and shut down."

4. Suspension: independent front, vibration, alignment. • "Vehicle's front suspension vibrates at moderate speeds, and vehicle intermittently pulls to right." • "Car began to veer to right; defect in suspension system." • "Front end misaligned; replaced right lower control arm and right ball joint, and realigned front end." • "Front end and dashboard vibrate at high speed; steering shimmies. Replaced constant velocity joints, balanced wheels, rotated tires." • "Front-end vibration between 50 and 60 mph; tires changed, balanced 3 times, aligned twice." • "Front-end vibration caused loss of steering, resulting in accident and death."

5. Power train: transmission: automatic, poor performance, difficulty shifting, slipping. • "Automatic floor transmission gearshift can be pushed through all gears while car in motion without depressing safety button on gearshift handle." • "Automatic transmission failure; aluminum case ruined; gear had fragments that had been ruined." • "Automatic transmission locked up while driving uphill; speed 25 mph; came to complete stop; vehicle was towed." • "Automatic transmission, moving from stop sign, transmission quit; car would not move." • "Automatic transmission is causing vibrations throughout car. Dealer cannot fix problem."

6. Fuel: fuel carburetion, stalling, hesitation. • "Severe hesitation problem at any time and at any speed; hesitates in traffic and highway driving too; slow pickup when entering expressway." • "Carburetor defective; car would stop dead cold on highway." • "Vehicle experiencing stalling, bucking and loss of power when attempting to accelerate." • "Vehicle bucks in drive; also backfires." • "Carburetor has air leak at base; rebuilt carburetor; vehicle surging and stalling when stopped; repaired/replaced JVS solenoid."

HYUNDAI EXCEL 1988

Complaint Severity: Typical. **Recall Alert:** See Recall Index. **Buyer's Summary:** Test the suspension by feeling for vibration or pulling while driving. Test the transmission thoroughly: Test transmission for slipping, locking up and performance.

Hot Spots and Owner/NHTSA Comments:

1. Power train: transmission: 5-speed and up, locking up. • "Five-speed manual transmission selector switch shorted: Transmission would temporarily disengage while traveling." • "Five-speed transmission locked, throwing driver into windshield and breaking it." • "Defective 5-speed manual transmission; while engine was still running, gear locked up in 1st and the stickshift will not come out." • "Shifted to 2nd gear and transmission totally locked up; was able to get vehicle into neutral. Parked vehicle overnight; transmission worked next day."

2. Exhaust/crankcase emission control devices: fire, failure. • "Reed valve subassembly failed, resulting in a fire and injury; prior to recall." • "Reed valve failure, causing other components to burn." • "Emission system exploded, causing fuel system and engine damage; prior to recall." • "Defective reed valve caused sluggishness and power failure; prior to recall." • "Defective reed valve; exhaust hose from emission control system blew off and plastic housing melted."

3. Engine: poor performance, fire, premature failure. • "Knocking and pinging; lack of power when accelerating." • "Premature engine malfunction; problems with bearings in engine." • "Fire broke out in engine compartment; could be the result of fuel leakage." • "Due to engine compartment fire, vehicle was totaled." • "While driving on freeway, car lost power and smoke was emanating from engine; by time vehicle came to a full stop, vehicle burned totally."

4. Power train: transmission: automatic, poor performance, difficulty shifting, slipping. • "Transmission jumps out of gear, and would not go into 2nd gear most of the time." • "Transmission shifts into passing gear too much; adjusted transmission shifter cable." • "Driving at 30 mph, vehicle's front wheels locked up in 3rd gear; difficult getting car into neutral out of way of traffic." • "Transmission locked up while shifting from 1st to 2nd gear; estimated speed was 15 mph." • "While driving, transmission locked up; caused vehicle to go out of control."

5. Suspension: independent front, vibration, leaks. • "Vibration felt through steering at low and high speeds; car wanders across lanes at highway speeds; wheels balanced to no avail." • "Repeated problems of vibration, felt in seats, steering wheel, etc.; several attempts to repair, problem still not solved." • "While traveling at highway speeds of 50-60 mph, vehicle experiences extreme front-end vibrations." • "Leaking front struts and bad shock absorbers caused alignment problems; tires worn, shocks on rear not attached; problems repaired." • "Serious vibration in front end; replaced tires and balanced front end; advised needs front suspension and/or shocks."

6. Power train: transmission: standard: manual, locking up, failure. • "Defective bearing stripped input shaft and rear bearing, causing transmission to lock up; prior to recall." • "Transmission noisy and failed to shift; prior to recall." • "Manual transmission failed, causing vehicle to lock up while moving, resulting in accident and injury." • "Transmission failed; prior to recall; also replaced axle constant velocity boot." • "Manual transmission failed prior to and after recall repairs; once resulting in an accident."

HYUNDAI EXCEL 1989

Complaint Severity: Typical. **Recall Alert:** See Recall Index. **Buyer's Summary:** Look carefully for any kind of leakage, especially under the car. Test the suspension by feeling for vibration or pulling while driving. Check the brakes—listen for noise, look for leaks and feel for vibration. They may fail, perform poorly or require frequent mechanical attention. Test the transmission thoroughly: Test transmission for slipping, locking up and performance.

Hot Spots and Owner/NHTSA Comments:

1. Power train: transmission: 5-speed and up, locking up, difficulty shifting. • "Driving at 15 mph in 2nd gear, the transmission locked up and stopped the front wheels. Car bucked 3 times then slid to stop, resulting in rear-end collision." • "Manual 5-speed transmission locked up without warning while shifting from drive to reverse and from 4th to 5th." • "Manual 5-speed transmission locked up while backing vehicle out of driveway. Replaced input shaft, seals and bearings." • "The transmission seized up twice; both times transmission was under 24 months and 30,000 miles." • "Manual 5-speed transmission jumps out of gear after shifting from 4th to 5th; also jumps out of reverse to no gear; speed 50 mph; no prior warning; could be recall related."

2. Power train: transmission: automatic, poor performance, difficulty shifting, slipping. • "After parking car in garage, driver removed key from ignition and exited car; turned around and noticed car starting to roll out of garage; when stopped, gear was in park." • "Sudden transmission lockup while shifting from 1st to 2nd gear, speed around 10 mph." • "While releasing emergency brake, car immediately began to roll down driveway, still in parking gear, full force on brake pedal; resulted in accident." • "Defective transmission seal tore due to improper installation on assembly line; oil leaked out; repaired/replaced seal." • "Vehicle was serviced for recall transmission oil change on July 18. On August 13, the 4th gear seized up and transmission locked up."

3. Engine: leaks, fire, noise. • "While driving, noticed strange smell; pulled to shoulder, popped hood and discovered that engine compartment was in flames." • "Engine failure; valve stem seals leaking oil; timing belt failure." • "While driving at 55 mph, vehicle came to abrupt stop with no acceleration power. Vehicle began to overheat, which has happened 3 times." • "While traveling 30 mph, engine started to make grinding noise and then ceased to function." • "Engine overheated and smoked, and blew smoke into the passenger compartment."

4. Suspension: independent front, vibration, tire wear. • "Problem with front-end vibration which ruins tires; problem caused by faulty design; all repair attempts to no avail." • "Experiencing front-end shimmy and very bad vibration; steering wheel jerks and doors shake; numerous repairs to no avail." • "Front-end shimmy in steering wheel becomes more apparent while driving interstate at 60 mph." • "At approximately 62 mph, front end started to vibrate." • "Vehicle shaking badly upon and during acceleration."

5. Exhaust: crankcase emission control devices: cracking, fire. • "Reed valve deterioration caused 2 engine fires; prior to recall; problem continues." • "Exhaust system clogs up and cracks exhaust manifold. Recall related." • "Defective exhaust/crankcase caused engine compartment fire while driving vehicle at 45 mph." • "Reed valve assembly failed, causing exhaust manifold to crack and resulting in an exhaust leak; prior to recall." • "Vehicle caught fire after recall work had been performed."

6. Brakes: hydraulic system, locking up, noise, vibration. • "Vehicle had brake loss on highway; after several pumping attempts, brakes regained slowly." • "Automatic brake adjuster failed; brakes adjusted manually." • "Grinding sound when applying brakes; brake light on dash stays on most of the time." • "Brakes locked, started smoking; smelled burning rubber; when car cooled, brakes worked again." • "Car in front suddenly stopped, driver hit brakes, which began to vibrate severely; could not control car due to front-end vibration; struck another vehicle."

HYUNDAI EXCEL 1990

Complaint Severity: Troublesome. **Recall Alert:** See Recall Index. **Buyer's Summary:** The fuel pump has received complaints. Make sure it doesn't make excessive noise and that you are experiencing adequate engine performance. Also, look for leaks. Test the suspension by feeling for vibration or pulling while driving. Check the brakes—listen for noise, look for leaks and feel for vibration. They may fail, perform poorly or require frequent mechanical attention. Test the transmission thoroughly. See "Sudden Accelerations" in Introduction.

Hot Spots and Owner/NHTSA Comments:

1. Power train: transmission: automatic, poor performance, difficulty shifting, slipping. • "Driver claims that vehicle moved into reverse without assistance; vehicle lost control, resulting in an accident." • "Automatic transmission starting to fail at 40,000 miles." • "Transmission slips out of gear." • "While driving, transmission slips out of gear as if car was in neutral." • "Transmission leaks and slips out of gear; also, transaxle rebuilt."

2. Suspension: independent front, alignment, tire wear. • "Misalignment, causing premature tire wear." • "Front end of vehicle vibrates and is hard to handle on the road." • "Front lower suspension is not lined up properly." • "Crunching noise in front end." • "Bad front-end alignment."

3. Visual systems: glass: window: door and side, breaking, poor performance. • "While driving, rear left-hand side window shattered." • "On 2 separate occasions, the back right and left windows spontaneously exploded; passengers in back seat were showered with glass, resulting in an injury." • "Driver's-side rear window exploded 3 times; replaced 3 times." • "The back seat side window exploded twice in 2 years; one was in cold weather, parked outside; second one, vehicle was parked in garage in hot weather and exploded." • "At stoplight, left rear passenger-side window shattered for no apparent reason."

4. Fuel: fuel pump, stalling, malfunction. • "Fuel pump malfunctioned and needed replacement." • "Fuel pump overheats and causes vehicle to stall without warning. Vehicle may restart once cooled." • "Fuel pump failed, causing vehicle to hesitate and/or stall after warming up." • "Fuel pump in gas tank faltering, making noises; inadequate gas to run car properly." • "Replaced fuel pump."

5. Fuel: throttle linkages and control, sudden accelerations. • "Rpm sensor failed, causing engine to run rough; item repaired under warranty." • "Upon applying the brakes, vehicle accelerated forward; resulted in accident." • "Upon shifting gear from park to drive with foot lightly on brake, vehicle accelerated, going into reverse and hitting car behind." • "Vehicle jumped into gear and accelerated."

6. Brakes: hydraulic system, locking up, failure. • "Applying brakes to make a stop, vehicle experienced complete brake lockup, causing an accident." • "Suspected brake lockup caused by marks on road; vehicle went out of control, which resulted in an accident." • "Brakes failed to respond while trying to slow vehicle down; resulted in an accident."

HYUNDAI EXCEL 1991

Complaint Severity: Typical. **Recall Alert:** See Recall Index. **Buyer's Summary:** Check the brakes—listen for noise, look for leaks and feel for vibration. They may fail, perform poorly or require frequent mechanical attention. Test the transmission thoroughly. See "Sudden Accelerations" in Introduction.

Hot Spots and Owner/NHTSA Comments:

1. Power train: transmission: automatic, poor performance, difficulty shifting, slipping. • "Defective transmission; car rolled back from parked position on a hill." • "Automatic transmission jerked hard and hesitated during acceleration. Vehicle rolls back, as if the transmission is a standard. Dealer said no problem found." • "Automatic transmission downshifts while driving; therefore, while still idling, car will not move; need to replace transmission." • "After driving a distance daily, automatic transmission would fail, resulting in vehicle not responding in drive." • "While traveling at 45 mph, automatic transmission failed. Dealer said that they replaced transmission in December 1992. Transmission shifting problems and stalled vehicle."

2. Visual systems: glass: window: door and side, breaking. • "Both rear quarter windows imploded into small pieces and sprayed glass over interior of vehicle. Passenger's side imploded 12 months before the driver's side." • "While driving at approximately 30-35 mph, the rear right-hand side window shattered; there were no cracks prior to incident." • "Rear window that pops out for ventilation shattered." • "Driver's window and rear left window exploded with no warning." • "While driving vehicle, driver's-side rear window exploded."

3. Fuel: fuel systems, noise, failure. • "Fuel system recall repairs refused due to unavailability of parts." • "Replaced noisy fuel pump."

4. Brakes: hydraulic system, locking up, rust, failure. • "Total loss of braking effectiveness when applying the brakes." • "Brake system failed completely 4 times; replaced master cylinder to no avail." • "Brakes locked up due to rust." • "Rear brakes locked, vehicle skidded 10 feet before stopping." • "When driving at 35 mph, brakes were applied very hard in a quick stop; rear brakes locked rear wheels and car skidded sideways for about 10 feet before coming to a stop."

5. Electrical system: ignition, stalling, hesitation. • "Numerous stalling and hesitation problems; repeated maintenance, problem still unsolved." • "Car cuts off in traffic without any prior warning." • " 'Check engine' light constantly comes on after starting up engine and remains on; causes stalling." • "Ignition failed, causing vehicle to stall." • "Vehicle stalls intermittently. This is the fifth occurrence."

6. Fuel: throttle linkages and control, sudden accelerations. • "Upon stopping and starting at intersection, vehicle hesitates, then surges forward." • "Sudden acceleration 4 times; once resulting in accident and injuries." • "The engine surged, but vehicle only seemed to roll, with no momentum." • "When the engine gets hot, the car bucks when starting again from a complete stop." • "Engine revving unusually high; placed into reverse and car suddenly accelerated into a wall; spring was found on garage floor."

HYUNDAI S COUPE 1991

Complaint Severity: Negligible. **Buyer's Summary:** Test the suspension by feeling for vibration or pulling while driving. Test the transmission thoroughly.

Hot Spots and Owner/NHTSA Comments:

1. Power train: transmission: automatic, poor performance, difficulty shifting, slipping. • "Automatic transmission slips out of gear at 30, 40 and 50 mph." • "Transmission overhauled; torque converter assembly replaced." • "Vehicle shifts up and down very hard; had it in shop 4 times, not fixed yet." • "Transmission sometimes slips from neutral to accelerate, causing it to surge forward." • "Automatic transmission skips gears at intervals. Lost 1½ quarts of transmission fluid."

2. Interior systems: active seat and shoulder belts and belt anchor, locking up, malfunction. • "Front shoulder seat belts lock up during normal driving; should only lock up upon impact or sudden stop." • "Right front seat belt was inoperable; replaced." • "Seat belt locks intermittently." • "Seat belts do not function properly; at times do not catch."

3. Suspension: independent front, alignment, noise, vibration. • "Instability of vehicle caused accident and death." • "Pulls to one direction; vibration in steering wheel at 30-40 mph." • "Poor alignment, causing vibration." • "Noise in both front and rear of vehicle."

HYUNDAI SONATA 1989

Complaint Severity: Harmless. **Recall Alert:** See Recall Index. **Buyer's Summary:** Look carefully for any kind of leakage, especially under the car. Check the brakes—listen for noise, look for leaks and feel for vibration. They may fail, perform poorly or require frequent mechanical attention. Test the transmission thoroughly. Make sure seat belts function correctly and fit comfortably. Make sure air conditioner works properly.

Hot Spots and Owner/NHTSA Comments:

1. Engine: leaks, failure. • "Engine seized." • "Oil leaks; repaired/replaced several engine parts, problem still exists." • "Recurring problem with engine oil leakage; installed oil leak stopper." • "Faulty flex plate and counterbalance shaft." • "Problem with oil consumption; having to put in 1 quart of oil every 1,000 miles."

2. Brakes: hydraulic system, pulling, leaks, excessive wear. • "Applied brakes gently; upon application, car jerked violently to right and began series of uncontrolled and swerving lane changes." • "Vehicle does not stop when brakes are applied; high-pitched sound continues, even after having been repaired." • "Master cylinder and rear wheel cylinders were leaking." • "Brakes slipping." • "Premature brake wear."

3. Power train: transmission: automatic, poor performance, difficulty shifting, slipping. • "Gears slipping; transmission rebuilt." • "Automatic transmission slips between gears; it would sometimes stay in 1st gear." • "Defective automatic transmission fluid, causing valves to stick." • "Defect in transmission system."

• "A transmission oil leak caused vehicle to stop in the midst of climbing on a hill; proceeded to roll back."
4. Interior systems: passive restraint: belts, malfunction, failure. • "Right passenger automatic seat belt went back and forth while vehicle in motion." • "Front seat belt harnesses, which are retractable, start to move rearward toward seat; halfway, then stop, continues toward seat; they push and keep shoulders pinned to seat." • "Driver's electronic seat belt retracts toward the window when brakes are applied for complete stop." • "Automatic seat belt fails constantly." • "Electric seat belts on driver's and passenger's sides broken and inoperative."
5. Air conditioner: leaks, failure. • "Freon leak." • "Air conditioner failure." • "Air conditioner failed; repaired/replaced."
6. Electrical system: battery, malfunction, failure. • "Battery failed." • "Battery malfunctioned." • "Battery died abruptly." • "Battery failed; couldn't start vehicle, had to jump-start twice."

HYUNDAI SONATA 1990

Complaint Severity: Best 3% in Guide. **Recall Alert:** See Recall Index. **Buyer's Summary:** Test the transmission thoroughly. Make sure seat belts function correctly and fit comfortably. See "Sudden Accelerations" in Introduction.

Hot Spots and Owner/NHTSA Comments:
1. Power train: transmission: automatic, poor performance, difficulty shifting, slipping. • "Transmission slips out of gear twice every month. Mechanic informed owner component was not built for this type of vehicle." • "When vehicle is in park, gears shift from park to drive without key being in ignition." • "Transmission fluid leak; gasket replaced." • "When shifting to 4th gear while driving, transmission slips out of gear into neutral." • "Automatic transmission leak."
2. Electrical system: battery, failure. • "Problem with battery." • "Defective battery." • "Battery failed." • "Dead battery caused car not to start." • "Replaced battery."
3. Interior systems: passive restraint: belts, malfunction, failure. • "Vehicle's driver's-side safety belt system gets stuck in middle position of mechanism." • "Driver's and passenger's automatic seat belts stopped halfway, blowing a fuse." • "Seat belts failed." • "Lubrication kit for automatic seat belts not mailed by manufacturer to complete recall." • "Automatic seat belt engagement fails."
4. Equipment: electric equipment: radio: tape deck, etc., malfunction, failure. • "Radio failed." • "Defective radio/cassette." • "Clock didn't work after purchase." • "Radio shorting out."
5. Fuel: throttle linkages and control, sudden accelerations. • "Owner can be sitting at a light with his foot on the brake and vehicle will still try to go." • "While downshifting and with speed cruise control on, vehicle suddenly accelerated." • "While driving on highway, engine surges; gas pedal would not depress." • "Vehicle can be going at 50 mph and will accelerate for no apparent reason to 80 mph; at times it has downshifted on its own."

HYUNDAI SONATA 1991

Complaint Severity: Negligible. **Recall Alert:** See Recall Index. **Buyer's Summary:** Test the transmission thoroughly. Make sure seat belts function correctly and fit comfortably.

Hot Spots and Owner/NHTSA Comments:
1. Interior systems: passive restraint: belts, uncomfortable, malfunction. • "Motorized shoulder belt will proceed to point where belt would choke occupant." • "Seat belt gets caught and will not travel on track." • "Seat belt did not come out from retractor assembly; prior to recall." • "Automatic seat belts failed prior to and after recall repairs." • "Motorized shoulder belt hung up in middle of frame above shoulder; wire that runs inside track came through framework between the two windows; wire off track."
2. Interior systems: active restraints: belt retractors, malfunction, failure. • "Driver and passenger seat belts do not retract properly." • "Seat belt retractor failed." • "Seat belt motor failed." • "Automatic seat belt retractor failed." • "Repaired 8 times, the seat belts still retract only 5 inches and jam. Warning light and buzzer do come on."
3. Power train: transmission: automatic, poor performance, difficulty shifting, slipping. • "Transmission leaks and/or slips, repaired, problem continues." • "Transmission leak." • "Vehicle shifts into reverse when idling at stop sign or light." • "Transmission does not stay in gear when accelerating." • "Leaking transmission." • "The automatic transmission changes gear; it happens when the car has not been driven in a while."
4. Electrical system: stalling, malfunction. • "Entire electrical system failure." • "Electrical problems cause car to stall." • "Electrical system malfunctioned, causing battery, alternator, fuse and ignition coil to fail." • "Electrical problems caused 4 batteries, 2 alternators and starter coil to fail."

Isuzu

ISUZU TRUCK RODEO 1991

Complaint Severity: Negligible. **Recall Alert:** See Recall Index. **Buyer's Summary:** Check the brakes—listen for noise, look for leaks and feel for vibration. They may fail, perform poorly or require frequent mechanical attention. Test the transmission thoroughly. Test the clutch.

Hot Spots and Owner/NHTSA Comments:
1. Power train: transmission: automatic, poor performance, difficulty shifting, slipping. • "Transmission dipstick recalled." • "Transmission fluid leak from dipstick tube." • "Vehicle caught on fire due to leakage of transmission fluid; leakage sprayed on driver, causing second degree burns to face and arms." • "Automatic transmission would not accelerate past 5 mph." • "Transmission leakage and false oil pressure reading."
2. Brakes: hydraulic: anti-skid system, poor performance, failure, locking up. • "Antilock brake failure 7 times; antilock brake system modules and speed sensor replaced, problem continues." • "Repeated antilock brake system failures." • "Antilock brake system failure." • "Antilock brake system malfunctioning." • "Wiring harness silicone sealer failed, causing antilock brake light to come on."
3. Brakes: hydraulic: disc: rotor: disc hub, vibration, excessive wear. • "Front brake rotors warped from overheating conditions, causing vibration." • "Front brakes inoperative due to warped rotors." • "Front brake rotors continue to wear at low mileage." • "Rotors warped; turned twice; replaced once; brake pedal pulsates; steering wheel shakes."
4. Electrical system: ignition, stalling. • "Vehicle stalls without warning, causing loss of control." • "Truck will stall without warning intermittently. Dealer has made attempts to resolve problem, but has not found cause of failure." • "Vehicle stalls after slowing down." • "Vehicle stalls out in traffic with no prior warning."
5. Power train: clutch assembly, excessive wear, stalling. • "After depressing clutch, transmission will downshift; stalls and cuts off. No prior warning. Happens about 3 times a day. Ceases for week, then happens again." • "When depressing the clutch

during normal driving, vehicle does one of two things: idles very high or stalls." • "Clutch failed." • "Premature clutch wear."

ISUZU TRUCK RODEO 1992

Complaint Severity: Minor. **Buyer's Summary:** The fuel injection system has been blamed for hesitation and stalling. Be sure the vehicle doesn't die in traffic or at stops. Check the brakes—listen for noise, look for leaks and feel for vibration. They may fail, perform poorly or require frequent mechanical attention. Test the clutch.

Hot Spots and Owner/NHTSA Comments:

1. Brakes: hydraulic: disc: rotor: disc hub, vibration, excessive wear. • "Front brake rotors keep warping; need to be replaced." • "Vibration when braking; rotors machined and turned." • "Brake rotors wear prematurely." • "Experiencing vibration in brakes and steering wheel due to defective rotors; replaced front rotor 7 times." • "Brake rotors replaced."

2. Electrical system: ignition, stalling. • "Vehicle will stall without prior warning while driving." • "Car stalls out while in deceleration mode or while attempting to make turns." • "Engine stalls from 55 mph and strands occupant in expressway traffic. On restart, all dash warning lights stay on; need dash removal to repair." • "While driving, vehicle stalls at any speed; dealer cannot find problem."

3. Fuel: fuel injection system, stalling, hesitation. • "Vehicle stalled on highway, causing accident and injury." • "Vehicle caught on fire." • "Engine stalls while decelerating; especially prevalent when clutch is depressed. Since car was new, dealer has not been able to correct defect." • "Intermittent stalling."

4. Brakes: hydraulic: anti-skid system, poor performance, failure, locking up. • "Antilock brakes locked up; antilock brake light stays on." • "Antilock brake system brake pedal on car vibrates." • "Vehicle antilock brake system failed 3 times; had master cylinder replaced." • "Antilock brake system failure; experienced pedal fading when applied, making a loud noise; pulsates when slowing down from 35-55 mph." • "Antilock brake lights constantly stayed on."

5. Power train: clutch assembly, stalling, poor performance. • "Vehicle experienced clutch problems." • "Vehicle shakes when clutch is released slowly while downshifting." • "When trying to slow down, you step on the clutch and the vehicle dies." • "Engine stalls while decelerating; especially prevalent when clutch is depressed. Since car was new, dealer has not been able to correct defect." • "Truck will stall when pushing clutch, affecting brakes and steering control. Dealer recognizes failure but unable to determine cause."

ISUZU TRUCK TROOPER 1988

Complaint Severity: Troublesome. **Recall Alert:** See Recall Index. **Buyer's Summary:** This vehicle has miscellaneous engine problems.

Hot Spots and Owner/NHTSA Comments:

1. Engine: other parts, failure. • "Air pockets in engine head allowed water to enter engine cylinders; engine emanating steam." • "Engine cylinder head cracked at weak point and was replaced; second cylinder head warped due to engine heat." • "Cylinder head cracked." • "Vehicle had defective engine oil seals; resulted in complete engine shutdown." • "Crack in cylinder head; repaired twice."

2. Wheels: lugs: nuts: bolts, breaking. • "Six wheel studs came off during tire changes." • "Two wheel studs broke." • "Wheel nuts and studs broke off during tire change." • "Lug nuts sheared off." • "Wheel nuts and studs splitting."

ISUZU TRUCK TROOPER 1990

Complaint Severity: Typical. **Recall Alert:** See Recall Index. **Buyer's Summary:** Check the brakes—listen for noise, look for leaks and feel for vibration. They may fail, perform poorly or require frequent mechanical attention. Test the transmission thoroughly.

Hot Spots and Owner/NHTSA Comments:

1. Power train: transmission: automatic, poor performance, difficulty shifting, slipping. • "Transmission problem caused lack of proper acceleration." • "Fire was caused by transmission leak." • "Automatic transmission oil comes up dipstick tube, leaking onto exhaust system; causing an under-hood fire." • "Vehicle caught on fire while driving due to transmission oil leakage." • "Automatic transmission fluid leaking out from dipstick hole dropped onto hot exhaust manifold; fire started; smoke discharged from engine."

2. Brakes: hydraulic system, excessive wear, noise. • "Premature wear of brakes caused grinding." • "Noisy brakes; replaced twice, problem continues." • "Squeaky brakes." • "Premature wear of brakes and rotors caused loud noise in rear." • "Brakes wear prematurely."

ISUZU TRUCK TROOPER 1991

Complaint Severity: Minor. **Recall Alert:** See Recall Index. **Buyer's Summary:** Check the brakes—listen for noise, look for leaks and feel for vibration. They may fail, perform poorly or require frequent mechanical attention. Test the transmission thoroughly.

Hot Spots and Owner/NHTSA Comments:

1. Power train: transmission: automatic, poor performance, difficulty shifting, slipping. • "Car was parked and off; owner noticed smoke and flames coming from hood. Transmission fluid overflowed from dipstick." • "Transmission would not downshift to lowest gear when stopping." • "Vehicle overflowed with transmission fluid. Resulted in vehicle fire. This is the second incident." • "Transmission seized."

2. Brakes: hydraulic system, noise, failure. • "Noisy brakes." • "Brake failure." • "Brakes do not hold when applied; brakes pop and squeak followed by tightness of pedal; no immediate brake support." • "Brakes grinding and squeaking."

ISUZU TRUCK TROOPER II 1988

Complaint Severity: Typical. **Recall Alert:** See Recall Index. **Buyer's Summary:** Look carefully for any kind of leakage, especially under the car. Check the brakes—listen for noise, look for leaks and feel for vibration. They may fail, perform poorly or require frequent mechanical attention. Test the transmission thoroughly.

Hot Spots and Owner/NHTSA Comments:

1. Engine: leaks, cracking. • "Noisy engine; leaking oil." • "Engine head replaced." • "Engine cylinder head cracked; also damaged radiator and fuel pump." • "Engine head cracked."

2. Brakes: hydraulic system, premature failure, poor performance, noise. • "Braking system defective; rear brakes premature failure; squeak." • "Poor performance of brakes." • "Howling sound when backing up and putting brakes on; replaced brake pads and bearing, but noise got worse." • "Noisy brakes." • "Brake pedal bleeds down to floor, primarily when car is not moving and pressure applied; requires long, hard braking to stop vehicle."

3. Brakes: hydraulic: shoe and drum system, premature failure, noise. • "Rear brakes wear excessively and are lost due to parking brake being inoperative." • "Faulty rear brakes." • "Noise when applying brakes; one time applied brakes and vehicle did not stop." • "Brakes screeched horrendously on slow reverse movement; replaced rear brakes."

4. Power train: transmission: automatic, poor performance, difficulty shifting, slipping. • "Transmission will not stay in 4th gear, constantly downshifts to 3rd gear for no apparent reason." • "Transmission stumbles over 45 mph; seems like downshifting." • "Noise in transmission when in reverse; leaking oil." • "Transmission downshifts sporadically."

Jaguar

JAGUAR XJ6 1989

Complaint Severity: Best 3% in Guide. **Recall Alert:** See Recall Index. **Buyer's Summary:** Look carefully for any kind of leakage, especially under the car. Test the suspension by feeling for vibration or pulling while driving.

Hot Spots and Owner/NHTSA Comments:

1. Electrical system: battery, leaks, failure. • "Defective battery; shorted 2 times." • "Battery problems." • "Battery acid leaks onto exhaust and engine area, vapor observed under hood." • "Boilover of battery acid to vehicle exterior engine area and exhaust system caused by faulty voltage regulator causing overcharging." • "Battery failure."

2. Suspension: independent front, alignment, tire wear. • "Defective front-end alignment; repaired/replaced by dealer." • "Misalignment caused premature tire wear; tires replaced." • "Load leveler solenoids failed." • "Suspension failure."

Jeep

JEEP CHEROKEE 1987

Complaint Severity: Negligible. **Recall Alert:** See Recall Index. **Buyer's Summary:** The electronic control unit has been blamed for engine performance problems, including stalling and surging. The fuel injection system has been blamed for hesitation and stalling. Be sure the vehicle doesn't die in traffic or at stops. Check the brakes—listen for noise, look for leaks and feel for vibration. They may fail, perform poorly or require frequent mechanical attention. Test the transmission thoroughly. See "Sudden Accelerations" in Introduction.

Hot Spots and Owner/NHTSA Comments:

1. Fuel: throttle linkages and control, sudden accelerations. • "Accelerator sticks on downshift; brakes had little effect; cleaned and lubricated pivot spring assembly." • "Engine runs uncontrolled at 3,000 rpm in neutral, extremely fast speed in drive; runs up to 53 mph without accelerating; loss of control; also stalls." • "Throttle position sensor defect occurs at various times, allowing engine to race up to 3,000 rpm at a stop." • "Vehicle suffers episodes of sudden acceleration due to throttle linkages failure; no way to stop vehicle except turn ignition off." • "Throttle linkages and controls causing car to suddenly accelerate without warning; sometimes engine won't accelerate at all."

2. Fuel: fuel injection system, stalling, hesitation. • "Engine stalls while idling, turning, slowing or stopping; repaired/replaced speed sensor, microprocessor, computer throttle positioning sensor; stalling continued." • "Fuel injection system; vehicle stalls frequently; going over speed bumps, upon deceleration, pulling into driveway or parking space or coming off freeway." • "Problem with fuel injection system—when starting engine, it will die when putting it into reverse or turning; sometimes will race to 2,000 rpm." • "On startup, engine idles between 2,800 and 3,400 rpm; pump accelerator and it only idles faster; takes 2-6 restarts to reach normal idling speed." • "Continuous stalling problems experienced; stalling occurs suddenly and intermittently; unable to locate cause."

3. Brakes: hydraulic system, poor performance, fade. • "Brake shoes needed replacing; rear wheel drums scored by dust and grit; needed to be turned." • "Brake failure; warning light comes on, brakes fade; replaced master cylinder." • "Brakes overheated, and pad glazing caused gradual loss of braking effect; installed new pads." • "Brake performance very poor; fades, spongy, low brake pedal." • "Lack of and unsafe brakes; brake light stays on."

4. Power train: transmission: automatic, poor performance, difficulty shifting, slipping. • "Transmission mount bolts were missing; were replaced." • "Automatic transmission module does not downshift car; goes into neutral while driving." • "Cannot remove key from ignition when vehicle in park; if gearshift is pushed firmly beyond park then released, key can be removed." • "Vehicle shifts gears from 1st to 2nd, then would not go into 3rd gear at high speed; could not get to speed limit; drove with flasher on."

5. Electrical system: ignition: electronic control unit, hesitation, stalling. • "Engine running rough, loggy, hesitating in motion; also, idle racing until throttle body replaced; computer replacement required to eliminate problem." • "Car repeatedly stalled and failed to restart on various occasions; replaced electronic control unit computer, ignition coil, distributor module and starter." • "Vehicle would totally stall out when pulling out into traffic; possible computer malfunction." • "Engine stalls and all power lost due to computer failure."

6. Electrical system: fire, failure. • "Electrical fire; battery exploded." • "Faulty electrical parts, especially fusible link/fuel injector and wiring under cooling system." • "Electrical shortages cause lighting failures and stalling." • "Electrical shorts causing battery voltage to be lowered to such a level that processors have difficulty controlling transmission; erratic shifting and engine stalling." • "Electrical problem caused brake failure; sudden loud noise, vehicle could not be controlled or steered; steering wheel appeared to be locked."

JEEP CHEROKEE 1988

Complaint Severity: Typical. **Buyer's Summary:** Look carefully for any kind of leakage, especially under the car. The fuel injection system has been blamed for hesitation and stalling. Be sure the vehicle doesn't die in traffic or at stops. Check the brakes—listen for noise, look for leaks and feel for vibration. They may fail, perform poorly or require frequent mechanical attention. Test the clutch. See "Sudden Accelerations" in Introduction.

Hot Spots and Owner/NHTSA Comments:

1. Fuel: throttle linkages and control, sudden accelerations. • "Serious sudden acceleration in parking lot; braking had no effect; hit several vehicles." • "Vehicle experiencing high-idle problem; surges back and forth from 500 up to 3,000 rpm, making it very difficult to judge a stop; repaired 7 times to no avail." • "Vehicle's engine increased to 4,000 rpm. Throttle position switch is defective." • "Throttle linkages and controls sticking; fuel injection sensor malfunctions caused engine racing." • "When driving at 40 mph, engine suddenly accelerated up to 6,000 rpm, no pressure on gas pedal; to stop acceleration, shut engine off."

2. Fuel: fuel injection system, stalling, hesitation. • "Vehicle stalls or dies while in motion at various speeds; repaired/replaced fuel pump, electrical harness, relays and computer, problem not corrected." • "Vehicle stalls while idling at low rpm; at highway speeds, kicks and bucks much like a backfire or crossfire." • "Engine stalling problems; reinstalled wiring, repaired/replaced all harnesses; problem not solved." • "Stalling problem only when engine cold; slight hesitation at all speeds and rpm." • "Vehicle has starting and stalling problems; stalling occurs when vehicle moving."
3. Exhaust system: manifold: engine, cracking, leaks. • "Exhaust manifold failed twice due to system being warped." • "Manifold has developed a crack for the third time in the same area." • "Crack in exhaust manifold." • "Exhaust manifold cracked; resulted in exhaust fumes leaking into passenger compartment." • "Exhaust manifold cracked and fumes come into passenger compartment. Thin metal welded at points that cracked."
4. Fuel: fuel injection: idle speed control unit, sudden acceleration. • "Unexpected high idling would occur when driving the vehicle at any speed." • "Vehicle suddenly surges after high engine idle." • "High idle speed control when first starting vehicle." • "Upon starting vehicle, experienced erratically full rpm idling." • "Idle accelerated to 1,500 rpm; after a few miles of running, idle returned to 400-500 rpm."
5. Power train: clutch assembly, difficulty shifting, leaks, failure. • "Approaching traffic signal, pushed clutch to take vehicle out of gear; pedal wouldn't respond; had to force gearshift out of 2nd without clutch in order to stop." • "Master and slave cylinder on clutch went out; failure occurred prematurely." • "Clutch problem; slave cylinder failed and leaked fluid on clutch disc, resulting in gears not shifting." • "Clutch quit operating, damaging bearings, pressure plate and slave cylinder." • "The master cylinder has been replaced 4 times; 2 slide cylinders and a new clutch."
6. Brakes: hydraulic: shoe and drum system, noise, poor performance. • "Poor performance of rear brakes; very soft, low and almost nonexistent; takes few seconds to stop while going backwards." • "Rear brakes failed to release, causing cylinders to malfunction; also, brake shoes and drums replaced." • "Cylinder frozen and rear brake shoe pads rusted, causing bad performance." • "Rear brakes inoperable; wheel cylinders were frozen and shoe pads were rusted." • "Brakes grabby and noisy; repaired/replaced shoes, drums and wheel cylinders."

JEEP CHEROKEE 1989

Complaint Severity: Negligible. **Recall Alert:** See Recall Index. **Buyer's Summary:** Verify that the cruise control system works properly, and that it doesn't cause the engine to surge. The electronic control unit has been blamed for engine performance problems, including stalling and surging. Check the brakes—listen for noise, look for leaks and feel for vibration. They may fail, perform poorly or require frequent mechanical attention. Test the transmission thoroughly. See "Sudden Accelerations" in Introduction.

Hot Spots and Owner/NHTSA Comments:

1. Brakes: hydraulic: anti-skid system, poor performance, failure, locking up. • "Antilock brake system failed at 41,000 miles. Recall had been performed. Subsequent total system failure occurred." • "Hydraulic system plugged due to contaminated brake fluid." • "Failure of antilock brake system has caused the vehicle to lose braking ability on several different occasions, forcing driver to use hand brake to stop vehicle." • "Antilock brake system is failing; vehicle pulls strongly to one side, resulting in loss of brake pressure and control." • "Antilock brake system failed and locked up; left vehicle with poor braking while driving."
2. Fuel: throttle linkages and control, sudden accelerations. • "Throttle position sensor allowed a fast idle condition; repaired." • "Involved in accident that was caused by mechanical and electrical defects of throttle position sensor." • "Motor revs very high when starting; possible throttle and linkage control malfunctions." • "Vehicle idles very high, causing vehicle to jump out of control after a stop."
3. Brakes: hydraulic system, locking up, excessive wear. • "When applying brakes on wet highway, wheels grabbed; loss of control occurred; resulted in a spinout." • "Ongoing brake disorder; upon braking, rear brakes tend to lock, putting rear of vehicle into skid on wet or dry pavement." • "Premature wearing of brake linings caused by brakes grabbing." • "Problem with brakes suddenly locking; causes vehicle to come to instant halt; parts not available for recall repair." • "Can push pedal all the way to the floor and vehicle still takes a while to stop."
4. Power train: transmission: automatic, poor performance, difficulty shifting, slipping. • "Problem with continuous change of gears; repaired/replaced transmission and computer, and rewired whole system." • "Constant problems, including transmission leaks and rough idling." • "Broken seals in automatic transmission system." • "Transmission loose, resulting from bolts not being installed during assembly." • "Automatic gearshift lever release button gets stuck intermittently in depressed position; unable to remove ignition key; also, can be shifted accidentally."
5. Electrical system: ignition: electronic control unit, stalling, sudden acceleration. • "Vehicle intermittently stalls at low speeds." • "When taking foot off gas pedal, vehicle stops running; same thing happens when approaching a stoplight." • "Engine surges; problem with computer sensor." • "Jeep bucks, backfires and then loses power while driving; once ignition is shut off, vehicle will not start; engine races when it is started." • "Computer would cause extensive high-speed revving of engine; tachometer would climb and stick at 5,000 rpm, sometimes, when idling or accelerating."
6. Equipment: speed control, malfunction, failure. • "Cruise control switch on brake failed; repaired." • "Cruise control system locks up when driving." • "Cruise control doesn't work; replaced regulator." • "Cruise control activated by 2 switches, both unlit and on turn signal lever; switches can be activated accidentally while disengaging turn signal." • "Cruise control performs improperly—speed oscillates back and forth."

JEEP CHEROKEE 1990

Complaint Severity: Typical. **Recall Alert:** See Recall Index. **Buyer's Summary:** Look carefully for any kind of leakage, especially under the car. Check the brakes—listen for noise, look for leaks and feel for vibration. They may fail, perform poorly or require frequent mechanical attention. Test the transmission thoroughly. See "Sudden Accelerations" in Introduction.

Hot Spots and Owner/NHTSA Comments:

1. Fuel: throttle linkages and control, sudden accelerations. • "Car idles at excessive rate at times, making it difficult to bring car to halt; estimated idle speed at 4,500-5,000 rpm, repaired 4 times to no avail." • "Throttle position sensor replaced; recall related. Distributor, fuel line and oxygen sensor failed." • "Throttle position sensor failed after recall repairs, causing accident." • "Unintended acceleration and racing of the motor required turning off the engine in order to stop vehicle, despite persistent braking." • "Faulty throttle position sensor causes engine to run at 3,000 rpm without touching gas pedal; causes undue wear and tear on engine, low gas mileage and very unsafe."
2. Brakes: hydraulic: anti-skid system, poor performance, failure, locking up. • "Antilock brake master cylinder and hy-

draulic pump failure." • "Antilock brake system failed upon application when proceeding from stop sign; coating from inside hose clogged up filter, preventing brake fluid from getting through." • "Antilock brake system malfunctioned; caused rear-end collision, which resulted in injuries." • "Brakes lock up and overheat; numerous repairs/replacements, including recall work, to no avail; several near-misses." • "While driving, experienced intermittent brake failure. Antilock and brake warning lights come on just prior to total failure."

3. Brakes: hydraulic system, vibration, failure. • "Vehicle has experienced brake problem; upon touching the brake with foot lightly, nothing happens." • "Three complete brake failures were experienced after recalls, fourth after latest repairs." • "Recurring brake failure; resulted in accident." • "Upon stopping, brakes pulsate and make a grinding noise." • "Brakes malfunctioning; do not stop vehicle at 30 mph without pulsing to floor; locks and vehicle skids; repaired to no avail."

4. Fuel: fuel injection: idle speed control unit, sudden acceleration. • "High engine idle speed prior to and after recall." • "Throttle position sensor failed, causing vehicle to accelerate out of control prior to and after recall repairs." • "Vehicle intermittently surges, sensor was replaced under recall." • "Engine idles high, causing vehicle to creep with brake pressure." • "Idle speed control unit failed, prior to recall."

5. Power train: transmission: automatic, poor performance, difficulty shifting, slipping. • "Transmission fluid lost." • "Transmission mount failed; repaired." • "Transmission leaking." • "Unable to put gear in park, first and 2nd gear." • "Automatic transmission leaks fluid."

6. Engine: stalling, leaks, failure. • "Recurring engine control problem; dies at start and at stop sign or light." • "Car running very rough; no overheating, oil changed at proper intervals; cylinders 3 and 4 lost all compression." • "Oil leak somewhere in the engine compartment." • "Engine leaking oil excessively." • "Engine exploded; hood was punched upwards and pulled off hinge. Cause of explosion unknown. Engine head, thermostat, head gasket and radiator to be replaced."

JEEP CHEROKEE 1991

Complaint Severity: Typical. **Recall Alert:** See Recall Index. **Buyer's Summary:** Check the brakes—listen for noise, look for leaks and feel for vibration. They may fail, perform poorly or require frequent mechanical attention. Test the transmission thoroughly. See "Sudden Accelerations" in Introduction.

Hot Spots and Owner/NHTSA Comments:

1. Brakes: hydraulic: anti-skid system, poor performance, failure, locking up. • "Antilock brake system fails with pedal to floor and pulsating. Antilock brake system warning light turns on to indicate failures: 2 master cylinders and antilock brake system booster pumps replaced." • "Antilock brake system would engage at cruising speed when brakes not applied; all 4 wheels freeze; resulted in loss of power and control." • "Antilock brakes locked up after recall work was performed. Replaced accumulator valve pump assembly." • "Complete failure of antilock brake system; pump, accumulator ball and hydraulic system. Brakes will hit or miss when applied. Response is unpredictable." • "Antilock brake system brake pedal traveled to floor, causing complete brake failure; no warning."

2. Fuel: throttle linkages and control, sudden accelerations. • "The throttle position sensor has malfunctioned 3 times because it does not have a weather seal." • "While backing out of shopping center parking lot, engine accelerated backward into 2 parked vehicles; back wheels continued to accelerate until stopped." • "Upon shifting from park to drive, vehicle suddenly surged without touching gas pedal; went out of control and resulted in an accident." • "Sudden acceleration caused loss of control and an accident." • "Vehicle suddenly accelerated when shifting into drive; applied brakes but couldn't stop car; resulted in an accident."

3. Brakes: hydraulic system, sudden acceleration, locking up, leaks. • "While driving and equipped with antilock brake system, made an attempt to stop by braking; however, brakes were inoperative; resulted in a multi-vehicle accident." • "Vehicle recalled for brake failure; assumed brakes were fixed; however, when driving, lost brakes without any warning; avoided accident by using curb to stop." • "In reverse, sudden acceleration occurred while brake was completely applied; key had to be removed to stop." • "Worn pads and inoperative actuator caused brakes to lock up." • "Internal seal leakage caused brake failure."

4. Electrical system: ignition, stalling. • "The night vehicle was picked up from dealer, it stalled approximately 10 times; replaced ignition module." • "Engine shuts off unexpectedly while driving at approximate speed of 65 mph." • "While driving vehicle on highway at 55 mph, it began to stall, then had complete engine shutdown." • "Vehicle has stalled 8 times at various speeds."

5. Power train: transmission: automatic, poor performance, difficulty shifting, slipping. • "Repaired transmission oil leak." • "Vehicle will not shift to reverse; when restarted, it stuck in drive." • "Vehicle would not go into park occasionally, would stick in neutral or reverse; difficult to remove the key." • "Transmission constantly fails to shift properly." • "Transmission cable cut."

6. Brakes: hydraulic: master cylinder, malfunction, failure. • "Master cylinder malfunctioned." • "Defective master cylinder and accumulator, causing brake failure; also caused brake and antilock brake lights to stay on." • "Replaced master cylinder, pads and rotors." • "After recall service done, service light came on; shortly after, antilock brake system failed. Master cylinder ring dissolved." • "Antilock brake system. Lost brakes while driving due to dirt getting into the master cylinder."

JEEP CHEROKEE 1992

Complaint Severity: Troublesome. **Recall Alert:** See Recall Index. **Buyer's Summary:** Look carefully for any kind of leakage, especially under the car. Check the brakes—listen for noise, look for leaks and feel for vibration. They may fail, perform poorly or require frequent mechanical attention. Test the transmission thoroughly. See "Sudden Accelerations" in Introduction.

Hot Spots and Owner/NHTSA Comments:

1. Brakes: hydraulic system, vibration, fade. • "Brakes fade." • "Extended stopping distance when applying the brakes." • "At 10 mph, the brakes vibrate, resulting in extra pressure to stop vehicle." • "Requires excessive effort to stop vehicle, extended stopping distance."

2. Brakes: hydraulic: anti-skid system, poor performance, failure, locking up. • "Antilock brakes vibrate, causing extended stopping when applied. Has been repaired previously." • "Consumer, on 3 different occasions, went to apply the brakes; antilock brake system locked up; there was no brake response." • "Vehicle pulls to left when brakes are applied; causes temporary loss of control." • "Antilock brake system: Complete loss of brake effectiveness after antilock brake system was applied." • "Antilock brake system failed, causing accident."

3. Fuel: throttle linkages and control, sudden accelerations. • "Vehicle was in park, put car in drive and it accelerated out of control; went through garage wall into dining room." • "Consumer was shifting into reverse and vehicle accelerated; caused an accident." • "While driving at approximately 45 mph, experienced intermittent throttle sticking; pedal goes to floor, then vehicle continues to accelerate; no prior warning." • "When driver pushed clutch into start, vehicle accelerated and crashed into garage."

4. Power train: transmission: automatic, poor performance, difficulty shifting, slipping. • "Transmission failed." • "Rear end clunks from reverse to drive." • "Transmission shift rod replaced due to transmission oil leak." • "Transmission gear sticks in park, will not engage in reverse from park." • "Transmission fluid leak creates potential for fire."

5. Exhaust system: muffler: resonator, leaks, failure. • "Muffler is leaking." • "Muffler failure." • "Problem with muffler heat shield."

6. Structure: door assembly: latches and locks, failure. • "Right door lock failed." • "Door latch bent; tailgate latch jammed." • "Latch on rear hatch failed." • "Recall repairs refused."

JEEP CHEROKEE 1993

Complaint Severity: Serious. **Theft Alert:** 17. **Recall Alert:** See Recall Index. **Buyer's Summary:** The airbags in this vehicle have experienced failures and malfunctions: You may need a professional evaluation on the condition of the airbags. Check the brakes—listen for noise, look for leaks and feel for vibration. They may fail, perform poorly or require frequent mechanical attention. Test the transmission thoroughly. See "Sudden Accelerations" in Introduction.

Hot Spots and Owner/NHTSA Comments:

1. Fuel: throttle linkages and control, sudden accelerations. • "Sudden acceleration, vehicle went into open throttle position, impact 1:00 position, speed 45 mph; lost control and hit a brick wall. Also, airbag deployed." • "Driver started vehicle and went from park into drive, and suddenly accelerated out of control. Driver put vehicle into neutral and stopped vehicle." • "Parked 1 hour, started engine and engaged reverse gear, car suddenly accelerated backwards, spinning the tires and hitting 2 vehicles." • "Accelerated when placed in reverse." • "Vehicle was parked, went from park to drive, experienced sudden acceleration, impact 11:00, hitting a parked vehicle; loss of brake effectiveness, speed unknown." • "Upon shifting from park to reverse, vehicle suddenly accelerated to unknown speeds, crashing into trees. Airbag did not deploy."

2. Brakes: hydraulic: anti-skid system, poor performance, failure, locking up. • "Antilock brake system: When applying brakes for panic stop, brakes will lock and vehicle will skid. Locking of brake system has reoccurred several times." • "Antilock brake system: When approaching stop at low speeds, hitting bump causes sensors to be confused, which locks one of the wheels and causes skidding." • "Vehicle equipped with antilock brake system. Upon application, the pedal is hard. This has occurred 4 times within 2,000 miles." • "At 40 mph, severe braking and severe pulling to the left. This is an antilock brake system-equipped vehicle." • "Vehicle has 5,000-pound tow package. Brakes are insufficient for backing down a grade with 2,200-pound trailer. Emergency brake application will help stopping."

3. Brakes: hydraulic system, noise, failure. • "Vehicle stalls out at any speed, causing brake and steering ability loss, replaced crankshaft, crank sensor, speed sensor (twice) and wiring to no avail." • "Noisy brakes." • "Owner started vehicle up, put foot on the gas and car went backwards; tried to apply the brakes and could not stop." • "Vehicle had complete brake loss and pedal went to floor." • "While driving, experienced total brake failure on 3 separate occasions; noticed grinding noise, then pedal went to the floor."

4. Interior systems: passive restraint: airbag: driver, malfunction, failure. • "Frontal collision, impact 12:00 position, hitting another vehicle, speed 35 mph, airbag did not deploy." • "Upon start, placed into reverse, then drive; engine surged and shot out of parking lot carrying another car with its two front wheels in air; airbag did not deploy." • "Vehicle had collision due to other driver making improper maneuver. Airbag did not deploy upon impact at approximately 25 mph." • "Driver hit another vehicle from behind at approximately 35-45 mph. Airbag did not deploy: seat belt does not fit properly." • "Airbag did not deploy during head-on collision at 15 mph. Driver received injuries."

5. Electrical system: ignition: coil, stalling, failure. • "Vehicle stalled while driving at a speed of 60 mph. Lost all power." • "Driving on a 2-lane road, tried to pass another car and the engine quit; due to ignition coil failure." • "Ignition coil was replaced 4 times. Improper design once, and the others burned out." • "Ignition coil failed."

6. Power train: transmission: automatic, poor performance, difficulty shifting, slipping. • "Experience intermittent transmission malfunction when placing in drive or reverse gear; vehicle acts as if in neutral." • "Automatic transmission does not engage when going from park to either drive or reverse, intermittently." • "Automatic transmission: Vehicle has a fluid leak in transmission. Transmission has had to be replaced already. The transmission sticks in gear, making it difficult to control." • "Parked on flat surface with engine running, vehicle slipped out of gear into reverse, hitting another vehicle. Dealer says annulus gear malfunctioned." • "Vehicle accelerated upon shifting from park to neutral, causing accident."

JEEP CHEROKEE 1994

Complaint Severity: Very Serious. **Recall Alert:** See Recall Index. **Buyer's Summary:** Look carefully for any kind of leakage, especially under the car. The airbags in this vehicle have experienced failures and malfunctions: You may need a professional evaluation on the condition of the airbags. Check the brakes—listen for noise, look for leaks and feel for vibration. They may fail, perform poorly or require frequent mechanical attention. Test the transmission thoroughly. See "Sudden Accelerations" in Introduction.

Hot Spots and Owner/NHTSA Comments:

1. Fuel: throttle linkages and control, sudden accelerations. • "Throttle stuck in reverse; engine roared; vehicle jetted backwards across street before stopping; brakes applied; driver used emergency brakes to stop vehicle." • "Vehicle was at a stop in idle position; when put into gear, vehicle went into open throttle position, impact 12:00 position, speed unknown, going through garage door." • "Vehicle in park; turned ignition on, vehicle went open throttle position in reverse, impact 6:00 position, speed unknown." • "Started engine; shifted from park to reverse; after gear engaged, engine accelerated uncontrollably; vehicle lurched backward; hit house; brakes applied; no warning." • "Started vehicle, put in reverse, accelerator stuck, car would not stop until it hit a wall."

2. Brakes: hydraulic system, noise, vibration, premature failure. • "Continuous knocking noise and pulsation from braking system after several repair attempts." • "Owner complains of having 3 sets of brakes put on within 7 months." • "Brake failure; unable to stop the vehicle even after pressing brake pedal all the way to the floor." • "Brakes failed, causing accident." • "Brakes failed to stop vehicle."

3. Power train: transmission: automatic, poor performance, difficulty shifting, slipping. • "When clutch and brake are depressed, engine idles roughly; becomes locked in 1st gear; after lifting foot off gas pedal, vehicle surges forward." • "Transmission leaks and makes loud noise when first starting vehicle; also, transfer case shattered." • "At 60 mph, transmission gearshift accidentally moved and was returned immediately; vehicle locked up a few minutes later." • "Went to stop going into a parking lot; transmission shifted from 1st to 2nd and went back and forth."

4. Brakes: hydraulic: anti-skid system, poor performance, failure, locking up. • "Antilock brake system failed, 12:00 position at 45 mph, resulting in accident." • "Antilock brakes made a knocking noise, and then there was no brake." • "Consumer was driving, tried to stop and went through a 4-way stop sign." • "Antilock brake failure."

5. Interior systems: passive restraint: airbag: driver, malfunction, failure. • "Driver's-side airbag did not deploy during accident, resulting in injury." • "When coming from a stoplight, driver's-side airbag deployed with no warning and no reason, causing driver injuries." • "Driver in auto accident and driver's airbag did not deploy." • "No deployment of airbag during accident." • "Airbag did not deploy."

6. Structure: door assembly: hinge and attachments, breaking, leaks, failure. • "Driver's-side lower door hinge broke, resulting in leakage of water onto the seat when it rains." • "The front door hinges were welded back to the door; there is a noise in the engine that sounds like a diesel—but it isn't." • "Driver's- and passenger-side door hinges are detaching from the welded area." • "Doors are not welded properly; pin came loose and doors are coming off." • "The driver's-side door hinges are not welded, can start car without using the clutch ; the horn outside the car not working on lower side."

JEEP CHEROKEE 1995

Complaint Severity: Very Serious. **Recall Alert:** See Recall Index. **Buyer's Summary:** The airbags in this vehicle have experienced failures and malfunctions: You may need a professional evaluation on the condition of your airbags. Check the brakes—listen for noise, look for leaks and feel for vibration. They may fail, perform poorly or require frequent mechanical attention. See "Sudden Accelerations" in Introduction.

Hot Spots and Owner/NHTSA Comments:

1. Fuel: throttle linkages and control, sudden accelerations. • "While vehicle was idling and then put into gear, it had sudden acceleration and hit building, resulting in accident and injury." • "While idling at stop, got back in vehicle and put foot on brakes, turned the key again although car was already on; vehicle suddenly accelerated backwards." • "Went to shift from park to drive; made loud noise and vehicle accelerated at high speed and airbag did not deploy on impact." • "Vehicle was parked in driveway, put vehicle into reverse, went into open throttle position; lost control, impact 6:00 position, whirled around and flipped over." • "Accelerator pedal stuck in neutral open position; vehicle lost control and hit a pole, impact 12:00 position, speed unknown."

2. Interior systems: passive restraint: airbag: driver, malfunction, failure. • "At 45 mph, 12:00 position, driver's-side airbag did not deploy; driver broke his neck." • "Airbag failed to deploy during accident." • "Went to shift from park to drive; made loud noise and vehicle accelerated at high speed; airbag did not deploy on impact." • "Driving 25 mph, vehicle tried to pass. Turned steering wheel; it would not respond, causing accident. Airbag did not totally deploy." • "Airbag did not deploy upon 12:00 position impact at 38 mph."

3. Brakes: hydraulic: anti-skid system, poor performance, failure, locking up. • "Applied the brake and it swerved to the left and into oncoming traffic." • "Antilock brake system has failed on 3 different occasions, with poor response to pedal travel." • "Antilock brake system failed, causing vehicle to go out of control." • "Vehicle vibrates when coming to a stop; rotors need to be replaced."

4. Engine: noise. • "The engine was knocking; it was replaced, and the new engine is doing the same thing." • "Engine makes metallic knocking noise when idling." • "Noisy engine." • "Discovered that vehicle was missing a retaining clip when it came out of the factory; manufacturer offered no assistance."

JEEP GRAND CHEROKEE 1993

Complaint Severity: Serious. **Recall Alert:** See Recall Index. **Buyer's Summary:** Test the suspension by feeling for vibration or pulling while driving. The airbags in this vehicle have experienced failures and malfunctions: You may need a professional evaluation on the condition of the airbags. Check the brakes—listen for noise, look for leaks and feel for vibration. They may fail, perform poorly or require frequent mechanical attention. See "Sudden Accelerations" in Introduction.

Hot Spots and Owner/NHTSA Comments:

1. Brakes: hydraulic: anti-skid system, poor performance, failure, locking up. • "Antilock brake system failure. Speed sensor on rear wheel failed, losing control and going into an embankment. Impact 6:00 position." • "Antilock brake system: Vehicle parked in driveway, when vehicle was put in reverse and brake pedal was applied, it felt as though it were frozen." • "When vehicle hits a bump in the road and brake pedal is depressed, the brakes lock up. Antilock brake system." • "Excessive braking effort is needed when applying the brakes." • "Antilock brake system had complete brake failure, with pedal going to the floor."

2. Interior systems: passive restraint: airbag: driver, malfunction, failure. • "Vehicle involved in a frontal collision and airbag did not deploy." • "Upon impact from other truck's left front to vehicle, airbag system didn't activate." • "Frontal collision, impact 11:00 position, speed 45 mph; airbag did not deploy." • "During a head-on collision, the vehicle's airbag (driver's side) did not deploy. Consumer filed a complaint with manufacturer." • "Airbag did not deploy during front-end collision at 20 mph. Driver received bruises."

3. Fuel: throttle linkages and control, sudden accelerations. • "After owner put truck into gear, she heard loud bang. Truck accelerated, hitting 4 cars. Airbag did not deploy. Estimated speed 15 mph." • "Vehicle had unwanted acceleration from park to reverse gear; hit a house." • "Vehicle suddenly surged forward, then shifted into reverse, crashing into another vehicle at unknown speed." • "After dealer has attempted repair, vehicle still has unintended acceleration from idling in gear situation. Foot on brake was not enough to prevent crash." • "Upon placing into reverse with foot on brake pedal, suddenly engine surged out of control, hitting a parked car."

4. Suspension: independent front, alignment, vibration. • "Independent front suspension failed, prior to recall, resulting in poor stability." • "Suspension misaligned." • "Front suspension lubricated due to noise when going over bumps." • "Vehicle is experiencing excessive vibration and has lost control several times." • "Front suspension bolt failed."

5. Electrical system: ignition: coil, stalling, failure. • "Ignition coil failed, preventing vehicle from starting." • "Ignition coil failed prior to recall." • "Ignition coil failed; prior to and after recall repair." • "Coil failed due to overheating, causing vehicle to stall."

6. Brakes: hydraulic system, vibration, failure. • "Upon placing into reverse with foot on brake pedal, suddenly engine surged out of control, hitting a parked car." • "Steering wheel intermittently shimmies and vibrates when brakes are applied." • "Brakes vibrated, causing loss of control." • "When brakes are applied, it is a delayed reaction; extended stopping distance." • "Brakes intermittently fail at different speeds."

JEEP GRAND CHEROKEE 1994

Complaint Severity: Troublesome. **Buyer's Summary:** Look carefully for any kind of leakage, especially under the car. The airbags in this vehicle have experienced failures and malfunctions: You may need a professional evaluation on the condition of the airbags. Check the brakes—listen for noise, look for leaks and feel for vibration. They may fail, perform poorly or require frequent mechanical attention. Test the transmission thoroughly. See "Sudden Accelerations" in Introduction.

Hot Spots and Owner/NHTSA Comments:

1. Fuel: throttle linkages and control, sudden accelerations. • "Started, shifted into reverse and vehicle took off out of control. Antilock brake system and parking brakes did not stop vehicle. Airbag did not inflate." • "When putting the vehicle into gear, the vehicle suddenly accelerated, causing an accident." • "While backing out of driveway in reverse gear, suddenly vehicle accelerated out of control at approximately 50 mph." • "Vehicle in reverse, high idle, impact 6:00 position; put vehicle in drive and experienced sudden acceleration, impact 12:00 position, speed unknown." • "Started vehicle, engaged in drive position, vehicle suddenly accelerated out of control, resulting in accident."

2. Brakes: hydraulic: anti-skid system, poor performance, failure, locking up. • "Antilock brake system failed to stop vehicle effectively when applied. Antilock brake system interior light stays on periodically when driving." • "When engaging antilock brake system at any speed less than 10 mph, even on dry pavement, pulls to the right; replaced antilock brake system hydraulic pump and antilock brake system sensor to no avail." • "Antilock brakes fail when vehicle is hot due to heat from exhaust manifold under antilock brake system pump system causing excessive heat and activating pump motor." • "Started, shifted into reverse and vehicle took off out of control. Antilock brake system and parking brakes did not stop vehicle. Airbag did not inflate." • "While driving, experience antilock failure; when on wet pavement, antilock brake system locks and grabs on vehicle equipped with all-wheel antilock brake system."

3. Interior systems: passive restraint: airbag: driver, malfunction, failure. • "Airbag did not deploy during front-end collision; vehicle was hit at left front by another vehicle traveling approximately 35 mph." • "No deployment of airbag in accident." • "Shifted into reverse, vehicle speed increased. Shifted car into park; car went into drive. Airbag did not deploy." • "From park to reverse position, engine surged then suddenly accelerated out of control at 30 mph, hitting a house." • "Airbag did not deploy."

4. Brakes: hydraulic system, locking up, failure. • "Replaced entire braking system; brakes are still inoperative." • "In hard braking, vehicle swerves left into oncoming traffic." • "When applying the brake, pedal hardened. Resulted from defective brake sensor." • "Brake pedal is difficult to depress, vehicle is hard to stop; intermittent problem." • "Place foot on brake and they freeze up and lock up as well."

5. Engine: noise, leaks, stalling. • "Vehicle hesitates when accelerating." • "Intermittent stalling when changing from reverse to drive." • "Noisy engine." • "Intermittent stalling and rough idling." • "Engine oil leak."

6. Power train: transmission: automatic, poor performance, difficulty shifting, slipping. • "Automatic transmission failed to hold vehicle while in park, resulting in accident." • "When you try to put it in gear, it will not go into gear." • "Passing gear engaged while cruise control was in use." • "Transmission revs in gear; rough gear changes; also, 4-wheel drive replaced." • "Automatic transmission; sudden acceleration; vehicle starts in 2nd gear; suddenly downshifts to 1st gear; lurches forward; slips into neutral; nearly caused accidents."

JEEP WRANGLER 1987

Complaint Severity: Negligible. **Recall Alert:** See Recall Index. **Buyer's Summary:** The carburetion system could contribute to stalling and hesitation. Look carefully for any kind of leakage, especially under the car.

Hot Spots and Owner/NHTSA Comments:

1. Visual systems: windshield wiper, breaking, poor performance. • "Windshield wipers broke where it's connected to frame; plastic nut popped." • "Received notification of safety recall for windshield frame and wipers; seek information concerning authorization to have repairs made." • "Manufacturer's design defect of wiper assembly caused windshield frame to break; replaced windshield frame." • "Windshield wipers never functioned properly; repaired under recall campaign notice." • "Windshield wiper and wiper delay inoperative at times; delay switch defective."

2. Engine: leaks, fire. • "Engine overhauled; replaced due to cracked heads and excessive oil consumption." • "Engine oil leaks after recall repairs." • "While parked, engine caught on fire; cause undetermined." • "Repaired/replaced following: camshaft and lifters, timing gear with chain, radiator, crankcase, pistons with rods and rod bearings." • "After driving car, parked approximately 10 minutes, fire coming from engine compartment."

3. Visual systems: glass: windshield, leaks, cracking. • "Windshield wiper motor makes grinding noise and jerks across windshield." • "Window frames incorrectly welded, causing misalignment of wiper linkages when wiper in operation; resulted in seizing; additional 31 vehicles have same problem." • "Large crack appeared in windshield; recall for windshield wiper assembly received, unable to repair." • "Windshield seal came loose, started leaking."

4. Electrical system: wiring: harness: front: under hood, malfunction, fire. • "Parked vehicle; noticed smoke coming from under hood; engine engulfed with flames; all plastic parts melted." • "After driving the vehicle, parked it and noticed smoke and fire coming from the engine compartment." • "Parked for approximately 10 minutes, came out and found vehicle burning under the hood; front wiring harness had caught fire on this vehicle and two others; same models." • "Engine compartment fire; electrical short; stopped motor control." • "Vehicle was parked and caught on fire. Resulted from wiring harness on fire wall shorting out."

5. Fuel: fuel carburetion, stalling, hesitation. • "Carburetor dumped fuel into exhaust system, which resulted in fire in catalytic converter." • "Experienced carburetor difficulties in fuel system shortly after purchase." • "Vehicle was parked; after 15 minutes, vehicle caught on fire, flames caused damage to 2 vehicles parked next to vehicle; engine and carburetor melted." • "Engine hesitation upon acceleration."

6. Visual systems: windshield wiper: motor, failure. • "Windshield wiper motor failed; replaced." • "Windshield wiper motor completely inoperative 12 months after recall was conducted." • "In pouring rain, windshield wipers suddenly stopped working." • "Windshield wiper motor faulty; wipers not working." • "Window wiper mechanism stuck at highway speeds; stuck wipers will not operate until they are manually lifted up."

JEEP WRANGLER 1988

Complaint Severity: Typical. **Recall Alert:** See Recall Index. **Buyer's Summary:** Look carefully for any kind of leakage, especially under the car. The fuel pump has received complaints. Make sure it doesn't make excessive noise and that you are experiencing adequate engine performance. Also, look for leaks. The fuel injection system has been blamed for hesitation and stalling. Be sure the vehicle doesn't die in traffic or at stops.

Hot Spots and Owner/NHTSA Comments:

1. Fuel: fuel injection system, stalling, hesitation. • "Upon deceleration, braking, engine rpm falls below factory-set idle rpm, then completely revs up to 1,000 rpm and then back down; sometimes causing stalling of engine." • "Engine stalled while braking in rush hour traffic; powerless until restarted engine; definite and immediate road hazard." • "Intermittent stalling." • "Engine stalling problems; stalls out immediately with no warning; goes dead instantly with no warning." • "Vehicle caught on fire while driving."

2. Exhaust system: catalytic converter system, malfunction, fire. • "Catalytic converter caught on fire." • "Catalytic converter overheated, melting fuel tank." • "Catalytic converter overheated, burned holes in carpet; caught on fire; vehicle was in motion; speed 55 mph." • "The catalytic converter overheated, resulting in a fire. Fire caused the brakes to melt."

3. Visual systems: windshield wiper, breaking, failure. • "Windshield wipers failed; had to be replaced." • "Defective windshield frame and wipers; unable to get assistance from manufacturer." • "Wiper flew off and cracked windshield; prior to recall notice." • "Twice, during storms, windshield wiper assembly flew off car." • "Received recall notice for repairs to be made to windshield wiper assembly; repeated attempts to solve have been unsuccessful."

4. Fuel: fuel pump, leaks, fire. • "Fuel sending unit gasket cracked, causing fuel to leak out of tank, resulting in fires; prior to recall." • "Had under-hood fire; checked with Chrysler to see if there was a recall; answer was vehicle identification number was not involved; 2 weeks later got recall notice for the problem." • "Recall repairs refused due to aftermarket hitch installed on vehicle."

5. Interior systems: active restraints: belt buckles, malfunction, failure. • "The driver's-side female portion of the seat belt will not except the male part of the seat belt." • "Vehicle rolled over while trying to avoid another vehicle; rolled several times, seat belt buckle failed, throwing driver from vehicle." • "Driver's-side shoulder and lap belt will not fasten when in use." • "Three point seat belt buckle plastic piece fell apart."

6. Visual systems: windshield wiper linkage: pivot: drive assembly, failure. • "Wiper arm came off due to faulty wiper assembly; prior to recall." • "Repair done on original wiper linkage; related to wiper linkage defect warned about in recall notification; caused by manufacturing defect." • "Windshield wiper pivot linkage defect; manufacturer will not comply with recall; also, a cracked windshield frame." • "Windshield frame metal cracked at wiper arm pivot mountings; caused binding of wiper linkage; problem previously corrected due to manufacturer's recall."

JEEP WRANGLER 1989

Complaint Severity: Harmless. **Recall Alert:** See Recall Index. **Buyer's Summary:** The carburetion system could contribute to stalling and hesitation. Look carefully for any kind of leakage, especially under the car. Test the clutch.

Hot Spots and Owner/NHTSA Comments:

1. Power train: clutch assembly, leaks, difficulty shifting, failure. • "Clutch leaks hydraulic fluid and doesn't function properly. Hydraulic cylinder seal keeps breaking. Throwout bearing is worn." • "Five-speed manual transmission has clutch assembly; clutch plate, master and slave cylinders have been replaced 3 times within ownership." • "Clutch slave cylinder gave out in middle of road, almost causing accident; not covered under warranty." • "Car won't go into gear; clutch pressure plate and slave cylinder worn; replaced warped pressure plate, clutch disc and throwout bearing." • "Clutch kit, shifter lever and slave cylinder replaced."

2. Visual systems: windshield wiper, cracking, failure. • "Wipers not functioning due to 1½-inch crack in metal where wiper connects to windshield." • "Received recall notice on windshield wiper assembly defect; repaired." • "Windshield frame metal too thin, causing wipers to fail." • "Wipers inoperable due to broken control arm." • "Metal around wiper connection cracked and loose; wiper arm does not stay connected to wipers."

3. Fuel: fuel carburetion, stalling, hesitation. • "Engine performed very sluggishly; dealer overhauled carburetor." • "Vehicle fire caused by gaskets on carburetor failing." • "At 55 mph, vehicle caught on fire around carburetor area. Vehicle is a complete loss." • "Carburetor caught fire after work done on fuel fume problem." • "Dirt entering carburetor destroyed needles, caused difficulty starting engine cold; strong smell of gasoline when engine turned off."

4. Visual systems: windshield wiper linkage: pivot: drive assembly, malfunction, failure. • "Wiper assembly swivel and bracket replaced prior to recall notification." • "Windshield wiper linkage recall not performed due to driver not having recall notification card." • "Windshield wiper assembly repaired prior to recall notification." • "Defective windshield wiper motor and linkage assembly replaced."

5. Electrical system: ignition, stalling, hesitation. • "Vehicle has been stalling at lights and stop signs." • "While driving, the engine cut off." • "Vehicle stalls when clutch is engaged." • "When driving, vehicle has loss of power, smell of overheating; vehicle will stall." • "While driving, vehicle will stall and/or hesitate without any warning."

6. Engine: leaks, noise. • "Problem with oil leak." • "Engine continues to rattle; repaired twice; also rough; burning smell occurs after highway driving." • "Experiencing continual oil leaks; had fixed 7 times." • "Engine replaced due to leakage." • "Oversized engine block caused oil leaks; replaced."

JEEP WRANGLER 1990

Complaint Severity: Minor. **Recall Alert:** See Recall Index. **Buyer's Summary:** The carburetion system could contribute to stalling and hesitation. Look carefully for any kind of leakage, especially under the car. The fuel pump has received complaints. Make sure it doesn't make excessive noise and that you are experiencing adequate engine performance. Also, look for leaks. Check the brakes—listen for noise, look for leaks and feel for vibration. They may fail, perform poorly or require frequent mechanical attention. Test the clutch.

Hot Spots and Owner/NHTSA Comments:

1. Power train: clutch assembly, leaks, failure. • "Clutch master cylinder, throwout bearing assembly and slave cylinder leaked." • "Master cylinder in clutch failed." • "Clutch slave cylinder failed." • "Clutch system contained leak, causing clutch to be inoperable." • "Failed slave cylinder in clutch assembly; clutch burned out."

2. Fuel: fuel carburetion, stalling, hesitation. • "Carburetor fuel adjuster is defective; causes vehicle to stall." • "Vehicle stalled and flooded in intersection; carburetor problems." • "Vehicle stalls and is hard to start, resulting from carburetor." • "Carburetor failed, causing vehicle to stall." • "Carburetor failure, causing intermittent stalling."

3. Electrical system: ignition, stalling. • "While slowing down to make turns or to stop, engine stalls; lose all power steering and brakes." • "Vehicle experiences starting trouble." • "Vehicle stalls at traffic lights, on freeways and secondary roads; loses power upon acceleration." • "Car stalls in traffic at high rates of speed."

4. Brakes: hydraulic system, leaks, stalling. • "Brake problems." • "While slowing down to make turns or to stop, engine stalls; lose all power steering and brakes." • "Brake fluid leaked and caused a loss of brakes."

5. Exhaust system: catalytic converter system, failure. • "Catalytic converter replaced." • "Catalytic converter failed; repaired." • "Catalytic converter failed."

6. Fuel: fuel pump, leaks, malfunction. • "Gas tank sending unit and gasket replaced twice, prior to recall, due to gasoline leak." • "Fuel pump recall repairs refused; no reason given." • "Fuel pump gasket recall repairs refused due to buying vehicle from another party."

JEEP WRANGLER 1991

Complaint Severity: Minor. **Recall Alert:** See Recall Index. **Buyer's Summary:** Look carefully for any kind of leakage, especially under the car. Test the clutch.

Hot Spots and Owner/NHTSA Comments:

1. Power train: clutch assembly, leaks, failure. • "Clutch failure; replaced 3 times in a 2-year period." • "Seals on slave cylinder leaked, causing clutch failure." • "Clutch inoperable due to hydraulic cylinder malfunction." • "Clutch slave cylinder leaks." • "Clutch assembly failed." • "Clutch slave cylinder failed."

JEEP WRANGLER 1992

Complaint Severity: Typical. **Recall Alert:** See Recall Index. **Buyer's Summary:** Look carefully for any kind of leakage, especially under the car. Check the brakes—listen for noise, look for leaks and feel for vibration. They may fail, perform poorly or require frequent mechanical attention. Test the clutch.

Hot Spots and Owner/NHTSA Comments:

1. Power train: clutch assembly: other parts, leaks, failure. • "Clutch slave cylinder assembly failed; interferes with gear change while driving." • "Slave seal on clutch failed." • "Clutch slave cylinder failed." • "Leak in clutch cylinder." • "Clutch master and slave cylinders failed."

2. Power train: clutch assembly, failure. • "Clutch slave cylinder failure." • "Slave cylinder failed." • "Clutch slave cylinder failed." • "Manual transmission clutch failure." • "Clutch assembly keeps falling off; replaced 3 times."

3. Power train: transmission: standard: manual, difficulty shifting, failure. • "Transmission failure." • "Vehicle grinds when shifting gears." • "Reverse gear failed." • "Unable to get into reverse."

4. Brakes: hydraulic system, locking up, failure. • "Slave cylinder failed." • "Recall delayed due to administrative problem." • "Brakes failed prior to recall, causing accident." • "Brakes locked up, causing accident."

JEEP WRANGLER 1994

Complaint Severity: Typical. **Recall Alert:** See Recall Index. **Buyer's Summary:** Look carefully for any kind of leakage, especially under the car.

Hot Spots and Owner/NHTSA Comments:

1. Emergency parking brake: mechanical, failure. • "Emergency parking brake failed to hold vehicle and it rolled into base of telephone pole." • "While parked on incline with emergency brake applied fully, vehicle rolled back, hitting another parked vehicle." • "Emergency brake failed." • "Emergency brake does not hold; pops out of engagement; dealer cannot locate problem."

2. Fuel: fuel tank assembly: tank, leaks, malfunction. • "Gas tank problems." • "Fuel tank seal leaks." • "Fuel tank leak." • "There are gas fumes from the gas tank."

3. Structure: hood assembly: latches, malfunction. • "At 65 mph, hood flew up. Windshield was smashed, vision was obstructed. Hood was latched securely, as hood obviously bounces when hood is not latched." • "Inside latch does not hold hood securely." • "While driving, safety latch that holds the hood down came loose; have to replace hood and windshield; dealer said safety latch needs padlock." • "Inside hood latch would not hold the hood down; flew up while driving."

Lexus

LEXUS 1992

Complaint Severity: Minor. **Buyer's Summary:** If there is a radio or CD player, be sure that it works.

Hot Spots and Owner/NHTSA Comments:

1. Equipment: electric equipment: radio: tape deck, etc., failure. • "Radio failed." • "Radio/tape player failed." • "Radio/cassette failed." • "Twelve-disc CD player failed." • "CD player failed."

Lincoln

LINCOLN CONTINENTAL 1988

Complaint Severity: Negligible. **Recall Alert:** See Recall Index. **Buyer's Summary:** Check the brakes—listen for noise, look for leaks and feel for vibration. They may fail, perform poorly or require frequent mechanical attention. Test the transmission thoroughly. See "Sudden Accelerations" in Introduction.

Hot Spots and Owner/NHTSA Comments:

1. Brakes: hydraulic system, vibration, failure. • "Brake system rendered inoperable due to intermittent electrical short circuit at steering column connector to ignition switch; already replaced per recall." • "Continual loss of brakes and vibration; antilock sensor replaced 6 to 7 times, as well as rear brakes and rotors." • "Intermittent braking failure; brakes failed to operate, collided with parked vehicle; second occurrence of failure within 37 days." • "Brakes applied, gear changed to reverse; car began to move only after turning car on and off many times; brakes began to engage." • "Continuous brake failures; replaced rear brakes; failed to operate when full strength applied to brake pedal; antilock brake lights on; accident occurred."

2. Power train: transmission: automatic, poor performance, difficulty shifting, slipping. • "While driving at speeds of 15-30 mph, transmission failed." • "Repeated automatic transmission problem; overhauled 4 times." • "Transmission shift cable broke; parked car with ignition turned off, car moved into busy street during rush hour." • "Transmission defective; leaks causing car to abruptly jump at low speeds." • "Automatic transmission defective; abrupt jumps at low speeds due to leak."

3. Brakes: hydraulic: anti-skid system, poor performance, failure, locking up. • "First occurrence, brake pedal went to the floor. Second occurrence, the brakes locked up, causing accident. Vehicle does have antilock brake system." • "Antilock brake system failed to stop vehicle effectively when applied, causing extended stopping. Electrical failure without backup systems." • "Antilock brake system: Total brake failure, including emergency brakes, while coming to stop; pedal went to floor; coasted to stop; speed 20 mph; no warning." • "Experienced total brake failure on the antilock brake system; problem in the ignition switch that

controls the electric to the antilock brake system." • "Antilock brake system malfunctioned; pedal goes down then it gets hard, resulting in total loss, replaced computer for antilock brake system to no avail."
4. Engine: mounts, breaking. • "Front and rear motor mounts broke." • "Motor mounts failed before and after recall repairs." • "Motor mounts broke after recall repair." • "When pulling out of driveway engine mounts failed and engine dropped to the ground." • "Broken motor mounts."
5. Fuel: throttle linkages and control, sudden accelerations. • "Vehicle goes into open throttle position after sitting in sun for a long period of time. To stop vehicle, press brakes real hard and hold." • "Shifted gear into drive and vehicle accelerated out of control; went through a wall and hit a truck." • "Vehicle experiencing sudden acceleration; car shoots forward at high speed without application to pedal." • "Engine accelerates from 0 to 55 mph without touching accelerator; engine roars with brakes applied; takes off on its own after taking foot off accelerator; no warning." • "Vehicle suddenly accelerated backward when shifting gear from park to reverse."
6. Interior systems: instruments and instrument panel, poor performance. • "Dashboard constructed and illuminated so that it's impossible for driver to read dashboard, gear indicator, turn signal when driving in broad daylight." • "Dashboard on 1988/1989 Lincoln Continental so constructed and illuminated that it's impossible for driver to read when driving in broad daylight." • "Problem with dashboard's lack of visibility; cannot read any information on dashboard during daytime." • "Instrument panel is impossible to read in daylight when sun is shining." • "Due to intensity of digitals, impossible to see other items on dash in daytime."

LINCOLN CONTINENTAL 1989

Complaint Severity: Negligible. **Recall Alert:** See Recall Index. **Buyer's Summary:** Check the brakes—listen for noise, look for leaks and feel for vibration. They may fail, perform poorly or require frequent mechanical attention. Test the transmission thoroughly.

Hot Spots and Owner/NHTSA Comments:
1. Power train: transmission: automatic, poor performance, difficulty shifting, slipping. • "Transmission does not shift smoothly; always jerks or hard shift from high to low gears." • "Recurring problem with rough transmission; all repair attempts to no avail." • "Automatic transmission shifts hard at low speeds, grinds; engine increases in rpm when upshifted during acceleration." • "The front strut was replaced 3 times and the rear was replaced 2 times, the transmission was replaced 4 times and the power steering and constant velocity joint replaced." • "Transmission shifts harshly from 1st to 2nd gear; also noisy."
2. Brakes: hydraulic system, vibration, failure. • "The digital dash lights don't light up and the brakes do not work. Once dash lights come on, everything is OK." • "Brakes failed completely 4 times; vehicle could only be stopped by manual emergency brakes; replaced brake pump assembly and brakes 3 times to no avail." • "Upon activation of brakes, steering control occurs, which causes warped rotors." • "Proceeded to an intersection, applied the brakes and found they were not operating." • "Entire brake system crystallizes continuously, causing vibrations."
3. Brakes: hydraulic: anti-skid system, poor performance, failure, locking up. • "Sensing switch and pump for the antilock braking system failed." • "Total loss of brakes on 2 different occasions; had to use hand brake to stop vehicle." • "Antilock brake system assembly on front; power brake hose rubs against bracket." • "Antilock valve block replaced due to vehicle pulling to right when brakes applied." • "The car has antilock brake system. When at the dealer, the pedal went all the way to the floor and did not stop the car."
4. Engine: mounts, noise, premature failure. • "Motor mounts are not holding engine down, causing loud noise and moving engine." • "Premature deterioration of right front and right rear engine mounts; prior to manufacturer recall." • "Motor mount wore out. Replaced at 51,000 miles." • "Replaced motor mounts." • "Replaced front cracked engine mounts."
5. Brakes: hydraulic: disc: rotor: disc hub, vibration, excessive wear. • "Front brakes warping; had rotors turned 3 times." • "Rotors on vehicle were replaced under recall; had to replace again under warranty; and now at 62,000 miles they need replacing again. Excessive wearing." • "Brakes fail on uneven surfaces; rotors warped." • "When stopping at highway speeds, front of car shakes and steering wheel vibrates; front brake rotors worn unevenly; no apparent wear in brake pads." • "Problem with front brakes pulsating under normal stopping use; repaired/replaced front brake rotors."
6. Electrical system: battery, malfunction, failure. • "Battery blew up." • "Battery had to be replaced." • "Battery in electrical system failed." • "Battery failure within 2 years." • "Battery failure 15 months after purchase of car and 21,000 miles."

LINCOLN CONTINENTAL 1990

Complaint Severity: Typical. **Recall Alert:** See Recall Index. **Buyer's Summary:** The steering may be stiff or not working correctly. Be sure to test the steering, especially on a cold start. Check the brakes—listen for noise, look for leaks and feel for vibration. They may fail, perform poorly or require frequent mechanical attention. See "Sudden Accelerations" in Introduction.

Hot Spots and Owner/NHTSA Comments:
1. Brakes: hydraulic: disc: rotor: disc hub, vibration, excessive wear. • "Warped front brake rotors caused vehicle to vibrate." • "Experience vibration in front end of car while braking; rotors warped." • "Front brake rotors warped; when brakes were applied; vehicle vibrated." • "Problem with vibration when applying brakes; repaired/replaced rotors." • "Warped rotors caused vehicle to pulsate; rotors were replaced twice."
2. Fuel: throttle linkages and control, sudden accelerations. • "Vehicle sticks at full throttle; only way to release is to shut off ignition and come to complete stop." • "Upon starting, vehicle accelerated at full rpm, slipped into reverse and crashed through garage door." • "Engine surges intermittently; car pulls without gas pedal being activated." • "Engine accelerated to approximately 80 mph, with no braking effectiveness when applied; vehicle was stopped by turning off ignition." • "Upon starting up with foot on brake and shifting gear into drive, throttle went wide open; vehicle accelerated forward over a curb, smashing into a bush."
3. Engine: mounts, breaking, corrosion. • "Front and rear engine mounts broke." • "Motor mounts were defective and were replaced by dealer; shift is now smoother." • "Engine mounts corroded and then broke." • "Defective motor mounts rubbed a hole in transmission fluid line and fluid was leaking under the vehicle." • "The front motor mounts had to be replaced at 60,000 miles." • "Motor mount on engine ruptured while driving."
4. Steering: linkages, breaking, pulling. • "While driving, vehicle makes snapping sound; pulls to right; front-end tie rods defective; replaced." • "While coming into toll booth, right front wheel flopped around with no control; sheared gas line; tie rod broke; loss of steering control." • "While driving at 40 mph, steering tie rod broke; lost control of vehicle til fully stopped." • "The tie rod broke and caused loss of steering control." • "Tie rods became loose; dealer had to replace all pieces at 71,000 miles. Previously the rotors warped and were replaced 3 times."

5. Steering: linkages: tie rod: inner, breaking, tire wear. • "Left and right front tie rods snapped off; ball joint froze and snapped while turning wheels." • "Tie rods failed, causing misalignment and premature tire wear." • "Inner end tie rods failed, causing premature tire wear." • "Tie rod broke, causing loss of steering control; rod moving back and forth severed gas line." • "Tie rods broke, causing loss of control."

6. Steering: linkages: tie rod: end, breaking, pulling. • "Failure of right and left tie rod ends." • "Left and right tie rod ends broke." • "Front tires turned toward each other. Steering locked up. Tie rod ends broke." • "In 30-degree weather, passenger tie rod end broke and caused a skid; right side broke 6 weeks later at 3 mph." • "Inner tie rod end coming out of the rack, causing vehicle to steer in 2 different directions."

LINCOLN CONTINENTAL 1991

Complaint Severity: Minor. **Recall Alert:** See Recall Index. **Buyer's Summary:** The steering may be stiff or not working correctly. Be sure to test the steering, especially on a cold start. Check the brakes—listen for noise, look for leaks and feel for vibration. They may fail, perform poorly or require frequent mechanical attention. Test the transmission thoroughly. See "Sudden Accelerations" in Introduction.

Hot Spots and Owner/NHTSA Comments:

1. Brakes: hydraulic: disc: rotor: disc hub, excessive wear. • "Recall repairs on front brake rotors were done, but problem reoccurred. Dealer says they will not fix." • "Front brake rotors continuously warp. When stopping, the front wheels skid on slippery surfaces." • "Driver heard loud noise. Pulled over and took off right front wheel. Four out of five lug nuts had sheared off. Dealer says vehicle had wrong rotor." • "Front brake rotors and pads failed, prior to recall." • "Replaced rear rotors."

2. Brakes: hydraulic: anti-skid system, poor performance, failure, locking up. • "Brakes locked up when applied; pedal went all the way to the floor." • "Antilock brake system front disc rotors continue to wear; when applying brake the front shakes." • "Vehicle has excessive vibration, to the point where driver has to pull over to gain control of vehicle. Dealer continues to replace antilock brake system components." • "Intermittent vibration of vehicle at high speeds and when braking." • "Experienced vibration in steering at 45 mph, losing stability. Also, antilock brake system, when applied, makes a loud grinding noise."

3. Power train: transmission: automatic, poor performance, difficulty shifting, slipping. • "Transmission gear would not engage." • "Transmission linkage is loose and vehicle slips out of park." • "Vehicle's automatic transmission slips intermittently and does not go into gears." • "Automatic transmission failure at 85,000 miles." • "Transmission failure, resulting in loss of control."

4. Fuel: throttle linkages and control, sudden accelerations. • "From 2 mph parking lot speed, engine suddenly accelerated and crashed into several other vehicles." • "Vehicle surged forward out of control." • "Vehicle suddenly accelerated and went out of control; resulted in an accident." • "Vehicle experienced sudden and uncontrolled acceleration when gear was shifted out of park." • "Driver put vehicle into drive from park and vehicle accelerated in parking lot; hit curb, sign and curb. Vehicle had to be turned off before it would stop."

5. Brakes: hydraulic: shoe: disc brake system, vibration, noise, pulling. • "Extreme vibration of frontal steering when braking at speeds of 30 to 40 mph; rotors have been replaced along with other parts 3 times." • "While driving, brakes squeaked and pedal went to the floor." • "Warped front brake rotors and pads, causing vehicle to vibrate upon braking." • "Vehicle pulled to right when brakes applied; prior to recall." • "Front brake assembly replaced."

6. Steering: linkages, locking up, breaking, failure. • "The outer tie rod end and the inner tie rod have been replaced twice, and now the end needs to be replaced." • "Front right tie rod failed due to metal fatigue, which resulted in tie rod and tire separating." • "Steering locked up when driver turned vehicle to the right." • "Both inner and outer tie rods on the driver's-side broke while making a left turn." • "Tie rod failed while turning into parking lot. Vehicle lost all control."

LINCOLN CONTINENTAL 1992

Complaint Severity: Typical. **Recall Alert:** See Recall Index. **Buyer's Summary:** Check the brakes—listen for noise, look for leaks and feel for vibration. They may fail, perform poorly or require frequent mechanical attention. See "Sudden Accelerations" in Introduction.

Hot Spots and Owner/NHTSA Comments:

1. Fuel: throttle linkages and control, sudden accelerations. • "Speed doesn't decrease once foot is removed from accelerator. When applying brakes, antilock brake system responds with possible lockup." • "Vehicle travels at approximately 24-31 mph with foot removed from gas pedal." • "While taking off from a stop sign, vehicle accelerated; stopped it by braking and turning off ignition." • "Sudden acceleration and high engine speeds result when stopped with vehicle in neutral." • "Engine idled to high speed with brakes applied. Surged with light touch to gas pedal. No warning. Impact 12:00 position, speed 15 mph. Airbag did not deploy."

2. Brakes: hydraulic: disc: rotor: disc hub, vibration, excessive wear. • "Antilock brake system failure; replaced; rotors warping and disc pads causing vibration of the front when making a stop." • "Front brake rotors warp constantly, causing brakes to vibrate when applied. Repaired 3 times." • "Brake rotors replaced. Travels 500 miles before brakes burn up." • "Front and back brake rotors replaced."

LINCOLN MARK VII 1988

Complaint Severity: Serious. **Recall Alert:** See Recall Index. **Buyer's Summary:** Check the brakes—listen for noise, look for leaks and feel for vibration. They may fail, perform poorly or require frequent mechanical attention. Test the transmission thoroughly. See "Sudden Accelerations" in Introduction.

Hot Spots and Owner/NHTSA Comments:

1. Fuel: throttle linkages and control, sudden accelerations. • "Problem with throttle and linkage controls; vehicle accelerated suddenly after putting into drive; resulted in accident with extensive damage." • "While in slowly moving traffic, vehicle accelerated wide open; resulted in collision." • "Upon putting vehicle into drive with foot on brakes, accelerated uncontrollably; resulted in accident." • "Vehicle hesitates, then takes off; unable to stop with application of brakes." • "While driving at low speed, engine suddenly jumped to full rpm; with both feet on brakes, could not stop; resulted in a collision."

2. Brakes: hydraulic system, noise, failure. • "Several occasions of brakes fading to the floor; dealer has replaced major components, but problem persists." • "Brakes grind, growl and squeak excessively; repaired/replaced rotors; noise ceased for short period of time, then returned." • "When driving in rain at highway speed, first application of brakes does not work as well as in clear weather." • "Brakes completely failed while driving; brake light went on; resulted in accident with injuries sustained." • "When it rains, brakes get very wet; push on brake and no brake until they dry out."

3. Brakes: hydraulic: anti-skid system, poor performance, failure, locking up. • "Defective antilock braking system; rubbing noise occurs when accelerating from complete stop; difficult to stop; repaired/replaced braking system." • "Antilock brake system failure; complete loss of braking ability while trying to stop. Had to use emergency brake to make vehicle stop." • "Brake failure caused car to skid; injuries." • "Front brake rotors warped, caused antilock brakes to grab unevenly."

4. Power train: transmission: automatic, poor performance, difficulty shifting, slipping. • "Unspecified transmission failure." • "Transmission slips, jumps and surges intermittently." • "Automatic transmission failure; assembled with parts missing." • "Transmission problems."

LINCOLN MARK VII 1989

Complaint Severity: Typical. **Buyer's Summary:** Check the brakes—listen for noise, look for leaks and feel for vibration. They may fail, perform poorly or require frequent mechanical attention. See "Sudden Accelerations" in Introduction.

Hot Spots and Owner/NHTSA Comments:

1. Fuel: throttle linkages and control, sudden accelerations. • "Vehicle placed in reverse gear; suddenly accelerated at full speed forward, burning rubber, without shifting gears, hitting a wall." • "Engine starts and dies on first attempt at starting." • "When started and shifted, barely touched gas pedal, car suddenly accelerated out of control; slammed on brake, had no effect; resulted in accident." • "Experienced a surge, then headlight went out while driving." • "Hesitation and/or stalls."

2. Brakes: hydraulic system, malfunction. • "Brake defect recall; have not had repairs, as dealer has not received necessary parts." • "Brakes grab and release alternately as you press on pedal." • "Occasional groan and shudder without using brake; comes from rear only."

LINCOLN TOWN CAR 1987

Complaint Severity: Very Serious. **Recall Alert:** See Recall Index. **Buyer's Summary:** Check the brakes—listen for noise, look for leaks and feel for vibration. They may fail, perform poorly or require frequent mechanical attention. See "Sudden Accelerations" in Introduction.

Hot Spots and Owner/NHTSA Comments:

1. Fuel: throttle linkages and control, sudden accelerations. • "Started vehicle, put in drive gear, took off at high rate of speed, resulting in severe damages." • "Upon starting, car took off like rocket, burned rubber; keeping foot on brake, shifted into neutral, turned ignition off." • "Car was put in drive and accelerated at an uncontrollable rate of speed until crashing, at which time the engine died and car stopped." • "Started car and moved gear into reverse; car spun wheels at excessive speed without warning; resulted in accident with 2 people injured." • "After being parked for an hour, when restarted without putting into any gear, vehicle surged back and forth extensively and hit parked vehicle."

2. Brakes: hydraulic system, locking up, noise, vibration. • "Brakes, when applied, went to the floor." • "Brakes lock up; car skids out of control in circles." • "Brake pedal must be pumped before car stops; pedal goes to floor." • "Defective brakes make grinding sound and, in some instances, just before coming to complete stop, car begins to vibrate." • "Problem with brake noise; repaired; a week later, noise returned; due to design—metal shoes were used rather than asbestos; problem cannot be solved."

LINCOLN TOWN CAR 1988

Complaint Severity: Typical. **Recall Alert:** See Recall Index. **Buyer's Summary:** Verify that the cruise control system works properly, and that it doesn't cause the engine to surge. The fuel injection system has been blamed for hesitation and stalling. Be sure the vehicle doesn't die in traffic or at stops. Check the brakes—listen for noise, look for leaks and feel for vibration. They may fail, perform poorly or require frequent mechanical attention. Test the transmission thoroughly. See "Sudden Accelerations" in Introduction.

Hot Spots and Owner/NHTSA Comments:

1. Fuel: throttle linkages and control, sudden accelerations. • "When pulled car onto highway, it took off; went across over curb, no control; hit cement base; resulted in 2 fatalities." • "Experienced 2 incidents of sudden acceleration, one in reverse and one in drive; both times resulted in accident, had no control over speed." • "Inserted key in ignition, started motor, car went completely out of control, surged back into other vehicle; applied brakes to no avail." • "Throttle body air bypass failure resulted in intermittent sudden acceleration; also prevented cruise control from disengaging." • "While pulling out of driveway, put vehicle in reverse, vehicle accelerated; stepped on brake but vehicle continued to surge; landed in neighbor's driveway."

2. Power train: transmission: automatic, poor performance, difficulty shifting, slipping. • "Car in parked position with engine on, gearshift selector moved from park position to reverse; car moved backward and struck brick column." • "Problems with shifting gears; severe jerking of shifting system; driving on freeway in slow traffic, must step down on gas pedal to kick into gear to speed up." • "Transmission has problems shifting gears; must step down on gas pedal to kick into gear; severe jerking of shifting system." • "Transmission downshifting many times; 2 new vacuum parts added to 1989 model." • "Transmission leak; replaced valve covers and intake gaskets."

3. Equipment: speed control, malfunction, sudden acceleration. • "Keyless entry and front door lock inoperable." • "Ongoing problem with cruise control; goes out suddenly on level ground; when going uphill, when needed to shift gears, automatically shifted then quit." • "While driving, speed cruise control turned on by itself and vehicle accelerated out of control." • "Difficulty getting car out of cruise by pressing 'off' button on steering wheel spoke; minor accident." • "Cruise control does not operate properly."

4. Fuel: fuel injection system, stalling, hesitation. • "Car hesitated, choked and jumped out of cruise control, then died." • "Engine missing and running badly; also, noise occurring at 55-60 mph; fix/insulation kit installed to correct noise and missing." • "Fuel injection system defective; does not idle properly, vibrates, burning gas excessively, stalls upon vibration." • "Stalling problem; repaired/replaced fuel pump, fuel pump relay, distributor, sensor and some wiring."

5. Electrical system: wiring: harness: under dash, malfunction, fire. • "Wiring harness from rear of car to front laid on top of gas tank; covering wore through and caused short." • "Steering column fire while vehicle was being driven; electrical short." • "Steering column caught on fire. Vehicle was totaled." • "Steering column started to smoke, resulting in a fire that burned up steering column." • "Vehicle began to smoke after moving back and forward in driveway. Smoke and flames were coming from dashboard on driver's side."

6. Brakes: hydraulic system, failure. • "Upon starting car, brake pedal normal; after driving, pedal hard, making car difficult to stop." • "Malfunction of brake system; applied brakes at stop, car didn't stop, pedal went to floor; replaced master cylinder." • "Defective brakes; upon starting or after sitting for an hour, brakes would not depress; in order to stop car, must turn ignition off." • "Brake system failure." • "Brake failure 4 times."

LINCOLN TOWN CAR 1989

Complaint Severity: Serious. **Recall Alert:** See Recall Index. **Buyer's Summary:** Look carefully for any kind of leakage, especially under the car. Verify that the cruise control system works properly, and that it doesn't cause the engine to surge. Test the transmission thoroughly. See "Sudden Accelerations" in Introduction. Make sure air conditioner works properly.

Hot Spots and Owner/NHTSA Comments:

1. Fuel: throttle linkages and control, sudden accelerations. • "While backing out of driveway, put gear in reverse and foot on brake, took foot off brake and vehicle accelerated out of control; resulted in an accident." • "Without touching the accelerator, vehicle accelerated out of control; resulted in an accident." • "Car accelerated at excessive rate of speed, brakes were ineffective in stopping car; accident occurred before finally stopping." • "Upon starting car and putting gear selector in drive, car suddenly accelerated to full power, completely out of control." • "Vehicle shifted into reverse with foot on brakes, raced to top speed; brakes failed to stop; resulted in accident."

2. Power train: transmission: automatic, poor performance, difficulty shifting, slipping. • "Erratic shifting of transmission." • "Transmission main control valve and front pump failed." • "Transmission failed in less than 1,000 miles." • "Less than 2 years and 25,000 miles, transmission needed replacement." • "Leaking transmission; gears slip; repaired/rebuilt 3 times."

3. Electrical system: wiring: harness: under dash, malfunction, fire. • "Car was parked, steering started smoking; burned steering column, dash and front seat." • "Car had not been driven for 2 days; noticed fire, possibly electrical." • "Car parked for 6 hours, caught fire and burned. Started from the dashboard wiring." • "There was a fire within the confines of the steering column. It is believed to be an electrical fire." • "Had electrical fire in steering column."

4. Engine: rust, leaks, premature failure. • "Freeze-out plug and water pump rusted out." • "Excessive use of oil; oil light continues to come on." • "Excessive use of oil." • "Excessive oil leak in engine; unknown problem." • "Less than 2 years and 25,000 miles, vehicle has had motor replaced twice."

5. Air conditioner: failure. • "Air conditioner would not operate." • "Air conditioning failed at 2,000 miles." • "Air conditioner temperature control/low idle relay problem." • "Air conditioner failed."

6. Equipment: speed control, malfunction. • "Intermittent cruise control problems." • "Car will go into or out of cruise control when not activated by driver." • "Car will go into or out of cruise control even if not activated by driver." • "Sluggish cruise control."

LINCOLN TOWN CAR 1990

Complaint Severity: Serious. **Recall Alert:** See Recall Index. **Buyer's Summary:** The airbags in this vehicle have experienced failures and malfunctions: You may need a professional evaluation on the condition of the airbags. Check the brakes—listen for noise, look for leaks and feel for vibration. They may fail, perform poorly or require frequent mechanical attention. See "Sudden Accelerations" in Introduction.

Hot Spots and Owner/NHTSA Comments:

1. Fuel: throttle linkages and control, sudden accelerations. • "While at stoplight or stop sign, engine races, causing car to lunge forward." • "Put car into reverse, leaped forward and traveled approximately 30 feet; smashed into double door of entryway of shopping mall before coming to stop." • "Upon starting vehicle, suddenly accelerated on its own, resulting in severe damages." • "Malfunction of the accelerator caused car to speed up to 80 mph when slight pressure was applied." • "Throttle sensor failed when engine started; car shifted into reverse, unintended acceleration occurred, hitting parked 18-wheel trailer."

2. Brakes: hydraulic system, locking up, vibration. • "Vehicle skids when brakes are applied." • "Right front brakes locked up; pulled to right while stopping." • "Black shavings coming from tire area; replaced pad and rotor." • "Brake rotors are out of round; vibration felt." • "Faulty brakes and computer failure caused accident."

3. Brakes: hydraulic: disc: rotor: disc hub, excessive wear, vibration. • "Front brake rotors wear out at approximately every 3,000 miles, causing brake failure." • "Vibration when braking; warping and thinning on front rotors." • "Front brake rotors warped; caused excessive vibration when braking." • "Brake rotors were out of round and not making contact with brake pads correctly." • "Rotors and drums worn out due to excessive heat, but pads remain in good condition."

4. Structure: hood assembly: latches, failure. • "Hood latch failed, causing hood to fly back and hit windshield." • "While driving, hood latch failure occurred and damaged the vehicle." • "Hood latch failed when driving at 55 mph on open highway." • "Defective hood latch caused hood to fly up while vehicle was in motion." • "Hood flew up while driving vehicle and broke front windshield."

5. Brakes: hydraulic: shoe: disc brake system, vibration, excessive wear. • "Front brake pads and rotors wore out completely and were replaced at 9,000 miles; caused vibration and lack of braking ability." • "When applying brakes, felt grinding and possible slipping of brakes; replaced brake pads and rotors." • "Rear brake lining and front pads and rotors problems." • "Excessive front brake wear; serviced many times; also, rear brake lining wearing out too soon." • "While pumping brakes, car kept moving; pulsation when braking; repaired/replaced front brake pads and turned rotors."

6. Interior systems: passive restraint: airbag: driver, malfunction, failure. • "Airbag did not deploy in an accident." • "Frontal crash with no airbag deployment. Dealer said the wiring and switches malfunctioned." • "At approximately 35 mph, airbag failed to deploy during accident, causing injury." • "Frontal collision. Driver's airbag did not deploy, but passenger's airbag did deploy. Rear passenger's seat belt did not lock up." • "Vehicle self-shifted from park to reverse upon starting, hitting fence and garage. Then suddenly accelerated in drive, hitting garage. Airbag did not deploy."

LINCOLN TOWN CAR 1991

Complaint Severity: Troublesome. **Recall Alert:** See Recall Index. **Buyer's Summary:** Check the brakes—listen for noise, look for leaks and feel for vibration. They may fail, perform poorly or require frequent mechanical attention. See "Sudden Accelerations" in Introduction.

Hot Spots and Owner/NHTSA Comments:

1. Brakes: hydraulic: disc: rotor: disc hub, excessive wear, premature failure. • "Brake booster is defective. Brakes come on when vehicle is in motion, and vehicle shakes. Brake rotors have been turned and new brakes installed." • "All 4 brake rotors wear out prematurely. Have been replaced 4 times in 30,000 miles; affects braking ability and could cause accident." • "Antilock brake system: All 4 rotors have warped; 4 sets from 10,000 miles apart. Vehicle vibrates extensively when applying brakes." • "Front brake rotors fail prematurely. Every 10,000 miles the rotors warp and need replacement." • "Warped rotors caused vibration when braking."

2. Brakes: hydraulic: anti-skid system, poor performance, failure, locking up. • "Antilock brake system reacts violently and throws driver's foot off the brake pedal; car also destroys front brake rotors." • "Foot was on brake, vehicle started to surge; no response from the antilock braking system. Airbag did not deploy." • "The antilock brake system has failed. When you press on the brake pedal, the pedal is hard and will not stop the car. Every time the car hits a bump, the antilock brake system light comes on." • "Electronic antilock brake system controllers failed, causing pump to pressurize master cylinder at wrong time and brakes to engage, resulting in loss of control, accident and injuries." • "Antilock brake system failed to stop vehicle effectively when applied, causing extended stopping. Brake pedal vibrates and shakes when applied."

3. Fuel: throttle linkages and control, sudden accelerations. • "While driving, throttle sticks, resulting in engine surge to 25 mph without pedal application." • "While backing out from a parking space, vehicle suddenly accelerated; applied brakes but couldn't stop vehicle; struck another vehicle in rear." • "While driving, vehicle throttle sticks, causing sudden acceleration; to stop vehicle, constantly pressed hard on brake pedal or put gear in neutral." • "Engine suddenly accelerated without depressing accelerator; brakes applied; no prior warning."

4. Brakes: hydraulic system, locking up, vibration, failure. • "Brakes, rotors, master cylinder and brake booster failed." • "In dealer's 11 times for brake service and changing other components. Brakes heat up, which results in lockup and slowing down." • "After passing a vehicle in middle lane, was in far left lane and attempted to return to middle lane; unable to stop vehicle by applying brakes or steer." • "Car unstable, with vibration and unacceptable jerking motion in front when trying to slow down or stop; original brake rotors replaced twice to no avail."

5. Equipment: electric power accessories: windows, malfunction, failure. • "All vehicle's electrical windows have become inoperative; replaced left front and rear and right rear." • "Left front and right rear and left front motors inside the doors that operate the window failed, resulting in windows coming down and locking in position; replaced 2 motors." • "All of the windows seem to stop working for no apparent reason; first there is a loud sound, then the window stops working." • "While driving in rain, left front and rear windows suddenly opened due to regulator failure, causing the vehicle to lose control and swerve." • "Left front power window inoperative due to broken cable."

6. Structure: hood assembly: latches, failure. • "Involved in recall on hood latch; makes appointment with dealer, goes to dealer at specified time, but dealer does not have parts to do repairs." • "Hood latch failed, causing hood to fly up." • "Hood latch failed while driving on highway at 60 mph, causing a vision problem and breaking windshield." • "While driving, hood latch disconnected; fell on windshield and smashed it." • "While driving, hood suddenly and without warning came up; safety latch did nothing; hood flew back, bent roof and shattered windshield."

LINCOLN TOWN CAR 1992

Complaint Severity: Very Serious. **Recall Alert:** See Recall Index. **Buyer's Summary:** The airbags in this vehicle have experienced failures and malfunctions: You may need a professional evaluation on the condition of the airbags. Check the brakes—listen for noise, look for leaks and feel for vibration. They may fail, perform poorly or require frequent mechanical attention. See "Sudden Accelerations" in Introduction.

Hot Spots and Owner/NHTSA Comments:

1. Fuel: throttle linkages and control, sudden accelerations. • "Started vehicle with foot on brake to enable a shift into reverse; engine went to full power, tires spun and vehicle crashed." • "Car accelerated in reverse while backing into parking place. Hit car behind it. Driver's seat back snapped off in accident." • "In reverse with brake pedal fully applied, car accelerated out of control, resulting in accident and injury." • "The accelerator stuck and vehicle accelerated on its own and caused an accident." • "When moving gears from park to drive, vehicle suddenly accelerated from 5 to 50 mph."

2. Brakes: hydraulic: anti-skid system, poor performance, failure, locking up. • "Antilock brakes don't release when foot is removed from brake pedal." • "Antilock brake system locks up on incline when applying brakes; brakes grab only when vehicle has been sitting for a period of time." • "Dealer replaced master cylinder once and front pads twice; car still has antilock brake system problems." • "Vehicle had antilock brake system lockup, causing spinout, landed in a ditch and caught on fire."

3. Brakes: hydraulic: disc: rotor: disc hub, vibration, excessive wear. • "Brake system failure; front disc rotors were defective; replaced 7 different rotors." • "Rotors continuously warp, causing brakes to pulsate." • "Left front brake rotor replaced." • "Antilock brake system front brakes lock up in low speed (5 mph). Failure of front rotors."

4. Interior systems: seat tracks and anchors, breaking, malfunction. • "Front seats of vehicle are off track. Loss of seat stability." • "Car brought back 3 times, nothing could be done until new design track is available; now available, dealer did not receive it." • "Driver's seat bolt broke, causing seat frame to separate from rail fastened to floor; driver thrown backwards." • "Driver's seat track keeps breaking while occupied; 3 times within 5,000 miles; not safe to drive—shakes, goes backwards and forwards. Antilock brake system failure; extended stopping." • "Driver's seat lifted off metal frame due to a bolt shearing through metal flange anchored to floor."

5. Interior systems: passive restraint: airbag: driver, malfunction, failure. • "Airbag prematurely deployed, causing loss of vehicle control and front-end collision at less than 50 mph." • "Car (rental) was involved in a frontal collision; airbag failed to deploy, despite impact with a speeding car." • "Upon impact, during frontal crash at approximately 40 mph, 1:00 position on front bumper, dual airbag failed to deploy." • "Dual airbags did not deploy."

LINCOLN TOWN CAR 1993

Complaint Severity: Best 3% in Guide. **Recall Alert:** See Recall Index. **Buyer's Summary:** Test the transmission thoroughly.

Hot Spots and Owner/NHTSA Comments:

1. Power train: transmission: automatic, poor performance, difficulty shifting, slipping. • "Noisy transmission." • "Traveling down the road, transmission slips out of gear." • "Transmission oil leak." • "Automatic transmission would not shift from 1st to 2nd gear as intended; should have shifted at 30 mph; almost caused head-on collision." • "Transmission slipped."

Mazda—Cars and Trucks

MAZDA 323 1987

Complaint Severity: Troublesome. **Buyer's Summary:** Test the clutch. See "Sudden Accelerations" in Introduction.

Hot Spots and Owner/NHTSA Comments:

1. Engine: pulley: crankshaft, breaking. • "Casting flow in crankshaft; harmonic balancer and pulley assembler broke off crankshaft at flow." • "Crankshaft in engine broke." • "End of crankshaft keyway goes bad, causing pulleys to become loose." • "While driving, the crankshaft broke in half, causing belts and pulleys to hang off and resulting in not being able to start vehicle." • "Crankshaft cracked where it is attached to the timing belt pulley."

2. Fuel: throttle linkages and control, sudden accelerations. • "Throttle stuck; placed gear in reverse and vehicle surged rearward; resulted in an accident." • "Sudden acceleration problem, especially when turning corners and going uphill, accelerating to approximately 2,500 rpm." • "Throttle linkage and control malfunction caused the engine to accelerate uncontrollably, resulting in an accident." • "Suddenly accelerated after taking foot off brake; gear in drive position." • "Upon starting and shifting to reverse, car suddenly propelled out of driveway; practically stood on brake trying to stop car; accident resulted."

3. Power train: clutch assembly, difficulty shifting. • "Chattering clutch, particularly when cold." • "Problems with clutch periodically in 1st gear." • "Clutch doesn't engage smoothly when moving car from standstill; loss of power causes clutch and car to chatter." • "Clutch chatters when engine is cold; occurs only when going from 1st to 2nd, 2nd to 3rd gears, etc."

MAZDA 323 1988

Complaint Severity: Troublesome. **Recall Alert:** See Recall Index. **Buyer's Summary:** Check the brakes—listen for noise, look for leaks and feel for vibration. They may fail, perform poorly or require frequent mechanical attention. Test the transmission thoroughly. See "Sudden Accelerations" in Introduction.

Hot Spots and Owner/NHTSA Comments:

1. Interior systems: active restraints: belt buckles, breaking, malfunction. • "Driver's seat belt buckle broke; it would release randomly before becoming inoperative; passenger's buckle broke until plastic particles removed from within." • "Driver's- and passenger-side seat belt buckles broke." • "Consumer was driving, made a quick stop and the seat belt buckle came loose." • "Driver seat belt buckle does not latch." • "Red release button cracked, rendering seat belt unlatchable." • "The driver's-side seat belt buckle is hard to lock."

2. Brakes: hydraulic system, excessive wear, locking up. • "Worn brakes replaced." • "At slow speeds on wet roads, car skids when applying brakes." • "Defective braking system; both front and rear brakes repaired/replaced." • "Front and rear brakes need replacement." • "Brakes wear down excessively; replaced very often."

3. Fuel: throttle linkages and control, sudden accelerations. • "Car accelerated immediately after startup; brakes didn't work, nor did car slow down or stop in neutral; resulted in accident." • "Vehicle suddenly accelerated when started in park; neither brakes nor shifting to neutral stopped car; hit another vehicle." • "Vehicle suddenly accelerated backwards when shifted into reverse gear, ran into foundation of a house; accelerator cable was sticking." • "Vehicle suddenly accelerated out of control in reverse; resulted in accident." • "Started ignition and car suddenly accelerated in park; resulted in accident but no damages."

4. Power train: transmission: automatic, poor performance, difficulty shifting, slipping. • "Numerous transmission replacements; vehicle hesitates when shifting gears." • "Transmission failed numerous times; shifting into reverse or drive, car would not move; gearshift sliding back and forth; replaced transmission, problems continued." • "Transmission thermostat failed." • "While driving on highway at 45 mph, transmission ceased to function." • "Transmission has failed on highway 3 times."

MAZDA 323 1989

Complaint Severity: Troublesome. **Recall Alert:** See Recall Index. **Buyer's Summary:** Look carefully for any kind of leakage, especially under the car. Check the brakes—listen for noise, look for leaks and feel for vibration. They may fail, perform poorly or require frequent mechanical attention. Test the transmission thoroughly. See "Sudden Accelerations" in Introduction.

Hot Spots and Owner/NHTSA Comments:

1. Interior systems: active restraints: belt buckles, breaking, malfunction. • "Vehicle's driver's-side seat belt female portion broke." • "The driver's-side latches are hard to unlatch, but passenger side won't latch at all." • "Driver's-side seat belt does not always buckle, and will not retract." • "A piece of the red release button has broken off and fallen into the latch well, causing the belt to be inoperative." • "Front passenger seat belt will not properly latch or unlatch for use."

2. Power train: transmission: automatic, poor performance, difficulty shifting, slipping. • "Automatic transmission with overdrive is not shifting correctly." • "Engine; car had 3 fires from transmission fluid falling on the transmission." • "Transmission stalled or hesitated while changing into lower gears." • "Brakes, transmission and electrical system have failed several times." • "Transmission makes grinding noise when shifting between gears."

3. Engine: noise, leaks, stalling, fire. • "Engine noise." • "Problem with minor oil leak." • "Heat sending sensor unit malfunctioned." • "Intermittent stalling." • "Engine; car had 3 fires from transmission fluid falling on the transmission."

4. Fuel: throttle linkages and control, sudden accelerations. • "Vehicle was started and shifted into reverse; sudden acceleration drove the car into a crash." • "Vehicle accelerated out of control when shifted into drive; after impact, vehicle still had high idling." • "After leaving drive-in, put auto into drive and suddenly darted into main street like a jet-propelled plane; hit parked car; damage total." • "Driver tapped accelerator pedal lightly to move forward; car suddenly accelerated at high rate of speed, striking pedestrian and causing whiplash to driver's neck." • "Vehicle experienced sudden acceleration; resulted in accident."

5. Interior systems: active restraints: belt retractors, breaking, malfunction, failure. • "Driver received serious head injuries upon impact with windshield due to failed seat belt retractor mechanism; impact velocity 25 mph, position 12:00." • "Seat belt retractor failed to tighten belt." • "Driver's-side seat belt retractor spring broke." • "Driver's-side seat belt does not always buckle; will not retract." • "Seat belt retractor failure."

6. Brakes: hydraulic system, noise, malfunction, failure. • "Brake wear indicator falsely causing noise." • "Brakes, transmission and electrical system have failed several times." • "Front disc brakes needed replacing." • "Brake system malfunctioned."

MAZDA 626 1987

Complaint Severity: Negligible. **Recall Alert:** See Recall Index. **Buyer's Summary:** Test the suspension by feeling for vibration or pulling while driving. Check the brakes—listen for noise, look for leaks and feel for vibration. They may fail, perform poorly or require frequent mechanical attention. Test the transmission thoroughly.

Hot Spots and Owner/NHTSA Comments:

1. Power train: transmission: automatic, poor performance, difficulty shifting, slipping. • "When turning corners and accelerating, transmission shifts into neutral for about a second; engine revs up and then shifts back into gear with a clunk." • "Vehicle experiences poor gas transition; shuddering during gear changes; replaced modified body valve and forward/reverse clutch plate." • "Defective transmission; when placed in drive, the car lurches forward or stalls; only idles in park or neutral." • "On occasion when slowing to turn corner and then accelerate, engine revs up for few seconds, as if transmission is slipping, before it finally grabs hold." • "When trying to accelerate, car does not shift into next gear; meter on dashboard shoots up past 3,000 rpm, yet car will not shift to next gear."

2. Electrical system: ignition: switch, failure. • "Vehicle exhibits all symptoms of recall on ignition switch terminal problem; replaced ignition switch." • "Ignition switch terminal failure caused windshield wipers, radio, engine cooling fan and air conditioner failures; engine came to complete halt." • "Recall for replacement of defective ignition switch received; replaced, owner paid for service; requesting reimbursement." • "Failure of recalled ignition switch caused problems with air conditioner." • "Faulty ignition switch resulted in engine breakdown, according to dealer."

3. Suspension: independent front, alignment, vibration. • "Independent front suspension faulty; car pulls toward the left and steering wheel vibrates." • "Suspension malfunction; car pulls to left, shimmies and shakes; aligned front end and straightened steering wheel. Continues to drift." • "Front suspension not correctly aligned; during highway driving, car pulls drastically to left." • "Vehicle pulls to left while driving; front-end alignment problem." • "When driving, car pulls to the left and right; front-end suspension problem to blame; left or right drifting depends where steering is turned."

4. Electrical system: ignition, malfunction, failure. • "Ignition switch malfunctioned; prior to recall." • "Ignition switch terminals shorted out, causing electrical burning smell and electrical failures." • "Ignition switch failure. Recall related." • "Short in ignition; repaired/replaced ignition assembly; recall on part, requesting reimbursement for repair."

5. Brakes: hydraulic system, noise, premature failure. • "Need front and rear brakes; grinding sound caused by not using asbestos in brakes." • "Premature failure of both rear and front brakes; have had to repair/replace pads and rear brakes." • "Faulty brakes; repaired/replaced rear brakes and front brakes at 29,000 miles." • "Front brake rotors failed." • "Worn brakes and pads replaced."

6. Electrical system: fire, failure. • "First failure, battery died, jump-started; second failure, entire electrical system failed, including battery; towed." • "Both alternator and battery failed at 35,000 miles." • "Electrical fire while parked overnight; found headliner burned following straight pattern out to left and right of dome light." • "When starting vehicle, wipers, radio, air conditioner and cassette player would not function." • "Electrical malfunction; windshield wipers would quit, took some time before getting them to work; at times, sunroof wouldn't come back unless using crank."

MAZDA 626 1988

Complaint Severity: Minor. **Recall Alert:** See Recall Index. **Buyer's Summary:** Make sure the shoulder belts don't cut across your neck and are well anchored. Test the transmission thoroughly. See "Sudden Accelerations" in Introduction.

Hot Spots and Owner/NHTSA Comments:

1. Power train: transmission: automatic, poor performance, difficulty shifting, slipping. • "Transmission leaking; does not shift properly; defective transmission." • "Transmission, computer-operated, erratically shifts gears; least difference in pressure on accelerator causes transmission to shift gears in jerky motion." • "Leaking transmission hoses replaced; shifting erratically at 60 mph." • "Transmission lines leaking." • "Automatic transmission slips into neutral, causing an increase in rpm."

2. Seat belts: malfunction, failure. • "Driver's-side seat belt on door track does not glide. When door closes, it should move to position; however, it does not." • "Vehicle's seat belt motorized retractor is inoperative on driver's-side." • "Motorized safety belt is stuck in position. This has happened after the recall work was performed." • "Driver's motorized seat belt is jammed and belt does not move." • "Automatic belt stopped midway when door was opened."

3. Structure: door assembly: handle: outside, breaking, malfunction. • "Door handle failed to open from the outside; would only open from inside." • "The driver's- and passenger-side door handles broke." • "Front door handles on driver's and passenger's sides will not open doors." • "Both front doors could not be opened from outside with handle. While stopped at light, rolled down electric window. Door popped open. Replaced handles."

4. Fuel: throttle linkages and control, sudden accelerations. • "Vehicle suddenly accelerated when putting car in drive; accelerator stuck; resulted in accident." • "Car took off backward at high speed, did not shift into reverse; applied brakes, no effect; resulted in accident; stick still in park position, finally got into neutral." • "Upon starting and before shifter was moved, engine started racing, car took off rapidly in reverse; rammed into pillar, then accelerated forward." • "When shifted in reverse with foot on brake, car shot backwards; hit a pole." • "Upon starting engine and shifting gear to reverse, vehicle suddenly accelerated out of control with loud engine racing sound; resulted in severe damages."

5. Interior systems: shoulder belts, malfunction, failure. • "During an accident, shoulder belts became unlatched at impact of less than 20 mph." • "Right front automatic shoulder belt failed to operate." • "Automatic shoulder belt loose; will not tighten even when pulling hard or jerking it; continues to sag." • "Automatic shoulder belt failed after recall repair." • "When driver's-side window is rolled down manually, automatic shoulder belt retracts and door pops open."

6. Equipment: electric power accessories: windows, malfunction. • "Power windows have a short and do not open." • "When power window is rolled down, the door latch releases and door opens." • "Driver's power window switch broke off, preventing window from going up or down." • "Driver's-side power window activator will not properly go up or down. Recall related." • "When the power windows are lowered, the door automatically pops open; this has happened while driving or while stationary."

MAZDA 626 1989

Complaint Severity: Typical. **Recall Alert:** See Recall Index. **Buyer's Summary:** Make sure the shoulder belts don't cut across your neck and are well anchored. Test the transmission thoroughly. Make sure seat belts function correctly and fit comfortably. See "Sudden Accelerations" in Introduction.

Hot Spots and Owner/NHTSA Comments:

1. Power train: transmission: automatic, poor performance, difficulty shifting, slipping. • "Upon accelerating, transmission shifts into neutral or misses a shift, causing vehicle to stall." • "Automatic transmission defect; removed key from ignition in drive gear, vehicle rolled forward; accident." • "Transmission will not lock in park." • "Heavy vibration when stopped in drive; reduced in neutral or park; unable to find cause." • "While driving at approximately 55-60 mph, suddenly vehicle became inoperative; engine revved and had no forward motion as though in neutral gear position; no warning."

2. Interior systems: passive restraint: belts, malfunction. • "Driver's motorized shoulder harness intermittently malfunctions; won't release, must disengage from closed position manually." • "The passenger-side seat belt retractor doesn't retract with door." • "Experienced intermittent failure of driver's motorized seat belt; won't go up once door opens, must operate manually." • "Driver's motorized shoulder belt will not release when door is opened." • "Passive restraint system malfunctions; fails to retract on opening of doors; happens occasionally."
3. Fuel: throttle linkages and control, sudden accelerations. • "Shifted to drive position, car surged at high rate of speed, brakes failed; accident occurred." • "Vehicle was in park. When driver turned ignition on, the vehicle jumped forward and hit another vehicle. Emergency brake was also on." • "When shifted from park to drive, had foot on brake, car suddenly accelerated, hitting a car and a pedestrian." • "Shifted from park to reverse; car suddenly accelerated through fence, hit a ditch; brake was applied and it locked." • "Sudden acceleration when braking; tested several times by dealer, but couldn't find anything wrong."
4. Interior systems: instrument panel: speedometer: odometer, inaccurate readings. • "Speedometer and odometer 10 percent fast, loss of 5,000 miles; incorrect speedometer gear installed." • "Speedometer off (miscalibrated) in excess of 10 percent of actual speed; replacement only marginally better, still off in excess; mileage overstated on odometer." • "Speedometer does not give accurate readings; it has been reading 10-15 percent too fast." • "Faulty speedometer; not related to accident." • "Original speedometer off 7-8 miles; repaired/replaced, second one also incorrect; repaired/replaced."
5. Structure: door assembly: handle: outside, failure. • "Driver's door handle would not open." • "Outside door handle failed; prior to recall." • "Door handle failed; prior to recall." • "Mazda has had no parts to fix door handle recall since January." • "Driver's outer door handle failed."
6. Interior systems: shoulder belts, malfunction, failure. • "Automatic shoulder belts fail to release." • "Seat belt design is inadequate; offers almost no effective restraint." • "Automatic shoulder belt doesn't move forward from locked position when door is opened." • "Front shoulder belt lock mechanism position, it's located directly next to one's head and protruding from door, could possibly cause skull injury during accident."

MAZDA 626 1990

Complaint Severity: Typical. **Recall Alert:** See Recall Index. **Buyer's Summary:** Make sure seat belts function correctly and fit comfortably.

Hot Spots and Owner/NHTSA Comments:
1. Interior systems: passive restraint: belts, malfunction. • "During rear-end accident, driver's-side shoulder and lap belt did not lock up to restrain; driver thrown into steering wheel, sustained injury." • "Driver's passive restraint shoulder belt may not complete cycle; stopping then starting." • "Primarily in cold weather, experiences intermittent malfunction of motorized shoulder harness when it goes backward or forward when opening door." • "Automatic passive restraint system failed; not completing cycle. Upon entry, owner struck eye, bruising it badly. Also, belt may not release on its own."
2. Structure: door assembly: handle: outside, failure. • "Right and rear door handles fell off due to the type of mechanisms used. This is an ongoing problem." • "Right front passenger's outside door handle latch failed, causing right-hand door mechanism to become very loose; prior to recall." • "Door assembly outer handles failed; prior to recall." • "Outside door handle on passenger's side is loose. Dealer didn't repair under recall notice." • "Outer door lock failed; prior to recall notification."
3. Structure: door assembly: latches and locks, malfunction, failure. • "Rear door latches do not stay secure." • "Driver door latch that controls all 4 doors will not lock or unlock with key." • "Door latches failed to hold." • "Driver's door latch disconnected when window was lowered."

MAZDA 626 1991

Complaint Severity: Typical. **Recall Alert:** See Recall Index. **Buyer's Summary:** Check the brakes—listen for noise, look for leaks and feel for vibration. They may fail, perform poorly or require frequent mechanical attention. Make sure seat belts function correctly and fit comfortably. See "Sudden Accelerations" in Introduction.

Hot Spots and Owner/NHTSA Comments:
1. Interior systems: passive restraint: belts, malfunction, failure. • "Automatic shoulder and lap belt did restrain driver upon impact; hit another vehicle head-on while moving into intersection, resulting in an injury." • "When rear-ended, with foot on brake, driver's shoulder belt didn't restrain from making contact, resulting in an injury. Estimated speed of impact 30 mph." • "Driver's automatic seat belt operated unpredictably, cutting driver's scalp." • "Passenger's automatic belt does not always move forward when door is open." • "Driver's and passenger's automatic seat belts fail to engage when vehicle is started."
2. Fuel: throttle linkages and control, sudden accelerations. • "Engine raced uncontrollably without foot on accelerator; throttle body stuck." • "While driving, throttle linkage became stuck." • "Throttle sticking occurred while driving, resulted in uncontrollable acceleration." • "While stopping, brake was depressed and vehicle surged and rolled forward; pedal went to the floor but couldn't stop car; caused an accident." • "While driving, experience intermittent sudden acceleration when throttle sticks and engine surges to high rpm, resulting in loss of control."
3. Engine: noise, fire, failure. • "Vehicle fire." • "Engine short block failed." • "Engine problems." • "While driving at 50-55 mph, on 2 different occasions within a week's time, heard a very loud noise; wonder if it could be backfiring." • "Engine overheated; defective head."
4. Interior systems: active seat and shoulder belts and belt anchor, malfunction, failure. • "Seat belts won't lock manually; only work on forward crash." • "Sometimes when coming to a stop, the seat belt tightens as if impacted with something." • "Vehicle was involved in a frontal collision in which the driver's-side seat belt did not restrain him from making contact with left panel." • "Seat belts restrain intermittently." • "At times, seat belt buckle across lap comes unbuckled; shoulder belt is too loose."
5. Brakes: hydraulic system, failure. • "Owner has had vehicle in 12 times for different parts of the brakes. Owner has had to replace everything dealing with the brakes." • "Brake shoes failed." • "Brake failure caused an accident; cruise control did not disengage." • "Excessive play in brake pedal, causing longer stopping distance."
6. Brakes: hydraulic: shoe: disc brake system, noise, failure. • "Brakes always make noise." • "Brakes repaired." • "Brake failure; pedal faded with grinding noise." • "Brake failure. Makes a loud grinding noise. Continues to wear front pads and rotors."

MAZDA 626 1993

Complaint Severity: Serious. **Buyer's Summary:** The airbags in this vehicle have experienced failures and malfunctions: You may need a professional evaluation on the condition of the airbags. Check the brakes—listen for noise, look for leaks, feel for vibration. They may fail, perform poorly or require frequent mechanical attention.

Hot Spots and Owner/NHTSA Comments:

1. Interior systems: passive restraint: airbag: driver, malfunction, failure. • "Frontal collision, speed 25 mph; lap and shoulder belt failed; airbag deployed after hitting the windshield." • "Airbag did not inflate during accident, causing injuries." • "Driver's-side shoulder belt began to unfasten upon side impact at 25 mph. Airbag did not deploy." • "During frontal impact, the airbag did not deploy." • "Airbag deployment was violent during accident, resulting in severe burns to driver's neck."

2. Electrical system: battery, failure. • "Battery failure." • "Battery dragging, due to dirty throttle chamber." • "Electrical problems; the alternator and the battery had to be replaced 3 times."

3. Brakes: hydraulic system, noise, failure. • "Pads failed." • "Brake linings failed, causing brakes to make noise when car stops." • "Noisy brakes." • "Extended stopping occurs when braking on icy or snowy road conditions." • "Noisy brakes."

4. Brakes: hydraulic: anti-skid system, poor performance, failure, locking up. • "Antilock brake system makes a grinding noise when pedal goes to the floor; parking brake was used to stop vehicle; 15-mph crash resulted on slippery surface." • "Brakes would not hold on a downhill ramp at 55 mph." • "Antilock brake system: When making turn, brakes lock up; failure of steering gear assembly, causing loss of control and going into embankment." • "Upon making a sharp turn, vehicle went into a skid. No response from brake and antilock braking system." • "Total loss of braking ability while driving at 20-30 mph twice; once resulting in an accident and injury."

5. Brakes: hydraulic: disc: pads and shoes, noise, vibration, failure. • "Front brake pads failed, causing grinding noise." • "Replaced front brake pads due to excessive vibration and noise." • "Front brake pads replaced with updated pads due to grinding noise when being applied." • "Brake pads failed." • "Noisy brakes; pads replaced, problem continues."

6. Engine: vibration, noise, failure. • "Loud tapping noise, caused by carbon buildup hitting valve and valve lifters." • "Noisy engine." • "Engine vibrates." • "Engine failure."

MAZDA 929 1988

Complaint Severity: Serious. **Recall Alert:** See Recall Index. **Buyer's Summary:** Check the brakes—listen for noise, look for leaks and feel for vibration. They may fail, perform poorly or require frequent mechanical attention. See "Sudden Accelerations" in Introduction.

Hot Spots and Owner/NHTSA Comments:

1. Fuel: throttle linkages and control, sudden accelerations. • "While engaged in reverse, car accelerated; then engaged in drive, car accelerated. Replaced water pump 6 months ago; possible moisture on computer chip." • "When started and shifted into drive, car suddenly accelerated very quickly with no pressure on gas; came to stop by hitting 2 cars head-on." • "Throttle got stuck in open position; vehicle accelerated out of control and hit a tree when pulling out of garage." • "Restarting engine, pressed gas pedal lightly, gained normal speed, then continued to gain speed on its own; resulted in accident; shifted to park to stop." • "Turned ignition on with gear in park; car suddenly accelerated and collided with house, causing severe injuries."

2. Structure: door assembly: handle: outside, breaking, malfunction. • "Exterior door handle failed; electric window activated, which resulted in door suddenly opening. Right rear passenger door handle broke due to same defect." • "Rear outer door handle assembly will not properly activate for use, to enter and exit vehicle." • "Right rear door does not open from the outside when the safety latch is in use. Door latch is breaking in the same position as front door locks." • "Right and left outer door handles broke; prior to recall; also handle rods in pathway of power window, causing misalignment and motor failure."

3. Brakes: hydraulic system, excessive wear, locking up, vibration. • "Engine shuts off when brakes are applied, and all warning lights come on, with loss of steering and brakes. Could cause an accident." • "While driving, experience total brake failure when pedal goes to floor and allows vehicle to proceed through intersection; without warning." • "Premature wearing of brakes; rotors needed in rear." • "After driving, vehicle experienced intermittent lockup of brakes." • "Brake problem caused vibration during acceleration."

4. Structure: door assembly: latches and locks, breaking, malfunction. • "Rear outer door handles broke; lowering window will release latch." • "Rear driver's-side door latch won't open from outside." • "Owner says rear doors on both sides are broken; he has a recall for the front doors, but feels the back doors are also a safety problem; outside handles and locks." • "Driver entrapment caused by broken door handle mechanism, jammed window and door egress." • "Driver's-side rear door opened by itself while locked or unlocked; would not latch shut."

5. Brakes: hydraulic: disc: rotor: disc hub, vibration, excessive wear. • "Replaced warped front brake rotors." • "Warped rotors and pads, causing vehicle to vibrate." • "Warped rotors and pads, causing vehicle to vibrate when braking." • "Brakes continue to vibrate due to defective rotors; repaired 3 times."

6. Fuel: fuel systems, fuel odor. • "Fuel fumes enter vehicle through vents. Replaced cracked fuel separator 3 times." • "Vehicle emitted strong fuel odor; checked by dealer, no leaks." • "When engine is cold and first started, fuel expels on the engine for a period of 5 minutes. In for repair and cannot find the problem." • "Recurring gasoline fumes."

MAZDA 929 1989

Complaint Severity: Typical. **Recall Alert:** See Recall Index. **Buyer's Summary:** Test the transmission thoroughly. See "Sudden Accelerations" in Introduction.

Hot Spots and Owner/NHTSA Comments:

1. Fuel: throttle linkages and control, sudden accelerations. • "While backing out of driveway, vehicle suddenly surged, then accelerated out of control; throttle stuck to the floor, resulting in hitting a retaining wall." • "When car is stopped with foot on brake, it will surge." • "Upon putting vehicle in drive with foot on brake, accelerated forward at high rate; wheels spun; struck brick wall." • "Vehicle went to full acceleration without depressing accelerator; brakes failed to slow car down; resulted in accident." • "Foot on brake, shifted to drive; wheels spun, car accelerated at high rate of speed; resulted in accident."

2. Structure: door assembly: handle: outside, breaking, malfunction, failure. • "Door handles recall has not been completed; dealer says parts not available; has been 3 months." • "Outside door handle failed, preventing door from opening." • "Left rear door handle does not operate; stuck in closed position due to defect in handle." • "Outside door handle failed, causing right rear door not to open from inside or outside; prior to recall, repairs refused—only pertains to front doors." • "Rear driver's-side door handle has broken; cannot open door from outside."

3. Structure: door assembly: latches and locks, breaking, malfunction. • "The rear door locks do not open from the outside. The owners had to take baby out of rear seat through the window. The problem is the same as for front door recall." • "Rear doors have the same problem as the front door locks had: They cannot be opened from the inside or outside." • "Door latch broke;

when rolling window down on driver's-side, the door opens." • "Inside lever latch has broken on both rear doors, which makes door locks inoperative and doors hard to open from outside." • "Rear passenger door will not open."

4. Power train: transmission: automatic, poor performance, difficulty shifting, slipping. • "Transmission slips and/or misses." • "Transmission will not lock in park." • "Vehicle experienced transmission problems." • "Defective transmission does not shift properly; revs up to 4,000 or 5,000 rpm and will not move with car in drive; overhauled but problem persists." • "Transmission clunks when shifting from one gear to another."

5. Structure: door assembly, malfunction, failure. • "Rear door handle child safety latch is engaged; you cannot open from inside or outside." • "Vehicle's doors become inoperative; unable to open; rear passenger door." • "Driver's-side door could not be opened due to outer door handle failure; prior to recall." • "The rear driver's-side door can't be opened from the outside; the driver's-side seat belt buckle will not lock."

MAZDA 929 1992

Complaint Severity: Dangerous (Worst 3% in Guide). **Recall Alert:** See Recall Index. **Buyer's Summary:** The airbags in this vehicle have experienced failures and malfunctions: You may need a professional evaluation on the condition of the airbags. See "Sudden Accelerations" in Introduction.

Hot Spots and Owner/NHTSA Comments:

1. Fuel: throttle linkages and control, sudden accelerations. • "Automatic transmission: continued forward movement after application of brakes at low speed; engine accelerated; jerked forward; rear-ended parked vehicle; no warning." • "Experienced sudden acceleration after vehicle was put in reverse; impact 6:00 position; put vehicle in drive; surged forward, hitting parked vehicle. Airbag did not deploy." • "Throttle went into open position, impact 12:00 position, speed 100 mph; vehicle crossed highway, hitting a guardrail and breaking steering wheel; had no brakes." • "While braking to stop, with gear in drive, engine accelerated forward; went into showroom of a building; impact 12:00 position; dual airbags did not deploy." • "Automatic transmission: While slowing down, engine suddenly accelerated; lurched forward; brakes applied; hit curb; speed 10 mph; impact position unknown."

2. Interior systems: passive restraint: airbag: driver, malfunction, failure. • "Frontal collision, impact 12:00 position, speed 30 mph, airbag did not deploy; lap and shoulder belt did not retract." • "While braking to stop, with gear in drive, engine accelerated forward; went into showroom of a building; impact 12:00 position; dual airbags did not deploy." • "Automatic transmission: While slowing down, engine suddenly accelerated; lurched forward; brakes applied; hit curb; speed 10 mph; impact position unknown." • "Vehicle accelerated forward; hit pole; impact 1:00 position; speed 20 mph; dual airbags did not deploy." • "Front-end crash at 25 mph; no airbag deployment."

MAZDA MX6 1989

Complaint Severity: Best 3% in Guide. **Recall Alert:** See Recall Index. **Buyer's Summary:** Look carefully for any kind of leakage, especially under the car. Check the brakes—listen for noise, look for leaks and feel for vibration. They may fail, perform poorly or require frequent mechanical attention. Test the transmission thoroughly.

Hot Spots and Owner/NHTSA Comments:

1. Power train: transmission: automatic, poor performance, difficulty shifting, slipping. • "Problem with transmission slipping on acceleration." • "Automatic transmission gets stuck in gear at times; upon entering highway, must come to complete stop and then accelerate." • "Transmission slipping; could not always duplicate problem." • "Problem with transmission slipping; repaired twice to no avail." • "Defective transmission; before complete failure, had problems with slipping; failed at 40,000 miles."

2. Brakes: hydraulic system, noise, failure. • "Defective braking system; repeated repairs made: calipers defective, rotors and pads repaired/replaced, ongoing problem with brakes." • "Front brakes wore out." • "On short stops when applying brakes, pedal gets hard and must be pumped to stop." • "Brakes are noisy; need front and rear brakes; several repair attempts, problem not always obvious." • "Brake failure."

3. Interior systems: active restraints: belt buckles, breaking, poor performance. • "Driver's seat belt buckle has broken 2 times." • "Driver's-side seat belt broke off completely; passenger-side is hard to latch and hard to unlatch." • "Driver's-side plastic tab to release fastener mechanism cracked, rendering buckle inoperative." • "Seat belt buckle failure on driver and passenger sides." • "Driver's seat belt buckle fails to latch."

4. Interior systems: seat tracks and anchors, breaking. • "Vehicle's front driver seat holding mechanism is broken, causing half the seat to move." • "Welds on left front seat slide; caused by broken controller." • "Driver's-side seat track anchor broke, causing the right side of the seat to rise up from the frame of the car when making a turn, resulting in handling problem." • "Seat adjustment bar welding broke." • "The front seat spot welds broke, causing the seat to tilt back and forth. This has been replaced before."

5. Engine: leaks, failure. • "Engine failure." • "Two bolts sheared off heat shield." • "Engine failure." • "Incorrect installation of crimp clamp caused hose to tear and leak, resulting in overheating and a blown head gasket."

MAZDA MX6 1993

Complaint Severity: Troublesome. **Recall Alert:** See Recall Index. **Buyer's Summary:** Verify that the cruise control system works properly, and that it doesn't cause the engine to surge. The airbags in this vehicle have experienced failures and malfunctions: You may need a professional evaluation on the condition of the airbags.

Hot Spots and Owner/NHTSA Comments:

1. Interior systems: passive restraint: airbag: driver, malfunction, failure. • "Accident at 5-10 mph, impact 3:00 position; driver seat belt did not work due to defective belt design. Driver thrown into passenger's side. Airbag failed to deploy." • "Had an accident, airbag deployed; thick black smoke came out and there was an awful smell." • "Vehicle was involved in a low-speed frontal accident. Airbag deployed, but inflated late. The seat belt did not hold driver back; face hit steering wheel." • "Frontal collision, impact 12:00 position; swerved to miss an object in road, hitting a guardrail, speed 50 mph. Airbag deployed, causing an injury." • "Airbag did not deploy."

2. Electrical system: battery, malfunction, failure. • "Battery shorted out; also, wiring problem." • "Battery failed." • "Battery failures."

3. Equipment: electric equipment: radio: tape deck etc., failure. • "Speaker failures." • "Cassette player failed." • "CD player failed."

4. Equipment: speed control, malfunction, failure. • "Hit brake pedal to deactivate cruise control, but received no response until shifting into neutral." • "Cruise control failed to disengage upon braking at 60 mph; resulted in an accident." • "Cruise control failed, causing accident." • "While driving, the cruise control was turned off; cruise control engaged and would not disengage; loss of control, flipped over, speed 65 mph; no impact."

MAZDA PROTEGE 1990

Complaint Severity: Typical. **Buyer's Summary:** Check the brakes—listen for noise, look for leaks and feel for vibration. They may fail, perform poorly or require frequent mechanical attention. Test the transmission thoroughly. Make sure seat belts function correctly and fit comfortably.

Hot Spots and Owner/NHTSA Comments:

1. Interior systems: passive restraint: belts, malfunction, poor performance. • "Driver's-side automatic seat belt does not work; it jams when door is closed." • "The driver's and front passenger's automatic seat belts do not work at all; driver's fails to retract and passenger's locks up in position." • "Most of the time during cold weather, passenger's automatic seat belt retractor gets stuck in both forward and backward positions." • "The seat belts will come up on you when you get into the vehicle, but will not retract when you try to exit." • "In accident, driver's seat belt did not restrain driver from hitting steering wheel; seat belt automatic device may not be effective for small person."

2. Brakes: hydraulic system, noise, poor performance. • "Brakes failed, causing an accident; vehicle totaled." • "Brakes squeal very loudly, grind, grab unevenly; pressure is inconsistent and unpredictable; sometimes almost skid to a stop." • "Brakes squeal." • "Brakes stick, causing hydroplaning; vehicle skidded." • "Brakes squeak; serviced twice, problem continues."

3. Power train: transmission: automatic, poor performance, difficulty shifting, slipping. • "Transmission had been rebuilt, broken down 4 times; picked up from dealer and car broke down 4 weeks later; dealer does not want to fix; still under warranty." • "Premature transmission failure." • "Vehicle's automatic transmission slips out of park and rolls." • "Hard to put in reverse; loud noise from front end." • "Vehicle began rolling in park; repeated servicing on problem; adjusted transmission control cables to no avail."

MAZDA PROTEGE 1991

Complaint Severity: Troublesome. **Buyer's Summary:** Make sure the shoulder belts don't cut across your neck and are well anchored. Check the brakes—listen for noise, look for leaks and feel for vibration. They may fail, perform poorly or require frequent mechanical attention. Test the transmission thoroughly. Make sure seat belts function correctly and fit comfortably.

Hot Spots and Owner/NHTSA Comments:

1. Brakes: hydraulic system, poor performance, locking up, noise. • "Poor brake performance causes pads and rear wheels to lock up; front rotors turned at 2,500 miles." • "Right front brake locked up, causing vehicle to flip over; resulted in injury." • "Brakes noisy and lock up; repaired/replaced front and rear shoes, pads and drums." • "Right rear brake grabs; noisy." • "Brakes grab."

2. Power train: transmission: automatic, poor performance, difficulty shifting, slipping. • "Transmission jumps out of gear." • "Transmission operates sluggishly and downshifts suddenly." • "Automatic transmission failure." • "Accident resulted when gear slipped out of park and vehicle rolled freely down an incline; emergency brake not engaged." • "Gearshift lever can be moved from drive to neutral and from neutral to drive without depressing the release button."

3. Interior systems: active restraints: belt retractors, breaking, malfunction. • "Front passenger and driver seat lap and shoulder belts will not retract." • "The passenger-side retractor doesn't retract forward; you need to pull it." • "Driver's-side seat belt retractor broke." • "Passenger-side lap belt disappears into the retractor. Requires the use of pliers to pull belt out of retractor." • "Seat belt does not retract properly."

4. Brakes: hydraulic: shoe and drum system, noise, failure. • "Rear brakes failed." • "Rear brake drum failed." • "Lemon law buyback for grabbing, grinding and noisy rear drum brakes."

5. Interior systems: passive restraint: belts, poor performance, malfunction. • "Both front automatic seat belts fit poorly." • "On the passenger's side, automatic seat belt does not slide forward, but sticks." • "The automatic seat belt system stops in mid-track and the door locks do not always open." • "Front left motorized shoulder belt will not move forward to the driver exit position; requires manually unlocking the tongue plate in order to exit."

6. Interior systems: shoulder belts, malfunction, failure. • "Driver's shoulder belt did not lock up as intended upon impact; speed 30 mph; driver injured." • "Passenger's seat belt, attached to the door, disconnected upon side impact." • "Shoulder belt shuttle mounted in the door hits you in the face." • "Vehicle was at complete stop, impact at 6:00 position; driver's-side lap and shoulder belt failed, throwing occupant into steering wheel."

MAZDA PROTEGE 1992

Complaint Severity: Typical. **Buyer's Summary:** Check the brakes—listen for noise, look for leaks and feel for vibration. They may fail, perform poorly or require frequent mechanical attention. Make sure seat belts function correctly and fit comfortably.

Hot Spots and Owner/NHTSA Comments:

1. Interior systems: passive restraint: belts, malfunction, failure. • "Driver's- and passenger-side automatic seat belts lock up and choke occupants." • "Front seat belts cannot be removed without using the emergency release button." • "Lap belt failed to secure driver in accident; caused automatic shoulder belt to sever driver's spinal cord, causing death." • "Automatic passive restraint indicator bell (motorized) constantly rings when driving or in use." • "Driver's-side shoulder belt gets stuck in different positions in door roller."

2. Brakes: hydraulic system, noise, failure. • "Bolt sitting between the hub brakes lodges between the tire and brakes, resulting in a loss of brakes." • "Took car to shop because brakes are very loud; could not find problem." • "Recurring brake failures; causes metal-to-metal contact or brake pedal going to the floor." • "When applying brakes and negotiating a turn, brakes make clunking sound. Dealer unable to detect cause." • "Brakes make a clunking noise when attempting to stop. Attempted to fix 5 times."

3. Brakes: hydraulic: shoe: disc brake system, poor performance, noise. • "Poor performance of rear brakes." • "Four-wheel drive, disc brake system; brakes go out without warning and rub metal to metal. Front caliper, cylinder and joint had to be replaced. Bolt has been stripped." • "Front rotors and pads warp, causing loss of brake effectiveness. Replaced once every year." • "Front brakes make a grinding noise."

MAZDA RX7 1987

Complaint Severity: Very Serious. **Buyer's Summary:** See "Sudden Accelerations" in Introduction.

Hot Spots and Owner/NHTSA Comments:

1. Fuel: throttle linkages and control, sudden accelerations. • "Accelerator hangs up or sticks at full throttle." • "Car suddenly accelerated without depressing gas pedal; car didn't stop with brakes; crashed through garage and caused extensive damage." •

"Repeated problem with car accelerating forward; foot on brake and car in drive, vehicle propelled forward; resulted in accident." • "Vehicle had 2 incidents of sudden acceleration; both times accident and injuries." • "Upon shifting gear from park to drive, vehicle suddenly accelerated and went out of control; resulted in accident."

MAZDA RX7 1993

Complaint Severity: Minor. **Recall Alert:** See Recall Index. **Buyer's Summary:** Look carefully for any kind of leakage, especially under the car. The electronic control unit has been blamed for engine performance problems, including stalling and surging.

Hot Spots and Owner/NHTSA Comments:

1. Electrical system: ignition: electronic control unit, stalling, failure. • "Ignition computer failed." • "Electronic control module failed." • "Electronic control unit failed." • "Intermittent stalling."

2. Fuel: fuel line fittings: nonmetallic, leaks, fire. • "Fuel lines and hoses, nonmetallic, leaked fuel on hot engine, resulting in a fire; prior to recall." • "After recall performed, owner noticed fumes." • "Vehicle caught fire." • "Fuel line, nonmetallic, failed prior to and after recall repairs." • "Recall related; in for repair, did not perform the corrected action properly."

MAZDA TRUCK MPV 1989

Complaint Severity: Typical. **Recall Alert:** See Recall Index. **Buyer's Summary:** Check the brakes—listen for noise, look for leaks and feel for vibration. They may fail, perform poorly or require frequent mechanical attention. Test the transmission thoroughly.

Hot Spots and Owner/NHTSA Comments:

1. Brakes: hydraulic system, poor performance, locking up. • "Intermittent loss of brake effectiveness in cold weather. Has been recalled and repaired numerous times." • "Brakes lock up, causing extended stopping distance and resulting in minor accident." • "Brakes locked up while vehicle was going 45 mph; caused loss of control, resulting in injury." • "Brake failure; complete brake lockup causes the vehicle to roll over; injuries resulted." • "Problem with brakes; slow and heavy, on wet day, had accident and slid into oncoming car, causing injuries to other driver; braking system totally locked up."

2. Brakes: hydraulic: shoe: disc brake system, excessive wear, noise, pulling. • "Excessive brake wear; out-of-round brake drums causing vibrations." • "Premature brake wear every 10,000 miles, pads had to be replaced." • "Intermittent brake lockup; also, increased stopping distance after recall performed." • "Front brakes wear out every 5,000 miles; replaced 7 times." • "When stopping vehicle, antilock brake system disc brakes squeal and pull the vehicle to the right. Replaced rotor, shims and pads."

3. Brakes: hydraulic: shoe and drum system, locking up, poor performance. • "Recall-related problem with brakes has been corrected twice; however, rear lockup and excessive brake pedal pressure are still problems." • "Rear brakes fail to engage when applied, resulting in heavy front brake wear." • "Rear brakes locked up; resulted in an accident; recall related." • "As a result of recall regarding rear brake lockup, rear brake shoes were replaced by dealer." • "Rear disc brakes did not operate; caused pressure on front disc brakes."

4. Engine: noise, fire. • "Vehicle caught fire; unsure as to cause, possible fuel leak or electrical malfunction." • "Engine knocks and/or pings." • "Oil passage blocked." • "Noisy engine." • "Hydraulic valve adjuster problems, causing clicking noise in engine."

5. Power train: transmission: automatic, poor performance, difficulty shifting, slipping. • "Stopped at stoplight; defective accumulator spring in transmission scrapes metal off casing, causing transmission to lock up intermittently." • "Driver heard noise like loose chain; damage to whole front half of transmission." • "Transmission broke down at 57,000 miles." • "Transmission makes noise when put in reverse, upon acceleration or when backing up." • "Transmission malfunction."

6. Brakes: hydraulic: disc: rotor: disc hub, excessive wear, vibration. • "Defective rotors in front disc brake system; replaced 6 times." • "Front brake rotors continue to warp, causing wheels to shimmy and/or shudder uncontrollably; may result in loss of control during emergency brake applications." • "Front brake rotors are warping; when braking, steering wheel shakes back and forth; problem is getting worse." • "Front brake rotors are warped for the fourth time." • "Front rotors had severe warpage; causes front end of vehicle to wobble."

MAZDA TRUCK MPV 1990

Complaint Severity: Serious. **Recall Alert:** See Recall Index. **Buyer's Summary:** Check the brakes—listen for noise, look for leaks and feel for vibration. They may fail, perform poorly or require frequent mechanical attention. Test the transmission thoroughly.

Hot Spots and Owner/NHTSA Comments:

1. Brakes: hydraulic: anti-skid system, poor performance, failure, locking up. • "Antilock brakes cause vehicle to vibrate or shimmy; replaced every 9,000 miles." • "Antilock brake system: Grabby braking; wheel locks up very easily, resulting in skidding and loss of control; corrected under recall; problem reoccurred." • "While traveling at low speeds, brakes locked up, resulting in loss of control; also caused minor injuries." • "Antilock brake system: While braking and when driving 50 mph and over, vehicle severely vibrates; sometimes, seems as if losing control of steering." • "Total brake failure resulted in delayed braking action and extended brake pedal travel."

2. Brakes: hydraulic system, vibration, noise, excessive wear. • "Had to apply brakes suddenly and forcefully; skidded on wet pavement into another vehicle." • "Returned van 4 times for recurring brake vibration; found a defective brake pin clip; repaired." • "Brakes were grabbing and not stopping vehicle properly; dealer replaced rear shoes and front pads, drums and rotors." • "Brakes were making a squeaking noise and were grabbing when applied; dealer replaced warped rotors and pads 7 times and readjusted rear brake shoes." • "Brake pads show excessive wear; turned rotors; repaired/replaced shoes and drums."

3. Power train: transmission: automatic, poor performance, difficulty shifting, slipping. • "The transmission in vehicle could not be put in reverse." • "Automatic transmission: Vehicle does not move or accelerate when stopped; transmission does not shift into gear." • "Transmission slips from 1st to 2nd gear; sluggish and noisy; resulted in failure." • "Transmission will not downshift on slight grade; poor acceleration." • "Transmission will not always downshift on hills; lack of power."

4. Brakes: hydraulic: shoe and drum system, locking up, malfunction. • "Rear brakes locked up on sudden stops, antilock brake system did not function because of a design problem; repaired/replaced several times." • "While going 15 mph, rear brakes malfunctioned; couldn't stop vehicle; resulted in an accident." • "Rear wheel brakes are locking, notwithstanding the antilock brake system, causing vehicle to skid." • "When transmission is in 1st or 2nd gear and speed is 5-10 mph, rear brakes lock up on dry or wet pavement." • "Antilock brakes pulsate and/or shimmy when used. Rear brakes lock up when brake pedal is depressed."

5. Brakes: hydraulic: shoe: disc brake system, excessive wear, poor performance. • "While driving, front brakes grab and cause irregular braking power and premature wear." • "Poor braking performance with extended stopping distance; various components replaced recently." • "Extreme wear of front brake pad linings resulted in poor brake performance; also, exhaust fume leakage into rear of passenger compartment." • "Front brake pads and rotors wore out, which caused vehicle to shimmy." • "Front disc brakes give off smell of burning and there is chattering at normal brake application."
6. Engine: noise, premature failure. • "Knocking sound from engine." • "Constant loud ticking from engine; could not find problem." • "Engine surge." • "Timing belt failed 3 times." • "Engine noise and knocking when engine is cold; engine replaced at 22,000 miles."

MAZDA TRUCK MPV 1991

Complaint Severity: Troublesome. **Recall Alert:** See Recall Index. **Buyer's Summary:** Check the brakes—listen for noise, look for leaks and feel for vibration. They may fail, perform poorly or require frequent mechanical attention. Test the transmission thoroughly.

Hot Spots and Owner/NHTSA Comments:
1. Brakes: hydraulic: anti-skid system, poor performance, failure, locking up. • "While driving, applied the brakes and antilock braking system failed, causing an accident and resulting in an injury to the other driver." • "Antilock brake system: During frontal collision, brakes failed at a speed of 55 mph, impact 11:00 position. Brakes locked up." • "Brakes sticking when applying pedal lightly; driver experienced lockup on 2 occasions." • "Antilock brakes squeak when applied." • "Antilock brake system locked up; caused vehicle to lose control."
2. Brakes: hydraulic system, excessive wear, malfunction, vibration. • "Depressing the brakes, pedal goes to the floor during wet conditions." • "Premature brake wear results in a knocking sound and inhibits safe vehicle stopping." • "Due to malfunctioning of the brakes, vehicle was involved in an accident." • "Vehicle vibrates when braking on incline, causing extended stopping distances." • "Brakes failed, causing accident." • "Premature wear of brakes."
3. Brakes: hydraulic: shoe: disc brake system, locking up, noise, failure. • "Brakes lock up intermittently." • "Recall repairs refused." • "Intermittent brake noise; repaired/replaced several times, problem continues." • "Front disc brake system failed after recall repairs." • "Continual replacement of front disc brakes between 13,000 and 17,000 miles."
4. Power train: transmission: automatic, poor performance, difficulty shifting, slipping. • "Vehicle rolled backwards, causing accident and injuries." • "Automatic transmission; while turning into intersection, transmission failed; vehicle became motionless." • "Transmission blew at 50,000 miles." • "Purchased truck used in April and the transmission blew out." • "Automatic transmission has gone out for the second time in 2 years."
5. Brakes: hydraulic: disc: rotor: disc hub, excessive wear, vibration. • "Front brake rotors wear prematurely." • "Continuous failure of brake rotors and pads, causing brakes to lock up when applied on wet roads." • "Experience vibration in the wheel when going downhill; replaced brake pads to no avail; dealer now says it is the rotors." • "Poor performance in rear antilock brakes causes front brake performance to decrease; rotors warped." • "Front brake rotors have worn out considerably with minimum mileage."
6. Brakes: hydraulic: disc: pads and shoes, excessive wear. • "Brake pads have to be changed every 15,000 miles; if not, a grinding sound comes from brake pads wearing. Replaced pads 6 times." • "Excessive wear on front brake pads; prior to recall." • "Premature wear of brake pads." • "Front brake pads wear prematurely."

MAZDA TRUCK MPV 1992

Complaint Severity: Serious. **Buyer's Summary:** Check the brakes—listen for noise, look for leaks and feel for vibration. They may fail, perform poorly or require frequent mechanical attention.

Hot Spots and Owner/NHTSA Comments:
1. Brakes: hydraulic: anti-skid system, poor performance, failure, locking up. • "Antilock brake system malfunction; car will skid 10-15 feet before stopping." • "Antilock brakes failed/locked up four times, causing loss of control/one accident/injury." • "Antilock brake system failed to stop vehicle when applied, causing two front-end collisions at 50-55 mph." • "Antilock brake system failure on wet road surface, experienced pedal fading, impact 12:00 position, 30 mph, no airbag." • "Antilock brake system: When applied, vehicle has delayed response and possible air getting into lines. Dealer has tried to fix with failure reoccurring."

MAZDA TRUCK NAVAJO 1991

Complaint Severity: Troublesome. **Recall Alert:** See Recall Index. **Buyer's Summary:** Check the brakes—listen for noise, look for leaks and feel for vibration. They may fail, perform poorly or require frequent mechanical attention.

Hot Spots and Owner/NHTSA Comments:
1. Brakes: hydraulic: anti-skid system, poor performance, failure, locking up. • "Rear brakes lock up in wet weather, causing vehicle to skid; loss of vehicle control and rear-end collision at 30 mph." • "Vehicle veers to the right when braking at any speed. Has been repaired 8 times due to brake problems." • "Vehicle's antilock brake system locks up with no warning at any speed. Premature brake wear, and antilock brake system light comes on." • "Antilock brakes locked up, causing accident." • "Antilock brake system seems to respond at different intervals; was not properly adjusted; resulted in the vehicle's loss of control."

Mercedes Benz

MERCEDES BENZ 190 1987

Complaint Severity: Dangerous (Worst 3% in Guide). **Recall Alert:** See Recall Index. **Buyer's Summary:** The airbags in this vehicle have experienced failures and malfunctions: You may need a professional evaluation on the condition of the airbags. See "Sudden Accelerations" in Introduction.

Hot Spots and Owner/NHTSA Comments:
1. Fuel: throttle linkages and control, sudden accelerations. • "Vehicle put into reverse from park position and accelerated in reverse. Driver's foot was on brake pedal." • "When shifted into reverse, car accelerated with such force that rear wheel broke traction and spun; no control; resulted in collision." • "Vehicle suddenly accelerated at full throttle, hitting building; injury; vehicle totaled." • "When shifting from park to drive, car shot forward at rapid speed; applied brakes to no avail." • "Car suddenly accelerates when gear placed in reverse; control lost; accident resulted."
2. Interior systems: passive restraint: airbag: driver, malfunction, failure. • "Airbag on driver's side defective." • "Involved in head-on collision, airbag did not come out; injuries sus-

tained." • "Airbag did not deploy." • "Airbag replaced due to cracked horn pad cover." • "During a frontal collision at 55 mph, impact at 12:00, airbag did not deploy."

MERCEDES BENZ 300 1987

Complaint Severity: Dangerous (Worst 3% in Guide). **Recall Alert:** See Recall Index. **Buyer's Summary:** The airbags in this vehicle have experienced failures and malfunctions: You may need a professional evaluation on the condition of the airbags. Check the brakes—listen for noise, look for leaks and feel for vibration. They may fail, perform poorly or require frequent mechanical attention. Test the transmission thoroughly. See "Sudden Accelerations" in Introduction.

Hot Spots and Owner/NHTSA Comments:

1. Fuel: throttle linkages and control, sudden accelerations. • "Vehicle shot forward at maximum acceleration, brakes failed; threw shift selector into park, which stopped vehicle." • "With foot on brake, put car into drive, car shot forward at incredible speed; crashed through rear wall of garage, ending up in basement of house." • "Upon putting gear lever into drive position, motor went into high speed and shot forward, completely out of control." • "When vehicle's shifter placed in drive, car suddenly accelerated; surged backwards when placed in reverse, resulting in accident." • "Shifted to drive, vehicle suddenly accelerated; turned off ignition to stop car."

2. Interior systems: passive restraint: airbag: driver, malfunction, failure. • "No deployment of driver's airbag during accident, causing injuries." • "No deployment of driver's or passenger's airbag; resulted in injuries." • "Front-end accident while traveling between 40 and 60 mph, impact at 11:00; airbag did not deploy." • "During a frontal collision at 50 mph, impact 12:00 position, airbag failed to deploy; driver suffered injuries." • "During a head-on collision while traveling at speed of 40 mph, impact at 12:00, airbag did not deploy; driver suffered injury."

3. Brakes: hydraulic system, locking up, noise, poor performance. • "Apparent brake lockup upon going around a turn, resulting in accident." • "Brakes make growling noise when stopping; braking action uneven, pulsates; antilock system activates with normal foot pressure on pedal coming to stop." • "Brakes make growling noise as car comes to a stop; braking action uneven or pulsates as comes to a stop." • "While backing out of garage in reverse, vehicle suddenly lurched forward at high speed, hitting kitchen and garage doors; brakes applied; no warning."

4. Interior systems: passive restraint: airbag, failure. • "Other vehicle traveled at 40 mph into a head-on crash while this vehicle was parked; injured this driver because the airbag did not deploy." • "Airbag did not deploy at time of accident." • "Airbag failed to function when vehicle involved in accident." • "The left front airbag failed to deploy during an accident."

5. Power train: transmission: automatic, poor performance, difficulty shifting, slipping. • "Automatic transmission in vehicle does not lock when parked with ignition off; child was able to move gear, causing vehicle to roll; accident." • "Transmission shifts roughly from gears." • "Transmission bad by design; moved gear from park to neutral in a parked car that had ignition off; caused an accident." • "Transmission shifts roughly from gear to gear."

MERCEDES BENZ 300 1989

Complaint Severity: Very Serious. **Recall Alert:** See Recall Index. **Buyer's Summary:** The airbags in this vehicle have experienced failures and malfunctions: You may need a professional evaluation on the condition of the airbags. See "Sudden Accelerations" in Introduction.

Hot Spots and Owner/NHTSA Comments:

1. Fuel: throttle linkages and control, sudden accelerations. • "Upon shifting vehicle into reverse and drive gears, accelerated at high rate of speed forward, striking several other vehicles; injuries sustained." • "Engine suddenly accelerated from stationary position; did not shift gears; caused accident and extensive damage." • "Starting the car, put it in reverse, car suddenly accelerated at great speed, resulting in accident." • "Vehicle suddenly accelerated out of control as soon as started car and put in forward gear; no braking response; accident." • "Accelerator automatically activated, causing vehicle to go from stop position into acceleration, striking parked vehicle."

2. Interior systems: passive restraint: airbag, malfunction, failure. • "Airbag indicator light came on and stayed on." • "Airbag control unit is defective and has to be replaced; car was never in accident." • "Red light shows on airbag; failure covered by warranty." • " 'Airbag' lights up on instrument panel." • "Balloon airbag did not inflate during head-on accident."

MERCEDES BENZ 300 1990

Complaint Severity: Typical. **Recall Alert:** See Recall Index. **Buyer's Summary:** Make sure air conditioner works properly.

Hot Spots and Owner/NHTSA Comments:

1. Air conditioner: noise, malfunction. • "Air conditioner system broke." • "Noisy sound in air conditioning." • "Air conditioning problem." • "Air circulation system has swishing sound from behind console, like liquid in air conditioner system; happens only when air conditioner is on."

2. Electrical system: battery, failure. • "Battery failure; replaced." • "Battery failure; replaced by manufacturer." • "Battery premature failure." • "Battery failed, replaced."

Mercury—Cars and Trucks

MERCURY CAPRI 1991

Complaint Severity: Typical. **Recall Alert:** See Recall Index. **Buyer's Summary:** The airbags in this vehicle have experienced failures and malfunctions: You may need a professional evaluation on the condition of the airbags. Test the transmission thoroughly.

Hot Spots and Owner/NHTSA Comments:

1. Structure: body roof: convertible top, poor performance. • "Convertible top torn from framework; mechanical defect." • "Convertible top replaced due to hole in back window; new top leaks." • "Glue came off bars that hold roof down when convertible top is up; decreased stability of canvas around roof top." • "Plastic window in convertible top clouded, impairing driver's view." • "Convertible: Poor visibility through rear window due to color deterioration."

2. Interior systems: passive restraint: airbag: driver, malfunction, failure. • "After colliding head-on with guardrail, airbag did not deploy." • "No deployment of driver's airbag during 2 separate accidents." • "Braking at panic stop, brakes locked up; speed estimation 35 mph. Airbag failed to deploy." • "No deployment of airbag in crash, causing injury." • "Rear-end accident sent vehicle head-on into another vehicle; airbag did not deploy; vehicle was totaled."

3. Power train: transmission: automatic, poor performance, difficulty shifting, slipping lines. • "Transmission cooling line leaked, which resulted in a fire." • "Engine compartment caught on fire; problem caused by transmission cooling line becoming unattached; sprayed fluid that ignited." • "Engine compartment fire resulted due to leak from cooling unit in the transmission." • "Vehicle fire originating at transmission cooler lines." • "Engine compartment fire; a cooler hose on transmission split and leaked fluid on hot exhaust, causing fire."

4. Electrical system: battery, failure. • "Battery failure." • "Battery failed twice." • "Battery exploded after vehicle was started; electrical short." • "Battery died."

5. Engine: noise, fire, leaks. • "Loud noise from engine." • "Unspecified engine problems." • "While driving, engine caught fire and vehicle burned." • "Engine caught fire, completely damaging the underhood." • "Vehicle caught on fire while making a right turn; related to recall notice received regarding transaxle oil inlet leakage of transmission fluid to other parts."

MERCURY COUGAR 1987

Complaint Severity: Troublesome. **Recall Alert:** See Recall Index. **Buyer's Summary:** The fuel injection system has been blamed for hesitation and stalling. Be sure the vehicle doesn't die in traffic or at stops. Test the suspension by feeling for vibration or pulling while driving. Check the brakes—listen for noise, look for leaks and feel for vibration. They may fail, perform poorly or require frequent mechanical attention. Test the transmission thoroughly. See "Sudden Accelerations" in Introduction.

Hot Spots and Owner/NHTSA Comments:

1. Fuel: throttle linkages and control, sudden accelerations. • "When the vehicle was put into reverse, the accelerator stuck and vehicle flew out of control." • "Vehicle suffered sudden acceleration due to apparent fuel linkage sticking and binding." • "Sudden, abrupt and at times gradual acceleration with or without foot on gas pedal; happened when car in gear, neutral and park; all repair attempts to no avail." • "Sudden, unintended full throttle acceleration occurred when shifted from park to drive; no control over speed; resulted in an accident." • "While driving, car ran through back wall; car jumped into gear from park to drive, or gas pedal stuck; resulted in accident."

2. Power train: transmission: automatic, poor performance, difficulty shifting, slipping. • "Shift sticks between reverse and neutral, have to reset; also gets stuck in park and drive; can't move." • "Automatic transmission leaking." • "Transmission malfunction; vehicle experienced bucking repeatedly." • "When shifted into reverse, car goes forward due to pin falling out of transmission." • "Automatic transmission jumps out of gear; hard to shift from reverse to drive."

3. Suspension: independent front, alignment, excessive wear, pulling. • "Front suspension misaligned; uneven and excessive wear of tires; front balance aligned 5 times by dealer." • "Vehicle pulls toward right when brakes are applied." • "Premature and excessive wear of outside tread of front tires; had tire rotated, balanced and aligned; showing signs of wear again at 8,000 miles." • "Rear end swung out to left, causing accident." • "Uneven and premature tire wear on front."

4. Brakes: hydraulic system, noise, failure. • "Brakes ineffective, soft." • "Grinding and squealing noise of brakes." • "Front brake rotors undersized for size of car; many repairs/replacements." • "Brake failures; replaced brake pads, turned rear brake drums, replaced front rotors." • "Brakes rubbing; refaced rotors and replaced cracked brake shoe."

5. Fuel: fuel injection system, stalling, hesitation. • "Idling car suddenly burst into flames; problem with the fuel injection system; car totaled." • "Engine caught fire when turned car on; fuel injection line leaked." • "Engine intermittently stalls in reverse, at stops or at low speeds." • "Vehicle stalled on top of hill; indicators on dash flashed, with foot on brake, car started rolling backwards at fast pace; braking to no avail; accident." • "When driving at 50-60 mph, or coming to stoplight or stop sign, car would stall; surged beyond accelerated speed; braking hard kept car in check."

6. Brakes: hydraulic: shoe: disc brake system, noise, failure. • "Front brakes worn and noisy; calipers, pads and drums replaced." • "Defective front brakes; repaired/replaced 6 times, all repair attempts to no avail." • "Front brakes wouldn't stop car fast enough; brake fades; excessive travel of brake pedal to floor; loss of control resulted in an accident." • "Front brakes noisy; replaced pads, noise continued." • "Defective braking system; rotors and brake shoes repaired/replaced due to loud squeaking, burning, rubbing noise after being in heavy traffic."

MERCURY COUGAR 1988

Complaint Severity: Troublesome. **Buyer's Summary:** Check the brakes—listen for noise, look for leaks and feel for vibration. They may fail, perform poorly or require frequent mechanical attention. See "Sudden Accelerations" in Introduction.

Hot Spots and Owner/NHTSA Comments:

1. Fuel: throttle linkages and control, sudden accelerations. • "Upon driving, car continues to accelerate after brake applied; when put in neutral, engine revs up until gas pedal tapped." • "Upon starting, car suddenly accelerated out of control, resulting in accident." • "Accelerator sticks wide open, making engine race; braking difficult and car travels at 35 mph without foot on gas pedal." • "Slowing down to enter a turn lane, vehicle decelerated but did not slow down enough; hit car, but had plenty of time to stop." • "Vehicle surges or suddenly accelerates when shifting gears from park to drive."

2. Brakes: hydraulic system, locking up, noise, failure. • "Defective braking system; repaired on 5 different occasions, problem persists." • "Braking problems, resulting in accident; brakes spongy; grinding; lock up." • "Brakes grabbing when hot; groan on release; rotated and balanced all 4 wheels." • "Brakes noisy when applied; also, drag or stick when starting from a stop." • "Brakes failed to slow or stop vehicle."

3. Brakes: hydraulic: shoe: disc brake system, noise, malfunction. • "Grinding noise in front right brake when brakes applied; replaced rotors, 4 disc pads and calipers, grinding continued; possible rebuilt calipers defective." • "Recurring front brake problem; replaced and resurfaced rotors, overhauled calipers, complete brake job and several repairs made; brakes have never worked properly." • "Cracked brake pads caused problem; repaired/replaced brake disc, pads and rotors." • "Brake rotors out of round; uneven tire wear; balanced tires and aligned." • "Recurring brake malfunctions; repaired/replaced rotor, caliper and master cylinder, problem continues."

4. Exhaust system: converter, malfunction, failure. • "Metallic noises on acceleration; repaired/replaced catalytic converter." • "Defective catalytic converter replaced." • "Faulty catalytic converter; only warning was slight rattle." • "Catalytic converter malfunctioned." • "Catalytic converter defective."

5. Interior systems: active restraints: belt buckles, breaking, malfunction. • "Seat belt buckle on driver's-side broke; replaced the complete seat belt unit, seat belt inoperative. Had ignition replaced." • "The spring within the buckle has broken, making the belt unusable." • "Seat belt buckle detached while driving." • "Driver's-side seat belt buckle failed; at first would latch, then would not lock at all; replaced by dealer." • "After putting on seat belts, snug against hips, buckle will release itself."

6. Engine: mounts, breaking, vibration. • "Engine mounts broke; replaced 2." • "Motor mount broke loose." • "Broken motor mounts." • "Vehicle will not start properly due to defective motor mounts." • "Motor mounts are loose, causing the vehicle to vibrate."

MERCURY COUGAR 1989

Complaint Severity: Troublesome. **Recall Alert:** See Recall Index. **Buyer's Summary:** Check the brakes—listen for noise, look for leaks and feel for vibration. They may fail, perform poorly or require frequent mechanical attention. Test the transmission thoroughly. See "Sudden Accelerations" in Introduction.

Hot Spots and Owner/NHTSA Comments:

1. Fuel: throttle linkages and control, sudden accelerations. • "Throttle stuck causing car to lunge forward and strike another vehicle." • "Car was in park, and accelerated once placed in reverse. Hit a tree and stopped. Engine had very high rpm before shifting gears." • "Attempting to start car, driver's foot on brake, put car into overdrive and car took off with hard acceleration; after striking 2 cars, shifted to park and stopped car." • "Upon putting car in drive, vehicle jumped out of gear; suddenly accelerated and went out of control, which caused accident and damage." • "Throttle is sticking; idling is extremely high, which results in constant brake wear."

2. Brakes: hydraulic: disc: rotor: disc hub, vibration, excessive wear. • "Braking problems at approximately 4,000 miles; both front rotors had to be replaced." • "Steering wheel vibrated when braking due to defective rotors; repaired/replaced, problem occurred again from bad rotors." • "Shimmy when brakes applied would nearly shake steering wheel out of hands; rotors repaired/replaced 3 times; original rotors too thin, thicker rotors installed." • "Brake rotors are warping, causing vibration and steering problems." • "When brakes are applied, front end starts to shimmy excessively; can feel through steering wheel; problem appears to be in rotors."

3. Brakes: hydraulic system, vibration, failure. • "Steering wheel vibrates when brakes are applied; repaired, problem continues." • "Recall on brakes for uneven wear; repaired, problem continues." • "The vehicle has been experiencing sudden acceleration. The vehicle has to be turned off in order to stop. Braking is ineffective." • "Brakes failed and pedal went all the way to the floor; dealer could not find anything wrong." • "Brakes failed to stop vehicle from accelerating backward."

4. Brakes: hydraulic: shoe: disc brake system, noise, excessive wear. • "Front rotors and disc pads replaced 3 times, problem continues." • "Grinding noise; shimmies and vibrates when brakes are applied at any speed." • "Front rotors and pads are warping continually; replaced; five sets have failed." • "Defective front brakes; front rotors have heat spot, calipers are sticking, brakes pulsate and vibrate when being applied at 45-55 mph." • "Brakes go to floor when making sharp turns; rotors replaced 3 times within 1 year."

5. Power train: transmission: automatic, poor performance, difficulty shifting, slipping. • "Problem with transmission oil leakage; repaired." • "Transmission does not shift into gear." • "Transmission slips out at different times, and downshifts." • "Transmission leak caused by loose front bolts and seals." • "Transmission drops out of cruise control when moving up steep hills; vehicle slows suddenly."

6. Brakes: hydraulic: power assist: vacuum system, failure. • "While driving, brakes failed; couldn't stop car; resulted in an accident, vehicle experienced 5 brake failures." • "Steering shakes and car shimmies at decreased speeds; adjusted brakes to no avail." • "Problem with air in brakes; repaired." • "Defective brakes; need to push with force to stop car; unsafe lifting of front of car at low speed." • "Failure of hydraulic power assist; no rear brakes."

MERCURY COUGAR 1990

Complaint Severity: Troublesome. **Recall Alert:** See Recall Index. **Buyer's Summary:** Check the brakes—listen for noise, look for leaks and feel for vibration. They may fail, perform poorly or require frequent mechanical attention. Test the transmission thoroughly. See "Sudden Accelerations" in Introduction.

Hot Spots and Owner/NHTSA Comments:

1. Fuel: throttle linkages and control, sudden accelerations. • "Driver's floor mat not fastened to seat rail to keep from sliding when entering and exiting, allowing mat to slide forward and jam gas pedal." • "While driving at 30-35 mph, vehicle suddenly accelerated; did not stop when brakes were applied; had to turn the ignition key off." • "While driving and applying emergency brakes to slow down, vehicle accelerated and then slowly dropped down in mileage." • "Vehicle went into open-throttle position while driving at 30 mph; could not stop vehicle. Applied brakes to stop vehicle, which caused brakes to overheat." • "Throttle stuck in open position; engine accelerated at rapid speed; plastic ring on linkage accelerator broke; linkage dangled loose."

2. Brakes: hydraulic: disc: rotor: disc hub, vibration, failure. • "Replaced front brake rotors twice within 21,000 miles." • "Defective rotors cause vibrations in steering control when braking." • "While braking, vehicle vibrates from the front end." • "As a result of bent rotors, extreme front-end shimmies and vibrations when brakes are applied." • "While driving car out of garage, brakes failed; rotors were warped; replaced."

3. Brakes: hydraulic system, vibration, failure. • "Warped rotors caused steering wheel shimmy; recall work done." • "When applying brakes, they completely malfunctioned, with the pedal hitting the floor." • "Brakes make a loud grinding noise; experienced a very low pressure when the brakes applied." • "When passing at 65 mph, vehicle failed to decrease in speed. Brakes had no impact with speed." • "Vehicle went into open-throttle position while driving at 30 mph; could not stop vehicle. Applied brakes to stop vehicle, which caused brakes to overheat."

4. Brakes: hydraulic: shoe: disc brake system, premature failure. • "Front disc brakes warped; replaced front rotors." • "Front brake problems; changed rotors and pads." • "Front brakes overheat, causing pads and rotors to wear out and score." • "Brake problems; replaced pads and rotors twice, still problems." • "Premature wear of rotors and pads; they were replaced."

5. Power train: transmission: automatic, poor performance, difficulty shifting, slipping. • "While shifting transmission into high gear, vehicle jumped out of gear and accelerated." • "Recurring problem with leak under car; repaired/replaced transmission pan gasket and seal pipe stick tube." • "Noisy when shifting gear to overdrive, and gearshift locked." • "Transmission shifts into neutral; dealer found nothing wrong."

6. Visual systems: windshield wiper, malfunction, failure. • "Windshield wipers inoperative." • "Windshield wipers recalled; repaired, problem with cleaning window continues." • "Noise from wipers, bent wipers; recalled." • "Windshield wiper assembly recalled." • "Windshield wipers work intermittently."

MERCURY COUGAR 1991

Complaint Severity: Negligible. **Recall Alert:** See Recall Index. **Buyer's Summary:** Check the brakes—listen for noise, look for leaks and feel for vibration. They may fail, perform poorly or require frequent mechanical attention. Test the transmission thoroughly. See "Sudden Accelerations" in Introduction.

Hot Spots and Owner/NHTSA Comments:

1. Fuel: throttle linkages and control, sudden accelerations. • "After backing onto roadway, shifted into drive and vehicle accelerated 200 feet. Driver threw into park and left vehicle." • "Whenever throttle is pushed, system may stick, resulting in full throttle." • "Vehicle accelerates when attempting to disengage cruise control, causing extreme pressure to be used on brake pedal to stop vehicle." • "While driving at 55 mph, throttle went into open position; put in neutral and turned ignition off, pulled off highway."

2. Power train: transmission: automatic, poor performance, difficulty shifting, slipping. • "When parked on incline, vehicle may jump out of gear and roll." • "Car rolls forward while engaged in park." • "Noise in transmission; gear set replaced."

3. Brakes: hydraulic: anti-skid system, poor performance, failure, locking up. • "Antilock brake system light came on and stayed on; vehicle had complete brake failure, which resulted in pedal fading." • "Antilock brake system brake pads need to be replaced every 6,000 miles. When driver applied brakes, pedal went to the floor and there was a grinding noise." • "Antilock brakes failed to stop vehicle properly; also, hard brake pedal." • "Constant vibration in steering wheel when brakes are applied; problem has existed since purchase of vehicle."

4. Brakes: hydraulic: disc: rotor: disc hub, vibration, excessive wear. • "Front brake rotors perform poorly, causing pulsation of brakes and vibration of steering wheel." • "The front rotor had to be replaced 3 times." • "Rotors replaced 2 times." • "Rotors warped twice."

5. Brakes: hydraulic: shoe: disc brake system, locking up, noise. • "Replacement of front brakes, rotors and pads." • "Front brake problems at 13,000 miles." • "Passing an 18-wheeler at 75 mph, came to a curve and tried to stop, but disc brakes had locked up." • "Right front brake squeals at low speeds."

6. Interior systems: instrument panel: speedometer: odometer, malfunction, failure. • "Odometer and trip odometer failure." • "Speedometer failure." • "If vehicle is parked in hot weather, upon driving, speedometer needle gets stuck at 40 mph." • "Speedometer failed."

MERCURY COUGAR 1992

Complaint Severity: Typical. **Buyer's Summary:** See "Sudden Accelerations" in Introduction.

Hot Spots and Owner/NHTSA Comments:

1. Fuel: throttle linkages and control, sudden accelerations. • "Engine accelerates to high speeds when applying brakes; no prior warning." • "Sudden acceleration, vehicle went into open-throttle position with high idle and surged forward, hitting workbench." • "Sudden acceleration, went into open-throttle position; put gear in neutral to stop vehicle." • "Owner is having problem with accelerating spring; vehicle just takes off with a great amount of speed; dealer can't find the problem." • "Defective throttle sensor causes vehicle to surge or suddenly accelerate when idling or driving at normal speeds. Crashed into a wall."

MERCURY COUGAR 1993

Complaint Severity: Typical. **Buyer's Summary:** Check the brakes—listen for noise, look for leaks and feel for vibration. They may fail, perform poorly or require frequent mechanical attention.

Hot Spots and Owner/NHTSA Comments:

1. Brakes: hydraulic system, vibration. • "When brakes are applied at any speed, vehicle will vibrate extensively." • "Motor shuts off while driving down road. Happens at low speed, with loss of steering and brakes." • "When applying the brakes, vehicle starts to vibrate." • "Vehicle intermittently vibrates when brakes applied." • "When brakes are applied, the steering wheel shakes from side to side, making vehicle difficult to control."

2. Brakes: hydraulic: disc: rotor: disc hub, excessive wear, vibration. • "Warped front brake rotors." • "Front brake rotors are warping, resulting in front wheel vibration." • "Antilock brake system: Continued wear of disc rotors; 5 times experienced extended stopping distance; making a loud noise." • "Power brakes fail to effectively stop vehicle when applied due to warped brake rotors." • "Vehicle shimmies; replacement of fourth set of brake rotors."

MERCURY GRAND MARQUIS 1987

Complaint Severity: Troublesome. **Recall Alert:** See Recall Index. **Buyer's Summary:** Look carefully for any kind of leakage, especially under the car. Verify that the cruise control system works properly, and that it doesn't cause the engine to surge. The electronic control unit has been blamed for engine performance problems, including stalling and surging. Check the brakes—listen for noise, look for leaks and feel for vibration. They may fail, perform poorly or require frequent mechanical attention. Test the transmission thoroughly. See "Sudden Accelerations" in Introduction.

Hot Spots and Owner/NHTSA Comments:

1. Fuel: throttle linkages and control, sudden accelerations. • "Uncontrolled sudden acceleration upon putting gear in drive; car shot forward with loud surge of power, resulting in accident." • "Intermittent acceleration problem; car accelerates into reverse and drive both; acceleration also very noisy, very hard to stop by brakes." • "While braking to stop, car suddenly accelerated; pushed brake hard, surged across street; hit building wall; resulted in extensive damage and injuries." • "Vehicle surges forward to high speeds when foot is removed from accelerator pedal, especially if weather is hot and air conditioner is on." • "When putting on the cruise control, vehicle accelerates."

2. Brakes: hydraulic system, noise, malfunction. • "Screeching and squealing of brakes; when tried to stop, accelerated." • "While in motion, brakes make grinding noise; when applied, brakes lock up." • "Presence of noise is due to an apparent brake system failure." • "Vehicle suddenly accelerated with brakes applied. Owner had to turn vehicle off to stop, and hit a tree." • "Constant loss of brake pressure and fluid."

3. Equipment: speed control, malfunction, failure. • "Cruise control problem; when resuming for 55 or 60 mph, car lunges rapidly forward to reach desired speed." • "Cruise control engaged on highways at 55 mph; tap brakes and slow down to 40 mph; when 'resume' button is pressed, accelerator pedal automatically shoots forward." • "Cruise control intermittent sensor replaced due to transmission dropping to passing gear when 'resume' button is hit after slowing down; accelerates car." • "Car will not stop accelerating until cruise control is shut off." • "Cruise control accelerated 20-25 mph higher than actual speed set; caused uncontrollable steering; resulted in an accident; no warning."

4. Power train: transmission: automatic, poor performance, difficulty shifting, slipping. • "Automatic transmission shifting rod loose; caused car to speed forward and backward with no control." • "When approaching 42-45 mph range, transmission jerks and lunges." • "Slipping or jerking problem in transmission at different speeds." • "Noise in transmission at 50-55 mph and in overdrive." • "Jerks and hesitates; defective."

5. Electrical system: ignition: electronic control unit, sudden acceleration, failure. • "Central computer failed at 35,000 miles." • "Vehicle experienced sudden acceleration; electronic control failed, engine went wide open; resulted in accident." • "Engine began racing, then slowed down several times after starting vehicle." • "Car suddenly accelerated and driver lost control; accident resulted; replaced failed processor in computer." • "Vehicle hard to start at initial startup, and then engine died altogether."

6. Engine: leaks, poor performance. • "Engine problem; knocking of bearings; rebuilt complete engine." • "One engine cylinder cracked; 2 replaced." • "Excessive oil consumption." • "Excessive oil consumption; adjusted several times, continued excessive oil loss." • "Two oil leaks from engine."

MERCURY GRAND MARQUIS 1988

Complaint Severity: Very Serious. **Recall Alert:** See Recall Index. **Buyer's Summary:** Check the brakes—listen for noise, look for leaks and feel for vibration. They may fail, perform poorly or require frequent mechanical attention. See "Sudden Accelerations" in Introduction.

Hot Spots and Owner/NHTSA Comments:

1. Fuel: throttle linkages and control, sudden accelerations. • "When stopped at stop sign, took foot off brake, car accelerated on its own to 50 mph. Dealer can't fix problem." • "Released accelerator, it stayed on floor with engine operating at maximum speed; stuck to floor." • "Manifold air pressure and throttle position sensors replaced twice; no power under load, occasional failure to accelerate." • "While driving, suddenly vehicle started accelerating from 35 to 70 mph without pressing gas pedal; to stop, turned off ignition." • "Vehicle was placed in reverse and it accelerated back into neighbor's house. Engine was racing."

2. Brakes: hydraulic system, locking up, malfunction. • "Vehicle surged forward after it was put in drive. Driver had foot on brake, but vehicle hit building." • "While driving on highway, car ahead suddenly stopped; upon applying brakes, car skidded, hitting median; resulted in injuries and car totaled." • "Brakes soft upon application, then locked; skidded across road into oncoming car." • "Brakes touchy, sometimes grab; not in any specific road condition or driving speed."

MERCURY GRAND MARQUIS 1989

Complaint Severity: Serious. **Buyer's Summary:** Look carefully for any kind of leakage, especially under the car. Verify that the cruise control system works properly, and that it doesn't cause the engine to surge. Test the transmission thoroughly. See "Sudden Accelerations" in Introduction. Make sure air conditioner works properly.

Hot Spots and Owner/NHTSA Comments:

1. Fuel: throttle linkages and control, sudden accelerations. • "Shifted gear into reverse, vehicle jolted backward full car length, then stopped." • "Fifteen-mile drive, parked 15 minutes; upon restarting and engaging reverse, car had sudden acceleration for about 10 feet, with wheels spinning." • "While parking at curb with brakes applied, engine accelerated to full speed; jumped curb and went through brick wall into restaurant; several persons were injured." • "Second crash from sudden acceleration; cruise control problems; restarted and shifted to drive, crashed into a car. Felt gas pedal pull to the floor." • "When shifting from reverse to drive, vehicle accelerated with great speed."

2. Power train: transmission: automatic, poor performance, difficulty shifting, slipping. • "Transmission stuck in 2nd gear." • "Automatic transmission failed at 46,000 miles; it does not engage in gear." • "Rough and/or jerky shifting transmission; recalled, problem continues." • "When braking, transmission does not decelerate as intended; engine lights come on prior to braking." • "Transmission lurching into passing gear on slight incline; car bogs down; continually shifts up and down with a great loss of momentum, causing dangerous or hazardous conditions."

3. Air conditioner: leaks, failure. • "Air conditioner releases fumes that cause nausea." • "Air conditioner relay failure." • "Air conditioning system emits unpleasant musty odor." • "Repeated repairs on air conditioner; when turned on low, terrible odor emanates, causing tearing of eyes and difficulty in breathing." • "Leaking air conditioner system in car; faulty O-ring."

4. Equipment: speed control, malfunction, failure. • "Cruise control wouldn't shut off; contacts cleaned." • "Cruise control failed." • "Once cruise completely disengaged by braking, cruise function may reactivate itself again by touching 'acceleration' button." • "While attempting to set cruise control, accelerator traveled to the floor and locked up. Accelerated from 65 to 85 mph. No prior warning."

MERCURY GRAND MARQUIS 1990

Complaint Severity: Serious. **Recall Alert:** See Recall Index. **Buyer's Summary:** The airbags in this vehicle have experienced failures and malfunctions: You may need a professional evaluation on the condition of the airbags. Check the brakes—listen for noise, look for leaks and feel for vibration. They may fail, perform poorly or require frequent mechanical attention. Test the transmission thoroughly. Make sure seat belts function correctly and fit comfortably. See "Sudden Accelerations" in Introduction.

Hot Spots and Owner/NHTSA Comments:

1. Fuel: throttle linkages and control, sudden accelerations. • "Backing out of garage, put foot on brake, slid gear into reverse, motor raced and shot back, doing damage to garage and car door." • "While driving vehicle intermittently surged without any warning." • "While driving, vehicle surged backward, causing an accident." • "Vehicle suddenly accelerated, went out of control and caused an accident." • "Upon putting vehicle in forward gear, shot forward at great speed and impacted into wall; sustained injuries."

2. Power train: transmission: automatic, poor performance, difficulty shifting, slipping. • "Transmission does not shift smoothly into overdrive or downshift out of overdrive." • "Transmission slipped out of gear; vehicle went out of control and hit a pillar." • "Car started moving backwards while in overdrive; put in drive, still went backwards; engine turned off and restarted, car accelerated out of control." • "Transmission does not shift properly; there is noise when gears are changing." • "Automatic transmission goes in and out of gear momentarily at different speeds without changing vehicle's speed."

3. Brakes: hydraulic system, locking up, failure. • "Brake failure." • "Right rear tire locks on medium brake application." • "Brakes; complete replacement of hub, etc." • "Rear brakes will lock up when applied and cause vehicle to skid and lose control." • "Brakes worn; replaced."

4. Interior systems: passive restraint: belts, uncomfortable, poor performance. • "Safety belt restraint system totally unsafe with removal of tension eliminator; shoulder strap comes across neck and collarbone, have to constantly pull loose." • "Front seat belts poorly positioned in a way that, when in use, they contact driver and passenger high on neck above collar, making belts very uncomfortable to wear." • "Persistent and continuing problem with seat belts; occupants suffer neck irritation, which constitutes danger when extended driving involved." • "No stop on seat belts; belts hit diagonally across throat." • "No matter how seats adjusted, seat and shoulder belt hits across throat; very dangerous and uncomfortable."

5. Interior systems: passive restraint: airbag: driver, malfunction, failure. • "Airbag exploded during a sudden-acceleration accident; driver suffered second and third degree burns on arm and fractured rib." • "Airbag inflated upon impact, causing hand burns and a bruised shoulder." • "No deployment of driver's airbag during accident." • "Airbag deployed during accident; burned both arms and face."

MERCURY GRAND MARQUIS 1991

Complaint Severity: Serious. **Recall Alert:** See Recall Index. **Buyer's Summary:** The airbags in this vehicle have experienced failures and malfunctions: You may need a professional evaluation on the condition of the airbags. Check the brakes—listen for noise, look for leaks and feel for vibration. They may fail, perform poorly or require frequent mechanical attention. See "Sudden Accelerations" in Introduction.

Hot Spots and Owner/NHTSA Comments:

1. Brakes: hydraulic system, vibration, failure. • "When brakes are applied, they vibrate; rotors and pads have had to be replaced." • "Vehicle lurches uncontrollably when applying brakes; replaced front caliper pistons." • "Brake failure 5 times; caused accident; several replacements." • "On a panic stop, vehicle veered sharply to right, then swung to left and hit divider." • "Brakes have been pulsating and grabbing."

2. Brakes: hydraulic: shoe: disc brake system, locking up, malfunction, poor performance. • "Front brake pads and rotors continually malfunction; repaired numerous times to no avail; they continue to malfunction." • "Front brakes lock up." • "Vehicle has had numerous replacements of brake components. Once only right front brake functioned. Vehicle has lost control when applying brakes; tire wear." • "Complete brake failure on front end. Brake ring retainers that hold bearings are made of plastic. Overheated." • "While traveling down a steep grade at 35-45 mph, vehicle shook and brakes performed poorly."

3. Brakes: hydraulic: disc: rotor: disc hub, vibration, excessive wear. • "Extreme vibration while braking; design flaw in rotors, no longer problem." • "Front rotors defective, causing steering and shimmying problems." • "Front rotors are warped at 27,000 miles and need replacement; cause vibration." • "The front brake rotors are warped, resulting in no braking ability." • "Defective front brake system; rotors get warped every 6,000-8,000 miles."

4. Fuel: throttle linkages and control, sudden accelerations. • "Upon shifting gears from park to drive, vehicle suddenly accelerated, causing loss of vehicle control. Driver shut vehicle off to stop." • "Upon shifting gears, a slight pause occurs between gear transition, then vehicle unexpectedly accelerates." • "Sudden acceleration caused a frontal crash; airbags prevented deaths." • "Sudden acceleration caused accident." • "Vehicle surged forward out of control, causing an accident; the airbag did not deploy."

5. Interior systems: passive restraint: airbag, malfunction, failure. • "Eye irritation caused by poisonous gas during airbag deployment." • "Airbag deployment was violent during accident, causing injuries." • "False deployment, causing loss of control and accident." • "During a collision at 50 mph, airbag deployed only partially due to steering wheel not opening completely; caused chest injury." • "In frontal collision, airbag deployed, but chemical gas emitted by inflator escaped through a hole that developed in middle of bag, causing facial burns."

6. Interior systems: passive restraint: airbag: driver, malfunction, failure. • "Upon starting vehicle, airbag deployed unexpectedly; caused injuries to driver." • "Frontal collision, impact 12:00 position, speed 20 mph, airbag deployed; did damage to driver." • "Vehicle surged forward out of control, causing an accident; the airbag did not deploy." • "Upon frontal impact, airbag deployed but failed to inflate." • "Driver's airbag repaired 4 times."

MERCURY GRAND MARQUIS 1992

Complaint Severity: Troublesome. **Buyer's Summary:** The airbags in this vehicle have experienced failures and malfunctions: You may need a professional evaluation on the condition of the airbags. Check the brakes—listen for noise, look for leaks and feel for vibration. They may fail, perform poorly or require frequent mechanical attention. Test the transmission thoroughly. See "Sudden Accelerations" in Introduction.

Hot Spots and Owner/NHTSA Comments:

1. Brakes: hydraulic: anti-skid system, poor performance, failure, locking up. • "Antilock brake system malfunctions due to defective wheel sensor." • "While driving, experienced brake lockup under normal deceleration on antilock brake system-equipped vehicle when warning light popped and went into skid, causing brake failure." • "Antilock brakes would pulsate when applied due to worn pads and warped rotors." • "Antilock brake system brake pedal locked up, which caused pedal to position halfway, diminished brake effectiveness and increased stopping distances; resulted in an accident." • "Antilock brake system: Vibration and pulsation in brakes and rotors; replacement of brakes every 5,000 miles."

2. Fuel: throttle linkages and control, sudden accelerations. • "Throttle position sensor sticks in open position without letting vehicle slow down." • "Shifter in park, engine started; car leaped forward while shift lever still in park, causing head and hand injuries." • "Throttle body grommet failed; prior to service recall."

3. Brakes: hydraulic system, vibration, noise, failure. • "Brakes failed, causing vehicle to lose control and slide into rear of another vehicle." • "Brakes dragging; noisy and vibrating." • "Brake pedal continues to depress closer to the floor, causing excessive brake wear and replacement every 13,000 miles." • "Vehicle vibrates when braking." • "While driving and approaching a stop sign, brakes failed; pedal went to floor, resulting in an accident."

4. Brakes: hydraulic: disc: rotor: disc hub, vibration, excessive wear. • "Front brake rotors, pads and calipers failed, causing vibration." • "Antilock brake system front rotors out of round, causing severe vibrations at highway speeds when braking." • "Brakes thump when applied. Dealer replaced rotors." • "Front brake rotors failed 5 times; also, brakes fade when used frequently." • "Front brake rotors and pads failed, causing vehicle to pulsate and vibrate; also, brakes fade and are hot when braking on long downhill slopes."

5. Power train: transmission: automatic, poor performance, difficulty shifting, slipping. • "Power steering; vehicle wanders while driving; also, failure of transmission, which locks up and is hard to shift while driving." • "Upon starting, without placing into gear, suddenly in reverse position vehicle accelerated out of control, jumping over another vehicle." • "When put in gear, car went into overdrive and moved forward and backward." • "Transmission overhauled." • "Replaced transmission."

6. Interior systems: passive restraint: airbag: driver, malfunction, failure. • "Hit a guardrail, and upon frontal impact the airbag did not deploy." • "During a frontal collision at 12:00 position, driving at 45 mph, airbag did not deploy; caused injuries to driver." • "Consumer was in between 2 trucks and her airbag involuntarily inflated; consumer caught on fire, lost control, ran into passing vehicle at 12:00 position." • "Driver's airbag failed to deploy during accident, resulting in a fatality." • "Airbag did not deploy during 35-mph frontal collision, resulting in an injury."

MERCURY GRAND MARQUIS 1994

Complaint Severity: Very Serious. **Recall Alert:** See Recall Index. **Buyer's Summary:** The airbags in this vehicle have experienced failures and malfunctions: You may need a professional evaluation on the condition of the airbags. See "Sudden Accelerations" in Introduction.

Hot Spots and Owner/NHTSA Comments:

1. Fuel: throttle linkages and control, sudden accelerations. • "Vehicle suddenly accelerated to unknown high speeds while idling, causing loss of vehicle control and a front-end collision. Dual airbags did not deploy." • "Vehicle was parked; when gear was shifted into drive, vehicle went into open-throttle position, hitting a building, impact 12:00 position; resulted in injuries." • "Increased acceleration when starting vehicle." • "Slowly entering school parking lot, vehicle automatically accelerated; driver jumped curb, hitting set of steps head-on." • "Vehicle accelerated out of control, resulting in accident; brake did not respond."

2. Interior systems: passive restraint: airbag: driver, malfunction, failure. • "While driving, noticed steering loss, due to missing bolt that connects steering wheel to the car; resulted in accident." • "Driver's airbag did not deploy." • "Driver's airbag did not deploy." • "Frontal collision, impact 12:00 position, speed 12 mph, airbag deployed, causing injuries to face and other parts of the body."

3. Interior systems: passive restraint: airbag: passenger, malfunction, failure. • "Passenger-side airbag assembly came out completely unassembled—wiring and all—during side impact." • "Passenger's airbag did not deploy."

MERCURY LYNX 1987

Complaint Severity: Typical. **Recall Alert:** See Recall Index. **Buyer's Summary:** The carburetion system could contribute to stalling and hesitation. The fuel injection system has been blamed for hesitation and stalling. Be sure the vehicle doesn't die in traffic or at stops. Check the brakes—listen for noise, look for leaks and feel for vibration. They may fail, perform poorly or require frequent mechanical attention. See "Sudden Accelerations" in Introduction.

Hot Spots and Owner/NHTSA Comments:

1. Fuel: fuel injection system, stalling, hesitation. • "Car hesitates as though it's going to cut off (but never does), while in backward and forward motion." • "Engine surges at different speeds." • "Engine stalls out when in operation; emits strong fuel odor, thick-film integrated unit repaired/replaced, stalling continues." • "Car sputters, stalls and becomes inoperative; replaced fuel sending unit, couplings and pump." • "Vehicle dies on takeoff and when making turns."

2. Fuel: fuel carburetion, stalling, hesitation. • "Engine cuts off, dies out when coming to a stop." • "Vehicle stalls at stop signs and on takeoff from stop signs." • "Getting gas backup in air conditioning system; problem with fuel carburetion system." • "Constant stalling due to defective processors." • "Car loses power intermittently; car surges; engine races at stop signs."

3. Fuel: throttle linkages and control, sudden accelerations. • "Car accelerates uncontrollably, jumps forward." • "Car races with foot on brakes; car plunges forward when foot is taken off." • "When throttle positioner at speeds of 55 mph, car jerks and shakes as if gas not going into engine." • "Car accelerating on its own; had to stamp on brake pedal to stop; occurred 8 times."

4. Brakes: hydraulic system, vibration, failure. • "Unspecified problem with brakes; no brakes in car, contamination of fluid in brakes." • "Brakes not do no work properly; pedal needs excessive pressure to slow in longer travel; when slowing right rear brake locks up; replaced cylinders and rotors." • "Faulty brakes; popping noise whenever brakes applied; replaced brakes and tightened right lower control arm bolts." • "Brake pulsation and clicking due to out-of-round drums and uneven wear."

5. Interior systems: active seat and shoulder belts and belt anchor, uncomfortable, failure. • "Defective front seat belt restraint, resulted in injury." • "During an accident as a result of the driver failing to yield the right-of-way, passive restraint system failed to work on passenger's side." • "Driver's-side seat belt does not fit properly."

MERCURY MARQUIS 1987

Complaint Severity: Troublesome. **Buyer's Summary:** See "Sudden Accelerations" in Introduction.

Hot Spots and Owner/NHTSA Comments:

1. Fuel: throttle linkages and control, sudden accelerations. • "Initial problem of stalling and misfiring at stops; car started accelerating unintentionally while driving." • "Vehicle idling, when engaged in drive, suddenly accelerated at full speed; hit brakes to regain control." • "Vehicle suddenly and without warning accelerated at very high speed, resulting in accident; occurred twice." • "Car's shift lever put in drive with foot on brake, car shot out uncontrollably, causing accident; hit parked car." • "While in park position, experienced sudden acceleration; resulted in accident."

MERCURY MARQUIS 1989

Complaint Severity: Troublesome. **Recall Alert:** See Recall Index. **Buyer's Summary:** Look carefully for any kind of leakage, especially under the car. See "Sudden Accelerations" in Introduction. Make sure air conditioner works properly.

Hot Spots and Owner/NHTSA Comments:

1. Air conditioner: leaks, poor performance. • "Air conditioner lines to condenser from compressor leaking freon; seals in lines are leaking refrigerant oil." • "Air conditioning has very bad odor, smells of mildew; as car gets older, gets worse." • "Air conditioning problem; doesn't cool properly when driving." • "Fumes emitted from air conditioner smell like chemicals; fumes are intermittent, but problem starts after car has been driven between 20 and 25 miles; burns eyes and nose and causes sore throat." • "Leaking O-ring seals in air conditioning system emitting strong odor."

2. Fuel: throttle linkages and control, sudden accelerations. • "Placed the vehicle in drive; without touching the gas pedal, the vehicle surged forward at a high rate of speed." • "Vehicle put in reverse, car accelerated from parking space, would not brake; lost control, hit building; caused damage." • "Car accelerated backwards, could not be stopped; damaged another vehicle." • "Vehicle put into reverse and suddenly accelerated, hitting another vehicle. Brakes didn't slow vehicle."

3. Interior systems: seat head restraints, poor performance. • "Problem with head restraint; too high, obstructs vision." • "Head restraints are very tall, obstructing rear and over-shoulder view." • "High-positioned headrests on front seats; not positioned in relation to rear side of car; hazardous checking approaching vehicle or pedestrian from rear." • "Driver's and passenger's headrests are too large, obstructing visibility."

MERCURY MARQUIS 1990

Complaint Severity: Harmless. **Recall Alert:** See Recall Index. **Buyer's Summary:** The fuel pump has received complaints. Make sure it doesn't make excessive noise and that you are experiencing adequate engine performance. Also, look for leaks.

Hot Spots and Owner/NHTSA Comments:

1. Fuel: fuel pump, noise, malfunction, fire. • "Constant whine and humming noise heard from vehicle. Possibly electronic fuel pump." • "Noise from rear of vehicle; suspect fuel pump inside fuel tank." • "Since purchase of vehicle, hear a bothersome hum; dealer indicates problem is fuel pump." • "Problem with constant nerve-wracking noise from fuel pump, which causes low acceleration, gasoline leaks and smells inside car; all repair attempts to no avail." • "Fuel pump shorted out wiring harness underneath the car, resulting in fire."

MERCURY SABLE 1987

Complaint Severity: Negligible. **Recall Alert:** See Recall Index. **Buyer's Summary:** Verify that the cruise control system works properly, and that it doesn't cause the engine to surge. The fuel injection system has been blamed for hesitation and stalling. Be sure the vehicle doesn't die in traffic or at stops. Check the brakes—listen for noise, look for leaks and feel for vibration. They may fail, perform poorly or require frequent mechanical attention. Test the transmission thoroughly. See "Sudden Accelerations" in Introduction.

Hot Spots and Owner/NHTSA Comments:

1. Brakes: hydraulic system, pulling, failure. • "While driving, pulled to right, brake pedal went to floor; installed anti-rattle springs." • "Brake system failures included booster, master cylinder and proportioning valve. These produced poor performance and reduced braking capability." • "Brake pedal goes to floor while braking; repaired/replaced master cylinder twice, adjusted brakes 3 times." • "Brakes intermittently very stiff; difficult to stop car, extreme foot pressure required." • "Brakes went to floor, unable to stop; brakes repaired twice, adjustments made, problem still exists."

2. Power train: transmission: automatic, poor performance, difficulty shifting, slipping. • "Transmission replaced 5 times due to slipping problems." • "Major problem with transmission; rebuilt at least 5 times—transmission went out at 20,000 miles, then 32,000 miles, third and fourth times at 37,000 and 43,000 miles." • "Transmission shifts roughly, especially when bringing vehicle to a stop; lurches forward when this happens." • "While driving at highway speed, heard single pop sound; vehicle came to complete halt without warning due to transmission failure."

3. Fuel: throttle linkages and control, sudden accelerations. • "Full-throttle application from standing stop; accelerator pedal remained on floor despite repeated tapping." • "Throttle sticking, causing unintended acceleration." • "Vehicle suffered sudden acceleration, apparently due to fuel linkage sticking; car accelerated while foot on brake." • "Vehicle suddenly accelerated while in operation; ran out of control, resulting in accident." • "Passing truck at 45 mph, accelerator stuck, car began to race; applied brakes to release stuck accelerator."

4. Fuel: fuel injection system, stalling, hesitation. • "Vehicle stalls and surges when accelerating and when less than one-third tank of gas." • "Intermittent hesitation and stalling; needed adjustment and cleaning of fuel injection system." • "Car stalls on acceleration and loses power; also, accelerator sticks and gas leaks." • "When fuel tank has one-quarter tank of gas or less, it stalls and/or hesitates when pulling out in traffic or going uphill." • "With a quarter tank of gas, engine stalls or loses power when accelerating from stop or slowing."

5. Brakes: hydraulic: disc: rotor: disc hub, vibration, excessive wear. • "Rotors are out of round, which results in poor stopping distances." • "Brake rotors completely rusted and fell apart; as a result, vehicle does not have any brakes left." • "Vehicle experienced front disk brake hub separation." • "Front brake rotors, pads and calipers failed; prior to recall." • "Recalled rotors were repaired twice; total brake failure occurred after recall."

6. Equipment: speed control, malfunction, failure. • "After braking to disengage cruise control, cruise control 'off' button pushed; car accelerated back to cruise speed." • "Speed cruise control failure; with speed control engaged, cruising, normal speed, push 'off' button and control disengages, then reengages upon release of button." • "While driving on the freeway with cruise control set for about 65 mph, cruise control turned off upon entering a ramp and went on its own; car accelerated." • "Upon attempting to brake, cruise control failed to disengage; throttle jammed, cruise control wouldn't release; caused acceleration." • "Cruise control causes car to accelerate even when switched to coast; resume does not hold set speed."

MERCURY SABLE 1988

Complaint Severity: Minor. **Recall Alert:** See Recall Index. **Buyer's Summary:** Check the brakes—listen for noise, look for leaks and feel for vibration. They may fail, perform poorly or require frequent mechanical attention. Test the transmission thoroughly. See "Sudden Accelerations" in Introduction.

Hot Spots and Owner/NHTSA Comments:

1. Fuel: throttle linkages and control, sudden accelerations. • "Intermittent stuck throttle; stopped vehicle by applying the brake and turning off the ignition." • "Car accelerated at about 30-35 mph, continued to accelerate without being able to slow it down. Sudden acceleration recurred after throttle position switch replaced." • "Vehicle surges forward and backward intermittently when shifting from drive to reverse." • "Car surges in reverse when fuel line cuts off; failed to start and stalled in operation."

2. Engine: mounts, breaking, vibration. • "Engine motor mounts broke, causing engine to become unstable." • "Three engine motor mounts have broken, causing poor performance." • "Engine was running rough; resulted in engine mount breakage." • "Due to defective motor mounts, which have been repaired 3 times, vehicle vibrates." • "Front motor mounts failed twice; also noisy engine and/or rough idling."

3. Power train: transmission: automatic, poor performance, difficulty shifting, slipping. • "Transmission failed after 36,000 miles while driving." • "Transmission problem with sluggish shifting and slipping between 2nd and 3rd gears, complete transmission failure while driving (lost all forward gears)." • "Lubricating circuit of transmission failed, causing transmission to freeze up and be completely destroyed." • "Automatic transmission linkage system failure; failed when overdrive transaxle was locked in parking position; vehicle unmoveable." • "Automatic transmission does not shift smoothly from low to high gear; roar in low gear, then shifts abruptly to 2nd and then 3rd gear."

4. Brakes: hydraulic: disc: rotor: disc hub, vibration, poor performance. • "Front brake rotor loose on right front side at point where hub joins rotor, which caused poor braking." • "Front brake rotors failed; prior to recall." • "Front brakes were replaced due to a recall; new rotors created grinding and squealing noises while stopping." • "Premature wear of rotors and pads; prior to recall." • "Warped rotors, causing poor brake performance."

5. Brakes: hydraulic system, corrosion, failure. • "Severe rear floor rust has corroded brake lines and caused total brake failure." • "Brakes failed to stop vehicle in time when applied; resulted in accident." • "Brakes not working properly; pedal needs to be pushed very strongly to stop car." • "Brakes failed to stop vehicle effectively; extended stopping, causing front-end collision at 35-40 mph."

6. Engine: vibration, fire, malfunction. • "Engine mounts failed; prior to recall; also, engine leaks oil." • "Excessive oil consumption." • "Engine vibrates; noise on left side when accelerating from stopped position." • "Three leaking motor mounts need to be replaced." • "Engine compartment fire broke out without warning; caused by an electrical short in the cooling system."

MERCURY SABLE 1989

Complaint Severity: Negligible. **Recall Alert:** See Recall Index. **Buyer's Summary:** Look carefully for any kind of leakage, especially under the car. The steering may be stiff or not working correctly. Be sure to test the steering, especially on a cold start. Check the brakes—listen for noise, look for leaks, feel for vibration. They may fail, perform poorly or require frequent mechanical attention. Test the transmission thoroughly. See "Sudden Accelerations" in Introduction.

Hot Spots and Owner/NHTSA Comments:

1. Brakes: hydraulic system, excessive wear, vibration, poor performance. • "Power steering and brakes went out, then smoke came through vents; power steering fluid caught fire on manifold." • "Brakes on left front excessively worn and grabbing." • "Brakes failed; vehicle went out of control, resulting in an accident." • "Brake vibration in steering column caused by poorly designed (too light) rotors; caused excessive caliper and pad wear." • "Power brakes have poor stopping ability, to the point of being dangerous, when stopping quickly."

2. Power train: transmission: automatic, poor performance, difficulty shifting, slipping. • "Automatic transmission shifts harshly; erratic and slips with jerking at low speed." • "When shifted into drive, pressed accelerator and car moved backwards; after 3 tries went into drive." • "Vehicle jerks while stopping; possible transmission defect." • "Automatic transmission erratic and not normal, jerks when accelerating from low speed of 10-20 mph." • "The automatic transmission planetary gear completely quit due to poor lubrication."

3. Interior systems: active restraints: belt buckles, malfunction, failure. • "While driving, driver and passanger shoulder and lap belts disengage; also stick in lock position." • "Seat belt buckle release button fails to pop back up after releasing, preventing buckles from relatching." • "Driver and passenger front and back shoulder and lap belts intermittently do not latch; other times, will latch and come undone while driving." • "Front passenger's and driver's seat belt anchor red push buttons get stuck in release position; and while in use release with no warning." • "Upon impact, passenger-side seat belt buckle detached; resulted in passenger hitting windshield."

4. Brakes: hydraulic: disc: rotor: disc hub, vibration, failure. • "Front brake rotors warped, causing vehicle to wobble when applying the brakes." • "Brake rotors started warping at 4,000 miles; braking problem persisted until whole car vibrated." • "Front brake rotors and pads failed; prior to recall."

5. Fuel: throttle linkages and control, sudden accelerations. • "Car suddenly accelerated, and when brakes were applied, spun, hitting a parked car." • "Car accelerates unexpectedly and for no reason when car is at idle." • "While driving, engine rpm increases without warning, causing vehicle to lurch forward." • "Engine suddenly surged forward; vehicle went out of control and caused an accident." • "While driving and coming to a red light, took foot of gas pedal and throttle stuck."

6. Steering: power assist: hose: fluid, leaks, fire. • "Leak in power steering pressure hose causes power steering fluid to leak out, results in steering vehicle manually; also, could cause a fire." • "Power steering hoses ruptured twice, resulting in vehicle losing steering without warning. Dealer states leakage could result in a fire." • "Defective power steering hose caused fire; while parking, heard popping sound; steering wheel froze; smoke started pouring from engine; opened hood, saw flames and smoke." • "The vehicle caught fire due to a leak in the power steering line leaking onto the engine." • "Engine compartment fire; power steering fluid leaked and caused fire."

MERCURY SABLE 1990

Complaint Severity: Typical. **Recall Alert:** See Recall Index. **Buyer's Summary:** The airbags in this vehicle have experienced failures and malfunctions: You may need a professional evaluation on the condition of the airbags. Check the brakes—listen for noise, look for leaks and feel for vibration. They may fail, perform poorly or require frequent mechanical attention. Test the transmission thoroughly. See "Sudden Accelerations" in Introduction.

Hot Spots and Owner/NHTSA Comments:

1. Fuel: throttle linkages and control, sudden accelerations. • "While driving at 30 mph, throttle disconnected and vehicle became inoperative." • "Throttle position sensor failed, causing high rpm and rapid acceleration." • "Engine accelerates out of range, and stalls unexpectedly while stopping for traffic; no warning." • "Engaged in drive with brake applied, vehicle accelerates rapidly out of control." • "Car accelerates while driving at any speed; rpm goes up to 3,000. Motor has to be turned off to get it to stop."

2. Brakes: hydraulic: disc: rotor: disc hub, vibration, excessive wear. • "Rotors warped, causing front end of vehicle to vibrate upon application of brakes." • "Warped front brake rotors caused pulsation and shuddering when brakes were applied." • "Front brake rotors became noisy, and stopping ability deteriorated." • "Rotors resurfaced at 19,000 miles." • "Front brake rotors warped, caused front end to shimmy." • "Front brake rotors warped; prior to recall."

3. Engine: mounts, breaking, premature failure. • "Vehicle had front motor mounts replaced, prior to recall, with approximately 34,000 miles on vehicle. Front motor mounts have broken again." • "Two motor mounts failed; resulted in engine movement; national back order at all dealerships." • "Defective motor mounts caused steering wheel to vibrate, and vehicle pulled to the right when driving." • "Front motor mounts failed, causing engine to have severe vibration and movement." • "Right front motor mount broke."

4. Interior systems: passive restraint: airbag: driver, malfunction, failure. • "Airbag failed to open when vehicle involved in front-end collision." • "Airbag did not deploy and seat belts did not work in an accident, impact 12:00 position, speed 60 mph." • "No deployment of driver's-side airbag in accident, causing injury." • "During accident, airbag did not deploy. Dealer did not replace it. Also, sensor light came on; took vehicle back and they changed the fuse." • "Airbag did not deploy during front-end collision. Shoulder harness seat belt failed to retract."

5. Brakes: hydraulic system, excessive wear, noise. • "Front and rear brakes replaced 4 times." • "Brakes resist and vehicle bucks when slowing down." • "Engaged in drive with brake applied, vehicle accelerates rapidly out of control." • "Problem with antilock brake; while turning with the brakes applied, there's a grinding noise and brake pedal forces your foot back."

6. Power train: transmission: automatic, poor performance, difficulty shifting, slipping. • "Car shifted very hard; replaced transmission, something broken inside." • "At times hard to shift from 1st to 2nd gear." • "Transmission seals failed." • "Transmission clunking and rough shifting gears."

MERCURY SABLE 1991

Complaint Severity: Typical. **Recall Alert:** See Recall Index. **Buyer's Summary:** Look carefully for any kind of leakage, especially under the car. The steering may be stiff or not working correctly. Be sure to test the steering, especially on a cold start. The airbags in this vehicle have experienced failures and malfunctions: You may need a professional evaluation on the condition of the airbags. Check the brakes—listen for noise, look for leaks and feel for vibration. They may fail, perform poorly or require frequent mechanical attention. Test the transmission thoroughly. See "Sudden Accelerations" in Introduction.

Hot Spots and Owner/NHTSA Comments:

1. Power train: transmission: automatic, poor performance, difficulty shifting, slipping. • "Ford has a transmission fix to prevent the planetary gears from exploding. These parts should be made available as a recall item to prevent personal injury." • "Four transmissions have failed with vehicle. Stalling in the middle of traffic, creating a target for a crash." • "Transmission slipped, then would not accelerate in gear." • "Transmission would not go into gear; dealer replaced, but transmission started slipping at 2,200 miles." • "Driving at 60 mph on turnpike, transmission planetary gears went out due to design of tubing for lubrication; safety hazard."

2. Brakes: hydraulic: disc: rotor: disc hub, vibration, excessive wear. • "Rotors failed, causing noise, wheel and brake control problems." • "Brake rotor continues to wear and gets replaced every 5,000 miles." • "Vibration on braking due to rusted brake rotors. Antilock brake system." • "Front brake made loud grinding noise and car pulled to side; dealer replaced both rotors." • "Warped rotors and pads replaced due to metal-to-metal brake system that can't dissipate the heat generated; caused brakes to pulsate; extended stopping distance."

3. Engine: mounts, breaking, leaks, corrosion. • "Excessive breaking of motor mounts, and malfunctioning transmission." • "Broken rear motor mount had to be replaced." • "Crack in engine mounts caused hydraulic fluid to leak out, resulting in rough engine surging." • "Corrosion of motor mounts; replaced; about 3 weeks later, transmission dropped out; replaced the rear right mounts again." • "Motor mounts are defective, requiring constant replacement and causing transmission to become inoperative."

4. Fuel: throttle linkages and control, sudden accelerations. • "Throttle position sensor replaced due to tachometer increasing from 800 to 2,000 rpm." • "Car took off uncontrollably in an acceleration." • "Engine accelerates while in motion; accelerator pedal traveled to floor, engine stopped racing after ignition was shut off." • "Vehicle has a tendency to surge forward in reverse and then stall." • "Put vehicle in drive and it surged, resulting in an accident."

5. Steering: linkages: tie rod: inner, premature failure. • "Left front tie rod broke, causing loss of steering." • "Left inner tie rod broke." • "While backing out of a parking stall, inner tie rod snapped, resulting in loss of control." • "Inner tie rod had to be replaced." • "Replaced left side inner tie rod."

6. Interior systems: passive restraint: airbag: driver, malfunction, failure. • "The driver's airbag did not deploy in a critical accident." • "Fifty-mph crash, through left front head lamp and grill, did not deploy the airbag." • "During a frontal collision, airbag deployed; first vehicle slid into vehicle 2, impact 12:00 position, speed 5 mph, injuries to hand and arm." • "During rear-end collision at 30 mph, front bumper impact 12:00 position, airbag failed to deploy; resulted in sustained injury when hit steering wheel." • "Vehicle was in a front-end accident and the airbag did not deploy."

MERCURY SABLE 1992

Complaint Severity: Typical. **Recall Alert:** See Recall Index. **Buyer's Summary:** The steering may be stiff or not working correctly. Be sure to test the steering, especially on a cold start. Check the brakes—listen for noise, look for leaks and feel for vibration. They may fail, perform poorly or require frequent mechanical attention. Test the transmission thoroughly. See "Sudden Accelerations" in Introduction.

Hot Spots and Owner/NHTSA Comments:

1. Power train: transmission: automatic, poor performance, difficulty shifting, slipping. • "Electronic-controlled automatic transmission will lose power when accelerating to merge into traffic. Transmission may downshift into lower gear." • "Microprocessor in transmission failed." • "Onboard computer controlling auto transmission has failed." • "Auto transmission failure at 68,000 miles." • "Transmission drops out of overdrive at highway speeds."

2. Brakes: hydraulic: disc: rotor: disc hub, vibration, excessive wear. • "Warped front brake rotors, causing vibration as brakes are applied at highway speeds." • "Fourth set of front brake rotors in 48,000 miles. Loss of steering control due to warped brake rotors; vibrating steering wheel." • "Rotors are warped on front brakes, caused vehicle to vibrate." • "Rear and front rotors warped prematurely due to defective design." • "Brake rotors warped, causing pulsation when stopping."

3. Fuel: throttle linkages and control, sudden accelerations. • "After making an attempt to stop, vehicle accelerated out of control, causing an accident." • "Sudden acceleration when driver attempted to depress accelerator caused loss of control." • "Upon shifting from park to drive, vehicle suddenly accelerated, causing accident."

4. Brakes: hydraulic: anti-skid system, poor performance, failure, locking up. • "When driving on gravel, the brakes automatically lock up for no reason." • "Antilock brakes shuddered at medium-high speed upon application of brakes." • "Intermittent brake failure caused accident." • "Antilock brakes malfunctioned; lost control of vehicle; vehicle veered from lane to lane but was able to avoid an accident because other cars were going slow." • "Antilock brake system light intermittently comes on; brake pedal went to floor; master cylinder replaced."

5. Steering: linkages, tire wear, pulling. • "Intermittent hangup or catch in steering system." • "Car has broken 2 of each item: steering tie rods, rack-and-pinion, and power steering pumps." • "Right front tie rod broke while driving very slowly in parking lot; speed 2 mph; noticed popping sound prior to breakage." • "Defective tie rod; vehicle veers from left to right, causing tracking problems and excessive tire wear; 10 sets of tires replaced within 23,000 miles." • "Front tie rod broke and allowed front wheels to go in opposite directions."

6. Brakes: hydraulic system, failure. • "While driving at approximately 35 mph and approaching an intersection, made attempt to stop, brake pedal went to floor; resulted in hitting vehicle in front." • "Brakes failed 3 times." • "After making an attempt to stop, brakes did not hold; vehicle accelerated out of control, causing an accident." • "Loose spring in brake." • "Rotors failed."

MERCURY SABLE 1993

Complaint Severity: Serious. **Recall Alert:** See Recall Index. **Buyer's Summary:** The fuel pump has received complaints. Make sure it doesn't make excessive noise and that you are experiencing adequate engine performance. Also, look for leaks. The airbags in this vehicle have experienced failures and malfunctions: You may need a professional evaluation on the condition of the airbags. Check the brakes—listen for noise, look for leaks and feel for vibration. They may fail, perform poorly or require frequent mechanical attention. Test the transmission thoroughly. See "Sudden Accelerations" in Introduction.

Hot Spots and Owner/NHTSA Comments:

1. Fuel: throttle linkages and control, sudden accelerations. • "Vehicle accelerated in reverse and hit another vehicle and building. Driver could not control vehicle. Tried to apply brake, but vehicle would not stop." • "While backing up, engine suddenly accelerated wide open; brakes applied; hit a tree before car could cross highway; impact 11:00 position; airbag did not deploy." • "Put car into reverse and it accelerated; car was totaled, no one was injured." • "After releasing brakes, engine idles high persistently while in gear, from 750 to 1,150 rpm; accelerates to 15 mph without depressing accelerator." • "Vehicle suddenly accelerated out of control; brake system did not respond, resulting in accident."

2. Power train: transmission: automatic, poor performance, difficulty shifting, slipping. • "Gear selector sometimes sticks." • "Vehicle was parked in gear, on incline; rolled forward 150 feet, hitting a house; automatic transmission." • "Transmission locks up; hesitates when driving on highway." • "Two loose bolts holding starter support caused transmission failure." • "Automatic transmission performs roughly when changing gears while in motion. Poor performance of transmission system shifting sensor."

3. Communications: horn assembly: button: ring, poor performance. • "Difficulty locating horn button in emergency situation." • "Poor location of horn button, causing difficulty locating button when turning wheel." • "Poor location of horn." • "Poor location of horn buttons."

4. Interior systems: passive restraint: airbag: driver, malfunction, failure. • "Front-end collision; dual airbag did not deploy." • "Airbag failed to deploy upon frontal impact." • "Frontal collision, impact 12:00 position, speed 55 mph, driver's and passenger's airbags did not deploy." • "Consumer was in an accident and driver's-side airbag deployed after she hit head on the steering wheel; broke arm in 3 places." • "While driving, chain reaction of vehicles, impact 12:00 position, speed 20 mph; lap and shoulder belt on driver's-side did not retract and airbag did not deploy."

5. Brakes: hydraulic: disc: rotor: disc hub, vibration, excessive wear. • "Vehicle's rotors warp every 10,000-12,000 miles due to defective design, causing brakes to vibrate." • "Front brake rotors and pads warped prematurely, causing vibration." • "Warped front brake rotors and pads, causing vibration." • "Owner says when he gets up to 50 mph, vehicle starts to vibrate due to rotors." • "Front brake rotors warped, prior to recall, causing vehicle to vibrate when brakes applied."

6. Fuel: fuel pump, stalling, failure. • "Fuel pump failed twice, causing vehicle to stall; prior to recall." • "Fuel pump failed, causing intermittent stalling." • "Fuel pump failed." • "Replaced fuel pump per service recall." • "Customer complains of fuel pump shutoff switch being located in trunk."

MERCURY TOPAZ 1987

Complaint Severity: Minor. **Buyer's Summary:** The carburetion system could contribute to stalling and hesitation. The electronic control unit has been blamed for engine performance problems, including stalling and surging. The fuel injection system has been blamed for hesitation and stalling. Be sure the vehicle doesn't die in traffic or at stops. Check the brakes—listen for noise, look for leaks and feel for vibration. They may fail, perform poorly or require frequent mechanical attention. Test the transmission thoroughly. See "Sudden Accelerations" in Introduction.

Hot Spots and Owner/NHTSA Comments:

1. Fuel: fuel injection system, stalling, hesitation. • "Fuel injection system erratic; engine revs up with no power, stalls and suddenly accelerates." • "Engine made loud screeching noise, vehicle stalled; no restart; replaced fuel pump, electronic throttle parts, thick-film integrated module and processor; continues to stall." • "Defect in fuel injection system; rough idling and stalling after starting." • "Fuel injection system failure; car does not start; replaced throttle position sensor." • "Fuel injector pump replaced twice."

2. Fuel: throttle linkages and control, sudden accelerations. • "Multiple problems with electronic fuel system; car accelerates to 3,000 rpm without warning while driving." • "Driving at 59 mph on highway, brakes applied, car continued to accelerate; pushed in clutch and tachometer revved to 6,000 rpm." • "No control over acceleration; speeds up or slows down, gaining speed until ignition turned off." • "Vehicle suffered sudden acceleration due to linkage failure."

3. Electrical system: ignition: electronic control unit, sudden acceleration, stalling. • "Vehicle suddenly accelerates and stalls; replaced sensor and electronic processor, problem continues." • "Engine control module failed; engine stalled in traffic." • "Reoccurring rapid acceleration incidents; repaired/replaced electronic computer 4 times." • "Electronic control module malfunctioned." • "Computer failed twice while traveling at highway speed."

4. Brakes: hydraulic system, excessive wear, noise, malfunction. • "Front and rear brakes replaced." • "Premature brake wear; repaired/replaced rear brakes and front rotors." • "Popping noise when brakes are applied." • "Brakes malfunctioned and had to be replaced." • "Brakes made loud, screeching, dragging noise when stopping; repairs rendered, problem continues."

5. Power train: transmission: automatic, poor performance, difficulty shifting, slipping. • "While in motion, car slipped out of gear and would not shift into any other gear; rebuilt transmission." • "Vehicle parked in gear, with emergency brake on; rolled backwards down a hill and into private property, still in park." • "Transmission slips on acceleration; will not shift out of 1st gear; also leaks; repaired/replaced transmission, O-ring seal and torque converter seal." • "Transmission leakage, rear drive axle joints; rear axle pinion and right rear differential failure."

6. Fuel: fuel carburetion, stalling, hesitation. • "Intermittent stalling." • "Engine lacks power; hesitates when in operation." • "Car stops like out of gas; defective air intake tube and carburetor." • "Vehicle cut off while at stop light." • "Engine stalls with no warning. Fuel pump replaced, but stalling continues."

MERCURY TOPAZ 1988

Complaint Severity: Typical. **Recall Alert:** See Recall Index. **Buyer's Summary:** The fuel pump has received complaints. Make sure it doesn't make excessive noise and that you are experiencing adequate engine performance. Also, look for leaks. The fuel injection system has been blamed for hesitation and stalling. Be sure the vehicle doesn't die in traffic or at stops. The steering may be stiff or not working correctly. Be sure to test the steering, especially on a cold start. Check the brakes—listen for noise, look for leaks and feel for vibration. They may fail, perform poorly or require frequent mechanical attention. Test the transmission thoroughly.

Hot Spots and Owner/NHTSA Comments:

1. Fuel: fuel pump, premature failure, stalling, vibration. • "Premature failure of fuel pump; national back order on this part." • "Fuel pump in gas tank emits terrible loud humming." • "Stalling problems due to failed fuel pump." • "Replaced the fuel pump inside tank 7 times. Pump was weak and caused vehicle to stall and die out; not getting enough fuel." • "Vibration noise heard with varying degree of loudness due to malfunctioning of fuel pump."

2. Fuel: fuel injection system, stalling, hesitation. • "Vehicle hesitates when accelerating; spits and sputters from stop position; occasional stalling on takeoff; repaired 7 times." • "Engine cuts off when accelerator is pushed, going from stop." • "Fuel injection malfunctions; repaired/replaced injectors, fuel pump and lines, vehicle still has poor mileage." • "Vehicle stalled; vapor lock; repaired/replaced fuel lines, injectors and fuel pump." • "Car stalls out continuously, especially if air conditioner is on."

3. Steering: linkages: tie rod: inner, breaking, premature failure. • "Inner tie rods were loose, which affected steering." • "Inner tie rod ends; joints loosened to point there was considerable play in steering wheel at highway speeds; front-end shimmy occurred." • "Teflon on tie rods; 2 inner and right outer spongy." • "Installed front inner tie rods." • "Right inner tie rod ball joint rusted, causing rod to break and resulting in loss of steering."

4. Power train: transmission: automatic, poor performance, difficulty shifting, slipping. • "While driving in drive gear, automatic transmission jumps into reverse gear; adjusted shift module." • "Transmission mount failed." • "Transmission will not shift smoothly; jerks when accelerating." • "Transmission does not shift smoothly, repaired." • "Transmission leaks; replaced housing."

5. Brakes: hydraulic system, excessive wear, noise. • "Brakes have been replaced 5 times, including rotors twice; also replaced tie rod." • "Problem with brakes squealing; found drum scorched inside and rotor damaged; spring, adjusting nut and other brake items were bouncing around freely." • "Brakes and pads replaced, rivets flattened and rotors replaced at 22,000 miles." • "Rear brakes repaired." • "Brakes wore out."

6. Electrical system: ignition, stalling. • "Engine stalling problem; engine dies out in heavy traffic; no problem restarting; when accelerate or depressed, dies out again." • "Recurring stalling problem since new." • "Vehicle stalls at highway speeds." • "Car stalls while driving and accelerating; difficult to start; diagnosed ignition problem, replaced distributor rotor, cap and spark plugs, problem still exists." • "While driving, vehicle is subject to stalling. Vehicle has been back and forth to dealer since 1991, with stalling resolved temporarily."

MERCURY TOPAZ 1989

Complaint Severity: Negligible. **Buyer's Summary:** Look carefully for any kind of leakage, especially under the car. The fuel pump has received complaints. Make sure it doesn't make excessive noise and that you are experiencing adequate engine performance. Also, look for leaks. The fuel injection system has been blamed for hesitation and stalling. Be sure the vehicle doesn't die in traffic or at stops. Check the brakes—listen for noise, look for leaks and feel for vibration. They may fail, perform poorly or require frequent mechanical attention. Test the transmission thoroughly. Make sure seat belts function correctly and fit comfortably.

Hot Spots and Owner/NHTSA Comments:

1. Fuel: fuel pump, noise, leaks, failure. • "Fuel pump; while driving, car makes a humming noise and cuts off in the middle of traffic." • "Car extremely slow in starting; repaired/replaced fuel pump." • "Fuel pump leakage occurred while fueling tank." • "Fuel pump stopped at 98,600 miles." • "Fuel pump failed."

2. Power train: transmission: automatic, poor performance, difficulty shifting, slipping. • "Transmission slipping." • "Transmission with plastic ball failure." • "Transmission growling noise twice; serviced, problem continues." • "Automatic transmission catches and sometimes hesitates when driving." • "Transmission failure; adjusted throttle control linkage and manual linkage; still not functioning normally."

3. Electrical system: ignition, stalling, hesitation. • "Engine stalls and hesitates when going from stop to go position after releasing brakes and depressing accelerator; no warning." • "Intermittent stalling and/or hesitation." • "Vehicle stalls intermittently loses power in all braking and steering." • "Engine stalls frequently without warning, causes loss of control." • "Engine stalls frequently without warning, causing loss of control."

4. Brakes: hydraulic system, noise, pulling, failure. • "Squeaking brakes because of material used in manufacture." • "Brake system problems; replaced breaks, rotors and calipers." • "Replaced brakes." • "Brakes are very squeaky and noisy." • "Brakes burning and pulling; after few weeks, brakes went out."

5. Fuel: fuel injection system, stalling, hesitation. • "Intermittent stalling." • "Hesitates and/or stalls when turning or accelerating." • "Intermittent stalling; replaced manifold air pressure sensor, processor and fuel pump." • "Engine stalls." • "Engine stalls on acceleration and when coming to a stop."

6. Interior systems: passive restraint: belts, malfunction, failure. • "Passenger passive restraint failed to engage properly." • "Rubber holding passenger seat belt on track torn away." • "Automatic shoulder belt tightened on passenger, causing injury." • "Finger became jammed in motorized shoulder seat belt on passenger's side after vehicle was started." • "Upon collision at approximately 45 mph, automatic restraint shoulder harness failed to hold; driver hit forehead on steering wheel, injuries sustained."

MERCURY TOPAZ 1990

Complaint Severity: Typical. **Recall Alert:** See Recall Index. **Buyer's Summary:** Check the brakes—listen for noise, look for leaks and feel for vibration. They may fail, perform poorly or require frequent mechanical attention. Test the transmission thoroughly. See "Sudden Accelerations" in Introduction.

Hot Spots and Owner/NHTSA Comments:

1. Power train: transmission: automatic, poor performance, difficulty shifting, slipping. • "Premature failure at 217 miles; transmission would not shift out of 1st gear." • "Vehicle would not accelerate beyond 20 mph and engine races; when accelerator released, vehicle would come to a stop." • "Numerous problems with transmission, including no shift; unable to resolve." • "Transmission locks in 1st gear, shifting problems for as long as a mile of driving." • "Transmission locks in 1st gear; in heavy traffic; overhauled."

2. Brakes: hydraulic system, locking up, noise, failure. • "Brakes intermittently lock up or soft; replaced, problem continues." • "Brakes fail upon initial application, don't respond until applied a second time." • "Brake failure caused an accident, impact at 12:00, while driving at 40 mph." • "Brakes squeal; problem seems to disappear when car warms up."

3. Fuel: throttle linkages and control, sudden accelerations. • "Intermittent speed control problems due to stuck throttle." • "From a standing start, vehicle would accelerate to 20 mph, then would not go any faster but engine would race; in 2nd gear it would accelerate to 30 mph." • "When vehicle gets up to 10 mph, gas pedal sticks." • "Sudden acceleration." • "Sudden acceleration, prior to recall, causing accident and injury."

4. Engine: stalling, vibration. • "Engine stalls while vehicle is in motion causing serious traffic problems." • "Ringing sound coming from motor; fuel pump changed, problem continues." • "Excessive engine oil consumption." • "Noise and vibration from engine when stopped in drive."

MERCURY TOPAZ 1991

Complaint Severity: Troublesome. **Buyer's Summary:** The car may have trouble with stalling and hesitation.

Hot Spots and Owner/NHTSA Comments:

1. Electrical system: ignition, stalling, poor performance. • "Intermittent stalling while driving." • "While driving, vehicle stalled several times with no warning." • "Vehicle stalls when coming to a stop or leaving a stop." • "Vehicle will stall without warning, intermittently, while driving." • "While driving at low to highway speeds, engine shuts down and won't restart. Must be towed into dealer."

MERCURY TOPAZ 1992

Complaint Severity: Typical. **Buyer's Summary:** Test the transmission thoroughly.

Hot Spots and Owner/NHTSA Comments:

1. Power train: transmission: automatic, poor performance, difficulty shifting, slipping. • "Automatic transmission; vehicle will not shift out of low gear." • "Automatic transmission defective; a loud noise when making a left or right turn." • "Transmission intermittently sticks in 1st gear." • "Hesitation when shifting transmission into gear. Fourth occurrence." • "Transmission stuck in 1st gear; shifts into neutral intermittently."

2. Engine: pulley: crankshaft, noise, excessive wear. • "Crankshaft moves excessively, making noise." • "Crankshaft pulley is coming loose possibly due to bolt coming off." • "Engine crankshaft pulley replaced 4 times." • "Valve body assembly, crankshaft pulley, damper assembly and belt replaced due to noise." • "Pulley on crankshaft split; dealer replaced for free; split again."

MERCURY TRACER 1988

Complaint Severity: Troublesome. **Recall Alert:** See Recall Index. **Buyer's Summary:** Look carefully for any kind of leakage, especially under the car. Check the brakes—listen for noise, look for leaks and feel for vibration. They may fail, perform poorly or require frequent mechanical attention. Test the transmission thoroughly. See "Sudden Accelerations" in Introduction.

Hot Spots and Owner/NHTSA Comments:

1. Interior systems: active restraints: belt retractors, malfunction, failure. • "Performed 2 years ago. Shoulder belt will no longer adjust or retract." • "Seat belt retractor works sometimes; belt keeps catching." • "Seat belts retract improperly." • "Driver's-side seat belt retractor inertia locking mechanism failed upon impact with guardrail, speed 30 mph, impact 1:00 position; injuries to head and neck." • "Seat belt does not retract properly."

2. Fuel: throttle linkages and control, sudden accelerations. • "When starting engine, moved gear from park to drive; engine started to whine and accelerate, then car bolted forward with foot on brake pedal, smashing into parked car." • "Vehicle suddenly accelerated while easing forward at gas pump; missed hitting person by making sharp turn; resulted in accident." • "Three times have been at complete standstill, put car in reverse to back up, car surged backwards at alarming speed." • "Shifted from park to reverse, car suddenly accelerated, lost control; and hit bus." • "Shifted from reverse to drive and car suddenly raced at high speed; after car stopped, started it in park and it raced again; worked fine on third trial."

3. Interior systems: active seat and shoulder belts and belt anchor, malfunction, failure. • "Driver's- and passenger-side seat belts failed; belts work about 2 times before jamming." • "Recall campaign issued on lap and shoulder seat belt replacement; parts not available at the dealer." • "Front seat belts inoperative; unless pulled out very slowly and evenly, cannot be completely extended." • "Right front seat belt began to lock up when drawn across to fasten; caused by angle at which mounted to body." • "While going down a hill, brakes didn't work and couldn't stop the car; seat belt failed; hit nose against steering wheel, and also badly bruised an arm."

4. Brakes: hydraulic system, failure. • "While driving, suddenly brakes failed; pedal went to floor; almost had a accident." • "While going down a small hill, brakes didn't work; vehicle veered off the main road; went through an open field and hit a parked garden tractor." • "Extended stopping distances due to defective hydraulic braking system." • "Accident resulted from a brake failure."

5. Power train: transmission: automatic, poor performance, difficulty shifting, slipping. • "Problem with transmission shifting very hard and making loud noise while changing gear." • "Gear would not shift into reverse; pushed back into neutral and then driven home." • "Transmission started leaking fluid; repaired/replaced." • "Vehicle shifted into gear, engine speed surged to over 6,000 rpm running into private property."

6. Brakes: hydraulic: master cylinder, leaks, failure. • "Three months after purchase, master cylinder went out, since then, brakes squeaked 3 times and still makes noises, but brakes are not faulty." • "Master cylinder failed; loss of braking." • "Master cylinder leaking fluid through seal, creating a possibility of loss of braking system." • "Near-accident; almost complete brake failure while approaching a light in heavy traffic; brake pedal hit floor; master cylinder failure." • "Brake master cylinder failed."

MERCURY TRACER 1989

Complaint Severity: Typical. **Recall Alert:** See Recall Index. **Buyer's Summary:** Look carefully for any kind of leakage, especially under the car. Check the brakes—listen for noise, look for leaks and feel for vibration. They may fail, perform poorly or require frequent mechanical attention. Test the transmission thoroughly.

Hot Spots and Owner/NHTSA Comments:

1. Brakes: hydraulic: master cylinder, leaks, failure. • "Brake master cylinder leaks." • "Master cylinder leaking." • "Brake failure; failure of master cylinder; surges while driving, pedal faded." • "Master cylinder leaks; rear brakes were never connected, which caused leaking problem."

2. Interior systems: active restraints: belt retractors, malfunction, failure. • "Upon pulling repaired/replaced seat belt out all way while cleaning car, would not retract back again." • "Driver's-side seat belt stuck inside wall of car." • "Seat belt retractors failed." • "Driver's seat belt stuck in retractor twice."

3. Power train: transmission: automatic, poor performance, difficulty shifting, slipping. • "While shifting gears, vehicle took off in reverse and went forward; lost control and caused accident." • "Transmissions shifts hard; gears grind." • "Vehicle failed to move while engine running; brakes off and in drive position when stepped on gas." • "Problem with transmission shifting hard and gears grinding; vibrating violently."

MERCURY TRACER 1991

Complaint Severity: Best 3% in Guide. **Recall Alert:** See Recall Index. **Buyer's Summary:** Check the brakes—listen for noise, look for leaks and feel for vibration. They may fail, perform poorly or require frequent mechanical attention.

Hot Spots and Owner/NHTSA Comments:

1. Brakes: hydraulic system, noise, excessive wear. • "Noisy brakes." • "Pads replaced twice in 10,000 miles." • "Brakes grind and squeak; very difficult to stop car at times; and reverse on several occasions." • "Noisy brakes—waiting on replacement parts." • "Brake and accelerator too close together."

2. Electrical system: wiring, malfunction, fire. • "Electrical system caught on fire near the gas tank." • "Wiring harness caught on fire and fuse did not protect the harness, this occurred while driving." • "Faulty wiring caused brake light to fail." • "Wiring harness under dash started to melt and black smoke came up from underneath. There are wire burns in the rear passenger seat." • "Smell of smoke prompted driver to pull to the side; smoke escaping from under dash and back seat; wires melted; foam under seat caught fire."

MERCURY TRACER 1993

Complaint Severity: Serious. **Recall Alert:** See Recall Index. **Buyer's Summary:** See "Sudden Accelerations" in Introduction.

Hot Spots and Owner/NHTSA Comments:

1. Fuel: throttle linkages and control, sudden accelerations. • "On 2 occasions, vehicle accelerated after reaching 35 mph. Emergency brakes had to be applied for extra brake effectiveness." • "Vehicle continues to idle when gas pedal is disengaged; no acceleration experienced." • "Shifted into reverse, vehicle surged and shifted into drive, vehicle surged forward into brick wall." • "While driving in low speed, vehicle will go into open-throttle position; to unstick the throttle, put gear into neutral."

MERCURY TRUCK VILLAGER 1993

Complaint Severity: Harmless. **Recall Alert:** See Recall Index. **Buyer's Summary:** Make sure air conditioner works properly.

Hot Spots and Owner/NHTSA Comments:

1. Air conditioner: hose: duct: air, malfunction. • "Smoke has entered the vehicle through the vents due to leaves and debris getting into the front blower assembly." • "Went back to start car after it cut off and smoke came out of the air conditioner vent." • "Had to replace blower because it had leaves in it and had a burning smell." • "Vehicle smokes due to debris in blower; area dealer is trying to charge to clear the area." • "Owner has on several occasions experienced the smell in the vehicle; the problem has been pinpointed to the vent system as the source of the smell."

2. Exhaust system: malfunction. • "Auto smells like something is burning." • "Burning smell inside vehicle; opened hood, saw no smoke or fire; started vehicle, drove away; smell went away." • "Smells like burning grass while driving down road; sort of scary; smell so heavy, have to keep windows rolled down." • "Vehicle was in for repair; burning smell in vehicle." • "Consumer leased car; there is an eggy smell and burns your eyes; have to drive with window down—if driving long distance, you will get a headache."

3. Heater: defroster: defogger and ventilation, malfunction. • "Consumer was driving when vehicle filled up with smoke; leaves got in the duct system and caused a fire." • "Owner detects burning smell coming from ventilation system." • "Smell of burning whenever air conditioner or heater is on; odor goes away after turning off heater/air conditioner." • "Intermittently owner notices burning smell when either air conditioner or heater used." • "Smelled odor coming from vents; possibly leaves trapped in vent system; dealer said resister array burnt out; blower motor only runs on high speed."

4. Air conditioner: motor: fan, malfunction, fire. • "When air conditioner is on, smell of burning out of the fan blower." • "Strong burning smell when blower is on." • "Experienced smoke from the blower motor." • "Have experienced smoke from the blower motor." • "Leaves collecting inside air conditioner blower motor, resulting in vehicle fire."

5. Air conditioner, malfunction, poor performance. • "Smells like rubber burning in the passenger compartment." • "On 3 occasions, owner has noticed burning smell when using air conditioner." • "Gas fumes coming out of the air conditioner when in operation." • "Air conditioner system emits burning odor." • "Gas smell inside of vehicle, especially using air conditioning and when restarting the engine."

6. Heater: water: defroster: defogger, malfunction. • "Any use of heater or defroster will fill the compartment with overheating electrical wire smoke." • "Window defroster does not properly defrost for visibility when driving in cold weather." • "Owner noticed rattling/burning smell occasionally." • "Auto smells like a brushfire when heat is turned on."

Mitsubishi

MITSUBISHI DIAMANTE 1992

Complaint Severity: Typical. **Buyer's Summary:** The airbags in this vehicle have experienced failures and malfunctions: You may need a professional evaluation on the condition of the airbags. Test the transmission thoroughly.

Hot Spots and Owner/NHTSA Comments:

1. Power train: transmission: automatic, poor performance, difficulty shifting, slipping. • "Automatic transmission jumped from park to drive, resulting in a head-on rollaway." • "Cold weather makes engaging into park impossible; it also makes it impossible to remove keys." • "While driving, passing at approximately 65 mph, slipped out of gear into neutral. Dealer can't reproduce." • "Transmission jolts in low gear; jumps when downshifting; hesitates upon acceleration."

2. Interior systems: passive restraint: airbag: driver, malfunction, failure. • "Vehicle was involved in an accident; the airbag did not deploy." • "Vehicle was at a complete stop when it was pushed into vehicle in front, impact 6:00 position, airbag did not deploy." • "Car crashed into a stopped vehicle, airbag did not deploy; driver and passenger injured." • "Airbag did not deploy." • "At approximately 25-30 mph, vehicle hit a dip in the road; the airbag deployed; caused bloody nose and broke eyeglasses."

3. Engine: noise, fire. • "Engine noise." • "Engine caught fire." • "Purchased car used; there is a noise in the car; took car to the dealer 7 times, can't find the problem."

MITSUBISHI ECLIPSE 1990

Complaint Severity: Typical. **Recall Alert:** See Recall Index. **Buyer's Summary:** Problems with the timing gear and chain can cause serious problems. Have the engine checked by a professional. Check the brakes—listen for noise, look for leaks and feel for vibration. They may fail, perform poorly or require frequent mechanical attention. Test the clutch.

Hot Spots and Owner/NHTSA Comments:

1. Brakes: hydraulic: disc: rotor: disc hub, vibration, excessive wear. • "Recurring problem with front-end wobble and steering wheel vibration; resurfaced front rotors several times." • "Brake rotor will warp between 6,000 and 10,000 miles; when brakes are applied they pulsate." • "Vibration in brake pedal and steering wheel when brakes applied at speeds greater than 35 mph; both front rotors replaced, problem reoccurred." • "Five incidents of front brake rotor failure, causing extreme vibration; loss of control upon braking makes car hazardous when brakes applied." • "Vehicle experiencing brake rotor warpage at 18,000 miles."

2. Brakes: hydraulic system, vibration, excessive wear. • "Upon approaching red light, no braking response; brakes failed, ran light; brakes returned after running light." • "Brakes malfunctioning; resulted in forward fast skid and an accident." • "Rotors

warp every few thousand miles." • "Brakes warped, causing pulsation and steering shimmy."
3. Electrical system: wiring, malfunction. • "Wires and plugs replaced." • "Electrical problems; headlights not working right, dome light doesn't come on when door is opened." • "Headlights and bright lights do not work. Received recall notice regarding failure of lights due to faulty wiring." • "Wiring of stereo speakers defective."
4. Engine: timing gear and chain, breaking, failure. • "Timing chain on engine broke and vehicle died on the highway." • "Plastic timing belt failed and destroyed engine." • "Timing belt failed." • "Timing belt broke twice."
5. Power train: clutch assembly, excessive wear, difficulty shifting. • "Clutch slips." • "Clutch requires excessive effort." • "Noisy clutch." • "Two clutch assemblies failed under normal driving conditions due to excessive wear."

MITSUBISHI ECLIPSE 1991

Complaint Severity: Typical. **Recall Alert:** See Recall Index. **Buyer's Summary:** Test the suspension by feeling for vibration or pulling while driving.

Hot Spots and Owner/NHTSA Comments:
1. Interior systems: active restraints: belt buckles, malfunction, failure. • "Front passenger seat belt sticks and will not unlatch." • "Driver's-side seat belt buckle is inoperative." • "Seat belt failure; Takata belt buckle failure." • "The driver lap belt is very hard to latch."
2. Suspension: independent front, pulling, failure. • "Vehicle pulls to right." • "Driving at approximately 28-30 mph, front left axle broke; resulted in an accident." • "While driving between 28-30 mph, front wheel and axle broke; vehicle went out of control over middle meridian and landed on opposite side of street." • "Steering wobble at 55 mph."

MITSUBISHI ECLIPSE 1992

Complaint Severity: Typical. **Buyer's Summary:** Problems with the timing gear and chain can cause serious problems. Have the engine checked by a professional. Make sure the shoulder belts don't cut across your neck and are well anchored.

Hot Spots and Owner/NHTSA Comments:
1. Engine: timing gear and chain, stalling, premature failure. • "Timing belt stripped, causing engine to stall." • "Timing belt broke, causing valves to bend." • "Timing belt broke while idling." • "Timing belt broke; also, lifters replaced due to tapping noise."
2. Interior systems: shoulder belts, malfunction, failure. • "Passenger-side seat belt retractor does not restrain." • "Driver's automatic shoulder belt failed/did not tighten up upon frontal collision; hit right front of stopped vehicle." • "Automatic shoulder belt locked up on passenger side."

MITSUBISHI GALANT 1994

Complaint Severity: Very Serious. **Buyer's Summary:** The airbags in this vehicle have experienced failures and malfunctions: You may need a professional evaluation on the condition of the airbags.

Hot Spots and Owner/NHTSA Comments:
1. Interior systems: passive restraint: airbag: driver, malfunction, failure. • "At 12:00 position at 30-35 mph, both driver's airbags did not deploy." • "While going forward out of the driveway, driver's airbag prematurely deployed; resulted in accident after airbags deployed." • "Right front control arm broke while driving; lost control, hitting curb, impact 10:00 position; airbag did not deploy." • "Dual airbags failed to deploy when striking another vehicle on side."
2. Interior systems: passive restraint: airbag: passenger, malfunction, failure. • "Dual airbags failed to deploy when striking another vehicle on side." • "Passenger's airbag deployment was violent upon impact, causing right eye injury." • "Car was in a head-on collision with a tree and the passenger's airbag did not deploy." • "While going forward out of the driveway, passenger's airbag prematurely deployed; resulted in accident after airbags deployed." • "Had an accident and the passenger's airbag did not deploy, causing injury."
3. Equipment: electric power accessories: windows, failure. • "Right front power window failed." • "Power window regulator fails when moisture is present on windows." • "Right front and left rear power windows failed." • "Experiencing electrical problem with all 4 windows."

MITSUBISHI PRECIS 1988

Complaint Severity: Troublesome. **Recall Alert:** See Recall Index. **Buyer's Summary:** Test transmission for slipping, locking up and performance.

Hot Spots and Owner/NHTSA Comments:
1. Power train: transmission: 5-speed and up, difficulty shifting, noise. • "Transmission not shifting into 5th gear." • "While driving in 2nd gear, transmission seized up, causing front wheels to lock up. Dealer says 4th gear was jammed." • "Vehicle's manual transmission while shift gear locked and loud noise was heard; transmission became inoperative." • "Transmission failure caused car to stop; skidded; speed 5 mph; while driving in 1st gear, heard loud noise, vehicle slowed down; loss of power." • "Transmission locked up in 2nd gear."
2. Exhaust/crankcase emission control devices: cracking, stalling. • "Catalytic converter and air tubes replaced twice." • "Reed valve subassembly failed prior to recall." • "Exhaust/crankcase emission cracked." • "Reed valve for emission control system failed, causing vehicle to stall; prior to recall; recall repairs refused due to vehicle identification number."

Nissan—Cars and Trucks

NISSAN 240SX 1989

Complaint Severity: Typical. **Recall Alert:** See Recall Index. **Buyer's Summary:** Problems with the timing gear and chain can cause serious problems. Have the engine checked by a professional. Test the transmission thoroughly.

Hot Spots and Owner/NHTSA Comments:
1. Engine: timing gear and chain, breaking, failure. • "Owner received letter from Nissan to bring vehicle in for timing chain guide. Vehicle has not run properly since work was done." • "Timing chain broke, causing problems." • "Timing chain broke; dealer claims parts were replaced under recall; driver never received any notice prior to this." • "There was a recall in 1989 for a timing chain guide; later, after the recall was done, the timing chain broke, causing the vehicle to lose power at highway speeds." • "The timing chain was replaced by the dealer, consumer says received a recall, couldn't find it, now is having a problem."
2. Power train: transmission: automatic, poor performance, difficulty shifting, slipping. • "Automatic transmission would slip into neutral after whining sound; caused by defect in transmis-

sion; replaced." • "Transmission failed." • "While driving, the transmission blew up." • "Transmission broke; premature failure."

NISSAN 300ZX 1987

Complaint Severity: Dangerous (Worst 3% in Guide). **Recall Alert:** See Recall Index. **Buyer's Summary:** See "Sudden Accelerations" in Introduction.

Hot Spots and Owner/NHTSA Comments:

1. Fuel: throttle linkages and control, sudden accelerations. • "Started car, put into reverse, started flying backwards, foot not on gas pedal, car ran into storage house, then put into drive, start flying forward." • "When shifted into reverse, vehicle accelerated backwards; brakes did not stop car; vehicle struck brick wall." • "Sudden violent acceleration, reached 100 mph; excessive braking to slow car down; replaced throttle cable." • "Shifted from park to reverse, car suddenly accelerated and hit neighbor's house; brakes ineffective." • "Shifted into reverse with foot on brake, engine opened up full throttle and suddenly accelerated backwards; brakes ineffective."

NISSAN 300ZX 1990

Complaint Severity: Troublesome. **Buyer's Summary:** Check the brakes—listen for noise, look for leaks and feel for vibration. They may fail, perform poorly or require frequent mechanical attention.

Hot Spots and Owner/NHTSA Comments:

1. Brakes: hydraulic: disc: rotor: disc hub, vibration, excessive wear. • "Pulsation upon braking; rotors warped; repeated problem." • "Front brake rotors go out of round, causing the steering wheel to vibrate." • "When brakes are applied on smooth road between 35-85 mph, the steering wheel and chassis vibrate due to rotors warping." • "Because of new materials put into the rotors there is no ventilation for the heat to escape; causes rotors to warp." • "Front brake disc hub and rotors were worn out; vehicle vibrated."

2. Brakes: hydraulic system, pulling, failure. • "When brakes applied on irregular road surface, steering wheel pulls to left or right; occasionally pulled violently enough to alter direction of wheel." • "Brakes, including rotors, worn enough to be replaced at 15,000 miles." • "Vehicle would not stop when brakes were applied; problem has been repaired 6-10 times." • "There was a brake recall, machines were not available to do work, had an accident in the meantime."

3. Brakes: hydraulic: shoe: disc brake system, vibration, pulling, excessive wear. • "Malfunctioning brakes; repaired/replaced front rotors, pads, front hubs and front antilock brake system sensor." • "Vehicle in shop for repairs of brake system 10 times and 44 days within 26,300 miles." • "Repaired/replaced brakes 6 times." • "When braking, severe vibration occurs in steering wheel, and car pulls to the left."

NISSAN 300ZX 1991

Complaint Severity: Typical. **Buyer's Summary:** Check the brakes—listen for noise, look for leaks and feel for vibration. They may fail, perform poorly or require frequent mechanical attention. Test the clutch.

Hot Spots and Owner/NHTSA Comments:

1. Brakes: hydraulic: disc: rotor: disc hub, vibration, excessive wear. • "Rotors replaced due to warpage; problem continues." • "Front brake rotors are constantly warping, causing extended stopping or no braking power when brakes are applied; repaired 4 times." • "Front brake rotors warped at 4,000 miles; braking performance decreased; resulted in an accident." • "Front brake rotors are warping upon braking at high speeds; brakes exhibit poor control."

2. Brakes: hydraulic: shoe: disc brake system, vibration, malfunction. • "Front brakes spin when applied; serviced 5 times, problem continues." • "Front brake failure." • "Brake pads and rotors failed." • "Brakes malfunctioned 4 times; repaired/replaced front pads and rotors." • "Disc brakes vibrate when braking from high speeds, causing steering wheel to vibrate."

3. Power train: clutch assembly, excessive wear. • "Loss of power to wheels due to clutch slippage or its inability to access gears; clutch system replaced." • "Clutch failed." • "Clutch master cylinder failed twice; emitting burning odor." • "Clutch failed 4 times."

NISSAN ALTIMA 1993

Complaint Severity: Serious. **Recall Alert:** See Recall Index. **Buyer's Summary:** Make sure the shoulder belts don't cut across your neck and are well anchored. The airbags in this vehicle have experienced failures and malfunctions: You may need a professional evaluation on the condition of the airbags. Check the brakes—listen for noise, look for leaks and feel for vibration. They may fail, perform poorly or require frequent mechanical attention. Make sure seat belts function correctly and fit comfortably. See "Sudden Accelerations" in Introduction.

Hot Spots and Owner/NHTSA Comments:

1. Interior systems: passive restraint: belts, locking up, malfunction. • "Front automatic shoulder harness prematurely locks up during normal driving without being activated." • "Automatic shoulder belts lock up, pinning occupants in seats; very frightening; excessive effort to release buckle." • "Driver's and passenger's automatic seat belt mechanisms are not properly releasing occupants; instead, seat belt is tightening, locking occupants in." • "While driving, turning or mostly applying brake, automatic seat belt retractor tightens, then locks up; won't release until ignition turned off." • "Motorized seat belts tighten; fail to release when attempting to exit vehicle."

2. Interior systems: passive restraint: airbag: driver, malfunction, failure. • "Passive restraint shoulder belt didn't restrain driver from making contact; no airbag deployment." • "During front-end collision at 25 mph, airbag did not deploy." • "Vehicle was at complete stop, hit from 6:00 position, impacted another vehicle at 12:00 position; airbag did not deploy." • "Airbag deployed; caused first and second degree burns on both hands; speed 15 mph; impact 12:00 position." • "Airbag did not inflate upon front-end collision."

3. Fuel: throttle linkages and control, sudden accelerations. • "Gasoline odor inside cab of vehicle, prior to recall, causing headaches; repairs refused due to being previously repaired." • "Engine movement caused throttle cable to pull out of wall, prior to recall, causing sudden acceleration, loss of control and an accident." • "Upon hitting the brakes, vehicle surged forward, causing me to total vehicle." • "Vehicle went open-throttle position, impact 12:00 position; vehicle was in drive, slowing down, when vehicle jerked forward from idle."

4. Visual systems: glass: windshield, cracking, poor performance. • "Crack in windshield on passenger's side; did not come from contact." • "Front windshield hit by a small pebble, causing the windshield to crack." • "Dashboard glare is so great that view through windshield is obstructed. Dash is tan with crackle finish." • "Dashboard reflects on windshield." • "Purchased car used; it was parked and the front windshield was cracked; dealer doesn't want to check it—not under warranty."

5. Brakes: hydraulic system, noise, failure. • "Noisy brakes." • "Brakes cannot hold car back." • "Brake failure." • "Upon hitting the brakes, vehicle surged forward, resulting in vehicle being totaled; airbag deployed."
6. Interior systems: shoulder belts, malfunction, failure. • "Driver's shoulder belt did not lock upon impact; driver lurched, hitting steering; airbag deployed; caused first- and second-degree burns on both hands; speed 15 mph; impact 12:00 position. Shoulder belt failed in accident." • "Driver's-side shoulder harness and lap belt locked up while trying to exit vehicle." • "Passive restraint shoulder belt didn't restrain driver from making contact; no airbag deployment."

NISSAN MAXIMA 1987

Complaint Severity: Troublesome. **Theft Alert:** 21. **Buyer's Summary:** Look carefully for any kind of leakage, especially under the car. The steering may be stiff or not working correctly. Be sure to test the steering, especially on a cold start. Test the transmission thoroughly. See "Sudden Accelerations" in Introduction.

Hot Spots and Owner/NHTSA Comments:
1. Fuel: throttle linkages and control, sudden accelerations. • "Car totally went out of control; accelerator stuck as if pushed to floor; crashed into house." • "Shifted gear into reverse with foot on brake, car instantly accelerated at high speed; resulted in accident." • "Problem of sudden uncontrollable acceleration; car shot forward at very high, uncontrollable speed; brakes did not stop car." • "Upon backing out of driveway, car totally went out of control; accelerator stuck as if pushed to floor; impact of crash stopped engine." • "Auto idling, engaged reverse and released brakes; vehicle jumped backwards at very high rate speed, hitting 2 parked cars."
2. Fuel: fuel injection: unknown type: injector, leaks, fire. • "Fuel injectors leaking; caused a fire; sparks from sparkplug caused fire." • "While driving, noticed smoke coming from hood, pulled to side, passerby extinguished fire in engine compartment; dealer says fuel injectors were the cause." • "Vehicle fuel injector caught on fire; engine burned." • "Fuel injectors are too close to spark plugs; injectors leaked on spark plugs, causing fire." • "Upon parking, smelled fuel, then found fuel leaking; had towed to dealer; after taking off, wrecker vehicle caught fire; #3 fuel injector was leaking."
3. Fuel: fuel systems, leaks, fire. • "Driver smelled gas fumes, followed by engine compartment fire." • "Turned on air conditioner; driving along and started to smell gas; vehicle burst into flames." • "Vehicle was parked hot; fire erupted from a suspected fuel leak." • "Engine fire occurred after a 90-minute drive on a 50-degree day." • "After parking, noticed white and gray smoke coming from engine compartment; engine on fire; vehicle totaled."
4. Power train: transmission: automatic, poor performance, difficulty shifting, slipping. • "Transmission; governor became jammed in casing, causing severe damage." • "Transmission malfunction; downshifts; also problems with passing gear." • "Automatic transmission slips badly, causing tremendous vibration; bangs when shifting gears." • "Transmission slipping; at speeds between 40-50 mph, experience sudden vibration in engine, car loses power; condition lasts 2 to 5 seconds." • "Automatic transmission hard to shift; replaced; governor shaft snapped."
5. Steering: gear: rack-and-pinion, stiffness, poor performance. • "Problem with power steering rack; difficult to steer, replaced rack." • "Premature failure of rack-and-pinion steering system." • "Defective rack-and-pinion steering gear, which resulted in loss of power steering; loss of vehicle control at any speed." • "Power steering fluid leaks; dirt scored seal, requiring replacement of rack-and-pinion steering assembly; loss of steering ability while vehicle in operation." • "Problem with power steering; upon first starting difficult to steer; sticks and/or grabs."
6. Engine: malfunction, fire. • "Owner says the vehicle was taken to school by daughter; vehicle was sitting when it caught fire; the entire engine burned up." • "Engine made loud popping noise, then caught on fire." • "Bolt inside engine fell off, cracking the camshaft and distorting rods; caused immediate stalling." • "Engine fire."

NISSAN MAXIMA 1988

Complaint Severity: Very Serious. **Buyer's Summary:** Look carefully for any kind of leakage, especially under the car. See "Sudden Accelerations" in Introduction.

Hot Spots and Owner/NHTSA Comments:
1. Fuel: throttle linkages and control, sudden accelerations. • "When ignition was turned on and gear thrown into reverse, vehicle suddenly and uncontrollably shot back at high speed." • "In reverse with foot on brake, vehicle suddenly shot backwards at a high rate of speed, hitting another vehicle." • "After starting vehicle, paused for 3 to 5 minutes, then placed into reverse; vehicle surged out of control; resulted in an accident." • "Upon turning on ignition, put gears in reverse and car suddenly bolted back uncontrollably; resulted in accident." • "Vehicle suddenly accelerated, lunged forward; pressed brake with no response; accident occurred."
2. Fuel: fuel systems, leaks, fire. • "Smell of gasoline coming from the air conditioner and heater when on." • "Consumer was driving and car caught on fire." • "Fire started either from fault in fuel injection system or electrical malfunction; engine compartment caught fire, destroying vehicle." • "Vehicle developed a fuel leak, which had to be repaired."
3. Electrical system: wiring: harness: front: underhood, fire. • "Vehicle fire, originating under hood." • "Vehicle caught fire in the engine compartment." • "Engine compartment fire under the hood while car was parked." • "Driver detected smoke; drove into service station; engine engulfed with smoke; all cables burned."

NISSAN MAXIMA 1989

Complaint Severity: Typical. **Buyer's Summary:** The fuel injection system has been blamed for hesitation and stalling. Be sure the vehicle doesn't die in traffic or at stops. Check the brakes—listen for noise, look for leaks and feel for vibration. They may fail, perform poorly or require frequent mechanical attention. Test the transmission thoroughly.

Hot Spots and Owner/NHTSA Comments:
1. Electrical system: battery, failure. • "Battery failed." • "Repeated battery failure; digital light for heating system started to flash and went out, car shut off and could not start; repaired/replaced battery, alternator, etc." • "Battery failed to produce power to start engine; replaced."
2. Power train: transmission: automatic, poor performance, difficulty shifting, slipping. • "Problem with transmission slipping; repaired." • "Transmission seal failure; replaced." • "With ignition switch locked, gearshift can be shifted and vehicle will roll." • "Transmission locked out of gear." • "Transmission reverse gear failed."
3. Brakes: hydraulic system, noise, failure. • "Two-month-old brakes began making loud noises and were hard to stop." • "Brake failure at 30,000 and 60,000 miles." • "Brake problem." • "While driving at 40 mph, brakes did not react when stopping; lost control, causing an accident; faulty brakes."

4. Equipment: electric power accessories: windows, malfunction, failure. • "Power windows don't work when vehicle is cold." • "Right power window jammed; replaced." • "Driver's-side window problem." • "Power window motor failed." • "Window track regulators, driver's front and rear and passenger front, malfunction; go down into door and will not roll up again; power windows."

5. Engine: noise, fire. • "Engine fire." • "Engine failed." • "Noisy engine." • "Oil pump housing defective." • "Engine defect; problem unspecified."

6. Fuel: fuel injection system, stalling, hesitation. • "Vehicle stalls from 500 to 2,000 rpm; several repairs made trying to find problem." • "Cold start hard starting; when started, stalls, idles." • "On first start of day, engine stutters, and as soon as transmission shifted into reverse, engine cuts off; repaired/replaced coolant temperature sensor and electronic control unit to no avail." • "Six repairs for hesitation, missing, rough idle; finally replaced all injectors, problems remain." • "Fuel injectors got blocked; repaired/replaced."

NISSAN MAXIMA 1990

Complaint Severity: Typical. **Buyer's Summary:** Check the brakes—listen for noise, look for leaks and feel for vibration. They may fail, perform poorly or require frequent mechanical attention. Test the transmission thoroughly.

Hot Spots and Owner/NHTSA Comments:

1. Power train: transmission: automatic, poor performance, difficulty shifting, slipping. • "Automatic transmission fluid leaking." • "Transmission shuddered and chattered when attempting to shift into overdrive." • "Transmission seal broke." • "Transmission has annoying whine at 40 mph." • "Rough shifting of transmission."

2. Brakes: hydraulic: shoe: disc brake system, malfunction, failure. • "Repaired/replaced brake system 5 times." • "Brake pads and rotors failed; replaced." • "Brake rotors machined smooth, replaced brake pads." • "While driving at 65 mph during a heavy rain, brakes malfunctioned and pedal went to the floor." • "Vehicle in shop for repairs of brake system 5 times and 25 days in first 23,000 miles."

3. Brakes: hydraulic system, noise, failure. • "Brakes fade." • "Noisy brakes. Serviced brakes; replaced pads and resurfaced rotors and drums." • "Brake failure. When slowing vehicle down at stop sign, experienced pedal fading; impact 12:00 position, speed 25 mph." • "Brakes failed." • "Noisy brakes."

4. Equipment: electric power accessories: windows, malfunction, failure. • "Power window on driver's side fails to go up." • "Front passenger-side power door window has failed; window will not open or close." • "Power windows on both front doors began closing very slowly when weather was cold." • "Front passenger-side power door window has failed; window will not open or close." • "Front driver's-side and left rear power window regulators failed, causing windows to slip."

NISSAN MAXIMA 1991

Complaint Severity: Typical. **Buyer's Summary:** Check the brakes—listen for noise, look for leaks and feel for vibration. They may fail, perform poorly or require frequent mechanical attention.

Hot Spots and Owner/NHTSA Comments:

1. Brakes: hydraulic system, noise. • "When driving at a low speed and going to stop, there's a grinding noise; checked out by dealer, who found nothing wrong with car." • "Noisy brakes; serviced 3 times, problem continues." • "Brakes feel soft and make grinding and/or squeaking noises." • "Brakes make a loud grinding noise when applied, resulting in extended stopping."

2. Brakes: hydraulic: shoe: disc brake system, noise, vibration, poor performance. • "Rear disc brakes shudder at low speed." • "First 3,000 miles, the car stopped acceptably. Front brakes wore away and were replaced several times; car will not stop without danger of frontal collision." • "Brakes grind, vibrate, squeal and fail to stop vehicle accurately." • "Noisy front brakes; pads replaced, problem continues." • "Noisy right front brakes; pads replaced and rotors resurfaced."

3. Brakes: hydraulic: power assist: vacuum system, noise. • "Brakes make grinding noise." • "Noisy brakes." • "Brakes make terrible sound when applied." • "Right front brake is noisy."

4. Interior systems: seat belts: lap: front, poor design. • "Front passenger seat belts do not fit properly because of their length." • "Front seat belts catch in recess; too deep on passenger and driver's sides, and it is difficult to get out of or loosen them." • "Driver's lap seat belt receptor is located in a cul-de-sac between the driver's and passenger's seat; this makes it very difficult to engage." • "Seat belt holders are deep in between seats and are hard to release."

NISSAN MAXIMA 1992

Complaint Severity: Troublesome. **Recall Alert:** See Recall Index. **Buyer's Summary:** The airbags in this vehicle have experienced failures and malfunctions: You may need a professional evaluation on the condition of the airbags. Check the brakes—listen for noise, look for leaks and feel for vibration. They may fail, perform poorly or require frequent mechanical attention.

Hot Spots and Owner/NHTSA Comments:

1. Interior systems: passive restraint: airbag: driver, malfunction, failure. • "Airbag deployed after hitting small hole in road; impact 11:00 position; speed 15 mph; driver received facial burns." • "Upon impact during frontal crash, 30-40 mph at 12:00 position on bumper, airbag failed to deploy (plowed into parked vehicle while being stolen)." • "Airbag deployed/exploded while driving; no accident or sudden impact; speed 20 mph; no apparent reason; no prior warning; first degree burns." • "Premature and improper deployment of airbag. Vehicle went partially off the road onto uneven shoulder, scraping bottom of vehicle. Driver was injured." • "Consumer received a recall on the airbag; had it fixed; and had an accident and head-on crash and the airbag didn't deploy."

2. Brakes: hydraulic system, noise, excessive wear. • "There is a knocking sound present when brakes are applied." • "Brakes are making a very loud noise. Had them fixed twice; still making noise." • "Vehicle experienced 8 brake failures; each time dealer fixed it, but problem has persisted." • "Turned into parking space in shopping area at less than 5 mph, brakes failed to stop vehicle; it accelerated into a furniture store." • "Front and rear brakes wear, causing squeaking noise, especially in wet weather."

NISSAN SENTRA 1987

Complaint Severity: Serious. **Recall Alert:** See Recall Index. **Buyer's Summary:** The carburetion system could contribute to stalling and hesitation. The fuel injection system has been blamed for hesitation and stalling. Be sure the vehicle doesn't die in traffic or at stops. Test the transmission thoroughly for slipping, locking up and performance. See "Sudden Accelerations" in Introduction.

Hot Spots and Owner/NHTSA Comments:

1. Fuel: throttle linkages and control, sudden accelerations. • "Vehicle suffers sudden acceleration due to malfunction of fuel linkage assembly." • "Car suddenly accelerates from cruising speed to 55 mph; brakes applied but failed; turned off ignition and used emergency brake to stop." • "Shifted from park to drive; vehicle suddenly accelerated, resulting in accident with injury." • "Engine surges up and down in speed frequently; sometimes takes off on its own without application to accelerator." • "On 2 occasions vehicle accelerated when shifted into reverse; lost control, resulting in an accident." • "Throttle stuck in open position, which resulted in an accident."

2. Interior systems: active restraints: belt buckles, breaking, malfunction. • "Driver's seat belt will not latch." • "Vehicle's driver's-side seat belt buckle broke and is inoperative." • "Right front shoulder and lap seat belt buckle failed while in use; restraint system is inoperative." • "Front passenger's seat belt buckle; plastic inside breaks and belt becomes inoperative." • "Passenger-side front seat belt buckle fails to latch properly."

3. Fuel: fuel injection system, stalling, hesitation. • "Engine stalls and hesitates, especially when air conditioner is on." • "Vehicle experiencing power surges; at high speeds car loses power when passing." • "Vehicle stalled constantly; replaced gas tank, fuel pump and fuel filter." • "Stalling and hesitation at stop signs, lights, yields and U-turns when accelerating." • "While driving downhill, car stalled; wheel locked at same time, causing accident; 5 tune-ups; fire in carburetor; carburetor overhauled, new fuel pump, car still stalling."

4. Power train: transmission: automatic, poor performance, difficulty shifting, slipping. • "Automatic transmission in reverse to back out of driveway, heard unusual noise, no noise in forward gear; something came loose and/or broke in transmission." • "Transmission slow to shift in cold weather." • "While driving at approximately 55 mph, the vehicle performed erratically and then the automatic transmission fell out from underneath." • "In park position, child was able to take vehicle out of park and place into gear without key in vehicle; rolled downhill, hitting a house."

5. Fuel: fuel carburetion, stalling, hesitation. • "Carburetor failed." • "Vehicle suffers stalling problems." • "Loss of power while accelerator is gently pressed in drive or neutral." • "Vehicle dies while driving, hesitates on acceleration." • "Engine stalls when coming to a stop."

6. Power train: transmission: 5-speed and up, poor performance, malfunction. • "Transmission will not stay in 5th gear." • "Five-speed manual transmission defective; pops out of 5th gear on freeway." • "Five-speed transmission failure; found case in transmission was torn due to metal fatigue in rack-and-pinion gears; substandard part used by manufacturer." • "Syncromesh faulty, 5-speed transmission; without warning, dropped out of 5th gear, stayed on for half an hour and dropped out again." • "Vehicle jumps out of 5th gear."

NISSAN SENTRA 1988

Complaint Severity: Troublesome. **Recall Alert:** See Recall Index. **Buyer's Summary:** Test the seat belt buckles carefully.

Hot Spots and Owner/NHTSA Comments:

1. Interior systems: active restraints: belt buckles, breaking, malfunction. • "Part in buckle cracked; mechanism would not release, causing front seat occupant to climb out of belt." • "A portion of the driver's seat belt release button broke off and fell into mechanism, jamming it up so it would not release." • "Passenger-side seat buckle will not latch for proper restraint." • "The passenger-side seat belt buckle is broken." • "The middle rear seat belt and the one behind the driver's seat do not latch at all."

NISSAN SENTRA 1989

Complaint Severity: Typical. **Recall Alert:** See Recall Index. **Buyer's Summary:** Check the brakes—listen for noise, look for leaks and feel for vibration. They may fail, perform poorly or require frequent mechanical attention. Test the transmission thoroughly. See "Sudden Accelerations" in Introduction.

Hot Spots and Owner/NHTSA Comments:

1. Brakes: hydraulic system, excessive wear, noise. • "Brakes replaced 4 times." • "Defective rear and front brakes, making grinding noise when brakes applied after approximately 15 to 20 minutes of driving." • "Hydraulic brake system faulty." • "While shifting car into reverse and applying the brakes to back out of gas station, brakes failed; vehicle went out of control; resulted in accident." • "If a quick stop required, brakes do not stop car as quickly as they should; appear to be crystallized."

2. Interior systems: active restraints: belt buckles, breaking, failure. • "Seat belt on driver's and passenger's sides do not buckle properly. Orange button breaks off into receptacle, making it difficult to latch." • "The driver's-side seat belt buckle will not release." • "Driver's-side red release button chips, causing pieces to fall inside latch holder and preventing fastener or latch from staying latched when driving." • "Passenger-side seat belt buckle locked in place and would not release, causing the belt to have to be replaced." • "Seat belt buckle failure while driving; will not latch properly."

3. Fuel: throttle linkages and control, sudden accelerations. • "Sudden acceleration caused accident and injury." • "Car surged while driving several times." • "Accident due to sudden acceleration in reverse." • "Vehicle suddenly accelerated uncontrollably, driver lost control of steering; brake applied to no avail; resulted in accident." • "Vehicle accelerated out of control, causing serious injuries."

4. Power train: transmission: automatic, poor performance, difficulty shifting, slipping. • "When trying to pass car, transmission will downshift to 1st at freeway speed, then shifts back to 3rd without going into 2nd; makes impossible to pass." • "Vehicle could roll freely in any gear, depending on the type of incline, only when emergency was not engaged; not mentioned in owner's manual." • "Vehicle vibrates in 1st gear." • "Transmission leaks, makes noise and does not lock when in gear; repaired/replaced gasket and transmission pan." • "Transmission malfunctioned, which resulted in several accidents."

5. Interior systems: active seat and shoulder belts and belt anchor, malfunction, failure. • "In a rear-end collision, front passenger seat belt did not hold and passenger hit the windshield." • "Seat belt failed to hold on sudden stop, causing driver to hit steering wheel and to hit head on window." • "During an accident, seat back broke; driver slipped out of seat belt and fell into the back of the car." • "Seat belt defective; will not hold at all if vehicle involved in rear-end collision; needs to be repaired."

6. Electrical system: battery, failure, fire. • "Defective battery in electrical system; replaced." • "Defective battery; repaired/replaced." • "Forty-five-minute drive, parked for 3 minutes, underhood fire in vicinity of battery consumed the car."

NISSAN SENTRA 1990

Complaint Severity: Troublesome. **Recall Alert:** See Recall Index. **Buyer's Summary:** Make sure the shoulder belts don't cut across your neck and are well anchored. Check the brakes—listen for noise, look for leaks and feel for vibration. They may fail, perform poorly or require frequent mechanical attention. Make sure seat belts function correctly and fit comfortably.

Hot Spots and Owner/NHTSA Comments:
1. Interior systems: active seat and shoulder belts and belt anchor, malfunction, failure. • "Driver seat belt failed in an accident, resulting in an injury." • "Design flaw, with over-the-shoulder unhook function of seat belt a primary concern." • "Shoulder and lap belts were repaired under recall, but still had slack and failed in an accident, causing serious injuries." • "Rear seat belt housing fell off; front seat casing causes excessive wear and regularly snags; passive safety restraint brings door to halt, causing minor contusions."
2. Interior systems: shoulder belts, malfunction, failure. • "Shoulder belt webbing problem." • "Shoulder belt failed, prior to recall; repairs refused due to unavailability of parts." • "Was rear-ended, seat belts did not restrain; later found out there is a recall that relates to failure." • "Seat belt failure; rear-ended and seat belt did not hold the driver." • "Seat belts lock up when opening door from outside and inside. Shut door to release belt lockup."
3. Brakes: hydraulic system, excessive wear, poor performance. • "Premature brake pad and shoe wear. Have to replace every 3,000-4,000 miles." • "Premature rotor wear." • "Braking system defective." • "Brakes seem to not function fully after initially starting car; seem to require a lot of pressure to stop the car."
4. Brakes: hydraulic: disc: rotor: disc hub, vibration, excessive wear. • "Brake rotor defect; entire steering system shook when braking." • "Experiencing brake problem; rotors possibly defective." • "Brake rotors overheated and warped, causing pulsation when braking." • "Vibrations from front axle, brake pedal and steering column; repaired/replaced rotors and calipers." • "Front disc brake rotors overheating and deteriorating."
5. Electrical system: ignition, stalling, fire. • "While driving, vehicle stalled and back trunk caught on fire; also, fuel pump fuse was blown." • "Vehicle experiencing engine stalling problems." • "Placement of ignition key; sunlight can hit key, causing bright reflection driver's eye." • "Engine shuts itself off at whim; while cruising in any gear or slowing with car in neutral, car will stall, usually without warning."
6. Interior systems: passive restraint: belts, malfunction, failure. • "The design of passive restraint can strangle occupant." • "Driver's-side seat belt malfunctions." • "Automatic shoulder belts failed to retract; frayed; recall repairs refused due to unavailability of parts." • "Passive shoulder belt apparently failed during head-on collision; sustained injuries."

NISSAN SENTRA 1991

Complaint Severity: Troublesome. **Recall Alert:** See Recall Index. **Buyer's Summary:** The fuel pump has received complaints. Make sure it doesn't make excessive noise and that you are experiencing adequate engine performance. Also, look for leaks. The fuel injection system has been blamed for hesitation and stalling. Be sure the vehicle doesn't die in traffic or at stops. Check the brakes—listen for noise, look for leaks and feel for vibration. They may fail, perform poorly or require frequent mechanical attention.

Hot Spots and Owner/NHTSA Comments:
1. Brakes: hydraulic system, poor performance, failure. • "Intermittent soft brake pedal, causing extended stopping distance." • "Brakes don't lock up, but there seems to be an increased stopping distance." • "Brakes failed, causing accident with extensive damage and injuries." • "Calipers and rotors failed." • "Four-wheel disc brakes perform sluggishly during panic stopping."
2. Fuel: fuel pump, stalling, failure. • "Fuel pump goes out at 55 mph on freeway. This is the third time." • "Fuel pump problems." • "While driving at high rate of speed, vehicle lost all power; dealer claimed that it was caused by a defective fuel pump." • "Fuel pump failure." • "Fuel pump causes vehicle to stall; vehicle will not start."
3. Interior systems: active restraints: belt buckles, malfunction, failure. • "Transmission went out; passenger seat belt buckle doesn't work, will not latch; emergency brake will not release; vehicle is inoperative." • "Seat belt buckles will not engage fully, but it is not recognizable until belt pops and unlatches." • "Both front seat belt buckles have failed. False latching, and pull apart or no click as it latches." • "Lap and shoulder belt failure; the driver's-side buckle will not latch or hold while driving." • "The driver's- and passenger-side seat belt buckles come loose when in use."
4. Fuel: fuel injection system, stalling, hesitation. • "Vehicle serviced 6 times for sluggishness; problem continues." • "Intermittent stalling." • "Vehicle hesitates when first starting." • "Intermittent stalling." • " 'Check engine' light comes on, seconds later car completely shuts down; this incident occurred several times."
5. Brakes: hydraulic: anti-skid system, poor performance, failure, locking up. • "The antilock brakes malfunction when vehicle is going over bumpy surface and brakes are applied." • "Antilock brake system activates upon hitting bumps, holes or slippery conditions, preventing vehicle from further braking, causing accident." • "Antilock brake system grabs, causing vehicle to vibrate." • "Braking at 55 mph caused all 4 wheels to lock up and initiated a 180-degree turn, driver's-side crash: 4 solid skid marks."
6. Electrical system: ignition, vibration, stalling. • "While driving, vehicle just cuts off." • "Unknown vibration, estimated speed 40-50 mph. Front starts to shimmy, with rpm dropping to a stall. Dealership unable to detect cause. Vehicle in shop 30 times." • "Bent component prevents removal of key." • "While driving, experience intermittent stalling; when engine shuts down at highway speed, vehicle seems to coast, then decelerate."

NISSAN SENTRA 1992

Complaint Severity: Typical. **Buyer's Summary:** Check the brakes—listen for noise, look for leaks and feel for vibration. They may fail, perform poorly or require frequent mechanical attention. Test the transmission thoroughly. See "Sudden Accelerations" in Introduction.

Hot Spots and Owner/NHTSA Comments:
1. Brakes: hydraulic system, noise, failure. • "When vehicle comes to a full stop, driver must maintain constant pressure on pedal; otherwise, a grinding noise is heard; dealer claims nothing wrong." • "Brakes were making squealing noises; owner took vehicle into dealer and they turned rotors and replaced pads twice within 18-month period." • "Brakes fade when applied in an emergency manner, causes sliding instead of stopping." • "Brakes malfunctioned and pedal went to the floor; couldn't stop vehicle."
2. Engine, stalling, fire. • "Overheating of engine." • "Vehicle stalled on highway, resulting in an accident." • "Engine module replaced due to poor gas mileage." • "Engine fire within 15 minutes of parking vehicle."
3. Fuel: throttle linkages and control, sudden accelerations. • "Vehicle accelerated forward, causing accident and injury." • "From a stop, in drive, foot on gas resulted in uncontrolled acceleration, which involved crashing into another vehicle before brakes could stop the car." • "Engine accelerated rapidly while driving at low speed (5 mph or less); no prior warning." • "Accelerator sticks and the brakes would not stop the vehicle."
4. Power train: transmission: automatic, poor performance, difficulty shifting, slipping. • "Transmission gasket failed." • "Brakes spongy; metal-to-metal malfunction, possible antilock brake system; transmission doesn't connect in gear. Smoke com-

ing from heater." • "Vehicle jerks when placed in 2nd through 4th gears; several repairs." • "Transmission failure."

NISSAN SENTRA 1993

Complaint Severity: Serious. **Buyer's Summary:** The airbags in this vehicle have experienced failures and malfunctions: You may need a professional evaluation on the condition of the airbags. Check the brakes—listen for noise, look for leaks and feel for vibration. They may fail, perform poorly or require frequent mechanical attention.

Hot Spots and Owner/NHTSA Comments:

1. Electrical system: ignition, stalling, hesitation. • " 'Check engine' light keeps coming on, causing vehicle to stall." • "Vehicle stalls when being driven on highway. Driver has difficult time restarting vehicle." • "Vehicle stalls without warning. Lost power in all gears." • "Vehicle periodically stalls; 3 times a day, 4 times a week." • "Vehicle stalls out at any speed and hesitates; replaced fuel filter to no avail."

2. Brakes: hydraulic system, noise, failure. • "Spongy brakes; vehicle hard to stop." • "Car surges forward with both feet on the brakes; engine accelerates very high, then it drops back down." • "Noisy brakes." • "Brakes do not work properly; difficulty stopping the car." • "Released cruise control; downshifted; applied brakes and brakes completely failed; hit another vehicle."

3. Interior systems: passive restraint: airbag: driver, malfunction, failure. • "Car hit a deer at 50 mph with brakes on; extensive damage but no airbag deployment. Car continued rolling after impact." • "Upon impact, driver's shoulder belt failed to retract, vehicle was hit at 10:00 position on bumper; airbag deployed after impact; sustained injury from steering and dash." • "At 30 mph, impact 12:00 position, driver's-side airbag did not deploy and bag (in package) fell out of steering wheel." • "Airbag did not deploy during frontal collision; shoulder and lap belt attached to door did not lock up; impact 11:00 position; speed 35 mph; car 1 swerved, hitting car 2."

NISSAN STANZA 1987

Complaint Severity: Typical. **Recall Alert:** See Recall Index. **Buyer's Summary:** Make sure the shoulder belts don't cut across your neck and are well anchored. The fuel injection system has been blamed for hesitation and stalling. Be sure the vehicle doesn't die in traffic or at stops. Test the transmission thoroughly. See "Sudden Accelerations" in Introduction.

Hot Spots and Owner/NHTSA Comments:

1. Fuel: throttle linkages and control, sudden accelerations. • "Upon placing transmission into drive with foot on brake, vehicle suddenly accelerated; caused an accident by hitting another vehicle." • "While in motion, engine revved, locked and propelled backwards at 20 mph; accident." • "Upon starting up vehicle and putting it into drive with foot on brake, vehicle suddenly accelerated out of control; hit another vehicle with 3 occupants." • "Car did not stop when backing out, causing accident that totaled the car." • "Upon starting, engine suddenly accelerated out of control, resulting in severe damages."

2. Power train: transmission: automatic, poor performance, difficulty shifting, slipping. • "Transmission problems; car downshifts or doesn't shift, poor pickup, jerks and pulling, noise on right side; replaced transmission." • "Automatic transmission has some shifting problems." • "Transmission does not downshift out of 3rd when stopping; when trying to accelerate in high gear, can barely move." • "Defect in automatic transmission; not changing gears at proper time, surges and refuses to back up when put in reverse." • "Automatic transmission shifts back and forth, particularly with cold start."

3. Engine: mounts, vibration, breaking. • "Extreme engine block vibration due to defective engine mounts; 2 sets of engine mounts have been replaced." • "Bracket attached to engine block broke, causing engine failure." • "Broken motor mount bolt (right side)." • "Motor mounts broken; car developed a very hard and fast bang each time car shifted gears." • "Engine motor mounts failed."

4. Fuel: fuel injection system, stalling, hesitation. • "Upon accelerating, car wouldn't exceed 45-50 mph; repairs rendered, problem continues." • "Vehicle stalls frequently when shifted into reverse." • "Car skips consistently at 65 mph and bucks." • "Vehicle stalls without warning while in traffic." • "Intermittent problems; car hesitating when trying to accelerate past 15-25 mph, then it surges."

5. Interior systems: shoulder belts, breaking, malfunction, uncomfortable. • "During head-on collision, the shoulder belt did not lock at 30 mph." • "Right front safety belt shoulder harness too short." • "Front shoulder seat belt restraints are improperly positioned. Could cause neck damage or severe injury to the trachea." • "The seat belt tightens up so that you cannot move, and also gets caught, trapping occupant in seat." • "Driver's-side seat belt broke off."

6. Interior systems: active restraints: belt buckles, malfunction, failure. • "Front driver's shoulder and lap belt buckle difficult to release; now, slips loose; owner moves belt from passenger to driver's side to be restrained." • "Passenger-side seat belt latch locked up and jammed, making it impossible unlatch seat belt; passenger was trapped inside vehicle." • "Seat belt assembly where you insert buckle would not release after pushing and moving assembly." • "Both front seat belt buckles experience inadvertent release. Vehicle involved with rollover, resulting in fatality."

NISSAN STANZA 1990

Complaint Severity: Typical. **Buyer's Summary:** Problems with the timing gear and chain can cause serious problems. Have the engine checked by a professional. Test the suspension by feeling for vibration or pulling while driving. Check the brakes—listen for noise, look for leaks and feel for vibration. They may fail, perform poorly or require frequent mechanical attention. Test the transmission thoroughly.

Hot Spots and Owner/NHTSA Comments:

1. Power train: transmission: automatic, poor performance, difficulty shifting, slipping. • "Sometimes from stop, only revs, then accelerates to 15 or 20 mph; unable to repair." • "Automatic transmission problem." • "Problem shifting gears; need to depress brake to shift." • "Transmission failed, causing vehicle to stall; also, torque converter failed." • "Transmission failed; replaced 3 times."

2. Suspension: independent front, vibration, alignment. • "Vehicle experiencing bad front-end vibration; car pulls to right." • "Vehicle front end veers to either side while driving; alignment doesn't stay within specifications, keeps coming off." • "Vehicle skips wildly when making turns or going over potholes." • "Front tires replaced due to misalignment." • "Problems with suspension."

3. Brakes: hydraulic system, noise, failure. • "Brake problems." • "Noisy brakes." • "Brake problems." • "Intermittent brake failures; braking potential compromised in emergency situations."

4. Engine: timing gear and chain, breaking, failure. • "Timing chain broke; vehicle would not drive properly." • "Timing chain broke; caused problems with valves and various other parts." • "The guide which holds the timing chain in place has broken. Low mileage vehicle. Vehicle stalls in traffic." • "Plastic guide to the timing belt broke, causing pistons to misfire and resulting in engine failure."

NISSAN TRUCK PATHFINDER 1990

Complaint Severity: Minor. **Recall Alert:** See Recall Index. **Buyer's Summary:** Test the transmission thoroughly.

Hot Spots and Owner/NHTSA Comments:

1. Power train: transmission: automatic, poor performance, difficulty shifting, slipping. • "Transmission failed; preventing gears from shifting." • "Transmission failed 2 times within 70,000 miles; the second time causing radiator contamination; replaced." • "Transmission lurched and/or revved, then started slipping and would not go into reverse." • "Transmission lubrication passage too small, resulting in lack of lubricant and slipping of transmission." • "Transmission problem."

2. Engine: stalling, poor performance. • "Loud noise from engine; vehicle stalled, smoke from engine; result of radiator contaminant?" • "Vehicle doesn't run due to engine losing power; keeps bogging down." • "Engine jerks, bogs down, loses power and hops; very unsafe." • "Engine warning light appeared several times; cause not determined." • "Oil sending switch failed."

NISSAN TRUCK QUEST 1993

Complaint Severity: Best 3% in Guide. **Recall Alert:** See Recall Index. **Buyer's Summary:** The rear window seems to shatter without reason.

Hot Spots and Owner/NHTSA Comments:

1. Visual systems: glass: window: rearview backlight, breaking. • "Vehicle parked; rear window exploded at 6:20 A.M." • "Rear window exploded from inside and/or outside; vehicle was parked; no apparent reason." • "Rear door window exploded, shattered; no apparent reason; vehicle parked in yard." • "Rear window broke without warning while driving."

NISSAN TRUCK VAN 1987

Complaint Severity: Best 3% in Guide. **Recall Alert:** See Recall Index. **Buyer's Summary:** Look carefully for any kind of leakage, especially under the car. The steering may be stiff or not working correctly. Be sure to test the steering, especially on a cold start. Test the transmission thoroughly.

Hot Spots and Owner/NHTSA Comments:

1. Engine: cooling system: hoses, leaks, fire. • "Cooling system hoses rotted due to power steering pump leakage of fluid; resulted in a blown head gasket." • "Coolant loss due to broken hoses; prior to and after recall." • "Engine caught fire; gasket failed, causing gas leak; prior to recall." • "Engine overheating; need to constantly refill overflow tank with coolant; replaced new engine hoses; vehicle on recall." • "Engine cooling hoses failed, prior to recall, causing a fire."

2. Engine: cooling system, leaks, overheating. • "Defective cooling system; repaired/replaced hose to radiator, belts, water pump and timing cover gasket." • " 'Low coolant' warning light on; coolant reservoir constantly empty, requiring refill every 500 miles; fear engine will overheat." • "Recurring problem with engine overheating; all repair attempts to no avail; van also leaks fluid." • "While driving, vehicle constantly overheated; twice was fixed under recall, but problem has persisted." • "Fourth recall was performed with radiator and fan, etc. One day truck sounded all alarms and overheated."

3. Engine: leaks, overheating. • "Vehicle was recalled on 3 separate occasions to remedy potential leaks and/or fires in engine compartment." • "Defective engine cooling system; failed prior to recall." • "Valve cover gasket leaks oil; cooling system hoses deteriorate because of overheating." • "Valve cover gasket, radiator hoses and water pump failed; prior to recall." • "Engine overheated; hose burst second time and leaked coolant; emergency brake became hot and turned leg hot; belts broke repeatedly, causing vehicle to stall."

4. Steering: power assist: hose: fluid, leaks, fire. • "Recurring problem with power steering hose leaking and making noise; repaired/replaced hose and tube assembly." • "Problem with leak in power steering hose; repaired." • "Recall notification for power steering hose leakage, which can be spread to exhaust manifold." • "Power steering hose broke, leaking fluid onto engine; after recall repair." • "Engine compartment; power steering fluid leak overheated causing a fire."

5. Power train: transmission: automatic, poor performance, difficulty shifting, slipping. • "Transmission malfunctioned; would not shift forward or reverse." • "Transmission cable failed." • "Transmission fails to shift in timely manner; noise when shifting from 2nd to 3rd gear." • "Automatic transmission problem; very hard shifting; also, when driving on ice or slippery roads, van slides during shifting." • "Transmission shifts improperly when cruise control engaged; also sticks in low gear; shifts violently."

6. Engine: cooling system: belts, breaking, fire, overheating. • "Fan belt/pulley installed incorrectly during recall repairs caused vehicle fire." • "Fan belt broke, prior to recall, causing engine to overheat and lose power." • "Fan belt broke twice." • "Recall related: Idler pulley seized up, causing power steering belt to burn. No problems having repair work performed." • "Fan belt broke after recall."

NISSAN TRUCK VAN 1988

Complaint Severity: Negligible. **Recall Alert:** See Recall Index. **Buyer's Summary:** Look carefully for any kind of leakage, especially under the car. The steering may be stiff or not working correctly. Be sure to test the steering, especially on a cold start. Test the transmission thoroughly.

Hot Spots and Owner/NHTSA Comments:

1. Engine: cooling system: hoses, leaks, fire, overheating. • "Defective radiator hose, causing antifreeze fluid to leak and vehicle to overheat; prior to recall notification." • "Cooling system malfunction caused overheating and ruptured upper radiator hose." • "Engine cooling problems, prior to and after recalls." • "Defective cooling system hose caused engine fire; prior to recall." • "Engine cooling hoses overheated prior to and after recall repairs."

2. Steering: power assist: hose: fluid, leaks, fire. • "Power steering fluid hose continues to leak after recall performed; repaired 3 times." • "Engine compartment fire occurred 2 weeks after recall work was performed. Power steering hose and cooling hose malfunctioned." • "Power steering fluid hose leakage, causing overheating of engine." • "Power steering hose leaking." • "Power steering hose clamps were leaking; had to add power steering fluid."

3. Engine: cooling system, overheating, leaks, fire. • "Vehicle has constantly overheated; was repaired 13 times, but continues to overheat." • "Engine cooling system overheated, causing fire." • "Vehicle has been running hot and constantly lost antifreeze fluid." • "Oil leaking from pressure switch." • "Engine heat radiates around front seats; high-pitched noise."

4. Steering: power assist, leaks. • "Constant smell of power steering fluid after recall." • "Power steering leak." • "Power steering leak." • "Power steering went out on vehicle and the steering

became difficult." • "Power steering pulley and belt failure caused smoke, no fire. Parts replaced."
5. Power train: transmission: automatic, poor performance, difficulty shifting, slipping. • "Transmission gears sticking." • "Reverse gear jumps back." • "Transmission problems." • "Engine overheating, causes transmission failure." • "Transmission failure."
6. Engine: leaks, overheating. • "Oil leakage caused rear window to film up hazardously; extremely difficult to see through rear window; also caused rear windshield wiper to deteriorate." • "Engine cylinder warped and blown; manifold cover damaged due to excessive heat; belt broke, noise and smoke came from engine; problem related to recall." • "Engine heats up to point of temperature reaching 'high'; inside of vehicle becomes very hot." • "Engine overheats when air conditioner is on." • "Engine compartment overheats while driving. Recall related. Vehicle was in for current recall."

Oldsmobile

OLDSMOBILE 88 1987

Complaint Severity: Serious. **Recall Alert:** See Recall Index. **Buyer's Summary:** The electronic control unit has been blamed for engine performance problems, including stalling and surging. The fuel injection system has been blamed for hesitation and stalling. Be sure the vehicle doesn't die in traffic or at stops. The steering may be stiff or not working correctly. Be sure to test the steering, especially on a cold start. Check the brakes—listen for noise, look for leaks and feel for vibration. They may fail, perform poorly or require frequent mechanical attention. Test the transmission thoroughly. See "Sudden Accelerations" in Introduction.

Hot Spots and Owner/NHTSA Comments:
1. Fuel: throttle linkages and control, sudden accelerations. • "When shifted into drive, vehicle suffers sudden acceleration. Occurrence appears due to fuel linkage failure." • "Accelerates from reverse to drive without touching gas pedal." • "Vehicle suffered sudden acceleration and loss of control; a spectacular noncollision accident resulted after putting into reverse with no foot on gas." • "Problem unwanted sudden acceleration resulted in an accident; when started car in gas station, after putting into drive car lurched forward and hit car in front." • "Repeated failure of fuel linkage resulted in frequent episodes of sudden acceleration; an accident resulted; brakes did not stop; extensive damage."
2. Fuel: fuel injection system, stalling, hesitation. • "Engine would stall when decelerating from stop signs or slow traffic." • "While traveling at highway speeds, engine sometimes shuts down (stalls), reducing steering and braking." • "Chronic engine stalling problems; stalls while accelerating from stop in heavy traffic." • "Car stalls intermittently on highway and at lower speeds too; when it stalls, power assist functions affected." • "Recurring stalling problem; repaired/replaced solenoid calibrator and crankshaft sensor."
3. Power train: transmission: automatic, poor performance, difficulty shifting, slipping. • "When car is put into reverse and accelerator is pressed, car hesitates then suddenly surges backwards; due to defective reverse pins; transmission replaced." • "Transmission always shifts rough when gear changed at higher speeds." • "Transmission malfunctioned; inability to upshift from 1st to 2nd gear prevents vehicle from maintaining adequate forward speed in ongoing traffic." • "Transmission slipping and stalling; replaced entire transmission." • "Transmission jerky; replaced torque converter, problem continues."
4. Steering: gear: rack-and-pinion, stiffness, poor performance. • "Rack-and-pinion replaced twice due to cold power steering." • "Rack-and-pinion steering malfunction; does not operate when car is first started, especially when engine or weather cold." • "Rack-and-pinion steering freezes up and needs replacing; has been replaced and rebuilt." • "Replaced rack-and-pinion steering mechanism due to stiffness." • "Problems with steering wheel; locks after overnight or short period of time parking."
5. Brakes: hydraulic system, failure. • "Spongy brake pedal goes almost to floor when depressing to brake; does not stop within reasonable distance." • "Brake failure; master cylinder and rear wheel cylinder leaking fluid; replacements made; front right rotor scratched; resurfaced rotors and pads." • "Brake pedal frequently goes to floor while waiting at lights, occasionally when stopping or slowing." • "Brake pedal gets very low; while driving and braking, pedal depressed, it drifted to floor, not stopping, causing rear-end collision." • "Brake failure; pedal faded, causing an accident, impact at 6:00 position, speed at 20 mph."
6. Electrical system: ignition: electronic control unit, stalling, malfunction. • "Stalling problem; total loss of power and diminished steering and braking control." • "Problem starting car; car dies while driving and sometimes at stops; repaired/replaced computer chips several times and fuel pump twice." • "Engine stalling problems; dies while driving, losing all engine power; repaired/replaced crank sensor and idle air control valve." • "Malfunction in computer; engine would die at any speed; repaired 4 times, problem still not corrected."

OLDSMOBILE 88 1988

Complaint Severity: Serious. **Buyer's Summary:** Verify that the cruise control system works properly, and that it doesn't cause the engine to surge. The fuel injection system has been blamed for hesitation and stalling. Be sure the vehicle doesn't die in traffic or at stops. The steering may be stiff or not working correctly. Be sure to test the steering, especially on a cold start. Check the brakes—listen for noise, look for leaks and feel for vibration. They may fail, perform poorly or require frequent mechanical attention. Test the transmission thoroughly. See "Sudden Accelerations" in Introduction.

Hot Spots and Owner/NHTSA Comments:
1. Fuel: throttle linkages and control, sudden accelerations. • "When shifter put in reverse, car suddenly accelerated; accident." • "Gas pedal suddenly went down by itself, car accelerated quickly; applied brakes and stopped acceleration." • "Engine surged unexpectedly, automobile plowed with great force into another, which, in turn, struck the one immediately in front of it." • "Upon shifting gear from park to drive, vehicle suddenly accelerated, resulting in accident." • "Car suddenly accelerated, would not stop upon braking; stopped only after collision resulted."
2. Fuel: fuel injection system, stalling, hesitation. • "Engine fails at various speeds; when fails there is loss of steering and braking; absolutely no control without physical effort." • "Vehicle stopped in motion, would not start, had to be towed; repaired/replaced fuel pump twice." • "Vehicle stalls at highway speed and in traffic; almost rear-ended." • "While driving, vehicle shuts down, causing all steering and brakes to fail." • "Constant stalling problems."
3. Equipment: speed control, malfunction. • "When using cruise control, while going downhill, control continually gains speed and doesn't hold to what it's set." • "Cruise control failure; it would surge when not placed in cruise position, slow down when cruise in 'on' position, repaired/replaced cruise control 'brain.' " • "Cruise control malfunctions on occasion and unpredictably, vehicle continues to accelerate beyond original speed set on cruise

control until brakes applied." • "Cruise control accelerates car; when placed on while driving at 30 mph, will accelerate very quickly to 75 mph." • "Car sometimes speeds up (surges) when cruise control set at highway speed of 55 mph, more or less."
4. Steering: gear: rack-and-pinion, stiffness, poor performance. • "Seems to have problems with front end—both idler arms have been replaced; now having problems with steering; seems to seize up on hard right and left turns." • "Rack-and-pinion steering locks up during cold start." • "Steering is very difficult; rack-and-pinion has gone bad." • "After vehicle has been parked for a few hours, steering wheel is difficult to turn, especially turning left. Once first turned, steering seems OK." • "Rack-and-pinion steering locks up during cold weather; becomes unlocked after engine has warmed up."
5. Power train: transmission: automatic, poor performance, difficulty shifting, slipping. • "Transmission vibrates when put into drive or reverse." • "Vehicle jerks when shifting gears; accelerating, it slips; 3rd gear seal broken; repaired." • "Slipping transmission." • "Transmission problems; replaced small ball bearing."
6. Brakes: hydraulic system, vibration, locking up, excessive wear. • "Defective braking system; front brake pads repaired/replaced 3 times in 52,000 miles, rotors have been turned 6 times." • "Front brake pads must be replaced every 13,000 miles." • "Vibration in front end when brakes are applied." • "When brakes are applied with some force, brakes lock up and vehicle skids." • "Loss of brakes is intermittent."

OLDSMOBILE 88 1989

Complaint Severity: Typical. **Recall Alert:** See Recall Index. **Buyer's Summary:** Verify that the cruise control system works properly, and that it doesn't cause the engine to surge. The electronic control unit has been blamed for engine performance problems, including stalling and surging. The fuel injection system has been blamed for hesitation and stalling. Be sure the vehicle doesn't die in traffic or at stops. Check the brakes—listen for noise, look for leaks and feel for vibration. They may fail, perform poorly or require frequent mechanical attention. Test the transmission thoroughly. See "Sudden Accelerations" in Introduction.

Hot Spots and Owner/NHTSA Comments:
1. Brakes: hydraulic system, noise, failure. • "Defective braking system; relay module failed; brake pump accumulator required repaired/replaced; also, brakes make squealing noise." • "Front brakes were replaced at 13,000 miles." • "Brake pedal requires excessive effort." • "Brakes went out entirely." • "Brakes failed, causing loss of control."
2. Electrical system: ignition: electronic control unit, stalling, failure. • "Engine stalls frequently while in motion and/or idling; replaced new computer." • "Intermittent stalling problems." • "Electronic control module defective; repaired/replaced." • "Computer program module failure." • "Starting car in morning after sitting all night, car would idle and shut off; replaced crankshaft sensor and electronic control module."
3. Equipment: speed control, malfunction, failure. • "Cruise control fails intermittently." • "Cruise control stops working on rough road." • "Vehicle jumps out of cruise control when in drive." • "Cruise control inoperative." • "Cruise control failure; reengaged after slowing down; vehicle accelerated violently; resulted in accident."
4. Fuel: fuel injection system, stalling, hesitation. • "Intermittent stalling caused by faulty engine computer module." • "Idle air valve caused engine to race." • "Car would misfire when accelerated, sometimes stop; repaired by dealer." • "Twice lost power when stopped at intersection, and lost power when driving at 40 mph." • "Engine stalls out on deceleration; also having starting difficulty in morning."
5. Fuel: throttle linkages and control, sudden accelerations. • "While in bank drive-in window, car accelerated to high rate of speed, plunging through brick wall; no control over speed; extensive damage." • "Throttle jamming, motor accelerated rapidly; threw off all fan belts; lost all power; fire on both sides of engine." • "At 50 mph, remove foot from accelerator speed drops to 30 mph, holds that speed; apply brakes, speed goes to 25 mph and stays there; condition hazardous."
6. Power train: transmission: automatic, poor performance, difficulty shifting, slipping. • "Transmission jumps when shifting from park into reverse." • "Transmission shudders at 35-45 mph." • "Transmission went out at about 9,500 miles; replaced by dealer." • "Defective transmission; could not pass a moving vehicle." • "Harsh reverse engagement in transmission; also, shifter knob came loose."

OLDSMOBILE 88 1990

Complaint Severity: Typical. **Recall Alert:** See Recall Index. **Buyer's Summary:** Make sure the shoulder belts don't cut across your neck and are well anchored. The electronic control unit has been blamed for engine performance problems, including stalling and surging. Check the brakes—listen for noise, look for leaks and feel for vibration. They may fail, perform poorly or require frequent mechanical attention. See "Sudden Accelerations" in Introduction.

Hot Spots and Owner/NHTSA Comments:
1. Fuel: throttle linkages and control, sudden accelerations. • "Upon shifting transmission into gear, vehicle accelerated without touching gas pedal; brakes could not stop; went out of control and caused accident." • "Pulled car in garage slowly; putting it in park, went into park harder than usual; suddenly jerked backwards very fast; accident." • "Vehicle in drive gear took off at high rate of speed; driver unable to get car under control; resulted in accident." • "Upon shifting transmission into gear, vehicle accelerated without touching gas pedal; brakes could not stop; went out of control and caused accident." • "Vehicle suddenly accelerated in drive and hit another car."
2. Electrical system: ignition: electronic control unit, stalling, malfunction. • "Onboard computer failure." • "Intermittent stalling; computer replaced." • "Worked for 20 minutes, then vehicle continued stalling; lost all power, with vehicle moving along; dealer replaced electronic control module." • "Vehicle stalls at random, sometimes every 2 weeks; dealer replaced electronic control module." • "Engine suddenly dies out on highway, in town, turning, etc."
3. Brakes: hydraulic system, vibration, noise, failure. • "Brakes failed, causing accident." • "Squeaky brakes." • "Brakes failed; master cylinder replaced, problem continued." • "Brakes vibrate when applied." • "Poor braking performance."
4. Brakes: hydraulic: anti-skid system, poor performance, failure, locking up. • "Failure of antilock brakes caused clicking sound and drainage of battery." • "Antilock brake system adds on an unacceptable stopping distance while hitting bumps below 40 mph." • "Intermittent antilock brake system failure." • "Antilock brake system failure; while driving vehicle, complete loss of brakes."
5. Interior systems: active seat and shoulder belts and belt anchor, uncomfortable, poor performance. • "Problems with driver's-side seat belt." • "Safety belts are attached to doors." • "Seat belts attached to door are too high on neck." • "Problem with seat belt; strap passes across throat."
6. Interior systems: shoulder belts, uncomfortable. • "Torso belt is routed under right arm of 5′5″-tall person, seat belt posi-

tioned across center of chest and diagonal strap passes across throat." • "Poor-fitting shoulder strap." • "Design of shoulder harness slides into neck of driver instead of across shoulder; causes extreme discomfort."

OLDSMOBILE 88 1991

Complaint Severity: Minor. **Recall Alert:** See Recall Index. **Buyer's Summary:** Make sure the shoulder belts don't cut across your neck and are well anchored. Verify that the cruise control system works properly, and that it doesn't cause the engine to surge. The electronic control unit has been blamed for engine performance problems, including stalling and surging. The fuel injection system has been blamed for hesitation and stalling. Be sure the vehicle doesn't die in traffic or at stops. Check the brakes—listen for noise, look for leaks and feel for vibration. They may fail, perform poorly or require frequent mechanical attention.

Hot Spots and Owner/NHTSA Comments:

1. Fuel: fuel injection system, stalling, hesitation. • "Intermittent stalling." • "Vehicle stalled while making exit on highway; all warning lights flashed." • "Intermittent stalling due to faulty air control system." • "Vehicle will stall with no warning. Dealer has made some adjustments to injection system, but correction is premature."

2. Brakes: hydraulic system, malfunction, failure. • "While driving experienced total brake failure when brake pedal went to the floor; resulted in hitting a sign." • "Vehicle's braking system malfunctions; have no brakes. A few hours later they return." • "Brake failure; loss of pressure, resulting in loss of control and an accident." • "When driving down road at 35 mph, engine dies, losing power steering and brakes. Dealer cannot fix." • "High-speed brake application with maximum pedal pressure applied resulted in total brake failure."

3. Electrical system: ignition, stalling. • "When driving down road at 35 mph; engine dies, losing power steering and brakes. Dealer cannot fix." • "While driving, vehicle stalls." • "Vehicle stalled without any warning." • "Car stalled out in idle on an incline, resulting in car drifting forward and total loss of brakes. Hit another vehicle 2 different times." • "Vehicle stalls out with no warning, usually at low speeds when turning."

4. Interior systems: shoulder belts, uncomfortable, poor performance. • "Shoulder belt comes across driver's neck; it is impossible to drive with it on." • "Shoulder belts rub against side of head and neck." • "Shoulder belt comes across neck." • "Shoulder belts fit unsafely under neck; design has no door pillar adjustment, they cross the upper and lower parts of driver's face." • "Driver's-side shoulder belt does not fit properly, cuts across bottom of face."

5. Electrical system: ignition: electronic control unit, stalling, malfunction. • "Electronic control module inoperative; replaced." • "Intermittent engine stalling without warning at highway speeds." • "Vehicle stopped dead in the middle of a high-speed 3-lane highway." • "Vehicle stalls."

6. Equipment: speed control, malfunction, failure. • "Vehicle sped up beyond cruise control speed setting." • "Cruise failures." • "Cruise control servo problem." • "Cruise control malfunctioning."

OLDSMOBILE 88 1992

Complaint Severity: Troublesome. **Buyer's Summary:** The airbags in this vehicle have experienced failures and malfunctions: You may need a professional evaluation on the condition of the airbags. Check the brakes—listen for noise, look for leaks and feel for vibration. They may fail, perform poorly or require frequent mechanical attention.

Hot Spots and Owner/NHTSA Comments:

1. Brakes: hydraulic: anti-skid system, poor performance, failure, locking up. • "Antilock brake system locks up while driving." • "Antilock brake-equipped car had brake pedal go to the floor. Car crashed into a truck as a result. Dealer can find no problem." • "Antilock brake system: When driver applied the brakes, the pedal went to the floor and vehicle did not stop." • "Pressed antilock brakes to stop at traffic light, brakes failed to stop vehicle, resulting in an accident and injury." • "The antilock brake system has failed. When brake was applied, the car would not stop."

2. Brakes: hydraulic system, locking up, failure. • "Driving down side street, heard loud bang, applied brakes and pedal went to the floor; coasted to a stop." • "Brakes failed, causing accident and injuries." • "Braking system is defective and causes wheel to lock up." • "Brakes are inadequate; increasing stopping distances. Feels like the brakes go off and on, making high-pitched noise or hum; hesitation while driving." • "Brakes failed, causing loss of control, accident and injuries."

3. Interior systems: passive restraint: airbag: driver, malfunction, failure. • "Frontal impact occurred from speed of 45 mph, the airbag did not deploy; driver's face hit steering wheel and broke nose." • "Vehicle was involved in a front-end accident and the airbag did not deploy." • "Driver airbag did not deploy during front-end collision." • "Driver's-side airbag did not deploy upon 12:00 (frontal) collision."

OLDSMOBILE 98 1987

Complaint Severity: Troublesome. **Recall Alert:** See Recall Index. **Buyer's Summary:** Verify that the cruise control system works properly, and that it doesn't cause the engine to surge. The electronic control unit has been blamed for engine performance problems, including stalling and surging. The fuel injection system has been blamed for hesitation and stalling. Be sure the vehicle doesn't die in traffic or at stops. Check the brakes—listen for noise, look for leaks and feel for vibration. They may fail, perform poorly or require frequent mechanical attention. Test the transmission thoroughly. See "Sudden Accelerations" in Introduction.

Hot Spots and Owner/NHTSA Comments:

1. Fuel: fuel injection system, stalling, hesitation. • "Fuel injector leaked; replaced; also replaced fuel injection pump twice." • "Fuel injection system malfunction; vehicle suffers stalling problems; unknown part in fuel injection system replaced, stalling ceased." • "While making left turn, motor died out; barely made turn; no power steering." • "Vehicle stalls in the middle of the road, driver loses power steering; potential hazard due to faulty fuel injection system."

2. Fuel: throttle linkages and control, sudden accelerations. • "Put car in reverse to back out of garage, car accelerated on its own; applied brakes, pedal went to floor; car collided with truck." • "Upon putting vehicle in reverse gear, suddenly accelerated and hit parked car; brakes failed to stop speed." • "Driver shifted from park to reverse with foot on brake and car bolted, hitting a truck; left skid marks." • "Driver making turn from highway at about 35 mph, took foot off gas pedal, and before brakes were applied, car accelerated." • "Driver took foot off brake and shifted into reverse, car suddenly accelerated nearly hitting people 3 times."

3. Brakes: hydraulic system, failure. • "Power brakes malfunction, at times brakes will not stop vehicle; repaired 3 times." • "Brake failure caused accident; master cylinder and pads replaced 5 times." • "Several rotor repairs for pulsating brakes." • "Brake failure; brakes unable to stop; rear-ended vehicle." • "Hit brakes, there were none; antilock brake light came on; brakes master cylinder fluid low."

4. Power train: transmission: automatic, poor performance, difficulty shifting, slipping. • "Transmission leak developed between 35,000 and 45,000 miles; replaced." • "Occasionally transmission doesn't respond, also jerks into gear at 35 mph." • "Low-speed transmission shifts are rough and jerky—like getting a poor tow job; seems to shift gears too often." • "Automatic transmission slips, has no engagement."
5. Electrical system: ignition: electronic control unit, stalling, malfunction. • "Defective computer caused engine to run rough, stall out and frequently smell of gasoline; repaired/replaced computer chip after 'service engine' light came on." • "Electronic control module failed, causing loss of power at highway speeds." • "Car stalls due to sensor failure." • "Stalling in intersection; replaced computer, problem persists." • "Driving 55 mph, all lights on instrument panel lit up, engine stopped; sensing switch missing, causing complete closing down of all operating systems."
6. Equipment: speed control, malfunction, failure. • "Location of speed reset lever causes driver to set speed when signaling, resulting in vehicle lurching forward into sudden acceleration." • "Cruise control causes vehicle to pick up speed, then drops out or won't engage at all." • "Cruise control stuck and would not release when brakes applied, vehicle stayed at same speed." • "Cruise control slipped out of control; would not engage or reengage." • "Intermittent operation of cruise control; would engage if left on; replaced servo control."

OLDSMOBILE 98 1988

Complaint Severity: Typical. **Buyer's Summary:** Verify that the cruise control system works properly, and that it doesn't cause the engine to surge. The steering may be stiff or not working correctly. Be sure to test the steering, especially on a cold start. Check the brakes—listen for noise, look for leaks and feel for vibration. They may fail, perform poorly or require frequent mechanical attention. See "Sudden Accelerations" in Introduction.

Hot Spots and Owner/NHTSA Comments:
1. Equipment: speed control, malfunction, sudden acceleration. • "Cruise control failed to work after approximately 11,000 miles; caused by open brake switch; replaced." • "Cruise control speed setting retains the last speed setting even after car turned off; easy to touch cruise control switch while using turn signal." • "On 5 occasions, car began at full-throttle acceleration when cruise control turned from off to on, or when 'resume' feature engaged." • "Cruise control sticks wide open; caused sudden acceleration; did not disengage by braking; turned off ignition to stop acceleration."
2. Fuel: throttle linkages and control, sudden accelerations. • "When accelerator released, vehicle continues to accelerate, requires hard braking to bring to control." • "Vehicle shot forward suddenly, driver lost control; hit parked car." • "Speed does not lessen when gas pedal released, continues at same speed until brakes applied; happens sporadically at different speeds." • "Car suddenly accelerated to 60 mph (running approximately 40 mph); fortunately No car in front." • "Engaged in drive, pressed gas pedal and it stuck, car took off very fast at high speed, resulting in accident."
3. Brakes: hydraulic system, vibration, excessive wear, failure. • "Master cylinder replaced." • "Uneven and excessive brake lining wear." • "When driver tried to stop for traffic light, brakes failed, resulting in accident; brake pedal went to floor, parking brake completely inoperable." • "Excessive vibration upon application of brakes; sometimes brakes do not work at all; replaced entire brake system."
4. Steering: gear: rack-and-pinion, stiffness, poor performance. • "Power steering goes out while driving; dealer said due to fluid being burned, replaced steering rack 2 times." • "The power steering is hard to turn; it is the rack-and-pinion." • "Cold power steering." • "Short steering rack leaks; power steering had to be replaced." • "Cold power steering."
5. Steering: power assist, failure. • "Power steering system failure." • "Cold power steering." • "Power steering malfunctioned; difficulty in steering vehicle." • "Power steering assist not functioning when cold."

OLDSMOBILE 98 1989

Complaint Severity: Typical. **Recall Alert:** See Recall Index. **Buyer's Summary:** Verify that the cruise control system works properly, and that it doesn't cause the engine to surge. The electronic control unit has been blamed for engine performance problems, including stalling and surging. The fuel injection system has been blamed for hesitation and stalling. Be sure the vehicle doesn't die in traffic or at stops. Check the brakes—listen for noise, look for leaks and feel for vibration. They may fail, perform poorly or require frequent mechanical attention. See "Sudden Accelerations" in Introduction.

Hot Spots and Owner/NHTSA Comments:
1. Fuel: fuel injection system, stalling, hesitation. • "Engine suffers lagging, hesitation; idle becomes erratic; accelerating and decelerating engine speed; at times, car vibrates excessively in park position." • "Vehicle burst into flames upon impact with a tree." • "Intermittent stalling when first started." • "Intermittent stalling, causing loss of power steering and brakes."
2. Fuel: throttle linkages and control, sudden accelerations. • "Vehicle surged forward while driving along at highway speed." • "Vehicle suddenly accelerated; upon putting car in reverse, car lurched violently. Resulted in accident." • "Motor jumps when engaged, and suddenly accelerates." • "Vehicle put into reverse, shot out of control in reverse." • "While backing out of garage, car uncontrollably accelerated in reverse; brakes did not work to stop speed; resulted in accident with injuries sustained."
3. Brakes: hydraulic system, malfunction, failure. • "Traveling about 25 mph, vehicle could not be stopped with maximum pressure on brake pedal; almost caused rear-end accident." • "In sudden panic stop, brakes failed to function properly; did not stop vehicle." • "Brakes applied in emergency stop, began to slide; brake pedal depressed all the way to floor; tires stopped sliding and collision occurred." • "Brake failure on highway; stopped with emergency brakes."
4. Electrical system: ignition, stalling, failure. • "Computer failed." • "Computer failures." • "Vehicle stalls in traffic with no warning when engine gets hot." • "Vehicle keeps stalling out at highway speeds and when coming to a stop. Open-throttle condition. Sometimes it will start again and sometimes it won't."
5. Electrical system: ignition: electronic control unit, malfunction. • "Electronic control module malfunctioned." • "Onboard computer problem." • "Faulty onboard computers in ignition system."
6. Equipment: speed control, malfunction, failure. • "Cruise control malfunction; replaced servo." • "Cruise control failure." • "Apparently sudden acceleration caused by cruise control; contributed to by lack of power steering and brakes." • "Cruise control disengages by itself."

OLDSMOBILE 98 1990

Complaint Severity: Typical. **Recall Alert:** See Recall Index. **Buyer's Summary:** Verify that the cruise control system works properly, and that it doesn't cause the engine to surge. Test the transmission thoroughly. See "Sudden Accelerations" in Introduction.

Hot Spots and Owner/NHTSA Comments:

1. Power train: transmission: automatic, poor performance, difficulty shifting, slipping. • "Automatic transmission passing gear malfunctioning; experiencing slowness or lag in activation of downshift of passing gear at various speeds." • "Transmission passing gear defect; slowness and/or lag in action of downshift of passing gear at various speeds, especially from 35-45 mph, delay takes from 3 to 4 seconds." • "Gears become stuck and cannot be shifted unless excessive force is applied." • "Problem with severe leak in transmission; tightened bolts around left drive axle and side cover gasket." • "Premature transmission failure at 3,695 miles."

2. Fuel: throttle linkages and control, sudden accelerations. • "Sudden accelerations, causing loss of control; two accidents and injuries." • "Put the car into gear and the car just accelerated twice for no reason." • "Vehicle suddenly accelerated upon changing from reverse to drive; crashed into a wall." • "While in park, suddenly car went in reverse; wheels squealed and then car went forward, causing an accident."

3. Equipment: speed control, malfunction. • "Cruise control repaired." • "No ground circuit to cruise control; repaired." • "Speed cruise control wouldn't always engage; once engaged, and disengaged when brakes were applied, couldn't get it to reengage by moving 'reengage' button."

OLDSMOBILE 98 1991

Complaint Severity: Troublesome. **Recall Alert:** See Recall Index. **Buyer's Summary:** Check the brakes—listen for noise, look for leaks and feel for vibration. They may fail, perform poorly or require frequent mechanical attention.

Hot Spots and Owner/NHTSA Comments:

1. Brakes: hydraulic system, vibration, failure. • "Brakes failed, resulting in an accident involving 2 other vehicles." • "While traveling between 40-50 mph, applied brakes and they went all the way to the floor; brought vehicle to a stop at shoulder by applying parking brake." • "While driving, brakes failed. Had an accident. Airbag did not deploy." • "Brakes vibrate excessively." • "Antirust solution was sprayed on brakes by manufacturer, which made brake lining defective; resulted in no brakes."

2. Brakes: hydraulic: anti-skid system, poor performance, failure, locking up. • "Brakes: Cruise control failure, causing overheating and failure of brake fluid." • "Antilock brake failure caused loss of control of vehicle, which resulted in an accident." • "Antilock brake-equipped brake pedal goes to floor, no extraneous noises; parking brake and running off the road averted a collision. No warning lights showed problems." • "While approaching slower traffic on highway, driver pushed brake pedal and it went to the floor; antilock brake system." • "The antilock brake system failed when applied, causing an accident."

3. Brakes: hydraulic: master cylinder, failure. • "Loss of brakes 3 different times; replaced master cylinder." • "Replaced master cylinder." • "Antilock brake system failed, causing accident." • "Antilock brake system: Dual master cylinder failed. Brake pedal went to the floor. No warning. Speed 35 mph." • "Estimated speed 55-60 mph, vehicle began reacting erratically. Driver applied antilock brake system and pedal went to the floor."

4. Visual systems: glass: windshield, cracking. • "Noisy lower right windshield when crossing bumps in road." • "Front windshield cracked 3 times due to stress; also, rear window separated from frame." • "Entire metal strip on top of windshield came off; resulted in wind sounds engulfing the vehicle." • "Windshield molding loose; replaced twice." • "Windshield cracked; replaced three times; also, rear window separated from the frame."

OLDSMOBILE ACHIEVA 1992

Complaint Severity: Typical. **Buyer's Summary:** Check the brakes—listen for noise, look for leaks and feel for vibration. They may fail, perform poorly or require frequent mechanical attention. Test the transmission thoroughly.

Hot Spots and Owner/NHTSA Comments:

1. Brakes: hydraulic: anti-skid system, poor performance, failure, locking up. • "Antilock brake system skids intermittently with no warning when braking." • "Antilock brake system brake pedal went to floor; after several seconds, brakes engaged; no brakes momentarily; increased stopping distances." • "Antilock brake system: On wet, snowy or icy conditions, wheels lock up; vehicle slides; slid through stop sign." • "Antilock brakes failed due to snow building up in wheels, resulting in accident and injuries." • "Antilock brake system failed; pedal faded; impact 11:00 position; lost control, hitting embankment at 30 mph."

2. Power train: transmission: automatic, poor performance, difficulty shifting, slipping. • "Squeak in transmission when changing from park to drive or when starting from a stop with car already in gear." • "Transmission failure." • "Transmission makes noise when shifting from park or reverse gears into drive." • "At 30 mph, transmission will not shift due to fuse melting. Related to computer; resulting in accident. replaced fuse twice."

OLDSMOBILE CALAIS 1987

Complaint Severity: Troublesome. **Recall Alert:** See Recall Index. **Buyer's Summary:** Look carefully for any kind of leakage, especially under the car. Problems with the timing gear and chain can cause serious problems. Have the engine checked by a professional. The electronic control unit has been blamed for engine performance problems, including stalling and surging. The fuel injection system has been blamed for hesitation and stalling. Be sure the vehicle doesn't die in traffic or at stops. Check the brakes—listen for noise, look for leaks and feel for vibration. They may fail, perform poorly or require frequent mechanical attention. See "Sudden Accelerations" in Introduction.

Hot Spots and Owner/NHTSA Comments:

1. Brakes: hydraulic system, pulling, poor performance. • "Apply brakes and car pulls to the left; brakes squeal." • "Brake system fails constantly; results in poor performance." • "Upon braking, vehicle pulled to right; brakes noisy and inadequate to stop; resulted in accident." • "Clunking and grinding sounds when brakes applied or released." • "When brakes are applied, gear jumps out of place."

2. Fuel: fuel injection system, stalling, hesitation. • "Cleaned fuel injection system; poor gas mileage." • "Car stalls continually at normal speeds, even at stops; seems to have an idle problem; idle air control valve replaced 3 times, continues to stall." • "Fuel injection system failure; poor acceleration; engine running hot." • "Car idling very rough; stalls when slowing down and/or trying to stop; all repair attempts to no avail." • "Engine quit starting when cold or warm; backfired terribly; wouldn't go 45 mph; stalled; rerouted fuel line from exhaust manifold to no avail."

3. Fuel: throttle linkages and control, sudden accelerations. • "Unintended sudden acceleration when shifted from park to reverse; resulted in accident and damages; replaced idle speed motor." • "Driver shifted car into drive with foot on brake, vehicle accelerated; brakes were applied with full force without any effect." • "Shifted vehicle into reverse, engine sounded erratic and accelerated at full speed, hitting the curb; brakes did not slow car down; repaired/replaced idle control motor." • "Backing out driveway, shifted from park to reverse, car became erratic and raced down driveway; brake failed to stop car; knocked down tree; accident occurred." • "Car made whistling sound, suddenly accelerated; brake and steering useless; accident resulted."

4. Engine: leaks, noise, stalling. • "Several engine repairs." • "Vehicle overheated twice; also oil leaked due to hole in oil pan." • "Noisy engine from purchase; timing gear needed replacing." • "Knocking noise when accelerating." • "Intermittent stalling."

5. Engine: timing gear and chain, breaking, noise, stalling. • "Timing chain broke and was replaced." • "Timing gear loose; rattles very noisily at idle." • "Noise in engine due to defective timing belt, which is made of plastic." • "Timing belt failed on freeway and vehicle stalled." • "Broken timing gears resulted in noises emanating from under the hood."

6. Electrical system: ignition: electronic control unit, stalling, malfunction. • "Vehicle experiencing stalling problem; usually occurs while driving at 45-50 mph; cuts out entirely when shifting into gear; resulted in accident." • "Vehicle suffers chronic stalling due to a faulty computer programmable read-only memory chip." • "Engine suffers stalling, programmable read-only memory replaced." • "Ignition module faulty; increased problems, with car running rough; eventually dies, possibly not restarting."

OLDSMOBILE CALAIS 1988

Complaint Severity: Typical. **Recall Alert:** See Recall Index. **Buyer's Summary:** Look carefully for any kind of leakage, especially under the car. Problems with the timing gear and chain can cause serious problems. Have the engine checked by a professional. The electronic control unit has been blamed for engine performance problems, including stalling and surging. Check the brakes—listen for noise, look for leaks and feel for vibration. They may fail, perform poorly or require frequent mechanical attention. See "Sudden Accelerations" in Introduction.

Hot Spots and Owner/NHTSA Comments:

1. Brakes: hydraulic system, excessive wear, failure. • "Excessive and premature wearing of brakes; repaired/replaced." • "Upon applying the brakes, there was no response." • "Brakes defective; unable to stop car to avoid accident, went through plate glass front window of a store." • "Continual problem with braking system; car does not stop as it should; under emergency conditions, brakes fade; repaired/replaced at 13,000 miles, still a problem." • "Power brakes hard to work, feel like no power assist, takes too long to stop."

2. Engine: timing gear and chain, breaking, malfunction. • "Timing gear making clicking sound; discovered not properly meshed; eventually fiberglass gear will disintegrate." • "Timing chain broke; engine makes constant rattling noise." • "When cold, engine stalls, spits and sputters; hot idle; misses when warms up due to installation of timing chain with 2 teeth off." • "Timing chain and gear knocked; dealers out of parts needed for repair." • "Malfunction in engine; lifters knock; timing belt bad."

3. Electrical system: ignition: electronic control unit, malfunction, failure. • "Computer failed 4 times." • "Electronic control module malfunctioned." • "Computer chip failure caused car to stall upon starting when cold." • "Faulty ignition module; cuts off at roadway speed; hard restart." • "Control module replaced."

4. Fuel: throttle linkages and control, sudden accelerations. • "Vehicle moves forward very fast and shoots back when in reverse; when brakes are applied does not stop fast; almost caused an accident several times." • "Motor races at idle; on level road with foot off gas pedal, car goes 30-35 miles per hour." • "Vehicle accelerated out of control, without touching gas pedal upon shifting into reverse." • "Vehicle goes 30 mph without touching gas pedal." • "Vehicle suddenly accelerated out of control 4 times causing an accident."

5. Engine: leaks, failure. • "Oil leakage problem; oil accumulates on top of engine block between sections of engine." • "Engine blown; replaced; replacement blown again." • "Head gasket leak." • "Engine failure caused by lack of oil to parts of the engine."

6. Engine: gaskets, leaks, failure. • "Head and oil gasket problems." • "Head gasket failed." • "Head gasket blew out, causing antifreeze to leak into engine cylinders; jerky acceleration and ticking noise." • "Blown head gaskets caused water to leak into fuel compartment."

OLDSMOBILE CALAIS 1989

Complaint Severity: Typical. **Recall Alert:** See Recall Index. **Buyer's Summary:** The electronic control unit has been blamed for engine performance problems, including stalling and surging. Check the brakes—listen for noise, look for leaks and feel for vibration. They may fail, perform poorly or require frequent mechanical attention. See "Sudden Accelerations" in Introduction.

Hot Spots and Owner/NHTSA Comments:

1. Fuel: throttle linkages and control, sudden accelerations. • "Gear shifted into drive, car went forward a little then suddenly accelerated, hitting a wall; slammed on brakes to no avail." • "Upon starting vehicle, it suddenly accelerated; shot through the parking lot into a field and then into a ditch; driver sustained injuries." • "Vehicle left in park with engine running; when shifted into drive, vehicle accelerated through garage wall; had no control over speed." • "Throttle sticks in open position while driving, causing vehicle to surge." • "Throttle stuck, causing vehicle to accelerate out of control; once resulting in an accident."

2. Brakes: hydraulic system, poor performance, failure. • "Rear brakes go out of adjustment very frequently, after only a few thousand miles, causing poor performance." • "Problem with brakes; when first brake, car slows down; can stand on brake pedal and brakes won't lock up." • "Experiencing continual brake system failure; seems like brakes not adequate for vehicle's weight; takes longer before stopping, especially going downhill." • "Failure of braking power while driving almost caused at least 2 accidents; brakes have been repaired twice."

3. Electrical system: ignition: electronic control unit, stalling, premature failure. • "Problem with module ignition sensor; car would turn over, but would not start." • "Problem with onboard computers." • "Engine stalls while traveling at 65 mph; loss of power; have to pull over for 10 to 15 minutes before restarting; problem caused by shorted electronic control module." • "Four replacements of electronic control module, which causes vehicle to suddenly accelerate on its own." • "Vehicle has ruined 7 electronic control modules, and is causing stalling during left turn from slow speed maneuver."

4. Brakes: hydraulic: power assist: vacuum system, poor performance. • "Unreliable brakes; need to maintain a good distance behind car ahead." • "When braking, car does not want to come to a complete stop at all times." • "Brake system requires excessive pedal force to achieve acceptable braking performance." • "Vehicle exhibits intermittent brake problems; hard to push." • "Excessive pressure required to push the brake pedal."

OLDSMOBILE CALAIS 1990

Complaint Severity: Typical. **Recall Alert:** See Recall Index. **Buyer's Summary:** Check the brakes—listen for noise, look for leaks and feel for vibration. They may fail, perform poorly or require frequent mechanical attention. See "Sudden Accelerations" in Introduction.

Hot Spots and Owner/NHTSA Comments:

1. Fuel: throttle linkages and control, sudden accelerations. • "Vehicle will surge and vibrate when in use." • "Shifted car into drive, suddenly it accelerated by itself and was totally out of control; jumped curb and crashed into wall." • "Sudden acceleration, causing injury." • "Vehicle suddenly accelerated forward when foot was removed from accelerator to slow down." • "Vehicle suddenly accelerated, hitting a wall."

2. Brakes: hydraulic system, noise, excessive wear. • "Brakes worn." • "Power brakes fail to effectively perform due to continuous grinding noise and chafing when applied. Brakes replaced 3 times." • "Grinding noise in brakes; smell of metal burning once in a while." • "Brakes sluggish, feels like it won't stop car."

OLDSMOBILE CIERA 1987

Complaint Severity: Typical. **Recall Alert:** See Recall Index. **Buyer's Summary:** The electronic control unit has been blamed for engine performance problems, including stalling and surging. The fuel injection system has been blamed for hesitation and stalling. Be sure the vehicle doesn't die in traffic or at stops. The steering may be stiff or not working correctly. Be sure to test the steering, especially on a cold start. Test the transmission thoroughly. See "Sudden Accelerations" in Introduction.

Hot Spots and Owner/NHTSA Comments:

1. Fuel: fuel injection system, stalling, hesitation. • "Fuel injection problem; car stalls, engine quit running without warning; loss of power steering and brakes." • "Fuel injection system faulty; car smokes and stalls; cleared clogged fuel injector, but stalling continues." • "Fuel injection problem, causing sudden acceleration and resulting in an accident; after putting into reverse, brakes did not stop acceleration." • "Fuel injector leak resulted in spraying gas onto the engine."

2. Fuel: throttle linkages and control, sudden accelerations. • "Sticking throttle; car runs up to 30 mph without stepping on gas." • "Accelerator jammed, causing car to exit driveway at high rate of speed; hit house across street, accelerated back, hit tree." • "While driving on highway, vehicle suddenly accelerated from 50 to 85 mph on its own." • "Upon putting gear into reverse, car went forward at high speed; sudden acceleration resulted in collision." • "Vehicle does not decelerate when foot removed from gas; very often must apply both feet on brake pedal to stop car."

3. Electrical system: ignition: electronic control unit, stalling, hesitation, sudden acceleration. • "Engine idles high, races, suddenly accelerates; bad programmable read-only memory; repaired/replaced programmable read-only memory, reset throttle position sensor, continues to accelerate out of control." • "While driving in high-speed lane, vehicle stalls out due to crankshaft sensor ignition module." • "Electronic control module defective, car loses power when slowing down." • "Engine stalled 6 times in 2-mile distance; car stopped dead accelerating up hill at 50-55 mph, repaired/replaced programmable read-only memory, manifold air pressure sensor and oxygen sensor." • "Recurring stalling and hesitation problem; repaired/replaced programmable read-only memory, pulsator, fuel sensor and pump; all repair attempts to no avail."

4. Power train: transmission: automatic, poor performance, difficulty shifting, slipping. • "Design flaw in transmission assembly; car would not move when weight on wheels; repaired/replaced transmission and converter." • "Transmission replaced at 13,000 miles." • "Automatic transmission jerks when downshift of transmission occurs." • "Transmission converter problem." • "Automatic transmission slips or jerks at times when starting off."

5. Electrical system: ignition, stalling, malfunction. • "While slowing down, car stalled, causing loss of power steering and brakes; car went into ditch, driver injured and another occupant killed." • "Vehicle stalled while going downhill; loss of brake and steering response resulted in accident; no injuries." • "Vehicle stalls, which causes loss of steering and brake controls." • "Engine stalls at high speed." • "Vehicle stalls intermittently, causing loss of control."

6. Steering: gear: rack-and-pinion, stiffness, poor performance. • "Power steering fluid began leaking; experienced difficulty with steering when engine cold; sticks and/or grabs." • "Problem with power steering binding; would not turn well first thing in the morning." • "Rack and pinion steering malfunctions in cold weather." • "Front end hard to steer when cold." • "When cold, power steering has flat spot; excessive fluid leak."

OLDSMOBILE CIERA 1988

Complaint Severity: Typical. **Recall Alert:** See Recall Index. **Buyer's Summary:** The fuel injection system has been blamed for hesitation and stalling. Be sure the vehicle doesn't die in traffic or at stops. Check the brakes—listen for noise, look for leaks and feel for vibration. They may fail, perform poorly or require frequent mechanical attention. Test the transmission thoroughly. See "Sudden Accelerations" in Introduction.

Hot Spots and Owner/NHTSA Comments:

1. Brakes: hydraulic system, vibration, excessive wear. • "Brakes pulsate; repaired at 10,000 miles; pulsating again at 21,000 miles." • "Brakes squeak; dealer claims nothing wrong." • "Car lurches back and forth when stopping; rotors warped." • "Recurring loss of braking power, despite replacement of front rotors and power assist unit." • "Brakes repaired."

2. Fuel: fuel injection system, stalling, hesitation. • "Car stalls and hesitates; condition started at 6,000 miles; 2 repairs attempted, at 11,000 miles and 13,000 miles, still experiencing problem." • "Engine stops while driving and will not restart; cause of problem unknown." • "Vehicle stalls in traffic without warning, which causes loss of steering and braking power; failed to locate problem." • "Intermittent stalling."

3. Electrical system: ignition, stalling, malfunction. • "Engine stalled and brakes grabbed; replaced electronic control module." • "Ignition switch replacement led to electrical short, which was repaired without charge." • "Vehicle has a tendency to stall. Failure occurs intermittently to constantly." • "Vehicle stalls while driving at 55 mph; causes loss of control."

4. Fuel: throttle linkages and control, sudden accelerations. • "Once reverse gear engaged, car suddenly accelerated backward, striking parked vehicles." • "Accident resulted from unintended sudden acceleration." • "Car takes off when cold and placed in reverse, idles rough." • "Car suddenly accelerates in drive or reverse; driver lost control; minor accident resulted." • "The accelerator stuck, causing sudden acceleration and resulting in loss of control and an accident."

5. Power train: transmission: automatic, poor performance, difficulty shifting, slipping. • "Transmission overhauled." • "Problem with automatic transmission since beginning." • "Car has no hill hold; when parked on hill, must hold foot brake and begin to give gas, or car drifts immediately when changing directions." • "Transmission goes into freewheeling and difficult to stop." • "Gear shift into reverse makes a horrible noise like it is going to fall apart."

6. Brakes: hydraulic: disc: rotor: disc hub, pulling, vibration. • "Rotors are warped from heat; jerking effect when braking." • "Defective or substandard brake rotors; pulsating brake pedal; car actually shakes while at stop." • "Brakes defective; chatter, slip;

problem with rotors." • "Front disc brakes rotors warped, causing uneven braking." • "Brake rotors have soft spots when applying the brakes, causing vehicle to jerk forward and pull to the right."

OLDSMOBILE CIERA 1989

Complaint Severity: Minor. **Recall Alert:** See Recall Index. **Buyer's Summary:** The electronic control unit has been blamed for engine performance problems, including stalling and surging. The fuel injection system has been blamed for hesitation and stalling. Be sure the vehicle doesn't die in traffic or at stops. Check the brakes—listen for noise, look for leaks and feel for vibration. They may fail, perform poorly or require frequent mechanical attention. Test the transmission thoroughly. See "Sudden Accelerations" in Introduction.

Hot Spots and Owner/NHTSA Comments:

1. Brakes: hydraulic system, noise, vibration. • "Master cylinder failed." • "Defect in braking system; brakes squeal from time to time." • "Repeated brake problems; brakes too small." • "Pulsating brakes; turned rotors." • "Pulsating brakes."

2. Fuel: throttle linkages and control, sudden accelerations. • "Turned ignition switch on, car suddenly accelerated; when stopped, found shift selector engaged in park position." • "Car at idle in park; when placed in reverse, car accelerated; it took very heavy braking to stop it in 15 feet." • "Irregular idle rpm causing a surge, which moves car unexpectedly if brakes not firmly engaged." • "After starting and putting car into reverse, car suddenly accelerated; brakes didn't work." • "Car was in drive and accelerated out of control. Stopped car by turning ignition off."

3. Electrical system: ignition, stalling, malfunction. • "Vehicle stalls out with no warning while driving." • "Defect in ignition system; fails to start." • "Engine stalling problems while traveling in heavy, slow traffic and when slowing to make turns." • "Intermittent stalling in traffic, resulting from defective ignition module." • "Computer inoperative during wet weather."

4. Electrical system: ignition: electronic control unit, stalling, malfunction. • "Vehicle stalls continuously while driving, even when warm; replaced programmable read-only memory." • "Computer equipment to spark went out; repaired." • "Driving out of driveway at a slow speed, vehicle stopped dead." • "Car loses total power and there is total loss of brakes." • "Replaced shorted ignition module for no start problem."

5. Fuel: fuel injection system, stalling, hesitation. • "Recurring fuel injector failure causes stalling; as soon as foot touches accelerator, the engine dies; loss of power steering and brakes; repaired/replaced fuel injector." • "Engine stalling problems in A.M. when cold; also, engine races sometimes." • "Car stalled out while in motion; repaired/replaced crank sensor and serpentine belt to no avail." • "Fuel injector cracked; repaired." • "Intermittent stalling."

6. Power train: transmission: automatic, poor performance, difficulty shifting, slipping. • "Transmission problems; car burned up; total loss." • "Transmission out after 178 miles." • "Car lost power; transmission replaced." • "Problem with automatic transmission." • "Premature and repeated transmission failure at 7,000 and 23,000 miles."

OLDSMOBILE CIERA 1990

Complaint Severity: Typical. **Recall Alert:** See Recall Index. **Buyer's Summary:** The fuel injection system has been blamed for hesitation and stalling. Be sure the vehicle doesn't die in traffic or at stops. Check the brakes—listen for noise, look for leaks and feel for vibration. They may fail, perform poorly or require frequent mechanical attention. Test the transmission thoroughly. Make sure seat belts function correctly and fit comfortably. See "Sudden Accelerations" in Introduction.

Hot Spots and Owner/NHTSA Comments:

1. Brakes: hydraulic system, noise, pulling, locking up. • "Brakes noisy and pull to right." • "While braking, vehicle will pull to left side and sometimes to right." • "Brakes lock up and are overheating." • "Repeated front brake chatter; repaired/replaced." • "Pulsating brakes."

2. Fuel: throttle linkages and control, sudden accelerations. • "While shifting gear into drive, vehicle suddenly accelerated; went out of control, resulting in an accident." • "Car surged forward at high rate of speed." • "Vehicle suddenly accelerated out of control, resulting in an accident and injury." • "Car suddenly accelerated in reverse gear and hit another vehicle." • "Vehicle suddenly accelerated to speeds of 40-50 mph while in reverse; vehicle crashed into a tree."

3. Power train: transmission: automatic, poor performance, difficulty shifting, slipping. • "Transmission failure at 10,000 miles." • "Transmission downshifts roughly." • "When key was out of ignition, vehicle rolled out of park into reverse, resulting in accident." • "Slippage in transmission from low to high." • "Transmission problem."

4. Fuel: fuel injection system, stalling, hesitation. • "Intermittent stalling." • "Noisy during acceleration." • "Vehicle went off road, hit a tree and immediately caught fire, causing death." • "Intake manifold gasket defective; caused engine leakage."

5. Interior systems: active seat and shoulder belts and belt anchor, malfunction, failure. • "Seat belt attached to the pillar; when turning, obstructs visibility of passenger-side window." • "Seat belts and shoulder harness attached to door." • "Seat belts failed during accident." • "During a frontal collision at approximately 35 mph, driver's and two passenger's lap and shoulder belts were inoperative."

6. Interior systems: passive restraint: belts, uncomfortable, poor performance. • "Design of automatic passive seat belt not adequate to protect passenger; if accident occurs and door flings open, passenger will be thrown out with belt on." • "Front seat belts (shoulder part) are uncomfortable; belts fit too close to neck." • "Seat belts attached to front door, blocks driver's view for over left shoulder viewing of oncoming cars."

OLDSMOBILE CIERA 1991

Complaint Severity: Typical. **Recall Alert:** See Recall Index. **Buyer's Summary:** Make sure seat belts function correctly and fit comfortably.

Hot Spots and Owner/NHTSA Comments:

1. Interior systems: passive restraint: belts, uncomfortable, poor performance. • "Poorly designed seat belts hit across driver's neck while driving, causing an uncomfortable fit." • "Door-mounted seat belts fit poorly on short drivers." • "Shoulder belts scrape neck."

OLDSMOBILE CUTLASS 1987

Complaint Severity: Typical. **Theft Alert:** 2. **Recall Alert:** See Recall Index. **Buyer's Summary:** Verify that the cruise control system works properly, and that it doesn't cause the engine to surge. The electronic control unit has been blamed for engine performance problems, including stalling and surging. The fuel injection system has been blamed for hesitation and stalling. Be sure the vehicle doesn't die in traffic or at stops. Check the brakes—listen for noise, look for leaks and feel for vibration. They may fail, perform poorly or require frequent mechanical attention. See "Sudden Accelerations" in Introduction.

Hot Spots and Owner/NHTSA Comments:

1. Fuel: throttle linkages and control, sudden accelerations. • "Vehicle in park position; turned on ignition; engine accelerated; lurched backward at high speed; no warning." • "After purchasing car, driver experienced sudden acceleration when braking; occurs at various speeds; near-accidents as a result." • "Engine suddenly accelerated after putting vehicle in gear with foot on brake." • "Vehicle suddenly accelerated out of control." • "Constant racing of engine after lifting foot from accelerator caused accident."

2. Brakes: hydraulic system, locking up, poor performance. • "Braking very erratic; first applied car does slow appreciably; pressure applied, brakes grab suddenly, leading to very uneven stopping." • "Excessive foot pedal pressure necessary to obtain braking power for near-normal response." • "Car drifts left when braking; replaced rotors, pads, calipers, master cylinder and proportion valve; still drifts." • "Brakes pulsating; rotor badly warped; pedal squeaking when pushed; clunk coming from rear end when brakes applied." • "Brakes locked up and vehicle lost control."

3. Electrical system: ignition: electronic control unit, stalling, malfunction, failure. • "Computer-related parts repaired/replaced, car dies while driving at low speeds, engine light comes on after driven; cannot restart until after sitting 3-5 minutes." • "Computer malfunction; car idle irregular; excessive engine vibrations; hesitation; acceleration; problems starting in morning." • "Stalling and high idle problems; electronic control module replaced 4 times." • "Electronic control module unit failed, causing erratic engine rpm."

4. Fuel: fuel injection system, stalling, hesitation. • "Vehicle stalls endlessly; cuts out while driving; problem with fuel injection system." • "Engine stalls unpredictably after short periods of surges; first time at 558 miles, 12,623 and 36,022 miles." • "Problem with fuel injection system; bad fast-idle condition; after cold start can drive car without touching gas pedal." • "When first started in morning, engine stalls out; cleaned injectors and throttle plate, adjusted throttle position sensor." • "Vehicle will stop completely at random for no reason; without warning, all power would suddenly cease."

5. Equipment: speed control, malfunction, failure. • "Recall on cruise control; working properly before recall repairs made; now, after repairs, inoperative." • "Cruise control erratic; jumps up and down; causes engine to pick up speed." • "Cruise control engages by itself." • "While driving with cruise control set, vehicle suddenly accelerates." • "Cruise control engaged and disengaged without warning on its own; engine runs rough; replaced cruise module."

6. Engine: noise, premature failure. • "Loss of oil pressure." • "At 30,000 miles vehicle needs a new engine." • "Engine noise when idling in drive." • "Engine problem; coolant and oil leaks." • "Knock, clattering and rattling noise inside engine at all times."

OLDSMOBILE CUTLASS 1988

Complaint Severity: Typical. **Recall Alert:** See Recall Index. **Buyer's Summary:** Verify that the cruise control system works properly, and that it doesn't cause the engine to surge. The electronic control unit has been blamed for engine performance problems, including stalling and surging. Check the brakes—listen for noise, look for leaks and feel for vibration. They may fail, perform poorly or require frequent mechanical attention. See "Sudden Accelerations" in Introduction.

Hot Spots and Owner/NHTSA Comments:

1. Brakes: hydraulic: shoe: disc brake system, vibration, corrosion, poor performance. • "Front brakes constantly shimmied; resulted in vehicle swaying all over the road; currently vehicle is parked in the garage." • "Front brake rotors were out of round, and pads came loose from metal backing and fell off; attempt to have dealer take care of problem fruitless." • "Hesitation and noise when brakes are applied due to defective pads and rotors; repaired/replaced, problem reoccurred." • "Corroded disc brakes, causing lack of brake reduction when applied. Previously repaired." • "Rear disc brakes lock up; replaced left rear brake pad and rotor 5 times."

2. Brakes: hydraulic system, malfunction, failure. • "Intermittent braking; when occurs, feel booster engage, brake pedal becomes hard and doesn't respond to additional pressure on pedal, which resulted in accident." • "Complete brake system failed at less than 12,000 miles." • "Brakes fail to stop vehicle effectively, causing extended or inoperative braking when applied." • "Parking emergency brake mechanism will not hold. Brakes fail to stop vehicle effectively, causing extended stopping; inoperative when applied."

3. Fuel: throttle linkages and control, sudden accelerations. • "Car occasionally surges forward, with foot on brakes, when stopped at light or parking." • "Put car into drive, accelerated on its own at very high speed with no vehicle control; previously, numerous engine stalling problems, which have not been resolved." • "Upon shifting transmission into proper gear, vehicle suddenly accelerated, went out of control and caused an accident." • "Upon shifting gear into reverse, vehicle accelerated at high speed, went out of control and caused an accident." • "Upon accelerating from standstill at traffic light, suspension in front right failed; vehicle lost steering control, jumped a curb and hit a utility pole."

4. Equipment: speed control, malfunction, poor performance. • "Cruise control stuck at 65 mph. Would not disengage with brakes, cruise off. Released after reducing to 20 mph. Could have caused an accident." • "On several occasions, accelerator suddenly receded away from foot, causing car to speed up and lunge forward; defect seems to be in cruise control." • "Occasionally when cruise control resumed, car exceeded previously set speed of 50-65 mph, approaching 90 mph; braked to slow down speed." • "Cruise control can't maintain appropriate speed."

5. Electrical system: ignition: electronic control unit, stalling, sudden acceleration. • "Broken ground circuit wire from computer caused uncontrollable acceleration when gears put into drive or reverse; resulted in accident." • "Engine stalls and cuts off while driving." • "Intermittent stalling from 45 mph; still stalls after new throttle position sensor, connectors and fan relays." • "Electrical and/or computer failure; car quit running; no warning signs; when it quit it would not start again for undetermined amount of time." • "Oil pressure gauge showed zero oil pressure when engine running; repaired/replaced computer chip; also, engine stalling problem."

6. Brakes: hydraulic: disc: rotor: disc hub, corrosion, poor performance. • "Rear disc brake and rotors; corrosion." • "Corroded rear disc brakes; rusted rotors in the rear; parking brake is frozen." • "Had 2 brake jobs done on antilock brake system because of corroded rear discs and rotors." • "Rotors corroded, calipers fractured; loss of brake fluid." • "Continual brake problems; warping of rotors."

OLDSMOBILE CUTLASS 1989

Complaint Severity: Negligible. **Recall Alert:** See Recall Index. **Buyer's Summary:** Verify that the cruise control system works properly, and that it doesn't cause the engine to surge. The electronic control unit has been blamed for engine performance problems, including stalling and surging. The fuel injection system has been blamed for hesitation and stalling. Be sure the vehicle doesn't die in traffic or at stops. Check the brakes—listen for noise, look for leaks and feel for vibration. They may fail, perform poorly or require frequent mechanical attention. Test the transmission thoroughly.

Hot Spots and Owner/NHTSA Comments:

1. Electrical system: ignition: electronic control unit, stalling, sudden acceleration. • "When decelerating, lost power completely because of computer chip failure." • "Defective computer caused sudden uncontrollable acceleration; turned off ignition to stop; repaired computer to the odometer." • "On freeway, engine stalls due to failure of ignition module." • "Electronic control module failed; caused vehicle to completely stall." • "While going 55-60 mph, vehicle suddenly stopped dead due to malfunctioning of the electronic control module."

2. Power train: transmission: automatic, poor performance, difficulty shifting, slipping. • "Vehicle jerks when shifting; fluid leaking." • "Transmission seals leaking." • "Automatic transmission 3rd gear failed, could only be driven in 2nd gear." • "Automatic transmission leaked oil; replaced filter adapter and gallery plugs." • "Between 25 and 35 mph, transmission downshifted roughly and/or hesitantly."

3. Equipment: speed control, sudden acceleration, failure. • "Sudden acceleration when applying brake when cruise control is on." • "Cruise control fails to disengage when brake applied." • "Due to faulty cruise control switch, engine intermittently surges." • "Use of cruise control below freezing temperatures causes vehicle to accelerate, causing loss of control." • "Cruise control would not maintain set speed; it gradually accelerates."

4. Brakes: hydraulic system, failure. • "Experiencing brake problems; difficult to press brake pedal to stop vehicle." • "Brakes become inoperative because bolts holding the calipers are too large for the holes; 1 set of pads is down to the metal, other set does not fit." • "Brake failure resulted in an accident." • "Poor braking; replaced, problem continues."

5. Fuel: fuel injection system, stalling, hesitation. • "Vehicle experiencing stalling problems at 65 mph or over." • "Stalling problems after fuel feed hose assembly recall repairs." • "Car stalling when stopped or just decelerating during the morning or after car sits for 45 minutes; also power steering lost, making control difficult." • "At 50-55 mph, car would stall; lose control of steering; keep foot on gas pedal (at stop) for it not to stall." • "Engine stalling at freeway speed of 55 mph while decelerating to go off ramp; occurred 3 times; adjustment made by dealer, condition worsened." • "Vehicle skipping; not getting enough gas." • "Defective fuel injection system." • "Engine stalls out; sometimes it dies out."

6. Electrical system: ignition, stalling, malfunction. • "Vehicle started sputtering like it would turn over, but would not start. Vehicle stalled in middle of road. There was also no speedometer or odometer reading." • "Engine stalling problem; stalls intermittently and without warning while car in motion; numerous repairs made but unable to solve problem." • "When approaching stop sign or signal, vehicle shakes, vibrates and/or stalls, won't accelerate; stuck at 25-30 mph; repaired/replaced computer and electronic module."

OLDSMOBILE CUTLASS 1990

Complaint Severity: Typical. **Recall Alert:** See Recall Index. **Buyer's Summary:** Check the brakes—listen for noise, look for leaks and feel for vibration. They may fail, perform poorly or require frequent mechanical attention. See "Sudden Accelerations" in Introduction.

Hot Spots and Owner/NHTSA Comments:

1. Brakes: hydraulic: shoe: disc brake system, corrosion, poor performance. • "Parking brake engaged, caliper stuck consistently; resulted in brake pads overheating." • "Four-wheel disc brakes, failure of wheel cylinder; will not release, causing pads to wear and causing damage to rotors." • "Experience long stopping distance; replaced pad 5 times, and 1 set of rotors on front brake system." • "Corroded disc brakes cause lack of brake reduction when applied." • "The rear disc brakes are completely corroded and do not work at all."

2. Fuel: throttle linkages and control, sudden accelerations. • "Upon shifting from park to drive, vehicle suddenly accelerated, crashing into 3 other vehicles." • "When shifting the vehicle into reverse, the vehicle unexpectedly accelerated rearward." • "Backing out of garage, sudden surge of power from motor; applied brakes, car kept going, resulting in accident." • "Upon starting up, vehicle accelerated on its own." • "Upon shifting gear into reverse, vehicle suddenly accelerated out of control; resulted in an accident."

3. Brakes: hydraulic system, locking up, failure. • "Brakes lock when pressure applied to pedal." • "Brakes failed to stop vehicle effectively when applied, causing extended stopping or becoming inoperative. Repaired 5 times." • "Brake pedal has caused 2 accidents because brakes go to the floor." • "Lost all brake capacity at one time; on several occasions, brakes smoked; certain times, seem to grab and/or pull; changed twice due to rust and corrosion." • "Continuous brake failure, with pedal fading."

4. Brakes: hydraulic: disc: caliper, locking up, corrosion, failure. • "The calipers keep freezing up on the back disc brakes." • "Poor braking ability; disc brake pad ate into rotor because pin housing would not slide back and forth; rusted inside, causing pad to rest on rotor." • "Corroded rear disc brakes; rusted caliper pin." • "Brake failure; rear corrosion of calipers and slide rail" • "Rear calipers rusted and/or corroded; calipers become fixed in one position; emergency brakes inoperative; extended stopping; rely on front brakes."

5. Brakes: hydraulic: disc: rotor: disc hub, vibration, excessive wear. • "Front brake discs warped; had difficult time controlling vehicle." • "Antilock brake system: Rear rotors have been replaced twice, turned down twice due to rust and/or corrosion." • "The front and rear rotor and caliper need to be replaced; dealer says to keep pumping the brake every time." • "Warped front disc rotors caused front brakes to vibrate." • "Repaired/replaced front brake rotors and pads 3 times."

6. Brakes: hydraulic: anti-skid system, poor performance, failure, locking up. • "Antilock brake system: Occasionally, complete brake failure when antilock brakes activate; warning light comes on occasionally." • "Antilock brakes failed, causing accident and injury." • "The antilock brake system didn't work, causing an accident." • "Upon touching the brake pedal 3 times lightly but not hard enough to activate the brake, the antilock braking system activated."

OLDSMOBILE CUTLASS 1991

Complaint Severity: Typical. **Recall Alert:** See Recall Index. **Buyer's Summary:** Look carefully for any kind of leakage, especially under the car. Make sure the shoulder belts don't cut across your neck and are well anchored. Check the brakes—listen for noise, look for leaks and feel for vibration. They may fail, perform poorly or require frequent mechanical attention. Test the transmission thoroughly. See "Sudden Accelerations" in Introduction.

Hot Spots and Owner/NHTSA Comments:

1. Brakes: hydraulic system, leaks, failure. • "Smoke coming from rear; brake fluid leaking, causing brake failure." • "Brake failure. Frontal collision. Impact 12:00 position." • "Complete loss of brake effectiveness when applying brakes." • "Applied brakes while slowing down; brakes failed without warning; stiff and firm." • "When coming to a stop, brakes are ineffective; must apply both feet on pedal sometimes to bring vehicle to a halt." • "Faulty brake accumulator caused brake failure."

2. Brakes: hydraulic: shoe: disc brake system, noise, premature failure. • "Antilock brake system failure; replaced pads, rotors, and calipers; experience lockup of brakes." • "Brakes will drag or severe noise when applied." • "The front brake had to be replaced; the third time, wore out at 15,000 miles." • "Four-wheel disc brakes; loss of brake effectiveness; rear brakes failed, had to use emergency brake." • "Brakes failed on 4-wheel discs; rear calipers froze and front faded when brake fluid boiled."

3. Fuel: throttle linkages and control, sudden accelerations. • "Throttle valve malfunctioned, caused engine runaway; repaired." • "While driving at 25 mph, vehicle suddenly accelerated; lost control and skidded; struck side of phone pole and rolled over on side of driveway." • "Vehicle surged forward out of control; resulted in an accident." • "While driving at 65 mph, transmission jumped out of gear and vehicle suddenly accelerated." • "Accelerator failure; when slowing down to make a turn, experienced pedal fading. Impact 12:00 position hitting a building. Speed unknown."

4. Power train: transmission: automatic, poor performance, difficulty shifting, slipping. • "Vehicle in reverse; surged forward twice before going into reverse." • "Transmission failed." • "Transmission fails to engage when first put into gear; repeated attempts resulted in sudden acceleration." • "Transmission jumped out of gear, causing accident and injury."

5. Brakes: hydraulic: anti-skid system, poor performance, failure, locking up. • "Brakes fade; antilock brake system malfunctioned." • "Brake light comes on intermittently. Brake pedal had to be pumped by driver in order to get antilock brake system to respond." • "Antilock brakes failed." • "Antilock brake system: When applying the brakes, pedal faded, causing the vehicle to rear-end another vehicle at impact 12:00 position."

6. Interior systems: shoulder belts, uncomfortable, failure. • "Front seat belts failed during accident." • "Vehicle equipped with door-mounted shoulder and seat belt failed to retain occupant. Door flew open and driver fell out." • "Seat belt cuts across the neck instead of across the shoulder." • "Driver's- and passenger-side seat belts have too much slack, preventing proper retainment of passenger in event of an accident." • "Shoulder belt fits poorly."

OLDSMOBILE CUTLASS 1992

Complaint Severity: Serious. **Recall Alert:** See Recall Index. **Buyer's Summary:** Make sure the shoulder belts don't cut across your neck and are well anchored. Check the brakes—listen for noise, look for leaks and feel for vibration. They may fail, perform poorly or require frequent mechanical attention. See "Sudden Accelerations" in Introduction.

Hot Spots and Owner/NHTSA Comments:

1. Brakes: hydraulic system, locking up, failure. • "Brake pedal failed when applying brakes. To stop vehicle, pulled off highway." • "Rear brakes locked on first occasion. Dealer replaced parts. Next problem was a lockup of the front brakes, which caused a skid off the road from 50 mph." • "Consumer was driving, tried to stop and car wouldn't stop; caused to rear-end the car in front." • "During stop, experienced brake failure; pedal went to floor and vehicle continued to roll forward; no prior warning."

2. Fuel: throttle linkages and control, sudden accelerations. • "Sudden acceleration, causing loss of control, accident and injuries." • "Backing out of driveway, vehicle suddenly accelerated with high idle, hitting vehicle, impact 6:00 position." • "While parking, placed gear into reverse position, vehicle lunged forward, without prior warning, hitting another vehicle." • "While driving at 25 mph, proceeded to stop with foot on the brakes when vehicle suddenly accelerated; swerved to the right and hit car in front." • "Vehicle was parked, went into drive; vehicle went open-throttle position, lost control; impact 12:00 position, speed unknown."

3. Brakes: hydraulic: anti-skid system, poor performance, failure, locking up. • "Antilock brake system not working." • "Faulty antilock brake system." • "Antilock brakes faded out, causing accident." • "Antilock brake system brake pedal traveled to the floor; caused loss of braking ability; no prior warning." • "Antilock brake system failed on wet pavement, resulting in loss of control and an accident."

4. Brakes: hydraulic: disc: pads and shoes, excessive wear, failure. • "Brake pads are wearing excessively quickly." • "Braking system failure; front brake pads are wearing excessively." • "Front brakes need pads." • "Brake failure; front disc pads and rotors replaced every 7,000 miles." • "Brakes failed due to worn brake pads."

5. Interior systems: shoulder belts, uncomfortable, poor performance. • "Poor fit on shoulder belts." • "Shoulder belt attached to door creates blind spot." • "Shoulder belt does not fit properly; when hooked up, it lies right across the passenger's face." • "Shoulder belts come across lower face and neck." • "Shoulder harness is too high for a smaller person."

6. Brakes: hydraulic: shoe: disc brake system, locking up, failure. • "Experienced pedal fading. Replaced disc pads and rotors; uneven wear in front brakes; front end shakes." • "Rear disc brakes do not work; front brakes lock up on ice or slippery conditions, causing vehicle to skid." • "Frontal collision, impact 12:00 position, speed 50 mph; experienced loss of front brake effectiveness." • "Replaced front brakes."

OLDSMOBILE CUTLASS 1993

Complaint Severity: Typical. **Recall Alert:** See Recall Index. **Buyer's Summary:** Carefully check the brakes—listen for noise, look for leaks and feel for vibration. They may fail, perform poorly or require frequent mechanical attention. See "Sudden Accelerations" in Introduction.

Hot Spots and Owner/NHTSA Comments:

1. Brakes: hydraulic system, vibration, failure. • "When owner applies brakes, there is a hard rubbing sound, squeaking and vibration. When bright lights and turn signal are on, brights won't dim." • "Brakes are very loud and pedal goes all the way to the floor." • "Brakes have failed on car 4 times. Engine died 3 times. Last time, lost brakes and hit house." • "Brake system failure; when making a sudden stop, experience pedal fading."

2. Brakes: hydraulic: shoe: disc brake system, vibration, poor performance, failure. • "When applying disc brakes, pedal goes to the floor." • "Antilock brake system: When applying brakes, experience a vibration in front end of vehicle; repaired vehicle 3 times." • "Brake failure; in cold start, experience loss of brake effectiveness; pedal goes completey to floor; repaired master cylinder, pads and rotors, and calipers." • "Front brakes operate poorly." • "Leased vehicle only stops with front pads. Back brakes don't engage when applied. Vehicle has 4-wheel disc brakes."

3. Brakes: hydraulic: anti-skid system, poor performance, failure, locking up. • "Antilock brake system light came on and brakes dragged." • "Antilock brake system failure; replaced the entire antilock brake system." • "At or below 30 mph, antilock brakes malfunctioned and caused 4-wheel lock-up to occur. Resulted in accident." • "Antilock brake system makes grinding noise when applying brakes; had complete brake lock-up while driving, losing control; skidded and rolled over, impact 3:00 position, speed 50 mph."

4. Fuel: throttle linkages and control, sudden accelerations. • "Started vehicle, while in park, vehicle accelerated in reverse and crashed." • "Placed car in reverse with foot on brake, and car accelerated on its own. Idle air control was installed." • "Vehicle went open-throttle position while driving. To stop vehicle, turned ignition off." • "On several occasions, vehicle accelerates unwantedly with excessive engine idle speed. Stopping power of brakes reduced to minimum."

OLDSMOBILE CUTLASS 1994

Complaint Severity: Minor. **Recall Alert:** See Recall Index. **Buyer's Summary:** The airbags in this vehicle have experienced failures and malfunctions: You may need a professional evaluation on the condition of the airbags. Check the brakes—listen for noise, look for leaks and feel for vibration. They may fail, perform poorly or require frequent mechanical attention.

Hot Spots and Owner/NHTSA Comments:

1. Brakes: hydraulic: anti-skid system, poor performance, failure, locking up. • "Rear antilock brakes replaced due to grabbing; antilock brake system light coming on." • "The brakes give and catch when being applied. They are antilock brakes." • "Antilock brake system failed when applied; pedal went to the floor; also, antilock brake system warning light stayed on." • "Intermittent antilock brake system failure; also, pedal faded."

2. Equipment: electric power accessories: locks: door, malfunction, failure. • "Power door lock switch failed, prior to manufacturer's recall." • "Power door locks failed." • "Water contacted power door relay, causing failure; prior to recall." • "Rear electrical door locks intermittently lock up, locking passenger inside vehicle."

3. Interior systems: passive restraint: airbag: driver, malfunction, failure. • "Driver hit vehicle head-on and airbag did not deploy, resulting in an injury." • "Upon impact, during front crash at approximately 25 mph, 10:00 position on front bumper, airbag failed to deploy." • "During front-end collision at 40 mph, airbag did not deploy, causing minor injuries to driver." • "Frontal collision, impact 12:00 position, speed 25 mph, airbag did not deploy."

Plymouth—Cars

PLYMOUTH ACCLAIM 1989

Complaint Severity: Typical. **Recall Alert:** See Recall Index. **Buyer's Summary:** Look carefully for any kind of leakage, especially under the car. The engine has experienced a variety of problems. Have it examined by a professional. Check the brakes—listen for noise, look for leaks and feel for vibration. They may fail, perform poorly or require frequent mechanical attention. Test the transmission thoroughly.

Hot Spots and Owner/NHTSA Comments:

1. Engine: gaskets: valve cover, leaks, fire. • "Valve cover gasket was leaking; problem was corrected by dealer, but was never notified by the manufacturer of any defect or recall." • "Engine compartment fire caused by faulty valve cover gasket." • "Valve cover gasket has been leaking; dealer tried to fix it, but did not solve problem." • "Engine valve cap or cover; factory recall because of danger of fire." • "Defective valve cover gasket; repaired/replaced several times."

2. Power train: transmission: automatic, poor performance, difficulty shifting, slipping. • "Automatic transmission; premature failure, vehicle only 3 months old." • "While driving, transmission ceased to function; rebuilt new transmission." • "Whistling noise coming from engine after driving at 60-65 mph; growling or chunking sound when shifting to reverse or overdrive before transmission moves car." • "Transmission jerks when shifting." • "Transmission does not downshift. Blown seal, with disc slipping."

3. Brakes: hydraulic system, malfunction, failure. • "Brakes malfunctioned 6 times and were replaced each time." • "Vehicle experienced a brake problem; dealer replaced master cylinder and vacuum booster, but brake problem persisted." • "Total brake failure resulted when brakes were applied." • "While driving, brakes failed completely; could not stop car, hit guardrail."

4. Brakes: hydraulic: master cylinder, leaks, failure. • "Defective master cylinder caused brake failure, which resulted in an accident." • "Internal leak in master cylinder causes brakes to quit working; brakes got soft and went to floor; skidded, hitting car in the rear end." • "Master cylinder failed with pedal going to the floor. Driver used emergency brake to stop. Replaced master cylinder and failure reoccurred. • "Master cylinder failed, causing an accident."

5. Engine: miscellaneous problems. • "Loss of engine oil: engine replaced." • "Vehicle experienced an engine fire from unknown source." • "Engine makes noise; dealer indicated it was a defective crankshaft." • "Valve failed."

PLYMOUTH ACCLAIM 1990

Complaint Severity: Troublesome. **Recall Alert:** See Recall Index. **Buyer's Summary:** The fuel injection system has been blamed for hesitation and stalling. Be sure the vehicle doesn't die in traffic or at stops. The airbags in this vehicle have experienced failures and malfunctions: You may need a professional evaluation on the condition of the airbags. Test the transmission thoroughly.

Hot Spots and Owner/NHTSA Comments:

1. Power train: transmission: automatic, poor performance, difficulty shifting, slipping. • "Transmission slips when shifting, or bangs into another gear periodically while driving." • "Four-speed automatic transmission fails to come out of 1st gear due to design flaw of new transmission; replacement transmission also shifts gears when car standing still." • "Problem with transmission controller; repaired/replaced." • "Transmission goes into 2nd gear from different gears; delays from reverse to drive; overhauled 3 times." • "Transmission jumps into neutral when stopped and slips out of gear."

2. Interior systems: passive restraint: airbag: driver, malfunction, failure. • "During an accident, impact at 12:00 position, speed 20 mph, airbag did not deploy." • "Vehicle was at a complete stop waiting for lights to change, airbag deployed without an impact; white smoke filled car and driver sustained burns to arms." • "Upon impact with a deer at approximately 30-35 mph, frontal crash, airbag deployed and emitted a smoke smell; powdery substance caused burns to wrist." • "Frontal collision. Impact 12:00 position. Speed 15 mph. Airbag deployed, but never inflated." • "While driving down street, airbag exploded, burning driver's face and hands."

3. Engine: gaskets: valve cover, leaks. • "Valve cover gasket leak; prior to recall." • "Defective value cover gasket leaks oil onto exhaust manifold. Potential risk of fire." • "Engine valve cover gasket dislocates, causing oil to leak and creating risk of potential fire." • "Recall; valve cover gasket." • "Oil leak from head gasket; repaired/replaced."

4. Electrical system: ignition, stalling, malfunction. • "While car was parked, ignition wiring burned in car." • "Experiencing

difficulty turning ignition system on or off; new ignition system slightly better." • "Vehicle stalls constantly, causing loss of control." • "Vehicle had a surge problem that was fixed by the dealer; now there is stalling that cannot be fixed."
5. Interior systems: passive restraint: airbag, malfunction, failure. • "Weak plastic airbag retainer clip, causing airbag module to become disconnected." • "Owner was driving down street and the vehicle's airbag deployed on its own." • "Airbag deployment in front-end collision caused severe hand burn." • "Premature airbag deployment upon low impact; deployed upon minor impact with parked car in parking garage at very low rate of speed (5-10 mph); injuries sustained." • "Vehicle went over a curb, airbag deployed but did not inflate; clothing was burned because of gases not being trapped."
6. Fuel: fuel injection system, stalling, hesitation. • "Fuel problems." • "While parking, vehicle suddenly accelerated and went out of control." • "Difficult to restart vehicle." • "Car died without any warning; could start, but once put in any gear, engine would jump, then stop again." • "Intermittent stalling and starting problems."

PLYMOUTH ACCLAIM 1991

Complaint Severity: Troublesome. **Recall Alert:** See Recall Index. **Buyer's Summary:** The airbags in this vehicle have experienced failures and malfunctions: You may need a professional evaluation on the condition of the airbags. Check the brakes—listen for noise, look for leaks and feel for vibration. They may fail, perform poorly or require frequent mechanical attention. Test the transmission thoroughly. See "Sudden Accelerations" in Introduction.

Hot Spots and Owner/NHTSA Comments:
1. Power train: transmission: automatic, poor performance, difficulty shifting, slipping. • "Without key in the ignition, transmission jumped out of gear; resulted in accident." • "Transmission would jump out of gear while starting or applying brakes." • "Vehicle was placed into park position with engine running; got out to wipe windshield, vehicle rolled out from driveway into yard in reverse position." • "Automatic transmission will downshift while traveling at highway speeds: ultradrive 4-speed." • "Transmission leaks, slips and won't change gears; also, gear selector broke."
2. Fuel: throttle linkages and control, sudden accelerations. • "Vehicle stops when owner is driving. Mechanic believes problem is the throttle body." • "While driving, vehicle accelerates by itself; have to put it in neutral, then park, to stop vehicle." • "Vehicle will surge or fast idle while driving at any speed." • "While idling in traffic at a stop sign and upon removing foot from the brake, vehicle suddenly accelerated to 55 mph." • "Stopped at an intersection and experienced intermittent engine surge; dealer cannot reproduce on computer."
3. Electrical system: ignition, stalling, failure. • "Engine intermittently cuts off during various types of driving conditions and speeds; no prior warning." • "Vehicle continually shuts down when driving on highway at 60 mph and over. Previously repaired." • "After warming up, engine stalls at 25 mph. Have a 2-minute delay before restart is possible." • "Ignition coil failure; replaced."
4. Interior systems: passive restraint: airbag: driver, malfunction, failure. • "Upon rear-ending a vehicle, the plastic casing around the airbag broke, but the airbag didn't deploy. Driver sustained cuts." • "Airbag deployment was violent during accident, resulting in burns to driver." • "Airbag partially deployed in a front-end collision at 40-50 mph into guardrail, causing minor injuries and burns to driver." • "Driver airbag deployed but did not inflate during an accident." • "Driver's-side airbag did not inflate properly during head-on collision, causing chemicals to spew into passenger compartment, burning driver."
5. Brakes: hydraulic system, locking up, failure. • "When brakes are cold, they take 3 or 4 times to work fully; once 3 or 4 applications have been made, brakes are very good to excellent in their response." • "Brake failure caused accident." • "Several brake failures and repairs after recall work done—2 near misses." • "Brake system failure." • "While driving during a rainstorm, applied brakes, the wheels locked up and vehicle skidded, striking the vehicle in front."
6. Interior systems: passive restraint: airbag, malfunction, failure. • "Airbag failed to deploy, impact at 11:00, speed 20 mph; driver was knocked unconscious and received head injuries." • "Airbag inflated without warning; caused accident." • "False deployment of driver's airbag resulted in injury." • "Airbag did not inflate during accident, causing injury." • "Brake pedal traveled to the floor. Caused complete loss of brake effectiveness. No prior warning. Resulting in accident. Airbag did not deploy. Impact 1:00 position."

PLYMOUTH ACCLAIM 1992

Complaint Severity: Very Serious. **Recall Alert:** See Recall Index. **Buyer's Summary:** The airbags in this vehicle have experienced failures and malfunctions: You may need a professional evaluation on the condition of the airbags. See "Sudden Accelerations" in Introduction.

Hot Spots and Owner/NHTSA Comments:
1. Interior systems: passive restraint: airbag: driver, malfunction, failure. • "Frontal collision. Impact 12:00 position. Airbag deployed at a speed of 8 mph." • "Vehicle was involved in a front-end collision and the airbag did not deploy." • "Airbag deployed when vehicle was involved in a minor accident, causing serious injuries to driver." • "While in park position with engine running, vehicle suddenly accelerated out of control, hitting 2 vehicles and then a building. Airbag failed to deploy." • "Had accident and the airbag did not deploy."
2. Electrical system: ignition, stalling, failure. • "While driving at highway speeds, experience intermittent sudden engine shutdown, rendering power steering and brake system inoperative; no warning." • "Stalled numerous times in traffic, and was almost rear-ended 4 times." • "Vehicle intermittently stalls out; prior to stalling, gives a chugging noise." • "Vehicle stalls without warning. Jerks real hard when coming to a stop."
3. Fuel: throttle linkages and control, sudden accelerations. • "While in park position with engine running, vehicle suddenly accelerated out of control, hitting 2 vehicles and then a building. Airbag failed to deploy." • "When pulling into parking space, vehicle accelerated out of control, jumping curb and hitting a wall. Airbag did deploy." • "While driving vehicle at low speed, vehicle will slow down and reaccelerate at high speed, causing loss of control; hitting curb; undercarriage damage."

PLYMOUTH ACCLAIM 1993

Complaint Severity: Serious. **Buyer's Summary:** The airbags in this vehicle have experienced failures and malfunctions: You may need a professional evaluation on the condition of the airbags. Check the brakes—listen for noise, look for leaks and feel for vibration. They may fail, perform poorly or require frequent mechanical attention.

Hot Spots and Owner/NHTSA Comments:
1. Electrical system: ignition, stalling. • "Engine and fuel components were replaced with no correction for stalling; cause of failure unknown." • "Vehicle stalls out while driving at any speed; dealer cannot find problem." • "Was driving over speed bump and

the car cut off; when this happens, have to wait 10 minutes before car will come on; this happens when it rains or is damp." • "Vehicle will stall at any time with no warning. Computers changed with same result. Dealer doesn't know what causes this."

2. Interior systems: passive restraint: airbag: driver, malfunction, failure. • "Airbag did not deploy; seat belts did not hold driver." • "Riding over bump in road, bottom scraped road; triggered airbag, and steering column bent." • "Brakes failed to stop vehicle when applied, caused extended stopping and rear-end collision at 35 mph. Also, airbag deployed." • "In accident, going 55 mph at 11:00 position, driver's-side airbag did not deploy." • "Airbag deployed during a 25-mph crash; caused more driver injuries than the crash itself."

3. Brakes: hydraulic: anti-skid system, poor performance, failure, locking up. • "Antilock brakes lock up intermittently." • "Brakes require extra effort before they will work." • "In a frontal collision, driver's-side airbag did not deploy; brakes would not stop vehicle; no antilock brake system." • "Fleet: Antilock brake failure due to Bendix module."

PLYMOUTH COLT 1987

Complaint Severity: Typical. **Recall Alert:** See Recall Index. **Buyer's Summary:** Check the brakes—listen for noise, look for leaks and feel for vibration. They may fail, perform poorly or require frequent mechanical attention. See "Sudden Accelerations" in Introduction.

Hot Spots and Owner/NHTSA Comments:

1. Brakes: hydraulic system, locking up, noise, failure. • "Applying brake sharply at speeds of 25 mph and above in emergency situations, brakes lock up." • "Continued brakes scraping and squealing upon depressing brake pedal." • "When brakes are wet they won't work." • "Brakes failed."

2. Fuel: throttle linkages and control, sudden accelerations. • "Sometimes when slowing down and moving, car will thrust forward on its own; hard to stop by braking." • "Car accelerates by itself without foot on gas pedal; gear placed into park while at red light to stop it from surging forward because brake does not keep car still." • "Engine surging while driving; stalls at stop." • "Sudden acceleration caused total loss of control, which resulted in an accident."

PLYMOUTH HORIZON 1987

Complaint Severity: Negligible. **Recall Alert:** See Recall Index. **Buyer's Summary:** The carburetion system could contribute to stalling and hesitation. Look carefully for any kind of leakage, especially under the car. The fuel injection system has been blamed for hesitation and stalling. Be sure the vehicle doesn't die in traffic or at stops. The steering may be stiff or not working correctly. Be sure to test the steering, especially on a cold start. See "Sudden Accelerations" in Introduction.

Hot Spots and Owner/NHTSA Comments:

1. Fuel: fuel injection system, stalling, hesitation. • "Recall work completed on the fuel flow regulator valve." • "Vehicle surges at speeds of 40 mph; dies or stalls at stop signs or turns." • "Fuel injection system faulty; car stalls when engine is hot or cold." • "Vehicle idles rough, won't start in cold weather; while driving, engine will stall and not restart." • "Engine surges and stalls; whenever engine gets down to idle, it starts surging even when moving in traffic."

2. Fuel: fuel carburetion, stalling, hesitation. • "Vehicle stalls frequently due to a fuel delivery system problem." • "Carburetor malfunctioned; stalling car, losing power; speed dropping until car stops; pushing down accelerator, speed continues to drop and engine dies." • "Fuel carburetion system malfunction caused the engine to become difficult to start." • "Vehicle stalls; sags; poor gas mileage; carburetor was changed and anti-vapor lock installed, still stalls out." • "Faulty carburetor caused gasoline fire; vehicle burned to ground after ignition was started to warm car."

3. Fuel: fuel injection: unknown type: regulator, leaks, fire. • "Pressure regulator in fuel supply system leaks oil onto engine; could result in fire." • "Defective fuel pressure regulator leak caused engine fire." • "Problem of fuel leakage due to defect in fuel pressure regulator; fuel foaming and vapor lock; installed driveability kit." • "Fuel injection regulator failed, causing vehicle to catch on fire; prior to recall." • "Smelling gas inside car; dealer says the fuel regulator needs replacing."

4. Fuel: fuel systems, leaks, stalling, fire. • "Fuel leakage from fuel pressure system; vehicle is smoking and could catch a fire." • "Car would stop abruptly anywhere; replaced gas tank, fuel lines, fuel pump and carburetor." • "Stalling caused by fuel systems contamination." • "Repairs completed; prior to recall." • "While driving, fire started under hood; vehicle caught fire."

5. Fuel: throttle linkages and control, sudden accelerations. • "Started engine, gear in reverse; motor raced, causing car to violently back up; gear in neutral, hit drive, lurched forward, hit wall; turned off motor." • "High rpm at start, odometer reading of 2,000 rpm; during cold weather, diesels, continues to run after key removed from ignition." • "Engine diesels and/or races when stopped for signal; goes to 30-35 mph from standstill; replaced spark plugs 3 times, rotor and cap to no avail." • "Vehicle suffered sudden acceleration and loss of control due to fuel linkage malfunction." • "Vehicle experiencing intermittent sudden acceleration while driving."

6. Steering: gear: rack-and-pinion, stiffness, poor performance. • "Steering is stiff while turning in cold, which could cause loss of control." • "Rack-and-pinion steering gets stiff until vehicle is warmed up." • "Rack-and-pinion steering binds in cold weather; causes loss of steering control." • "Rack-and-pinion steering needs to be replaced." • "Replaced rack-and-pinion steering system."

PLYMOUTH HORIZON 1988

Complaint Severity: Serious. **Recall Alert:** See Recall Index. **Buyer's Summary:** Check the brakes—listen for noise, look for leaks and feel for vibration. They may fail, perform poorly or require frequent mechanical attention. See "Sudden Accelerations" in Introduction.

Hot Spots and Owner/NHTSA Comments:

1. Fuel: throttle linkages and control, sudden accelerations. • "Sudden acceleration and bucking caused by faulty manifold air pressure sensors; replaced, problem continues." • "While vehicle is in motion, the vehicle accelerates to a higher speed without driver applying accelerator pedal. Vehicle idles at a higher rate." • "While driving 45-55 mph, vehicle would suddenly surge forward for about 2 seconds at a time." • "Vehicle surges, mostly on highways after driving about 30 mph." • "Engine experienced unwanted acceleration until the ignition was turned off in gear; no prior warning."

2. Brakes: hydraulic system, locking up, poor performance. • "Driving 25 mph, vehicle brakes locked; skidded and rear-ended, causing injury." • "Front and rear brakes required with less than 17,000 miles; wore prematurely." • "Poor performance of brakes; have had to replace 3 times or more; sometimes won't stop car." • "Unspecified brake failure; noise; ground down to rotor."

PLYMOUTH LASER 1990

Complaint Severity: Minor. **Recall Alert:** See Recall Index. **Buyer's Summary:** Problems with the timing gear and chain can cause serious problems. Have the engine checked by a professional. The fuel injection system has been blamed for hesitation and stalling. Be sure the vehicle doesn't die in traffic or at stops. Test the suspension by feeling for vibration or pulling while driving. Check the brakes—listen for noise, look for leaks and feel for vibration. They may fail, perform poorly or require frequent mechanical attention. Test transmission for slipping, locking up and performance.

Hot Spots and Owner/NHTSA Comments:

1. Brakes: hydraulic system, noise, poor performance, failure. • "Problem with defective brakes; warped rotors and pads." • "Master cylinder defective; braking performance poor." • "Brakes make loud noise when depressed, or when vehicle is in reverse and brakes are pressed." • "When braking at 35 mph, vehicle would not slow down after pumping the brakes; then brake pedal went down to the floor." • "Warped brakes and rotors; replaced."

2. Power train: transmission: 5-speed and up, difficulty shifting. • "Vehicle exhibits transmission problem; vehicle often pops out of gear, and at times has difficulty shifting gears." • "Transmission pops out of gear; hard to put back into gear." • "Second gear grinds; dealer notified and parts are being redesigned." • "Five-speed manual transmission difficult to shift in all gears."

3. Fuel: fuel injection system, stalling, hesitation. • "Chronic problem with rough idle and stalling; smell of gas." • "Engine hesitates after car has been sitting idle for a few hours; also occurs when car is put into drive after backing." • "Intermittent stalling." • "Engine misses; stalls when cold." • "At beginning, vehicle would not accelerate due to defective air flow sensor."

4. Engine: timing gear and chain, breaking, failure. • "Timing belt broke, causing valve damage." • "Timing belt broke, damaging engine." • "Timing belt slipped off." • "Timing belt slipped, resulting in damaged valves."

5. Suspension: independent front, tire wear, alignment. • "Left rear wheel toed in, causing uneven tire wear." • "Alignment problem caused tire problem." • "Front end pulls to right when driving; balanced tires." • "Poor directional control; car veers and dances to the right when accelerating; all repair attempts to no avail."

6. Visual systems: glass: windshield, cracking. • "Windshield repaired/replaced 4 times; 2 windshields shattered while driving." • "Plastic strip on upper windshield warped; crack in windshield." • "Windshield failed." • "Windshield stress cracks."

PLYMOUTH NEON 1995

Complaint Severity: Dangerous (Worst 3% in Guide). **Recall Alert:** See Recall Index. **Buyer's Summary:** The airbags in this vehicle have experienced failures and malfunctions: You may need a professional evaluation on the condition of the airbags. Check the brakes—listen for noise, look for leaks and feel for vibration. They may fail, perform poorly or require frequent mechanical attention.

Hot Spots and Owner/NHTSA Comments:

1. Interior systems: passive restraint: airbag: driver, malfunction, failure. • "Car was in an accident; driver's-side airbag didn't deploy, and seat belt didn't restrain." • "Upon impact during frontal crash at approximately 10 mph, 2:00 position on front bumper, both driver airbags deployed with such force that driver and passenger windows exploded." • "Driver's airbag deployed upon 30-mph collision; side windows shattered, spreading glass all over vehicle; resulted in an injury." • "During front-end collision, driver's airbag did not deploy."

2. Interior systems: passive restraint: airbag: passenger, malfunction, failure. • "Frontal impact 12:00 position, speed 35 mph, airbag deployed on passenger side, causing injuries." • "Passenger side airbag deployed upon 30-mph collision; side windows shattered, spreading glass all over vehicle; resulted in an injury." • "During front-end collision, passenger's airbag did not deploy." • "Upon impact during frontal crash at approximately 10 mph, 2:00 position on front bumper, passenger's airbag deployed with such force that driver and passenger windows exploded." • "Hit another vehicle at 25 mph and passenger's airbag did not deploy."

3. Brakes: hydraulic: anti-skid system, poor performance, failure, locking up. • "Antilock brake system brake pedal went down to floor; have to pump the brakes to get them up. Replaced master cylinder and hydraulic assembly." • "While driving, experienced intermittent brake failure when pedal went to floor, without prior warning; dealer can't reproduce." • "Antilock brake system made a clicking noise; would not stop the car. Felt like there were no power brakes. Replaced antilock brake system module and brake pads, problem still exists."

PLYMOUTH RELIANT 1987

Complaint Severity: Typical. **Buyer's Summary:** The electronic control unit has been blamed for engine performance problems, including stalling and surging. The fuel injection system has been blamed for hesitation and stalling. Be sure the vehicle doesn't die in traffic or at stops. Test the transmission thoroughly. See "Sudden Accelerations" in Introduction.

Hot Spots and Owner/NHTSA Comments:

1. Exhaust system: manifold: oxygen sensor, stalling, premature failure. • "Vehicle stalled on highway due to a defective manifold air pressure sensor; replaced 4 times." • "Vehicle would stall; if it sat overnight, it wouldn't start in the mornings." • "The manifold air pressure sensor burned out 4 times; caused vehicle to stall." • "Manifold air pressure sensors malfunctioned 3 times; caused vehicle to stall." • "Intermittent stalling and hesitation; replaced manifold air pressure sensor to no avail."

2. Power train: transmission: automatic, poor performance, difficulty shifting, slipping. • "Car motor running, vehicle in park, went into reverse on its own; slammed into parked car." • "Transmission stick shift hard to move; smelled something burning, suddenly radio, fan, and indicator went out, then engine stopped completely." • "Car stopped in drive, drifted backward; hit brake and put transmission in 1st gear." • "While vehicle in park, automatic transmission slipped into reverse and rolled, resulting in an accident." • "Car idling in park position started to move in reverse; rolled into a house."

3. Electrical system: ignition: electronic control unit, stalling, malfunction. • "At low speeds, vehicle stalls and shuts down; failed to start; replaced logic module and fuel pump." • "Malfunction of computer chip; giving false signals to car indicating loss of power." • "Computer went bad; skip in engine; car died." • "Computer chip manifold air pressure sensor; engine dies out." • "Attempting to accelerate and going up hills, vehicle hits high rpm with no acceleration; vehicle hesitated then accelerated."

4. Fuel: fuel injection system, stalling, hesitation. • "Vehicle vibrates and stalls out at signals." • "Intermittent stalling and/or hesitation." • "Defect in fuel injection system; bucking and rough running of engine; smell of raw gas." • "During 15 minutes of cold start, car loses power and/or idles rough; sometimes not enough power to operate brakes; almost caused 2 accidents." • "While going on highway, car suddenly stalled; power brakes and steering failed; spun around and hit guardrail."

5. Engine: stalling, premature failure. • "Car parked overnight, wouldn't start up next day; discovered fire or meltdown had taken place." • "Engine problems; fan that cools engine; 'power loss' light stayed on." • "Knock in motor." • "Engine failed; replaced 4 times." • "Engine overheated and stalled."
6. Fuel: throttle linkages and control, sudden accelerations. • "Sudden surge of power when ignition turned on." • "When ignition turned on and car put in drive, barely put foot on accelerator when car jumped forward fast; brake wouldn't stop; collision occurred with 5 cars." • "When first starting car, motor races high; slows up after pumping gas pedal several times; also occurs while traveling." • "Throttle linkages faulty; caused uncontrolled acceleration." • "While driving and coming to a stop, then starting out, pressed gas pedal and vehicle suddenly accelerated out of control, even with application of brakes."

PLYMOUTH RELIANT 1988

Complaint Severity: Typical. **Buyer's Summary:** The engine has experienced a variety of problems. Have it examined by a professional. The fuel injection system has been blamed for hesitation and stalling. Be sure the vehicle doesn't die in traffic or at stops. The steering may be stiff or not working correctly. Be sure to test the steering, especially on a cold start. Check the brakes—listen for noise, look for leaks and feel for vibration. They may fail, perform poorly or require frequent mechanical attention. Test the transmission thoroughly.

Hot Spots and Owner/NHTSA Comments:
1. Power train: transmission: automatic, poor performance, difficulty shifting, slipping. • "When shifting from park to drive, will jerk forward." • "Key can be removed from ignition without transmission being in park." • "Automatic transmission jumped from park to reverse, running over driver; injuries sustained." • "Each time car brakes to a stop, it rocks back and forth a few times." • "When vehicle standing and put in forward gear, grabs very hard; seems as if going to tear." • "When transmission in park position, car rolls backward." • "Transaxle clunks when shifting from neutral or park."
2. Brakes: hydraulic system, excessive wear, noise, poor performance. • "While driving, applied brakes, pedal went to floor; brakes increased with pumping effort." • "Defect in braking system; squeals." • "Excessive wear on brake pads; replaced rotors and pads." • "Applied brakes to no avail; skidded into a car, which in turn rear-ended another car." • "Brake rotors turned, disc pads and master cylinder replaced at 2,336 miles." • "Rotors and shoes make squeaking noise; replaced rotors 3 times, shoes once within 90 days of replacement."
3. Engine: miscellaneous problems. • "Experiencing excessive oil use." • "Engine noise." • "Major engine overhaul twice." • "Engine replaced twice." • "Oil indicator light did not alert driver in time to avoid engine damage."
4. Fuel: fuel injection system, stalling, hesitation. • "Engine stalling problems; stalls when brakes applied; difficult to control; caused by faulty injector." • "Erratic idling." • "While driving, vehicle jerks, engine light comes on; have to stop and turn engine off." • "Car surging, fast and/or rough idle; when foot off gas pedal, vehicle surges forward."
5. Steering: gear: rack-and-pinion, stiffness, poor performance. • "Steering makes noise when turning; repaired/replaced rack-and-pinion steering mechanism twice." • "Rack-and-pinion assembly, which is held by 4 bolts to the cross member, became loose, which caused loss of steering." • "Rack-and-pinion steering binds when vehicle is turned to left at certain point." • "Welded bolts broke away from rack-and-pinion; difficulty in steering." • "Rack-and-pinion failed twice."
6. Brakes: hydraulic: shoe: disc brake system, malfunction, failure. • "Front brake defect; front pads, calipers and shoe lining repaired/replaced." • "Front brakes malfunctioned and were replaced." • "Front brake faulty; brake rubbing noise heard; replaced front brakes and turned rotors." • "Brakes completely worn out; when driving forward, no braking power, resulted in accident." • "Front brake pads and rotors failed."

PLYMOUTH RELIANT 1989

Complaint Severity: Typical. **Recall Alert:** See Recall Index. **Buyer's Summary:** The fuel injection system has been blamed for hesitation and stalling. Be sure the vehicle doesn't die in traffic or at stops. See "Sudden Accelerations" in Introduction.

Hot Spots and Owner/NHTSA Comments:
1. Engine: gaskets: valve cover, leaks. • "Defective valve cover gasket, causing oil leak." • "Valve cover gasket failure; possible engine oil leak." • "Engine gaskets and valve cover are leaking; previous repair work had been conducted." • "Engine cylinder head cover gasket dislocated; caused oil leakage; repaired/replaced cylinder head cover using silicone rubber adhesive sealant in place of gasket." • "Valve cover gasket replaced twice due to oil leak; after recall repair." • "Leak due to dislocation of engine cylinder head cover gasket caused fire while in motion with occupants; recall campaign initiated."
2. Fuel: fuel injection system, stalling, hesitation. • "Gas fumes in car; leakage." • "Intermittent hesitation and/or stalling." • "Problem with car not starting; repaired/replaced defective fuel injector." • "Fuel system defective." • "Hesitation in motor when accelerating from slower speeds."
3. Fuel: throttle linkages and control, sudden accelerations. • "Started car and it immediately accelerated, jumped forward over concrete curb." • "Intermittent sudden acceleration while driving." • "Vehicle suddenly surged forward, resulting in a vehicle accident." • "Turned car on, vehicle jumped forward into wall."

PLYMOUTH SUNDANCE 1987

Complaint Severity: Typical. **Recall Alert:** See Recall Index. **Buyer's Summary:** Look carefully for any kind of leakage, especially under the car. The fuel injection system has been blamed for hesitation and stalling. Be sure the vehicle doesn't die in traffic or at stops. Check the brakes—listen for noise, look for leaks and feel for vibration. They may fail, perform poorly or require frequent mechanical attention. Test the transmission thoroughly. See "Sudden Accelerations" in Introduction.

Hot Spots and Owner/NHTSA Comments:
1. Fuel: throttle linkages and control, sudden accelerations. • "While driving, vehicle suddenly surged; brakes failed, resulting in accident." • "In parking lot, started car and took foot off gas pedal; pedal stayed down and car continued to accelerate; brakes no help in speed control; forced to hit into curb." • "No deceleration when applying brakes; accident." • "Throttle control system malfunction, resulting in sudden acceleration." • "Engine surge problem occurs; after cold start, will suddenly quit between 5 to 10 minutes; surge also causes engine to ramp up to high speed in 2-4 seconds."
2. Fuel: fuel injection system, stalling, hesitation. • "Car engine speeds; very slow to return to specified idle; most annoying while shifting gears." • "Stalling problems occur while idling, mostly while driving, resulting in power loss." • "Car stalls continually when raining, at all speeds." • "Speed sensor problem." • "Engine hesitating and stalling; speed sensor defective." • "Recently

needed to have injector, logic chip and converter replaced under warranty."

3. Power train: transmission: automatic, poor performance, difficulty shifting, slipping. • "Shifting problems into 1st and 2nd gears; 1st sometimes doesn't work at all." • "Automatic transmission; gears stick when attempting to change gears." • "Slow oil leak; removed transmission, had to install torque converter and reseal transmission oil pump." • "When put automatic transmission in park, can move in any gear; vehicle rolls as if in neutral." • "Transmission shift locking device fails to function properly. This allows shifter to move freely between gears."

4. Brakes: hydraulic system, vibration, failure. • "Brakes gave out; almost caused accident." • "Brake failed, causing loss of control and resulting in accident." • "Excessive vibration upon braking." • "Vehicle experiences complete brake failure." • "Defective brakes; grabbing, grating and slipping; eventually caused accident."

5. Fuel: fuel systems, leaks, fire. • "Fuel filter and injector replaced." • "While driving, vehicle caught on fire; dealer could not pinpoint cause." • "Fuel leakage caused fire and injury; prior to recall notification.". • "While driving at 25 mph, a noise occurred; vehicle engulfed in flames 5 minutes after parking." • "Gasoline fumes enter cab of vehicle; recall repairs refused by dealer due to vehicle identification number."

PLYMOUTH SUNDANCE 1988

Complaint Severity: Typical. **Recall Alert:** See Recall Index. **Buyer's Summary:** Make sure the shoulder belts don't cut across your neck and are well anchored. The engine has experienced a variety of problems. Have it examined by a professional. Test the transmission thoroughly. Make sure seat belts function correctly and fit comfortably. See "Sudden Accelerations" in Introduction.

Hot Spots and Owner/NHTSA Comments:

1. Interior systems: passive restraint: belts, malfunction, failure. • "Automatic shoulder belts do not function." • "Automatic shoulder restraint; car was fixed under recall and it failed again; dealer wants to charge consumer to fix." • "Driver's-side motorized seat belt stays in the closed position; not activated when door or key is used. This is the second failure." • "Automatic shoulder belt inoperative." • "Driver's and passenger's motorized seat belts failed before and after recall."

2. Fuel: throttle linkages and control, sudden accelerations. • "Car accelerated on numerous occasions; when started up, can hear engine racing and rpm will go as high as 4,000." • "Vehicle intermittently surges, especially in warm weather." • "Engine idle increased from normal to about 800-1,200 rpm at stop; increased car speed when driving and foot taken from accelerator." • "Car races when in gear." • "Vehicle in park position; shifted into drive, then jumped forward, hitting a wall." • "Idle surges for few minutes after startup."

3. Interior systems: active restraints: belt retractors, malfunction, failure. • "Left and right shoulder belts failed." • "Both seat belt retractors jammed. Seat belts are inoperative." • "Seat belt track jammed." • "Seat and shoulder belts do not tighten when locked." • "Automatic seat belts failed twice."

4. Power train: transmission: automatic, poor performance, difficulty shifting, slipping. • "Problem with transmission slipping; overhauled." • "Automatic transmission jumps in and out of 1st, chatters in reverse when cold." • "Chronic transmission leak." • "Problem with transmission slipping." • "Transmission failure."

5. Engine: miscellaneous problems. • "Engine rod failure." • "Defective engine; repaired/replaced cam, lifters and timing belt twice." • "Engine knocks." • "Engine mounted incorrectly; oil leak; replaced head gasket and valves." • "Engine oil leak beneath crankcase." • "Engine was found to have been mounted incorrectly at factory; removed and remounted."

6. Interior systems: shoulder belts, malfunction, failure. • "Driver rear-ended another vehicle; seat belt failed to lock, causing driver to strike steering wheel with chest." • "Driver's shoulder belt stuck in locked position." • "Shoulder belt moved to center of door and then stalled in that position and would not move to base position. Had shoulder belt replaced." • "Shoulder belt failed on driver's side." • "Motorized seat belt failed; prior to recall."

PLYMOUTH SUNDANCE 1989

Complaint Severity: Minor. **Recall Alert:** See Recall Index. **Buyer's Summary:** Look carefully for any kind of leakage, especially under the car. Make sure the shoulder belts don't cut across your neck and are well anchored. Make sure seat belts function correctly and fit comfortably.

Hot Spots and Owner/NHTSA Comments:

1. Interior systems: passive restraint: belts, malfunction, failure. • "Passenger's automatic seat belt failed; prior to recall." • "Motorized driver shoulder belt cable twisted, not allowing belt to complete distance." • "Automatic seat belts were not working; failed to move on track." • "Front automatic seat belts failed 3 times." • "Driver's automatic seat belt would only move about 1 foot; this made it impossible to get into the vehicle without disconnecting the seat belt."

2. Engine: gaskets: valve cover, leaks, fire. • "Problem with continual oil leak; recall repair of valve cover gasket, problem persists." • "Defect in cylinder head cover gasket." • "Engine valve cover leaking; replaced." • "Fire occurred due to oil leak from faulty valve cover gasket; less than 1 month after vehicle fire, received safety recall notice for cylinder head cover gasket." • "Faulty valve cover seal; leaking oil in engine; first repair unsuccessful; consumer says bad part put back in, waiting on correct part under recall for replacement."

3. Interior systems: active restraints: belt retractors, malfunction, failure. • "Front and rear passenger's retractors failed to hold." • "Driver's shoulder belt locked up midtravel; passenger shoulder belt works intermittently." • "Shoulder belt retractor will not retract." • "Lap and shoulder belt will not retract on passenger's side of vehicle." • "Automatic shoulder belt retractor locked inadvertently, leaving slack in belt that contributed to occupant's injuries in accident."

4. Interior systems: shoulder belts, breaking, failure. • "Driver's seat belt failure during accident; repaired/replaced, replacement also defective." • "Vehicle was hit from a 6:00 position while stopped, driver's lap and shoulder belt broke from impact and seat broke and fell backwards." • "Automatic shoulder restraints do not function when closing the doors." • "Faulty automatic shoulder restraints." • "Driver and passenger automatic shoulder belts malfunctioned; motor does not work; has been repaired once."

PLYMOUTH SUNDANCE 1990

Complaint Severity: Dangerous (Worst 3% in Guide). **Recall Alert:** See Recall Index. **Buyer's Summary:** Look carefully for any kind of leakage, especially under the car. The airbags in this vehicle have experienced failures and malfunctions: You may need a professional evaluation on the condition of the airbags.

Hot Spots and Owner/NHTSA Comments:

1. Interior systems: passive restraint: airbag: driver, malfunction, failure. • "Airbag deployed; no accident; no sudden impact; speed 5-10 mph; absolutely no warning." • "Upon impact during frontal crash at approximately 38 mph, 12:00 position on

bumper, airbag failed to deploy; also, driver's shoulder harness failed to retract." • "Hit raised sewer cover lid in road, causing car to stop short. Seat belts retracted and airbag didn't inflate." • "Airbag inflated and ruptured during collision, causing burns." • "During front-end collision at 20 mph, airbag deployed, injuring driver, causing burns." • "Frontal collision, impact 12:00 position, speed 35 mph, airbag deployed, causing third degree burns."
2. Interior systems: passive restraint: airbag, malfunction, failure. • "Airbag did not deploy during accident." • "Gas escaping through vents in airbag burned driver during deflation." • "Driver burned by airbag during accident." • "Airbag activated during collision, but didn't inflate and hit into driver's neck; caused severe injuries." • "Airbag malfunctioned during an accident."
3. Engine: leaks, fire. • "Vehicle fire." • "Defective oil sending unit leaking; replaced." • "Has an oil leak." • "Engine fire." • "Fire in engine compartment for no apparent reason."

PLYMOUTH SUNDANCE 1991

Complaint Severity: Very Serious. **Recall Alert:** See Recall Index. **Buyer's Summary:** The airbags in this vehicle have experienced failures and malfunctions: You may need a professional evaluation on the condition of the airbags. Test the transmission thoroughly. See "Sudden Accelerations" in Introduction.

Hot Spots and Owner/NHTSA Comments:
1. Interior systems: passive restraint: airbag: driver, malfunction, failure. • "During a frontal collision, impact at 12:00, at 15 mph, airbag deployed and caused injuries." • "Airbag did not deploy during a front-end collision, impact 12:00 position, speed 40 mph." • "Another vehicle moved over into same lane and caused first vehicle to go into gravel and hit a guardrail; airbag did not deploy, impact 1:00 position." • "Airbag did not deploy during front-end collision, causing neck injuries to driver." • "While driving vehicle at 50 mph, it hit a patch of ice and lost control; vehicle rolled over; airbag did not deploy."
2. Fuel: throttle linkages and control, sudden accelerations. • "Stopping on ramp to await decrease in oncoming traffic, vehicle accelerated and went out of control. Second time, resulted in an accident." • "Upon braking, vehicle suddenly accelerated." • "While driving, vehicle surges." • "When trying to stop for a stop sign or light, vehicle accelerates out of control; almost ran into the back of cars." • "Sudden acceleration when vehicle is in neutral."
3. Interior systems: bucket: backrest, breaking, malfunction. • "While driving vehicle at normal speed, applied brakes and driver experienced seat back failure." • "Seat back support bolt failed, causing seat to collapse." • "Driver's seat backrest bolt sheared. Caused driver to fall backward while entering vehicle. Also, engine surges without accelerating and with foot on brakes." • "Driver's seat back bolt failed while driving, causing seat back to fall backwards." • "Consumer was driving, the seat back bolt broke and seat went back." • "Driver's reclining seat backrest does not stay up on its own; stabilized by a milk carton; allegedly fixed twice."
4. Electrical system: ignition, stalling, failure. • "Intermittent stalling due to ignition module failure." • "Intermittent stalling while car is in motion." • "Car stalled in middle of highway, resulting in a collision. Driver's airbag deployed." • "Replaced fuel filler and checked electric system because 'check engine' light comes on, then vehicle stalls out at any speed."
5. Power train: transmission: automatic, poor performance, difficulty shifting, slipping. • "Transmission broke down twice." • "Automatic transmission gear selector will shift gears without pressing the button." • "Car was put into gear when key was not in ignition; vehicle took off; resulted in an accident." • "Concerned about safety of being able to shift out of park when engine off."

PLYMOUTH SUNDANCE 1992

Complaint Severity: Very Serious. **Recall Alert:** See Recall Index. **Buyer's Summary:** The airbags in this vehicle have experienced failures and malfunctions: You may need a professional evaluation on the condition of the airbags. Check the brakes—listen for noise, look for leaks and feel for vibration. They may fail, perform poorly or require frequent mechanical attention.

Hot Spots and Owner/NHTSA Comments:
1. Interior systems: bucket: backrest, breaking, failure. • "Seat back failed due to a bolt breaking while driving." • "Bolt in driver's-side seat back broke, and seat back fell into rear seat." • "Consumer was parking the car; the driver's-side seat fell backwards." • "Usually when braking, rear seat backrest flops forward; does not stay in upright position; if occupied, could cause injury." • "Vehicle was hit from behind and propelled into 2 other vehicles. Airbag did not deploy and driver's seat back broke."
2. Interior systems: passive restraint: airbag: driver, malfunction, failure. • "Premature inflation of airbag caused an accident." • "Vehicle was hit from behind and propelled into 2 other vehicles. Airbag did not deploy and driver's seat back broke." • "Airbag deployment upon frontal impact with deer at 50 mph; smoke came out, obstructing vision." • "Airbag deployment was violent during accident, causing injury." • "Was involved in accident; airbag set body and clothing on fire."
3. Brakes: hydraulic system, noise, failure. • "Brakes would not stop vehicle with excessive force; smoking." • "Brakes squeal when stopping or applying any pressure to brake pedal (ever since accident)." • "While driving, brakes completely malfunctioned; vehicle went out of control, resulting in an accident; daughter and friend suffered injuries." • "Brakes failed; could not stop vehicle from going out of control, resulting in an accident."

PLYMOUTH SUNDANCE 1993

Complaint Severity: Dangerous (Worst 3% in Guide). **Buyer's Summary:** The airbags in this vehicle have experienced failures and malfunctions: You may need a professional evaluation on the condition of the airbags.

Hot Spots and Owner/NHTSA Comments:
1. Interior systems: passive restraint: airbag: driver, malfunction, failure. • "Driver airbag did not deploy after a head-on collision." • "Car was in an accident and the driver's-side airbag didn't deploy." • "The driver's-side airbag deployed at 12:00 (frontal) collision at 30 mph; airbag failed to inflate." • "Airbag failed to deploy in a front-end collision." • "Hit a deer and then hit a embankment head-on, vehicle flipped over; airbag did not deploy."

PLYMOUTH TURISMO 1987

Complaint Severity: Minor. **Recall Alert:** See Recall Index. **Buyer's Summary:** The carburetion system could contribute to stalling and hesitation. Look carefully for any kind of leakage, especially under the car. The fuel injection system has been blamed for hesitation and stalling. Be sure the vehicle doesn't die in traffic or at stops. Check the brakes—listen for noise, look for leaks and feel for vibration. They may fail, perform poorly or require frequent mechanical attention.

Hot Spots and Owner/NHTSA Comments:
1. Fuel: fuel carburetion, stalling, hesitation. • "Defective carburetor; vehicle loses all power when traveling up incline; hesitates." • "Vehicle experienced stalling problems and hesitation; defective carburetor worked on." • "Defective carburetor; hesitation problems experienced." • "Severe engine stalling problems; vehicle involved in rear-end collision due to stalling; also has er-

ratic idle and misfiring." • "Crack in internal portion of carburetor caused immediate loss of speed at 55 mph; replaced carburetor." • "Intermittent stalling; replaced carburetor 3 times."

2. Fuel: fuel injection system, stalling, hesitation. • "Intermittent stalling, then surging." • "Car stalls in traffic, as well as cold start in the morning; have replaced a timing belt and repaired a wire in the electrical system. Car still stalls." • "Engine died on major highway; no prior warning." • "Car stalls periodically, takes 2-4 minutes to start; does not accelerate properly at times; speed drops from 65 mph to 35 mph while driving." • "Fuel pressure regulator failure caused engine fire; prior to recall."

3. Electrical system: malfunction, fire. • "Parked vehicle caught fire; chief of fire department ruled electrical fire." • "Battery replaced 3 times; alternator replaced." • "Defect in electrical system; repaired/replaced batteries 4 times." • "Electrical malfunction; battery had to be repaired/replaced twice in less than 2 years; starter failed." • "Computer module, ignition and oxygen sensor all failed."

4. Fuel: fuel injection: unknown type: regulator, leaks, fire. • "Serious fuel leak exists at loose fuel regulator fitting." • "Faulty fuel pressure regulator, causing fire; prior to recall." • "Engine fire; prior to recall." • "Vehicle caught on fire; prior to recall." • "Fuel leakage resulted in engine fire; prior to recall."

5. Brakes: hydraulic system, malfunction, excessive wear. • "Front brakes binding; get very hot and could smell hot metal; brakes warped rotors." • "Brake malfunction; repaired several times." • "Brakes perform poorly due to failure of various brake system components such as calipers." • "Brake shoes wear out every 300 miles; repaired/replaced rotors and caliper once at 20,000 miles, now needs again at 28,000."

Plymouth—Trucks

PLYMOUTH TRUCK VOYAGER 1987

Complaint Severity: Typical. **Recall Alert:** See Recall Index. **Buyer's Summary:** The carburetion system could contribute to stalling and hesitation. The fuel injection system has been blamed for hesitation and stalling. Be sure the vehicle doesn't die in traffic or at stops. The steering may be stiff or not working correctly. Be sure to test the steering, especially on a cold start. Test the transmission thoroughly.

Hot Spots and Owner/NHTSA Comments:

1. Power train: transmission: automatic, poor performance, difficulty shifting, slipping. • "Transmission shifted into neutral when accelerator pushed to floor." • "Transmission slipped out of gear and rolled, causing an accident." • "Problem with transmission slipping out of gear; rolled down and hit tree while parked; repaired." • "Vehicle rolled about 10 yards and hit a car wash; vehicle was in park gear." • "Car placed in park while idling, started moving in reverse, resulted in accident with injuries sustained."

2. Engine: mounts, breaking, excessive wear. • "Engine mount broke twice and was replaced." • "Two motor mounts, which keep engine from rotating as motor accelerates and decelerates, sheared off; engine rotated 15 degrees; repaired/replaced both motor mounts." • "Engine mounting came loose; causes various transmission and electrical problems." • "Front motor mount busted; 2 months afterwards, busted again; sheared bolts off block." • "Engine makes noise due to broken motor mount; repaired."

3. Steering: gear: rack-and-pinion, stiffness, poor performance. • "Power steering failed; replaced." • "Rack-and-pinion steering has been replaced 3 times." • "Loss of power steering fluid causes difficulty in steering; repaired/replaced rack-and-pinion steering system." • "Problem with power steering; steering makes loud hissing noise." • "Power steering fluid leaks from rack-and-pinion assembly."

4. Fuel: fuel carburetion, stalling, hesitation. • "Intermittent stalling." • "Car stalls when decelerating; repaired 4 times, problem continues to exist." • "Struck rear of another car; 10 seconds later, engine compartment burst into flames." • "Car stalled and stopped in middle of traffic with air conditioner on." • "Vehicle stalls constantly without warning." • "Stalled at 65 mph; when at stoplight, would stall and had to wait 3 to 5 minutes to restart; new carburetor installed, problem still occurs."

5. Structure: hatchback locks and latches, failure. • "In collision, causing hatch to open; resulted in person falling out and dying from injuries." • "Rear hatch unlatched and opened following 10 mph rear-end collision." • "Liftgate opened upon 35-mph impact; 14- and 16-year-old kids ejected." • "Experienced difficulty in latching hatchback due to screws becoming loose and backing out of latch mechanism." • "Rear hatch latch failed; hatch does not stay up; falls and hits person on head."

6. Fuel: fuel injection system, stalling, hesitation. • "Intermittent stalling." • "Vehicle intermittently stalls." • "Vehicle stalls on occasion." • "Car stalled while feeding gas to engine."

PLYMOUTH TRUCK VOYAGER 1988

Complaint Severity: Minor. **Recall Alert:** See Recall Index. **Buyer's Summary:** The fuel pump has received complaints. Make sure it doesn't make excessive noise and that you are experiencing adequate engine performance. Also, look for leaks. Verify that the cruise control system works properly, and that it doesn't cause the engine to surge. The fuel injection system has been blamed for hesitation and stalling. Be sure the vehicle doesn't die in traffic or at stops. The steering may be stiff or not working correctly. Be sure to test the steering, especially on a cold start. Test the transmission thoroughly.

Hot Spots and Owner/NHTSA Comments:

1. Fuel: fuel pump, noise, stalling, vibration. • "One month after purchasing car, fuel pump started making noises; dealer said was normal; then in middle of nowhere, fuel pump went out." • "While driving on freeway, fuel pump failed; caused stalling." • "Car began cutting in and out, surging, then finally died." • "Had to replace fuel pump because pump vibrated loudly." • "Vehicle has no acceleration due to fuel system. Fuel pump changed 5 times with no change in condition."

2. Steering: gear: rack-and-pinion, stiffness, poor performance. • "Rack-and-pinion steering is leaking oil (1 pint a week) and causing fear of an oil-fed fire. Steering replaced for leakage also." • "Rack-and-pinion assembly failure; steering difficult to turn." • "Rack-and-pinion failure; repaired/replaced at 11,400 miles; failed again 5 months later." • "Defective rack-and-pinion steering system; repaired/replaced." • "Power rack-and-pinion steering unit; shaft end packing seals failed; leaked." • "Defective rack-and-pinion assembly, which caused steering to become very hard and difficult to control."

3. Power train: transmission: automatic, poor performance, difficulty shifting, slipping. • "Automatic transmission malfunctioned." • "Difficulties with gear shifter when trying to shift into park; stopped with gear in park, van moved in reverse; injured person by pinning her to gate and wall." • "Transmission hesitates when shifting from park to drive; shifts hard." • "Transmission bangs into gears." • "While driving, transmission would not shift into passing gear; jerked and jumped; complete transmission overhaul."

4. Fuel: fuel injection system, stalling, hesitation. • "Vehicle stalls during deceleration." • "Engine stalls frequently when slowing to a stop or while idling at light; happens intermittently." • "Engine stalled in motion; problem reoccurred after computer system and fuel pump replaced." • "Intermittent stalling." • "Engine stalls at all speeds."
5. Structure: hatchback locks and latches, failure. • "Rear hatch door is loose. Owner has had latch tightened, with looseness recurring." • "While driving, liftgate opened; road under construction and bumpy." • "The rear hatch latch doesn't close right." • "Liftgate opened within first months of ownership. Latch needed constant tightening. While driving, back gate would open periodically." • "Rear latch came open while driving along."
6. Equipment: speed control, malfunction, failure. • "Cruise would not disengage until third application of brakes; cruise stopped working completely." • "Cruise control failed to maintain a constant speed; tries to recover but overshoots, then it suddenly gains speed." • "Car accelerated unexpectedly up to speed set on cruise control; cruise control was not in 'on' position." • "Cruise control doesn't hold set speed; slows down and then all of a sudden will speed up, at times reaching speeds of 80 mph; at times car travels in a jerking motion." • "Cruise control inoperative."

PLYMOUTH TRUCK VOYAGER 1989

Complaint Severity: Minor. **Recall Alert:** See Recall Index. **Buyer's Summary:** Look carefully for any kind of leakage, especially under the car. The fuel injection system has been blamed for hesitation and stalling. Be sure the vehicle doesn't die in traffic or at stops. Check the brakes—listen for noise, look for leaks and feel for vibration. They may fail, perform poorly or require frequent mechanical attention. Test the transmission thoroughly.

Hot Spots and Owner/NHTSA Comments:
1. Power train: transmission: automatic, poor performance, difficulty shifting, slipping. • "Vehicle in shop 9 times due to automatic transmission downshifts." • "Transmission replaced 4 times." • "Transmission replaced due to forward, reverse and overdrive gear failure." • "Transmission went out; would not downshift; after coming to complete stop car would lurch forward, then would remain in 2nd gear until turned off." • "While driving, truck would not disengage out of 1st gear. Automatic transmission disintegrated; full of metal debris." • "Experiencing transmission problems; had 12 different repairs done on the transmission."
2. Structure: hatchback locks and latches, failure. • "Rear hatch latch flew open without impact, spilling contents all over the road." • "Rear latch came open while driving; no impact involved." • "The latch broke on the hatchback door." • "Indicator light for the rear liftgate; rear liftgate opened by itself when making a turn." • "While driving up to driveway, rear tailgate raised up; surface leading to driveway slightly bumpy."
3. Engine: leaks, fire, failure. • "Fire developed under hood; prior to fire, noticed vapor from under hood but could not find source." • "Engine locked up; 2 bent connecting rods; water got into engine and on top of pistons, causing problem; bad design of air intake hose." • "Oil leak repaired, prior to recall of valve cover seal; several parts replaced/repaired since to no avail." • "Engine stopped working; new one was installed." • "Engine smoking and coolant leaking."
4. Engine: gaskets: valve cover, leaks, fire. • "Rear valve cover gasket leaks; recall refused for engine size." • "Valve cover gasket leaking." • "Ten minutes after parking, engine compartment caught fire; dealer replaced valve cover gasket; was also replaced 3 other times by nondealers due to leaks." • "Replaced valve cover gasket; resealed (factory recall)."
5. Brakes: hydraulic system, failure. • "Upon pressing, brakes go down to the floor and become spongy." • "Brake cylinder leaking water into hydraulic system, causing contamination." • "Brake failure." • "Brakes grab in erratic fashion."
6. Fuel: fuel injection system, stalling, hesitation. • "Intermittent stalling." • "Intermittent stalling; restarts after engine cools." • "Intermittent stalling problem; results in loss of power steering and brakes." • "Vehicle intermittently stalls, which causes loss of steering control and braking power." • "Cold starting problems; sometimes warm starting problems."

PLYMOUTH TRUCK VOYAGER 1990

Complaint Severity: Minor. **Recall Alert:** See Recall Index. **Buyer's Summary:** Test the transmission thoroughly.

Hot Spots and Owner/NHTSA Comments:
1. Power train: transmission: automatic, poor performance, difficulty shifting, slipping. • "Transmission shifts with extreme jerk and clunks in reverse; gears have high-pitched noise; third set of gears and new transmission have been ordered." • "When stopping, transmission downshifts; makes vehicle jerk and leap forward; a few times when accelerating transmission wouldn't shift gears, seemed to be stuck in 2nd." • "Transmission sounds strange; jumps into gear suddenly when at stop sign, requiring immediate braking; also slips gear; all repair attempts to no avail." • "Transmission discharging too much fluid from either seals or vent; fluid blowing over entire engine area; may cause improper shifting or possible engine fire." • "Automatic transmission locked up in 1st gear; transmission replaced."
2. Structure: hatchback locks and latches, failure. • "Rear latch mechanism causing electrical shortage and other components to come on and off periodically. Repaired 4 times." • "While driving, rear hatch liftgate would open frequently. Latch failed to close completely; repaired 3 times." • "While driving at 70 mph on highway, rear hatch liftgate opened with no warning." • "Vehicle's rear hatch gate pops open while driving with no prior warning." • "Rear hatch latch failed on impact, causing hatch to fall backwards; all contents fell out of the rear."
3. Structure: door assembly, poor performance, failure. • "Passenger-side sliding door slid completely off track while opening; door almost fell on passenger's foot." • "Sliding door fell off when it was opened." • "Sliding door separated from its track and caused damage to the vehicle." • "Went to open sliding door in icy conditions and the whole door fell off the track." • "Sliding side door (electrical) sticks; locks intermittently. Problem hasn't been identified. Occupants climb over other seats to exit."
4. Structure: hatchback support, malfunction, failure. • "Rear hatch latch liftgate is difficult to open; when open, hydraulic cylinders do not keep it open." • "Hydraulic lift does not hold door." • "Hydraulic lifts failed in the rear liftgate." • "Rear liftgate support rods replaced." • "Hatch door doesn't stay up."

PLYMOUTH TRUCK VOYAGER 1991

Complaint Severity: Typical. **Recall Alert:** See Recall Index. **Buyer's Summary:** Check the brakes—listen for noise, look for leaks and feel for vibration. They may fail, perform poorly or require frequent mechanical attention. Test the transmission thoroughly.

Hot Spots and Owner/NHTSA Comments:
1. Brakes: hydraulic: anti-skid system, poor performance, failure, locking up. • "After coming off freeway and turning onto a side road, the antilock brake warning lights came on; put foot on brakes and got no braking power." • "Brake fluid leaking; antilock brake failure." • "Antilock brake system completely failed; pedal

would not move." • "While driving vehicle at any speed, antilock brake light would come on; lack of braking effectiveness would occur." • "Antilock brake system brake light came on and brakes failed when driver tried to stop vehicle. Brake pedal went to the floor; vehicle did not stop."

2. Power train: transmission: automatic, poor performance, difficulty shifting, slipping. • "While driving on freeway, noticed a downshifting sound; vehicle began to decelerate, then suddenly saw smoke coming from rear. Found engine compartment on fire." • "Automatic transmission does not automatically shift into gear while driving on freeway." • "The transmission will not downshift; it needs to be rebuilt." • "The electronic automatic transmission had to be replaced at 14,000 miles, and now has to be replaced again at owners expense." • "Transmission jumps out of gear in reverse when vehicle is stopped."

3. Brakes: hydraulic system, noise, failure. • "Brake failure caused accident." • "Fluid leak, causing loss of brake." • "Brakes do not stop the vehicle properly; adjusted several times." • "While driving, attempted to brake, but brakes were mushy." • "Brakes failed 3 times, resulting in accidents prior to and after recall repairs." • "Noise is heard when braking; brakes perform erratically, with mushy feeling when applied."

4. Structure: door assembly, poor performance, failure. • "While parked on an incline, upon opening, the sliding door fell off track on 2 occasions." • "Sliding door came off of track when attempting to close." • "Driver's- and passenger-side doors fall off and get caught in the fender while driving." • "Sliding door has a tendency to come off track." • "Passenger sliding door fell off."

5. Interior systems: active restraints: belt buckles, malfunction, failure. • "Driver's seat belt mechanism does not lock." • "Both front seat belts are hard to close; feels like there are things stuck in there." • "All seat belts can release with a soft touch." • "Driver's seat belt buckle fails to remain engaged. Owner has had dealer replace buckle 3 times." • "The seat belts in rear seat middle position lap belt unlatched. Belt in middle seat on right came loose from floor bolt." • "Airbag did not deploy."

6. Brakes: power assist: primary: pump, malfunction, failure. • "Antilock brake system failure; experience extended stopping distance; antilock brake system light comes on; power assist pump failure." • "Antilock brake system malfunctioned, resulting in long stopping distance. Replaced antilock brake system pump." • "Antilock brake system brake pump failed, causing ineffective braking ability; replaced twice." • "Antilock brake system hydraulic pump caused brakes to fail, resulting in extended stopping distance; slowly guide to stop." • "Antilock brake system: Pedal went to the floor, gradually increasing stopping distances. Multiple repairs, and replaced motor and pump assembly."

PLYMOUTH TRUCK VOYAGER 1992

Complaint Severity: Typical. **Recall Alert:** See Recall Index. **Buyer's Summary:** The airbags in this vehicle have experienced failures and malfunctions: You may need a professional evaluation on the condition of the airbags. Check the brakes—listen for noise, look for leaks and feel for vibration. They may fail, perform poorly or require frequent mechanical attention. Test the transmission thoroughly.

Hot Spots and Owner/NHTSA Comments:

1. Brakes: hydraulic: anti-skid system, poor performance, failure, locking up. • "Antilock brake system: Master brake cylinder failed, making brake pedal unable to be depressed. Replaced part, but problem reoccurs." • "Antilock brake system: While applying brakes, very difficult to stop vehicle; excessive effort; caused extended stopping distances." • "Antilock brake system: On panic stop, vehicle responds with delay. Driver ran off road due to extended stopping distance." • "Estimated speed 25 mph; in snowy conditions, antilock brake system didn't respond to brake application. No airbag deployment." • "Loss of brakes; antilock brake system; no brake pressure."

2. Interior systems: passive restraint: airbag: driver, malfunction, failure. • "Airbag did not deploy in an accident." • "Driver was bruised when airbag did not deploy during a 45-mph head-on crash." • "Airbag did not deploy in front-end collision; vehicle went into a snowbank at 35 mph, causing internal injuries to driver." • "Frontal collision, impact 11:00 position, 50 mph, airbag did not deploy." • "Airbag did not deploy during front-end collision; speed 15 mph; impact 12:00 position."

3. Power train: transmission: automatic, poor performance, difficulty shifting, slipping. • "Transmission does not shift out of 1st gear." • "Transmission replaced 3 times due to rapid downshifting and/or vibrations; caused loss of control." • "Automatic transmission: shifted from drive to park; left car running while parked on incline; driver noticed car coming toward him; driver pinned between car and workbench." • "The transmission does not shift properly and makes a banging noise." • "Had transmission replaced once, repaired twice; it slips and skips gears."

4. Brakes: hydraulic system, failure. • "Entire antilock and dual brake systems were not working; dealer replaced entire brake system." • "Brakes disengaged at 5 mph when applied, causing vehicle to run a stop sign; crashed into a bus." • "Brakes failed, causing accident." • "When vehicle is at altitude higher than 5,280 feet, brakes and steering go out." • "When brakes were applied, driver lost steering control, hitting concrete median."

5. Brakes: power assist: primary: pump, malfunction, failure. • "Antilock brake system: When entering highway, applied brakes, pedal went to the floor. Replaced pump and relay." • "Antilock brake system brake pump failed, reducing pressure to nothing. Pump replaced, and the following day failure reoccurred. • "Antilock brake system malfunctioned, resulting in excessively long stopping distance. In some cases, braking ability is lost. Replaced pump and motor assembly." • "Experienced extended stopping distance on several occasions due to antilock brake system pump assembly failure." • "Antilock system pump failed, causing complete loss of braking power. Antilock brake system warning light and regular brake light came on prior to failure. No other warning."

6. Structure: hatchback locks and latches, failure. • "Rear liftgate opened upon impact; vehicle rear-ended by another vehicle at low speed; bent bumper; knocked rear seat out." • "Whenever attempting to close liftgate, experience difficulty; latch keeps popping open; finally must use key to lock." • "Vehicle's rear liftgate opened while driving when going over a bump. The rear hatch flew open and glass shattered." • "Van was in an accident; hit from the rear and the rear hatch latch came open." • "The rear hatch latch is hard to close."

PLYMOUTH TRUCK VOYAGER 1993

Complaint Severity: Typical. **Recall Alert:** See Recall Index. **Buyer's Summary:** Check the brakes—listen for noise, look for leaks and feel for vibration. They may fail, perform poorly or require frequent mechanical attention. Test the transmission thoroughly.

Hot Spots and Owner/NHTSA Comments:

1. Brakes: hydraulic: anti-skid system, poor performance, failure, locking up. • "Antilock brake system went out; experiencing long stopping distance; almost resulting in accident." • "Antilock brake system: Applied brakes; second time, brakes locked up; vehicle slid; hit by another; vehicle totaled." • "Went to stop the truck and experienced total brake failure." • "Had 9 experiences with having to shift into lower gear because antilock brake system would not work." • "Antilock brake system light lit up within 1 mile; brakes became stiff; great deal of force applied in order to stop." • "The van has experienced complete brake failure of the antilock brake system on the vehicle."

2. Power train: transmission: automatic, poor performance, difficulty shifting, slipping. • "Transmission does not shift correctly, and causes vehicle to stall." • "Transmission vibration." • "Transmission failure." • "Transmission noise when shifting gears from 1st to 2nd." • "Automatic transmission; owners heard loud noise; vehicle no longer responded to acceleration."

3. Electrical system: ignition, stalling, failure. • "While driving, engine suddenly died without warning; lost all vehicle power; cause unknown; speed 35-40 mph; curvy roads." • "Vehicle stalls out while in motion." • "Intermittent stalling." • "Vehicle stops without warning; problem will not duplicate for dealer." • "Vehicle can be driven for about 5 minutes and then dies." • "While driving, vehicle will shut down with no warning."

4. Brakes: hydraulic system, poor performance, failure. • "Experiencing extended stopping distance." • "Consumer was driving with 2 children in van, tried to stop at a stop sign and van wouldn't stop; went through the stop sign; had to drive van in low gear." • "Wheels will not lock up on dry roads when brakes are applied in panic situation." • "Brakes are still failing, after having them looked at 8 times." • "Heavy-duty brakes; upon application, brake pedal went to the floor, with vehicle responding slowly. Incident occurred twice; cause unknown."

5. Structure: hatchback locks and latches, failure. • "Rear hatch latch opened while driving; no impact involved." • "Had a rear-end collision; rear door popped open." • "Rear liftgate opened up while driving." • "While driving and attempting to slow down, rear door clicks, with warning light possibly illuminating. Driver got out to reclose." • "Rental vehicle; lost control of vehicle, rolled over; rear latch liftgate came open."

6. Equipment: child seat: integral part of seat, poor design. • "The built-in child seat came undone in a sudden stop." • "The plastic buckle on the child safety seat came loose when vehicle was in an accident. Child's arms and torso came out of seat." • "Built-in child safety seat does not keep the final strap tight when vehicle is in motion." • "Integrated child safety seat does not keep child upright when he or she is sleeping." • "Integrated child safety seat option does not recline, leaving child in an upright position and allowing child's head to lean forward so that neck is vulnerable."

PLYMOUTH TRUCK VOYAGER 1994

Complaint Severity: Serious. **Recall Alert:** See Recall Index. **Buyer's Summary:** The airbags in this vehicle have experienced failures and malfunctions: You may need a professional evaluation on the condition of the airbags. Check the brakes—listen for noise, look for leaks and feel for vibration. They may fail, perform poorly or require frequent mechanical attention. Test the transmission thoroughly.

Hot Spots and Owner/NHTSA Comments:

1. Structure: hatchback locks and latches, failure. • "Vehicle rear hatch latch is difficult to close; have to slam down 4 or 5 times to shut." • "Rear door latch pops open while driving on regular road conditions." • "Back hatch has opened several times and contents of van spilled onto highway." • "Rear liftgate opened by itself while driving." • "While driving, the rear hatch latch came open."

2. Interior systems: passive restraint: airbag: driver, malfunction, failure. • "During frontal collision, driver's-side airbag did not deploy." • "Airbag failed to deploy when driver rear-ended another vehicle." • "Vehicle was in an accident and driver's airbag didn't deploy; consumer hit passenger side of another car." • "In a vehicle crash, the airbags did not deploy." • "The vehicle was involved in a frontal collision at 55 mph and driver's airbag did not deploy."

3. Brakes: hydraulic: anti-skid system, poor performance, failure, locking up. • "Antilock brake system failed to stop vehicle effectively when applied; caused extended stopping or became inoperative." • "Antilock brake system: Owner indicates brakes perform erratically, on wet surfaces with pedal going to floor." • "Antilock brake system malfunctioned during normal stopping; pedal got soft and antilock brake system light came on; dealer cannot locate the problem." • "Antilock brake system continually fails. Brakes catch and then let go." • "The brakes go to the floor and do not work; lock up."

4. Power train: transmission: automatic, poor performance, difficulty shifting, slipping. • "Transmission makes clunking noise; jumps forward upon stopping or accelerating." • "Automatic transmission failure; would not shift into gear." • "Gear shifted while being parked on an incline; transmission popped out of park; vehicle rolled into another piece of equipment and smashed rear end." • "Excessive effort required to shift into drive." • "Automatic transmission has failed completely; occasionally hesitates before going into reverse, then slams into reverse; does not move when applying gas pedal."

5. Interior systems: passive restraint: airbag: passenger, failure. • "Vehicle was involved in an accident and the airbags did not deploy." • "Dual airbags did not deploy during frontal collision; vehicle broadsided another vehicle; impact 12:00 position; speed 40 mph." • "Frontal collision, impact 12:00 position, speed 45 mph, lost control; went into embankment; passenger's airbag did not deploy and lap and shoulder belt failed." • "Upon frontal collision to a rear-ender, dual airbags failed to deploy." • "During frontal collision, passenger-side airbag did not deploy."

6. Electrical system: ignition, stalling, failure. • "Vehicle stalled on railroad tracks and at other times, with no warning. Numerous tests by dealer with no change in condition." • "Auto stops while driving; told that they have found the problem, but the auto keeps doing the same thing." • "Vehicle stalls; loss of power steering." • "Ignition sticks." • "Key fails to move in ignition."

Pontiac

PONTIAC 6000 1987

Complaint Severity: Typical. **Recall Alert:** See Recall Index. **Buyer's Summary:** Look carefully for any kind of leakage, especially under the car. The electronic control unit has been blamed for engine performance problems, including stalling and surging. The fuel injection system has been blamed for hesitation and stalling. Be sure the vehicle doesn't die in traffic or at stops. The steering may be stiff or not working correctly. Be sure to test the steering, especially on a cold start. Check the brakes—listen for noise, look for leaks and feel for vibration. They may fail, perform poorly or require frequent mechanical attention. See "Sudden Accelerations" in Introduction.

Hot Spots and Owner/NHTSA Comments:

1. Fuel: fuel injection system, stalling, hesitation. • "Car stalls; sometimes accelerates and difficult to stop." • "Engine stalls at all speeds up to 50 mph; car loses power to steering and brakes." • "When gas tank half full or less, noise increases; car stalls, quits, conks out; continual problem." • "Intermittent stalling." • "Intermittent stalling and/or surging."

2. Brakes: hydraulic system, locking up, failure. • "Vehicle has had continual brake problems." • "Heavy rain conditions; applied brakes, brakes locked, car swerved and spun around, careening all over the road." • "Must depress pedal with extra energy or pump pedal several times to stop vehicle."
3. Fuel: throttle linkages and control, sudden accelerations. • "While backing out of parking space, car suddenly accelerated backwards at an increasing speed until it hit a building; brakes seem ineffective." • "On several occasions car accelerated without driver's assistance." • "In reverse, car surges backward uncontrollably without any warning." • "Car suddenly accelerated in reverse; brakes applied but not effective; control lost, hitting a building." • "Attempted to accelerate normally, car rapidly accelerated on its own; car did not downshift, braking to no avail."
4. Steering: gear: rack-and-pinion, stiffness, poor performance. • "Rack-and-pinion steering locks up during cold start." • "Rack-and-pinion steering failed, causing excessive effort in steering." • "In cold weather, steering wheel turns in jerks, makes popping noise in column; improves when vehicle warms up, but does not function normally." • "Rack-and-pinion steering sticks and vibrates at low speeds; power steering was replaced; condition improved, now have loud noise when wheel is turned." • "Rack-and-pinion steering locks up; seals are wearing out against the aluminum housing."
5. Electrical system: ignition: electronic control unit, sudden acceleration, stalling. • "Engine has tendency to speed up, even when no pressure is applied; occurs sporadically; 2 modules were repaired/replaced, problem still exists." • "Attempting to back out of parking place in congested parking lot, car suddenly accelerated backward at an increasing rate of speed until it hit a building." • "Defective programmable read-only memory; causes car to stall out; surges at high and low speeds, idles rough and rough shifting into gear." • "Intermittent stalling."
6. Engine: leaks, fire, excessive wear. • "Problem with coolant leaking from engine." • "Problem with car not starting; caught on fire approximately 30 minutes later, engulfed entire car." • "Coolant leak from engine; repaired twice, problem not corrected." • "High oil consumption." • "Car burns oil excessively (every 1,000 miles)."

PONTIAC 6000 1988

Complaint Severity: Typical. **Recall Alert:** See Recall Index. **Buyer's Summary:** Verify that the cruise control system works properly, and that it doesn't cause the engine to surge. The electronic control unit has been blamed for engine performance problems, including stalling and surging. The fuel injection system has been blamed for hesitation and stalling. Be sure the vehicle doesn't die in traffic or at stops. The steering may be stiff or not working correctly. Be sure to test the steering, especially on a cold start. Check the brakes—listen for noise, look for leaks and feel for vibration. They may fail, perform poorly or require frequent mechanical attention. See "Sudden Accelerations" in Introduction.

Hot Spots and Owner/NHTSA Comments:
1. Brakes: hydraulic system, vibration, excessive wear. • "Vibration when applying the brakes to slow down or stop." • "Premature brake wear; replaced 3 times by 25,000 miles." • "Brakes failed completely upon application, resulting in accident." • "Brakes squeal when lightly applied; noise disappears when pressure applied." • "Power brakes lose their boost at times; don't work properly."
2. Electrical system: ignition: electronic control unit, stalling, malfunction. • "Sometimes car wouldn't start, at other times car would die out trying to complete a turn; car would lurch forward without foot on gas; third programmable read-only memory replacement." • "Engine stalls from zero to 60 mph with no warning." • "Engine continually stalls; shuts off while driving at any speed or at stoplight." • "Car frequently loses power and stalls for no apparent reason; has to be restarted, 'service engine' light comes on; repaired/replaced electronic control module, electronic control module calibrator and programmable read-only memory." • "Had to replace 8 computers due to rough idle/stalling."
3. Steering: gear: rack-and-pinion, stiffness, poor performance. • "Difficult to turn steering wheel upon starting in cold weather due to rack-and-pinion steering binding; brought to dealer and had to pay for labor, but not parts." • "Noisy power steering when turning." • "Fluid level gets low from leak at rack-and-pinion area, causing wheel to lock up while turning." • "Power steering failure; seals leak and steering growls and vibrates when steering wheel turned sharply; worse upon first startup." • "Power steering very hard; needs excessive effort to turn steering wheel."
4. Fuel: throttle linkages and control, sudden accelerations. • "Sudden acceleration in reverse at startup with foot on brake pedal." • "Backing from parking space, vehicle suddenly accelerated uncontrollably, smashing into other cars." • "Car accelerated at such speed that car literally went flying through back of garage, airborne; took drop of 12 feet." • "Vehicle accelerated uncontrollably, while backing up, smashing into cars behind." • "Two accidents due to sudden acceleration."
5. Fuel: fuel injection system, stalling, hesitation. • "Idles extremely fast when starting cold." • "Engine runs rough and jerks at 30-35 mph." • "Car would not start when hot." • "Repeated stalling." • "Stalling problems." • "Intermittent stalling; several repairs to no avail."
6. Equipment: speed control, sudden acceleration, malfunction. • "Set cruise control, car accelerated; continued to accelerate out of control, as though foot pedal stuck." • "While in cruise control mode, vehicle surged ahead suddenly at a fast speed, giving feeling of being out of control." • "Cruise control sticks, will not release upon hitting brakes; quit operating completely." • "When cruise control is used or going up incline, and even driving away from stop sign, car pings every time accelerate."

PONTIAC 6000 1989

Complaint Severity: Minor. **Recall Alert:** See Recall Index. **Buyer's Summary:** The electronic control unit has been blamed for engine performance problems, including stalling and surging. The fuel injection system has been blamed for hesitation and stalling. Be sure the vehicle doesn't die in traffic or at stops. Check the brakes—listen for noise, look for leaks and feel for vibration. They may fail, perform poorly or require frequent mechanical attention. Test the transmission thoroughly. See "Sudden Accelerations" in Introduction.

Hot Spots and Owner/NHTSA Comments:
1. Electrical system: ignition: electronic control unit, stalling, malfunction. • "Engine shuts down while driving on interstate or at stop signs; no warning given." • "Repeated failures of the electronic computer module caused vehicle to stall." • "Experienced stalling at high or low speeds, resulting in loss of power steering and braking capability; replaced electronic control module." • "Vehicle serviced the day before an accident due to stalling; replaced chip in engine." • "Car stalls and loses all power when applying brakes."
2. Fuel: fuel injection system, stalling, hesitation. • "Vehicle loses its ability to idle when taking foot off accelerator pedal; engine dies." • "Car stopped when driving; engine would die every 100 feet." • "Intermittent stalling problem; usually car will stall or not start after driving 1-2 hours, and will stall driving 40 mph; no warning prior to condition." • "Repeated stalls when slowing." •

"Engine quits suddenly, without warning, while driving; lose power brakes and steering in traffic."
3. Fuel: throttle linkages and control, sudden accelerations. • "When gear placed into reverse, car accelerated with foot on brake; skidded, collided with and stopped by concrete planter; revving and racing until ignition turned off." • "Upon starting vehicle and shifting gear into reverse, vehicle suddenly accelerated out of control, resulting in an accident." • "Vehicle surges forward and driver lost control of vehicle." • "Sudden acceleration in reverse."
4. Brakes: hydraulic system, sudden acceleration, failure. • "As approached red light, brakes failed; accident." • "Vehicle accelerated, allowing uncontrollable braking ability; brakes burned out; possible fuel injection system problem."
5. Power train: transmission: automatic, poor performance, difficulty shifting, slipping. • "Transmission was not shifting properly." • "Transmission slipping; rebuilt." • "While driving at 55 mph, transmission failed; vehicle's speed cut back to 25-35 mph and wouldn't accelerate." • "Transmission shifts improperly; leaking." • "Automatic transmission failure at 50,000 miles."
6. Electrical system: ignition, stalling. • "Engine stalling problem; when at low speed, as in turns or entering or leaving parking space, car stalls; will lurch or surge when foot not on accelerator." • "While driving along in traffic, vehicle stalls." • "Vehicle constantly stalled without warning." • "While driving at 55 mph, vehicle stalled; problem lasted over 1-week period."

PONTIAC BONNEVILLE 1987

Complaint Severity: Troublesome. **Recall Alert:** See Recall Index. **Buyer's Summary:** The electronic control unit has been blamed for engine performance problems, including stalling and surging. The fuel injection system has been blamed for hesitation and stalling. Be sure the vehicle doesn't die in traffic or at stops. The steering may be stiff or not working correctly. Be sure to test the steering, especially on a cold start. Test the transmission thoroughly. See "Sudden Accelerations" in Introduction.

Hot Spots and Owner/NHTSA Comments:
1. Fuel: throttle linkages and control, sudden accelerations. • "While parked and slowly moving forward, shifted into drive vehicle suddenly accelerated." • "Started the vehicle and shifted into gear, car went into full throttle." • "Vehicle suddenly accelerated backward upon starting, resulting in severe damages." • "Continual unintended acceleration problems; brakes unable to stop when acceleration occurs; finally resulted in accident." • "Unintended sudden acceleration seems to occur at downshift from 4th to 3rd gear; pump on brakes to stop." • "Vehicle suddenly accelerated as topped hill, making it impossible to stop car in time to prevent hitting vehicles stopped ahead."
2. Fuel: fuel injection system, stalling, hesitation. • "While driving, car has stalled, causing all power to shut off, including power to steer; swerved to one side." • "Vehicle suffers chronic stalling due to failure of various fuel system components, such as fuel pump, mass air flow sensor and throttle position sensor." • "Vehicle stalled several times at various speeds; problem with the fuel injection system." • "Engine stalling problems while driving; complete loss of brakes and steering when stalling occurs." • "Engine dies when either slowing down or at full stop."
3. Electrical system: ignition: electronic control unit, stalling, malfunction. • "While driving, engine would die for no reason at all." • "Computer system failed; car went completely dead driving highway speed; no steering or brakes; hard stopping; after 30 minutes, restarted; repaired/replaced microchip." • "Electric failure; car suddenly stalls; replaced mass air flow sensor and programmable read-only memory, stalling continues." • "While traveling at 60-65 miles an hour, engine would die in middle of traffic; installed electronic control module and calibrator, problem still not resolved." • "Engine stalls at slow or high speeds; replaced programmable read-only memory in computer and exhaust gas recirculation valve, problem remains."
4. Power train: transmission: automatic, poor performance, difficulty shifting, slipping. • "Vehicle goes backward when in drive rolls backward between removing foot from brake and application to accelerator." • "Vehicle installed with undersized transmission from factory, resulting in transmission failure." • "Automatic transmission jumps and drags while in gear." • "Car shudders at 45 mph; vibrates; gear sticking; replaced transmission." • "Vehicle downshifts into 2nd gear very rough, particularly when climbing hills; happens sometimes on the upshift."
5. Steering: gear: rack-and-pinion, stiffness, poor performance. • "Rack-and-pinion steering binds during cold start; replaced." • "Rack-and-pinion steering is very hard for first 5 minutes, and then has hard spots at different speeds." • "Vehicle pulls to left and power steering binds at cold start due to rack-and-pinion malfunction." • "Steering locks up in cold weather; wheel would not turn for 5-10 minutes, then would free up." • "Failure of power steering; repaired 5 times; 4 major repairs done."
6. Electrical system: ignition, stalling, failure. • "Ignition module failed, causing intermittent stalling." • "While driving, car loses all power." • "Engine stalling; would stop running at high speeds." • "Vehicle constantly stalls; various parts have been replaced and vehicle was repaired numerous times." • "Vehicle stalls at highway speeds."

PONTIAC BONNEVILLE 1988

Complaint Severity: Serious. **Buyer's Summary:** Verify that the cruise control system works properly, and that it doesn't cause the engine to surge. The steering may be stiff or not working correctly. Be sure to test the steering, especially on a cold start. Check the brakes—listen for noise, look for leaks and feel for vibration. They may fail, perform poorly or require frequent mechanical attention. Test the transmission thoroughly. See "Sudden Accelerations" in Introduction.

Hot Spots and Owner/NHTSA Comments:
1. Fuel: throttle linkages and control, sudden accelerations. • "After shifting out of park, vehicle suddenly accelerated; resulted in accident." • "Throttle will not return to idle after removing foot from accelerator pedal, causing acceleration; it works properly on uphill grades." • "Vehicle seemed to be accelerating; before could regain control of car, struck rear of vehicle in front." • "Vehicle suddenly accelerated out of control upon shifting gear into drive." • "Upon starting car and shifting gear to drive, suddenly accelerated out of control, resulting in an accident."
2. Power train: transmission: automatic, poor performance, difficulty shifting, slipping. • "Premature failure of reverse gear in automatic transmission." • "Transmission problems when shifting into overdrive." • "Replaced automatic transmission fluid, filter and pan gasket." • "Automatic transmission slipping in 2nd gear." • "Transmission does not come out of 1st gear at times; other times will not come out of 2nd; must stop and start up again."
3. Steering: gear: rack-and-pinion, stiffness, poor performance. • "Rack-and-pinion steering binds when engine is cold." • "Power steering mechanism fails to work immediately after ignition in cold weather." • "Rack-and-pinion binds and locks up, especially in the mornings or after the vehicle sits for any length of time." • "Power steering does not work properly when vehicle is first started in cold weather." • "While starting up vehicle, rack-and-pinion steering locks up during cold weather."

4. Brakes: hydraulic: shoe: disc brake system, locking up, excessive wear, vibration. • "Front brakes locked up." • "Brakes jerk when applied; feels like brakes might lock up." • "Front disc brakes seem to have excessive wear; repaired/replaced original at 17,000 miles, brakes repaired/replaced approximately every 10,000 miles." • "Premature brake wear; pads replaced at 12,000 miles." • "Defective front disc brakes warped rotors, which causes chattering and front-end vibration when brakes are applied; repaired/replaced, problem reoccurring."

5. Equipment: speed control, sudden acceleration, malfunction. • "With cruise control on, vehicle surged forward twice while going up grade and once on level road." • "Cruise control malfunctioning; causes car to speed up." • "Cruise control randomly accelerates to wide-open throttle when activated. Pontiac cannot solve problem." • "Cruise control sets intermittently; when it does set, it allows speed to vary from 50-75 mph; modulator module diagnosed as defective."

PONTIAC BONNEVILLE 1989

Complaint Severity: Typical. **Recall Alert:** See Recall Index. **Buyer's Summary:** Verify that the cruise control system works properly, and that it doesn't cause the engine to surge. The fuel injection system has been blamed for hesitation and stalling. Be sure the vehicle doesn't die in traffic or at stops. Check the brakes—listen for noise, look for leaks and feel for vibration. They may fail, perform poorly or require frequent mechanical attention. Test the transmission thoroughly.

Hot Spots and Owner/NHTSA Comments:

1. Brakes: hydraulic system, excessive wear, failure. • "Premature brake wear." • "Two very close calls where car could not stop within normal distance; in both cases, wheels simply wouldn't stop, or skidded." • "Brakes inadequate; takes too long to stop; fades." • "Brake failure at approximately 35-40 mph caused vehicle to lose control and rear-end another vehicle." • "Accident due to brake failure; both occupants hurt badly; factory defect."

2. Fuel: fuel injection system, stalling, hesitation. • "Defective fuel injection caused engine to run bad; added cleaner to gas to correct problem." • "Engine stalling in traffic when fuel low." • "Hard starting problem; many repairs, problem continues." • "Intermittent stalling, despite many repairs." • "Intermittent stalling."

3. Power train: transmission: automatic, poor performance, difficulty shifting, slipping. • "Transmission slips in reverse and 1st gear." • "Difficult downshifting of transmission." • "Premature failure of transmission." • "Defective transmission; repaired/replaced." • "Transmission failure."

4. Equipment: speed control, malfunction, failure. • "Cruise control failure." • "Cruise control goes on and off when set." • "Cruise control inoperative." • "Cruise control malfunction."

5. Brakes: hydraulic: anti-skid system, poor performance, failure, locking up. • "Antilock brake system locking up at slow speeds in winter driving; caused accident." • "Antilock brake system failed; essentially total brake failure; pedal nearly impossible to push; antilock brake system warning light did come on." • "Antilock brake system: Pedal faded; to stop vehicle, had to pump the pedal several times to build up pressure." • "Antilock brake system brake pedal gets rock hard when stopping; 2 occasions; one at 45 mph and one at 60 mph; dealer cannot duplicate to repair."

PONTIAC BONNEVILLE 1990

Complaint Severity: Minor. **Buyer's Summary:** The fuel injection system has been blamed for hesitation and stalling. Be sure the vehicle doesn't die in traffic or at stops. Check the brakes—listen for noise, look for leaks and feel for vibration. They may fail, perform poorly or require frequent mechanical attention. See "Sudden Accelerations" in Introduction.

Hot Spots and Owner/NHTSA Comments:

1. Brakes: hydraulic: anti-skid system, poor performance, failure, locking up. • "Antilock brake system: Rotors, calipers and pads constantly go out—approximately every 2 months; caliper sticks; hear grinding noise; loss of brakes." • "Was driving on the freeway, trying to slow down and the brake pedal wouldn't go down." • "When applying the brake, sometimes it will not stop the car." • "Consumer had to make an emergency stop; the antilock brake system failed." • "Antilock brake system failure; intermittent loss of braking."

2. Electrical system: ignition, stalling, malfunction. • "Sensor failure in engine causes vehicle to stall, causing the front wheel to lock up." • "Vehicle stalls without warning, causing loss of control." • "Vehicle stalled without warning; while driving and when coming to stop, to keep vehicle running, foot has to be on accelerator." • "While driving 60 mph on expressway, at city speeds, slow speeds or idling, engine stalls and/or cuts out and has absolutely no power." • "Poor cold starting; ignition blackouts during acceleration."

3. Fuel: fuel injection system, stalling, hesitation. • "Fuel injection failed; caused vehicle to stall." • "Injection problem." • "Fuel injector sensor failed." • "Vehicle hesitated while going up hill, got uphill; and stalled down other slope."

4. Fuel: throttle linkages and control, sudden accelerations. • "While shifting gear from park to drive, vehicle suddenly accelerated out of control; resulted in an accident." • "While backing out of a parking space, vehicle accelerated forward and out of control without foot on accelerator pedal; resulted in an accident." • "Experienced sudden acceleration; lost control, hitting a parked vehicle, impact 1:00 position." • "Vehicle stalls with warning; in for repair of computer, throttle position sensor and fuel pump."

PONTIAC BONNEVILLE 1992

Complaint Severity: Typical. **Recall Alert:** See Recall Index. **Buyer's Summary:** Look carefully for any kind of leakage, especially under the car. The airbags in this vehicle have experienced failures and malfunctions: You may need a professional evaluation on the condition of the airbags. Check the brakes—listen for noise, look for leaks and feel for vibration. They may fail, perform poorly or require frequent mechanical attention.

Hot Spots and Owner/NHTSA Comments:

1. Brakes: hydraulic system, locking up, failure. • "Antilock brake system: Brake adjustment broke off; caused brake pads to tear up whole brake system; made loud noise like a blowout; entire system was replaced at 41,000 miles." • "Brakes failed, causing loss of control and an accident." • "Three brake failures; twice within half an hour, pedal went to the floor; accident happened once, speed 30 mph." • "Applied brakes to avoid accident; brakes locked up, could not release."

2. Interior systems: passive restraint: airbag: driver, malfunction, failure. • "Frontal collision, impact 12:00 position, speed 55 mph, airbag did not deploy; lap and shoulder belt did not retract on driver's side." • "Airbag did not deploy during an accident; car has history of electrical problems; insurance adjuster said the airbag sensors did function properly." • "Airbag did not deploy during front-end impact; vehicle hit tree head-on; speed 25-30 mph." • "Airbag did not deploy during front-end collision. Driver lost control. Hit tree head-on. Speed 35 mph on impact." • "Frontal collision, impact 12:00 position, speed 35 mph, airbag did not deploy."

3. Engine: stalling, fire. • "Engine fire." • "Vehicle stalled, resulting in accident and injuries." • "Engine compartment fire while driving at 30 mph; prior to fire, vehicle was serviced for fuel line leak; no warning." • "Vehicle fire." • "While parked in garage, vehicle burst into flames coming from engine compartment after being parked for approximately 15 minutes."
4. Visual systems: glass: windshield, cracking, poor performance. • "Windshield cracked when defroster was turned on." • "Mist forms on windshield when operating defroster. Obstructs visibility." • "While driving at 55 mph and higher, wind gusts in; causes vibration on floorboards and steering wheel; produces strange sound, startling driver." • "Windshield design causes poor visibility."
5. Brakes: hydraulic: shoe and drum system, locking up, leaks, failure. • "Spring broke in rear brake assembly." • "Rear brake lockup on passenger-side." • "Master cylinder leaking due to nothing holding pistons back, causing complete collapse of hardware holding brakes in place." • "Antilock brake system: While driving at moderate speed, applied brakes; no braking effect; right rear brake assembly broke; no warning."

PONTIAC BONNEVILLE 1993

Complaint Severity: Troublesome. **Buyer's Summary:** The airbags in this vehicle have experienced failures and malfunctions: You may need a professional evaluation on the condition of the airbags. Test the transmission thoroughly.

Hot Spots and Owner/NHTSA Comments:
1. Interior systems: passive restraint: airbag: driver, malfunction, failure. • "Frontal collision, impact 12:00 position, speed 15 mph, dual airbags did not deploy." • "Other driver jumped the stop sign and vehicle was forced into a telephone pole; driver's airbag did not deploy." • "Airbag did not deploy during head-on collision." • "Hit vehicle broadside and airbag did not deploy."
2. Power train: transmission: automatic, poor performance, difficulty shifting, slipping. • "Transmission would not shift past 2nd gear. Had to have it replaced 1 month after purchase date." • "While driving, noticed smoke in rear; passing driver indicated vehicle was on fire. Pulled to side to put out fire. Dealer says transmission caught fire." • "Automatic transmission failure." • "Cooling unit leaks."

PONTIAC FIERO 1987

Complaint Severity: Harmless. **Recall Alert:** See Recall Index. **Buyer's Summary:** The electronic control unit has been blamed for engine performance problems, including stalling and surging. The fuel injection system has been blamed for hesitation and stalling. Be sure the vehicle doesn't die in traffic or at stops. Check the brakes—listen for noise, look for leaks and feel for vibration. They may fail, perform poorly or require frequent mechanical attention.

Hot Spots and Owner/NHTSA Comments:
1. Engine: stalling, fire. • "Constant engine problems; smoke from engine." • " 'Service engine soon' light wouldn't go off; engine backfiring; smoking bad in engine compartment." • "Engine lost power and stalled, then caught on fire." • "Engine compartment fire." • "Potential for engine compartment fire; recall repair done."
2. Brakes: hydraulic system, noise, pulling, poor performance. • "While driving 45 mph, a truck stopped suddenly; applied brake, traveled 300 feet before brakes activated; caused rear-end collision with truck." • "Brakes make a very loud clunking and grinding noise." • "Brakes making loud clunking and/or grinding noise; vehicle often pulls to left or whips when hitting deformities in road; driver experiencing loss of control of car." • "Brakes make high, piercing cricket sound upon application."
3. Fuel: fuel injection system, stalling, hesitation. • "Car took off at intersection, then lost all power and stalled." • "Vehicle misses and/or stalls; repairs rendered, problem continues." • "Vehicle totally cuts out and stalls; loses all warning signals and steering; resulted in accident." • "Engine fire after recall repairs." • "Engine caught on fire after recall repairs."
4. Electrical system: stalling, fire, failure. • "Problem with stalling and hard start; engine gets very hot; sensors and electrical components continuously burn out; smoke and sparks came out of air filter and engine." • "Electrical failure." • "Engine replaced; shortly thereafter, wiring around engine caught fire." • "Recall notice not received for defective electrical system." • "Fire in electrical system caused major damages."
5. Electrical system: ignition: electronic control unit, stalling, malfunction. • "Stalling problem; car went dead and did not restart; problem caused by defect in electronic control module and manifold air pressure sensor." • "Electronic control module replaced." • "Electronic control module inoperative." • "Engine rpm increases by itself; races and will not idle down."
6. Engine cooling system: overheating. • "Engine always overheating and burning too much oil." • "Engine overheats." • "Engine frequently overheats." • "Engine overheats; water pump and head gasket replaced."

PONTIAC FIERO 1988

Complaint Severity: Typical. **Recall Alert:** See Recall Index. **Buyer's Summary:** The electronic control unit has been blamed for engine performance problems, including stalling and surging. Test the suspension by feeling for vibration or pulling while driving. Check the brakes—listen for noise, look for leaks and feel for vibration. They may fail, perform poorly or require frequent mechanical attention. Test the clutch. See "Sudden Accelerations" in Introduction.

Hot Spots and Owner/NHTSA Comments:
1. Engine: overheating, fire. • "Overheating of engine due to loss of coolant and sludge buildup." • "Excessive oil consumption; smoke coming from exhaust." • "Defective engine; potential engine fire." • "Defect in engine; fire completely destroyed." • "Always smelling smoke while traveling; engine always seems hot or burning."
2. Fuel: throttle linkages and control, sudden accelerations. • "Car started with roar; upon releasing hand brake, went forward at tremendous speed straight through garage door into pole and stopped." • "Accelerator sticks; car speeds up on its own without pressing accelerator." • "Two accidents due to vehicle reversing directions at full speed." • "Engine accelerated to full speed while driving; from 55 to 100 mph on one occasion, again from 35 mph, resulting in an accident. No prior warning."
3. Brakes: hydraulic: disc: caliper, breaking, failure. • "Rear brake calipers failed." • "The bolts were missing from the rear caliper; the rim was damaged; the emergency brake bracket pads were no good; the brake pad on the left rear was split." • "Rear brake calipers failed twice." • "Caliper broke; brake pad and rotor wore on one side; hubcap ruined."
4. Electrical system: ignition: electronic control unit, hesitation, failure. • "Hesitation on acceleration; stalling; erratic idle; continual loss of power; replaced programmable read-only memory for electronic control module." • "Defective computer replaced." • "Electronic control module failed."
5. Power train: clutch assembly, failure. • "Clutch failure." • "Replaced clutch." • "Clutch hard to depress; chatters when pushed; replaced clutch master cylinder."

6. Suspension: independent front, vibration, failure. • "Front-end suspension assembly disconnected from frame; loss of steering capacity; veered off road to avoid collision." • "Front-end suspension disconnected from frame; lost steering capacity." • "Vehicle experiencing severe vibration through steering column." • "Front-end suspension system became disconnected from frame; steering capacity lost."

PONTIAC FIREBIRD 1987

Complaint Severity: Troublesome. **Recall Alert:** See Recall Index. **Buyer's Summary:** The electronic control unit has been blamed for engine performance problems, including stalling and surging. The fuel injection system has been blamed for hesitation and stalling. Be sure the vehicle doesn't die in traffic or at stops. The steering may be stiff or not working correctly. Be sure to test the steering, especially on a cold start. See "Sudden Accelerations" in Introduction.

Hot Spots and Owner/NHTSA Comments:

1. Fuel: throttle linkages and control, sudden accelerations. • "Accelerator pedal sticks momentarily in depressed position when traveling at 25-35 mph; problem intermittent." • "Vehicle experiencing chronic sudden acceleration problems." • "After accelerating to pass another vehicle, car continued to accelerate when foot taken off gas pedal; key turned off and steering wheel locked; resulted in an accident." • "While driving, vehicle suddenly accelerated to high speed; went out of control; resulted in an accident." • "Car unable to decelerate; applied brakes, car maintained its speed; resulted in an accident."

2. Steering: power assist: pump, breaking, failure. • "Broke away from its mounting plate twice, causing fluid to fly around under hood." • "Power steering became inoperable; lost all power; received recall letter concerning steering pump mounting bracket and/or loss of serpentine drive belt." • "Loss of power steering while driving 55 mph on turnpike; due to fractured power steering pump support brace." • "Power steering bracket breaks repeatedly; throwing belt; causing all power to be lost; bracket and belt replaced." • "Bracket and bolt suddenly fractured, causing loss of power steering; replaced broken power steering bracket and bolt."

3. Fuel: fuel injection system, stalling, hesitation. • "Car dying or stalling." • "Vehicle stalls at all speeds." • "Intermittent stalling; irregular noise during acceleration." • " 'Service engine' light comes on intermittently, car begins to sputter and hesitate; idles very erratically from high to low, stalls; unable to solve problem." • "Engine stalls, hesitates, lunges, and misses when in operation."

4. Steering: power assist, breaking, excessive wear. • "Power steering bracket broke 2 times." • "Inadequate power steering unit." • "Breakage of power steering." • "Power steering system failed; repaired/replaced power steering bracket, pressure hose, pump, pulley, bracket and bolt." • "Power steering bracket failed in traffic; caused complete loss of power steering; belt was ejected from car; second occurrence."

5. Electrical system: ignition: electronic control unit, stalling, hesitation, failure. • "Engine stalling problems; shuts off while driving at almost any speed and without warning; repaired/replaced electronic control module, mass air flow and valve seals, did not solve problem." • "Electronic control module burned out; replaced 4 times to no avail." • "Car motor hesitates; loss of power and poor performance." • "Incorrect computer chip from factory, causing hesitation at low speed." • "Car speeds up and slows down on its own, regardless of how much gas put in; popping noise under passenger-side; car jumps and/or bucks, then quits totally."

PONTIAC FIREBIRD 1988

Complaint Severity: Typical. **Recall Alert:** See Recall Index. **Buyer's Summary:** Check the brakes—listen for noise, look for leaks and feel for vibration. They may fail, perform poorly or require frequent mechanical attention. See "Sudden Accelerations" in Introduction.

Hot Spots and Owner/NHTSA Comments:

1. Fuel: throttle linkages and control, sudden accelerations. • "The throttle began to stick at about 46,000 miles; vehicle was serviced for this problem 32 times, but problem persists." • "Accident due to sudden acceleration." • "Throttle stuck after taking foot off accelerator; accelerated to more than 100 mph, while overheating brakes; no accident." • "Car suddenly accelerates when started up; control lost; accident resulted." • "Vehicle suddenly accelerated out of control backwards, resulting in an accident."

2. Brakes: hydraulic: shoe: disc brake system, pulling, malfunction. • "Inadequate braking system; brakes pull left so hard that it is difficult to drive." • "Total brake system failure; smoking front brakes; soft pedal; loss of brake pedal at highway speed." • "Car sometimes doesn't have good stopping ability; brakes squeak; when applied, take a while to grab; car propels itself a long way before stopping." • "Front brakes threw off metallic shavings onto wheels, making vehicle noisy."

PONTIAC FIREBIRD 1989

Complaint Severity: Typical. **Recall Alert:** See Recall Index. **Buyer's Summary:** The engine has experienced a variety of problems. Have it examined by a professional. The electronic control unit has been blamed for engine performance problems, including stalling and surging. Check the brakes—listen for noise, look for leaks and feel for vibration. They may fail, perform poorly or require frequent mechanical attention. Test the transmission thoroughly. See "Sudden Accelerations" in Introduction.

Hot Spots and Owner/NHTSA Comments:

1. Fuel: throttle linkages and control, sudden accelerations. • "Idled down, then suddenly accelerated, causing a runaway engine; unable to control at high speed." • "Vehicle suddenly accelerated by itself; problems controlling and bringing to a stop; second incident resulted in accident; repaired/replaced 3 times to no avail." • "Attorney's office representing client; vehicle was stopped at traffic light behind another car; lifting foot off brake pedal, car suddenly accelerated into second car." • "Accelerator pedal sticks open; overrevs to point that car becomes hazardous to operate." • "Upon shifting gear from park to drive, vehicle accelerated out of control; resulted in an accident."

2. Brakes: hydraulic system, noise, failure. • "When making a right turn, applied brakes and foot went down to floor while on pedal; car would not stop." • "Brake cable lying across exhaust pipe; plastic coating melted through; metal rattling against exhaust." • "Brakes failed within 2 years." • "Noisy rear brakes." • "Brakes inoperative; pedal constantly hits the floor."

3. Power train: transmission: automatic, poor performance, difficulty shifting, slipping. • "Every time car was put into drive, it would go into reverse." • "Hard shift or clunk in transmission." • "Transmission overhauled, problems continue." • "While driving, shifted from drive to overdrive; car went into reverse, fishtailed, spun completely around and went backward; accident." • "Transmission replaced."

4. Electrical system: ignition: electronic control unit, stalling, failure. • "Vehicle continually stalled, and would die out in traffic." • "Vehicle stalls intermittently due to electronic control module failure; problem not remedied." • "Engine stalled; replaced electronic control module and rotor." • "Failure of engine computer chip that controls engine, fuel intake, rpm and fuel usage."

5. Electrical system: ignition, malfunction, failure. • "Difficulty starting; rough engine idle." • "Ignition system malfunctioned and caused vehicle not to start; repaired." • "Ignition switch and/or computer failed." • "Ignition system needed complete replacement, as car would no longer start."

6. Engine: miscellaneous problems. • "Excessive oil consumption." • "Blown head gaskets." • "Engine caught on fire while driving." • "Engine (2.8L) not adequate for car."

PONTIAC FIREBIRD 1991

Complaint Severity: Serious. **Recall Alert:** See Recall Index. **Buyer's Summary:** Look carefully for any kind of leakage, especially under the car. The electronic control unit has been blamed for engine performance problems, including stalling and surging. Test the suspension by feeling for vibration or pulling while driving. The airbags in this vehicle have experienced failures and malfunctions: You may need a professional evaluation on the condition of the airbags.

Hot Spots and Owner/NHTSA Comments:

1. Interior systems: passive restraint: airbag: driver, malfunction, failure. • "During an accident while driving at approximately 50 mph, impact at 12:00, the airbag failed to deploy." • "Upon impact at approximately 10-15 mph, airbag did not deploy; rear-ended another vehicle; with frontal crash at 12:00." • "No deployment of airbag during accident; caused neck, back and kidney injuries." • "Horn assembly ceased to operate. Airbag failed to deploy upon frontal impact." • "Head-on collision into another vehicle's side; airbag did not deploy."

2. Fuel: fuel tank assembly: tank, leaks, failure. • "Gas tank leak." • "Recalled for pinholes in gas tank." • "Leak in fuel tank or in the area of tank leaks raw gas onto the exhaust, which could result in an explosion." • "Gas tank leaked; replaced." • "Gas tank leaks."

3. Suspension: single axle: rear, noise, poor performance. • "Banging noise in rear end." • "A noise is emanating from rear of vehicle." • "Vehicle's rear end makes loud noises." • "Noise coming from rear end." • "Rear end would go opposite on wet street; making a left turn, when turn signal came on, vehicle lost control, resulting in an accident and injury."

4. Electrical system: ignition: electronic control unit, stalling, malfunction. • "Computer sensor failed." • "Electronic control module and ignition module failure." • "Engine stalls on deceleration or at stops." • "Engine stalling when pulling away from stops into traffic."

5. Emergency parking brake: mechanical, failure. • "Parking brake will not set properly; causes the vehicle to roll." • "Parking brake pulls up too far." • "Parking brake pulls all the way up." • "Hand brake failed."

PONTIAC GRAND AM 1987

Complaint Severity: Troublesome. **Recall Alert:** See Recall Index. **Buyer's Summary:** Problems with the timing gear and chain can cause serious problems. Have the engine checked by a professional. The electronic control unit has been blamed for engine performance problems, including stalling and surging. The fuel injection system has been blamed for hesitation and stalling. Be sure the vehicle doesn't die in traffic or at stops. Check the brakes—listen for noise, look for leaks and feel for vibration. They may fail, perform poorly or require frequent mechanical attention. Test the transmission thoroughly.

Hot Spots and Owner/NHTSA Comments:

1. Fuel: fuel injection system, stalling, hesitation. • "Constant engine stalling; several repairs; repaired/replaced electronic control module, camshaft sensor, fuel pump, relay and oil pressure switch, continues to stall." • "Vehicle cuts off while driving or coming to a stop." • "Engine dying at stops or lights; accelerates; throttles up and down and vibrates terribly." • "When accelerating, car totally shuts itself off; repairs rendered, problems continued." • "Vehicle cuts out while driving 30 mph or when slowing down; cleaned fuel injection system often."

2. Brakes: hydraulic system, malfunction, failure. • "Braking ability is inadequate in emergency situations; extended brake distance; fades; braking improved in rear when emergency brake activated." • "Brake goes to floor sometimes; need to pump brake to make pedal come up." • "Braking distance poor; must press pedal to floor; previously caused 1 rear-end accident." • "Brake ineffectiveness; checked 3 times in first year; resulted in accident." • "Brake pedal has little or no cushion; must use excessive pressure to stop car; must press pedal until it hits the floor before stopping car, even at slow speeds."

3. Electrical system: ignition: electronic control unit, stalling, hesitation. • "Car stalls after deceleration; fails to restart and accelerates by itself." • "Idles rough; stalling, hesitating and bucking; races, hard to stop; replaced updated programmable read-only memory, problem continues." • "Intermittent stalling, possibly caused by a faulty electronic control module." • "While driving on interstate at 55 mph, vehicle suddenly stalled." • "While driving, engine constantly died."

4. Engine: timing gear and chain, breaking, failure. • "Timing gear replaced; 3 teeth broken off." • "Replaced engine 3 times; timing gear failed." • "Engine makes a clanking noise due to defective timing gears." • "Timing gears stripped at 50,000 miles; motor always noisy; replaced new gears."

5. Power train: transmission: automatic, poor performance, difficulty shifting, slipping. • "Automatic transmission shifts up and down with such force it jerks car back and forth." • "Car's automatic transmission jumped out of gear; accident." • "Transmission shifter failed to lock in park." • "Vehicle jumped out of park into reverse while standing in driveway; owner dragged by car when entangled in seat belt trying to reenter car." • "Transmission problem; with engine running, vehicle suddenly moved backwards from park position; resulted in accident."

6. Interior systems: active restraints: belt retractors, locking up, failure. • "Front seat belts lock up." • "Driver's-side seat belt retractor failed." • "Wearing of seat belt; retractor spring unraveled, causing permanent loss of tension and no restraining power." • "Front seat belt binding and inoperable; faulty retractor." • "Front passenger seat belt retractor failed."

PONTIAC GRAND AM 1988

Complaint Severity: Typical. **Recall Alert:** See Recall Index. **Buyer's Summary:** The electronic control unit has been blamed for engine performance problems, including stalling and surging. Check the brakes—listen for noise, look for leaks and feel for vibration. They may fail, perform poorly or require frequent mechanical attention. Test the transmission thoroughly. See "Sudden Accelerations" in Introduction.

Hot Spots and Owner/NHTSA Comments:

1. Brakes: hydraulic system, locking up, failure. • "Brakes locked up while driving; threw the driver forward, causing injury." • "Brakes failed." • "Brakes go to floor when stopping; front brake caliper grips, then loosens, causing sudden motion in other direction." • "Too much free travel of brake pedal; extra pressure needed to stop vehicle." • "Poor brakes, which require pumping to get some reaction; also, must leave emergency brakes on to build up pressure to assist in braking." • "Accident resulted twice due to improper function of brakes."

2. Fuel: throttle linkages and control, sudden accelerations. • "While in reverse, vehicle suddenly surged out of control." • "Vehicle suddenly accelerated forward, causing collision." • "Vehicle suddenly accelerated 3 times with foot on brakes; once out of control and resulting in accident." • "Placed car in reverse, it suddenly accelerated in reverse; after tapping accelerator, brakes inoperative." • "Violent forward surging of vehicle led to accident."

3. Electrical system: ignition: electronic control unit, stalling, malfunction. • "Vehicle shut off completely at speed of 45-50 mph; keeps stalling out." • "Intermittent stalling when slowing down or stopped; also when engine is warm." • "While driving on highway, vehicle would suddenly slow down." • "Failure of electronic control module causes engine to run rough and surge when first started; car runs fine after 5 miles of driving." • "Electronic control module malfunctioned; resulted in total loss of instrumentation and acceleration control."

4. Engine: stalling, overheating. • "Engine ran rough and vehicle stalled." • "Blown head gasket." • "Engine surged; replaced crank sensor position." • "Engine problems; overheating, knocking and vibrating; antifreeze leak." • "Engine constantly overheats; either stalls or stops."

5. Power train: transmission: automatic, poor performance, difficulty shifting, slipping. • "Automatic transmission failure; jumped into reverse on its own." • "While turning, automobile transmission failed; caused no brakes and steering wheel lockup; resulted in an accident." • "Transmission would not shift into 3rd gear." • "Transmission malfunctions."

6. Engine: other parts, miscellaneous problems. • "Started engine, 'check gauge' light came on; checked gauges; showed no oil pressure; engine could have seized up. Also, ignition coil cover goes bad." • "Head gasket failure; cracked heads." • "Cracked camshaft." • "Crankshaft pulley bolts fell off." • "Problem with inconsistent idling; replaced main seal in rear of engine." • "Problems getting oil filters; special little filter that goes inside of oil pan." • "No oil getting to engine."

PONTIAC GRAND AM 1989

Complaint Severity: Typical. **Recall Alert:** See Recall Index. **Buyer's Summary:** Look carefully for any kind of leakage, especially under the car. The electronic control unit has been blamed for engine performance problems, including stalling and surging. The fuel injection system has been blamed for hesitation and stalling. Be sure the vehicle doesn't die in traffic or at stops. Check the brakes—listen for noise, look for leaks and feel for vibration. They may fail, perform poorly or require frequent mechanical attention. Test the transmission thoroughly.

Hot Spots and Owner/NHTSA Comments:

1. Brakes: hydraulic system, noise, failure. • "When applying the brakes, they do not grab. Excessive stopping distance and brake wear." • "Brakes were pressed but didn't catch; car slid and hit embankment, resulting in fatality of 12-year-old girl; also, just before the accident had no steering." • "Brake failure, causing 2 separate accidents." • "Brake failure; brake pedal goes almost to floor." • "Brakes make strange noise."

2. Electrical system: ignition: electronic control unit, stalling, hesitation, failure. • "Computer control module failed." • "While driving, vehicle continually hesitates and suddenly stops without warning; dealer would not take responsibility." • "Computer sensor failed twice." • "Computer for ignition quit; replaced."

3. Engine: gaskets: valve cover, leaks, malfunction. • "Valve cover gasket started leaking." • "Head gasket blew out; dealer paid half and admits there is a problem." • "Head and head gasket failed." • "Defective head gasket leaks onto engine, creating risk of fire; causing overheating." • "The head gasket went, causing the antifreeze to go into the oil."

4. Fuel: fuel injection system, stalling, hesitation. • "Intermittent stalling." • "Engine hard to start due to fuel injection problem." • "Intermittent stalling, especially when coming to stop while going downhill." • "Hesitation on acceleration at speeds of 40-50 mph, and when at idle." • "Foot on brake, car in parking gear, 'check engine light' came on; car started to vibrate and surge forward, almost striking public property; problem still exists." • "Car runs poorly when cold, hesitates, stalls and backfires."

5. Fuel: fuel line fittings and pump, breaking, failure. • "Fuel line that attaches to fuel injection rail breaks and fuel pours over engine." • "Fuel line that attaches to fuel injection rail breaks without warning; fuel pours out over engine; could cause fire if engine hot." • "Fuel feed line became disconnected at fuel rail, causing gasoline to pour all over engine."

6. Power train: transmission: automatic, poor performance, difficulty shifting, slipping. • "Driver put car in park; car rolled backwards with gearshift still in park position." • "Malfunction occurred that caused car to go into reverse while shift lever securely in park position." • "Transmission slips at high speeds; knocking noise when vehicle turns to right." • "With key out of ignition and transmission in park, vehicle jumped out of gear; rolled over and caused accident." • "Upon shifting into 2nd gear, vehicle experiences serious hesitation; replaced once before for similar problem."

PONTIAC GRAND AM 1990

Complaint Severity: Troublesome. **Buyer's Summary:** Check the brakes—listen for noise, look for leaks and feel for vibration. They may fail, perform poorly or require frequent mechanical attention. Test the transmission thoroughly. See "Sudden Accelerations" in Introduction.

Hot Spots and Owner/NHTSA Comments:

1. Brakes: hydraulic system, malfunction, failure. • "Driver was approaching a light and applied brakes; pedal went to the floor; vehicle did not stop or slow down; accident resulted." • "Braking system malfunctioned; foot took brake pedal down to floor when brakes applied while approaching traffic light; caused accident with injury sustained." • "There is a high-pitched noise coming from the brakes; problem has been repaired 4 times." • "Inadequate braking power resulted in an accident." • "Brake pedal traveled to the floor, causing extended stopping distances and resulting in an accident. No prior warning."

2. Fuel: throttle linkages and control, sudden accelerations. • "Vehicle had sudden full acceleration with no warning when put into gear with brake fully applied. Ignition had to be turned off and car put into park to stop." • "Upon shifting from park to reverse, vehicle suddenly accelerated, crashing into a pole at an unknown speed. Driver received injuries." • "Vehicle started accelerating by itself at 55 mph; brakes could not slow speed fast enough; resulted in accident." • "While making a turn, vehicle accelerated; throttle stuck at 100 mph, almost causing an accident; brake wear." • "Placed foot on brake, started vehicle and shifted gear into reverse position; vehicle suddenly accelerated at full throttle."

3. Interior systems: active seat and shoulder belts and belt anchor, malfunction, failure. • "Seat belts were loose and did not keep occupants in seats." • "Seat belt material is shredding." • "Seat belts do not hold driver or passenger in place when seats move forward unexpectedly." • "Right front impact; seat belts tore out of door, causing driver and passenger to hit windshield." • "Seat belt failed to restrain in an accident."

4. Power train: transmission: automatic, poor performance, difficulty shifting, slipping. • "Transmission noisy in reverse; shifts slow in forward gears." • "Transmission failed twice; vehicle was pulling to the right while driving." • "The transmission gets hot and the fluid boils up, covering the valves and making car shut off; this could cause an accident." • "Slipping when shifting gears."

PONTIAC GRAND AM 1991

Complaint Severity: Typical. **Recall Alert:** See Recall Index. **Buyer's Summary:** The fuel injection system has been blamed for hesitation and stalling. Be sure the vehicle doesn't die in traffic or at stops. The steering may be stiff or not working correctly. Be sure to test the steering, especially on a cold start. Check the brakes—listen for noise, look for leaks and feel for vibration. They may fail, perform poorly or require frequent mechanical attention. See "Sudden Accelerations" in Introduction.

Hot Spots and Owner/NHTSA Comments:

1. Fuel: throttle linkages and control, sudden accelerations. • "Had foot on brake, car accelerated anyway." • "Backing out of parking lot, accelerator stuck; put vehicle in drive; lost control, going across a median strip and hitting a tree, impact 12:00 position, 30 mph." • "Sudden acceleration, causing accident and injury." • "While driving at 35 mph, vehicle went open-throttle position; lost control, impact 12:00 position." • "Sudden acceleration; vehicle went out of control, which resulted in an accident."

2. Fuel: fuel injection system, stalling, hesitation. • "Engine cuts off at low speeds; intermittent problem." • "Intermittent stalling." • "Intermittent loss of power." • "Intermittent stalling." • "When driving in heavy rain and avoiding as many puddles as possible, vehicle runs rough and loses power."

3. Steering: wheel and column, vibration, failure. • "While turning, the steering wheel would vibrate; dealer replaced steering wheel hose; vibration, however, returned." • "Loose steering; requires oversteering to keep vehicle from wandering." • "Rubbing sound when turning steering wheel." • "When steering wheel is turned left on a rough road, the steering wheel itself will vibrate rapidly in driver's hand." • "Steering failed."

4. Brakes: hydraulic system, excessive wear, failure. • "Excessive brake wear." • "Front brakes failed." • "Applied brakes when road was wet and the car swerved and did a 360-degree spin around; car ended up in opposite lane." • "While driving, brakes failed; resulted in loss of control."

5. Electrical system: ignition, stalling, failure. • "Vehicle stalls out with no warning." • "Vehicle stalls out any speed; updated programmable read-only memory, tuneup, dealer cannot locate problem." • "Electrical short in ignition system. Failure of manifold air pressure sensor." • "Failure of automatic transmission when shifting into reverse." • "While driving, car stalls out with no warning."

PONTIAC GRAND AM 1992

Complaint Severity: Typical. **Recall Alert:** See Recall Index. **Buyer's Summary:** Check the brakes—listen for noise, look for leaks and feel for vibration. They may fail, perform poorly or require frequent mechanical attention. See "Sudden Accelerations" in Introduction.

Hot Spots and Owner/NHTSA Comments:

1. Brakes: hydraulic: anti-skid system, poor performance, failure, locking up. • "Antilock brake system failure; brakes lose power if on slight incline; pedal went to floor while traveling 45 mph; master cylinder replaced." • "Antilock brake failure; also, misaligned emergency parking brake." • "Antilock brakes locked up, resulting in accidents." • "Malfunction with antilock brake system, causing complete loss of braking ability. Replaced speed sensor and computer to no avail." • "Antilock brake system brake pedal hesitates; traveled to floor; caused extended stopping distances; resulted in accident; car rolled into another car; impact 12:00 position, 5 mph."

2. Brakes: hydraulic: disc: pads and shoes, excessive wear, failure. • "Premature wear of front brake pads." • "Premature wear of brakes because they are not heavy enough." • "Brake pads have been replaced several times and the brakes are wearing down." • "Front brake pads machined and rotors replaced due to grinding noise; brakes pulsating." • "Purchased new car and had to replace the front rotor and pads about 4 times."

3. Equipment: electric power accessories: locks: door, malfunction, failure. • "Door locks intermittently fail." • "Power door locks inoperative." • "Power door locks failed intermittently after repair attempts, causing vehicle to be stuck in unlocked position." • "Power door lock does not work; replaced electrical parts and switch twice."

4. Fuel: throttle linkages and control, sudden accelerations. • "At the end of a 33-minute drive, reduced speed; slow rolling resulted in a sudden acceleration and frontal crash situation." • "Vehicle suddenly accelerated upon moving gears from park to drive, causing vehicle to crash into a telephone pole." • "Antilock brake system gone out on right front wheel." • "When coming to complete stop, car made gurgling noise, then lurched forward 5-10 feet." • "Intermittent engine surging." • "Engine surges."

5. Electrical system: ignition, hesitation, stalling. • "Vehicle loses power." • "The lights keep coming on and the car will cut off while driving." • "Vehicle hesitates when you give it gas." • "Vehicle periodically shuts down or cuts off when driving at highway speeds, 40 mph and up." • "While driving, engine dies."

6. Interior systems: bucket: backrest, breaking, failure. • "Was rear-ended; driver's-side seat back collapsed." • "Driver's-side seat back collapsed into the back seat during an accident." • "Driver and passenger seat backs collapsed during rear-end collision, causing injuries to driver and passenger." • "Driver's seat back broke; tilted backwards during accident." • "Experienced seat back failure; seat would not lock in place, sliding backwards while driving."

PONTIAC GRAND AM 1993

Complaint Severity: Typical. **Recall Alert:** See Recall Index. **Buyer's Summary:** Check the brakes—listen for noise, look for leaks and feel for vibration. They may fail, perform poorly or require frequent mechanical attention. Test the transmission thoroughly. See "Sudden Accelerations" in Introduction.

Hot Spots and Owner/NHTSA Comments:

1. Brakes: hydraulic: anti-skid system, poor performance, failure, locking up. • "Antilock brake system grabs when applied; brake pedal goes to floor; hesitates; causes extended stopping." • "Antilock brake system failed to stop vehicle, causing front-end collision at 5-10 mph. No airbag." • "Brake pads and rotors wear out prematurely; antilock brakes fail to work properly in snow or rain, causing vehicle to skid." • "Antilock brake system failed completely; resulted in total brake failure; dealer cannot find problem, but said they will replace motor pack if this happens again." • "In wintry and wet weather, antilock brakes, when applied, jerk and do not stop."

2. Power train: transmission: automatic, poor performance, difficulty shifting, slipping. • "Vehicle rolls too much when on hill; caused accident." • "Automatic transmission failure; while driving, the vehicle's transmission seized." • "Transmission clutch housing failed." • "Replaced transmission due to internal fluid leak in the low reverse clutch circuit." • "Vehicle periodically pulls to the left or right when driving at high speeds due to defective drivetrain. Repaired 3 times." • "When stopping on a hill, vehicle rolls back when foot taken off brake."

3. Fuel: throttle linkages and control, sudden accelerations. • "Automatic transmission; after shifting to park, vehicle surges to approximately 5,000 rpm with gear lever still in park position; no warning." • "Twice, when cruise control was applied, vehicle suddenly accelerated out of control due to throttle body assembly being stuck open." • "Sudden acceleration, causing loss of control and an accident." • "Throttle body stuck in open position, causing vehicle to accelerate out of control." • "Sudden acceleration as vehicle was slowing, causing an accident; hit a wall."

4. Interior systems: seat tracks and anchors, malfunction, failure. • "Seat adjustment problems." • "After making sudden stop, experienced driver's and passenger's seats sliding forward, causing accident, impact 1:00 position, speed 5 mph." • "Passenger seat won't move forward on track." • "Front passenger's seat does not stay in locked position, causing seat to move back and forth; passenger hit windshield."

5. Electrical system: ignition, stalling, failure. • "Engine stalled while driving 45-50 mph." • "Vehicle stalls out with no warning." • "Ignition switch failure, causing intermittent cranking and starting problems." • "Vehicle stalls without warning. Air conditioner unit releases fuel fumes into vehicle; replaced fuel canister."

PONTIAC GRAND AM 1994

Complaint Severity: Serious. **Recall Alert:** See Recall Index. **Buyer's Summary:** The airbags in this vehicle have experienced failures and malfunctions: You may need a professional evaluation on the condition of the airbags. Check the brakes—listen for noise, look for leaks and feel for vibration. They may fail, perform poorly or require frequent mechanical attention. Test the transmission thoroughly. See "Sudden Accelerations" in Introduction.

Hot Spots and Owner/NHTSA Comments:

1. Interior systems: passive restraint: airbag: driver, malfunction, failure. • "Antilock brake system failed to stop vehicle when applied, causing rear-end collision at 35-40 mph. Airbag did not deploy." • "No deployment of airbag during accident, resulting in injury." • "At 12:00 position at 30-40 mph, driver's-side airbag did not deploy, resulting in an injury." • "No deployment of driver's airbag during accident." • "Airbag did not deploy during front-end collision; vehicle hit another moving vehicle."

2. Brakes: hydraulic: anti-skid system, poor performance, failure, locking up. • "The antilock brakes on the car are contaminated and make a squeaking noise." • "Antilock brake system failed to stop vehicle when applied, causing rear-end collision at 35-40 mph. Airbag did not deploy." • "Antilock brakes grind." • "Antilock brake system locked up, resulting in loss of control; vehicle spun and slid into a curb; dealer found no problem; owner said possible problem in antilock brake system chip." • "Antilock brake system: Owner applied brakes in panic stop, vehicle continued forward until impact."

3. Power train: transmission: automatic, poor performance, difficulty shifting, slipping. • "Automatic transmission locks up in passing gear and cannot be disengaged." • "Driving vehicle at 35 mph, cruise control engaged itself to high rpm; to disengage shifted gears up and down; replaced transmission." • "While driving, transmission jumps into neutral and car loses speed." • "Transmission stuck in passing gear."

4. Fuel: throttle linkages and control, sudden accelerations. • "While foot was on brake, engine surged and vehicle lunged forward." • "Sudden accelerations, causing loss of control and an accident." • "Vehicle surges and stalls above 40 mph. Throttle position sensor replaced to no avail." • "Sudden acceleration problem."

PONTIAC GRAND PRIX 1988

Complaint Severity: Minor. **Recall Alert:** See Recall Index. **Buyer's Summary:** Verify that the cruise control system works properly, and that it doesn't cause the engine to surge. Check the brakes—listen for noise, look for leaks and feel for vibration. They may fail, perform poorly or require frequent mechanical attention.

Hot Spots and Owner/NHTSA Comments:

1. Brakes: hydraulic system, excessive wear, failure. • "Power brakes constantly replaced due to premature wear." • "Front and rear brakes have been replaced twice within 18 months; grinding noise leading up to breakdown." • "Repeated brake repairs." • "Brakes malfunctioned; replaced pads and rotors, long-term problem; repaired/replaced to no avail." • "Brakes squealing upon application."

2. Brakes: hydraulic: switch: brake light, malfunction, failure. • "Brake light switch failed on numerous occasions; replaced twice." • "Inoperative brake light; repaired/replaced brake light switch." • "Brake light switch failed twice in traffic, nearly causing an accident." • "Brake light switch malfunctioned; resulted in no brake lights." • "Brake light switch failed; failure allows cruise control to remain engaged after brake has been activated; replaced switch has also failed."

3. Brakes: hydraulic: shoe and drum system, corrosion, failure. • "Rear brakes froze and are not working; dealer indicated it was a common problem." • "Corroded rear disc brakes." • "Rear brakes freeze up, resulting in brake failure." • "Rear brake pads fell off vehicle; caused loss of braking effectiveness." • "Rear brakes malfunctioned due to frozen calipers."

4. Equipment: speed control, malfunction, failure. • "Cruise control module inoperative." • "Malfunction of cruise control; does not automatically shut off when brake is applied." • "Cruise control malfunctioned at 29,000 miles." • "The cruise control system slipped; causes throttle to stick at high speed; failure also causes chain reaction that resulted in jammed accelerator." • "Cruise control would surge about 5 miles after being engaged."

PONTIAC GRAND PRIX 1989

Complaint Severity: Minor. **Recall Alert:** See Recall Index. **Buyer's Summary:** Verify that the cruise control system works properly, and that it doesn't cause the engine to surge. The electronic control unit has been blamed for engine performance problems, including stalling and surging. Check the brakes—listen for noise, look for leaks and feel for vibration. They may fail, perform poorly or require frequent mechanical attention.

Hot Spots and Owner/NHTSA Comments:

1. Brakes: hydraulic: disc: caliper, excessive wear, malfunction, failure. • "Rear calipers rusted, causing premature wear on front pads." • "Right and left rear brake sliders on the caliper freeze; not closing or opening when brakes are applied." • "A defective caliper caused loss of braking effectiveness, which resulted in an accident." • "Within 2 weeks, both front brake caliper guide pins broke, causing wheel lockup and grinding. Brakes had been serviced earlier in vehicle's life." • "Front disc brake caliper bolts were missing; brake pads flew out and blew the tire."

2. Electrical system: ignition: electronic control unit, stalling. • "Defective computer control in fuel injection system (electronic control module) causes stalling problem." • "Experiencing continual stalling problems; car quits operating while in motion;

each time let up on accelerator while in neutral, key turned and it restarted." • "On 2 different occasions, while driving, lost all power; would not start until engine cooled off; due to failure of memory calibration; replaced." • "Vehicle constantly stalls at cold starts and engine quits; dealer replaced the electronic control module several times." • "Repeated stalling on turns and when slowing down due to failure of the electronic control module."

3. Brakes: hydraulic: shoe: disc brake system, corrosion, excessive wear. • "Rear brake calipers have corroded and quit exerting braking force. Lack of friction has allowed the rear rotor to corrode also." • "Excessive wear of front brake rotors due to warping." • "Front brakes wore out twice and were replaced." • "Rusted rear calipers, causing excessive wear of front brake pads and rotors." • "Corroded rear disc brakes cause reduction in braking ability. Repaired 3-4 times." • "Front brakes became extremely hot, causing smoke to be emitted from under hood."

4. Equipment: speed control, malfunction, failure. • "Cruise control module malfunctioned." • "Cruise control pops out while driving." • "Switch controlling cruise control shut off." • "Inoperative cruise control." • "When speed control shut off or brakes, applied would continue at maximum speed." • "Brake did not disengage cruise control when applied; almost hit car in front; brake light failed and brake switch was going bad; repaired."

5. Brakes: hydraulic: shoe and drum system, excessive wear, noise, corrosion. • "Front brakes have premature wear because rear brakes do not work properly." • "A part of the rear brakes is inoperative, resulting in the rear brake functioning improperly." • "Heard a terrible noise when backing up; found the back brakes were corroded." • "Heard a noise and developed extended stopping distance due to rear brake corrosion." • "Right rear brake locked up, causing vehicle to spin out of control; resulted in an accident."

6. Brakes: hydraulic: switch: brake light, failure. • "Brake light switch broke; resulted in no brake lights." • "Brake light switch failed when brakes applied at stop signs or traffic lights; almost resulted in rear-end accident." • "Brake lights stopped functioning; discovered problem was a failed brake switch under pedal; repaired/replaced." • "Problem with electrical short in brake light switch; causes brake lights to come on."

PONTIAC GRAND PRIX 1990

Complaint Severity: Typical. **Recall Alert:** See Recall Index. **Buyer's Summary:** Check the brakes—listen for noise, look for leaks and feel for vibration. They may fail, perform poorly or require frequent mechanical attention. See "Sudden Accelerations" in Introduction.

Hot Spots and Owner/NHTSA Comments:

1. Brakes: hydraulic: disc: caliper, excessive wear, malfunction. • "Rear brake calipers are wearing prematurely; repaired/replaced twice." • "Rear calipers froze when driver applied brakes; slid into another lane." • "Brake caliper freezes, rendering rear brakes inoperative. 'Slider kit' used to fix problem." • "Rear brake caliper sliders froze, causing uneven wear of rotors and pads." • "Rear brake calipers seize, causing pads to separate from pad plates; premature wear and noise." • "Left and right rear brake calipers gave out completely while driving."

2. Brakes: hydraulic: shoe: disc brake system, corrosion, excessive wear. • "Front disk brakes wore out at about 5,000 miles." • "Corroded rear disc brakes, which caused reduction in braking ability." • "Owner complains of having to replace a number of brake pads, rotors and calipers since the purchase of this vehicle." • "Corroded rear disc brakes, causing lack of brake effectiveness when applied at any speed." • "Left rear caliper inoperative; rotors rusted; front brakes replaced." • "Front brakes are worn out."

3. Brakes: hydraulic: shoe and drum system, malfunction, failure. • "Rear brake caliper froze, causing loss of braking power." • "While driving on highway, noticed a burning smell inside of vehicle; right rear caliper was frozen, and pedal went to the floor; caliper needed replacement." • "Rear brakes fail to stop vehicle effectively when applied at any time; excessive force is necessary." • "Rear brakes inoperative." • "Rear brake slider kit seized up and became inoperative. This put extra pressure on functioning front brakes."

4. Fuel: throttle linkages and control, sudden accelerations. • "Engine accelerated at approximately 20-30 mph; while coming to a stop ignition had to be cut off before vehicle came to a stop; resulted in loss of control." • "When foot is removed from gas pedal, car accelerates." • "When shifting gear from park to drive, vehicle suddenly accelerated out of control, hitting and injuring a person." • "Upon shifting gear into reverse vehicle accelerated out of control; caused an accident." • "While driving and when removing speed cruise control, vehicle would suddenly accelerate."

5. Brakes: hydraulic system, noise, failure. • "Brake failure; pedal faded when coming down a steep downgrade hill; pumped the pedal to build up pressure to stop vehicle." • "When driver depressed brakes coming off exit, brake pedal went to floor. Brake fluid boiled due to extent of pressure. Brake rotors, calipers and sliders failed." • "Noisy brakes; replaced." • "Rear brakes are inoperative. Replaced front disc pads and rotors." • "Brake failure, causing extended stopping distance; twice resulted in loss of control, accident and injury."

PONTIAC GRAND PRIX 1991

Complaint Severity: Typical. **Recall Alert:** See Recall Index. **Buyer's Summary:** Check the brakes—listen for noise, look for leaks and feel for vibration. They may fail, perform poorly or require frequent mechanical attention.

Hot Spots and Owner/NHTSA Comments:

1. Brakes: hydraulic: disc: caliper, poor performance, failure. • "Dealer cannot fix the spongy brakes after 3 tries; 4-wheel disc brakes." • "Rear calipers do not engage all the way, causing more load on and excessive wear of front brakes." • "Brake caliper slides, causing brake failure." • "Rear disc brakes pads fell completely off; caliper slide pins were frozen on both wheels; bonding did not hold brake pads to metal retainer; loss of braking." • "Noticed long stopping distance due to caliper sliding on rear brakes being frozen in place; replaced disc braking system 2 times." • "Extremely poor braking performance due to rear caliper slide freezing. Rendered rear brakes inoperative."

2. Brakes: hydraulic system, excessive wear, vibration. • "Had 10 sets of brakes replaced." • "Brakes wear out prematurely." • "When applying brakes intermittently, pressure is lost, causing long and extended stopping distances." • "Brake size insufficient for vehicle weight, causing premature brake wear." • "Brakes make metal-to-metal noise; no cause or cure." • "Vehicle pulsates when braking at a speed of 35 mph."

3. Electrical system: ignition, stalling, malfunction. • "Vehicle stalls with no warning while driving." • "Engine dies while going around curves; accelerator pulsates while slowing down; speed 30 mph and under." • "Vehicle will stall without warning at a speed of 10 mph." • "Vehicle stalls while driving or when making a sudden stop. Replaced idle air control and programmable read-only memory. • "Vehicle stalls in traffic without prior warning, losing power steering and brakes."

4. Brakes: hydraulic: shoe and drum system, corrosion, failure. • "Rear brakes are inoperative from corrosion. Front brakes wear out prematurely. Increased stopping distance could cause accident." • "Rear brakes are corroding. Steering smokes due to turn signal switch shorting." • "Rear brakes froze, causing extended stopping distance; previously repaired." • "Corrosion of rear disc brake, causing loss of brake effectiveness." • "Vehicle's rear brakes malfunction, causing premature wear and tear of front brakes."

PONTIAC GRAND PRIX 1992

Complaint Severity: Troublesome. **Recall Alert:** See Recall Index. **Buyer's Summary:** Check the brakes—listen for noise, look for leaks and feel for vibration. They may fail, perform poorly or require frequent mechanical attention. See "Sudden Accelerations" in Introduction.

Hot Spots and Owner/NHTSA Comments:

1. Brakes: hydraulic system, excessive wear, failure. • "Loss of braking power when driving on wet roads." • "While driving, experienced total brake failure when pedal went to floor; resulted in an accident; dealer had worked on brake system twice before." • "Brake failure; frontal collision; experienced faded pedal, impact 12:00 position, 40 mph." • "The vehicle has had excessive wearing of the brakes, and does not stop properly." • "Brakes failed, causing an accident."

2. Fuel: throttle linkages and control, sudden accelerations. • "The car keeps accelerating and has been in 3 accidents." • "Automatic transmission failure; gears slip and sudden acceleration of the vehicle." • "Consumer put into reverse and it accelerated." • "Sudden acceleration caused accident." • "Vehicle had uncontrolled acceleration and caused an accident."

3. Brakes: hydraulic: anti-skid system, poor performance, failure, locking up. • "Antilock brake system failed, causing accident and injury." • "While applying brakes, pedal becomes hard; results in approximately 50 percent braking power; exact cause unknown; no prior warning." • "Rear antilock brakes fail to stop vehicle effectively when applied. Replaced front pads 11 times and rear only once." • "Antilock brake system keeps locking up and experienced long stopping distance; replaced rotor, slides and caliper to no avail."

4. Brakes: hydraulic: disc: pads and shoes, excessive wear, locking up, malfunction. • "Front brake pads wear out prematurely." • "Premature wear of brake pads and rotors." • "Antilock brake system locked up during sudden braking, then released; then a loud noise was heard; replaced pad; noticed black dust on brake after driving 200 miles." • "Antilock brake system malfunctioned; pedal hard; noticed smoke coming out of front wheel; replaced 4 sets of brake pads."

PONTIAC GRAND PRIX 1994

Complaint Severity: Negligible. **Buyer's Summary:** Test the horn and the windshield wipers.

Hot Spots and Owner/NHTSA Comments:

1. Communications: horn assembly: button: ring, poor performance. • "Horn button requires excessive effort." • "Use of horn requires excessive effort." • "Difficulty blowing horn." • "Excessive pressure required to press horn button." • "The location of the button to sound the horn does not allow for safe usage."

2. Visual systems: windshield wiper/washer switch, failure. • "The windshield wipers do not operate properly due to failure of the wiper/washer switch." • "Windshield wiper switch fails to work unless turn signal is on."

PONTIAC LEMANS 1988

Complaint Severity: Typical. **Recall Alert:** See Recall Index. **Buyer's Summary:** The electronic control unit has been blamed for engine performance problems, including stalling and surging. Check the brakes—listen for noise, look for leaks and feel for vibration. They may fail, perform poorly or require frequent mechanical attention. See "Sudden Accelerations" in Introduction.

Hot Spots and Owner/NHTSA Comments:

1. Brakes: hydraulic: shoe: disc brake system, malfunction, failure. • "Front disc brakes are too small for vehicle; inability to stop, resulting in vehicle accident." • "Front brakes fail to stop vehicle effectively. Have replaced brake calipers, rotors and brake pads 5 times." • "Front brakes froze up; had to replace rotors, pads and calipers." • "Front brakes worn out prematurely at 26,000 miles; replaced with new brakes." • "Calipers are not releasing and are eating up the pads and rotors."

2. Fuel: throttle linkages and control, sudden accelerations. • "Upon starting car and putting in reverse, instead of going backward, went forward at great speed, resulting in an accident." • "After hearing knocking sound, vehicle suddenly accelerated out of control." • "Engine and air conditioner on, put gear in drive, car shot forward at a great speed; had no control." • "Shifted car from park to drive, moved foot from brake, car was going at high rate of speed; car continued to go after gear was moved to park." • "Stopped at drive-through; when accelerated, car took off (accelerated fast); could not stop by braking; accident occurred."

3. Electrical system: ignition: electronic control unit, sudden acceleration, stalling, malfunction. • "Car suddenly accelerated by itself; very high rpm; repaired/replaced sensors for computer, problem not corrected." • "Vehicle died in middle of street and was towed away by the police." • "Vehicle stalls out with no warning." • "Electronic control module malfunctioned." • "Electronic control module failed 3 times, causing stalling."

4. Brakes: hydraulic: disc: pads and shoes, excessive wear, noise, poor performance. • "Brake pads failed 4 times." • "Premature brake pad wear causes loss of braking effectiveness; had to replace pads as recently as 1 month ago, now need new ones." • "Grinding noise from front brakes; replaced front brake pads." • "Inadequate brake performance; replaced 3 sets of brake pads." • "Excessive front brake pad wear; pads wear out every 10,000 miles."

PONTIAC LEMANS 1989

Complaint Severity: Negligible. **Recall Alert:** See Recall Index. **Buyer's Summary:** The electronic control unit has been blamed for engine performance problems, including stalling and surging. The fuel injection system has been blamed for hesitation and stalling. Be sure the vehicle doesn't die in traffic or at stops. Check the brakes—listen for noise, look for leaks and feel for vibration. They may fail, perform poorly or require frequent mechanical attention.

Hot Spots and Owner/NHTSA Comments:

1. Brakes: hydraulic: shoe: disc brake system, excessive wear, locking up, failure. • "Excessive brake wear." • "Premature wear of brakes." • "Brake system problems; replaced 9 sets of brakes in 26,000 miles." • "Brakes locked up once applied, forcing car back to left and causing rollover." • "Complete front brake failure; replaced pads 7 times, calipers 4 times and rotors 3 times." • "Premature wear of front brakes; have been replaced 4 times and continue to fail."

2. Electrical system: ignition: electronic control unit, stalling, failure. • "Computer module has been replaced 3 times. Vehicle stalls excessively." • "Electrical system failed; replaced twice; causes vehicle to perform sluggishly upon acceleration." • "Complete power loss while driving." • "Onboard computer failure; fails to start." • "Computer system defect."

3. Fuel: fuel injection system, stalling, hesitation. • "Engine bucking and stalling problems." • "Vehicle stalls and driver loses control of brakes." • "Fuses (of the fuel injection system) blew out for no apparent reason." • "Starting difficulties." • "Vehicle intermittently stalls."

4. Interior systems: active restraints: belt buckles, breaking, failure. • "The driver's seat belt has broken. The red tab in the middle of the buckle came out, and now buckle does not latch." • "Seat belt buckle failure; seat belt will not latch properly." • "Seat belt latch will not unlock once locked; hard to latch (lock)." • "Seat belt buckle on driver's-side fell apart."

5. Interior systems: active restraints: belt retractors, malfunction, failure. • "Shoulder belts fail to retract properly; also cut into driver's neck." • "Seat belt fails to retract." • "Driver's and passenger's seat belts are not retracting properly." • "Shoulder belts do not retract; also, harness guides snapped off."

PONTIAC LEMANS 1990

Complaint Severity: Troublesome. **Recall Alert:** See Recall Index. **Buyer's Summary:** Make sure the shoulder belts don't cut across your neck and are well anchored. See "Sudden Accelerations" in Introduction.

Hot Spots and Owner/NHTSA Comments:

1. Interior systems: shoulder belts, malfunction, failure. • "Shoulder seat belt light stays on." • "False latching of driver's-side shoulder belt strap resulted in harness becoming detached from tracking system; seat belt warning light is on." • "Rear shoulder belt failed during accident, causing injuries." • "Occupant had to be cut from front passenger's shoulder and lap belt after being involved in front-end collision at 35 mph."

2. Fuel: throttle linkages and control, sudden accelerations. • "Shifted from park to reverse and car accelerated." • "While parking, heard noise from engine, then car took off on its own; no help from brakes; ran into building." • "Upon shifting from park to reverse, vehicle accelerated backwards, causing an accident." • "Driving vehicle at low speed, vehicle went into open-throttle position, impact 12:00 position, speed unknown; no failure found after repaired."

3. Interior systems: active restraints: belt retractors, malfunction, failure. • "Passenger's shoulder belt does not retract or restrain." • "Driver's-side seat belt retractor failed." • "Seat belt retractor does not lock properly." • "Driver's-side belt will not retract."

PONTIAC LEMANS 1991

Complaint Severity: Typical. **Recall Alert:** See Recall Index. **Buyer's Summary:** Make sure the shoulder belts don't cut across your neck, work properly and are well anchored. Check the brakes—listen for noise, look for leaks and feel for vibration. They may fail, perform poorly or require frequent mechanical attention.

Hot Spots and Owner/NHTSA Comments:

1. Interior systems: shoulder belts, failure. • "Automatic shoulder harness failed." • "Shoulder belt failed twice." • "Third occasion of shoulder belt mechanisms jamming. Seat belts are not working again." • "Driver's seat belt did not restrain in an accident." • "Shoulder belts failed to release upon impact; resulted in 2 fatalities and injury."

2. Brakes: hydraulic system, noise, failure. • "While driving to a game, was forced to make a quick stop due to a truck attempting to turn left; brakes failed; involved in a rear-end collision." • "Noisy brakes." • "Brakes are noisy, and there's pulsation in pedal." • "Brakes will not stop the car. Push very hard on pedal and car will not stop. Can't lock wheels."

PONTIAC SUNBIRD 1987

Complaint Severity: Typical. **Recall Alert:** See Recall Index. **Buyer's Summary:** Look carefully for any kind of leakage, especially under the car. The fuel injection system has been blamed for hesitation and stalling. Be sure the vehicle doesn't die in traffic or at stops. Check the brakes—listen for noise, look for leaks and feel for vibration. They may fail, perform poorly or require frequent mechanical attention. See "Sudden Accelerations" in Introduction.

Hot Spots and Owner/NHTSA Comments:

1. Engine: leaks, malfunction. • "Engine oil leakage." • "Experienced pinging in engine; adjusted timing, pinging reduced slightly." • "Started car; in few seconds, small 'boom' sounded and smoke and fire came from under hood; car completely destroyed." • "Overheating and blown head gasket." • "Engine damage due to lack of oil." • "Several engine problems; repaired/replaced rocker gasket and belts; also, engine is noisy."

2. Brakes: hydraulic system, poor performance, failure. • "Brakes extremely spongy, almost as if only half-working; even after adjustments, still poor." • "Brake failure resulted in accident and injury." • "Brakes failed to grab; avoided hitting car in front, but rear-ended instead; brakes adjusted." • "Poor performance of brakes; would not stop at times." • "Poor performance of brakes; make thumping sound when applied." • "Attempting to stop quickly, brakes would not lock, causing greatly increased stopping distance."

3. Engine: gaskets: valve cover, leaks, failure. • "Engine valve cover leaking oil." • "Valve cover gasket leaks oil, causing car not to idle properly." • "Car was smoking very bad; told that head gasket had been blown and head was bad." • "Oil leak; valve cover gasket replaced." • "Head gasket blown."

4. Fuel: fuel injection system, stalling, hesitation. • "Engine turns over slowly when cold; surges and hesitates." • "Fire resulted due to dirt within fuel line; dislodged, causing fuel injection unit to overflow; fuel leaked on hot engine manifold, with eventual ignition." • "Continual problem with car failing to start; will turn over but not catch; 2 attempts must be made before it finally takes hold." • "Engine hesitates, runs rough, backfires and misses; replaced throttle position sensor." • "Engine cuts out and stalls; keeps reoccurring; when stalls, loses both power steering and brakes."

5. Fuel: throttle linkages and control, sudden accelerations. • "Throttle linkages stuck at 85 mph when in passing gear." • "Runaway engine; car drove itself, no need for pressure on gas pedal to accelerate car." • "Car suddenly accelerated forward; applied brakes to no avail; used emergency brakes, which slowed car down but did not stop it; resulted in accident." • "When driving at 40 mph, foot off gas pedal to decrease speed, instead of slowing down, car speeded up." • "At highway speeds when taking foot off gas pedal to slow down, sometimes it works, sometimes car speeds up very fast on its own."

PONTIAC SUNBIRD 1989

Complaint Severity: Serious. **Recall Alert:** See Recall Index. **Buyer's Summary:** Check the brakes—listen for noise, look for leaks and feel for vibration. They may fail, perform poorly or require frequent mechanical attention. See "Sudden Accelerations" in Introduction.

Hot Spots and Owner/NHTSA Comments:

1. Brakes: hydraulic system, poor performance, failure. • "While engaging the brakes vehicle lost complete control; caused accident, which resulted in injuries and property damage." • "Extended braking distance; excessive brake pedal distance is noted before engagement of system." • "Poor performance of brakes."

2. Electrical system: ignition, stalling, sudden acceleration. • "Electronic control module, coil and 2 ignition wires failed." • "When vehicle is brought to a full stop but engine and transmission are still engaged in drive, engine will stall; engine restarts in neutral or park." • "While passing, car continued to accelerate; turned ignition off to stop."

3. Fuel: throttle linkages and control, sudden accelerations. • "Car accelerated at full rpm in reverse; peeling out with blue smoke off tires; hit a pedestrian; locked onto front bumper of parked truck to prevent killing man." • "Driver started shifting gears, car suddenly accelerated at full speed, resulting in accident; when car finally stopped, it was noted that gear was in park." • "Engine surges intermittently." • "Car in reverse with foot on brakes, engine revved; went into reverse by itself; brake pedal went to floor when applied; resulted in accident."

PONTIAC SUNBIRD 1990

Complaint Severity: Typical. **Buyer's Summary:** Look carefully for any kind of leakage, especially under the car. Check the brakes—listen for noise, look for leaks and feel for vibration. They may fail, perform poorly or require frequent mechanical attention.

Hot Spots and Owner/NHTSA Comments:

1. Brakes: hydraulic system, poor performance, failure. • "Total brake failure; pedal went to floor; had to use emergency brake to stop vehicle." • "Brake problems." • "Five or six brake repairs; still unsatisfactory." • "Brake pedal went to floor without brake power on 2 occasions; unable to determine cause."

2. Engine: leaks, fire. • "Oil leak; engine light comes on and car is smoking." • "The engine is leaking oil; can smell gas fumes." • "In engine and passenger compartment, fumes of gasoline and oil are present." • "Engine caught on fire and burned from windshield area to the front."

PONTIAC SUNBIRD 1991

Complaint Severity: Serious. **Recall Alert:** See Recall Index. **Buyer's Summary:** See "Sudden Accelerations" in Introduction.

Hot Spots and Owner/NHTSA Comments:

1. Fuel: throttle linkages and control, sudden accelerations. • "Going from park to drive, vehicle went into high idle and open-throttle position, impact 12:00 position, speed unknown; in for repair of faulty alternator." • "Vehicle accelerated in reverse with minimum effect of brakes; gas pedal was not depressed." • "Sudden acceleration in reverse, causing accident." • "In reverse position, vehicle accelerated out of control on 2 occasions for no apparent reason." • "In wet weather, driver proceeded to brake. When foot was removed from accelerator, vehicle speeded up. Brakes and steering became difficult."

PONTIAC SUNBIRD 1992

Complaint Severity: Typical. **Recall Alert:** See Recall Index. **Buyer's Summary:** See "Sudden Accelerations" in Introduction.

Hot Spots and Owner/NHTSA Comments:

1. Fuel: throttle linkages: accelerator, sudden accelerations. • "Accelerator cable replaced." • "Broken throttle cable." • "Vehicle accelerated while in motion with brakes applied; caused replacement of accelerator cable." • "When taking off from a stopping position, vehicle continued to accelerate; applied brakes but vehicle would not stop; cable broke."

2. Fuel: throttle linkages and control, sudden accelerations. • "Throttle linkage and control failed, prior to recall, causing cruise control failure." • "Unsafe condition with throttle mechanism caused sudden acceleration." • "Throttle stuck open while driving; became very hard to stop." • "Sudden acceleration due to hole in vacuum hose after recall repairs."

PONTIAC SUNBIRD 1993

Complaint Severity: Serious. **Recall Alert:** See Recall Index. **Buyer's Summary:** Check the brakes—listen for noise, look for leaks and feel for vibration. They may fail, perform poorly or require frequent mechanical attention.

Hot Spots and Owner/NHTSA Comments:

1. Brakes: hydraulic: anti-skid system, poor performance, failure, locking up. • "When applying brakes at 35 mph, antilock brake system failed to respond; struck vehicle in front. Seat belt didn't prevent head and knees from hitting windshield." • "Defective antilock brakes." • "Antilock brakes periodically lock up when driving, causing loss of vehicle control." • "Poor performance of antilock brake system, causing extended stops." • "Brakes failed, causing accident and injuries."

Renault

RENAULT ALLIANCE 1987

Complaint Severity: Typical. **Recall Alert:** See Recall Index. **Buyer's Summary:** Look carefully for any kind of leakage, especially under the car. The electronic control unit has been blamed for engine performance problems, including stalling and surging. The fuel injection system has been blamed for hesitation and stalling. Be sure the vehicle doesn't die in traffic or at stops. Check the brakes—listen for noise, look for leaks and feel for vibration. They may fail, perform poorly or require frequent mechanical attention.

Hot Spots and Owner/NHTSA Comments:

1. Heater: water: defroster: defogger: heater core: water, malfunction, failure. • "While driving on interstate, suddenly hot fluid and steam spilled into interior of vehicle; couldn't stop or see road; lost control and sustained injury." • "Heater core overheated, causing liquid substance to spray out with a hissing noise while defroster was on; stopped when defroster was turned off." • "Heater coil exploded; caused burns to legs and face." • "Vehicle fire caused by heater core; vehicle is involved in recall."

2. Brakes: hydraulic system, excessive wear, noise, rust. • "Replacement of front and rear brake pads and shoes, turned drums and rotors; unspecified brake problems." • "Grease on bushings ate bushings, letting rust in on metal." • "Excessive and premature brake wear." • "Brakes squeal." • "Brakes and emergency brake cables malfunctioned; repaired/replaced brake cables and shoes."

3. Fuel: fuel injection system, stalling, hesitation. • "Vehicle stops without notice on highway." • "Vehicle shutting off while in motion." • "Car stalls anytime, at any speed; once stalled on railroad, on an incline; repaired/replaced motor, manifold air pressure sensor 5 times." • "Car repeatedly dies without warning while in motion, turning or at stop positions; caused near-accidents at 3 different times." • "While making turn, car would stall without warning."

4. Electrical system: ignition: electronic control unit, stalling, failure. • "Electronic control module failed; caused stalling; replaced sensor and electronic control module." • "When coming to stop, car surges forward; hard to start; replaced electronic control unit unit." • "Computer failed, causing transmission to jump into neutral gear and/or stall." • "Electrical short caused computer failure."
5. Engine: poor performance, overheating. • "Engine not powerful enough for acceleration; replaced." • "Engine problems, causing engine to overheat." • "While driving, noticed that engine was on fire." • "Head gasket busted; engine overheated due to cooling system pressure."
6. Engine: cooling system, leaks, overheating. • "Cooling system intermittently leaks." • "Engine cooling system leaks and overheats; repaired/replaced thermostat and coolant." • "Cooling system pressures overheated engine due to inadequate venting." • "Loss of power and exploding noise, causing car to fill with steam."

RENAULT MEDALLION 1988

Complaint Severity: Harmless. **Recall Alert:** See Recall Index. **Buyer's Summary:** The electronic control unit has been blamed for engine performance problems, including stalling and surging. The fuel injection system has been blamed for hesitation and stalling. Be sure the vehicle doesn't die in traffic or at stops. Check the brakes—listen for noise, look for leaks and feel for vibration. They may fail, perform poorly or require frequent mechanical attention. See "Sudden Accelerations" in Introduction.

Hot Spots and Owner/NHTSA Comments:
1. Brakes: hydraulic system, poor performance, excessive wear, noise. • "Brakes continue to wear rotors and pads to nothing every few months." • "Poor performance of brakes; low pedal and excessive squeaking in damp weather; pads and shoes repaired/replaced more than once." • "Defective braking system; had to repair/replace 2 sets of front rotors and 4 sets of front brake pads; brakes grind." • "Eight brake repairs; fails after every repair; cause undetermined." • "Brakes squeak excessively when applied, sounds like rubbing metal to metal; repaired/replaced brake pads, rotors and rear shoes numerous times to no avail."
2. Electrical system: ignition: electronic control unit, stalling, hesitation, malfunction. • "When going around corners and merging into traffic, vehicle would not accelerate immediately; stalls; replaced sensor." • "During warmup, engine hesitates, especially when applying brakes or making turns; engine seems to go to idle speed mode." • "Computer failure; when started, on acceleration, hesitates and stalls." • "While driving, lights began fading, vehicle stalled in traffic; engine dead; almost rear-ended; replaced onboard computer and alternator." • "Vehicle hesitates due to computer problems; replaced microprocessor."
3. Brakes: hydraulic: disc: pads and shoes, excessive wear, poor performance. • "Front brake pads (original) were defective and wore out prematurely." • "Front disc brake pads have been replaced 5 times within 60,000 miles." • "Noise in front end caused by pads having worn down and cut into rotors; replaced twice." • "Excessive brake pressure required to stop; car bucks when brakes applied; replaced pads and adjustments made, problem continues." • "Brakes' defective design causes excessive and/or unusual wear on pads, damaging rotors; make extreme noises when applied."
4. Fuel: fuel injection system, stalling, hesitation. • "Erratic engine problems; engine stalls on many occasions." • "Engine sputters, cuts out then accelerates and lunges forward; generally occurs when engine has warmed up; car jumps when put into gear." • "Car continually cuts off while driving; no acceleration when pressing gas pedal." • "Engine hesitation and missing problem; rough idle, especially when it's cold." • "While driving, vehicle loses power without warning."
5. Fuel: throttle linkages and control, sudden accelerations. • "Upon putting vehicle in drive gear, shot forward at high speed to 80 mph; excessive brake applications controlled speed." • "While driving, vehicle started accelerating on its own; was unable to stop car; accident." • "While pulling into garage, vehicle suddenly surged; crashed through kitchen and back out of garage." • "Problem with throttle malfunction; idles extremely fast upon starting engine; almost resulted in accident." • "Accident resulted from vehicle suddenly accelerating while backing." • "Car kept climbing in speed and lurched forward; car accelerated on its own at intersection."

Saab

SAAB 900 1987

Complaint Severity: Negligible. **Recall Alert:** See Recall Index. **Buyer's Summary:** The fuel injection system has been blamed for hesitation and stalling. Be sure the vehicle doesn't die in traffic or at stops. Check the brakes—listen for noise, look for leaks and feel for vibration. They may fail, perform poorly or require frequent mechanical attention. Test the transmission thoroughly.

Hot Spots and Owner/NHTSA Comments:
1. Fuel: fuel injection system, stalling, hesitation. • "Car loses power; not getting enough gas; slows down to 10 mph, experienced 4 breakdowns." • "Car will stall at 30 mph; problem not corrected after several repairs." • "Gasoline fumes inside car; problems starting; stalls when engine cold." • "Cold start; engine has no power; stumbles and stalls." • "Poor starting and hesitation problems." • "Constant hesitation in engine." • "Car does not accelerate adequately from stop position nor when driving at slow speed; does not pick up speed immediately."
2. Power train: transmission: automatic, poor performance, difficulty shifting, slipping. • "Shift cable seal failure resulted in oil leak; also, pinion bearings failed." • "Automatic transmission leaks." • "Cracked transmission, pan causing loss of fluids on 2 separate occasions." • "Transmission slips." • "Transmission housing broken."
3. Brakes: hydraulic: shoe: disc brake system, excessive wear, failure. • "Squealing and/or sticking brakes." • "Repeated failure of pads, calipers and master cylinder produced severe overheating, intense noise and excessive wear; entire front brakes were replaced." • "Front brakes wore out after 15,000 miles; second pair wore out at 31,000 miles; front brakes now have worn to 3/32 of an inch; in need of third replacement." • "Brake system defect; caliper or hydraulic problem on both front wheels." • "Front inner disc brakes wear out and fail."
4. Brakes: hydraulic: disc: caliper, locking up, failure. • "Repeated front brake failure resulted in accident when calipers locked up." • "Front caliper locked up, causing accident; also, premature wear of front brake rotors and pads." • "Defective brake caliper." • "Brake caliper locked up, causing loss of control."

SAAB 900 1994

Complaint Severity: Typical. **Recall Alert:** See Recall Index. **Buyer's Summary:** The steering may be stiff or not working correctly. Be sure to test the steering, especially on a cold start. Check the brakes—listen for noise, look for leaks and feel for vibration. They may fail, perform poorly or require frequent mechanical attention.

Hot Spots and Owner/NHTSA Comments:
1. Brakes: hydraulic: anti-skid system, poor performance, failure, locking up. • "Driver applied brakes and found there were none. The antilock brake system light and fluid light came on and stayed on." • "Antilock brake system didn't respond properly, with delay in reaction; vehicle plowed into truck. No airbag deployment, but extensive front damage." • "When car is on hill, there are no brakes for 5 minutes." • "Antilock brake system failed to stop vehicle effectively when applied, causing front-end collision at 10 mph. Dual airbags did not deploy." • "Antilock brake system failed when applied, causing vehicle to slide into curb, no impact; airbag did not deploy."
2. Steering: wheel and column, vibration. • "Steering wheel oscillates on smooth roads between 55-65 mph." • "Steering wheel vibration at highway speeds."

SAAB 9000 1988

Complaint Severity: Best 3% in Guide. **Recall Alert:** See Recall Index. **Buyer's Summary:** Check the brakes—listen for noise, look for leaks and feel for vibration. They may fail, perform poorly or require frequent mechanical attention. Test the transmission thoroughly.

Hot Spots and Owner/NHTSA Comments:
1. Power train: transmission: automatic, poor performance, difficulty shifting, slipping. • "Transmission makes hooting or chirping sound when shifting." • "Automatic transmission does not function properly; rubbing sound during gear changes; hard to engage in park; car rolled back in garage while in park." • "Automatic transmission started slipping at 7,000 miles." • "Transmission leaks fluid; repaired/replaced transmission; cooling system contaminated by transmission fluid." • "Transmission failure."
2. Brakes: hydraulic: anti-skid system, poor performance, failure, locking up. • "Defect in seal surrounding antilock braking system caused brakes to fail; required replacement." • "The antilock brake system failed; and to that, the antilock brake system light comes on and the brakes make noise when applied; dealer can find nothing wrong." • "Antilock brakes fail intermittently."
3. Wheels: vibration, premature failure. • "Bent wheels cause vibration in automobile; several repair attempts before problem was corrected." • "Three of four wheels were bent to such a great extent that car shimmied too much on highway; total of 6 wheels and 1 tire replaced." • "Repeated failure of wheels and rims; rims severely bent and causing abnormal wear and tear on tires; 7 wheels and/or rims needed to be replaced by 30,000 miles." • "Three of alloy wheels bent; replaced."

SAAB 9000 1989

Complaint Severity: Typical. **Recall Alert:** See Recall Index. **Buyer's Summary:** Check the brakes—listen for noise, look for leaks and feel for vibration. They may fail, perform poorly or require frequent mechanical attention.

Hot Spots and Owner/NHTSA Comments:
1. Brakes: hydraulic: anti-skid system, poor performance, failure, locking up. • "Upon brake application, pedal went completely to floor; hydraulic failure; brake fluid and antilock warning lights came on; stopped with hand brakes." • "Sudden total brake failure; brake pedal went completely to floor; brake fluid and antilock warning lights came on; appears to be electrical failure." • "Recurring brake and/or antilock brake failure." • "Traveling down the highway at 60 mph, no response from braking system resulting in failure of the antilock brakes." • "Antilock brake system has gone out 2 times without warning; pedal goes to floor with no braking effect; no warning; extended stopping; 45 mph."
2. Electrical system: wiring: harness: under dash, malfunction, fire. • "Electrical wiring problem, causing fire." • "Vehicle backed out of driveway and placed on street in front of house. Upon starting, smoke emanated from under dashboard. Fire consumed vehicle." • "Fire broke out in passenger compartment; probable cause an electrical short." • "Recall related. Electrical short; smell of smoke in console; vehicle caught on fire."

Saturn

SATURN 1992

Complaint Severity: Typical. **Buyer's Summary:** The fuel injection system has been blamed for hesitation and stalling. Be sure the vehicle doesn't die in traffic or at stops. Check the brakes—listen for noise, look for leaks and feel for vibration. They may fail, perform poorly or require frequent mechanical attention.

Hot Spots and Owner/NHTSA Comments:
1. Brakes: hydraulic system, failure. • "Brake failure." • "Brakes failed, resulting in extended stopping distance, loss of control, accident and injury." • "Spongy brakes." • "Brake failure." • "Noisy brakes; repaired 4 times, problem continues."
2. Fuel: fuel injection system, stalling, hesitation. • "Vehicle fire." • "Electronic fuel component failed." • "Intermittent backfire." • "Intermittent stalling." • "Intermittent hesitation when air conditioner is on."
3. Engine: mounts, vibration, failure. • "Broken motor mounts, causing vibration." • "Engine mount failed." • "Engine mounts failed; also, valves replaced." • "Motor mounts failed." • "Top engine mount collapsed, causing vehicle to vibrate."
4. Engine: stalling, vibration, failure. • "Intermittent stalling; also, vehicle vibrates, hesitates and runs rough; oil not filtering correctly through engine." • "Engine failure." • "Oil pressure incorrect; engine overheated and misfired." • "While driving, noticed smoke coming from engine compartment."
5. Equipment: electric power accessories: windows, failure. • "Electric window control failed." • "Power window in rear door failed." • "Power windows failed." • "Driver's power window regulator failed, causing power window failure."

SATURN 1993

Complaint Severity: Typical. **Recall Alert:** See Recall Index. **Buyer's Summary:** Check the brakes—listen for noise, look for leaks and feel for vibration. They may fail, perform poorly or require frequent mechanical attention. Test the transmission thoroughly.

Hot Spots and Owner/NHTSA Comments:
1. Brakes: hydraulic system, failure. • "Brakes failed; brake pedal went to the floor; resulting in extended stopping distance." • "Brakes failed while test-driving vehicle; resulted in accident and injuries." • "Brakes failed, causing an accident." • "Brakes failed on wet road, causing an accident." • "Brakes failed, causing an accident and injury."
2. Visual systems: glass: windshield, breaking. • "While standing still, rear windshield exploded for no apparent reason." • "Windshield noise due to faulty windshield garnish molding." • "Windshield cracked." • "Windshield broke twice." • "Windshield cracked very easily when struck by small stone."
3. Brakes: hydraulic: disc: rotor: disc hub, vibration, failure. • "Brake rotors failed causing vehicle to vibrate." • "Front brake

rotors and pads replaced due to noise." • "Both front brake discs out of round; shimmy."
4. Interior systems: active seat and shoulder belts and belt anchor, failure. • "Seat belt failed in accident, causing injury." • "Temporary seat belt latch plate was not provided." • "Seat belt cover failed." • "No seat belt."
5. Power train: transmission: automatic, poor performance, difficulty shifting, slipping. • "Transmission shifts roughly." • "Transmission failed; slipped in lower gears." • "Vehicle rolls backwards when foot is removed from gas pedal to brake."

SATURN SL2 1993

Complaint Severity: Serious. **Recall Alert:** See Recall Index. **Buyer's Summary:** Verify that the cruise control system works properly, and that it doesn't cause the engine to surge. The airbags in this vehicle have experienced failures and malfunctions: You may need a professional evaluation on the condition of the airbags. Check the brakes—listen for noise, look for leaks and feel for vibration. They may fail, perform poorly or require frequent mechanical attention. Make sure seat belts function correctly and fit comfortably.

Hot Spots and Owner/NHTSA Comments:
1. Equipment: speed control, sudden acceleration, failure. • "Cruise control fails to engage upon first attempt; also will disengage on its own." • "Vehicle suddenly accelerated upon setting cruise control." • "Cruise control failed to disengage when the brakes applied." • "Cruise control; after engaged, has loss of power while driving." • "Cruise control intermittently disengages while driving." • "Cruise control would not engage."
2. Brakes: hydraulic: anti-skid system, poor performance, failure, locking up. • "When making a stop, no response from antilock braking system." • "Complete antilock brake system failure occurred with pedal to floor; had to jam into park to stop." • "Antilock brake system failed on incline. Experienced pedal fading. Stopped vehicle by using emergency brake." • "Antilock brake system rotors had to be replaced twice." • "Brakes failed, driver applied brakes and pedal went to the floor." • "Antilock brake system: Experienced pedal fading when applying brakes; complete loss of brake effectiveness, impact 5:00 position, speed 5 mph."
3. Interior systems: passive restraint: airbag: driver, malfunction, failure. • "In 12:00 position in 25-35-mph accident, driver's-side airbag did not deploy." • "Airbag did not deploy." • "Airbag did not deploy at minimum speed of of 40 mph." • "In a vehicle accident at approximately 45 mph, the driver's-side airbag did not deploy."
4. Brakes: hydraulic system, failure. • "Total brake loss at 35-40 mph." • "Both front rotors and rear drums burned out, resulting in no braking power when applied." • "Hydraulic brakes do not stop the vehicle; increased stopping distances; had the brakes serviced 6 times and problem still exists." • "Had 2 incidents when brakes would not stop vehicle."
5. Interior systems: passive restraint: belts, malfunction, uncomfortable. • "Driver's motorized shoulder belt will release while driving; passenger's belt will lock up." • "Automatic door-frame-mounted shoulder harness seat belt tightens instead of releasing occupant when exiting vehicle." • "Occupant's finger got caught in automatic seat belt track." • "Due to height and fastening of seat belt, belt cuts across the neck."

SATURN SL2 1994

Complaint Severity: Typical. **Buyer's Summary:** Verify that the cruise control system works properly, and that it doesn't cause the engine to surge. Check the brakes—listen for noise, look for leaks and feel for vibration. They may fail, perform poorly or require frequent mechanical attention.

Hot Spots and Owner/NHTSA Comments:
1. Equipment: speed control, malfunction, failure. • "Driver had cruise control on; came to stoplight and applied brakes (spongy). Vehicle cruise control did not disengage." • "Cruise control disengages itself while driving. Unintended acceleration occurs when engaging cruise control." • "Intermittently, cruise control wouldn't engage. Replaced module and adjusted clutch switch." • "Cruise control fails to disengage when driving, causing surging and/or sudden acceleration; loss of vehicle control." • "While driving at approximately 60 mph, experience intermittent cruise control failure; cruise control may not engage, or may disengage without application of brake."
2. Brakes: hydraulic system, noise, locking up. • "Brakes are grinding." • "During brake application, brakes failed completely." • "When coming to slow stop, squeaking noise follows." • "While coming to stop, brake pedal traveled to floor momentarily; extended stopping; speed 20 mph; no warning." • "Under certain driving conditions, brakes lock up."

Sterling

STERLING 825 1987

Complaint Severity: Harmless. **Recall Alert:** See Recall Index. **Buyer's Summary:** Check the brakes—listen for noise, look for leaks and feel for vibration. They may fail, perform poorly or require frequent mechanical attention. See "Sudden Accelerations" in Introduction.

Hot Spots and Owner/NHTSA Comments:
1. Brakes: hydraulic: shoe: disc brake system, excessive wear, poor performance. • "Front brake rotors and pads replaced 4 times." • "Defective front brakes; repaired 3 times; pads wear unevenly and rotors bend out of shape; car shudders." • "Front end shimmies upon braking; antilock brakes not working properly; car skids when applied; replaced parts and rotors." • "Defective braking system; excessive and repeated brake failures; front brake pulsating; repaired/replaced rotors, pads resurfaced repeatedly." • "Car vibrates when braking; worse when brake pedal is depressed at speeds of 65-70 mph; front brakes changed and resurfaced 7 times, problem still exists."
2. Interior systems: instrument panel: speedometer: odometer, malfunction, failure. • "Unspecified odometer problems." • "Odometer inoperative; repaired twice." • "Speedometer inoperative; replaced." • "Speedometer/odometer inoperative." • "Speedometer/trip computer had difference of 10 percent; replaced speedometer."
3. Brakes: hydraulic system, vibration, excessive wear. • "Brakes and steering column vibrate upon applying brakes." • "Without warning, car suddenly began to shake violently in front end when brakes applied; extremely difficult to bring car to safe stop." • "Premature wear of all brake pads results in poor braking potential and rotor replacements." • "Consistent problem with vibration when braking, especially at higher speeds." • "Brakes very dangerous; been replaced, rotated and worked on, and continue to cause severe shimmy."
4. Electrical system: malfunction, failure. • "Electrical system failure caused air conditioner, windshield wipers and defogger to fail during rainstorm." • "Trouble with electrical system; malfunctioning remote door locks, cruise control, vanity mirror and dashboard lights." • "Defect in electrical system; many erratic things

happen due to shortage in electrical system." • "Electrical controls don't always work."

5. Fuel: throttle linkages and control, sudden accelerations. • "While driving, vehicle surged forward out of control; caused an accident." • "With foot on brake, changed gear from park position, vehicle engine roared then accelerated, hitting another vehicle." • "After driving 135 miles with air conditioner running, then parking car, upon startup after 15 minutes, rpm went to maximum and car started racing backward; brakes failed." • "Accelerator button under hood sticks, causing vehicle to accelerate with foot off gas pedal."

Subaru

SUBARU GL 1987

Complaint Severity: Typical. **Recall Alert:** See Recall Index. **Buyer's Summary:** Problems with the timing gear and chain can cause serious problems. Have the engine checked by a professional. The steering may be stiff or not working correctly. Be sure to test the steering, especially on a cold start. Test the transmission thoroughly. See "Sudden Accelerations" in Introduction.

Hot Spots and Owner/NHTSA Comments:

1. Engine: timing gear and chain, breaking, failure. • "While driving, vehicle suddenly lost power without warning; timing belt failure." • "While in travel, timing belt broke." • "Engine cam belts and timing belt broke; caused vehicle to stall." • "While driving on freeway, engine suddenly went out with no warning due to timing belt failure; nearly caused accident." • "Failure of timing belt at highway speed caused immediate loss of power." • "Timing belt failed while driving at 40 mph; car backfired and stopped very quickly."

2. Engine: camshaft, noise, failure. • "Rubber cam belt failure; car lost complete power." • "Overhead camshaft problem; belt broke; car stopped with no warning." • "Engine noisy when cold, loose cam belts adjusted." • "Cam belts adjusted several times; engine knock." • "Noise from exhaust caused by camshaft drive belt failing." • "Camshaft belt in imminent danger of breaking; repairs made."

3. Fuel: throttle linkages and control, sudden accelerations. • "Unintended sudden acceleration, even while vehicle in neutral; still roaring in full throttle; resulted in accident 2 times." • "When shifted into reverse, engine roared and car suddenly accelerated, went out of control; hit parked car and came to stop after hitting wall." • "Car had sudden acceleration when shifted into reverse; foot was on brake; car stopped only after it flew backwards over a retaining wall." • "In process of parking, vehicle suddenly accelerated on its own, forcing forward; resulted in accident." • "Vehicle suddenly accelerated in parking lot after shifted into reverse; braking did not stop acceleration, crashed into chain-link fence."

4. Engine: other parts, noise, failure. • "Engine heads defective; had to be replaced several times due to problem with original design." • "Vehicle has been running hot due to a cracked cylinder head; dealer replaced cylinder head, but car still ran hot; needs new radiator." • "Timing belt noisy; repaired/replaced." • "The aluminum heads cracked due to excessive heat."

5. Steering: power assist: pump, breaking, malfunction. • "Erratic steering and handling of car; power steering pump support bracket broken; failure due to metal fatigue." • "Bracket that holds steering pump cracked, chirping noise made." • "Aluminum alloy bracket that holds power steering pump cracked; broke off in hand." • "Power steering bracket broke while in operation." • "Power steering bracket cracked by mounting bolts; metal was inadequate strength."

6. Power train: transmission: automatic, poor performance, difficulty shifting, slipping. • "Transmission grinds when shifting from 2nd to 3rd gear." • "Roughness with transmission." • "Automatic transmission won't go into 2nd gear when accelerating, goes 15 mph." • "Car will not shift to 2nd when it is cold." • "Transmission would not shift; noise coming from control."

SUBARU GL 1988

Complaint Severity: Typical. **Recall Alert:** See Recall Index. **Buyer's Summary:** Carefully check the brakes—listen for noise, look for leaks and feel for vibration. They may fail, perform poorly or require frequent mechanical attention. See "Sudden Accelerations" in Introduction.

Hot Spots and Owner/NHTSA Comments:

1. Fuel: throttle linkages and control, sudden accelerations. • "When started with foot on brake, shifted into drive and car took off like jet; hit embankment and tree, flipped over; car totaled." • "Uncontrolled sudden acceleration upon starting vehicle and putting gear into drive, resulting in accident." • "While cruising, vehicle suddenly accelerated at full throttle; driver lost control; brakes locked up; accident resulted." • "Vehicle suddenly accelerated; motor went full power, causing car to race near 100 mph; driver lost control and crashed into guardrail." • "Upon shifting transmission into reverse, vehicle accelerated out of control; caused damage."

2. Interior systems: active restraints: belt buckles, malfunction, failure. • "Seat belt buckle is sometimes difficult to fasten; pressure applied may falsely indicate that it is securely fastened." • "Passenger buckle fails to engage; cause unknown." • "Driver's-side seat belt failure; unable to unlatch seat belt." • "The front passenger and driver's-side seat belt buckles sometimes appear to be locked, but come loose." • "Seat belts do not latch properly." • "The seat belts are very difficult to latch."

3. Brakes: hydraulic: shoe: disc brake system, excessive wear, vibration. • "Excessive brake wear; many repairs, problem continues." • "When brakes applied, front-end shimmy; press down hard to stop vehicle; makes steering difficult." • "Malfunction in brake, rubs and vibrates; replaced rotor and brake pads."

4. Interior systems: active restraints: belt retractors, malfunction, failure. • "Driver's-side lap and shoulder belts will not retract." • "Front seat 3-point harness system will not release from pillar." • "Seat belt retractor in back seat did not hold on impact of accident, causing injury; holds only if the brakes are applied first." • "Passenger-side seat belt not working properly; would seem to latch, then without warning would simply release, seat belt turned wrong; needed replacement."

SUBARU JUSTY 1988

Complaint Severity: Typical. **Recall Alert:** See Recall Index. **Buyer's Summary:** Test transmission for slipping, locking up and performance.

Hot Spots and Owner/NHTSA Comments:

1. Power train: transmission: 5-speed and up, difficulty shifting. • "Transmission grinds." • "Five-speed manual transmission defective; have had several repairs made." • "Recurring problem with transmission; repaired twice; presently grinds into 3rd and 5th gears; also, intermittently will not shift in or out of 2nd gear."

SUBARU LEGACY 1990

Complaint Severity: Minor. **Recall Alert:** See Recall Index. **Buyer's Summary:** Check the brakes—listen for noise, look for leaks and feel for vibration. They may fail, perform poorly or require frequent mechanical attention. Test the transmission thoroughly. See "Sudden Accelerations" in Introduction.

Hot Spots and Owner/NHTSA Comments:

1. Power train: transmission: automatic, poor performance, difficulty shifting, slipping. • "Vehicle would not move from park to reverse." • "Extensive transmission problems; vehicle experiences delayed reaction when going into reverse; also, intermittent sudden acceleration." • "Transmission completely failed, making vehicle inoperative in drive or reverse." • "Car will intermittently not engage in gear when shifting from park to reverse; dealer has attempted to fix trouble 3 times, but problem still exists." • "Transmission shifts hard; jerks when shifting; fluid leaking; dipstick broken; replaced main pressure valve and solenoid; also, noisy when shifts warm."

2. Fuel: throttle linkages and control, sudden accelerations. • "Problem of sudden unintended acceleration." • "Car suddenly accelerates forward while braking at very low speeds, attempting to stop at light, sign or intersection." • "When placing vehicle from park into reverse, a brief delay occurred, then vehicle suddenly accelerated." • "While pulling into driveway to park, vehicle suddenly accelerated, jumped over a motor and finally hit a house." • "Transmission in park with foot on brakes when car shot backwards."

3. Brakes: hydraulic: disc: rotor: disc hub, vibration, corrosion, poor performance. • "Rear disc rotor corroded, causing loss of brake effectiveness." • "Front brake rotors had a crack after they were replaced." • "Rear rotors and pads worn." • "Rear brake rotors rusted; failed to stop vehicle." • "While applying brakes, vehicle vibrates; caused by corrosion of rear brake rotors. Also causes increased brake pad wear."

4. Structure: door assembly: latches and locks, malfunction, failure. • "Manual door locks locked with baby trapped inside; locks appear to be in unlocked position." • "Poor latches and locks due to design. Door-switch assembly pushing on either side locks or unlocks doors." • "When trying to open doors, they lock themselves." • "Driver's door locked and could not be opened." • "Lock on passenger's side gets stuck."

5. Brakes: hydraulic system, poor performance. • "Car has tendency to skid to side when brakes applied in panic stop; brakes seem to lock unevenly." • "When vehicle is first started after being parked overnight or for several hours, upon applying, brakes freeze and cannot be depressed." • "Weak brake pedal, causing extended stopping distance."

6. Equipment: electric power accessories: locks: door, malfunction, failure. • "Power door lock button on driver's and passenger's doors, when moved to lock position, will not let passengers out of vehicle; forced the doors open with lever." • "When trying to open doors from inside, doors will lock." • "Owner complains of not being able to open the doors all the way. Relay door locks failed." • "Passenger-side rear door locking mechanism failed." • "When trying to open doors from inside, doors will lock."

SUBARU LEGACY 1991

Complaint Severity: Serious. **Recall Alert:** See Recall Index. **Buyer's Summary:** Test the transmission thoroughly. Make sure seat belts function correctly and fit comfortably.

Hot Spots and Owner/NHTSA Comments:

1. Power train: transmission: automatic, poor performance, difficulty shifting, slipping. • "Vehicle would not come out of park; when it did, it surged and crashed into house." • "Transmission failed while driving; difficult to shift gears; no warning." • "Transmission failed to go over 45 mph or in reverse gear; also, transmission locked up twice." • "Transmission replaced due to noise and sticking in 3rd gear." • "Vehicle hesitates when shifted into reverse gear." • "While parked in front of a business with gear in park position, transmission jumped out of gear; vehicle accelerated out of control and hit a tree."

2. Steering: locking up, failure. • "Poor steering caused vehicle to veer from lane to lane and then skid." • "To avoid impact of other vehicle, car swerved, lost control and hit a barrier, then caught on fire and exploded." • "In downgrading conditions, steering failed on right curve." • "Attempting to change into center lane from left lane on divided highway, was involved in an accident when a car in right lane also changed into center lane." • "While going around a right curve, steering locked up and pulled vehicle to left, hitting curve guard."

3. Interior systems: passive restraint: belts, malfunction, failure. • "Driver's-side automatic seat belt does not return." • "Driver's- and passenger-side retractors sometimes don't retract back." • "Child on passenger's side of vehicle got thumb caught in automatic seat belt track." • "Passenger-side automatic shoulder seat belt did not restrain passenger during accident."

Suzuki—Trucks

SUZUKI TRUCK SAMURAI 1987

Complaint Severity: Dangerous (Worst 3% in Guide). **Buyer's Summary:** Look carefully for any kind of leakage, especially under the car. Test the suspension by feeling for vibration or pulling while driving.

Hot Spots and Owner/NHTSA Comments:

1. Suspension: poor stability. • "While turning steering wheel sharply left, vehicle toppled over on left side." • "Car unsafe to drive; possibility of rolling over while in motion." • "Poor stability; when going around curve vehicle went up on 2 wheels at normal speed." • "When driving on highway, swift wind makes vehicle out of control; poor stability; tips on turns at any speed." • "When driving in wind, feel like vehicle going to tip over; poor stability." • "Vehicle turned to right, lost control and rolled once; poor stability."

2. Suspension: independent front, poor performance. • "When hit a small patch of ice, vehicle skidded onto dry pavement; wheel tucked under and vehicle turned over due to weak suspension." • "Owner unhappy with stability of vehicle." • "Due to poor stability of vehicle, driver lost control; vehicle rolled over several times; one fatality resulted." • "When bumped fender of parked car at 15-20 mph, vehicle turned over on its side due to poor stability." • "Slightest pressure on brakes caused vehicle to swerve to side of road to a complete stop."

3. Engine: leaks, failure. • "Complete engine failure, including head gaskets leaking antifreeze into cylinders, destroying bearings." • "Complete engine shutdown due to spontaneous oil evaporation." • "Experienced severe loss of power (55-30 mph)." • "Engine blew while in motion due to oil leak."

4. Structure: frame: members and body, poor stability. • "Rear end slid on 25-mph curve; vehicle almost rolled over." • "Entering and exiting interstates, vehicle tilts; driver almost lost control." • "Car fishtailed to right; tumbled down an embankment." • "Come close to flipping when going around turns at 10 mph."

SUZUKI TRUCK SAMURAI 1988

Complaint Severity: Dangerous (Worst 3% in Guide). **Recall Alert:** See Recall Index. **Buyer's Summary:** Test the suspension by feeling for vibration or pulling while driving.

Hot Spots and Owner/NHTSA Comments:

1. Suspension: poor stability. • "Poorly designed suspension, causing unit to flip upon swerving, hitting bump or making quick turn." • "Vehicle gives very rough, bumpy ride; poor handling around corners." • "Impossible to control at speeds above 40 mph; went out of control after going over small hill; accident." • "Poor stability; unsafe distance between tires; when going around curve, lifting of 2 wheels." • "Driver lost complete control; skidded sideways, then rolled 6 times down embankment; poor stability." • "Vehicle spun out of control on patch of ice, rolled over into 7-foot ditch; poor stability."

2. Suspension: independent front, poor stability. • "Swerved to avoid object on road; rolled over several times." • "Very light suspension; poor stability when going around a curve, feels as if going to roll over." • "When made hard left turn to avoid hitting deer, felt like right side came off ground." • "Attempting to make U-turn, vehicle rolled over onto roof." • "Truck flipped over going 35 mph; it also has spun around."

3. Interior systems: active restraints: belt buckles, breaking, malfunction. • "The passenger seat belt buckle is broken." • "The driver's-side seat belt buckle broke and was replaced." • "Front lap and shoulder belt buckle is jamming, making it very difficult to open belt."

Toyota—Cars and Trucks

TOYOTA CAMRY 1987

Complaint Severity: Typical. **Recall Alert:** See Recall Index. **Buyer's Summary:** Verify that the cruise control system works properly, and that it doesn't cause the engine to surge. Check the brakes—listen for noise, look for leaks and feel for vibration. They may fail, perform poorly or require frequent mechanical attention. Test the transmission thoroughly. Make sure seat belts function correctly and fit comfortably. See "Sudden Accelerations" in Introduction.

Hot Spots and Owner/NHTSA Comments:

1. Brakes: hydraulic system, noise, vibration. • "Shimmy in brake pedal progressively worsened, causing steering wheel to vibrate." • "Brakes make grinding sound when stopping at low speeds." • "Vehicle vibrating during braking; replaced brake pads and rotors." • "Excessive squealing in braking system; can't be corrected." • "Vehicle seems to slide when brakes are applied during wet weather; spins completely around; brakes replaced." • "Brakes pulsate badly, can be felt through steering wheel and brake pedal."

2. Fuel: throttle linkages and control, sudden accelerations. • "Shifted car to drive, lightly tapped gas pedal, vehicle rapidly propelled at fastest speed possible, racing at maximum capacity out of control." • "Upon turning on ignition and putting gearshift into reverse, suddenly car ran backward with great speed, crashing into block wall." • "Turned on ignition, put gearshift into reverse, vehicle suddenly ran backwards with great speed, did semicircle and crashed into brick wall." • "Shifted from park to drive with foot on brakes, released parking brake and car suddenly accelerated 50-75 feet, hitting wall." • "Gearshift in drive with foot depressing brakes, car shot forward without any intervention from driver; resulted in accident and injuries."

3. Equipment: electric power accessories: locks: door, malfunction, failure. • "Power door locks intermittently stick and/or lock up; causes occupants to manually unlock doors." • "Electronic door locks stick, resulting in difficulty in opening the vehicle." • "Experienced inside and outside power door lockup intermittently." • "Driver's-side electronic door locks jam intermittently." • "Relays for all power door locks burned, making doors inoperative." • "Power door locks intermittently lock themselves; temporary."

4. Interior systems: passive restraint: belts, malfunction, failure. • "Automatic seat belts inoperative due to a short in the computer system." • "Vehicle was involved in a rollover accident. Passenger-side passive restraint system did not hold occupant in place; occupant hit windshield." • "Automatic front shoulder belt computer started acting erratically; warning light goes on when belts are on tight, and later quit moving totally; repaired/replaced." • "Passive restraint on driver's-side reacts erratically; sticks." • "Automatic seat belts in front do not work."

5. Equipment: speed control, malfunction, failure. • "Cruise control switch failed." • "Defective cruise control; when off, car accelerated to about 90 mph; whenever it was turned on, it would not resume or hold preset speed; slows down." • "When on cruise control, car keeps accelerating, especially at over 50 mph." • "Speed control does not engage; however, when it does engage it will turn off by itself." • "Cruise control difficult to engage; engages by itself at approximately 65 mph." • "Cruise control slips off while in use."

6. Power train: transmission: automatic, poor performance, difficulty shifting, slipping. • "Vehicle pulls and jerks going through gears on both acceleration and deceleration." • "Transmission shifter moved without key in ignition, resulting in accident." • "Automatic transmission shifts roughly from lower to higher gears." • "Gear sticks (grinding)." • "Automatic transmission jumps out of gear; when on a incline, shifter in drive and engine running, car rolls backwards." • "Automatic transmission sounds like it is slipping when shifting between 2nd and 3rd; also takes long time to shift into 3rd."

TOYOTA CAMRY 1988

Complaint Severity: Typical. **Theft Alert:** 47. **Recall Alert:** See Recall Index. **Buyer's Summary:** Verify that the cruise control system works properly, and that it doesn't cause the engine to surge. Check the brakes—listen for noise, look for leaks and feel for vibration. They may fail, perform poorly or require frequent mechanical attention. Test the transmission thoroughly. See "Sudden Accelerations" in Introduction.

Hot Spots and Owner/NHTSA Comments:

1. Equipment: electric power accessories: locks: door, malfunction, failure. • "Power door locks failed to unlock, preventing entry into vehicle." • "Power door locks stick, causing driver to be locked inside or preventing entry at different times." • "Power door lock jammed, resulting in passengers being trapped inside." • "Driver's-side power door locks will not lock." • "Controls malfunctioned, causing power windows and power door locks not to work." • "Power door locks failed to open from outside; occupant climbed over front seat to get to driver's seat."

2. Fuel: throttle linkages and control, sudden accelerations. • "Vehicle suddenly accelerated when shifted from park position, causing loss of control and an accident." • "Put vehicle into drive and reverse, vehicle went open-throttle position, impact 6:00 position, hitting a brick wall, speed unknown." • "At stoplight with gear in drive, car surged forward into truck; caused extensive damage." • "Shifted from park to drive, vehicle roared full throttle and leaped forward 20 feet; jumped 18-inch dirt mound and crashed into tree." • "Shifted into drive, unexpectedly car went into fast forward motion; resulted in accident." • "Parked vehicle idling for about 45-60 seconds, then shifted to drive; vehicle suddenly accelerated out of control, resulting in accident."

3. Brakes: hydraulic system, vibration, failure. • "Brake problems, causing vibration after applying brakes." • "Vehicle experienced total brake failure; brake functions normal after standing overnight." • "Power brakes failed to stop vehicle at 45 mph, causing vehicle to crash into embankment. Brake pedal faded to the floor." • "There have been 2 occurrences where vehicle accelerated out of control: throttle failure. Brakes failed, resulting in a hitting tree." • "Defective braking system; brakes do not perform as should; braking action delayed." • "Severe squeaking and/or grinding in both front and rear brakes when applied; repaired/replaced pads, front brakes and drums."

4. Equipment: speed control, malfunction, failure. • "Erratic cruise control operation." • "Cruise control stuck at 60 mph; to turn off, must shift to neutral, braking does not work; almost caused collision." • "Cruise control stuck on; would not disengage, even after brake and cruise control switch had been applied; resulted in accident." • "Faulty cruise control caused vehicle to accelerate forward; went over embankment into river." • "Cruise control occasionally does strange things, like going off when I haven't hit the brakes."

5. Brakes: hydraulic: shoe: disc brake system, excessive wear, vibration. • "Front brake pads and rotors worn out; prematurely repaired/replaced at less than 16,000 miles." • "New brake pads and rotors replaced under 16,000 miles." • "Disc brake pads, rotors and calipers continue to wear due to massive heat buildup." • "Premature wear of front brakes." • "Premature brake wear resulted in poor brake performance." • "Front brake vibration; repaired/replaced rotors and pads."

6. Power train: transmission: automatic, poor performance, difficulty shifting, slipping. • "Automatic transmission failed; bearings and gears wore out and broke. Vehicle went from 65 to 10 mph on highway." • "Ongoing problem of transmission leakage." • "Turned motor off, removed key, vehicle rolled down hill and smashed into driver's side of another car." • "In 2 separate occurrences, the automatic transmission reverse gear went out." • "While at highway speed of 65 mph, automatic transmission disintegrated internally. Vehicle stopped dead."

TOYOTA CAMRY 1989

Complaint Severity: Negligible. **Recall Alert:** See Recall Index. **Buyer's Summary:** Check the brakes—listen for noise, look for leaks and feel for vibration. They may fail, perform poorly or require frequent mechanical attention. Test the transmission thoroughly. Make sure seat belts function correctly and fit comfortably. See "Sudden Accelerations" in Introduction.

Hot Spots and Owner/NHTSA Comments:

1. Equipment: electric power accessories: locks: door, malfunction, failure. • "Driver's and passenger's power door locks failed to release, preventing exit from or entry into vehicle." • "Right rear door locks froze; remaining door locks still functioning." • "Power door lock jammed; resulted in not being able to enter vehicle." • "Power door locks failed before and after recall repair." • "Seven minutes after electric door lock acted erratically, smelled electrical burning; fire occurred under dashboard. Odor." • "Power door lock stuck and failed to open; trapped occupants inside vehicle."

2. Fuel: throttle linkages and control, sudden accelerations. • "While driving 50 mph, car lurched forward; lost control of steering wheel and hit concrete barrier." • "Automatic transmission: Throttle stuck in open position twice while in traffic; driver immediately shifted to neutral to avoid accident; speed 40 mph; no prior warning." • "Vehicle accelerated forward when put into drive; revved; hit and leaped 9-inch curbing without stopping; brakes failed to function." • "Increased car speed to 50 mph, at which point car lurched forward; could not control steering wheel; hit concrete barrier." • "When air conditioner is on, car moves forward a little bit, even after brake is applied." • "Vehicle suddenly accelerated and went out of control; resulted in an accident."

3. Brakes: hydraulic system, vibration, excessive wear. • "Excessive vibration, since purchase, when braking; vibration also felt through steering wheel; unable to find cause and/or cure." • "Vibration from brake and steering wheel." • "Brakes wear quickly." • "While driving, another vehicle ran a stop sign and hit first vehicle; brakes were ineffective in stopping vehicle; resulted in serious injuries and damage." • "Brakes prematurely wore out within 7,000 miles; caused extended stopping distances." • "Noisy brakes."

4. Power train: transmission: automatic, poor performance, difficulty shifting, slipping. • "Does not stay in drive and slips out of gear. When car slows down, it shifts out of drive and won't go forward anymore." • "Transmission slipped." • "Transmission hesitates; replaced." • "Transmission jerks when placed in 1st gear." • "Transmission would not change into 3rd gear when cold."

5. Interior systems: passive restraint: belts, uncomfortable, malfunction. • "Chest belts need more adjustment for short people to keep belt from crossing over neck area." • "Right front passenger automatic seat belt harness repeatedly failed to retract around passenger." • "Automatic seat belts were inoperative; replaced fuse and everything was back to normal." • "Driver's-side shoulder belt motor failed." • "Motorized seat belts fail to tighten up around occupants as intended; remain in retractor position toward front of door."

TOYOTA CAMRY 1990

Complaint Severity: Typical. **Recall Alert:** See Recall Index. **Buyer's Summary:** Look carefully for any kind of leakage, especially under the car. Check the brakes—listen for noise, look for leaks and feel for vibration. They may fail, perform poorly or require frequent mechanical attention. Make sure seat belts function correctly and fit comfortably. See "Sudden Accelerations" in Introduction.

Hot Spots and Owner/NHTSA Comments:

1. Equipment: electric power accessories: locks: door, malfunction, failure. • "The rear passenger power door locks on the driver's side will not open from the inside." • "Automatic door locks do not unlock, trapping occupants inside for a brief period." • "When power door locks were pushed down, they popped up on their own; unable to unlock passenger door with driver door." • "Temporary failure of power door locks, windows and moonroof 3 different times." • "Power door locks failed to work; occupants crawled out through the trunk."

2. Fuel: throttle linkages and control, sudden accelerations. • "Slowed to 15 mph while braking to a stop; vehicle surged ahead with full engine power and crashed." • "Sudden acceleration, resulting in 2 separate accidents." • "Sudden surge at high speed into concrete wall." • "While parking in garage, vehicle accelerated out of control; caused accident; no injuries or damage incurred." • "Throttle sticks; dealer cleaned and temporarily fixed 12 months ago, problem just returned."

3. Brakes: hydraulic system, vibration, excessive wear, failure. • "During trip, rear wheel started to smoke; all wheel covers became extremely hot; indicates defects in braking system." • "Pulsating brakes failed." • "Brake lining replaced." • "Brakes lose fluid and brake pads wear down very fast." • "Have to press brakes hard; car jerks to a stop."

4. Electrical system: battery, leaks, fire, failure. • "Battery exploded when vehicle was started." • "Acid leaks from defective battery." • "Loose connection caused battery and alternator failure." • "Original car battery exploded while attempting to start vehicle." • "Battery exploded, resulting in a fire." • "Vehicle battery exploded and acid spilled over onto engine."

5. Interior systems: passive restraint: belts, uncomfortable, failure. • "Seat belt location and fit bothersome; fits right under chin; driver must keep adjusting location of strap; also threat of injury." • "Safety belts on driver's seat misaligned." • "Seat belts do not secure occupants properly; loose." • "Driver's-side seat belt did not hold during front-end collision, causing driver to hit head on windshield." • "Driver's and passenger's automatic seat belts failed; erratic operation; finally they stopped working."

TOYOTA CAMRY 1991

Complaint Severity: Harmless. **Recall Alert:** See Recall Index. **Buyer's Summary:** Check the brakes—listen for noise, look for leaks and feel for vibration. They may fail, perform poorly or require frequent mechanical attention. See "Sudden Accelerations" in Introduction.

Hot Spots and Owner/NHTSA Comments:

1. Equipment: electric power accessories: locks: door, malfunction, failure. • "The rear power door lock on the passenger-side will not open from the inside." • "Electronic door locks jammed, resulting in difficulty in entering vehicle." • "Intermittent operation of power door locks; can't depend on safe exit from car." • "Power door locks failed, trapping occupant inside vehicle." • "Power door locks are hard to open from the outside sometimes."

2. Equipment: electric equipment: radio: tape deck, etc., fire, malfunction. • "Radio smoked and failed." • "Electrical component in the radio shorted out, causing a fire." • "Vehicle radio malfunction; originally a recall problem."

3. Brakes: hydraulic system, vibration, pulling, poor performance. • "Brakes have severe grinding and excessive stopping distance. Problem began at 29,000 miles." • "While driving, brake pulsation occurs, which causes vibration, also when stopped entire vehicle vibrates; dealer can't correct." • "Brakes pull to the left." • "While driving, noticed smoke coming from wheel, then brakes began to stick due to contamination of brake fluid."

4. Electrical system: wiring: harness: under dash, fire, malfunction. • "Wiring under the dash caused spontaneous combustion; vehicle completely burned from dash to trunk area within 4 minutes." • "While parked in driveway, interior caught on fire in dashboard; vehicle totaled." • "Electrical short resulted in fire in dashboard of vehicle." • "While parked, vehicle caught on fire; originated from dashboard area." • "Driven 2 hours and parked 1 hour; fire started in dash and burned the car." • "Electrical fire in dashboard caused meltdown and vehicle fire."

5. Fuel: throttle linkages and control, sudden accelerations. • "While driving, experienced throttle sticking; vehicle hesitates, then suddenly surges forward." • "While pulling into the garage, vehicle accelerated and went out of control; caused a great deal of damage." • "Accelerator pedal sticks, causing increases in speed and loss of vehicle control." • "Intermittent surging at any speed." • "While parking, vehicle suddenly accelerated and went into tree; caused accident that resulted in broken feet and ankle injuries."

6. Brakes: hydraulic: shoe: disc brake system, excessive wear. • "Dealer replaced rotors and pads at only 200 miles; 50 percent pad wear reported." • "Brakes overheated while trying to control engine surge." • "Premature brake wear." • "Excessive brake wear; the brake pedal is too low." • "Front brakes wear out prematurely, with little to no wear on rear brakes."

TOYOTA CAMRY 1992

Complaint Severity: Serious. **Buyer's Summary:** The airbags in this vehicle have experienced failures and malfunctions: You may need a professional evaluation on the condition of the airbags. See "Sudden Accelerations" in Introduction. Make sure air conditioner works properly.

Hot Spots and Owner/NHTSA Comments:

1. Interior systems: passive restraint: airbag: driver, malfunction, failure. • "Airbag prematurely deployed while driving at 55 mph on highway, causing a front-end collision and burn injuries." • "Vehicle was involved in a head-on collision and the airbag did not deploy." • "Upon impact during frontal crash, 2:00 position on front bumper, airbag failed to deploy." • "Multiple-car expressway crash at 60 mph in the rain; had front bumper direct hit, but no airbag deployment. Driver suffered a head injury." • "Estimated 25-30 mph, vehicle hit an ice slick. Driver lost control, going down embankment. Airbag failed to deploy when striking tree." • "Airbag exploded, no crash; cornea sustained injury, skin suffered abrasions and burns."

2. Equipment: electric power accessories: locks: door, malfunction, failure. • "Power right rear door lock would not open on the inside or outside." • "Right rear door lock failed to unlock; buzzing noise." • "Power door lock switch from the inside is defective, making it difficult to exit." • "Power door locks have failed to work 3 times when the ignition switch was off." • "While driving, power door locks engaged by themselves." • "Power door lock switch failed; locks will not open from inside; driver was trapped inside vehicle; only way to open is with key from the outside."

3. Fuel: throttle linkages and control, sudden accelerations. • "Upon leaving car wash, shifted gear from neutral to drive and vehicle suddenly accelerated; sped down a wet incline of 45 feet into street traffic." • "The accelerator on vehicle sticks on occasion. When driver steps on pedal, there is resistance." • "Throttle valve design causes buildup from evaporated fuel around 30,000 miles, causing throttle valve to stick." • "While driving experienced sudden acceleration on 2 occasions when vehicle engine surged; rendered brakes ineffective." • "Upon starting, with foot on brake, vehicle surged, then suddenly shot out of garage with emergency brake still engaged in reverse position."

4. Air conditioner: failure, poor performance. • "Windshield fogs up when air conditioner is on, limiting visibility." • "Sharp, musty odor emitted through ventilation." • "Air conditioner failed 2 times." • "Air conditioner failed."

5. Engine: vibration, fire, leaks. • "Oil leak; repaired." • "Engine expelling dark smoke." • "Vehicle fire." • "Engine vibrates." • "The engine failed and caused the car to stop."

6. Interior systems: passive restraint: airbag, malfunction, failure. • "Airbag did not deploy." • "Airbag deployed when vehicle passed over debris." • "Vehicle was hit head-on by another vehicle. Driver had seat belt on; the airbag deployed but did not inflate. Driver went through windshield." • "No deployment of airbag in accident, causing injuries."

TOYOTA CAMRY 1993

Complaint Severity: Serious. **Buyer's Summary:** The airbags in this vehicle have experienced failures and malfunctions: You may need a professional evaluation on the condition of the airbags. Check the brakes—listen for noise, look for leaks and feel for vibration. They may fail, perform poorly or require frequent mechanical attention.

Hot Spots and Owner/NHTSA Comments:

1. Interior systems: passive restraint: airbag: driver, malfunction, failure. • "Airbag inflated while owner was driving on a highway; driver injured." • "At 45-50 mph, 11:00 position, during accident, driver's-side airbag did not deploy and driver's seat belt did not hold. She hit steering wheel." • "Driver's airbag inflator installed improperly, causing airbag to release hot gas and chemicals into driver's face during accident; burns and injury." • "Driver's airbag did not inflate; also, no deployment of passenger's airbag during accident." • "Airbag did not inflate during deployment, resulting in injuries."

2. Brakes: hydraulic system, excessive wear, noise, poor performance. • "When applying the brakes, vehicle slid 8 feet." • "Braking system failure; excessive wear of brakes." • "Noisy and/or grinding brakes upon coming to a stop." • "When coming to a complete stop on a wet surface, the brakes lock up and act as if they are crystallized." • "When brakes are applied, they fade, as though they are not going to hold."

3. Brakes: hydraulic: anti-skid system, poor performance, failure, locking up. • "Antilock brake system failed to stop vehicle when applied, causing front-end collision at 45 mph. Airbag did not deploy. Driver injured." • "Antilock brakes squeaking when applied." • "Antilock brake system locked up twice, causing vehicle to lose control; resulted in 2 accidents." • "When it is cold outside, antilock brake system does not work." • "Antilock brake system failed to stop vehicle causing front-end collision at 5 mph. Airbag did not deploy." • "Airbag did not deploy during front-end collision at 40 mph. Driver received injuries; antilock brake system."

4. Interior systems: passive restraint: airbag, malfunction, failure. • "No deployment of airbag in rear-end crash." • "Airbag did not deploy." • "Airbag deployment was violent, causing nose, neck and face injury." • "Vehicle was involved in a front-end accident and the airbag did not deploy." • "Slowing down for stoplight, vehicle rear-ended another vehicle at 5-10 mph. After driving 1.1 miles after accident, airbag deployed." • "Airbag did not deploy."

5. Brakes: hydraulic: shoe: disc brake system, noise, failure. • "When applying brakes, a clunking and grinding sound persists. Dealer has no idea what the cause is." • "Noisy front brakes." • "Brake rotors and pads failed." • "Front brakes grind." • "Noisy front brake rotors and pads."

6. Engine: noise, fire, vibration. • "Noisy engine." • "Engine fire, causing injuries." • "Noisy and/or vibrating engine." • "Engine noise and/or vibration." • "Vehicle designed without engine shut off device for emergency purposes." • "Engine idles rough; noisy."

TOYOTA CAMRY 1994

Complaint Severity: Very Serious. **Theft Alert:** 6. **Buyer's Summary:** The airbags in this vehicle have experienced failures and malfunctions: You may need a professional evaluation on the condition of the airbags. Check the brakes—listen for noise, look for leaks and feel for vibration. They may fail, perform poorly or require frequent mechanical attention. Test the transmission thoroughly.

Hot Spots and Owner/NHTSA Comments:

1. Interior systems: passive restraint: airbag: driver, malfunction, failure. • "In accident at 40 mph at 1:00/2:00 position; driver's-side airbag did not deploy." • "Hit other vehicle from behind at 20 mph and driver's airbag did not deploy." • "No deployment of airbag during accident, resulting in injury." • "Airbag did not deploy during an accident at 12:00, resulting in an injury." • "Frontal collision; driver's airbag did not deploy. Hit van broadside." • "Estimated speed 25 mph; driver's airbag failed to deploy."

2. Interior systems: passive restraint: airbag: passenger, malfunction, failure. • "Dual airbag did not deploy." • "Had frontal collision, passenger-side airbag exploded and cut cornea." • "Frontal collision, impact 12:00 position position, speed 20 mph, dual airbags did not deploy." • "No deployment of passenger's airbag; resulted in injury to passenger during accident." • "Passenger airbag did not deploy during a frontal 45-mph collision." • "Hit other vehicle from behind at 20 mph; passenger's airbag did not deploy."

3. Brakes: hydraulic system, noise, locking up, failure. • "Front brake system failure; when braking there is a grinding noise." • "Wife was driving; when she went to hit brakes, the car kept speeding up, which caused her to total her car and another." • "Total loss of braking ability 4 different times." • "Touched braked pedal lightly; heard grinding noise and stopping distance increased." • "Brakes locked up twice upon sudden stopping, causing 2 accidents."

4. Power train: transmission: automatic, poor performance, difficulty shifting, slipping. • "Vehicle sporadically will not move when placed into gear." • "Will not move forward or backwards, as if in neutral. When vehicle put in reverse, it jumps forward. Locks locked." • "Transmission case cracked." • "Premature transmission failure." • "Transmission front pump seal replaced." • "Started vehicle, shifted gears to reverse; backed up, then shifted to drive and gears locked up, preventing vehicle from going into any other gears."

5. Brakes: hydraulic: anti-skid system, poor performance, failure, locking up. • "Noisy antilock brakes." • "Consumer had car tuned up, went to pick up car and was driving car home, started to get off the exit and there was no brake (antilock brake system); dealer say no one messed with the brakes." • "Antilock brake system did not stop vehicle, even though stepped on pedal hard." • "Antilock brake system failed; vehicle lost control, resulting in an accident; speed 25 mph." • "When applying brakes, car speeds up instead of slowing down. antilock brake system is malfunctioning." • "Antilock brake system failed, causing accident."

6. Brakes: hydraulic: shoe: disc brake system, excessive wear, failure. • "Vehicle's braking system does not stop in panic stopping, causing freewheeling due to fact disc pads cannot grip rotor or hydraulic problems." • "Premature brake wear." • "Front disc brakes failed."

TOYOTA CELICA 1987

Complaint Severity: Serious. **Buyer's Summary:** Check the brakes—listen for noise, look for leaks and feel for vibration. They may fail, perform poorly or require frequent mechanical attention. See "Sudden Accelerations" in Introduction.

Hot Spots and Owner/NHTSA Comments:

1. Fuel: throttle linkages and control, sudden accelerations. • "Faulty throttle linkage causes the gas pedal to stick, causing sudden acceleration." • "Car accelerated through intersection; both feet slammed on brake, car kept going; hit a pole." • "Unintended acceleration, resulting in accident." • "Car suddenly began to accelerate on its own; went through stop sign, nearly hitting a car." • "While driving, accelerator sticks, accelerating car at full speed; only way to stop is to turn off ignition." • "While driving, accelerator sticks wide open; only way to correct is to turn ignition off."

2. Brakes: hydraulic: shoe: disc brake system, vibration, poor performance. • "Front disc brakes out of round; brakes pulsate when used at 35 mph, felt in brake pedal; continual problem." • "Front disc brakes vibrate." • "Rotors on the front disc-type braking system were faulty; had to be turned; still rubbing."

• "Vehicle experiences problems with front disc brakes, pads and rotors; car pulsates; unsmooth when applying brakes; repairs."

TOYOTA CELICA 1990

Complaint Severity: Dangerous (Worst 3% in Guide). **Recall Alert:** See Recall Index. **Buyer's Summary:** The airbags in this vehicle have experienced failures and malfunctions: You may need a professional evaluation on the condition of the airbags. See "Sudden Accelerations" in Introduction.

Hot Spots and Owner/NHTSA Comments:

1. Interior systems: passive restraint: airbag: driver, malfunction, failure. • "Head-on collision resulted in substantial front-end damage and personal injuries; failed to trigger and/or inflate airbag system." • "While driving at 35 mph, vehicle hit another car, which resulted in an accident; airbag failed to deploy during accident." • "At 45 mph, frontal collision; airbag did not deploy." • "Driver's airbag supplemental restraint system failed to provide protection when accident occurred; driver sustained injuries." • "Airbag failed to deploy upon impact; point of impact 12:00 position, velocity 40 mph." • "While driving at 50 mph, during a front-end collision, impact at 11:00, airbag did not deploy."

2. Interior systems: passive restraint: airbag, malfunction, failure. • "Airbag inoperative during collision." • "Airbag did not deploy in head-on collision at 40 mph." • "Airbag warning light stays on during operation of vehicle; suspect electrical short." • "Airbag inflated with force, knocking individual unconscious and causing accident." • "Airbag did not deploy during accident, causing injuries." • "Airbag failed to deploy in front-end collision that caused accident and injury."

3. Fuel: throttle linkages and control, sudden accelerations. • "Sudden acceleration occurred as soon as brake pedal was released; vehicle was stopped by placing transmission into park." • "Vehicle experienced sudden acceleration, which caused accident." • "Suspects throttle stuck when vehicle drove forward instead of stopping; crashed into oncoming traffic, killing 2 people." • "Slow-speed turn caused throttle to open and car suddenly accelerated. After the crash, the engine was still racing and the ignition was turned off."

4. Interior systems: passive restraint: airbag impact sensor, failure. • "During an accident at 10-20 mph, airbag did not deploy." • "During frontal collision at 35 mph, airbag did not deploy." • "No deployment of airbag during accident, causing injury." • "During an accident with impact at 12:00, airbag did not deploy from decreasing speed (55 to 40 mph)."

TOYOTA CELICA 1991

Complaint Severity: Dangerous (Worst 3% in Guide). **Buyer's Summary:** The airbags in this vehicle have experienced failures and malfunctions: You may need a professional evaluation on the condition of the airbags.

Hot Spots and Owner/NHTSA Comments:

1. Interior systems: passive restraint: airbag: driver, malfunction, failure. • "Airbag did not deploy during front-end accident at 12:00, speed 10-12 mph." • "In course of an accident while going 45 mph, impact at 12:00, airbag did not deploy." • "During rear-end collision, vehicle slammed into a tree at approximately 40 mph, impact 12:00 position on front bumper, airbag failed to deploy." • "During a frontal collision, airbag deployed and burned driver's neck and left side of face; also burned a hole in shirt." • "Airbag did not deploy during accident, causing injuries."

2. Interior systems: passive restraint: airbag, failure. • "Driver's-side airbag didn't inflate on front-end impact with a dirt embankment." • "Airbag did not inflate in accident because sensors are in the front fenders." • "While driving at approximately 25-30 mph, driver slammed on brakes; vehicle skidded, then crashed head-on into a tree; airbag failed to deploy." • "Frontal impact at 35 mph, at 3:00, airbag failed to deploy." • "Airbag failed to deploy upon frontal collision at estimated 50 mph. Vehicle in front was at a dead stop. Four-vehicle accident."

TOYOTA COROLLA 1987

Complaint Severity: Very Serious. **Buyer's Summary:** The carburetion system could contribute to stalling and hesitation. Verify that the cruise control system works properly, and that it doesn't cause the engine to surge. The fuel injection system has been blamed for hesitation and stalling. Be sure the vehicle doesn't die in traffic or at stops. See "Sudden Accelerations" in Introduction.

Hot Spots and Owner/NHTSA Comments:

1. Fuel: fuel carburetion, stalling, hesitation. • "Slowing down or stopping, car cuts off; at high idle, vehicle vibrates." • "Vehicle suffers hesitation, rough idling and loud exhaust sound; several attempts to repair to no avail." • "Vehicle suffers hesitation and stalling problems; repaired/replaced carburetor and stalling kit, stalling continues." • "Car cuts off while driving, stopping, or slowing down; also hesitates and cuts back." • "Engine experiencing stalling; hesitation upon acceleration; installed carburetor hesitation kit, did not solve problem." • "Severe hesitation when coming to and taking off from stop." • "Hesitation in acceleration."

2. Fuel: throttle linkages and control, sudden accelerations. • "Uncontrolled sudden acceleration, resulting in accident; brakes did not stop speed; loss of control." • "When shifted into reverse from park, vehicle suffered sudden acceleration and loss of control." • "While driving, vehicle suddenly accelerated; went out of control and caused minor accident." • "Shifted to reverse position to back out, suddenly car accelerated backward; resulted in accident." • "Upon starting engine, accelerated immediately without shifting into gear; went forward until it struck a steel beam." • "Upon shifting gear from park to reverse, vehicle suddenly accelerated; jumped 3 curbs and landed on opposite side of street; an incline stopped vehicle."

3. Equipment: speed control, sudden acceleration, malfunction. • "Intermittent cruise control problems." • "Car suddenly self-accelerated at very high speed; stopped after hitting brick wall; brakes ineffective." • "Shifted from park to reverse with foot on brakes and car suddenly accelerated; brakes ineffective, turned off ignition to stop car." • "Recurring sudden acceleration problem resulted in accident." • "Cruise control malfunctioned and caused vehicle to accelerate out of control."

4. Fuel: fuel injection system, stalling, hesitation. • "Having difficulty starting car; at stop, car idles at higher extreme, shakes a lot." • "While accelerating, vehicle hesitates; installed a hesitation kit to prevent further problems; accelerates intermittently as well." • "Vehicle stalls out and hesitates when stopped; also, suddenly accelerates without warning; installed restrictor valve." • "Problem with hesitation when cold." • "Spontaneous acceleration, car suddenly jumped from 600 rpm to 1,100 rpm; also, stalling problem."

TOYOTA COROLLA 1988

Complaint Severity: Serious. **Buyer's Summary:** Verify that the cruise control system works properly, and that it doesn't cause the engine to surge. See "Sudden Accelerations" in Introduction.

Hot Spots and Owner/NHTSA Comments:

1. Equipment: speed control, sudden acceleration, malfunction. • "While in motion with cruise control on, braked to disen-

gage cruise control to no avail; accelerated under a tractor trailer; severe injuries." • "Cruise control continues to perform intermittently; engine accelerates beyond set point or stops functioning; repaired/replaced computer, dash and stalk switches." • "Cruise control causing transmission downshift and erratic speed control." • "Problem disengaging cruise control while in motion; brakes and switch were ineffective; resulted in accident with both driver and passenger severely injured." • "Cruise control malfunction; shuts itself off when engaged; replaced cruise computer and switch."
2. Fuel: throttle linkages and control, sudden accelerations. • "While driving, vehicle suddenly accelerated; lost control and caused accident." • "When placed in drive, vehicle accelerated and hit a concrete barricade." • "While driving downhill car accelerated; brakes failed; lost control, hitting tree." • "While idling with foot on brake pedal, upon placing transmission into drive position, engine suddenly surged, accelerating out of control and hitting a parked car."

TOYOTA COROLLA 1989

Complaint Severity: Typical. **Buyer's Summary:** Look carefully for any kind of leakage, especially under the car. Test the suspension by feeling for vibration or pulling while driving. Check the brakes—listen for noise, look for leaks and feel for vibration. They may fail, perform poorly or require frequent mechanical attention. Test the transmission thoroughly. See "Sudden Accelerations" in Introduction. Make sure air conditioner works properly.

Hot Spots and Owner/NHTSA Comments:
1. Fuel: throttle linkages and control, sudden accelerations. • "Vehicle went into sudden acceleration; motor roared and car took off; shifted into park and turned off ignition to bring under control." • "Started engine and shifted gear into drive; car suddenly lurched forward and hit a moving car." • "While driving, vehicle suddenly accelerated forward out of control; resulted in an accident." • "While driving, vehicle suddenly accelerated; went out of control, which resulted in an accident." • "Vehicle suddenly lost control, crashing into brick wall; faulty throttle linkage; injury." • "Car's accelerator cable snapped and caused it to stall out."
2. Power train: transmission: automatic, poor performance, difficulty shifting, slipping. • "While in drive, can take key out of ignition, resulting in car running away and striking another vehicle." • "While driving, vehicle starts bucking as slipping in and out of gear." • "Automatic transmission failed prematurely." • "Premature transmission failure." • "Transmission failure." • "Transmission jerks when going into 2nd gear."
3. Suspension: independent front, excessive wear, tire wear, vibration. • "Problem with premature wear of front and back tire treads; repaired/replaced." • "Problem with uneven wear and twisting of tire treads; realigned, balanced and rotated tires to no avail; no problem found with shocks." • "Frequent rotation of tires due to uneven tire wear." • "Front end vibrates and makes noise, causing tires to wear excessively; unbalanced." • "Front end cannot be aligned because of possible frame damage from accident before purchase."
4. Air conditioner: leaks, malfunction. • "Air conditioning not working correctly." • "Air conditioning works intermittently." • "Air conditioner leaks." • "Air conditioner leaked due to hole in system."
5. Brakes: hydraulic system, poor performance, failure. • "Brakes failed." • "Rear brake problems." • "Defective braking system." • "Vehicle returned twice to dealer for adjustment of brakes because inconsistent."
6. Interior systems: active seat and shoulder belts and belt anchor, poor performance. • "Driver's seat belt started to unravel, until seat belt was no longer usable." • "Tag on driver's-side seat belt indicated warning to replace seat belt; 3 months later, tag on new belt was exposed." • "Right rear seat belt too tight." • "Premature replacement of driver's-side seat belt."

TOYOTA COROLLA 1990

Complaint Severity: Typical. **Buyer's Summary:** Test the suspension by feeling for vibration or pulling while driving. Test the transmission thoroughly. Make sure seat belts function correctly and fit comfortably. Make sure air conditioner works properly.

Hot Spots and Owner/NHTSA Comments:
1. Power train: transmission: automatic, poor performance, difficulty shifting, slipping. • "During brake application, total loss of brakes and transmission." • "Transmission gasket pan leak." • "Transmission valve body burned up." • "Vehicle bucks; transmission repaired." • "Automatic transmission failed, causing the front wheels to lock while traveling 75 mph." • "Automatic transmission failure; vehicle seized without warning."
2. Interior systems: active restraints: belt retractors, malfunction, failure. • "Frontal collision impact 1:00 position, speed 35 mph, lap and shoulder belt on driver's-side did not retract." • "Driver and passenger seat belts do not retract and are loose." • "Vehicle was at complete stop and hit from a 6:00 position. Lap and shoulder belt did not retract." • "Upon rear-end collision, shoulder harness failed to restrain; resulted in head impact with steering column." • "Safety belt does not return properly." • "Passenger shoulder harness jammed; replaced."
3. Suspension: independent front, alignment, tire wear. • "Bad alignment, causing tires to cup and ride rough." • "Front axle cracked; boots around axle broke; brake pad wore out." • "Alignment problems; 4 sets of tires installed, problem continues." • "Front wheel alignment problem." • "Wheel alignment problem." • "Four tires wore out; uneven tire wear; alignment checked."
4. Equipment: electric equipment: radio: tape deck, etc., failure. • "Radio works erratically." • "Stereo didn't work properly; replaced." • "Radio replaced 3 times." • "Stereo tape player failed."
5. Interior systems: passive restraint: belts, malfunction, failure. • "Automatic seat belt failed upon being involved in a vehicle accident; driver broke her neck." • "Shoulder strap stays attached to door; doesn't move; very inconvenient connecting 2 straps from opposite directions, and detaching 2 belts, not 1, in an emergency." • "Poor seat belt design; does not restrain, designed so person can move around in car." • "Front seat safety belt jammed once." • "Seat belts should be automatic, but have never worked that way."
6. Air conditioner: noise, poor performance. • "Air conditioner squeaking." • "Air conditioning problems." • "Odor when air conditioner is on." • "Air conditioner doesn't get cold enough."

TOYOTA COROLLA 1991

Complaint Severity: Typical. **Buyer's Summary:** Test the suspension by feeling for vibration or pulling while driving.

Hot Spots and Owner/NHTSA Comments:
1. Suspension: independent front, alignment, vibration, tire wear. • "Wheels not aligned properly." • "Vehicle misaligned, causing tire wear." • "Roaring noise and vibration; front and rear wheels aligned." • "Premature wear of front tires due to misalignment." • "Misalignment on driver's side, causing excessive wear on tires." • "Alignment problems, causing severe tire wear and damage." • "Tires badly worn."
2. Equipment: electric equipment: radio: tape deck, etc., malfunction, failure. • "Radio shorted out, causing smoke." •

"Radio shorted out, leaving some circuits; out of order, as well as a strong odor inside the vehicle." • "While driving, car radio caught fire, causing fire in passenger compartment." • "Car radio does not perform due to electrical shortage; smell of plastic burning." • "Replacement of radio tape player caused short in dash lights."

3. Exhaust system: manifold: engine, cracking, failure. • "Exhaust manifold cracked. Caused lack of acceleration and stalling; no apparent reason; could have been caused by cold weather." • "Cracked exhaust manifold." • "Car was purchased used; the exhaust manifold to the engine was cracked." • "Exhaust manifold cracked due to poor design." • "The exhaust manifold has cracked for no apparent reason."

4. Interior systems: active seat and shoulder belts and belt anchor, poor performance, failure. • "Seat belts failed to restrain occupants; both seat backs fell back." • "Unsatisfied with seat and shoulder belt system." • "During an accident, seat belt did not secure driver; he fell out of seat and landed in passenger's seat; suffered injury." • "Driver's-side seat belt failed in an accident." • "Seat belts do not provide adequate protection for children in car seats or boosters; a child in a tantrum can move seat, and seat belt would lock up."

5. Structure: door assembly, malfunction, failure. • "Rubber door insulators loose." • "Passenger door edge-protecting band failure." • "Door lock failed." • "Door moldings failed." • "Door edging separated, preventing door from closing."

6. Electrical system: ignition, stalling, malfunction. • "Four occasions of stalling; mostly after 60 minutes run time, from idle speed to 50 mph. Vehicle will restart." • "Replaced ring around ignition." • "Power problems when traveling uphill." • "When cut off car with engine hot and try to start car again, it will not start."

TOYOTA COROLLA 1992

Complaint Severity: Troublesome. **Recall Alert:** See Recall Index. **Buyer's Summary:** Test the transmission thoroughly.

Hot Spots and Owner/NHTSA Comments:

1. Power train: transmission: automatic, poor performance, difficulty shifting, slipping. • "Plastic works its way into the gears when you shift into drive." • "Coming to a stop after 50 miles, when in reverse, transmission sounds like it is racing and causes the car to creep. The engine is not racing." • "Automatic transmission jumps out of gear while driving; various speeds and weather conditions; no warning." • "Transmission jumped out of park into reverse gear."

TOYOTA COROLLA 1993

Complaint Severity: Dangerous (Worst 3% in Guide). **Recall Alert:** See Recall Index. **Buyer's Summary:** The airbags in this vehicle have experienced failures and malfunctions: You may need a professional evaluation on the condition of the airbags.

Hot Spots and Owner/NHTSA Comments:

1. Interior systems: passive restraint: airbag: driver, malfunction, failure. • "No deployment of airbag during front-end collision." • "In accident, airbag deployed, filling car with smoke; burned face." • "Airbag deployed, causing severe burns on driver's face; frontal collision; vehicle hit an embankment; 30 mph; impact 12:00 position." • "Airbag did not deploy during frontal impact." • "Collision possibly caused airbag to deploy resulting in face and neck injury." • "False deployment of airbag; also, deployment was violent, causing facial, right hip and shoulder injuries." • "At 30 mph, 12:00 position, driver's-side airbag did not deploy."

TOYOTA COROLLA 1994

Complaint Severity: Dangerous (Worst 3% in Guide). **Theft Alert:** 26. **Recall Alert:** See Recall Index. **Buyer's Summary:** The airbags in this vehicle have experienced failures and malfunctions: You may need a professional evaluation on the condition of the airbags.

Hot Spots and Owner/NHTSA Comments:

1. Interior systems: passive restraint: airbag: driver, malfunction, failure. • "In a vehicle collision, the airbag did not deploy." • "Upon head-on collision, neither of driver's airbags deployed, resulting in extensive injuries." • "No deployment of airbag during collision." • "Car driving at 20 mph; truck backing out of driveway hit car on passenger-side; airbags deployed and hit driver in the face; injury—eye has an abrasion (owned vehicle 4 months)." • "Car was in an accident; airbag deployed, causing the right arm to strike the windshield; injury." • "Airbag deployment was violent during accident, resulting in knee, neck and back injuries."

2. Interior systems: passive restraint: airbag: passenger, failure. • "Upon impact, during frontal crash in stopped position, speed 35 mph, 10:00 position on front bumper, dual airbags failed to deploy." • "Dual airbags did not deploy during front-end collision at 55 mph. Injuries received." • "Passenger-side airbag did not deploy." • "In a head-on collision, the passenger's airbag did not deploy. This is the second collision where airbags did not deploy." • "The passenger-side airbag did not deploy on impact, and the driver's did."

TOYOTA CRESSIDA 1987

Complaint Severity: Dangerous (Worst 3% in Guide). **Buyer's Summary:** See "Sudden Accelerations" in Introduction.

Hot Spots and Owner/NHTSA Comments:

1. Fuel: throttle linkages and control, sudden accelerations. • "Shifted gear into reverse, engine rapidly accelerated on its own, striking a motor home." • "Vehicle suddenly accelerated; lunged forward, crashing through garage wall; stopped halfway into family room." • "While backing up, vehicle suddenly accelerated out of control, even when brakes were applied." • "Vehicle suddenly accelerated when shifted from park to reverse after starting engine; brakes did not work; hit telephone pole 60 feet away." • "Pulled away from curb, car surged and hit tree." • "Started car, placed gearshift from park to drive; car took off with great speed and hit building."

TOYOTA CRESSIDA 1989

Complaint Severity: Troublesome. **Buyer's Summary:** Make sure seat belts function correctly and fit comfortably. See "Sudden Accelerations" in Introduction.

Hot Spots and Owner/NHTSA Comments:

1. Air conditioner: poor performance, failure. • "Fumes and vapors from air conditioning unit, causing odor and possible unhealthy toxic fumes to be inhaled." • "Problem with air conditioning unit." • "Air conditioning unit faulty; replaced." • "Air conditioner failure."

2. Fuel: throttle linkages and control, sudden accelerations. • "Vehicle surged forward out of control when gear shifted." • "Accelerator stuck while parking; vehicle hit curb; steering system broke." • "Upon left turn uphill, vehicle accelerated uncontrollably; attempts to brake were unsuccessful; climbed embankment; accident." • "While in motion, car suddenly accelerated, hitting pillar; throttle seemed wide open; occupant seriously injured."

3. Interior systems: passive restraint: belts, uncomfortable, failure. • "Design has no effective adjustments provided to prevent belt from crossing and remaining across face and neck of a short person." • "No way to adjust automatic passive restraint seat belt (shoulder harness) to fit short people; belt rides on face and neck of driver." • "Vehicle rear-ended by another vehicle; seat belts were not activated and driver hit steering wheel; passenger hit windshield; automatic shoulder belt defect." • "Driver's-side shoulder and lap belt did not retain occupant during front-end and rear-end collision at 45 mph, causing injuries to driver."

TOYOTA TERCEL 1987

Complaint Severity: Very Serious. **Recall Alert:** See Recall Index. **Buyer's Summary:** The carburetion system could contribute to stalling and hesitation. See "Sudden Accelerations" in Introduction.

Hot Spots and Owner/NHTSA Comments:

1. Fuel: fuel carburetion, stalling, hesitation. • "Car stalls all the time." • "Fuel carburetion problems; severe hesitation and stalling that is unpredictable in heavy traffic." • "Engine hesitates; no acceleration; stalls." • "Car has erratic hesitation and surges, as well as dead spots in engine; replaced carburetor 3 times to no avail." • "Car hesitating; running rough; engine missing on acceleration; repaired/replaced carburetor, switch, wire and enrichment compensator." • "Carburetor was defective; replaced 4 times; caused hesitation and lack of speed."

2. Fuel: throttle linkages and control, sudden accelerations. • "Sudden acceleration, impact at 11:00 position, speed 20 mph, hit a brick wall." • "Two incidents of sudden acceleration; shifted gear into drive, car accelerated at very high speed on its own." • "Car dangerously picked up speed while in motion; turning off ignition did not stop car; crashed, causing extensive injuries to occupants." • "Problem sudden acceleration resulted in an accident; after shifting to reverse, car shot out, hit heavy truck; extensive damage." • "Problem sudden acceleration, causing accident." • "Sudden acceleration, loss of steering. Stopped car by using emergency brake and hitting curb."

TOYOTA TERCEL 1988

Complaint Severity: Very Serious. **Recall Alert:** See Recall Index. **Buyer's Summary:** The carburetion system could contribute to stalling and hesitation. See "Sudden Accelerations" in Introduction.

Hot Spots and Owner/NHTSA Comments:

1. Electrical system: ignition, stalling, hesitation. • "Vehicle intermittently stalls." • "Vehicle keeps hesitating and losing power when getting into traffic pattern. Carburetor has been replaced several times, but problem still persists." • "Vehicle stalls at any speed; dealer cannot find problem." • "Intermittent hesitation at all speeds." • "Computer failed." • "While driving, engine shut off and started smoking."

2. Fuel: fuel carburetion, stalling, hesitation. • "Carburetor is feeding gas to the exhaust system in excessive amounts." • "Exhaust emissions and carburetor: Vehicle will not run properly; it hesitates and stalls." • "Carburetor failure; also caused carbon buildup on brakes." • "Car hesitates and loses power at 55 mph, cuts off when coming to stop; in heavy traffic, car came to stop and the car coming behind barely avoided collision." • "Defect in carburetor; car would hesitate a lot when first starting out and sputter; jerking and stalling; not able to go over 45 mph." • "At 55 mph, engine stalls and cuts out; carburetor replaced, problem corrected."

3. Engine: fire, failure. • "During accident, engine compartment came inside cab of car, pushing into drivers and passenger's feet, causing injury." • "Fire started in engine; passenger's compartment and vehicle totaled." • "Engine caught fire; total loss." • "Engine failure while in motion." • "Engine failure."

4. Fuel: throttle linkages and control, sudden accelerations. • "Vehicle surged backward out of control; vehicle was stopped by placing in park; vehicle surged forward after being placed in drive." • "Vehicle constantly surged." • "Put car in drive, released brake, car suddenly accelerated; resulted in accident." • "Started to back out of the garage, when suddenly the car accelerated backwards at a high rate of speed, hitting corner of the house." • "Car began accelerating in reverse; lost control."

TOYOTA TERCEL 1989

Complaint Severity: Typical. **Recall Alert:** See Recall Index. **Buyer's Summary:** The carburetion system could contribute to stalling and hesitation. The fuel injection system has been blamed for hesitation and stalling. Be sure the vehicle doesn't die in traffic or at stops.

Hot Spots and Owner/NHTSA Comments:

1. Fuel: fuel carburetion, stalling, hesitation. • "Carburetor defective." • "Problem starting car; need to replace defective carburetor." • "Carburetor design causes poor performance and stalling on roads." • "Engine skips and fuel leaks due to malfunctioning carburetor." • "Faulty enrichment kit caused hesitation; after recall." • "Vehicle loses 90 percent power while in transit, especially after making turns, at stop signs and at lights, creating rear-end accident potential."

2. Fuel: fuel injection system, stalling, hesitation. • "Hard starting when cold or hot due to fuel problem." • "Vehicle performs sluggishly when cold." • "Car hesitates when accelerating from a stopped position." • "Vehicle misses." • "During certain periods of warmup, acceleration of vehicle extremely poor; worst case is when has operated to normal temperature and then allowed to cool." • "Engine carbon buildup, causing stalling."

3. Electrical system: ignition, stalling. • "Engine stalls shortly after start; sometimes while driving." • "Vehicle failed to accelerate safely; it stalls intermittently." • "While driving, engine stalls, which causes lack of acceleration." • "Vehicle stalls when cold; very sluggish when driving at beginning." • "Car keeps cutting off."

4. Fuel: carburetor: unknown type, hesitation, stalling. • "Carburetor fails, causing hesitations." • "Carburetor failed." • "Intermittent stalling due to carbon buildup in carburetor." • "Carburetor causes the car not to accelerate when accelerator is pressed, and then the car takes off."

TOYOTA TRUCK 4RUNNER 1990

Complaint Severity: Typical. **Buyer's Summary:** Test the suspension by feeling for vibration or pulling while driving. Check the brakes—listen for noise, look for leaks and feel for vibration. They may fail, perform poorly or require frequent mechanical attention.

Hot Spots and Owner/NHTSA Comments:

1. Brakes: hydraulic system, excessive wear, poor performance. • "Brakes replaced every 12,000 to 15,000 miles." • "When putting foot on brake, vehicle will slow down but will not come to a full stop; pedal will go to the floor." • "Brakes failed twice." • "After driving nonstop for a while, brakes begin to pulsate." • "Poor braking system; master cylinder replaced by dealer, but no change in performance." • "Failed brake switch circuit; brakes seem to lose pressure; in hard stops, pedal goes to floor with little effect."

2. Brakes: hydraulic: anti-skid system, poor performance, failure, locking up. • "Problems with rear antilock brake system caused accident." • "Vehicle equipped with antilock brake system; during brake application, pedal goes to floor; seems there is no control over vehicle." • "Consumer states no confidence in antilock braking system on dry roads." • "Brakes chatter upon braking; told this was normal vibration due to antilock brake system." • "While going down steep grade, vehicle experienced loss of braking ability. Antilock brake system did not interact." • "Vehicle has a defective antilock braking system, causes long stopping distance and pedal going to the floor."

3. Suspension: independent front, vibration, pulling, noise. • "Noisy suspension; difficult when turning left." • "Vehicle vibrates and pulls left; had defective front end, or frame slightly bent that could not be straightened." • "Car make popping and/or clicking noise when making hard, slow turns." • "Front end shimmies."

TOYOTA TRUCK 4RUNNER 1991

Complaint Severity: Typical. **Buyer's Summary:** Test the suspension by feeling for vibration or pulling while driving. Check the brakes—listen for noise, look for leaks and feel for vibration. They may fail, perform poorly or require frequent mechanical attention.

Hot Spots and Owner/NHTSA Comments:

1. Suspension: independent front, noise, alignment. • "Noisy suspension." • "Noise when turning left." • "Poor alignment causes premature tire wear." • "Doesn't handle well in winds." • "Front-end alignment problem." • "Vehicle squeals when first accelerating while cold."

2. Brakes: hydraulic: disc: rotor: disc hub, vibration, excessive wear. • "Front rotor replaced every 3,000 to 4,000 miles, when brakes are applied, vehicle pulsates." • "Warped front brake rotors, causing vibration in steering." • "Brake rotors failed, causing severe vibration when applying brakes." • "Replaced front brake rotors."

3. Engine: stalling, failure. • "Engine block and head gasket replaced." • "Intermittent stalling." • "Engine failed." • "Rear main seal on engine failed."

TOYOTA TRUCK PICKUP 1989

Complaint Severity: Minor. **Buyer's Summary:** Test the suspension by feeling for vibration or pulling while driving. Check the brakes—listen for noise, look for leaks and feel for vibration. They may fail, perform poorly or require frequent mechanical attention. Test the clutch.

Hot Spots and Owner/NHTSA Comments:

1. Brakes: hydraulic system, excessive wear, failure. • "Noisy brakes in reverse; excessive caliper wear." • "Noisy rear brakes when in reverse; replaced." • "Brake problem, causing tire damage." • "Brakes failed." • "Brake rotors unstable." • "Brake failure."

2. Suspension: independent front, alignment, poor performance. • "Center support bearing failed." • "Shocks failed." • "Vehicle rollover while swerving for animal." • "Bad wheel alignment, causing tire wear." • "Problems with suspension." • "Suspension problem."

3. Power train: clutch assembly, failure. • "Clutch failed." • "Replaced clutch assembly." • "Clutch failed." • "Throwout bearing failed."

TOYOTA TRUCK PICKUP 1991

Complaint Severity: Negligible. **Buyer's Summary:** Test the suspension by feeling for vibration or pulling while driving. Check the brakes—listen for noise, look for leaks and feel for vibration. They may fail, perform poorly or require frequent mechanical attention.

Hot Spots and Owner/NHTSA Comments:

1. Suspension: independent front, alignment, tire wear. • "Vehicle out of alignment." • "Vehicle misaligned." • "Misalignment, causing tire wear." • "Vehicle misaligned." • "Front end aligned." • "Shimmy at 50 mph."

2. Brakes: hydraulic system, failure. • "Brakes." • "Brake problems." • "Brakes failed." • "Brakes failed twice."

TOYOTA TRUCK PREVIA 1991

Complaint Severity: Typical. **Recall Alert:** See Recall Index. **Buyer's Summary:** Check the brakes—listen for noise, look for leaks and feel for vibration. They may fail, perform poorly or require frequent mechanical attention.

Hot Spots and Owner/NHTSA Comments:

1. Structure: door assembly, malfunction, poor performance. • "The driver's-side door will open occasionally due to the vehicle being jarred by bumps." • "Driver's-side door doesn't close properly; needs to be closed 3-4 times before it catches." • "Defective handle on sliding door." • "Right side sliding door stuck." • "Difficulty opening and closing sliding door." • "When entering sliding side door, door slipped on son's foot, resulting in the door jamming."

2. Equipment: electric equipment: radio: tape deck, etc., fire, failure. • "Car radio shorted out, resulting in a passenger's compartment fire." • "Radio smoked after recall repairs." • "CD player inoperative." • "Radio failed; prior to recall." • "Electrical short in radio burned all electrical wires, resulting in a fire prior to and after recall repairs."

3. Visual systems: sunroof assembly, noise, failure. • "Simultaneous operation of both moonroofs causes extreme noise and vibration, especially at high speeds." • "The electrical sunroof not working; it's the cable." • "Sunroof failure." • "Sunroof won't open." • "Sunroof motor failed."

4. Brakes: hydraulic system, poor performance, failure. • "Brakes replaced." • "Brake problem." • "Poor brake performance; resulted in extended stopping distance; brake cylinder replaced." • "Upon application of brake pressure, pedal drops down approximately 1 inch and becomes hard; braking power is lost."

5. Visual systems: windshield wiper: motor, malfunction, failure. • "Windshield wiper motor failed during heavy snow due to plastic gears; design problem." • "Windshield wiper motor failed; prior to recall." • "Windshield wipers stop working during a rainstorm due to a defective motor." • "Windshield wiper motor failures occurred in a very hard rain on the interstate during very heavy traffic."

Volkswagen—Cars and Trucks

VOLKSWAGEN FOX 1988

Complaint Severity: Typical. **Recall Alert:** See Recall Index. **Buyer's Summary:** Look carefully for any kind of leakage, especially under the car.

Hot Spots and Owner/NHTSA Comments:

1. Heater: water: defroster: defogger: heater core: water, leaks, malfunction. • "Hole in heater core." • "Car parked and was idling when there was an explosion; filled car with hot steam, which slightly burned the legs of both passengers and the right leg of driver." • "While driving, heard a hissing sound and saw coolant leaking into passenger compartment; caused by a defective heater core." • "Heater core has been replaced once; coolant is leaking inside of compartment and fogging windows."

VOLKSWAGEN GOLF 1987

Complaint Severity: Serious. **Recall Alert:** See Recall Index. **Buyer's Summary:** Look carefully for any kind of leakage, especially under the car. The fuel injection system has been blamed for hesitation and stalling. Be sure the vehicle doesn't die in traffic or at stops. See "Sudden Accelerations" in Introduction.

Hot Spots and Owner/NHTSA Comments:

1. Heater: water: defroster: defogger: heater core: water, leaks, malfunction. • "Heater core leaks inside, causing all windows to steam up and making driving extremely dangerous." • "Defective heater core caused windows to be covered with a film that was oily to touch." • "Heater core failed, prior to recall, causing steam from vents to accumulate on inside windows, impairing vision." • "Vehicle overheats and gives off odor when heater in use." • "Vehicle filled with steam; heater core replaced prior to recall." • "Heater core defective; has not gotten a satisfactory explanation from dealer; fears a possible accident."

2. Fuel: throttle linkages and control, sudden accelerations. • "Vehicle's suddenly accelerated once ignition was engaged, resulting in an accident." • "Vehicle sudden acceleration due to stuck throttle." • "While pulling away from ATM machine, car leaped forward, hitting lamppost." • "Accelerator jammed; vehicle suddenly out of control." • "Gas pedal stuck and driver lost control; stopped by snowbank." • "Sudden acceleration occurred upon starting vehicle, resulting in an accident."

3. Fuel: fuel injection system, stalling, hesitation. • "Chronic stalling resulted from fuel injection system failure." • "Vehicle hesitates during acceleration and driving around corners." • "Fuel injection system failure; vehicle stalls and hesitates during acceleration." • "Vehicle will not start."

VOLKSWAGEN JETTA 1987

Complaint Severity: Typical. **Recall Alert:** See Recall Index. **Buyer's Summary:** Look carefully for any kind of leakage, especially under the car. The fuel pump has received complaints. Make sure it doesn't make excessive noise and that you are experiencing adequate engine performance. Also, look for leaks. The fuel injection system has been blamed for hesitation and stalling. Be sure the vehicle doesn't die in traffic or at stops. Check the brakes—listen for noise, look for leaks and feel for vibration. They may fail, perform poorly or require frequent mechanical attention. See "Sudden Accelerations" in Introduction.

Hot Spots and Owner/NHTSA Comments:

1. Heater: water: defroster: defogger: heater core: water, leaks, malfunction. • "Antifreeze fumes penetrated vehicle due to defective heater core, which caused nausea and vomiting." • "While driving at 10-15 mph, the heater core exploded; caused leakage through vents and resulted in the driver's right foot receiving second-degree burns." • "Heater core failed, causing windows to fog and have smell inside." • "Heater core failure; smoke was coming out of heater." • "Heater core burst while driving; sent hot radiator coolant into passenger compartment; fluid poured over driver's foot, causing second-degree burns." • "Heater core malfunctioned; smoke built up inside car and caused poor visibility."

2. Fuel: fuel injection system, stalling, hesitation. • "Car lacks power; fuel injection system contaminated by dirty gas." • "Car hesitates at cold start; fuel injectors repaired/replaced 3 times; will not accelerate properly, especially when pulling out into traffic." • "Car developed a potentially dangerous hesitation when cold; car would start up right away, but engine hesitates or stalls when stepping on gas." • "Vehicle loses performance when accelerating, even when shifting gears; gas given but engine won't respond; happens more frequently when air conditioning is on." • "Vehicle suffers stalling problems when hot; cuts out while driving; repaired/replaced injectors, ignitor, transfer pump and fuel filter." • "Car stalls on highway; vibrates considerably; replaced injectors."

3. Fuel: fuel pump, stalling, failure. • "Continuous engine stalling; repaired/replaced transfer fuel pump 3 times, also fuel tank, did not solve problem; continues to stall." • "Fuel transfer pump failure occurred 3 times, with resulting sudden power loss, and then car difficult to restart." • "Electric fuel pump made of plastic cracked; all fuel leaked out." • "Car stalled in heavy traffic due to fuel pump failure." • "Fuel pump failure." • "Fuel pump failed after recall repairs."

4. Fuel: throttle linkages and control, sudden accelerations. • "Vehicle suddenly accelerated when put gear into drive, smashing through garage door." • "While in park, car proceeded to move gate; on 2 occasions shifted from park to reverse; car accelerated forward then reversed while foot on brakes." • "Attempting to move, car in gear, foot on brake, car accelerated; hit rear of van; brakes unable to stop car; car stopped by turning off key and activating emergency brake." • "Pushing continuously on brake pedal, vehicle accelerated at a high rate of speed, resulting in accident." • "Upon releasing hand brakes, car suddenly moved backward and swerved to left at great speed, hitting 2 parked cars."

5. Interior systems: active seat and shoulder belts and belt anchor, uncomfortable, failure. • "Poor fit of seat belts across neck; potential hazard." • "Attorney's office representing man killed when car impacted on left front fender, causing floor to buckle and push driver's seat to tilt backward." • "Seat belts lock before getting a chance to secure them, and stay locked for over 20 twenty minutes." • "Driver's seat belt torn when caught in seat back adjustment mechanism. Seat no longer adjusts."

6. Brakes: hydraulic system, excessive wear, malfunction. • "Excessive front and rear brake wear." • "Brakes squeak." • "Brakes malfunctioned; vehicle went out of control; resulted in an accident." • "Upon braking application, brakes faded, resulting in an accident." • "Unbearable shrieking noise in brake system."

VOLKSWAGEN JETTA 1988

Complaint Severity: Minor. **Recall Alert:** See Recall Index. **Buyer's Summary:** The fuel injection system has been blamed for hesitation and stalling. Be sure the vehicle doesn't die in traffic or at stops. Check the brakes—listen for noise, look for leaks and feel for vibration. They may fail, perform poorly or require frequent mechanical attention. Test the transmission thoroughly. See "Sudden Accelerations" in Introduction.

Hot Spots and Owner/NHTSA Comments:

1. Heater: water: defroster: defogger: heater core: water, failure. • "Heater core failed, causing hot water to spew into the passenger's compartment." • "Heater core failed, causing windshield to be coated with coolant." • "Heater core failed; prior to recall." • "Heater core replaced; prior to recall."

2. Fuel: fuel injection system, stalling, hesitation. • "Engine fire; prior to recall." • "Vehicle stalls because of faulty fuel injection system." • "Car stalls at fast speeds, causing steering and braking failure." • "Unspecified problems with fuel injection system; repaired/replaced idle stabilizer valve, timing and fuel pump relay." • "Idles very rough; often stalls out in traffic and while warming up during hot weather." • "Stalling and rpm instability; occurs when car driven and then not used for 2 to 5 hours." • "Engine stalling problem; repaired 6 times to no avail."

3. Interior systems: seat belts: lap: front, poor performance. • "Vehicle has shoulder belts but no lap belts." • "Driver and front passenger seats are not equipped with lap belts." • "Design defect; there is no lap belt." • "Missing lap belt, would like one installed." • "Child safety seat restraints in front passenger seat inadequate."

4. Fuel: throttle linkages and control, sudden accelerations. • "Vehicle went into open-throttle position, speed 90 mph; to stop, applied brakes real hard." • "Automatic transmission: After shifting from park to drive, engine accelerated to highest rpm; brakes applied; no warning before or after." • "Vehicle suddenly accelerated when car was in reverse; accident occurred." • "After starting and changing gears, vehicle suddenly accelerated to approximately 60 mph; went out of control and hit street sign and fence." • "Engine revved up; loss of control; caused accident."

5. Power train: transmission: automatic, poor performance, difficulty shifting, slipping. • "Problems with reverse gear." • "Prior to 23,000 miles, transmission replaced or repaired at least 3 times." • "Transmission failure; repaired/replaced 3 times." • "While driving, vehicle downshifting from 3rd to 2nd gear almost caused accident." • "Rpm races to 5, but car at 20 mph; engine roar extremely hard, car stays in 1st gear too long, then jerks into 2nd gear." • "Transmission wore out."

6. Brakes: hydraulic system, noise, premature failure. • "While driving downhill, applied brakes; brake pedal dropped to floor; able to stop after putting car in low gear; repaired/replaced master cylinder, drums and seals." • "Unspecified problem with brakes, causing them to squeal." • "Brakes keep going bad; repaired 3 times." • "Brakes failed." • "Vehicle went into open-throttle position, speed 90 mph; to stop, applied brakes real hard."

VOLKSWAGEN JETTA 1989

Complaint Severity: Minor. **Recall Alert:** See Recall Index. **Buyer's Summary:** The fuel injection system has been blamed for hesitation and stalling. Be sure the vehicle doesn't die in traffic or at stops. Check the brakes—listen for noise, look for leaks and feel for vibration. They may fail, perform poorly or require frequent mechanical attention. Test the transmission thoroughly. See "Sudden Accelerations" in Introduction.

Hot Spots and Owner/NHTSA Comments:

1. Interior systems: seat belts: lap: front, no lap belts. • "Vehicle was built without lap belts in the driver and front passenger-sides." • "Vehicle has no front-seat lap belts." • "Vehicle not equipped with lap belts." • "Lap belt not installed."

2. Fuel: fuel injection system, stalling, hesitation. • "Engine stalls when cold." • "Car exhibits intermittent starting problems; also cuts off unexpectedly without warning." • "Vehicle stalls after starting and also in traffic." • "Intermittent stalling." • "Engine began sputtering, jerking and hesitating while driving; cause of stalling problems unknown." • "Vehicle stalls and/or bucks."

3. Fuel: throttle linkages and control, sudden accelerations. • "Throttle linkages accelerate; car accelerates only in cold weather; dealer changed the accelerator cable; car is still doing the same thing." • "Throttle sticks at midrange engine speeds in extremely cold weather." • "Transmission severely damaged; accelerator stuck in open position, car accelerated to speed in excess of 100 mph; unable to decelerate, even when in park." • "Accelerator became lodged in open position; car accelerated to speed in excess of 100 mph." • "While engine idling and when letting out clutch, car will accelerate faster than expected."

4. Interior systems: active seat and shoulder belts and belt anchor, failure, no lap belts. • "The passive restraint seat belts did not function properly when vehicle involved in rear-end collision; failed to lock." • "Upon impact, seat belt failed to hold, throwing driver into steering wheel." • "Lap belts omitted." • "Front passive restraints consist of 2-point shoulder belt; no lap belt, knee bolster installed under dashboard." • "Vehicle is equipped only with shoulder belts; no lap belts in the front seat." • "Feels shoulder belts without lap belts unsafe."

5. Power train: transmission: automatic, poor performance, difficulty shifting, slipping. • "Transmission and/or differential failure." • "Transmission fluid mixed with water, giving fluid a frothy strawberry color." • "Transmission slips gears at high speeds; requires replacement of entire transmission; also, noise in engine coming from torque converter." • "Transmission failure." • "Trouble with transmission; sometimes when stopped, can't put transmission in gear."

6. Brakes: hydraulic system, excessive wear, poor performance. • "Premature brake wear." • "Brake problems." • "Replaced squeaky brakes." • "Premature brake rotor wear; replaced pads and rotors serviced." • "Front passive seat belts do not grab and/or lock in place as designed upon braking; occupants could move forward and go through windshield during an accident."

VOLKSWAGEN JETTA 1990

Complaint Severity: Best 3% in Guide. **Recall Alert:** See Recall Index. **Buyer's Summary:** The electronic control unit has been blamed for engine performance problems, including stalling and surging. The fuel injection system has been blamed for hesitation and stalling. Be sure the vehicle doesn't die in traffic or at stops. Check the brakes—listen for noise, look for leaks and feel for vibration. They may fail, perform poorly or require frequent mechanical attention.

Hot Spots and Owner/NHTSA Comments:

1. Electrical system: ignition, stalling, malfunction. • "Battery exploded while turning on ignition." • "While driving at high speed, car slows to about 10 mph by itself." • "Intermittent stalling, mostly after engine has been turned off for a few hours or more and vehicle has been idle; results in steering wheel lockup." • "Problem with idle stabilizer." • "Steering wheel locks when hitting water puddles of any size; engine stalls; no warning." • "Vehicle periodically shuts down when driving at any speed. Repaired 4 times."

2. Electrical system: ignition: electronic control unit, stalling, sudden acceleration. • "Car has sudden surges in acceleration; runs rough; rpm needle jumps up and down between 1,000 and 3,000 rpm; frequently stalls; repaired 3 times to no avail." • "Engine computer improperly controls engine speed; engine jumps from 1,000 rpm to 3,300 rpm without having foot on gas pedal." • "Electronic fuel injection operates by computer; the system will cause stalling without any warning while traveling or braking." • "Continuous stalling when idling at a stoplight or stop sign." • "Loss of power when slowing down to make a turn; repeated repairs/replacements. • "Sudden acceleration caused by electronic control module problem."

3. Fuel: fuel injection: idle speed control unit, stalling, malfunction. • "Replaced idle stabilizer valve." • "Repeated stalling problem; caused by defective idle adjustment." • "Vehicle stalls; caused by erratic idle speed control unit." • "Vehicle experiences erratic idling at different rpm." • "When started cold, engine idles normal for about 5 seconds, then goes up to about 2,000 rpm." • "Rpm fluctuates under driving conditions; symptom occurs during neutral state."

4. Brakes: hydraulic system, locking up, leaks. • "Problem with brake fluid." • "Brakes worn; replaced." • "Brakes stick and/or lock up." • "Brake valve leak." • "Throttle sticks while driving, rapidly accelerating vehicle at various speeds; ride brakes to slow down."
5. Electrical system: starter, failure. • "Starter coil failed." • "Starter failure." • "Problem with starter." • "Starter intermittently inoperative; one hour to a few minutes; repaired/replaced, now replaced starter not engaging."
6. Fuel: fuel injection system, stalling, hesitation. • "Vehicle stalls; lack of power." • "Stalling and surging problems." • "Fuel injection system failed twice."

VOLKSWAGEN JETTA 1991

Complaint Severity: Negligible. **Recall Alert:** See Recall Index. **Buyer's Summary:** Look carefully for any kind of leakage, especially under the car. See "Sudden Accelerations" in Introduction.

Hot Spots and Owner/NHTSA Comments:

1. Fuel: throttle linkages and control, sudden accelerations. • "Throttle cable has poor design where it attaches to the gas pedal. Cable separates easily and causes lack of throttle control." • "Vehicle will speed up or slow down on its own." • "Throttle servo bracket bent, causing throttle to stay open." • "Vehicle went into open-throttle position while driving at 65 mph; when ignition is turned off, engine continues to run."
2. Engine: malfunction, fire. • "Vehicle will not start when engine is hot." • "Engine failure caused loss of steering and resulted in a collision with guardrail." • "Fire broke out in engine compartment; vehicle totaled; driver's hand injured; caused damage."
3. Fuel: fuel systems, leaks, fire. • "While in motion, vehicle started to lose speed; smoke began to come out; caught on fire." • "Vehicle caught on fire." • "Fuel leak; odor."
4. Structure: bumper assembly, failure. • "Faulty front bumper cover caused front signal to disconnect." • "Front bumpers keep dropping off without warning while driving." • "Front bumper fell off." • "While driving, front bumper fell off."

VOLKSWAGEN JETTA 1992

Complaint Severity: Minor. **Recall Alert:** See Recall Index. **Buyer's Summary:** The ignition or speed control unit may contribute to stalling and hesitation.

Hot Spots and Owner/NHTSA Comments:

1. Electrical system: ignition, stalling, failure. • "Vehicle shorted out; made vehicle inoperative." • "In hot weather with air conditioning on, vehicle will stall; very hard to restart. Will not start on cool mornings." • "Owner says he was coming over a hill when his engine died; vehicle runs very hot." • "Intermittent stalling."

VOLKSWAGEN TRUCK VANAGON 1987

Complaint Severity: Best 3% in Guide. **Recall Alert:** See Recall Index. **Buyer's Summary:** The fuel injection system has been blamed for hesitation and stalling. Be sure the vehicle doesn't die in traffic or at stops.

Hot Spots and Owner/NHTSA Comments:

1. Engine: malfunction, leaks. • "When temperature 98 degrees or more, vehicle dies out at stop signs, signal lights or in heavy traffic." • "Engine replaced due to oil loss damaging key components in engine compartment." • "Engine malfunctions: water pump, head cylinders and head gasket replaced." • "Continuous loss of coolant and engine oil." • "Engine losing coolant."
2. Fuel: fuel injection system, stalling, hesitation. • "Intermittent stalling and/or loss of power." • "Engine dies at stops with air conditioner on; other times, hesitates and tries to stall; loses power while driving." • "Fuel shuts off, engine fails; unable to locate cause." • "Malfunction of fuel injection system; engine hesitates, bucks and stalls under heavy load; unresolvable problem."
3. Structure: door assembly: latches and locks, failure. • "Sliding door opens by itself, even when locked." • "Side-mounted door will open intermittently, especially while driving at highway speeds." • "Side sliding door flies open while driving." • "Cargo door latch continually needs to be replaced."

Volvo

VOLVO 240 1987

Complaint Severity: Serious. **Buyer's Summary:** Test the suspension by feeling for vibration or pulling while driving. Check the brakes—listen for noise, look for leaks and feel for vibration. They may fail, perform poorly or require frequent mechanical attention. Test the transmission thoroughly. See "Sudden Accelerations" in Introduction.

Hot Spots and Owner/NHTSA Comments:

1. Fuel: throttle linkages and control, sudden accelerations. • "Power surge; started car, had foot on brake when placing car in reverse (since on grade); car shot backward and lost control in U-turn, hitting 2 parked cars." • "When stopping and proceeding forward, lunges forward uncontrollably." • "Vehicle suddenly accelerated when shifted into park from drive; accident and injury." • "Car in reverse; engine made loud sound, backed up at high speed; hit car; placed in drive, car moved without stepping on accelerator; hit another car." • "Experience sudden acceleration; vehicle goes into open-throttle position when turn ignition on and put into drive."
2. Suspension: independent front, vibration, tire wear, poor performance. • "Excessive vibration of entire car during operation; vibration in steering wheel so bad almost impossible to control." • "While traveling on slightly wet or icy road, a 35-mph wind struck right rear of vehicle; vehicle began to skid, resulting in an accident." • "Front suspension unstable; when driving on wet road, wind struck to right rear of car, vehicle spun out of control; struck wall." • "Excessive steering wheel vibration; right front tire out of balance due to suspension design." • "At moderate speeds, vehicle suffers severe vibration, rendering vehicle inoperable."
3. Brakes: hydraulic system, excessive wear, failure. • "When attempting to stop, brakes won't react immediately; loud grinding metal-to-metal sound from front of car; brake pedal shakes." • "Brakes have been replaced on numerous occasions; safety compromised in braking situations due to extending stopping distances." • "Brakes went to floor after 2 pumps; returned in short period of time; replaced cylinder, problem still occurs." • "Sudden acceleration, along with loud thumping sounds coming from rear of car when brakes are applied." • "Brakes failed; after 2 pumps of brakes, pedal pressed to floor."
4. Power train: transmission: automatic, poor performance, difficulty shifting, slipping. • "Automatic transmission does not shift smoothly; pops or jumps into position; also makes a metal grinding noise when shifting." • "Gearshift lever improperly adjusted; pops and/or jumps out of gear." • "Transmission jumps out of gear when in park and emergency brake on; also, loud noise from transmission." • "Automatic transmission jumped out of gear; accident."

VOLVO 740 1987

Complaint Severity: Serious. **Recall Alert:** See Recall Index. **Buyer's Summary:** The fuel injection system has been blamed for hesitation and stalling. Be sure the vehicle doesn't die in traffic or at stops. Check the brakes—listen for noise, look for leaks and feel for vibration. They may fail, perform poorly or require frequent mechanical attention. Test the transmission thoroughly. See "Sudden Accelerations" in Introduction.

Hot Spots and Owner/NHTSA Comments:

1. Fuel: throttle linkages and control, sudden accelerations. • "Started car in parking place, shifted to reverse, car shot backwards into busy street; brakes did not work; car hit another vehicle." • "Vehicle suddenly accelerated while trying to park; jumped curb and went across sidewalk, hitting a wall." • "Car accelerated rapidly and smashed another car." • "After shifting into drive with brakes applied; vehicle lurched forward out of garage at 40-50 mph; hit fence; impact 12:00 position." • "While in park position, car accelerated when engine was turned on; smashed through storefront window."

2. Brakes: hydraulic system, noise, poor performance. • "Brakes noisy when applied at all speeds to stop." • "Brakes offer poor performance; make unusual noises; don't stop satisfactorily. Wear out with less than 25,000 miles." • "Once shifted into reverse, vehicle accelerated, crossing road. Brakes had no effect on acceleration." • "Front brakes lock up when stopping hard." • "Brakes squeaking; front brake pads were replaced, but did not solve problem; noise louder; rear brakes were needed."

3. Fuel: fuel injection system, stalling, hesitation. • "Car stalls when shifting into gear and slowing for stops; hesitates while cruising on highway." • "Intermittent engine stalling." • "Engine stalling problems; stalls when hot or cold." • "Engine stalling problems; also, fails to start."

4. Power train: transmission: automatic, poor performance, difficulty shifting, slipping. • "Car parked on slight incline, parking brakes not engaged; child pulled gearshift lever without depressing knob, car rolled in street." • "Bad and faulty transmission; replaced with new transmission system." • "Automatic transmission faulty; runs forwards in neutral." • "Transmission failed."

VOLVO 740 1988

Complaint Severity: Serious. **Recall Alert:** See Recall Index. **Buyer's Summary:** Check the brakes—listen for noise, look for leaks and feel for vibration. They may fail, perform poorly or require frequent mechanical attention. See "Sudden Accelerations" in Introduction.

Hot Spots and Owner/NHTSA Comments:

1. Fuel: throttle linkages and control, sudden accelerations. • "Vehicle suddenly accelerates after foot taken off gas pedal; also has high idle coming to stops." • "This vehicle accelerated from a parked position out of control; first forward, and then backwards." • "Started car and placed into reverse; car took off at a high rate of speed out of control. No braking response; accident resulted." • "Upon placing gear into drive position, vehicle suddenly accelerated uncontrollably; no braking response; accident resulted." • "Vehicle suddenly accelerated while idling at stoplight, crashing into another vehicle at unknown speed." • "Vehicle suddenly accelerated out of control upon shifting gear into drive."

2. Brakes: hydraulic system, locking up, poor performance. • "Brakes sometimes grind and feel like they are not grabbing properly." • "Binding and grinding of brakes; repaired/replaced brakes." • "Brakes lock when coming to a stop; lose brakes and pedal goes in 3 or 4 inches and locks." • "Discs and rotors failed." • "Motor mounts replaced twice in 5 years; replaced brakes twice in a year."

VOLVO 740 1989

Complaint Severity: Serious. **Recall Alert:** See Recall Index. **Buyer's Summary:** The electronic control unit has been blamed for engine performance problems, including stalling and surging. The fuel injection system has been blamed for hesitation and stalling. Be sure the vehicle doesn't die in traffic or at stops. Check the brakes—listen for noise, look for leaks and feel for vibration. They may fail, perform poorly or require frequent mechanical attention. See "Sudden Accelerations" in Introduction.

Hot Spots and Owner/NHTSA Comments:

1. Fuel: throttle linkages and control, sudden accelerations. • "Started vehicle, put it in drive with foot on the brakes, and vehicle suddenly accelerated." • "From park position, when started and shifted into drive, sudden acceleration occurred, resulting in collision." • "Upon shifting gear from park to reverse, vehicle suddenly accelerated backwards; did not stop when brakes were applied; hit a house." • "When shifted into reverse, car shot backwards; before tried to control the speed, hit parked car." • "Car shifted from park into drive, went out of control from dead stop to high speed; crashed into another parking car." • "Vehicle was started, shifted gear from park to reverse; vehicle accelerated in reverse, jumped an 8-inch curb and knocked over a tree."

2. Brakes: hydraulic system, vibration, premature failure. • "While leaving a private parking lot, collided with car in front that was going very slow; applied brakes but couldn't stop; fatalities, injury and damage." • "Brakes wore out pads at 30,000 miles." • "Brakes wore out prematurely; steel rotors on front badly worn." • "Vehicle vibrates and shakes when brakes are applied. Brakes have been replaced 5 times." • "Numerous replacements of hydraulic braking system; extreme vibration upon application of brake pedal." • "Complete brake failure caused pedal to fade." • "Started vehicle, put it in drive with foot on the brakes, and vehicle suddenly accelerated."

3. Electrical system: ignition: electronic control unit, stalling, failure. • "Electrical; the ignition electronic control unit failed." • "Defect in computer system, causing car to stall intermittently." • "Onboard computers failed." • "While driving, vehicle constantly stalled and engine died; dealer could not determine problem." • "Computer ignition system replaced." • "Continual engine stalling problem; replaced computer to no avail."

4. Electrical system: ignition, stalling, malfunction. • "Intermittent stalling while driving or stopping in front of traffic light or traffic sign." • "Key can be removed when vehicle is in gear." • "Stalling in traffic while accelerating." • "Ignition system malfunction." • "Vehicle intermittently stalls." • "Problem with ignition system; have to turn key several times to start engine."

5. Fuel: fuel injection system, stalling, hesitation. • "Intermittent stalling." • "Problem with engine; intermittently dies while stopping." • "Replaced speed sensor and coolant temperature sensor." • "Fuel system failure." • "Vehicle intermittently stalls at highway speeds, and sometimes stops on surface streets completely." • "Recurring problem with engine intermittently stalling out during braking, at stop signs and signals."

6. Brakes: hydraulic: anti-skid system, poor performance, failure, locking up. • "Upon applying antilock brake system, front end vibrated due to excessive brake wear." • "Brakes fail at low speeds; very slow for brakes." • "Antilock brake system problem; brakes started making grunting noise." • "Antilock brake system: Brakes failed to stop in normal manner; required excessive force on pedal to stop; replaced major components." • "Intermittent problem with antilock brake system; cleaned sensor to no avail."

VOLVO 740 1990

Complaint Severity: Very Serious. **Recall Alert:** See Recall Index. **Buyer's Summary:** The electronic control unit has been blamed for engine performance problems, including stalling and surging. The fuel injection system has been blamed for hesitation and stalling. Be sure the vehicle doesn't die in traffic or at stops. The airbags in this vehicle have experienced failures and malfunctions: You may need a professional evaluation on the condition of the airbags. Check the brakes—listen for noise, look for leaks and feel for vibration. They may fail, perform poorly or require frequent mechanical attention. See "Sudden Accelerations" in Introduction.

Hot Spots and Owner/NHTSA Comments:

1. Fuel: throttle linkages and control, sudden accelerations. • "Recurring sudden acceleration problem; resulted in accident 1 time." • "While leaving a stop sign, vehicle suddenly accelerated to 70-80 mph; went out of control, ran into a concrete wall and hit another vehicle." • "When gear was shifted into reverse, vehicle accelerated out of control, resulting in an accident." • "Started car, put into reverse, and vehicle lunged into drive." • "Vehicle suddenly accelerated in reverse while attempting to make U-turn; resulted in severe damages." • "Unintended acceleration resulted when shifting into drive; hit concrete barrier; airbag did not deploy, impact 12:00 position, speed approximately 40 mph."

2. Brakes: hydraulic system, malfunction, poor performance. • "Started vehicle while in park, it went into reverse; had no brakes." • "Traveling 40 mph or over and applying the brakes, steering starts to vibrate." • "Total loss of brakes when trying to make a stop." • "Brakes have excessive free play before activation." • "Continually having braking problems on intermittent basis; when brake applied, makes loud grinding noise, then pedal continues to jerk down." • "Entire braking system had to be replaced twice due to temporary loss of braking power caused by vibration of steering wheel."

3. Electrical system: ignition: electronic control unit, stalling, failure. • "One person was injured and three people died in an accident when onboard computer failed." • "Electronic control module malfunctioned; vehicle would not start." • "Engine experiences severe stalling; repaired/replaced computer chips, problem still exists." • "On 3 separate occasions, vehicle suddenly lost power." • "Problem with onboard computers; 'service engine' light came on; dealer reset." • "Computer failed, causing vehicle to stall."

4. Interior systems: passive restraint: airbag: driver, malfunction, failure. • "Vehicle was rear-ended by other vehicle; driver's airbag failed to deploy." • "Frontal collision, impact 12:00 position, speed 45 mph, airbag did deploy, causing injuries and burns." • "No deployment of the airbag during rear-end collision." • "Upon impact during frontal crash at approximately 40 mph, steering column popped open; airbag failed to deploy with 12:00 hit to front bumper." • "Frontal collision, speed 55 mph, impact 12:00 position, airbag did not deploy." • "Frontal collision, impact 12:00 position, speed unknown, vehicle going through intersection; airbag partially deployed."

5. Fuel: fuel injection system, stalling, hesitation. • "Cold starting problems." • "Intermittent stalling; sudden acceleration, causing accident." • "Vehicle hard to start." • "Intermittent stalling." • "Car idles rough and stalls." • "Vehicle hesitates intermittently."

6. Brakes: hydraulic: anti-skid system, poor performance, failure, locking up. • "On antilock brake system-equipped vehicle, when coming to stop, hear grinding sound, like metal-to-metal; brake pedal pushes up, then pulls to right; dealer says this is normal." • "Speed sensor failed." • "When applying brakes, antilock brake system made clunking noise; resulted in no engagement."

Yugo

YUGO GV 1987

Complaint Severity: Negligible. **Buyer's Summary:** The carburetion system could contribute to stalling and hesitation. Look carefully for any kind of leakage, especially under the car. Check the brakes—listen for noise, look for leaks and feel for vibration. They may fail, perform poorly or require frequent mechanical attention. Test the clutch.

Hot Spots and Owner/NHTSA Comments:

1. Fuel: fuel carburetion, stalling, hesitation. • "Every time at takeoff vehicle stalls; backfiring; no warning." • "Carburetion system faulty; carburetor floods when shifting to 2nd, causing car to stall." • "Car backfires and stalls; died in middle of traffic; repaired/replaced carburetor." • "When hot, hard time starting, then dies when stopped; car stalls on expressway; fixed by adjusting float in carburetor." • "Faulty fuel carburetion system causes the engine to keep running after key is removed from the ignition." • "Intermittent stalling problem; lost all power and engine dies."

2. Brakes: hydraulic system, noise, locking up, poor performance. • "Defective braking system; loss of effectiveness." • "Severe and continuous brake problems; brakes squeak; brake light comes on continually; grinds; repaired/replaced rotors and pad, problems still exist." • "Brakes grind, go to floor and then pump up; have locked up twice; various brake system parts replaced." • "On sudden stops, brakes don't stop vehicle completely or fast enough." • "Poor performance of brakes; brake light comes on; squeals; grinds; repaired/replaced front rotors and pads, problem continues."

3. Engine: leaks, premature failure. • "Car will not start if temperature outside less than 40 degrees." • "Gas leaking around engine; black smoke coming from under hood; vehicle starts slowing down; decreases speed; due to defective rings in engine." • "Engine problems; valves bent; repaired/replaced cylinder heads with gaskets and installed timing belt." • "Oil in air filter; discovered 2 cylinders were ruined and block was pitted." • "Premature failure of engine."

4. Brakes: hydraulic: shoe: disc brake system, noise, locking up, failure. • "Brake problems; noisy; replaced pads and rotors." • "Braking system defective; repaired/replaced pads and rotors at 11,000 miles." • "Front brakes locked and froze up." • "Front brakes squeak; replaced front brakes and pads and turned rotors." • "Brake pad on left front wheel falling out; lost brakes; wheels locked completely; pad was jammed between what holds pad and the disc."

5. Structure: door assembly: handle: inside, breaking, failure. • "Driver door window crank broke." • "Driver and passenger door handles broke; replaced." • "Door handles broke off; exit from car through windows." • "Driver's door handle broken." • "Broken door handles."

6. Power train: clutch assembly, malfunction, premature failure. • "Clutch malfunctioning; repaired." • "Clutch needs to be replaced." • "New clutch needed every 10,000 miles." • "Clutch sticks; will not go into gear with ease." • "Complete clutch failure, replaced clutch cables."

YUGO GV 1988

Complaint Severity: Best 3% in Guide. **Buyer's Summary:** The carburetion system could contribute to stalling and hesitation. Look carefully for any kind of leakage, especially under the car. Check the brakes—listen for noise, look for leaks and feel for vibration. They may fail, perform poorly or require frequent mechanical attention.

Hot Spots and Owner/NHTSA Comments:

1. Brakes: hydraulic system, leaks, locking up, excessive wear. • "Unspecified brake failure; brake leaks." • "Brakes grinding upon application." • "Driving 55 mph, all at once came to screeching stop; brakes locked up without touching them." • "Complained about brake problem at 1,000-3,000 miles; brakes failed at 8,000 miles."

2. Fuel: fuel carburetion, stalling, hesitation. • "Engine stalls while slowing down or when going around curves." • "Fuel carburetion system defective; unspecified failure or problems in carburetor; catalytic converter, purged canister; exhaust gas recirculation valve." • "Vehicle stalls out turning corners; idles rough; has burning smell under car; replaced carburetor." • "At highway speeds, hesitating, jerking and loss of power; also, poor gas mileage."

3. Interior systems: active seat and shoulder belts and belt anchor, malfunction, failure. • "Seat belt are inoperative." • "Latching system of seat belt inadequate for securing child restraints; pulling belt sharply to latch, pulling force removed; belt unlatches." • "Seat belts inoperative." • "Left seat belt won't tighten."

SECTION II:
Safety Comparisons

Comparing Complaint Severity: What the Numbers Mean

One of the assumptions of *The Used Car Reliability and Safety Guide* is that all cars, despite reputations, mechanical quality and manufacturing, will eventually develop troubles. The questions that remain are: What exactly is going to go wrong? and how do these problems contribute to safety concerns?

The complaints section of the guide answers the first question outright by providing testimony from car owners. The second question is answered, in part, by the accident-based "Complaint Severity Rating."

The "Complaint Severity Rating" tells you how worried you should be about the problems associated with a car—should they develop. Every car in this guide is compared to all other cars and rated.

Take, for example, a car that receives a large number of complaints about squeaky brakes, door locks, trunk latches, air conditioning and uncomfortable seats. This array of problems may be annoying, but not at all dangerous. In fact, they may be irrelevant in regard to safety, and have never been associated with an accident. This car would have an excellent complaint severity rating, despite the fact that it has numerous problems.

Then, as another example, imagine a car that's received complaints about only two problems, engine runaway and brake failure. This car would likely have a poor rating, even if the car has an excellent reputation for quality in every other regard, because the complaints received by NHTSA are so frequently associated with accidents.

The "Complaint Severity Rating" is based on a simple comparison of the number of total complaints to the number of complaints associated with accidents. A car that received 100 complaints, only a few of which are accident related, will have a good rating. A car that received 100 complaints, many of which were accident related, will have a poor rating. In other words, the rating separates the bothersome from the dangerous.

This section of the Guide looks more closely at these ratings, compares like automobiles and lists what NHTSA has determined to be the five primary causes of each car's most frequently occurring accident-related problems.

The Top 10, All Makes and Models

Following are the ten cars with the worst "Complaint Severity Ratings." The percentages on the right-hand side of the table represent what portion of complaints about the car were associated with accidents. For example, in the case of the Suzuki Samurai, which tops the list, just over half (51 percent) of all the complaints filed about the vehicle were directly related to accidents. That's the highest percentage of any vehicle in the Guide.

To some extent, the Top 10 comparison is more of a curiosity than an informative resource, because the cars are so different from each other. It's hard to rationalize comparing the Geo Storm, a minicompact economy vehicle, with the Mercedes Benz 300.

The comparison does show some overall relativity of the cars that have experienced the most severe problems, which some people may find useful. For each of the Top 10, there is breakdown of the causes of the accidents experienced by the cars and a brief explanation.

Model	% of Complaints Associated With Accidents
1. Suzuki Samurai	51%
2. Geo Storm	42%
3. Toyota Celica	41%
4. Mercedes Benz 300	39%
5. Acura Legend	37%
6. Plymouth Neon	36%
7. Nissan 300ZX	30%
8. BMW 318	29%
9. Toyota Cressida	28%
10. Mercedes Benz 190	28%

CAUSES OF ACCIDENTS IN THE TOP 10

Suzuki Samurai

NHTSA's Causes for Malfunction or Accident	
1. Stability	73.6%
2. Design	8.3%
3. Broken, shattered, cracked or split parts	4.2%
4. Erratic operation, poor performance	3.5%
5. Loss of control, poor direction, wanders	2.8%

The Suzuki Samurai is number one on this list (again) for one simple reason: rollover accidents. The owners of this vehicle have complained in large numbers about the vehicle's suspension, which is blamed for causing a dangerous lack of stability. Many of the "design" problems can also be construed as problems with stability. The structure of the truck's frame, for example, was also listed by NHTSA as a cause of rollover accidents. The other categories are irrelevant in comparison.

If safety is your primary concern when buying a used car, relatively speaking and based on consumer testimony, there is no vehicle in any category that is worse than the Samurai.

Geo Storm

NHTSA's Causes for Malfunction or Accident	
1. Erratic operation, poor performance	36.4%
2. Assembly, parts improperly installed or located	26.4%
3. Broken, shattered, cracked or split parts	6.4%
4. Parts inoperative	5.7%
5. Design	4.3%

The 1990, 1991 and 1992 Geo Storms received numerous complaints that were inherently accident-related. The difficulties reported were that the airbags would either fail to deploy in an accident, deploy unwantedly or release burning chemicals onto passengers, even when the airbags deployed properly. These problems were so frequently complained about that the Storm currently ranks second among all vehicles for complaint severity. Some accidents were also caused by the Storm's problem with stalling and hesitation.

Toyota Celica

NHTSA's Causes for Malfunction or Accident	
1. Assembly, parts improperly installed or located	29.1%
2. Erratic operation, poor performance	29.1%
3. Engine runaway, sudden acceleration	9.4%
4. Parts lock up, stick or grab	7.1%
5. Design	5.5%

The Celica represents a car that seems to grow worse each year for complaint severity. The 1988 and 1989 Celicas already had problems with sudden accelerations, according to car owners. A description of this problem can be found in the Introduction. Add to the engine runaway difficulties of the 1980s the airbag failures in the 1990s, and the Celica appears in the Top 10 for the first time.

Mercedes Benz 300

NHTSA's Causes for Malfunction or Accident	
1. Engine runaway, sudden acceleration	56.5%
2. Erratic operation, poor performance	21.4%
3. Assembly, parts improperly installed or located	5.3%
4. Parts lock up, stick or grab	3.8%
5. Design	3.1%

The 1986, 1987 and 1989 Mercedes 300 owners complained about a combination of malfunctions that are not only common in quite a few reputable luxury automobiles, but also frequently responsible for propelling their "Complaint Severity Ratings" way up: sudden accelerations and brake trouble. About 1 in every 5 complaints filed against this model involved engine runaway, and again, a full description of the sudden accelerations issue is included in the Introduction to this Guide.

The good news is that beyond sudden accelerations, brakes and airbags, the Mercedes did not receive many complaints in other areas. The more recently manufactured Mercedes 300s, in particular, received few complaints.

Acura Legend

NHTSA's Causes for Malfunction or Accident	
1. Engine runaway, sudden acceleration	58.4%
2. Erratic operation, poor performance	25.6%
3. Assembly, parts improperly installed or located	3.6%
4. Parts lock up, stick or grab	2.5%
5. Parts inoperative	2.5%

According to the owners of Acura Legends from 1986 through 1991, sudden accelerations have plagued this vehicle. Unlike some of the other vehicles that have problems with engine runaway, however, there have been other significant problems that have contributed to accidents in the Legend. Most notable are problems with the transmission in the 1986, 1987 and 1988 models. Owners complained that the transmission would slip out of gear or operate poorly, and this could lead to accidents. Also, the fact that airbags began to fail in the 1990 and 1991 models didn't help to lower the car's "Complaint Severity Rating."

Plymouth Neon

NHTSA's Causes for Malfunction or Accident	
1. Erratic operation, poor performance	47.4%
2. Parts inoperative	42.0%
3. Parts disconnected or fell off	5.3%
4. Stalls	5.3%
5. No other causes	

First a clarification. Dealers say that the Plymouth Neon and the Dodge Neon are the same car, but for the trim and other aesthetic differences. Although only the Plymouth Neon made it into the Top 10 list, the Dodge version was not far behind. In fact, the difficulties reported for the Dodge version are almost exactly the same as for the Plymouth, and both are ranked in the worst 3 percent in the guide for complaint severity.

The owners complain that the 1995 Neons (the only one that could appear in this guide) have problems with airbag failures. Testimony of failure to deploy appeared with surprising frequency in less than one complete year.

Nissan 300ZX

NHTSA's Causes for Malfunction or Accident	
1. Engine runaway, sudden acceleration	65.2%
2. Erratic operation, poor performance	15.5%
3. Parts lock up, stick or grab	5.8%
4. Loss of control, poor direction, wanders	2.6%
5. Excessive wear	1.3%

The 1990 and 1991 Nissan 300ZXs actually have fared well against consumer complaints. The 1985, 1986 and 1987 versions, on the other hand, continue to endure complaints about sudden accelerations and engine fires. More information about sudden accelerations, the leading cause for concern in this vehicle, is available in the Guide Introduction.

Meanwhile, the fuel system has been blamed for a variety of leaking problems that NHTSA says can cause the car to erupt in flames. Were it not for the more typical severity record of the more recent models of 300ZX, this car would probably appear a few notches higher on the Top 10 list.

BMW 318

NHTSA's Causes for Malfunction or Accident	
1. Erratic operation, poor performance	43.8%
2. Assembly, parts improperly installed or located	31.3%
3. Design	12.5%
4. Recall problem not fixed	6.2%
5. Parts fade	6.2%

Only one model year of this car made it into this Guide, the 1991. And the only real complaint about this automobile concerns the airbags. They would either fail to deploy or deploy unexpectedly.

Toyota Cressida

NHTSA's Causes for Malfunction or Accident	
1. Engine runaway, sudden acceleration	63.3%
2. Erratic operation, poor performance	17.7%
3. Parts lock up, stick or grab	5.1%
4. Broken, shattered, cracked or split parts	2.5%

The Toyota Cressida, especially the early models, received severe complaints in a number of areas. The most significant, year after year, was sudden accelerations, for which there is more information in the Guide's Introduction. Engine runaway was compounded with cruise control malfunctions and engine fires due to oil leaks in the 1985 model.

One item of note with this vehicle: There was a nine-way tie for the fifth most common cause of component failure, and the percentage was just slightly above 1 percent for each. So only four cause descriptions were included in the cause chart.

Mercedes Benz 190

NHTSA's Causes for Malfunction or Accident

1. Engine runaway, sudden acceleration	56.7%
2. Erratic operation, poor performance	16.7%
3. Parts inoperative	6.7%
4. Design	5.0%
5. Jumped out of gear	3.3%

The Mercedes Benz 190 also has had significant problems with engine runaway, like the 300 model listed previously. In addition to this, however, are the owner complaints about faulty parking brakes in the 1986 models that would allow their cars to roll into accidents.

Also listed in both the 1986 and 1987 models are complaints about airbag failure.

Minicompact and Subcompact Cars

Model	% of Complaints Associated With Accidents
1. Geo Storm	42%
2. Toyota Celica	41%
3. Plymouth Neon	36%
4. Nissan 300ZX	30%
5. BMW 318	29%
6. Geo Metro	23%
7. Dodge Neon	23%
8. Geo Prizm	20%
9. Honda Civic	19%
10. Chevrolet Chevette	19%
11. Honda Prelude	18%
12. Toyota Tercel	16%
13. Dodge Shadow	16%
14. Toyota Corolla	16%
15. Chevrolet Sprint	16%
16. Toyota MR2	15%
17. Ford Mustang	15%
18. Nissan Sentra	14%
19. Ford Festiva	14%
20. Isuzu Impulse	13%
21. Acura Integra	13%
22. Dodge Daytona	13%
23. Mazda Protégé	13%
24. Mercury Capri	12%
25. Hyundai Excel	12%
26. Chevrolet Cavalier	11%
27. Plymouth Colt	11%
28. Pontiac Firebird	11%
29. Pontiac Sunbird	11%
30. Chrysler LeBaron	10%
31. Chevrolet Camaro	10%
32. Subaru Justy	10%
33. Dodge Colt	10%
34. Mitsubishi Eclipse	10%
35. Nissan 240SX	9%
36. Buick Skylark	9%
37. Renault Alliance	9%
38. Renault Encore	7%
39. Plymouth Horizon	7%
40. Hyundai S Coupe	5%
41. Dodge Charger	5%
42. Mercury Lynx	5%
43. Dodge Omni	4%
44. Yugo GV	4%
45. Subaru XT	3%
46. Oldsmobile Firenza	2%

Geo Storm

NHTSA's Causes for Malfunction or Accident

1. Erratic operation, poor performance	36.4%
2. Assembly, parts improperly installed or located	26.4%
3. Broken, shattered, cracked or split parts	6.4%
4. Parts inoperative	5.7%
5. Design	4.3%

See Top 10 list for review.

Toyota Celica

NHTSA's Causes for Malfunction or Accident

1. Assembly, parts improperly installed or located	29.1%
2. Erratic operation, poor performance	29.1%
3. Engine runaway, sudden acceleration	9.4%
4. Parts lock up, stick or grab	7.1%
5. Design	5.5%

See Top 10 list for review.

Plymouth Neon

NHTSA's Causes for Malfunction or Accident

1. Erratic operation, poor performance	47.4%
2. Parts inoperative	42.0%
3. Parts disconnected or fell off	5.3%
4. Stalls	5.3%
5. No other causes	

See Top 10 list for review.

Nissan 300ZX

NHTSA's Causes for Malfunction or Accident

1. Engine runaway, sudden acceleration	65.2%
2. Erratic operation, poor performance	15.5%
3. Parts lock up, stick or grab	5.8%
4. Loss of control, poor direction, wanders	2.6%
5. Excessive wear	1.3%

See Top 10 list for review.

BMW 318

NHTSA's Causes for Malfunction or Accident

1. Erratic operation, poor performance	43.8%
2. Assembly, parts improperly installed or located	31.3%
3. Design	12.5%
4. Recall problem not fixed	6.2%
5. Parts fade	6.2%

See Top 10 list for review.

Compact Cars

Model	% of Complaints Associated With Accidents
1. Toyota Cressida	28%
2. Honda Accord	26%
3. Nissan Altima	21%
4. Volvo 240	19%
5. Plymouth Sundance	18%
6. Dodge Shadow	16%
7. Saturn SL2	16%
8. Mazda 323	15%
9. Mitsubishi Precis	14%
10. Chevrolet Beretta	13%
11. Mitsubishi Galant	12%
12. Pontiac Grand Am	12%
13. Mercury Tracer	12%
14. Oldsmobile Calais	11%
15. Toyota Camry	11%
16. Ford Probe	10%
17. Chrysler LeBaron	10%
18. Mitsubishi Diamante	10%
19. Volkswagen Quantum	10%
20. Chevrolet Nova	10%
21. Chevrolet Citation	10%
22. Oldsmobile Achieva	10%
23. Pontiac LeMans	10%
24. Volkswagen Golf	10%
25. Subaru Legacy	9%
26. Nissan Stanza	9%
27. Saturn	9%
28. Volkswagen Fox	9%
29. Buick Skylark	9%
30. Subaru GL	9%
31. Mercury Topaz	9%
32. Ford Tempo	8%
33. Ford Escort	8%
34. Chevrolet Spectrum	8%
35. Plymouth Reliant	8%
36. Chrysler Encore	8%
37. Hyundai Elantra	8%
38. Mazda MX6	7%
39. Dodge Aries	7%
40. Oldsmobile Ciera	7%
41. Volkswagen Jetta	6%
42. Renault Medallion	4%

Toyota Cressida

NHTSA's Causes for Malfunction or Accident

1. Engine runaway, sudden acceleration	63.3%
2. Erratic operation, poor performance	17.7%
3. Parts lock up, stick or grab	5.1%
4. Broken, shattered, cracked or split parts	2.5%

See Top 10 list for review.

Honda Accord

NHTSA's Causes for Malfunction or Accident

1. Engine runaway, sudden acceleration	43.2%
2. Erratic operation, poor performance	31.8%
3. Parts lock up, stick or grab	4.1%
4. Parts inoperative	3.8%
5. Assembly, parts improperly installed or located	2.3%

Engine runaway has been the haunting factor leading to accidents in the Honda Accord in the earlier models. The worst of it seems to occur in the 1987 and 1988 models. In the 1990s, the complaints most often associated with accidents concern airbags. Failure to deploy or deploying when not needed is a problem that needs to be checked professionally.

The only other lingering problems in the Accord are the brakes and the transmission. But these problems are not nearly as worrisome as those of sudden accelerations and airbag failure, based on the complaints filed by owners.

Nissan Altima

NHTSA's Causes for Malfunction or Accident

1. Erratic operation, poor performance	52.4%
2. Parts inoperative	14.3%
3. Broken, shattered, cracked or split parts	9.5%
4. Assembly, parts improperly installed or located	9.5%
5. Engine runaway, sudden acceleration	9.5%

Although engine runaway is a concern with the Altima, most of the complaints (all for the 1993 model) were directed at the car's seat belt and airbag systems.

Buyers should make sure the seat belts function properly, are securely anchored and fit comfortably. As for the airbags, the only real way to check them is to get a professional examination.

Volvo 240

NHTSA's Causes for Malfunction or Accident

1. Engine runaway, sudden acceleration	38.1%
2. Erratic operation, poor performance	38.1%
3. Parts lock up, stick or grab	9.5%

The 1987 Volvo 240 has serious problems with sudden accelerations. Engine runaway is clearly responsible for putting this car high on the list of accident-related complaints. The car also has difficulties with stalling in traffic, a poorly operating transmission and brakes that lock up.

Plymouth Sundance

NHTSA's Causes for Malfunction or Accident

1. Erratic operation, poor performance	32.9%
2. Assembly, parts improperly installed or located	12.0%
3. Parts inoperative	11.4%
4. Broken, shattered, cracked or split parts	10.8%
5. Engine runaway, sudden acceleration	4.8%

From 1990 on, the Plymouth Sundance has had a large number of complaints associated with the airbags. Again, airbag-related complaints are destined to be associated with accidents, because one can't know they're not working until they're put to the test. Nonetheless, this vehicle has had problems with proper deployment of airbags year after year. A professional evaluation is a must in these later models.

One other problem of note: The 1992 model of the Sundance had a problem with seat backs breaking. Buyers should give this a good test.

Earlier Sundance models have had a variety of problems to consider, including sudden acceleration and engine fires.

Midsized or Intermediate Cars

Model	% of Complaints Associated With Accidents
1. Mazda 929	22%
2. Volvo 740	18%
3. Lincoln Mark VII	18%
4. Plymouth Acclaim	17%
5. Chevrolet Corsica	15%
6. Chevrolet Monte Carlo	14%
7. Nissan Maxima	14%
8. Mercury Cougar	14%
9. Dodge Spirit	13%
10. Mercury Marquis	12%
11. Chrysler Imperial	12%
12. Cadillac Cimarron	12%
13. Ford Thunderbird	10%
14. Oldsmobile Cutlass	10%
15. Dodge 600	10%
16. Chrysler Concorde	9%
17. Buick Regal	8%
18. Mazda 626	8%
19. Dodge Lancer	8%
20. Cadillac Eldorado	8%
21. Pontiac Grand Prix	8%
22. Oldsmobile Toronado	8%
23. Dodge Intrepid	8%
24. Ford Taurus	7%
25. Chevrolet Lumina	7%
26. Buick Skyhawk	7%
27. Chrysler Alliance	7%
28. Pontiac 6000	7%
29. Mercury Sable	7%
30. Dodge Diplomat	7%
31. Buick Century	7%
32. Dodge Dynasty	7%
33. Chevrolet Celebrity	6%
34. Lexus	6%
35. Dodge Monaco	6%
36. Chrysler New Yorker	6%
37. Eagle Medallion	5%
38. Hyundai Sonata	3%
39. Buick Riviera	3%
40. Peugeot 505	3%

Mazda 929

NHTSA's Causes for Malfunction or Accident	
1. Engine runaway, sudden acceleration	57.7%
2. Erratic operation, poor performance	25.0%
3. Stability	3.8%

The Mazda 929, as the above percentages suggest, appears on the top of the list in this vehicle class almost entirely because of sudden accelerations; almost three out of five accident-related complaints filed against this automobile were because of engine runaway.

The 1992 model ranks as the worst in the bunch because of added problems with the airbags. With more than one in five complaints filed against this automobile directly related to accidents, one should definitely consider having the car thoroughly evaluated by a professional.

Other areas to consider for safety are the brakes and the transmission. Buyers should make sure that both are working properly.

Volvo 740

NHTSA's Causes for Malfunction or Accident	
1. Engine runaway, sudden acceleration	53.2%
2. Erratic operation, poor performance	17.4%
3. Assembly, parts improperly installed or located	6.4%
4. Parts inoperative	3.7%
5. Broken, shattered, cracked or split parts	2.8%

Once again, sudden accelerations are the culprit with the Volvo. Engine runaway is the leading complaint for 740s in 1988, 1989 and 1990 model years. Plus there were additional complaints regarding faulty airbags in the 1990 model year. Both problems could be addressed by a professional evaluation.

Earlier model years had more typical problems with transmissions, brakes, hesitation and stalling.

Lincoln Mark VII

NHTSA's Causes for Malfunction or Accident	
1. Engine runaway, sudden acceleration	48.7%
2. Erratic operation, poor performance	20.5%
3. Broken, shattered, cracked or split parts	5.1%
4. Design	5.1%
5. Parts inoperative	5.1%

Complaints filed against the Lincoln Mark VII, which also appears in the luxury automobile category, range from typical to serious, but never fall in the worst categories of concern.

Engine runaway, brake trouble and transmission failures do appear in the cars' complaint summaries. Overall, though, there weren't enough complaints filed against the automobile to compensate for this handful of severe difficulties, which explains its high ranking on this list. That said, the biggest concern is clearly engine runaway, and there is more on this topic in the Guide's Introduction.

Plymouth Acclaim

NHTSA's Causes for Malfunction or Accident	
1. Erratic operation, poor performance	35.0%
2. Broken, shattered, cracked or split parts	12.6%
3. Engine runaway, sudden acceleration	10.7%
4. Parts inoperative	8.7%
5. Assembly, parts improperly installed or located	6.7%

The Plymouth Acclaim has had a variety of troublesome complaints since 1989. Engine fires, transmission failures, stalling and other concerns are prevalent.

The car ranks highly compared to other automobiles, mostly because of the 1992 and 1993 models, which have had troubles with airbags and stalling in traffic. Buyers should carefully test the transmission when test driving the car, but if one is going to seriously consider the car, it should have the airbags and transmission checked by a pro.

Chevrolet Corsica

NHTSA's Causes for Malfunction or Accident	
1. Erratic operation, poor performance	34.7%
2. Parts inoperative	17.9%
3. Assembly, parts improperly installed or located	7.7%
4. Broken, shattered, cracked or split parts	7.1%
5. Part fades	6.1%

From 1990 on, the Corsica has been haunted by a different severe problem each year. In the 1990 Corsica, it's seat belts that aren't anchored, engine runaway and wiring problems. In 1991, airbags enter the picture. In 1992, the brakes become the leading concern. And in 1993, airbags still lead the way, but also seat back failures appear for the first time.

Buyers should pay close attention to the owner testimonies in the complaint summary section of this Guide. Each Corsica seems to be different.

Large Cars

Model	% of Complaints Associated With Accidents
1. Mercury Grand Marquis	20%
2. Lincoln Town Car	18%
3. Buick Park Avenue	16%
4. Buick Roadmaster	15%
5. Ford Crown Victoria	14%
6. Ford LTD	14%
7. Pontiac Bonneville	13%
8. Oldsmobile 88	13%
9. Chevrolet Caprice	13%
10. Buick LeSabre	12%
11. Cadillac DeVille	9%
12. Eagle Vision	9%
13. Oldsmobile 98	8%
14. Buick Electra	8%
15. Cadillac Fleetwood	8%
16. Pontiac Parisienne	7%
17. Lincoln Continental	6%
18. Chrysler Fifth Avenue	6%
19. Chrysler New Yorker	6%
20. Oldsmobile Custom Cruiser	4%
21. Eagle Premier	4%

Mercury Grand Marquis

NHTSA's Causes for Malfunction or Accident	
1. Engine runaway, sudden acceleration	46.3%
2. Erratic operation, poor performance	25.8%
3. Parts lock up, stick or grab	5.7%
4. Parts inoperative	3.7%
5. Broken, shattered, cracked or split parts	2.9%

Based on the testimony of Grand Marquis owners, it seems as if this vehicle can never snap out of its difficulties. In model years from 1987 through 1994, two Grand Marquis had a complaint severity rating of "Troublesome," and all others ranked worse.

The main problems owners complain about are engine runaway and transmission failure. In later years, the airbags also experience problems. One in every five complaints is associated with accidents in the Grand Marquis, which is as bad as it gets among large automobiles.

Lincoln Town Car

NHTSA's Causes for Malfunction or Accident	
1. Engine runaway, sudden acceleration	43.5%
2. Erratic operation, poor performance	23.8%
3. Assembly, parts improperly installed or located	6.8%
4. Parts inoperative	6.8%
5. Parts lock up, stick or grab	3.6%

The only reason the Lincoln Town Car hasn't topped the Mercury Grand Marquis among large cars for complaint severity is the fact that the 1993 model hasn't received many worrisome complaints. Most every other model back to 1987 has had serious problems with engine runaway, stalling, transmissions that don't work properly, hood latches that release and other miscellaneous problems.

Sudden accelerations, in particular, are of concern, and buyers should be sure to read more about this problem in the Guide's Introduction.

Buick Park Avenue

NHTSA's Causes for Malfunction or Accident	
1. Parts inoperative	36.6%
2. Erratic operation, poor performance	29.3%
3. Assembly, parts improperly installed or located	14.6%
4. Broken, shattered, cracked or split parts	7.3%
5. Parts lock up, stick or grab	4.9%

The 1991 and 1992 Buick Park Avenues have had notable problems with the brakes. Although many automobiles have brake trouble, the complaints about the Park Avenue's brakes are more frequently associated with accidents. A thorough test of the brakes is a must.

The other reason the Park Avenue ranks so highly among big cars is because owners have complained that the airbags don't work properly. This is going to require a professional evaluation.

Buick Roadmaster

NHTSA's Causes for Malfunction or Accident	
1. Erratic operation, poor performance	50.0%
2. Engine runaway, sudden acceleration	14.7%
3. Assembly, parts improperly installed or located	8.8%
4. Broken, shattered, cracked or split parts	5.9%
5. Design	5.9%

Like many other vehicles with the most severe complaint ratings, the Roadmaster has problems with airbags, brakes, sudden accelerations and transmissions. But the leading problem with this vehicle is seeing out the windshield.

Numerous owners complained that the windshield would fog up and stay that way, with the defroster not helping at all: Certainly something worth testing or asking about.

Ford Crown Victoria

NHTSA's Causes for Malfunction or Accident

1. Engine runaway, sudden acceleration	42.6%
2. Erratic operation, poor performance	26.0%
3. Design	5.4%
4. Assembly, parts improperly installed or located	5.4%
5. Parts lock up, stick or grab	5.4%

With the Ford Crown Victoria, it almost isn't worth mentioning anything other than the huge numbers of complaints about sudden accelerations. Brakes and transmissions have been associated with accidents in this car, but there is nowhere near the degree of the throttle linkages and control problems, which are most frequently blamed for engine runaway.

There is more about sudden accelerations in the Introduction.

Sports, Performance and Luxury Cars

Model	% of Complaints Associated With Accidents
1. Mercedes Benz 300	39%
2. Acura Legend	37%
3. Mercedes Benz 190	28%
4. BMW 325	27%
5. Lincoln Mark VII	18%
6. Mazda RX7	17%
7. Audi 5000	14%
8. Chevrolet Corvette	13%
9. Cadillac Seville	12%
10. Cadillac DeVille	9%
11. Oldsmobile Toronado	8%
12. Lincoln Continental	6%
13. Saab 900	6%
14. Lexus	6%
15. Eagle Talon	6%
16. Chrysler Fifth Avenue	6%
17. Saab 9000	6%
18. Jaguar XJ6	2%

Mercedes Benz 300

NHTSA's Causes for Malfunction or Accident

1. Engine runaway, sudden acceleration	56.5%
2. Erratic operation, poor performance	21.4%
3. Assembly, parts improperly installed or located	5.3%
4. Parts lock up, stick or grab	3.8%
5. Design	3.1%

See Top 10 list for review.

Acura Legend

NHTSA's Causes for Malfunction or Accident

1. Engine runaway, sudden acceleration	58.4%
2. Erratic operation, poor performance	25.6%
3. Assembly, parts improperly installed or located	3.6%
4. Parts lock up, stick or grab	2.5%
5. Parts inoperative	2.5%

See Top 10 list for review.

Mercedes Benz 190

NHTSA's Causes for Malfunction or Accident

1. Engine runaway, sudden acceleration	56.7%
2. Erratic operation, poor performance	16.7%
3. Parts inoperative	6.7%
4. Design	5.0%
5. Jumped out of gear	3.3%

See Top 10 list for review.

BMW 325

NHTSA's Causes for Malfunction or Accident

1. Engine runaway, sudden acceleration	54.2%
2. Erratic operation, poor performance	23.7%
3. Parts inoperative	6.8%
4. Parts lock up, stick or grab	5.1%
5. Parts improperly adjusted or routed	3.4%

Although the BMW 325 shows improvement over the years, the improvement hasn't been enough to overcome the numerous complaints about sudden accelerations, transmission failures, stalling in traffic and brake troubles that are frequently associated with accidents.

Another problem of note in the 1987 model is exploding windshields which NHTSA says is caused by faulty defroster wiring.

Lincoln Mark VII

NHTSA's Causes for Malfunction or Accident

1. Engine runaway, sudden acceleration	48.7%
2. Erratic operation, poor performance	20.5%
3. Broken, shattered, cracked or split parts	5.1%
4. Design	5.1%
5. Parts inoperative	5.1%

See Midsized or Intermediate Cars for review.

Pickup Trucks

Model	% of Complaints Associated With Accidents
1. Chevrolet S10	14%
2. GMC Sonoma	12%
3. Dodge Dakota	9%
4. Ford F150	9%
5. Ford F250	7%
6. Ford F350	6%
7. Chevrolet C10	6%
8. Toyota Pickup	6%
9. Chevrolet C20	6%
10. Chevrolet C15	5%
11. Chevrolet G20	4%
12. Chevrolet C25	3%
13. Jeep Comanche	1%

Chevrolet S10

NHTSA's Causes for Malfunction or Accident	
1. Erratic operation, poor performance	24.3%
2. Parts inoperative	14.1%
3. Parts lock up, stick or grab	12.8%
4. Parts fade	10.2%
5. Engine runaway, sudden acceleration	9.2%

There are a variety of reasons why the Chevrolet S10 tops the list among pickup trucks for complaint severity.

The problems start with the 1986 model—a truck with serious transmission and engine troubles. The next model year then developed problems with sudden accelerations, steering failure and stalling in traffic. The 1988 and 1989 trucks had negligible complaint severity ratings, but problems return in the 1990s.

Brakes, as well as sudden accelerations, are a troublesome to very serious problem in all of the S10s in the 1990s. And finally, in the 1995 model, complaints about airbags have started to pile up.

When combined, the S10 ranks worst among pickups for complaint severity.

GMC Sonoma

NHTSA's Causes for Malfunction or Accident	
1. Parts inoperative	88.9%
2. Excessive effort (to operate)	11.1%

The problem with the Sonoma is that, relative to all the incredibly popular pickups that have been on the market for years, the solitary 1994 Sonoma is doomed to rank poorly in comparison. This single model year has had a disproportionate amount of complaints associated with its brakes and transmission. But overall, there haven't been that many accident-related complaints filed against the automobile—as of yet.

It's going to take another few years to determine if the Sonoma is going to keep this ranking. In the meantime, test the brakes thoroughly.

Dodge Dakota

NHTSA's Causes for Malfunction or Accident	
1. Erratic operation, poor performance	22.3%
2. Parts lock up, stick or grab	17.0%
3. Jumped out of gear	13.8%
4. Broken, shattered, cracked or split parts	11.7%
5. Engine runaway, sudden acceleration	6.4%

The Dodge Dakota, over an eight-year period, never really qualifies as one of the worst of the worst when it comes to complaint severity. The reason it ranks so highly among pickup trucks is because of the ongoing occurrence of problems, as opposed to one or two model years making the difference. Transmission difficulties, brake problems, sudden accelerations and stalling in traffic start to add up in comparison to other trucks.

Ford F150

NHTSA's Causes for Malfunction or Accident	
1. Erratic operation, poor performance	22.3%
2. Parts inoperative	17.0%
3. Parts lock up, stick or grab	13.8%
4. Parts fade	11.7%
5. Engine runaway, sudden acceleration	6.4%

Like the Dakota, the Ford F150 and F250 aren't really that bad in comparison to vehicles in other car categories. Problem severity never exceeds "Typical" in any model year. However, one should pay special attention to the brakes in this truck. Brakes represent the number one problem with F150s for nine of the past ten years.

Ford F250

NHTSA's Causes for Malfunction or Accident	
1. Parts inoperative	18.3%
2. Erratic operation, poor performance	17.0%
3. Parts lock up, stick or grab	12.4%
4. Parts fade	11.8%
5. Engine runaway, sudden acceleration	9.2%

Same as the Ford F150.

Passenger/All-Purpose Trucks

Model	% of Complaints Associated With Accidents
1. Suzuki Samurai	51%
2. GMC Jimmy	20%
3. Ford Bronco II	17%
4. Mazda Navajo	14%
5. Chevrolet Blazer	13%
6. Jeep Grand Cherokee	13%
7. Toyota 4Runner	11%
8. Jeep Cherokee	11%
9. Chevrolet Suburban	11%
10. Isuzu Trooper	11%
11. GMC C1500	10%
12. Ford Ranger	10%
13. Ford Explorer	10%
14. Ford Bronco	10%
15. Dodge Ram	9%
16. Jeep Wrangler	6%
17. Isuzu Trooper II	6%
18. Ford Econoline	6%
19. GMC S15	6%
20. Isuzu Rodeo	6%
21. Chrysler Town and Country	4%
22. Mercury Villager	3%
23. Winnebago Lesharo	2%
24. Jeep Wagoneer	2%

Suzuki Samurai

NHTSA's Causes for Malfunction or Accident	
1. Stability	73.6%
2. Design	8.3%
3. Broken, shattered, cracked or split parts	4.2%
4. Erratic operation, poor performance	3.5%
5. Loss of control, poor direction, wanders	2.8%

See Top 10 list for review.

GMC Jimmy

NHTSA's Causes for Malfunction or Accident	
1. Parts inoperative	25.6%
2. Erratic operation, poor performance	16.7%
3. Parts lock up, stick or grab	14.1%
4. Engine runaway, sudden acceleration	10.3%
5. Parts fade	9.0%

The Jimmy has difficulties in several areas, most notably the brakes, which represent the number one complaint in all but one model year. The only remaining question with the Jimmy is: What, besides the brakes, is wrong this year?

Each year from 1989 through 1994, there is something different that owners complain about with regularity, starting with sudden accelerations in 1989, then seat belts in 1991 (there is no listing in the Guide for the 1990 model year), the seat backs in 1992 and the transmission in 1993. The jury is still out for 1994.

Ford Bronco II

NHTSA's Causes for Malfunction or Accident	
1. Stability	28.7%
2. Parts lock up, stick or grab	11.2%
3. Erratic operation, poor performance	9.8%
4. Broken, shattered, cracked or split parts	7.0%
5. Parts slip, loose	6.3%

The lingering problem for the Ford Bronco II is stability. Although the transmission comes and goes as a frequent accident-related Hot Spot, the suspension appears again and again as a problem for the Bronco II. The suspension is what leads to stability difficulties and rollover accidents.

Another worrisome problem is the reoccurring problem with engine fires. Leaks of various kinds have most often caused Broncos II to ignite, NHTSA records report.

Mazda Navajo

NHTSA's Causes for Malfunction or Accident	
1. Parts lock up, stick or grab	37.5%
2. Part disconnected or fell off	12.5%
3. Engine runaway, sudden acceleration	12.5%
4. Parts inoperative	12.5%
5. Erratic operation, poor performance	12.5%

The 1991 Mazda Navajo (the only one listed in the Guide) had a large proportion of its brake problems lead to accidents. Owners complained that the brakes would seize, leading to an accident.

Chevrolet Blazer

NHTSA's Causes for Malfunction or Accident	
1. Erratic operation, poor performance	21.9%
2. Parts inoperative	18.5%
3. Engine runaway, sudden acceleration	13.8%
4. Parts fade	11.2%
5. Parts lock up, stick or grab	9.2%

The Chevrolet Blazer never had complaint severity ratings above "Typical" until the 1992 model. Thereafter, there are several severity problems worth noting.

The two biggest culprits are the brakes and engine runaway. Following that, owners have complained over the years of transmission difficulties, airbag failures and stalling. But clearly, checking the brakes and reading the section about sudden accelerations in the Introduction should be priorities for people interested in buying a Blazer.

Minivans and Vans

Model	% of Complaints Associated With Accidents
1. Mazda MPV	17%
2. Chevrolet Lumina	13%
3. Chevrolet Astro	13%
4. Toyota Van	12%
5. Ford Aerostar	11%
6. GMC Safari	9%
7. Dodge Caravan	9%
8. Plymouth Voyager	9%
9. Toyota Previa	8%
10. Ford Windstar	6%
11. Ford E150	4%
12. Ford E350	4%
13. Nissan Quest	2%
14. Volkswagen Vanagon	2%
15. Nissan Van	2%

Mazda MPV

NHTSA's Causes for Malfunction or Accident	
1. Parts lock up, stick or grab	23.0%
2. Parts inoperative	21.0%
3. Recall problem not fixed	15.0%
4. Erratic operation, poor performance	7.0%
5. Broken, shattered, cracked or split parts	5.0%

The complaints filed with NHTSA about the Mazda MPV van make it simple to identify the cause of the high complaint severity rating: brakes and transmission.

With the exception of some engine fires caused by leaks in the 1989 model, the brakes and the transmission are the only other sources of accident-related complaints. Both should be given a thorough test, and a detailed maintenance history should be made available by the seller.

Chevrolet Lumina

NHTSA's Causes for Malfunction or Accident	
1. Broken, shattered, cracked or split parts	40.0%
2. Design	20.0%
3. Parts disconnected or fell off	20.0%
4. Parts fade	10.0%
5. Erratic operation, poor performance	10.0%

After the MPV, van troubles are generally reasonable. Only 13 percent of the 1,600 complaints filed with NHTSA about the Lumina were accident related, and yet it's second on the list for vans and minivans for accident troubles.

In fact, only the brakes are listed as the primary accident-related complaints in the Lumina. They should be given a careful test, and perhaps a professional evaluation.

Chevrolet Astro

NHTSA's Causes for Malfunction or Accident	
1. Erratic operation, poor performance	25.0%
2. Engine runaway, sudden acceleration	18.4%
3. Parts inoperative	9.4%
4. Parts lock up, stick or grab	8.2%
5. Design	7.4%

The Astro, like the Lumina, has brake trouble year after year. But added to that are troubles with sudden accelerations, which frequently lead to accidents.

Another troublesome trend with the Astro is the steering. Between 1987 and 1991, the Astro had serious problems with the steering not working properly and causing abnormal tire wear. In later models, the steering problems are replaced with transmission difficulties, airbag failures and stalling. All can be easily associated with accidents.

Toyota Van

NHTSA's Causes for Malfunction or Accident	
1. Erratic operation, poor performance	57.1%
2. Broken, shattered, cracked or split parts	14.3%
3. Loss of control, wanders	14.3%
4. Parts lock up, stick or grab	14.3%

NHTSA listed one year of "Toyota Van," a 1985 model which after more than ten years on the road has eked out a place in the Guide with a grand total of 58 complaints. Seven of those complaints were accident-related, and were associated either with poor brakes or a stiff steering wheel.

Ford Aerostar

NHTSA's Causes for Malfunction or Accident	
1. Engine runaway, sudden acceleration	25.4%
2. Erratic operation, poor performance	23.1%
3. Parts lock up, stick or grab	10.3%
4. Jumped out of gear	7.0%
5. Broken, shattered, cracked or split parts	4.8%

Unlike the Toyota van, the Aerostar is one of the most complained about vehicles on the road, but not number one among minivans (the Dodge Caravan holds that title).

The accident-related complaints were mostly related to sudden accelerations and the transmission. Owners complain that the transmission can slip out of gear or can have difficulty changing gears, both of which can lead to accidents. Airbags and brakes have also been a problem.

SECTION III: Recall Index

Acura

Note: If your Acura is presented to an authorized dealer at an agreed-upon service date and the remedy is not provided free of charge within a reasonable time, please contact Honda/Acura at (800) 999-1009. Also contact the NHTSA's Auto Safety Hotline at (800) 424-9393.

ACURA INTEGRA 1989

System: Interior; seat belts; belt buckles. **Vehicle:** 2-door, 4-door and 5-door passenger vehicles equipped with safety belts made by Takata Corporation. **Defect:** The front safety belt buckle release buttons can break. These red plastic release buttons are marked "press." If a button breaks, pieces can fall into the buckle assembly, causing the buckle to operate improperly. **Consequence:** The safety belts would not provide adequate protection to an occupant in a vehicle crash. **Corrective Action:** Owners should promptly check the condition and operation of both front safety belt buckles. Carefully inspect the red release button for any breaks or cracks. Check that both buckles are operating properly by inserting each latch plate into its buckle, tugging on the belt to make sure the latch is securely locked and then pressing the release button. The latch plate should pop out of the buckle when the button is pressed. If either release button shows any sign of breakage or cracking, or if either buckle fails to operate properly, promptly contact your authorized Honda/Acura dealer to schedule an appointment to have the buckle replaced or repaired, free of charge. The manufacturer is developing a remedy designed to prevent the failure of the buttons that are not currently broken.

ACURA INTEGRA 1990

System: Trailer hitch installed on 1990 and 1991 Acura Integra. **Defect:** Fatigue failure of the trailer hitch vertical mounting plate caused by cyclic stress from extended use under overloaded conditions, in the zone adjacent to a weld. **Consequence:** Hitch tow bar could separate from the vertical mounting plate, resulting in tow bar attachment failure and separation of trailer from tow vehicle without warning. **Corrective Action:** A component will be supplied to customer to be attached to the vehicle towing loop to eliminate cyclic stress in the vertical load plate. Units found with existing fatigue fractures will be replaced with modified hitches. **Note:** This recall is being conducted by Carrol Smith Consulting, Inc.

System: Interior; seat belts; belt buckles. **Vehicle:** 2-door, 4-door and 5-door passenger vehicles equipped with safety belts made by Takata Corporation. **Defect:** The front safety belt buckle release buttons can break. These red plastic release buttons are marked "press." If a button breaks, pieces can fall into the buckle assembly, causing the buckle to operate improperly. **Consequence:** The safety belts would not provide adequate protection to an occupant in a vehicle crash. **Corrective Action:** Owners should promptly check the condition and operation of both front safety belt buckles. Carefully inspect the red release button for any breaks or cracks. Check that both buckles are operating properly by inserting each latch plate into its buckle, tugging on the belt to make sure the latch is securely locked and then pressing the release button. The latch plate should pop out of the buckle when the button is pressed. If either release button shows any sign of breakage or cracking, or if either buckle fails to operate properly, promptly contact your authorized Honda/Acura dealer to schedule an appointment to have the buckle replaced or repaired, free of charge. The manufacturer is developing a remedy designed to prevent the failure of the buttons that are not currently broken.

ACURA INTEGRA 1991

System: Trailer hitch installed on 1990 and 1991 Acura Integra. **Defect:** Fatigue failure of the trailer hitch vertical mounting plate caused by cyclic stress from extended use under overloaded conditions, in the zone adjacent to a weld. **Consequence:** Hitch tow bar could separate from the vertical mounting plate, resulting in tow bar attachment failure and separation of trailer from tow vehicle without warning. **Corrective Action:** A component will be supplied to customer to be attached to the vehicle towing loop, to eliminate cyclic stress in the vertical load plate. Units found with existing fatigue fractures will be replaced with modified hitches. **Note:** This recall is being conducted by Carrol Smith Consulting, Inc.

System: Interior; seat belts; belt buckles. **Vehicle:** 2-door, 4-door and 5-door passenger vehicles equipped with safety belts made by Takata Corporation. **Defect:** The front safety belt buckle release buttons can break. These red plastic release buttons are marked "press." If a button breaks, pieces can fall into the buckle assembly, causing the buckle to operate improperly. **Consequence:** The safety belts would not provide adequate protection to an occupant in a vehicle crash. **Corrective Action:** Owners should promptly check the condition and operation of both front safety belt buckles. Carefully inspect the red release button for any breaks or cracks. Check that both buckles are operating properly by inserting each latch plate into its buckle, tugging on the belt to make sure the latch is securely locked and then pressing the release button. The latch plate should pop out of the buckle when the button is pressed. If either release button shows any sign of breakage or cracking, or if either buckle fails to operate properly, promptly contact your authorized Honda/Acura dealer to schedule an appointment to have the buckle replaced or repaired, free of charge. The manufacturer is developing a remedy designed to prevent the failure of the buttons that are not currently broken.

ACURA INTEGRA 1994

System: Power train; transmission; automatic. **Vehicle:** Passenger vehicles equipped with automatic transmissions. **Defect:** A retaining clip that connects the transmission shift cable to the shift lever actuating rod can have insufficient retention pressure and may eventually come off after repeated shift lever operation. If this happens, the position of the shift lever may not match the actual transmission gear position. **Consequence:** This could result in unanticipated vehicle movement and accident. **Corrective Action:** Dealers will install an improved retaining clip.

ACURA LEGEND 1987

System: Interior; seat belts; belt buckles. **Vehicle:** 2-door, 4-door and 5-door passenger vehicles equipped with safety belts made by Takata Corporation. **Defect:** The front safety belt buckle release buttons can break. These red plastic release buttons are marked "press." If a button breaks, pieces can fall into the buckle assembly, causing the buckle to operate improperly. **Consequence:** The safety belts would not provide adequate protection to an occupant in a vehicle crash. **Corrective Action:** Owners should promptly check the condition and operation of both front safety belt buckles. Carefully inspect the red release button for any breaks or cracks. Check that both buckles are operating properly by inserting each latch plate into its buckle, tugging on the belt to make sure the latch is securely locked and then pressing the release button. The latch plate should pop out of the buckle when the button is pressed. If either release button shows any sign of breakage or cracking, or if either buckle fails to operate properly, promptly contact your authorized Honda/Acura dealer to schedule an appointment to have the buckle replaced or repaired, free of charge. The manufacturer is developing a remedy designed to prevent the failure of the buttons that are not currently broken.

ACURA LEGEND 1988

System: Owners manual information—FMVSS 210. **Vehicle:** Passenger cars and wagons. **Defect:** Owners manual information required by FMVSS 210, sections 6a and 6b, was omitted from the manual. **Consequence:** Vehicle's manual information does not comply with FMVSS 210. **Corrective Action:** Upgrade existing manuals by inserting adhesive-backed correction pages.

System: Interior; seat belts; belt buckles. **Vehicle:** 2-door, 4-door and 5-door passenger vehicles equipped with safety belts made by Takata Corporation. **Defect:** The front safety belt buckle release buttons can break. These red plastic release buttons are marked "press." If a button breaks, pieces can fall into the buckle assembly, causing the buckle to operate improperly. **Consequence:** The safety belts would not provide adequate protection to an occupant in a vehicle crash. **Corrective Action:** Owners should promptly check the condition and operation of both front safety belt buckles. Carefully inspect the red release button for any breaks or cracks. Check that both buckles are operating properly by inserting each latch plate into its buckle, tugging on the belt to make sure the latch is securely locked and then pressing the release button. The latch plate should pop out of the buckle when the button is pressed. If either release button shows any sign of breakage or cracking, or if either buckle fails to operate properly, promptly contact your authorized Honda/Acura dealer to schedule an appointment to have the buckle replaced or repaired, free of charge. The manufacturer is developing a remedy designed to prevent the failure of the buttons that are not currently broken.

ACURA LEGEND 1989

System: Airbag modules. **Vehicle:** Passenger cars equipped with driver's-side supplemental airbag modules. **Defect:** Threaded inflator components may have been damaged during assembly, which may allow components to separate when inflator receives a signal to deploy the airbag. **Consequence:** Inflator component separation allows hot combustion gases to escape into the passenger compartment, which could result in injuries to vehicle occupants. **Corrective Action:** Replace air bag modules containing potentially defective inflators. **Note:** This campaign was initiated by TRW, Inc., manufacturer of the airbag module.

System: Interior; seat belts; belt buckles. **Vehicle:** 2-door, 4-door and 5-door passenger vehicles equipped with safety belts made by Takata Corporation. **Defect:** The front safety belt buckle release buttons can break. These red plastic release buttons are marked "press." If a button breaks, pieces can fall into the buckle assembly, causing the buckle to operate improperly. **Consequence:** The safety belts would not provide adequate protection to an occupant in a vehicle crash. **Corrective Action:** Owners should promptly check the condition and operation of both front safety belt buckles. Carefully inspect the red release button for any breaks or cracks. Check that both buckles are operating properly by inserting each latch plate into its buckle, tugging on the belt to make sure the latch is securely locked and then pressing the release button. The latch plate should pop out of the buckle when the button is pressed. If either release button shows any sign of breakage or cracking, or if either buckle fails to operate properly, promptly contact your authorized Honda/Acura dealer to schedule an appointment to have the buckle replaced or repaired, free of charge. The manufacturer is developing a remedy designed to prevent the failure of the buttons that are not currently broken.

ACURA LEGEND 1990

System: Airbag modules. **Vehicle:** Passenger cars equipped with driver's-side supplemental airbag modules. **Defect:** Threaded inflator components may have been damaged during assembly, which may allow components to separate when inflator receives a signal to deploy the airbag. **Consequence:** Inflator component separation allows hot combustion gases to escape into the passenger compartment, which could result in injuries to vehicle occupants. **Corrective Action:** Replace airbag modules containing potentially defective inflators. **Note:** This campaign was initiated by TRW, Inc., manufacturer of the airbag module.

System: Interior; seat belts; belt buckles. **Vehicle:** 2-door, 4-door and 5-door passenger vehicles equipped with safety belts made by Takata Corporation. **Defect:** The front safety belt buckle release buttons can break. These red plastic release buttons are marked "press." If a button breaks, pieces can fall into the buckle assembly, causing the buckle to operate improperly. **Consequence:** The safety belts would not provide adequate protection to an occupant in a vehicle crash. **Corrective Action:** Owners should promptly check the condition and operation of both front safety belt buckles. Carefully inspect the red release button for any breaks or cracks. Check that both buckles are operating properly by inserting each latch plate into its buckle, tugging on the belt to make sure the latch is securely locked and then pressing the release button. The latch plate should pop out of the buckle when the button is pressed. If either release button shows any sign of breakage or cracking, or if either buckle fails to operate properly, promptly contact your authorized Honda/Acura dealer to schedule an appointment to have the buckle replaced or repaired, free of charge. The manufacturer is developing a remedy designed to prevent the failure of the buttons that are not currently broken.

ACURA LEGEND 1991

System: Airbag modules. **Vehicle:** Passenger cars equipped with driver's-side supplemental airbag modules. **Defect:** Threaded inflator components may have been damaged during assembly, which may allow components to separate when inflator receives a signal to deploy the airbag. **Consequence:** Inflator component separation allows hot combustion gases to escape into the passenger compartment, which could result in injuries to vehicle occupants. **Corrective Action:** Replace airbag modules containing potentially defective inflators. **Note:** This campaign was initiated by TRW, Inc., manufacturer of the airbag module.

System: Transmission shift cable bracket. **Vehicle:** 4-door passenger cars. **Defect:** Transmission shift cable bracket can be damaged by the engine rocking forward on engine mounts in a minor collision. **Consequence:** When the shift cable bracket is damaged, the shift lever position may not correctly indicate the transmission gear position. This could result in unanticipated movement of the car and an accident. **Corrective Action:** Replace the transmission shift cable and attaching hardware with redesigned assemblies.

AUDI

AUDI 5000 1987

System: Fuel tank. **Vehicle:** Turbo and turbo Quattro passenger cars. **Defect:** Repeated topping off of fuel tank during refueling reduces the expansion space within the tank, allowing vapors to escape from the charcoal filter to the outside rather than being inducted into the engine. **Consequence:** Escaping vapors could ignite by heat emitted by the exhaust system. **Corrective Action:** Install redesigned filler neck and a new vent valve and hose for charcoal filter. Also, stop refueling when pump nozzle shuts off.

System: Rear brake caliper. **Vehicle:** Passenger cars. **Defect:** Certain rear brake calipers could bind and consequently overheat. **Consequence:** Overheated calipers could cause brake pedal to feel spongy and could result in one brake circuit becoming inoperative. Braking ability would be affected. **Corrective Action:** Requires inspection of brake calipers and replacement of calipers as necessary.

System: Fuel. **Vehicle:** Passenger cars with turbo. **Defect:** Fuel injection seals may harden, due to high temperature and alcohol in some fuels, and allow fuel to escape into the engine compartment. **Consequence:** Fuel dripping onto hot engine components could cause an engine compartment fire. **Corrective Action:** Replace engine's fuel injector seals with improved seals plus improvements designed to better insulate the engine against fire risk.

System: Power train. **Vehicle:** Passenger cars with automatic 3-speed transmissions. **Defect:** The differential oil of the transaxle is lost over time due to evaporation. Low oil levels cause premature bearing and gear wear and eventual failure of the differential. **Consequence:** In the event of failure, the vehicle's drive wheels could lose power. In extreme circumstances, the front wheels lock, causing rapid deceleration and resulting in possible loss of vehicle control and an accident. **Corrective Action:** Drain and replace the differential gear oil with oil having higher performance characteristics.

BMW

Note: If your BMW is presented to an authorized dealer on an agreed-upon service date and the remedy is not provided within a reasonable time and free of charge, or the remedy does not correct the defect or noncompliance, please contact BMW at (800) 831-1117. Also contact the NHTSA's Auto Safety Hotline at (800) 424-9393.

BMW 318 1991

System: Throttle linkages and control. **Vehicle:** Passenger vehicles. **Defect:** The crankcase ventilation system, vented into the intake tract of the engine at the bellows boot ahead of the throttle housing, allows warm water vapor from the crankcase vent to condense and freeze in the colder bellows boot when the ambient air temperature is 15 degrees Fahrenheit or less. The buildup of ice can dislodge and move into the throttle housing, preventing the throttle plate from fully closing when the driver releases the gas pedal. **Consequence:** If the throttle plate is prevented from closing, there is an increase in idle speed, as well as slower than normal deceleration, which occurs without prior warning and could result in an accident. **Corrective Action:** Replace the throttle housing with a version containing a modified heating system along with rerouting of the CVS hose. This will prevent ice buildup in the intake tract.

System: Coolant system. **Vehicle:** Passenger cars. **Defect:** The malfunction or failure of a coolant system component results in significantly increased coolant temperature and a resulting increase in system pressure. **Consequence:** Vehicles operated under this increased cooling system pressure condition can suffer damage or failure of parts of the cooling system, such as (1) leakage from a coolant hose, (2) leakage of the radiator or expansion tank, (3) disconnection of a hose from a pipe or a fitting, and (4) cracks in the heater core end piece, resulting in coolant leakage. In some cases, boiling coolant can contact the lower right leg of the driver, resulting in burns. Also, escaping coolant in the passenger compartment can cause vapor fogging of the interior surface of the windows, reducing driver visibility. **Corrective Action:** BMW is currently developing an engineering solution to the problem of excessive pressure in the coolant system.

System: Fuel; fuel line fittings; metallic. **Vehicle:** Passenger vehicles; models 318i, 318si, 318ic, 325i, 325is, 325ix, 325ic, 525i, 535i, 735i and 735il. **Defect:** Feed fuel hoses can harden and "set" over time, allowing a seepage of fuel at the connection between the hose and the engine fitting. The clamp used to hold the hose to the fitting is unable to compensate for the hardening of the feed fuel hose. **Consequence:** Fuel seepage between the feed fuel hose and the engine fitting can result in free fuel in the engine compartment, which could result in a fire when exposed to a source of ignition. **Corrective Action:** A redesigned feed fuel hose and hose clamp will be installed to alleviate the fuel seepage.

BMW 325 1987

System: Brake light switch. **Vehicle:** Passenger cars with high brake lights. **Defect:** Brake light switch could overheat, eventually leading to melting of plastic internal parts in the area of electrical contacts. **Consequence:** Switch plunger could jam, rendering brake lights either inoperative or continuously illuminated regardless of brake pedal operation. **Corrective Action:** Replace brake light switch with revised switch with increased electrical load capacity.

System: Coolant system. **Vehicle:** Passenger cars. **Defect:** The malfunction or failure of a coolant system component results in significantly increased coolant temperature and a resulting increase in system pressure. **Consequence:** Vehicles operated under this increased cooling system pressure condition can suffer damage or failure of parts of the cooling system, such as (1) leakage from a coolant hose, (2) leakage of the radiator or expansion tank, (3) disconnection of a hose from a pipe or a fitting, and (4) cracks in the heater core end piece, resulting in coolant leakage. In some cases, boiling coolant can contact the lower right leg of the driver, resulting in burns. Also, escaping coolant in the passenger compartment can cause vapor fogging of the interior surface of the windows, reducing driver visibility. **Corrective Action:** BMW is currently developing an engineering solution to the problem of excessive pressure in the coolant system.

BMW 325 1989

System: Coolant system. **Vehicle:** Passenger cars. **Defect:** The malfunction or failure of a coolant system component results in significantly increased coolant temperature and a resulting increase in system pressure. **Consequence:** Vehicles operated under this increased cooling system pressure condition can suffer damage or failure of parts of the cooling system, such as (1) leakage from a coolant hose, (2) leakage of the radiator or expansion tank, (3) disconnection of a hose from a pipe or a fitting, and (4) cracks in the heater core end piece, resulting in coolant leakage. In some cases, boiling coolant can contact the lower right leg of the driver, resulting in burns. Also, escaping coolant in the passenger compartment can cause vapor fogging of the interior surface of the windows, reducing driver visibility. **Corrective Action:** BMW is currently developing an engineering solution to the problem of excessive pressure in the coolant system.

System: Fuel; fuel line fittings; metallic. **Vehicle:** Passenger vehicles; models 318i, 318si, 318ic, 325i, 325is, 325ix, 325ic, 525i, 535i, 735i and 735il. **Defect:** Feed fuel hoses can harden and "set" over time, allowing a seepage of fuel at the connection between the hose and the engine fitting. The clamp used to hold the hose to the fitting is unable to compensate for the hardening of the feed fuel hose. **Consequence:** Fuel seepage between the feed fuel hose and the engine fitting can result in free fuel in the engine compartment, which could result in a fire when exposed to a source of ignition. **Corrective Action:** A redesigned feed fuel hose and hose clamp will be installed to alleviate the fuel seepage.

BUICK

Note: Owners who take their Buick to an authorized dealer on an agreed-upon service date and do not receive the free remedy within a reasonable time should contact Buick at (800) 521-7300; Chevrolet at (800) 222-1020; Pontiac at (800) 762-2737; or Oldsmobile at (800) 442-6537. Also contact the NHTSA's Auto Safety Hotline at (800) 424-9393.

BUICK CENTURY 1988

System: Seat belt assembly anchorage information—FMVSS 210. **Vehicle:** Passenger cars. **Defect:** Owner's manual did not include statement on child restraint systems. **Consequence:** Vehicles do not conform to FMVSS 210. **Corrective Action:** Furnish owners with updated owner's manuals that contain the omitted instructions.

System: Suspension—lower control front arm bracket. **Vehicle:** Passenger cars. **Defect:** Front suspension lower control arm bracket could develop metal cracks. **Consequence:** These cracks may result in disengagement of the lower control arm. If this occurs while vehicle is in motion, it could result in loss of steering control, and a vehicle crash could occur without prior warning. **Corrective Action:** Inspect all vehicles and replace engine cradle assembly on all suspect vehicles.

System: Fuel feed hose. **Vehicle:** Passenger cars equipped with a 2.8L V6 engine. **Defect:** Fuel feed hose could leak at the coupling on the engine end of the hose assembly. **Consequence:** Fuel leakage into the engine compartment could result in an engine compartment fire that could spread to the passenger compartment. **Corrective Action:** Install new fuel feed hose assembly.

BUICK CENTURY 1989

System: Interior; active restraints; belt anchor and attachment—FMVSS 210. **Vehicle:** Passenger vehicles. **Description of Noncompliance:** These vehicles were assembled with rear outboard safety belt anchorages that may not withstand the required load. This does not comply with FMVSS 210, "Seat belt assembly anchorages." **Consequence of Noncompliance:** In a collision, stress can cause the attachment metal to tear and allow the anchorage to separate from the body of the vehicle. The safety belt may not protect an occupant in the event of a vehicle crash. **Corrective Action:** Dealers will replace the existing anchor bolts with a new shoulder bolt and thread-locking adhesive. Additionally, noise control patches will be applied at each anchorage.

BUICK CENTURY 1990

System: Interior: seating. **Vehicle:** Passenger cars with 6-way power seats or power recliners. **Defect:** The power seat or recliner wiring harness can be pinched or can chafe on the seat frame or spring support rod, wearing through the wire insulation and causing an electrical short. **Consequence:** The high current caused by the electrical short welds the circuit breaker elements together in the closed position, leaving the circuit unprotected and generating sufficient heat to burn the wire insulation and ignite the seat cushion material. **Corrective Action:** Repair any abraded wiring and reroute the wiring harness using a wiring harness clip.

System: Interior; active restraints; belt anchor and attachment—FMVSS 210. **Vehicle:** Passenger vehicles. **Description of Noncompliance:** These vehicles were assembled with rear outboard safety belt anchorages that may not withstand the required load. This does not comply with FMVSS 210, "Seat belt assembly anchorages." **Consequence of Noncompliance:** In a collision, stress can cause the attachment metal to tear and allow the anchorage to separate from the body of the vehicle. The safety belt may not protect an occupant in the event of a vehicle crash. **Corrective Action:** Dealers will replace the existing anchor bolts with a new shoulder bolt and thread-locking adhesive. Additionally, noise control patches will be applied at each anchorage.

BUICK CENTURY 1991

System: Interior: seating. **Vehicle:** Passenger cars with 6-way power seats or power recliners. **Defect:** The power seat or recliner wiring harness can be pinched or can chafe on the seat frame or spring support rod, wearing through the wire insulation and causing an electrical short. **Consequence:** The high current caused by the electrical short welds the circuit breaker elements together in the closed position, leaving the circuit unprotected and generating sufficient heat to burn the wire insulation and ignite the seat cushion material. **Corrective Action:** Repair any abraded wiring and reroute the wiring harness using a wiring harness clip.

System: Lighting; lamp or socket; park lights—FMVSS 108. **Vehicle:** Passenger cars. **Description of Noncompliance:** These vehicles were equipped with the wrong bulbs for the front park/turn signal lamps. This does not conform to the requirements of FMVSS 108, "Lamps, reflective devices and associated equipment." **Consequence of Noncompliance:** Reduced lighting on the park/turn signal lights decreases the likelihood of the vehicle operator's intent of being seen by other motorists. **Corrective Action:** General Motors has not submitted a corrective action for this noncompliance. **Note:** The manufacturer has petitioned the NHTSA for a determination that this matter is inconsequential with respect to motor vehicle safety. The manufacturer is not obligated to conduct an owner notification and remedy campaign until NHTSA has resolved the petition.

System: Interior; active restraints; belt anchor and attachment—FMVSS 210. **Vehicle:** Passenger vehicles. **Description of Noncompliance:** These vehicles were assembled with rear outboard safety belt anchorages that may not withstand the required load. This does not comply with FMVSS 210, "Seat belt assembly anchorages." **Consequence of Noncompliance:** In a collision, stress can cause the attachment metal to tear and allow the anchorage to separate from the body of the vehicle. The safety belt may not protect an occupant in the event of a vehicle crash. **Corrective Action:** Dealers will replace the existing anchor bolts with a new shoulder bolt and thread-locking adhesive. Additionally, noise control patches will be applied at each anchorage.

BUICK CENTURY 1992

System: Transmission and transmission shift indicator. **Vehicle:** 1992 "A" and "W" body passenger cars with 4-speed automatic transmissions. **Defect:** The reverse servo apply pin may bind in the case, which could cause reverse band distress (loss or slipping of reverse), reverse band drag in drive range (poor performance/poor power) or the transmission to remain in reverse while the shift indicator shows neutral gear position. **Consequence:** If the transmission remains in reverse while the shift indicator shows neutral, the vehicle may unexpectedly move rearward, resulting in a vehicle accident. **Corrective Action:** Replace the transaxle where required.

System: Electrical; remote entry modules. **Vehicle:** Passenger cars (station wagons) with remote entry modules. **Defect:** The optional remote entry module may have a fault that causes random actuation of interior lamps, door locks and/or tailgate release. This actuation may occur while the vehicle is in use or unattended. **Consequence:** If the tailgate release actuates, the tailgate will open. Unrestrained passengers in the rear seat area could fall out of the vehicle while the car is in motion and receive serious injuries. **Corrective Action:** Replace the remote entry module with a newly revised module to prevent random actuation.

System: Lighting; lamp or socket; park lights—FMVSS 108. **Vehicle:** Passenger cars. **Description of Noncompliance:** These vehicles were equipped with the wrong bulbs for the front park/turn signal lamps. This does not conform to the requirements of FMVSS 108, "Lamps, reflective devices and associated equipment." **Consequence of Noncompliance:** Reduced lighting on the park/turn signal lights decreases the likelihood of the vehicle operator's intent of being seen by other motorists. **Corrective Action:** General Motors has not submitted a corrective action for this noncompliance. **Note:** The manufacturer has petitioned the NHTSA for a determination that this matter is inconsequential with respect to motor vehicle safety. The manufacturer is not obligated to conduct an owner notification and remedy campaign until NHTSA has resolved the petition.

System: Interior; active restraints; belt anchor and attachment—FMVSS 210. **Vehicle:** Passenger vehicles. **Description of Noncompliance:** These vehicles were assembled with rear outboard safety belt anchorages that may not withstand the required load. This does not comply with FMVSS 210, "Seat belt assembly anchorages." **Consequence of Noncompliance:** In a collision, stress can cause the attachment metal to tear and allow the anchorage to separate from the body of the vehicle. The safety belt may not protect an occupant in the event of a vehicle crash. **Corrective Action:** Dealers will replace the existing anchor bolts with a new shoulder bolt and thread-locking adhesive. Additionally, noise control patches will be applied at each anchorage.

BUICK CENTURY 1993

System: Brakes; hydraulic; hose. **Vehicle:** Passenger vehicles. **Defect:** The brake hoses were manufactured incorrectly, and do not comply with FMVSS 106, "Brake hoses." **Consequence:** The improperly manufactured brake hoses can cause reduced brake effectiveness and/or uneven braking, which could result in an accident. **Corrective Action:** Replace the right front brake hose assembly on Ciera and Century models, and both rear brake hoses on Cavalier and Sunbird models.

System: Lighting; lamp or socket; park lights—FMVSS 108. **Vehicle:** Passenger cars. **Description of Noncompliance:** These vehicles were equipped with the wrong bulbs for the front park/turn signal lamps. This does not conform to the requirements of FMVSS 108, "Lamps, reflective devices and associated equipment." **Consequence of Noncompliance:** Reduced lighting on the park/turn signal lights decreases the likelihood of the vehicle operator's intent of being seen by other motorists. **Corrective Action:** General Motors has not submitted a corrective action for this noncompliance. **Note:** The manufacturer has petitioned the NHTSA for a determination that this matter is inconsequential with respect to motor vehicle safety. The manufacturer is not obligated to conduct an owner notification and remedy campaign until NHTSA has resolved the petition.

System: Interior; active restraints; belt anchor and attachment—FMVSS 210. **Vehicle:** Passenger vehicles. **Description of Noncompliance:** These vehicles were assembled with rear outboard safety belt anchorages that may not withstand the required load. This does not comply with FMVSS 210, "Seat belt assembly anchorages." **Consequence of Noncompliance:** In a collision, stress can cause the attachment metal to tear and allow the anchorage to separate from the body of the vehicle. The safety belt may not protect an occupant in the event of a vehicle crash. **Corrective Action:** Dealers will replace the existing anchor bolts with a new shoulder bolt and thread-locking adhesive. Additionally, noise control patches will be applied at each anchorage.

BUICK CENTURY 1994

System: Equipment; speed control. **Vehicle:** Passenger cars with 3.1L engines and cruise control. **Defect:** The cruise control cable may separate from the conduit end fitting while engaged, and accelerator control could be lost. **Consequence:** Loss of accelerator control may not reduce engine speed to a level anticipated by the driver. Although the vehicle can still be stopped with the service brake, loss of accelerator control could result in a vehicle crash without prior warning. **Corrective Action:** Replace the cruise control cable.

System: Fuel; throttle linkages and control return spring—FMVSS 124. **Vehicle:** Passenger cars equipped with 3.1L L82 engines. **Description of Noncompliance:** In the event of a primary accelerator control spring failure, the secondary (backup) accelerator control return spring will not return the throttle to the fully closed position, as required by FMVSS 124, "Accelerator control system." **Consequence of Noncompliance:** Loss of throttle control could result in a vehicle crash without prior warning. **Corrective Action:** Dealers will replace the secondary throttle return spring.

System: Fuel; throttle linkages; accelerator; flexible. **Vehicle:** Passenger vehicles. **Defect:** During assembly, water may have entered the accelerator control cable conduit, causing it to develop a high effort and/or binding condition in very cold weather. **Consequence:** High effort or binding conditions cause loss of normal throttle control, or the throttle may not return to idle when the accelerator pedal is released. If this were to occur while the vehicle is in motion, a vehicle crash could occur. **Corrective Action:** The dealer will purge the throttle cable of any internally trapped water, if it is present.

System: Structure; door assembly; latches and locks. **Vehicle:** Passenger vehicles with power door locks. **Defect:** Water intrusion can cause a short circuit in the power door lock assembly. **Consequence:** A short circuit in the power door lock assembly can result in a vehicle fire. **Corrective Action:** Dealers will replace the power door lock relay and any corroded terminals. In addition, the new relay will be relocated to an area where water intrusion is less likely.

System: Suspension; independent front; spindle; knuckle; steering. **Vehicle:** Passenger cars. **Defect:** The right-hand spindle nut was not properly tightened during assembly. This can cause premature wheel bearing failure and, over time, the spindle can fracture. **Consequence:** This would cause the wheel to separate from the axle and result in a vehicle crash. **Corrective Action:** Dealers will inspect the torque on the right-hand front spindle nut. If the spindle nut is undertorqued, the dealer will replace the right-hand front wheel bearing assembly and the spindle nut will be replaced.

System: Lighting; lamp or socket; park lights—FMVSS 108. **Vehicle:** Passenger cars. **Description of Noncompliance:** These vehicles were equipped with the wrong bulbs for the front park/turn signal lamps. This does not conform to the requirements of FMVSS 108, "Lamps, reflective devices and associated equipment." **Consequence of Noncompliance:** Reduced lighting on the park/turn signal lights decreases the likelihood of the vehicle operator's intent of being seen by other motorists. **Corrective Action:** General Motors has not submitted a corrective action for this noncompliance. **Note:** The manufacturer has petitioned the NHTSA for a determination that this matter is inconsequential with respect to motor vehicle safety. The manufacturer is not obligated to conduct an owner notification and remedy campaign until NHTSA has resolved the petition.

System: Interior; active restraints; belt anchor and attachment—FMVSS 210. **Vehicle:** Passenger vehicles. **Description of Noncompliance:** These vehicles were assembled with rear outboard safety belt anchorages that may not withstand the required load. This does not comply with FMVSS 210, "Seat belt assembly anchorages." **Consequence of Noncompliance:** In a collision, stress can cause the attachment metal to tear and allow the anchorage to separate from the body of the vehicle. The safety belt may not protect an occupant in the event of a vehicle crash. **Corrective Action:** Dealers will replace the existing anchor bolts with a new shoulder bolt and thread-locking adhesive. Additionally, noise control patches will be applied at each anchorage.

BUICK ELECTRA 1987

System: Electrical—in-line fusible link. **Vehicle:** Passenger cars. **Defect:** An in-line fusible link may melt down and cause a fire. **Consequence:** The in-line fusible link located in the area of the plastic windshield washer bottle bracket may, under a high resistance load, melt down and ignite the washer bottle bracket, resulting in an engine compartment fire. **Corrective Action:** The windshield washer bottle bracket will be replaced.

System: Accelerator cable. **Vehicle:** Passenger cars. **Defect:** Excessive accelerator cable friction may restrict the cable's free movement between the accelerator pedal and the throttle body. **Consequence:** This could prevent throttle from returning to closed (idle) position when accelerator pedal is released; thus, engine speed would not decrease, and loss of accelerator control could result in an accident. **Corrective Action:** Replace accelerator cable.

BUICK LESABRE 1987

System: Brakes. **Vehicle:** Passenger cars with antilock brakes. **Defect:** The antilock brake system (ABS) pressure/warning switch may exhibit brake fluid seepage, which eventually can lead to loss of the brake system hydraulic pump motor. Additionally, the hydraulic pump motor and ABS electrical relays may have been exposed to water contamination during vehicle assembly. This condition can cause loss of the hydraulic pump motor and/or loss of the ABS function. **Consequence:** Loss of the hydraulic pump motor would result in a total loss of rear brakes, as well as power assist to the front brakes. The red "brake" warning light would illuminate and stay on. If this warning is not heeded, a loss of rear brakes at a time when minimum stopping distance is required could result in a vehicle crash. An inoperative ABS electrical relay could cause loss of the ABS function, but normal power-assisted braking would be retained. The amber "antilock" warning light would illuminate and stay on. **Corrective Action:** The ABS and hydraulic pump motor electrical relays and 30 amp fuses will be replaced. In addition, the hydraulic pump motor assembly and pressure/warning switch will be inspected and, if required, replaced.

System: Electrical—in-line fusible link. **Vehicle:** Passenger cars. **Defect:** An in-line fusible link may melt down and cause a fire. **Consequence:** The in-line fusible link located in the area of the plastic windshield washer bottle bracket may, under a high resistance load, melt down and ignite the washer bottle bracket, resulting in an engine compartment fire. **Corrective Action:** The windshield washer bottle bracket will be replaced.

System: Brakes. **Vehicle:** Passenger cars equipped with antilock brake system. **Defect:** Low torque of the brake hydraulic unit mounting bolts could cause increased brake pedal travel and/or poor pedal feel if attachment loosens. **Consequence:** This condition could lead to separation of the brake hydraulic unit from its mounting bracket, and result in loss of brake function and an accident. **Corrective Action:** Replace hydraulic unit mounting bolts.

System: Cruise control. **Vehicle:** Passenger vehicles equipped with cruise control and certain gasoline and diesel engines. **Defect:** A small nylon bushing in the cruise control servo bail may slip out of place, causing intermittent and unexpected increases in engine speed or dieseling (engine run-on with ignition off). **Consequence:** Servo rod assembly could catch on engine components and result in a stuck throttle, with potential for a vehicle crash. **Corrective Action:** Install a new bushing in cruise control servo bail.

BUICK LESABRE 1988

System: Rear seat belt instructions—FMVSS 209. **Vehicle:** Passenger cars. **Defect:** Owner's manual did not include instructions on proper usage of rear seat safety belt systems. **Consequence:** Vehicles do not conform to FMVSS 209. **Corrective Action:** Furnish owners with updated owner's manuals that contain the omitted instructions.

System: Brakes. **Vehicle:** Passenger cars equipped with antilock brake system. **Defect:** Low torque of the brake hydraulic unit mounting bolts could cause increased brake pedal travel and/or poor pedal feel if attachment loosens. **Consequence:** This condition could lead to separation of the brake hydraulic unit from its mounting bracket, and result in loss of brake function and an accident. **Corrective Action:** Replace hydraulic unit mounting bolts.

System: Cruise control. **Vehicle:** Passenger vehicles equipped with cruise control and certain gasoline and diesel engines. **Defect:** A small nylon bushing in the cruise control servo bail may slip out of place, causing intermittent and unexpected increases in engine speed or dieseling (engine run-on with ignition off). **Consequence:** Servo rod assembly could catch on engine components and result in a stuck throttle, with potential for a vehicle crash. **Corrective Action:** Install a new bushing in cruise control servo bail.

BUICK LESABRE 1989

System: Fuel rollover valve—FMVSS 301. **Vehicle:** Passenger cars. **Defect:** Fuel rollover valve assembly may not have been installed. **Consequence:** In event of an accident in which vehicle becomes inverted, missing valve could allow fuel spillage in excess of amount allowed by FMVSS 301, which could result in a fire. **Corrective Action:** Replace fuel sender and pump assembly.

System: Structure; frame—FMVSS 301. **Vehicle:** Passenger cars. **Defect:** Welds in the left rear rocker panel area may break loose and cause excessive forward movement of the rear suspension. **Consequence:** This could result in damage to the fuel tanks or lines that could result in a fuel leak during or after a crash, which would result in a fire. This is in violation of FMVSS 301. **Corrective Action:** Install a reinforcement kit.

BUICK LESABRE 1992

System: Brakes—FMVSS 105. **Vehicle:** Passenger cars. **Defect:** When applied, the parking brake lever assembly may release one or more teeth, reducing the cable load to the rear brakes. **Consequence:** Depending on the extent of the lever release and road level, the parking brake may not hold the vehicle, allowing it to roll, which could result in an accident. Vehicle does not comply with FMVSS 105. **Corrective Action:** Replace parking brake lever assembly.

BUICK PARK AVENUE 1991

System: Brakes—FMVSS 105. **Vehicle:** Passenger cars. **Defect:** When applied, the parking brake lever assembly may release one or more teeth, reducing the cable load to the rear brakes. **Consequence:** Depending on the extent of the lever release and road level, the parking brake may not hold the vehicle, allowing it to roll, which could result in an accident. Vehicle does not comply with FMVSS 105. **Corrective Action:** Replace parking brake lever assembly.

BUICK REGAL 1987

System: Transmission. **Vehicle:** Passenger cars and wagons with 200 4R transmissions. **Defect:** Manual valve link in the transmission may have been improperly formed. **Consequence:** The valve link could separate, resulting in a gear selection different from what the driver selects. Also, car could be started with transmission in gear, allowing vehicle to move in an unanticipated direction. **Corrective Action:** Replace the manual valve detent lever link.

System: Cruise control. **Vehicle:** Passenger vehicles equipped with cruise control and certain gasoline and diesel engines. **Defect:** A small nylon bushing in the cruise control servo bail may slip out of place, causing intermittent and unexpected increases in engine speed or dieseling (engine run-on with ignition off). **Consequence:** Servo rod assembly could catch on engine components and result in a stuck throttle, with potential for a vehicle crash. **Corrective Action:** Install a new bushing in cruise control servo bail.

BUICK REGAL 1988

System: Electrical—stoplamp switch. **Vehicle:** Passenger cars. **Defect:** The stoplamp switch may have a loose electrical contact. The loose contact can overheat and melt the surrounding plastic, causing the contact to stick open. **Consequence:** An open contact would render the brake lights inoperative when the brake pedal is depressed. Also, the transmission clutch control and cruise control contacts would remain closed. This condition would result in cruise resuming upon brake pedal release if the cruise control is in the "on" position. Either an unexpected cruise resume or inoperative brake lights could result in a vehicle crash without prior warning. **Corrective Action:** The rotary stoplamp switch will be replaced on all involved vehicles.

System: Transmission—shift linkage. **Vehicle:** Passenger cars. **Defect:** An interference between the transmission shift cable and the bellcrank clip in the steering column can result in disengagement of the transmission cable. **Consequence:** This condition could allow the transmission to be in a gear other than that displayed by the shift indicator. The vehicle could move in an unexpected direction and cause a vehicle crash without prior warning. **Corrective Action:** A newly designed bellcrank clip will be installed.

System: Hood latch. **Vehicle:** Passenger cars. **Defect:** The secondary hood latch may not properly engage. **Consequence:** If primary latch disengages, hood could unexpectedly open. If car was in motion, hood could contact the windshield and reduce the driver's forward vision area, and could result in an accident. **Corrective Action:** Replace secondary latch with a new latch.

System: Steering—suspension. **Vehicle:** Passenger cars. **Defect:** Lower control arm to ball joint attachment can become loose. Also, certain cars could have tie rod ball stud nuts that were not properly torqued and could loosen. **Consequence:** Continued operation of a car with either condition could result in separation of that joint and possible loss of steering control, and could result in an accident. **Corrective Action:** Replace both lower control arms; also, check tie rod ball stud nut torque.

System: Left front brake hose. **Vehicle:** Passenger cars. **Defect:** Twisted components could allow the left front brake hose to contact the fender lining and rail area; over time, the brake hose could wear through. **Consequence:** This could result in a loss of brake fluid and a partial loss of braking capability, which could result in an accident. **Corrective Action:** Inspect left front brake hose for proper installation and replace, as necessary.

System: Seat belt anchorage—FMVSS 210. **Vehicle:** Passenger cars. **Defect:** Front shoulder belt guide loop attachment fastener may pull through door-mounted anchor plate. **Consequence:** Seat belt may not sustain loads required by FMVSS 210, and the seat belt may not properly restrain a passenger in a vehicle accident, resulting in increased risk of injury to an occupant. **Corrective Action:** Replace front shoulder belt guide loop attachment nuts and install new guide cover.

System: Wheels. **Vehicle:** Passenger vehicles equipped with Kelsey Hayes steel wheels; models RPO PB6 14″ and RPO PG1 15″. **Defect:** Cracks develop in the wheel mounting surface. If these cracks become severe enough, the wheel will completely separate from the vehicle. **Consequence:** If wheel separation occurs while the vehicle is in motion, loss of steering and brake control of the vehicle occurs, and a vehicle crash could result without prior warning. **Corrective Action:** Dealers will inspect the manufacturing date codes stamped on each wheel of the vehicle, and if a wheel falls within the specified date code range, the dealer will replace that wheel assembly.

System: Wheels. **Vehicle:** Passenger vehicles equipped with Kelsey Hayes steel wheels; models RPO PB9 14″ and RPO PG1 15″. **Defect:** Cracks develop in the wheel mounting surface. If these cracks become severe enough, the wheel will completely separate from the vehicle. **Consequence:** If wheel separation occurs while the vehicle is in motion, loss of steering and brake control of the vehicle occurs, and a vehicle crash could result without prior warning. **Corrective Action:** Dealers will inspect the manufacturing date codes stamped on each wheel of the vehicle, and if a wheel falls within the specified date code range, the dealer will replace that wheel assembly. **Note:** Vehicles previously inspected that had less than four wheels replaced are to be reinspected.

BUICK REGAL 1989

System: Fuel return pipe assembly. **Vehicle:** Passenger cars. **Defect:** Fuel return lines could fracture and allow fuel to leak in the area of the fuel tank. **Consequence:** In presence of an ignition source, this condition could result in a fire. **Corrective Action:** Install new fuel return pipe assembly.

System: Seat belt anchorage—FMVSS 210. **Vehicle:** Passenger cars. **Defect:** Front shoulder belt guide loop attachment fastener may pull through door-mounted anchor plate. **Consequence:** Seat belt may not sustain loads required by FMVSS 210, and the seat belt may not properly restrain a passenger in a vehicle accident, resulting in increased risk of injury to an occupant. **Corrective Action:** Replace front shoulder belt guide loop attachment nuts and install new guide cover.

System: Brake stoplamp switch. **Vehicle:** Passenger cars. **Defect:** Brake stoplamps may not illuminate or, in some cases, stoplamps will not stay illuminated all the time when brakes are applied due to a faulty stoplamp switch. Also, in vehicles equipped with cruise control, a faulty stoplamp switch can result in resumption of the cruise control function upon release of the brake pedal. **Consequence:** A trailing vehicle may not recognize a braking action in time to respond appropriately. Also, cruise control will reengage upon release of the brake pedal and resume the set speed. In either case, it could result in a crash without prior warning. **Corrective Action:** Install an improved design stoplamp switch.

System: Wheels. **Vehicle:** Passenger vehicles equipped with Kelsey Hayes steel wheels; models RPO PB6 14″ and RPO PG1 15″. **Defect:** Cracks develop in the wheel mounting surface. If these cracks become severe enough, the wheel will completely separate from the vehicle. **Consequence:** If wheel separation occurs while the vehicle is in motion, loss of steering and brake control of the vehicle occurs, and a vehicle crash could result without prior warning. **Corrective Action:** Dealers will inspect the manufacturing date codes stamped on each wheel of the vehicle, and if a wheel falls within the specified date code range, the dealer will replace that wheel assembly.

System: Wheels. **Vehicle:** Passenger vehicles equipped with Kelsey Hayes steel wheels; models RPO PB9 14″ and RPO PG1 15″. **Defect:** Cracks develop in the wheel mounting surface. If these cracks become severe enough, the wheel will completely separate from the vehicle. **Consequence:** If wheel separation occurs while the vehicle is in motion, loss of steering and brake control of the vehicle occurs, and a vehicle crash could result without prior warning. **Corrective Action:** Dealers will inspect the manufacturing date codes stamped on each wheel of the vehicle, and if a wheel falls within the specified date code range, the dealer will replace that wheel assembly. **Note:** Vehicles previously inspected that had less than four wheels replaced are to be reinspected.

BUICK REGAL 1990

System: Seat belt anchorage—FMVSS 210. **Vehicle:** Passenger cars. **Defect:** Front shoulder belt guide loop attachment fastener may pull through door-mounted anchor plate. **Consequence:** Seat belt may not sustain loads required by FMVSS 210, and the seat belt may not properly restrain a passenger in a vehicle accident, resulting in increased risk of injury to an occupant. **Corrective Action:** Replace front shoulder belt guide loop attachment nuts and install new guide cover.

System: Safety belts—FMVSS 208. **Vehicle:** Passenger cars. **Defect:** Owner's manuals did not fully explain how front shoulder belt comfort feature works. **Consequence:** Cars would not comply with FMVSS 208, and incorrect use of safety restraints could lead to personal injury to occupants if an accident should occur. **Corrective Action:** Insert sticker that provides missing information in owner's manuals.

System: Brake stoplamp switch. **Vehicle:** Passenger cars. **Defect:** Brake stoplamps may not illuminate or, in some cases, stoplamps will not stay illuminated all the time when brakes are applied, due to a faulty stoplamp switch. Also, in vehicles equipped with cruise control, a faulty stoplamp switch can result in resumption of the cruise control function upon release of the brake pedal. **Consequence:** A trailing vehicle may not recognize a braking action in time to respond appropriately. Also, cruise control will reengage upon release of the brake pedal and resume the set speed. In either case, it could result in a crash without prior warning. **Corrective Action:** Install an improved design stoplamp switch.

System: Front shoulder safety belt. **Vehicle:** Passenger cars. **Defect:** Front shoulder safety belt webbing may separate at front belt upper guide loops on either side of the front seat. **Consequence:** Webbing separation could occur without prior warning and increase the risk of injury to belted front outboard occupants in a high-energy crash. **Corrective Action:** Install a controlled rotation bracket on driver's- and passenger-side front seat belt guide loops.

System: Wheels. **Vehicle:** Passenger vehicles equipped with Kelsey Hayes steel wheels; models RPO PB6 14″ and RPO PG1 15″. **Defect:** Cracks develop in the wheel mounting surface. If these cracks become severe enough, the wheel will completely separate from the vehicle. **Consequence:** If wheel separation occurs while the vehicle is in motion, loss of steering and brake control of the vehicle occurs, and a vehicle crash could result without prior warning. **Corrective Action:** Dealers will inspect the manufacturing date codes stamped on each wheel of the vehicle, and if a wheel falls within the specified date code range, the dealer will replace that wheel assembly.

System: Wheels. **Vehicle:** Passenger vehicles equipped with Kelsey Hayes steel wheels; models RPO PB9 14″ and RPO PG1 15″. **Defect:** Cracks develop in the wheel mounting surface. If these cracks become severe enough, the wheel will completely separate from the vehicle. **Consequence:** If wheel separation occurs while the vehicle is in motion, loss of steering and brake control of the vehicle occurs, and a vehicle crash could result without prior warning. **Corrective Action:** Dealers will inspect the manufacturing date codes stamped on each wheel of the vehicle, and if a wheel falls within the specified date code range, the dealer will replace that wheel assembly. **Note:** Vehicles previously inspected that had less than four wheels replaced are to be reinspected.

BUICK REGAL 1991

System: Front shoulder safety belt. **Vehicle:** Passenger cars. **Defect:** Front shoulder safety belt webbing may separate at front belt upper guide loops on either side of the front seat. **Consequence:** Webbing separation could occur without prior warning and increase the risk of injury to belted front outboard occupants in a high-energy crash. **Corrective Action:** Install a controlled rotation bracket on driver's- and passenger-side front seat belt guide loops.

System: Safety belts—FMVSS 208. **Vehicle:** Passenger vehicles; 1991 GMC "J" and "W" model cars. **Defect:** The front door shoulder belt guide loops may be cracked and are not in compliance with FMVSS 208. **Consequence:** The seat occupant faces increased risk of injury in the event of a sudden stop or accident. **Corrective Action:** Install reinforcing plates on the cracked shoulder belt guides.

System: Fuel; fuel lines. **Vehicle:** Passenger cars with 3.8L V6 engines. **Defect:** The fuel feed hose can pull out of the crimped coupling at the engine end of the hose assembly, causing fuel leakage. **Consequence:** If the coupling were to separate and an ignition source is present, an engine compartment fire could occur. **Corrective Action:** Install a new fuel feed hose.

BUICK REGAL 1992

System: Transmission and transmission shift indicator. **Vehicle:** 1992 "A" and "W" body passenger cars with 4-speed automatic transmissions. **Defect:** The reverse servo apply pin may bind in the case, which could cause reverse band distress (loss or slipping of reverse), reverse band drag in drive range (poor performance/poor power) or the transmission to remain in reverse while the shift indicator shows neutral gear position. **Consequence:** If the transmission remains in reverse while the shift indicator shows neutral, the vehicle may unexpectedly move rearward, resulting in a vehicle accident. **Corrective Action:** Replace the transaxle where required.

BUICK REGAL 1993

System: Front seat manual recliner mechanisms—FMVSS 207. **Vehicle:** Passenger cars. **Defect:** The driver and passenger front seat manual reclining mechanisms do not comply with the requirements of FMVSS 207, "Seating systems." The seat back mechanisms will not latch under certain conditions. **Consequence:** The seats may recline without prior warning, resulting in a hazard to seat occupants and possible loss of vehicle control. **Corrective Action:** Replace the manual seat recliner mechanism with a mechanism that complies with FMVSS 207.

System: Lighting; lamp; side marker lights—FMVSS 108. **Vehicle:** Passenger vehicles. **Description of Noncompliance:** Incorrect clear front side marker bulbs were installed rather than amber bulbs. This does not conform to the requirements of FMVSS 108, "Lamps, reflective devices and associated equipment." **Consequence of Noncompliance:** During illumination, the bulbs will show clear rather than amber and could momentarily confuse other drivers. **Corrective Action:** Dealers will replace the clear bulbs with the correct amber bulbs.

BUICK RIVIERA 1990

System: Airbag modules. **Vehicle:** Passenger cars equipped with driver's-side supplemental airbag modules. **Defect:** Threaded inflator components may have been damaged during assembly, which may allow components to separate when inflator receives a signal to deploy the airbag. **Consequence:** Inflator component separation allows hot combustion gases to escape into the passenger compartment, which could result in injuries to vehicle occupants. **Corrective Action:** Replace airbag modules containing potentially defective inflators. **Note:** This campaign was initiated by TRW, Inc., manufacturer of the airbag module.

System: Rear seat shoulder safety belt retractor. **Vehicle:** Passenger cars. **Defect:** Misaligned rear seat safety belt shoulder retractor assemblies could cause pendulum interference, causing the belt to remain in locked position or to travel freely without locking. **Consequence:** In the event of a panic stop or accident, if the belt retractor inertia lock does not engage, the rear seat occupant would have an increased likelihood of injury. **Corrective Action:** Realign rear shoulder belt retractor assembly.

System: Transaxle; shift control cable. **Vehicle:** Passenger cars. **Defect:** Transaxle shift control cable may disengage from the floor shift control, with loss of gear indicator reference and shift selector operation. **Consequence:** Driver would not be able to determine actual gear position the transaxle is in, which could result in unexpected vehicle movement and an accident without prior warning. **Corrective Action:** Install a transaxle shift control cable retaining clip to prevent cable disengagement.

System: Control displays—FMVSS 101 and 105. **Vehicle:** Passenger cars. **Defect:** Brake indicator light may not light when ignition is in the "on" position, the parking brake is applied and the shift selector is in the park or neutral gear range. **Consequence:** Vehicles would not meet the requirements of FMVSS 101 and 105. **Corrective Action:** Replace the programmable read-only memory in the body computer module to prevent this condition from occurring.

System: Interior; shoulder belts. **Vehicle:** Passenger vehicles. **Defect:** The front outer shoulder belt web sewn stop can become stuck in the retractor. The belt can be difficult to pull out of the retractor, and some occupants may not be able to fasten the belt. **Consequence:** This condition can prevent a person from using their restraint system, resulting in an increased risk of injury in an accident. **Corrective Action:** Dealer will install a webbing stop button if the customer requests repair.

BUICK ROADMASTER 1992

System: Secondary hood latch. **Vehicle:** Passenger cars. **Defect:** Secondary hood latch assemblies can corrode, causing a high latch release effort and possibly preventing the hood from latching properly when it is closed. **Consequence:** If the secondary hood latch is not properly engaged, and the primary hood latch was also not engaged, the hood could open and contact the windshield while the vehicle was in motion, reducing the forward vision area of the driver and resulting in a possible vehicle accident without prior warning. **Corrective Action:** Install a new secondary hood latch assembly.

System: Active safety belt. **Vehicle:** Passenger cars; General Motors "B" series. **Defect:** The shoulder belt guide loop plastic covering may crack and expose the steel subplate. **Consequence:** In the event of a vehicle crash, the exposed steel subplate can cut the safety belt webbing, resulting in increased possibility and/or severity of injury to the affected seat occupant. **Corrective Action:** Install new shoulder belt guide loops.

BUICK ROADMASTER 1994

System: Engine cooling hoses. **Vehicle:** Passenger vehicles equipped with engine oil coolers and 5.7L or 4.3L engines. **Defect:** The engine oil cooler inlet hose may have been installed too close to the steering gear, causing chafing. The chafing can eventually wear through the hose's protective sleeve, resulting in engine oil leaking onto the engine. **Consequence:** If this occurs, the oil leak onto the engine can result in an engine compartment fire.

System: Wheels; lug nuts; bolts. **Vehicle:** Passenger cars. **Defect:** Paint on the wheel mounting surfaces can act as a shim between the wheel and the rotor and drum. As the vehicle is driven, the wheel imbeds into the paint, loosening the lug nut and causing a loss of clamp load. **Consequence:** Once clamp load is lost, all tire loads are taken by the wheel studs, resulting in a fracture of the wheel studs. This could cause the wheel to separate from the vehicle and could result in a vehicle crash without prior warning. **Corrective Action:** Dealers will clean the wheel mounting surfaces for all four wheels. Also, the wheel studs will be inspected for damage and will be replaced as necessary.

System: Fuel; fuel tank assembly; attachments. **Vehicle:** Passenger vehicles. **Defect:** The fuel tank attachment strap fasteners were not properly tightened. The fasteners can completely detach, eventually allowing the fuel tank to sag and the bottom of the tank to strike the roadway. **Consequence:** This can result in a fuel tank leak and fire if the leaking fuel is exposed to a source of ignition. **Corrective Action:** Dealers will retighten the fuel tank strap fasteners.

System: Fuel; throttle linkages and control; return spring—FMVSS 124. **Vehicle:** Passenger vehicles. **Description of Noncompliance:** These vehicles fail to conform to FMVSS 124, "Accelerator control systems." At low temperatures, excessive friction can occur in the accelerator pedal assembly. **Consequence of Noncompliance:** In the event of a failure of the throttle return spring, if there is excessive friction in the pedal assembly, the engine speed may not return to idle, increasing the potential for a vehicle crash. **Corrective Action:** Dealers will replace the accelerator pedal assembly.

BUICK SKYHAWK 1987

System: Brakes—FMVSS 105. **Vehicle:** Passenger cars. **Defect:** Parking brake lever mechanisms may not properly engage when applied as required by FMVSS 105. **Consequence:** Vehicle could unexpectedly roll away uncontrolled, which could result in a vehicle crash. **Corrective Action:** Replace parking brake lever assembly.

System: Fuel. **Vehicle:** Vehicles built with 2.0L engines. **Defect:** The fuel feed and/or return hose and pipe assemblies could crack or separate, allowing fuel to leak into the underhood area. **Consequence:** This could result in an underhood fire without prior warning, and cause injury to occupants. **Corrective Action:** Replace both fuel feed and return hose and pipe assemblies.

BUICK SKYLARK 1987

System: Fuel/hose. **Vehicle:** Passenger cars. **Defect:** The fuel feed or fuel return hose at the engine may rub against a shift lever on the 5-speed transaxle. **Consequence:** In time, a hole could be rubbed through the hose and fuel could leak into the engine compartment. This could result in an underhood fire. **Corrective Action:** Replace the fuel feed and return hose and pipe assemblies.

BUICK SKYLARK 1988

System: Headlight switch panel. **Vehicle:** Passenger cars with electronic digital instrument cluster. **Defect:** Unexpected loss of tail lamp and side marker lamp function may occur, reducing other drivers' ability to see the vehicle. **Consequence:** This could lead to a vehicle crash without prior warning in conditions of poor visibility, severe weather or nighttime. **Corrective Action:** Replace headlight switch panel.

System: Front fuel feed hose. **Vehicle:** Passenger cars equipped with quad 4 engines. **Defect:** Front fuel feed hose assembly could crack or separate at the coupling on the engine end of the hose assembly, allowing fuel to leak into the engine compartment. **Consequence:** Leaking fuel in the engine compartment could result in a fire. **Corrective Action:** Replace front fuel feed hose assembly.

System: Fuel hose. **Vehicle:** Passenger cars equipped with quad 4 engines. **Defect:** Front fuel feed hose assembly could crack or separate at the coupling on the engine end of the hose assembly, allowing fuel to leak into the engine compartment. **Consequence:** Fuel leaking in the engine compartment could result in an underhood fire. **Corrective Action:** Replace front fuel feed hose assembly.

BUICK SKYLARK 1989

System: Front fuel feed hose. **Vehicle:** Passenger cars equipped with quad 4 engines. **Defect:** Front fuel feed hose assembly could crack or separate at the coupling on the engine end of the hose assembly, allowing fuel to leak into the engine compartment. **Consequence:** Leaking fuel in the engine compartment could result in a fire. **Corrective Action:** Replace front fuel feed hose assembly.

System: Fuel hose. **Vehicle:** Passenger cars equipped with quad 4 engines. **Defect:** Front fuel feed hose assembly could crack or separate at the coupling on the engine end of the hose assembly, allowing fuel to leak into the engine compartment. **Consequence:** Fuel leaking in the engine compartment could result in an underhood fire. **Corrective Action:** Replace front fuel feed hose assembly.

BUICK SKYLARK 1990

System: Front fuel feed and return hoses. **Vehicle:** Passenger cars. **Defect:** Improperly torqued connections of front fuel feed and return hoses to fuel pipes at the body rail could loosen and leak fuel into the underhood area. **Consequence:** Fuel leaks in the presence of an ignition source could result in an underhood fire. **Corrective Action:** Properly torque the front fuel feed and return hoses at the body rail lines to prevent fuel leakage.

BUICK SKYLARK 1991

System: Visual systems. **Vehicle:** Passenger cars equipped with power windows. **Defect:** Moisture can enter the express-down electronic control module and cause a short circuit that causes window operation without operator control and leaves the window in the down position. **Consequence:** The electronic control module will fail from overheating and could result in a fire hazard inside the door panel. **Corrective Action:** Replace the window express-down electronic control module.

BUICK SKYLARK 1992

System: Interior systems: seat back. **Vehicle:** Passenger cars; "N" coupe models. **Defect:** The passenger-side easy-entry seat adjuster may fail—fully lock into position after the seat back has been tilted forward and the seat slid forward and then returned to its original position. **Consequence:** If the seat adjuster fails to lock into position, the passenger seat would slide forward in the event of a sudden stop or accident. Occupants of the passenger seat would face increased risk of serious injury. **Corrective Action:** Replace the adjuster assembly on the seat. **Note:** General Motors has informed this agency that all repairs will be made before the vehicle is offered for sale.

System: Steering column. **Vehicle:** Passenger cars with column shift. **Defect:** A misadjustment of the park lock cable in the column shift assembly makes it possible for the steering column to lock while the vehicle is in motion and the ignition switch is in the "off" position. **Consequence:** Locking of the steering column while the vehicle is in motion results in loss of control and increased risk of a vehicle crash. **Corrective Action:** Adjust the park lock cable, and reroute and restrain the brake transmission shift interlock harness and connector. **Note:** General Motors informed this agency that all repairs will be made before vehicles are offered for sale.

System: Fuel—FMVSS 301. **Vehicle:** Passenger cars. **Defect:** The vehicles were assembled with an incorrect suspension upper spring seat at the right-rear position. If the vehicle is involved in a rear-impact accident, the right-hand rear wheel house flange could sever the fuel tank filler pipe and spill fuel. **Consequence:** These vehicles are not in compliance with FMVSS 301, "Fuel system integrity." Spilled fuel in a low-speed accident can result in a fire. **Corrective Action:** Inspect and replace incorrect upper spring seat with the correct part.

System: Transmission—FMVSS 102. **Vehicle:** Passenger cars with an electronic PRNDL—(gear) indicator. **Defect:** Rotating the lock cylinder and ignition switch from "run" to the "off" position with the transmission shift lever in any position other than park will shut off the illuminated PRNDL indicator. This does not comply with FMVSS 102, "Transmission shift lever sequence." **Consequence:** A non-illuminated PRNDL indicator left in any gear other than park would not clearly show the engaged transmission gear and could result in unexpected vehicle motion. **Corrective Action:** See note. **Note:** The manufacturer's petition which requested that NHTSA determine that this FMVSS noncompliance does not create an unreasonable risk to motor vehicle safety has been granted. Therefore, the manufacturer is not obligated to conduct an owner notification and remedy campaign.

CADILLAC

Note: If your Cadillac is presented to an authorized dealer on an agreed-upon service date and the remedy is not provided free of charge within a reasonable time, or the remedy does not correct the defect, please contact Cadillac at (800) 458-8006. Also contact the NHTSA's Auto Safety Hotline at (800) 424-9393.

CADILLAC DEVILLE 1987

System: Brakes. **Vehicle:** Passenger cars with antilock brakes. **Defect:** The antilock brake system (ABS) pressure/warning switch may exhibit brake fluid seepage, which eventually can lead to loss of the brake system hydraulic pump motor. Additionally, the hydraulic pump motor and ABS electrical relays may have been exposed to water contamination during vehicle assembly. This condition can cause loss of the hydraulic pump motor and/or loss of the ABS function. **Consequence:** Loss of the hydraulic pump motor would result in a total loss of rear brakes, as well as power assist to the front brakes. The red "brake" warning light would illuminate and stay on. If this warning is not heeded, a loss of rear brakes at a time when minimum stopping distance is required could result in a vehicle crash. An inoperative ABS electrical relay could cause loss of the ABS function, but normal power-assisted braking would be retained. The amber "antilock" warning light would illuminate and stay on. **Corrective Action:** The ABS and hydraulic pump motor electrical relays and 30 amp fuses will be replaced. In addition, the hydraulic pump motor assembly and pressure/warning switch will be inspected and, if required, replaced.

CADILLAC DEVILLE 1990

System: Airbag modules. **Vehicle:** Passenger cars equipped with driver's-side supplemental airbag modules. **Defect:** Threaded inflator components may have been damaged during assembly, which may allow components to separate when inflator receives a signal to deploy the airbag. **Consequence:** Inflator component separation allows hot combustion gases to escape into the passenger compartment, which could result in injuries to vehicle occupants. **Corrective Action:** Replace airbag modules containing potentially defective inflators. **Note:** This campaign was initiated by TRW, Inc., manufacturer of the airbag module.

CADILLAC DEVILLE 1991

System: Power train; axle assembly. **Vehicle:** Passenger vehicles. **Defect:** The upper transaxle oil cooler hose can pull out of the crimped coupling at the transaxle end of the line assembly. **Consequence:** In the event of separation of the coupling, an oil leak can occur which, when exposed to an ignition source, could result in an engine compartment fire. **Corrective Action:** Dealers will install a new upper transaxle oil cooler line to the transaxle.

CADILLAC DEVILLE 1992

System: Power train; axle assembly. **Vehicle:** Passenger vehicles. **Defect:** The upper transaxle oil cooler hose can pull out of the crimped coupling at the transaxle end of the line assembly. **Consequence:** In the event of separation of the coupling, an oil leak can occur which, when exposed to an ignition source, could result in an engine compartment fire. **Corrective Action:** Dealers will install a new upper transaxle oil cooler line to the transaxle.

CADILLAC DEVILLE 1993

System: Power train; axle assembly. **Vehicle:** Passenger vehicles. **Defect:** The upper transaxle oil cooler hose can pull out of the crimped coupling at the transaxle end of the line assembly. **Consequence:** In the event of separation of the coupling, an oil leak can occur which, when exposed to an ignition source, could result in an engine compartment fire. **Corrective Action:** Dealers will install a new upper transaxle oil cooler line to the transaxle.

CADILLAC DEVILLE 1994

System: Lighting; high-mounted stoplamp assembly—FMVSS 108. **Vehicle:** Passenger vehicles. **Description of Noncompliance:** Because of the interference from "blackout" paint designed to "frame" the center high-mounted stoplamp in the vehicle's rear window, these vehicles do not meet the photometric requirements of FMVSS 108, "Lamps, reflective devices and associated equipment." **Consequence of Noncompliance:** This can result in decreased notice to following drivers of the vehicle's braking activities. **Corrective Action:** General Motors has not submitted a corrective action for this noncompliance. **Note:** The manufacturer has petitioned NHTSA for a determination that this matter is inconsequential with respect to motor vehicle safety. The manufacturer is not obligated to conduct an owner notification and remedy campaign until NHTSA has resolved that the matter is consequential.

CADILLAC ELDORADO 1989

System: Antilock brake mounting bolts. **Vehicle:** Passenger cars equipped with antilock brakes (ABS). **Defect:** One or both ABS hydraulic unit mounting bolts may not be properly seated and could loosen. **Consequence:** This condition could lead to separation of the ABS hydraulic unit from the mounting bracket, and result in loss of brake function and a crash without prior warning. **Corrective Action:** Replace both ABS hydraulic unit mounting bolts.

CADILLAC ELDORADO 1990

System: Airbag modules. **Vehicle:** Passenger cars equipped with driver's-side supplemental airbag modules. **Defect:** Threaded inflator components may have been damaged during assembly, which may allow components to separate when inflator receives a signal to deploy the airbag. **Consequence:** Inflator component separation allows hot combustion gases to escape into the passenger compartment, which could result in injuries to vehicle occupants. **Corrective Action:** Replace airbag modules containing potentially defective inflators. **Note:** This campaign was initiated by TRW, Inc., manufacturer of the airbag module.

System: Rear seat shoulder safety belt retractor. **Vehicle:** Passenger cars. **Defect:** Misaligned rear seat safety belt shoulder retractor assemblies could cause pendulum interference, causing the belt to remain in locked position or to travel freely without locking. **Consequence:** In the event of a panic stop or accident, if the belt retractor inertia lock does not engage, the rear seat occupant would have an increased likelihood of injury. **Corrective Action:** Realign rear shoulder belt retractor assembly.

System: Transaxle; shift control cable. **Vehicle:** Passenger cars. **Defect:** Transaxle shift control cable may disengage from the floor shift control with loss of gear indicator reference and shift selector operation. **Consequence:** Driver would not be able to determine actual gear position the transaxle is in, which could result in unexpected vehicle movement and an accident without prior warning. **Corrective Action:** Install a transaxle shift control cable retaining clip to prevent cable disengagement.

System: Interior; shoulder belts. **Vehicle:** Passenger vehicles. **Defect:** The front outer shoulder belt web sewn stop can become stuck in the retractor. The belt can be difficult to pull out of the retractor and some occupants may not be able to fasten the belt. **Consequence:** This condition can prevent a person from using their restraint system, resulting in an increased risk of injury in an accident. **Corrective Action:** Dealer will install a webbing stop button if the customer requests repair.

CADILLAC ELDORADO 1992

System: Steering. **Vehicle:** Passenger cars. **Defect:** The intermediate shaft to steering rack lower coupling pinch bolt may be missing. **Consequence:** If this condition exists and shaft disengagement occurs, loss of steering control will be experienced by the driver, which could result in an accident. **Corrective Action:** Install pinch bolt. **Note:** General Motors has identified this as a predelivery recall campaign. All vehicles will be corrected before they are sold.

CADILLAC FLEETWOOD 1989

System: Stoplamp—FMVSS 108. **Vehicle:** Coach limousines. **Defect:** Center high-mounted stoplamp may be obstructed or absent. **Consequence:** The obstruction or lack of a center high-mounted stoplamp would increase the hazard of a rear-end collision, and the vehicle would not comply with FMVSS 108. **Corrective Action:** Remove obstructing window tinting or install high center stoplamp when missing.

System: Safety belts—FMVSS 208. **Vehicle:** Coach limousines. **Defect:** Safety belts may not have been installed for rear-facing seats. **Consequence:** Occupants of these seats would be subject to increased injury in the event of a sudden stop or accident, and vehicles do not comply with FMVSS 208. **Corrective Action:** Install additional safety belts.

System: Compliance label; part 567. **Vehicle:** Coach limousines. **Defect:** Vehicle alterers' label may be missing or incomplete. **Consequence:** Vehicles do not comply with part 567. **Corrective Action:** Add compliance label.

System: Tire placard—FMVSS 110. **Vehicle:** Limousine conversions. **Defect:** Tire placard listing recommended tire pressures can be absent or can contain incorrect information. **Consequence:** Use of incorrect tire pressures could cause increased tire wear, which could result in difficulty in vehicle handling or steering. **Corrective Action:** Install label with correct tire information.

System: Alterers' placard; 49 CFR, part 567. **Vehicle:** Limousine conversions. **Defect:** Alterers' label stating that vehicle complies with standards, including weight of vehicle, may be absent or incomplete. **Consequence:** Owner would not be aware of correct weight rating and tire size as required by 49 CFR, part 567. **Corrective Action:** Install correct alterers' placard.

CADILLAC FLEETWOOD 1990

System: Tire placard—FMVSS 110. **Vehicle:** Limousine conversions. **Defect:** Tire placard listing recommended tire pressures can be absent or can contain incorrect information. **Consequence:** Use of incorrect tire pressures could cause increased tire wear, which could result in difficulty in vehicle handling or steering. **Corrective Action:** Install label with correct tire information.

System: Alterers' placard; 49 CFR part 567. **Vehicle:** Limousine conversions. **Defect:** Alterers' label stating that vehicle complies with standards, including weight of vehicle, may be absent or incomplete. **Consequence:** Owner would not be aware of correct weight rating and tire size as required by 49 CFR, part 567. **Corrective Action:** Install correct alterer's placard.

CADILLAC SEVILLE 1989

System: Antilock brake mounting bolts. **Vehicle:** Passenger cars equipped with antilock brakes (ABS). **Defect:** One or both ABS hydraulic unit mounting bolts may not be properly seated and could loosen. **Consequence:** This condition could lead to separation of the ABS hydraulic unit from the mounting bracket, and result in loss of brake function and a crash without prior warning. **Corrective Action:** Replace both ABS hydraulic unit mounting bolts.

CADILLAC SEVILLE 1990

System: Airbag modules. **Vehicle:** Passenger cars equipped with driver's-side supplemental airbag modules. **Defect:** Threaded inflator components may have been damaged during assembly, which may allow components to separate when inflator receives a signal to deploy the airbag. **Consequence:** Inflator component separation allows hot combustion gases to escape into the passenger compartment, which could result in injuries to vehicle occupants. **Corrective Action:** Replace airbag modules containing potentially defective inflators. **Note:** This campaign was initiated by TRW, Inc., manufacturer of the airbag module.

System: Rear seat shoulder safety belt retractor. **Vehicle:** Passenger cars. **Defect:** Misaligned rear seat safety belt shoulder retractor assemblies could cause pendulum interference, causing the belt to remain in locked position or to travel freely without locking. **Consequence:** In the event of a panic stop or accident, if the belt retractor inertia lock does not engage, the rear seat occupant would have an increased likelihood of injury. **Corrective Action:** Realign rear shoulder belt retractor assembly.

System: Transaxle; shift control cable. **Vehicle:** Passenger cars. **Defect:** Transaxle shift control cable may disengage from the floor shift control, with loss of gear indicator reference and shift selector operation. **Consequence:** Driver would not be able to determine actual gear position the transaxle is in, which could result in unexpected vehicle movement and an accident without prior warning. **Corrective Action:** Install a transaxle shift control cable retaining clip to prevent cable disengagement.

CADILLAC SEVILLE 1993

System: Fuel; fuel lines. **Vehicle:** Passenger cars with 4.6L engines. **Defect:** The fuel feed and return lines to the engine fuel injection system were not fully assembled and locked. The lines can work loose, causing a fuel leak in the engine compartment. **Consequence:** Fuel leaks in the engine compartment can result in underhood fires if exposed to a source of ignition. **Corrective Action:** Dealer will inspect vehicle and, if necessary, adjust or replace the fuel feed and return lines to the engine fuel injection system.

System: Air conditioner; compressor. **Vehicle:** Passenger vehicles with 4.6L engines. **Defect:** If the air conditioner compressor clutch assembly contacts the auxiliary engine oil cooler outlet hose, the hose may wear through, allowing engine oil to leak into the engine compartment. **Consequence:** An oil leak that contacts the hot exhaust system can result in an engine compartment fire. **Corrective Action:** Dealers will install a tie strap to retain the auxiliary engine oil cooler outlet hose to the auxiliary engine oil cooler inlet hose at the bottom of the radiator, ensuring adequate clearance of the affected hose from the air conditioner compressor clutch assembly.

CHEVROLET

Note: If your Chevrolet is presented to an authorized dealer on an agreed-upon service date and the remedy is not provided within a reasonable amount of time, or the remedy does not correct the noncompliance, please contact Chevrolet at (800) 222-1020 or Pontiac at (800) 762-2737. Also contact the NHTSA's Auto Safety Hotline at (800) 424-9393.

CHEVROLET BERETTA 1988

System: Hood latch—secondary. **Vehicle:** Passenger cars. **Defect:** Secondary hood latch assembly may not have been properly adjusted, resulting in latch becoming bent. **Consequence:** A bent secondary hood latch could cause the primary latch to malfunction. If this occurred, the hood could unexpectedly open. If this happened while vehicle is in motion, reduction of forward visibility could cause a vehicle crash without prior warning. **Corrective Action:** Inspect and replace secondary hood latch assemblies as required.

System: Door hinges. **Vehicle:** Passenger cars. **Defect:** A door hinge (upper or lower) may break while opening or closing the door, making it difficult to reposition and close properly. **Consequence:** Hinge separation may reduce the structural integrity of the side of the car and increase risk of injury in certain types of accidents. **Corrective Action:** Replace door hinges on both doors.

System: Hood. **Vehicle:** Passenger vehicles. **Defect:** Secondary hood latch assembly on these vehicles may not be properly adjusted and could become bent. This will lead to a condition where full primary latch engagement is not attained. **Consequence:** A bent secondary hood latch could lead to the primary latch not being fully engaged, allowing the hood to unexpectedly open. If this were to occur while the vehicle was in motion, the hood may contact the windshield, reducing the forward vision area of the driver, and a vehicle crash could occur without prior warning. **Corrective Action:** Replace the primary hood latch assembly, the secondary hood latch assembly and the support bracket.

System: Safety belts (passive restraint). **Vehicle:** Passenger cars equipped with door-mounted shoulder and lap safety belt systems. **Defect:** The front shoulder belt retractors may have reduced sensitivity of the lockup feature and would not function in a sudden deceleration or crash. **Consequence:** Failure of the shoulder belt retractor would result in the seat occupant only being restrained by the lap belt in a crash or sudden stop, and an increased possibility of injury. **Corrective Action:** Replace the front shoulder belt retractors and assemblies.

CHEVROLET BERETTA 1989

System: Fuel tank. **Vehicle:** Passenger cars with 2.0L or 2.8L engines. **Defect:** A fuel tank leak could occur due to small creases on the tank underside cracking during pressure cycling that occurs during normal operation. **Consequence:** In presence of an ignition source, this condition could result in a fire. **Corrective Action:** Replace fuel tank.

System: Front seat belt latch—FMVSS 209. **Vehicle:** Passenger cars. **Defect:** Front seat belt latchplates may not engage the buckle assemblies. **Consequence:** In event of an accident, unbelted or improperly belted occupants are more at risk of injury than if belts are properly buckled. **Corrective Action:** Replace improperly functioning buckle assemblies.

System: Front seat frame. **Vehicle:** Passenger cars. **Defect:** The front seat frame assembly may contain an improper, missing and/or mislocated weld that could fracture. **Consequence:** This could cause unexpected seat movement and result in personal injury and/or loss of control of the car. **Corrective Action:** Replace both front seat assemblies.

System: Safety belts (passive restraint). **Vehicle:** Passenger cars equipped with door-mounted shoulder and lap safety belt systems. **Defect:** The front shoulder belt retractors may have reduced sensitivity of the lockup feature and would not function in a sudden deceleration or crash. **Consequence:** Failure of the shoulder belt retractor would result in the seat occupant only being restrained by the lap belt in a crash or sudden stop, and an increased possibility of injury. **Corrective Action:** Replace the front shoulder belt retractors and assemblies.

CHEVROLET BERETTA 1990

System: Seat belt assemblies—FMVSS 209. **Vehicle:** Passenger cars. **Defect:** Owner's manuals were printed with rear center seat belt information omitted. **Consequence:** This would not comply with FMVSS 209. **Corrective Action:** Insert missing information into owner's manual.

System: Safety belts (passive restraint). **Vehicle:** Passenger cars equipped with door-mounted shoulder and lap safety belt systems. **Defect:** The front shoulder belt retractors may have reduced sensitivity of the lockup feature and would not function in a sudden deceleration or crash. **Consequence:** Failure of the shoulder belt retractor would result in the seat occupant only being restrained by the lap belt in a crash or sudden stop, and an increased possibility of injury. **Corrective Action:** Replace the front shoulder belt retractors and assemblies.

CHEVROLET BERETTA 1991

System: Steering wheel nut. **Vehicle:** Passenger cars. **Defect:** Nut attaching steering wheel may not have been properly tightened during installation. **Consequence:** This could allow steering wheel to separate from steering column; loss of vehicle control and a crash could occur without prior warning. **Corrective Action:** Tighten the nut to the proper torque as necessary.

CHEVROLET BERETTA 1992

System: Lighting; stoplamps. **Vehicle:** Passenger cars. **Defect:** The service brake stoplamp switch becomes inoperative. **Consequence:** The inoperative stoplamp switch will not illuminate the stoplamps when the brake pedal is depressed. This would not adequately inform other drivers of the vehicle operator's intent to stop or slow down. **Corrective Action:** Replace the stoplamp switch and correct the wiring in the connector of the stoplamp switch wiring harness. **Note:** If the failure occurs during three consecutive service brake applications, the amber "antilock" brake system (ABS) telltale lamp may illuminate, indicating a problem with the system.

CHEVROLET CAMARO 1987

System: Seat belt buckle. **Vehicle:** Passenger cars. **Defect:** Plastic components of seat belt buckle assemblies do not contain an ultraviolet stabilizer, and exposure to direct sunlight and elevated interior temperatures could weaken the plastic components. **Consequence:** This could result in breakage of plastic components, which could prevent buckle from latching and protecting occupant in a sudden stop or accident. **Corrective Action:** Replace or repair seat belt buckle.

CHEVROLET CAMARO 1988

System: Seat belt buckle. **Vehicle:** Passenger cars. **Defect:** Plastic components of seat belt buckle assemblies do not contain an ultraviolet stabilizer, and exposure to direct sunlight and elevated interior temperatures could weaken the plastic components. **Consequence:** This could result in breakage of plastic components, which could prevent buckle from latching and protecting occupant in a sudden stop or accident. **Corrective Action:** Replace or repair seat belt buckle.

System: Fuel feed hoses. **Vehicle:** Passenger cars with 2.8L V6 engines. **Defect:** Fuel feed hoses may pull out of the crimped coupling at the engine end of the hose assembly. **Consequence:** If this coupling separated, allowing gasoline to leak, and an ignition source is present, an engine compartment fire could occur. **Corrective Action:** Install a redesigned fuel feed hose.

CHEVROLET CAMARO 1989

System: Rear inboard seat belt. **Vehicle:** Convertible passenger cars. **Defect:** Webbing on the buckle portion of the rear lap and shoulder belts may be too long. **Consequence:** In the event of a severe vehicle crash, the effectiveness of the lap and shoulder belt may be reduced. **Corrective Action:** Replace rear inboard seat belts with belts of the proper length.

System: Seat belt buckle. **Vehicle:** Passenger cars. **Defect:** Plastic components of seat belt buckle assemblies do not contain an ultraviolet stabilizer, and exposure to direct sunlight and elevated interior temperatures could weaken the plastic components. **Consequence:** This could result in breakage of plastic components, which could prevent buckle from latching and protecting occupant in a sudden stop or accident. **Corrective Action:** Replace or repair seat belt buckle.

System: Fuel feed hoses. **Vehicle:** Passenger cars with 2.8L V6 engines. **Defect:** Fuel feed hoses may pull out of the crimped coupling at the engine end of the hose assembly. **Consequence:** If this coupling separated, allowing gasoline to leak, and an ignition source is present, an engine compartment fire could occur. **Corrective Action:** Install a redesigned fuel feed hose.

CHEVROLET CAMARO 1990

System: Seat belt buckle. **Vehicle:** Passenger cars. **Defect:** Plastic components of seat belt buckle assemblies do not contain an ultraviolet stabilizer, and exposure to direct sunlight and elevated interior temperatures could weaken the plastic components. **Consequence:** This could result in breakage of plastic components, which could prevent buckle from latching and protecting occupant in a sudden stop or accident. **Corrective Action:** Replace or repair seat belt buckle.

System: Fuel return hoses. **Vehicle:** Passenger cars equipped with 5.0L and 5.7L V8 engines. **Defect:** Fuel return hoses may break at either crimped coupling. **Consequence:** If this coupling separated, allowing gasoline to leak, and an ignition source was present, an engine compartment fire could occur. **Corrective Action:** Install a properly crimped fuel return hose.

CHEVROLET CAMARO 1991

System: Windshield mounting—FMVSS 212. **Vehicle:** Passenger cars. **Defect:** Poor bond adhesion between the windshield glass and the mounting, which could allow the windshield to separate from the vehicle during a collision. This fails to conform with FMVSS 212. **Consequence:** If windshield separation occurs in a collision, an unbelted occupant could be ejected from the vehicle, and personal injury could occur. **Corrective Action:** Remove all sealer from windshield and mounting; apply new bonding and sealant material, and reinstall windshield.

System: Safety belt assembly—FMVSS 209. **Vehicle:** Passenger cars; coupes and convertibles. **Defect:** The metal latchplates may not engage the buckle assemblies, causing a "no latch" condition. Movement of the seat occupant in this condition could cause latchplate to release from the buckle. **Consequence:** Unbelted or incorrectly belted seat occupants are subjected to increased risk of injury in the event of sudden stop or accident. **Corrective Action:** Replace the retractor assembly for the safety belt (front and rear in coupes, and front only in convertibles).

System: Front bucket seat latch—FMVSS 207. **Vehicle:** Passenger cars. **Defect:** The front seat upper hinge cover screws are too long, and interfere with the seat back inertia lock. This prevents the seat back from locking properly. **Consequence:** In the event of a sudden stop or vehicle impact, an unlocked seat back would increase the risk of injury to the seat occupant. **Corrective Action:** Replace screws securing upper hinge trim cover with correct-length screws.

System: Fuel; fuel tank assembly; pipe; filler; neck—FMVSS 301. **Vehicle:** Passenger vehicles. **Description of Noncompliance:** The fuel filler neck solder joint can develop cracks or pinhole leaks, which does not comply with FMVSS 301, "Fuel system integrity." The cracks and holes can allow fuel vapor and fuel leakage. **Consequence of Noncompliance:** Gasoline vapor and fuel leaks can result in a fire if exposed to a source of ignition. **Corrective Action:** Dealers will inspect the fuel tank assembly and replace those which exhibit the cracks or pinhole leaks.

CHEVROLET CAMARO 1992

System: Transmission. **Vehicle:** Passenger cars with automatic transmissions. **Defect:** The automatic transmission shift control cable can separate. **Consequence:** Separation of the transmission shift cable can prevent the transmission from being shifted into the proper position. This condition can cause unexpected vehicle movement when the transmission indicator is in park or neutral position and the transmission is in a drive mode; this could result in a vehicle crash without prior warning. **Corrective Action:** The dealer will replace the shift cable.

System: Fuel; fuel tank assembly; pipe; filler; neck—FMVSS 301. **Vehicle:** Passenger vehicles. **Description of Noncompliance:** The fuel filler neck solder joint can develop cracks or pinhole leaks, which does not comply with FMVSS 301, "Fuel system integrity." The cracks and holes can allow fuel vapor and fuel leakage. **Consequence of Noncompliance:** Gasoline vapor and fuel leaks can result in a fire if exposed to a source of ignition. **Corrective Action:** Dealers will inspect the fuel tank assembly and replace those which exhibit the cracks or pinhole leaks.

CHEVROLET CAMARO 1993

System: VIN plate—FMVSS 115. **Vehicle:** Passenger cars. **Defect:** The VIN plate character height is 3.55mm, instead of the 4mm minimum height established in FMVSS 115. This does not comply with FMVSS 115, "Vehicle Identification Numbers (VIN)." **Consequence:** VIN plate characters are too small to be readily discernible. **Corrective Action:** See note. **Note:** The manufacturer's petition which requested that NHTSA determine that this FMVSS noncompliance does not create an unreasonable risk to motor vehicle safety has been granted. Therefore, the manufacturer is not obligated to conduct an owner notification and remedy campaign.

CHEVROLET CAMARO 1994

System: Fuel; fuel lines; hoses; nonmetallic. **Vehicle:** Passenger cars with 5.7L V8 engines. **Defect:** The fuel lines on these vehicles may have been misrouted and may contact the "air" check valve. The high temperatures from the air check valve could allow it to melt through and damage a fuel line. **Consequence:** A fuel line that has been damaged by the heat of the air check valve may leak fuel into the engine compartment, where it could result in a fire if exposed to a source of ignition. **Corrective Action:** Reroute any misrouted fuel lines to the proper position, and replace any fuel line bundle where the outer shell has been melted through.

CHEVROLET CAPRICE 1987

System: Transmission **Vehicle:** Passenger cars and wagons with 200 4R transmissions. **Defect:** Manual valve link in the transmission may have been improperly formed. **Consequence:** The valve link could separate, resulting in a gear selection different from what the driver selects. Also car could be started with transmission in gear, allowing vehicle to move in an unanticipated direction. **Corrective Action:** Replace the manual valve detent lever link.

System: Cruise control. **Vehicle:** Passenger vehicles equipped with cruise control and certain gasoline and diesel engines. **Defect:** A small nylon bushing in the cruise control servo bail may slip out of place, causing intermittent and unexpected increases in engine speed or dieseling (engine run-on with ignition off). **Consequence:** Servo rod assembly could catch on engine components and result in a stuck throttle, with potential for a vehicle crash. **Corrective Action:** Install a new bushing in cruise control servo bail.

CHEVROLET CAPRICE 1988

System: Cruise control. **Vehicle:** Passenger vehicles equipped with cruise control and certain gasoline and diesel engines. **Defect:** A small nylon bushing in the cruise control servo bail may slip out of place, causing intermittent and unexpected increases in engine speed or dieseling (engine run-on with ignition off). **Consequence:** Servo rod assembly could catch on engine components and result in a stuck throttle, with potential for a vehicle crash. **Corrective Action:** Install a new bushing in cruise control servo bail.

CHEVROLET CAPRICE 1990

System: Plastic fuel filter. **Vehicle:** Police and taxi model passenger cars. **Defect:** Plastic fuel filter assemblies may develop leaks. **Consequence:** Fuel leaks could result in a vehicle fire due to static charge buildups found in the plastic fuel lines and fuel filter, which may act as an ignition source. **Corrective Action:** Replace plastic assembly with metal fuel filter and bracket.

CHEVROLET CAPRICE 1991

System: Secondary hood latch. **Vehicle:** Passenger cars. **Defect:** Secondary hood latch assemblies can corrode, causing a high latch release effort and possibly preventing the hood from latching properly when it is closed. **Consequence:** If the secondary hood latch is not properly engaged, and the primary hood latch was also not engaged, the hood could open and contact the windshield while the vehicle was in motion, reducing the forward vision area of the driver, and resulting in a possible vehicle accident without prior warning. **Corrective Action:** Install a new secondary hood latch assembly.

System: Wheels. **Vehicle:** Police cars equipped with special police package, which includes 15″×7″ steel wheels with wheel code RDL. **Defect:** The steel wheels exhibit fatigue cracking around the circumference of the wheel lug nut mounting surface due to wheel bending caused by frequent misuse of tire mounting equipment, lug nut overtorquing, and the unusual operating conditions experienced by police vehicles. **Consequence:** The cracking can cause wheel fracturing and subsequent separation from the axle, which could result in a vehicle accident. **Corrective Action:** Replace the defective wheels with redesigned steel wheels.

System: Active safety belt. **Vehicle:** Passenger cars; General Motors "B" series. **Defect:** The shoulder belt guide loop plastic covering may crack and expose the steel subplate. **Consequence:** In the event of a vehicle crash, the exposed steel subplate can cut the safety belt webbing, resulting in increased possibility and/or severity of injury to the affected seat occupant. **Corrective Action:** Install new shoulder belt guide loops.

System: Electrical. **Vehicle:** SEQ 9C1 police cars in corrosion areas of the United States and Canada only. **Defect:** An electrical groundout condition may exist between the 12 volt junction block and the metal inner fender skirt. **Consequence:** This condition can cause a melted junction block, smoke and burned underhood wiring, resulting in a disabled vehicle or a vehicle fire. This condition can occur while the vehicle is in operation or while the vehicle is parked and the ignition is in the "off" position. **Corrective Action:** Install a shielding insulator under the junction block. **Note:** The states GM considers part of the corrosion area are: CT, IL, IN, ME, MA, MI, NH, NJ, NY, OH, PA, RI, VT and WI.

CHEVROLET CAPRICE 1992

System: Secondary hood latch. **Vehicle:** Passenger cars. **Defect:** Secondary hood latch assemblies can corrode, causing a high latch release effort and possibly preventing the hood from latching properly when it is closed. **Consequence:** If the secondary hood latch is not properly engaged, and the primary hood latch was also not engaged, the hood could open and contact the windshield while the vehicle was in motion, reducing the forward vision area of the driver, and resulting in a possible vehicle accident without prior warning. **Corrective Action:** Install a new secondary hood latch assembly.

System: Wheels. **Vehicle:** Police cars equipped with special police package that includes 15″×7″ steel wheels with wheel code RDL. **Defect:** The steel wheels exhibit fatigue cracking around the circumference of the wheel lug nut mounting surface due to wheel bending caused by frequent misuse of tire mounting equipment, lug nut overtorquing, and the unusual operating conditions experienced by police vehicles. **Consequence:** The cracking can cause wheel fracturing and subsequent separation from the axle, which could result in a vehicle accident. **Corrective Action:** Replace the defective wheels with redesigned steel wheels.

System: Fuel system. **Vehicle:** Passenger cars with 4.3L engines (RPO LB4). **Defect:** The engine-mounted fuel feed and return pipes may fracture due to contact with the engine frame during operation. **Consequence:** If the fuel pipe fractures, gasoline will be forced at pressure from the fuel pipes into the engine compartment, resulting in an underhood fire if the gasoline is exposed to a source of ignition. **Corrective Action:** Replace the fuel feed and return pipes using new pipe assemblies.

System: Electrical. **Vehicle:** SEQ 9C1 police cars in corrosion areas of the United States and Canada only. **Defect:** An electrical groundout condition may exist between the 12 volt junction block and the metal inner fender skirt. **Consequence:** This condition can cause a melted junction block, smoke and burned underhood wiring, resulting in a disabled vehicle or a vehicle fire. This condition can occur while the vehicle is in operation or while the vehicle is parked and the ignition is in the "off" position. **Corrective Action:** Install a shielding insulator under the junction block. **Note:** The states GM considers part of the corrosion area are: CT, IL, IN, ME, MA, MI, NH, NJ, NY, OH, PA, RI, VT and WI.

CHEVROLET CAPRICE 1994

System: Engine cooling hoses. **Vehicle:** Passenger vehicles equipped with engine oil coolers and 5.7L or 4.3L engines. **Defect:** The engine oil cooler inlet hose may have been installed too close to the steering gear, causing chafing. The chafing can eventually wear through the hose's protective sleeve, resulting in engine oil leaking onto the engine. **Consequence:** If this occurs, the oil leak onto the engine can result in an engine compartment fire. **Corrective Action:** None provided.

System: Wheels; lug nuts; bolts. **Vehicle:** Passenger cars. **Defect:** Paint on the wheel mounting surfaces can act as a shim between the wheel and the rotor and drum. As the vehicle is driven, the wheel imbeds into the paint, loosening the lug nut and causing a loss of clamp load. **Consequence:** Once clamp load is lost, all tire loads are taken by the wheel studs, resulting in fracture of the wheel studs. This could cause the wheel to separate from the vehicle and could result in the vehicle's crash without prior warning. **Corrective Action:** Dealers will clean the wheel mounting surfaces for all four wheels. Also, the wheel studs will be inspected for damage and will be replaced as necessary.

System: Fuel; fuel tank assembly; attachments. **Vehicle:** Passenger vehicles. **Defect:** The fuel tank attachment strap fasteners were not properly tightened. The fasteners can completely detach, eventually allowing the fuel tank to sag and the bottom of the tank to strike the roadway. **Consequence:** This can result in a fuel tank leak and fire if the leaking fuel is exposed to a source of ignition. **Corrective Action:** Dealers will retighten the fuel tank strap fasteners.

System: Fuel; throttle linkages and control; return spring—FMVSS 124. **Vehicle:** Passenger vehicles. **Description of Noncompliance:** These vehicles fail to conform to FMVSS 124, "Accelerator control systems." At low temperatures, excessive friction can occur in the accelerator pedal assembly. **Consequence of Noncompliance:** In the event of a failure of the throttle return spring, if there is excessive friction in the pedal assembly, the engine speed may not return to idle, increasing the potential for a vehicle crash. **Corrective Action:** Dealers will replace the accelerator pedal assembly.

CHEVROLET CAVALIER 1987

System: Brakes—FMVSS 105. **Vehicle:** Passenger cars. **Defect:** Parking brake lever mechanisms may not properly engage when applied, as required by FMVSS 105. **Consequence:** Vehicle could unexpectedly roll away uncontrolled, which could result in a vehicle crash. **Corrective Action:** Replace parking brake lever assembly.

System: Accelerator control cable. **Vehicle:** Passenger vehicles equipped with 2.0L engines. **Defect:** Accelerator control cable may contain water, which could freeze while vehicle is parked, causing travel of accelerator control cable to become restricted when throttle is initially opened. **Consequence:** Engine speed may not decrease, which could result in loss of accelerator control and a crash without prior warning. **Corrective Action:** Replace accelerator control cable.

CHEVROLET CAVALIER 1988

System: Rear lamp wiring harness—FMVSS 108. **Vehicle:** Coupe and convertible passenger cars. **Defect:** Rear lamp wiring harness may contain open or intermittent circuits affecting backup lamp or license plate lamp operation. **Consequence:** Lamps would flash or be inoperative; cars would not comply with FMVSS 108. **Corrective Action:** Install new wiring harness.

System: Windshield—FMVSS 212. **Vehicle:** Passenger cars. **Defect:** There may be poor bond adhesion between windshield glass and mounting. **Consequence:** Windshield could separate during a 30 mph frontal barrier test required by FMVSS 212. Such separation during an accident could result in an unbelted occupant being ejected and injured. **Corrective Action:** Reinstall windshield ensuring proper adhesion.

CHEVROLET CAVALIER 1989

System: Fuel tank. **Vehicle:** Passenger cars with 2.0L or 2.8L engines. **Defect:** A fuel tank leak could occur due to small creases on the tank underside cracking during pressure cycling that occurs during normal operation. **Consequence:** In the presence of an ignition source, this condition could result in a fire. **Corrective Action:** Replace fuel tank.

CHEVROLET CAVALIER 1991

System: Seat belt anchorage—FMVSS 210. **Vehicle:** Passenger vehicles. **Defect:** Front door interlock striker may fail, causing door frame collapse and insufficient strength for the shoulder belt anchorage. **Consequence:** The door frame would collapse. Vehicle does not comply with FMVSS 210. **Corrective Action:** Replace the passive restraint interlock striker studs on front doors.

System: Safety belts—FMVSS 208. **Vehicles:** Passenger vehicles; 1991 GMC "J" and "W" model cars. **Defect:** The front door shoulder belt guide loops may be cracked, and are not in compliance with FMVSS 208. **Consequence:** The seat occupant faces increased risk of injury in the event of a sudden stop or accident. **Corrective Action:** Install reinforcing plates on the cracked shoulder belt guides.

CHEVROLET CAVALIER 1992

System: Hood latch. **Vehicle:** Passenger cars. **Defect:** The secondary hood latch spring is improperly installed or missing, leading to a condition where the secondary hood latch does not engage the secondary striker. **Consequence:** If the secondary hood latch is not engaged, and the primary hood latch was also not engaged, the hood could open unexpectedly. If this occurs while the vehicle is in motion, the hood may contact the windshield, reducing the forward vision area of the driver, and a vehicle crash could occur. **Corrective Action:** Inspect hood latch assemblies and, where necessary, install a new secondary hood latch spring.

CHEVROLET CAVALIER 1993

System: Brakes; hydraulic; hose. **Vehicle:** Passenger vehicles. **Defect:** The brake hoses were manufactured incorrectly, and do not comply with FMVSS 106, "Brake hoses." **Consequence:** The improperly manufactured brake hoses can cause reduced brake effectiveness and/or uneven braking, which could result in an accident. **Corrective Action:** Replace the right front brake hose assembly on Ciera and Century models, and both rear brake hoses on Cavalier and Sunbird models.

CHEVROLET CAVALIER 1994

System: Suspension; independent front spindle; knuckle; steering. **Vehicle:** Passenger cars. **Defect:** These vehicles were built with overtorqued drive axle spindle nuts. This condition can cause excessive loads on the spindle nut and drive axle resulting in failure of the drive axle, or the spindle nut. Failure of either of these components can result in separation of the steering knuckle tire-wheel assembly from the drive axle. **Consequence:** This can result in loss of vehicle control and a vehicle accident. **Corrective Action:** Dealers will replace the left and right-hand drive axles, bearing-hub assemblies, spindle nuts and washers on all involved vehicles.

CHEVROLET CELEBRITY 1988

System: Suspension—lower control front arm bracket. **Vehicle:** Passenger cars. **Defect:** Front suspension lower control arm bracket could develop metal cracks. **Consequence:** These cracks may result in disengagement of the lower control arm. If this occurs while vehicle is in motion, it could result in loss of steering control, and a vehicle crash could occur without prior warning. **Corrective Action:** Inspect all vehicles and replace engine cradle assembly on all suspect vehicles.

System: Fuel feed hose. **Vehicle:** Passenger cars equipped with a 2.8L V6 engine. **Defect:** Fuel feed hose could leak at the coupling on the engine end of the hose assembly. **Consequence:** Fuel leakage into the engine compartment could result in an engine compartment fire that could spread to the passenger compartment. **Corrective Action:** Install new fuel feed hose assembly.

CHEVROLET CELEBRITY 1989

System: Interior; active restraints; belt anchor and attachment—FMVSS 210. **Vehicle:** Passenger vehicles. **Description of Noncompliance:** These vehicles were assembled with rear outboard safety belt anchorages that may not withstand the required load. This does not comply with FMVSS 210, "Seat belt assembly anchorages." **Consequence of Noncompliance:** In a collision, stress can cause the attachment metal to tear and allow the anchorage to separate from the body of the vehicle. The safety belt may not protect an occupant in the event of a vehicle crash. **Corrective Action:** Dealers will replace the existing anchor bolts with a new shoulder bolt and thread-locking adhesive. Additionally, noise control patches will be applied at each anchorage.

CHEVROLET CORSICA 1988

System: Hood latch—secondary. **Vehicle:** Passenger cars. **Defect:** Secondary hood latch assembly may not have been properly adjusted, resulting in latch becoming bent. **Consequence:** A bent secondary hood latch could cause the primary latch to malfunction. If this occurred, the hood could unexpectedly open. If this happened while vehicle is in motion, reduction of forward visibility could cause a vehicle crash without prior warning. **Corrective Action:** Inspect and replace secondary hood latch assemblies as required.

System: Door hinges. **Vehicle:** Passenger cars. **Defect:** A door hinge (upper or lower) may break while opening or closing the door, making the door difficult to reposition and close properly. **Consequence:** Hinge separation may reduce the structural integrity of the side of the car and increase risk of injury in certain types of accidents. **Corrective Action:** Replace door hinges on both doors.

System: Hood. **Vehicle:** Passenger vehicles. **Defect:** Secondary hood latch assembly on these vehicles may not be properly adjusted and could become bent. This will lead to a condition where full primary latch engagement is not attained. **Consequence:** A bent secondary hood latch could lead to the primary latch not being fully engaged, allowing the hood to unexpectedly open. If this were to occur while the vehicle was in motion, the hood may contact the windshield, reducing the forward vision area of the driver, and a vehicle crash could occur without prior warning. **Corrective Action:** Replace the primary hood latch assembly, the secondary hood latch assembly and the support bracket.

System: Safety belts (passive restraint). **Vehicle:** Passenger cars equipped with door-mounted shoulder and lap safety belt systems. **Defect:** The front shoulder belt retractors may have reduced sensitivity of the lockup feature and would not function in a sudden deceleration or crash. **Consequence:** Failure of the shoulder belt retractor would result in the seat occupant only being restrained by the lap belt in a crash or sudden stop, and an increased possibility of injury.

Corrective Action: Replace the front shoulder belt retractors and assemblies.

CHEVROLET CORSICA 1989

System: Fuel tank. **Vehicle:** Passenger cars with 2.0L or 2.8L engines. **Defect:** A fuel tank leak could occur due to small creases on the tank underside cracking during pressure cycling that occurs during normal operation. **Consequence:** In the presence of an ignition source, this condition could result in a fire. **Corrective Action:** Replace fuel tank.

System: Front seat belt latch—FMVSS 209. **Vehicle:** Passenger cars. **Defect:** Front seat belt latchplates may not engage the buckle assemblies. **Consequence:** In the event of an accident, unbelted or improperly belted occupants are more at risk to injury than if belts are properly buckled. **Corrective Action:** Replace improperly functioning buckle assemblies.

System: Front seat frame. **Vehicle:** Passenger cars. **Defect:** The front seat frame assembly may contain an improper, missing and/or mislocated weld that could fracture. **Consequence:** This could cause unexpected seat movement and result in personal injury and/or loss of control of the car. **Corrective Action:** Replace both front seat assemblies.

System: Safety belts (passive restraint). **Vehicle:** Passenger cars equipped with door-mounted shoulder and lap safety belt systems. **Defect:** The front shoulder belt retractors may have reduced sensitivity of the lockup feature and would not function in a sudden deceleration or crash. **Consequence:** Failure of the shoulder belt retractor would result in the seat occupant only being restrained by the lap belt in a crash or sudden stop, and an increased possibility of injury. **Corrective Action:** Replace the front shoulder belt retractors and assemblies.

System: Wheels. **Vehicle:** Passenger cars with styled steel wheels. **Defect:** The styled steel wheels can have cracks developing at the outer edges of the wheel where the spokes meet the rim. The cracks propagate from each side of a spoke toward each other, and eventually meet. The meeting of the cracks results in complete separation of a spoke from the wheel. **Consequence:** The cracking condition can occur on every spoke on the wheel, causing complete separation of the wheel from the vehicle and resulting in loss of steering and braking control. **Corrective Action:** Replace the involved wheel assemblies.

CHEVROLET CORSICA 1990

System: Seat belt assemblies—FMVSS 209. **Vehicle:** Passenger cars. **Defect:** Owner's manuals were printed with rear center seat belt information omitted. **Consequence:** This would not comply with FMVSS 209. **Corrective Action:** Insert missing information into owner's manual.

System: Safety belts (passive restraint). **Vehicle:** Passenger cars equipped with door-mounted shoulder and lap safety belt systems. **Defect:** The front shoulder belt retractors may have reduced sensitivity of the lockup feature and would not function in a sudden deceleration or crash. **Consequence:** Failure of the shoulder belt retractor would result in the seat occupant only being restrained by the lap belt in a crash or sudden stop, and an increased possibility of injury. **Corrective Action:** Replace the front shoulder belt retractors and assemblies.

CHEVROLET CORSICA 1991

System: Steering wheel nut. **Vehicle:** Passenger cars. **Defect:** Nut attaching steering wheel may not have been properly tightened during installation. **Consequence:** This could allow steering wheel to separate from steering column; loss of vehicle control and a crash could occur without prior warning. **Corrective Action:** Tighten the nut to the proper torque as necessary.

CHEVROLET CORSICA 1992

System: Lighting; stoplamps. **Vehicle:** Passenger cars. **Defect:** The service brake stoplamp switch becomes inoperative. **Consequence:** The inoperative stoplamp switch will not illuminate the stoplamps when the brake pedal is depressed. This would not adequately inform other drivers of the vehicle operator's intent to stop or slow down. **Corrective Action:** Replace the stoplamp switch and correct the wiring in the connector of the stoplamp switch wiring harness. **Note:** If the failure occurs during three consecutive service brake applications, the amber "antilock" brake system (ABS) telltale lamp may illuminate, indicating a problem with the system.

CHEVROLET CORVETTE 1988

System: Wheel welds. **Vehicle:** Passenger cars equipped with 17-inch wheels. **Defect:** Missing weld that attaches wheel center to the rim could allow wheel center to separate from the rim. **Consequence:** This could result in partial loss of steering control and brakes, loss of tire air pressure and sudden change in vehicle direction, which could result in crash without prior warning. **Corrective Action:** Replace wheels with missing welds.

System: Rear wheel tie rods. **Vehicle:** Passenger cars. **Defect:** Rear wheel tie rod assembly may fatigue and could fracture at the inboard bearing due to high inner joint rocking torque. **Consequence:** Fracture in this assembly could result in loss of vehicle control and a crash without prior warning. **Corrective Action:** Replace faulty tie rod assemblies.

System: Safety belts. **Vehicle:** Passenger cars. **Defect:** Under certain vehicle operations and occupant usage conditions, the safety belts can lock up or jam in the safety belt retractor. **Consequence:** If lockup occurs, it is impossible to pull the belt out of the retractor. The occupant of a seat with an unusable safety belt is subject to increased risk of injury or death in the event of a sudden stop or accident. **Corrective Action:** Replace the safety belts if the lockup occurs.

CHEVROLET CORVETTE 1989

System: Rear wheel tie rods. **Vehicle:** Passenger cars. **Defect:** Rear wheel tie rod assembly may fatigue and could fracture at the inboard bearing due to high inner joint rocking torque. **Consequence:** Fracture in this assembly could result in loss of vehicle control and a crash without prior warning. **Corrective Action:** Replace faulty tie rod assemblies.

System: Safety belts. **Vehicle:** Passenger cars. **Defect:** Under certain vehicle operations and occupant usage conditions, the safety belts can lock up or jam in the safety belt retractor. **Consequence:** If lockup occurs, it is impossible to pull the belt out of the retractor. The occupant of a seat with an unusable safety belt is subject to increased risk of injury or death in the event of a sudden stop or accident. **Corrective Action:** Replace the safety belts if the lockup occurs.

CHEVROLET CORVETTE 1990

System: Fuel lines. **Vehicle:** Passenger cars with LT5 engines. **Defect:** Fuel feed and return line connectors have incorrect line end flare configurations. **Consequence:** Line ends could crack, causing a fuel leak that could result in an engine compartment fire. **Corrective Action:** Install new fuel lines with correct end flare configuration.

System: Safety belts. **Vehicle:** Passenger cars. **Defect:** Under certain vehicle operations and occupant usage conditions, the safety belts can lock up or jam in the safety belt retractor. **Consequence:** If lockup occurs, it is impossible to pull the belt out of the retractor. The occupant of a seat with an unusable safety belt is subject to increased risk of injury or death in the event of a sudden stop or accident. **Corrective Action:** Replace the safety belts if the lockup occurs.

CHEVROLET CORVETTE 1991

System: Safety belts. **Vehicle:** Passenger cars. **Defect:** Under certain vehicle operations and occupant usage conditions, the safety belts can lock up or jam in the safety belt retractor. **Consequence:** If lockup occurs, it is impossible to pull belt out of the retractor. The occupant of a seat with an unusable safety belt is subject to increased risk of injury or death in the event of a sudden stop or accident. **Corrective Action:** Replace the safety belts if the lockup occurs.

CHEVROLET LUMINA 1990

System: Seat belt anchorage—FMVSS 210. **Vehicle:** Passenger cars. **Defect:** Front shoulder belt guide loop attachment fastener may pull through door-mounted anchor plate. **Consequence:** Seat belt may not sustain loads required by FMVSS 210, and in a vehicle accident, the seat belt may not properly restrain a passenger, resulting in increased risk of injury to an occupant. **Corrective Action:** Replace front shoulder belt guide loop attachment nuts and install new guide cover.

System: Brake stoplamp switch. **Vehicle:** Passenger cars. **Defect:** Brake stoplamps may not illuminate or, in some cases, stoplamps will not stay illuminated all the time when brakes are applied due to a faulty stoplamp switch. Also, in vehicles equipped with cruise control, a faulty stoplamp switch can result in resumption of the cruise control function upon release of the brake pedal. **Consequence:** A trailing vehicle may not recognize a braking action in time to respond appropriately. Also, cruise control will reengage upon release of the brake pedal and resume the set speed. Either case could result in a crash without prior warning. **Corrective Action:** Install an improved design stoplamp switch.

System: Front shoulder safety belt. **Vehicle:** Passenger cars. **Defect:** Front shoulder safety belt webbing may separate at front belt upper guide loops on either side of the front seat. **Consequence:** Webbing separation could occur without prior warning and increase the risk of injury to belted front outboard occupants in a high-energy crash. **Corrective Action:** Install a controlled rotation bracket on driver's- and passenger-side front seat belt guide loops.

System: Wheels. **Vehicle:** Passenger vehicles equipped with Kelsey Hayes steel wheels; models RPO PB6 14″ and RPO PG1 15″. **Defect:** Cracks develop in the wheel mounting surface. If these cracks become severe enough, the wheel will completely separate from the vehicle. **Consequence:** If wheel separation occurs while the vehicle is in motion, loss of steering and brake control of the vehicle occurs, and a vehicle crash could result without prior warning. **Corrective Action:** Dealers will inspect the manufacturing date codes stamped on each wheel of the vehicle, and if a wheel falls within the specified date code range, the dealer will replace that wheel assembly.

System: Wheels. **Vehicle:** Passenger vehicles equipped with Kelsey Hayes steel wheels; models RPO PB9 14″ and RPO PG1 15″. **Defect:** Cracks develop in the wheel mounting surface. If these cracks become severe enough, the wheel will completely separate from the vehicle. **Consequence:** If wheel separation occurs while the vehicle is in motion, loss of steering and brake control of the vehicle occurs, and a vehicle crash could result without prior warning. **Corrective Action:** Dealers will inspect the manufacturing date codes stamped on each wheel of the vehicle, and if a wheel falls within the specified date code range, the dealer will replace that wheel assembly. **Note:** Vehicles previously inspected that had less than four wheels replaced are to be reinspected.

CHEVROLET LUMINA 1991

System: Safety belts—FMVSS 208. **Vehicles:** Passenger vehicles; 1991 GMC "J" and "W" model cars. **Defect:** The front door shoulder belt guide loops may be cracked and are not in compliance with FMVSS 208. **Consequence:** The seat occupant faces increased risk of injury in the event of a sudden stop or accident. **Corrective Action:** Install reinforcing plates on the cracked shoulder belt guides.

CHEVROLET LUMINA 1992

System: Transmission and transmission shift indicator. **Vehicle:** 1992 "A" and "W" body passenger cars with 4-speed automatic transmissions. **Defect:** The reverse servo apply pin may bind in the case, which could cause reverse band distress (loss or slipping of reverse), reverse band drag in drive range (poor performance/poor power) or the transmission to remain in reverse while the shift indicator shows neutral gear position. **Consequence:** If the transmission remains in reverse while the shift indicator shows neutral, the vehicle may unexpectedly move rearward, resulting in a vehicle accident. **Corrective Action:** Replace the transaxle where required.

System: Fuel system. **Vehicle:** Passenger cars with methanol/ethanol fuel systems. **Defect:** There is fuel leakage at the fuel tank fill and/or vent pipe extension solder joints. **Consequence:** Fuel leaks can lead to a vehicle fire if exposed to a source of ignition. **Corrective Action:** Replace the fuel tank.

CHEVROLET LUMINA 1993

System: Front seat manual recliner mechanisms—FMVSS 207. **Vehicle:** Passenger cars. **Defect:** The driver and passenger front seat manual reclining mechanisms do not comply with the requirements of FMVSS 207, "Seating systems." The seat back mechanisms will not latch under certain conditions. **Consequence:** The seats may recline without prior warning, resulting in a hazard to seat occupants and possible loss of vehicle control. **Corrective Action:** Replace the manual seat recliner mechanism with a mechanism that complies with FMVSS 207.

CHEVROLET MONTE CARLO 1987

System: Transmission. **Vehicle:** Passenger cars and wagons with 200 4R transmissions. **Defect:** Manual valve link in the transmission may have been improperly formed. **Consequence:** The valve link could separate, resulting in a gear selection different from what the driver selects. Also, car could be started with transmission in gear, allowing vehicle to move in an unanticipated direction. **Corrective Action:** Replace the manual valve detent lever link.

CHEVROLET SPECTRUM 1987

System: Fuel tank or fuel feed pipe. **Vehicle:** Passenger cars. **Defect:** Perforation of the fuel tank or the attached fuel feed pipe due to corrosion of the tank or fuel feed pipe materials. **Consequence:** This condition could allow fuel to leak from the fuel tank, and ultimately result in a fire without prior warning. Such a fire could spread to the passenger compartment. **Corrective Action:** The fuel tank will be replaced on all involved vehicles.

System: Engine. **Vehicle:** Passenger cars. **Defect:** The positive crankcase ventilation (PCV) valve may provide inadequate air flow under low engine load conditions. **Consequence:** This condition can allow water/oil mixture to build up in the hose from the oil separator to the air inlet duct. After the engine is stopped, this water/oil mixture can, under cold weather conditions, freeze and completely block the oil separator air duct hose. This blockage will result in increased pressure within the crankcase. This can cause oil leaks; if a sufficient quantity of oil came in contact with the hot exhaust system, an engine compartment fire could result without prior warning. **Corrective Action:** The PCV valve will be replaced with a new valve.

CHEVROLET TRUCK ASTRO 1987

System: Safety belt—FMVSS 209. **Vehicle:** Van conversions. **Defect:** The seat belts for the front and midship seats did not rest on pelvis as required by FMVSS 209. **Consequence:** Seat belts may not restrain seat occupant, and could injure the seat occupant in the event of a sudden stop or accident. **Corrective Action:** Relocate seat belt anchor bolts to adjust belts for seat locations.

System: Interior systems; seat tracks, anchors and seats. **Vehicle:** Vans and utility vehicles equipped with bucket seats with knob-type recliner mechanisms. **Defect:** The recliner mechanism and the seat frame may have foam and/or vinyl between them, creating a "soft" joint. This soft joint results in lower than specified bolt torque, which leads to joint looseness, causing bolt fatigue and eventual bolt failure. **Consequence:** If bolt failure occurs to the driver's seat, it would allow the seat back to suddenly recline, and could result in loss of vehicle control and a vehicle crash without prior warning. **Corrective Action:** Dealers will remove the foam and/or vinyl from between the recliner mechanism and the seat frame soft joint and replace the recliner bolts.

CHEVROLET TRUCK ASTRO 1988

System: Safety belt—FMVSS 209. **Vehicle:** Van conversions. **Defect:** The seat belts for the front and midship seats did not rest on pelvis as required by FMVSS 209. **Consequence:** Seat belts may not restrain seat occupant, and could injure the seat occupant in the event of a sudden stop or accident. **Corrective Action:** Relocate seat belt anchor bolts to adjust belts for seat locations.

System: Interior systems; seat tracks, anchors and seats. **Vehicle:** Vans and utility vehicles equipped with bucket seats with knob-type recliner mechanisms. **Defect:** The recliner mechanism and the seat frame may have foam and/or vinyl between them, creating a "soft" joint. This soft joint results in lower than specified bolt torque, which leads to joint looseness, causing bolt fatigue and eventual bolt failure. **Consequence:** If bolt failure occurs to the driver's seat, it would allow the seat back to suddenly recline, and could result in loss of vehicle control and a vehicle crash without prior warning. **Corrective Action:** Dealers will remove the foam and/or vinyl from between the recliner mechanism and the seat frame soft joint and replace the recliner bolts.

CHEVROLET TRUCK ASTRO 1989

System: Safety belt—FMVSS 209. **Vehicle:** Van conversions. **Defect:** The seat belts for the front and midship seats did not rest on pelvis as required by FMVSS 209. **Consequence:** Seat belts may not restrain seat occupant, and could injure the seat occupant in the event of a sudden stop or accident. **Corrective Action:** Relocate seat belt anchor bolts to adjust belts for seat locations.

System: Seat belt anchorage—FMVSS 210. **Vehicle:** Vans. **Defect:** Seat belt anchorage bar for rear sofa failed to sustain loads required by FMVSS 210. **Consequence:** Vehicles would not comply with FMVSS 210. **Corrective Action:** Replace noncomplying sofa bar with bar that meets requirements. **Note:** This recall is being conducted by Sherrod Vans, Inc.

System: Interior systems; seat tracks, anchors and seats. **Vehicle:** Vans and utility vehicles equipped with bucket seats with knob-type recliner mechanisms. **Defect:** The recliner mechanism and the seat frame may have foam and/or vinyl between them, creating a "soft" joint. This soft joint results in lower than specified bolt torque, which leads to joint looseness, causing bolt fatigue and eventual bolt failure. **Consequence:** If bolt failure occurs to the driver's seat, it would allow the seat back to suddenly recline, and could result in loss of vehicle control and a vehicle crash without prior warning. **Corrective Action:** Dealers will remove the foam and/or vinyl from between the recliner mechanism and the seat frame soft joint and replace the recliner bolts.

CHEVROLET TRUCK ASTRO 1990

System: Fuel return hoses. **Vehicle:** School buses and truck vans equipped with 6.0L TBI gas engines and 60-gallon fuel tanks. **Defect:** Fuel return hoses may break at either crimped coupling, causing a leakage of fuel. **Consequence:** In the event of a fuel return line separation, a fuel leak occurring in the presence of an ignition source could cause a fire. **Corrective Action:** Install a properly crimped fuel return hose.

System: Safety belt—FMVSS 209. **Vehicle:** Van conversions. **Defect:** The seat belts for the front and midship seats did not rest on pelvis as required by FMVSS 209. **Consequence:** Seat belts may not restrain seat occupant, and could injure the seat occupant in the event of a sudden stop or accident. **Corrective Action:** Relocate seat belt anchor bolts to adjust belts for seat locations.

System: Seat belt anchorage—FMVSS 210. **Vehicle:** Vans. **Defect:** Seat belt anchorage bar for rear sofa failed to sustain loads required by FMVSS 210. **Consequence:** Vehicles would not comply with FMVSS 210. **Corrective Action:** Replace noncomplying sofa bar with bar that meets requirements. **Note:** This recall is being conducted by Sherrod Vans, Inc.

System: Interior systems; seat tracks, anchors and seats. **Vehicle:** Vans and utility vehicles equipped with bucket seats with knob-type recliner mechanisms. **Defect:** The recliner mechanism and the seat frame may have foam and/or vinyl between them, creating a "soft" joint. This soft joint results in lower than specified bolt torque, which leads to joint looseness, causing bolt fatigue and eventual bolt failure. **Consequence:** If bolt failure occurs to the driver's seat, it would allow the seat back to suddenly recline, and could result in loss of vehicle control and a vehicle crash without prior warning. **Corrective Action:** Dealers will remove the foam and/or vinyl from between the recliner mechanism and the seat frame soft joint and replace the recliner bolts.

CHEVROLET TRUCK ASTRO 1991

System: Safety belt—FMVSS 209. **Vehicle:** Van conversions. **Defect:** The seat belts for the front and midship seats did not rest on pelvis as required by FMVSS 209. **Consequence:** Seat belts may not restrain seat occupant, and could injure the seat occupant in the event of a sudden stop or accident. **Corrective Action:** Relocate seat belt anchor bolts to adjust belts for seat locations.

System: Seat belt anchorage—FMVSS 210. **Vehicle:** Vans. **Defect:** Seat belt anchorage bar for rear sofa failed to sustain loads required by FMVSS 210. **Consequence:** Vehicles would not comply with FMVSS 210. **Corrective Action:** Replace noncomplying sofa bar with bar that meets requirements. **Note:** This recall is being conducted by Sherrod Vans, Inc.

System: Interior systems; seat tracks, anchors and seats. **Vehicle:** Vans and utility vehicles equipped with bucket seats with knob-type recliner mechanisms. **Defect:** The recliner mechanism and the seat frame may have foam and/or vinyl between them, creating a "soft" joint. This soft joint results in lower than specified bolt torque, which leads to joint looseness, causing bolt fatigue and eventual bolt failure. **Consequence:** If bolt failure occurs to the driver's seat, it would allow the seat back to suddenly recline, and could result in loss of vehicle control and a vehicle crash without prior warning. **Corrective Action:** Dealers will remove the foam and/or vinyl from between the recliner mechanism and the seat frame soft joint and replace the recliner bolts.

CHEVROLET TRUCK ASTRO 1992

System: Interior systems; seat head restraints. **Vehicle:** Conversion vans. **Description of Noncompliance:** The front driver and passenger seat back heights do not conform to the requirements of FMVSS 202, "Head restraints." **Consequence of Noncompliance:** Seat occupants are subject to increased risk of injury in the event of a sudden stop or accident. **Corrective Action:** Sherry Designs will provide an attachable headrest for the dealer or customer to add to the seats.

CHEVROLET TRUCK ASTRO 1993

System: Interior systems; seat head restraints. **Vehicle:** Conversion vans. **Description of Noncompliance:** The front driver and passenger seat back heights do not conform to the requirements of FMVSS 202, "Head restraints." **Consequence of Noncompliance:** Seat occupants are subject to increased risk of injury in the event of a sudden stop or accident. **Corrective Action:** Sherry Designs will provide an attachable headrest for the dealer or customer to add to the seats.

System: Interior systems; seat belts; lap; front. **Vehicle:** Chevrolet and GMC conversion vans. **Description of Noncompliance:** The safety belt length does not meet the requirements to fit a 95th percentile dummy in the driver's seat position if the seat is in full forward position. This does not comply with the requirements of FMVSS 208, "Occupant crash protection." **Consequence of Noncompliance:** Large persons in the driver's seat would be exposed to increased risk of injury in a sudden stop or crash. **Corrective Action:** Dealers will replace the shorter safety belt with a longer belt that offers the protection set forth in the standard.

CHEVROLET TRUCK ASTRO 1994

System: Equipment; certification labels. **Vehicle:** Conversion vans. **Description of Noncompliance:** The manufacturer's certification label and/or the driver airbag advisory label may be missing from the vehicles, which does not conform to the requirements of 49 CFR 567. **Consequence of Noncompliance:** Owners of the vehicle would be unaware of the load capacity of the vans and the van build date, and would not have any assurance that the vans meet the federal motor vehicle safety standards. **Corrective Action:** The labels will be furnished to owners for installation on the vehicles. **Note:** If you have any questions regarding the distribution of these labels, please contact Explorer Van Service Center at (800) 828-2056. Also contact the NHTSA's Auto Safety Hotline at (800) 424-9393.

System: Interior systems; seat head restraints. **Vehicle:** Conversion vans. **Description of Noncompliance:** The front driver and passenger seat back heights do not conform to the requirements of FMVSS 202, "Head restraints." **Consequence of Noncompliance:** Seat occupants are subject to increased risk of injury in the event of a sudden stop or accident. **Corrective Action:** Sherry Designs will provide an attachable headrest for the dealer or customer to add to the seats.

CHEVROLET TRUCK BLAZER 1988

System: Brakes; hydraulic; disc rotors. **Vehicle:** Light trucks and vans sold or registered in the following states: CT, IL, IN, MA, ME, MI,

NH, NJ, NY, OH, PA, RI, VT and WI. **Defect:** Severe corrosion due to road salt at the joint of the stamped steel center section and the cast outer section can cause the sections to separate. **Consequence:** Separation of the rotor sections can cause loss of braking ability in the affected wheel. This could result in increased stopping distance and/ or loss of vehicle control and an accident. **Corrective Action:** Replace the front brake rotors with new rotors with a corrosion protection coating. However, if replacement of brake linings is necessary, it will be done at owner's expense, since brake linings are normal maintenance items. **Note:** The vehicles involved can be identified by the following: the 5th character of the vehicle identification number must be a *K* or *L*, and the 7th character must be *3, 4, 5, 6* or *9*. If your vehicle is presented to an authorized dealer on an agreed-upon service date, and the remedy is not provided within a reasonable amount of time and free of charge or the remedy does not correct the safety-related defect or noncompliance, please contact your nearest GMC Truck zone office. The telephone numbers of the zone offices are listed in your warranty and owner's assistance information manuals. Also contact the NHTSA's Auto Safety Hotline at (800) 424-9393.

CHEVROLET TRUCK BLAZER 1989

System: Brakes; hydraulic; disc rotors. **Vehicle:** Light trucks and vans sold or registered in the following states: CT, IL, IN, MA, ME, MI, NH, NJ, NY, OH, PA, RI, VT and WI. **Defect:** Severe corrosion due to road salt at the joint of the stamped steel center section and the cast outer section can cause the sections to separate. **Consequence:** Separation of the rotor sections can cause loss of braking ability in the affected wheel. This could result in increased stopping distance and/ or loss of vehicle control and an accident. **Corrective Action:** Replace the front brake rotors with new rotors with a corrosion protection coating. However, if replacement of brake linings is necessary, it will be done at owner's expense, since brake linings are normal maintenance items. **Note:** The vehicles involved can be identified by the following: the 5th character of the vehicle identification number must be a *K* or *L*, and the 7th character must be *3, 4, 5, 6* or *9*. If your vehicle is presented to an authorized dealer on an agreed-upon service date, and the remedy is not provided within a reasonable amount of time and free of charge or the remedy does not correct the safety-related defect or noncompliance, please contact your nearest GMC Truck zone office. The telephone numbers of the zone offices are listed in your warranty and owner's assistance information manuals. Also contact the NHTSA's Auto Safety Hotline at (800) 424-9393.

CHEVROLET TRUCK BLAZER 1990

System: Brakes; hydraulic; disc rotors. **Vehicle:** Light trucks and vans sold or registered in the following states: CT, IL, IN, MA, ME, MI, NH, NJ, NY, OH, PA, RI, VT and WI. **Defect:** Severe corrosion due to road salt at the joint of the stamped steel center section and the cast outer section can cause the sections to separate. **Consequence:** Separation of the rotor sections can cause loss of braking ability in the affected wheel. This could result in increased stopping distance and/ or loss of vehicle control and an accident. **Corrective Action:** Replace the front brake rotors with new rotors with a corrosion protection coating. However, if replacement of brake linings is necessary, it will be done at owner's expense since brake linings are normal maintenance items. **Note:** The vehicles involved can be identified by the following: the 5th character of the vehicle identification number must be a *K* or *L*, and the 7th character must be *3, 4, 5, 6* or *9*. If your vehicle is presented to an authorized dealer on an agreed-upon service date, and the remedy is not provided within a reasonable amount of time and free of charge or the remedy does not correct the safety-related defect or noncompliance, please contact your nearest GMC Truck zone office. The telephone numbers of the zone offices are listed in your warranty and owner's assistance information manuals. Also contact the NHTSA's Auto Safety Hotline at (800) 424-9393.

CHEVROLET TRUCK BLAZER 1991

System: Fuel systems—FMVSS 301. **Vehicle:** Light trucks and multipurpose vehicles. **Defect:** Vehicles have been shipped with the fuel tank sender seal out of position. **Consequence:** In the event of rollover accident, an out of position seal could allow fuel spillage in excess of the amount prescribed by FMVSS 301. Spilled fuel could ignite near an ignition source. **Corrective Action:** Replace sender seals.

System: Brakes; hydraulic; disc rotors. **Vehicle:** Light trucks and vans sold or registered in the following states: CT, IL, IN, MA, ME, MI, NH, NJ, NY, OH, PA, RI, VT and WI. **Defect:** Severe corrosion due to road salt at the joint of the stamped steel center section and the cast outer section can cause the sections to separate. **Consequence:** Separation of the rotor sections can cause loss of braking ability in the affected wheel. This could result in increased stopping distance and/ or loss of vehicle control and an accident. **Corrective Action:** Replace the front brake rotors with new rotors with a corrosion protection coating. However, if replacement of brake linings are necessary, it will be done at owner's expense, since brake linings are normal maintenance items. **Note:** The vehicles involved can be identified by the following: the 5th character of the vehicle identification number must be a *K* or *L*, and the 7th character must be *3, 4, 5, 6* or *9*. If your vehicle is presented to an authorized dealer on an agreed-upon service date, and the remedy is not provided within a reasonable amount of time and free of charge or the remedy does not correct the safety-related defect or noncompliance, please contact your nearest GMC Truck zone office. The telephone numbers of the zone offices are listed in your warranty and owner's assistance information manuals. Also contact the NHTSA's Auto Safety Hotline at (800) 424-9393.

CHEVROLET TRUCK BLAZER 1992

System: Brakes; hydraulic; disc rotors. **Vehicle:** Light trucks and vans sold or registered in the following states: CT, IL, IN, MA, ME, MI, NH, NJ, NY, OH, PA, RI, VT and WI. **Defect:** Severe corrosion due to road salt at the joint of the stamped steel center section and the cast outer section can cause the sections to separate. **Consequence:** Separation of the rotor sections can cause loss of braking ability in the affected wheel. This could result in increased stopping distance and/ or loss of vehicle control and an accident. **Corrective Action:** Replace the front brake rotors with new rotors with a corrosion protection coating. However, if replacement of brake linings is necessary, it will be done at owner's expense since brake linings are normal maintenance items. **Note:** The vehicles involved can be identified by the following: the 5th character of the vehicle identification number must be a *K* or *L*, and the 7th character must be *3, 4, 5, 6* or *9*. If your vehicle is presented to an authorized dealer on an agreed-upon service date, and the remedy is not provided within a reasonable amount of time and free of charge or the remedy does not correct the safety-related defect or noncompliance, please contact your nearest GMC Truck zone office. The telephone numbers of the zone offices are listed in your warranty and owner's assistance information manuals. Also contact the NHTSA's Auto Safety Hotline at (800) 424-9393.

CHEVROLET TRUCK BLAZER 1993

System: Power train; transmission; automatic. **Vehicle:** Light-duty pickup trucks and utility vehicles equipped with 4-wheel drive. **Note:** The "S" series trucks are not included because they are only 2-wheel drive. **Defect:** Significant wear can develop on the low and reverse clutch, preventing the park pawl from engaging. This can allow a "no park" condition to occur while the engine is running, causing unintentional movement of the vehicle without operator action. (The "no park" condition will not occur while the engine is off.) **Consequence:** Unintentional vehicle movement could result in a vehicle accident and injury to persons in the path of the vehicle. **Corrective Action:** Dealers will check the transmission fluid for contamination, which will indicate if the low or reverse clutch is worn. If the transmission fluid shows contamination, the transmission will be replaced.

CHEVROLET TRUCK BLAZER 1994

System: Equipment; other pieces; trailer hitches and attachments. **Vehicle:** Light-duty 4-door multipurpose vehicles equipped with a weight distribution trailer hitch (VR4) option. **Defect:** The trailer hitch attaching bolts were not tightened to the specified torque. This can lead to loosening and subsequent breakage of the fasteners. **Consequence:** If this were to occur while the trailer was being pulled, the hitch and trailer could separate from the vehicle. **Corrective Action:** Dealers will torque all eight trailer hitch bolts to the correct torque.

CHEVROLET TRUCK BLAZER 1995

System: Brakes; hydraulic; linkage; pedal. **Vehicle:** Light-duty utility vehicles. **Defect:** The brake pedal pivot bolt was hand-started in the weld nut, but was not torqued correctly, causing the bolt to disengage from the weld nut. **Consequence:** This condition can result in a total loss of braking capability. **Corrective Action:** Dealers will inspect for hand-started brake pedal bolts and torque them to correct specifications.

System: Suspension; front control arm; upper; ball joint. **Vehicle:** Multipurpose vehicles equipped with 4-wheel drive. **Defect:** The upper ball joint nuts were undertorqued, resulting in improper seating in the steering knuckle. **Consequence:** This condition can cause the ball joint stud to loosen and fracture, resulting in a loss of steering control. **Corrective Action:** Dealers will retorque the upper ball joint nut on both sides of the vehicle to the correct torque values.

System: Engine; cooling system; fan. **Vehicle:** Light-duty pickup trucks and utility vehicles equipped with air conditioning and 4.3L engines. **Defect:** Fan blade rivet breakage can occur, causing the fan blade to separate from the spider. **Consequence:** If this occurred while the hood was open, a person working under the hood of the vehicle or in the vicinity of the vehicle could be struck by the fan blade and injured. **Corrective Action:** Dealers will inspect and replace the fan with a newer fan having thicker-headed rivets, if necessary.

CHEVROLET TRUCK C10 1988

System: Cruise control. **Vehicle:** Light- and medium-duty pickup trucks with cruise control. **Defect:** Cruise control cable lock mechanism may self-disengage, causing erratic operation or throttle not returning to idle. **Consequence:** Engine speed would not decrease; loss of accelerator control could result in a crash without prior warning. **Corrective Action:** Install a clamp around the lock tab of cruise control.

System: Steering—tie rod nuts. **Vehicle:** Light- and medium-duty pickup trucks. **Defect:** One or both outer tie rod nuts may be loose and not crimped. **Consequence:** Loss of one or both nuts could lead to tie rod disengaging from steering knuckle; resulting in possible loss of steering control and possibly a crash. **Corrective Action:** Replace tie rod and knuckle and set toe-in.

System: Door locks—FMVSS 206. **Vehicle:** Light-and medium-duty pickup trucks. **Description of Noncompliance:** Trucks may have cracked or broken door striker nuts, which do not conform to FMVSS 206. **Consequence of Noncompliance:** In a collision, a cracked or broken striker nut could allow door to open unexpectedly and possibly cause injury to occupants. **Corrective Action:** Replace existing door striker nuts.

System: Brake—hose. **Vehicle:** Trucks. **Defect:** Right- and left-hand brake hose may contact the wheel or tire in a full turn. **Consequence:** If the hose makes contact with the wheel or tire, it will eventually wear the hose to a point of rupture, resulting in a loss of the front brakes. Loss of front brakes would increase the stopping distance when minimum time is required, and could result in a vehicle crash. **Corrective Action:** Install new repositioning brackets for the front brake hoses.

System: Power train. **Vehicle:** Light trucks with 5.0L, 5.7L and 7.4L engines and 4l60, 4l60-E and 3l80 automatic transmissions. **Defect:** Unanticipated heat in the transmission can force the transmission fluid out of the vent tube. **Consequence:** The vented transmission fluid can catch fire if exposed to a source of ignition. **Corrective Action:** Install a longer transmission vent hose routed to the left side of the engine compartment of the vehicle.

CHEVROLET TRUCK C10 1989

System: Trailer hitch fasteners. **Vehicle:** Extended-cab trucks with optional trailer hitch (VR4). **Defect:** There may be below specified torque on the trailer hitch attaching fasteners, allowing the trailer hitch to move under towing loads. **Consequence:** Fasteners could fail; if this occurs while trailer is being pulled, hitch and trailer could separate and a vehicle crash could occur without prior warning. **Corrective Action:** Correct torque in trailer hitch fasteners to prevent trailer separation.

System: Power train. **Vehicle:** Light trucks with 5.0L, 5.7L and 7.4L engines and 4l60, 4l60-E and 3l80 automatic transmissions. **Defect:** Unanticipated heat in the transmission can force the transmission fluid out of the vent tube. **Consequence:** The vented transmission fluid can catch fire if exposed to a source of ignition. **Corrective Action:** Install a longer transmission vent hose routed to the left side of the engine compartment of the vehicle.

CHEVROLET TRUCK C15 1990

System: Brake pedal support. **Vehicle:** Light trucks. **Defect:** Loose pivot bolt holding the brake pedal to its support bracket could disengage from the nut. **Consequence:** This could cause loss of braking activity that could result in a truck crash without prior warning. **Corrective Action:** Retorque brake pedal pivot bolts to specifications to prevent loosening.

CHEVROLET TRUCK LUMINA APV 1990

System: Rear seat anchorage—FMVSS 207. **Vehicle:** Multipurpose passenger vehicle. **Defect:** The rear modular seat frame hold-down hooks may not meet the required pull force at the rear set anchorage. **Consequence:** Vehicles would not conform to FMVSS 207. **Corrective Action:** Replace rear hold-down hooks and pivot rivets with heat-treated hardware.

System: Safety belt assembly—FMVSS 209. **Vehicle:** Passenger vans with gray interiors. **Defect:** A right-hand seat and shoulder belt retractor may have been installed in the second row left-hand seat position (directly behind driver). **Consequence:** The incorrect retractor may cause the belts to lock up if the van is parked on a steep grade. As a result of this, the occupant could not extend the belt for use. **Corrective Action:** Replace shoulder belt assembly.

CHEVROLET TRUCK S10 1987

System: Steering linkage. **Vehicle:** Light-duty trucks. **Defect:** Inner tie rod to relay rod nuts on steering linkage may be improperly torqued and not crimped. **Consequence:** Loss of one or both nuts could lead to inner tie rod disengagement, which could result in loss of steering control and a truck crash. **Corrective Action:** Replace steering linkage assembly.

CHEVROLET TRUCK S10 1989

System: Engine. **Vehicle:** Light trucks with 2.5L engines without air conditioning. **Defect:** The engine cooling fan blades break as a result of fatigue and/or vehicle induced stress. **Consequence:** If the blade breakage occurs while the hood is open, a person working under the hood or in the vicinity of the vehicle could be struck and injured by the blade segment. **Corrective Action:** Install a newly designed fan assembly.

CHEVROLET TRUCK S10 1990

System: Engine. **Vehicle:** Light trucks with 2.5L engines without air conditioning. **Defect:** The engine cooling fan blades break as a result of fatigue and/or vehicle-induced stress. **Consequence:** If the blade breakage occurs while the hood is open, a person working under the hood or in the vicinity of the vehicle could be struck and injured by the blade segment. **Corrective Action:** Install a newly designed fan assembly.

CHEVROLET TRUCK S10 1991

System: Windshield and side window mounting—FMVSS 212. **Vehicle:** Utility, pickup and extended-cab pickup trucks. **Defect:** Use of improper primer on metal surfaces of windshield and side window openings could cause low adhesion to the metal surface and would not provide retention required by FMVSS 212. **Consequence:** Windshield and side window glass would not prevent the ejection of vehicle occupants during a vehicle crash, which could cause serious injuries and fatalities. **Corrective Action:** Remove and reinstall glass using proper primer.

System: Lower control arm attaching nuts. **Vehicle:** Light-duty trucks. **Defect:** Nuts used to attach lower control arms, rear spring and shackle and rear shock absorbers do not meet specifications and could "strip." **Consequence:** Stripping of the nuts in the rear suspension could reduce clamp load on the lower control arm, which could allow the arm to detach, resulting in loss of vehicle control and an accident. **Corrective Action:** Replace lower control arm attachment nuts, as well as rear spring and shackle and rear shock absorber nuts.

System: Fuel systems—FMVSS 301. **Vehicle:** Light trucks and multipurpose vehicles. **Defect:** Vehicles have been shipped with the fuel tank sender seal out of position. **Consequence:** In the event of rollover accident, an out of position seal could allow fuel spillage in excess of the amount prescribed by FMVSS 301. Spilled fuel could ignite near an ignition source. **Corrective Action:** Replace sender seals.

System: Engine. **Vehicle:** Light trucks with 2.5L engines without air conditioning. **Defect:** The engine cooling fan blades break as a result of fatigue and/or vehicle-induced stress. **Consequence:** If the blade breakage occurs while the hood is open, a person working under the hood or in the vicinity of the vehicle could be struck and injured by the blade segment. **Corrective Action:** Install a newly designed fan assembly.

CHEVROLET TRUCK S10 1992

System: Engine. **Vehicle:** Light trucks with 2.5L engines without air conditioning. **Defect:** The engine cooling fan blades break as a result of fatigue and/or vehicle-induced stress. **Consequence:** If the blade breakage occurs while the hood is open, a person working under the hood or in the vicinity of the vehicle could be struck and injured by the blade segment. **Corrective Action:** Install a newly designed fan assembly.

CHEVROLET TRUCK S10 1993

System: Interior systems—FMVSS 209. **Vehicle:** 2-door compact utility trucks with folding rear seats. **Defect:** The outboard rear safety belt assembly will not release the webbing from the retracted position. This does not meet the requirements of FMVSS 209, "Seat belt assemblies." **Consequence:** If the outboard rear safety belt assembly will not release the webbing from the retracted position, safety belt use for the seat occupant is impossible, increasing the risk of injury in an accident. **Corrective Action:** Replace any belt that does not freely extend from the retracted position.

CHEVROLET TRUCK S10 1994

System: Fuel; fuel tank assembly; pipe; filler; neck. **Vehicle:** Light-duty pickup trucks. **Defect:** The fuel tank filler pipes were not manufactured to specification, which caused loss of fuel between the fuel tank filler pipe and the vent tube during a test. The loss of fuel was in excess of the amount permitted by FMVSS 301, "Fuel system integrity." **Consequence:** If a vehicle crash were to occur, causing the joint between the fuel tank filler pipes and the vent tube to crack, and if the vehicle overturned, fuel leakage would occur, which could result in a post-crash fire. **Corrective Action:** Dealers will replace the fuel filler pipe on these vehicles.

System: Brakes; hydraulic; power assist; check valve. **Vehicle:** Light-duty pickup trucks equipped with 2.2L engines. **Defect:** A vacuum hose can detach from the power brake booster check valve as a result of engine backfire. **Consequence:** This can result in increased engine idle and loss of power brake assist after depletion of the booster vacuum reserve. **Corrective Action:** Dealers will install a clamp on the power brake booster assist.

CHEVROLET TRUCK S10 1995

System: Engine; cooling system; fan. **Vehicle:** Light-duty pickup trucks and utility vehicles equipped with air conditioning and 4.3L engines. **Defect:** Fan blade rivet breakage can occur, causing the fan blade to separate from the spider. **Consequence:** If this occurred while the hood was open, a person working under the hood of the vehicle or in the vicinity of the vehicle could be struck by the fan blade and injured. **Corrective Action:** Dealers will inspect and replace the fan with a newer fan having thicker-headed rivets, if necessary.

CHEVROLET TRUCK SUBURBAN 1988

System: Seat belt. **Vehicle:** Van-type passenger vehicle equipped with bucket seats and gray interior trim. **Defect:** Driver's seat and/or shoulder belt locking mechanism may not operate. **Consequence:** In a crash, affected belts would not lock, thereby increasing the possibility of injury to the seat occupant. **Corrective Action:** Install a new driver's seat belt assembly.

System: Brakes; hydraulic; disc rotors. **Vehicle:** Light trucks and vans sold or registered in the following states: CT, IL, IN, MA, ME, MI, NH, NJ, NY, OH, PA, RI, VT and WI. **Defect:** Severe corrosion due to road salt at the joint of the stamped steel center section and the cast outer section can cause the sections to separate. **Consequence:** Separation of the rotor sections can cause loss of braking ability in the affected wheel. This could result in increased stopping distance and/or loss of vehicle control and an accident. **Corrective Action:** Replace the front brake rotors with new rotors with a corrosion protection coating. However, if replacement of brake linings is necessary, it will be done at owner's expense, since brake linings are normal maintenance items. **Note:** The vehicles involved can be identified by the following: the 5th character of the vehicle identification number must be a *K* or *L*, and the 7th character must be *3, 4, 5, 6* or *9*. If your vehicle is presented to an authorized dealer on an agreed-upon service date, and the remedy is not provided within a reasonable amount of time and free of charge or the remedy does not correct the safety-related defect or noncompliance, please contact your nearest GMC Truck zone office. The telephone numbers of the zone offices are listed in your warranty and owner's assistance information manuals. Also contact the NHTSA's Auto Safety Hotline at (800) 424-9393.

CHEVROLET TRUCK SUBURBAN 1989

System: Brakes; hydraulic; disc rotors. **Vehicle:** Light trucks and vans sold or registered in the following states: CT, IL, IN, MA, ME, MI, NH, NJ, NY, OH, PA, RI, VT and WI. **Defect:** Severe corrosion due to road salt at the joint of the stamped steel center section and the cast outer section can cause the sections to separate. **Consequence:** Separation of the rotor sections can cause loss of braking ability in the affected wheel. This could result in increased stopping distance and/or loss of vehicle control and an accident. **Corrective Action:** Replace the front brake rotors with new rotors with a corrosion protection coating. However, if replacement of brake linings is necessary, it will be done at owner's expense since brake linings are normal maintenance items. **Note:** The vehicles involved can be identified by the following: the 5th character of the vehicle identification number must be a *K* or *L*, and the 7th character must be *3, 4, 5, 6* or *9*. If your vehicle is presented to an authorized dealer on an agreed-upon service date, and the remedy is not provided within a reasonable amount of time and free of charge or the remedy does not correct the safety-related defect or noncompliance, please contact your nearest GMC Truck zone office. The telephone numbers of the zone offices are listed in your warranty and owner's assistance information manuals. Also contact the NHTSA's Auto Safety Hotline at (800) 424-9393.

System: Interior systems; seat tracks, anchors and seats. **Vehicle:** Vans and utility vehicles equipped with bucket seats with knob-type recliner mechanisms. **Defect:** The recliner mechanism and the seat frame may have foam and/or vinyl between them, creating a "soft" joint. This soft joint results in lower than specified bolt torque, which leads to joint looseness, causing bolt fatigue and eventual bolt failure. **Consequence:** If bolt failure occurs to the driver's seat, it would allow the seat back to suddenly recline, and could result in loss of vehicle control and a vehicle crash without prior warning. **Corrective Action:** Dealers will remove the foam and/or vinyl from between the recliner mechanism and the seat frame soft joint and replace the recliner bolts.

CHEVROLET TRUCK SUBURBAN 1990

System: Brakes; hydraulic; disc rotors. **Vehicle:** Light trucks and vans sold or registered in the following states: CT, IL, IN, MA, ME, MI, NH, NJ, NY, OH, PA, RI, VT and WI. **Defect:** Severe corrosion due to road salt at the joint of the stamped steel center section and the cast outer section can cause the sections to separate. **Consequence:** Separation of the rotor sections can cause loss of braking ability in the affected wheel. This could result in increased stopping distance and/or loss of vehicle control and an accident. **Corrective Action:** Replace the front brake rotors with new rotors with a corrosion protection coating. However, if replacement of brake linings is necessary, it will be done at owner's expense since brake linings are normal maintenance items. **Note:** The vehicles involved can be identified by the following: the 5th character of the vehicle identification number must be a *K* or *L*, and the 7th character must be *3, 4, 5, 6* or *9*. If your vehicle is presented to an authorized dealer on an agreed-upon service date, and the remedy is not provided within a reasonable amount of time and free of charge or the remedy does not correct the safety-related defect or noncompliance, please contact your nearest GMC Truck zone office. The telephone numbers of the zone offices are listed in your warranty and owner's assistance information manuals. Also contact the NHTSA's Auto Safety Hotline at (800) 424-9393.

System: Interior systems; seat tracks, anchors and seats. **Vehicle:** Vans and utility vehicles equipped with bucket seats with knob-type recliner mechanisms. **Defect:** The recliner mechanism and the seat frame may have foam and/or vinyl between them, creating a "soft" joint. This soft joint results in lower than specified bolt torque, which leads to joint looseness, causing bolt fatigue and eventual bolt failure. **Consequence:** If bolt failure occurs to the driver's seat, it would allow the seat back to suddenly recline, and could result in loss of vehicle control and a vehicle crash without prior warning. **Corrective Action:** Dealers will remove the foam and/or vinyl from between the recliner mechanism and the seat frame soft joint and replace the recliner bolts.

CHEVROLET TRUCK SUBURBAN 1991

System: Brakes; hydraulic; disc rotors. **Vehicle:** Light trucks and vans sold or registered in the following states: CT, IL, IN, MA, ME, MI, NH, NJ, NY, OH, PA, RI, VT and WI. **Defect:** Severe corrosion due to road salt at the joint of the stamped steel center section and the cast outer section can cause the sections to separate. **Consequence:** Separation of the rotor sections can cause loss of braking ability in the affected wheel. This could result in increased stopping distance and/or loss of vehicle control and an accident. **Corrective Action:** Replace the front brake rotors with new rotors with a corrosion protection coating. However, if replacement of brake linings is necessary, it will be done at owner's expense since brake linings are normal maintenance items. **Note:** The vehicles involved can be identified by the following: the 5th character of the vehicle identification number must be a *K* or *L*, and the 7th character must be *3, 4, 5, 6* or *9*. If your vehicle is presented to an authorized dealer on an agreed-upon service date, and the remedy is not provided within a reasonable amount of time and free of charge or the remedy does not correct the safety-related defect or noncompliance, please contact your nearest GMC Truck zone office. The telephone numbers of the zone offices are listed in your warranty and owner's assistance information manuals. Also contact the NHTSA's Auto Safety Hotline at (800) 424-9393.

CHEVROLET TRUCK SUBURBAN 1992

System: Brakes; hydraulic; disc rotors. **Vehicle:** Light trucks and vans sold or registered in the following states: CT, IL, IN, MA, ME, MI, NH, NJ, NY, OH, PA, RI, VT and WI. **Defect:** Severe corrosion due to road salt at the joint of the stamped steel center section and the cast outer section can cause the sections to separate. **Consequence:** Separation of the rotor sections can cause loss of braking ability in the affected wheel. This could result in increased stopping distance and/or loss of vehicle control and an accident. **Corrective Action:** Replace the front brake rotors with new rotors with a corrosion protection coating. However, if replacement of brake linings is necessary, it will be done at owner's expense since brake linings are normal maintenance items. **Note:** The vehicles involved can be identified by the following: the 5th character of the vehicle identification number must be a *K* or *L*, and the 7th character must be *3, 4, 5, 6* or *9*. If your vehicle is presented to an authorized dealer on an agreed-upon service date, and the remedy is not provided within a reasonable amount of time and free of charge or the remedy does not correct the safety-related defect or noncompliance, please contact your nearest GMC Truck zone office. The telephone numbers of the zone offices are listed in your warranty and owner's assistance information manuals. Also contact the NHTSA's Auto Safety Hotline at (800) 424-9393.

CHRYSLER

Note: If your Chrysler is presented to an authorized dealer on an agreed-upon service date and the remedy is not provided within a reasonable time and free of charge or the remedy does not correct the defect or noncompliance, please contact Chrysler Service Center at (800) 992-1997. Also contact the NHTSA's Auto Safety Hotline at (800) 424-9393.

CHRYSLER CONCORDE 1994

System: Electrical system; wiring. **Vehicle:** Passenger cars. **Defect:** The right steering tie rod can rub through the automatic transmission wiring harness, causing a short circuit that results in electrical system malfunctions, including engine stalling and an inoperative park/starter interlock system. **Consequence:** Electrical system malfunction, causing stalling while in motion, or an inoperative park/starter interlock system, which allows engine start while the transmission is not in the park position, may result in an accident. **Corrective Action:** Install a revised wiring harness and a convoluted sleeve to protect the transmission wiring harness.

CHRYSLER FIFTH AVENUE 1988

System: Electrical—engine wiring harness. **Vehicle:** Passenger cars equipped with automatic speed control. **Defect:** Engine compartment wiring harness fusible link wires may be trapped under the speed control servo bracket. **Consequence:** Trapped wires may eventually cause a high-resistance electrical short that can result in an underhood fire. **Corrective Action:** Free any trapped wiring; then secure wiring with a tie strap to keep away from speed control bracket.

CHRYSLER FIFTH AVENUE 1990

System: Airbag inflator modules. **Vehicle:** Passenger cars with gray interior. **Defect:** Airbag inflator modules may not contain diffuser holes between the igniter and propellant chambers. **Consequence:** Airbags would not deploy in an impact situation, which could lead to driver injury. **Corrective Action:** Replace airbag inflator modules with properly machined modules.

CHRYSLER IMPERIAL 1990

System: Brakes. **Vehicle:** Passenger cars and vans with antilock brake systems (ABS). **Defect:** The antilock brake system high-pressure hose may leak or detach at its crimped end fitting, resulting in the discharge of hydraulic fluid. **Consequence:** Fluid discharge eventually causes the loss of both the antilock brake system and hydraulic assist for the brake system, resulting in increased likelihood of brake lockup and increased stopping distances, which could result in a vehicle accident. **Corrective Action:** Replace the ABS high-pressure hose with a hose of different design and construction.

CHRYSLER IMPERIAL 1991

System: Safety belt. **Vehicle:** Passenger vehicles. **Defect:** Front outboard safety belt may become difficult to latch and or unlatch due to a webbing stiffener entering the buckle housing and dislodging the buckle latch guide. **Consequence:** Latch may open during accident or sudden stop, exposing seat occupant to increased risk of injury. **Corrective Action:** Replace buckle latch engagement.

System: Brakes. **Vehicle:** Passenger cars and vans with antilock brake systems (ABS). **Defect:** The antilock brake system high-pressure hose may leak or detach at its crimped end fitting, resulting in the discharge of hydraulic fluid. **Consequence:** Fluid discharge eventually causes the loss of both the antilock brake system and hydraulic assist for the brake system, resulting in increased likelihood of brake lockup and increased stopping distances, which could result in a vehicle accident. **Corrective Action:** Replace the ABS high-pressure hose with a hose of different design and construction.

CHRYSLER LEBARON 1987

System: Throttle linkage. **Vehicle:** Passenger cars. **Defect:** Driver's floor mat mispositioned so as to interfere with accelerator pedal. **Consequence:** Floor mat may restrict return of accelerator pedal to the idle position. **Corrective Action:** Floor mat will be replaced with a redesigned mat to eliminate the interference.

System: Fuel. **Vehicle:** Vehicles equipped with 2.2L turbocharged engine. **Defect:** Fuel leakage may occur in low ambient temperature operation at connections of an engine compartment fuel supply hose to the pressure regulator and to the fuel rail. **Consequence:** In the presence of an ignition source, fuel leakage could result in a fire. **Corrective Action:** Relocate pressure regulator; replace fuel supply with formed hose with revised routing configuration to ensure sealing integrity.

CHRYSLER LEBARON 1989

System: Engine valve cover gasket. **Vehicle:** Passenger cars, light trucks and minivans. **Defect:** The engine valve cover gasket may dislocate and allow an engine oil leak at the gasket. **Consequence:** The leakage of oil in the engine compartment could cause a fire. **Corrective Action:** Replace gasket cover with revised cover; RTV sealant will be applied in place of a gasket.

System: Disc brakes. **Vehicle:** Passenger cars. **Defect:** The bonded disc brake linings may separate from the shoes due to a bonding deficiency, which may allow corrosion degradation of the bond attachment. **Consequence:** Separation of the disc brake linings results in an increase in stopping distance. **Corrective Action:** Replace the front and rear linings on vehicles with 15-inch brakes. Replace only the rear brake linings on vehicles with 14-inch brakes because the front linings on these vehicles are riveted. **Note:** This recall applies only to cars registered in the "salt belt" states that use large quantities of road salt for snow and ice removal. Chrysler includes the following states: CT, DE, IL, IN, IA, ME, MA, MD, MI, MN, MO, NH, NJ, NY, OH, PA, RI, VT, VA, DC, WV and WI.

CHRYSLER LEBARON 1990

System: Engine valve cover gasket. **Vehicle:** Passenger cars, light trucks and minivans. **Defect:** The engine valve cover gasket may dislocate and allow an engine oil leak at the gasket. **Consequence:** The leakage of oil in the engine compartment could cause a fire. **Corrective Action:** Replace gasket cover with revised cover; RTV sealant will be applied in place of a gasket.

System: Airbag inflator modules. **Vehicle:** Passenger cars with gray interior. **Defect:** Airbag inflator modules may not contain diffuser holes between the igniter and propellant chambers. **Consequence:** Airbags would not deploy in an impact situation, which could lead to driver injury. **Corrective Action:** Replace airbag inflator modules with properly machined modules.

CHRYSLER LEBARON 1991

System: Front disc brake caliper guide pin bolts. **Vehicle:** Passenger cars. **Defect:** Front disc brake caliper guide pin bolts may not have been adequately torqued and could loosen. **Consequence:** This could cause reduced braking effectiveness and could result in an accident. **Corrective Action:** Properly torque front brake caliper guide pin bolts to 250 pounds.

System: Airbag sensors. **Vehicle:** Passenger cars. **Defect:** The two airbag system front impact sensors may not be secured to their mounting brackets. **Consequence:** Airbag will not deploy in a frontal collision if the front impact sensors are not attached. **Corrective Action:** Repair to ensure proper attachment of front impact sensors to brackets.

System: Parking brake assembly—FMVSS 105. **Vehicle:** Passenger cars. **Defect:** Mismatched parking brake cable lengths to the rear wheels reduce braking ability of one of the rear wheels, in violation of FMVSS 105. **Consequence:** Insufficient braking ability could result in inadvertent vehicle rollaway, which could result in a vehicle accident. **Corrective Action:** Replace mismatched parking brake cable with one of correct length.

System: Safety belt. **Vehicle:** Passenger vehicle. **Defect:** Front outboard safety belt may become difficult to latch and/or unlatch due to a webbing stiffener entering the buckle housing and dislodging the buckle latch guide. **Consequence:** Latch may open during accident or sudden stop, exposing seat occupant to increased risk of injury. **Corrective Action:** Replace buckle latch engagement.

System: Door assembly. **Vehicle:** Passenger cars; sedans, coupes and convertibles. **Defect:** The owner's manual incorrectly states that the front passenger door cannot be opened from the inside if the door is locked until the lock control handle has been pulled up. On these vehicles, the front passenger door can be opened by the inside door handle even if the door is locked. **Consequence:** The error in the owner's manual may lead a front seat passenger to mistakenly open the car door while the vehicle is in motion, believing the inside door handle would not open if the door was locked. This could result in an injury to the front seat passenger. **Corrective Action:** Notify the vehicle owners of the error in the owner's manual and inform them of the actual operation of the front door lock system.

CHRYSLER LEBARON 1992

System: Steering; upper steering column coupling bolt. **Vehicle:** Passenger vehicles; sedans, convertibles and minivans. **Defect:** The zinc-plating operation performed on the upper steering column shaft coupling bolt caused hydrogen embrittlement and breakage of the bolt. **Consequence:** Fractures of the upper steering column shaft coupling bolt result in a lack of coupling load on the shaft and loss of steering control. **Corrective Action:** Replace the zinc-plated bolt with a phosphate-plated bolt.

System: Hood latch. **Vehicle:** Passenger cars. **Defect:** The hood latch assembly may not have been properly installed, and the secondary hood latch may be prevented from engaging when the hood is closed. **Consequence:** If the primary hood latch engagement fails, the lack of engagement by the secondary hood latch could cause the hood to open while the vehicle is in motion, reducing operator's ability to see the road and oncoming traffic, and possibly resulting in a vehicle accident. **Corrective Action:** Adjust the secondary hood latch to allow the latch assembly to properly engage when the hood is closed.

CHRYSLER NEW YORKER 1987

System: Fuel. **Vehicle:** Vehicles equipped with 2.2L turbocharged engine. **Defect:** Fuel leakage may occur in low ambient temperature operation at connections of an engine compartment fuel supply hose to the pressure regulator and to the fuel rail. **Consequence:** In the presence of an ignition source, fuel leakage could result in a fire. **Corrective Action:** Relocate pressure regulator; replace fuel supply with formed hose with revised routing configuration to ensure sealing integrity.

CHRYSLER NEW YORKER 1990

System: Heater blower motor resistor block. **Vehicle:** Passenger cars without automatic temperature control system. **Defect:** Water leaking under windshield cowl in area above the heater blower motor resistor block results in corrosion of the resistor terminals. **Consequence:** Corrosion of the resistor terminals increases electrical resistance, leading to overheating and possible ignition of the wiring connectors and insulation, causing a fire in the cowl area. **Corrective Action:** The blower motor resistor block will be replaced, and a mastic patch applied to seal the cowl against water entry. Damaged wire connectors will be replaced.

System: Brakes. **Vehicle:** Passenger cars and vans with antilock brake systems (ABS). **Defect:** The antilock brake system high-pressure hose may leak or detach at its crimped end fitting, resulting in the discharge of hydraulic fluid. **Consequence:** Fluid discharge eventually causes the loss of both the antilock brake system and hydraulic assist for the brake system, resulting in increased likelihood of brake lockup and increased stopping distances, which could result in a vehicle accident. **Corrective Action:** Replace the antilock brake system high-pressure hose with a hose of different design and construction.

CHRYSLER NEW YORKER 1991

System: Heater blower motor resistor block. **Vehicle:** Passenger cars without automatic temperature control system. **Defect:** Water leaking under windshield cowl in area above the heater blower motor resistor block results in corrosion of the resistor terminals. **Consequence:** Corrosion of the resistor terminals increases electrical resistance, leading to overheating and possible ignition of the wiring connectors and insulation, causing a fire in the cowl area. **Corrective Action:** The blower motor resistor block will be replaced, and a mastic patch applied to seal the cowl against water entry. Damaged wire connectors will be replaced.

System: Safety belt. **Vehicle:** Passenger vehicle. **Defect:** Front outboard safety belt may become difficult to latch and/or unlatch due to a webbing stiffener entering the buckle housing and dislodging the buckle latch guide. **Consequence:** Latch may open during accident or sudden stop, exposing seat occupant to increased risk of injury. **Corrective Action:** Replace buckle latch engagement.

System: Brakes. **Vehicle:** Passenger cars and vans with antilock brake systems (ABS). **Defect:** The antilock brake system high-pressure hose may leak or detach at its crimped end fitting, resulting in the discharge of hydraulic fluid. **Consequence:** Fluid discharge eventually causes the loss of both the antilock brake system and hydraulic assist for the brake system, resulting in increased likelihood of brake lockup and increased stopping distances, which could result in a vehicle accident. **Corrective Action:** Replace the antilock brake system high-pressure hose with a hose of different design and construction.

CHRYSLER NEW YORKER 1994

System: Electrical system; wiring. **Vehicle:** Passenger cars. **Defect:** The right steering tie rod can rub through the automatic transmission wiring harness, causing a short circuit that results in electrical system malfunctions, including engine stalling and an inoperative park/starter interlock system. **Consequence:** Electrical system malfunction causing stalling while in motion, or an inoperative park/starter interlock system, which allows engine start while the transmission is not in the park position, may result in an accident. **Corrective Action:** Install a revised wiring harness and a convoluted sleeve to protect the transmission wiring harness.

CHRYSLER TRUCK TOWN AND COUNTRY 1992

System: Safety belts—FMVSS 209. **Vehicle:** Vans, light trucks and multipurpose vehicles. **Defect:** Front outboard seat belt assemblies do not have the properly marked label with manufacturer information. **Consequence:** The seat belt assemblies do not comply with FMVSS 209. **Corrective Action:** Chrysler has not proposed a corrective action for this safety defect. **Note:** The manufacturer's petition, which requested that NHTSA determine that this FMVSS noncompliance does not create an unreasonable risk to motor vehicle safety, has been granted. Therefore, the manufacturer is not obligated to conduct an owner notification and remedy campaign.

System: Fuel tank. **Vehicle:** Passenger vans. **Defect:** Fuel tank flanges were not bent as required to allow the specified clearance for the fuel tank mounting straps and fuel lines at the tank. **Consequence:** The unbent flanges to the fuel tank will damage the mounting straps and/or fuel lines. The damaged mounting straps may break, causing the tank to drop, and the damaged fuel line will leak fuel. In either case, a fire could result if the spilled fuel is exposed to an ignition source. **Corrective Action:** Repair the flange by bending to the correct angle; replace damaged fuel lines and mounting straps.

System: Structure; hatchback locks and latches. **Vehicle:** Light-duty passenger minivans; 1984 through 1995 models without remote release; 1984 through 1995 models with remote release. **Description of Alleged Defect:** This is not a safety recall. There has been no determination that a safety defect exists with the minivan latches. Chrysler is conducting a service campaign to replace the liftgate latch assembly of the affected minivans. In a collision, the rear liftgate latch assembly could open. **Consequence of Alleged Defect:** If the liftgate latch opens, occupants can be ejected, resulting in significantly increased risk of injury or death. **Corrective Action:** Chrysler dealers will replace the liftgate latch with a new, stronger latch assembly without charge. The replacement latch assemblies are currently being produced for this service action. Chrysler will renotify owners when parts are available. **Note:** This is not a safety recall. There has been no determination that a safety defect exists with the minivan latches. However, Chrysler has decided to provide a stronger latch without charge. Owners can contact Chrysler at (800) MINIVAN [(800) 646-4826].

CHRYSLER TRUCK TOWN AND COUNTRY 1993

System: Wheels. **Vehicle:** Passenger minivans with 15-inch stamped steel road wheels or stamped steel spare wheels. **Defect:** The 15-inch wheels have a malformed lug nut seat configuration that causes poor nut-to-wheel contact and centering of the wheel during installation. **Consequence:** Poor nut-to-wheel contact during installation can lead to possible loss of a wheel, resulting in loss of vehicle control and an accident. **Corrective Action:** The road and spare wheels with the malformed lug nut seat configuration will be replaced.

System: Structure; hatchback locks and latches. **Vehicle:** Light-duty passenger minivans; 1984 through 1995 models without remote release; 1984 through 1995 models with remote release. **Description of Alleged Defect:** This is not a safety recall. There has been no determination that a safety defect exists with the minivan latches. Chrysler is conducting a service campaign to replace the liftgate latch assembly of the affected minivans. In a collision, the rear liftgate latch assembly could open. **Consequence of Alleged Defect:** If the liftgate latch opens, occupants can be ejected, resulting in significantly increased risk of injury or death. **Corrective Action:** Chrysler dealers will replace the liftgate latch with a new, stronger latch assembly without charge. The replacement latch assemblies are currently being produced for this service action. Chrysler will renotify owners when parts are available. **Note:** This is not a safety recall. There has been no determination that a safety defect exists with the minivan latches. However, Chrysler has decided to provide a stronger latch without charge. Owners can contact Chrysler at (800) MINIVAN [(800) 646-4826].

DODGE

Note: If your Dodge is presented to an authorized dealer on an agreed-upon service date and the remedy is not provided free of charge within a reasonable time, please contact Chrysler at (800) 853-1403. Also contact the NHTSA's Auto Safety Hotline at (800) 424-9393.

DODGE ARIES 1989

System: Engine valve cover gasket. **Vehicle:** Passenger cars, light trucks and minivans. **Defect:** The engine valve cover gasket may dislocate, allowing an engine oil leak at the gasket. **Consequence:** The leakage of oil in the engine compartment could cause a fire. **Corrective Action:** Replace gasket cover with revised cover; RTV sealant will be applied in place of a gasket.

DODGE CHARGER 1987

System: Fuel. **Vehicle:** Passenger vehicles. **Defect:** Pressure regulator installed in the fuel supply plumbing system leaks fuel into the engine compartment. **Consequence:** Fuel leaks can result in a fire when near a source of ignition. **Corrective Action:** The fuel supply pressure regulator assembly will be replaced with a new assembly to ensure integrity of the fuel supply system.

DODGE COLT 1987

System: Interior; seat belts; belt buckles. **Vehicle:** Passenger, multipurpose vehicles and light-duty trucks equipped with safety belts made by Takata Corporation. **Defect:** The front safety belt buckle release buttons can break. These red plastic release buttons are marked "press." If a button breaks, pieces can fall into the buckle assembly, causing the buckle to operate improperly. **Consequence:** The safety belts would not provide adequate protection to an occupant in a vehicle crash. **Corrective Action:** Owners should promptly check the condition and operation of both front safety belt buckles and carefully inspect the red release button for any breaks or cracks. They should ensure that both buckles are operating properly by inserting each latchplate into its buckle, tugging on the belt to make sure the latch is securely locked and then pressing the release button. The latchplate should pop out of the buckle when the button is pressed. If either release button shows a sign of breaking or cracking, or if either buckle fails to operate properly, owners should promptly contact their authorized dealer to schedule an appointment to have the buckle replaced or repaired, free of charge. The manufacturer is developing a remedy designed to prevent failure of the buttons that are not currently broken.

DODGE COLT 1988

System: Interior; seat belts; belt buckles. **Vehicle:** Passenger, multipurpose vehicles and light-duty trucks equipped with safety belts made by Takata Corporation. **Defect:** The front safety belt buckle release buttons can break. These red plastic release buttons are marked "press." If a button breaks, pieces can fall into the buckle assembly, causing the buckle to operate improperly. **Consequence:** The safety belts would not provide adequate protection to an occupant in a vehicle crash. **Corrective Action:** Owners should promptly check the condition and operation of both front safety belt buckles and carefully inspect the red release button for any breaks or cracks. They should ensure that both buckles are operating properly by inserting each latchplate into its buckle, tugging on the belt to make sure the latch is securely locked and then pressing the release button. The latchplate should pop out of the buckle when the button is pressed. If either release button shows a sign of breaking or cracking, or if either buckle fails to operate properly, owners should promptly contact their authorized dealer to schedule an appointment to have the buckle replaced or repaired, free of charge. The manufacturer is developing a remedy designed to prevent failure of the buttons that are not currently broken.

DODGE COLT 1989

System: Interior; seat belts; belt buckles. **Vehicle:** Passenger, multipurpose vehicles and light-duty trucks equipped with safety belts made by Takata Corporation. **Defect:** The front safety belt buckle release buttons can break. These red plastic release buttons are marked "press." If a button breaks, pieces can fall into the buckle assembly, causing the buckle to operate improperly. **Consequence:** The safety belts would not provide adequate protection to an occupant in a vehicle crash. **Corrective Action:** Owners should promptly check the condition and operation of both front safety belt buckles and carefully inspect the red release button for any breaks or cracks. They should ensure that both buckles are operating properly by inserting each latchplate into its buckle, tugging on the belt to make sure the latch is securely locked and then pressing the release button. The latchplate should pop out of the buckle when the button is pressed. If either release button shows a sign of breaking or cracking, or if either buckle fails to operate properly, owners should promptly contact their authorized dealer to schedule an appointment to have the buckle replaced or repaired, free of charge. The manufacturer is developing a remedy designed to prevent failure of the buttons that are not currently broken.

DODGE DAYTONA 1987

System: Fuel. **Vehicle:** Vehicles equipped with 2.2L turbocharged engine. **Defect:** Fuel leakage may occur in low ambient temperature operation at connections of an engine compartment fuel supply hose to the pressure regulator and to the fuel rail. **Consequence:** In the presence of an ignition source, fuel leakage could result in a fire. **Corrective Action:** Relocate pressure regulator; replace fuel supply with formed hose with revised routing configuration to ensure sealing integrity.

DODGE DAYTONA 1989

System: Engine valve cover gasket. **Vehicle:** Passenger cars, light trucks and minivans. **Defect:** The engine valve cover gasket may dislocate, allowing an engine oil leak at the gasket. **Consequence:** The leakage of oil in the engine compartment could cause a fire. **Corrective Action:** Replace gasket cover with revised cover; RTV sealant will be applied in place of a gasket.

System: Disc brakes. **Vehicle:** Passenger cars. **Defect:** The bonded disc brake linings may separate from the shoes due to a bonding deficiency that may allow corrosion degradation of the bond attachment. **Consequence:** Separation of the disc brake linings results in an increase in stopping distance. **Corrective Action:** Replace the front and rear linings on vehicles with 15-inch brakes. Replace only the rear brake linings on vehicles with 14-inch brakes because the front linings on these vehicles are riveted. **Note:** This recall applies only to cars registered in the "salt belt" states that use large quantities of road salt for snow and ice removal. Chrysler includes the following states: CT, DE, IL, IN, IA, ME, MA, MD, MI, MN, MO, NH, NJ, NY, OH, PA, RI, VT, VA, DC, WV and WI.

DODGE DAYTONA 1990

System: Engine valve cover gasket. **Vehicle:** Passenger cars, light trucks and minivans. **Defect:** The engine valve cover gasket may dislocate, allowing an engine oil leak at the gasket. **Consequence:** The leakage of oil in the engine compartment could cause a fire. **Corrective Action:** Replace gasket cover with revised cover; RTV sealant will be applied in place of a gasket.

System: Airbag inflator modules. **Vehicle:** Passenger cars with gray interior. **Defect:** Airbag inflator modules may not contain diffuser holes between the igniter and propellant chambers. **Consequence:** Airbags would not deploy in an impact situation, which could lead to driver injury. **Corrective Action:** Replace airbag inflator modules with properly machined modules.

DODGE DYNASTY 1989

System: Engine valve cover gasket. **Vehicle:** Passenger cars, light trucks and minivans. **Defect:** The engine valve cover gasket may dislocate, allowing an engine oil leak at the gasket. **Consequence:** The leakage of oil in the engine compartment could cause a fire. **Corrective Action:** Replace gasket cover with revised cover; RTV sealant will be applied in place of a gasket.

DODGE DYNASTY 1990

System: Engine valve cover gasket. **Vehicle:** Passenger cars, light trucks and minivans. **Defect:** The engine valve cover gasket may dislocate, allowing an engine oil leak at the gasket. **Consequence:** The leakage of oil in the engine compartment could cause a fire. **Corrective Action:** Replace gasket cover with revised cover; RTV sealant will be applied in place of a gasket.

System: Airbag inflator modules. **Vehicle:** Passenger cars with gray interior. **Defect:** Airbag inflator modules may not contain diffuser holes between the igniter and propellant chambers. **Consequence:** Airbags would not deploy in an impact situation, which could lead to driver injury. **Corrective Action:** Replace airbag inflator modules with properly machined modules.

System: Heater blower motor resistor block. **Vehicle:** Passenger cars without automatic temperature control system. **Defect:** Water leaking under windshield cowl in the area above heater blower motor resistor block results in corrosion of the resistor terminals. **Consequence:** Corrosion of the resistor terminals increases electrical resistance, leading to overheating and possible ignition of the wiring connectors and insulation, causing a fire in the cowl area. **Corrective Action:** The blower motor resistor block will be replaced, and a mastic patch applied to seal the cowl against water entry. Damaged wire connectors will be replaced.

System: Brakes. **Vehicle:** Passenger cars and vans with antilock brake systems (ABS). **Defect:** The antilock brake system high-pressure hose may leak or detach at its crimped end fitting, resulting in the discharge of hydraulic fluid. **Consequence:** Fluid discharge eventually causes the loss of both the antilock brake system and hydraulic assist for the brake system, resulting in increased likelihood of brake lockup and increased stopping distances, which could result in a vehicle accident. **Corrective Action:** Replace the antilock brake system high-pressure hose with a hose of different design and construction.

DODGE DYNASTY 1991

System: Front disc brake caliper guide pin bolts. **Vehicle:** Passenger cars. **Defect:** Front disc brake caliper guide pin bolts may not have been adequately torqued and could loosen. **Consequence:** This could cause reduced braking effectiveness and could result in an accident. **Corrective Action:** Properly torque front brake caliper guide pin bolts to 250 pounds.

System: Heater blower motor resistor block. **Vehicle:** Passenger cars without automatic temperature control system. **Defect:** Water leaking under windshield cowl in the area above heater blower motor resistor block results in corrosion of the resistor terminals. **Consequence:** Corrosion of the resistor terminals increases electrical resistance, leading to overheating and possible ignition of the wiring connectors and insulation, causing a fire in the cowl area. **Corrective Action:** The blower motor resistor block will be replaced, and a mastic patch applied to seal the cowl against water entry. Damaged wire connectors will be replaced.

System: Safety belt. **Vehicle:** Passenger vehicle. **Defect:** Front outboard safety belt may become difficult to latch and/or unlatch due to a webbing stiffener entering the buckle housing and dislodging the buckle latch guide. **Consequence:** Latch may open during accident or sudden stop, exposing seat occupant to increased risk of injury. **Corrective Action:** Replace buckle latch engagement.

System: Brakes. **Vehicle:** Passenger cars and vans with antilock brake systems (ABS). **Defect:** The antilock brake system high-pressure hose may leak or detach at its crimped end fitting, resulting in the discharge of hydraulic fluid. **Consequence:** Fluid discharge eventually causes the loss of both the antilock brake system and hydraulic assist for the brake system, resulting in increased likelihood of brake lockup and increased stopping distances, which could result in a vehicle accident. **Corrective Action:** Replace the antilock brake system high-pressure hose with a hose of different design and construction.

DODGE DYNASTY 1992

System: Steering; upper steering column coupling bolt. **Vehicle:** Passenger vehicles; sedans, convertibles and minivans. **Defect:** The zinc-plating operation performed on the upper steering column shaft coupling bolt caused hydrogen embrittlement and breakage of the bolt. **Consequence:** Fractures of the upper steering column shaft coupling bolt result in a lack of coupling load on the shaft and loss of steering control. **Corrective Action:** Replace the zinc-plated bolt with a phosphate-plated bolt.

DODGE INTREPID 1993

System: Suspension: front lower control arm. **Vehicle:** Passenger cars. **Defect:** The front suspension lower control arm tension strut washers can crack and fall off due to hydrogen embrittlement. **Consequence:** Loss of a washer will cause a clunking sound, heard during braking. If left unattended, the loss of the washer will eventually result in tension strut attachment failure, which can result in loss of steering control and an accident. **Corrective Action:** Replace the front and rear strut bar washers and nuts.

DODGE INTREPID 1994

System: Electrical system; wiring. **Vehicle:** Passenger cars. **Defect:** The right steering tie rod can rub through the automatic transmission wiring harness, causing a short circuit that results in electrical system malfunctions, including engine stalling and an inoperative park/starter interlock system. **Consequence:** Electrical system malfunction, causing stalling while in motion, or an inoperative park/starter interlock system, which allows engine start while the transmission is not in the park position, may result in an accident. **Corrective Action:** Install a revised wiring harness and a convoluted sleeve to protect the transmission wiring harness.

DODGE LANCER 1987

System: Fuel. **Vehicle:** Vehicles equipped with 2.2L turbocharged engine. **Defect:** Fuel leakage may occur in low ambient temperature operation at connections of an engine compartment fuel supply hose to the pressure regulator and to the fuel rail. **Consequence:** In the presence of an ignition source, fuel leakage could result in a fire. **Corrective Action:** Relocate pressure regulator; replace fuel supply with formed hose with revised routing configuration to ensure sealing integrity.

System: Parking brake. **Vehicle:** Passenger cars. **Defect:** Parking brake mechanism component may disengage. **Consequence:** This could result in loss of parking brake function; also, loose component could jam in the parking brake assembly. **Corrective Action:** Replace parking brake assembly.

DODGE MONACO 1990

System: Steering column shaft. **Vehicle:** Passenger cars. **Defect:** Lower intermediate steering shaft may separate at the rubber isolated coupling of the shaft. **Consequence:** This could result in loss of steering control and an accident. **Corrective Action:** Replace intermediate steering shaft with a shaft containing a restrained coupling.

System: Front brake hose. **Vehicle:** Passenger cars. **Defect:** Routing of the front brake hose may cause excessive hose flexing, resulting in premature fatigue cracking of the outer hose cover. **Consequence:** This could lead to hose failure and loss of brake fluid, reducing braking effectiveness. **Corrective Action:** Replace front brake hoses with hoses redesigned to provide a modified routing configuration.

System: Rear brake tube. **Vehicle:** Passenger cars. **Defect:** Rear brake tube routing is contacted by fuel tank heat shield when suspension is in full jounce position. This damages the brake fluid tube, causing a leak. **Consequence:** Loss of fluid from half of the diagonally split brake hydraulic system affects braking capability, which could result in an accident. **Corrective Action:** Modify the heat shield to eliminate potential for the shield contacting brake tube.

System: Heater; water; defroster; heater core. **Vehicle:** Passenger vehicles. **Defect:** The end cap connecting the heat exchanger's core to the engine cooling system could rupture and allow hot coolant to escape into the passenger compartment. **Consequence:** The coolant escaping into the passenger compartment could contact the driver's feet and injure the driver. Also, steam from the heater liquid will cloud on the window surfaces and impair the driver's vision. In either case, failure of the heater core end cap could result in a vehicle accident. **Corrective Action:** A coolant temperature-controlled heater core fluid bypass valve will be installed.

DODGE MONACO 1991

System: Rear brake tube. **Vehicle:** Passenger cars. **Defect:** Rear brake tube routing is contacted by fuel tank heat shield when suspension is in full jounce position. This damages the brake fluid tube, causing a leak. **Consequence:** Loss of fluid from half of the diagonally split brake hydraulic system affects braking capability, which could result in an accident. **Corrective Action:** Modify the heat shield to eliminate potential for the shield contacting brake tube.

System: Battery feed wiring. **Vehicle:** Passenger cars. **Defect:** Routing of battery main feed wiring may allow it to contact the air cleaner bracket, and continued contact may lead to an electrical short circuit. **Consequence:** The electrical short circuit caused by continuous contact could result in the ignition of the wiring insulation, and an underhood fire. **Corrective Action:** The main feed on all involved vehicles will be rerouted and secured with tie straps away from the air cleaner bracket.

System: Brakes. **Vehicle:** Passenger cars and vans with antilock brake systems (ABS). **Defect:** The antilock brake system high-pressure hose may leak or detach at its crimped end fitting, resulting in the discharge of hydraulic fluid. **Consequence:** Fluid discharge eventually causes the loss of both the antilock brake system and hydraulic assist for the brake system, resulting in increased likelihood of brake lockup and increased stopping distances, which could result in a vehicle accident. **Corrective Action:** Replace the antilock brake system high-pressure hose with a hose of different design and construction.

System: Heater; water; defroster; heater core. **Vehicle:** Passenger vehicles. **Defect:** The end cap connecting the heat exchanger's core to the engine cooling system could rupture and allow hot coolant to escape into the passenger compartment. **Consequence:** The coolant escaping into the passenger compartment could contact the driver's feet and injure the driver. Also, steam from the heater liquid will cloud on the window surfaces and impair the driver's vision. In either case, failure of the heater core end cap could result in a vehicle accident. **Corrective Action:** A coolant temperature-controlled heater core fluid bypass valve will be installed.

DODGE NEON 1995

System: Brakes; hydraulic; anti-skid system. **Vehicle:** Passenger cars. **Defect:** The antilock brake system master cylinder rear seal allows air to enter the brake system, causing spongy brakes or partial brake system loss. **Consequence:** Air entering the brake system causes extended stopping distance or partial loss of brakes, which may result in an accident. **Corrective Action:** Master cylinders will be inspected for the suspect build date code range and will be replaced if necessary.

System: Transmission. **Vehicle:** Passenger vehicles. **Defect:** Moisture can get into the power train control module (PCM), causing driveability malfunctions, including stalling. **Consequence:** Should driveability malfunctions or stalling occur while the vehicle is in motion, a traffic accident may occur. **Corrective Action:** The power train control modules on these vehicles will be replaced.

System: Brakes; hydraulic; lines; fittings. **Vehicle:** Passenger vehicles. **Defect:** The rear brake hose mounting bracket screws can fail, allowing the brake hoses to move out of position. The unrestrained hoses are then susceptible to damage, which could result in brake fluid leakage. **Consequence:** Brake fluid leakage will reduce the braking performance of the vehicle and extend stopping distances, and could result in an accident. **Corrective Action:** The rear brake line hose bracket screws on these vehicles will be replaced.

DODGE OMNI 1987

System: Fuel. **Vehicle:** Vehicles equipped with 2.2L turbocharged engine. **Defect:** Fuel leakage may occur in low ambient temperature operation at connections of an engine compartment fuel supply hose to the pressure regulator and to the fuel rail. **Consequence:** In the presence of an ignition source, fuel leakage could result in a fire. **Corrective Action:** Relocate pressure regulator; replace fuel supply with formed hose with revised routing configuration to ensure sealing integrity.

System: Fuel. **Vehicle:** Passenger vehicles. **Defect:** Pressure regulator installed in the fuel supply plumbing system leaks fuel into the engine compartment. **Consequence:** Fuel leaks can result in a fire when near a source of ignition. **Corrective Action:** The fuel supply pressure regulator assembly will be replaced with a new assembly to ensure integrity of the fuel supply system.

DODGE OMNI 1989

System: Engine valve cover gasket. **Vehicle:** Passenger cars, light trucks and minivans. **Defect:** The engine valve cover gasket may dislocate, allowing an engine oil leak at the gasket. **Consequence:** The leakage of oil in the engine compartment could cause a fire. **Corrective Action:** Replace gasket cover with revised cover; RTV sealant will be applied in place of a gasket.

DODGE SHADOW 1987

System: Fuel. **Vehicle:** Vehicles equipped with 2.2L turbocharged engine. **Defect:** Fuel leakage may occur in low ambient temperature operation at connections of an engine compartment fuel supply hose to the pressure regulator and to the fuel rail. **Consequence:** In the presence of an ignition source, fuel leakage could result in a fire. **Corrective Action:** Relocate pressure regulator; replace fuel supply with formed hose with revised routing configuration to ensure sealing integrity.

System: Parking brake. **Vehicle:** Passenger cars. **Defect:** Parking brake mechanism component may disengage. **Consequence:** This could result in loss of parking brake function; also, loose component could jam in the parking brake assembly. **Corrective Action:** Replace parking brake assembly.

DODGE SHADOW 1988

System: Front passenger seat lap belt. **Vehicle:** Passenger cars. **Defect:** Front passenger seat lap belt retractor, which incorporates a child seat belt locking feature, may malfunction. **Consequence:** Seat belt lock could retract and child seat may move out of its restrained position. **Corrective Action:** Replace front passenger seat lap retractor with a redesigned retractor.

System: Automatic shoulder restraints. **Vehicle:** Passenger cars with automatic shoulder restraints. **Defect:** The automatic shoulder restraint systems can malfunction and become inoperative. **Consequence:** Seat occupants without shoulder restraints are subject to increased risk of injury in the event of a sudden stop or vehicle crash. **Corrective Action:** Replace the system drive and rail assembly with revised components. **Note:** While the automatic shoulder restraint system may not function, the restraint system can be operated manually, and should be used to preserve the safety of the seat occupant.

DODGE SHADOW 1989

System: Engine valve cover gasket. **Vehicle:** Passenger cars, light trucks and minivans. **Defect:** The engine valve cover gasket may dislocate, allowing an engine oil leak at the gasket. **Consequence:** The leakage of oil in the engine compartment could cause a fire. **Corrective Action:** Replace gasket cover with revised cover; RTV sealant will be applied in place of a gasket.

System: Automatic shoulder restraints. **Vehicle:** Passenger cars with automatic shoulder restraints. **Defect:** The automatic shoulder restraint systems can malfunction and become inoperative. **Consequence:** Seat occupants without shoulder restraints are subject to increased risk of injury in the event of a sudden stop or vehicle crash. **Corrective Action:** Replace the system drive and rail assembly with revised components. **Note:** While the automatic shoulder restraint system may not function, the restraint system can be operated manually, and should be used to preserve the safety of the seat occupant.

DODGE SHADOW 1990

System: Engine valve cover gasket. **Vehicle:** Passenger cars, light trucks and minivans. **Defect:** The engine valve cover gasket may dislocate, allowing an engine oil leak at the gasket. **Consequence:** The leakage of oil in the engine compartment could cause a fire. **Corrective Action:** Replace gasket cover with revised cover; RTV sealant will be applied in place of a gasket.

DODGE SHADOW 1991

System: Front disc brake caliper guide pin bolts. **Vehicle:** Passenger cars. **Defect:** Front disc brake caliper guide pin bolts may not have been adequately torqued and could loosen. **Consequence:** This could cause reduced braking effectiveness and could result in an accident. **Corrective Action:** Properly torque front brake caliper guide pin bolts to 250 pounds.

System: Airbag sensors. **Vehicle:** Passenger cars. **Defect:** The two airbag system front impact sensors may not be secured to their mounting brackets. **Consequence:** Airbag will not deploy in a frontal collision if the front impact sensors are not attached. **Corrective Action:** Repair to ensure proper attachment of front impact sensors to brackets.

DODGE SHADOW 1992

System: Steering; upper steering column coupling bolt. **Vehicle:** Passenger vehicles; sedans, convertibles and minivans. **Defect:** The zinc-plating operation performed on the upper steering column shaft coupling bolt caused hydrogen embrittlement and breakage of the bolt. **Consequence:** Fractures of the upper steering column shaft coupling bolt result in a lack of coupling load on the shaft and loss of steering control. **Corrective Action:** Replace the zinc-plated bolt with a phosphate-plated bolt.

DODGE SPIRIT 1989

System: Engine valve cover gasket. **Vehicle:** Passenger cars, light trucks and minivans. **Defect:** The engine valve cover gasket may dislocate, allowing an engine oil leak at the gasket. **Consequence:** The leakage of oil in the engine compartment could cause a fire. **Corrective Action:** Replace gasket cover with revised cover; RTV sealant will be applied in place of a gasket.

DODGE SPIRIT 1990

System: Engine valve cover gasket. **Vehicle:** Passenger cars, light trucks and minivans. **Defect:** The engine valve cover gasket may dislocate, allowing an engine oil leak at the gasket. **Consequence:** The leakage of oil in the engine compartment could cause a fire. **Corrective Action:** Replace gasket cover with revised cover; RTV sealant will be applied in place of a gasket.

DODGE SPIRIT 1991

System: Front disc brake caliper guide pin bolts. **Vehicle:** Passenger cars. **Defect:** Front disc brake caliper guide pin bolts may not have been adequately torqued and could loosen. **Consequence:** This could cause reduced braking effectiveness and could result in an accident. **Corrective Action:** Properly torque front brake caliper guide pin bolts to 250 pounds.

System: Airbag sensors. **Vehicle:** Passenger cars. **Defect:** The two airbag system front impact sensors may not be secured to their mounting brackets. **Consequence:** Airbag will not deploy in a frontal collision if the front impact sensors are not attached. **Corrective Action:** Repair to ensure proper attachment of front impact sensors to brackets.

System: Safety belt. **Vehicle:** Passenger vehicle. **Defect:** Front outboard safety belt may become difficult to latch and/or unlatch due to a webbing stiffener entering the buckle housing and dislodging the buckle latch guide. **Consequence:** Latch may open during accident or sudden stop, exposing seat occupant to increased risk of injury. **Corrective Action:** Replace buckle latch engagement.

DODGE SPIRIT 1992

System: Steering; upper steering column coupling bolt. **Vehicle:** Passenger vehicles; sedans, convertibles and minivans. **Defect:** The zinc-plating operation performed on the upper steering column shaft coupling bolt caused hydrogen embrittlement and breakage of the bolt. **Consequence:** Fractures of the upper steering column shaft coupling bolt result in a lack of coupling load on the shaft and loss of steering control. **Corrective Action:** Replace the zinc-plated bolt with a phosphate-plated bolt.

DODGE TRUCK CARAVAN 1987

System: Structure; hatchback locks and latches. **Vehicle:** Light-duty passenger minivans; 1984 through 1995 models without remote release; 1984 through 1995 models with remote release. **Description of Alleged Defect:** This is not a safety recall. There has been no determination that a safety defect exists with the minivan latches. Chrysler is conducting a service campaign to replace the liftgate latch assembly of the affected minivans. In a collision, the rear liftgate latch assembly could open. **Consequence of Alleged Defect:** If the liftgate latch opens, occupants can be ejected, resulting in significantly increased risk of injury or death. **Corrective Action:** Chrysler dealers will replace the liftgate latch with a new, stronger latch assembly without charge. The replacement latch assemblies are currently being produced for this service action. Chrysler will renotify owners when parts are available. **Note:** This is not a safety recall. There has been no determination that a safety defect exists with the minivan latches. However, Chrysler has decided to provide a stronger latch without charge. Owners can contact Chrysler at (800) MINIVAN [(800) 646-4826].

DODGE TRUCK CARAVAN 1988

System: Fuel tanks. **Vehicle:** Vans. **Defect:** Fuel tanks may have been damaged during tank manufacture. **Consequence:** This could result in fuel leakage, with the potential for a fire. **Corrective Action:** Replace fuel tanks as necessary.

System: Fuel tanks. **Vehicle:** Vans. **Defect:** Fuel tanks may be constructed of improper material. **Consequence:** Fuel could leak at the tank seam, which, in presence of an ignition source, could result in a fire. **Corrective Action:** Replace suspect fuel tanks.

System: Structure; hatchback locks and latches. **Vehicle:** Light-duty passenger minivans; 1984 through 1995 models without remote release; 1984 through 1995 models with remote release. **Description of Alleged Defect:** This is not a safety recall. There has been no determination that a safety defect exists with the minivan latches. Chrysler is conducting a service campaign to replace the liftgate latch assembly of the affected minivans. In a collision, the rear liftgate latch assembly could open. **Consequence of Alleged Defect:** If the liftgate latch opens, occupants can be ejected, resulting in significantly increased risk of injury or death. **Corrective Action:** Chrysler dealers will replace the liftgate latch with a new, stronger latch assembly without charge. The replacement latch assemblies are currently being produced for this service action. Chrysler will renotify owners when parts are available. **Note:** This is not a safety recall. There has been no determination that a safety defect exists with the minivan latches. However, Chrysler has decided to provide a stronger latch without charge. Owners can contact Chrysler at (800) MINIVAN [(800) 646-4826].

DODGE TRUCK CARAVAN 1989

System: Engine valve cover gasket. **Vehicle:** Passenger cars, light trucks and minivans. **Defect:** The engine valve cover gasket may dislocate, allowing an engine oil leak at the gasket. **Consequence:** The leakage of oil in the engine compartment could cause a fire. **Corrective Action:** Replace gasket cover with revised cover; RTV sealant will be applied in place of a gasket.

System: Safety belt buckle assembly. **Vehicle:** Passenger vans and cars. **Defect:** Inboard front seat belt buckle assembly straps can suffer fatigue failure of the strap near its anchor position. **Consequence:** Fatigue failure of safety belts in a sudden stop or accident condition results in increased likelihood of injury to seat occupant. **Corrective Action:** Replace fatigued straps, or retrofit straps with a reinforcement plate and remove an antirotation tab to prevent fatigue failure.

System: Structure; hatchback locks and latches. **Vehicle:** Light-duty passenger minivans; 1984 through 1995 models without remote release; 1984 through 1995 models with remote release. **Description of Alleged Defect:** This is not a safety recall. There has been no determination that a safety defect exists with the minivan latches. Chrysler is conducting a service campaign to replace the liftgate latch assembly of the affected minivans. In a collision, the rear liftgate latch assembly could open. **Consequence of Alleged Defect:** If the liftgate latch opens, occupants can be ejected, resulting in significantly increased risk of injury or death. **Corrective Action:** Chrysler dealers will replace the liftgate latch with a new, stronger latch assembly without charge. The replacement latch assemblies are currently being produced for this service action. Chrysler will renotify owners when parts are available. **Note:** This is not a safety recall. There has been no determination that a safety defect exists with the minivan latches. However, Chrysler has decided to provide a stronger latch without charge. Owners can contact Chrysler at (800) MINIVAN [(800) 646-4826].

DODGE TRUCK CARAVAN 1990

System: Engine valve cover gasket. **Vehicle:** Passenger cars, light trucks and minivans. **Defect:** The engine valve cover gasket may dislocate, allowing an engine oil leak at the gasket. **Consequence:** The leakage of oil in the engine compartment could cause a fire. **Corrective Action:** Replace gasket cover with revised cover; RTV sealant will be applied in place of a gasket.

System: Brakes; proportioning valve screw. **Vehicle:** Truck van. **Defect:** Incorrect screws may have been used in installing the load-sensing brake proportioning valve to its bracket causing the clamping load to be less than intended. **Consequence:** This could result in inconsistent front-to-rear brake balance, with potential for rear brake skid under heavy braking conditions. **Corrective Action:** Replace proportioning valve bracket screws with proper length screws.

System: Safety belt buckle assembly. **Vehicle:** Passenger vans and cars. **Defect:** Inboard front seat belt buckle assembly straps can suffer fatigue failure of the strap near its anchor position. **Consequence:** Fatigue failure of safety belts in a sudden stop or accident condition results in increased likelihood of injury to seat occupant. **Corrective Action:** Replace fatigued straps, or retrofit straps with a reinforcement plate and remove an antirotation tab to prevent fatigue failure.

System: Structure; hatchback locks and latches. **Vehicle:** Light-duty passenger minivans; 1984 through 1995 models without remote release; 1984 through 1995 models with remote release. **Description of Alleged Defect:** This is not a safety recall. There has been no determination that a safety defect exists with the minivan latches. Chrysler is conducting a service campaign to replace the liftgate latch assembly of the affected minivans. In a collision, the rear liftgate latch assembly could open. **Consequence of Alleged Defect:** If the liftgate latch opens, occupants can be ejected, resulting in significantly increased risk of injury or death. **Corrective Action:** Chrysler dealers will replace the liftgate latch with a new, stronger latch assembly without charge. The replacement latch assemblies are currently being produced for this service action. Chrysler will renotify owners when parts are available. **Note:** This is not a safety recall. There has been no determination that a safety defect exists with the minivan latches. However, Chrysler has decided to provide a stronger latch without charge. Owners can contact Chrysler at (800) MINIVAN [(800) 646-4826].

DODGE TRUCK CARAVAN 1991

System: Turn signal flasher—FMVSS 108. **Vehicle:** Commercial vans. **Defect:** Incorrect turn signal flasher inhibits indication of signal lamp outage. **Consequence:** Inoperative turn signal lamps would not inform driver that a lamp was out, or warn other drivers of intent to turn, creating a risk of accident; vehicle does not comply with FMVSS 108. **Corrective Action:** Replace turn signal flasher with proper flasher.

System: Brakes. **Vehicle:** Passenger cars and vans with antilock brake systems (ABS). **Defect:** The antilock brake system high-pressure hose may leak or detach at its crimped end fitting, resulting in the discharge of hydraulic fluid. **Consequence:** Fluid discharge eventually causes the loss of both the antilock brake system and hydraulic assist for the brake system, resulting in increased likelihood of brake lockup and increased stopping distances, which could result in a vehicle accident. **Corrective Action:** Replace the antilock brake system high-pressure hose with a hose of different design and construction.

System: Brakes; antilock brake system system. **Vehicle:** Passenger minivans with antilock braking systems (ABS). **Defect:** The antilock brake system high-pressure pump may be porous, which will result in brake fluid leakage. **Consequence:** Fluid leakage eventually causes the loss of both the antilock brake system and hydraulic assist for the brake system, resulting in increased likelihood of brake lockup and increased stopping distances, which could result in a vehicle accident. **Corrective Action:** Replace the antilock brake system high-pressure pump and high pressure hose if the last six digits of the bar code label on the pump are between 052300 and 059262.

System: Structure; hatchback locks and latches. **Vehicle:** Light-duty passenger minivans; 1984 through 1995 models without remote release; 1984 through 1995 models with remote release. **Description of Alleged Defect:** This is not a safety recall. There has been no determination that a safety defect exists with the minivan latches. Chrysler is conducting a service campaign to replace the liftgate latch assembly of the affected minivans. In a collision, the rear liftgate latch assembly could open. **Consequence of Alleged Defect:** If the liftgate latch opens, occupants can be ejected, resulting in significantly increased risk of injury or death. **Corrective Action:** Chrysler dealers will replace the liftgate latch with a new, stronger latch assembly without charge. The replacement latch assemblies are currently being produced for this service action. Chrysler will renotify owners when parts are available. **Note:** This is not a safety recall. There has been no determination that a safety defect exists with the minivan latches. However, Chrysler has decided to provide a stronger latch without charge. Owners can contact Chrysler at (800) MINIVAN [(800) 646-4826].

DODGE TRUCK CARAVAN 1992

System: Brakes; pedal. **Vehicle:** Minivan. **Defect:** The brake pedal pad attachment to the pedal arm may not have adequate strength due to mislocation of welds, and could break. **Consequence:** Failure of the pedal pad to pedal arm attachment results in loss of braking ability, and could result in an accident. **Corrective Action:** Replace inadequate brake pedals with properly manufactured pedals.

System: Steering; upper steering column coupling bolt. **Vehicle:** Passenger vehicles; sedans, convertibles and minivans. **Defect:** The zinc-plating operation performed on the upper steering column shaft coupling bolt caused hydrogen embrittlement and breakage of the bolt. **Consequence:** Fractures of the upper steering column shaft coupling bolt result in a lack of coupling load on the shaft and loss of steering control. **Corrective Action:** Replace the zinc-plated bolt with a phosphate-plated bolt.

System: Safety belts—FMVSS 209. **Vehicle:** Vans, light trucks and multipurpose vehicles. **Defect:** Front outboard seat belt assemblies do not have the properly marked label with manufacturer information. **Consequence:** The seat belt assemblies do not comply with FMVSS 209. **Corrective Action:** Chrysler has not proposed a corrective action for this safety defect. **Note:** The manufacturer's petition, which requested that NHTSA determine that this FMVSS noncompliance does not create an unreasonable risk to motor vehicle safety, has been granted. Therefore, the manufacturer is not obligated to conduct an owner notification and remedy campaign.

System: Fuel tank. **Vehicle:** Passenger vans. **Defect:** Fuel tank flanges were not bent as required to allow the specified clearance for the fuel tank mounting straps and fuel lines at the tank. **Consequence:** The unbent flanges to the fuel tank will damage the mounting straps and/or fuel lines. The damaged mounting straps may break, causing the tank to drop, and the damaged fuel line will leak fuel. In either case, a fire could result if the spilled fuel is exposed to an ignition source. **Corrective Action:** Repair the flange by bending to the correct angle; replace damaged fuel lines and mounting straps.

System: Structure; hatchback locks and latches. **Vehicle:** Light-duty passenger minivans; 1984 through 1995 models without remote release; 1984 through 1995 models with remote release. **Description of Alleged Defect:** This is not a safety recall. There has been no determination that a safety defect exists with the minivan latches. Chrysler is conducting a service campaign to replace the liftgate latch assembly of the affected minivans. In a collision, the rear liftgate latch assembly could open. **Consequence of Alleged Defect:** If the liftgate latch opens, occupants can be ejected, resulting in significantly increased risk of injury or death. **Corrective Action:** Chrysler dealers will replace the liftgate latch with a new, stronger latch assembly without charge. The replacement latch assemblies are currently being produced for this service action. Chrysler will renotify owners when parts are available. **Note:** This is not a safety recall. There has been no determination that a safety defect exists with the minivan latches. However, Chrysler has decided to provide a stronger latch without charge. Owners can contact Chrysler at (800) MINIVAN [(800) 646-4826].

DODGE TRUCK CARAVAN 1993

System: Wheels. **Vehicle:** Passenger minivans with 15-inch stamped steel road wheels or stamped steel spare wheels. **Defect:** The 15-inch wheels have a malformed lug nut seat configuration, which causes poor nut-to-wheel contact and centering of the wheel during installation. **Consequence:** Poor nut-to-wheel contact during installation can lead to possible loss of a wheel, resulting in loss of vehicle control and an accident. **Corrective Action:** The road and spare wheels with the malformed lug nut seat configuration will be replaced.

System: Structure; hatchback locks and latches. **Vehicle:** Light-duty passenger minivans; 1984 through 1995 models without remote release; 1984 through 1995 models with remote release. **Description of Alleged Defect:** This is not a safety recall. There has been no determination that a safety defect exists with the minivan latches. Chrysler is conducting a service campaign to replace the liftgate latch assembly of the affected minivans. In a collision, the rear liftgate latch assembly could open. **Consequence of Alleged Defect:** If the liftgate latch opens, occupants can be ejected, resulting in significantly increased risk of injury or death. **Corrective Action:** Chrysler dealers will replace the liftgate latch with a new, stronger latch assembly without charge. The replacement latch assemblies are currently being produced for this service action. Chrysler will renotify owners when parts are available. **Note:** This is not a safety recall. There has been no determination that a safety defect exists with the minivan latches. However, Chrysler has decided to provide a stronger latch without charge. Owners can contact Chrysler at (800) MINIVAN [(800) 646-4826].

DODGE TRUCK CARAVAN 1994

System: Structure; hatchback locks and latches. **Vehicle:** Light-duty passenger minivans; 1984 through 1995 models without remote release; 1984 through 1995 models with remote release. **Description of Alleged Defect:** This is not a safety recall. There has been no determination that a safety defect exists with the minivan latches. Chrysler is conducting a service campaign to replace the liftgate latch assembly of the affected minivans. In a collision, the rear liftgate latch assembly could open. **Consequence of Alleged Defect:** If the liftgate latch opens, occupants can be ejected, resulting in significantly increased risk of injury or death. **Corrective Action:** Chrysler dealers will replace the liftgate latch with a new, stronger latch assembly without charge. The replacement latch assemblies are currently being produced for this service action. Chrysler will renotify owners when parts are available. **Note:** This is not a safety recall. There has been no determination that a safety defect exists with the minivan latches. However, Chrysler has decided to provide a stronger latch without charge. Owners can contact Chrysler at (800) MINIVAN [(800) 646-4826].

DODGE TRUCK DAKOTA 1987

System: Rear parking brake cables—FMVSS 105. **Vehicle:** Pickup trucks equipped with standard 9″×2½″ rear brakes. **Defect:** These trucks were equipped with rear parking brake cables that caused limited rear brake shoe travel, resulting in the parking brake system not holding the vehicle in the reverse direction when parked on a 20 percent grade, as required by FMVSS 105. **Consequence:** If the truck is parked on an incline and the parking brake is set, it may roll back, causing damage or an accident. **Corrective Action:** Replace both rear parking brake cables.

System: Speed control cables. **Vehicle:** Pickup trucks equipped with V6 engine and automatic speed control. **Defect:** Speed control system cables may partially disengage and bind at the carburetor throttle lever attachment. **Consequence:** Throttle would stay partially open when accelerator pedal is released. **Corrective Action:** Install a washer at speed control cable to carburetor throttle lever attachment to eliminate potential for this condition.

DODGE TRUCK DAKOTA 1988

System: Parking—gearshift. **Vehicle:** Light trucks, vans and wagons. **Defect:** Automatic transmission may contain a park sprag rod assembly that may stick in the tooth butt unengaged position. **Consequence:** This condition could allow the vehicle to roll with the gearshift lever in park position. **Corrective Action:** All involved vehicles will have the park sprag rod assemblies replaced.

System: Rear wheel stud nuts. **Vehicle:** Pickup trucks. **Defect:** Machining error in locating wheel stud holes may prevent full seating of the brake drum to shaft flange. **Consequence:** Wheel studs could loosen, allowing wheel to separate from the truck. **Corrective Action:** Replace axle shafts as necessary.

DODGE TRUCK DAKOTA 1989

System: Engine valve cover gasket. **Vehicle:** Passenger cars, light trucks and minivans. **Defect:** The engine valve cover gasket may dislocate, allowing an engine oil leak at the gasket. **Consequence:** The leakage of oil in the engine compartment could cause a fire. **Corrective Action:** Replace gasket cover with revised cover; RTV sealant will be applied in place of a gasket.

DODGE TRUCK DAKOTA 1990

System: Engine valve cover gasket. **Vehicle:** Passenger cars, light trucks and minivans. **Defect:** The engine valve cover gasket may dislocate, allowing an engine oil leak at the gasket. **Consequence:** The leakage of oil in the engine compartment could cause a fire. **Corrective Action:** Replace gasket cover with revised cover; RTV sealant will be applied in place of a gasket.

DODGE TRUCK DAKOTA 1991

System: Fuel hose. **Vehicle:** Pickup trucks equipped with 4-speed automatic transmissions. **Defect:** Steel-braided fuel hose routing may allow contact between the hose and transmission wiring harness. **Consequence:** This contact could cause hose damage and fuel leakage that, in the presence of an ignition source, could result in a fire. **Corrective Action:** Install a tie strap to secure the transmission wiring away from the fuel hose.

System: Brakes. **Vehicle:** Regular cab and club cab pickup trucks with 2-wheel drive. **Defect:** The right front brake hose may rub against the tire during a full-lock left turn, which may eventually cause wear-through of the brake hose on the right front side. **Consequence:** Wear-through of the right front brake hose would cause fluid loss from half of the split brake hydraulic system and increase stopping distance, which could result in an accident. **Corrective Action:** If clearance between the brake hose and tire on the right front is inadequate, replace brake hose with a modified version to ensure adequate clearance.

System: Steering; wheel and column. **Vehicle:** Light-duty trucks, vans and wagons equipped with "premium" steering wheels. **Defect:** The steering wheel armature stamping can crack, due to fatigue, and separate from the center hub attachment to the steering column. **Consequence:** This condition can cause separation of the center hub attachment to the steering column, resulting in a loss of control and an accident. **Corrective Action:** Dealers will inspect the steering wheel for armature cracks and replace any wheels exhibiting cracks. All other vehicles will have a reinforcement plate installed to prevent steering wheel separation if cracking occurs.

DODGE TRUCK DAKOTA 1992

System: Safety belts—FMVSS 209. **Vehicle:** Vans, light trucks and multipurpose vehicles. **Defect:** Front outboard seat belt assemblies do not have the properly marked label with manufacturer information. **Consequence:** The seat belt assemblies do not comply with FMVSS 209. **Corrective Action:** Chrysler has not proposed a corrective action for this safety defect. **Note:** The manufacturer's petition, which requested that NHTSA determine that this FMVSS noncompliance does not create an unreasonable risk to motor vehicle safety, has been granted. Therefore, the manufacturer is not obligated to conduct an owner notification and remedy campaign.

DODGE TRUCK DAKOTA 1993

System: Brakes; antilock brakes (ABS). **Vehicle:** Pickup trucks with optional 4-wheel antilock brake systems. **Defect:** Some of the antilock brake system-equipped vehicles were built with an undersized brake return check valve. In incidents where hard brake pedal effort is applied on low-friction road surfaces, like rain-covered streets, the valves may fail, causing the antilock brake system to become inoperative. This creates excess brake pedal travel and may cause the antilock brake system warning light to come on. **Consequence:** Lack of front-wheel antilock brake system could cause the front wheel brakes to lock, increasing stopping distance, which may result in an accident. **Corrective Action:** Replace the return check valve with the correct valve.

DODGE TRUCK DAKOTA 1994

System: Fuel; fuel tank assembly; attachment. **Vehicle:** Light-duty trucks. **Defect:** Two fuel tank support strap attaching studs were not adequately tightened, which could cause one or both of the straps to separate, mislocating the fuel tanks, or allow complete separation of the fuel tank from the vehicle. **Consequence:** In either case, fuel tank support straps failure results in fuel leakage, which could result in a fire. **Corrective Action:** The fuel tank support strap attaching studs will be properly tightened. **Note:** If your vehicle is presented to an authorized dealer on an agreed-upon service date and the remedy is not provided within a reasonable time and free of charge, or the remedy does not correct the defect or noncompliance, please contact Chrysler Service Center at (800) 992-1997. Also contact the NHTSA's Auto Safety Hotline at (800) 424-9393.

System: Suspension; independent front control arm. **Vehicle:** Light-duty pickup truck with 4-wheel drive. **Defect:** Some upper control arm attaching bolts can fail due to improper heat treatment. The bolts are too soft to withstand the stresses in the steering system and can break. **Consequence:** If the attaching bolts of the upper control arm break, the vehicle can experience loss of steering control, which could result in an accident. **Corrective Action:** Replace the upper control arm attaching bolts. **Note:** If your vehicle is presented to an authorized dealer on an agreed-upon service date and the remedy is not provided within a reasonable time and free of charge, or the remedy does not correct the defect or noncompliance, please contact Chrysler Service Center at (800) 992-1997. Also contact the NHTSA's Auto Safety Hotline at (800) 424-9393.

System: Steering wheel and column. **Vehicle:** Light-duty pickup trucks. **Defect:** While making a turn, the extra keys on a vehicle operator's key ring can become temporarily lodged in the screw access holes in the back cover of the steering wheel. **Consequence:** This condition can hamper the steering wheel return or cause the ignition to be turned off, resulting in loss of vehicle control and an accident. **Corrective Action:** Chrysler dealers will install plugs in the screw access holes in the steering wheel back cover. **Note:** This recall campaign has been superseded by the following recall. If your vehicle is presented to an authorized dealer on an agreed-upon service date and the remedy is not provided within a reasonable time free of charge, or the remedy does not correct the defect, please contact the Chrysler Service Center at (800) 853-1403. Also contact the NHTSA's Auto Safety Hotline at (800) 424-9393.

System: Steering wheel and column. **Vehicle:** Light-duty trucks and club cab trucks. **Defect:** While making a turn, the extra keys on a vehicle operator's key ring can become temporarily lodged in the screw access holes in the back cover of the steering wheel. **Consequence:** This condition can hamper the steering wheel return or cause the ignition to be turned off, resulting in loss of vehicle control and an accident. **Corrective Action:** Dealers will replace the steering wheel back cover with a redesigned cover. **Note:** This campaign supersedes the previous recall. If your vehicle is presented to an authorized dealer on an agreed-upon service date and the remedy is not provided free of charge within a reasonable time, please contact Chrysler at (800) 853-1403. Also contact the NHTSA's Auto Safety Hotline at (800) 424-9393.

DODGE TRUCK RAM 1989

System: Visual systems; mirror; rearview; exterior. **Vehicle:** Light-duty pickup and chassis trucks; 10,000 pounds gross vehicle weight rating or more. **Description of Noncompliance:** The right outside rearview mirror contains convex glass rather than flat. Therefore, these vehicles fail to comply with FMVSS 111, "Rearview mirrors." **Consequence of Noncompliance:** See note. **Corrective Action:** See note. **Note:** The manufacturer's petition, which requested that NHTSA determine that this FMVSS noncompliance does not create an unreasonable risk to motor vehicle safety, has been partially granted. NHTSA denied Chrysler's petition with respect to the 1994 cab/chassis vehicles. Chrysler will conduct an owner notification and remedy campaign for these 90 vehicles. Chrysler is not obligated to conduct an owner notification and remedy campaign for the remaining 1988 through 1993 cab/chassis vehicles.

System: Visual systems; mirror; rearview; exterior. **Vehicle:** Light-duty pickup and chassis trucks; 10,000 pounds gross vehicle weight rating or more. **Description of Noncompliance:** The right outside rearview mirror contains convex glass rather than flat. Therefore, these vehicles fail to comply with FMVSS 111, "Rearview mirrors." **Consequence of Noncompliance:** See note. **Corrective Action:** See note. **Note:** The manufacturer's petition, which requested that NHTSA determine that this FMVSS noncompliance does not create an unreasonable risk to motor vehicle safety, has been partially granted. Chrysler is not obligated to conduct an owner notification and remedy campaign for these 26,600 cab/chassis vehicles.

DODGE TRUCK RAM 1990

System: Visual systems; mirror; rearview; exterior. **Vehicle:** Light-duty pickup and chassis trucks; 10,000 pounds gross vehicle weight rating or more. **Description of Noncompliance:** The right outside rearview mirror contains convex glass rather than flat. Therefore, these vehicles fail to comply with FMVSS 111, "Rearview mirrors." **Consequence of Noncompliance:** See note. **Corrective Action:** See note. **Note:** The manufacturer's petition, which requested that NHTSA determine that this FMVSS noncompliance does not create an unreasonable risk to motor vehicle safety, has been partially granted. NHTSA denied Chrysler's petition with respect to the 1994 cab/chassis vehicles. Chrysler will conduct an owner notification and remedy campaign for these 90 vehicles. Chrysler is not obligated to conduct an owner notification and remedy campaign for the remaining 1988 through 1993 cab/chassis vehicles.

System: Visual systems; mirror; rearview; exterior. **Vehicle:** Light-duty pickup and chassis trucks; 10,000 pounds gross vehicle weight rating or more. **Description of Noncompliance:** The right outside rearview mirror contains convex glass rather than flat. Therefore these vehicles fail to comply with FMVSS 111, "Rearview mirrors." **Consequence of Noncompliance:** See note. **Corrective Action:** See note. **Note:** The manufacturer's petition, which requested that NHTSA determine that this FMVSS noncompliance does not create an unreasonable risk to motor vehicle safety, has been partially granted. Chrysler is not obligated to conduct an owner notification and remedy campaign for these 26,600 cab/chassis vehicles.

DODGE TRUCK RAM 1991

System: Tires—FMVSS 120. **Vehicle:** Vans, maxivans, wagons and maxiwagons. **Defect:** The tire selection and rims certification label may have incorrect information. **Consequence:** The certification label fails to meet the requirements of FMVSS 120. **Corrective Action:** An overlay of the correct tire and rim selection information certificate will be provided.

System: Fuel; fuel pump. **Equipment Description:** Cummins intercooled turbo-diesel engine using Bosch fuel pumps. **Defect:** Bosch distributor-type fuel pumps have a manufacturing defect that can cause the ball pin, which is part of the pump's control lever assembly, to break, causing the link between the control sleeve and the control lever to become inoperative. **Consequence:** When the link between the control lever and the control sleeve breaks, the speed control no longer responds to movement of the accelerator pedal, resulting in loss of speed control and a possible accident. **Corrective Action:** The fuel pumps will be inspected and, if necessary, repaired or replaced. **Note:** If you have any problem obtaining the needed repair, please contact the Chrysler zone service office in your area. It is listed under "Service Assistance" in your owner's manual. A zone representative will arrange for prompt attention to your vehicle. Also contact the NHTSA's Auto Safety Hotline at (800) 424-9393.

System: Visual systems; mirror; rearview; exterior. **Vehicle:** Light-duty pickup and chassis trucks; 10,000 pounds gross vehicle weight rating or more. **Description of Noncompliance:** The right outside rearview mirror contains convex glass rather than flat. Therefore, these vehicles fail to comply with FMVSS 111, "Rearview mirrors." **Consequence of Noncompliance:** See note. **Corrective Action:** See note. **Note:** The manufacturer's petition, which requested that NHTSA determine that this FMVSS noncompliance does not create an unreasonable risk to motor vehicle safety, has been partially granted. NHTSA denied Chrysler's petition with respect to the 1994 cab/chassis vehicles. Chrysler will conduct an owner notification and remedy campaign for these 90 vehicles. Chrysler is not obligated to conduct an owner notification and remedy campaign for the remaining 1988 through 1993 cab/chassis vehicles.

System: Visual systems; mirror; rearview; exterior. **Vehicle:** Light-duty pickup and chassis trucks; 10,000 pounds gross vehicle weight rating or more. **Description of Noncompliance:** The right outside rearview mirror contains convex glass rather than flat. Therefore, these vehicles fail to comply with FMVSS 111, "Rearview mirrors." **Consequence of Noncompliance:** See note. **Corrective Action:** See note. **Note:** The manufacturer's petition, which requested that NHTSA determine this FMVSS noncompliance does not create an unreasonable risk to motor vehicle safety, has been partially granted. Chrysler is not obligated to conduct an owner notification and remedy campaign for these 26,600 cab/chassis vehicles.

System: Steering; wheel and column. **Vehicle:** Light duty-trucks, vans and wagons equipped with "premium" steering wheels. **Defect:** The steering wheel armature stamping can crack, due to fatigue, and separate from the center hub attachment to the steering column. **Consequence:** This condition can cause separation of the center hub attachment to the steering column, resulting in a loss of control and an accident. **Corrective Action:** Dealers will inspect the steering wheel for armature cracks and replace any wheels exhibiting cracks. All other vehicles will have a reinforcement plate installed to prevent steering wheel separation if cracking occurs. **Note:** If your vehicle is presented to an authorized dealer on an agreed-upon service date and the remedy is not provided free of charge within a reasonable time, please contact Chrysler at (800) 853-1403. Also contact the NHTSA's Auto Safety Hotline at (800) 424-9393.

DODGE TRUCK RAM 1992

System: Tires—FMVSS 120. **Vehicle:** Vans, maxivans, wagons and maxiwagons. **Defect:** The tire selection and rims certification label may have incorrect information. **Consequence:** The certification label fails to meet the requirements of FMVSS 120. **Corrective Action:** An overlay of the correct tire and rim selection information certificate will be provided.

System: Fuel; fuel pump. **Equipment Description:** Cummins intercooled turbo-diesel engine using Bosch fuel pumps. **Defect:** Bosch distributor-type fuel pumps have a manufacturing defect that can cause the ball pin, which is part of the pump's control lever assembly, to break, causing the link between the control sleeve and the control lever to become inoperative. **Consequence:** When the link between the control lever and the control sleeve breaks, the speed control no longer responds to movement of the accelerator pedal, resulting in loss of speed control and a possible accident. **Corrective Action:** The fuel pumps will be inspected and, if necessary, repaired or replaced. **Note:** If you have any problem obtaining the needed repair, please contact the Chrysler zone service office in your area. It is listed under "Service Assistance" in your owner's manual. A zone representative will arrange for prompt attention to your vehicle. Also contact the NHTSA's Auto Safety Hotline at (800) 424-9393.

System: Visual systems; mirror; rearview; exterior. **Vehicle:** Light-duty pickup and chassis trucks; 10,000 pounds gross vehicle weight rating or more. **Description of Noncompliance:** The right outside rearview mirror contains convex glass rather than flat. Therefore, these vehicles fail to comply with FMVSS 111, "Rearview mirrors." **Consequence of Noncompliance:** See note. **Corrective Action:** See note. **Note:** The manufacturer's petition, which requested that NHTSA determine this FMVSS noncompliance does not create an unreasonable risk to motor vehicle safety, has been partially granted. NHTSA denied Chrysler's petition with respect to the 1994 cab/chassis vehicles. Chrysler will conduct an owner notification and remedy campaign for these 90 vehicles. Chrysler is not obligated to conduct an owner notification and remedy campaign for the remaining 1988 through 1993 cab/chassis vehicles.

System: Visual systems; mirror; rearview; exterior. **Vehicle:** Light-duty pickup and chassis trucks; 10,000 pounds gross vehicle weight rating or more. **Description of Noncompliance:** The right outside rearview mirror contains convex glass rather than flat. Therefore these vehicles fail to comply with FMVSS 111, "Rearview mirrors." **Consequence of Noncompliance:** See note. **Corrective Action:** See note. **Note:** The manufacturer's petition, which requested that NHTSA determine this FMVSS noncompliance does not create an unreasonable risk to motor vehicle safety, has been partially granted. Chrysler is not obligated to conduct an owner notification and remedy campaign for these 26,600 cab/chassis vehicles.

DODGE TRUCK RAM 1994

System: Suspension; independent front. **Vehicle:** Light-duty pickup trucks equipped with 4-wheel drive. **Defect:** Front suspension track bar attachment to the axle may not be adequately tightened. **Consequence:** Loss of the track bar attachment can cause axle vibration and directional control difficulty, which could result in loss of vehicle control and an accident. **Corrective Action:** Tighten front suspension track bar axle attachment to the specified torque.

System: Interior systems; seat latch—FMVSS 207. **Vehicle:** Light trucks. **Description of Noncompliance:** The seat back latch lever pivot rivets are susceptible to distortion. The distorted assemblies allow the seat back release latch lever to remain in the released position, which is in noncompliance with FMVSS 207, "Seating systems." **Consequence of Noncompliance:** In the event of a sudden stop or accident, the forces on the seat back may subject seat occupants to an increased risk of injury. **Corrective Action:** Dealers will replace the suspect seat back latch assembly with a revised assembly. **Note:** If you have any problem obtaining the needed repair, please contact the Chrysler zone service office in your area. It is listed under "Service Assistance" in your owner's manual. A zone representative will arrange for prompt attention to your vehicle. Also contact the NHTSA's Auto Safety Hotline at (800) 424-9393.

System: Visual systems; mirror; rearview; exterior. **Vehicle:** Light-duty pickup and chassis trucks; 10,000 pounds gross vehicle weight rating or more. **Description of Noncompliance:** The right outside rearview mirror contains convex glass rather than flat. Therefore, these vehicles fail to comply with FMVSS 111, "Rearview mirrors." **Consequence of Noncompliance:** See note. **Corrective Action:** See note. **Note:** The manufacturer's petition, which requested that NHTSA determine this FMVSS noncompliance does not create an unreasonable risk to motor vehicle safety, has been partially granted. NHTSA denied Chrysler's petition with respect to the 1994 cab/chassis vehicles. Chrysler will conduct an owner notification and remedy campaign for these 90 vehicles. Chrysler is not obligated to conduct an owner notification and remedy campaign for the remaining 1988 through 1993 cab/chassis vehicles.

System: Visual systems; mirror; rearview; exterior. **Vehicle:** Light-duty pickup and chassis trucks; 10,000 pounds gross vehicle weight rating or more. **Description of Noncompliance:** The right outside rearview mirror contains convex glass rather than flat. Therefore, these vehicles fail to comply with FMVSS 111, "Rearview mirrors." **Consequence of Noncompliance:** The images presented in the mirror are closer than they appear, which may cause the driver to misjudge the distance from the object to the rear of the vehicle, and could result in an accident. **Corrective Action:** Dealers will replace the right outside rearview mirror with a mirror having a flat surface. **Note:** If your vehicle is presented to an authorized dealer on an agreed-upon service date and the remedy is not provided free of charge within a reasonable time, contact Chrysler at (800) 853-1403. Also contact the NHTSA's Auto Safety Hotline at (800) 424-9393.

System: Suspension; independent front. **Vehicle:** Light-duty vans; 3500 series 4-wheel drive models only (10,500 and 11,000 pounds gross vehicle weight). **Defect:** The front suspension track bar has inadequate fatigue strength. **Consequence:** Failure of the track bar can result in front axle vibration and loss of steering control. **Corrective Action:** Dealers will replace the front suspension track bar. **Note:** If your vehicle is presented to an authorized dealer on an agreed-upon service date and the remedy is not provided within a reasonable time and free of charge, or the remedy does not correct the defect or noncompliance, please contact the Chrysler Service Center at (800) 853-1403. Also contact the NHTSA's Auto Safety Hotline at (800) 424-9393.

System: Fuel; fuel systems. **Vehicle:** Light-duty pickup trucks built without a rear bumper. **Description of Noncompliance:** These vehicles do not meet the rear impact test requirements of FMVSS 301, "Fuel system integrity." **Consequence of Noncompliance:** These vehicles have an increased risk of a fuel spill in the event of a rear-end collision. **Corrective Action:** Chrysler has not finalized repair procedures for these vehicles. **Note:** If your vehicle is presented to an authorized dealer on an agreed-upon service date and the remedy is not provided within a reasonable time and free of charge, or the remedy does not correct the defect or noncompliance, please contact the Chrysler Service Center at (800) 853-1403. Also contact the NHTSA's Auto Safety Hotline at (800) 424-9393.

System: Lighting; lamp or socket; courtesy lights. **Vehicle:** Long wheelbase conversion vans with a neon center light beam. **Defect:** The transformer used to power the neon center light beam can overheat and catch on fire. **Consequence:** The overheating and fires caused by the neon transformer can result in damage to the light beam assembly and the roof of the vehicle, and could result in a vehicle fire. **Corrective Action:** Mark III dealers will modify the assemblies to eliminate the neon lighting fixture in the vehicle and replace it with incandescent lights operating directly from the vehicle 12-volt battery. **Note:** If your vehicle is presented to an authorized dealer on an agreed-upon service date and the remedy is not provided within a reasonable time and free of charge, or the remedy does not correct the defect or noncompliance, please contact the Mark III Service Center at (800) 903-8267. Also contact the NHTSA's Auto Safety Hotline at (800) 424-9393.

System: Steering wheel and column. **Vehicle:** Light-duty pickup trucks. **Defect:** While making a turn, the extra keys on a vehicle operator's key ring can become temporarily lodged in the screw access holes in the back cover of the steering wheel. **Consequence:** This condition can hamper the steering wheel return or cause the ignition to be turned off, resulting in loss of vehicle control and an accident. **Corrective Action:** Chrysler dealers will install plugs in the screw access holes in the steering wheel back cover. **Note:** This recall campaign has been superseded by the following recall. If your vehicle is presented to an authorized dealer on an agreed-upon service date and the remedy is not provided within a reasonable time free of charge, or the remedy does not correct the defect, please contact the Chrysler service center at (800) 853-1403. Also contact the NHTSA's Auto Safety Hotline at (800) 424-9393.

System: Steering wheel and column. **Vehicle:** Light-duty trucks and club cab trucks. **Defect:** While making a turn, the extra keys on a vehicle operator's key ring can become temporarily lodged in the screw access holes in the back cover of the steering wheel. **Consequence:** This condition can hamper the steering wheel return or cause the ignition to be turned off, resulting in loss of vehicle control and an accident. **Corrective Action:** Dealers will replace the steering wheel back cover with a redesigned cover. **Note:** This campaign supersedes the previous recall.

System: Suspension; independent front. **Vehicle:** Cab and chassis trucks; 3500 series 4-wheel drive models only; 11,000 pounds gross vehicle weight. **Defect:** The front suspension track bar bracket attachment has inadequate fatigue strength and can fail, causing front axle vibration. **Consequence:** This can result in loss of steering control and an accident. **Corrective Action:** A front suspension track bar bracket reinforcement strut will be installed. **Note:** If the vehicle is presented to an authorized dealer on an agreed-upon service date and the remedy is not provided free of charge within a reasonable time, or the remedy does not correct the defect, please contact Chrysler at (800) 853-1403. Also contact the NHTSA's Auto Safety Hotline at (800) 424-9393.

System: Interior systems; active restraints; belt buckles. **Vehicle:** Light-duty pickup trucks. **Defect:** The cinch bar component within the passenger-side safety belt buckle assembly shatters, causing the belt to release. **Consequence:** The passenger would not be properly restrained and could be injured in the event of a sudden stop or accident. **Corrective Action:** Dealers will replace the cinch bar with a newly designed part. **Note:** If the vehicle is presented to an authorized dealer on an agreed-upon service date and the remedy is not provided free of charge within a reasonable time, please contact Chrysler at (800) 853-1403. Also contact the NHTSA's Auto Safety Hotline at (800) 424-9393.

System: Structure; hood assembly; latches. **Vehicle:** Light-duty pickup trucks. **Defect:** The secondary hood latch rod can bind on the guide bracket and prevent engagement of the secondary latch. **Consequence:** This condition can cause the hood to fly up, obstructing the driver's vision and increasing the potential for a vehicle accident. **Corrective Action:** Dealers will replace the secondary hood latch bracket. **Note:** If your vehicle is presented to an authorized dealer on an agreed-upon service date and the remedy is not provided free of charge within a reasonable time, please contact Chrysler at (800) 853-1403. Also contact the NHTSA's Auto Safety Hotline at (800) 424-9393.

DODGE TRUCK RAM 1995

System: Steering wheel and column. **Vehicle:** Light-duty pickup trucks. **Defect:** While making a turn, the extra keys on a vehicle operator's key ring can become temporarily lodged in the screw access holes in the back cover of the steering wheel. **Consequence:** This condition can hamper the steering wheel return or cause the ignition to be turned off, resulting in loss of vehicle control and an accident. **Corrective Action:** Chrysler dealers will install plugs in the screw access holes in the steering wheel back cover. **Note:** This recall campaign has been superseded by the following recall. If your vehicle is presented to an authorized dealer on an agreed-upon service date and the remedy is not provided free of charge within a reasonable period of time, please contact Chrysler at (800) 853-1403. Also contact the NHTSA's Auto Safety Hotline at (800) 424-9393.

System: Steering wheel and column. **Vehicle:** Light duty trucks and club cab trucks. **Defect:** While making a turn, the extra keys on a vehicle operator's key ring can become temporarily lodged in the screw access holes in the back cover of the steering wheel. **Consequence:** This condition can hamper the steering wheel return or cause the ignition to be turned off, resulting in loss of vehicle control and an accident. **Corrective Action:** Dealers will replace the steering wheel back cover with a redesigned cover. **Note:** This campaign supersedes the previous recall. If your vehicle is presented to an authorized dealer on an agreed-upon service date and the remedy is not provided free of charge within a reasonable period of time, please contact Chrysler at (800) 853-1403. Also contact the NHTSA's Auto Safety Hotline at (800) 424-9393.

System: Structure; hood assembly; latches. **Vehicle:** Light-duty pickup trucks. **Defect:** The secondary hood latch rod can bind on the guide bracket and prevent engagement of the secondary latch. **Consequence:** This condition can cause the hood to fly up, obstructing the driver's vision and increasing the potential for a vehicle accident. **Corrective Action:** Dealers will replace the secondary hood latch bracket.

EAGLE

Note: If your Eagle is presented to an authorized dealer on an agreed-upon service date and the remedy is not provided within a reasonable time and free of charge, or the remedy does not correct the defect or noncompliance, please contact the Chrysler Service Center at (800) 992-1997. Also contact the NHTSA's Auto Safety Hotline at (800) 424-9393.

EAGLE MEDALLION 1988

System: Cooling system—heater core. **Vehicle:** Passenger cars. **Defect:** Cooling system pressures during overheated engine operation may exceed the strength capability of certain components due to inadequate venting capacity of the system pressure cap. **Consequence:** The buildup of pressure may cause heater core to rupture and discharge hot coolant and steam in the proximity of the driver's legs. **Corrective Action:** Replace all coolant system pressure caps with caps having adequate venting capacity.

EAGLE MEDALLION 1989

System: Cooling system—heater core. **Vehicle:** Passenger cars. **Defect:** Cooling system pressures during overheated engine operation may exceed the strength capability of certain components due to inadequate venting capacity of the system pressure cap. **Consequence:** The buildup of pressure may cause heater core to rupture and discharge hot coolant and steam in the proximity of the driver's legs. **Corrective Action:** Replace all coolant system pressure caps with caps having adequate venting capacity.

EAGLE PREMIER 1988

System: Brake master cylinder. **Vehicle:** Passenger cars. **Defect:** Master cylinder may have been misassembled, causing a blocked hydraulic fluid outlet port and restricted fluid flow. **Consequence:** This could result in increased brake pedal travel and partial loss of braking capability. **Corrective Action:** Replace master brake cylinder.

System: Cooling system—heater core. **Vehicle:** Passenger cars. **Defect:** Cooling system pressures during overheated engine operation may exceed the strength capability of certain components due to inadequate venting capacity of the system pressure cap. **Consequence:** The buildup of pressure may cause heater core to rupture and discharge hot coolant and steam in the proximity of the driver's legs. **Corrective Action:** Replace all coolant system pressure caps with caps having adequate venting capacity.

System: Automatic transmission. **Vehicle:** Passenger cars equipped with 4-cylinder engines. **Defect:** Automatic transmissions experienced endurance failures of park mechanism components during severe testing. **Consequence:** Vehicles would be subject to transmission failures. **Corrective Action:** Retrofit transmission.

System: Front brake hose. **Vehicle:** Passenger cars. **Defect:** Routing of the front brake hose may cause excessive hose flexing, resulting in premature fatigue cracking of the outer hose cover. **Consequence:** This could lead to hose failure and loss of brake fluid, reducing braking effectiveness. **Corrective Action:** Replace front brake hoses with hoses redesigned to provide a modified routing configuration.

System: Heater; water; defroster; heater core. **Vehicle:** Passenger vehicles. **Defect:** The end cap connecting the heat exchanger's core to the engine cooling system could rupture and allow hot coolant to escape into the passenger compartment. **Consequence:** The coolant escaping into the passenger compartment could contact the driver's feet and injure the driver. Also, steam from the heater liquid will cloud on the window surfaces and impair the driver's vision. In either case, failure of the heater core end cap could result in a vehicle accident.

Corrective Action: A coolant temperature-controlled heater core fluid bypass valve will be installed.

EAGLE PREMIER 1989

System: Front brake hose. **Vehicle:** Passenger cars. **Defect:** Routing of the front brake hose may cause excessive hose flexing, resulting in premature fatigue cracking of the outer hose cover. **Consequence:** This could lead to hose failure and loss of brake fluid, reducing braking effectiveness. **Corrective Action:** Replace front brake hoses with hoses redesigned to provide a modified routing configuration.

System: Rear brake tube. **Vehicle:** Passenger cars. **Defect:** Rear brake tube routing is contacted by fuel tank heat shield when suspension is in full jounce position. This damages the brake fluid tube, causing a leak. **Consequence:** Loss of fluid from half of the diagonally split brake hydraulic system affects braking capability, which could result in an accident. **Corrective Action:** Modify the heat shield to eliminate the potential for shield contacting brake tube.

System: Heater; water; defroster; heater core. **Vehicle:** Passenger vehicles. **Defect:** The end cap connecting the heat exchanger's core to the engine cooling system could rupture and allow hot coolant to escape into the passenger compartment. **Consequence:** The coolant escaping into the passenger compartment could contact the driver's feet and injure the driver. Also, steam from the heater liquid will cloud on the window surfaces and impair the driver's vision. In either case, failure of the heater core end cap could result in a vehicle accident. **Corrective Action:** A coolant temperature-controlled heater core fluid bypass valve will be installed.

EAGLE PREMIER 1990

System: Steering column shaft. **Vehicle:** Passenger cars. **Defect:** Lower intermediate steering shaft may separate at the rubber isolated coupling of the shaft. **Consequence:** This could result in loss of steering control and an accident. **Corrective Action:** Replace intermediate steering shaft with a shaft containing a restrained coupling.

System: Front brake hose. **Vehicle:** Passenger cars. **Defect:** Routing of the front brake hose may cause excessive hose flexing, resulting in premature fatigue cracking of the outer hose cover. **Consequence:** This could lead to hose failure and loss of brake fluid, reducing braking effectiveness. **Corrective Action:** Replace front brake hoses with hoses redesigned to provide a modified routing configuration.

System: Rear brake tube. **Vehicle:** Passenger cars. **Defect:** Rear brake tube routing is contacted by fuel tank heat shield when suspension is in full jounce position. This damages the brake fluid tube, causing a leak. **Consequence:** Loss of fluid from half of the diagonally split brake hydraulic system affects braking capability, which could result in an accident. **Corrective Action:** Modify the heat shield to eliminate the potential for shield contacting brake tube.

System: Heater; water; defroster; heater core. **Vehicle:** Passenger vehicles. **Defect:** The end cap connecting the heat exchanger's core to the engine cooling system could rupture and allow hot coolant to escape into the passenger compartment. **Consequence:** The coolant escaping into the passenger compartment could contact the driver's feet and injure the driver. Also, steam from the heater liquid will cloud on the window surfaces and impair the driver's vision. In either case, failure of the heater core end cap could result in a vehicle accident. **Corrective Action:** A coolant temperature-controlled heater core fluid bypass valve will be installed.

EAGLE PREMIER 1991

System: Rear brake tube. **Vehicle:** Passenger cars. **Defect:** Rear brake tube routing is contacted by fuel tank heat shield when suspension is in full jounce position. This damages the brake fluid tube, causing a leak. **Consequence:** Loss of fluid from half of the diagonally split brake hydraulic system affects braking capability, which could result in an accident. **Corrective Action:** Modify the heat shield to eliminate the potential for shield contacting brake tube.

System: Battery feed wiring. **Vehicle:** Passenger cars. **Defect:** Routing of battery main feed wiring may allow it to contact the air cleaner bracket, and continued contact may lead to an electrical short circuit. **Consequence:** The electrical short circuit caused by continuous contact could result in the ignition of the wiring insulation, and an underhood fire. **Corrective Action:** The main feed on all involved vehicles will be rerouted and secured with tie straps away from the air cleaner bracket.

System: Brakes. **Vehicle:** Passenger cars and vans with antilock brake systems (ABS). **Defect:** The antilock brake system high-pressure hose may leak or detach at its crimped end fitting, resulting in the discharge of hydraulic fluid. **Consequence:** Fluid discharge eventually causes the loss of both the antilock brake system and hydraulic assist for the brake system, resulting in increased likelihood of brake lockup and increased stopping distances, which could result in a vehicle accident. **Corrective Action:** Replace the antilock brake system high-pressure hose with a hose of different design and construction.

System: Heater; water; defroster; heater core. **Vehicle:** Passenger vehicles. **Defect:** The end cap connecting the heat exchanger's core to the engine cooling system could rupture and allow hot coolant to escape into the passenger compartment. **Consequence:** The coolant escaping into the passenger compartment could contact the driver's feet and injure the driver. Also, steam from the heater liquid will cloud on the window surfaces and impair the driver's vision. In either case, failure of the heater core end cap could result in a vehicle accident. **Corrective Action:** A coolant temperature-controlled heater core fluid bypass valve will be installed.

EAGLE TALON 1990

System: Sunroof hinges. **Vehicle:** Passenger cars equipped with DSM-manufactured sunroofs. **Defect:** Operation of sunroof in "non-standard" manner may cause male hinge disengagement from the roof hinge receiver. **Consequence:** The sunroof glass could detach from the roof and result in injury to occupants or persons in the vicinity, especially if this occurs while the vehicle is in motion. **Corrective Action:** Replace male hinge with a modified version to increase roof hinge receiver retention ability. **Note:** This recall applies only to Diamond Star Motors-installed sunroofs. Chrysler Corporation's Plymouth and Eagle dealerships and Mitsubishi Motor Sales of America will implement the recall action.

System: Windshield mounting—FMVSS 212. **Vehicle:** Passenger cars. **Defect:** Diluted primer may have been used on the windshield-opening flanges prior to windshield glass installation, which would not provide the retention required by FMVSS 212. **Consequence:** Windshields would not prevent ejection of vehicle occupants during a vehicle crash, which causes serious injuries and fatalities. **Corrective Action:** Replace windshields, associated parts and primer.

System: Interior; seat belts; belt buckles. **Vehicle:** Passenger, multipurpose vehicles and light-duty trucks equipped with safety belts made by Takata Corporation. **Defect:** The front safety belt buckle release buttons can break. These red plastic release buttons are marked "press." If a button breaks, pieces can fall into the buckle assembly, causing the buckle to operate improperly. **Consequence:** The safety belts would not provide adequate protection to an occupant in a vehicle crash. **Corrective Action:** Owners should promptly check the condition and operation of both front safety belt buckles and carefully inspect the red release button for any breaks or cracks. They should ensure that both buckles are operating properly by inserting each latchplate into its buckle, tugging on the belt to make sure the latch is securely locked and then pressing the release button. The latchplate should pop out of the buckle when the button is pressed. If either release button shows a sign of breaking or cracking, or if either buckle fails to operate properly, owners should promptly contact their authorized dealer to schedule an appointment to have the buckle replaced or repaired, free of charge. The manufacturer is developing a remedy designed to prevent failure of the buttons that are not currently broken.

EAGLE VISION 1993

System: Suspension: front lower control arm. **Vehicle:** Passenger cars. **Defect:** The front suspension lower control arm tension strut washers can crack and fall off due to hydrogen embrittlement. **Consequence:** Loss of a washer will cause a clunking sound, heard during braking. If left unattended, the loss of the washer will eventually result in tension strut attachment failure that can result in loss of steering control and an accident. **Corrective Action:** Replace the front and rear strut bar washers and nuts.

FLEETWOOD

FLEETWOOD BOUNDER 1990

System: Other equipment—TV. **Vehicle:** Motor homes. **Defect:** The television mounted in the front overhead cabinet may be insecurely mounted, and could vibrate loose and fall. **Consequence:** Falling TV could strike the driver or front seat passenger, or could distract the driver's attention, creating the potential for an accident. **Corrective Action:** Add two retaining brackets to prevent the TV from moving out of its cabinet. **Note:** Kustom Fit, a division of Bostrom Seating, Inc., initiated this recall and will implement the recall action on the seats installed in motorhomes at Fleetwood Enterprises, Inc., dealerships.

System: Seat belt anchorages. **Vehicle:** Motor homes. **Defect:** Metal-formed ends of seat belt anchorage bar may be cracked. **Consequence:** Seat belt anchorages would not sustain seat belt loads in a crash, increasing the risk of injury to the occupant. **Corrective Action:** Replace top plate weldment, including seat belt anchorage bar, on seat pedestals.

System: Steering. **Vehicle:** Motor homes built on a General Motors P30 chassis. **Defect:** The steering column shaft nut retaining clip may be missing. Under certain conditions, the lack of a retaining clip will allow the nut to work loose and the steering wheel to separate from the steering column. **Consequence:** Steering wheel separation from the steering column can result in complete loss of steering control and a vehicle accident. **Corrective Action:** Inspect steering assembly for a steering wheel nut retaining clip. If clip is missing, install a steering wheel nut retaining clip, or have a dealer inspect and install a clip. Fleetwood advises owners not to operate the motor homes until a steering wheel nut inspection and clip installation is completed. **Note:** Fleetwood Enterprises, Inc. indicates that someone other than the dealer can inspect the motor home and install the missing clips. Should the corrective action be accomplished by someone other than a Fleetwood dealer, the instructions provided must be followed carefully.

FORD

Note: If your Ford is presented to an authorized dealer on an agreed-upon service date and the remedy is not provided within a reasonable time and free of charge, or the remedy does not correct the defect or noncompliance, please contact the Ford Service Center at (800) 392-3673. Also contact the NHTSA's Auto Safety Hotline at (800) 424-9393.

FORD CROWN VICTORIA 1987

System: Steering centerlinks. **Vehicle:** Passenger vehicles with 5.0L engines. **Defect:** Steering centerlinks may break at a bend location. **Consequence:** Steering control would be diminished, with reduced control of left wheel only and considerable steering wheel free play. **Corrective Action:** Replace steering centerlink.

System: Fuel rails. **Vehicle:** Passenger cars equipped with 5.0L fuel-injected engines. **Defect:** Fuel rails may be bent so that #5 injector cups are out of design position. **Consequence:** Bent fuel rail could cause a fuel leak, which, in the presence of an ignition source, could result in an engine fire. **Corrective Action:** Replace fuel rail assemblies as necessary.

System: Fuel line coupling. **Vehicle:** Passenger cars and light trucks equipped with fuel injection. **Defect:** Spring lock fuel line coupling may not be properly engaged. **Consequence:** Coupling could disengage due to fuel pressure, vibration and engine movements; this would cause loss of fuel which, in the presence of an ignition source, creates a fire risk. **Corrective Action:** Install retainer clips over the couplings to prevent coupling separation and fuel leakage.

System: Seat belts. **Vehicle:** Station wagons equipped with optional dual rear-facing seats. **Defect:** Automatic retractor for seat belts for dual rear-facing seats may be installed in an improper location. **Consequence:** Seat belt could bind between seat cushion and seat back, causing the retractor to be sluggish or unable to take up excess belt slack. **Corrective Action:** Remove, and properly install the right auxiliary seat belts.

FORD CROWN VICTORIA 1988

System: Seat belts. **Vehicle:** Station wagons equipped with optional dual rear-facing seats. **Defect:** Automatic retractor for seat belts for dual rear-facing seats may be installed in an improper location. **Consequence:** Seat belt could bind between seat cushion and seat back causing the retractor to be sluggish or unable to take up excess belt slack. **Corrective Action:** Remove, and properly install the right auxiliary seat belts.

FORD CROWN VICTORIA 1989

System: Fuel; optical sensors. **Vehicle:** Flexible-fuel passenger cars with fuel systems modified to operate with gasoline, methanol or combinations of the two fuels. **Defect:** Glass element that separates electronic circuitry from pressurized fuel may loosen and create an opening that could allow pressurized fuel to enter the body of sensor. **Consequence:** Under these conditions of seal deterioration, the housing cover would not contain fuel, causing a fuel leak which, in the presence of a source of ignition, could result in a fire. **Corrective Action:** Install new optical sensors.

FORD CROWN VICTORIA 1990

System: Airbag modules. **Vehicle:** Passenger cars equipped with driver's-side supplemental airbag modules. **Defect:** Threaded inflator components may have been damaged during assembly, which may allow components to separate when inflator receives a signal to deploy the airbag. **Consequence:** Inflator component separation allows hot combustion gases to escape into the passenger compartment, which could result in injuries to vehicle occupants. **Corrective Action:** Replace airbag modules containing potentially defective inflators. **Note:** This campaign was initiated by TRW, Inc., manufacturer of the airbag module.

System: Rear brakes. **Vehicle:** Passenger cars with 5.8L engines and police performance packages. **Defect:** The rear brake lines have inadequate clearance between the brake tube and the vehicle underbody in the area of the left rear wheel opening. **Consequence:** Inadequate clearance can cause abrasion of the brake line and a leak can develop, resulting in loss of brake fluid to the rear brake system and increased stopping distances. **Corrective Action:** Repair any brake lines that have an indication of contact or have the potential for contact with the body of the vehicle. Relocate lines, if necessary.

FORD CROWN VICTORIA 1991

System: Airbag modules. **Vehicle:** Passenger cars equipped with driver's-side supplemental airbag modules. **Defect:** Threaded inflator components may have been damaged during assembly, which may allow components to separate when inflator receives a signal to deploy the airbag. **Consequence:** Inflator component separation allows hot combustion gases to escape into the passenger compartment, which could result in injuries to vehicle occupants. **Corrective Action:** Replace airbag modules containing potentially defective inflators. **Note:** This campaign was initiated by TRW, Inc., manufacturer of the airbag module.

System: Automatic transmission park rod assembly. **Vehicle:** Passenger cars with automatic overdrive transmissions. **Defect:** The park rod assembly contains a park cam with inadequate surface hardness, which could lead to park disengagement or no park engagement when the lever is placed in park. **Consequence:** If park is not engaged and the parking brake is off, a vehicle rollaway could result. **Corrective Action:** Replace park rod assembly on automatic transmissions.

System: Rear brakes. **Vehicle:** Passenger cars with 5.8L engines and police performance packages. **Defect:** The rear brake lines have inadequate clearance between the brake tube and the vehicle underbody in the area of the left rear wheel opening. **Consequence:** Inadequate clearance can cause abrasion of the brake line and a leak can develop, resulting in loss of brake fluid to the rear brake system and increased stopping distances. **Corrective Action:** Repair any brake lines that have an indication of contact or have the potential for contact with the body of the vehicle. Relocate lines, if necessary.

FORD CROWN VICTORIA 1992

System: Instrument panel; antilock brake warning lights—FMVSS 105. **Vehicle:** Passenger cars. **Defect:** Incorrect instrument panel wiring assemblies in some vehicles will not actuate the "antilock" brake warning lights. **Consequence:** The vehicles do not meet the specifications of FMVSS 105. The driver would not be aware when the antilock brake system is malfunctioning. **Corrective Action:** Modify the wire assembly to allow actuation of the antilock brake warning lights.

System: Interior systems; tracks and anchors; front seat; power. **Vehicle:** Police or fleet vehicles equipped with rubber floor mats and non-powered front seats. **Defect:** An unused power seat harness connector is positioned on the rubber floor mat under the seat. If the vehicle is operated in cold weather in areas that have large amounts of salt used for snow and ice control, a puddle of saltwater can accumulate on the rubber floor mats, repeatedly wetting the connector. This will result in corrosion of the connector, causing a current to flow between the terminals without tripping the circuit breaker. **Consequence:** If this occurs, current flow can heat the connector and release fumes into the passenger compartment, and can result in a vehicle fire. **Corrective Action:** Dealers will remove the unused connector and install a sealed heat shrink cap over the affected wires.

FORD CROWN VICTORIA 1993

System: Interior systems; tracks and anchors; front seat; power. **Vehicle:** Police or fleet vehicles equipped with rubber floor mats and non-powered front seats. **Defect:** An unused power seat harness connector is positioned on the rubber floor mat under the seat. If the vehicle is operated in cold weather in areas that have large amounts of salt used for snow and ice control, a puddle of saltwater can accumulate on the rubber floor mats, repeatedly wetting the connector. This will result in corrosion of the connector, causing a current to flow between the terminals without tripping the circuit breaker. **Consequence:** If this occurs, current flow can heat the connector and release fumes into the passenger compartment, and can result in a vehicle fire. **Corrective Action:** Dealers will remove the unused connector and install a sealed heat shrink cap over the affected wires.

FORD CROWN VICTORIA 1994

System: Brakes; hydraulic system. **Vehicle:** Passenger cars. **Defect:** The nuts and bolts that attach the rear brake adapter to the axle housing flange can loosen and eventually separate. If one or more of the nuts come off the bolts, damage to the parking brake assembly or to the antilock brake system (ABS) sensor and sensor ring (if so equipped) will occur. If all four nuts on one end of the axle come off the bolts, damage to the brake hydraulic line or the parking brake cable can occur. **Consequence:** Occurrence of any of these conditions can result in a loss of braking capability and possible accident. **Corrective Action:** Dealers will inspect and, if needed, install new bolts. If any of the fasteners are disconnected, the parking brake and antilock brake system components will be inspected and serviced.

FORD ESCORT 1987

System: Wheel lug nuts. **Vehicle:** Passenger cars equipped with stainless steel decorative lug nuts included with styled steel, polycast and cast aluminum wheels. **Defect:** Lug nuts could gall and possibly seize on the wheel studs without providing adequate clamping load on the wheels. **Consequence:** Wheel studs could fracture, creating a risk of a wheel separating with little forewarning. **Corrective Action:** Replace wheel lug nuts and, if necessary, replace wheels and wheel studs.

System: Fuel line coupling. **Vehicle:** Passenger cars and light trucks equipped with fuel injection. **Defect:** Spring lock fuel line coupling may not be properly engaged. **Consequence:** Coupling could disengage due to fuel pressure, vibration and engine movements; this would cause loss of fuel which, in the presence of an ignition source, creates a fire risk. **Corrective Action:** Install retainer clips over the couplings to prevent coupling separation and fuel leakage.

System: Seat track pedestal. **Vehicle:** Passenger cars. **Defect:** The forward outboard pedestal of the seat track of the driver's seat may be susceptible to fatigue fracture. **Consequence:** This could result in a limited degree of rocking motion of the driver's seat assembly upon acceleration or deceleration, which could cause an accident. **Corrective Action:** Install a reinforcement on all models and a new seat track as necessary.

FORD ESCORT 1988

System: Fuel line coupling. **Vehicle:** Passenger cars and light trucks equipped with fuel injection. **Defect:** Spring lock fuel line coupling may not be properly engaged. **Consequence:** Coupling could disengage due to fuel pressure, vibration and engine movements; this would cause loss of fuel which, in the presence of an ignition source, creates a fire risk. **Corrective Action:** Install retainer clips over the couplings to prevent coupling separation and fuel leakage.

FORD ESCORT 1990

System: Windshield—FMVSS 212. **Vehicle:** Passenger cars. **Defect:** Special primer that promotes the bonding of a urethane adhesive to the glass was not applied to the windshields before installation. **Consequence:** Omission of the primer could cause the windshield not to be properly adhered to the car body, and vehicle would not comply with FMVSS 212. **Corrective Action:** Remove and properly reinstall windshield using special primer.

FORD ESCORT 1991

System: Throttle linkages. **Vehicle:** Passenger cars. **Defect:** Interference occurs between the bolt that secures a fuel line shield to the lower portion of the dash panel and the accelerator pedal. **Consequence:** This could cause the accelerator pedal to stick at the wide-open throttle position, and result in loss of control, with the risk of a vehicle accident. **Corrective Action:** Cut off extra length of bolt that protrudes above surface of the weld nut to prevent interference.

System: Fuel system. **Vehicle:** Passenger vehicles equipped with fuel pump sending assemblies produced by Ford Electrical and Fuel Handling Division (FEHD). **Defect:** Fatigue cracks can develop in the solder joint between the fuel return tube and the fuel pump sending unit located at the top of the fuel tank. **Consequence:** Should a crack develop, fuel vapor can escape from the tank when the tank is full, and a small amount of fuel can leak from the crack. Fuel leaks can result in fire when exposed to a source of ignition. **Corrective Action:** Install a new fuel pump sending assembly.

System: Steering. **Vehicle:** Passenger cars. **Defect:** The roll pins securing the ignition lock in the steering column housing can separate or move out of position. **Consequence:** The ignition lock cylinder may disengage from the steering column housing, which could cause the steering column to lock up, resulting in loss of vehicle control and a possible accident. **Corrective Action:** If one or both of the roll pins are missing or not fully inserted, the ignition lock housing will be replaced, along with the door locks and the liftgate or deck-lid locks, so that key compatibility is maintained. If both pins are present and fully inserted, a plastic snap-on sleeve will be installed as a precaution to prevent the roll pins from coming out.

System: Suspension; independent front. **Equipment Description:** Offset rear toe adjusting pin. **Defect:** The offset toe adjusting pin can fracture under conditions such as torsional loads, flexing motion, impact loads and overtorquing. **Consequence:** This can result in loss of vehicle steering control and an accident. **Corrective Action:** Dana will pay for replacement and labor costs of the adjustment pin without charge to the installing facility and the vehicle owner. These pins should be replaced by a Ford original equipment pin assembly. Owner or installer inquiries concerning this recall campaign should contact Dana Service Center at (800) 248-9606. **Note:** If you have any problems with the pin replacement reimbursement program, please contact Dana Service Center at (800) 248-9606. Also contact the NHTSA's Auto Safety Hotline at (800) 424-9393.

FORD ESCORT 1992

System: Stoplamps. **Vehicle:** Passenger cars. **Defect:** The stoplamp switches could intermittently malfunction, resulting in the stoplamps not illuminating when the brakes are applied. **Consequence:** This could result in following motorists not being signaled that the vehicle is braking, and could result in a collision. **Corrective Action:** Replace the faulty stoplamp switches.

System: Fuel. **Vehicle:** Passenger vehicles equipped with fuel pump sending assemblies produced by Ford Electrical and Fuel Handling Division (FEHD). **Defect:** Fatigue cracks can develop in the solder joint between the fuel return tube and the fuel pump sending unit located at the top of the fuel tank. **Consequence:** Should a crack develop, fuel vapor can escape from the tank when the tank is full, and a small amount of fuel can leak from the crack. Fuel leaks can result in fire when exposed to a source of ignition. **Corrective Action:** Install a new fuel pump sending assembly.

System: Suspension; independent front. **Equipment Description:** Offset rear toe adjusting pin. **Defect:** The offset toe adjusting pin can fracture under conditions such as torsional loads, flexing motion, impact loads and overtorquing. **Consequence:** This can result in loss of vehicle steering control and an accident. **Corrective Action:** Dana will pay for replacement and labor costs of the adjustment pin without charge to the installing facility and the vehicle owner. These pins should be replaced by a Ford original equipment pin assembly. Owner or installer inquiries concerning this recall campaign should contact Dana Service Center at (800) 248-9606. **Note:** If you have any problems with the pin replacement reimbursement program, please contact Dana Service Center at (800) 248-9606. Also contact the NHTSA's Auto Safety Hotline at (800) 424-9393.

FORD ESCORT 1993

System: Suspension; independent front. **Equipment Description:** Offset rear toe adjusting pin. **Defect:** The offset toe adjusting pin can fracture under conditions such as torsional loads, flexing motion, impact loads and overtorquing. **Consequence:** This can result in loss of vehicle steering control and an accident. **Corrective Action:** Dana will pay for replacement and labor costs of the adjustment pin without charge to the installing facility and the vehicle owner. These pins should be replaced by a Ford original equipment pin assembly. Owner or installer inquiries concerning this recall campaign should contact Dana Service Center at (800) 248-9606. **Note:** If you have any problems with the pin replacement reimbursement program, please contact Dana Service Center at (800) 248-9606. Also contact the NHTSA's Auto Safety Hotline at (800) 424-9393.

System: Interior systems; seat tracks and anchors. **Vehicle:** Passenger vehicles. **Defect:** The lock plates of the driver's-side inboard seat track adjusters were manufactured with an unauthorized modification to the fabrication process that causes the seat not to fully engage in certain seating positions near the midpoint of the seat track travel. **Consequence:** In the event of a crash, the seat can move, which would result in reduced occupant protection. **Corrective Action:** Dealers will replace the driver's-side inboard seat track.

FORD ESCORT 1994

System: Interior systems; passive restraint; airbag; driver's-side. **Vehicle:** Passenger cars. **Defect:** The driver's-side airbag module can have an inadequately welded inflator canister. **Consequence:** In the event of a collision, the weld seam can separate, causing the airbag to fail to deploy properly and hot gases to be expelled from the back of the steering wheel. This can result in an increased risk of personal injury from the hot gases and the airbag failure. **Corrective Action:** Dealers will install a new airbag module.

FORD FESTIVA 1988

System: Interior; seat belts; belt buckles. **Vehicle:** Passenger vehicles equipped with safety belts made by Takata Corporation. **Defect:** The front safety belt buckle release buttons can break. These red plastic release buttons are marked "press." If a button breaks, pieces can fall into the buckle assembly, causing the buckle to operate improperly. **Consequence:** The safety belts would not provide adequate protection to an occupant in a vehicle crash. **Corrective Action:** Owners should promptly check the condition and operation of both front safety belt buckles, and carefully inspect the red release button for any breaks or cracks. They should ensure that both buckles are operating properly by inserting each latchplate into its buckle, tugging on the belt to make sure that the latch is securely locked and then pressing the release button. The latchplate should pop out of the buckle when the button is pressed. If either release button shows a sign of breaking or cracking, or if either buckle fails to operate properly, owners should promptly contact their authorized dealer to schedule an appointment to have the buckle replaced or repaired, free of charge. The manufacturer is developing a remedy designed to prevent failure of the buttons that are not currently broken. **Note:** The 1987 through 1989 4-door Mercury Tracers involved in this recall campaign were only sold in Canada. No Tracers sold in the United States are involved.

FORD FESTIVA 1989

System: Interior; seat belts; belt buckles. **Vehicle:** Passenger vehicles equipped with safety belts made by Takata Corporation. **Defect:** The front safety belt buckle release buttons can break. These red plastic release buttons are marked "press." If a button breaks, pieces can fall into the buckle assembly, causing the buckle to operate improperly. **Consequence:** The safety belts would not provide adequate protection to an occupant in a vehicle crash. **Corrective Action:** Owners should promptly check the condition and operation of both front safety belt buckles, and carefully inspect the red release button for any breaks or cracks. They should ensure that both buckles are operating properly by inserting each latchplate into its buckle, tugging on the belt to make sure that the latch is securely locked and then pressing the release button. The latchplate should pop out of the buckle when the button is pressed. If either release button shows a sign of breaking or cracking or if either buckle fails to operate properly, owners should promptly contact their authorized dealer to schedule an appointment to have the buckle replaced or repaired, free of charge. The manufacturer is developing a remedy designed to prevent failure of the buttons that are not currently broken. **Note:** The 1987 through 1989 4-door Mercury Tracers involved in this recall campaign were only sold in Canada. No Tracers sold in the United States are involved.

FORD MUSTANG 1987

System: Fuel line coupling. **Vehicle:** Passenger cars and light trucks equipped with fuel injection. **Defect:** Spring lock fuel line coupling may not be properly engaged. **Consequence:** Coupling could disengage due to fuel pressure, vibration and engine movements; this would cause loss of fuel which, in the presence of an ignition source, creates a fire risk. **Corrective Action:** Install retainer clips over the couplings to prevent coupling separation and fuel leakage.

FORD MUSTANG 1991

System: Automatic transmission park rod assembly. **Vehicle:** Passenger cars with automatic overdrive transmissions. **Defect:** The park rod assembly contains a park cam with inadequate surface hardness, which could lead to park disengagement or no park engagement when the lever is placed in park. **Consequence:** If park is not engaged and the parking brake is off, a vehicle rollaway could result. **Corrective Action:** Replace park rod assembly on automatic transmissions.

FORD MUSTANG 1993

System: Fuel; fuel injection system. **Vehicle:** Passenger cars equipped with 5.0L engines. **Defect:** The fuel rail that provides the fuel supply to the fuel injectors has an improperly formed tube that has the potential to fracture, causing fuel to leak. **Consequence:** Fuel leakage in the presence of an ignition source can result in a fire. **Corrective Action:** The engine fuel rail will be replaced.

FORD MUSTANG 1994

System: Interior; seat; material. **Vehicle:** GT model passenger vehicles equipped with the power lumbar feature on the front seats. **Defect:** The wire harness on these seats is banded to the front seat cushion supports. The end of one of the supports can puncture the harness, resulting in a high-resistance electrical short. **Consequence:** Overheating can result, and melting, smoke and possible ignition of the surrounding materials can occur. **Corrective Action:** Dealers will remove the tie strap from each of the front seats.

System: Interior; instrument panel; speedometer; odometer—FMVSS 101. **Vehicle:** Passenger cars, light-duty trucks and multipurpose vehicles. **Description of Noncompliance:** These vehicles were built with speedometers registering speed in mph (miles per hour), but odometers indicating distance in kilometers. The odometers were intended to indicate distance in miles, and were not identified with the metric "km" designation. This does not comply with FMVSS 101, "Controls and displays." **Consequence of Noncompliance:** The different readings of the speedometer and the odometer may confuse a driver. **Corrective Action:** Ford has not submitted a corrective action for this noncompliance. **Note:** The manufacturer has petitioned the NHTSA for a determination that this matter is inconsequential with respect to motor vehicle safety. The manufacturer is not obligated to conduct an owner notification and remedy campaign until NHTSA has resolved the petition.

FORD PROBE 1989

System: Brakes; hydraulic; shoe and drum systems; drum. **Equipment Description:** Replacement brake drums for passenger vehicles, Midas part BD 1552. **Defect:** The groove for the rear wheel bearing retainer ring was incorrectly machined. **Consequence:** If the retaining ring does not sit correctly in the groove, the axle lug nuts will break, causing the brake drum, wheel and tire assembly to separate from the vehicle. **Corrective Action:** Midas shops will replace the brake drums with other brake drums from another supplier. **Note:** If your vehicle is presented to an authorized dealer on an agreed-upon service date and the remedy is not provided within a reasonable time and free of charge, or the remedy does not correct the defect or noncompliance, please contact the NHTSA's Auto Safety Hotline at (800) 424-9393. Empire Motor Company, Ltd., of Tokyo, Japan, manufactured these brake drums. The U.S. representative is EMC of America, Los Angeles, CA. These brake drums were installed on vehicles from July 13, 1993 through September 30, 1993.

FORD PROBE 1990

System: Throttle. **Defect:** Throttle levers may have been bent during assembly. **Consequence:** Throttle may stick and not return fully to idle position. **Corrective Action:** Place affected vehicles on delivery hold until repaired.

System: Brakes; hydraulic; shoe and drum systems; drum. **Equipment Description:** Replacement brake drums for passenger vehicles, Midas part BD 1552. **Defect:** The groove for the rear wheel bearing retainer ring was incorrectly machined. **Consequence:** If the retaining ring does not sit correctly in the groove, the axle lug nuts will break, causing the brake drum, wheel and tire assembly to separate from the vehicle. **Corrective Action:** Midas shops will replace the brake drums with other brake drums from another supplier. **Note:** If your vehicle is presented to an authorized dealer on an agreed-upon service date and the remedy is not provided within a reasonable time and free of charge, or the remedy does not correct the defect or noncompliance, please contact the NHTSA's Auto Safety Hotline at (800) 424-9393. Empire Motor Company, Ltd., of Tokyo, Japan, manufactured these brake drums. The U.S. representative is EMC of America, Los Angeles, CA. These brake drums were installed on vehicles from July 13, 1993 through September 30, 1993.

FORD PROBE 1991

System: Safety belt retractor bracket attachment. **Vehicle:** Passenger cars; Probe GL models only. **Defect:** Brackets mounting automatic shoulder belt retractor assembly may have an understrength spot weld. **Consequence:** Shoulder belt could fail in a collision increasing the risk of injury to the occupant. **Corrective Action:** Install two bolts in the brackets to prevent shoulder belt failure.

System: Brakes; hydraulic; shoe and drum systems; drum. **Equipment Description:** Replacement brake drums for passenger vehicles, Midas part BD 1552. **Defect:** The groove for the rear wheel bearing retainer ring was incorrectly machined. **Consequence:** If the retaining ring does not sit correctly in the groove, the axle lug nuts will break, causing the brake drum, wheel and tire assembly to separate from the vehicle. **Corrective Action:** Midas shops will replace the brake drums with other brake drums from another supplier. **Note:** If your vehicle is presented to an authorized dealer on an agreed-upon service date and the remedy is not provided within a reasonable time and free of charge, or the remedy does not correct the defect or noncompliance, please contact the NHTSA's Auto Safety Hotline at (800) 424-9393. Empire Motor Company, Ltd., of Tokyo, Japan, manufactured these brake drums. The U.S. representative is EMC of America, Los Angeles, CA. These brake drums were installed on vehicles from July 13, 1993 through September 30, 1993.

FORD TAURUS 1987

System: Steering shaft assembly. **Vehicle:** Passenger cars. **Defect:** Steering shaft assemblies contain lower shafts of insufficient length for proper attachment to the shaft insulator flange. **Consequence:** Shaft could separate, resulting in total loss of steering control and a possible accident. **Corrective Action:** Replace steering shaft assembly, as necessary.

System: Rear spindle. **Vehicle:** Passenger cars. **Defect:** Left and/or right rear spindle assemblies may have been improperly heat treated. **Consequence:** If spindle stem separates, loss of vehicle control could occur without prior warning. **Corrective Action:** Replace rear spindle.

System: Rear window wiper motor. **Vehicle:** Station wagons equipped with optional rear window wiper motors. **Defect:** Road salt-induced erosion of the wiper motor conductor strips could cause localized thermal stress within the glass. **Consequence:** Glass could fracture while station wagon is being driven or parked, creating a risk of injury to occupants or sudden distraction to the driver. **Corrective Action:** Apply sealant to conductor strips and protective tape to lower back lights.

System: Fuel line coupling. **Vehicle:** Passenger cars and light trucks equipped with fuel injection. **Defect:** Spring lock fuel line coupling may not be properly engaged. **Consequence:** Coupling could disengage due to fuel pressure, vibration and engine movements; this would cause loss of fuel which, in the presence of an ignition source, creates a fire risk. **Corrective Action:** Install retainer clips over the couplings to prevent coupling separation and fuel leakage.

System: Brakes. **Vehicle:** Passenger vehicles sold or registered in the following states: CT, IL, IN, ME, MA, MI, NH, NJ, NY, OH, PA, RI, VT and WI. **Defect:** Front disc brake rotors of the subject vehicles may experience severe corrosion if operated in areas where calcium chloride and sodium chloride are used extensively. **Consequence:** Severely corroded rotors may fracture or separate near the inner edges of the brake discs, resulting in reduced braking effectiveness, higher than normal pedal efforts, loud grinding noises and moderate pulls when the brakes are applied. Reduced braking effectiveness may increase minimum stopping distances, possibly resulting in an accident. **Corrective Action:** Replace front brake rotors with full cast front brake rotors.

System: Structure: storage compartments. **Vehicle:** Passenger cars (station wagons). **Defect:** Children can accidentally lock themselves in the footwell area of the rear-facing third seat, or in the storage compartment in station wagons not equipped with an optional third seat. Once the compartment is closed, it cannot be opened from the inside. **Consequence:** There is a danger of air deprivation, hypothermia and/or panic response to a child who has locked himself or herself into the compartment, with the possibility of asphyxiation. **Corrective Action:** Replace the self-latching assembly currently used in the rear storage compartment with a latch assembly that can only be closed with a key. **Note:** Until the latch assembly is replaced, Ford recommends owners lock the storage compartment when not in use. Also, Ford advises that the latch striker can be removed to disable the current latch until revised latch assemblies are available.

System: Structure; rear subframe mounts. **Vehicle:** Taurus and Sables built from October 14, 1985 through August 19, 1988 and Lincoln Continentals built from November 4, 1987 through September 30, 1988 (except 1989-1991 2.5L Taurus and 1989-1992 SHO). The affected cars were sold or registered in the following states: CT, IL, IN, ME, MA, MI, NH, NJ, NY, OH, PA, RI, VT and WI. **Defect:** The body mounts at the rear corners of the subframe, which supports the engine and transmission, may become detached due to corrosion of the subframe mount retaining plate. This would allow the rear corners of the subframe to drop. **Consequence:** If one of the rear corners drops, only minor indications of a malfunction, such as a clunking noise or slight change in steering wheel alignment, are noticeable. However, if both rear corners of the subframe drop, steering becomes very difficult, which could adversely affect vehicle control and possibly result in an accident. **Corrective Action:** Install a corrosion-resistant reinforcing plate and a new bolt on both rear subframe mounts.

System: Suspension; independent front shock absorber. **Equipment Description:** Aftermarket shock absorbers for 1986-1994 Ford Taurus and Mercury Sable passenger cars; parts 71780 and 81780. **Defect:** The arc welds on the sway bar bracket, where it attaches to the strut reserve tube, did not fuse properly. **Consequence:** Over time, a portion of the bracket can tear away from the strut, falling into and puncturing the tire or causing damage to the wheel, which could result in an accident. **Corrective Action:** Monroe dealers will replace the strut free of charge. **Note:** If the vehicle is presented to an authorized dealer on an agreed-upon service date and the remedy is not provided free of charge within a reasonable time, or the remedy does not correct the defect, please contact Monroe at (800) 521-6754. Also contact the NHTSA's Auto Safety Hotline at (800) 424-9393.

FORD TAURUS 1988

System: Power seat switch wiring. **Vehicle:** Passenger cars. **Defect:** The power seat switch wiring is routed over rather than under the front seat support brace, allowing damage by seat cushion spring ends when the seat is occupied. **Consequence:** Power seat switch wiring insulation may become abraded or punctured, and an electrical short could occur that could result in a fire in the seat cushion material. **Corrective Action:** Revise routing of power seat wiring to prevent damage from seat cushion spring contact.

System: Brakes. **Vehicle:** Passenger vehicles sold or registered in the following states: CT, IL, IN, ME, MA, MI, NH, NJ, NY, OH, PA, RI, VT and WI. **Defect:** Front disc brake rotors of the subject vehicles may experience severe corrosion if operated in areas where calcium chloride and sodium chloride are used extensively. **Consequence:** Severely corroded rotors may fracture or separate near the inner edges of the brake discs, resulting in reduced braking effectiveness, higher than normal pedal efforts, loud grinding noises and moderate pulls when the brakes are applied. Reduced braking effectiveness may increase minimum stopping distances, possibly resulting in an accident. **Corrective Action:** Replace front brake rotors with full cast front brake rotors.

System: Structure: storage compartments. **Vehicle:** Passenger cars (station wagons). **Defect:** Children can accidentally lock themselves in the footwell area of the rear-facing third seat, or in the storage compartment in station wagons not equipped with an optional third seat. Once the compartment is closed, it cannot be opened from the inside. **Consequence:** There is a danger of air deprivation, hypothermia and/or panic response to a child who has locked himself or herself into the compartment, with the possibility of asphyxiation. **Corrective Action:** Replace the self-latching assembly currently used in the rear storage compartment with a latch assembly that can only be closed with a key. **Note:** Until the latch assembly is replaced, Ford recommends owners lock the storage compartment when not in use. Also, Ford advises that the latch striker can be removed to disable the current latch until revised latch assemblies are available.

System: Structure; rear subframe mounts. **Vehicle:** Taurus and Sables built from October 14, 1985 through August 19, 1988, and Lincoln Continentals built from November 4, 1987 through September 30, 1988 (except 1989-1991 2.5L Taurus and 1989-1992 SHO). The affected cars were sold or registered in the following states: CT, IL, IN, ME, MA, MI, NH, NJ, NY, OH, PA, RI, VT and WI. **Defect:** The body mounts at the rear corners of the subframe, which supports the engine and transmission, may become detached due to corrosion of the subframe mount retaining plate. This would allow the rear corners of the subframe to drop. **Consequence:** If one of the rear corners drops, only minor indications of a malfunction, such as a clunking noise or slight change in steering wheel alignment, are noticeable. However, if both rear corners of the subframe drop, steering becomes very difficult, which could adversely affect vehicle control and possibly result in an accident. **Corrective Action:** Install a corrosion-resistant reinforcing plate and a new bolt on both rear subframe mounts.

System: Suspension; independent front shock absorber. **Equipment Description:** Aftermarket shock absorbers for 1986-1994 Ford Taurus and Mercury Sable passenger cars; parts 71780 and 81780. **Defect:** The arc welds on the sway bar bracket, where it attaches to the strut reserve tube, did not fuse properly. **Consequence:** Over time, a portion of the bracket can tear away from the strut, falling into and puncturing the tire or causing damage to the wheel, which could result in an accident. **Corrective Action:** Monroe dealers will replace the strut free of charge. **Note:** If the vehicle is presented to an authorized dealer on an agreed-upon service date and the remedy is not provided free of charge within a reasonable time or the remedy does not correct the defect, please contact Monroe at (800) 521-6754. Also contact the NHTSA's Auto Safety Hotline at (800) 424-9393.

FORD TAURUS 1989

System: Power seat switch wiring. **Vehicle:** Passenger cars. **Defect:** The power seat switch wiring is routed over rather than under the front seat support brace, allowing damage by seat cushion spring ends when the seat is occupied. **Consequence:** Power seat switch wiring insulation may become abraded or punctured, and an electrical short could occur that could result in a fire in the seat cushion material. **Corrective Action:** Revise routing of power seat wiring to prevent damage from seat cushion spring contact.

System: Brakes. **Vehicle:** Passenger vehicles sold or registered in the following states: CT, IL, IN, ME, MA, MI, NH, NJ, NY, OH, PA, RI, VT and WI. **Defect:** Front disc brake rotors of the subject vehicles may experience severe corrosion if operated in areas where calcium chloride and sodium chloride are used extensively. **Consequence:** Severely corroded rotors may fracture or separate near the inner edges of the brake discs, resulting in reduced braking effectiveness, higher than normal pedal efforts, loud grinding noises and moderate pulls when the brakes are applied. Reduced braking effectiveness may increase minimum stopping distances, possibly resulting in an accident. **Corrective Action:** Replace front brake rotors with full cast front brake rotors.

System: Structure: storage compartments. **Vehicle:** Passenger cars (station wagons). **Defect:** Children can accidentally lock themselves in the footwell area of the rear-facing third seat, or in the storage compartment in station wagons not equipped with an optional third seat. Once the compartment is closed, it cannot be opened from the inside. **Consequence:** There is a danger of air deprivation, hypothermia and/or panic response to a child who has locked himself or herself into the compartment, with the possibility of asphyxiation. **Corrective Action:** Replace the self-latching assembly currently used in the rear storage compartment with a latch assembly that can only be closed with a key. **Note:** Until the latch assembly is replaced, Ford recommends owners lock the storage compartment when not in use. Also, Ford advises that the latch striker can be removed to disable the current latch until revised latch assemblies are available.

System: Safety belt buckle. **Vehicle:** Passenger cars and utility vehicles. **Defect:** The rigid mounted safety belt buckles are defective in three ways. First, a fastened safety belt buckle will not unlatch when the release button is depressed. This results from interference between the buckle ejector finger and the buckle tongue window. The second defect is the safety belt buckle may not latch. The third possible defect is that the tongue may be retained by the buckle, but it may not be latched sufficiently to provide occupant protection. **Consequence:** An insufficiently latched or unlatched safety belt increases the risk of injury to seat occupants in the event of a sudden stop or accident. If the safety belt buckle will not unlatch, it will not allow the occupant to get out of the vehicle in an emergency situation. **Corrective Action:** Ford will replace the rigid mounted safety belt buckles with end release safety belt buckles designed to prevent latch problems. **Note:** Only the end release buckles on "rigid" mountings are susceptible to this malfunction; the web-mounted front center end release buckles and the web-mounted rear-facing third seat end release buckles in Taurus or Sable vehicles will not be replaced. Also, the web-mounted front center buckles in Explorer vehicles will not be replaced.

System: Structure; rear subframe mounts. **Vehicle:** Taurus and Sables built from August 1, 1988 through December 23, 1992 and Lincoln Continentals built from October 3, 1988 through December 23, 1992. The affected cars were sold or registered in the following states: CT,

IL, IN, ME, MA, MI, NH, NJ, NY, OH, PA, RI, VT and WI. **Defect:** The body mounts at the rear corners of the subframe, which supports the engine and transmission, may become detached due to corrosion of the subframe mount retaining plate. This would allow the rear corners of the subframe to drop. **Consequence:** If one of the rear corners drops, only minor indications of a malfunction, such as a clunking noise or slight change in steering wheel alignment, are noticeable. However, if both rear corners of the subframe drop, steering becomes very difficult, which could adversely affect vehicle control and possibly result in an accident. **Corrective Action:** Install a corrosion-resistant reinforcing plate and a new bolt on both rear subframe mounts.

System: Suspension; independent front shock absorber. **Equipment Description:** Aftermarket shock absorbers for 1986-1994 Ford Taurus and Mercury Sable passenger cars; parts 71780 and 81780. **Defect:** The arc welds on the sway bar bracket, where it attaches to the strut reserve tube, did not fuse properly. **Consequence:** Over time, a portion of the bracket can tear away from the strut, falling into and puncturing the tire or causing damage to the wheel, which could result in an accident. **Corrective Action:** Monroe dealers will replace the strut free of charge. **Note:** If the vehicle is presented to an authorized dealer on an agreed-upon service date and the remedy is not provided free of charge within a reasonable time, or the remedy does not correct the defect, please contact Monroe at (800) 521-6754. Also contact the NHTSA's Auto Safety Hotline at (800) 424-9393.

FORD TAURUS 1990

System: Autolamp headlamp control. **Vehicle:** Passenger cars with autolamp headlamp control system. **Defect:** An incorrect transistor may cause autolamp system light sensor module malfunction. **Consequence:** Headlamps could turn off while vehicle is being driven or remain on after vehicle is parked. Loss of headlights while driving at night could be hazardous to the driver and other traffic. **Corrective Action:** Replace light sensor modules.

System: Airbag modules. **Vehicle:** Passenger cars equipped with driver's-side supplemental airbag modules. **Defect:** Threaded inflator components may have been damaged during assembly, which may allow components to separate when inflator receives a signal to deploy the airbag. **Consequence:** Inflator component separation allows hot combustion gases to escape into the passenger compartment, which could result in injuries to vehicle occupants. **Corrective Action:** Replace airbag modules containing potentially defective inflators. **Note:** This campaign was initiated by TRW, Inc., manufacturer of the airbag module.

System: Steel wheels. **Vehicle:** Passenger cars equipped with police vehicle option package and 14″ × 5.5″ heavy-duty steel wheel. **Defect:** Wheels may contain cracks that could propagate in raised portion of wheel center. **Consequence:** Under severe duty, this could result in eventual separation of wheel rim from center, with loss of control and possibly a collision. **Corrective Action:** Replace wheels with wheels of a revised design.

System: Brakes. **Vehicle:** Passenger vehicles sold or registered in the following states: CT, IL, IN, ME, MA, MI, NH, NJ, NY, OH, PA, RI, VT and WI. **Defect:** Front disc brake rotors of the subject vehicles may experience severe corrosion if operated in areas where calcium chloride and sodium chloride are used extensively. **Consequence:** Severely corroded rotors may fracture or separate near the inner edges of the brake discs, resulting in reduced braking effectiveness, higher than normal pedal efforts, loud grinding noises and moderate pulls when the brakes are applied. Reduced braking effectiveness may increase minimum stopping distances, possibly resulting in an accident. **Corrective Action:** Replace front brake rotors with full cast front brake rotors.

System: Structure; storage compartments. **Vehicle:** Passenger cars (station wagons). **Defect:** Children can accidentally lock themselves in the footwell area of the rear-facing third seat, or in the storage compartment in station wagons not equipped with an optional third seat. Once the compartment is closed, it cannot be opened from the inside. **Consequence:** There is a danger of air deprivation, hypothermia and/or panic response to a child who has locked himself or herself into the compartment, with the possibility of asphyxiation. **Corrective Action:** Replace the self-latching assembly currently used in the rear storage compartment with a latch assembly that can only be closed with a key. **Note:** Until the latch assembly is replaced, Ford recommends owners lock the storage compartment when not in use. Also, Ford advises that the latch striker can be removed to disable the current latch until revised latch assemblies are available.

System: Safety belt buckle. **Vehicle:** Passenger cars and utility vehicles. **Defect:** The rigid mounted safety belt buckles are defective in three ways. First, a fastened safety belt buckle will not unlatch when the release button is depressed. This results from interference between the buckle ejector finger and the buckle tongue window. The second defect is the safety belt buckle may not latch. The third possible defect is that the tongue may be retained by the buckle, but it may not be latched sufficiently to provide occupant protection. **Consequence:** An insufficiently latched or unlatched safety belt increases the risk of injury to seat occupants in the event of a sudden stop or accident. If the safety belt buckle will not unlatch, it will not allow the occupant to get out of the vehicle in an emergency situation. **Corrective Action:** Ford will replace the rigid mounted safety belt buckles with end release safety belt buckles designed to prevent latch problems. **Note:** Only the end release buckles on "rigid" mountings are susceptible to this malfunction; the web-mounted front center end release buckles and the web-mounted rear-facing third seat end release buckles in Taurus or Sable vehicles will not be replaced. Also, the web-mounted front center buckles in Explorer vehicles will not be replaced.

System: Structure; rear subframe mounts. **Vehicle:** Taurus and Sables built from August 1, 1988 through December 23, 1992 and Lincoln Continentals built from October 3, 1988 through December 23, 1992. The affected cars were sold or registered in the following states: CT, IL, IN, ME, MA, MI, NH, NJ, NY, OH, PA, RI, VT and WI. **Defect:** The body mounts at the rear corners of the subframe, which supports the engine and transmission, may become detached due to corrosion of the subframe mount retaining plate. This would allow the rear corners of the subframe to drop. **Consequence:** If one of the rear corners drops, only minor indications of a malfunction, such as a clunking noise or slight change in steering wheel alignment, are noticeable. However, if both rear corners of the subframe drop, steering becomes very difficult, which could adversely affect vehicle control and possibly result in an accident. **Corrective Action:** Install a corrosion-resistant reinforcing plate and a new bolt on both rear subframe mounts.

System: Suspension; independent front shock absorber. **Equipment Description:** Aftermarket shock absorbers for 1986-1994 Ford Taurus and Mercury Sable passenger cars; parts 71780 and 81780. **Defect:** The arc welds on the sway bar bracket, where it attaches to the strut reserve tube, did not fuse properly. **Consequence:** Over time, a portion of the bracket can tear away from the strut, falling into and puncturing the tire or causing damage to the wheel, which could result in an accident. **Corrective Action:** Monroe dealers will replace the strut free of charge.

FORD TAURUS 1991

System: Brakes. **Vehicle:** Passenger vehicles sold or registered in the following states: CT, IL, IN, ME, MA, MI, NH, NJ, NY, OH, PA, RI, VT and WI. **Defect:** Front disc brake rotors of the subject vehicles may experience severe corrosion if operated in areas where calcium chloride and sodium chloride are used extensively. **Consequence:** Severely corroded rotors may fracture or separate near the inner edges of the brake discs, resulting in reduced braking effectiveness, higher than normal pedal efforts, loud grinding noises and moderate pulls when the brakes are applied. Reduced braking effectiveness may increase minimum stopping distances, possibly resulting in an accident. **Corrective Action:** Replace front brake rotors with full cast front brake rotors.

System: Structure; storage compartments. **Vehicle:** Passenger cars (station wagons). **Defect:** Children can accidentally lock themselves in the footwell area of the rear-facing third seat, or in the storage compartment in station wagons not equipped with an optional third seat. Once the compartment is closed, it cannot be opened from the inside. **Consequence:** There is a danger of air deprivation, hypothermia and/or panic response to a child who has locked himself or herself into the compartment, with the possibility of asphyxiation. **Corrective Action:** Replace the self-latching assembly currently used in the rear storage compartment with a latch assembly that can only be closed with a key. **Note:** Until the latch assembly is replaced, Ford recommends owners lock the storage compartment when not in use. Also, Ford advises that the latch striker can be removed to disable the current latch until revised latch assemblies are available.

System: Structure; rear subframe mounts. **Vehicle:** Taurus and Sables built from August 1, 1988 through December 23, 1992 and Lincoln Continentals built from October 3, 1988 through December 23, 1992. The affected cars were sold or registered in the following states: CT, IL, IN, ME, MA, MI, NH, NJ, NY, OH, PA, RI, VT and WI. **Defect:** The body mounts at the rear corners of the subframe, which supports the engine and transmission, may become detached due to corrosion of the subframe mount retaining plate. This would allow the rear corners of the subframe to drop. **Consequence:** If one of the rear corners drops, only minor indications of a malfunction, such as a clunking noise or slight change in steering wheel alignment, are noticeable. However, if both rear corners of the subframe drop, steering becomes very difficult, which could adversely affect vehicle control and possibly result in an accident. **Corrective Action:** Install a corrosion-resistant reinforcing plate and a new bolt on both rear subframe mounts.

System: Suspension; independent front shock absorber. **Equipment Description:** Aftermarket shock absorbers for 1986-1994 Ford Taurus and Mercury Sable passenger cars; parts 71780 and 81780. **Defect:** The arc welds on the sway bar bracket, where it attaches to the strut reserve tube, did not fuse properly. **Consequence:** Over time, a portion of the bracket can tear away from the strut, falling into and puncturing the tire or causing damage to the wheel, which could result in an accident. **Corrective Action:** Monroe dealers will replace the strut free of charge.

FORD TAURUS 1992

System: Liftgate. **Vehicle:** Passenger cars (station wagons). **Defect:** Manufacturing errors by the supplier of the liftgate latch mechanism may cause the secondary portion of the liftgate latch not to function. If the latch is not in the primary latch position, the liftgate could open without operator action. **Consequence:** If the liftgate were to open during vehicle operation, passengers or cargo could fall from the open liftgate. **Corrective Action:** Replace malfunctioning liftgate latches.

System: Structure; storage compartments. **Vehicle:** Passenger cars (station wagons). **Defect:** Children can accidentally lock themselves in the footwell area of the rear-facing third seat, or in the storage compartment in station wagons not equipped with an optional third seat. Once the compartment is closed, it cannot be opened from the inside. **Consequence:** There is a danger of air deprivation, hypothermia and/or panic response to a child who has locked himself or herself into the compartment, with the possibility of asphyxiation. **Corrective Action:** Replace the self-latching assembly currently used in the rear storage compartment with a latch assembly that can only be closed with a key. **Note:** Until the latch assembly is replaced, Ford recommends owners lock the storage compartment when not in use. Also, Ford advises that the latch striker can be removed to disable the current latch until revised latch assemblies are available.

System: Structure; rear subframe mounts. **Vehicle:** Taurus and Sables built from August 1, 1988 through December 23, 1992 and Lincoln Continentals built from October 3, 1988 through December 23, 1992. The affected cars were sold or registered in the following states: CT, IL, IN, ME, MA, MI, NH, NJ, NY, OH, PA, RI, VT and WI. **Defect:** The body mounts at the rear corners of the subframe, which supports the engine and transmission, may become detached due to corrosion of the subframe mount retaining plate. This would allow the rear corners of the subframe to drop. **Consequence:** If one of the rear corners drops, only minor indications of a malfunction, such as a clunking noise or slight change in steering wheel alignment, are noticeable. However, if both rear corners of the subframe drop, steering becomes very difficult, which could adversely affect vehicle control and possibly result in an accident. **Corrective Action:** Install a corrosion-resistant reinforcing plate and a new bolt on both rear subframe mounts.

System: Suspension; independent front shock absorber. **Equipment Description:** Aftermarket shock absorbers for 1986-1994 Ford Taurus and Mercury Sable passenger cars; parts 71780 and 81780. **Defect:** The arc welds on the sway bar bracket, where it attaches to the strut reserve tube, did not fuse properly. **Consequence:** Over time, a portion of the bracket can tear away from the strut, falling into and puncturing the tire or causing damage to the wheel, which could result in an accident. **Corrective Action:** Monroe dealers will replace the strut free of charge. **Note:** If the vehicle is presented to an authorized dealer on an agreed-upon service date and the remedy is not provided free of charge within a reasonable time, or the remedy does not correct the defect, please contact Monroe at (800) 521-6754. Also contact the NHTSA's Auto Safety Hotline at (800) 424-9393.

FORD TAURUS 1993

System: Brakes. **Vehicle:** Passenger cars with optional antilock brake systems (ABS). **Defect:** Antilock brake system controllers designed for rear wheel drive cars may have been installed on these front wheel drive cars. **Consequence:** This could result in reduced braking ability and possible vehicle accident. **Corrective Action:** Replace the rear wheel drive antilock brake system controller with a front wheel drive antilock brake system controller.

System: Structure; rear subframe mounts. **Vehicle:** Taurus and Sables built from August 1, 1988 through December 23, 1992 and Lincoln Continentals built from October 3, 1988 through December 23, 1992. The affected cars were sold or registered in the following states: CT, IL, IN, ME, MA, MI, NH, NJ, NY, OH, PA, RI, VT and WI. **Defect:** The body mounts at the rear corners of the subframe, which supports the engine and transmission, may become detached due to corrosion of the subframe mount retaining plate. This would allow the rear corners of the subframe to drop. **Consequence:** If one of the rear corners drops, only minor indications of a malfunction, such as a clunking noise or slight change in steering wheel alignment, are noticeable. However, if both rear corners of the subframe drop, steering becomes very difficult, which could adversely affect vehicle control and possibly result in an accident. **Corrective Action:** Install a corrosion-resistant reinforcing plate and a new bolt on both rear subframe mounts.

System: Suspension; independent front shock absorber. **Equipment Description:** Aftermarket shock absorbers for 1986-1994 Ford Taurus and Mercury Sable passenger cars; parts 71780 and 81780. **Defect:** The arc welds on the sway bar bracket, where it attaches to the strut reserve tube, did not fuse properly. **Consequence:** Over time, a portion of the bracket can tear away from the strut, falling into and puncturing the tire or causing damage to the wheel, which could result in an accident. **Corrective Action:** Monroe dealers will replace the strut free of charge.

FORD TAURUS 1994

System: Suspension; independent front shock absorber. **Equipment Description:** Aftermarket shock absorbers for 1986-1994 Ford Taurus and Mercury Sable passenger cars; parts 71780 and 81780. **Defect:** The arc welds on the sway bar bracket, where it attaches to the strut reserve tube, did not fuse properly. **Consequence:** Over time, a portion of the bracket can tear away from the strut, falling into and puncturing the tire or causing damage to the wheel, which could result in an accident. **Corrective Action:** Monroe dealers will replace the strut free of charge. **Note:** If the vehicle is presented to an authorized dealer on an agreed-upon service date and the remedy is not provided free of charge within a reasonable time, or the remedy does not correct the defect, please contact Monroe at (800) 521-6754. Also contact the NHTSA's Auto Safety Hotline at (800) 424-9393.

FORD TEMPO 1987

System: Wheel lug nuts. **Vehicle:** Passenger cars equipped with stainless steel decorative lug nuts included with styled steel, polycast and cast aluminum wheels. **Defect:** Lug nuts could gall and possibly seize on the wheel studs without providing adequate clamping load on the wheels. **Consequence:** Wheel studs could fracture, creating a risk of a wheel separating with little warning. **Corrective Action:** Replace wheel lug nuts and, if necessary, replace wheels and wheel studs.

FORD TEMPO 1988

System: Throttle. **Vehicle:** Passenger cars with 2.3L engines. **Defect:** Two attachment screws for the throttle position sensors could loosen and back out. **Consequence:** If both screws come out, sensors could disengage from the throttle shaft, preventing return of the throttle from midposition. **Corrective Action:** Replace attachment screws with screws with pre-applied adhesive that will be tightened to a higher torque specification.

FORD TEMPO 1990

System: Airbag modules. **Vehicle:** Passenger cars equipped with driver's-side supplemental airbag modules. **Defect:** Threaded inflator components may have been damaged during assembly, which may allow components to separate when inflator receives a signal to deploy the airbag. **Consequence:** Inflator component separation allows hot combustion gases to escape into the passenger compartment, which could result in injuries to vehicle occupants. **Corrective Action:** Replace airbag modules containing potentially defective inflators. **Note:** This campaign was initiated by TRW, Inc., manufacturer of the airbag module.

FORD THUNDERBIRD 1987

System: Fuel line coupling. **Vehicle:** Passenger cars and light trucks equipped with fuel injection. **Defect:** Spring lock fuel line coupling may not be properly engaged. **Consequence:** Coupling could disengage due to fuel pressure, vibration and engine movements; this would cause loss of fuel which, in the presence of an ignition source, creates a fire risk. **Corrective Action:** Install retainer clips over the couplings to prevent coupling separation and fuel leakage.

FORD THUNDERBIRD 1988

System: Axle rear shaft flange—suspension. **Vehicle:** Passenger cars. **Defect:** A design change to facilitate changeover in rear axle shaft flanges inadvertently produced the possibility for interference between the flange and disc brake rotor. **Consequence:** The interference could prevent proper seating of the rotor. Also, an improperly seated rotor could in time result in a reduction in the clamping forces of the wheel studs, possibly leading to fractured studs and rear wheel separation. **Corrective Action:** Inspection of vehicles and, where necessary, replacement of rear axle shafts and rear brake rotors.

FORD THUNDERBIRD 1989

System: Fuel tank. **Vehicle:** Passenger cars. **Defect:** Plastic rollover valve mounting plate may not be properly sealed to the plastic fuel tank. **Consequence:** Fuel or vapor could leak, which could result in a vehicle fire. **Corrective Action:** Replace fuel tank.

System: Rear suspension knuckles. **Vehicle:** Passenger cars. **Defect:** Improperly heat-treated rear suspension knuckles could experience high-mileage fatigue cracks and eventual fracture. **Consequence:** This could result in rear suspension failure at the affected wheel, with an adverse affect on control of the car, which could cause an accident. **Corrective Action:** Replace knuckles that have the affected lot codes.

System: Brakes—suspension. **Vehicle:** Passenger cars. **Defect:** Due to contact between the brake caliper of the inboard front wheel and the front stabilizer bar, there may be increased brake pedal travel following low-speed turning maneuvers. **Consequence:** This could cause a reduction in brake performance that could result in an accident. **Corrective Action:** Install acorn-type front suspension strut nuts to eliminate stabilizer bar-to-brake caliper contact.

FORD THUNDERBIRD 1990

System: Battery-to-starter cable. **Vehicle:** Passenger cars equipped with 3.8L engines. **Defect:** Battery-to-starter cables are longer than specified; excessive cable length could contact engine damper pulley. **Consequence:** Cable protective covering and insulation could wear through and cause a direct short to ground, resulting in overheating of the cable insulation and possibly an underhood fire. **Corrective Action:** Replace battery-to-starter cable with correct length cable.

System: Windshield wiper assembly. **Vehicle:** Passenger cars. **Defect:** The nuts that hold the windshield wiper motor to the wiper module may not have been sufficiently tightened, and may loosen or come off. This causes changed wiper patterns, or the wipers may jam if two of the three nuts come off. **Consequence:** Changes in the wiper pattern or jamming of the wipers would result in reduced driver visibility in inclement weather conditions. **Corrective Action:** Apply torque-retention material to wiper motor studs and nuts and retorque.

FORD THUNDERBIRD 1991

System: Automatic transmission park rod assembly. **Vehicle:** Passenger cars with automatic overdrive transmissions. **Defect:** The park rod assembly contains a park cam with inadequate surface hardness, which could lead to park disengagement or no park engagement when the lever is placed in park. **Consequence:** If park is not engaged and the parking brake is off, a vehicle rollaway could result. **Corrective Action:** Replace park rod assembly on automatic transmissions.

System: Windshield wiper assembly. **Vehicle:** Passenger cars. **Defect:** The nuts which hold windshield wiper motor to the wiper module may not have been sufficiently tightened and may loosen or come off. This causes changed wiper patterns, or the wipers may jam if two of the three nuts come off. **Consequence:** Changes in the wiper pattern or jamming of the wipers would result in reduced driver visibility in inclement weather conditions. **Corrective Action:** Apply torque-retention material to wiper motor studs and nuts and retorque.

FORD TRUCK AEROSTAR 1987

System: Fuel line coupling. **Vehicle:** Passenger cars and light trucks equipped with fuel injection. **Defect:** Spring lock fuel line coupling may not be properly engaged. **Consequence:** Coupling could disengage due to fuel pressure, vibration and engine movements; this would cause loss of fuel which, in the presence of an ignition source, creates a fire risk. **Corrective Action:** Install retainer clips over the couplings to prevent coupling separation and fuel leakage.

System: Electrical. **Vehicle:** Multipurpose vehicles and vans, equipped with optional trailer tow package. **Defect:** Vehicles equipped with trailer tow package have a trailer taillight relay assembly that contains wires of smaller gauge than the fuse link which protects the circuit. **Consequence:** Should a short circuit occur in the wiring within the relay, or if water intrusion occurs, the smaller gauge wire in the relay will function as a fuse link and overheat. The possibility exists for a fire if the wires are exposed to combustible materials. **Corrective Action:** Installation of a relay with wires of gauge adequate to protect the circuit.

System: Safety belts. **Vehicle:** Vans equipped with captain's chairs. **Defect:** Vans were produced without plastic cover designed to cover outboard seat back pivot hinge allowing webbing of front passenger-side safety belts to become abraded or cut due to contact with exposed hinge. **Consequence:** Damage to belt webbing could weaken belts to the point of failure, increasing risk of injury in an accident or a sudden stop. **Corrective Action:** Install plastic pivot cover; replace belts as necessary.

System: Rear liftgate. **Vehicle:** Vans built at the St. Louis assembly plant. **Defect:** Some liftgate gas cylinder-to-body attachment ball studs may fracture in either the open or closed position. **Consequence:** If a ball stud fractures, the liftgate will not remain in the open position. Bodily injury could result if the liftgate drops while someone is under it. **Corrective Action:** Replace the gas cylinder-to-body attachment ball studs.

FORD TRUCK AEROSTAR 1988

System: Electrical. **Vehicle:** Multipurpose vehicles and vans, equipped with optional trailer tow package. **Defect:** Vehicles equipped with trailer tow package have a trailer taillight relay assembly that contains wires of smaller gauge than the fuse link that protects the circuit. **Consequence:** Should a short circuit occur in the wiring within the relay, or if water intrusion occurs, the smaller gauge wire in the relay will function as a fuse link and overheat. The possibility exists for a fire if the wires are exposed to combustible materials. **Corrective Action:** Installation of a relay with wires of gauge adequate to protect the circuit.

System: Rear liftgate. **Vehicle:** Vans built at the St. Louis assembly plant. **Defect:** Some liftgate gas cylinder-to-body attachment ball studs may fracture in either the open or closed position. **Consequence:** If a ball stud fractures, the liftgate will not remain in the open position. Bodily injury could result if the liftgate drops while someone is under it. **Corrective Action:** Replace the gas cylinder-to-body attachment ball studs.

FORD TRUCK AEROSTAR 1989

System: Seat assembly. **Vehicle:** Truck-vans equipped with quad captain's chairs. **Defect:** The second row right-hand seat assembly has a tilt-forward function. A latch retains the seat in the normal ride position, and this latch may release under severe frontal impact conditions, allowing the seat to pivot forward. **Consequence:** In the event of vehicle accident, the seat could pivot forward, increasing the risk of injury to the occupant. **Corrective Action:** Replace seat pawl assembly with a revised-design assembly.

System: Seat belt anchorage—FMVSS 210. **Vehicle:** Vans. **Defect:** Seat belt anchorage bar for rear sofa failed to sustain loads required by FMVSS 210. **Consequence:** Vehicles would not comply with FMVSS 210. **Corrective Action:** Replace noncomplying sofa bar with bar that meets requirements. **Note:** This recall is being conducted by Sherrod Vans, Inc.

System: Transmission. **Vehicle:** Pickup trucks, vans and multipurpose vehicles equipped with A4lD automatic transmissions. **Defect:** When the automatic transmission shift lever is placed in the park position, the park pawl does not always abut or engage the park gear. **Consequence:** Driver may believe the vehicle is safely engaged in park when the gear is not truly engaged. This can lead to the vehicle jumping out of gear unintentionally, vehicle rollaway when parked on a sloped surface and inadvertent motion when the vehicle is started. All of these conditions can result in a vehicle accident. **Corrective Action:** Repair the transmission with a new park pawl.

FORD TRUCK AEROSTAR 1990

System: Brakes; master cylinder. **Vehicle:** Trucks and vans. **Defect:** Inability to maintain pressure in the secondary system of the master cylinder (controls braking of rear wheels) could increase brake pedal travel and reduce brake performance at temperatures less than 40 degrees. **Consequence:** This would cause reduced braking effectiveness and increased stopping distance, which could result in a crash or collision. **Corrective Action:** Install new-design master cylinder incorporating a redesigned seal.

System: Seat assembly. **Vehicle:** Truck-vans equipped with quad captain's chairs. **Defect:** The second row right-hand seat assembly has a tilt-forward function. A latch retains the seat in the normal ride position, and this latch may release under severe frontal impact conditions, allowing the seat to pivot forward. **Consequence:** In the event of vehicle accident, the seat could pivot forward, increasing the risk of injury to the occupant. **Corrective Action:** Replace seat pawl assembly with a revised-design assembly.

System: Seat belt anchorage—FMVSS 210. **Vehicle:** Vans. **Defect:** Seat belt anchorage bar for rear sofa failed to sustain loads required by FMVSS 210. **Consequence:** Vehicles would not comply with FMVSS 210. **Corrective Action:** Replace noncomplying sofa bar with bar that meets requirements. **Note:** This recall is being conducted by Sherrod Vans, Inc.

System: Transmission. **Vehicle:** Pickup trucks, vans and multipurpose vehicles equipped with A4lD automatic transmissions. **Defect:** When the automatic transmission shift lever is placed in the park position, the park pawl does not always abut or engage the park gear. **Consequence:** Driver may believe the vehicle is safely engaged in park when the gear is not truly engaged. This can lead to the vehicle jumping out of gear unintentionally, vehicle rollaway when parked on a sloped surface and inadvertent motion when the vehicle is started. All of these conditions can result in a vehicle accident. **Corrective Action:** Repair the transmission with a new park pawl.

FORD TRUCK AEROSTAR 1991

System: Seat belt anchorage—FMVSS 210. **Vehicle:** Vans. **Defect:** Seat belt anchorage bar for rear sofa failed to sustain loads required by FMVSS 210. **Consequence:** Vehicles would not comply with FMVSS 210. **Corrective Action:** Replace noncomplying sofa bar with bar that meets requirements. **Note:** This recall is being conducted by Sherrod Vans, Inc.

System: Transmission. **Vehicle:** Pickup trucks, vans and multipurpose vehicles equipped with A4lD automatic transmissions. **Defect:** When the automatic transmission shift lever is placed in the park position, the park pawl does not always abut or engage the park gear. **Consequence:** Driver may believe the vehicle is safely engaged in park when the gear is not truly engaged. This can lead to the vehicle jumping out of gear unintentionally, vehicle rollaway when parked on a sloped surface and inadvertent motion when the vehicle is started. All of these conditions can result in a vehicle accident. **Corrective Action:** Repair the transmission with a new park pawl.

FORD TRUCK BRONCO 1987

System: Fuel line coupling. **Vehicle:** Passenger cars and light trucks equipped with fuel injection. **Defect:** Spring lock fuel line coupling may not be properly engaged. **Consequence:** Coupling could disengage due to fuel pressure, vibration and engine movements; this would cause loss of fuel which, in the presence of an ignition source, creates a fire risk. **Corrective Action:** Install retainer clips over the couplings to prevent coupling separation and fuel leakage.

System: Visual systems; glass; windshield. **Vehicle:** Aftermarket windshields for light-duty trucks. **Defect:** The windshields do not meet the marking requirements of FMVSS 205, "Glazing materials." **Consequence:** The windshields are not identified as to the type of glass used. However, the windshields comply fully with the performance requirements of FMVSS 205. **Corrective Action:** See note. **Note:** The manufacturer's petition, which requested that NHTSA determine that this FMVSS noncompliance does not create an unreasonable risk to motor vehicle safety, has been granted. Therefore, the manufacturer is not obligated to conduct an owner notification and remedy campaign.

FORD TRUCK BRONCO 1988

System: Visual systems; glass; windshield. **Vehicle:** Aftermarket windshields for light-duty trucks. **Defect:** The windshields do not meet the marking requirements of FMVSS 205, "Glazing materials." **Consequence:** The windshields are not identified as to the type of glass used. However, the windshields comply fully with the performance requirements of FMVSS 205. **Corrective Action:** See note. **Note:** The manufacturer's petition, which requested that NHTSA determine that this FMVSS noncompliance does not create an unreasonable risk to motor vehicle safety has been granted. Therefore, the manufacturer is not obligated to conduct an owner notification and remedy campaign.

FORD TRUCK BRONCO 1989

System: Tire reserve load label—FMVSS 110. **Vehicle:** Passenger vehicle. **Defect:** Tire reserve load label may not have been installed. **Consequence:** Vehicle would not comply with FMVSS 110. **Corrective Action:** Install proper label.

System: Visual systems; glass; windshield. **Vehicle:** Aftermarket windshields for light-duty trucks. **Defect:** The windshields do not meet the marking requirements of FMVSS 205, "Glazing materials." **Consequence:** The windshields are not identified as to the type of glass used. However, the windshields comply fully with the performance requirements of FMVSS 205. **Corrective Action:** See note. **Note:** The manufacturer's petition, which requested that NHTSA determine that this FMVSS noncompliance does not create an unreasonable risk to motor vehicle safety, has been granted. Therefore, the manufacturer is not obligated to conduct an owner notification and remedy campaign.

FORD TRUCK BRONCO 1990

System: Visual systems; glass; windshield. **Vehicle:** Aftermarket windshields for light-duty trucks. **Defect:** The windshields do not meet the marking requirements of FMVSS 205, "Glazing materials." **Consequence:** The windshields are not identified as to the type of glass used. However, the windshields comply fully with the performance requirements of FMVSS 205. **Corrective Action:** See note. **Note:** The manufacturer's petition, which requested that NHTSA determine that this FMVSS noncompliance does not create an unreasonable risk to motor vehicle safety, has been granted. Therefore, the manufacturer is not obligated to conduct an owner notification and remedy campaign.

FORD TRUCK BRONCO 1991

System: Visual systems; glass; windshield. **Vehicle:** Aftermarket windshields for light-duty trucks. **Defect:** The windshields do not meet the marking requirements of FMVSS 205, "Glazing materials." **Consequence:** The windshields are not identified as to the type of glass used. However, the windshields comply fully with the performance requirements of FMVSS 205. **Corrective Action:** See note. **Note:** The manufacturer's petition, which requested that NHTSA determine that this FMVSS noncompliance does not create an unreasonable risk to motor vehicle safety, has been granted. Therefore, the manufacturer is not obligated to conduct an owner notification and remedy campaign.

FORD TRUCK BRONCO 1992

System: Structure; door latch. **Vehicle:** Multipurpose vehicles, light trucks and medium trucks. **Defect:** Water can enter the door latch release cable. If the vehicle is operated in below-freezing temperatures, the water in the door latch release cable can freeze and cause the latch mechanism to malfunction. **Consequence:** The malfunction of the door latch release can result in three different problems: The door will not be able to be relatched; the inside door handle can become inoperative; and the door could appear to be latched when it is not, allowing the door to open unexpectedly if it is jarred, and increasing the risk of injury to the adjacent seat occupant. **Corrective Action:** Revised door release cables and water shields will be installed.

System: Visual systems; glass; windshield. **Vehicle:** Aftermarket windshields for light-duty trucks. **Defect:** The windshields do not meet the marking requirements of FMVSS 205, "Glazing materials." **Consequence:** The windshields are not identified as to the type of glass used. However, the windshields comply fully with the performance requirements of FMVSS 205. **Corrective Action:** See note. **Note:** The manufacturer's petition, which requested that NHTSA determine that this FMVSS noncompliance does not create an unreasonable risk to motor vehicle safety, has been granted. Therefore, the manufacturer is not obligated to conduct an owner notification and remedy campaign.

System: Emergency parking brake; mechanical. **Vehicle:** Light-duty pickup trucks and multipurpose vehicles with manual transmissions. **Defect:** The parking brake control self-adjust pawl does not line up properly with the self-adjust ratchet, causing the pawl to slip over one or more teeth in the ratchet. **Consequence:** When this occurs, it can result in parking brake system ineffectiveness. The parking brake will not hold the vehicle, causing the vehicle to roll freely, if the transmission is not left in gear. **Corrective Action:** A wedge will be installed which will serve to lock the parking brake self-adjust mechanism pawl into engagement with the ratchet. Also, owners will be advised to release and reapply the parking brake whenever tooth skip occurs, and will be reminded to always turn off the engine and leave the vehicle in gear when the vehicle is parked.

FORD TRUCK BRONCO 1994

System: Visual systems; glass; windshield. **Vehicle:** Aftermarket windshields for light-duty trucks. **Defect:** The windshields do not meet the marking requirements of FMVSS 205, "Glazing materials." **Consequence:** The windshields are not identified as to the type of glass used. However, the windshields comply fully with the performance requirements of FMVSS 205. **Corrective Action:** See note. **Note:** The manufacturer's petition, which requested that NHTSA determine that this FMVSS noncompliance does not create an unreasonable risk to motor vehicle safety, has been granted. Therefore, the manufacturer is not obligated to conduct an owner notification and remedy campaign.

System: Structure; bumper assembly. **Vehicle:** Light-duty pickup trucks and multipurpose vehicles. **Defect:** The U-clip-style nuts that retain the front bumpers to the front bumper inner arms can fracture. **Consequence:** If one of the U-clip nuts fractures, the bumper will loosen and rattle, causing fracture of the remaining U-clip nuts and resulting in separation of the bumper from the vehicle. If the bumper were to detach from the vehicle while it is being driven, a vehicle collision could result. **Corrective Action:** Inspection and replacement of the four U-clip nuts and the associated bolts.

System: Emergency parking brake; mechanical. **Vehicle:** Light-duty pickup trucks and multipurpose vehicles with manual transmissions. **Defect:** The parking brake control self-adjust pawl does not line up properly with the self-adjust ratchet, causing the pawl to slip over one or more teeth in the ratchet. **Consequence:** When this occurs, it can result in parking brake system ineffectiveness. The parking brake will not hold the vehicle, causing the vehicle to roll freely, if the transmission is not left in gear. **Corrective Action:** A wedge will be installed which will serve to lock the parking brake self-adjust mechanism pawl into engagement with the ratchet. Also, owners will be advised to release and reapply the parking brake whenever tooth skip occurs, and will be reminded to always turn off the engine and leave the vehicle in gear when the vehicle is parked.

FORD TRUCK BRONCO II 1987

System: Wheel lug nuts. **Vehicle:** Van conversion-type trucks. **Defect:** Aluminum wheels may have been installed with improper lug nuts. **Consequence:** Wheel could become loose, or even separate from the hub and axle assembly, while the vehicle is in motion. **Corrective Action:** Change tapered-style lug nuts to short shank-style lug nuts.

System: Utility vehicle stickers—parts 573 and 579. **Vehicle:** Multipurpose 4×4 passenger. **Defect:** Stickers concerning handling and maneuverability, which are affixed to driver's sun visor sleeves do not meet criteria for permanent adhesion. **Consequence:** Vehicles do not meet formats specified by parts 573 and 579 of 49 CFR. **Corrective Action:** Owners will be mailed new sun visor sleeves with all applicable decal information permanently affixed.

System: Fuel line coupling. **Vehicle:** Passenger cars and light trucks equipped with fuel injection. **Defect:** Spring lock fuel line coupling may not be properly engaged. **Consequence:** Coupling could disengage due to fuel pressure, vibration and engine movements; this would cause loss of fuel which, in the presence of an ignition source, creates a fire risk. **Corrective Action:** Install retainer clips over the couplings to prevent coupling separation and fuel leakage.

FORD TRUCK BRONCO II 1989

System: Front wheel bearing. **Vehicle:** 4×4 multipurpose vehicles and trucks equipped with front axle automatic locking hubs. **Defect:** Front wheel bearing adjusting nut retaining keys may be missing from front axle assemblies, allowing the nut to loosen. **Consequence:** This could result in detachment of the wheel and hub assembly from the axle, loss of vehicle control and an accident. **Corrective Action:** Install retaining keys in front wheel hub assemblies where missing.

FORD TRUCK E150 1989

System: Park gear snap ring. **Vehicle:** 4×2 light trucks and vans equipped with one-piece driveshaft and an E40D transmission. **Defect:** Under certain conditions, the snap ring that locates the park gear on the output shaft of the transmission may fracture. **Consequence:** When the gear is placed in park, the park gear will not engage, allowing the truck to roll freely if the parking brake is not properly set. This could result in an accident. **Corrective Action:** Install improved snap ring and revised transmission extension housing.

FORD TRUCK E350 1987

System: Fuel—tank vapor valve. **Vehicle:** Ambulance, Econoline E350 vans and cutaway chassis with 7.5L engines. **Defect:** Fuel leak at the top of the front fuel tank in the area of the vapor valve grommet. Grommet may split due to compressive load when installed in the fuel tank. **Consequence:** Fuel may leak from vapor valve and become the source of fuel for a fire. **Corrective Action:** Installation of a newly designed vapor valve grommet.

System: Fuel. **Vehicle:** Ambulance, Ford Econoline E350 cutaway chassis and vans equipped with 7.5L engines. **Defect:** Expulsion of fuel due to overpressurization. **Consequence:** Fuel or fuel vapors in the presence of an ignition source can cause a fire. **Corrective Action:** Modification of the base fuel venting and emission control system to reduce operating temperatures and fuel system pressures.

System: Fuel. **Vehicle:** 1983-1987 E250, E350, club wagons and Econoline vans and chassis equipped with 7.5L engines and 1985-1987 E250, E350, club wagons and Econoline vans equipped with 5.8L engines. **Defect:** Vehicles are subject to excessive underhood temperatures and fuel system pressures in severe-duty applications. **Consequence:** This creates potential for fuel expulsion from the fuel filler pipe which, in the presence of an ignition source, could result in a fire. **Corrective Action:** Install modification kits to minimize possibility of fuel expulsion and to shield underbody components from exhaust system heat.

System: Engine hoses. **Vehicle:** Ambulance vehicles manufactured from Ford cutaway chassis and vans. **Defect:** Extreme operating conditions could cause premature deterioration of the engine compartment heater hoses or engine bypass hoses. **Consequence:** Engine coolant could discharge onto the engine and its exhaust manifold, creating the potential for a fire due to the high engine exhaust manifold temperatures. **Corrective Action:** Replace hoses and radiator caps; install high heat resistance aluminized stainless steel mufflers.

System: Electrical wiring—harness. **Vehicle:** Type II and III ambulances built on Ford chassis. **Defect:** Nylon ties that support the main wiring harness to the chassis could wear and break due to excessive vibration. Thus, the wiring harness could fall on engine components and short-circuit. **Consequence:** This could cause loss of electrical system, which could result in an underhood fire. **Corrective Action:** Install retrofit of plastic-coated metal clamps, loom for positive battery cables and reroute wiring.

System: Heater hose. **Vehicle:** Buses built on Ford E350 chassis. **Defect:** Heater hose may be incorrectly routed. **Consequence:** Hose could wear through and leak, which could result in an underhood fire. **Corrective Action:** Reroute and splice hose as necessary.

System: Heater hose. **Vehicle:** Gas chassis—cutaway and van ambulances. **Defect:** Heater hose may be incorrectly routed. **Consequence:** Hose could wear through and leak, which could result in an underhood fire. **Corrective Action:** Reroute and repair hose as necessary.

System: Heater hose. **Vehicle:** Ambulances built on Ford E350 chassis. **Defect:** Heater hose may be incorrectly routed. **Consequence:** Hose could wear through and leak which could result in an underhood fire. **Corrective Action:** Reroute hose as necessary.

FORD TRUCK E350 1988

System: Electrical wiring—harness. **Vehicle:** Type II and III ambulances built on Ford chassis. **Defect:** Nylon ties that support the main wiring harness to the chassis could wear and break due to excessive vibration. Thus, the wiring harness could fall on engine components and short-circuit. **Consequence:** This could cause loss of electrical system, which could result in an underhood fire. **Corrective Action:** Install retrofit of plastic-coated metal clamps, loom for positive battery cables and reroute wiring.

FORD TRUCK E350 1989

System: Electrical wiring—harness. **Vehicle:** Type II and III ambulances built on Ford chassis. **Defect:** Nylon ties that support the main wiring harness to the chassis could wear and break due to excessive vibration. Thus, the wiring harness could fall on engine components and short-circuit. **Consequence:** This could cause loss of electrical system, which could result in an underhood fire. **Corrective Action:** Install retrofit of plastic-coated metal clamps, loom for positive battery cables and reroute wiring.

System: Park gear snap ring. **Vehicle:** 4×2 light trucks and vans equipped with one-piece driveshaft and an E40D transmission. **Defect:** Under certain conditions, the snap ring that locates the park gear on the output shaft of the transmission may fracture. **Consequence:** When the gear is placed in park, the park gear would not engage, allowing the truck to roll freely if the parking brake is not properly set. This could result in an accident. **Corrective Action:** Install improved snap ring and revised transmission extension housing.

FORD TRUCK E350 1990

System: Park gear snap ring. **Vehicle:** 4×2 light trucks and vans equipped with one-piece driveshaft and an E40D transmission. **Defect:** Under certain conditions, the snap ring that locates the park gear on the output shaft of the transmission may fracture. **Consequence:** When the gear is placed in park, the park gear would not engage, allowing the truck to roll freely if the parking brake is not properly set. This could result in an accident. **Corrective Action:** Install improved snap ring and revised transmission extension housing.

FORD TRUCK ECONOLINE 1987

System: Fuel—tank vapor valve. **Vehicle:** Ambulance, Econoline E350 vans and cutaway chassis with 7.5L engines. **Defect:** Fuel leak at the top of the front fuel tank in the area of the vapor valve grommet. Grommet may split due to compressive load when installed in the fuel tank. **Consequence:** Fuel may leak from vapor valve and become the source of fuel for a fire. **Corrective Action:** Installation of a newly designed vapor valve grommet.

System: Fuel. **Vehicle:** Ambulance, Ford Econoline E350 cutaway chassis and vans equipped with 7.5L engines. **Defect:** Expulsion of fuel due to overpressurization. **Consequence:** Fuel or fuel vapors in the presence of an ignition source can cause a fire. **Corrective Action:** Modification of the base fuel venting and emission control system to reduce operating temperatures and fuel system pressures.

System: Fuel line coupling. **Vehicle:** Passenger cars and light trucks equipped with fuel injection. **Defect:** Spring lock fuel line coupling may not be properly engaged. **Consequence:** Coupling could disengage due to fuel pressure, vibration and engine movements; this would cause loss of fuel which, in the presence of an ignition source, creates a fire risk. **Corrective Action:** Install retainer clips over the couplings to prevent coupling separation and fuel leakage.

System: Fuel. **Vehicle:** 1983-1987 E250, E350, club wagons and Econoline vans and chassis equipped with 7.5L engines and 1985-1987 E250, E350, club wagons and Econoline vans equipped with 5.8L engines. **Defect:** Vehicles are subject to excessive underhood temperatures and fuel system pressures in severe-duty applications. **Consequence:** This creates potential for fuel expulsion from the fuel filler pipe which, in the presence of an ignition source, could result in a fire. **Corrective Action:** Install modification kits to minimize possibility of fuel expulsion and to shield underbody components from exhaust system heat.

FORD TRUCK ECONOLINE 1989

System: Park gear snap ring. **Vehicle:** 4×2 light trucks and vans equipped with one-piece driveshaft and an E40D transmission. **Defect:** Under certain conditions, the snap ring that locates the park gear on the output shaft of the transmission may fracture. **Consequence:** When the gear is placed in park, the park gear would not engage, allowing the truck to roll freely if the parking brake is not properly set. This could result in an accident. **Corrective Action:** Install improved snap ring and revised transmission extension housing.

System: Fuel tank; auxiliary. **Vehicle:** Vans and light trucks with dual fuel tanks produced in the following periods: F150, F250 and F350 light trucks built between February 28, 1989, and July, 1989; Econoline built between February 28, 1989, and February 11, 1991. **Defect:** The dual fuel tank selector valve may malfunction and cause an overfill condition in one of the fuel tanks, resulting in an overflow of fuel past the filler cap. **Consequence:** The overflow of fuel past the filler cap causes a fuel leakage, which can result in a fire when exposed to a source of ignition. **Corrective Action:** Replace the dual fuel tank selector valve. **Note:** Ford has agreed to recall these vehicles, but parts are not yet available. Parts will be available in December 1991. You will receive a letter from Ford advising you when to schedule an appointment with your dealer to have the recall work performed. In the meantime, you can take the following precautions: fill each tank to only one-third full. If your vehicle leaks fuel or if you smell fuel, stop using the vehicle and call Ford at (313) 446-4654 and advise them of your problem. Refer to Ford Safety Recall 91S39. An operator will take your name and telephone number. A Ford representative will call you back.

FORD TRUCK ECONOLINE 1990

System: Park gear snap ring. **Vehicle:** 4×2 light trucks and vans equipped with one-piece driveshaft and an E40D transmission. **Defect:** Under certain conditions, the snap ring that locates the park gear on the output shaft of the transmission may fracture. **Consequence:** When the gear is placed in park, the park gear would not engage, allowing the truck to roll freely if the parking brake is not properly set. This could result in an accident. **Corrective Action:** Install improved snap ring and revised transmission extension housing.

System: Fuel tank; auxiliary. **Vehicle:** Vans and light trucks with dual fuel tanks produced in the following periods: F150, F250 and F350 light trucks built between February 28, 1989, and July, 1989; Econoline built between February 28, 1989, and February 11, 1991. **Defect:** The dual fuel tank selector valve may malfunction and cause an overfill condition in one of the fuel tanks, resulting in an overflow of fuel past the filler cap. **Consequence:** The overflow of fuel past the filler cap causes a fuel leakage, which can result in a fire when exposed to a source of ignition. **Corrective Action:** Replace the dual fuel tank selector valve. **Note:** Ford has agreed to recall these vehicles, but parts are not yet available. Parts will be available in December 1991. You will receive a letter from Ford advising you when to schedule an appointment with your dealer to have the recall work performed. In the meantime, you can take the following precautions: fill each tank to only one-third full. If your vehicle leaks fuel or if you smell fuel, stop using the vehicle and call Ford at (313) 446-4654 and advise them of your problem. Refer to Ford Safety Recall 91S39. An operator will take your name and telephone number. A Ford representative will call you back.

System: Rear bench seat: safety belt anchorage, FMVSS 210. **Vehicle:** Full-size van (Econoline) conversions. **Defect:** The safety belt anchorage for the rear bench seat failed to comply with the standards of FMVSS 210. **Consequence:** Failure to meet the load requirements of FMVSS 210 places the seat occupants in increased risk of injury in the event of a sudden stop or accident. **Corrective Action:** The manufacturer will replace the noncomplying safety belt anchorage with a new anchorage that meets the requirements of FMVSS 210. **Note:** This recall is being conducted by Glaval Corporation, 29340 Lexington Park Drive, Elkhart, Indiana 46515.

System: Suspension. **Vehicle:** Vans; model E250 Econoline. **Defect:** The rear shock crossmember of the frame can crack and separate from the frame. **Consequence:** Separation of the rear shock crossmember from the frame can result in loss of vehicle control and an accident. **Corrective Action:** Replace the rear chock crossmember with a shock crossmember made of high-strength steel.

FORD TRUCK ECONOLINE 1992

System: Safety compliance certification labels. **Vehicle:** Vans. **Defect:** The tire certification labels incorrectly identify the vehicle tire requirements as P235/75R15 SL (standard load), rather than as P235/75R15 XL (extra load). **Consequence:** The certification labels on the affected vehicles do not comply with FMVSS 120, "Tire selection and rims for motor vehicles other than passenger cars." Incorrect tire selection could result in sudden failure of a tire while the vehicle is in motion, and result in a vehicle accident. **Corrective Action:** Correct tire information labels and installation instructions will be mailed to the owners of these vehicles. Owners will be instructed that dealers can install the label provided if they prefer.

System: Fuel system. **Vehicle:** Cargo vans with Sears Fleet DSO package. **Defect:** The fuel filler hose or fuel filler vent hose was damaged by a drill bit used to install the DSO package attaching hardware onto the floor pan. **Consequence:** If either of the hoses was penetrated by the drill bit, fuel leakage could result, particularly during fueling of the vehicle. In the presence of an ignition source, this could result in fire. **Corrective Action:** Replace the fuel filler and vent hoses and relocate the mounting hardware in the floor pan.

FORD TRUCK ECONOLINE 1993

System: Fuel system. **Vehicle:** Cargo vans with Sears Fleet DSO package. **Defect:** The fuel filler hose or fuel filler vent hose was damaged by a drill bit used to install the DSO package attaching hardware onto the floor pan. **Consequence:** If either of the hoses was penetrated by the drill bit, fuel leakage could result, particularly during fueling of the vehicle. In the presence of an ignition source, this could result in fire. **Corrective Action:** Replace the fuel filler and vent hoses and relocate the mounting hardware in the floor pan.

System: Lighting; lamp or socket; courtesy lights. **Vehicle:** Long-wheelbase conversion vans with a neon center light beam. **Defect:** The transformer used to power the neon center light beam can overheat and catch on fire. **Consequence:** The overheating and fires caused by the neon transformer can result in damage to the light beam assembly and the roof of the vehicle, and could result in a vehicle fire. **Corrective Action:** Mark III dealers will modify the assemblies to eliminate the neon lighting fixture in the vehicle, and replace it with incandescent lights operating directly from the vehicle 12-volt battery. **Note:** If your vehicle is presented to an authorized dealer on an agreed-upon service date and the remedy is not provided within a reasonable time and free of charge, or the remedy does not correct the defect or noncompliance, please contact Mark III Service Center at (800) 903-8267. Also contact the NHTSA's Auto Safety Hotline at (800) 424-9393.

FORD TRUCK EXPLORER 1991

System: Sunroof hinges. **Vehicle:** Multipurpose passenger 4-door vehicles with sunroofs. **Defect:** If sunroof glass is removed and reinstalled by vehicle operator, hinge assemblies can be accidentally improperly mated. **Consequence:** Sunroof could detach from the vehicle while being driven, creating a risk to following vehicles, to people in the vicinity or to vehicle occupants if the glass should fall into the cabin. **Corrective Action:** Install revised sunroof hinges that will adequately retain sunroof assembly.

System: Fuel tank and heat shield. **Vehicle:** Multipurpose passenger vehicle. **Defect:** The front heat shield may contact the front of the plastic fuel tank, causing cuts or other damage to the extent of penetration. **Consequence:** This penetration of the fuel tank causes vapors to escape and possibly fuel to spill, which could catch fire in the presence of an ignition source. **Corrective Action:** Relocate the heat shield; inspect and replace damaged fuel tanks.

System: Vapor vent valve carrier weld to plastic fuel tank. **Vehicle:** Multipurpose passenger vehicles. **Defect:** The hot-plate weld which attaches the vapor vent valve carrier to the top of the plastic fuel tank may partially fracture, allowing vapor of fuel to escape from the top of the tank. **Consequence:** The escaped vapor or leaked fuel could cause a fire in the presence of a source of ignition. **Corrective Action:** Fuel tank will be removed and inspected for weld integrity. Fuel tanks with inadequate welds will be replaced.

System: Rear bumper reinforcement. **Vehicle:** Multipurpose passenger vehicle. **Defect:** Rear bumper reinforcement may be subject to fatigue cracking under extended trailer tow service when using a bumper-mounted trailer hitch ball. **Consequence:** Under extreme conditions, bumper could separate from the vehicle when using a bumper-mounted trailer hitch ball. **Corrective Action:** Install two brackets to reinforce the bumper. **Note:** Bumper-mounted trailer hitch ball assembly should not be used until repair procedure is completed.

System: Transmission. **Vehicle:** Pickup trucks, vans and multipurpose vehicles equipped with A4lD automatic transmissions. **Defect:** When the automatic transmission shift lever is placed in the park position, the park pawl does not always abut or engage the park gear. **Consequence:** Driver may believe the vehicle is safely engaged in park when the gear is not truly engaged. This can lead to the vehicle jumping out of gear unintentionally, vehicle rollaway when parked on a sloped surface and inadvertent motion when the vehicle is started. All of these conditions can result in a vehicle accident. **Corrective Action:** Repair the transmission with a new park pawl.

System: Safety belt buckle. **Vehicle:** Passenger cars and utility vehicles. **Defect:** The rigid mounted safety belt buckles are defective in three ways. First, a fastened safety belt buckle will not unlatch when the release button is depressed. This results from interference between the buckle ejector finger and the buckle tongue window. The second defect is the safety belt buckle may not latch. The third possible defect is that the tongue may be retained by the buckle, but it may not be latched sufficiently to provide occupant protection. **Consequence:** An insufficiently latched or unlatched safety belt increases the risk of injury to seat occupants in the event of a sudden stop or accident. If the safety belt buckle will not unlatch, it will not allow the occupant to get out of the vehicle in an emergency situation. **Corrective Action:** Ford will replace the rigid mounted safety belt buckles with end release safety belt buckles designed to prevent latch problems. **Note:** Only the end release buckles on "rigid" mountings are susceptible to this malfunction; the web-mounted front center end release buckles and the web-mounted rear-facing third seat end release buckles in Taurus or Sable vehicles will not be replaced. Also, the web-mounted front center buckles in Explorer vehicles will not be replaced.

FORD TRUCK EXPLORER 1992

System: Structure; hatchback hydraulic cylinder. **Vehicle:** Multipurpose passenger vehicles. **Defect:** The hydraulic lift cylinders are attached to brackets that are welded to the liftgate. The bracket welds can fracture. **Consequence:** With a broken bracket weld, there is a potential for the liftgate bracket to gradually bend inward, allowing the lift cylinder ball stud to disengage. **Corrective Action:** Dealers will install reinforcement brackets.

FORD TRUCK EXPLORER 1993

System: Equipment; other labels. **Vehicle:** Light trucks and multipurpose vehicles. **Defect:** The instrument panel cluster contains components intended for vehicles to be exported to Europe. The brake display telltale is identified by the International Standards Organization (ISO) symbol, but not the word *brake*, as specified in FMVSS 101 and 105. **Consequence:** The operators of these vehicles may not identify the ISO brake symbol as an indication of a brake problem, and may not heed the warning of an immediate or impending brake failure. **Corrective Action:** Ford has not submitted a corrective action for this recall. **Note:** The manufacturer's petition, which requested that NHTSA determine that this FMVSS noncompliance does not create an unreasonable risk to motor vehicle safety, has been granted. Therefore, the manufacturer is not obligated to conduct an owner notification and remedy campaign.

System: Emergency parking brake; mechanical. **Vehicle:** Light-duty pickup trucks and multipurpose vehicles with manual transmissions. **Defect:** The parking brake control self-adjust pawl does not line up properly with the self-adjust ratchet, causing the pawl to slip over one or more teeth in the ratchet. **Consequence:** When this occurs, it can result in parking brake system ineffectiveness. The parking brake will not hold the vehicle, causing the vehicle to roll freely, if the transmission is not left in gear. **Corrective Action:** A wedge will be installed that will serve to lock the parking brake self-adjust mechanism pawl into engagement with the ratchet. Also, owners will be advised to release and reapply the parking brake whenever tooth skip occurs, and will be reminded to always turn off the engine and leave the vehicle in gear when the vehicle is parked.

System: Structure; hatchback hydraulic cylinder. **Vehicle:** Multipurpose passenger vehicles. **Defect:** The hydraulic lift cylinders are attached to brackets that are welded to the liftgate. The bracket welds can fracture. **Consequence:** With a broken bracket weld, there is a potential for the liftgate bracket to gradually bend inward, allowing the lift cylinder ball stud to disengage. **Corrective Action:** Dealers will install reinforcement brackets.

FORD TRUCK EXPLORER 1994

System: Emergency parking brake; mechanical. **Vehicle:** Light-duty pickup trucks and multipurpose vehicles with manual transmissions. **Defect:** The parking brake control self-adjust pawl does not line up properly with the self-adjust ratchet, causing the pawl to slip over one or more teeth in the ratchet. **Consequence:** When this occurs, it can result in parking brake system ineffectiveness. The parking brake will not hold the vehicle, causing the vehicle to roll freely, if the transmission is not left in gear. **Corrective Action:** A wedge will be installed that will serve to lock the parking brake self-adjust mechanism pawl into engagement with the ratchet. Also, owners will be advised to release and reapply the parking brake whenever tooth skip occurs, and will be reminded to always turn off the engine and leave the vehicle in gear when the vehicle is parked.

FORD TRUCK F SERIES (LIGHT) 1987

System: Engine governor lever assemblies—throttle linkage. **Vehicle:** Truck and bus chassis with 6.6L and 7.8L diesel engines. **Defect:** Diesel engine governor lever assemblies may have been improperly assembled so that one or more of three retaining prongs may not be engaged in the governor lever pivot shafts. **Consequence:** Separation of accelerator linkage and return springs could occur, causing the time for the engine to return to idle from an open throttle position to substantially increase. **Corrective Action:** Replace governor lever assemblies.

FORD TRUCK F150 1987

System: Suspension. **Vehicle:** F150 pickup trucks. **Defect:** Front inner wheel bearings may not have been lubricated adequately at time of assembly. **Consequence:** If this condition were to occur, friction will cause premature deterioration of the wheel bearings, and steering control could be affected adversely. **Corrective Action:** Inspect and replace any bearing showing signs of galling or heat spots.

System: Fuel line coupling. **Vehicle:** Passenger cars and light trucks equipped with fuel injection. **Defect:** Spring lock fuel line coupling may not be properly engaged. **Consequence:** Coupling could disengage due to fuel pressure, vibration and engine movements; this would cause loss of fuel which, in the presence of an ignition source, creates a fire risk. **Corrective Action:** Install retainer clips over the couplings to prevent coupling separation and fuel leakage.

System: Wheels—lug nuts. **Vehicle:** Pickup trucks modified into Bigfoot cruisers by Scherer Truck Equipment, Inc. **Defect:** Wheel lug nut cone angles do not match lug nut seating angles. **Consequence:** Nuts could loosen in service, creating potential for wheels to separate from truck. **Corrective Action:** Repair to prevent loosening of lug nuts.

System: Visual systems; glass; windshield. **Vehicle:** Aftermarket windshields for light-duty trucks. **Defect:** The windshields do not meet the marking requirements of FMVSS 205, "Glazing materials." **Consequence:** The windshields are not identified as to the type of glass used. However, the windshields comply fully with the performance requirements of FMVSS 205. **Corrective Action:** See note. **Note:** The manufacturer's petition, which requested that NHTSA determine that this FMVSS noncompliance does not create an unreasonable risk to motor vehicle safety, has been granted. Therefore, the manufacturer is not obligated to conduct an owner notification and remedy campaign.

FORD TRUCK F150 1988

System: Rear window glazing—FMVSS 205. **Vehicle:** Light-duty trucks equipped with optional sliding rear window. **Defect:** Sliding rear window may contain glazing panels that do not meet requirements of FMVSS 205. **Consequence:** A fractured window may contain fragments that are larger than the 425 grams allowed. **Corrective Action:** Replace suspect window panels.

System: Visual systems; glass; windshield. **Vehicle:** Aftermarket windshields for light-duty trucks. **Defect:** The windshields do not meet the marking requirements of FMVSS 205, "Glazing materials." **Consequence:** The windshields are not identified as to the type of glass used. However, the windshields comply fully with the performance requirements of FMVSS 205. **Corrective Action:** See note below. **Note:** The manufacturer's petition, which requested that NHTSA determine that this FMVSS noncompliance does not create an unreasonable risk to motor vehicle safety, has been granted. Therefore, the manufacturer is not obligated to conduct an owner notification and remedy campaign.

FORD TRUCK F150 1989

System: Fuel tank shields—FMVSS 301. **Vehicle:** 4×2 pickup trucks with 133-inch wheelbase and manual transmissions. **Defect:** Shields on the fronts of the midship-mounted fuel tanks were omitted during assembly. **Consequence:** Trucks could not comply with 30 mph impact test of FMVSS 301, "Fuel system integrity." **Corrective Action:** Install fuel tank shields.

System: Park gear snap ring. **Vehicle:** 4×2 light trucks and vans equipped with one-piece driveshaft and an E40D transmission. **Defect:** Under certain conditions, the snap ring that locates the park gear on the output shaft of the transmission may fracture. **Consequence:** When the gear is placed in park, the park gear would not engage, allowing the truck to roll freely if the parking brake is not properly set. This could result in an accident. **Corrective Action:** Install improved snap ring and revised transmission extension housing.

System: Fuel tank; auxiliary. **Vehicle:** Vans and light trucks with dual fuel tanks produced in the following periods: F150, F250 and F350 light trucks built between February 28, 1989, and July, 1989; Econoline built between February 28, 1989, and February 11, 1991. **Defect:** The dual fuel tank selector valve may malfunction and cause an overfill condition in one of the fuel tanks, resulting in an overflow of fuel past the filler cap. **Consequence:** The overflow of fuel past the filler cap causes a fuel leakage, which can result in a fire when exposed to a source of ignition. **Corrective Action:** Replace the dual fuel tank selector valve. **Note:** Ford has agreed to recall these vehicles, but parts are not yet available. Parts will be available in December 1991. You will receive a letter from Ford advising you when to schedule an appointment with your dealer to have the recall work performed. In the meantime, you can take the following precautions: Fill each tank to only one-third full. If your vehicle leaks fuel or if you smell fuel, stop using the vehicle and call Ford at (313) 446-4654 and advise them of your problem. Refer to Ford Safety Recall 91S39. An operator will take your name and telephone number. A Ford representative will call you back.

System: Visual systems; glass; windshield. **Vehicle:** Aftermarket windshields for light-duty trucks. **Defect:** The windshields do not meet the marking requirements of FMVSS 205, "Glazing materials." **Consequence:** The windshields are not identified as to the type of glass used. However, the windshields comply fully with the performance requirements of FMVSS 205. **Corrective Action:** See note. **Note:** The manufacturer's petition, which requested that NHTSA determine this FMVSS noncompliance does not create an unreasonable risk to motor vehicle safety, has been granted. Therefore, the manufacturer is not obligated to conduct an owner notification and remedy campaign.

FORD TRUCK F150 1990

System: Fuel line assembly. **Vehicle:** Light-duty trucks equipped with dual fuel tanks. **Defect:** Incorrectly installed fuel line connectors have fuel supply and return lines crossed. **Consequence:** Fuel could be transferred from one tank to the other, possibly resulting in fuel overflow and spillage; in the presence of an ignition source, a fire could occur. **Corrective Action:** Replace fuel line assembly.

System: Park gear snap ring. **Vehicle:** 4×2 light trucks and vans equipped with one-piece driveshaft and an E40D transmission. **Defect:** Under certain conditions, the snap ring that locates the park gear on the output shaft of the transmission may fracture. **Consequence:** When the gear is placed in park, the park gear would not engage, allowing the truck to roll freely if the parking brake is not properly set. This could result in an accident. **Corrective Action:** Install improved snap ring and revised transmission extension housing.

System: Visual systems; glass; windshield. **Vehicle:** Aftermarket windshields for light-duty trucks. **Defect:** The windshields do not meet the marking requirements of FMVSS 205, "Glazing materials." **Consequence:** The windshields are not identified as to the type of glass used. However, the windshields comply fully with the performance requirements of FMVSS 205. **Corrective Action:** See note. **Note:** The manufacturer's petition, which requested that NHTSA determine that this FMVSS noncompliance does not create an unreasonable risk to motor vehicle safety, has been granted. Therefore, the manufacturer is not obligated to conduct an owner notification and remedy campaign.

System: Fuel; fuel tank assembly. **Vehicle:** Light trucks and chassis cabs with gasoline engines and dual fuel tanks. **Defect:** A malfunctioning check valve within the fuel pump assembly causes a portion of the unused fuel from one tank to be returned to the second tank. When this occurs, the capacity of the second tank can be exceeded, causing fuel spillage. **Consequence:** Spilled fuel can result in a fire when exposed to a source of ignition. **Corrective Action:** Replacement of the fuel pressure regulator and installation of redundant check valves.

FORD TRUCK F150 1991

System: Visual systems; glass; windshield. **Vehicle:** Aftermarket windshields for light-duty trucks. **Defect:** The windshields do not meet the marking requirements of FMVSS 205, "Glazing materials." **Consequence:** The windshields are not identified as to the type of glass used. However, the windshields comply fully with the performance requirements of FMVSS 205. **Corrective Action:** See note. **Note:** The manufacturer's petition, which requested that NHTSA determine that this FMVSS noncompliance does not create an unreasonable risk to motor vehicle safety, has been granted. Therefore, the manufacturer is not obligated to conduct an owner notification and remedy campaign.

System: Fuel; fuel tank assembly. **Vehicle:** Light trucks and chassis cabs with gasoline engines and dual fuel tanks. **Defect:** A malfunctioning check valve within the fuel pump assembly causes a portion of the unused fuel from one tank to be returned to the second tank. When this occurs, the capacity of the second tank can be exceeded, causing fuel spillage. **Consequence:** Spilled fuel can result in a fire when exposed to a source of ignition. **Corrective Action:** Replacement of the fuel pressure regulator and installation of redundant check valves.

FORD TRUCK F150 1992

System: Structure; door latch. **Vehicle:** Multipurpose vehicles, light trucks and medium trucks. **Defect:** Water can enter the door latch release cable. If the vehicle is operated in below-freezing temperatures, the water in the door latch release cable can freeze and cause the latch mechanism to malfunction. **Consequence:** The malfunction of the door latch release can result in three different problems: The door will not be able to be relatched; the inside door handle can become inoperative; and the door could appear to be latched when it is not, allowing the door to open unexpectedly if it is jarred, and increasing the risk of injury to the adjacent seat occupant. **Corrective Action:** Revised door release cables and water shields will be installed.

System: Visual systems; glass; windshield. **Vehicle:** Aftermarket windshields for light-duty trucks. **Defect:** The windshields do not meet the marking requirements of FMVSS 205, "Glazing materials." **Consequence:** The windshields are not identified as to the type of glass used. However, the windshields comply fully with the performance requirements of FMVSS 205. **Corrective Action:** See note. **Note:** The manufacturer's petition, which requested that NHTSA determine that this FMVSS noncompliance does not create an unreasonable risk to motor vehicle safety, has been granted. Therefore, the manufacturer is not obligated to conduct an owner notification and remedy campaign.

System: Fuel; fuel tank assembly. **Vehicle:** Light trucks and chassis cabs with gasoline engines and dual fuel tanks. **Defect:** A malfunctioning check valve within the fuel pump assembly causes a portion of the unused fuel from one tank to be returned to the second tank. When this occurs, the capacity of the second tank can be exceeded, causing fuel spillage. **Consequence:** Spilled fuel can result in a fire when exposed to a source of ignition. **Corrective Action:** Replacement of the fuel pressure regulator and installation of redundant check valves.

System: Emergency parking brake; mechanical. **Vehicle:** Light-duty pickup trucks and multipurpose vehicles with manual transmissions. **Defect:** The parking brake control self-adjust pawl does not line up properly with the self-adjust ratchet, causing the pawl to slip over one or more teeth in the ratchet. **Consequence:** When this occurs, it can result in parking brake system ineffectiveness. The parking brake will not hold the vehicle, causing the vehicle to roll freely, if the transmission is not left in gear. **Corrective Action:** A wedge will be installed which will serve to lock the parking brake self-adjust mechanism pawl into engagement with the ratchet. Also, owners will be advised to release and reapply the parking brake whenever tooth skip occurs, and will be reminded to always turn off the engine and leave the vehicle in gear when the vehicle is parked.

FORD TRUCK F150 1993

System: Visual systems; glass; windshield. **Vehicle:** Aftermarket windshields for light-duty trucks. **Defect:** The windshields do not meet the marking requirements of FMVSS 205, "Glazing materials." **Consequence:** The windshields are not identified as to the type of glass used. However, the windshields comply fully with the performance requirements of FMVSS 205. **Corrective Action:** See note. **Note:** The manufacturer's petition, which requested that NHTSA determine that this FMVSS noncompliance does not create an unreasonable risk to motor vehicle safety, has been granted. Therefore, the manufacturer is not obligated to conduct an owner notification and remedy campaign.

System: Power train; transfer case. **Vehicle:** 4-wheel drive light trucks and multipurpose passenger vehicles with touch-drive electric shift transfer cases. **Defect:** The transfer cases have been built with the wrong electric shift motor. The transfer cases can slip out of the 4×4 high gear position during coasting in forward gears or with power applied in reverse gear. **Consequence:** If this occurs, the vehicle can roll freely as if in neutral position, regardless of the transmission gear selector position. This can result in loss of vehicle control and an accident. **Corrective Action:** Replace defective transfer cases with the correct version.

System: Fuel; fuel tank assembly. **Vehicle:** Light trucks and chassis cabs with gasoline engines and dual fuel tanks. **Defect:** A malfunctioning check valve within the fuel pump assembly causes a portion of the unused fuel from one tank to be returned to the second tank. When this occurs, the capacity of the second tank can be exceeded, causing fuel spillage. **Consequence:** Spilled fuel can result in a fire when exposed to a source of ignition. **Corrective Action:** Replacement of the fuel pressure regulator and installation of redundant check valves.

System: Structure; bumper assembly. **Vehicle:** Light-duty pickup trucks and multipurpose vehicles. **Defect:** The U-clip-style nuts that retain the front bumpers to the front bumper inner arms can fracture. **Consequence:** If one of the U-clip nuts fractures, the bumper will loosen and rattle, causing fracture of the remaining U-clip nuts, resulting in separation of the bumper from the vehicle. If the bumper were to detach from the vehicle while it is being driven, a vehicle collision could result. **Corrective Action:** Inspection and replacement of the four U-clip nuts and the associated bolts.

System: Emergency parking brake; mechanical. **Vehicle:** Light-duty pickup trucks and multipurpose vehicles with manual transmissions. **Defect:** The parking brake control self-adjust pawl does not line up properly with the self-adjust ratchet, causing the pawl to slip over one or more teeth in the ratchet. **Consequence:** When this occurs, it can result in parking brake system ineffectiveness. The parking brake will not hold the vehicle, causing the vehicle to roll freely, if the transmission is not left in gear. **Corrective Action:** A wedge will be installed, which will serve to lock the parking brake self-adjust mechanism pawl into engagement with the ratchet. Also, owners will be advised to release and reapply the parking brake whenever tooth skip occurs, and will be reminded to always turn off the engine and leave the vehicle in gear when the vehicle is parked.

FORD TRUCK F150 1994

System: Visual systems; glass; windshield. **Vehicle:** Aftermarket windshields for light-duty trucks. **Defect:** The windshields do not meet the marking requirements of FMVSS 205, "Glazing materials." **Consequence:** The windshields are not identified as to the type of glass used. However, the windshields comply fully with the performance requirements of FMVSS 205. **Corrective Action:** See note. **Note:** The manufacturer's petition, which requested that NHTSA determine that this FMVSS noncompliance does not create an unreasonable risk to motor vehicle safety, has been granted. Therefore, the manufacturer is not obligated to conduct an owner notification and remedy campaign.

System: Interior systems: passive restraints; airbag. **Vehicle:** Light trucks equipped with airbag occupant protection systems. **Defect:** The design of the airbag diagnostic monitor causes the driver's-side airbag to deploy when the passenger door is slammed while the ignition key is turned to the start position. **Consequence:** Inadvertent deployment of the air bag can result in injury to the driver. **Corrective Action:** Install a redesigned airbag diagnostic monitor. **Note:** These vehicles have not been sold to retailers; the vehicles should still be at the dealer locations.

System: Interior systems; passive restraints; airbag; driver. **Vehicle:** Light-duty trucks under 8,500 pounds GVWR. **Defect:** These vehicles were built with nonfunctional airbag diagnostic modules intended for certain vehicles over 8,500 pounds GVWR. **Consequence:** The airbag supplemental restraint and the airbag warning light will not function. This could result in reduced occupant protection in the event of a collision that should activate the airbag supplemental restraint system. **Corrective Action:** Dealers will inspect these vehicles and, if necessary, install the correct airbag diagnostic module.

System: Structure; bumper assembly. **Vehicle:** Light-duty pickup trucks and multipurpose vehicles. **Defect:** The U-clip-style nuts that retain the front bumpers to the front bumper inner arms can fracture. **Consequence:** If one of the U-clip nuts fractures, the bumper will loosen and rattle, causing fracture of the remaining U-clip nuts and resulting in separation of the bumper from the vehicle. If the bumper were to detach from the vehicle while it is being driven, a vehicle collision could result. **Corrective Action:** Inspection and replacement of the four U-clip nuts and the associated bolts.

System: Emergency parking brake; mechanical. **Vehicle:** Light-duty pickup trucks and multipurpose vehicles with manual transmissions. **Defect:** The parking brake control self-adjust pawl does not line up properly with the self-adjust ratchet, causing the pawl to slip over one or more teeth in the ratchet. **Consequence:** When this occurs, it can result in parking brake system ineffectiveness. The parking brake will not hold the vehicle, causing the vehicle to roll freely, if the transmission is not left in gear. **Corrective Action:** A wedge will be installed, which will serve to lock the parking brake self-adjust mechanism pawl into engagement with the ratchet. Also, owners will be advised to release and reapply the parking brake whenever tooth skip occurs and will be reminded to always turn off the engine and leave the vehicle in gear when the vehicle is parked.

FORD TRUCK F250 1987

System: Fuel line coupling. **Vehicle:** Passenger cars and light trucks equipped with fuel injection. **Defect:** Spring lock fuel line coupling may not be properly engaged. **Consequence:** Coupling could disengage due to fuel pressure, vibration and engine movements; this would cause loss of fuel which, in the presence of an ignition source, creates a fire risk. **Corrective Action:** Install retainer clips over the couplings to prevent coupling separation and fuel leakage.

System: Wheels—lug nuts **Vehicle:** Pickup trucks modified into Bigfoot cruisers by Scherer Truck Equipment, Inc. **Defect:** Wheel lug nut cone angles do not match lug nut seating angles. **Consequence:** Nuts could loosen in service, creating potential for wheels to separate from truck. **Corrective Action:** Repair to prevent loosening of lug nuts.

System: Visual systems; glass; windshield. **Vehicle:** Aftermarket windshields for light-duty trucks. **Defect:** The windshields do not meet the marking requirements of FMVSS 205, "Glazing materials." **Consequence:** The windshields are not identified as to the type of glass used. However, the windshields comply fully with the performance requirements of FMVSS 205. **Corrective Action:** See note. **Note:** The manufacturer's petition, which requested that NHTSA determine that this FMVSS noncompliance does not create an unreasonable risk to motor vehicle safety, has been granted. Therefore, the manufacturer is not obligated to conduct an owner notification and remedy campaign.

FORD TRUCK F250 1988

System: Rear window glazing—FMVSS 205. **Vehicle:** Light-duty trucks equipped with optional sliding rear window. **Defect:** Sliding rear window may contain glazing panels that do not meet requirements of FMVSS 205. **Consequence:** A fractured window may contain fragments that are larger than the 425 grams allowed. **Corrective Action:** Replace suspect window panels.

System: Brakes; front brake lining. **Vehicle:** F250 and F350 trucks with 7.3L diesel and 7.5L EFI engines; F250 and F350 4×4 models with 5.8L EFI engines. **Defect:** A revised brake lining noise insulator resulted in a decrease in the thermal insulation between the brake lining and the front brake caliper piston. This caused greater heat transfer to the caliper pistons, with the potential to overheat the brake fluid and diminish brake effectiveness during severe braking conditions. **Consequence:** Increased stopping distances and inability to hold vehicles on a steep grade results in increased risk of accident in the event of a sudden stop or when constant braking is needed to maneuver through areas with steep grades. **Corrective Action:** Add snap-in insulators that attach to each of the front brake caliper pistons. In addition, vehicles with 7.5L engines will have insulation added to the engine compartment brake lines. **Note:** Ford recommends vehicle operators do not exceed the GCWR and GVWR of their vehicles, and also recommend proper maintenance of the brakes on these vehicles and any trailer, particularly when operating in mountainous areas with long, steep grades.

System: Visual systems; glass; windshield. **Vehicle:** Aftermarket windshields for light-duty trucks. **Defect:** The windshields do not meet the marking requirements of FMVSS 205, "Glazing materials." **Consequence:** The windshields are not identified as to the type of glass used. However, the windshields comply fully with the performance requirements of FMVSS 205. **Corrective Action:** See note. **Note:** The manufacturer's petition, which requested that NHTSA determine this FMVSS noncompliance does not create an unreasonable risk to motor vehicle safety, has been granted. Therefore, the manufacturer is not obligated to conduct an owner notification and remedy campaign.

FORD TRUCK F250 1989

System: Fuel reservoir shield—FMVSS 301. **Vehicle:** Light-duty trucks with GVWR over 8,500 pounds. **Defect:** Fuel reservoir shields, which protect the reservoir from contact by the transfer case in certain frontal impacts, were not installed. **Consequence:** Fuel spillage in excess of that permitted by FMVSS 301 could occur. **Corrective Action:** Install fuel reservoir protective shields.

System: Fuel tank shields—FMVSS 301. **Vehicle:** 4×2 pickup trucks with 133-inch wheelbase and manual transmissions. **Defect:** Shields on the fronts of the midship-mounted fuel tanks were omitted during assembly. **Consequence:** Trucks would not comply with 30 mph impact test of FMVSS 301, "Fuel system integrity." **Corrective Action:** Install fuel tank shields.

System: Park gear snap ring. **Vehicle:** 4×2 light trucks and vans equipped with one-piece driveshaft and an E40D transmission. **Defect:** Under certain conditions, the snap ring that locates the park gear on the output shaft of the transmission may fracture. **Consequence:** When the gear is placed in park, the park gear would not engage, allowing the truck to roll freely if the parking brake is not properly set. This could result in an accident. **Corrective Action:** Install improved snap ring and revised transmission extension housing.

System: Fuel tank; auxiliary. **Vehicle:** Vans and light trucks with dual fuel tanks produced in the following periods: F150, F250 and F350 light trucks built between February 28, 1989, and July, 1989; Econoline built between February 28, 1989, and February 11, 1991. **Defect:** The dual fuel tank selector valve may malfunction and cause an overfill condition in one of the fuel tanks, resulting in an overflow of fuel past the filler cap. **Consequence:** The overflow of fuel past the filler cap causes a fuel leakage, which can result in a fire when exposed to a source of ignition. **Corrective Action:** Replace the dual fuel tank selector valve. **Note:** Ford has agreed to recall these vehicles, but parts are not yet available. Parts will be available in December 1991. You will receive a letter from Ford advising you when to schedule an appointment with your dealer to have the recall work performed. In the meantime, you can take the following precautions: Fill each tank to only one-third full. If your vehicle leaks fuel or if you smell fuel, stop using the vehicle and call Ford at (313) 446-4654 and advise them of your problem. Refer to Ford Safety Recall 91S39. An operator will take your name and telephone number. A Ford representative will call you back.

System: Brakes; front brake lining. **Vehicle:** F250 and F350 trucks with 7.3L diesel and 7.5L EFI engines; F250 and F350 4×4 models with 5.8L EFI engines. **Defect:** A revised brake lining noise insulator resulted in a decrease in the thermal insulation between the brake lining and the front brake caliper piston. This caused greater heat transfer to the caliper pistons, with the potential to overheat the brake fluid and diminish brake effectiveness during severe braking conditions. **Consequence:** Increased stopping distances and inability to hold vehicles on a steep grade result in increased risk of accident in the event of a sudden stop or when constant braking is needed to maneuver through areas with steep grades. **Corrective Action:** Add snap-in insulators that attach to each of the front brake caliper pistons. In addition, vehicles with 7.5L engines will have insulation added to the engine compartment brake lines. **Note:** Ford recommends vehicle operators do not exceed the GCWR and GVWR of their vehicles, and also recommend proper maintenance of the brakes on these vehicles and any trailer, particularly when operating in mountainous areas with long, steep grades.

System: Visual systems; glass; windshield. **Vehicle:** Aftermarket windshields for light-duty trucks. **Defect:** The windshields do not meet the marking requirements of FMVSS 205, "Glazing materials." **Consequence:** The windshields are not identified as to the type of glass used. However, the windshields comply fully with the performance requirements of FMVSS 205. **Corrective Action:** See note. **Note:** The manufacturer's petition, which requested that NHTSA determine that this FMVSS noncompliance does not create an unreasonable risk to motor vehicle safety, has been granted. Therefore, the manufacturer is not obligated to conduct an owner notification and remedy campaign.

FORD TRUCK F250 1990

System: Fuel line assembly. **Vehicle:** Light-duty trucks equipped with dual fuel tanks. **Defect:** Incorrectly installed fuel line connectors have fuel supply and return lines crossed. **Consequence:** Fuel could be transferred from one tank to the other, possibly resulting in fuel overflow and spillage; in presence of an ignition source, a fire could occur. **Corrective Action:** Replace fuel line assembly.

System: Park gear snap ring. **Vehicle:** 4×2 light trucks and vans equipped with one-piece driveshaft and an E40D transmission. **Defect:** Under certain conditions, the snap ring that locates the park gear on the output shaft of the transmission may fracture. **Consequence:** When the gear is placed in park, the park gear would not engage, allowing the truck to roll freely if the parking brake is not properly set. This could result in an accident. **Corrective Action:** Install improved snap ring and revised transmission extension housing.

System: Brakes; front brake lining. **Vehicle:** F250 and F350 trucks with 7.3L diesel and 7.5L EFI engines ; F250 and F350 4×4 models with 5.8L EFI engines. **Defect:** A revised brake lining noise insulator resulted in a decrease in the thermal insulation between the brake lining and the front brake caliper piston. This caused greater heat transfer to the caliper pistons, with the potential to overheat the brake fluid and diminish brake effectiveness during severe braking conditions. **Consequence:** Increased stopping distances and inability to hold vehicles on a steep grade result in increased risk of accident in the event of a sudden stop or when constant braking is needed to maneuver through areas with steep grades. **Corrective Action:** Add snap-in insulators that attach to each of the front brake caliper pistons. In addition, vehicles with 7.5L engines will have insulation added to the engine compartment brake lines. **Note:** Ford recommends vehicle operators do not exceed the GCWR and GVWR of their vehicles, and also recommends proper maintenance of the brakes on these vehicles and any trailer, particularly when operating in mountainous areas with long, steep grades.

System: Visual systems; glass; windshield. **Vehicle:** Aftermarket windshields for light-duty trucks. **Defect:** The windshields do not meet the marking requirements of FMVSS 205, "Glazing materials." **Consequence:** The windshields are not identified as to the type of glass used. However, the windshields comply fully with the performance requirements of FMVSS 205. **Corrective Action:** See note. **Note:** The manufacturer's petition, which requested that NHTSA determine that this FMVSS noncompliance does not create an unreasonable risk to motor vehicle safety, has been granted. Therefore, the manufacturer is not obligated to conduct an owner notification and remedy campaign.

System: Fuel; fuel tank assembly. **Vehicle:** Light trucks and chassis cabs with gasoline engines and dual fuel tanks. **Defect:** A malfunctioning check valve within the fuel pump assembly causes a portion of the unused fuel from one tank to be returned to the second tank. When this occurs, the capacity of the second tank can be exceeded, causing fuel spillage. **Consequence:** Spilled fuel can result in a fire when exposed to a source of ignition. **Corrective Action:** Replacement of the fuel pressure regulator and installation of redundant check valves.

System: Fuel; fuel lines; metallic. **Vehicle:** Light-duty and super-duty pickup trucks and chassis over 8,500 pounds GVWR rating equipped with 7.5L engines. **Defect:** The steel fuel return tubes that connect the frame fuel return lines with the engine fuel rail can contact the pinch weld flange connecting the dash panel to the floor pan. Continued contact leads to abrasion of the steel fuel return tube, and eventually results in a fuel leak. **Consequence:** Abrasion of the steel tube wall that eventually causes a fuel leak may result in a fire, if a source of ignition is present. **Corrective Action:** Ford dealers will replace the fuel return tubes with flexible stainless steel braided/Teflon tubes. Dealers will also inspect the fuel supply tubes.

FORD TRUCK F250 1991

System: Brakes; front brake lining. **Vehicle:** F250 and F350 trucks with 7.3L diesel and 7.5L EFI engines; F250 and F350 4×4 models with 5.8L EFI engines. **Defect:** A revised brake lining noise insulator resulted in a decrease in the thermal insulation between the brake lining and the front brake caliper piston. This caused greater heat transfer to the caliper pistons, with the potential to overheat the brake fluid and diminish brake effectiveness during severe braking conditions. **Consequence:** Increased stopping distances and inability to hold vehicles on a steep grade result in increased risk of accident in the event of a sudden stop or when constant braking is needed to maneuver through areas with steep grades. **Corrective Action:** Add snap-in insulators that attach to each of the front brake caliper pistons. In addition, vehicles with 7.5L engines will have insulation added to the engine compartment brake lines. **Note:** Ford recommends vehicle operators do not exceed the GCWR and GVWR of their vehicles, and also recommend proper maintenance of the brakes on these vehicles and any trailer, particularly when operating in mountainous areas with long, steep grades.

System: Visual systems; glass; windshield. **Vehicle:** Aftermarket windshields for light-duty trucks. **Defect:** The windshields do not meet the marking requirements of FMVSS 205, "Glazing materials." **Consequence:** The windshields are not identified as to the type of glass used. However, the windshields comply fully with the performance requirements of FMVSS 205. **Corrective Action:** See note. **Note:** The manufacturer's petition, which requested that NHTSA determine that this FMVSS noncompliance does not create an unreasonable risk to motor vehicle safety, has been granted. Therefore, the manufacturer is not obligated to conduct an owner notification and remedy campaign.

System: Fuel; fuel tank assembly. **Vehicle:** Light trucks and chassis cabs with gasoline engines and dual fuel tanks. **Defect:** A malfunctioning check valve within the fuel pump assembly causes a portion of the unused fuel from one tank to be returned to the second tank. When this occurs, the capacity of the second tank can be exceeded, causing fuel spillage. **Consequence:** Spilled fuel can result in a fire when exposed to a source of ignition. **Corrective Action:** Replacement of the fuel pressure regulator and installation of redundant check valves.

System: Fuel; fuel lines; metallic. **Vehicle:** Light-duty and super-duty pickup trucks and chassis over 8,500 pounds GVWR equipped with 7.5L engines. **Defect:** The steel fuel return tubes that connect the frame fuel return lines with the engine fuel rail can contact the pinch weld flange connecting the dash panel to the floor pan. Continued contact leads to abrasion of the steel fuel return tube and eventually results in a fuel leak. **Consequence:** Abrasion of the steel tube wall, which eventually causes a fuel leak, may result in a fire if a source of ignition is present. **Corrective Action:** Ford dealers will replace the fuel return tubes with flexible stainless steel braided/Teflon tubes. Dealers will also inspect the fuel supply tubes.

FORD TRUCK F250 1992

System: Structure; door latch. **Vehicle:** Multipurpose vehicles, light trucks and medium trucks. **Defect:** Water can enter the door latch release cable. If the vehicle is operated in below-freezing temperatures, the water in the door latch release cable can freeze and cause the latch mechanism to malfunction. **Consequence:** The malfunction of the door latch release can result in three different problems: The door will not be able to be relatched; the inside door handle can become inoperative; and the door could appear to be latched when it is not, allowing the door to open unexpectedly if it is jarred, and increasing the risk of injury to the adjacent seat occupant. **Corrective Action:** Revised door release cables and water shields will be installed.

System: Engine compartment; sound insulation. **Vehicle:** Trucks and chassis cabs equipped with 7.3L diesel engines. **Defect:** The sound insulation on the engine side of the dash panel can contact the exhaust manifold. **Consequence:** Contact between the insulation and the hot exhaust manifold may result in a engine compartment fire. **Corrective Action:** Dealers will modify the sound insulator at no cost to owners.

System: Visual systems; glass; windshield. **Vehicle:** Aftermarket windshields for light-duty trucks. **Defect:** The windshields do not meet the marking requirements of FMVSS 205, "Glazing materials." **Consequence:** The windshields are not identified as to the type of glass used. However, the windshields comply fully with the performance requirements of FMVSS 205. **Corrective Action:** See note. **Note:** The manufacturer's petition, which requested that NHTSA determine that this FMVSS noncompliance does not create an unreasonable risk to motor vehicle safety, has been granted. Therefore, the manufacturer is not obligated to conduct an owner notification and remedy campaign.

System: Fuel; fuel tank assembly. **Vehicle:** Light trucks and chassis cabs with gasoline engines and dual fuel tanks. **Defect:** A malfunctioning check valve within the fuel pump assembly causes a portion of the unused fuel from one tank to be returned to the second tank. When this occurs, the capacity of the second tank can be exceeded, causing fuel spillage. **Consequence:** Spilled fuel can result in a fire when exposed to a source of ignition. **Corrective Action:** Replacement of the fuel pressure regulator and installation of redundant check valves.

System: Emergency parking brake; mechanical. **Vehicle:** Light-duty pickup trucks and multipurpose vehicles with manual transmissions. **Defect:** The parking brake control self-adjust pawl does not line up properly with the self-adjust ratchet causing the pawl to slip over one or more teeth in the ratchet. **Consequence:** When this occurs, it can result in parking brake system ineffectiveness. The parking brake will not hold the vehicle, causing the vehicle to roll freely, if the transmission is not left in gear. **Corrective Action:** A wedge will be installed, which will serve to lock the parking brake self-adjust mechanism pawl into engagement with the ratchet. Also, owners will be advised to release and reapply the parking brake whenever tooth skip occurs, and will be reminded to always turn off the engine and leave the vehicle in gear when the vehicle is parked.

FORD TRUCK F250 1993

System: Visual systems; glass; windshield. **Vehicle:** Aftermarket windshields for light-duty trucks. **Defect:** The windshields do not meet the marking requirements of FMVSS 205, "Glazing materials." **Consequence:** The windshields are not identified as to the type of glass used. However, the windshields comply fully with the performance requirements of FMVSS 205. **Corrective Action:** See note. **Note:** The manufacturer's petition, which requested that NHTSA determine that this FMVSS noncompliance does not create an unreasonable risk to motor vehicle safety, has been granted. Therefore, the manufacturer is not obligated to conduct an owner notification and remedy campaign.

System: Fuel; fuel tank assembly. **Vehicle:** Light trucks and chassis cabs with gasoline engines and dual fuel tanks. **Defect:** A malfunctioning check valve within the fuel pump assembly causes a portion of the unused fuel from one tank to be returned to the second tank. When this occurs, the capacity of the second tank can be exceeded, causing fuel spillage. **Consequence:** Spilled fuel can result in a fire when exposed to a source of ignition. **Corrective Action:** Replacement of the fuel pressure regulator and installation of redundant check valves.

System: Structure; bumper assembly. **Vehicle:** Light-duty pickup trucks and multipurpose vehicles. **Defect:** The U-clip-style nuts that retain the front bumpers to the front bumper inner arms can fracture. **Consequence:** If one of the U-clip nuts fractures, the bumper will loosen and rattle, causing fracture of the remaining U-clip nuts and resulting in separation of the bumper from the vehicle. If the bumper were to detach from the vehicle while it is being driven, a vehicle collision could result. **Corrective Action:** Inspection and replacement of the four U-clip nuts and the associated bolts.

System: Emergency parking brake; mechanical. **Vehicle:** Light-duty pickup trucks and multipurpose vehicles with manual transmissions. **Defect:** The parking brake control self-adjust pawl does not line up properly with the self-adjust ratchet, causing the pawl to slip over one or more teeth in the ratchet. **Consequence:** When this occurs, it can result in parking brake system ineffectiveness. The parking brake will not hold the vehicle, causing the vehicle to roll freely, if the transmission is not left in gear. **Corrective Action:** A wedge will be installed, which will serve to lock the parking brake self-adjust mechanism pawl into engagement with the ratchet. Also, owners will be advised to release and reapply the parking brake whenever tooth skip occurs, and will be reminded to always turn off the engine and leave the vehicle in gear when the vehicle is parked.

FORD TRUCK F350 1987

System: Fuel line coupling. **Vehicle:** Passenger cars and light trucks equipped with fuel injection. **Defect:** Spring lock fuel line coupling may not be properly engaged. **Consequence:** Coupling could disengage due to fuel pressure, vibration and engine movements; this would cause loss of fuel which, in the presence of an ignition source, creates a fire risk. **Corrective Action:** Install retainer clips over the couplings to prevent coupling separation and fuel leakage.

System: Steering—suspension. **Vehicle:** Trucks and chassis cabs. **Defect:** Steering and suspension systems may not adequately control steering-type wobble, allowing the front end to shimmy. **Consequence:** Severe shimmy could damage the vehicle frame or steering gear, creating potential for loss of steering control. **Corrective Action:** Modify and/or replace front suspension and steering components, tires and frames.

System: Visual systems; glass; windshield. **Vehicle:** Aftermarket windshields for light duty-trucks. **Defect:** The windshields do not meet the marking requirements of FMVSS 205, "Glazing materials." **Consequence:** The windshields are not identified as to the type of glass used. However, the windshields comply fully with the performance requirements of FMVSS 205. **Corrective Action:** See note. **Note:** The manufacturer's petition, which requested that NHTSA determine that this FMVSS noncompliance does not create an unreasonable risk to motor vehicle safety, has been granted. Therefore, the manufacturer is not obligated to conduct an owner notification and remedy campaign.

FORD TRUCK F350 1988

System: Steering—suspension. **Vehicle:** Trucks and chassis cabs. **Defect:** Steering and suspension systems may not adequately control steering-type wobble, allowing the front end to shimmy. **Consequence:** Severe shimmy could damage the vehicle frame or steering gear, creating potential for loss of steering control. **Corrective Action:** Modify and/or replace front suspension and steering components, tires and frames.

System: Rear window glazing—FMVSS 205. **Vehicle:** Light-duty trucks equipped with optional sliding rear window. **Defect:** Sliding rear window may contain glazing panels that do not meet requirements of FMVSS 205. **Consequence:** A fractured window may contain fragments that are larger than the 425 grams allowed. **Corrective Action:** Replace suspect window panels.

System: Brakes; front brake lining. **Vehicle:** F250 and F350 trucks with 7.3L diesel and 7.5L EFI engines; F250 and F350 4×4 models with 5.8L EFI engines. **Defect:** A revised brake lining noise insulator resulted in a decrease in the thermal insulation between the brake lining and the front brake caliper piston. This caused greater heat transfer to the caliper pistons, with the potential to overheat the brake fluid and diminish brake effectiveness during severe braking conditions. **Consequence:** Increased stopping distances and inability to hold vehicles on a steep grade result in increased risk of accident in the event of a sudden stop or when constant braking is needed to maneuver through areas with steep grades. **Corrective Action:** Add snap-in insulators that attach to each of the front brake caliper pistons. In addition, vehicles with 7.5L engines will have insulation added to the engine compartment brake lines. **Note:** Ford recommends vehicle operators do not exceed the GCWR and GVWR of their vehicles, and also recommend proper maintenance of the brakes on these vehicles and any trailer, particularly when operating in mountainous areas with long, steep grades.

System: Visual systems; glass; windshield. **Vehicle:** Aftermarket windshields for light-duty trucks. **Defect:** The windshields do not meet the marking requirements of FMVSS 205, "Glazing materials." **Consequence:** The windshields are not identified as to the type of glass used. However, the windshields comply fully with the performance requirements of FMVSS 205. **Corrective Action:** See note. **Note:** The manufacturer's petition, which requested that NHTSA determine that this FMVSS noncompliance does not create an unreasonable risk to motor vehicle safety, has been granted. Therefore, the manufacturer is not obligated to conduct an owner notification and remedy campaign.

FORD TRUCK F350 1989

System: Fuel tank shields—FMVSS 301. **Vehicle:** 4×2 pickup trucks with 133-inch wheelbase and manual transmissions. **Defect:** Shields on the fronts of the midship-mounted fuel tanks were omitted during assembly. **Consequence:** Trucks would not comply with 30 mph impact test of FMVSS 301, "Fuel system integrity." **Corrective Action:** Install fuel tank shields.

System: Park gear snap ring. **Vehicle:** 4×2 light trucks and vans equipped with one-piece driveshaft and an E40D transmission. **Defect:** Under certain conditions, the snap ring that locates the park gear on the output shaft of the transmission may fracture. **Consequence:** When the gear is placed in park, the park gear would not engage, allowing the truck to roll freely if the parking brake is not properly set. This could result in an accident. **Corrective Action:** Install improved snap ring and revised transmission extension housing.

System: Fuel tank; auxiliary. **Vehicle:** Vans and light trucks with dual fuel tanks produced in the following periods: F150, F250 and F350 light trucks built between February 28, 1989, and July, 1989; Econoline built between February 28, 1989, and February 11, 1991. **Defect:** The dual fuel tank selector valve may malfunction and cause an overfill condition in one of the fuel tanks, resulting in an overflow of fuel past the filler cap. **Consequence:** The overflow of fuel past the filler cap causes a fuel leakage, which can result in a fire when exposed to a source of ignition. **Corrective Action:** Replace the dual fuel tank selector valve. **Note:** Ford has agreed to recall these vehicles, but parts are not yet available. Parts will be available in December 1991. You will receive a letter from Ford advising you when to schedule an appointment with your dealer to have the recall work performed. In the meantime, you can take the following precautions: Fill each tank to only one-third full. If your vehicle leaks fuel or if you smell fuel, stop using the vehicle and call Ford at (313) 446-4654 and advise them of your problem. Refer to Ford Safety Recall 91S39. An operator will take your name and telephone number. A Ford representative will call you back.

System: Brakes; front brake lining. **Vehicle:** F250 and F350 trucks with 7.3L diesel and 7.5L EFI engines; F250 and F350 4×4 models with 5.8L EFI engines. **Defect:** A revised brake lining noise insulator resulted in a decrease in the thermal insulation between the brake lining and the front brake caliper piston. This caused greater heat transfer to the caliper pistons, with the potential to overheat the brake fluid and diminish brake effectiveness during severe braking conditions. **Consequence:** Increased stopping distances and inability to hold vehicles on a steep grade result in increased risk of accident in the event of a sudden stop or when constant braking is needed to maneuver through areas with steep grades. **Corrective Action:** Add snap-in insulators that attach to each of the front brake caliper pistons. In addition, vehicles with 7.5L engines will have insulation added to the engine compartment brake lines. **Note:** Ford recommends vehicle operators do not exceed the GCWR and GVWR of their vehicles, and also recommend proper maintenance of the brakes on these vehicles and any trailer, particularly when operating in mountainous areas with long, steep grades.

System: Visual systems; glass; windshield. **Vehicle:** Aftermarket windshields for light-duty trucks. **Defect:** The windshields do not meet the marking requirements of FMVSS 205, "Glazing materials." **Consequence:** The windshields are not identified as to the type of glass used. However, the windshields comply fully with the performance requirements of FMVSS 205. **Corrective Action:** See note. **Note:** The manufacturer's petition, which requested that NHTSA determine that this FMVSS noncompliance does not create an unreasonable risk to motor vehicle safety, has been granted. Therefore, the manufacturer is not obligated to conduct an owner notification and remedy campaign.

FORD TRUCK F350 1990

System: Fuel line assembly. **Vehicle:** Light-duty trucks equipped with dual fuel tanks. **Defect:** Incorrectly installed fuel line connectors have fuel supply and return lines crossed. **Consequence:** Fuel could be transferred from one tank to the other, possibly resulting in fuel overflow and spillage; in the presence of an ignition source, a fire could occur. **Corrective Action:** Replace fuel line assembly.

System: Park gear snap ring. **Vehicle:** 4×2 light trucks and vans equipped with one-piece driveshaft and an E40D transmission. **Defect:**

Under certain conditions, the snap ring that locates the park gear on the output shaft of the transmission may fracture. **Consequence:** When the gear is placed in park, the park gear would not engage, allowing the truck to roll freely if the parking brake is not properly set. This could result in an accident. **Corrective Action:** Install improved snap ring and revised transmission extension housing.

System: Brakes; front brake lining. **Vehicle:** F250 and F350 trucks with 7.3L diesel and 7.5 L EFI engines; F250 and F350 4×4 models with 5.8L EFI engines. **Defect:** A revised brake lining noise insulator resulted in a decrease in the thermal insulation between the brake lining and the front brake caliper piston. This caused greater heat transfer to the caliper pistons, with the potential to overheat the brake fluid and diminish brake effectiveness during severe braking conditions. **Consequence:** Increased stopping distances and inability to hold vehicles on a steep grade result in increased risk of accident in the event of a sudden stop or when constant braking is needed to maneuver through areas with steep grades. **Corrective Action:** Add snap-in insulators that attach to each of the front brake caliper pistons. In addition, vehicles with 7.5L engines will have insulation added to the engine compartment brake lines. **Note:** Ford recommends vehicle operators do not exceed the GCWR and GVWR of their vehicles, and also recommend proper maintenance of the brakes on these vehicles and any trailer, particularly when operating in mountainous areas with long, steep grades.

System: Visual systems; glass; windshield. **Vehicle:** Aftermarket windshields for light-duty trucks. **Defect:** The windshields do not meet the marking requirements of FMVSS 205, "Glazing materials." **Consequence:** The windshields are not identified as to the type of glass used. However, the windshields comply fully with the performance requirements of FMVSS 205. **Corrective Action:** See note. **Note:** The manufacturer's petition, which requested that NHTSA determine that this FMVSS noncompliance does not create an unreasonable risk to motor vehicle safety, has been granted. Therefore, the manufacturer is not obligated to conduct an owner notification and remedy campaign.

System: Fuel; fuel tank assembly. **Vehicle:** Light trucks and chassis cabs with gasoline engines and dual fuel tanks. **Defect:** A malfunctioning check valve within the fuel pump assembly causes a portion of the unused fuel from one tank to be returned to the second tank. When this occurs, the capacity of the second tank can be exceeded, causing fuel spillage. **Consequence:** Spilled fuel can result in a fire when exposed to a source of ignition. **Corrective Action:** Replacement of the fuel pressure regulator and installation of redundant check valves.

System: Fuel; fuel lines; metallic. **Vehicle:** Light-duty and super-duty pickup trucks and chassis over 8,500 pounds GVWR equipped with 7.5L engines. **Defect:** The steel fuel return tubes that connect the frame fuel return lines with the engine fuel rail can contact the pinch weld flange connecting the dash panel to the floor pan. Continued contact leads to abrasion of the steel fuel return tube, and eventually results in a fuel leak. **Consequence:** Abrasion of the steel tube wall, which eventually causes a fuel leak, may result in a fire if a source of ignition is present. **Corrective Action:** Ford dealers will replace the fuel return tubes with flexible stainless steel braided/Teflon tubes. Dealers will also inspect the fuel supply tubes.

FORD TRUCK F350 1991

System: Brakes; front brake lining. **Vehicle:** F250 and F350 trucks with 7.3L diesel and 7.5L EFI engines; F250 and F350 4×4 models with 5.8L EFI engines. **Defect:** A revised brake lining noise insulator resulted in a decrease in the thermal insulation between the brake lining and the front brake caliper piston. This caused greater heat transfer to the caliper pistons, with the potential to overheat the brake fluid and diminish brake effectiveness during severe braking conditions. **Consequence:** Increased stopping distances and inability to hold vehicles on a steep grade result in increased risk of accident in the event of a sudden stop or when constant braking is needed to maneuver through areas with steep grades. **Corrective Action:** Add snap-in insulators that attach to each of the front brake caliper pistons. In addition, vehicles with 7.5L engines will have insulation added to the engine compartment brake lines. **Note:** Ford recommends vehicle operators do not exceed the GCWR and GVWR of their vehicles, and also recommend proper maintenance of the brakes on these vehicles and any trailer, particularly when operating in mountainous areas with long, steep grades.

System: Visual systems; glass; windshield. **Vehicle:** Aftermarket windshields for light-duty trucks. **Defect:** The windshields do not meet the marking requirements of FMVSS 205, "Glazing materials." **Consequence:** The windshields are not identified as to the type of glass used. However, the windshields comply fully with the performance requirements of FMVSS #205. **Corrective Action:** See note. **Note:** The manufacturer's petition, which requested that NHTSA determine that this FMVSS noncompliance does not create an unreasonable risk to motor vehicle safety, has been granted. Therefore, the manufacturer is not obligated to conduct an owner notification and remedy campaign.

System: Fuel; fuel tank assembly. **Vehicle:** Light trucks and chassis cabs with gasoline engines and dual fuel tanks. **Defect:** A malfunctioning check valve within the fuel pump assembly causes a portion of the unused fuel from one tank to be returned to the second tank. When this occurs, the capacity of the second tank can be exceeded, causing fuel spillage. **Consequence:** Spilled fuel can result in a fire when exposed to a source of ignition. **Corrective Action:** Replacement of the fuel pressure regulator and installation of redundant check valves.

System: Fuel; fuel lines; metallic. **Vehicle:** Light-duty and super-duty pickup trucks and chassis over 8,500 pounds GVWR equipped with 7.5L engines. **Defect:** The steel fuel return tubes that connect the frame fuel return lines with the engine fuel rail can contact the pinch weld flange connecting the dash panel to the floor pan. Continued contact leads to abrasion of the steel fuel return tube, and eventually results in a fuel leak. **Consequence:** Abrasion of the steel tube wall, which eventually causes a fuel leak, may result in a fire if a source of ignition is present. **Corrective Action:** Ford dealers will replace the fuel return tubes with flexible stainless steel braided/Teflon tubes. Dealers will also inspect the fuel supply tubes.

FORD TRUCK F350 1992

System: Structure; door latch. **Vehicle:** Multipurpose vehicles, light trucks and medium trucks. **Defect:** Water can enter the door latch release cable. If the vehicle is operated in below-freezing temperatures, the water in the door latch release cable can freeze and cause the latch mechanism to malfunction. **Consequence:** The malfunction of the door latch release can result in three different problems: The door will not be able to be relatched; the inside door handle can become inoperative; and the door could appear to be latched when it is not, allowing the door to open unexpectedly if it is jarred, and increasing the risk of injury to the adjacent seat occupant. **Corrective Action:** Revised door release cables and water shields will be installed.

System: Engine compartment; sound insulation. **Vehicle:** Trucks and chassis cabs equipped with 7.3L diesel engines. **Defect:** The sound insulation on the engine side of the dash panel can contact the exhaust manifold. **Consequence:** Contact between the insulation and the hot exhaust manifold may result in a engine compartment fire. **Corrective Action:** Dealers will modify the sound insulator at no cost to owners.

System: Visual systems; glass; windshield. **Vehicle:** Aftermarket windshields for light-duty trucks. **Defect:** The windshields do not meet the marking requirements of FMVSS 205, "Glazing materials." **Consequence:** The windshields are not identified as to the type of glass used. However, the windshields comply fully with the performance requirements of FMVSS 205. **Corrective Action:** See note. **Note:** The manufacturer's petition, which requested that NHTSA determine that this FMVSS noncompliance does not create an unreasonable risk to motor vehicle safety, has been granted. Therefore, the manufacturer is not obligated to conduct an owner notification and remedy campaign.

System: Fuel; fuel tank assembly. **Vehicle:** Light trucks and chassis cabs with gasoline engines and dual fuel tanks. **Defect:** A malfunctioning check valve within the fuel pump assembly causes a portion of the unused fuel from one tank to be returned to the second tank. When this occurs, the capacity of the second tank can be exceeded, causing fuel spillage. **Consequence:** Spilled fuel can result in a fire when exposed to a source of ignition. **Corrective Action:** Replacement of the fuel pressure regulator and installation of redundant check valves.

System: Emergency parking brake; mechanical. **Vehicle:** Light-duty pickup trucks and multipurpose vehicles with manual transmissions. **Defect:** The parking brake control self-adjust pawl does not line up properly with the self-adjust ratchet, causing the pawl to slip over one or more teeth in the ratchet. **Consequence:** When this occurs, it can result in parking brake system ineffectiveness. The parking brake will not hold the vehicle, causing the vehicle to roll freely, if the transmission is not left in gear. **Corrective Action:** A wedge will be installed, which will serve to lock the parking brake self-adjust mechanism pawl into engagement with the ratchet. Also, owners will be advised to release and reapply the parking brake whenever tooth skip occurs, and will be reminded to always turn off the engine and leave the vehicle in gear when the vehicle is parked.

FORD TRUCK F350 1993

System: Visual systems; glass; windshield. **Vehicle:** Aftermarket windshields for light-duty trucks. **Defect:** The windshields do not meet the marking requirements of FMVSS 205, "Glazing materials." **Consequence:** The windshields are not identified as to the type of glass used. However, the windshields comply fully with the performance requirements of FMVSS 205. **Corrective Action:** See note. **Note:** The manufacturer's petition, which requested that NHTSA determine that this FMVSS noncompliance does not create an unreasonable risk to motor vehicle safety, has been granted. Therefore, the manufacturer is not obligated to conduct an owner notification and remedy campaign.

System: Fuel; fuel tank assembly. **Vehicle:** Light trucks and chassis cabs with gasoline engines and dual fuel tanks. **Defect:** A malfunctioning check valve within the fuel pump assembly causes a portion of the unused fuel from one tank to be returned to the second tank. When this occurs, the capacity of the second tank can be exceeded, causing fuel spillage. **Consequence:** Spilled fuel can result in a fire when exposed to a source of ignition. **Corrective Action:** Replacement of the fuel pressure regulator and installation of redundant check valves.

System: Structure; bumper assembly. **Vehicle:** Light-duty pickup trucks and multipurpose vehicles. **Defect:** The U-clip-style nuts that retain the front bumpers to the front bumper inner arms can fracture. **Consequence:** If one of the U-clip nuts fractures, the bumper will loosen and rattle, causing fracture of the remaining U-clip nuts and resulting in separation of the bumper from the vehicle. If the bumper were to detach from the vehicle while it is being driven, a vehicle collision could result. **Corrective Action:** Inspection and replacement of the four U-clip nuts and the associated bolts.

System: Emergency parking brake; mechanical. **Vehicle:** Light-duty pickup trucks and multipurpose vehicles with manual transmissions. **Defect:** The parking brake control self-adjust pawl does not line up properly with the self-adjust ratchet, causing the pawl to slip over one or more teeth in the ratchet. **Consequence:** When this occurs, it can result in parking brake system ineffectiveness. The parking brake will not hold the vehicle, causing the vehicle to roll freely, if the transmission is not left in gear. **Corrective Action:** A wedge will be installed, which will serve to lock the parking brake self-adjust mechanism pawl into engagement with the ratchet. Also, owners will be advised to release and reapply the parking brake whenever tooth skip occurs, and will be reminded to always turn off the engine and leave the vehicle in gear when the vehicle is parked.

FORD TRUCK RANGER 1987

System: Utility vehicle stickers—parts 573 and 579. **Vehicle:** Multipurpose 4×4 passenger. **Defect:** Stickers concerning handling and maneuverability, which are affixed to driver's sun visor sleeves, do not meet criteria for permanent adhesion. **Consequence:** Vehicles do not meet formats specified by parts 573 and 579 of 49 CFR. **Corrective Action:** Owners will be mailed new sun visor sleeves with all applicable decal information permanently affixed.

System: Seat belt anchorage. **Vehicle:** Pickup trucks. **Defect:** The buckle portion of the seat belt assembly may not have been properly anchored to the floor. **Consequence:** If this condition exists, the seat belt assembly would not withstand a substantial impact load and would have the potential for personal injury. **Corrective Action:** Inspect and make proper installation of seat belt and buckle anchor bolts, if necessary.

System: Fuel line coupling. **Vehicle:** Passenger cars and light trucks equipped with fuel injection. **Defect:** Spring lock fuel line coupling may not be properly engaged. **Consequence:** Coupling could disengage due to fuel pressure, vibration and engine movements; this would cause loss of fuel which, in the presence of an ignition source, creates a fire risk. **Corrective Action:** Install retainer clips over the couplings to prevent coupling separation and fuel leakage.

System: Wheels—lug nuts. **Vehicle:** Pickup trucks modified into Bigfoot cruisers by Scherer Truck Equipment, Inc. **Defect:** Wheel lug nut cone angles do not match lug nut seating angles. **Consequence:** Nuts could loosen in service, creating potential for wheels to separate from truck. **Corrective Action:** Repair to prevent loosening of lug nuts.

System: Visual systems; glass; window; door and side—FMVSS 205. **Vehicle:** Light-duty pickup trucks. **Description of Noncompliance:** The quarter windows were incorrectly marked "AS2" rather than "AS3." The vehicles do not conform to the requirements of FMVSS 205, "Glazing standards." **Consequence of Noncompliance:** The windows installed in these vehicles meet all the requirements for "AS3." However, the markings are incorrect, which causes the vehicle to be in noncompliance with FMVSS 205. **Corrective Action:** Ford has not submitted a corrective action for this recall. **Note:** The manufacturer's petition, which requested that NHTSA determine that this FMVSS noncompliance does not create an unreasonable risk to motor vehicle safety, has been granted. Therefore, the manufacturer is not obligated to conduct an owner notification and remedy campaign.

FORD TRUCK RANGER 1988

System: Rear brake assembly. **Vehicle:** Regular cab pickup trucks equipped with limited-slip rear axles. **Defect:** Trucks were built with incorrect rear brake assemblies. **Consequence:** A tendency for rear brake lockup would exist, particularly during heavy brake application with a lightly loaded truck. Also, increased stopping distance would be required if brake modulation (pumping the brakes) is used to control the vehicle during a hard brake stop. **Corrective Action:** Replace rear brake assemblies.

System: Visual systems; glass; window; door and side; FMVSS 205. **Vehicle:** Light-duty pickup trucks. **Description of Noncompliance:** The quarter windows were incorrectly marked "AS2" rather than "AS3." The vehicles do not conform to the requirements of FMVSS 205, "Glazing standards." **Consequence of Noncompliance:** The windows installed in these vehicles meet all the requirements for "AS3." However, the markings are incorrect, which causes the vehicle to be in noncompliance with FMVSS 205. **Corrective Action:** Ford has not submitted a corrective action for this recall. **Note:** The manufacturer's petition, which requested that NHTSA determine that this FMVSS noncompliance does not create an unreasonable risk to motor vehicle safety, has been granted. Therefore, the manufacturer is not obligated to conduct an owner notification and remedy campaign.

FORD TRUCK RANGER 1989

System: Front wheel bearing. **Vehicle:** 4×4 multipurpose vehicles and trucks equipped with front axle automatic locking hubs. **Defect:** Front wheel bearing adjusting nut retaining keys may be missing from front axle assemblies, allowing the nut to loosen. **Consequence:** This could result in detachment of the wheel and hub assembly from the axle, loss of vehicle control and an accident. **Corrective Action:** Install retaining keys in front wheel hub assemblies where missing.

System: Visual systems; glass; window; door and side—FMVSS 205. **Vehicle:** Light-duty pickup trucks. **Description of Noncompliance:** The quarter windows were incorrectly marked "AS2" rather than "AS3." The vehicles do not conform to the requirements of FMVSS 205, "Glazing standards." **Consequence of Noncompliance:** The windows installed in these vehicles meet all the requirements for "AS3." However, the markings are incorrect, which causes the vehicle to be in noncompliance with FMVSS 205. **Corrective Action:** Ford has not submitted a corrective action for this recall. **Note:** The manufacturer's petition, which requested that NHTSA determine that this FMVSS noncompliance does not create an unreasonable risk to motor vehicle safety, has been granted. Therefore, the manufacturer is not obligated to conduct an owner notification and remedy campaign.

FORD TRUCK RANGER 1990

System: Throttle linkages and control. **Vehicle:** Light trucks. **Defect:** Throttle lever may contact throttle body air inlet tube, with the potential for throttle remaining open following release of the accelerator pedal from the full-throttle position in trucks with 4.0L engines. **Consequence:** Uncontrolled acceleration could create lack of control and cause an accident. **Corrective Action:** Manufacturer will replace air inlet tube with newly designed replacement with an increased throttle lever-to-inlet tube clearance.

System: Transmission. **Vehicle:** Pickup trucks, vans and multipurpose vehicles equipped with A4lD automatic transmissions. **Defect:** When the automatic transmission shift lever is placed in the park position, the park pawl does not always abut or engage the park gear. **Consequence:** Driver may believe the vehicle is safely engaged in park when the gear is not truly engaged. This can lead to the vehicle jumping out of gear unintentionally, vehicle rollaway when parked on a sloped surface and inadvertent motion when the vehicle is started. All of these conditions can result in a vehicle accident. **Corrective Action:** Repair the transmission with a new park pawl.

System: Visual systems; glass; window; door and side—FMVSS 205. **Vehicle:** Light-duty pickup trucks. **Description of Noncompliance:** The quarter windows were incorrectly marked "AS2" rather than "AS3." The vehicles do not conform to the requirements of FMVSS 205, "Glazing standards." **Consequence of Noncompliance:** The windows installed in these vehicles meet all the requirements for "AS3." However, the markings are incorrect, which causes the vehicle to be in noncompliance with FMVSS 205. **Corrective Action:** Ford has not submitted a corrective action for this recall. **Note:** The manufacturer's petition, which requested that NHTSA determine that this FMVSS noncompliance does not create an unreasonable risk to motor vehicle safety, has been granted. Therefore, the manufacturer is not obligated to conduct an owner notification and remedy campaign.

FORD TRUCK RANGER 1991

System: Transmission. **Vehicle:** Pickup trucks, vans and multipurpose vehicles equipped with A4lD automatic transmissions. **Defect:** When the automatic transmission shift lever is placed in the park position, the park pawl does not always abut or engage the park gear. **Consequence:** Driver may believe the vehicle is safely engaged in park when the gear is not truly engaged. This can lead to the vehicle jumping out of gear unintentionally, vehicle rollaway when parked on a sloped surface and inadvertent motion when the vehicle is started. All of these conditions can result in a vehicle accident. **Corrective Action:** Repair the transmission with a new park pawl.

System: Visual systems; glass; window; door and side—FMVSS 205. **Vehicle:** Light-duty pickup trucks. **Description of Noncompliance:** The quarter windows were incorrectly marked "AS2" rather than "AS3." The vehicles do not conform to the requirements of FMVSS 205, "Glazing standards." **Consequence of Noncompliance:** The windows installed in these vehicles meet all the requirements for "AS3." However, the markings are incorrect, which causes the vehicle to be in noncompliance with FMVSS 205. **Corrective Action:** Ford has not submitted a corrective action for this recall. **Note:** The manufacturer's petition, which requested that NHTSA determine that this FMVSS noncompliance does not create an unreasonable risk to motor vehicle safety, has been granted. Therefore, the manufacturer is not obligated to conduct an owner notification and remedy campaign.

FORD TRUCK RANGER 1992

System: Structure; door latch. **Vehicle:** Multipurpose vehicles, light trucks and medium trucks. **Defect:** Water can enter the door latch release cable. If the vehicle is operated in below-freezing temperatures, the water in the door latch release cable can freeze and cause the latch mechanism to malfunction. **Consequence:** The malfunction of the door latch release can result in three different problems: The door will not be able to be relatched; the inside door handle can become inoperative; and the door could appear to be latched when it is not, allowing the door to open unexpectedly if it is jarred, and increasing the risk of injury to the adjacent seat occupant. **Corrective Action:** Revised door release cables and water shields will be installed.

System: Visual systems; glass; window; door and side—FMVSS 205. **Vehicle:** Light-duty pickup trucks. **Description of Noncompliance:** The quarter windows were incorrectly marked "AS2" rather than "AS3." The vehicles do not conform to the requirements of FMVSS 205, "Glazing standards." **Consequence of Noncompliance:** The windows installed in these vehicles meet all the requirements for "AS3." However, the markings are incorrect, which causes the vehicle to be in noncompliance with FMVSS 205. **Corrective Action:** Ford has not submitted a corrective action for this recall. **Note:** The manufacturer's petition, which requested that NHTSA determine that this FMVSS noncompliance does not create an unreasonable risk to motor vehicle safety, has been granted. Therefore, the manufacturer is not obligated to conduct an owner notification and remedy campaign.

FORD TRUCK RANGER 1993

System: Equipment; other labels. **Vehicle:** Light trucks and multipurpose vehicles. **Defect:** The instrument panel cluster contains components intended for vehicles to be exported to Europe. The brake display telltale is identified by the International Standards Organization (ISO) symbol, but not the word brake, as specified in FMVSS 101 and 105. **Consequence:** The operators of these vehicles may not identify the ISO brake symbol as an indication of a brake problem, and may not heed the warning of an immediate or impending brake failure. **Corrective Action:** Ford has not submitted a corrective action for this recall. **Note:** The manufacturer's petition, which requested that NHTSA determine that this FMVSS noncompliance does not create an unreasonable risk to motor vehicle safety, has been granted. Therefore, the manufacturer is not obligated to conduct an owner notification and remedy campaign.

System: Visual systems; glass; window; door and side—FMVSS 205. **Vehicle:** Light-duty pickup trucks. **Description of Noncompliance:** The quarter windows were incorrectly marked "AS2" rather than "AS3." The vehicles do not conform to the requirements of FMVSS 205, "Glazing standards." **Consequence of Noncompliance:** The windows installed in these vehicles meet all the requirements for "AS3." However, the markings are incorrect, which causes the vehicle to be in noncompliance with FMVSS 205. **Corrective Action:** Ford has not submitted a corrective action for this recall. **Note:** The manufacturer's petition, which requested that NHTSA determine that this FMVSS noncompliance does not create an unreasonable risk to motor vehicle safety, has been granted. Therefore, the manufacturer is not obligated to conduct an owner notification and remedy campaign.

System: Emergency parking brake; mechanical. **Vehicle:** Light-duty pickup trucks and multipurpose vehicles with manual transmissions. **Defect:** The parking brake control self-adjust pawl does not line up properly with the self-adjust ratchet, causing the pawl to slip over one or more teeth in the ratchet. **Consequence:** When this occurs, it can result in parking brake system ineffectiveness. The parking brake will not hold the vehicle, causing the vehicle to roll freely, if the transmission is not left in gear. **Corrective Action:** A wedge will be installed, which will serve to lock the parking brake self-adjust mechanism pawl into engagement with the ratchet. Also, owners will be advised to release and reapply the parking brake whenever tooth skip occurs, and will be reminded to always turn off the engine and leave the vehicle in gear when the vehicle is parked.

FORD TRUCK RANGER 1994

System: Fuel; fuel lines; hoses; nonmetallic. **Vehicle:** Light-duty pickup trucks equipped with 3.0L and 4.0L engines. **Defect:** The front fuel lines have a section of flexible hose that is susceptible to cracking, which can allow fuel leakage. **Consequence:** Leaking fuel can result in a fire when exposed to a source of ignition. **Corrective Action:** Dealers will inspect and, if necessary, replace the front fuel line assembly. **Note:** Ford Motor Company is the manufacturer of both the Ford Ranger and the Mazda B-Series light pickup trucks. Ford Motor Company and Mazda (North America) will be performing the corrective actions for their own trucks. If your vehicle is presented to an authorized dealer on an agreed-upon service date and the remedy is not provided within a reasonable time and free of charge, or the remedy does not correct the defect or noncompliance, please contact Ford Service Center at (800) 392-3673; or Mazda Service Center at (800)

222-5500. Also contact the NHTSA's Auto Safety Hotline at (800) 424-9393.

System: Visual systems; glass; window; door and side—FMVSS 205. **Vehicle:** Light-duty pickup trucks. **Description of Noncompliance:** The quarter windows were incorrectly marked "AS2" rather than "AS3." The vehicles do not conform to the requirements of FMVSS 205, "Glazing standards." **Consequence of Noncompliance:** The windows installed in these vehicles meet all the requirements for "AS3." However, the markings are incorrect, which causes the vehicle to be in noncompliance with FMVSS 205. **Corrective Action:** Ford has not submitted a corrective action for this recall. **Note:** The manufacturer's petition, which requested that NHTSA determine that this FMVSS noncompliance does not create an unreasonable risk to motor vehicle safety, has been granted. Therefore, the manufacturer is not obligated to conduct an owner notification and remedy campaign.

System: Emergency parking brake; mechanical. **Vehicle:** Light-duty pickup trucks and multipurpose vehicles with manual transmissions. **Defect:** The parking brake control self-adjust pawl does not line up properly with the self-adjust ratchet, causing the pawl to slip over one or more teeth in the ratchet. **Consequence:** When this occurs, it can result in parking brake system ineffectiveness. The parking brake will not hold the vehicle, causing the vehicle to roll freely, if the transmission is not left in gear. **Corrective Action:** A wedge will be installed, which will serve to lock the parking brake self-adjust mechanism pawl into engagement with the ratchet. Also, owners will be advised to release and reapply the parking brake whenever tooth skip occurs, and will be reminded to always turn off the engine and leave the vehicle in gear when the vehicle is parked.

FORD TRUCK WINDSTAR 1995

System: Electrical system; wiring harness; front; underhood. **Vehicle:** Light-duty van. **Defect:** The wiring harness insulation can abrade on a brace that runs from the instrument panel to the cowl. **Consequence:** This condition can result in an electrical short and possibly a vehicle fire. **Corrective Action:** Dealers will install a shield on the instrument panel to the cowl brace, and install of a piece of convolute wrap material on one of the adjacent harnesses.

System: Electrical system; alternator; regulator; starter. **Vehicle:** Light-duty van. **Defect:** The alternator output wire was not connected tightly to the power distribution box. **Consequence:** This can result in overheating of the connection and a possible vehicle fire. **Corrective Action:** Dealers will inspect and tighten the connection. Vehicles with visible damage to the plastic power distribution box housing will have the underhood harness, including the power distribution box, replaced.

System: Interior; passive restraints; airbag; passenger. **Vehicle:** Passenger cars, vans and multipurpose vehicles. **Defect:** The passenger-side airbag has an inflator body that cracked during forming of the curl that retains the igniter plug in the end of the inflator. Also the igniter end cap can separate from the inflator. **Consequence:** The passenger-side airbag may not inflate properly, resulting in reduced occupant protection in a vehicle accident. If the igniter end cap separates in a frontal collision, hot gases can be released and ignite flammable material or cause burn injuries. **Corrective Action:** Dealers will remove and replace the passenger-side airbag module.

GEO

Note: If your Geo is presented to an authorized dealer on an agreed-upon service date and the remedy is not provided within a reasonable time and free of charge, or the remedy does not correct the defect or noncompliance, please contact Chevrolet Service Center at (800) 222-1020. Also please contact the NHTSA's Auto Safety Hotline at (800) 424-9393.

GEO METRO 1989

System: Structure; hood assembly. **Vehicle:** Passenger cars. **Defect:** Mislocated attaching spot welds of the hood striker assembly cause cracks to start on the hood inner panel. If cracks occur, the hood striker assembly may not properly engage the hood latch when the hood is closed. **Consequence:** An improperly engaged hood latch may result in a hood fly-up while the vehicle is in motion. This would obstruct the driver's view and could cause a vehicle crash. **Corrective Action:** GMC dealers will install two bolts and nuts to secure the striker assembly to the hood inner panel, and ensure that the hood latch assembly fasteners are properly tightened.

System: Interior; seat belts; belt buckles. **Vehicle:** Passenger and multipurpose vehicles equipped with safety belts made by Takata Corporation. **Defect:** The front safety belt buckle release buttons can break. These red plastic release buttons are marked "press." If a button breaks, pieces can fall into the buckle assembly, causing the buckle to operate improperly. **Consequence:** The safety belts would not provide adequate protection to an occupant in a vehicle crash. **Corrective Action:** Owners should promptly check the condition and operation of both front safety belt buckles and carefully inspect the red release buttons for any breaks or cracks. They should ensure that both buckles are operating properly by inserting each latchplate into its buckle, tugging on the belt to make sure the latch is securely locked and then pressing the release button. The latchplate should pop out of the buckle when the button is pressed. If either release button shows a sign of breaking or cracking, or if either buckle fails to operate properly, owners should promptly contact their authorized dealer to schedule an appointment to have the buckle replaced or repaired, free of charge. The manufacturer is developing a remedy designed to prevent failure of the buttons that are not currently broken.

GEO METRO 1990

System: Structure; hood assembly. **Vehicle:** Passenger cars. **Defect:** Mislocated attaching spot welds of the hood striker assembly cause cracks to start on the hood inner panel. If cracks occur, the hood striker assembly may not properly engage the hood latch when the hood is closed. **Consequence:** An improperly engaged hood latch may result in a hood fly-up while the vehicle is in motion. This would obstruct the driver's view and could cause a vehicle crash. **Corrective Action:** GMC dealers will install two bolts and nuts to secure the striker assembly to the hood inner panel, and ensure that the hood latch assembly fasteners are properly tightened.

System: Interior; seat belts; belt buckles. **Vehicle:** Passenger and multipurpose vehicles equipped with safety belts made by Takata Corporation. **Defect:** The front safety belt buckle release buttons can break. These red plastic release buttons are marked "press." If a button breaks, pieces can fall into the buckle assembly, causing the buckle to operate improperly. **Consequence:** The safety belts would not provide adequate protection to an occupant in a vehicle crash. **Corrective Action:** Owners should promptly check the condition and operation of both front safety belt buckles and carefully inspect the red release buttons for any breaks or cracks. They should ensure that both buckles are operating properly by inserting each latchplate into its buckle, tugging on the belt to make sure the latch is securely locked and then pressing the release button. The latchplate should pop out of the buckle when the button is pressed. If either release button shows a sign of breaking or cracking, or if either buckle fails to operate properly, owners should promptly contact their authorized dealer to schedule an appointment to have the buckle replaced or repaired, free of charge. The manufacturer is developing a remedy designed to prevent failure of the buttons that are not currently broken.

GEO METRO 1991

System: Structure; hood assembly. **Vehicle:** Passenger cars. **Defect:** Mislocated attaching spot welds of the hood striker assembly cause cracks to start on the hood inner panel. If cracks occur, the hood striker assembly may not properly engage the hood latch when the hood is closed. **Consequence:** An improperly engaged hood latch may result in a hood fly-up while the vehicle is in motion. This would obstruct the driver's view and could cause a vehicle crash. **Corrective Action:** GMC dealers will install two bolts and nuts to secure the striker assembly to the hood inner panel, and ensure that the hood latch assembly fasteners are properly tightened.

System: Interior; seat belts; belt buckles. **Vehicle:** Passenger and multipurpose vehicles equipped with safety belts made by Takata Corporation. **Defect:** The front safety belt buckle release buttons can break. These red plastic release buttons are marked "press." If a button breaks, pieces can fall into the buckle assembly, causing the buckle to operate improperly. **Consequence:** The safety belts would not provide adequate protection to an occupant in a vehicle crash. **Corrective Action:** Owners should promptly check the condition and operation of both front safety belt buckles and carefully inspect the red release buttons for any breaks or cracks. They should ensure that both buckles are operating properly by inserting each latchplate into its buckle, tugging on the belt to make sure the latch is securely locked and then pressing the release button. The latchplate should pop out of the buckle when the button is pressed. If either release button shows a sign of breaking or cracking, or if either buckle fails to operate properly, owners should promptly contact their authorized dealer to schedule an appointment to have the buckle replaced or repaired, free of charge. The manufacturer is developing a remedy designed to prevent failure of the buttons that are not currently broken.

GEO METRO 1992

System: Structure; hood assembly. **Vehicle:** Passenger cars. **Defect:** Mislocated attaching spot welds of the hood striker assembly cause cracks to start on the hood inner panel. If cracks occur, the hood striker assembly may not properly engage the hood latch when the hood is closed. **Consequence:** An improperly engaged hood latch may result in a hood fly-up while the vehicle is in motion. This would obstruct the driver's view and could cause a vehicle crash. **Corrective Action:** GMC dealers will install two bolts and nuts to secure the striker assembly to the hood inner panel, and ensure that the hood latch assembly fasteners are properly tightened.

GEO METRO 1993

System: Structure; hood assembly. **Vehicle:** Passenger cars. **Defect:** Mislocated attaching spot welds of the hood striker assembly cause cracks to start on the hood inner panel. If cracks occur, the hood striker assembly may not properly engage the hood latch when the hood is closed. **Consequence:** An improperly engaged hood latch may result in a hood fly-up while the vehicle is in motion. This would obstruct the driver's view and could cause a vehicle crash. **Corrective Action:** GMC dealers will install two bolts and nuts to secure the striker assembly to the hood inner panel, and ensure that the hood latch assembly fasteners are properly tightened.

GEO PRIZM 1991

System: Wheel lug nuts. **Vehicle:** Passenger cars. **Defect:** Lug nuts that retain wheels and wheel covers may have been torqued to lower than recommended specifications. **Consequence:** Insufficient clamping of lug nuts retaining the wheel cover and wheel could result in a loose wheel that could fall off, with potential for loss of control and an accident. **Corrective Action:** Remove original wheel cover, torque lug to specification and install full wheel covers that are retained by spring clips.

GEO PRIZM 1994

System: Safety belt assemblies. **Equipment:** Safety belt assemblies used on 1994 Toyota Corollas and GEO Prizms. **Description of Noncompliance:** The anchor straps installed in the belt assemblies (front inner, left- and right-hand sides) were improperly heat treated and can break, which will not sufficiently restrain seat occupants in the event of a sudden stop or accident. This does not comply with FMVSS 209, "Seat belt assemblies." **Consequence of Noncompliance:** Insufficient restraints for seat occupants increases the risk of injury in the event of an accident. **Corrective Action:** The manufacturer will provide replacement safety belt anchor straps. **Note:** If your vehicle is presented to an authorized dealer on an agreed-upon service date and the remedy is not provided within a reasonable time and free of charge, or the remedy does not correct the defect or noncompliance, please contact Quality Safety Systems at (519) 973-7400. Also contact the NHTSA's Auto Safety Hotline at (800) 424-9393.

System: Interior system; active restraints; belt buckles—FMVSS 209. **Vehicle:** Passenger vehicles. **Description of Noncompliance:** The front seat belt buckle anchor straps were not properly heat treated. In the event of an accident, the seat belt buckle can separate from the anchor strap. This does not conform to the requirements of FMVSS 209, "Seat belt assemblies." **Consequence:** If the seat belt buckle separates from the anchor strap in a sudden stop or accident, the seat occupant is exposed to increased risk of personal injury. **Corrective Action:** Dealers will inspect the buckle assembly anchor straps and replace those with suspect date codes 52733D 032 or 52733D 042.

GEO STORM 1990

System: Seat back hinge mechanism. **Vehicle:** Passenger cars. **Defect:** When using front seat back release levers to tip front seat back forward to gain entry to, or exit from, the rear seat, it is possible to insert a finger into the seat back hinge mechanism. **Consequence:** This could result in the finger being pinched, and possibly seriously injured. **Corrective Action:** Repair to prevent condition that would permit finger injury.

System: Steering wheel hub airbag system. **Vehicle:** Passenger cars equipped with airbags in the steering wheel hub. **Defect:** The steering wheel center hub can fracture during certain frontal and near-frontal vehicle collisions. **Consequence:** Fracturing of the steering wheel hub can decrease the driver's control of the vehicle, and could reduce the crash protection of the steering system and the driver's-side airbag. **Corrective Action:** A steering wheel reinforcement plate and nut will be added to the steering wheel hub.

System: Interior; seat belts; belt buckles. **Vehicle:** Passenger and multipurpose vehicles equipped with safety belts made by Takata Corporation. **Defect:** The front safety belt buckle release buttons can break. These red plastic release buttons are marked "press." If a button breaks, pieces can fall into the buckle assembly, causing the buckle to operate improperly. **Consequence:** The safety belts would not provide adequate protection to an occupant in a vehicle crash. **Corrective Action:** Owners should promptly check the condition and operation of both front safety belt buckles and carefully inspect the red release buttons for any breaks or cracks. They should ensure that both buckles are operating properly by inserting each latchplate into its buckle, tugging on the belt to make sure the latch is securely locked and then pressing the release button. The latchplate should pop out of the buckle when the button is pressed. If either release button shows a sign of breaking or cracking, or if either buckle fails to operate properly, owners should promptly contact their authorized dealer to schedule an appointment to have the buckle replaced or repaired, free of charge. The manufacturer is developing a remedy designed to prevent failure of the buttons that are not currently broken.

GEO STORM 1991

System: Steering wheel hub airbag system. **Vehicle:** Passenger cars equipped with airbags in the steering wheel hub. **Defect:** The steering wheel center hub can fracture during certain frontal and near-frontal vehicle collisions. **Consequence:** Fracturing of the steering wheel hub can decrease the driver's control of the vehicle, and could reduce the crash protection of the steering system and the driver's-side airbag. **Corrective Action:** A steering wheel reinforcement plate and nut will be added to the steering wheel hub.

System: Interior; seat belts; belt buckles. **Vehicle:** Passenger and multipurpose vehicles equipped with safety belts made by Takata Corporation. **Defect:** The front safety belt buckle release buttons can break. These red plastic release buttons are marked "press." If a button breaks, pieces can fall into the buckle assembly, causing the buckle to operate improperly. **Consequence:** The safety belts would not provide adequate protection to an occupant in a vehicle crash. **Corrective Action:** Owners should promptly check the condition and operation of both front safety belt buckles, and carefully inspect the red release buttons for any breaks or cracks. They should ensure that both buckles are operating properly by inserting each latchplate into its buckle, tugging on the belt to make sure the latch is securely locked and then pressing the release button. The latchplate should pop out of the buckle when the button is pressed. If either release button shows a sign of breaking or cracking, or if either buckle fails to operate properly, owners should promptly contact their authorized dealer to schedule an appointment to have the buckle replaced or repaired, free of charge. The manufacturer is developing a remedy designed to prevent failure of the buttons that are not currently broken.

GEO STORM 1992

System: Steering wheel hub airbag system. **Vehicle:** Passenger cars equipped with airbags in the steering wheel hub. **Defect:** The steering wheel center hub can fracture during certain frontal and near-frontal vehicle collisions. **Consequence:** Fracturing of the steering wheel hub can decrease the driver's control of the vehicle, and could reduce the crash protection of the steering system and the driver's-side airbag. **Corrective Action:** A steering wheel reinforcement plate and nut will be added to the steering wheel hub.

GMC

Note: If your GMC is presented to an authorized dealer on an agreed-upon service date and the remedy is not provided within a reasonable time and free of charge, or the remedy does not correct the defect or noncompliance, please contact Chevrolet Service Center at (800) 222-1020; or GMC Service Center at (313) 456-4547. Also contact the NHTSA's Auto Safety Hotline at (800) 424-9393.

GMC C1500 1988

System: Power train. **Vehicle:** Light trucks with 5.0L, 5.7L, and 7.4L engines and 4160, 4160-E and 3180 automatic transmissions. **Defect:** Unanticipated heat in the transmission can force the transmission fluid out of the vent tube. **Consequence:** The vented transmission fluid can catch fire if exposed to a source of ignition. **Corrective Action:** Install a longer transmission vent hose routed to the left side of the engine compartment of the vehicle.

GMC JIMMY 1991

System: Windshield and side window mounting—FMVSS 212. **Vehicle:** Utility, pickup and extended cab pickup trucks. **Defect:** Use of improper primer on metal surfaces of windshield and side window openings could cause low adhesion to the metal surface and would not provide retention required by FMVSS 212. **Consequence:** Windshield and side window glass would not prevent the ejection of vehicle occupants during a vehicle crash, which causes serious injuries and fatalities. **Corrective Action:** Remove and reinstall glass using proper primer.

System: Fuel systems—FMVSS 301. **Vehicle:** Light trucks and multipurpose vehicles. **Defect:** Vehicles have been shipped with the fuel tank sender seal out of position. **Consequence:** In the event of rollover accident, an out of position seal could allow fuel spillage in excess of the amount prescribed by FMVSS 301. Spilled fuel could ignite near an ignition source. **Corrective Action:** Replace sender seals.

GMC JIMMY 1993

System: Power train; transmission; automatic. **Vehicle:** Light-duty pickup trucks and utility vehicles equipped with 4-wheel drive. **Note:** The "S" series trucks are not included because they are only 2-wheel drive. **Defect:** Significant wear can develop on the low and reverse clutch, preventing the park pawl from engaging. This can allow a "no park" condition to occur while the engine is running, causing unintentional movement of the vehicle without operator action. (The "no park" condition will not occur while the engine is off.) **Consequence:** Unintentional vehicle movement could result in a vehicle accident and injury to persons in the path of the vehicle. **Corrective Action:** Dealers will check the transmission fluid for contamination, which will indicate if the low or reverse clutch is worn. If the transmission fluid shows contamination, the transmission will be replaced.

GMC JIMMY 1994

System: Equipment; other pieces; trailer hitches and attachments. **Vehicle:** Light-duty 4-door multipurpose vehicles equipped with a weight distribution trailer hitch (VR4) option. **Defect:** The trailer hitch attaching bolts were not tightened to the specified torque. This can lead to loosening and subsequent breakage of the fasteners. **Consequence:** If this were to occur while the trailer was being pulled, the hitch and trailer could separate from the vehicle. **Corrective Action:** Dealers will torque all eight trailer hitch bolts to the correct torque.

GMC S15 1989

System: Engine. **Vehicle:** Light trucks with 2.5L engines without air conditioning. **Defect:** The engine cooling fan blades break as a result of fatigue and/or vehicle-induced stress. **Consequence:** If the blade breakage occurs while the hood is open, a person working under the hood or in the vicinity of the vehicle could be struck and injured by the blade segment. **Corrective Action:** Install a newly designed fan assembly.

GMC SAFARI 1987

System: Interior systems; seat tracks, anchors and seats. **Vehicle:** Vans and utility vehicles equipped with bucket seats with knob-type recliner mechanisms. **Defect:** The recliner mechanism and the seat frame may have foam and/or vinyl between them, creating a "soft" joint. This soft joint results in lower than specified bolt torque, which leads to joint looseness, causing bolt fatigue and eventual bolt failure. **Consequence:** If bolt failure occurs to the driver's seat, it would allow the seat back to suddenly recline, and could result in loss of vehicle control and a vehicle crash without prior warning. **Corrective Action:** Dealers will remove the foam and/or vinyl from between the recliner mechanism and the seat frame soft joint and replace the recliner bolts.

GMC SAFARI 1988

System: Brakes; hydraulic; disc rotors. **Vehicle:** Light trucks and vans sold or registered in the following states: CT, IL, IN, MA, ME, MI, NH, NJ, NY, OH, PA, RI, VT and WI. **Defect:** Severe corrosion due to road salt at the joint of the stamped steel center section and the cast outer section can cause the sections to separate. **Consequence:** Separation of the rotor sections can cause loss of braking ability in the affected wheel. This could result in increased stopping distance and/or loss of vehicle control and an accident. **Corrective Action:** Replace the front brake rotors with new rotors with a corrosion-protection coating. However, if replacement of brake linings is necessary, it will be done at owner's expense, since brake linings are normal maintenance items. **Note:** The vehicles involved can be identified by the following: the 5th character of the vehicle identification number must be a *K* or *L*, and the 7th character must be *3*, *4*, *5*, *6* or *9*. If your vehicle is presented to an authorized dealer on an agreed-upon service date, and the remedy is not provided within a reasonable amount of time and free of charge or the remedy does not correct the safety-related defect or noncompliance, please contact your nearest GMC Truck zone office. The telephone numbers of the zone offices are listed in your warranty and owner's assistance information manuals. Also contact the NHTSA's Auto Safety Hotline at (800) 424-9393.

System: Interior systems; seat tracks, anchors and seats. **Vehicle:** Vans and utility vehicles equipped with bucket seats with knob-type recliner mechanisms. **Defect:** The recliner mechanism and the seat frame may have foam and/or vinyl between them, creating a "soft" joint. This soft joint results in lower than specified bolt torque, which leads to joint looseness, causing bolt fatigue and eventual bolt failure. **Consequence:** If bolt failure occurs to the driver's seat, it would allow the seat back to suddenly recline, and could result in loss of vehicle control and a vehicle crash without prior warning. **Corrective Action:** Dealers will remove the foam and/or vinyl from between the recliner mechanism and the seat frame soft joint and replace the recliner bolts.

GMC SAFARI 1989

System: Seat belt anchorage—FMVSS 210. **Vehicle:** Vans. **Defect:** Seat belt anchorage bar for rear sofa failed to sustain loads required by FMVSS 210. **Consequence:** Vehicles would not comply with FMVSS 210. **Corrective Action:** Replace noncomplying sofa bar with bar that meets requirements. **Note:** This recall is being conducted by Sherrod Vans, Inc.

System: Brakes; hydraulic; disc rotors. **Vehicle:** Light trucks and vans sold or registered in the following states: CT, IL, IN, MA, ME, MI, NH, NJ, NY, OH, PA, RI, VT and WI. **Defect:** Severe corrosion due to road salt at the joint of the stamped steel center section and the cast outer section can cause the sections to separate. **Consequence:** Separation of the rotor sections can cause loss of braking ability in the affected wheel. This could result in increased stopping distance and/or loss of vehicle control and an accident. **Corrective Action:** Replace the front brake rotors with new rotors with a corrosion-protection coating. However, if replacement of brake linings is necessary, it will be done at owner's expense, since brake linings are normal maintenance items. **Note:** The vehicles involved can be identified by the following: the 5th character of the vehicle identification number must be a *K* or *L*, and the 7th character must be *3, 4, 5, 6* or *9*. If your vehicle is presented to an authorized dealer on an agreed-upon service date, and the remedy is not provided within a reasonable amount of time and free of charge or the remedy does not correct the safety-related defect or noncompliance, please contact your nearest GMC Truck zone office. The telephone numbers of the zone offices are listed in your warranty and owner's assistance information manuals. Also contact the NHTSA's Auto Safety Hotline at (800) 424-9393.

System: Interior systems; seat tracks, anchors and seats. **Vehicle:** Vans and utility vehicles equipped with bucket seats with knob-type recliner mechanisms. **Defect:** The recliner mechanism and the seat frame may have foam and/or vinyl between them, creating a "soft" joint. This soft joint results in lower than specified bolt torque, which leads to joint looseness, causing bolt fatigue and eventual bolt failure. **Consequence:** If bolt failure occurs to the driver's seat, it would allow the seat back to suddenly recline, and could result in loss of vehicle control and a vehicle crash without prior warning. **Corrective Action:** Dealers will remove the foam and/or vinyl from between the recliner mechanism and the seat frame soft joint and replace the recliner bolts.

GMC SAFARI 1990

System: Fuel return hoses. **Vehicle:** School buses and truck vans equipped with 6.0L TBI gas engines and 60-gallon fuel tanks. **Defect:** Fuel return hoses may break at either crimped coupling, causing a leakage of fuel. **Consequence:** In the event of a fuel return line separation, a fuel leak occurring in the presence of an ignition source could cause a fire. **Corrective Action:** Install a properly crimped fuel return hose.

System: Seat belt anchorage—FMVSS 210. **Vehicle:** Vans. **Defect:** Seat belt anchorage bar for rear sofa failed to sustain loads required by FMVSS 210. **Consequence:** Vehicles would not comply with FMVSS 210. **Corrective Action:** Replace noncomplying sofa bar with bar that meets requirements. **Note:** This recall is being conducted by Sherrod Vans, Inc.

System: Brakes; hydraulic; disc rotors. **Vehicle:** Light trucks and vans sold or registered in the following states: CT, IL, IN, MA, ME, MI, NH, NJ, NY, OH, PA, RI, VT and WI. **Defect:** Severe corrosion due to road salt at the joint of the stamped steel center section and the cast outer section can cause the sections to separate. **Consequence:** Separation of the rotor sections can cause loss of braking ability in the affected wheel. This could result in increased stopping distance and/or loss of vehicle control and an accident. **Corrective Action:** Replace the front brake rotors with new rotors with a corrosion-protection coating. However, if replacement of brake linings is necessary, it will be done at owner's expense, since brake linings are normal maintenance items. **Note:** The vehicles involved can be identified by the following: the 5th character of the vehicle identification number must be a *K* or *L*, and the 7th character must be *3, 4, 5, 6* or *9*. If your vehicle is presented to an authorized dealer on an agreed-upon service date, and the remedy is not provided within a reasonable amount of time and free of charge or the remedy does not correct the safety-related defect or noncompliance, please contact your nearest GMC Truck zone office. The telephone numbers of the zone offices are listed in your warranty and owner's assistance information manuals. Also contact the NHTSA's Auto Safety Hotline at (800) 424-9393.

System: Interior systems; seat tracks, anchors and seats. **Vehicle:** Vans and utility vehicles equipped with bucket seats with knob-type recliner mechanisms. **Defect:** The recliner mechanism and the seat frame may have foam and/or vinyl between them, creating a "soft" joint. This soft joint results in lower than specified bolt torque, which leads to joint looseness, causing bolt fatigue and eventual bolt failure. **Consequence:** If bolt failure occurs to the driver's seat, it would allow the seat back to suddenly recline, and could result in loss of vehicle control and a vehicle crash without prior warning. **Corrective Action:** Dealers will remove the foam and/or vinyl from between the recliner mechanism and the seat frame soft joint and replace the recliner bolts.

GMC SAFARI 1994

System: Equipment; certification labels. **Description of Noncompliance:** The manufacturer's certification label and/or the driver airbag advisory label may be missing from the vehicles, which does not conform to the requirements of 49 CFR 567. **Consequence of Noncompliance:** Owners of the vehicle would be unaware of the load capacity of the vans, the van build date, and would not have any assurance that the vans meet the federal motor vehicle safety standards. **Corrective Action:** The labels will be furnished to owners for installation on the vehicles. **Note:** If you have any questions regarding the distribution of these labels, please contact Explorer Van Service Center at (800) 828-2056. Also contact the NHTSA's Auto Safety Hotline at (800) 424-9393.

GMC SUBURBAN 1989

System: Interior systems; seat tracks, anchors and seats. **Vehicle:** Vans and utility vehicles equipped with bucket seats with knob-type recliner mechanisms. **Defect:** The recliner mechanism and the seat frame may have foam and/or vinyl between them, creating a "soft" joint. This soft joint results in lower than specified bolt torque, which leads to joint looseness, causing bolt fatigue and eventual bolt failure. **Consequence:** If bolt failure occurs to the driver's seat, it would allow the seat back to suddenly recline, and could result in loss of vehicle control and a vehicle crash without prior warning. **Corrective Action:** Dealers will remove the foam and/or vinyl from between the recliner mechanism and the seat frame soft joint and replace the recliner bolts.

HONDA

Note: If your Honda is presented to an authorized dealer at an agreed-upon service date and the remedy is not provided free of charge within a reasonable time, please contact Honda/Acura at (800) 999-1009. Also contact the NHTSA's Auto Safety Hotline at (800) 424-9393.

HONDA ACCORD 1987

System: Owner's manual information—FMVSS 210. **Vehicle:** Passenger cars and wagons. **Defect:** Owner's manual information required by FMVSS 210, sections 6a and 6b, was omitted from the manual. **Consequence:** Vehicle's manual information does not comply with FMVSS 210. **Corrective Action:** Upgrade existing manuals by inserting adhesive-backed correction pages.

System: Fuel system. **Vehicle:** Passenger cars in areas where salt and calcium chloride are used in snow and ice control. **Defect:** If the plastic coating of the fuel filler and/or breather pipe is damaged, saltwater may accumulate between the plastic coating and the steel pipes, and the accumulation could cause corrosion, which would eventually rust through the affected pipes, allowing gasoline fumes and fuel to leak. **Consequence:** Gasoline fumes and/or fuel leakage through the filler or breather pipes could result in a fire when exposed to a source of ignition. **Corrective Action:** Repairs will be made to vehicles with corroded filler or breather pipes. **Note:** Honda has included 1986 and 1987 Accords built between June 13, 1985, and September 15, 1987, as well as 1983, 1984, 1985, 1986 and 1987 Preludes built between September 9, 1982, and May 7, 1987.

HONDA ACCORD 1988

System: Owner's manual information—FMVSS 210. **Vehicle:** Passenger cars and wagons. **Defect:** Owner's manual information required by FMVSS 210, sections 6a and 6b, was omitted from the manual. **Consequence:** Vehicle's manual information does not comply with FMVSS 210. **Corrective Action:** Upgrade existing manuals by inserting adhesive-backed correction pages.

System: Interior; seat belts; belt buckles. **Vehicle:** 2-door, 4-door and 5-door passenger vehicles equipped with safety belts made by Takata Corporation. **Defect:** The front safety belt buckle release buttons can break. These red plastic release buttons are marked "press." If a button breaks, pieces can fall into the buckle assembly, causing the buckle to operate improperly. **Consequence:** The safety belts would not provide adequate protection to an occupant in a vehicle crash. **Corrective Action:** Owners should promptly check the condition and operation of both front safety belt buckles. Carefully inspect the red release buttons for any breaks or cracks. Check that both buckles are operating properly by inserting each latchplate into its buckle, tugging on the belt to make sure the latch is securely locked and then pressing the release button. The latchplate should pop out of the buckle when the button is pressed. If either release button shows any sign of breakage or cracking, or if either buckle fails to operate properly, promptly contact your authorized Honda/Acura dealer to schedule an appointment to have the buckle replaced or repaired, free of charge. The manufacturer is developing a remedy designed to prevent the failure of the buttons that are not currently broken.

HONDA ACCORD 1989

System: Interior; seat belts; belt buckles. **Vehicle:** 2-door, 4-door and 5-door passenger vehicles equipped with safety belts made by Takata Corporation. **Defect:** The front safety belt buckle release buttons can break. These red plastic release buttons are marked "press." If a button breaks, pieces can fall into the buckle assembly, causing the buckle to operate improperly. **Consequence:** The safety belts would not provide adequate protection to an occupant in a vehicle crash. **Corrective Action:** Owners should promptly check the condition and operation of both front safety belt buckles. Carefully inspect the red release buttons for any breaks or cracks. Check that both buckles are operating properly by inserting each latchplate into its buckle, tugging on the belt to make sure the latch is securely locked and then pressing the release button. The latchplate should pop out of the buckle when the button is pressed. If either release button shows any sign of breakage or cracking, or if either buckle fails to operate properly, promptly contact your authorized Honda/Acura dealer to schedule an appointment to have the buckle replaced or repaired, free of charge. The manufacturer is developing a remedy designed to prevent the failure of the buttons that are not currently broken.

HONDA ACCORD 1990

System: Safety belt. **Vehicle:** Passenger cars. **Defect:** The rear outside seating position safety belts may lock up at angles other than those required by FMVSS 209, "Seat belt assemblies." This does not conform to the motor vehicle safety standard. **Consequence:** Nonconforming safety belts cause an increased risk of injury in the event of a sudden stop or accident. **Corrective Action:** Replace the sensor in the rear seat belt retractor. **Note:** The manufacturer's petition, which requested that NHTSA determine that this FMVSS noncompliance does not create an unreasonable risk to motor vehicle safety, has been granted. Therefore, the manufacturer is not obligated to conduct an owner notification and remedy campaign.

System: Safety belt. **Vehicle:** Passenger cars; 2-door and 4-door sedans. **Defect:** The rear outside seating position safety belts may lock up at angles other than those required by FMVSS 209, "Seat belt assemblies." This does not conform to the motor vehicle safety standard. **Consequence:** Nonconforming safety belts cause an increased risk of injury in the event of a sudden stop or accident. **Corrective Action:** See note. **Note:** The manufacturer's petition, which requested that NHTSA determine that this FMVSS noncompliance does not create an unreasonable risk to motor vehicle safety, has been granted. Therefore, the manufacturer is not obligated to conduct an owner notification and remedy campaign.

System: Interior; seat belts; belt buckles. **Vehicle:** 2-door, 4-door and 5-door passenger vehicles equipped with safety belts made by Takata Corporation. **Defect:** The front safety belt buckle release buttons can break. These red plastic release buttons are marked "press." If a button breaks, pieces can fall into the buckle assembly, causing the buckle to operate improperly. **Consequence:** The safety belts would not provide adequate protection to an occupant in a vehicle crash. **Corrective Action:** Owners should promptly check the condition and operation of both front safety belt buckles. Carefully inspect the red release buttons for any breaks or cracks. Check that both buckles are operating properly by inserting each latchplate into its buckle, tugging on the belt to make sure the latch is securely locked and then pressing the release button. The latchplate should pop out of the buckle when the button is pressed. If either release button shows any sign of breakage or cracking, or if either buckle fails to operate properly, promptly contact your authorized Honda/Acura dealer to schedule an appointment to have the buckle replaced or repaired, free of charge. The manufacturer is developing a remedy designed to prevent the failure of the buttons that are not currently broken.

HONDA ACCORD 1991

System: Cargo lights. **Vehicle:** Passenger cars; station wagons. **Defect:** A washer in the cargo area light may not be properly attached, and may have fallen in the cargo light during assembly. If this occurred, and the 3-position light switch is in the middle position and the tailgate is open, the washer can cause a short circuit in the light. **Consequence:** The light short circuit could cause the switch to overheat, resulting in a cargo compartment fire. **Corrective Action:** Remove the washers behind the cargo area light and replace any damaged light assemblies.

System: Safety belt. **Vehicle:** Passenger cars. **Defect:** The rear outside seating position safety belts may lock up at angles other than those required by FMVSS 209, "Seat belt assemblies." This does not conform to the motor vehicle safety standard. **Consequence:** Nonconforming safety belts cause an increased risk of injury in the event of a sudden stop or accident. **Corrective Action:** Replace the sensor in the rear seat belt retractor. **Note:** The manufacturer's petition, which requested that NHTSA determine that this FMVSS noncompliance does not create an unreasonable risk to motor vehicle safety, has been granted. Therefore, the manufacturer is not obligated to conduct an owner notification and remedy campaign.

System: Safety belt. **Vehicle:** Station wagons. **Defect:** The rear outside seating position safety belts may lock up at angles other than those required by FMVSS 209, "Seat belt assemblies." This does not conform to the motor vehicle safety standard. **Consequence:** Nonconforming safety belts cause an increased risk of injury in the event of a sudden stop or accident. **Corrective Action:** Replace the sensor in the rear seat belt retractor.

System: Safety belt. **Vehicle:** Passenger cars; 2-door and 4-door sedans. **Defect:** The rear outside seating position safety belts may lock up at angles other than those required by FMVSS 209, "Seat belt assemblies." This does not conform to the motor vehicle safety standard. **Consequence:** Nonconforming safety belts cause an increased risk of injury in the event of a sudden stop or accident. **Corrective Action:** See note. **Note:** The manufacturer's petition, which requested that NHTSA determine that this FMVSS noncompliance does not create an unreasonable risk to motor vehicle safety, has been granted. Therefore, the manufacturer is not obligated to conduct an owner notification and remedy campaign.

System: Interior; seat belts; belt buckles. **Vehicle:** 2-door, 4-door and 5-door passenger vehicles equipped with safety belts made by Takata Corporation. **Defect:** The front safety belt buckle release buttons can break. These red plastic release buttons are marked "press." If a button breaks, pieces can fall into the buckle assembly, causing the buckle to operate improperly. **Consequence:** The safety belts would not provide adequate protection to an occupant in a vehicle crash. **Corrective Action:** Owners should promptly check the condition and operation of both front safety belt buckles. Carefully inspect the red release buttons for any breaks or cracks. Check that both buckles are operating properly by inserting each latchplate into its buckle, tugging on the belt to make sure the latch is securely locked and then pressing the release button. The latchplate should pop out of the buckle when the button is pressed. If either release button shows any sign of breakage or cracking, or if either buckle fails to operate properly, promptly contact your authorized Honda/Acura dealer to schedule an appointment to have the buckle replaced or repaired, free of charge. The manufacturer is developing a remedy designed to prevent the failure of the buttons that are not currently broken.

HONDA ACCORD 1992

System: Front seat safety belts. **Vehicle:** Passenger cars. **Defect:** The left and right seat safety belt assemblies are not interchangeable. Some left seat safety belt assemblies were installed on the right side of the car. **Consequence:** A safety belt assembly installed on the wrong side of the car can not be pulled out of the retractor because of the mounting angle, making the safety belt unusable, and the seat occupant of an unusable seat belt would be exposed to increased risk of injury in a sudden stop or accident. **Corrective Action:** Install correct seat belt assemblies on the correct side of the car. **Note:** Honda America informed this agency that all corrections were made at the factory.

System: Safety belt. **Vehicle:** Passenger cars. **Defect:** The rear outside seating position safety belts may lock up at angles other than those required by FMVSS 209, "Seat belt assemblies." This does not conform to the motor vehicle safety standard. **Consequence:** Nonconforming safety belts cause an increased risk of injury in the event of a sudden stop or accident. **Corrective Action:** Replace the sensor in the rear seat belt retractor. **Note:** The manufacturer's petition, which requested that NHTSA determine that this FMVSS noncompliance does not create an unreasonable risk to motor vehicle safety, has been granted. Therefore, the manufacturer is not obligated to conduct an owner notification and remedy campaign.

System: Safety belt. **Vehicle:** Station wagons. **Defect:** The rear outside seating position safety belts may lock up at angles other than those required by FMVSS 209, "seat belt assemblies." This does not conform to the motor vehicle safety standard. **Consequence:** Nonconforming safety belts cause an increased risk of injury in the event of a sudden stop or accident. **Corrective Action:** Replace the sensor in the rear seat belt retractor.

System: Safety belt. **Vehicle:** Passenger cars; 2-door and 4-door sedans. **Defect:** The rear outside seating position safety belts may lock up at angles other than those required by FMVSS 209, "Seat belt assemblies." This does not conform to the motor vehicle safety standard. **Consequence:** Nonconforming safety belts cause an increased risk of injury in the event of a sudden stop or accident. **Corrective Action:** See note. **Note:** The manufacturer's petition, which requested that NHTSA determine that this FMVSS noncompliance does not create an unreasonable risk to motor vehicle safety, has been granted. Therefore, the manufacturer is not obligated to conduct an owner notification and remedy campaign.

HONDA ACCORD 1993

System: Safety belt. **Vehicle:** Passenger cars. **Description of Noncompliance:** The rear outside seating position safety belts may lock up at angles other than those required by FMVSS 209, "Seat belt assemblies." This does not conform to the motor vehicle safety standard. **Consequence of Noncompliance:** Nonconforming safety belts cause an increased risk of injury in the event of a sudden stop or accident. **Corrective Action:** Replace the sensor in the rear seat belt retractor. **Note:** The manufacturer's petition, which requested that NHTSA determine that this FMVSS noncompliance does not create an unreasonable risk to motor vehicle safety, has been granted. Therefore, the manufacturer is not obligated to conduct an owner notification and remedy campaign.

System: Safety belt. **Vehicle:** Station wagons. **Defect:** The rear outside seating position safety belts may lock up at angles other than those required by FMVSS 209, "Seat belt assemblies." This does not conform to the motor vehicle safety standard. **Consequence:** Nonconforming safety belts cause an increased risk of injury in the event of a sudden stop or accident. **Corrective Action:** Replace the sensor in the rear seat belt retractor.

System: Safety belt. **Vehicle:** Passenger cars; 2-door and 4-door sedans. **Description of Noncompliance:** The rear outside seating position safety belts may lock up at angles other than those required by FMVSS 209, "Seat belt assemblies." This does not conform to the motor vehicle safety standard. **Consequence of Noncompliance:** Nonconforming safety belts cause an increased risk of injury in the event of a sudden stop or accident. **Corrective Action:** See note. **Note:** The manufacturer's petition, which requested that NHTSA determine that this FMVSS noncompliance does not create an unreasonable risk to motor vehicle safety, has been granted. Therefore, the manufacturer is not obligated to conduct an owner notification and remedy campaign.

HONDA ACCORD 1994

System: Tires; valve stem. **Vehicle:** 2-door coupes and 4-door sedans. **Defect:** The tire valve stems were damaged during the assembly process. This can cause the tire to lose air pressure. **Consequence:** Significant air loss can result in steering pull, tire overheating and eventual tire failure, which could result in an accident. **Corrective Action:** Dealer will inspect all tires to determine if the valve stems were damaged. Any damaged tire stems will be replaced. **Note:** All vehicles have been inspected and tires with damaged valve stems have been replaced. This campaign is completed.

HONDA CIVIC 1987

System: Owner's manual information—FMVSS 210. **Vehicle:** Passenger cars and wagons. **Defect:** Owner's manual information required by FMVSS 210, sections 6a and 6b, was omitted from the manual. **Consequence:** Vehicle's manual information does not comply with FMVSS 210. **Corrective Action:** Upgrade existing manuals by inserting adhesive-backed correction pages.

System: Front windshield wiper assembly. **Vehicle:** Passenger cars. **Defect:** Under high ambient temperatures, front windshield wiper contact unit could loosen and become dislodged. **Consequence:** This could result in windshield wiper failure and would affect driver visibility. **Corrective Action:** Install a contact unit holder that would prevent loosening.

System: Interior; seat belts; belt buckles. **Vehicle:** 2-door, 4-door and 5-door passenger vehicles equipped with safety belts made by Takata Corporation. **Defect:** The front safety belt buckle release buttons can break. These red plastic release buttons are marked "press." If a button breaks, pieces can fall into the buckle assembly, causing the buckle to operate improperly. **Consequence:** The safety belts would not provide adequate protection to an occupant in a vehicle crash. **Corrective Action:** Owners should promptly check the condition and operation of both front safety belt buckles. Carefully inspect the red release buttons for any breaks or cracks. Check that both buckles are operating properly by inserting each latchplate into its buckle, tugging on the belt to make sure the latch is securely locked and then pressing the release button. The latchplate should pop out of the buckle when the button is pressed. If either release button shows any sign of breakage or cracking, or if either buckle fails to operate properly, promptly contact your authorized Honda/Acura dealer to schedule an appointment to have the buckle replaced or repaired, free of charge. The manufacturer is developing a remedy designed to prevent the failure of the buttons that are not currently broken.

HONDA CIVIC 1988

System: Owner's manual information—FMVSS 210. **Vehicle:** Passenger cars and wagons. **Defect:** Owner's manual information required by FMVSS 210, sections 6a and 6b, was omitted from the manual. **Consequence:** Vehicle's manual information does not comply with FMVSS 210. **Corrective Action:** Upgrade existing manuals by inserting adhesive-backed correction pages.

System: Electronic fuel injection control unit. **Vehicle:** Passenger cars equipped with automatic transmissions. **Defect:** Electronic fuel injection control unit may cause idle speed to increase by about 550 rpm while car is stopped in gear. **Consequence:** Higher than normal idle could create potential for loss of vehicle control. **Corrective Action:** Replace electronic fuel injection control unit.

System: Interior; seat belts; belt buckles. **Vehicle:** 2-door, 4-door and 5-door passenger vehicles equipped with safety belts made by Takata Corporation. **Defect:** The front safety belt buckle release buttons can break. These red plastic release buttons are marked "press." If a button breaks, pieces can fall into the buckle assembly, causing the buckle to operate improperly. **Consequence:** The safety belts would not provide adequate protection to an occupant in a vehicle crash. **Corrective Action:** Owners should promptly check the condition and operation of both front safety belt buckles. Carefully inspect the red release buttons for any breaks or cracks. Check that both buckles are operating properly by inserting each latchplate into its buckle, tugging on the belt to make sure the latch is securely locked and then pressing the release button. The latchplate should pop out of the buckle when the button is pressed. If either release button shows any sign of breakage or cracking, or if either buckle fails to operate properly, promptly contact your authorized Honda/Acura dealer to schedule an appointment to have the buckle replaced or repaired, free of charge. The manufacturer is developing a remedy designed to prevent the failure of the buttons that are not currently broken.

HONDA CIVIC 1989

System: Interior; seat belts; belt buckles. **Vehicle:** 2-door, 4-door and 5-door passenger vehicles equipped with safety belts made by Takata Corporation. **Defect:** The front safety belt buckle release buttons can break. These red plastic release buttons are marked "press." If a button breaks, pieces can fall into the buckle assembly, causing the buckle to operate improperly. **Consequence:** The safety belts would not provide adequate protection to an occupant in a vehicle crash. **Corrective Action:** Owners should promptly check the condition and operation of both front safety belt buckles. Carefully inspect the red release buttons for any breaks or cracks. Check that both buckles are operating properly by inserting each latchplate into its buckle, tugging on the belt to make sure the latch is securely locked and then pressing the release button. The latchplate should pop out of the buckle when the button is pressed. If either release button shows any sign of breakage or cracking, or if either buckle fails to operate properly, promptly contact your authorized Honda/Acura dealer to schedule an appointment to have the buckle replaced or repaired, free of charge. The manufacturer is developing a remedy designed to prevent the failure of the buttons that are not currently broken.

HONDA CIVIC 1990

System: Windshield—FMVSS 212. **Vehicle:** Passenger cars; DX and LX sedans. **Defect:** Poor adhesion may occur between paint layers in the windshield mounting area due to defective paint batches or overspraying. **Consequence:** Paint separation in the windshield areas would lead to noncompliance with FMVSS 212 retention requirements. Loss of windshield retention ability could cause windshield to separate from vehicle without warning and harm vehicle occupants and others in the vicinity. **Corrective Action:** Reinstall windshield to ensure proper retention.

System: Transmission; park pawl. **Vehicle:** DX and LX sedans with automatic transmissions. **Defect:** Due to an improperly machined internal shaft in the transmission, the pawl mechanism may not fully engage when transmission is in the park position. **Consequence:** Vehicle could roll while the transmission is in the park position and a crash could result. **Corrective Action:** Install an improved parking pawl shaft.

System: Interior; seat belts; belt buckles. **Vehicle:** 2-door, 4-door and 5-door passenger vehicles equipped with safety belts made by Takata Corporation. **Defect:** The front safety belt buckle release buttons can break. These red plastic release buttons are marked "press." If a button breaks, pieces can fall into the buckle assembly, causing the buckle to operate improperly. **Consequence:** The safety belts would not provide adequate protection to an occupant in a vehicle crash. **Corrective Action:** Owners should promptly check the condition and operation of both front safety belt buckles. Carefully inspect the red release buttons for any breaks or cracks. Check that both buckles are operating properly by inserting each latchplate into its buckle, tugging on the belt to make sure the latch is securely locked and then pressing the release button. The latchplate should pop out of the buckle when the button is pressed. If either release button shows any sign of breakage or cracking, or if either buckle fails to operate properly, promptly contact your authorized Honda/Acura dealer to schedule an appointment to have the buckle replaced or repaired, free of charge. The manufacturer is developing a remedy designed to prevent the failure of the buttons that are not currently broken.

HONDA CIVIC 1991

System: Interior; seat belts; belt buckles. **Vehicle:** 2-door, 4-door and 5-door passenger vehicles equipped with safety belts made by Takata Corporation. **Defect:** The front safety belt buckle release buttons can break. These red plastic release buttons are marked "press." If a button breaks, pieces can fall into the buckle assembly, causing the buckle to operate improperly. **Consequence:** The safety belts would not provide adequate protection to an occupant in a vehicle crash. **Corrective Action:** Owners should promptly check the condition and operation of both front safety belt buckles. Carefully inspect the red release buttons for any breaks or cracks. Check that both buckles are operating properly by inserting each latchplate into its buckle, tugging on the belt to make sure the latch is securely locked and then pressing the release button. The latchplate should pop out of the buckle when the button is pressed. If either release button shows any sign of breakage or cracking, or if either buckle fails to operate properly, promptly contact your authorized Honda/Acura dealer to schedule an appointment to have the buckle replaced or repaired, free of charge. The manufacturer is developing a remedy designed to prevent the failure of the buttons that are not currently broken.

HONDA CIVIC 1992

System: Power train; transmission; automatic. **Vehicle:** Passenger vehicles equipped with automatic transmissions. **Defect:** A retaining clip that connects the transmission shift cable to the shift lever actuating rod can have insufficient retention pressure, and may eventually come off after repeated shift lever operation. If this happens, the position of the shift lever may not match the actual transmission gear position. **Consequence:** This could result in unanticipated vehicle movement and an accident. **Corrective Action:** Dealers will install an improved retaining clip.

HONDA CIVIC 1993

System: Power train; transmission; automatic. **Vehicle:** Passenger vehicles equipped with automatic transmissions. **Defect:** A retaining clip that connects the transmission shift cable to the shift lever actuating rod can have insufficient retention pressure, and may eventually come off after repeated shift lever operation. If this happens, the position of the shift lever may not match the actual transmission gear position. **Consequence:** This could result in unanticipated vehicle movement and an accident. **Corrective Action:** Dealers will install an improved retaining clip.

HONDA CIVIC 1994

System: Interior systems; passive restraints; airbag; passenger. **Vehicle:** Passenger cars. **Defect:** The passenger-side airbag modules contain incorrect inflators that are out of specification for the passenger-side airbag. **Consequence:** In the event of a collision, the airbag may not provide adequate protection to the passenger. **Corrective Action:** Honda dealers will replace the passenger airbag module with a module containing the correct inflator.

System: Power train; transmission; automatic. **Vehicle:** Passenger vehicles equipped with automatic transmissions. **Defect:** A retaining clip that connects the transmission shift cable to the shift lever actuating rod can have insufficient retention pressure, and may eventually come off after repeated shift lever operation. If this happens, the position of the shift lever may not match the actual transmission gear position. **Consequence:** This could result in unanticipated vehicle movement and an accident. **Corrective Action:** Dealers will install an improved retaining clip.

HONDA PRELUDE 1988

System: Throttle valve. **Vehicle:** Passenger cars. **Defect:** A small amount of coolant seepage may occur, and eventually residue may accumulate on the throttle valve. **Consequence:** Residue may cause throttle valve return-to-idle speed to be slower than normal when accelerator pedal is released. **Corrective Action:** Replace throttle body assembly.

System: Owner's manual information—FMVSS 210. **Vehicle:** Passenger cars and wagons. **Defect:** Owner's manual information required by FMVSS 210, sections 6a and 6b, was omitted from the manual. **Consequence:** Vehicle's manual information does not comply with FMVSS 210. **Corrective Action:** Upgrade existing manuals by inserting adhesive-backed correction pages.

System: Power steering. **Vehicle:** Passenger cars. **Defect:** Vibration and high underhood temperatures could cause power steering supply hose at the connector clamp seal to develop a fluid leak. **Consequence:** If the fluid contacts the hot exhaust manifold, it may cause smoke and possibly an underhood fire. **Corrective Action:** Install an improved power steering supply hose assembly.

System: Front seat anchorage brackets—FMVSS 207. **Vehicle:** Passenger cars. **Defect:** The rear inboard seat anchorage bracket for the front seats may not withstand the force required by FMVSS 207. **Consequence:** Bracket failure could result in seats becoming loose; vehicles would not comply with FMVSS 207. **Corrective Action:** Install a reinforcing plate to rear inboard seat anchorage bracket for each front seat.

System: Accelerator pedal stopper. **Vehicle:** Passenger cars. **Defect:** The accelerator pedal stopper may be bent when excessive downward force is applied after pedal has contacted the stopper. **Consequence:** This could result in loss of accelerator control should the pedal be caught and held down by the bent stopper, which could cause an accident. **Corrective Action:** Install a support to prevent stopper from bending.

System: Interior; seat belts; belt buckles. **Vehicle:** 2-door, 4-door and 5-door passenger vehicles equipped with safety belts made by Takata Corporation. **Defect:** The front safety belt buckle release buttons can break. These red plastic release buttons are marked "press." If a button breaks, pieces can fall into the buckle assembly, causing the buckle to operate improperly. **Consequence:** The safety belts would not provide adequate protection to an occupant in a vehicle crash. **Corrective Action:** Owners should promptly check the condition and operation of both front safety belt buckles. Carefully inspect the red release buttons for any breaks or cracks. Check that both buckles are operating properly by inserting each latchplate into its buckle, tugging on the belt to make sure the latch is securely locked and then pressing the release button. The latchplate should pop out of the buckle when the button is pressed. If either release button shows any sign of breakage or cracking, or if either buckle fails to operate properly, promptly contact your authorized Honda/Acura dealer to schedule an appointment to have the buckle replaced or repaired, free of charge. The manufacturer is developing a remedy designed to prevent the failure of the buttons that are not currently broken.

HYUNDAI

Note: If your Hyundai is presented to an authorized dealer on an agreed-upon service date and the remedy is not provided free of charge within a reasonable time, please contact Hyundai at (800) 829-9956. Also contact the NHTSA's Auto Safety Hotline at (800) 424-9393.

HYUNDAI EXCEL 1987

System: Brakes—FMVSS 105. **Vehicle:** Vehicles with 4- or 5-speed manual transmissions and automatic transmissions. **Defect:** Vehicle may fail to conform to the brake fade and recovery portion of FMVSS 105. **Consequence:** There may be a loss of braking efficiency during repeated hard application of brakes, which could result in a crash without prior warning. **Corrective Action:** Replace front brake pads with newly designed semimetallic brake pads.

System: Cruise control. **Vehicle:** Passenger cars with specific cruise systems (SCS). **Defect:** If cruise control main switch is in the "on" position when engine is started, system can be affected by a short-duration voltage drop caused by optional hi-power (H340) radio. **Consequence:** This could cause erratic cruise control operation, which could result in an accident. **Corrective Action:** Replace electronic control module.

System: Exhaust system. **Vehicle:** Passenger vehicles. **Defect:** Deterioration of the reed valve subassembly may lead to a malfunction within the secondary air supply portion of the emission control system. The screws that attach the reeds to the reed valve subassembly may rust and, if the rusting becomes severe, the screw heads will erode and allow the reeds to separate from the reed valve subassembly. Corrosion may also occur on the reed valve subassembly, deforming the reed seats and preventing the reeds from closing properly. Separation of the reeds from the reed valve subassembly or improper closing of the reeds allows hot exhaust gases to flow backward into the plastic secondary air filter case when the vehicle is being driven. These hot exhaust gases may melt the secondary plastic air filter case. **Consequence:** The melting plastic air filter case may lead to a fire in the engine compartment. **Corrective Action:** Replace the reed valve subassembly with one whose metal components are fabricated from corrosion-resistant stainless steel. **Note:** Hyundai Motor Company will be performing this recall for the Hyundai Excel and for the Mitsubishi Precis.

System: Power train; transmission; standard; manual. **Vehicle:** Passenger cars equipped with manual 4- or 5-speed transmissions. **Defect:** The manual transmissions may lock up from insufficient lubrication of the gears in the transmission case. This can cause the drive wheels to seize and the vehicle to come to a sudden stop. **Consequence:** Sudden stops without prior warning can cause vehicle occupants to be thrown around in the car, and also cause loss of vehicle control, which could result in an accident. **Corrective Action:** Hyundai will perform a free transmission oil change.

HYUNDAI EXCEL 1988

System: Cruise control. **Vehicle:** Passenger cars with specific cruise systems (SCS). **Defect:** If cruise control main switch is in the "on" position when engine is started, system can be affected by a short-duration voltage drop caused by optional hi-power (H340) radio. **Consequence:** This could cause erratic cruise control operation, which could result in an accident. **Corrective Action:** Replace electronic control module.

System: Exhaust system. **Vehicle:** Passenger vehicles. **Defect:** Deterioration of the reed valve subassembly may lead to a malfunction within the secondary air supply portion of the emission control system. The screws that attach the reeds to the reed valve subassembly may rust and, if the rusting becomes severe, the screw heads will erode and allow the reeds to separate from the reed valve subassembly. Corrosion may also occur on the reed valve subassembly, deforming the reed seats and preventing the reeds from closing properly. Separation of the reeds from the reed valve subassembly or improper closing of the reeds allows hot exhaust gases to flow backward into the plastic secondary air filter case when the vehicle is being driven. These hot exhaust gases may melt the secondary plastic air filter case. **Consequence:** The melting plastic air filter case may lead to a fire in the engine compartment. **Corrective Action:** Replace the reed valve subassembly with one whose metal components are fabricated from corrosion-resistant stainless steel. **Note:** Hyundai Motor Company will be performing this recall for the Hyundai Excel and for the Mitsubishi Precis.

System: Power train; transmission; standard; manual. **Vehicle:** Passenger cars equipped with manual 4- or 5-speed transmissions. **Defect:** The manual transmission may lock up from insufficient lubrication of the gears in the transmission case. This can cause the drive wheels to seize and the vehicle to come to a sudden stop. **Consequence:** Sudden stops without prior warning can cause vehicle occupants to be thrown around in the car, and also cause loss of vehicle control, which could result in an accident. **Corrective Action:** Hyundai will perform a free transmission oil change.

System: Heater; water; defroster; heater core. **Vehicle:** Passenger cars. **Defect:** The heater control valve stem does not meet the material specifications. High coolant temperatures can cause the stem to leak. **Consequence:** This can result in a burn injury to the front seat passenger's feet and legs. **Corrective Action:** Dealers will inspect and replace defective valve stems.

HYUNDAI EXCEL 1989

System: Cruise control. **Vehicle:** Passenger cars with specific cruise systems (SCS). **Defect:** If cruise control main switch is in the "on" position when engine is started, system can be affected by a short-duration voltage drop caused by optional hi-power (H340) radio. **Consequence:** This could cause erratic cruise control operation, which could result in an accident. **Corrective Action:** Replace electronic control module.

System: Exhaust system. **Vehicle:** Passenger vehicles. **Defect:** Deterioration of the reed valve subassembly may lead to a malfunction within the secondary air supply portion of the emission control system. The screws that attach the reeds to the reed valve subassembly may rust and, if the rusting becomes severe, the screw heads will erode and allow the reeds to separate from the reed valve subassembly. Corrosion may also occur on the reed valve subassembly, deforming the reed seats and preventing the reeds from closing properly. Separation of the reeds from the reed valve subassembly or improper closing of the reeds allows hot exhaust gases to flow backward into the plastic secondary air filter case when the vehicle is being driven. These hot exhaust gases may melt the secondary plastic air filter case. **Consequence:** The melting plastic air filter case may lead to a fire in the engine compartment. **Corrective Action:** Replace the reed valve subassembly with one whose metal components are fabricated from corrosion-resistant stainless steel. **Note:** Hyundai Motor Company will be performing this recall for the Hyundai Excel and for the Mitsubishi Precis.

System: Power train; transmission; standard; manual. **Vehicle:** Passenger cars equipped with manual 4- or 5-speed transmissions. **Defect:** The manual transmission may lock up from insufficient lubrication of the gears in the transmission case. This can cause the drive wheels to seize and the vehicle to come to a sudden stop. **Consequence:** Sudden stops without prior warning can cause vehicle occupants to be thrown around in the car, and also cause loss of vehicle control, which could result in an accident. **Corrective Action:** Hyundai will perform a free transmission oil change.

System: Heater; water; defroster; heater core. **Vehicle:** Passenger cars. **Defect:** The heater control valve stem does not meet the material specifications. High coolant temperatures can cause the stem to leak. **Consequence:** This can result in a burn injury to the front seat passenger's feet and legs. **Corrective Action:** Dealers will inspect and replace defective valve stems.

HYUNDAI EXCEL 1990

System: Front wheels. **Vehicle:** Passenger cars. **Defect:** Lock washer located under the nut that secures the front hub to the driveshaft may have had improper heat treatment and could crack. **Consequence:** This could cause wheel bearing freeplay, and could result in bearing damage and possible loss of vehicle control through wheel failure. **Corrective Action:** Replace lock washer on each front wheel and repair area around lock washer as necessary.

System: Fuel; fuel systems—FMVSS 301. **Vehicle:** 3- and 4-door passenger vehicles. **Defect:** The vehicles failed the lateral moving barrier impact test requirements of FMVSS 301, "Fuel system integrity." The fuel leakage from the gas tank exceeded the maximum allowable amount of spillage. **Consequence:** In the event of an accident, the fuel spillage can result in a fire if exposed to a source of ignition. **Corrective Action:** Hyundai has developed an appropriate countermeasure that will comply with all requirements of FMVSS 301.

HYUNDAI EXCEL 1991

System: Fuel; fuel systems—FMVSS 301. **Vehicle:** 3- and 4-door passenger vehicles. **Defect:** The vehicles failed the lateral moving barrier impact test requirements of FMVSS 301, "Fuel system integrity." The fuel leakage from the gas tank exceeded the maximum allowable amount of spillage. **Consequence:** In the event of an accident, the fuel spillage can result in a fire if exposed to a source of ignition. **Corrective Action:** Hyundai has developed an appropriate countermeasure that will comply with all requirements of FMVSS 301.

HYUNDAI SONATA 1989

System: Engine cooling hose clamp. **Vehicle:** Passenger cars with 2.4L engines. **Defect:** The spring clamp tangs on the coolant bypass hose may contact and possibly damage the engine fuel supply hose. **Consequence:** Fuel could leak from the damaged hose into the engine compartment and could result in a fire. **Corrective Action:** Rotate spring clamp to prevent contact with fuel hose; replace damaged hoses.

System: Secondary hood latch. **Vehicle:** Passenger cars. **Defect:** Insufficient clearance could cause the safety catch on the secondary hood latch striker to bind. **Consequence:** If primary latch is released or if hood is not completely closed, hood could fly open while vehicle is in motion; this would block driver's vision and could result in an accident. **Corrective Action:** Replace hood latch striker assembly.

System: Interior systems; passive restraint; belts. **Vehicle:** Passenger vehicles equipped with motorized passive restraint systems. **Defect:** The motorized shoulder belt can travel slowly or chatter in the track, and may eventually stop tracking and become inoperative. **Consequence:** Slowing, chattering or failure of the motorized shoulder belt may discourage use of the restraint system, increasing the risk of injury in the event of a sudden stop or accident. **Corrective Action:** Dealers will lubricate the track assembly and, if any systems are found inoperative, the system will be repaired or replaced as required.

HYUNDAI SONATA 1990

System: Engine cooling hose clamp. **Vehicle:** Passenger cars with 2.4L engines. **Defect:** The spring clamp tangs on the coolant bypass hose may contact and possibly damage the engine fuel supply hose. **Consequence:** Fuel could leak from the damaged hose into the engine compartment and could result in a fire. **Corrective Action:** Rotate spring clamp to prevent contact with fuel hose; replace damaged hoses.

System: Secondary hood latch. **Vehicle:** Passenger cars. **Defect:** Insufficient clearance could cause the safety catch on the secondary hood latch striker to bind. **Consequence:** If primary latch is released or if hood is not completely closed, hood could fly open while vehicle is in motion; this would block driver's vision and could result in an accident. **Corrective Action:** Replace hood latch striker assembly.

System: Interior systems; passive restraint; belts. **Vehicle:** Passenger vehicles equipped with motorized passive restraint systems. **Defect:** The motorized shoulder belt can travel slowly or chatter in the track, and may eventually stop tracking and become inoperative. **Consequence:** Slowing, chattering or failure of the motorized shoulder belt may discourage use of the restraint system, increasing the risk of injury in the event of a sudden stop or accident. **Corrective Action:** Dealers will lubricate the track assembly and, if any systems are found inoperative, the system will be repaired or replaced as required.

HYUNDAI SONATA 1991

System: Interior systems; passive restraint; belts. **Vehicle:** Passenger vehicles equipped with motorized passive restraint systems. **Defect:** The motorized shoulder belt can travel slowly or chatter in the track, and may eventually stop tracking and become inoperative. **Consequence:** Slowing, chattering or failure of the motorized shoulder belt may discourage use of the restraint system, increasing the risk of injury in the event of a sudden stop or accident. **Corrective Action:** Dealers will lubricate the track assembly and, if any systems are found inoperative, the system will be repaired or replaced as required.

ISUZU

Note: If your Isuzu is presented to the dealer from whom you purchased the item on an agreed-upon service date and the remedy is not provided or the remedy does not correct the safety-related defect or noncompliance, please contact Reese Products Warranty Department at (800) 326-1090, ext. 203. Also contact the NHTSA's Auto Safety Hotline at (800) 424-9393.

ISUZU TRUCK RODEO 1991

System: Transmission. **Vehicle:** Multipurpose passenger vehicles with V6 engines, and automatic transmission vehicles. **Defect:** The transmission fluid level gauges (dipsticks) installed in these vehicles are not to designed specifications. The gauge indicates that transmission fluid should be added when it is at the correct level. **Consequence:** Adding more transmission fluid than required will cause the fluid to leak through the fluid level gauge tube onto the manifold as the engine temperature rises. This creates a potential for a fire. **Corrective Action:** Replace oil level gauge and notify owners to use only the specified amount of automatic transmission fluid.

ISUZU TRUCK TROOPER 1988

System: Rear heater. **Vehicle:** Multipurpose vehicles equipped with rear heaters. **Defect:** Due to insufficient clearance between a bolt that fixes the heater to the vehicle body and a fuel delivery pipe, and between a rear heater hose clip, use under severe conditions could cause pipe rupture and fuel leakage. **Consequence:** This could result in a fire. **Corrective Action:** Install new lines and a clip.

System: Trailer hitch. **Equipment Description:** Reese class II trailer hitch, part 06070. **Defect:** The weld on the receiver unit of the trailer hitch can break. **Consequence:** If the failure occurs, the trailer can separate from the towing vehicle, which could result in a vehicle crash without warning. **Corrective Action:** Replace the trailer hitch.

ISUZU TRUCK TROOPER 1990

System: Engine oil cooler hose. **Vehicle:** Multipurpose passenger vehicles with V6 engines. **Defect:** Improperly installed hose on the oil cooler could come in contact with the exhaust manifold and could melt. **Consequence:** Engine oil could leak out, with potential for engine seizure and damage, which could result in a fire. **Corrective Action:** Properly install cooler hose clip to prevent contact with exhaust manifold.

System: Transmission oil level gauge. **Vehicle:** Multipurpose passenger vehicles with V6 engines and only automatic transmission vehicles. **Defect:** Putting in more transmission oil than specified can cause oil to bleed through the air groove onto the exhaust manifold if oil temperature rises. **Consequence:** This could cause smoke emission from the manifold, which could ignite rubber hoses and result in a fire. **Corrective Action:** Replace oil level gauge and notify owners to use only the specified amount of automatic transmission fluid.

System: Trailer hitch. **Equipment Description:** Reese class II trailer hitch, part 06070. **Defect:** The weld on the receiver unit of the trailer hitch can break. **Consequence:** If the failure occurs, the trailer can separate from the towing vehicle, which could result in a vehicle crash without warning. **Corrective Action:** Replace the trailer hitch.

ISUZU TRUCK TROOPER 1991

System: Engine oil cooler hose. **Vehicle:** Multipurpose passenger vehicles with V6 engines. **Defect:** Improperly installed hose on the oil cooler could come in contact with the exhaust manifold and could melt. **Consequence:** Engine oil could leak out, with potential for engine seizure and damage, which could result in a fire. **Corrective Action:** Properly install cooler hose clip to prevent contact with exhaust manifold.

System: Transmission oil level gauge. **Vehicle:** Multipurpose passenger vehicles with V6 engines and only automatic transmission vehicles. **Defect:** Putting in more transmission oil than specified can cause oil to bleed through the air groove onto the exhaust manifold if oil temperature rises. **Consequence:** This could cause smoke emission from the manifold, which could ignite rubber hoses and result in a fire. **Corrective Action:** Replace oil level gauge and notify owners to use only the specified amount of automatic transmission fluid.

System: Trailer hitch. **Equipment Description:** Reese class II trailer hitch, part 06070. **Defect:** The weld on the receiver unit of the trailer hitch can break. **Consequence:** If the failure occurs, the trailer can separate from the towing vehicle, which could result in a vehicle crash without warning. **Corrective Action:** Replace the trailer hitch.

ISUZU TRUCK TROOPER II 1988

System: Rear disc brakes. **Vehicle:** Multipurpose vehicles. **Defect:** Guide pin on rear disc brake caliper support could have loosened during transport and would no longer hold the caliper in correct position. **Consequence:** This could result in brake drag, premature brake pad wear and partial loss of braking power, with the potential for an accident. **Corrective Action:** Install brake caliper guide pin kit.

System: Rear heater. **Vehicle:** Multipurpose vehicles equipped with rear heaters. **Defect:** Due to insufficient clearance between a bolt that fixes the heater to the vehicle body and a fuel delivery pipe, and between a rear heater hose clip, use under severe conditions could cause pipe rupture and fuel leakage. **Consequence:** This could result in a fire. **Corrective Action:** Install new lines and a clip.

System: Trailer hitch. **Equipment Description:** Reese class II trailer hitch, part 06070. **Defect:** The weld on the receiver unit of the trailer hitch can break. **Consequence:** If the failure occurs, the trailer can separate from the towing vehicle, which could result in a vehicle crash without warning. **Corrective Action:** Replace the trailer hitch.

JAGUAR

Note: If your Jaguar is presented to an authorized dealer on an agreed-upon service date and the remedy is not provided within a reasonable time and free of charge, or the remedy does not correct the defect or noncompliance, please contact the NHTSA's Auto Safety Hotline at (800) 424-9393.

JAGUAR XJ6 1989

System: High-pressure hose. **Vehicle:** Passenger cars; 4-door sedans. **Defect:** High-pressure fluid supply hose could rupture, causing loss of fluid of the brake power assist system. **Consequence:** Loss of fluid could lead to loss of power assist to the braking system, which may result in loss of vehicle control and an accident; the expelled fluid from the hose failure could cause an engine compartment fire. **Corrective Action:** Install new power hydraulic hose of a different specification.

System: Brake accumulator switch. **Vehicle:** Passenger cars. **Defect:** Brake accumulator switch, which controls hydraulic fluid flow to and from the engine-driven pump, could leak, causing loss of fluid in the power brake assist system. This leak is also in the vicinity of electrical wiring. **Consequence:** The leaking brake accumulator switch could cause electrical power interruption and could cause the assist feature of brakes not to recharge. Also, fluid loss could lead to sudden loss of power assistance to the braking system, which could result in loss of vehicle control and an accident. **Corrective Action:** Replace brake accumulator switches with revised seals.

System: Interior systems; passive restraints; belts. **Vehicle:** Sedan and coupe passenger vehicles. **Defect:** The normal lockup function of the automatic (passive) belt reel can cause the belt motor winch assembly to lock up such that the passive belt system will not deploy and/or function or gets stuck at various points along the track, causing kinking or breaking of its cable or detachment of the tongue. **Consequence:** If this occurs, the occupants of the vehicle cannot use the safety belts, increasing the risk of injury in the event of a sudden stop or accident. **Corrective Action:** Jaguar will repair the passive belt system if this problem occurs or has occurred. Jaguar will notify owners of the existence of a lifetime warranty on components of the automatic (passive) belt system.

JEEP

Note: If your Jeep is presented to an authorized dealer on an agreed-upon service date and the remedy is not provided free of charge within a reasonable time, please contact Chrysler at (800) 853-1403. Also contact the NHTSA's Auto Safety Hotline at (800) 424-9393.

JEEP CHEROKEE 1987

System: Steering linkage couplers. **Vehicle:** Multipurpose passenger vehicles. **Defect:** Steering linkage couplers remained in acid etching bath too long. **Consequence:** Couplers could be out of tolerance, resulting in steering wheel misalignment, with eventual loss of vehicle control. **Corrective Action:** Replace out-of-tolerance steering linkage couplers.

System: Engine manifold—fuel hose. **Vehicle:** Multipurpose vehicles equipped with I-6 engines. **Defect:** A stud may have been installed on top of the intake manifold of engine that could contact the fuel supply hose. **Consequence:** Chafing of the fuel hose could occur, which could result in a fuel leak. **Corrective Action:** Remove stud and replace fuel supply hose and line assembly on vehicles with accumulated mileage.

System: Cruise control. **Vehicle:** Multipurpose vehicles with cruise control. **Defect:** Cruise control module could have inconsistent cruise control operation. **Consequence:** Inconsistent cruise control operation could result in loss of control and an accident. **Corrective Action:** Replace module, as necessary.

System: Throttle—accelerator. **Vehicle:** Multipurpose vehicles equipped with 4.0L engines. **Defect:** Vehicle may contain an out-of-tolerance throttle body. **Consequence:** This could prevent the accelerator from returning to idle when released. **Corrective Action:** Replace suspect throttle bodies.

System: Power brakes. **Vehicle:** Vehicles equipped with 2.1L turbo diesel engine. **Defect:** Brake booster vacuum reservoir canisters may develop leaks due to bumper impact. **Consequence:** This would result in loss of power brake assist and an increase in stopping distance. **Corrective Action:** Replace brake booster vacuum canisters with new type canisters; also install a restriction orifice to ensure sufficient vacuum in event canister leakage occurs.

JEEP CHEROKEE 1989

System: Throttle position sensor. **Vehicle:** Multipurpose vehicles equipped with 4.0L engine and automatic transmission. **Defect:** Malfunction of fuel injection system throttle position sensor could cause intermittent high engine idle speed. **Consequence:** High engine idle when car is first placed in gear could result in unexpected acceleration. **Corrective Action:** Replace throttle position sensors with sensors that will send correct signals to the fuel injection system.

System: Hydraulic fluid contamination; antilock brake system (ABS). **Vehicle:** Multipurpose vehicles equipped with antilock brake system. **Defect:** There may be hydraulic fluid contamination from condensation formation that can plug the antilock brake system booster pump filter; stress corrosion of the master cylinder snap ring has been traced to chlorine leaking from the low-pressure hydraulic hose, which may cause it to break; front brake hose to tire interference may cause failure of the brake hose. **Consequence:** Contamination of the hydraulic fluid can cause malfunctioning of the antilock brake system; low-pressure hose leakage causes loss of brake fluid and also results in corrosion and failure of the master cylinder snap ring, resulting in complete brake failure; failure of the front brake hose due to hose to tire interference will cause failure of one-half of the brake system, resulting in a longer stopping distance than expected. **Corrective Action:** Replace antilock brake system low-pressure hose; rebuild master brake cylinder; inspect and service interference problems; replace front brake hose as necessary.

JEEP CHEROKEE 1990

System: Throttle position sensor. **Vehicle:** Multipurpose vehicles equipped with 4.0L engine and automatic transmission. **Defect:** Malfunction of fuel injection system throttle position sensor could cause intermittent high engine idle speed. **Consequence:** High engine idle when car is first placed in gear could result in unexpected acceleration. **Corrective Action:** Replace throttle position sensors with sensors that will send correct signals to the fuel injection system.

System: Hydraulic fluid contamination; antilock brake system (ABS). **Vehicle:** Multipurpose vehicles equipped with antilock brake system. **Defect:** There may be hydraulic fluid contamination from condensation formation that can plug the antilock brake system booster pump filter; stress corrosion of the master cylinder snap ring has been traced to chlorine leaking from the low-pressure hydraulic hose, which may cause it to break; front brake hose to tire interference may cause failure of the brake hose. **Consequence:** Contamination of the hydraulic fluid can cause malfunctioning of the antilock brake system; low-pressure hose leakage causes loss of brake fluid and also results in corrosion and failure of the master cylinder snap ring, resulting in complete brake failure; failure of the front brake hose due to hose to tire interference will cause failure of one-half of the brake system, resulting in a longer stopping distance than expected. **Corrective Action:** Replace antilock brake system low-pressure hose; rebuild master brake cylinder; inspect and service interference problems; replace front brake hose as necessary.

System: Antilock brake system; antilock brake system high-pressure hose attachment to end unit. **Vehicle:** Multipurpose passenger vehicle. **Defect:** Improper insertion and/or crimping of the hose-to-end fittings of the high-pressure hose on the antilock brake system can cause detachment of the hose from the antilock brake system, and discharge of hydraulic fluid. **Consequence:** Detachment of the hose from the antilock brake system causes the loss of the antilock brake system function and hydraulic brake assist, leaving only manual brakes and decreasing stopping ability, which could result in an accident. Discharge of hydraulic fluid in the area of the hot exhaust system could result in an engine compartment fire. **Corrective Action:** Replace the antilock brake system high-pressure hose.

JEEP CHEROKEE 1991

System: Rear wheel brake tube. **Vehicle:** Multipurpose 4-wheel drive vehicles. **Defect:** Suspension jounce (bounce) bumper could contact left rear wheel brake tube when suspension is at full jounce. **Consequence:** Contact at full jounce may cause the brake tube to collapse and restrict the hydraulic brake fluid pressure to the left rear brake, which affects the braking capability of the vehicle. **Corrective Action:** Replace left rear brake tube with tube designed to eliminate contact with bumper.

System: Brake tubes. **Vehicle:** Multipurpose passenger vehicles equipped with antilock brake system (ABS). **Defect:** Improperly installed brake fluid tube may allow the tube to contact the steering intermediate shaft, damaging the tube. **Consequence:** Brake fluid leakage could occur and result in partial loss of braking capability. **Corrective Action:** Reposition brake tube to avoid contact with steering shaft; also replace any damaged brake tubes.

System: Antilock brake system; antilock brake system high-pressure hose attachment to end unit. **Vehicle:** Multipurpose passenger vehicle. **Defect:** Improper insertion and/or crimping of the hose-to-end fittings of the high-pressure hose on the antilock brake system can cause detachment of the hose from the antilock brake system, and discharge of hydraulic fluid. **Consequence:** Detachment of the hose from the antilock brake system causes the loss of the antilock brake system function and hydraulic brake assist, leaving only manual brakes and decreasing stopping ability, which could result in an accident. Discharge of hydraulic fluid in the area of the hot exhaust system could result in an engine compartment fire. **Corrective Action:** Replace the antilock brake system high pressure hose.

JEEP CHEROKEE 1992

System: Safety belts—FMVSS 209. **Vehicle:** Vans, light trucks and multipurpose vehicles. **Defect:** Front outboard seat belt assemblies do not have the properly marked label with manufacturer information. **Consequence:** The seat belt assemblies do not comply with FMVSS 209. **Corrective Action:** Chrysler has not proposed a corrective action for this safety defect. **Note:** The manufacturer's petition, which requested that NHTSA determine that this FMVSS noncompliance does not create an unreasonable risk to motor vehicle safety, has been granted. Therefore, the manufacturer is not obligated to conduct an owner notification and remedy campaign.

JEEP CHEROKEE 1993

System: Tire certification labels—FMVSS 120. **Vehicle:** Utility vehicles with 4.0L engines. **Defect:** The tire and wheel specification information on the certification label indicates a minimum tire size larger than the tire actually fitted to the vehicle. This does not comply with FMVSS 120, "Tire selection and rims." **Consequence:** Installation of the wrong size tires to the rim could result in loss of vehicle control. **Corrective Action:** Provide correct certification labels to vehicle owners for application to the vehicles.

JEEP CHEROKEE 1994

System: Interior systems: restraint safety belt anchor and attachment— FMVSS 210. **Vehicle:** Multipurpose passenger vehicle. **Defect:** The two rear inboard safety belt attachment bolts may have inadequate thread engagement into the floor pan anchor nuts. **Consequence:** The safety belt attachment bolts may not support the load of rear seat passengers in the event of a sudden stop or accident; the assembly fails to comply with the static load requirements of FMVSS 210, "Seat belt assembly anchorages." The inability to support the load of rear seat passengers increases the risk of injury to seat occupants. **Corrective Action:** Replace the two inboard safety belt anchor bolts with longer bolts on all vehicles. **Note:** If you have any problem obtaining the needed repair, please contact the Chrysler zone service office in your area. (It is listed under "Service Assistance" in your owner's manual.) A zone representative will arrange for prompt attention to your vehicle. Also, please contact the NHTSA's Auto Safety Hotline at (800) 424-9393.

JEEP CHEROKEE 1995

System: Interior systems; passive restraint; airbag; driver. **Vehicle:** Multipurpose passenger vehicles. **Defect:** Certain of the driver's-side airbag modules were assembled without an arming lever. **Consequence:** This condition will cause the airbag to not deploy in the event of a vehicle accident, increasing the potential for personal injury. **Corrective Action:** Dealers will inspect the vehicles for the presence of the airbag module arming lever and will replace those airbag modules that are missing a lever.

System: Emergency parking brake; mechanical; release. **Vehicle:** Multipurpose passenger vehicles. **Defect:** The parking brake handle release button can separate from the parking brake handle assembly, causing the parking brake to be inoperative. **Consequence:** The parking brake may not hold, causing the vehicle to roll inadvertently. **Corrective Action:** Dealers will replace the parking brake handle assembly.

JEEP GRAND CHEROKEE 1993

System: Brakes. **Vehicle:** Grand Cherokee and Grand Wagoneer utility vehicles. **Defect:** The retainer clip that secures the master cylinder input rod to the brake pedal was not installed properly, and could work loose. **Consequence:** Disengagement of the retainer clip will allow free play in the attachment and can allow the input rod to separate from the brake pedal, causing complete loss of brake application, which could result in an accident. **Corrective Action:** Improperly installed retainer clips will be removed and new retainer clips will be properly installed.

System: Front suspension. **Vehicle:** Sport utility vehicles. **Defect:** The eccentric cam adjuster bolts in both front lower suspension arm-to-front axle bracket attachments may fail due to assembly misalignment. **Consequence:** Cam bolt failures cause the vehicle to pull to one side when the brakes are applied, resulting in a possible loss of vehicle control and an accident. **Corrective Action:** Replace the front suspension cam bolts, cam washers, and nuts with components of a different design.

System: Structure; liftgate. **Vehicle:** Utility vehicles; Grand Cherokee and Grand Wagoneer. **Defect:** Grease applied to the liftgate latch rubber bumpers to ease component assembly caused the bumper to swell, interfering with the movement of the liftgate latch pawl. This prevents the liftgate from latching when closed and difficult to open when latched. **Consequence:** An unlatched liftgate can open while the vehicle is in motion, and could result in an occupant falling out. **Corrective Action:** Replace the liftgate assembly on affected vehicles.

System: Steering; column shaft; upper. **Vehicle:** Multipurpose passenger vehicles. **Defect:** The molded plastic pin that connects the upper steering column shaft and the lower column shaft may have been sheared prior to installation of the steering column assembly into the vehicle. If this occurred, the upper steering shaft will separate from the lower steering shaft. **Consequence:** If the upper and lower steering shafts separate, complete loss of steering control will occur, which could result in an accident. **Corrective Action:** A restraining sleeve will be added to the intermediate shaft to limit the amount of steering shaft movement available. **Note:** If you have a problem obtaining the needed repair, please contact the Chrysler zone office in your area. It is listed under "Service Assistance" in your owner's manual. A zone representative will arrange for prompt attention to your vehicle. Also contact the NHTSA's Auto Safety Hotline at (800) 424-9393.

JEEP WRANGLER 1987

System: Wheel lug nuts—steering shaft—clamp bolts. **Vehicle:** Multipurpose passenger vehicle. **Defect:** The wheel lug nuts may have been improperly tightened. Also, the steering shaft clamp bolts may not be properly tightened. **Consequence:** Improperly tightened wheel lug nuts may cause the lugs to break, and eventually result in the wheel falling off. Improperly tightened steering shaft clamp bolt may cause complete loss of steering ability. Either of these conditions could result in a loss of steering control, and a crash could occur without prior warning. **Corrective Action:** Properly tighten both wheel lug nuts and steering shaft clamp bolts.

System: Cruise control. **Vehicle:** Multipurpose vehicles with cruise control. **Defect:** Cruise control module could have inconsistent cruise control operation. **Consequence:** Inconsistent cruise control operation could result in loss of control and an accident. **Corrective Action:** Replace module as necessary.

System: Visual; windshield frame and wiper linkage. **Vehicle:** Multipurpose vehicles. **Defect:** Windshield frame metal may crack at the wiper arm pivot mountings due to metal stress during wiper operation. **Consequence:** This can cause dislocation and binding of the wiper system linkage which, in inclement weather, could affect driver visibility and result in an accident. **Corrective Action:** Retrofit with a windshield frame reinforcement at the wiper pivot locations, and redesigned linkage components to reduce stress at the pivot mountings. **Note:** The manufacturer began including a windshield frame reinforcement in its vehicle production as of October 13, 1988. 1989 models produced before October 13, 1988, are eligible for this recall.

System: Brakes. **Vehicle:** Utility vehicles. **Defect:** On 1987 through early 1990 models, both front brake hoses can wear due to direct contact with the wheel-opening splash shields. On the late 1990 through 1992 models, periodic rubbing contact of the left front brake hose can occur due to movement of the splash shield in certain vehicle operating conditions. **Consequence:** Either condition can cause loss of front brake system functions, resulting in increased stopping distances and an increased risk of vehicle accident. **Corrective Action:** The 1987 to 1990 model vehicles will have both splash shields replaced, and both front brake hoses replaced as necessary. All affected late 1990 through 1992 model year vehicles will have additional fasteners installed to further secure the left side splash shield. Also, the left front brake hose will be inspected and replaced as necessary.

System: Fuel; fuel pump. **Vehicle:** Multipurpose passenger vehicles equipped with plastic fuel tanks. **Defect:** The fuel tank sending unit gasket can crack, causing fuel and fuel vapor leaks. **Consequence:** Fuel and fuel vapor leaked from the fuel tank can result in fire when exposed to a source of ignition. **Corrective Action:** Replace the fuel tank sending unit gasket.

JEEP WRANGLER 1988

System: Visual; windshield frame and wiper linkage. **Vehicle:** Multipurpose vehicles. **Defect:** Windshield frame metal may crack at the wiper arm pivot mountings due to metal stress during wiper operation. **Consequence:** This can cause dislocation and binding of the wiper system linkage which, in inclement weather, could affect driver visibility and result in an accident. **Corrective Action:** Retrofit with a windshield frame reinforcement at the wiper pivot locations, and redesigned linkage components to reduce stress at the pivot mountings. **Note:** The manufacturer began including a windshield frame reinforcement in its vehicle production as of October 13, 1988. 1989 Models produced before October 13, 1988, are eligible for this recall.

System: Brakes. **Vehicle:** Utility vehicles. **Defect:** On 1987 through early 1990 models, both front brake hoses can wear due to direct contact with the wheel-opening splash shields. On the late 1990 through 1992 models, periodic rubbing contact of the left front brake hose can occur due to movement of the splash shield in certain vehicle operating conditions. **Consequence:** Either condition can cause loss of front brake system functions, resulting in increased stopping distances and an increased risk of vehicle accident. **Corrective Action:** The 1987 to 1990 model vehicles will have both splash shields replaced, and both front brake hoses replaced as necessary. All affected late 1990 through 1992 model year vehicles will have additional fasteners installed to further secure the left side splash shield. Also, the left front brake hose will be inspected and replaced as necessary.

System: Fuel; fuel pump. **Vehicle:** Multipurpose passenger vehicles equipped with plastic fuel tanks. **Defect:** The fuel tank sending unit gasket can crack, causing fuel and fuel vapor leaks. **Consequence:** Fuel and fuel vapor leaked from the fuel tank can result in fire when exposed to a source of ignition. **Corrective Action:** Replace the fuel tank sending unit gasket.

JEEP WRANGLER 1989

System: Fuel tank—FMVSS 301. **Vehicle:** Multipurpose vehicles equipped with metal fuel tanks. **Defect:** In a rear-impact collision, fuel tank may leak fuel in excess of amount allowed by FMVSS 301 because of misbuilt fuel tank skid plates. **Consequence:** In the presence of an ignition source, this could result in a fire. Vehicle would not comply with FMVSS 301. **Corrective Action:** Install flange on fuel tank skid plate.

System: Brakes. **Vehicle:** Utility vehicles. **Defect:** On 1987 through early 1990 models, both front brake hoses can wear due to direct contact with the wheel-opening splash shields. On the late 1990 through 1992 models, periodic rubbing contact of the left front brake hose can occur due to movement of the splash shield in certain vehicle operating conditions. **Consequence:** Either condition can cause loss of front brake system functions, resulting in increased stopping distances and an increased risk of vehicle accident. **Corrective Action:** The 1987 to 1990 model vehicles will have both splash shields replaced, and both front brake hoses replaced as necessary. All affected late 1990 through 1992 model year vehicles will have additional fasteners installed to further secure the left side splash shield. Also, the left front brake hose will be inspected and replaced as necessary.

System: Visual; windshield frame and wiper linkage. **Vehicle:** Multipurpose vehicles. **Defect:** Windshield frame metal may crack at the wiper arm pivot mountings due to metal stress during wiper operation. **Consequence:** This can cause dislocation and binding of the wiper system linkage which, in inclement weather, could affect driver visibility and result in an accident. **Corrective Action:** Retrofit with a windshield frame reinforcement at the wiper pivot locations, and install new redesigned linkage components to reduce stress at the pivot mountings. **Note:** The manufacturer began including a windshield frame reinforcement in its vehicle production as of October 13, 1988. 1989 models produced before October 13, 1988, are eligible for this recall.

System: Fuel; fuel pump. **Vehicle:** Multipurpose passenger vehicles equipped with plastic fuel tanks. **Defect:** The fuel tank sending unit gasket can crack, causing fuel and fuel vapor leaks. **Consequence:** Fuel and fuel vapor leaked from the fuel tank can result in fire when exposed to a source of ignition. **Corrective Action:** Replace the fuel tank sending unit gasket.

JEEP WRANGLER 1990

System: Brakes. **Vehicle:** Utility vehicles. **Defect:** On 1987 through early 1990 models, both front brake hoses can wear due to direct contact with the wheel-opening splash shields. On the late 1990 through 1992 models, periodic rubbing contact of the left front brake hose can occur due to movement of the splash shield in certain vehicle operating conditions. **Consequence:** Either condition can cause loss of front brake system functions, resulting in increased stopping distances and an increased risk of vehicle accident. **Corrective Action:** The 1987 to 1990 model vehicles will have both splash shields replaced, and both front brake hoses replaced as necessary. All affected late 1990 through 1992 model year vehicles will have additional fasteners installed to further secure the left side splash shield. Also, the left front brake hose will be inspected and replaced as necessary.

System: Fuel; fuel pump. **Vehicle:** Multipurpose passenger vehicles equipped with plastic fuel tanks. **Defect:** The fuel tank sending unit gasket can crack, causing fuel and fuel vapor leaks. **Consequence:** Fuel and fuel vapor leaked from the fuel tank can result in fire when exposed to a source of ignition. **Corrective Action:** Replace the fuel tank sending unit gasket.

JEEP WRANGLER 1991

System: Certification label—FMVSS 120. **Vehicle:** Multipurpose passenger vehicle. **Defect:** Certification label does not contain required tire and wheel information. **Consequence:** Vehicles would not comply with FMVSS 120. **Corrective Action:** Install supplemental tire information labels adjacent to certification labels.

System: Brakes. **Vehicle:** Utility vehicles. **Defect:** On 1987 through early 1990 models, both front brake hoses can wear due to direct contact with the wheel-opening splash shields. On the late 1990 through 1992 models, periodic rubbing contact of the left front brake hose can occur due to movement of the splash shield in certain vehicle operating conditions. **Consequence:** Either condition can cause loss of front brake system functions, resulting in increased stopping distances and an increased risk of vehicle accident. **Corrective Action:** The 1987 to 1990 model vehicles will have both splash shields replaced, and both front brake hoses replaced as necessary. All affected late 1990 through 1992 model year vehicles will have additional fasteners installed to further secure the left side splash shield. Also, the left front brake hose will be inspected and replaced as necessary.

System: Ignition system. **Vehicle:** Multipurpose passenger vehicles equipped with manual transmissions. **Defect:** Salt corrosion products between the starter solenoid wire and the adjacent battery feed in the bulkhead connector may short these connections, causing the circuit to bypass the ignition key control of the starter motor solenoid. The car can start without the starter sequence being initiated by the ignition key in the ignition lock. **Consequence:** The unintended start of a vehicle with a manual transmission left in a drive gear can result in a runaway vehicle. **Corrective Action:** The starter solenoid wiring will be separated from the battery feed wire by relocating it within the bulkhead connector on affected vehicles.

System: Fuel; fuel pump. **Vehicle:** Multipurpose passenger vehicles equipped with plastic fuel tanks. **Defect:** The fuel tank sending unit gasket can crack, causing fuel and fuel vapor leaks. **Consequence:** Fuel and fuel vapor leaked from the fuel tank can result in fire when exposed to a source of ignition. **Corrective Action:** Replace the fuel tank sending unit gasket.

JEEP WRANGLER 1992

System: Brakes. **Vehicle:** Utility vehicles. **Defect:** On 1987 through early 1990 models, both front brake hoses can wear due to direct contact with the wheel-opening splash shields. On the late 1990 through 1992 models, periodic rubbing contact of the left front brake hose can occur due to movement of the splash shield in certain vehicle operating conditions. **Consequence:** Either condition can cause loss of front brake system functions, resulting in increased stopping distances and an increased risk of vehicle accident. **Corrective Action:** The 1987 to 1990 model vehicles will have both splash shields replaced, and both front brake hoses replaced as necessary. All affected late 1990 through 1992 model year vehicles will have additional fasteners installed to further secure the left side splash shield. Also, the left front brake hose will be inspected and replaced as necessary.

System: Ignition system. **Vehicle:** Multipurpose passenger vehicles equipped with manual transmissions. **Defect:** Salt corrosion products between the starter solenoid wire and the adjacent battery feed in the bulkhead connector may short these connections, causing the circuit to bypass the ignition key control of the starter motor solenoid. The car can start without the starter sequence being initiated by the ignition key in the ignition lock. **Consequence:** The unintended start of a vehicle with a manual transmission left in a drive gear can result in a runaway vehicle. **Corrective Action:** The starter solenoid wiring will be separated from the battery feed wire by relocating it within the bulkhead connector on affected vehicles.

System: Fuel; fuel pump. **Vehicle:** Multipurpose passenger vehicles equipped with plastic fuel tanks. **Defect:** The fuel tank sending unit gasket can crack, causing fuel and fuel vapor leaks. **Consequence:** Fuel and fuel vapor leaked from the fuel tank can result in fire when exposed to a source of ignition. **Corrective Action:** Replace the fuel tank sending unit gasket.

JEEP WRANGLER 1993

System: Ignition system. **Vehicle:** Multipurpose passenger vehicles equipped with manual transmissions. **Defect:** Salt corrosion products between the starter solenoid wire and the adjacent battery feed in the bulkhead connector may short these connections, causing the circuit to bypass the ignition key control of the starter motor solenoid. The car can start without the starter sequence being initiated by the ignition key in the ignition lock. **Consequence:** The unintended start of a vehicle with a manual transmission left in a drive gear can result in a runaway vehicle. **Corrective Action:** The starter solenoid wiring will be separated from the battery feed wire by relocating it within the bulkhead connector on affected vehicles.

System: Fuel; fuel pump. **Vehicle:** Multipurpose passenger vehicles equipped with plastic fuel tanks. **Defect:** The fuel tank sending unit gasket can crack, causing fuel and fuel vapor leaks. **Consequence:** Fuel and fuel vapor leaked from the fuel tank can result in fire when exposed to a source of ignition. **Corrective Action:** Replace the fuel tank sending unit gasket.

JEEP WRANGLER 1994

System: Fuel; fuel pump. **Vehicle:** Multipurpose passenger vehicles equipped with plastic fuel tanks. **Defect:** The fuel tank sending unit gasket can crack, causing fuel and fuel vapor leaks. **Consequence:** Fuel and fuel vapor leaked from the fuel tank can result in fire when exposed to a source of ignition. **Corrective Action:** Replace the fuel tank sending unit gasket.

LINCOLN

Note: If your Lincoln is presented to an authorized dealer on an agreed-upon service date and the remedy is not provided within a reasonable time and free of charge, or the remedy does not correct the defect or noncompliance, please contact the Ford Service Center at (800) 392-3673. Also contact the NHTSA's Auto Safety Hotline at (800) 424-9393.

LINCOLN CONTINENTAL 1988

System: Seat belts. **Vehicle:** Passenger cars. **Defect:** Driver and right front passenger inboard seat belts may be improperly anchored due to loose nuts that could back off. **Consequence:** Belt anchor could disengage the stud; an unattached belt assembly would not withstand an impact load. **Corrective Action:** Inboard seat belt anchorages will be corrected to prevent loosening.

System: Suspension—torsion springs. **Vehicle:** Passenger cars. **Defect:** Two torsion springs attached to rear suspension control arms may fracture and rub against a rear tire. **Consequence:** This could result in sudden loss of tire inflation pressure, with potential for an accident. **Corrective Action:** Install torsion spring seats to restrict the springs from contacting the tire if they should fracture.

System: Transmission shift cable. **Vehicle:** Passenger cars. **Defect:** Transmission shift cables may not meet Ford's pullout load specifications for the swivel tube portion of the cable, which could allow the swivel tube to separate from the shift cable assembly. **Consequence:** Operator would not be able to shift from one of the drive gears into park position. **Corrective Action:** Replace shift cable.

System: Wiring harness. **Vehicle:** Passenger cars. **Defect:** Nylon-shielded wiring harness, located in the engine compartment, is susceptible to heat damage and melting of the nylon material in 100-degree-plus weather. **Consequence:** Melted nylon shield could drip onto the exhaust manifold and result in an underhood fire. **Corrective Action:** Wrap wiring harness with heat-resistant Fiberglass tape.

System: Electrical. **Vehicle:** Passenger cars. **Defect:** Electrical circuit that controls current to brake pump motor relay, heater and air conditioning blower motor, turn signals and an electronic message center may overheat due to inability of ignition circuit wiring connections to dissipate heat generated by electrical loads. **Consequence:** Brake pump motor will not operate, substantially reducing braking capability; brake warning light will come on. **Corrective Action:** Replace ignition switch and modify switch wiring.

System: Gas lines. **Vehicle:** Extended-wheelbase limousines. **Defect:** Process used for connecting the gas lines was substandard. **Consequence:** A gas leak could develop, creating a fire potential. **Corrective Action:** Install standard gas line compression fittings.

System: Brakes. **Vehicle:** Passenger vehicles sold or registered in the following states: CT, IL, IN, ME, MA, MI, NH, NJ, NY, OH, PA, RI, VT and WI. **Defect:** Front disc brake rotors of the subject vehicles may experience severe corrosion if operated in areas where calcium chloride and sodium chloride are used extensively. **Consequence:** Severely corroded rotors may fracture or separate near the inner edges of the brake discs, resulting in reduced braking effectiveness, higher than normal pedal efforts, loud grinding noises and moderate pulls when the brakes are applied. Reduced braking effectiveness may increase minimum stopping distances, possibly resulting in an accident. **Corrective Action:** Replace front brake rotors with full cast front brake rotors.

System: Structure; rear subframe mounts. **Vehicle:** Taurus and Sables built from October 14, 1985 through August 19, 1988, and Lincoln Continentals built from November 4, 1987 through September 30, 1988 (except 1989—1991 2.5L Taurus and 1989—1992 SHO). The affected cars were sold or registered in the following states: CT, IL, IN, ME, MA, MI, NH, NJ, NY, OH, PA, RI, VT and WI. **Defect:** The body mounts at the rear corners of the subframe, which supports the engine and transmission, may become detached due to corrosion of the subframe mount retaining plate. This would allow the rear corners of the subframe to drop. **Consequence:** If one of the rear corners drops, only minor indications of a malfunction, such as a clunking noise or slight change in steering wheel alignment, are noticeable. However, if both rear corners of the subframe drop, steering becomes very difficult, which could adversely affect vehicle control and possibly result in an accident. **Corrective Action:** Install a corrosion-resistant reinforcing plate and a new bolt on both rear subframe mounts.

System: Structure; rear subframe mounts. **Vehicle:** Taurus and Sables built from August 1, 1988 through December 23, 1992 and Lincoln Continentals built from October 3, 1988 through December 23, 1992. The affected cars were sold or registered in the following states: CT, IL, IN, ME, MA, MI, NH, NJ, NY, OH, PA, RI, VT and WI. **Defect:** The body mounts at the rear corners of the subframe, which supports the engine and transmission, may become detached due to corrosion of the subframe mount retaining plate. This would allow the rear corners of the subframe to drop. **Consequence:** If one of the rear corners drops, only minor indications of a malfunction such as a clunking noise or slight change in steering wheel alignment are noticeable. However, if both rear corners of the subframe drop, steering becomes very difficult, which could adversely affect vehicle control and possibly result in an accident. **Corrective Action:** Install a corrosion-resistant reinforcing plate and a new bolt on both rear subframe mounts.

LINCOLN CONTINENTAL 1989

System: Rear seat belt retractor. **Vehicle:** Passenger cars. **Defect:** The left side, rear seat belt retractor assembly may be improperly secured and could pull free of its mounting location. **Consequence:** Occupant, though still restrained by the lap portion of the belt, would not have upper body protection. **Corrective Action:** Reinstall the retractor attachment bolt.

System: Brakes. **Vehicle:** Passenger vehicles sold or registered in the following states: CT, IL, IN, ME, MA, MI, NH, NJ, NY, OH, PA, RI, VT and WI. **Defect:** Front disc brake rotors of the subject vehicles may experience severe corrosion if operated in areas where calcium chloride and sodium chloride are used extensively. **Consequence:** Severely corroded rotors may fracture or separate near the inner edges of the brake discs, resulting in reduced braking effectiveness, higher than normal pedal efforts, loud grinding noises and moderate pulls when the brakes are applied. Reduced braking effectiveness may increase minimum stopping distances, possibly resulting in an accident. **Corrective Action:** Replace front brake rotors with full cast front brake rotors.

System: Structure; rear subframe mounts. **Vehicle:** Taurus and Sables built from August 1, 1988 through December 23, 1992 and Lincoln Continentals built from October 3, 1988 through December 23, 1992. The affected cars were sold or registered in the following states: CT, IL, IN, ME, MA, MI, NH, NJ, NY, OH, PA, RI, VT and WI. **Defect:** The body mounts at the rear corners of the subframe, which supports the engine and transmission, may become detached due to corrosion of the subframe mount retaining plate. This would allow the rear corners of the subframe to drop. **Consequence:** If one of the rear corners drops, only minor indications of a malfunction, such as a clunking noise or slight change in steering wheel alignment, are noticeable. However, if both rear corners of the subframe drop, steering becomes very difficult, which could adversely affect vehicle control and possibly result in an accident. **Corrective Action:** Install a corrosion-resistant reinforcing plate and a new bolt on both rear subframe mounts.

LINCOLN CONTINENTAL 1990

System: Airbag modules. **Vehicle:** Passenger cars equipped with driver's-side supplemental airbag modules. **Defect:** Threaded inflator components may have been damaged during assembly, which may allow components to separate when inflator receives a signal to deploy the airbag. **Consequence:** Inflator component separation allows hot combustion gases to escape into the passenger compartment, which could result in injuries to vehicle occupants. **Corrective Action:** Replace airbag modules containing potentially defective inflators. **Note:** This campaign was initiated by TRW, Inc., manufacturer of the airbag module.

System: Brakes. **Vehicle:** Passenger vehicles sold or registered in the following states: CT, IL, IN, ME, MA, MI, NH, NJ, NY, OH, PA, RI, VT and WI. **Defect:** Front disc brake rotors of the subject vehicles may experience severe corrosion if operated in areas where calcium chloride and sodium chloride are used extensively. **Consequence:** Severely corroded rotors may fracture or separate near the inner edges of the brake discs, resulting in reduced braking effectiveness, higher than normal pedal efforts, loud grinding noises and moderate pulls when the brakes are applied. Reduced braking effectiveness may increase minimum stopping distances, possibly resulting in an accident. **Corrective Action:** Replace front brake rotors with full cast front brake rotors.

System: Structure; rear subframe mounts. **Vehicle:** Taurus and Sables built from August 1, 1988 through December 23, 1992 and Lincoln Continentals built from October 3, 1988 through December 23, 1992. The affected cars were sold or registered in the following states: CT, IL, IN, ME, MA, MI, NH, NJ, NY, OH, PA, RI, VT and WI. **Defect:** The body mounts at the rear corners of the subframe, which supports the engine and transmission, may become detached due to corrosion of the subframe mount retaining plate. This would allow the rear corners of the subframe to drop. **Consequence:** If one of the rear corners drops, only minor indications of a malfunction, such as a clunking noise or slight change in steering wheel alignment, are noticeable. However, if both rear corners of the subframe drop, steering becomes very difficult, which could adversely affect vehicle control and possibly result in an accident. **Corrective Action:** Install a corrosion-resistant reinforcing plate and a new bolt on both rear subframe mounts.

LINCOLN CONTINENTAL 1991

System: Brakes. **Vehicle:** Passenger vehicles sold or registered in the following states: CT, IL, IN, ME, MA, MI, NH, NJ, NY, OH, PA, RI, VT and WI. **Defect:** Front disc brake rotors of the subject vehicles may experience severe corrosion if operated in areas where calcium chloride and sodium chloride are used extensively. **Consequence:** Severely corroded rotors may fracture or separate near the inner edges of the brake discs, resulting in reduced braking effectiveness, higher than normal pedal efforts, loud grinding noises and moderate pulls when the brakes are applied. Reduced braking effectiveness may increase minimum stopping distances, possibly resulting in an accident. **Corrective Action:** Replace front brake rotors with full cast front brake rotors.

System: Structure; rear subframe mounts. **Vehicle:** Taurus and Sables built from August 1, 1988 through December 23, 1992 and Lincoln Continentals built from October 3, 1988 through December 23, 1992. The affected cars were sold or registered in the following states: CT, IL, IN, ME, MA, MI, NH, NJ, NY, OH, PA, RI, VT and WI. **Defect:** The body mounts at the rear corners of the subframe, which supports the engine and transmission, may become detached due to corrosion of the subframe mount retaining plate. This would allow the rear corners of the subframe to drop. **Consequence:** If one of the rear corners drops, only minor indications of a malfunction, such as a clunking noise or slight change in steering wheel alignment, are noticeable. However, if both rear corners of the subframe drop, steering becomes very difficult, which could adversely affect vehicle control and possibly result in an accident. **Corrective Action:** Install a corrosion-resistant reinforcing plate and a new bolt on both rear subframe mounts.

LINCOLN CONTINENTAL 1992

System: Structure; rear subframe mounts. **Vehicle:** Taurus and Sables built from August 1, 1988 through December 23, 1992 and Lincoln Continentals built from October 3, 1988 through December 23, 1992. The affected cars were sold or registered in the following states: CT, IL, IN, ME, MA, MI, NH, NJ, NY, OH, PA, RI, VT and WI. **Defect:** The body mounts at the rear corners of the subframe, which supports the engine and transmission, may become detached due to corrosion of the subframe mount retaining plate. This would allow the rear corners of the subframe to drop. **Consequence:** If one of the rear corners drops, only minor indications of a malfunction, such as a clunking noise or slight change in steering wheel alignment, are noticeable. However, if both rear corners of the subframe drop, steering becomes very difficult, which could adversely affect vehicle control and possibly result in an accident. **Corrective Action:** Install a corrosion-resistant reinforcing plate and a new bolt on both rear subframe mounts.

LINCOLN MARK VII 1988

System: Fuel line coupling. **Vehicle:** Passenger cars and light trucks equipped with fuel injection. **Defect:** Spring lock fuel line coupling may not be properly engaged. **Consequence:** Coupling could disengage due to fuel pressure, vibration and engine movements; this would cause loss of fuel which, in the presence of an ignition source, creates a fire risk. **Corrective Action:** Install retainer clips over the couplings to prevent coupling separation and fuel leakage.

LINCOLN TOWN CAR 1987

System: Electrical—wiring harness. **Vehicle:** Passenger cars. **Defect:** Wiring harness in the engine compartment may be misrouted and subject to damage. **Consequence:** A short circuit could occur (during use or when parked), which could result in a vehicle fire. **Corrective Action:** Properly route wiring harnesses, as necessary.

System: Steering centerlinks. **Vehicle:** Passenger vehicles with 5.0L engines. **Defect:** Steering centerlinks may break at a bend location. **Consequence:** Steering control would be diminished, with reduced control of left wheel only and considerable steering wheel free play. **Corrective Action:** Replace steering centerlink.

System: Idler arm brackets. **Vehicle:** Passenger cars. **Defect:** Idler arm brackets may fracture at the threaded shafts due to improper heat treatment. **Consequence:** Driver would experience a clunking noise on turns and a loose feeling in the steering wheel; steering control would be maintained. **Corrective Action:** Replace idler arm assembly.

System: Fuel line coupling. **Vehicle:** Passenger cars and light trucks equipped with fuel injection. **Defect:** Spring lock fuel line coupling may not be properly engaged. **Consequence:** Coupling could disengage due to fuel pressure, vibration and engine movements; this would cause loss of fuel which, in the presence of an ignition source, creates a fire risk. **Corrective Action:** Install retainer clips over the couplings to prevent coupling separation and fuel leakage.

System: Windows—FMVSS 205. **Vehicle:** Limousine conversions. **Defect:** Window film does not meet light requirement of not less than 70 percent. **Consequence:** Limousines will not comply with FMVSS 205. **Corrective Action:** Remove window film to ensure compliance with standard.

System: Rear safety belts. **Vehicle:** Limousine conversions equipped with rear-facing seats. **Defect:** Safety belts (type 1 lap belts) for rear-facing seats were not installed. **Consequence:** Lack of restraints could contribute to otherwise preventable injury, and vehicles would not comply with FMVSS 209 and 210. **Corrective Action:** Install safety belts for rear-facing seats.

System: Stoplamp—FMVSS 108. **Vehicle:** Coach limousines. **Defect:** Center high-mounted stoplamp may be obstructed or absent. **Consequence:** The obstruction or lack of a center high-mounted stoplamp would increase the hazard of a rear-end collision, and the vehicle would not comply with FMVSS 108. **Corrective Action:** Remove obstructing window tinting or install high center stoplamp when missing.

System: Safety belts—FMVSS 208. **Vehicle:** Coach limousines. **Defect:** Safety belts may not have been installed for rear-facing seats. **Consequence:** Occupant of these seats would be subject to increased injury in the event of a sudden stop or accident, and vehicles do not comply with FMVSS 208. **Corrective Action:** Install additional safety belts.

System: Compliance label—part 567. **Vehicle:** Coach limousines. **Defect:** Vehicle alterer's label may be missing or incomplete. **Conse-**

quence: Vehicles do not comply with part 567. **Corrective Action:** Add compliance label.

System: Tire placard—FMVSS 110. **Vehicle:** Limousine conversions. **Defect:** Tire placard listing recommended tire pressures can be absent or can contain incorrect information. **Consequence:** Use of incorrect tire pressures could cause increased tire wear, which could result in difficulty in vehicle handling or steering. **Corrective Action:** Install label with correct tire information.

System: Alterer's placard; 49 CFR part 567. **Vehicle:** Limousine conversions. **Defect:** Alterer's label stating that vehicle complies with standards, including weight of vehicle, may be absent or incomplete. **Consequence:** Owner would not be aware of correct weight rating and tire size as required by 49 CFR part 567. **Corrective Action:** Install correct alterer's placard.

LINCOLN TOWN CAR 1988

System: Fuel rails. **Vehicle:** Passenger cars equipped with 5.0L fuel-injected engines. **Defect:** Fuel rails may be bent so that #5 Injector cups are out of design position. **Consequence:** Bent fuel rail could cause a fuel leak, which in the presence of an ignition source could result in an engine fire. **Corrective Action:** Replace fuel rail assemblies as necessary.

System: Fuel line coupling. **Vehicle:** Passenger cars and light trucks equipped with fuel injection. **Defect:** Spring lock fuel line coupling may not be properly engaged. **Consequence:** Coupling could disengage due to fuel pressure, vibration and engine movements; this would cause loss of fuel which, in the presence of an ignition source, creates a fire risk. **Corrective Action:** Install retainer clips over the couplings to prevent coupling separation and fuel leakage.

System: Windows—FMVSS 205. **Vehicle:** Limousine conversions. **Defect:** Window film does not meet light requirement of not less than 70 percent. **Consequence:** Limousines will not comply with FMVSS 205. **Corrective Action:** Remove window film to ensure compliance with standard.

System: Rear safety belts. **Vehicle:** Limousine conversions equipped with rear-facing seats. **Defect:** Safety belts (type 1 lap belts) for rear-facing seats were not installed. **Consequence:** Lack of restraints could contribute to otherwise preventable injury, and vehicles would not comply with FMVSS 209 and 210. **Corrective Action:** Install safety belts for rear-facing seats.

System: Stoplamp—FMVSS 108. **Vehicle:** Coach limousines. **Defect:** Center high-mounted stoplamp may be obstructed or absent. **Consequence:** The obstruction or lack of a center high-mounted stoplamp would increase the hazard of a rear-end collision, and the vehicle would not comply with FMVSS 108. **Corrective Action:** Remove obstructing window tinting or install high center stoplamp when missing.

System: Safety belts—FMVSS 208. **Vehicle:** Coach limousines. **Defect:** Safety belts may not have been installed for rear-facing seats. **Consequence:** Occupant of these seats would be subject to increased injury in the event of a sudden stop or accident, and vehicles do not comply with FMVSS 208. **Corrective Action:** Install additional safety belts.

System: Compliance label—part 567. **Vehicle:** Coach limousines. **Defect:** Vehicle alterer's label may be missing or incomplete. **Consequence:** Vehicles do not comply with part 567. **Corrective Action:** Add compliance label.

System: Tire placard—FMVSS 110. **Vehicle:** Limousine conversions. **Defect:** Tire placard listing recommended tire pressures can be absent or can contain incorrect information. **Consequence:** Use of incorrect tire pressures could cause increased tire wear, which could result in difficulty in vehicle handling or steering. **Corrective Action:** Install label with correct tire information.

System: Alterer's placard; 49 CFR part 567. **Vehicle:** Limousine conversions. **Defect:** Alterer's label stating that vehicle complies with standards, including weight of vehicle, may be absent or incomplete. **Consequence:** Owner would not be aware of correct weight rating and tire size as required by 49 CFR part 567. **Corrective Action:** Install correct alterer's placard.

LINCOLN TOWN CAR 1989

System: Windows—FMVSS 205. **Vehicle:** Limousine conversions. **Defect:** Window film does not meet light requirement of not less than 70 percent. **Consequence:** Limousines will not comply with FMVSS 205. **Corrective Action:** Remove window film to ensure compliance with standard.

System: Rear safety belts. **Vehicle:** Limousine conversions equipped with rear-facing seats. **Defect:** Safety belts (type 1 lap belts) for rear-facing seats were not installed. **Consequence:** Lack of restraints could contribute to otherwise preventable injury, and vehicles would not comply with FMVSS 209 and 210. **Corrective Action:** Install safety belts for rear-facing seats.

System: Stoplamp—FMVSS 108. **Vehicle:** Coach limousines. **Defect:** Center high-mounted stoplamp may be obstructed or absent. **Consequence:** The obstruction or lack of a center high-mounted stoplamp would increase the hazard of a rear-end collision, and the vehicle would not comply with FMVSS 108. **Corrective Action:** Remove obstructing window tinting or install high center stoplamp when missing.

System: Safety belts—FMVSS 208. **Vehicle:** Coach limousines. **Defect:** Safety belts may not have been installed for rear-facing seats. **Consequence:** Occupant of these seats would be subject to increased injury in the event of a sudden stop or accident, and vehicles do not comply with FMVSS 208. **Corrective Action:** Install additional safety belts.

System: Compliance label—part 567. **Vehicle:** Coach limousines. **Defect:** Vehicle alterer's label may be missing or incomplete. **Consequence:** Vehicles do not comply with part 567. **Corrective Action:** Add compliance label.

System: Tire placard—FMVSS 110. **Vehicle:** Stretch limousines. **Defect:** Tire placard may contain incorrect gross vehicle weight ratings and tire information. **Consequence:** Limousines would not comply with FMVSS 110, and consumer might unknowingly overload the vehicle because of placard misinformation. **Corrective Action:** Install revised tire placards.

System: Alterer's certification label; 49 CFR part 567. **Vehicle:** Stretch limousines. **Defect:** Gross vehicle weight ratings and tire information may be incorrect on labels. **Consequence:** Vehicles would not comply with 49 CFR part 567. **Corrective Action:** Install revised certification labels.

System: Window tint—FMVSS 205. **Vehicle:** Stretch limousines. **Defect:** Window tint does not meet luminous transmittance requirements of FMVSS 205. **Consequence:** Limousines do not comply with standards; also, increased potential for accidents because of limited visibility. **Corrective Action:** Remove window film, as necessary.

System: Tire placard—FMVSS 110. **Vehicle:** Limousine conversions. **Defect:** Tire placard listing recommended tire pressures can be absent or can contain incorrect information. **Consequence:** Use of incorrect tire pressures could cause increased tire wear, which could result in difficulty in vehicle handling or steering. **Corrective Action:** Install label with correct tire information.

System: Alterer's placard; 49 CFR part 567. **Vehicle:** Limousine conversions. **Defect:** Alterer's label stating that vehicle complies with standards, including weight of vehicle, may be absent or incomplete. **Consequence:** Owner would not be aware of correct weight rating and tire size as required by 49 CFR part 567. **Corrective Action:** Install correct alterer's placard.

LINCOLN TOWN CAR 1990

System: Tire placard—FMVSS 110. **Vehicle:** Stretch limousines. **Defect:** Tire placard may contain incorrect gross vehicle weight ratings and tire information. **Consequence:** Limousines would not comply with FMVSS 110, and consumer might unknowingly overload the vehicle because of placard misinformation. **Corrective Action:** Install revised tire placards.

System: Alterer's certification label; 49 CFR part 567. **Vehicle:** Stretch limousines. **Defect:** Gross vehicle weight ratings and tire information may be incorrect on labels. **Consequence:** Vehicles would not comply with 49 CFR part 567. **Corrective Action:** Install revised certification labels.

System: Window tint—FMVSS 205. **Vehicle:** Stretch limousines. **Defect:** Window tint does not meet luminous transmittance requirements of FMVSS 205. **Consequence:** Limousines do not comply with standards; also, increased potential for accidents because of limited visibility. **Corrective Action:** Remove window film, as necessary.

System: Tire placard—FMVSS 110. **Vehicle:** Limousine conversions. **Defect:** Tire placard listing recommended tire pressures can be absent or can contain incorrect information. **Consequence:** Use of incorrect tire pressures could cause increased tire wear, which could result in difficulty in vehicle handling or steering. **Corrective Action:** Install label with correct tire information.

System: Alterer's placard; 49 CFR part 567. **Vehicle:** Limousine conversions. **Defect:** Alterer's label stating that vehicle complies with standards, including weight of vehicle, may be absent or incomplete. **Consequence:** Owner would not be aware of correct weight rating and tire size as required by 49 CFR part 567. **Corrective Action:** Install correct alterer's placard.

System: Structure; hood assembly; latches. **Vehicle:** Passenger vehicles registered or sold in the following states: AL, CT, DE, FL, GA, IL, IN, LA, ME, MD, MA, MI, MS, NH, NJ, NY, NC, OH, PA, RI, SC, TX, VT, VA, WI and DC. **Defect:** Corrosion of the hood latch striker plate causes detachment of the plate from the hood assembly, resulting in an unexpected opening of the hood while the vehicle is being driven. **Consequence:** This condition can reduce the driver's view of the road, increasing the potential of a vehicle accident. **Corrective Action:** Dealers will install a new hood inner panel reinforcement and a new, galvanized hood latch striker plate.

LINCOLN TOWN CAR 1991

System: Fuel lines. **Vehicle:** Passenger cars. **Defect:** Distorted fuel lines in engine compartment may contact the steering column universal joint and cause damage to the fuel line. **Consequence:** Fuel leakage could occur from the damaged fluid line and, in the presence of an ignition source, could result in a fire. **Corrective Action:** Reposition fuel line to prevent contact with the universal joint; if fuel lines are already damaged, repair or replace fuel lines.

System: Hood. **Vehicle:** Passenger cars. **Defect:** The secondary hood latch may not engage when the hood is closed. **Consequence:** In the event the primary hood latch releases when the vehicle is in motion, the hood could fly up, obstructing the operator's vision and increasing the potential for a vehicle accident. **Corrective Action:** Install a new hood latching assembly. **Note:** You will receive a letter from Ford advising you when to schedule an appointment with your dealer to have the recall performed. Refer to Ford Safety Campaign 91S40. To find out if your car is involved in this recall, call Ford's toll-free line [(800) 392-3673] and provide them with your vehicle identification number. If you are experiencing a hood latch problem, call Ford at (313) 446-4654. An operator will take your name and telephone number. A Ford representative will call you back.

System: Structure; hood assembly; latches. **Vehicle:** Passenger vehicles registered or sold in the following states: AL, CT, DE, FL, GA, IL, IN, LA, ME, MD, MA, MI, MS, NH, NJ, NY, NC, OH, PA, RI, SC, TX, VT, VA, WI and DC. **Defect:** Corrosion of the hood latch striker plate causes detachment of the plate from the hood assembly, resulting in an unexpected opening of the hood while the vehicle is being driven. **Consequence:** This condition can reduce the driver's view of the road, increasing the potential of a vehicle accident. **Corrective Action:** Dealers will install a new hood inner panel reinforcement and a new, galvanized hood latch striker plate.

System: Structure; hood; latches. **Vehicle:** Passenger vehicles. **Defect:** The secondary hood latch may not engage when the hood is closed. **Consequence:** In the event the primary hood latch releases or is not properly latched when the vehicle is in motion, the hood could fly up, obstructing the operator's vision and increasing the potential for a vehicle accident. **Corrective Action:** Dealers will replace the hood latch assembly.

LINCOLN TOWN CAR 1992

System: Equipment; tire reserve load label—FMVSS 110. **Vehicle:** Stretch limousine. **Description of Noncompliance:** The tire placard is not correct due to modifications made by the limousine conversion company. This does not comply with FMVSS 110, "Tire selection and rims." **Consequence of Noncompliance:** This can result in premature wear of the tires. **Corrective Action:** Craftsmen will send correct tire placards to owners. **Note:** If you do not receive correct tire placards for your vehicle, please contact Craftsmen Limousine at (417) 865-2999. Also contact the NHTSA's Auto Safety Hotline at (800) 424-9393.

System: Structure; hood; latches. **Vehicle:** Passenger vehicles. **Defect:** The secondary hood latch may not engage when the hood is closed. **Consequence:** In the event the primary hood latch releases or is not properly latched when the vehicle is in motion, the hood could fly up, obstructing the operator's vision and increasing the potential for a vehicle accident. **Corrective Action:** Dealers will replace the hood latch assembly.

LINCOLN TOWN CAR 1993

System: Equipment; tire reserve load label—FMVSS 110. **Vehicle:** Stretch limousine. **Description of Noncompliance:** The tire placard is not correct due to modifications made by the limousine conversion company. This does not comply with FMVSS 110, "Tire selection and rims." **Consequence of Noncompliance:** This can result in premature wear of the tires. **Corrective Action:** Craftsmen will send correct tire placards to owners. **Note:** If you do not receive correct tire placards for your vehicle, please contact Craftsmen Limousine at (417) 865-2999. Also contact the NHTSA's Auto Safety Hotline at (800) 424-9393.

MAZDA

Note: If your Mazda is presented to an authorized dealer on an agreed-upon service date and the remedy is not provided free of charge within a reasonable time, please contact Mazda at (800) 222-5500. Also contact the NHTSA's Auto Safety Hotline at (800) 424-9393.

MAZDA 323 1988

System: Interior; seat belts; belt buckles. **Vehicle:** Passenger vehicles equipped with safety belts made by Takata Corporation. **Defect:** The front safety belt buckle release buttons can break. These red plastic release buttons are marked "press." If a button breaks, pieces can fall into the buckle assembly, causing the buckle to operate improperly. **Consequence:** The safety belts would not provide adequate protection to an occupant in a vehicle crash. **Corrective Action:** Owners should promptly check the condition and operation of both front safety belt buckles, and carefully inspect the red release buttons for any breaks or cracks. They should ensure that both buckles are operating properly by inserting each latchplate into its buckle, tugging on the belt to make sure the latch is securely locked and then pressing the release button. The latchplate should pop out of the buckle when the button is pressed. If either release button shows a sign of breaking or cracking, or if either buckle fails to operate properly, owners should promptly contact their authorized dealer to schedule an appointment to have the buckle replaced or repaired, free of charge. The manufacturer is developing a remedy designed to prevent failure of the buttons that are not currently broken.

MAZDA 323 1989

System: Interior; seat belts; belt buckles. **Vehicle:** Passenger vehicles equipped with safety belts made by Takata Corporation. **Defect:** The front safety belt buckle release buttons can break. These red plastic release buttons are marked "press." If a button breaks, pieces can fall into the buckle assembly, causing the buckle to operate improperly. **Consequence:** The safety belts would not provide adequate protection to an occupant in a vehicle crash. **Corrective Action:** Owners should promptly check the condition and operation of both front safety belt buckles, and carefully inspect the red release buttons for any breaks or cracks. They should ensure that both buckles are operating properly by inserting each latchplate into its buckle, tugging on the belt to make sure the latch is securely locked and then pressing the release button. The latchplate should pop out of the buckle when the button is pressed. If either release button shows a sign of breaking or cracking, or if either buckle fails to operate properly, owners should promptly contact their authorized dealer to schedule an appointment to have the buckle replaced or repaired, free of charge. The manufacturer is developing a remedy designed to prevent failure of the buttons that are not currently broken.

MAZDA 626 1987

System: Ignition switch terminal. **Vehicle:** Passenger cars. **Defect:** Ignition switch terminal may malfunction. **Consequence:** This could result in failure of windshield wipers, windshield washer, engine cooling fan, heater blower and air conditioning compressor. Failure of windshield-clearing devices could cause reduced visibility, which could result in an accident. **Corrective Action:** Replace ignition switches.

MAZDA 626 1988

System: Floor mat—accelerator pedal **Vehicle:** Passenger cars. **Defect:** Floor mat could interfere with release of the accelerator pedal due to improper shape of mat. **Consequence:** This could result in loss of accelerator control and create the potential for an accident. **Corrective Action:** Remove present mat and replace with new, improved mat.

System: Fuel tank. **Vehicle:** Passenger cars. **Defect:** Fuel tank fixing band retention is not sufficient, allowing the band to rub against the fuel tank by vehicle vibrations. **Consequence:** This could wear a hole in the fuel tank, which could result in fuel leakage. **Corrective Action:** Repair fuel fixing band by installing a rubber sheet.

System: Brakes—dust boot. **Vehicle:** Passenger cars. **Defect:** Vehicles equipped with rear brake drums transported by train may experience separation of the brake shoe from the wheel brake cylinder piston. **Consequence:** Should separation occur, repeated brake operation may damage the wheel brake cylinder dust boot, allowing water or dust intrusion and subsequent piston contamination. **Corrective Action:** All vehicles will be inspected, and if no separation is found, grease will be applied to the component interface to lower friction and avoid subsequent relative motion. If separation is found, the wheel brake cylinder dust boot will be replaced.

System: Throttle. **Vehicle:** Passenger cars. **Defect:** At ambient temperatures below zero degree Fahrenheit, frost may accumulate within the throttle body under extended constant-speed operation. **Consequence:** Frost accumulation on the throttle valve may prevent the valve from returning smoothly. **Corrective Action:** Install a new type thermostat designed to raise the coolant temperature and warm the throttle body to a level above freezing.

System: Seat belts. **Vehicle:** Passenger cars with automatic shoulder belt. **Defect:** The drive spring that drives the automatic belt may break. **Consequence:** This would prevent full forward movement of the seat belt anchorage from the lock position when the door is opened. **Corrective Action:** Replace automatic shoulder belt.

System: Structure; door assembly; handle; outer. **Vehicle:** Passenger vehicles. **Defect:** Resin-molded handles fail at the door latch actuating rod attachment, freeing the rod to fall inside the door frame. Subsequent lowering of the associated window may force the actuating rod downward and release the door latch. **Consequence:** Inadvertent actuation of the door latch causes the door to open unexpectedly, which could result in an occupant falling out of the vehicle. **Corrective Action:** Dealers will replace the door handle and latch assembly.

MAZDA 626 1989

System: Brakes; hydraulic; shoe and drum systems; drum. **Equipment Description:** Replacement brake drums for passenger vehicles, Midas part BD 1552. **Defect:** The groove for the rear wheel bearing retainer ring was incorrectly machined. **Consequence:** If the retaining ring does not sit correctly in the groove, the axle lug nuts will break, causing the brake drum, wheel and tire assembly to separate from the vehicle. **Corrective Action:** Midas shops will replace the brake drums with brake drums from another supplier. **Note:** Empire Motor Company, Ltd., of Tokyo, Japan, manufactured these brake drums. The U.S. representative is EMC of America, Los Angeles, CA. These brake drums were installed on vehicles from July 13, 1993, through September 30, 1993.

System: Structure; door assembly; handle; outer. **Vehicle:** Passenger vehicles. **Defect:** Resin-molded handles fail at the door latch actuating rod attachment, freeing the rod to fall inside the door frame. Subsequent lowering of the associated window may force the actuating rod downward and release the door latch. **Consequence:** Inadvertent actuation of the door latch causes the door to open unexpectedly, which could result in an occupant falling out of the vehicle. **Corrective Action:** Dealers will replace the door handle and latch assembly.

MAZDA 626 1990

System: Brakes; hydraulic; shoe and drum systems; drum. **Equipment Description:** Replacement brake drums for passenger vehicles, Midas part BD 1552. **Defect:** The groove for the rear wheel bearing retainer ring was incorrectly machined. **Consequence:** If the retaining ring does not sit correctly in the groove, the axle lug nuts will break, causing the brake drum, wheel and tire assembly to separate from the vehicle. **Corrective Action:** Midas shops will replace the brake drums with brake drums from another supplier. **Note:** Empire Motor Company, Ltd., of Tokyo, Japan, manufactured these brake drums. The U.S. representative is EMC of America, Los Angeles, CA. These brake drums were installed on vehicles from July 13, 1993, through September 30, 1993.

System: Structure; door assembly; handle; outer. **Vehicle:** Passenger vehicles. **Defect:** Resin-molded handles fail at the door latch actuating rod attachment, freeing the rod to fall inside the door frame. Subsequent lowering of the associated window may force the actuating rod downward and release the door latch. **Consequence:** Inadvertent actuation of the door latch causes the door to open unexpectedly, which could result in an occupant falling out of the vehicle. **Corrective Action:** Dealers will replace the door handle and latch assembly.

MAZDA 626 1991

System: Brakes; hydraulic; shoe and drum systems; drum. **Equipment Description:** Replacement brake drums for passenger vehicles, Midas part BD 1552. **Defect:** The groove for the rear wheel bearing retainer ring was incorrectly machined. **Consequence:** If the retaining ring does not sit correctly in the groove, the axle lug nuts will break, causing the brake drum, wheel and tire assembly to separate from the vehicle. **Corrective Action:** Midas shops will replace the brake drums with brake drums from another supplier. **Note:** Empire Motor Company, Ltd., of Tokyo, Japan, manufactured these brake drums. The U.S. representative is EMC of America, Los Angeles, CA. These brake drums were installed on vehicles from July 13, 1993, through September 30, 1993.

System: Structure; door assembly; handle; outer. **Vehicle:** Passenger vehicles. **Defect:** Resin-molded handles fail at the door latch actuating rod attachment, freeing the rod to fall inside the door frame. Subsequent lowering of the associated window may force the actuating rod downward and release the door latch. **Consequence:** Inadvertent actuation of the door latch causes the door to open unexpectedly, which could result in an occupant falling out of the vehicle. **Corrective Action:** Dealers will replace the door handle and latch assembly.

MAZDA 929 1988

System: Structure; door assembly; handle; outer. **Vehicle:** Passenger vehicles. **Defect:** Resin-molded handles fail at the door latch actuating rod attachment, freeing the rod to fall inside the door frame. Subsequent lowering of the associated window may force the actuating rod downward and release the door latch. **Consequence:** Inadvertent actuation of the door latch causes the door to open unexpectedly, which could result in an occupant falling out of the vehicle. **Corrective Action:** Dealers will replace the door handle and latch assembly.

System: Interior; seat belts; belt buckles. **Vehicle:** Passenger vehicles equipped with safety belts made by Takata Corporation. **Defect:** The front safety belt buckle release buttons can break. These red plastic release buttons are marked "press." If a button breaks, pieces can fall into the buckle assembly, causing the buckle to operate improperly. **Consequence:** The safety belts would not provide adequate protection to an occupant in a vehicle crash. **Corrective Action:** Owners should promptly check the condition and operation of both front safety belt buckles, and carefully inspect the red release buttons for any breaks or cracks. They should ensure that both buckles are operating properly by inserting each latchplate into its buckle, tugging on the belt to make sure the latch is securely locked and then pressing the release button. The latchplate should pop out of the buckle when the button is pressed. If either release button shows a sign of breaking or cracking, or if either buckle fails to operate properly, owners should promptly contact their authorized dealer to schedule an appointment to have the buckle replaced or repaired, free of charge. The manufacturer is developing a remedy designed to prevent failure of the buttons that are not currently broken.

MAZDA 929 1989

System: Structure; door assembly; handle; outer. **Vehicle:** Passenger vehicles. **Defect:** Resin-molded handles fail at the door latch actuating rod attachment, freeing the rod to fall inside the door frame. Subsequent lowering of the associated window may force the actuating rod downward and release the door latch. **Consequence:** Inadvertent actuation of the door latch causes the door to open unexpectedly, which could result in an occupant falling out of the vehicle. **Corrective Action:** Dealers will replace the door handle and latch assembly.

System: Interior; seat belts; belt buckles. **Vehicle:** Passenger vehicles equipped with safety belts made by Takata Corporation. **Defect:** The front safety belt buckle release buttons can break. These red plastic release buttons are marked "press." If a button breaks, pieces can fall into the buckle assembly, causing the buckle to operate improperly. **Consequence:** The safety belts would not provide adequate protection to an occupant in a vehicle crash. **Corrective Action:** Owners should promptly check the condition and operation of both front safety belt buckles, and carefully inspect the red release buttons for any breaks or cracks. They should ensure that both buckles are operating properly by inserting each latchplate into its buckle, tugging on the belt to make sure the latch is securely locked and then pressing the release button. The latchplate should pop out of the buckle when the button is pressed. If either release button shows a sign of breaking or cracking, or if either buckle fails to operate properly, owners should promptly contact their authorized dealer to schedule an appointment to have the buckle replaced or repaired, free of charge. The manufacturer is developing a remedy designed to prevent failure of the buttons that are not currently broken.

MAZDA 929 1992

System: Headlamps—FMVSS 108. **Equipment Description:** Headlamps for passenger vehicles. **Defect:** An *o* mark that is required on both vertical and horizontal vehicle headlamp aiming devices is missing. **Consequence:** This does not comply with FMVSS 108, "Lamps, reflective devices and associated equipment." **Corrective Action:** None provided. **Note:** The manufacturer's petition, which requested that NHTSA determine that this FMVSS noncompliance does not create an unreasonable risk to motor vehicle safety, has been granted. Therefore, the manufacturer is not obligated to conduct an owner notification and remedy campaign.

MAZDA MX6 1989

System: Brakes; hydraulic; shoe and drum systems; drum. **Equipment Description:** Replacement brake drums for passenger vehicles, Midas part BD 1552. **Defect:** The groove for the rear wheel bearing retainer ring was incorrectly machined. **Consequence:** If the retaining ring does not sit correctly in the groove, the axle lug nuts will break, causing the brake drum, wheel and tire assembly to separate from the vehicle. **Corrective Action:** Midas shops will replace the brake drums with brake drums from another supplier. **Note:** Empire Motor Company, Ltd., of Tokyo, Japan, manufactured these brake drums. The U.S. representative is EMC of America, Los Angeles, CA. These brake drums were installed on vehicles from July 13, 1993, through September 30, 1993.

MAZDA MX6 1993

System: Suspension. **Vehicle:** Passenger cars produced at Flat Rock, Michigan. **Defect:** The lower arm ball joints on both sides of the front suspension may not have been torqued to specification. **Consequence:** The insufficient torque of the lower ball joint retaining bolt can result in the suspension failing while the car is in motion and subsequent loss of steering control without warning, which can result in an accident. **Corrective Action:** Inspect the lower ball joint retaining bolts and tighten loose bolts to the correct torque.

MAZDA RX7 1993

System: Fuel; fuel lines; hoses; nonmetallic. **Vehicle:** Passenger vehicles. **Defect:** Residual engine heat can cause premature deterioration of the fuel hose, causing the hose to leak. Also, removing and reinstalling the deteriorated fuel hoses increases the likelihood of a leak. **Consequence:** This condition can result in an engine compartment fire. **Corrective Action:** Dealers will install an additional control unit for the electric cooling fan. The fan will then activate after the engine is turned off when the coolant exceeds a specified temperature. The fuel hoses will also be replaced with revised hoses.

MAZDA TRUCK MPV 1989

System: Safety belts—FMVSS 210. **Vehicle:** Seven-passenger van. **Defect:** The center safety belt attachment hardware brackets for the third seat may not withstand the specified tensile load. **Consequence:** Vans would not comply with FMVSS 210. **Corrective Action:** Replace safety belt assemblies with brackets.

System: Brake vacuum hose. **Vehicle:** Multipurpose vehicle. **Defect:** When the vehicle is exposed to temperatures below 5° Fahrenheit (−15° Celsius), the neutral detergent used as an assembly lubricant may stick to the check valve, preventing valve from functioning. **Consequence:** This could cause an inoperative brake power assist, which decreases braking ability and presents a potential for an accident. **Corrective Action:** Replace vacuum hose assembly.

System: Brakes. **Vehicle:** Multipurpose vehicles. **Defect:** When applying the foot (service) brake in the low vehicle speed condition, the braking power produced may be more than expected. **Consequence:** The unexpected braking power could result in rear brake lockup and the vehicle becoming difficult to control. **Corrective Action:** Replace brake shoe assembly with improved assembly.

System: Interior; seat belts; belt buckles. **Vehicle:** Passenger vehicles equipped with safety belts made by Takata Corporation. **Defect:** The front safety belt buckle release buttons can break. These red plastic release buttons are marked "press." If a button breaks, pieces can fall into the buckle assembly, causing the buckle to operate improperly. **Consequence:** The safety belts would not provide adequate protection to an occupant in a vehicle crash. **Corrective Action:** Owners should promptly check the condition and operation of both front safety belt buckles, and carefully inspect the red release buttons for any breaks or cracks. They should ensure that both buckles are operating properly by inserting each latchplate into its buckle, tugging on the belt to make sure the latch is securely locked and then pressing the release button. The latchplate should pop out of the buckle when the button is pressed. If either release button shows a sign of breaking or cracking, or if either buckle fails to operate properly, owners should promptly contact their authorized dealer to schedule an appointment to have the buckle replaced or repaired, free of charge. The manufacturer is developing a remedy designed to prevent failure of the buttons that are not currently broken.

MAZDA TRUCK MPV 1990

System: Brakes. **Vehicle:** Passenger van. **Defect:** The rear brake linings can change over time. As the brakes wear, the coefficient of friction can increase, producing inconsistent rear brake performance and premature activation of the antilock brake system. **Consequence:** Inconsistent braking and premature activation of the antilock brake system can cause sudden stops or increased braking distances, resulting in increased risk of vehicle accident. **Corrective Action:** Replace the rear brake assemblies with assemblies whose friction characteristics do not change. This will reduce the risk of premature antilock brake system activation.

System: Interior; seat belts; belt buckles. **Vehicle:** Passenger vehicles equipped with safety belts made by Takata Corporation. **Defect:** The front safety belt buckle release buttons can break. These red plastic release buttons are marked "press." If a button breaks, pieces can fall into the buckle assembly, causing the buckle to operate improperly. **Consequence:** The safety belts would not provide adequate protection to an occupant in a vehicle crash. **Corrective Action:** Owners should promptly check the condition and operation of both front safety belt buckles, and carefully inspect the red release buttons for any breaks or cracks. They should ensure that both buckles are operating properly by inserting each latchplate into its buckle, tugging on the belt to make sure the latch is securely locked and then pressing the release button. The latchplate should pop out of the buckle when the button is pressed. If either release button shows a sign of breaking or cracking, or if either buckle fails to operate properly, owners should promptly contact their authorized dealer to schedule an appointment to have the buckle replaced or repaired, free of charge. The manufacturer is developing a remedy designed to prevent failure of the buttons that are not currently broken.

MAZDA TRUCK MPV 1991

System: Brakes. **Vehicle:** Passenger van. **Defect:** The rear brake linings can change over time. As the brakes wear, the coefficient of friction can increase, producing inconsistent rear brake performance and premature activation of the antilock brake system. **Consequence:** Inconsistent braking and premature activation of the antilock brake system can cause sudden stops or increased braking distances, resulting in increased risk of vehicle accident. **Corrective Action:** Replace the rear brake assemblies with assemblies whose friction characteristics do not change. This will reduce the risk of premature antilock brake system activation.

System: Interior; seat belts; belt buckles. **Vehicle:** Passenger vehicles equipped with safety belts made by Takata Corporation. **Defect:** The front safety belt buckle release buttons can break. These red plastic release buttons are marked "press." If a button breaks, pieces can fall into the buckle assembly, causing the buckle to operate improperly. **Consequence:** The safety belts would not provide adequate protection to an occupant in a vehicle crash. **Corrective Action:** Owners should promptly check the condition and operation of both front safety belt buckles, and carefully inspect the red release buttons for any breaks or cracks. They should ensure that both buckles are operating properly by inserting each latchplate into its buckle, tugging on the belt to make sure the latch is securely locked and then pressing the release button. The latchplate should pop out of the buckle when the button is pressed. If either release button shows a sign of breaking or cracking, or if either buckle fails to operate properly, owners should promptly contact their authorized dealer to schedule an appointment to have the buckle replaced or repaired, free of charge. The manufacturer is developing a remedy designed to prevent failure of the buttons that are not currently broken.

MAZDA TRUCK NAVAJO 1991

System: Fuel tank. **Vehicle:** Light-duty trucks built by Ford Motor Company. **Defect:** Front heat shield extension may contact the upper front corner of plastic fuel tank, damaging or puncturing the fuel tank. **Consequence:** Such fuel tank damage could allow vapor and/or fuel to escape; this could result in a fire if a source of ignition is present. **Corrective Action:** Relocate heat shield; replace fuel tank if damaged or punctured.

System: Rear bumper reinforcement. **Vehicle:** Light-duty trucks built by Ford Motor Company. **Defect:** Rear bumper may be susceptible to fatigue cracking under extended trailer tow service when using a bumper-mounted trailer hitch. **Consequence:** Bumper could separate from vehicle when using a bumper-mounted trailer hitch ball. **Corrective Action:** Install two additional brackets, one additional bar and associated fasteners to prevent bumper separation. **Note:** Bumper-mounted trailer hitch ball assembly should not be used until repair procedure is completed.

System: Transmission. **Vehicle:** Pickup trucks, vans and multipurpose vehicles equipped with A4LD automatic transmissions. **Defect:** When the automatic transmission shift lever is placed in the park position, the park pawl does not always abut or engage the park gear. **Consequence:** Driver may believe the vehicle is safely engaged in park when the gear is not truly engaged. This can lead to the vehicle jumping out of gear unintentionally, vehicle rollaway when parked on a sloped surface, and inadvertent motion when the vehicle is started. All of these conditions can result in a vehicle accident. **Corrective Action:** Repair the transmission with a new park pawl.

MERCEDES BENZ

MERCEDES BENZ 190 1987

System: Airbag unit. **Vehicle:** Passenger cars equipped with airbag units. **Defect:** Push-pull forces of electrical connection between the airbag unit and steering wheel are not within specifications. **Consequence:** Plug may get disconnected, which could result in failure of airbag to be deployed in case of a major accident, increasing potential for injury to the driver, especially if driver is not belted. **Corrective Action:** Inspect and replace airbag unit where necessary.

System: Parking brake. **Vehicle:** Passenger cars. **Defect:** The design of the parking brake grip makes it possible to distort the grip and pinch the brake release knob. If the release knob sticks in a partial engage/release position because of the pinched grip, it is possible for the lever to release unintentionally, with a corresponding reduction in parking brake force. **Consequence:** If the vehicle is not properly parked, with the transmission in the correct position, and if the vehicle is parked on a grade, reduction in parking brake force could lead to unintentional rollaway and an accident. **Corrective Action:** Replace the parking brake grip with a new grip type.

MERCEDES BENZ 300 1987

System: Airbag unit. **Vehicle:** Passenger cars equipped with airbag units. **Defect:** Push-pull forces of electrical connection between the airbag unit and steering wheel are not within specifications. **Consequence:** Plug may get disconnected, which could result in failure of airbag to be deployed in case of a major accident, increasing potential for injury to the driver, especially if driver is not belted. **Corrective Action:** Inspect and replace airbag unit where necessary.

System: Airbag. **Vehicle:** Passenger cars. **Defect:** Airbag gas generator may not ignite at low ambient temperatures. **Consequence:** If airbag does not deploy in a major accident, potential for injury to driver is increased, especially if driver is not belted. **Corrective Action:** Replace airbag units.

System: Fuel system; throttle linkages. **Vehicle:** Passenger cars. **Defect:** Due to heat effects, the throttle bushing located on the accelerator control cable can fatigue and break, causing the throttle linkage to separate. **Consequence:** If the throttle linkage separates, the engine will return to idle speed and remain at idle, with no acceleration ability. Loss of engine speed without prior warning could lead to loss of vehicle control and an accident. **Corrective Action:** Replace the throttle bushing with a new bushing made from more heat-resistant materials.

MERCEDES BENZ 300 1989

System: Fuel system; throttle linkages. **Vehicle:** Passenger cars. **Defect:** Due to heat effects, the throttle bushing located on the accelerator control cable can fatigue and break, causing the throttle linkage to separate. **Consequence:** If the throttle linkage separates, the engine will return to idle speed and remain at idle, with no acceleration ability. Loss of engine speed without prior warning could lead to loss of vehicle control and an accident. **Corrective Action:** Replace the throttle bushing with a new bushing made from more heat-resistant materials.

MERCEDES BENZ 300 1990

System: Brake strut support hex nut bolts. **Vehicle:** Passenger cars. **Defect:** Bolts used for the brake strut support do not meet specifications and may break. **Consequence:** The failure of the bolts may result in a deterioration of vehicle steering and braking, which could result in loss of control and an accident. **Corrective Action:** Replace hex nut bolts with bolts that meet specifications.

System: Tires. **Vehicle:** Passenger cars; 300SL and 500SL. **Defect:** Left front and left rear tires may have been damaged by a worn chain drive of the conveyor system. **Consequence:** Damaged or cut tires could fail during use, and result in an accident with possible injuries. **Corrective Action:** Replace damaged tires with tires of the same brand name.

System: Air conditioning, preresistor for auxiliary fan. **Vehicle:** Passenger cars; 300E, CE, TE, D, E4M and TE4M. **Defect:** Under certain operating conditions, the plastic cover of the preresistor for the auxiliary fan may melt, possibly igniting the preresistor. **Consequence:** This results in an underhood fire that would be hazardous to occupants. **Corrective Action:** Replace the preresistor with a version having a metal cover. **Warning:** The climate control system should be operated in the EC (economy) mode until the preresistor is changed.

System: Fuel system; throttle linkages. **Vehicle:** Passenger cars. **Defect:** Due to heat effects, the throttle bushing located on the accelerator control cable can fatigue and break, causing the throttle linkage to separate. **Consequence:** If the throttle linkage separates, the engine will return to idle speed and remain at idle, with no acceleration ability. Loss of engine speed without prior warning could lead to loss of vehicle control and an accident. **Corrective Action:** Replace the throttle bushing with a new bushing made from more heat-resistant materials.

MERCURY

Note: If your Mercury is presented to an authorized dealer on an agreed-upon service date and the remedy is not provided free of charge within a reasonable time, or the remedy does not correct the defect, please contact Ford Service Center at (800) 392-3673. Also contact the NHTSA's Auto Safety Hotline at (800) 424-9393.

MERCURY CAPRI 1991

System: Transmission oil cooler line. **Vehicle:** Passenger cars. **Defect:** The rubber tube that connects the transmission to the transmission oil cooler (in the radiator) may disconnect, causing discharge of fluid. **Consequence:** Discharged transmission fluid may strike the exhaust manifold or the exhaust pipe, resulting in a fire. **Corrective Action:** Install revised line and clamps to improve line retention to the transmission.

System: Airbags. **Vehicle:** Passenger cars manufactured in Australia. **Defect:** The airbag modules do not meet the Ford specifications for high ambient temperature performance. **Consequence:** At high ambient interior vehicle temperatures (above 140° Fahrenheit), the airbag may tear and malfunction upon deployment. **Corrective Action:** Replace the airbag modules with modules that meet specifications.

MERCURY COUGAR 1987

System: Fuel line coupling. **Vehicle:** Passenger cars and light trucks equipped with fuel injection. **Defect:** Spring lock fuel line coupling may not be properly engaged. **Consequence:** Coupling could disengage due to fuel pressure, vibration and engine movements; this would cause loss of fuel which, in the presence of an ignition source, creates a fire risk. **Corrective Action:** Install retainer clips over the couplings to prevent coupling separation and fuel leakage.

MERCURY COUGAR 1989

System: Fuel tank. **Vehicle:** Passenger cars. **Defect:** Plastic rollover valve mounting plate may not be properly sealed to the plastic fuel tank. **Consequence:** Fuel or vapor could leak, which could result in a vehicle fire. **Corrective Action:** Replace fuel tank.

System: Rear suspension knuckles. **Vehicle:** Passenger cars. **Defect:** Improperly heat-treated rear suspension knuckles could experience high-mileage fatigue cracks and eventual fracture. **Consequence:** This could result in rear suspension failure at the affected wheel, with an adverse effect on control of the car, which could cause an accident. **Corrective Action:** Replace knuckles that have the affected lot codes.

System: Brakes—suspension. **Vehicle:** Passenger cars. **Defect:** Due to contact between the brake caliper of the inboard front wheel and the front stabilizer bar, there may be increased brake pedal travel following low-speed turning maneuvers. **Consequence:** This could cause a reduction in brake performance, which could result in an accident. **Corrective Action:** Install acorn-type front suspension strut nuts to eliminate stabilizer bar-to-brake caliper contact.

MERCURY COUGAR 1990

System: Battery to starter cable. **Vehicle:** Passenger cars equipped with 3.8L engines. **Defect:** Battery to starter cables are longer than specified; excessive cable length could contact engine damper pulley. **Consequence:** Cable protective covering and insulation could wear through and cause a direct short to ground, resulting in overheating of the cable insulation, and possibly an underhood fire. **Corrective Action:** Replace battery to starter cable with correct length cable.

System: Windshield wiper assembly. **Vehicle:** Passenger cars. **Defect:** The nuts which hold the windshield wiper motor to the wiper module may not have been sufficiently tightened, and may loosen or come off. This causes changed wiper patterns, or the wipers may jam if two of the three nuts come off. **Consequence:** Changes in the wiper pattern or jamming of the wipers would result in reduced driver visibility in inclement weather conditions. **Corrective Action:** Apply torque-retention material to wiper motor studs and nuts, and retorque.

MERCURY COUGAR 1991

System: Automatic transmission park rod assembly. **Vehicle:** Passenger cars with automatic overdrive transmissions. **Defect:** The park rod assembly contains a park cam with inadequate surface hardness, which could lead to park disengagement or "no park" engagement when the lever is placed in park. **Consequence:** If park is not engaged and the parking brake is off, a vehicle rollaway could result. **Corrective Action:** Replace park rod assembly on automatic transmissions.

System: Windshield wiper assembly. **Vehicle:** Passenger cars. **Defect:** The nuts which hold the windshield wiper motor to the wiper module may not have been sufficiently tightened, and may loosen or come off. This causes changed wiper patterns, or the wipers may jam if two of the three nuts come off. **Consequence:** Changes in the wiper pattern or jamming of the wipers would result in reduced driver visibility in inclement weather conditions. **Corrective Action:** Apply torque-retention material to wiper motor studs and nuts, and retorque.

MERCURY GRAND MARQUIS 1987

System: Steering centerlinks. **Vehicle:** Passenger vehicles with 5.0L engines. **Defect:** Steering centerlinks may break at a bend location. **Consequence:** Steering control would be diminished, with reduced control of left wheel only and considerable steering wheel free play. **Corrective Action:** Replace steering centerlink.

System: Fuel rails. **Vehicle:** Passenger cars equipped with 5.0L fuel-injected engines. **Defect:** Fuel rails may be bent so that #5 injector cups are out of design position. **Consequence:** Bent fuel rail could cause a fuel leak, which in the presence of an ignition source could result in an engine fire. **Corrective Action:** Replace fuel rail assemblies as necessary.

System: Fuel line coupling. **Vehicle:** Passenger cars and light trucks equipped with fuel injection. **Defect:** Spring lock fuel line coupling may not be properly engaged. **Consequence:** Coupling could disengage due to fuel pressure, vibration and engine movements; this would cause loss of fuel which, in the presence of an ignition source, creates a fire risk. **Corrective Action:** Install retainer clips over the couplings to prevent coupling separation and fuel leakage.

System: Seat belts. **Vehicle:** Station wagons equipped with optional dual rear-facing seats. **Defect:** Automatic retractor for seat belts for dual rear-facing seats may be installed in an improper location. **Consequence:** Seat belt could bind between seat cushion and seat back, causing the retractor to be sluggish or unable to take up excess belt slack. **Corrective Action:** Remove belts and properly install the right auxiliary seat belts.

MERCURY GRAND MARQUIS 1988

System: Seat belts. **Vehicle:** Station wagons equipped with optional dual rear-facing seats. **Defect:** Automatic retractor for seat belts for dual rear-facing seats may be installed in an improper location. **Consequence:** Seat belt could bind between seat cushion and seat back, causing the retractor to be sluggish or unable to take up excess belt slack. **Corrective Action:** Remove belts and properly install the right auxiliary seat belts.

MERCURY GRAND MARQUIS 1990

System: Airbag modules. **Vehicle:** Passenger cars equipped with driver's-side supplemental airbag modules. **Defect:** Threaded inflator components may have been damaged during assembly, which may allow components to separate when inflator receives a signal to deploy the airbag. **Consequence:** Inflator component separation allows hot combustion gases to escape into the passenger compartment, which could result in injuries to vehicle occupants. **Corrective Action:** Replace airbag modules containing potentially defective inflators. **Note:** This campaign was initiated by TRW, Inc., manufacturer of the airbag module.

MERCURY GRAND MARQUIS 1991

System: Airbag modules. **Vehicle:** Passenger cars equipped with driver's-side supplemental airbag modules. **Defect:** Threaded inflator components may have been damaged during assembly, which may allow components to separate when inflator receives a signal to deploy the airbag. **Consequence:** Inflator component separation allows hot combustion gases to escape into the passenger compartment, which could result in injuries to vehicle occupants. **Corrective Action:** Replace airbag modules containing potentially defective inflators. **Note:** This campaign was initiated by TRW, Inc., manufacturer of the airbag module.

System: Automatic transmission park rod assembly. **Vehicle:** Passenger cars with automatic overdrive transmissions. **Defect:** The park rod assembly contains a park cam with inadequate surface hardness, which could lead to park disengagement or "no park" engagement when the lever is placed in park. **Consequence:** If park is not engaged and the parking brake is off, a vehicle rollaway could result. **Corrective Action:** Replace park rod assembly on automatic transmissions.

MERCURY GRAND MARQUIS 1994

System: Brakes; hydraulic system. **Vehicle:** Passenger cars. **Defect:** The nuts and bolts that attach the rear brake adapter to the axle housing flange can loosen and eventually separate. If one or more of the nuts come off the bolts, damage to the parking brake assembly or to the antilock brake system (ABS) sensor and sensor ring (if so equipped) will occur. If all four nuts on one end of the axle come off the bolts, damage to the brake hydraulic line or the parking brake cable can occur. **Consequence:** Occurrence of any of these conditions can result in a loss of braking capability and possible accident. **Corrective Action:** Dealers will inspect and, if needed, install new bolts. If any of the fasteners are disconnected, the parking brake and antilock brake system components will be inspected and serviced.

MERCURY LYNX 1987

System: Wheel lug nuts. **Vehicle:** Passenger cars equipped with stainless steel decorative lug nuts included with styled steel, polycast and cast aluminum wheels. **Defect:** Lug nuts could gall and possibly seize on the wheel studs, without providing adequate clamping load on the wheels. **Consequence:** Wheel studs could fracture, creating a risk of a wheel separating with little forewarning. **Corrective Action:** Replace wheel lug nuts and, if necessary, replace wheels and wheel studs.

System: Fuel line coupling. **Vehicle:** Passenger cars and light trucks equipped with fuel injection. **Defect:** Spring lock fuel line coupling may not be properly engaged. **Consequence:** Coupling could disengage due to fuel pressure, vibration and engine movements; this would cause loss of fuel which, in the presence of an ignition source, creates a fire risk. **Corrective Action:** Install retainer clips over the couplings to prevent coupling separation and fuel leakage.

System: Seat track pedestal. **Vehicle:** Passenger cars. **Defect:** The forward outboard pedestal of the seat track of the driver's seat may be susceptible to fatigue fracture. **Consequence:** This could result in a limited degree of rocking motion of the driver's seat assembly upon acceleration or deceleration, which could cause an accident. **Corrective Action:** Install a reinforcement on all models, and a new seat track as necessary.

MERCURY MARQUIS 1989

System: Tire placard—FMVSS 110. **Vehicle:** Limousine conversions. **Defect:** Tire placard listing recommended tire pressures can be absent or can contain incorrect information. **Consequence:** Use of incorrect tire pressures could cause increased tire wear, which could result in difficulty in vehicle handling or steering. **Corrective Action:** Install label with correct tire information.

System: Alterer's placard; 49 CFR part 567. **Vehicle:** Limousine conversions. **Defect:** Alterer's label stating that vehicle complies with standards, including weight of vehicle, may be absent or incomplete. **Consequence:** Owner would not be aware of correct weight rating and tire size as required by 49 CFR part 567. **Corrective Action:** Install correct alterer's placard.

MERCURY MARQUIS 1990

System: Tire placard—FMVSS 110. **Vehicle:** Limousine conversions. **Defect:** Tire placard listing recommended tire pressures can be absent or can contain incorrect information. **Consequence:** Use of incorrect tire pressures could cause increased tire wear, which could result in difficulty in vehicle handling or steering. **Corrective Action:** Install label with correct tire information.

System: Alterer's placard; 49 CFR part 567. **Vehicle:** Limousine conversions. **Defect:** Alterer's label stating that vehicle complies with standards, including weight of vehicle, may be absent or incomplete. **Consequence:** Owner would not be aware of correct weight rating and tire size as required by 49 CFR part 567. **Corrective Action:** Install correct alterer's placard.

MERCURY SABLE 1987

System: Steering shaft assembly. **Vehicle:** Passenger cars. **Defect:** Steering shaft assemblies contain lower shafts of insufficient length for proper attachment to the shaft insulator flange. **Consequence:** Shaft could separate, resulting in total loss of steering control and a possible accident. **Corrective Action:** Replace steering shaft assembly, as necessary.

System: Rear spindle. **Vehicle:** Passenger cars. **Defect:** Left and/or right rear spindle assemblies may have been improperly heat treated. **Consequence:** If spindle stem separates, loss of vehicle control could occur without prior warning. **Corrective Action:** Replace rear spindle.

System: Rear window wiper motor. **Vehicle:** Station wagons equipped with optional rear window wiper motors. **Defect:** Road salt-induced erosion of the wiper motor conductor strips could cause localized thermal stress within the glass. **Consequence:** Glass could fracture while station wagon is being driven or parked, creating a risk of injury to occupants or sudden distraction to the driver. **Corrective Action:** Apply sealant to conductor strips, and protective tape to lower back lights.

System: Fuel line coupling. **Vehicle:** Passenger cars and light trucks equipped with fuel injection. **Defect:** Spring lock fuel line coupling may not be properly engaged. **Consequence:** Coupling could disengage due to fuel pressure, vibration and engine movements; this would cause loss of fuel which, in the presence of an ignition source, creates a fire risk. **Corrective Action:** Install retainer clips over the couplings to prevent coupling separation and fuel leakage.

System: Brakes. **Vehicle:** Passenger vehicles sold or registered in the following states: CT, IL, IN, ME, MA, MI, NH, NJ, NY, OH, PA, RI, VT and WI. **Defect:** Front disc brake rotors of the subject vehicles may experience severe corrosion if operated in areas where calcium chloride and sodium chloride are used extensively. **Consequence:** Severely corroded rotors may fracture or separate near the inner edges of the brake discs, resulting in reduced braking effectiveness, higher than normal pedal efforts, loud grinding noises and moderate pulls when the brakes are applied. Reduced braking effectiveness may increase minimum stopping distances, possibly resulting in an accident. **Corrective Action:** Replace front brake rotors with full cast front brake rotors.

System: Structure; storage compartments. **Vehicle:** Passenger cars (station wagons). **Defect:** Children can accidentally lock themselves in the footwell area of the rear-facing third seat, or in the storage compartment in station wagons not equipped with an optional third seat. Once the compartment is closed, it cannot be opened from the inside. **Consequence:** There is a danger of air deprivation, hypothermia and/or panic response to a child who has locked himself or herself into the compartment, with the possibility of asphyxiation. **Corrective Action:** Replace the self-latching assembly currently used in the rear storage compartment with a latch assembly that can only be closed with a key. **Note:** Until the latch assembly is replaced, Ford recommends owners lock the storage compartment when not in use. Also, Ford advises that the latch striker can be removed to disable the current latch until revised latch assemblies are available.

System: Structure; rear subframe mounts. **Vehicle:** Taurus and Sables built from October 14, 1985 through August 19, 1988, and Lincoln Continentals built from November 4, 1987 through September 30, 1988 (except 1989-1991 2.5L Taurus and 1989–1992 SHO). The affected cars were sold or registered in the following states: CT, IL, IN, ME, MA, MI, NH, NJ, NY, OH, PA, RI, VT and WI. **Defect:** The body mounts at the rear corners of the subframe, which supports the engine and transmission, may become detached due to corrosion of the subframe mount retaining plate. This would allow the rear corners of the subframe to drop. **Consequence:** If one of the rear corners drops, only minor indications of a malfunction, such as a clunking noise or slight change in steering wheel alignment, are noticeable. However, if both rear corners of the subframe drop, steering becomes very difficult, which could adversely affect vehicle control and possibly result in an accident. **Corrective Action:** Install a corrosion-resistant reinforcing plate and a new bolt on both rear subframe mounts.

System: Suspension; independent front shock absorber. **Equipment Description:** Aftermarket shock absorbers for 1986-1994 Ford Taurus and Mercury Sable passenger cars; parts 71780 and 81780. **Defect:** The arc welds on the sway bar bracket, where it attaches to the strut reserve tube, did not fuse properly. **Consequence:** Over time, a portion of the bracket can tear away from the strut, falling into and puncturing the tire or causing damage to the wheel, which could result in an accident. **Corrective Action:** Monroe dealers will replace the strut free of charge.

MERCURY SABLE 1988

System: Power seat switch wiring. **Vehicle:** Passenger cars. **Defect:** The power seat switch wiring is routed over, rather than under, the front seat support brace, allowing damage by seat cushion spring ends when seat is occupied. **Consequence:** Power seat switch wiring insulation may become abraded or punctured, and an electrical short could occur that could result in a fire in the seat cushion material. **Corrective Action:** Revise routing of power seat wiring to prevent damage from seat cushion spring contact.

System: Brakes. **Vehicle:** Passenger vehicles sold or registered in the following states: CT, IL, IN, ME, MA, MI, NH, NJ, NY, OH, PA, RI, VT and WI. **Defect:** Front disc brake rotors of the subject vehicles may experience severe corrosion if operated in areas where calcium chloride and sodium chloride are used extensively. **Consequence:** Severely corroded rotors may fracture or separate near the inner edges of the brake discs, resulting in reduced braking effectiveness, higher than normal pedal efforts, loud grinding noises and moderate pulls when the brakes are applied. Reduced braking effectiveness may increase minimum stopping distances, possibly resulting in an accident. **Corrective Action:** Replace front brake rotors with full cast front brake rotors.

System: Structure; storage compartments. **Vehicle:** Passenger cars (station wagons). **Defect:** Children can accidentally lock themselves in the footwell area of the rear-facing third seat, or in the storage compartment in station wagons not equipped with an optional third seat. Once the compartment is closed, it cannot be opened from the inside. **Consequence:** There is a danger of air deprivation, hypothermia and/or panic response to a child who has locked himself or herself into the compartment, with the possibility of asphyxiation. **Corrective Action:** Replace the self-latching assembly currently used in the rear storage compartment with a latch assembly that can only be closed with a key. **Note:** Until the latch assembly is replaced, Ford recommends owners lock the storage compartment when not in use. Also, Ford advises that the latch striker can be removed to disable the current latch until revised latch assemblies are available.

System: Structure; rear subframe mounts. **Vehicle:** Taurus and Sables built from October 14, 1985 through August 19, 1988, and Lincoln Continentals built from November 4, 1987 through September 30, 1988 (except 1989-1991 2.5L Taurus and 1989-1992 SHO). The affected cars were sold or registered in the following states: CT, IL, IN, ME, MA, MI, NH, NJ, NY, OH, PA, RI, VT and WI. **Defect:** The body mounts at the rear corners of the subframe, which supports the engine and transmission, may become detached due to corrosion of the subframe mount retaining plate. This would allow the rear corners of the subframe to drop. **Consequence:** If one of the rear corners drops, only minor indications of a malfunction, such as a clunking noise or slight change in steering wheel alignment, are noticeable. However, if both rear corners of the subframe drop, steering becomes very difficult, which could adversely affect vehicle control and possibly result in an accident. **Corrective Action:** Install a corrosion-resistant reinforcing plate and a new bolt on both rear subframe mounts.

System: Suspension; independent front shock absorber. **Equipment Description:** Aftermarket shock absorbers for 1986-1994 Ford Taurus and Mercury Sable passenger cars; parts 71780 and 81780. **Defect:** The arc welds on the sway bar bracket, where it attaches to the strut reserve tube, did not fuse properly. **Consequence:** Over time, a portion of the bracket can tear away from the strut, falling into and puncturing the tire or causing damage to the wheel, which could result in an accident. **Corrective Action:** Monroe dealers will replace the strut free of charge.

MERCURY SABLE 1989

System: Front side marker lamps—FMVSS 108. **Vehicle:** Passenger cars. **Defect:** Front side marker lamps were unintentionally equipped with clear bulbs instead of amber-colored bulbs, as specified in FMVSS 108. **Consequence:** Vehicles would not comply with standard. **Corrective Action:** Replace clear bulbs with amber-colored bulbs.

System: Power seat switch wiring. **Vehicle:** Passenger cars. **Defect:** The power seat switch wiring is routed over, rather than under, the front seat support brace, allowing damage by seat cushion spring ends when seat is occupied. **Consequence:** Power seat switch wiring insulation may become abraded or punctured, and an electrical short could occur that could result in a fire in the seat cushion material. **Corrective Action:** Revise routing of power seat wiring to prevent damage from seat cushion spring contact.

System: Brakes. **Vehicle:** Passenger vehicles sold or registered in the following states: CT, IL, IN, ME, MA, MI, NH, NJ, NY, OH, PA, RI, VT and WI. **Defect:** Front disc brake rotors of the subject vehicles may experience severe corrosion if operated in areas where calcium chloride and sodium chloride are used extensively. **Consequence:** Severely corroded rotors may fracture or separate near the inner edges of the brake discs, resulting in reduced braking effectiveness, higher than normal pedal efforts, loud grinding noises and moderate pulls when the brakes are applied. Reduced braking effectiveness may increase minimum stopping distances, possibly resulting in an accident. **Corrective Action:** Replace front brake rotors with full cast front brake rotors.

System: Structure; storage compartments. **Vehicle:** Passenger cars (station wagons). **Defect:** Children can accidentally lock themselves in the footwell area of the rear-facing third seat, or in the storage compartment in station wagons not equipped with an optional third seat. Once the compartment is closed, it cannot be opened from the inside. **Consequence:** There is a danger of air deprivation, hypothermia and/or panic response to a child who has locked himself or herself into the compartment, with the possibility of asphyxiation. **Corrective Action:** Replace the self-latching assembly currently used in the rear storage compartment with a latch assembly that can only be closed with a key. **Note:** Until the latch assembly is replaced, Ford recommends owners lock the storage compartment when not in use. Also, Ford advises that the latch striker can be removed to disable the current latch until revised latch assemblies are available.

System: Safety belt buckle. **Vehicle:** Passenger cars and utility vehicles. **Defect:** The rigid mounted safety belt buckles are defective in three ways. First, a fastened safety belt buckle will not unlatch when the release button is depressed. This results from interference between the buckle ejector finger and the buckle tongue window. The second defect is the safety belt buckle may not latch. The third possible defect is that the tongue may be retained by the buckle, but it may not be latched sufficiently to provide occupant protection. **Consequence:** An insufficiently latched or unlatched safety belt increases the risk of injury to seat occupants in the event of a sudden stop or accident. If the safety belt buckle will not unlatch, it will not allow the occupant to get out of the vehicle in an emergency situation. **Corrective Action:** Ford will replace the rigid mounted safety belt buckles with end release safety belt buckles designed to prevent latch problems. **Note:** Only the end release buckles on "rigid" mountings are susceptible to this malfunction; the web-mounted front center end release buckles and the web-mounted rear facing third seat end release buckles in Taurus or Sable vehicles will not be replaced. Also, the web-mounted front center buckles in Explorer vehicles will not be replaced.

System: Structure; rear subframe mounts. **Vehicle:** Taurus and Sables built from August 1, 1988 through December 23, 1992 and Lincoln Continentals built from October 3, 1988 through December 23, 1992. The affected cars were sold or registered in the following states: CT, IL, IN, ME, MA, MI, NH, NJ, NY, OH, PA, RI, VT and WI. **Defect:** The body mounts at the rear corners of the subframe, which supports the engine and transmission, may become detached due to corrosion of the subframe mount retaining plate. This would allow the rear corners of the subframe to drop. **Consequence:** If one of the rear corners drops, only minor indications of a malfunction, such as a clunking noise or slight change in steering wheel alignment, are noticeable. However, if both rear corners of the subframe drop, steering becomes very difficult, which could adversely affect vehicle control and possibly result in an accident. **Corrective Action:** Install a corrosion-resistant reinforcing plate and a new bolt on both rear subframe mounts.

System: Suspension; independent front shock absorber. **Equipment Description:** Aftermarket shock absorbers for 1986-1994 Ford Taurus and Mercury Sable passenger cars; parts 71780 and 81780. **Defect:** The arc welds on the sway bar bracket, where it attaches to the strut reserve tube, did not fuse properly. **Consequence:** Over time, a portion of the bracket can tear away from the strut, falling into and puncturing the tire or causing damage to the wheel, which could result in an accident. **Corrective Action:** Monroe dealers will replace the strut free of charge. **Note:** If the vehicle is presented to an authorized dealer on an agreed-upon service date and the remedy is not provided free of charge within a reasonable time, or the remedy does not correct the defect, please contact Monroe at (800) 521-6754. Also contact the NHTSA's Auto Safety Hotline at (800) 424-9393.

MERCURY SABLE 1990

System: Autolamp headlamp control. **Vehicle:** Passenger cars with autolamp headlamp control system. **Defect:** An incorrect transistor may cause autolamp system light sensor module malfunction. **Consequence:** Headlamps could turn off while vehicle is being driven, or remain on after vehicle is parked. Loss of headlights while driving at night could be hazardous to the driver and other traffic. **Corrective Action:** Replace light sensor modules.

System: Airbag modules. **Vehicle:** Passenger cars equipped with driver's-side supplemental airbag modules. **Defect:** Threaded inflator components may have been damaged during assembly, which may allow components to separate when inflator receives a signal to deploy the airbag. **Consequence:** Inflator component separation allows hot combustion gases to escape into the passenger compartment, which could result in injuries to vehicle occupants. **Corrective Action:** Replace airbag modules containing potentially defective inflators. **Note:** This campaign was initiated by TRW, Inc., manufacturer of the airbag module.

System: Brakes. **Vehicle:** Passenger vehicles sold or registered in the following states: CT, IL, IN, ME, MA, MI, NH, NJ, NY, OH, PA, RI, VT and WI. **Defect:** Front disc brake rotors of the subject vehicles may experience severe corrosion if operated in areas where calcium chloride and sodium chloride are used extensively. **Consequence:** Severely corroded rotors may fracture or separate near the inner edges of the brake discs, resulting in reduced braking effectiveness, higher than normal pedal efforts, loud grinding noises and moderate pulls when the brakes are applied. Reduced braking effectiveness may increase minimum stopping distances, possibly resulting in an accident. **Corrective Action:** Replace front brake rotors with full cast front brake rotors.

System: Structure; storage compartments. **Vehicle:** Passenger cars (station wagons). **Defect:** Children can accidentally lock themselves in the footwell area of the rear-facing third seat, or in the storage compartment in station wagons not equipped with an optional third seat. Once the compartment is closed, it cannot be opened from the inside. **Consequence:** There is a danger of air deprivation, hypothermia and/or panic response to a child who has locked himself or herself into the compartment, with the possibility of asphyxiation. **Corrective Action:** Replace the self-latching assembly currently used in the rear storage compartment with a latch assembly that can only be closed with a key. **Note:** Until the latch assembly is replaced, Ford recommends owners lock the storage compartment when not in use. Also, Ford advises that the latch striker can be removed to disable the current latch until revised latch assemblies are available.

System: Safety belt buckle. **Vehicle:** Passenger cars and utility vehicles. **Defect:** The rigid mounted safety belt buckles are defective in three ways. First, a fastened safety belt buckle will not unlatch when the release button is depressed. This results from interference between the buckle ejector finger and the buckle tongue window. The second defect is the safety belt buckle may not latch. The third possible defect is that the tongue may be retained by the buckle, but it may not be latched sufficiently to provide occupant protection. **Consequence:** An insufficiently latched or unlatched safety belt increases the risk of injury to seat occupants in the event of a sudden stop or accident. If the safety belt buckle will not unlatch, it will not allow the occupant to get out of the vehicle in an emergency situation. **Corrective Action:** Ford will replace the rigid mounted safety belt buckles with end release safety belt buckles designed to prevent latch problems. **Note:** Only the end release buckles on "rigid" mountings are susceptible to this malfunction; the web-mounted front center end release buckles and the web-mounted rear-facing third seat end release buckles in Taurus or Sable vehicles will not be replaced. Also, the web-mounted front center buckles in Explorer vehicles will not be replaced.

System: Structure; rear subframe mounts. **Vehicle:** Taurus and Sables built from August 1, 1988 through December 23, 1992 and Lincoln Continentals built from October 3, 1988 through December 23, 1992. The affected cars were sold or registered in the following states: CT, IL, IN, ME, MA, MI, NH, NJ, NY, OH, PA, RI, VT and WI. **Defect:** The body mounts at the rear corners of the subframe, which supports the engine and transmission, may become detached due to corrosion of the subframe mount retaining plate. This would allow the rear corners of the subframe to drop. **Consequence:** If one of the rear corners drops, only minor indications of a malfunction, such as a clunking noise or slight change in steering wheel alignment, are noticeable. However, if both rear corners of the subframe drop, steering becomes very difficult, which could adversely affect vehicle control and possibly result in an accident. **Corrective Action:** Install a corrosion-resistant reinforcing plate and a new bolt on both rear subframe mounts.

System: Suspension; independent front shock absorber. **Equipment Description:** Aftermarket shock absorbers for 1986-1994 Ford Taurus and Mercury Sable passenger cars; parts 71780 and 81780. **Defect:** The arc welds on the sway bar bracket, where it attaches to the strut reserve tube, did not fuse properly. **Consequence:** Over time, a portion of the bracket can tear away from the strut, falling into and puncturing the tire or causing damage to the wheel, which could result in an accident. **Corrective Action:** Monroe dealers will replace the strut free of charge. **Note:** If the vehicle is presented to an authorized dealer on an agreed-upon service date and the remedy is not provided free of charge within a reasonable time, or the remedy does not correct the defect, please contact Monroe at (800) 521-6754. Also contact the NHTSA's Auto Safety Hotline at (800) 424-9393.

MERCURY SABLE 1991

System: Brakes. **Vehicle:** Passenger vehicles sold or registered in the following states: CT, IL, IN, ME, MA, MI, NH, NJ, NY, OH, PA,

RI, VT and WI. **Defect:** Front disc brake rotors of the subject vehicles may experience severe corrosion if operated in areas where calcium chloride and sodium chloride are used extensively. **Consequence:** Severely corroded rotors may fracture or separate near the inner edges of the brake discs, resulting in reduced braking effectiveness, higher than normal pedal efforts, loud grinding noises and moderate pulls when the brakes are applied. Reduced braking effectiveness may increase minimum stopping distances, possibly resulting in an accident. **Corrective Action:** Replace front brake rotors with full cast front brake rotors.

System: Structure; storage compartments. **Vehicle:** Passenger cars (station wagons). **Defect:** Children can accidentally lock themselves in the footwell area of the rear-facing third seat, or in the storage compartment in station wagons not equipped with an optional third seat. Once the compartment is closed, it cannot be opened from the inside. **Consequence:** There is a danger of air deprivation, hypothermia and/or panic response to a child who has locked himself or herself into the compartment, with the possibility of asphyxiation. **Corrective Action:** Replace the self-latching assembly currently used in the rear storage compartment with a latch assembly that can only be closed with a key. **Note:** Until the latch assembly is replaced, Ford recommends owners lock the storage compartment when not in use. Also, Ford advises that the latch striker can be removed to disable the current latch until revised latch assemblies are available.

System: Structure; rear subframe mounts. **Vehicle:** Taurus and Sables built from August 1, 1988 through December 23, 1992 and Lincoln Continentals built from October 3, 1988 through December 23, 1992. The affected cars were sold or registered in the following states: CT, IL, IN, ME, MA, MI, NH, NJ, NY, OH, PA, RI, VT and WI. **Defect:** The body mounts at the rear corners of the subframe, which supports the engine and transmission, may become detached due to corrosion of the subframe mount retaining plate. This would allow the rear corners of the subframe to drop. **Consequence:** If one of the rear corners drops, only minor indications of a malfunction, such as a clunking noise or slight change in steering wheel alignment, are noticeable. However, if both rear corners of the subframe drop, steering becomes very difficult, which could adversely affect vehicle control and possibly result in an accident. **Corrective Action:** Install a corrosion-resistant reinforcing plate and a new bolt on both rear subframe mounts.

System: Suspension; independent front shock absorber. **Equipment Description:** Aftermarket shock absorbers for 1986-1994 Ford Taurus and Mercury Sable passenger cars; parts 71780 and 81780. **Defect:** The arc welds on the sway bar bracket, where it attaches to the strut reserve tube, did not fuse properly. **Consequence:** Over time, a portion of the bracket can tear away from the strut, falling into and puncturing the tire or causing damage to the wheel, which could result in an accident. **Corrective Action:** Monroe dealers will replace the strut free of charge. **Note:** If the vehicle is presented to an authorized dealer on an agreed-upon service date and the remedy is not provided free of charge within a reasonable time, or the remedy does not correct the defect, please contact Monroe at (800) 521-6754. Also contact the NHTSA's Auto Safety Hotline at (800) 424-9393.

MERCURY SABLE 1992

System: Structure; storage compartments. **Vehicle:** Passenger cars (station wagons). **Defect:** Children can accidentally lock themselves in the footwell area of the rear-facing third seat, or in the storage compartment in station wagons not equipped with an optional third seat. Once the compartment is closed, it cannot be opened from the inside. **Consequence:** There is a danger of air deprivation, hypothermia and/or panic response to a child who has locked himself or herself into the compartment, with the possibility of asphyxiation. **Corrective Action:** Replace the self-latching assembly currently used in the rear storage compartment with a latch assembly that can only be closed with a key. **Note:** Until the latch assembly is replaced, Ford recommends owners lock the storage compartment when not in use. Also, Ford advises that the latch striker can be removed to disable the current latch until revised latch assemblies are available.

System: Structure; rear subframe mounts. **Vehicle:** Taurus and Sables built from August 1, 1988 through December 23, 1992 and Lincoln Continentals built from October 3, 1988 through December 23, 1992. The affected cars were sold or registered in the following states: CT, IL, IN, ME, MA, MI, NH, NJ, NY, OH, PA, RI, VT and WI. **Defect:** The body mounts at the rear corners of the subframe, which supports the engine and transmission, may become detached due to corrosion of the subframe mount retaining plate. This would allow the rear corners of the subframe to drop. **Consequence:** If one of the rear corners drops, only minor indications of a malfunction such as a clunking noise or slight change in steering wheel alignment are noticeable. However, if both rear corners of the subframe drop, steering becomes very difficult, which could adversely affect vehicle control and possibly result in an accident. **Corrective Action:** Install a corrosion-resistant reinforcing plate and a new bolt on both rear subframe mounts.

System: Suspension; independent front shock absorber. **Equipment Description:** Aftermarket shock absorbers for 1986-1994 Ford Taurus and Mercury Sable passenger cars; parts 71780 and 81780. **Defect:** The arc welds on the sway bar bracket, where it attaches to the strut reserve tube, did not fuse properly. **Consequence:** Over time, a portion of the bracket can tear away from the strut, falling into and puncturing the tire or causing damage to the wheel, which could result in an accident. **Corrective Action:** Monroe dealers will replace the strut free of charge. **Note:** If the vehicle is presented to an authorized dealer on an agreed upon service date and the remedy is not provided free of charge within a reasonable time, or the remedy does not correct the defect, please contact Monroe at (800) 521-6754. Also contact the NHTSA's Auto Safety Hotline at (800) 424-9393.

MERCURY SABLE 1993

System: Brakes **Vehicle:** Passenger cars with optional antilock brake systems (ABS). **Defect:** Antilock brake system controllers designed for rear-wheel drive cars may have been installed on these front-wheel drive cars. **Consequence:** This could result in reduced braking ability and possible vehicle accident. **Corrective Action:** Replace the rear-wheel drive antilock brake system controller with a front-wheel drive antilock brake system controller.

System: Structure; rear subframe mounts. **Vehicle:** Taurus and Sables built from August 1, 1988 through December 23, 1992 and Lincoln Continentals built from October 3, 1988 through December 23, 1992. The affected cars were sold or registered in the following states: CT, IL, IN, ME, MA, MI, NH, NJ, NY, OH, PA, RI, VT and WI. **Defect:** The body mounts at the rear corners of the subframe, which supports the engine and transmission, may become detached due to corrosion of the subframe mount retaining plate. This would allow the rear corners of the subframe to drop. **Consequence:** If one of the rear corners drops, only minor indications of a malfunction, such as a clunking noise or slight change in steering wheel alignment, are noticeable. However, if both rear corners of the subframe drop, steering becomes very difficult, which could adversely affect vehicle control and possibly result in an accident. **Corrective Action:** Install a corrosion-resistant reinforcing plate and a new bolt on both rear subframe mounts.

System: Suspension; independent front shock absorber. **Equipment Description:** Aftermarket shock absorbers for 1986-1994 Ford Taurus and Mercury Sable passenger cars; parts 71780 and 81780. **Defect:** The arc welds on the sway bar bracket, where it attaches to the strut reserve tube, did not fuse properly. **Consequence:** Over time, a portion of the bracket can tear away from the strut, falling into and puncturing the tire or causing damage to the wheel, which could result in an accident. **Corrective Action:** Monroe dealers will replace the strut free of charge. **Note:** If the vehicle is presented to an authorized dealer on an agreed-upon service date and the remedy is not provided free of charge within a reasonable time or the remedy does not correct the defect, please contact Monroe at (800) 521-6754. Also, contact the NHTSA's Auto Safety Hotline at (800) 424-9393.

MERCURY TOPAZ 1988

System: Throttle. **Vehicle:** Passenger cars with 2.3L engines. **Defect:** Two attachment screws for the throttle position sensors could loosen and back out. **Consequence:** If both screws come out, sensors could disengage from the throttle shaft, preventing return of the throttle from midposition. **Corrective Action:** Replace attachment screws with screws with pre-applied adhesive that will be tightened to a higher torque specification.

MERCURY TOPAZ 1990

System: Airbag modules. **Vehicle:** Passenger cars equipped with driver's-side supplemental airbag modules. **Defect:** Threaded inflator components may have been damaged during assembly, which may allow components to separate when inflator receives a signal to deploy the airbag. **Consequence:** Inflator component separation allows hot combustion gases to escape into the passenger compartment, which could result in injuries to vehicle occupants. **Corrective Action:** Replace airbag modules containing potentially defective inflators. **Note:** This campaign was initiated by TRW, Inc., manufacturer of the airbag module.

MERCURY TRACER 1988

System: Fuel filler neck screws. **Vehicle:** Passenger cars. **Defect:** Incorrect fuel filler neck attachment screws were used to attach the neck to the rear quarter panels. **Consequence:** This condition could cause a rattle between the fuel filler pipe and the surrounding body structure. **Corrective Action:** Replace incorrect screws with new bolt and washer assemblies.

System: Front lap shoulder belts. **Vehicle:** Passenger cars. **Defect:** Some lap shoulder belt retractors were built with certain out-of-tolerance components. **Consequence:** Retractors may lock at low belt pull-out rates; this could discourage seat belt usage. **Corrective Action:** Replace front lap shoulder belt assemblies, as necessary.

System: Interior; seat belts; belt buckles. **Vehicle:** Passenger vehicles equipped with safety belts made by Takata Corporation. **Defect:** The front safety belt buckle release buttons can break. These red plastic release buttons are marked "press." If a button breaks, pieces can fall into the buckle assembly, causing the buckle to operate improperly. **Consequence:** The safety belts would not provide adequate protection to an occupant in a vehicle crash. **Corrective Action:** Owners should promptly check the condition and operation of both front safety belt buckles, and carefully inspect the red release buttons for any breaks or cracks. They should ensure that both buckles are operating properly by inserting each latchplate into its buckle, tugging on the belt to make sure that latch is securely locked and then pressing the release button. The latchplate should pop out of the buckle when the button is pressed. If either release button shows a sign of breaking or cracking, or if either buckle fails to operate properly, owners should promptly contact their authorized dealer to schedule an appointment to have the buckle replaced or repaired, free of charge. The manufacturer is developing a remedy designed to prevent failure of the buttons that are not currently broken. **Note:** The 1987 through 1989 four-door Mercury Tracers involved in this recall campaign were only sold in Canada. No Tracers sold in the United States are involved.

MERCURY TRACER 1989

System: Interior; seat belts; belt buckles. **Vehicle:** Passenger vehicles equipped with safety belts made by Takata Corporation. **Defect:** The front safety belt buckle release buttons can break. These red plastic release buttons are marked "press." If a button breaks, pieces can fall into the buckle assembly, causing the buckle to operate improperly. **Consequence:** The safety belts would not provide adequate protection to an occupant in a vehicle crash. **Corrective Action:** Owners should promptly check the condition and operation of both front safety belt buckles, and carefully inspect the red release buttons for any breaks or cracks. They should ensure that both buckles are operating properly by inserting each latchplate into its buckle, tugging on the belt to make sure that latch is securely locked and then pressing the release button. The latchplate should pop out of the buckle when the button is pressed. If either release button shows a sign of breaking or cracking, or if either buckle fails to operate properly, owners should promptly contact their authorized dealer to schedule an appointment to have the buckle replaced or repaired, free of charge. The manufacturer is developing a remedy designed to prevent failure of the buttons that are not currently broken. **Note:** The 1987 through 1989 four-door Mercury Tracers involved in this recall campaign were only sold in Canada. No Tracers sold in the United States are involved.

MERCURY TRACER 1991

System: Fuel system. **Vehicle:** Passenger vehicles equipped with fuel pump sending assemblies produced by Ford Electrical and Fuel Handling Division (FEHD). **Defect:** Fatigue cracks can develop in the solder joint between the fuel return tube and the fuel pump sending unit located at the top of the fuel tank. **Consequence:** Should a crack develop, fuel vapor can escape from the tank when the tank is full, and a small amount of fuel can leak from the crack. Fuel leaks can result in fire when exposed to a source of ignition. **Corrective Action:** Install a new fuel pump sending assembly.

System: Steering. **Vehicle:** Passenger cars. **Defect:** The roll pins securing the ignition lock in the steering column housing can separate or move out of position. **Consequence:** The ignition lock cylinder may disengage from the steering column housing, which could cause the steering column to lock up, resulting in loss of vehicle control and a possible accident. **Corrective Action:** If one or both of the roll pins are missing or not fully inserted, the ignition lock housing will be replaced, along with the doorlocks and the liftgate or deck-lid locks, so that key compatibility is maintained. If both pins are present and fully inserted, a plastic snap-on sleeve will be installed as a precaution to prevent the roll pins from coming out.

System: Suspension; independent front. **Equipment Description:** Offset rear toe adjusting pin. **Defect:** The offset toe adjusting pin can fracture under conditions such as torsional loads, flexing motion, impact loads and overtorquing. **Consequence:** This can result in loss of vehicle steering control and an accident. **Corrective Action:** Dana will pay for replacement and labor costs of the adjustment pin without charge to the installing facility or the vehicle owner. These pins should be replaced by a Ford original equipment pin assembly. Owner or installer inquiries concerning this recall campaign should contact Dana Service Center at (800) 248-9606. **Note:** If you have any problems with the pin replacement reimbursement program, please contact Dana Service Center at (800) 248-9606. Also contact the NHTSA's Auto Safety Hotline at (800) 424-9393.

MERCURY TRACER 1993

System: Suspension; independent front. **Equipment Description:** Offset rear toe adjusting pin. **Defect:** The offset toe adjusting pin can fracture under conditions such as torsional loads, flexing motion, impact loads and overtorquing. **Consequence:** This can result in loss of vehicle steering control and an accident. **Corrective Action:** Dana will pay for replacement and labor costs of the adjustment pin without charge to the installing facility or the vehicle owner. These pins should be replaced by a Ford original equipment pin assembly. Owner or installer inquiries concerning this recall campaign should contact Dana Service Center at (800) 248-9606. **Note:** If you have any problems with the pin replacement reimbursement program, please contact Dana Service Center at (800) 248-9606. Also contact the NHTSA's Auto Safety Hotline at (800) 424-9393.

MERCURY TRUCK VILLAGER 1993

System: Brakes: master cylinder. **Vehicle:** Passenger minivans. **Defect:** The service brake master cylinder was not properly assembled, or could have been damaged by the evacuation and filling of the brake system at the assembly plant. **Consequence:** This can result in a partial brake system failure due to internal master cylinder leakage, which can cause loss of braking on two of the four wheels. If this occurs, there would be increased brake pedal travel, higher pedal efforts and increased stopping distances. **Corrective Action:** A new brake master cylinder will be installed. **Note:** Ford Motor Company and Nissan Motors Corporation will conduct separate recall campaigns for this safety defect.

System: Interior: passenger restraint. **Vehicle:** Passenger minivans. **Defect:** One or both of the bolts securing the automatic seat belt restraint system tracks to the b-pillars were not adequately tightened. **Consequence:** This condition can result in the automatic seat belt system track joints having less than design strength, and increase the risk of injury to the seat occupant in the event of a collision or sudden stop. **Corrective Action:** Dealers will tighten the passive restraint system track mounting bolts. **Note:** Ford Motor Company and Nissan

Motors Corporation will conduct separate recall campaigns for this safety defect.

System: Fuel system. **Vehicle:** Passenger vans. **Defect:** Fuel filler hoses may have been cut prior to installation by a utility knife used to open the shipping box. **Consequence:** Fuel leakage can result if the cut extended through the thickness of the hose wall. Leaking fuel can result in a fire if exposed to a source of ignition. **Corrective Action:** Replace the fuel filler hose. **Note:** Ford Motor Company and Nissan Motors Corporation will each be handling this recall for their own vehicles.

MITSUBISHI

Note: If your Mitsubishi is presented to an authorized dealer on an agreed-upon service date and the remedy is not provided free of charge within a reasonable time, please contact Mitsubishi at (800) 222-0037. Also contact the NHTSA's Auto Safety Hotline at (800) 424-9393.

MITSUBISHI ECLIPSE 1990

System: Electrical—underhood wiring harness. **Vehicle:** Passenger cars. **Defect:** Wiring harness for the headlamps may break due to the stress created by the headlamp popup devices. **Consequence:** Breakage of the wiring harness causes loss of headlamp illumination, which could have a potential for an accident. **Corrective Action:** Headlamp wiring harness routing will be modified and damaged wires repaired.

System: Sunroof hinges. **Vehicle:** Passenger cars equipped with DSM-manufactured sunroofs. **Defect:** Operation of sunroof in "non-standard" manner may cause male hinge disengagement from the roof hinge receiver. **Consequence:** The sunroof glass could detach from the roof and result in injury to occupants or persons in the vicinity, especially if this occurs while the vehicle is in motion. **Corrective Action:** Replace male hinge with a modified version to increase roof hinge receiver retention ability. **Note:** This recall applies only to Diamond Star Motors-installed sunroofs. Chrysler Corporation's Plymouth and Eagle dealerships and Mitsubishi Motor Sales of America will implement the recall action.

System: Windshield mounting—FMVSS 212. **Vehicle:** Passenger cars. **Defect:** Diluted primer may have been used on the windshield opening flanges prior to windshield glass installation, which would not provide the retention required by FMVSS 212. **Consequence:** Windshields would not prevent ejection of vehicle occupants during a vehicle crash, which causes serious injuries and fatalities. **Corrective Action:** Replace windshields, associated parts and primer.

System: Interior; seat belts; belt buckles. **Vehicle:** Passenger vehicles and light-duty trucks and vans equipped with safety belts made by Takata Corporation. **Defect:** The front safety belt buckle release buttons can break. These red plastic release buttons are marked "press." If a button breaks, pieces can fall into the buckle assembly, causing the buckle to operate improperly. **Consequence:** The safety belts would not provide adequate protection to an occupant in a vehicle crash. **Corrective Action:** Owners should promptly check the condition and operation of both front safety belt buckles, and carefully inspect the red release buttons for any breaks or cracks. They should ensure that both buckles are operating properly by inserting each latchplate into its buckle, tugging on the belt to make sure the latch is securely locked and then pressing the release button. The latchplate should pop out of the buckle when the button is pressed. If either release button shows a sign of breaking or cracking, or if either buckle fails to operate properly, owners should promptly contact their authorized dealer to schedule an appointment to have the buckle replaced or repaired, free of charge. The manufacturer is developing a remedy designed to prevent failure of the buttons that are not currently broken.

MITSUBISHI ECLIPSE 1991

System: Interior; seat belts; belt buckles. **Vehicle:** Passenger vehicles and light-duty trucks and vans equipped with safety belts made by Takata Corporation. **Defect:** The front safety belt buckle release buttons can break. These red plastic release buttons are marked "press." If a button breaks, pieces can fall into the buckle assembly, causing the buckle to operate improperly. **Consequence:** The safety belts would not provide adequate protection to an occupant in a vehicle crash. **Corrective Action:** Owners should promptly check the condition and operation of both front safety belt buckles, and carefully inspect the red release buttons for any breaks or cracks. They should ensure that both buckles are operating properly by inserting each latchplate into its buckle, tugging on the belt to make sure the latch is securely locked and then pressing the release button. The latchplate should pop out of the buckle when the button is pressed. If either release button shows a sign of breaking or cracking, or if either buckle fails to operate properly, owners should promptly contact their authorized dealer to schedule an appointment to have the buckle replaced or repaired, free of charge. The manufacturer is developing a remedy designed to prevent failure of the buttons that are not currently broken. **Note:** If your vehicle is presented to an authorized dealer on an agreed-upon service date and the remedy is not provided free of charge within a reasonable time, please contact Mitsubishi at (800) 222-0037. Also contact the NHTSA's Auto Safety Hotline at (800) 424-9393.

MITSUBISHI PRECIS 1988

System: Exhaust system. **Vehicle:** Passenger vehicles. **Defect:** Deterioration of the reed valve subassembly may lead to a malfunction within the secondary air supply portion of the emission control system. The screws which attach the reeds to the reed valve subassembly may rust and, if the rusting becomes severe, the screw heads will erode and allow the reeds to separate from the reed valve subassembly. Corrosion may also occur on the reed valve subassembly, deforming the reed seats and preventing the reeds from closing properly. Separation of the reeds from the reed valve subassembly or improper closing of the reeds allows hot exhaust gases to flow backward into the plastic secondary air filter case when the vehicle is being driven. These hot exhaust gases may melt the secondary plastic air filter case. **Consequence:** The melting plastic air filter case may lead to a fire in the engine compartment. **Corrective Action:** Replace the reed valve subassembly with one whose metal components are fabricated from corrosion-resistant stainless steel. **Note:** Hyundai Motor Company will be performing this recall for the Hyundai Excel and for the Mitsubishi Precis.

System: Heater; water; defroster; heater core. **Vehicle:** Passenger cars. **Defect:** The heater control valve stem does not meet the material specifications. High coolant temperatures can cause the stem to leak. **Consequence:** This can result in a burn injury to the front seat passenger's feet and legs. **Corrective Action:** Dealers will inspect and replace defective valve stems.

System: Heater; water; defroster; heater core. **Vehicle:** Passenger cars. **Defect:** Vehicles involved are those that had the heater valve stems replaced in an earlier Mitsubishi recall. Certain vehicles had an incorrect valve stem installed, which could cause the incorrect stem to leak after a period of time. **Consequence:** This can result in a burn injury to the front seat passenger's feet and legs. **Corrective Action:** Dealers will inspect and replace incorrect valve stems.

NISSAN

Note: If your Nissan is presented to an authorized dealer on an agreed-upon service date and the remedy is not provided free of charge within a reasonable time, please contact Nissan at (800) 647-7261. Also contact the NHTSA's Auto Safety Hotline at (800) 424-9393.

NISSAN 240SX 1989

System: Interior; seat belts; belt buckles. **Vehicle:** Passenger, multi-purpose vehicles and light-duty trucks equipped with safety belts made by Takata Corporation. **Defect:** The front safety belt buckle release buttons can break. These red plastic release buttons are marked "press." If a button breaks, pieces can fall into the buckle assembly, causing the buckle to operate improperly. **Consequence:** The safety belts would not provide adequate protection to an occupant in a vehicle crash. **Corrective Action:** Owners should promptly check the condition and operation of both front safety belt buckles, and carefully inspect the red release buttons for any breaks or cracks. They should ensure that both buckles are operating properly by inserting each latchplate into its buckle, tugging on the belt to make sure the latch is securely locked and then pressing the release button. The latchplate should pop out of the buckle when the button is pressed. If either release button shows a sign of breaking or cracking, or if either buckle fails to operate properly, owners should promptly contact their authorized dealer to schedule an appointment to have the buckle replaced or repaired free of charge.

NISSAN 300ZX 1987

System: Accelerator—transmission. **Vehicle:** Passenger cars equipped with automatic transmission. **Defect:** Unintended acceleration may occur, for example, when shifting from the park position. **Consequence:** This could result in a vehicle accident. **Corrective Action:** Install a shift interlock system which prevents the transmission shift lever from being moved from the park position unless the brake pedal is depressed.

NISSAN ALTIMA 1993

System: Fuel; throttle linkages and control. **Vehicle:** Passenger vehicles. **Defect:** Engine movement can be transmitted to the airflow meter/filter housing and support bracket, which is mounted in the engine air duct, causing the throttle cable housing to pull out of the cable guide. This may prevent the throttle from returning to the idle position when the gas pedal is released. **Consequence:** If this were to occur while the vehicle is in motion, loss of throttle control could result in an accident. **Corrective Action:** Nissan will reposition the throttle cable housing in the support bracket to provide additional slack for engine movement. A rubber stopper will be clamped to the cable to maintain the correct position for the cable at the support bracket. In addition, the throttle cable will be tested for pullout resistance from the guide in the event the cable was damaged. The throttle assembly will be replaced, if necessary.

NISSAN MAXIMA 1992

System: Interior systems; passive restraints; airbags. **Vehicle:** Passenger cars with driver's-side airbags. **Defect:** In some underbody impacts, the airbag sensor activates and sends a signal to the airbag, located in the center of the steering wheel, causing the driver's-side airbag to inflate. **Consequence:** Airbag inflation may occur when it is not needed to protect the driver, and may result in minor injuries to the driver from the inflating airbag. **Corrective Action:** A tunnel sensor of different design will be installed on the affected vehicles.

NISSAN SENTRA 1987

System: Interior; seat belts; belt buckles. **Vehicle:** Passenger, multipurpose vehicles and light-duty trucks equipped with safety belts made by Takata Corporation. **Defect:** The front safety belt buckle release buttons can break. These red plastic release buttons are marked "press." If a button breaks, pieces can fall into the buckle assembly, causing the buckle to operate improperly. **Consequence:** The safety belts would not provide adequate protection to an occupant in a vehicle crash. **Corrective Action:** Owners should promptly check the condition and operation of both front safety belt buckles, and carefully inspect the red release buttons for any breaks or cracks. They should ensure that both buckles are operating properly by inserting each latchplate into its buckle, tugging on the belt to make sure the latch is securely locked and then pressing the release button. The latchplate should pop out of the buckle when the button is pressed. If either release button shows a sign of breaking or cracking, or if either buckle fails to operate properly, owners should promptly contact their authorized dealer to schedule an appointment to have the buckle replaced or repaired free of charge.

NISSAN SENTRA 1988

System: Interior; seat belts; belt buckles. **Vehicle:** Passenger, multipurpose vehicles and light duty trucks equipped with safety belts made by Takata Corporation. **Defect:** The front safety belt buckle release buttons can break. These red plastic release buttons are marked "press." If a button breaks, pieces can fall into the buckle assembly, causing the buckle to operate improperly. **Consequence:** The safety belts would not provide adequate protection to an occupant in a vehicle crash. **Corrective Action:** Owners should promptly check the condition and operation of both front safety belt buckles, and carefully inspect the red release buttons for any breaks or cracks. They should ensure that both buckles are operating properly by inserting each latchplate into its buckle, tugging on the belt to make sure the latch is securely locked and then pressing the release button. The latchplate should pop out of the buckle when the button is pressed. If either release button shows a sign of breaking or cracking, or if either buckle fails to operate properly, owners should promptly contact their authorized dealer to schedule an appointment to have the buckle replaced or repaired free of charge.

NISSAN SENTRA 1989

System: Interior; seat belts; belt buckles. **Vehicle:** Passenger, multipurpose vehicles and light-duty trucks equipped with safety belts made by Takata Corporation. **Defect:** The front safety belt buckle release buttons can break. These red plastic release buttons are marked "press." If a button breaks, pieces can fall into the buckle assembly, causing the buckle to operate improperly. **Consequence:** The safety belts would not provide adequate protection to an occupant in a vehicle crash. **Corrective Action:** Owners should promptly check the condition and operation of both front safety belt buckles, and carefully inspect the red release buttons for any breaks or cracks. They should ensure that both buckles are operating properly by inserting each latchplate into its buckle, tugging on the belt to make sure the latch is securely locked and then pressing the release button. The latchplate should pop out of the buckle when the button is pressed. If either release button shows a sign of breaking or cracking, or if either buckle fails to operate properly, owners should promptly contact their authorized dealer to schedule an appointment to have the buckle replaced or repaired free of charge.

NISSAN SENTRA 1990

System: Shoulder safety belts. **Vehicle:** Passenger cars; Sentra B12 model equipped with 2-point nonmotorized passive front shoulder belts. **Defect:** Improper belt guide performance can cause fraying of the shoulder safety belts near the retractor. **Consequence:** The fraying of the shoulder safety belt webbing can cause improper retraction of the belt, which would lead to inadequate protection of seat occupant during a sudden stop or accident, and could result in increased risk of injury. **Corrective Action:** Modify the safety belt guides to prevent fraying and/or replace retractor assembly if fraying is present.

System: Interior; seat belts; belt buckles. **Vehicle:** Passenger, multipurpose vehicles and light-duty trucks equipped with safety belts made by Takata Corporation. **Defect:** The front safety belt buckle release buttons can break. These red plastic release buttons are marked "press." If a button breaks, pieces can fall into the buckle assembly, causing the buckle to operate improperly. **Consequence:** The safety belts would not provide adequate protection to an occupant in a vehicle crash. **Corrective Action:** Owners should promptly check the condition and operation of both front safety belt buckles, and carefully inspect the red release buttons for any breaks or cracks. They should ensure that both buckles are operating properly by inserting each latchplate into its buckle, tugging on the belt to make sure the latch is securely locked and then pressing the release button. The latchplate should pop out of the buckle when the button is pressed. If either release button shows a sign of breaking or cracking, or if either buckle fails to operate properly, owners should promptly contact their authorized dealer to schedule an appointment to have the buckle replaced or repaired free of charge.

NISSAN SENTRA 1991

System: Shoulder safety belts. **Vehicle:** Passenger cars; Sentra B12 model equipped with 2-point nonmotorized passive front shoulder belts. **Defect:** Improper belt guide performance can cause fraying of the shoulder safety belts near the retractor. **Consequence:** The fraying of the shoulder safety belt webbing can cause improper retraction of the belt, which would lead to inadequate protection of seat occupant during a sudden stop or accident, and could result in increased risk of injury. **Corrective Action:** Modify the safety belt guides to prevent fraying and/or replace retractor assembly if fraying is present.

System: Interior; seat belts; belt buckles. **Vehicle:** Passenger, multipurpose vehicles and light-duty trucks equipped with safety belts made by Takata Corporation. **Defect:** The front safety belt buckle release buttons can break. These red plastic release buttons are marked "press." If a button breaks, pieces can fall into the buckle assembly, causing the buckle to operate improperly. **Consequence:** The safety belts would not provide adequate protection to an occupant in a vehicle crash. **Corrective Action:** Owners should promptly check the condition and operation of both front safety belt buckles, and carefully inspect the red release buttons for any breaks or cracks. They should ensure that both buckles are operating properly by inserting each latchplate into its buckle, tugging on the belt to make sure the latch is securely locked and then pressing the release button. The latchplate should pop out of the buckle when the button is pressed. If either release button shows a sign of breaking or cracking, or if either buckle fails to operate properly, owners should promptly contact their authorized dealer to schedule an appointment to have the buckle replaced or repaired free of charge.

NISSAN STANZA 1987

System: Tire information label—FMVSS 120. **Vehicle:** Light trucks, multipurpose passenger vehicles and passenger cars. **Defect:** Incorrect tire inflation pressures were printed on certification labels. **Consequence:** Incorrect tire inflation could result in loss of vehicle control and an accident. **Corrective Action:** Install corrected tire information label on doorpost certification label.

NISSAN TRUCK PATHFINDER 1990

System: Tire information label—FMVSS 120. **Vehicle:** Light trucks, multipurpose passenger vehicles and passenger cars. **Defect:** Incorrect tire inflation pressures were printed on certification labels. **Consequence:** Incorrect tire inflation could result in loss of vehicle control and an accident. **Corrective Action:** Install corrected tire information label on doorpost certification label.

System: Interior; seat belts; belt buckles. **Vehicle:** Passenger, multipurpose vehicles and light-duty trucks equipped with safety belts made by Takata Corporation. **Defect:** The front safety belt buckle release buttons can break. These red plastic release buttons are marked "press." If a button breaks, pieces can fall into the buckle assembly, causing the buckle to operate improperly. **Consequence:** The safety belts would not provide adequate protection to an occupant in a vehicle crash. **Corrective Action:** Owners should promptly check the condition and operation of both front safety belt buckles, and carefully inspect the red release buttons for any breaks or cracks. They should ensure that both buckles are operating properly by inserting each latchplate into its buckle, tugging on the belt to make sure the latch is securely locked and then pressing the release button. The latchplate should pop out of the buckle when the button is pressed. If either release button shows a sign of breaking or cracking, or if either buckle fails to operate properly, owners should promptly contact their authorized dealer to schedule an appointment to have the buckle replaced or repaired free of charge.

NISSAN TRUCK QUEST 1993

System: Brakes: master cylinder. **Vehicle:** Passenger minivans. **Defect:** The service brake master cylinder was not properly assembled, or could have been damaged by the evacuation and filling of the brake system at the assembly plant. **Consequence:** This can result in a partial brake system failure due to internal master cylinder leakage, which can cause loss of braking on two of the four wheels. If this occurs, there would be increased brake pedal travel, higher pedal efforts and increased stopping distances. **Corrective Action:** A new brake master cylinder will be installed. **Note:** Ford Motor Company and Nissan Motors Corporation will conduct separate recall campaigns for this safety defect.

System: Interior: passenger restraint. **Vehicle:** Passenger minivans. **Defect:** One or both of the bolts securing the automatic seat belt restraint system tracks to the b-pillars were not adequately tightened. **Consequence:** This condition can result in the automatic seat belt system track joints having less than design strength, and increase the risk of injury to the seat occupant in the event of a collision or sudden stop. **Corrective Action:** Dealers will tighten the passive restraint system track mounting bolts. **Note:** Ford Motor Company and Nissan Motors Corporation will conduct separate recall campaigns for this safety defect.

System: Fuel system. **Vehicle:** Passenger vans. **Defect:** Fuel filler hoses may have been cut, prior to installation, by a utility knife used to open the shipping box. **Consequence:** Fuel leakage can result if the cut extended through the thickness of the hose wall. Leaking fuel can result in a fire if exposed to a source of ignition. **Corrective Action:** Replace the fuel filler hose. **Note:** Ford Motor Company and Nissan Motors Corporation will each be handling this recall for their own vehicles.

NISSAN TRUCK VAN 1987

System: Engine. **Vehicle:** Van. **Defect:** Valve cover gasket may leak oil. **Consequence:** Oil may drip on exhaust manifold, and if engine is operated under severe conditions, or operated at continuously high speeds, the manifold may become hot enough to ignite the oil. This could result in an engine compartment fire. **Corrective Action:** The valve cover gasket will be replaced, with a new gasket redesigned to correct the oil leak.

System: Power steering hose. **Vehicle:** Truck van. **Defect:** Power steering hoses may leak fluid that can spread to the exhaust manifold. **Consequence:** Under certain conditions, the manifold may become hot enough to ignite the power steering fluid and result in an engine compartment fire. **Corrective Action:** Install new heat-resistant power steering hoses. Also install new fan coupling to increase air flow volume through engine compartment, and replace any other damaged components.

System: Cooling system. **Vehicle:** Passenger vans. **Defect:** The cooling system hoses deteriorate and fail because of inadequate heat resistance. Failure first occurs at the clamp connections, causing coolant fluid to be leaked or sprayed onto the engine compartment components. **Consequence:** If the vehicle is operated with a low coolant level, the cooling system temperature and pressure would rise very quickly. Coolant reaching the hot exhaust manifold can ignite and cause an engine compartment fire. **Corrective Action:** Replace the defective cooling system hoses with improved heat-resistant hoses, modify the coolant recovery system to prevent sudden increases in cooling system temperature and pressure, and replace engine compartment components which may have been damaged or would deteriorate with time. **Note:** Included in the campaign service will be an engine oil and filter change, as well as a complete cooling system service. Also, your dealer is authorized to provide a loaner car, at no charge, while van is being serviced. The warranty on all power train components is extended to 6 years or 100,000 miles. Previously extended power train warranty costs will be reimbursed, if requested.

System: Engine compartment. **Vehicle:** Passenger vans. **Defect:** Nissan has made a preliminary determination that a defect exists in engine compartment component(s) that may fail due to the engine compartment heat. **Consequence:** The undetermined engine compartment component(s) can cause an engine compartment fire, resulting in possible injury to vehicle occupants. **Corrective Action:** Dealers will install a new design cooling system including fan belts, radiator, water pump, alternator, freeze plug shields and associated hoses. The remedy will also include a new auxiliary electric fan and power steering fluid cooler. To complete the remedy, a warning system to monitor cooling system performance will be installed to detect potential engine overheating.

System: Engine cooling system; hoses. **Vehicle:** Passenger, C22 vans. **Defect:** Engine compartment fires and other thermal incidents have occurred on vehicles which had received all of the remedies provided by a previous safety-related recall. The fires are attributed to errors in installing the remedy specified in the recall. **Consequence:** If the remedy specified for previous recall was not performed correctly or the vehicle has not received the remedy, a fire could occur. **Corrective Action:** Nissan will offer to repurchase these vehicles from the owners. The vehicles will then be destroyed. For owners that decline the repurchase offer, Nissan will provide a reinspection of their vehicle, free of charge, to confirm the prior recall was completed properly. Also, Nissan will perform any recall-related repairs that may be needed at no charge to the owner. **Note:** Please contact Nissan Service Center at (800) 677-7822 for more information concerning this recall. Consumers can also contact the NHTSA's Auto Safety Hotline at (800) 424-9393.

NISSAN TRUCK VAN 1988

System: Power steering hose. **Vehicle:** Truck van. **Defect:** Power steering hoses may leak fluid that can spread to the exhaust manifold. **Consequence:** Under certain conditions, the manifold may become hot enough to ignite the power steering fluid and result in an engine compartment fire. **Corrective Action:** Install new heat-resistant power steering hoses. Also, install new fan coupling to increase air flow volume through the engine compartment, and replace any other damaged components.

System: Cooling system. **Vehicle:** Passenger vans. **Defect:** The cooling system hoses deteriorate and fail because of inadequate heat resistance. Failure first occurs at the clamp connections, causing coolant fluid to be leaked or sprayed onto the engine compartment components. **Consequence:** If the vehicle is operated with a low coolant level, the cooling system temperature and pressure would rise very quickly. Coolant reaching the hot exhaust manifold can ignite and cause an engine compartment fire. **Corrective Action:** Replace the defective cooling system hoses with improved heat-resistant hoses, modify the coolant recovery system to prevent sudden increases in cooling system temperature and pressure, and replace engine compartment components that may have been damaged or would deteriorate with time. **Note:** Included in the campaign service will be an engine oil and filter change as well as a complete cooling system service. Also, your dealer is authorized to provide a loaner car, at no charge, while van is being serviced. The warranty on all power train components is extended to 6 years or 100,000 miles. Previously extended power train warranty costs will be reimbursed, if requested.

System: Engine compartment. **Vehicle:** Passenger vans. **Defect:** Nissan has made a preliminary determination that a defect exists in engine compartment component(s) that may fail due to the engine compartment heat. **Consequence:** The undetermined engine compartment component(s) can cause an engine compartment fire, resulting in possible injury to vehicle occupants. **Corrective Action:** Dealers will install a new design cooling system including fan belts, radiator, water pump, alternator, freeze plug shields and associated hoses. The remedy will also include a new auxiliary electric fan and power steering fluid cooler. To complete the remedy, a warning system to monitor cooling system performance will be installed to detect potential engine overheating.

System: Engine cooling system; hoses. **Vehicle:** Passenger, C22 vans. **Defect:** Engine compartment fires and other thermal incidents have occurred on vehicles which had received all of the remedies provided by a previous safety-related recall. The fires are attributed to errors in installing the remedy specified in the recall. **Consequence:** If the remedy specified for previous recall was not performed correctly, or the vehicle has not received the remedy, a fire could occur. **Corrective Action:** Nissan will offer to repurchase these vehicles from the owners. The vehicles will then be destroyed. For owners that decline the repurchase offer, Nissan will provide a reinspection of their vehicle, free of charge, to confirm the prior recall was completed properly. Also, Nissan will perform any recall-related repairs that may be needed at no charge to the owner. **Note:** Please contact Nissan Service Center at (800) 677-7822 for more information concerning this recall. Consumers can also contact the NHTSA's Auto Safety Hotline at (800) 424-9393.

OLDSMOBILE

Note: Owners who take their Oldsmobile to an authorized dealer on an agreed-upon service date and do not receive the free remedy within a reasonable time, should contact Buick at (800) 521-7300; Chevrolet at (800) 222-1020; Pontiac at (800) 762-2737; or Oldsmobile at (800) 442-6537. Also contact the NHTSA's Auto Safety Hotline at (800) 424-9393.

OLDSMOBILE 88 1987

System: Electrical—in-line fusible link. **Vehicle:** Passenger cars. **Defect:** An in-line fusible link may melt down and cause a fire. **Consequence:** The in-line fusible link located in the area of the plastic windshield washer bottle bracket may, under a high-resistance load, melt down and ignite the washer bottle bracket, resulting in an engine compartment fire. **Corrective Action:** The windshield washer bottle bracket will be replaced.

System: Accelerator cable. **Vehicle:** Passenger cars. **Defect:** Excessive accelerator cable friction may restrict the cable's free movement between the accelerator pedal and the throttle body. **Consequence:** This could prevent throttle from returning to closed (idle) position when accelerator pedal is released; thus, engine speed would not decrease, and loss of accelerator control could result in an accident. **Corrective Action:** Replace accelerator cable.

OLDSMOBILE 88 1989

System: Fuel rollover valve—FMVSS 301. **Vehicle:** Passenger cars. **Defect:** Fuel rollover valve assembly may not have been installed. **Consequence:** In event of an accident in which vehicle becomes inverted, missing valve could allow fuel spillage in excess of amount allowed by FMVSS 301, which could result in a fire. **Corrective Action:** Replace fuel sender and pump assembly.

System: Structure; frame—FMVSS 301. **Vehicle:** Passenger cars. **Defect:** Welds in the left rear rocker panel area may break loose and cause excessive forward movement of the rear suspension. **Consequence:** This could result in damage to the fuel tanks or lines, that could result in a fuel leak during or after a crash which would result in a fire. This is in violation of FMVSS 301. **Corrective Action:** Install a reinforcement kit.

System: Rear safety belts—FMVSS 210. **Vehicle:** Passenger cars. **Defect:** Welds in the left rear rocker panel may break loose and cause excessive forward movement of the rear suspension. **Consequence:** This could result in damage to the fuel tanks or lines, which could result in a fuel leak during or after a crash that would result in a fire. This is in violation of FMVSS 301. **Corrective Action:** Install a reinforcement kit.

OLDSMOBILE 88 1990

System: Airbag modules. **Vehicle:** Passenger cars equipped with driver's-side supplemental airbag modules. **Defect:** Threaded inflator components may have been damaged during assembly, which may allow components to separate when inflator receives a signal to deploy the airbag. **Consequence:** Inflator component separation allows hot combustion gases to escape into the passenger compartment, which could result in injuries to vehicle occupants. **Corrective Action:** Replace airbag modules containing potentially defective inflators. **Note:** This campaign was initiated by TRW, Inc., manufacturer of the airbag module.

System: Digital (electronic) instrument cluster—FMVSS 101. **Vehicle:** Delta 88 Royale cars equipped with digital (electronic) instrument cluster. **Defect:** Cars were built missing a wire between the digital cluster and the dimmer control, thereby failing to provide at least two levels of lighting. **Consequence:** Vehicles would not comply with requirements of FMVSS 101. **Corrective Action:** Rewire connection between the dimmer switch and the digital cluster.

OLDSMOBILE 88 1991

System: Brakes—FMVSS 105. **Vehicle:** Passenger cars. **Defect:** When applied, the parking brake lever assembly may release one or more teeth, reducing the cable load to the rear brakes. **Consequence:** Depending on the extent of the lever release and road level, the parking brake may not hold the vehicle, allowing it to roll, which could result in an accident. Vehicle does not comply with FMVSS 105. **Corrective Action:** Replace parking brake lever assembly.

OLDSMOBILE 98 1987

System: Brakes. **Vehicle:** Passenger cars with antilock brakes. **Defect:** The antilock brake system (ABS) pressure/warning switch may exhibit brake fluid seepage, which eventually can lead to loss of the brake system hydraulic pump motor. Additionally, the hydraulic pump motor and antilock brake system electrical relays may have been exposed to water contamination during vehicle assembly. This condition can cause loss of the hydraulic pump motor and/or loss of the antilock brake system function. **Consequence:** Loss of the hydraulic pump motor would result in a total loss of rear brakes, as well as power assist to the front brakes. The red "brake" warning light would illuminate and stay on. If this warning is not heeded, a loss of rear brakes at a time when minimum stopping distance is required could result in a vehicle crash. An inoperative antilock brake system electrical relay could cause loss of the antilock brake system function, but normal power-assisted braking would be retained. The amber "antilock" warning light would illuminate and stay on. **Corrective Action:** The antilock brake system and hydraulic pump motor electrical relays and 30 amp fuses will be replaced. In addition, the hydraulic pump motor assembly and pressure/warning switch will be inspected and, if required, replaced.

System: Electrical—in-line fusible link. **Vehicle:** Passenger cars. **Defect:** An in-line fusible link may melt down and cause a fire. **Consequence:** The in-line fusible link located in the area of the plastic windshield washer bottle bracket may, under a high-resistance load, melt down and ignite the washer bottle bracket, resulting in an engine compartment fire. **Corrective Action:** The windshield washer bottle bracket will be replaced.

System: Accelerator cable. **Vehicle:** Passenger cars. **Defect:** Excessive accelerator cable friction may restrict the cable's free movement between the accelerator pedal and the throttle body. **Consequence:** This could prevent throttle from returning to closed (idle) position when accelerator pedal is released; thus, engine speed would not decrease, and loss of accelerator control could result in an accident. **Corrective Action:** Replace accelerator cable.

OLDSMOBILE 98 1989

System: Supplemental inflatable restraint. **Vehicle:** Passenger cars equipped with AJ3 supplemental inflatable restraint. **Defect:** The standard (base) pad assembly for the supplemental inflatable restraint may have been incorrectly installed. **Consequence:** In event of a crash, lack of benefit of this special pad assembly (or knee bolster) could result in greater injury to driver than might otherwise occur. **Corrective Action:** Replace parts as required, and perform an electrical test.

OLDSMOBILE 98 1990

System: Airbag modules. **Vehicle:** Passenger cars equipped with driver's-side supplemental airbag modules. **Defect:** Threaded inflator components may have been damaged during assembly, which may allow components to separate when inflator receives a signal to deploy the airbag. **Consequence:** Inflator component separation allows hot combustion gases to escape into the passenger compartment, which could result in injuries to vehicle occupants. **Corrective Action:** Replace airbag modules containing potentially defective inflators. **Note:** This campaign was initiated by TRW, Inc., manufacturer of the airbag module.

OLDSMOBILE 98 1991

System: Brakes—FMVSS 105. **Vehicle:** Passenger cars. **Defect:** When applied, the parking brake lever assembly may release one or more teeth, reducing the cable load to the rear brakes. **Consequence:** Depending on the extent of the lever release and road level, the parking brake may not hold the vehicle, allowing it to roll, which could result in an accident. Vehicle does not comply with FMVSS 105. **Corrective Action:** Replace parking brake lever assembly.

System: Transmission shift lever. **Vehicle:** Passenger vehicles with automatic transmissions. **Defect:** The console-mounted shift lever may disengage from the shift control cable bracket, causing loss of gear indicator reference and shift selector operation. **Consequence:** The driver can place the gear shifter in the park position without setting the parking brake, but the transaxle may not actually be in park, resulting in unexpected vehicle movement if the vehicle is stopped on a grade. Also, the driver can place the gear selector in drive or reverse without turning the engine off, and the transaxle may not be in the position indicated, causing the vehicle to move in the opposite direction. Both conditions can result in a vehicle accident without prior warning. **Corrective Action:** Install two transaxle shift control cable retaining clips.

OLDSMOBILE CALAIS 1987

System: Fuel—hose. **Vehicle:** Passenger cars. **Defect:** The fuel feed or fuel return hose at the engine may rub against a shift lever on the 5-speed transaxle. **Consequence:** In time, a hole could be rubbed through the hose and fuel could leak into the engine compartment. This could result in an underhood fire. **Corrective Action:** Replace the fuel feed and return hose and pipe assemblies.

OLDSMOBILE CALAIS 1988

System: Front fuel feed hose. **Vehicle:** Passenger cars equipped with quad 4 engines. **Defect:** Front fuel feed hose assembly could crack or separate at the coupling on the engine end of the hose assembly, allowing fuel to leak into the engine compartment. **Consequence:** Leaking fuel in the engine compartment could result in a fire. **Corrective Action:** Replace front fuel feed hose assembly.

System: Fuel hose. **Vehicle:** Passenger cars equipped with quad 4 engines. **Defect:** Front fuel feed hose assembly could crack or separate at the coupling on the engine end of the hose assembly, allowing fuel to leak into the engine compartment. **Consequence:** Fuel leaking in the engine compartment could result in an underhood fire. **Corrective Action:** Replace front fuel feed hose assembly. **Note:** GMC has expanded previous NHTSA Recall to include an additional 108,836 vehicles.

OLDSMOBILE CALAIS 1989

System: Front fuel feed hose. **Vehicle:** Passenger cars equipped with quad 4 engines. **Defect:** Front fuel feed hose assembly could crack or separate at the coupling on the engine end of the hose assembly, allowing fuel to leak into the engine compartment. **Consequence:** Leaking fuel in the engine compartment could result in a fire. **Corrective Action:** Replace front fuel feed hose assembly.

System: Fuel hose. **Vehicle:** Passenger cars equipped with quad 4 engines. **Defect:** Front fuel feed hose assembly could crack or separate at the coupling on the engine end of the hose assembly, allowing fuel to leak into the engine compartment. **Consequence:** Fuel leaking in the engine compartment could result in an underhood fire. **Corrective Action:** Replace front fuel feed hose assembly. **Note:** GMC has expanded previous NHTSA Recall to include an additional 108,836 vehicles.

OLDSMOBILE CALAIS 1990

System: Front fuel feed and return hoses. **Vehicle:** Passenger cars. **Defect:** Improperly torqued connections of front fuel feed and return hoses to fuel pipes at the body rail could loosen and leak fuel into the underhood area. **Consequence:** Fuel leaks, in the presence of an ignition source, could result in an underhood fire. **Corrective Action:** Properly torque the front fuel feed and return hoses at the body rail lines to prevent fuel leakage.

OLDSMOBILE CIERA 1987

System: Windshield—FMVSS 212. **Vehicle:** Passenger cars. **Defect:** Poor bond adhesion between the windshield glass and mounting could allow the windshield to separate during a 30 mph frontal barrier test required by FMVSS 212. **Consequence:** If windshield glass separation occurs during an accident, an unbelted occupant could be ejected from the vehicle and injured. **Corrective Action:** Reinstall windshields to ensure proper bond adhesion.

OLDSMOBILE CIERA 1988

System: Fuel feed hose. **Vehicle:** Passenger cars equipped with a 2.8L V6 engine. **Defect:** Fuel feed hose could leak at the coupling on the engine end of the hose assembly. **Consequence:** Fuel leakage into the engine compartment could result in an engine compartment fire that could spread to the passenger compartment. **Corrective Action:** Install new fuel feed hose assembly.

OLDSMOBILE CIERA 1989

System: Interior; active restraints; belt anchor and attachment—FMVSS 210. **Vehicle:** Passenger vehicles. **Description of Noncompliance:** These vehicles were assembled with rear outboard safety belt anchorages that may not withstand the required load. This does not comply with FMVSS 210, "Seat belt assembly anchorages." **Consequence of Noncompliance:** In a collision, stress can cause the attachment metal to tear and allow the anchorage to separate from the body of the vehicle. The safety belt may not protect an occupant in the event of a vehicle crash. **Corrective Action:** Dealers will replace the existing anchor bolts with a new shoulder bolt and thread-locking adhesive. Additionally, noise control patches will be applied at each anchorage.

OLDSMOBILE CIERA 1990

System: Interior: seating. **Vehicle:** Passenger cars with 6-way power seats or power recliners. **Defect:** The power seat or recliner wiring harness can be pinched or can chafe on the seat frame or spring support rod, wearing through the wire insulation and causing an electrical short. **Consequence:** The high current caused by the electrical short welds the circuit breaker elements together in the closed position, leaving the circuit unprotected and generating sufficient heat to burn the wire insulation and ignite the seat cushion material. **Corrective Action:** Repair any abraded wiring and reroute the wiring harness using a wiring harness clip.

System: Interior; active restraints; belt anchor and attachment—FMVSS 210. **Vehicle:** Passenger vehicles. **Description of Noncompliance:** These vehicles were assembled with rear outboard safety belt anchorages that may not withstand the required load. This does not comply with FMVSS 210, "Seat belt assembly anchorages." **Consequence of Noncompliance:** In a collision, stress can cause the attachment metal to tear and allow the anchorage to separate from the body of the vehicle. The safety belt may not protect an occupant in the event of a vehicle crash. **Corrective Action:** Dealers will replace the existing anchor bolts with a new shoulder bolt and thread-locking adhesive. Additionally, noise control patches will be applied at each anchorage.

OLDSMOBILE CIERA 1991

System: Interior: seating. **Vehicle:** Passenger cars with 6-way power seats or power recliners. **Defect:** The power seat or recliner wiring harness can be pinched or can chafe on the seat frame or spring support rod, wearing through the wire insulation and causing an electrical short. **Consequence:** The high current caused by the electrical short welds the circuit breaker elements together in the closed position, leaving the circuit unprotected and generating sufficient heat to burn the wire insulation and ignite the seat cushion material. **Corrective Action:** Repair any abraded wiring and reroute the wiring harness using a wiring harness clip.

System: Interior; active restraints; belt anchor and attachment—FMVSS 210. **Vehicle:** Passenger vehicles. **Description of Noncompliance:** These vehicles were assembled with rear outboard safety belt anchorages that may not withstand the required load. This does not comply with FMVSS 210, "Seat belt assembly anchorages." **Consequence of Noncompliance:** In a collision, stress can cause the attachment metal to tear and allow the anchorage to separate from the body of the vehicle. The safety belt may not protect an occupant in the event of a vehicle crash. **Corrective Action:** Dealers will replace the existing anchor bolts with a new shoulder bolt and thread-locking adhesive. Additionally, noise control patches will be applied at each anchorage.

OLDSMOBILE CUTLASS 1987

System: Transmission **Vehicle:** Passenger cars and wagons with 200 4R transmissions. **Defect:** Manual valve link in the transmission may have been improperly formed. **Consequence:** The valve link could separate, resulting in a gear selection different from what the driver selects. Also, car could be started with transmission in gear, allowing vehicle to move in an unanticipated direction. **Corrective Action:** Replace the manual valve detent lever link.

System: Cruise control. **Vehicle:** Passenger vehicles equipped with cruise control, and certain gasoline and diesel engines. **Defect:** A small nylon bushing in the cruise control servo bail may slip out of place, causing intermittent and unexpected increases in engine speed or dieseling (engine run-on with ignition off). **Consequence:** Servo rod assembly could catch on engine components and result in a stuck throttle, with potential for a vehicle crash. **Corrective Action:** Install a new bushing in cruise control servo bail.

OLDSMOBILE CUTLASS 1988

System: Brakes—FMVSS 105. **Vehicle:** Passenger cars. **Defect:** The parking brake cable may be disconnected from the left rear brake caliper. **Consequence:** Parking brake cannot be properly applied and vehicle will not meet the grade-holding requirements of FMVSS 105. **Corrective Action:** Install a retainer on left rear caliper, if cable is not already retained with a cotter pin, and adjust parking brake system.

System: Cruise control. **Vehicle:** Passenger vehicles equipped with cruise control, and certain gasoline and diesel engines. **Defect:** A small nylon bushing in the cruise control servo bail may slip out of place, causing intermittent and unexpected increases in engine speed or dieseling (engine run-on with ignition off). **Consequence:** Servo rod assembly could catch on engine components and result in a stuck throttle, with potential for a vehicle crash. **Corrective Action:** Install a new bushing in cruise control servo bail.

System: Seat belt anchorage—FMVSS 210. **Vehicle:** Passenger cars. **Defect:** Front shoulder belt guide loop attachment fastener may pull through door-mounted anchor plate. **Consequence:** Seat belt may not sustain loads required by FMVSS 210, and in a vehicle accident, the seat belt may not properly restrain a passenger, resulting in increased risk of greater injury to an occupant. **Corrective Action:** Replace front shoulder belt guide loop attachment nuts and install new guide cover.

System: Wheels. **Vehicle:** Passenger vehicles equipped with Kelsey Hayes steel wheels; models RPO PB6 14″ and RPO PG1 15″. **Defect:** Cracks develop in the wheel mounting surface. If these cracks become severe enough, the wheel will completely separate from the vehicle. **Consequence:** If wheel separation occurs while the vehicle is in motion, loss of steering and brake control of the vehicle occurs, and a vehicle crash could result without prior warning. **Corrective Action:** Dealers will inspect the manufacturing codes stamped on each wheel of the vehicle, and if a wheel falls within the specified date code range, the dealer will replace that wheel assembly.

System: Wheels. **Vehicle:** Passenger vehicles equipped with Kelsey Hayes steel wheels; models RPO PB9 14″ and RPO PG1 15″. **Defect:** Cracks develop in the wheel mounting surface. If these cracks become severe enough, the wheel will completely separate from the vehicle. **Consequence:** If wheel separation occurs while the vehicle is in motion, loss of steering and brake control of the vehicle occurs, and a vehicle crash could result without prior warning. **Corrective Action:** Dealers will inspect the manufacturing date codes stamped on each wheel of the vehicle, and if a wheel falls within the specified date code range, the dealer will replace that wheel assembly. **Note:** Vehicles previously inspected that had less than four wheels replaced are to be reinspected.

OLDSMOBILE CUTLASS 1989

System: Air conditioner control—FMVSS 103. **Vehicle:** Passenger cars equipped with electronic comfort control air conditioning. **Defect:** The electronic air conditioning control may not function in car that has been parked for a few hours with ignition off. **Consequence:** Windshield may not defrost and car would not conform with FMVSS 103. **Corrective Action:** Replace electronic comfort control assembly.

System: Seat belt anchorage—FMVSS 210. **Vehicle:** Passenger cars. **Defect:** Front shoulder belt guide loop attachment fastener may pull through door-mounted anchor plate. **Consequence:** Seat belt may not sustain loads required by FMVSS 210, and in a vehicle accident, the seat belt may not properly restrain a passenger, resulting in increased risk of greater injury to an occupant. **Corrective Action:** Replace front shoulder belt guide loop attachment nuts and install new guide cover.

System: Brake stoplamp switch. **Vehicle:** Passenger cars. **Defect:** Brake stoplamps may not illuminate or, in some cases, stoplamps will not stay illuminated all the time when brakes are applied due to a faulty stoplamp switch. Also, in vehicles equipped with cruise control, a faulty stoplamp switch can result in resumption of the cruise control function upon release of the brake pedal. **Consequence:** A trailing vehicle may not recognize a braking action in time to respond appropriately. Also, cruise control will reengage upon release of the brake pedal and resume the set speed. In either case, it could result in a crash without prior warning. **Corrective Action:** Install an improved-design stoplamp switch.

System: Wheels. **Vehicle:** Passenger vehicles equipped with Kelsey Hayes steel wheels; models RPO PB6 14″ and RPO PG1 15″. **Defect:**

Cracks develop in the wheel mounting surface. If these cracks become severe enough, the wheel will completely separate from the vehicle. **Consequence:** If wheel separation occurs while the vehicle is in motion, loss of steering and brake control of the vehicle occurs, and a vehicle crash could result without prior warning. **Corrective Action:** Dealers will inspect the manufacturing codes stamped on each wheel of the vehicle, and if a wheel falls within the specified date code range, the dealer will replace that wheel assembly.

System: Wheels. **Vehicle:** Passenger vehicles equipped with Kelsey Hayes steel wheels; models RPO PB9 14″ and RPO PG1 15″. **Defect:** Cracks develop in the wheel mounting surface. If these cracks become severe enough, the wheel will completely separate from the vehicle. **Consequence:** If wheel separation occurs while the vehicle is in motion, loss of steering and brake control of the vehicle occurs, and a vehicle crash could result without prior warning. **Corrective Action:** Dealers will inspect the manufacturing date codes stamped on each wheel of the vehicle, and if a wheel falls within the specified date code range, the dealer will replace that wheel assembly. **Note:** Vehicles previously inspected that had less than four wheels replaced are to be reinspected.

OLDSMOBILE CUTLASS 1990

System: Seat belt anchorage—FMVSS 210. **Vehicle:** Passenger cars. **Defect:** Front shoulder belt guide loop attachment fastener may pull through door-mounted anchor plate. **Consequence:** Seat belt may not sustain loads required by FMVSS 210, and in a vehicle accident, the seat belt may not properly restrain a passenger, resulting in increased risk of injury to an occupant. **Corrective Action:** Replace front shoulder belt guide loop attachment nuts and install new guide cover.

System: Brake stoplamp switch. **Vehicle:** Passenger cars. **Defect:** Brake stoplamps may not illuminate or, in some cases, stoplamps will not stay illuminated all the time when brakes are applied due to a faulty stoplamp switch. Also, in vehicles equipped with cruise control, a faulty stoplamp switch can result in resumption of the cruise control function upon release of the brake pedal. **Consequence:** A trailing vehicle may not recognize a braking action in time to respond appropriately. Also, cruise control will reengage upon release of the brake pedal and resume the set speed. In either case, it could result in a crash without prior warning. **Corrective Action:** Install an improved-design stoplamp switch.

System: Front shoulder safety belt. **Vehicle:** Passenger cars. **Defect:** Front shoulder safety belt webbing may separate at front belt upper guide loops on either side of the front seat. **Consequence:** Webbing separation could occur without prior warning, and increase the risk of injury to belted front outboard occupants in a high-energy crash. **Corrective Action:** Install a controlled rotation bracket on driver's- and passenger-side front seat belt guide loops.

System: Wheels. **Vehicle:** Passenger vehicles equipped with Kelsey Hayes steel wheels; models RPO PB6 14″ and RPO PG1 15″. **Defect:** Cracks develop in the wheel mounting surface. If these cracks become severe enough, the wheel will completely separate from the vehicle. **Consequence:** If wheel separation occurs while the vehicle is in motion, loss of steering and brake control of the vehicle occurs, and a vehicle crash could result without prior warning. **Corrective Action:** Dealers will inspect the manufacturing codes stamped on each wheel of the vehicle, and if a wheel falls within the specified date code range, the dealer will replace that wheel assembly.

System: Wheels. **Vehicle:** Passenger vehicles equipped with Kelsey Hayes steel wheels; models RPO PB9 14″ and RPO PG1 15″. **Defect:** Cracks develop in the wheel mounting surface. If these cracks become severe enough, the wheel will completely separate from the vehicle. **Consequence:** If wheel separation occurs while the vehicle is in motion, loss of steering and brake control of the vehicle occurs, and a vehicle crash could result without prior warning. **Corrective Action:** Dealers will inspect the manufacturing date codes stamped on each wheel of the vehicle, and if a wheel falls within the specified date code range, the dealer will replace that wheel assembly. **Note:** Vehicles previously inspected that had less than four wheels replaced are to be reinspected.

OLDSMOBILE CUTLASS 1991

System: Safety belts—FMVSS 208. Description of vehicles: Passenger vehicles; 1991 GMC "J" and "W" model cars. **Defect:** The front door shoulder belt guide loops may be cracked, and are not in compliance with FMVSS 208. **Consequence:** The seat occupant faces increased risk of injury in the event of a sudden stop or accident. **Corrective Action:** Install reinforcing plates on the cracked shoulder belt guides.

OLDSMOBILE CUTLASS 1992

System: Transmission and transmission shift indicator. **Vehicle:** 1992 "A" and "W" body passenger cars with 4-speed automatic transmissions. **Defect:** The reverse servo apply pin may bind in the case, which could cause reverse band distress (loss or slipping of reverse), reverse band drag in drive range (poor performance/poor power) or the transmission to remain in reverse while the shift indicator shows neutral gear position. **Consequence:** If the transmission remains in reverse while the shift indicator shows neutral, the vehicle may unexpectedly move rearward and result in a vehicle accident. **Corrective Action:** Replace the transaxle where required.

OLDSMOBILE CUTLASS 1993

System: Front seat manual recliner mechanisms—FMVSS 207. **Vehicle:** Passenger cars. **Defect:** The driver and passenger front seat manual reclining mechanisms do not comply with the requirements of FMVSS 207, "Seating systems." The seat back mechanisms will not latch under certain conditions. **Consequence:** The seats may recline without prior warning, resulting in a hazard to seat occupants and possible loss of vehicle control. **Corrective Action:** Replace the manual seat recliner mechanism with a mechanism that complies with FMVSS 207.

System: Brakes; hydraulic; lines; nonmetallic. **Vehicle:** Passenger vehicles. **Defect:** The brake lines can contact the transmission mounting bracket of the frame side rail. The lines can wear through, resulting in loss of brake fluid, and eventual loss of half the vehicle braking system. **Consequence:** A leak in the hydraulic brake line will cause a loss of one-half the vehicle braking system and extended braking distances that can result in an accident. **Corrective Action:** Dealers will inspect for proper brake line clearance and reposition the brake lines. Brake lines found to have indentations will be replaced.

OLDSMOBILE CUTLASS 1994

System: Equipment; speed control. **Vehicle:** Passenger cars with 3.1L engines and cruise control. **Defect:** The cruise control cable may separate from the conduit end fitting while engaged, and accelerator control could be lost. **Consequence:** Loss of accelerator control may not reduce engine speed to a level anticipated by the driver. Although the vehicle can still be stopped with the service brake, loss of accelerator control could result in a vehicle crash without prior warning. **Corrective Action:** Replace the cruise control cable.

System: Brakes; hydraulic; lines; nonmetallic. **Vehicle:** Passenger vehicles. **Defect:** The brake lines can contact the transmission mounting bracket of the frame side rail. The lines can wear through, resulting in loss of brake fluid, and eventual loss of half the vehicle braking system. **Consequence:** A leak in the hydraulic brake line will cause a loss of one-half the vehicle braking system and extended braking distances that can result in an accident. **Corrective Action:** Dealers will inspect for proper brake line clearance and reposition the brake lines. Brake lines found to have indentations will be replaced.

System: Brakes; hydraulic; lines; hose; nonmetallic. **Vehicle:** Passenger vehicles. **Defect:** The rear wheel brake hose(s) can contact the rear suspension components, causing the brake hose(s) to wear through. **Consequence:** This condition can cause loss of brake fluid and eventual loss of the vehicle braking system, increasing the potential for a vehicle accident. **Corrective Action:** Dealers will inspect for proper brake hose position and replace those hoses in an incorrect position with correctly routed new hoses.

PLYMOUTH

Note: If your Plymouth is presented to an authorized dealer on an agreed-upon service date and the remedy is not provided free of charge within a reasonable time, please contact Chrysler at (800) 853-1403. Also contact the NHTSA's Auto Safety Hotline at (800) 424-9393.

PLYMOUTH ACCLAIM 1989

System: Engine valve cover gasket. **Vehicle:** Passenger cars, light trucks and minivans. **Defect:** The engine valve cover gasket may dislocate and allow an engine oil leak at the gasket. **Consequence:** The leakage of oil in the engine compartment could cause a fire. **Corrective Action:** Replace gasket cover with revised cover; RTV sealant will be applied in place of a gasket.

PLYMOUTH ACCLAIM 1990

System: Engine valve cover gasket. **Vehicle:** Passenger cars, light trucks and minivans. **Defect:** The engine valve cover gasket may dislocate and allow an engine oil leak at the gasket. **Consequence:** The leakage of oil in the engine compartment could cause a fire. **Corrective Action:** Replace gasket cover with revised cover; RTV sealant will be applied in place of a gasket.

PLYMOUTH ACCLAIM 1991

System: Front disc brake caliper guide pin bolts. **Vehicle:** Passenger cars. **Defect:** Front disc brake caliper guide pin bolts may not have been adequately torqued and could loosen. **Consequence:** This could cause reduced braking effectiveness and could result in an accident. **Corrective Action:** Properly torque front brake caliper guide pin bolts to 250 pounds.

System: Airbag sensors. **Vehicle:** Passenger cars. **Defect:** The two airbag system front impact sensors may not be secured to their mounting brackets. **Consequence:** Airbag will not deploy in a frontal collision if the front impact sensors are not attached. **Corrective Action:** Repair to ensure proper attachment of front impact sensors to brackets.

System: Safety belt. **Vehicle:** Passenger vehicle. **Defect:** Front outboard safety belt may become difficult to latch and/or unlatch due to a webbing stiffener entering the buckle housing and dislodging the buckle latch guide. **Consequence:** Latch may open during accident or sudden stop, exposing seat occupant to increased risk of injury. **Corrective Action:** Replace buckle latch engagement.

PLYMOUTH ACCLAIM 1992

System: Steering; upper steering column coupling bolt. **Vehicle:** Passenger vehicles; sedans, convertibles and minivans. **Defect:** The zinc-plating operation performed on the upper steering column shaft coupling bolt caused hydrogen embrittlement and breakage of the bolt. **Consequence:** Fractures of the upper steering column shaft coupling bolt result in a lack of coupling load on the shaft and loss of steering control. **Corrective Action:** Replace the zinc-plated bolt with a phosphate-plated bolt.

PLYMOUTH COLT 1987

System: Interior; seat belts; belt buckles. **Vehicle:** Passenger, multi-purpose vehicles and light-duty trucks equipped with safety belts made by Takata Corporation. **Defect:** The front safety belt buckle release buttons can break. These red plastic release buttons are marked "press." If a button breaks, pieces can fall into the buckle assembly, causing the buckle to operate improperly. **Consequence:** The safety belts would not provide adequate protection to an occupant in a vehicle crash. **Corrective Action:** Owners should promptly check the condition and operation of both front safety belt buckles, and carefully inspect the red release buttons for any breaks or cracks. They should ensure that both buckles are operating properly by inserting each latchplate into its buckle, tugging on the belt to make sure the latch is securely locked and then pressing the release button. The latchplate should pop out of the buckle when the button is pressed. If either release button shows a sign of breaking or cracking, or if either buckle fails to operate properly, owners should promptly contact their authorized dealer to schedule an appointment to have the buckle replaced or repaired, free of charge. The manufacturer is developing a remedy designed to prevent failure of the buttons that are not currently broken.

PLYMOUTH HORIZON 1987

System: Fuel. **Vehicle:** Passenger vehicles. **Defect:** Pressure regulator installed in the fuel supply plumbing system leaks fuel into the engine compartment. **Consequence:** Fuel leaks can result in a fire when near a source of ignition. **Corrective Action:** The fuel supply pressure regulator assembly will be replaced with a new assembly to ensure integrity of the fuel supply system.

PLYMOUTH HORIZON 1988

System: Horn symbol display—FMVSS 101. **Vehicle:** Passenger cars. **Defect:** Steering wheel horn pads do not contain the horn symbol display, as required by FMVSS 101. **Consequence:** Vehicles do not comply with FMVSS 101, "Controls and displays." **Corrective Action:** Send notification postcard to owners to assist any future owners who might be unsure of horn location.

PLYMOUTH LASER 1990

System: Electrical, underhood wiring harness. **Vehicle:** Passenger cars. **Defect:** Wiring harness for the headlamps may break due to the stress created by the headlamp popup devices. **Consequence:** Breakage of the wiring harness causes loss of headlamp illumination, which could have a potential for an accident. **Corrective Action:** Headlamp wiring harness routing will be modified, and damaged wires repaired.

System: Sunroof hinges. **Vehicle:** Passenger cars equipped with DSM-manufactured sunroofs. **Defect:** Operation of sunroof in "non-standard" manner may cause male hinge disengagement from the roof hinge receiver. **Consequence:** The sunroof glass could detach from the roof and result in injury to occupants or persons in the vicinity, especially if this occurs while the vehicle is in motion. **Corrective Action:** Replace male hinge with a modified version to increase roof hinge receiver retention ability. **Note:** This recall applies only to Diamond Star Motors-installed sunroofs. Chrysler Corporation's Plymouth and Eagle dealerships and Mitsubishi Motor Sales of America will implement the recall action.

System: Windshield mounting—FMVSS 212. **Vehicle:** Passenger cars. **Defect:** Diluted primer may have been used on the windshield-opening flanges prior to windshield glass installation, which would not provide the retention required by FMVSS 212. **Consequence:** Windshields would not prevent ejection of vehicle occupants during a vehicle crash, which causes serious injuries and fatalities. **Corrective Action:** Replace windshields, associated parts and primer.

System: Interior; seat belts; belt buckles. **Vehicle:** Passenger, multi-purpose vehicles and light-duty trucks equipped with safety belts made by Takata Corporation. **Defect:** The front safety belt buckle release buttons can break. These red plastic release buttons are marked "press." If a button breaks, pieces can fall into the buckle assembly, causing the buckle to operate improperly. **Consequence:** The safety belts would not provide adequate protection to an occupant in a vehicle crash. **Corrective Action:** Owners should promptly check the condition and operation of both front safety belt buckles, and carefully inspect the red release buttons for any breaks or cracks. They should ensure that both buckles are operating properly by inserting each latchplate into its buckle, tugging on the belt to make sure the latch is securely locked and then pressing the release button. The latchplate should pop out of the buckle when the button is pressed. If either release button shows a sign of breaking or cracking, or if either buckle fails to operate properly, owners should promptly contact their authorized dealer to schedule an appointment to have the buckle replaced or repaired, free of charge. The manufacturer is developing a remedy designed to prevent failure of the buttons that are not currently broken.

PLYMOUTH NEON 1995

System: Brakes; hydraulic; anti-skid system. **Vehicle:** Passenger cars. **Defect:** The antilock brake system master cylinder rear seal allows air to enter the brake system, causing spongy brakes or partial brake system loss. **Consequence:** Air entering the brake system caused extended stopping distance or partial loss of brakes, which may result in an accident. **Corrective Action:** Master cylinders will be inspected for the suspect build date code range and will be replaced if necessary.

System: Transmission. **Vehicle:** Passenger vehicles. **Defect:** Moisture can get into the power train control module (PCM), causing driveability malfunctions, including stalling. **Consequence:** Should driveability malfunctions or stalling occur while the vehicle is in motion, a traffic accident may occur. **Corrective Action:** The power train control modules on these vehicles will be replaced.

System: Brakes; hydraulic; lines; fittings. **Vehicle:** Passenger vehicles. **Defect:** The rear brake hose mounting bracket screws can fail, allowing the brake hoses to move out of position. The unrestrained hoses are then susceptible to damage, which could result in brake fluid leakage. **Consequence:** Brake fluid leakage will reduce the braking performance of the vehicle and extend stopping distances, and could result in an accident. **Corrective Action:** The rear brake line hose bracket screws on these vehicles will be replaced.

PLYMOUTH RELIANT 1989

System: Engine valve cover gasket. **Vehicle:** Passenger cars, light trucks and minivans. **Defect:** The engine valve cover gasket may dislocate, allowing an engine oil leak at the gasket. **Consequence:** The leakage of oil in the engine compartment could cause a fire. **Corrective Action:** Replace gasket cover with revised cover; RTV sealant will be applied in place of a gasket.

PLYMOUTH SUNDANCE 1987

System: Fuel. **Vehicle:** Vehicles equipped with 2.2L turbocharged engine. **Defect:** Fuel leakage may occur in low ambient temperature operation at connections of an engine compartment fuel supply hose to the pressure regulator and to the fuel rail. **Consequence:** In the presence of an ignition source, fuel leakage could result in a fire. **Corrective Action:** Relocate pressure regulator; replace fuel supply with formed hose with revised routing configuration to ensure sealing integrity.

PLYMOUTH SUNDANCE 1988

System: Front passenger seat lap belt. **Vehicle:** Passenger cars. **Defect:** Front passenger seat lap belt retractor, which incorporates a child seat belt locking feature, may malfunction. **Consequence:** Seat belt lock would extract, and child seat may move out of its restrained position. **Corrective Action:** Replace front passenger seat lap retractor with a redesigned retractor.

System: Automatic shoulder restraints. **Vehicle:** Passenger cars with automatic shoulder restraints. **Defect:** The automatic shoulder restraint systems can malfunction and become inoperative. **Consequence:** Seat occupants without shoulder restraints are subject to increased risk of injury in the event of a sudden stop or vehicle crash. **Corrective Action:** Replace the system drive and rail assembly with revised components. **Note:** While the automatic shoulder restraint system may not function, the restraint system can be operated manually, and should be used to preserve the safety of the seat occupant.

PLYMOUTH SUNDANCE 1989

System: Engine valve cover gasket. **Vehicle:** Passenger cars, light trucks and minivans. **Defect:** The engine valve cover gasket may dislocate, allowing an engine oil leak at the gasket. **Consequence:** The leakage of oil in the engine compartment could cause a fire. **Corrective Action:** Replace gasket cover with revised cover; RTV sealant will be applied in place of a gasket.

System: Automatic shoulder restraints. **Vehicle:** Passenger cars with automatic shoulder restraints. **Defect:** The automatic shoulder restraint systems can malfunction and become inoperative. **Consequence:** Seat occupants without shoulder restraints are subject to increased risk of injury in the event of a sudden stop or vehicle crash. **Corrective Action:** Replace the system drive and rail assembly with revised components. **Note:** While the automatic shoulder restraint system may not function, the restraint system can be operated manually, and should be used to preserve the safety of the seat occupant.

PLYMOUTH SUNDANCE 1990

System: Engine valve cover gasket. **Vehicle:** Passenger cars, light trucks and minivans. **Defect:** The engine valve cover gasket may dislocate, allowing an engine oil leak at the gasket. **Consequence:** The leakage of oil in the engine compartment could cause a fire. **Corrective Action:** Replace gasket cover with revised cover; RTV sealant will be applied in place of a gasket.

PLYMOUTH SUNDANCE 1991

System: Front disc brake caliper guide pin bolts. **Vehicle:** Passenger cars. **Defect:** Front disc brake caliper guide pin bolts may not have been adequately torqued and could loosen. **Consequence:** This could cause reduced braking effectiveness and could result in an accident. **Corrective Action:** Properly torque front brake caliper guide pin bolts to 250 pounds.

PLYMOUTH SUNDANCE 1992

System: Steering; upper steering column coupling bolt. **Vehicle:** Passenger vehicles; sedans, convertibles and minivans. **Defect:** The zinc-plating operation performed on the upper steering column shaft coupling bolt caused hydrogen embrittlement and breakage of the bolt. **Consequence:** Fractures of the upper steering column shaft coupling bolt result in a lack of coupling load on the shaft and loss of steering control. **Corrective Action:** Replace the zinc-plated bolt with a phosphate-plated bolt.

PLYMOUTH TURISMO 1987

System: Fuel. **Vehicle:** Passenger vehicles. **Defect:** Pressure regulator installed in the fuel supply plumbing system leaks fuel into the engine compartment. **Consequence:** Fuel leaks can result in a fire when near a source of ignition. **Corrective Action:** The fuel supply pressure regulator assembly will be replaced with a new assembly to ensure integrity of the fuel supply system.

PLYMOUTH TRUCK VOYAGER 1987

System: Structure; hatchback locks and latches. **Vehicle:** Light-duty passenger minivans; 1984 through 1995 models without remote release; 1984 through 1995 models with remote release. **Description of Alleged Defect:** This is not a safety recall. There has been no determination that a safety defect exists with the minivan latches. Chrysler is conducting a service campaign to replace the liftgate latch assembly of the affected minivans. In a collision, the rear liftgate latch assembly could open. **Consequence of Alleged Defect:** If the liftgate latch opens, occupants can be ejected, resulting in significantly increased risk of injury or death. **Corrective Action:** Chrysler dealers will replace the liftgate latch with a new, stronger latch assembly without charge. **Note:** This is not a safety recall. There has been no determination that a safety defect exists with the minivan latches. However, Chrysler has decided to provide a stronger latch without charge. Owners can contact Chrysler at (800) MINIVAN [(800) 646-4826].

PLYMOUTH TRUCK VOYAGER 1988

System: Fuel tanks. **Vehicle:** Vans. **Defect:** Fuel tanks may have been damaged during tank manufacture. **Consequence:** This could result in fuel leakage, with the potential for a fire. **Corrective Action:** Replace fuel tanks as necessary.

System: Fuel tanks. **Vehicle:** Vans. **Defect:** Fuel tanks may be constructed of improper material. **Consequence:** Fuel could leak at the tank seam which, in the presence of an ignition source, could result in a fire. **Corrective Action:** Replace suspect fuel tanks.

System: Structure; hatchback locks and latches. **Vehicle:** Light-duty passenger minivans; 1984 through 1995 models without remote release; 1984 through 1995 models with remote release. **Description of Alleged Defect:** This is not a safety recall. There has been no determination that a safety defect exists with the minivan latches. Chrysler is conducting a service campaign to replace the liftgate latch assembly of the affected minivans. In a collision, the rear liftgate latch assembly could open. **Consequence of Alleged Defect:** If the liftgate latch opens, occupants can be ejected, resulting in significantly increased risk of injury or death. **Corrective Action:** Chrysler dealers will replace the liftgate latch with a new, stronger latch assembly without charge. **Note:** This is not a safety recall. There has been no determination that a safety defect exists with the minivan latches. However, Chrysler has decided to provide a stronger latch without charge. Owners can contact Chrysler at (800) MINIVAN [(800) 646-4826].

PLYMOUTH TRUCK VOYAGER 1989

System: Engine valve cover gasket. **Vehicle:** Passenger cars, light trucks and minivans. **Defect:** The engine valve cover gasket may dislocate, allowing an engine oil leak at the gasket. **Consequence:** The leakage of oil in the engine compartment could cause a fire. **Corrective Action:** Replace gasket cover with revised cover; RTV sealant will be applied in place of a gasket.

System: Safety belt buckle assembly. **Vehicle:** Passenger vans and cars. **Defect:** Inboard front seat belt buckle assembly straps can suffer fatigue failure of the strap near its anchor position. **Consequence:** Fatigue failure of safety belts in a sudden stop or accident condition results in increased likelihood of injury to seat occupant. **Corrective Action:** Replace fatigued straps, or retrofit straps with a reinforcement plate and removal of an antirotation tab to prevent fatigue failure.

System: Structure; hatchback locks and latches. **Vehicle:** Light-duty passenger minivans; 1984 through 1995 models without remote release; 1984 through 1995 models with remote release. **Description of Alleged Defect:** This is not a safety recall. There has been no determination that a safety defect exists with the minivan latches. Chrysler is conducting a service campaign to replace the liftgate latch assembly of the affected minivans. In a collision, the rear liftgate latch assembly could open. **Consequence of Alleged Defect:** If the liftgate latch opens, occupants can be ejected, resulting in significantly increased risk of injury or death. **Corrective Action:** Chrysler dealers will replace the liftgate latch with a new, stronger latch assembly without charge. **Note:** This is not a safety recall. There has been no determination that a safety defect exists with the minivan latches. However, Chrysler has decided to provide a stronger latch without charge. Owners can contact Chrysler at (800) MINIVAN [(800) 646-4826].

PLYMOUTH TRUCK VOYAGER 1990

System: Engine valve cover gasket. **Vehicle:** Passenger cars, light trucks and minivans. **Defect:** The engine valve cover gasket may dislocate, allowing an engine oil leak at the gasket. **Consequence:** The leakage of oil in the engine compartment could cause a fire. **Corrective Action:** Replace gasket cover with revised cover; RTV sealant will be applied in place of a gasket.

System: Brakes; proportioning valve screw. **Vehicle:** Truck van. **Defect:** Incorrect screws may have been used in installing the load-sensing brake proportioning valve to its bracket, causing the clamping load to be less than intended. **Consequence:** This could result in inconsistent front-to-rear brake balance, with potential for rear brake skid under heavy braking conditions. **Corrective Action:** Replace proportioning valve-to-bracket screws with proper length screws.

System: Safety belt buckle assembly. **Vehicle:** Passenger vans and cars. **Defect:** Inboard front seat belt buckle assembly straps can suffer fatigue failure of the strap near its anchor position. **Consequence:** Fatigue failure of safety belts in a sudden stop or accident condition results in increased likelihood of injury to seat occupant. **Corrective Action:** Replace fatigued straps, or retrofit straps with a reinforcement plate and removal of an antirotation tab to prevent fatigue failure.

System: Structure; hatchback locks and latches. **Vehicle:** Light-duty passenger minivans; 1984 through 1995 models without remote release; 1984 through 1995 models with remote release. **Description of Alleged Defect:** This is not a safety recall. There has been no determination that a safety defect exists with the minivan latches. Chrysler is conducting a service campaign to replace the liftgate latch assembly of the affected minivans. In a collision, the rear liftgate latch assembly could open. **Consequence of Alleged Defect:** If the liftgate latch opens, occupants can be ejected, resulting in significantly increased risk of injury or death. **Corrective Action:** Chrysler dealers will replace the liftgate latch with a new, stronger latch assembly without charge. **Note:** This is not a safety recall. There has been no determination that a safety defect exists with the minivan latches. However, Chrysler has decided to provide a stronger latch without charge. Owners can contact Chrysler at (800) MINIVAN [(800) 646-4826].

PLYMOUTH TRUCK VOYAGER 1991

System: Brakes. **Vehicle:** Passenger cars and vans with antilock brake systems (ABS). **Defect:** The antilock brake system high-pressure hose may leak or detach at its crimped end fitting, resulting in the discharge of hydraulic fluid. **Consequence:** Fluid discharge eventually causes the loss of both the antilock brake system and hydraulic assist for the brake system, resulting in increased likelihood of brake lockup and increased stopping distances, which could result in a vehicle accident. **Corrective Action:** Replace the antilock brake system high-pressure hose with a hose of different design and construction.

System: Brakes; antilock brake system. **Vehicle:** Passenger minivans with antilock braking systems (ABS). **Defect:** The antilock brake system high-pressure pump may be porous, which will result in brake fluid leakage. **Consequence:** Fluid leakage eventually causes the loss of both the antilock brake system and hydraulic assist for the brake system, resulting in increased likelihood of brake lockup and increased stopping distances, which could result in a vehicle accident. **Corrective Action:** Replace the antilock brake system high-pressure pump and high-pressure hose if the last six digits of the bar code label on the pump are between 052300 and 059262.

System: Structure; hatchback locks and latches. **Vehicle:** Light-duty passenger minivans; 1984 through 1995 models without remote release; 1984 through 1995 models with remote release. **Description of Alleged Defect:** This is not a safety recall. There has been no determination that a safety defect exists with the minivan latches. Chrysler is conducting a service campaign to replace the liftgate latch assembly of the affected minivans. In a collision, the rear liftgate latch assembly could open. **Consequence of Alleged Defect:** If the liftgate latch opens, occupants can be ejected, resulting in significantly increased risk of injury or death. **Corrective Action:** Chrysler dealers will replace the liftgate latch with a new, stronger latch assembly without charge. **Note:** This is not a safety recall. There has been no determination that a safety defect exists with the minivan latches. However, Chrysler has decided to provide a stronger latch without charge. Owners can contact Chrysler at (800) MINIVAN [(800) 646-4826].

PLYMOUTH TRUCK VOYAGER 1992

System: Brakes; pedal. **Vehicle:** Minivan. **Defect:** The brake pedal pad attachment to the pedal arm may not have adequate strength, due to mislocation of welds, and could break. **Consequence:** Failure of the pedal pad to pedal arm attachment results in loss of braking ability, and could result in an accident. **Corrective Action:** Replace inadequate brake pedals with properly manufactured pedals.

System: Steering; upper steering column coupling bolt. **Vehicle:** Passenger vehicles; sedans, convertibles and minivans. **Defect:** The zinc-plating operation performed on the upper steering column shaft coupling bolt caused hydrogen embrittlement and breakage of the bolt. **Consequence:** Fractures of the upper steering column shaft coupling bolt result in a lack of coupling load on the shaft and loss of steering control. **Corrective Action:** Replace the zinc-plated bolt with a phosphate-plated bolt.

System: Safety belts—FMVSS 209. **Vehicle:** Vans, light trucks and multipurpose vehicles. **Defect:** Front outboard seat belt assemblies do not have the properly marked label with manufacturer information. **Consequence:** The seat belt assemblies do not comply with FMVSS 209. **Corrective Action:** Chrysler has not proposed a corrective action for this safety defect. **Note:** The manufacturer's petition, which requested that NHTSA determine this FMVSS noncompliance does not create an unreasonable risk to motor vehicle safety, has been granted. Therefore, the manufacturer is not obligated to conduct an owner notification and remedy campaign.

System: Fuel tank. **Vehicle:** Passenger vans. **Defect:** Fuel tank flanges were not bent as required to allow the specified clearance for the fuel tank mounting straps and fuel lines at the tank. **Consequence:** The unbent flanges to the fuel tank will damage the mounting straps and/or fuel lines. The damaged mounting straps may break, causing the tank to drop, and the damaged fuel line will leak fuel. In either case a fire could result if the spilled fuel is exposed to an ignition source. **Corrective Action:** Repair the flange by bending to the correct angle; replace damaged fuel lines and mounting straps.

System: Structure; hatchback locks and latches. **Vehicle:** Light-duty passenger minivans; 1984 through 1995 models without remote release; 1984 through 1995 models with remote release. **Description of Alleged Defect:** This is not a safety recall. There has been no determination that a safety defect exists with the minivan latches. Chrysler is conducting a service campaign to replace the liftgate latch assembly of the affected minivans. In a collision, the rear liftgate latch assembly could open. **Consequence of Alleged Defect:** If the liftgate latch opens, occupants can be ejected, resulting in significantly increased risk of injury or death. **Corrective Action:** Chrysler dealers will replace the liftgate latch with a new, stronger latch assembly without charge. **Note:** This is not a safety recall. There has been no determination that a safety defect exists with the minivan latches. However, Chrysler has decided to provide a stronger latch without charge. Owners can contact Chrysler at (800) MINIVAN [(800) 646-4826].

PLYMOUTH TRUCK VOYAGER 1993

System: Wheels. **Vehicle:** Passenger minivans with 15-inch stamped steel road wheels or stamped steel spare wheels. **Defect:** The 15-inch wheels have malformed lug nut seat configuration which causes poor nut-to-wheel contact and centering of the wheel during installation. **Consequence:** Poor nut-to-wheel contact during installation can lead to possible loss of a wheel, resulting in loss of vehicle control and an accident. **Corrective Action:** The road and spare wheels with the malformed lug nut seat configuration will be replaced.

System: Structure; hatchback locks and latches. **Vehicle:** Light-duty passenger minivans; 1984 through 1995 models without remote release; 1984 through 1995 models with remote release. **Description of Alleged Defect:** This is not a safety recall. There has been no determination that a safety defect exists with the minivan latches. Chrysler is conducting a service campaign to replace the liftgate latch assembly of the affected minivans. In a collision, the rear liftgate latch assembly could open. **Consequence of Alleged Defect:** If the liftgate latch opens, occupants can be ejected, resulting in significantly increased risk of injury or death. **Corrective Action:** Chrysler dealers will replace the liftgate latch with a new, stronger latch assembly without charge. **Note:** This is not a safety recall. There has been no determination that a safety defect exists with the minivan latches. However, Chrysler has decided to provide a stronger latch without charge. Owners can contact Chrysler at (800) MINIVAN [(800) 646-4826].

PLYMOUTH TRUCK VOYAGER 1994

System: Structure; hatchback locks and latches. **Vehicle:** Light-duty passenger minivans; 1984 through 1995 models without remote release; 1984 through 1995 models with remote release. **Description of Alleged Defect:** This is not a safety recall. There has been no determination that a safety defect exists with the minivan latches. Chrysler is conducting a service campaign to replace the liftgate latch assembly of the affected minivans. In a collision, the rear liftgate latch assembly could open. **Consequence of Alleged Defect:** If the liftgate latch opens, occupants can be ejected, resulting in significantly increased risk of injury or death. **Corrective Action:** Chrysler dealers will replace the liftgate latch with a new, stronger latch assembly without charge. **Note:** This is not a safety recall. There has been no determination that a safety defect exists with the minivan latches. However, Chrysler has decided to provide a stronger latch without charge. Owners can contact Chrysler at (800) MINIVAN [(800) 646-4826].

PONTIAC

Note: Owners who take their Pontiac to an authorized dealer on an agreed-upon service date and do not receive the free remedy within a reasonable time should contact Buick at (800) 521-7300; Chevrolet at (800) 222-1020; Pontiac at (800) 762-2737; or Oldsmobile at (800) 442-6537. Also contact the NHTSA's Auto Safety Hotline at (800) 424-9393.

PONTIAC 6000 1987

System: Windshield—FMVSS 212. **Vehicle:** Passenger cars. **Defect:** Poor bond adhesion between the windshield glass and mounting could allow the windshield to separate during a 30 mph frontal barrier test required by FMVSS 212. **Consequence:** If windshield glass separation occurs during an accident, an unbelted occupant could be ejected from the vehicle and injured. **Corrective Action:** Reinstall windshields to ensure proper bond adhesion.

System: Brakes. **Vehicle:** Passenger cars with antilock brakes. **Defect:** The antilock brake system (ABS) pressure/warning switch may exhibit brake fluid seepage, which eventually can lead to loss of the brake system hydraulic pump motor. Additionally, the hydraulic pump motor and antilock brake system electrical relays may have been exposed to water contamination during vehicle assembly. This condition can cause loss of the hydraulic pump motor and/or loss of the antilock brake system function. **Consequence:** Loss of the hydraulic pump motor would result in a total loss of rear brakes, as well as power assist to the front brakes. The red "brake" warning light would illuminate and stay on. If this warning is not heeded, a loss of rear brakes at a time when minimum stopping distance is required could result in a vehicle crash. An inoperative antilock brake system electrical relay could cause loss of the antilock brake system function, but normal power-assisted braking would be retained. The amber "antilock" warning light would illuminate and stay on. **Corrective Action:** The antilock brake system and hydraulic pump motor electrical relays and 30 amp fuses will be replaced. In addition, the hydraulic pump motor assembly and pressure/warning switch will be inspected and, if required, replaced.

PONTIAC 6000 1988

System: Suspension—lower control front arm bracket. **Vehicle:** Passenger car. **Defect:** Front suspension lower control arm bracket could develop metal cracks. **Consequence:** These cracks may result in disengagement of the lower control arm. If this occurs while vehicle is in motion, it could result in loss of steering control, and a vehicle crash could occur without prior warning. **Corrective Action:** Inspect all vehicles and replace engine cradle assembly on all suspect vehicles.

System: Fuel feed hose. **Vehicle:** Passenger cars equipped with a 2.8L V6 engine. **Defect:** Fuel feed hose could leak at the coupling on the engine end of the hose assembly. **Consequence:** Fuel leakage into the engine compartment could result in an engine compartment fire that could spread to the passenger compartment. **Corrective Action:** Install new fuel feed hose assembly.

PONTIAC 6000 1989

System: Interior; active restraints; belt anchor and attachment—FMVSS 210. **Vehicle:** Passenger vehicles. **Description of Noncompliance:** These vehicles were assembled with rear outboard safety belt anchorages that may not withstand the required load. This does not comply with FMVSS 210, "Seat belt assembly anchorages." **Consequence of Noncompliance:** In a collision, stress can cause the attachment metal to tear and allow the anchorage to separate from the body of the vehicle. The safety belt may not protect an occupant in the event of a vehicle crash. **Corrective Action:** Dealers will replace the existing anchor bolts with a new shoulder bolt and thread-locking adhesive. Additionally, noise control patches will be applied at each anchorage.

PONTIAC BONNEVILLE 1987

System: Headlamp circuit. **Vehicle:** Passenger cars equipped with foglamps. **Defect:** The headlamp circuit breaker may overheat at low beam, causing an intermittent headlamp circuit. **Consequence:** Headlamp and foglamps would go out suddenly, reducing driver visibility, which could result in a vehicle crash. **Corrective Action:** Revise foglamp circuit to prevent overheating of headlamp circuit.

System: Electrical—in-line fusible link. **Vehicle:** Passenger cars. **Defect:** An in-line fusible link may melt down and cause a fire. **Consequence:** The in-line fusible link located in the area of the plastic windshield washer bottle bracket may, under a high-resistance load, melt down and ignite the washer bottle bracket, resulting in an engine compartment fire. **Corrective Action:** The windshield washer bottle bracket will be replaced.

System: Accelerator cable. **Vehicle:** Passenger cars. **Defect:** Excessive accelerator cable friction may restrict the cable's free movement between the accelerator pedal and the throttle body. **Consequence:** This could prevent throttle from returning to closed (idle) position when accelerator pedal is released; thus, engine speed would not decrease, and loss of accelerator control could result in an accident. **Corrective Action:** Replace accelerator cable.

PONTIAC BONNEVILLE 1989

System: Fuel rollover valve—FMVSS 301. **Vehicle:** Passenger cars. **Defect:** Fuel rollover valve assembly may not have been installed.

Consequence: In event of an accident in which vehicle becomes inverted, missing valve could allow fuel spillage in excess of amount allowed by FMVSS 301, which could result in a fire. **Corrective Action:** Replace fuel sender and pump assembly.

PONTIAC BONNEVILLE 1992

System: Transaxle shift control. **Vehicle:** Passenger cars with console-shift automatic transmission. **Defect:** Transaxle shift control cable may disengage from shift control cable bracket, causing loss of gear indicator reference and shift selector operation. **Consequence:** The disengaged cable could falsely indicate transmission gear position, and the vehicle might be left in reverse or drive when the driver moved the gear selector to park or the opposite direction. A vehicle left on an incline without parking brakes when the gear selector is placed in park could move. Either case results in unexpected vehicle movement without prior warning, and could cause a vehicle accident. **Corrective Action:** Install a transaxle shift control cable retaining clip on the shift control cable bracket on top of transaxle.

System: Brakes—FMVSS 105. **Vehicle:** Passenger cars. **Defect:** When applied, the parking brake lever assembly may release one or more teeth, reducing the cable load to the rear brakes. **Consequence:** Depending on the extent of the lever release and road level, the parking brake may not hold the vehicle, allowing it to roll, which could result in an accident. Vehicle does not comply with FMVSS 105. **Corrective Action:** Replace parking brake lever assembly.

PONTIAC FIERO 1987

System: Engine. **Vehicle:** Passenger cars with 4-cylinder engines. **Defect:** Due to an interaction of the engine compartment environment and maintenance- or service-related factors, there is a risk of engine compartment fires. **Consequence:** An engine compartment fire can spread to the passenger compartment and injure occupants. **Corrective Action:** Correct or install new engine components to prevent unreasonable fire risk.

System: Engine. **Vehicle:** Fiero passenger cars with 2.8L 6-cylinder engines. **Defect:** PCV grommet oil leaks, transmission oil cooler leaks, piston connecting rod failures breaking through engine wall causing oil spillage, fuel rail leaks, coolant leaks, rocker cover oil leaks, and maintenance- or service-related factors could cause engine compartment fires. **Consequence:** An engine compartment fire can spread to the passenger compartment and injure occupants. **Corrective Action:** Correct or install new components to prevent unreasonable fire risk.

PONTIAC FIERO 1988

System: Engine. **Vehicle:** Passenger cars with 4-cylinder engines. **Defect:** Due to an interaction of the engine compartment environment and maintenance- or service-related factors, there is a risk of engine compartment fires. **Consequence:** An engine compartment fire can spread to the passenger compartment and injure occupants. **Corrective Action:** Correct or install new engine components to prevent unreasonable fire risk.

System: Engine. **Vehicle:** Fiero passenger cars with 2.8L 6-cylinder engines. **Defect:** PCV grommet oil leaks, transmission oil cooler leaks, piston connecting rod failures breaking through engine wall causing oil spillage, fuel rail leaks, coolant leaks, rocker cover oil leaks, and maintenance- or service-related factors could cause engine compartment fires. **Consequence:** An engine compartment fire can spread to the passenger compartment and injure occupants. **Corrective Action:** Correct or install new components to prevent unreasonable fire risk.

PONTIAC FIREBIRD 1987

System: Seat belt buckle. **Vehicle:** Passenger cars. **Defect:** Plastic components of seat belt buckle assemblies do not contain an ultraviolet stabilizer, and exposure to direct sunlight and elevated interior temperatures could weaken the plastic components. **Consequence:** This could result in breakage of plastic components, which could prevent buckle from latching and protecting occupant in a sudden stop or accident. **Corrective Action:** Replace or repair seat belt buckle.

PONTIAC FIREBIRD 1988

System: Seat belt buckle. **Vehicle:** Passenger cars. **Defect:** Plastic components of seat belt buckle assemblies do not contain an ultraviolet stabilizer, and exposure to direct sunlight and elevated interior temperatures could weaken the plastic components. **Consequence:** This could result in breakage of plastic components, which could prevent buckle from latching and protecting occupant in a sudden stop or accident. **Corrective Action:** Replace or repair seat belt buckle.

System: Fuel feed hoses. **Vehicle:** Passenger cars with 2.8L V6 engines. **Defect:** Fuel feed hoses may pull out of the crimped coupling at the engine end of the hose assembly. **Consequence:** If this coupling separated, allowing gasoline to leak, and an ignition source is present, an engine compartment fire could occur. **Corrective Action:** Install a redesigned fuel feed hose.

PONTIAC FIREBIRD 1989

System: Seat belt buckle. **Vehicle:** Passenger cars. **Defect:** Plastic components of seat belt buckle assemblies do not contain an ultraviolet stabilizer, and exposure to direct sunlight and elevated interior temperatures could weaken the plastic components. **Consequence:** This could result in breakage of plastic components, which could prevent buckle from latching and protecting occupant in a sudden stop or accident. **Corrective Action:** Replace or repair seat belt buckle.

System: Fuel feed hoses. **Vehicle:** Passenger cars with 2.8L V6 engines. **Defect:** Fuel feed hoses may pull out of the crimped coupling at the engine end of the hose assembly. **Consequence:** If this coupling separated, allowing gasoline to leak, and an ignition source is present, an engine compartment fire could occur. **Corrective Action:** Install a redesigned fuel feed hose.

PONTIAC FIREBIRD 1991

System: Windshield mounting—FMVSS 212. **Vehicle:** Passenger cars. **Defect:** Poor bond adhesion between the windshield glass and the mounting, which could allow the windshield to separate from the vehicle during a collision. This fails to conform with FMVSS 212. **Consequence:** If windshield separation occurs in a collision, an unbelted occupant could be ejected from the vehicle, and personal injury could occur. **Corrective Action:** Remove all sealer from windshield and mounting; apply new bonding and sealant material, and reinstall windshield.

System: Safety belt assembly—FMVSS 209. **Vehicle:** Passenger cars; coupes and convertibles. **Defect:** The metal latchplates may not engage the buckle assemblies, causing a "no latch" condition. Movement of the seat occupant in this condition could cause latchplate release from the buckle. **Consequence:** Unbelted or incorrectly belted seat occupants are subjected to increased risk of injury in the event of sudden stop or accident. **Corrective Action:** Replace the retractor assembly for the safety belt (front and rear in coupes and front only in convertibles).

System: Fuel; fuel tank assembly; pipe; filler; neck—FMVSS 301. **Vehicle:** Passenger vehicles. **Description of Noncompliance:** The fuel filler neck solder joint can develop cracks or pinhole leaks, which does not comply with FMVSS 301, "Fuel system integrity." The cracks and holes can allow fuel vapor and fuel leakage. **Consequence of Noncompliance:** Gasoline vapor and fuel leaks can result in a fire if exposed to a source of ignition. **Corrective Action:** Dealers will inspect the fuel tank assembly and replace those which exhibit the cracks or pinhole leaks.

PONTIAC GRAND AM 1987

System: Fuel **Vehicle:** Vehicles built with 2.0L engines. **Defect:** The fuel feed and/or return hose and pipe assemblies could crack or separate, allowing fuel to leak into the underhood area. **Consequence:** This could result in an underhood fire, without prior warning, and cause injury to occupants. **Corrective Action:** Replace both fuel feed and return hose and pipe assemblies.

System: Fuel and hose. **Vehicle:** Passenger cars. **Defect:** The fuel feed or fuel return hose at the engine may rub against a shift lever on the 5-speed transaxle. **Consequence:** In time, a hole could be rubbed through the hose and fuel could leak into the engine compartment. This could result in an underhood fire. **Corrective Action:** Replace the fuel feed and return hose and pipe assemblies.

PONTIAC GRAND AM 1988

System: Front fuel feed hose. **Vehicle:** Passenger cars equipped with quad 4 engines. **Defect:** Front fuel feed hose assembly could crack or separate at the coupling on the engine end of the hose assembly, allowing fuel to leak into the engine compartment. **Consequence:** Leaking fuel in the engine compartment could result in a fire. **Corrective Action:** Replace front fuel feed hose assembly.

System: Fuel hose. **Vehicle:** Passenger cars equipped with quad 4 engines. **Defect:** Front fuel feed hose assembly could crack or separate at the coupling on the engine end of the hose assembly, allowing fuel to leak into the engine compartment. **Consequence:** Fuel leaking in the engine compartment could result in an underhood fire. **Corrective Action:** Replace front fuel feed hose assembly. **Note:** GMC has expanded previous NHTSA Recall to include an additional 108,836 vehicles.

PONTIAC GRAND AM 1989

System: Front fuel feed hose. **Vehicle:** Passenger cars equipped with quad 4 engines. **Defect:** Front fuel feed hose assembly could crack or separate at the coupling on the engine end of the hose assembly, allowing fuel to leak into the engine compartment. **Consequence:** Leaking fuel in the engine compartment could result in a fire. **Corrective Action:** Replace front fuel feed hose assembly.

System: Fuel hose. **Vehicle:** Passenger cars equipped with quad 4 engines. **Defect:** Front fuel feed hose assembly could crack or separate at the coupling on the engine end of the hose assembly, allowing fuel to leak into the engine compartment. **Consequence:** Fuel leaking in the engine compartment could result in an underhood fire. **Corrective Action:** Replace front fuel feed hose assembly. **Note:** GMC has expanded previous NHTSA Recall to include an additional 108,836 vehicles.

PONTIAC GRAND AM 1991

System: Steering column jackets. **Vehicle:** Passenger cars. **Defect:** Steering column jackets may be 10 mm short in overall length, causing inadequate retention of the column to the column support bracket. **Consequence:** In the event of a front-end collision, improper compression of the steering column may increase likelihood of injury to the driver. **Corrective Action:** Replace steering column assembly.

System: Visual systems. **Vehicle:** Passenger cars equipped with power windows. **Defect:** Moisture can enter the express-down electronic control module and cause a short circuit that causes window operation without operator control and leaves the window in the down position. **Consequence:** The electronic control module will fail from overheating and could result in a fire hazard inside the door panel. **Corrective Action:** Replace the window express-down electronic control module.

PONTIAC GRAND AM 1992

System: Interior systems; seat back. **Vehicle:** Passenger cars; "N" coupe models. **Defect:** The passenger-side easy-entry seat adjuster may fail to fully lock into position after the seat back has been tilted forward and the seat slid forward, then returned to its original position. **Consequence:** If the seat adjuster fails to lock into position, the passenger seat would slide forward in the event of a sudden stop or accident. Occupants of the passenger seat would face increased risk of serious injury. **Corrective Action:** Replace the adjuster assembly on the seat. **Note:** GMC has informed this agency that all repairs will be made before the vehicle is offered for sale.

System: Rear axle. **Vehicle:** Passenger cars. **Defect:** The bolts and nuts which attach the bearing-hub assembly to the rear axle flange are not sufficiently tightened on some vehicles. **Consequence:** This would allow excessive movement of the bearing-hub assembly relative to the rear axle flange and could cause elongation and eventual separation of the attaching bolts from the rear axle flange. If this were to occur while the vehicle was in motion, the affected tire and wheel could track erratically, eventually causing failure of the other attaching bolts. The tire and wheel assembly could separate from the vehicle, which could result in a vehicle accident. **Corrective Action:** Tighten rear axle bearing-hub assembly fasteners, and replace all the fasteners on a wheel if two or more bolts are found to be loose. **Note:** GMC reports that all subject vehicles were held and repaired before any owner took possession, so there will be no owner notification.

System: Fuel—FMVSS 301. **Vehicle:** Passenger cars. **Defect:** The vehicles were assembled with an incorrect suspension upper spring seat at the right rear position. If the vehicle is involved in a rear-impact accident, the right-hand rear wheel house flange could sever the fuel tank filler pipe and spill fuel. **Consequence:** These vehicles are not in compliance with FMVSS 301, "Fuel system integrity." Spilled fuel in a low-speed accident can result in a fire. **Corrective Action:** Inspect and replace incorrect upper spring seat with the correct part.

PONTIAC GRAND AM 1993

System: Electrical; ignition switch. **Vehicle:** Passenger cars with automatic transaxles. **Defect:** The neutral safety switch could have been fractured during installation. **Consequence:** A fractured switch can result in a no-start condition. Also, a vehicle with a fractured switch can be started in gear, causing the vehicle to move unexpectedly and possibly resulting in an accident. **Corrective Action:** The dealer will replace the neutral switch. The manual switch of the automatic transaxle assembly will be inspected and replaced if an oversized condition exists.

PONTIAC GRAND AM 1994

System: Fuel; fuel tank assembly—FMVSS 301. **Vehicle:** Passenger vehicles. **Description of Noncompliance:** These vehicles were constructed with welds in the rear compartment pan assembly that are not sufficient to comply with the requirements pertaining to fuel tank leakage in the event of a rear-impact collision. The fuel tank assemblies do not comply with FMVSS 301, "Fuel system integrity." **Consequence:** This can result in an increased risk of a vehicle fire in the event of a rear-impact collision. **Corrective Action:** Dealer will install rivets adjacent to the locations where the suspect welds are located.

PONTIAC GRAND PRIX 1988

System: Wheel lug nuts. **Vehicle:** Passenger cars. **Defect:** Wheel lug nuts were not properly torqued to specifications. **Consequence:** Wheel lug nuts could loosen and/or come off the wheel studs. This could eventually result in the wheel separating from the vehicle. Loss of vehicle control and a vehicle crash could occur. **Corrective Action:** Inspect vehicle and ensure proper torque, replace any missing lug nuts or loose studs.

System: Transmission—shift linkage. **Vehicle:** Passenger cars. **Defect:** An interference between the transmission shift cable and the bellcrank clip in the steering column can result in disengagement of the transmission cable. **Consequence:** This condition could allow the transmission to be in a gear other than that displayed by the shift indicator. The vehicle could move in an unexpected direction and cause a vehicle crash without prior warning. **Corrective Action:** A newly designed bellcrank clip will be installed.

System: Seat belts. **Vehicle:** Passenger cars. **Defect:** The front shoulder belt guide loop attached to the upper rear corner of the door may interfere with the garnish molding. **Consequence:** This interference could limit the rotation of the guide loop. If this condition exists and vehicle is involved in a crash, it could be possible for the shoulder belt welding to be cut by the guide. Loss of the shoulder belt function during a vehicle crash could increase the risk of injuries to occupants. **Corrective Action:** A newly designed guide loop nut and spacer will be installed to eliminate the potential for interference conditions.

System: Hood latch. **Vehicle:** Passenger cars. **Defect:** The secondary hood latch may not properly engage. **Consequence:** If primary latch disengages, hood could unexpectedly open. If car was in motion, hood could contact the windshield and reduce the driver's forward vision area, and could result in an accident. **Corrective Action:** Replace secondary latch with a new latch.

System: Brakes—FMVSS 105. **Vehicle:** Passenger cars. **Defect:** The parking brake cable may be disconnected from the left rear brake caliper. **Consequence:** Parking brake cannot be properly applied and vehicle will not meet the grade-holding requirements of FMVSS 105.

Corrective Action: Install a retainer on left rear caliper, if cable is not already retained with a cotter pin, and adjust parking brake system.

System: Seat belt anchorage—FMVSS 210. **Vehicle:** Passenger cars. **Defect:** Front shoulder belt guide loop attachment fastener may pull through door-mounted anchor plate. **Consequence:** Seat belt may not sustain loads required by FMVSS 210, and in a vehicle accident, the seat belt may not properly restrain a passenger, resulting in increased risk of greater injury to an occupant. **Corrective Action:** Replace front shoulder belt guide loop attachment nuts and install new guide cover.

System: Brake stoplamp switch. **Vehicle:** Passenger cars. **Defect:** Brake stoplamps may not illuminate or, in some cases, stoplamps may not stay illuminated all the time when brakes are applied due to a faulty stoplamp switch. Also, in vehicles with cruise control, a faulty stoplamp switch can result in resumption of the cruise control function upon release of the brake pedal. **Consequence:** A trailing vehicle may not recognize a braking action in time to respond appropriately. Also, cruise control will reengage upon release of the brake pedal and resume the set speed. In either case, it could result in a crash without prior warning. **Corrective Action:** Install an improved-design stoplamp switch.

System: Wheels. **Vehicle:** Passenger vehicles equipped with Kelsey Hayes steel wheels; models RPO PB6 14″ and RPO PG1 15″. **Defect:** Cracks develop in the wheel mounting surface. If these cracks become severe enough, the wheel will completely separate from the vehicle. **Consequence:** If wheel separation occurs while the vehicle is in motion, loss of steering and brake control of the vehicle occurs, and a vehicle crash could result without prior warning. **Corrective Action:** Dealers will inspect the manufacturing codes stamped on each wheel of the vehicle, and if a wheel falls within the specified date code range, the dealer will replace that wheel assembly.

System: Wheels. **Vehicle:** Passenger vehicles equipped with Kelsey Hayes steel wheels; models RPO PB9 14″ and RPO PG1 15″. **Defect:** Cracks develop in the wheel mounting surface. If these cracks become severe enough, the wheel will completely separate from the vehicle. **Consequence:** If wheel separation occurs while the vehicle is in motion, loss of steering and brake control of the vehicle occurs, and a vehicle crash could result without prior warning. **Corrective Action:** Dealers will inspect the manufacturing date codes stamped on each wheel of the vehicle, and if a wheel falls within the specified date code range, the dealer will replace that wheel assembly. **Note:** Vehicles previously inspected that had less than four wheels replaced are to be reinspected.

PONTIAC GRAND PRIX 1989

System: Fuel return pipe assembly. **Vehicle:** Passenger cars. **Defect:** Fuel return lines could fracture and allow fuel to leak in the area of the fuel tank. **Consequence:** In the presence of an ignition source, this condition could result in a fire. **Corrective Action:** Install new fuel return pipe assembly.

System: Engine oil cooler line. **Vehicle:** Passenger cars with LG5 3.1L turbocharger engines. **Defect:** Misrouting of turbocharger oil feed pipe could allow pipe to contact the positive battery cable connecting stud on the starter motor. **Consequence:** This could cause an electrical ground that could result in an engine compartment fire. **Corrective Action:** Reroute oil feed pipe; also install a newly designed clamp and bracket to locate pipe away from the starter.

System: Seat belt anchorage—FMVSS 210. **Vehicle:** Passenger cars. **Defect:** Front shoulder belt guide loop attachment fastener may pull through door-mounted anchor plate. **Consequence:** Seat belt may not sustain loads required by FMVSS 210, and in a vehicle accident, the seat belt may not properly restrain a passenger, resulting in increased risk of injury to an occupant. **Corrective Action:** Replace front shoulder belt guide loop attachment nuts and install new guide cover.

System: Brake stoplamp switch. **Vehicle:** Passenger cars. **Defect:** Brake stoplamps may not illuminate or, in some cases, stoplamps will not stay illuminated all the time when brakes are applied due to a faulty stoplamp switch. Also, in vehicles equipped with cruise control, a faulty stoplamp switch can result in resumption of the cruise control function upon release of the brake pedal. **Consequence:** A trailing vehicle may not recognize a braking action in time to respond appropriately. Also, cruise control will reengage upon release of the brake pedal and resume the set speed. In either case, it could result in a crash without prior warning. **Corrective Action:** Install an improved-design stoplamp switch.

System: Brake stoplamp switch. **Vehicle:** Passenger cars. **Defect:** Brake stoplamps may not illuminate or, in some cases, stoplamps may not stay illuminated all the time when brakes are applied due to a faulty stoplamp switch. Also, in vehicles with cruise control, a faulty stoplamp switch can result in resumption of the cruise control function upon release of the brake pedal. **Consequence:** A trailing vehicle may not recognize a braking action in time to respond appropriately. Also, cruise control will reengage upon release of the brake pedal and resume the set speed. In either case, it could result in a crash without prior warning. **Corrective Action:** Install an improved-design stoplamp switch. **Note:** This recall augments the previous NHTSA Recall.

System: Wheels. **Vehicle:** Passenger vehicles equipped with Kelsey Hayes steel wheels; models RPO PB6 14″ and RPO PG1 15″. **Defect:** Cracks develop in the wheel mounting surface. If these cracks become severe enough, the wheel will completely separate from the vehicle. **Consequence:** If wheel separation occurs while the vehicle is in motion, loss of steering and brake control of the vehicle occurs, and a vehicle crash could result without prior warning. **Corrective Action:** Dealers will inspect the manufacturing codes stamped on each wheel of the vehicle, and if a wheel falls within the specified date code range, the dealer will replace that wheel assembly.

System: Wheels. **Vehicle:** Passenger vehicles equipped with Kelsey Hayes steel wheels; models RPO PB9 14″ and RPO PG1 15″. **Defect:** Cracks develop in the wheel mounting surface. If these cracks become severe enough, the wheel will completely separate from the vehicle. **Consequence:** If wheel separation occurs while the vehicle is in motion, loss of steering and brake control of the vehicle occurs, and a vehicle crash could result without prior warning. **Corrective Action:** Dealers will inspect the manufacturing date codes stamped on each wheel of the vehicle, and if a wheel falls within the specified date code range, the dealer will replace that wheel assembly. **Note:** Vehicles previously inspected that had less than four wheels replaced are to be reinspected.

PONTIAC GRAND PRIX 1990

System: Fuel tank—exhaust heat shield. **Vehicle:** Passenger cars; SE Turbo models only. **Defect:** During a rear-end collision, the rear exhaust system heat shield, which is welded to the tailpipe assembly, may puncture the fuel tank. **Consequence:** In the presence of an external source of ignition, this could result in a fire. **Corrective Action:** Remove rear exhaust system heat shield from the pipe assembly.

System: Seat belt anchorage—FMVSS 210. **Vehicle:** Passenger cars. **Defect:** Front shoulder belt guide loop attachment fastener may pull through door-mounted anchor plate. **Consequence:** Seat belt may not sustain loads required by FMVSS 210, and in a vehicle accident, the seat belt may not properly restrain a passenger, resulting in increased risk of greater injury to an occupant. **Corrective Action:** Replace front shoulder belt guide loop attachment nuts and install new guide cover.

System: Brake stoplamp switch. **Vehicle:** Passenger cars. **Defect:** Brake stoplamps may not illuminate or, in some cases, stoplamps will not stay illuminated all the time when brakes are applied due to a faulty stoplamp switch. Also, in vehicles equipped with cruise control, a faulty stoplamp switch can result in resumption of the cruise control function upon release of the brake pedal. **Consequence:** A trailing vehicle may not recognize a braking action in time to respond appropriately. Also, cruise control will reengage upon release of the brake pedal and resume the set speed. In either case, it could result in a crash without prior warning. **Corrective Action:** Install an improved design stoplamp switch.

System: Front shoulder safety belt. **Vehicle:** Passenger cars. **Defect:** Front shoulder safety belt webbing may separate at front belt upper guide loops on either side of the front seat. **Consequence:** Webbing separation could occur without prior warning, and increase the risk of injury to belted front outboard occupants in a high-energy crash. **Corrective Action:** Install a controlled-rotation bracket on driver's- and passenger-side front seat belt guide loops.

System: Wheels. **Vehicle:** Passenger vehicles equipped with Kelsey Hayes steel wheels; models RPO PB6 14" and RPO PG1 15". **Defect:** Cracks develop in the wheel mounting surface. If these cracks become severe enough, the wheel will completely separate from the vehicle. **Consequence:** If wheel separation occurs while the vehicle is in motion, loss of steering and brake control of the vehicle occurs, and a vehicle crash could result without prior warning. **Corrective Action:** Dealers will inspect the manufacturing codes stamped on each wheel of the vehicle, and if a wheel falls within the specified date code range, the dealer will replace that wheel assembly.

System: Wheels. **Vehicle:** Passenger vehicles equipped with Kelsey Hayes steel wheels; models RPO PB9 14" and RPO PG1 15". **Defect:** Cracks develop in the wheel mounting surface. If these cracks become severe enough, the wheel will completely separate from the vehicle. **Consequence:** If wheel separation occurs while the vehicle is in motion, loss of steering and brake control of the vehicle occurs, and a vehicle crash could result without prior warning. **Corrective Action:** Dealers will inspect the manufacturing date codes stamped on each wheel of the vehicle, and if a wheel falls within the specified date code range, the dealer will replace that wheel assembly. **Note:** Vehicles previously inspected that had less than four wheels replaced are to be reinspected.

PONTIAC GRAND PRIX 1991

System: Safety belts—FMVSS 208. **Vehicle:** Passenger vehicles; 1991 GMC "J" and "W" model cars. **Defect:** The front door shoulder belt guide loops may be cracked and are not in compliance with FMVSS 208. **Consequence:** The seat occupant faces increased risk of injury in the event of a sudden stop or accident. **Corrective Action:** Install reinforcing plates on the cracked shoulder belt guides.

System: Lighting; headlamps. **Vehicle:** Passenger cars; coupes only. **Defect:** The fog lamps, low beam headlamps and high beam headlamps can be operated simultaneously. This can cause the headlamp circuit breaker to overload and trip, resulting in loss of headlamps (low and high beam) and fog lights. **Consequence:** Loss of headlamps without prior warning reduces driver visibility in inclement weather conditions or at night, and could result in a vehicle accident. In addition, the use of more than four white lights on a vehicle at the same time violates the law in some states. **Corrective Action:** Install new fog lamp relays, new circuit breakers and new circuit breaker terminals. Also modify the lighting circuit to prevent the fog lamps and high beam lamps from operating simultaneously.

PONTIAC GRAND PRIX 1992

System: Transmission and transmission shift indicator. **Vehicle:** 1992 "A" and "W" body passenger cars with 4-speed automatic transmissions. **Defect:** The reverse servo apply pin may bind in the case, which could cause reverse band distress (loss or slipping of reverse), reverse band drag in drive range (poor performance/poor power) or the transmission to remain in reverse while the shift indicator shows neutral gear position. **Consequence:** If the transmission remains in reverse while the shift indicator shows neutral, the vehicle may unexpectedly move rearward and result in a vehicle accident. **Corrective Action:** Replace the transaxle where required.

PONTIAC LEMANS 1988

System: Fuel filler neck—FMVSS 301. **Vehicle:** Passenger cars. **Defect:** Fuel filler neck may have been incompletely welded, allowing fuel to leak from the neck assembly. **Consequence:** In the event of a collision impact, fuel spillage in excess of amount allowed by FMVSS 301 could result in a fire. **Corrective Action:** Replace fuel filler neck assembly.

System: Seat belts. **Vehicle:** Passenger cars. **Defect:** Seat belt buckles may not properly latch, allowing the latchplate to be removed from the buckle without pressing the release button. **Consequence:** In event of a sudden stop or collision, seat belt could release, increasing the risk of injury to occupants. **Corrective Action:** Replace seat belt buckles.

System: Interior systems; safety belt buckles. **Vehicle:** Passenger cars. **Defect:** The safety belt buckle assemblies may not latch or may not release due to the fracture of the red release push button. **Consequence:** The buckle malfunction would prevent the use of the safety belt system, placing the front seat occupant in increased risk of injury in the event of a sudden stop or accident. **Corrective Action:** Replace or repair the safety belt buckles.

PONTIAC LEMANS 1989

System: Interior systems; safety belt buckles. **Vehicle:** Passenger cars. **Defect:** The safety belt buckle assemblies may not latch or may not release due to the fracture of the red release push button. **Consequence:** The buckle malfunction would prevent the use of the safety belt system, placing the front seat occupant in increased risk of injury in the event of a sudden stop or accident. **Corrective Action:** Replace or repair the safety belt buckles.

PONTIAC LEMANS 1990

System: Interior systems; safety belt buckles. **Vehicle:** Passenger cars. **Defect:** The safety belt buckle assemblies may not latch or may not release due to the fracture of the red release push button. **Consequence:** The buckle malfunction would prevent the use of the safety belt system, placing the front seat occupant in increased risk of injury in the event of a sudden stop or accident. **Corrective Action:** Replace or repair the safety belt buckles.

System: Interior; shoulder belts. **Vehicle:** Passenger cars. **Defect:** Insufficient lubrication in the guide track rail in which the shoulder belt carrier moves, causing a chattering noise, momentary binding while traveling, cycling back and forth or stops completely. **Consequence:** This condition can prevent a person from using their restraint system, resulting in an increased risk of injury in an accident. **Corrective Action:** Dealers will lubricate the track system on these vehicles.

PONTIAC LEMANS 1991

System: Interior systems; safety belt buckles. **Vehicle:** Passenger cars. **Defect:** The safety belt buckle assemblies may not latch or may not release due to the fracture of the red release push button. **Consequence:** The buckle malfunction would prevent the use of the safety belt system, placing the front seat occupant in increased risk of injury in the event of a sudden stop or accident. **Corrective Action:** Replace or repair the safety belt buckles.

System: Interior; shoulder belts. **Vehicle:** Passenger cars. **Defect:** Insufficient lubrication in the guide track rail in which the shoulder belt carrier moves, causing a chattering noise, momentary binding while traveling, cycling back and forth or stops completely. **Consequence:** This condition can prevent a person from using their restraint system, resulting in an increased risk of injury in an accident. **Corrective Action:** Dealers will lubricate the track system on these vehicles.

PONTIAC SUNBIRD 1987

System: Fuel. **Vehicle:** Vehicles built with 2.0L engines. **Defect:** The fuel feed and/or return hose and pipe assemblies could crack or separate, allowing fuel to leak into the underhood area. **Consequence:** This could result in an underhood fire, without prior warning, and cause injury to occupants. **Corrective Action:** Replace both fuel feed and return hose/pipe assemblies.

PONTIAC SUNBIRD 1989

System: Fuel tank. **Vehicle:** Passenger cars with 2.0L or 2.8L engines. **Defect:** A fuel tank leak could occur due to small creases on the tank underside cracking during pressure cycling that occurs during normal operation. **Consequence:** In the presence of an ignition source, this condition could result in a fire. **Corrective Action:** Replace fuel tank.

PONTIAC SUNBIRD 1991

System: Seat belt anchorage—FMVSS 210. **Vehicle:** Passenger vehicles. **Defect:** Front door interlock striker may fail, causing door frame collapse and insufficient strength for the shoulder belt anchorage. **Consequence:** The door frame would collapse. Vehicle does not comply with FMVSS 210. **Corrective Action:** Replace the passive restraint interlock striker studs on front doors.

System: Safety belts—FMVSS 208. **Vehicle:** Passenger vehicles; 1991 GMC "J" and "W" model cars. **Defect:** The front door shoulder belt guide loops may be cracked and are not in compliance with FMVSS 208. **Consequence:** The seat occupant faces increased risk of injury in the event of a sudden stop or accident. **Corrective Action:** Install reinforcing plates on the cracked shoulder belt guides.

PONTIAC SUNBIRD 1992

System: Hood latch. **Vehicle:** Passenger cars. **Defect:** The secondary hood latch spring is improperly installed or missing, leading to a condition where the secondary hood latch does not engage the secondary striker. **Consequence:** If the secondary hood latch is not engaged, and the primary hood latch was also not engaged, the hood could open unexpectedly. If this occurs while the vehicle is in motion, the hood may contact the windshield, reducing the forward vision area of the driver, and a vehicle crash could occur. **Corrective Action:** Inspect hood latch assemblies and, where necessary, install a new secondary hood latch spring.

System: Accelerator control. **Vehicle:** Passenger car. **Defect:** The accelerator cable may have been kinked during vehicle assembly. The kink in the cable can cause either a high-effort accelerator cable, sticking accelerator cable or a broken accelerator cable. **Consequence:** If the accelerator control cable sticks or breaks, it can result in loss of throttle control. If loss of throttle control occurs while the vehicle is in motion, a vehicle crash could occur without prior warning. **Corrective Action:** Replace the accelerator control cable assembly.

System: Fuel; throttle linkages; accelerator; flexible. **Vehicle:** During very cold weather, water that enters the accelerator control cable conduit freezes and causes the accelerator cable to develop a high-effort or binding condition. **Consequence:** If this occurs, loss of normal throttle control can result, or the throttle will not return to idle when the accelerator pedal is released, causing possible loss of control and an accident. **Corrective Action:** Dealers will replace the accelerator control assembly.

PONTIAC SUNBIRD 1993

System: Brakes; hydraulic; hose. **Vehicle:** Passenger vehicles. **Description of Noncompliance:** The brake hoses were manufactured incorrectly, and do not comply with FMVSS 106, "Brake hoses." **Consequence of Noncompliance:** The improperly manufactured brake hoses can cause reduced brake effectiveness and/or uneven braking, which could result in an accident. **Corrective Action:** Replace the right front brake hose assembly on Ciera and Century models, and both rear brake hoses on Cavalier and Sunbird models.

System: Fuel; throttle linkages; accelerator; flexible. **Vehicle:** During very cold weather, water that enters the accelerator control cable conduit freezes and causes the accelerator cable to develop a high-effort or binding condition. **Consequence:** If this occurs, loss of normal throttle control can result, or the throttle will not return to idle when the accelerator pedal is released, causing possible loss of control and an accident. **Corrective Action:** Dealers will replace the accelerator control assembly.

RENAULT

RENAULT ALLIANCE 1987

System: Cooling system; heater core. **Vehicle:** Passenger cars. **Defect:** Cooling system pressures during overheated engine operation may exceed the strength capability of certain components due to inadequate venting capacity of the system pressure cap. **Consequence:** The buildup of pressure may cause heater core to rupture and discharge hot coolant and steam in the proximity of the driver's legs. **Corrective Action:** Replace all coolant system pressure caps with caps having adequate venting capacity.

System: Water heater; heater core. **Vehicle:** Passenger automobiles. **Defect:** The end cap connecting the heat exchanger's core to the engine cooling system could rupture and allow hot coolant to escape into the passenger compartment. **Consequence:** The coolant escaping into the passenger compartment could contact the driver's feet and injure the driver. Also, steam from the heated liquid will cloud on the window surfaces and impair the driver's vision, and could result in a vehicle accident. **Corrective Action:** Replace the heater core with a core of different design that will not rupture and leak in the passenger compartment.

RENAULT MEDALLION 1988

System: Throttle cable. **Vehicle:** Passenger cars. **Defect:** Loss of retention of an integral overtravel spring on throttle cable could cause spring dislocation. **Consequence:** A dislocated spring can cause increased idle position throttle opening and higher than normal idle speed. **Corrective Action:** Replace throttle cables with cables designed to provide positive retention of the overtravel spring.

System: Heater blower motor. **Vehicle:** Passenger cars. **Defect:** Fuse block wiring terminals may not adequately clamp the positive electrical connection of heater blower motor fuse blades. **Consequence:** This could increase electrical resistance that could overheat and ignite the fuse block and terminal wiring, resulting in an instrument panel fire. **Corrective Action:** Modify fuse block terminal to ensure adequate retention clamp load on heater blower fuse blades.

SAAB

Note: If your Saab is presented to an authorized dealer on an agreed-upon service date and the remedy is not provided within a reasonable amount of time and free of charge, or the remedy does not correct the defect or noncompliance, please contact Saab at (800) 955-9007. Also contact the NHTSA's Auto Safety Hotline at (800) 424-9393.

SAAB 900 1987

System: Engine—fuel injection hose. **Vehicle:** Passenger cars. **Defect:** The fuel hose between the pressure regulator and the injector fuel rail may rupture due to stress. **Consequence:** This could result in a fuel leak and possibly a fire. **Corrective Action:** Replace fuel hose with new preformed plastic hose.

System: Electrical—wiring harness. **Vehicle:** Passenger cars. **Defect:** Wiring harness may chafe against sharp edges under the dashboard and against a support under the rear seat (1988 models only). **Consequence:** This could cause a short circuit; the resulting heat buildup could cause smoke or a fire in the passenger compartment. **Corrective Action:** Install rubber protective strips to sharp edges and completely encase wire harness in a protective plastic tube.

SAAB 900 1988

System: Front suspension control arm bolts. **Vehicle:** Passenger cars. **Defect:** Bolts used in the attachments of the front suspension system control arms may be defective. **Consequence:** If more than one of the three bolts should fail, lower front control arm could come loose, leading to loss of directional control of a front wheel. **Corrective Action:** Replace bolts with proper specification bolts.

System: Electrical—wiring harness. **Vehicle:** Passenger cars. **Defect:** Wiring harness may chafe against sharp edges under the dashboard and against a support under the rear seat (1988 models only). **Consequence:** This could cause a short circuit; the resulting heat buildup could cause smoke or a fire in the passenger compartment. **Corrective Action:** Install rubber protective strips to sharp edges and completely encase wire harness in a protective plastic tube.

SAAB 900 1994

System: Brakes; hydraulic; shoe; disc brake system. **Vehicle:** Passenger cars. **Defect:** The original front brake discs and/or pad shields do not protect the assemblies from being coated with a layer of slush, road salt or water while driving in snow or heavy rain. This can result in a delay in braking action that increases normal stopping distance. **Consequence:** Increased stopping distance could result in an accident. **Corrective Action:** Dealers will replace the original front brake shields with a new design. An additional hole will be drilled in the steering kingpin housing to attach a larger cover plate. A smaller protection plate will also be attached to the existing two bolts in the hub.

System: Interior systems; seats. **Vehicle:** Passenger cars; hatchbacks with nonpower front driver seats. **Defect:** A weld in the seat rails was not made, increasing the risk of fatigue cracks forming around the attachment bushings on the height-adjustment mechanism, causing the possibility of the height adjuster breaking in a rear-end collision and allowing the seat to fold backwards. **Consequence:** This can increase the risk of injury to seat occupants. **Corrective Action:** Dealers will install new front seat frame rails.

System: Interior systems; tracks and anchors; front seat. **Vehicle:** Passenger cars equipped with nonpower front seats. **Defect:** Two trigger springs mounted to the fore and aft adjustment lever do not develop sufficient force to properly lock the seat rails. After the seat is adjusted, this does not allow the seat rail lock to properly engage, which can cause the seat to move in a sudden stop or collision. **Consequence:** This can increase the possibility of injury to a seat occupant in the event of a sudden stop or accident. **Corrective Action:** Dealers will remove both front seats and the two springs on each seat will be replaced with new springs with proper tension to ensure proper engagement.

System: Structure; door assembly; frame and panel. **Vehicle:** Passenger vehicles. **Description of Noncompliance:** The two weld points in the rearward attachment bracket for the side impact protection beam in the rear door may be out of position. If the welds are out of position, the vehicles will not meet the requirements of FMVSS 214, S5, "Side door strength." **Consequence of Noncompliance:** Passengers sitting in the rear seats will be subject to an increased risk of injury in the event of a side collision. **Corrective Action:** Dealers will install support brackets at the support weld locations.

System: Interior systems; seat; bucket; seat back. **Vehicle:** Passenger cars. **Defect:** One or more of the arc welds can be missing on the seat back frame recliner. **Consequence:** This can result in a seat back falling backwards under a load. **Corrective Action:** Both front seat backs will be inspected with the use of a hook to pull back the seat back upholstery. For any seat with missing welds, the seat back frame/recliner will be replaced.

System: Power train; transmission; standard; manual. **Vehicle:** Passenger vehicles equipped with manual transmissions. **Defect:** It is possible to move the shift lever into the reverse gear position, remove the ignition key and still have the transmission in neutral, or to accidentally disengage reverse by striking the gear lever. **Consequence:** If the parking brake is not applied, the car can roll from its original parked position, increasing the potential for a vehicle accident. **Corrective Action:** Dealers will replace transmission linkage components and complete a specially developed service adjustment procedure that will ensure that when the shift is moved to the reverse position, the reverse gear is actually engaged.

SAAB 9000 1988

System: Cruise control. **Vehicle:** Passenger cars. **Defect:** The ball chain between the cruise control vacuum regulator and the accelerator pedal arm may catch on the vacuum regulator attachment clip. **Consequence:** If the chain gets caught, the throttle could be prevented from returning to fully closed position when the accelerator pedal is released. **Corrective Action:** A plastic cap will be installed over the vacuum regulator clip to cover the openings.

System: Hydraulic brake lines—throttle cable. **Vehicle:** Passenger cars equipped with automatic transmissions. **Defect:** The routing of the throttle kickdown cable could allow chafing to occur between the cable and any one of three steel brake fluid lines near the valve block of the hydraulic brake unit. **Consequence:** This could cause brake fluid leakage; thus, the brake circuit supplied by that line would become inoperative and result in decreased braking effectiveness and an accident. **Corrective Action:** Change cable routing and install new attachment bracket to prevent chafing.

System: Electrical. **Vehicle:** Passenger cars equipped with automatic transmissions. **Defect:** Abrasion on the printed circuit card in the combination neutral safety/backup lamp switch operated by the automatic transmission gear selector may cause residue to collect in electrical area on the circuit card. **Consequence:** This could cause overheating of the switch assembly, with smoke and possibly a fire in the center console area. **Corrective Action:** Add an electrical circuit, including a relay, to the backup lamp circuit to reduce the current that can flow through the combination switch.

SAAB 9000 1989

System: Fuel filter. **Vehicle:** Passenger cars. **Defect:** Fuel filter may not meet the specification concerning leakage criteria due to low temperature during the gluing process. **Consequence:** Fuel filter may leak, creating a potential fire hazard. **Corrective Action:** Replace fuel filter.

System: Hydraulic brake lines—throttle cable. **Vehicle:** Passenger cars equipped with automatic transmissions. **Defect:** The routing of the throttle kickdown cable could allow chafing to occur between the cable and any one of three steel brake fluid lines near the valve block of the hydraulic brake unit. **Consequence:** This could cause brake fluid leakage; thus, the brake circuit supplied by that line would become inoperative and result in decreased braking effectiveness and an accident. **Corrective Action:** Change cable routing and install new attachment bracket to prevent chafing.

System: Electrical. **Vehicle:** Passenger cars equipped with automatic transmissions. **Defect:** Abrasion on the printed circuit card in the combination neutral safety/backup lamp switch operated by the automatic transmission gear selector may cause residue to collect in electrical area on the circuit card. **Consequence:** This could cause overheating of the switch assembly, with smoke and possibly a fire in the center console area. **Corrective Action:** Add an electrical circuit, including a relay, to the backup lamp circuit to reduce the current that can flow through the combination switch.

SATURN

SATURN 1993

System: Brakes. **Vehicle:** Passenger cars with 034 or 035 as the last three digits of the date code tag on the brake master cylinder. **Defect:** The brake booster assemblies were improperly manufactured. This can cause the separation of the brake booster housing during a high-effort braking maneuver. **Consequence:** The separation of the brake booster housing can result in total loss of brake application, without prior warning, and a vehicle accident. **Corrective Action:** Replace defective brake booster assemblies.

SATURN SL2 1993

System: Electrical. **Vehicle:** Sedans, coupes and station wagons equipped with twin cam 16V engines. **Defect:** The positive battery cable terminal at the starter solenoid may be formed incorrectly. Incorrectly formed terminals can contact the starter solenoid housing and cause an electric short circuit. **Consequence:** An electrical short circuit between the battery cable and the starter housing can result in an underhood fire. **Corrective Action:** Inspect and, if necessary, adjust the clearance between the positive battery cable terminal so that it does not contact the starter solenoid housing.

System: Electrical; generator; wire harness. **Vehicle:** Passenger vehicles. **Defect:** The generator electrical wiring is not protected against excessive current flow, which may be caused by an electrical short circuit in the generator. **Consequence:** Should an electrical short circuit occur in the generator, the generator wiring harness would experience excessive current flow. Under certain conditions, enough heat could be generated to ignite surrounding materials. If this occurs, an underhood fire could result with or without the engine running and without prior warning. **Corrective Action:** The generator wiring harness will be replaced with one that will open as a fuse would under certain excessive current flow conditions.

STERLING

STERLING 825 1987

System: Ignition switch. **Vehicle:** Passenger cars. **Defect:** Fault in the ignition switch can interrupt power supply to various electrical systems and components. **Consequence:** Electrical systems, including headlamps and windshield wipers, may become inoperative, resulting in reduced visibility, which could result in an accident. **Corrective Action:** Replace ignition switch and attached electrical subharness. Also lubricate ignition lock mechanism.

System: Automatic front safety belt assemblies equipped with a retractor having web- and vehicle-sensitive lockup mechanisms. **Vehicle:** Passenger cars with automatic shoulder belt systems. **Defect:** Automatic shoulder belt assembly may malfunction during abrupt braking or cornering. The assembly may tighten against the occupant, restricting movement. Also, the retractor driver unit may stall in any position, leaving the belt loose. In either case, the belt would not retract when the door is opened. **Consequence:** The automatic shoulder restraint system would not allow seat occupant to exit the vehicle without disconnecting the safety belt. **Corrective Action:** Replace the automatic safety belt assemblies.

SUBARU

Note: If your Subaru is presented to an authorized dealer on an agreed-upon service date and the remedy is not provided free of charge within a reasonable time, please contact Subaru at (800) 782-2783. Also contact the NHTSA's Auto Safety Hotline at (800) 424-9393.

SUBARU GL 1987

System: Engine—preheat tubes. **Vehicle:** 4-door sedan, 3-door coupe and station wagon, 4-wheel drive (4WD) carburetor-equipped vehicles. **Defect:** The composition of certain nongenuine replacement preheat tubes can cause combustion. **Consequence:** This could result in an engine compartment fire. **Corrective Action:** Install a modified design preheat tube.

System: Rear suspension. **Vehicle:** Passenger cars. **Defect:** The inner arms of the rear suspension are subject to corrosion in areas where road salt is used heavily in winter. **Consequence:** Operation and control of the vehicle can be adversely affected by corrosion of the inner control arms. **Corrective Action:** Rustproof or replace the inner control arms as necessary.

SUBARU GL 1988

System: Owner manual—FMVSS 210. **Vehicle:** Passenger cars. **Defect:** Omission of information specified by FMVSS 210 from owner manual. **Consequence:** Fails to meet requirements of FMVSS 210 regarding child restraint systems. **Corrective Action:** Adhesive-backed inserts will be furnished with the correct information.

System: Interior; seat belts; belt buckles. **Vehicle:** Passenger vehicles equipped with safety belts made by Takata Corporation: Dl, GL and Loyale models involve only 3-door coupes, other models in these series are not involved. **Defect:** The front safety belt buckle release buttons can break. These red plastic release buttons are marked "press." If a button breaks, pieces can fall into the buckle assembly, causing the buckle to operate improperly. **Consequence:** The safety belts would not provide adequate protection to an occupant in a vehicle crash. **Corrective Action:** Owners should promptly check the condition and operation of both front safety belt buckles, and carefully inspect the red release buttons for any breaks or cracks. They should ensure that both buckles are operating properly by inserting each latchplate into its buckle, tugging on the belt to make sure the latch is securely locked and then pressing the release button. The latchplate should pop out of the buckle when the button is pressed. If either release button shows a sign of breaking or cracking, or if either buckle fails to operate properly, owners should promptly contact their authorized dealer to schedule an appointment to have the buckle replaced or repaired, free of charge. The manufacturer is developing a remedy designed to prevent failure of the buttons that are not currently broken. **Note:** The manufacturer has not supplied the model vehicles included in this campaign.

SUBARU JUSTY 1988

System: Alternator. **Vehicle:** 4-wheel drive vehicles equipped with an accessory Subaru air conditioning system. **Defect:** Insufficient clearance between the relocated alternator wiring and the solenoid hose alternator wiring stay bracket can cause wire chafing and an electrical short. **Consequence:** An electrical short could result in smoke and possibly an engine compartment fire. **Corrective Action:** Modify by removing the solenoid hose and alternator stay bracket.

System: Owner manual—FMVSS 210. **Vehicle:** Passenger cars. **Defect:** Omission of information specified by FMVSS 210 from owner manual. **Consequence:** Fails to meet requirements of FMVSS 210 regarding child restraint systems. **Corrective Action:** Adhesive-backed inserts will be furnished with the correct information.

System: Transmission fluid. **Vehicle:** Five-speed manual transmission, four-wheel drive vehicles. **Defect:** Due to the design of the transmission case dipstick and the fluid level checking method, there may be insufficient lubrication of the 4-wheel drive extension housing bearing. **Consequence:** This could cause bearing seizure and possible rear wheel lockup, which could result in an accident. **Corrective Action:** Install modified dipstick and insert information in owner's manual on the correct fluid level checking procedures.

System: Interior; seat belts; belt buckles. **Vehicle:** Passenger vehicles equipped with safety belts made by Takata Corporation: Dl, GL and Loyale models involve only 3-door coupes, other models in these series are not involved. **Defect:** The front safety belt buckle release buttons can break. These red plastic release buttons are marked "press." If a button breaks, pieces can fall into the buckle assembly, causing the buckle to operate improperly. **Consequence:** The safety belts would not provide adequate protection to an occupant in a vehicle crash. **Corrective Action:** Owners should promptly check the condition and operation of both front safety belt buckles, and carefully inspect the red release buttons for any breaks or cracks. They should ensure that both buckles are operating properly by inserting each latchplate into its buckle, tugging on the belt to make sure the latch is securely locked and then pressing the release button. The latchplate should pop out of the buckle when the button is pressed. If either release button shows a sign of breaking or cracking, or if either buckle fails to operate properly, owners should promptly contact their authorized dealer to schedule an appointment to have the buckle replaced or repaired, free of charge. The manufacturer is developing a remedy designed to prevent failure of the buttons that are not currently broken. **Note:** The manufacturer has not supplied the model vehicles included in this campaign.

SUBARU LEGACY 1990

System: Defroster. **Vehicle:** Passenger cars—4-door sedans and station wagons. **Defect:** The defroster lever pin of the defroster shutter door may become dislocated and allow the shutter to close, preventing defroster from functioning. **Consequence:** Nonfunctioning defroster would adversely affect driver visibility. **Corrective Action:** Install a positioning stopper device to prevent dislocation of defroster lever pin to ensure defroster operation.

System: Front door latch screws. **Vehicle:** Four-door sedans and station wagons. **Defect:** Torque of latch screws on front doors may loosen over time due to a gap between the latch baseplate and inner door panel under the screw head. **Consequence:** The affected door may not be opened from inside, preventing exit from that door. **Corrective Action:** Replace front door latch screws with "lock-tight" screws.

System: Transmission park gear. **Vehicle:** Passenger cars with electronically controlled automatic transmissions. **Defect:** Under certain load conditions, the park gear may not disengage immediately when the transmission lever is moved from park to reverse. **Consequence:** Delayed release of transmission from park causes delayed and possibly abrupt vehicle movement that could result in loss of vehicle control and an accident. **Corrective Action:** Install a modified parking brake pawl to prevent delayed release into reverse gear.

System: Power train; transmission; 5-speed. **Vehicle:** XT-6 and Legacy all-wheel drive 5-speed manual transmissions and Loyale equipped with an on-demand 4-wheel drive 5-speed transmission; registered in the following states: AK, CT, DE, IL, IN, IA, ME, MD, MA, MI, MN, NH, NJ, NY, OH, PA, RI, VT and WI. **Defect:** When the vehicle is driven continuously under extremely cold temperatures (−22° F) and high humidity weather conditions, the transmission breathing (air) vent can be blocked due to moisture freezing at the oil level gauge. If this occurs, pressure inside the transmission case will increase and push out the rear oil seal, causing transmission oil leakage. The lack of lubrication can burn the internal components of the transmission, cause the transmission to seize and the vehicle to come to a sudden stop. **Consequence:** Sudden stops without prior warning can cause vehicle occupants to be thrown around the vehicle and cause loss of vehicle control, which can result in an accident. **Corrective Action:**

Dealers will modify the oil gauge pipe and modify the oil level gauge (dipstick) or replace it, depending on the type of dipstick in the vehicle.

SUBARU LEGACY 1991

System: Front door latch screws. **Vehicle:** Four-door sedans and station wagons. **Defect:** Torque of latch screws on front doors may loosen over time due to a gap between the latch baseplate and inner door panel under the screw head. **Consequence:** The affected door may not be opened from inside, preventing exit from that door. **Corrective Action:** Replace front door latch screws with "lock-tight" screws.

System: Transmission park gear. **Vehicle:** Passenger cars with electronically controlled automatic transmissions. **Defect:** Under certain load conditions, the park gear may not disengage immediately when the transmission lever is moved from park to reverse. **Consequence:** Delayed release of transmission from park causes delayed and possibly abrupt vehicle movement that could result in loss of vehicle control and an accident. **Corrective Action:** Install a modified parking brake pawl to prevent delayed release into reverse gear.

System: Power train; transmission; 5-speed. **Vehicle:** XT-6 and Legacy all-wheel drive 5-speed manual transmissions and Loyale equipped with an on-demand 4-wheel drive 5-speed transmission; registered in the following states: AK, CT, DE, IL, IN, IA, ME, MD, MA, MI, MN, NH, NJ, NY, OH, PA, RI, VT and WI. **Defect:** When the vehicle is driven continuously under extremely cold temperatures (−22° F) and high humidity weather conditions, the transmission breathing (air) vent can be blocked due to moisture freezing at the oil level gauge. If this occurs, pressure inside the transmission case will increase and push out the rear oil seal, causing transmission oil leakage. The lack of lubrication can burn the internal components of the transmission, cause the transmission to seize and the vehicle to come to a sudden stop. **Consequence:** Sudden stops without prior warning can cause vehicle occupants to be thrown around the vehicle and cause loss of vehicle control, which can result in an accident. **Corrective Action:** Dealers will modify the oil gauge pipe and modify the oil level gauge (dipstick) or replace it, depending on the type of dipstick in the vehicle.

SUZUKI

SUZUKI TRUCK SAMURAI 1988

System: Interior; seat belts; belt buckles. **Vehicle:** Passenger and multipurpose vehicles equipped with safety belts made by Takata Corporation. **Defect:** The front safety belt buckle release buttons can break. These red plastic release buttons are marked "press." If a button breaks, pieces can fall into the buckle assembly, causing the buckle to operate improperly. **Consequence:** The safety belts would not provide adequate protection to an occupant in a vehicle crash. **Corrective Action:** Owners should promptly check the condition and operation of both front safety belt buckles, and carefully inspect the red release buttons for any breaks or cracks. They should ensure that both buckles are operating properly by inserting each latchplate into its buckle, tugging on the belt to make sure the latch is securely locked and then pressing the release button. The latchplate should pop out of the buckle when the button is pressed. If either button shows a sign of breaking or cracking, or if either buckle fails to operate properly, owners should promptly contact their authorized dealer to schedule an appointment to have the buckle replaced or repaired, free of charge. The manufacturer is developing a remedy designed to prevent failure of the buttons that are not currently broken.

TOYOTA

Note: If your Toyota is presented to an authorized dealer on an agreed-upon service date and the remedy is not provided free of charge within a reasonable time, please contact Toyota at (800) 331-4331. Also contact the NHTSA's Auto Safety Hotline at (800) 424-9393.

TOYOTA CAMRY 1987

System: Front lap belt. **Vehicle:** Passenger cars. **Defect:** Occupant release of the lap belt in a certain manner could cause the belt retractor to lock at the retracted and stowed position. **Consequence:** Seat belts may be unusable or occupants may be discouraged from using belts, increasing their potential for injury in an accident or sudden stop. **Corrective Action:** Replace lap belt with a redesigned belt guide.

System: Passive restraint; automatic seat belts. **Vehicle:** Passenger car. **Defect:** Liquid spilled in the console area can penetrate to the housing of the electronic control unit for the front seat automatic seat belts. Liquid contamination of the electronic control unit can cause failure of the unit signal needed to activate the movement of the motorized safety belt anchorage. **Consequence:** The motorized safety belt anchorages may not move properly, resulting in lack of safety belt protection for seat occupants of the front seat, and increasing the risk of injury in the event of a sudden stop or accident. **Corrective Action:** Install a protective cover to the electronic control unit of the automatic safety belt system.

System: Structure; power door locks. **Vehicle:** Passenger cars with power door locks. **Defect:** The electronic control unit (ECU) for the power door lock system can fail, causing the contacts to "weld" and resulting in door lock solenoid damage, with failure of the door to lock or unlock, even under manual operation. **Consequence:** If the door fails to open after electronic control unit failure, vehicle occupants would have increased difficulty exiting the vehicle in an emergency. **Corrective Action:** Install an additional subcircuit relay control to prevent malfunction of original relays in the ECU.

TOYOTA CAMRY 1988

System: Car jack. **Vehicle:** Station wagons. **Defect:** Due to a design defect in the thread profile of the car jack, when the wagon is raised, the jack may be unable to sustain the vehicle. **Consequence:** Jack could lower itself with potential to cause personal injury. **Corrective Action:** Replace jack.

System: Front lap belt. **Vehicle:** Passenger cars. **Defect:** Occupant release of the lap belt in a certain manner could cause the belt retractor to lock at the retracted and stowed position. **Consequence:** Seat belts may be unusable or occupants may be discouraged from using belts, increasing their potential for injury in an accident or sudden stop. **Corrective Action:** Replace lap belt with a redesigned belt guide.

System: Structure; power door locks. **Vehicle:** Passenger cars with power door locks. **Defect:** The electronic control unit (ECU) for the power door lock system can fail, causing the contacts to "weld" and resulting in door lock solenoid damage, with failure of the door to lock or unlock, even under manual operation. **Consequence:** If the door fails to open after electronic control unit failure, vehicle occupants would have increased difficulty exiting the vehicle in an emergency. **Corrective Action:** Install an additional subcircuit relay control to prevent malfunction of original relays in the ECU.

TOYOTA CAMRY 1989

System: Front lap belt. **Vehicle:** Passenger cars. **Defect:** Occupant release of the lap belt in a certain manner could cause the belt retractor to lock at the retracted and stowed position. **Consequence:** Seat belts may be unusable or occupants may be discouraged from using belts, increasing their potential for injury in an accident or sudden stop. **Corrective Action:** Replace lap belt with a redesigned belt guide.

System: Structure; power door locks. **Vehicle:** Passenger cars with power door locks. **Defect:** The electronic control unit (ECU) for the power door lock system can fail, causing the contacts to "weld" and resulting in door lock solenoid damage, with failure of the door to lock or unlock, even under manual operation. **Consequence:** If the door fails to open after electronic control unit failure, vehicle occupants would have increased difficulty exiting the vehicle in an emergency. **Corrective Action:** Install an additional subcircuit relay control to prevent malfunction of original relays in the ECU.

TOYOTA CAMRY 1990

System: Structure: power door locks. **Vehicle:** Passenger cars with power door locks. **Defect:** The electronic control unit (ECU) for the power door lock system can fail, causing the contacts to "weld" and resulting in door lock solenoid damage, with failure of the door to lock or unlock, even under manual operation. **Consequence:** If the door fails to open after electronic control unit failure, vehicle occupants would have increased difficulty exiting the vehicle in an emergency.

Corrective Action: Install an additional subcircuit relay control to prevent malfunction of original relays in the ECU.

TOYOTA CAMRY 1991

System: Equipment: car radio. **Vehicle:** Passenger cars and minivans with Fujitsu Ten radios. **Defect:** Failure of a specific electronic component in the radios causes an electrical short circuit. **Consequence:** If the failure occurs, it could result in a passenger compartment fire. **Corrective Action:** Repair the radio.

TOYOTA CELICA 1990

System: Airbag. **Vehicle:** Passenger cars. **Defect:** Airbag inflator case was incorrectly machined. **Consequence:** In an accident, the airbag may not deploy, which could result in increased injury to the driver. **Corrective Action:** Replace airbag inflator unit.

TOYOTA COROLLA 1992

System: Certification label; 49 CFR part 567. **Vehicle:** Passenger cars. **Defect:** Due to a computer program error, certain digits of the GVWR and the GAWR appeared in incorrect locations on the certification label located on the left front door of the subject vehicles. **Consequence:** The certification label would not comply with the standards of 49 CFR part 576. **Corrective Action:** Return the vehicle to the Toyota dealer for exchange of the certification label.

TOYOTA COROLLA 1993

System: Electrical—Wiring. **Vehicle:** Corolla passenger vehicles built in Japan or Canada not equipped with power windows, power door locks and sunroof, registered in the following states: CT, IL, IN, ME, MA, MI, NH, NJ, NY, OH, PA, RI, VT and WI. **Defect:** An unused harness connector for power windows, power door locks and sunroof was improperly routed under the floor carpet in the left kick panel. If the vehicle is operated in cold weather conditions where large amounts of road salts are used, the saltwater or snow carried into the vehicle by the driver's shoes can penetrate the carpet and drip onto the connector, resulting in the formation of a salt bridge between the terminals. **Consequence:** This causes an electrical short inside the harness, and can result in a vehicle fire. **Corrective Action:** Dealers will remove the unused harness connector.

TOYOTA COROLLA 1994

System: Safety belt assemblies. **Equipment Description:** Safety belt assemblies used on 1994 Toyota Corollas and Geo Prizms. **Description of Noncompliance:** The anchor straps installed in the belt assemblies (front inner, left- and right-hand sides) were improperly heat treated and can break, which will not sufficiently restrain seat occupants in the event of a sudden stop or accident. This does not comply with FMVSS 209, "Seat belt assemblies." **Consequence of Noncompliance:** Insufficient restraints for seat occupants increases the risk of injury in the event of an accident. **Corrective Action:** The manufacturer will provide replacement safety belt anchor straps.

System: Electrical—wiring. **Vehicle:** Corolla passenger vehicles built in Japan or Canada not equipped with power windows, power door locks and sunroof, registered in the following states: CT, IL, IN, ME, MA, MI, NH, NJ, NY, OH, PA, RI, VT and WI. **Defect:** An unused harness connector for power windows, power door locks and sunroof was improperly routed under the floor carpet in the left kick panel. If the vehicle is operated in cold weather conditions where large amounts of road salts are used, the saltwater or snow carried into the vehicle by the driver's shoes can penetrate the carpet and drip onto the connector, resulting in the formation of a salt bridge between the terminals. **Consequence:** This causes an electrical short inside the harness, and can result in a vehicle fire. **Corrective Action:** Dealers will remove the unused harness connector.

TOYOTA MR2 1991

System: Steering wheel and airbag—FMVSS 208. **Vehicle:** Passenger vehicles. **Defect:** The driver's occupant protection system (steering wheel and airbag) exceeds the 60g thorax criterion in NHTSA crash tests. **Consequence:** The occupant protection system does not comply with the energy absorption requirements of FMVSS 208. This reduces the crash protection afforded by the steering wheel and airbag systems in event of an accident. **Corrective Action:** Replace the steering wheel with a modified wheel designed for increased energy absorption.

TOYOTA TERCEL 1987

System: Headlamps—FMVSS 108. **Vehicle:** Passenger cars equipped with Koito headlamps. **Defect:** There can be interference with the headlamp housing if headlamp bulbs are replaced with any brand other than Koito brand bulbs. **Consequence:** The interference with the headlamp housing caused by other than Koito brand lamp bulbs does not comply with FMVSS 108, "Lamps, reflective devices and associated equipment." **Corrective Action:** Toyota dealers will provide a new Koito brand bulb with no charge if a non-Koito brand bulb is now installed, or should a headlamp bulb burn out in the future. "Caution" labels will also be placed on each headlamp housing.

TOYOTA TERCEL 1988

System: Headlamps—FMVSS 108. **Vehicle:** Passenger cars equipped with Koito headlamps. **Defect:** There can be interference with the headlamp housing if headlamp bulbs are replaced with any brand other than Koito brand bulbs. **Consequence:** The interference with the headlamp housing caused by other than Koito brand lamp bulbs does not comply with FMVSS 108, "Lamps, reflective devices and associated equipment." **Corrective Action:** Toyota dealers will provide a new Koito brand bulb with no charge if a non-Koito brand bulb is now installed, or should a headlamp bulb burn out in the future. "Caution" labels will also be placed on each headlamp housing.

TOYOTA TERCEL 1989

System: Headlamps—FMVSS 108. **Vehicle:** Passenger cars equipped with Koito headlamps. **Defect:** There can be interference with the headlamp housing if headlamp bulbs are replaced with any brand other than Koito brand bulbs. **Consequence:** The interference with the headlamp housing caused by other than Koito brand lamp bulbs does not comply with FMVSS 108, "Lamps, reflective devices and associated equipment." **Corrective Action:** Toyota dealers will provide a new Koito brand bulb for no charge if a non-Koito brand bulb is now installed, or should a headlamp bulb burn out in the future. "Caution" labels will also be placed on each headlamp housing.

TOYOTA TRUCK PREVIA 1991

System: Visual systems; windshield wiper and washer. **Vehicle:** 2-wheel drive and 4-wheel drive minivans. **Defect:** Certain windshield wiper components are subject to premature failure due to insufficient strength to function under high load levels. **Consequence:** The windshield wiper assembly can fail and cease operation entirely, resulting in reduced driver visibility in inclement weather. **Corrective Action:** Install new wiper motors, certain wiper arm components and retorque the wiper arm pivot.

System: Equipment: car radio. **Vehicle:** Passenger cars and minivans with Fujitsu Ten radios. **Defect:** Failure of a specific electronic component in the radios causes an electrical short circuit. **Consequence:** If the failure occurs, it could result in a passenger compartment fire. **Corrective Action:** Repair the radio.

VOLKSWAGEN

VOLKSWAGEN FOX 1988

System: Steering. **Vehicle:** Passenger cars. **Defect:** Steering wheel and shaft, designed to use surface friction, may lose this friction if grease or oil is present on the cone-shaped surface of the steering shaft. **Consequence:** If the above condition is present and the steering wheel nut is torqued lower than specified, break of the friction lock could result in loosening and separation of the steering wheel. **Corrective Action:** Remove the steering wheel of vehicles and clean friction surface and install a spring retainer; replace the steering wheel nut with a self-locking nut.

System: Engine cooling system. **Vehicle:** Passenger cars. **Defect:** In the event of a cooling system component failure while the vehicle is being driven, the coolant can overheat, causing the cooling system pressure to rise to a level where a leak in the heat exchanger can occur. **Consequence:** A leak or failure of the heat exchanger located under the dashboard can allow hot coolant to escape and cause injury to the feet of a passenger. Hot coolant can also steam up the interior of the vehicle, temporarily impairing the driver's visibility, increasing the potential for a vehicle accident. **Corrective Action:** Dealers will install a bypass valve kit which is designed to route excessively hot coolant to the engine without flowing through the heat exchanger. Dealers will also install a plastic cover underneath the dashboard on the passenger side to ensure that the passenger is not exposed to hot coolant in the event of a leak.

VOLKSWAGEN GOLF 1987

System: Fuel pump. **Vehicle:** Passenger cars equipped with a dual fuel pump system. **Defect:** Fuel pump, located inside fuel tank, could seize during high ambient temperatures because of an extremely fine mesh fuel filter, restricting the fuel flow. **Consequence:** Fuel supply to engine would be partially interrupted, resulting in stalling. **Corrective Action:** Install a modified fuel pump and filter.

System: Wheels and lug nuts. **Vehicle:** Passenger cars equipped with alloy wheels. **Defect:** The front left wheel lug nuts may have been improperly torqued. **Consequence:** An improperly torqued wheel may loosen over a period of time and could eventually separate, causing an accident. **Corrective Action:** Inspect and retorque left front wheel lug nuts.

System: Water heater; heater core. **Vehicle:** Passenger automobiles. **Defect:** The end cap connecting the heat exchanger's core to the engine cooling system could rupture and allow hot coolant to escape into the passenger compartment. **Consequence:** The coolant escaping into the passenger compartment could contact the driver's feet and injure the driver. Also, steam from the heated liquid will cloud on the window surfaces and impair the driver's vision, and could result in a vehicle accident. **Corrective Action:** Replace the heater core with an improved heater core.

VOLKSWAGEN GOLF 1989

System: Water heater; heater core. **Vehicle:** Passenger automobiles. **Defect:** The end cap connecting the heat exchanger's core to the engine cooling system could rupture and allow hot coolant to escape into the passenger compartment. **Consequence:** The coolant escaping into the passenger compartment could contact the driver's feet and injure the driver. Also, steam from the heated liquid will cloud on the window surfaces and impair the driver's vision, and could result in a vehicle accident. **Corrective Action:** Replace the heater core with an improved heater core.

System: Fuel lines. **Vehicle:** Passenger cars. **Defect:** The fuel hose attached to the fuel distribution rail on the engine may shrink beyond the clamp force of the fuel hose clamps, allowing fuel to leak. **Consequence:** Fuel leakage in the engine compartment can cause an underhood fire if the fuel comes in contact with a source of ignition. **Corrective Action:** Replace the fuel hose attached to the fuel rail and install a new spring-type self-tightening clamp.

System: Fuel lines. **Vehicle:** Passenger cars. **Defect:** The fuel hose attached to the fuel distribution rail on the engine may shrink beyond the clamp force of the fuel hose clamps, allowing fuel to leak. **Consequence:** Fuel leakage in the engine compartment can cause an underhood fire if the fuel comes in contact with a source of ignition. **Corrective Action:** Replace the fuel hose attached to the fuel rail and install a new spring-type self-tightening clamp.

System: Brakes; hydraulic lines. **Vehicle:** Passenger cars equipped with Digifant engine management systems. **Defect:** An engine preheating tube may not be properly supported due to a missing support bracket, causing the preheating tube to chafe against the right front metal brake line. This can damage the hydraulic line, causing brake fluid leakage and diminished braking in one brake circuit. **Consequence:** Diminished braking can result in increased stopping distances and a possible accident. **Corrective Action:** Dealers will install a preheating tube support bracket to ensure proper positioning relative to the right front metal brake line.

VOLKSWAGEN JETTA 1987

System: Fuel pump. **Vehicle:** Passenger cars equipped with a dual fuel pump system. **Defect:** Fuel pump, located inside fuel tank, could seize during high ambient temperatures because of an extremely fine mesh fuel filter, restricting the fuel flow. **Consequence:** Fuel supply to engine would be partially interrupted, resulting in stalling. **Corrective Action:** Install a modified fuel pump and filter.

System: Right front brake line. **Vehicle:** Passenger cars. **Defects:** An incorrectly contoured metal brake line leading to the right front wheel could be damaged by a preheating tube chafing against it. **Consequence:** Prolonged chafing could eventually cause a leaking brake line, resulting in diminished braking in one brake circuit, which would increase the stopping distances and result in an accident. **Corrective Action:** Curve or replace right front brake line.

System: Water heater; heater core. **Vehicle:** Passenger automobiles. **Defect:** The end cap connecting the heat exchanger's core to the engine cooling system could rupture and allow hot coolant to escape into the passenger compartment. **Consequence:** The coolant escaping into the passenger compartment could contact the driver's feet and injure the driver. Also, steam from the heated liquid will cloud on the window surfaces and impair the driver's vision, and could result in a vehicle accident. **Corrective Action:** Replace the heater core with an improved heater core.

VOLKSWAGEN JETTA 1988

System: Cruise control switch—FMVSS 101. **Vehicle:** Passenger cars equipped with cruise control. **Defect:** Certain vehicles may not be marked with letters *RES* to identify the resume function as required by FMVSS 101. **Consequence:** Vehicles do not comply with FMVSS 101. **Corrective Action:** Replace part of cruise switch portion.

System: Front seat belt. **Vehicle:** Passenger vehicles equipped with passive restraint seat belt systems. **Defect:** Seat belt retractor pawl may not meet hardening specifications contained in Volkswagen's design standard. **Consequence:** Vehicles do not meet Volkswagen's design standard. **Corrective Action:** Replace front passive restraint seat belt assembly as necessary.

System: Brake boosters. **Vehicle:** Passenger cars. **Defect:** Brake boosters have been improperly assembled, with the two halves of the booster unit insufficiently connected. **Consequence:** Brake booster halves could separate under heavy brake application and braking power would suddenly diminish, which could result in an accident. **Corrective Action:** Replace brake boosters as necessary.

System: Right front brake line. **Vehicle:** Passenger cars. **Defect:** An incorrectly contoured metal brake line leading to the right front wheel could be damaged by a preheating tube chafing against it. **Consequence:** Prolonged chafing could eventually cause a leaking brake line, resulting in diminished braking in one brake circuit, which would increase the stopping distances and result in an accident. **Corrective Action:** Curve or replace right front brake line.

System: Water heater; heater core. **Vehicle:** Passenger automobiles. **Defect:** The end cap connecting the heat exchanger's core to the engine cooling system could rupture and allow hot coolant to escape into the passenger compartment. **Consequence:** The coolant escaping into the passenger compartment could contact the driver's feet and injure the driver. Also, steam from the heated liquid will cloud on the window surfaces and impair the driver's vision, and could result in a vehicle accident. **Corrective Action:** Replace the heater core with an improved heater core.

System: Fuel lines. **Vehicle:** Passenger cars. **Defect:** The fuel hose attached to the fuel distribution rail on the engine may shrink beyond the clamp force of the fuel hose clamps, allowing fuel to leak. **Consequence:** Fuel leakage in the engine compartment can cause an underhood fire if the fuel comes in contact with a source of ignition. **Corrective Action:** Replace the fuel hose attached to the fuel rail and install a new spring-type self-tightening clamp.

System: Brakes; hydraulic lines. **Vehicle:** Passenger cars equipped with Digifant engine management systems. **Defect:** An engine preheating tube may not be properly supported due to a missing support bracket, causing the preheating tube to chafe against the right front metal brake line. This can damage the hydraulic line, causing brake fluid leakage and diminished braking in one brake circuit. **Consequence:** Diminished braking can result in increased stopping distances and a possible accident. **Corrective Action:** Dealers will install a preheating tube support bracket to ensure proper positioning relative to the right front metal brake line.

VOLKSWAGEN JETTA 1989

System: Right front brake line. **Vehicle:** Passenger cars. **Defect:** An incorrectly contoured metal brake line leading to the right front wheel could be damaged by a preheating tube chafing against it. **Consequence:** Prolonged chafing could eventually cause a leaking brake line, resulting in diminished braking in one brake circuit, which would increase the stopping distances and result in an accident. **Corrective Action:** Curve or replace right front brake line.

System: Water heater; heater core. **Vehicle:** Passenger automobiles. **Defect:** The end cap connecting the heat exchanger's core to the engine cooling system could rupture and allow hot coolant to escape into the passenger compartment. **Consequence:** The coolant escaping into the passenger compartment could contact the driver's feet and injure the driver. Also, steam from the heated liquid will cloud on the window surfaces and impair the driver's vision, and could result in a vehicle accident. **Corrective Action:** Replace the heater core with an improved heater core.

System: Fuel lines. **Vehicle:** Passenger cars. **Defect:** The fuel hose attached to the fuel distribution rail on the engine may shrink beyond the clamp force of the fuel hose clamps, allowing fuel to leak. **Consequence:** Fuel leakage in the engine compartment can cause an underhood fire if the fuel comes in contact with a source of ignition. **Corrective Action:** Replace the fuel hose attached to the fuel rail and install a new spring-type self-tightening clamp.

System: Brakes; hydraulic lines. **Vehicle:** Passenger cars equipped with Digifant engine management systems. **Defect:** An engine preheating tube may not be properly supported due to a missing support bracket, causing the preheating tube to chafe against the right front metal brake line. This can damage the hydraulic line, causing brake fluid leakage and diminished braking in one brake circuit. **Consequence:** Diminished braking can result in increased stopping distances and a possible accident. **Corrective Action:** Dealers will install a preheating tube support bracket to ensure proper positioning relative to the right front metal brake line.

VOLKSWAGEN JETTA 1990

System: Steering power assist. **Vehicle:** Passenger cars. **Defect:** Power steering pump bracket is subject to breakage due to excessive tension caused by a lack of clearance between the pump mounting bracket and sealing flange edge of the oil pan. **Consequence:** Bracket breakage could allow power steering pump to loosen and drive belt to slip, resulting in the need for unexpected increased steering force with the potential for an accident. **Corrective Action:** Replace power steering pump bracket.

System: Brake caliper air ducts. **Vehicle:** Passenger cars. **Defect:** Omission of air ducts intended to guide flow of cooling air to left and right front brake calipers could allow brake fluid to exceed allowable operating temperature under certain operating conditions. **Consequence:** If brake fluid boils, this could result in reduced braking pressure, with potential for an accident. **Corrective Action:** Install missing left and right front air ducts.

System: Water heater; heater core. **Vehicle:** Passenger automobiles. **Defect:** The end cap connecting the heat exchanger's core to the engine cooling system could rupture and allow hot coolant to escape into the passenger compartment. **Consequence:** The coolant escaping into the passenger compartment could contact the driver's feet and injure the driver. Also, steam from the heated liquid will cloud on the window surfaces and impair the driver's vision, and could result in a vehicle accident. **Corrective Action:** Replace the heater core with an improved heater core.

System: Fuel lines. **Vehicle:** Passenger cars. **Defect:** The fuel hose attached to the fuel distribution rail on the engine may shrink beyond the clamp force of the fuel hose clamps, allowing fuel to leak. **Consequence:** Fuel leakage in the engine compartment can cause an underhood fire if the fuel comes in contact with a source of ignition. **Corrective Action:** Replace the fuel hose attached to the fuel rail and install a new spring-type self-tightening clamp.

System: Brakes; hydraulic lines. **Vehicle:** Passenger cars equipped with Digifant engine management systems. **Defect:** An engine preheating tube may not be properly supported due to a missing support bracket, causing the preheating tube to chafe against the right front metal brake line. This can damage the hydraulic line, causing brake fluid leakage and diminished braking in one brake circuit. **Consequence:** Diminished braking can result in increased stopping distances and a possible accident. **Corrective Action:** Dealers will install a preheating tube support bracket to ensure proper positioning relative to the right front metal brake line.

VOLKSWAGEN JETTA 1991

System: Front brake hoses. **Vehicle:** Passenger cars. **Defect:** Front brake hoses of insufficient length were installed in some vehicles. These short hoses could stretch and develop cracks. **Consequence:** This could result in brake fluid leakage, with loss of fluid pressure and braking ability. **Corrective Action:** Replace both brake hoses.

System: Cruise control. **Vehicle:** Passenger cars; California models equipped with cruise control. **Defect:** The lock nut of the cruise control rod for the operating servo may not have been properly torqued during manufacture. **Consequence:** Inadequate torque of the lock nut could allow the rod adjustment to change. This could increase the engine idle speed, and possibly increase stopping distance, with a potential for a vehicle accident. **Corrective Action:** Check and ensure proper lock nut torque on the cruise control rod.

System: Fuel lines. **Vehicle:** Passenger cars. **Defect:** The fuel hose attached to the fuel distribution rail on the engine may shrink beyond the clamp force of the fuel hose clamps, allowing fuel to leak. **Consequence:** Fuel leakage in the engine compartment can cause an underhood fire if the fuel comes in contact with a source of ignition. **Corrective Action:** Replace the fuel hose attached to the fuel rail and install a new spring-type self-tightening clamp.

System: Brakes; hydraulic lines. **Vehicle:** Passenger cars equipped with Digifant engine management systems. **Defect:** An engine preheating tube may not be properly supported due to a missing support bracket, causing the preheating tube to chafe against the right front metal brake line. This can damage the hydraulic line, causing brake fluid leakage and diminished braking in one brake circuit. **Consequence:** Diminished braking can result in increased stopping distances and a possible accident. **Corrective Action:** Dealers will install a preheating tube support bracket to ensure proper positioning relative to the right front metal brake line.

VOLKSWAGEN JETTA 1992

System: Fuel lines. **Vehicle:** Passenger cars. **Defect:** The fuel hose attached to the fuel distribution rail on the engine may shrink beyond the clamp force of the fuel hose clamps, allowing fuel to leak. **Consequence:** Fuel leakage in the engine compartment can cause an underhood fire if the fuel comes in contact with a source of ignition. **Corrective Action:** Replace the fuel hose attached to the fuel rail and install a new spring-type self-tightening clamp.

VOLKSWAGEN TRUCK VANAGON 1987

System: Fuel tank. **Vehicle:** Van-type vehicles. **Defect:** Usage of fuel with Reid pressure up to 14 PSI could, under high engine load and high ambient temperatures, lead to stalling. **Consequence:** Fuel flow could become restricted and cause the engine to stall. **Corrective Action:** Install a new fuel tank containing a redesigned fuel filter, as well as modified control units.

System: Rearward passenger seat. **Vehicle:** Van-type vehicles. **Defect:** Seat brackets that anchor rearward passenger seats may not engage properly. **Consequence:** Seat could break loose during acceleration and cause injury to the seat occupant. **Corrective Action:** Ensure that seat brackets are properly engaged.

System: Shift locking pawl. **Vehicle:** Van-type vehicles with automatic transmissions. **Defect:** Pin in shift locking pawl may not be properly welded to the pawl. **Consequence:** If pin separates from pawl, during driving, driver would be able to move the shift lever into any position without pressing safety release button. **Corrective Action:** Replace shift locking pawl.

System: Fuel; in-line filter. **Vehicle:** Van-type vehicles. **Defect:** In-line fuel filter located between the fuel tank and fuel pump could seep fuel at the seam of the plastic casing. **Consequence:** Should seepage occur, leaking fuel can cause a risk of fire in the presence of an ignition source. **Corrective Action:** The in-line fuel filter will be replaced with a straight fuel hose.

System: Wheels/tires. **Vehicle:** Van- and camper-type vehicles. **Defect:** Due to improper mounting process, Semperit tires 20570R14 mounted on alloy wheel size 6J × 14 could experience tiny cracks in the bead area. **Consequence:** Tires could lose air, creating potential for loss of vehicle control. **Corrective Action:** Replace tires as necessary.

System: Cruise control. **Vehicle:** Van/camper-type vehicles. **Defect:** When using the cruise control, the accelerator cable tension may allow the cable to sag and become entangled with the water pipe bracket, impeding its return to idle position. **Consequence:** Failure to return to idle position could lead to an accident. **Corrective Action:** The present accelerator cable bracket will be replaced.

System: Fuel lines. **Vehicle:** Passenger cars. **Defect:** The fuel hose attached to the fuel distribution rail on the engine may shrink beyond the clamp force of the fuel hose clamps, allowing fuel to leak. **Consequence:** Fuel leakage in the engine compartment can cause an underhood fire if the fuel comes in contact with a source of ignition. **Corrective Action:** Replace the fuel hose attached to the fuel rail and install a new spring-type self-tightening clamp.

System: Air conditioner hose; duct; air. **Vehicle:** Vans equipped with factory air conditioning. **Defect:** The plastic material of the center airflow duct, which is fastened by 2 mounting screws to the ceiling of the passenger compartment, can crack and eventually break. **Consequence:** If the plastic breaks where it is held at the 2 mounting screws, the center airflow duct can separate from its supports and cause injury to the passengers sitting in the center seat of the vehicle. **Corrective Action:** Dealers will install a reinforcement plate at the connections of both the center and rear airflow ducts.

VOLVO

VOLVO 740 1987

System: Engine wiring harness. **Vehicle:** Passenger sedans and wagons. **Defect:** Engine wiring harness could chafe against an air conditioning pipe. **Consequence:** A short circuit and malfunctioning of the electrical system, as well as charring of the wiring insulation, could result. **Corrective Action:** Relocate wiring harness and secure with a new bracket and clamp.

System: Driveshaft—fuel tank. **Vehicle:** Passenger cars. **Defect:** Driveshaft could contact the fuel tank and score and scrape outer surfaces of the tank at the point of contact. **Consequence:** A small leak could develop, which could, in the presence of an ignition source, result in a fire. **Corrective Action:** Replace fuel tank and/or install protective device between driveshaft and the tank.

System: Safety belts for auxiliary seats. **Vehicle:** Station wagons. **Defect:** Safety belts are designed to be routed under a diagonal cross brace during fastening. The instructional labels for the belt routing are inadequate, and can result in inadvertent release of the belt buckle. **Consequence:** Safety belt misuse could cause the seat occupant to face greater risk of injury in a sudden stop or vehicle accident if an inadvertent release of the safety belt occurred. **Corrective Action:** Install labels to instruct the user in proper safety belt routing; also replace safety belt buckles.

VOLVO 740 1988

System: Driveshaft—fuel tank. **Vehicle:** Passenger cars. **Defect:** Driveshaft could contact the fuel tank and score and scrape outer surfaces of the tank at the point of contact. **Consequence:** A small leak could develop, which could, in the presence of an ignition source, result in a fire. **Corrective Action:** Replace fuel tank and/or install protective device between driveshaft and the tank.

System: Safety belts for auxiliary seats. **Vehicle:** Station wagons. **Defect:** Safety belts are designed to be routed under a diagonal cross brace during fastening. The instructional labels for the belt routing are inadequate, and can result in inadvertent release of the belt buckle. **Consequence:** Safety belt misuse could cause the seat occupant to face greater risk of injury in a sudden stop or vehicle accident if an inadvertent release of the safety belt occurred. **Corrective Action:** Install labels to instruct the user in proper safety belt routing; also replace safety belt buckles.

VOLVO 740 1989

System: Safety belts for auxiliary seats. **Vehicle:** Station wagons. **Defect:** Safety belts are designed to be routed under a diagonal cross brace during fastening. The instructional labels for the belt routing are inadequate, and can result in inadvertent release of the belt buckle. **Consequence:** Safety belt misuse could cause the seat occupant to face greater risk of injury in a sudden stop or vehicle accident if an inadvertent release of the safety belt occurred. **Corrective Action:** Install labels to instruct the user in proper safety belt routing; also replace safety belt buckles.

VOLVO 740 1990

System: Fuel damper. **Vehicle:** Passenger cars equipped with B234F (16-valve) engines. **Defect:** Fuel damper located behind the fuel line and the fuel rail may be improperly assembled. Over time, the solder joints could allow a small amount of fuel to leak. **Consequence:** Fuel leakage, in the presence of an ignition source, could result in a fire. **Corrective Action:** Replace fuel damper.

System: Safety belts for auxiliary seats. **Vehicle:** Station wagons. **Defect:** Safety belts are designed to be routed under a diagonal cross brace during fastening. The instructional labels for the belt routing are inadequate, and can result in inadvertent release of the belt buckle. **Consequence:** Safety belt misuse could cause the seat occupant to face greater risk of injury in a sudden stop or vehicle accident if an inadvertent release of the safety belt occurred. **Corrective Action:** Install labels to instruct the user in proper safety belt routing; also replace safety belt buckles.